Lecture Notes in Artificial Intelligence 3066

Edited by J. G. Carbonell and J. Siekmann

Subseries of Lecture Notes in Computer Science

Springer
Berlin
Heidelberg
New York
Hong Kong
London
Milan
Paris
Tokyo

Shusaku Tsumoto Roman Słowiński
Jan Komorowski Jerzy W. Grzymala-Busse (Eds.)

Rough Sets and Current Trends in Computing

4th International Conference, RSCTC 2004
Uppsala, Sweden, June 1-5, 2004
Proceedings

Springer

Series Editors

Jaime G. Carbonell, Carnegie Mellon University, Pittsburgh, PA, USA
Jörg Siekmann, University of Saarland, Saarbrücken, Germany

Volume Editors

Shusaku Tsumoto
Shimane University
School of Medicine, Department of Medical Informatics
89-1 Enya-cho, Izumo, Shimane 693-8501, Japan
E-mail: tsumoto@computer.org

Roman Slowiński
Poznan University of Technology
Institute of Computing Science
Piotrowo 3a, 60-965 Poznan, Poland
E-mail: slowinsk@sol.put.poznan.pl

Jan Komorowski
Uppsala University
The Linnaeus Centre for Bioinformatics, BMC
Box 598, Husargatan 3, 751 24 Uppsala, Sweden
E-mail: Jan.Komorowski@lcb.uu.se

Jerzy W. Grzymala-Busse
University of Kansas
Department of Electrical Engineering and Computer Science
Lawrence, KS 66045, USA
E-mail: Jerzy@ku.edu

Library of Congress Control Number: 2004106316

CR Subject Classification (1998): I.2, F.4.1, F.1, I.5.1, I.4, H.2.8, H.3, H.4

ISSN 0302-9743
ISBN 3-540-22117-4 Springer-Verlag Berlin Heidelberg New York

Springer-Verlag is a part of Springer Science+Business Media

springeronline.com

Printed in Germany

Typesetting: Camera-ready by author, data conversion by Olgun Computergrafik
Printed on acid-free paper SPIN: 11008972 06/3142 5 4 3 2 1 0

Foreword

In recent years rough set theory has attracted the attention of many researchers and practitioners all over the world, who have contributed essentially to its development and applications.

We are observing a growing research interest in the foundations of rough sets, including the various logical, mathematical and philosophical aspects of rough sets. Some relationships have already been established between rough sets and other approaches, and also with a wide range of hybrid systems. As a result, rough sets are linked with decision system modeling and analysis of complex systems, fuzzy sets, neural networks, evolutionary computing, data mining and knowledge discovery, pattern recognition, machine learning, and approximate reasoning. In particular, rough sets are used in probabilistic reasoning, granular computing (including information granule calculi based on rough mereology), intelligent control, intelligent agent modeling, identification of autonomous systems, and process specification.

Methods based on rough set theory alone or in combination with other approaches have been discovered with a wide range of applications in such areas as: acoustics, bioinformatics, business and finance, chemistry, computer engineering (e.g., data compression, digital image processing, digital signal processing, parallel and distributed computer systems, sensor fusion, fractal engineering), decision analysis and systems, economics, electrical engineering (e.g., control, signal analysis, power systems), environmental studies, informatics, medicine, molecular biology, musicology, neurology, robotics, social science, software engineering, spatial visualization, Web engineering, and Web mining.

The conferences on Rough Sets and Current Trends in Computing foster the gathering of researchers from different areas actively engaged in the theory and application of rough sets. A large number of high quality submissions from many countries to the Fourth International Conference on Rough Sets and Current Trends in Computing (RSCTC 2004) has proved that the decision made in 1998 to start such a series of conferences was very beneficial not only to the rough set community but also to other research communities.

We would like to thank all colleagues for submitting papers to the conference.

On behalf of the whole rough set community we would like to express our deep appreciation to our colleagues, especially to the Chairs, the members of the Program Committee and the members of the Organizing Committee for their excellent work in organizing the RSCTC 2004 conference in Uppsala, Sweden.

We hope that all participants of the RSCTC 2004 conference enjoyed a very successful meeting, which led to the discovery of new research directions, stimulating scientific cooperation, and will bring about further development of the rough set foundations, methods, and real-life applications in many areas, including bioinformatics.

June 2004 Zdzisław Pawlak Andrzej Skowron

Preface

This volume contains the papers selected for presentation at the Fourth International Conference on Rough Sets and Current Trends in Computing (RSCTC 2004) held at Uppsala University, Uppsala, Sweden, June 1–5, 2004. There were 248 online submissions for RSCTC 2004, excluding for three keynote papers and one paper on our bibliography project, which was the largest number of submissions in this conference series. Papers went through a rigorous review process. Each paper was reviewed by at least three program committee members. Whenever the reviews were conflicting, another PC member was asked to review the paper again.

After the reviews, the four PC chairs reviewed the papers again and checked all the comments of the reviewers. Since we had 248 good papers, we had to select them carefully. Of the 248 papers submitted, 45 were accepted as full papers, and an additional 60 were accepted as short papers. In total, 105 papers were accepted, the acceptance ratio was only 42.3%.

RSCTC 2004 provided a forum for exchanging ideas among many researchers in the International Rough Set Society (IRSS, URL: http://www.roughsets.org) and in various areas of soft computing and served as a stimulus for mutual understanding and cooperation. In recent years, there have been a number of advances in rough set theory and applications. Hence, we have witnessed a growing number of international workshops/conferences on rough sets and their applications. In addition, it should be observed that one of the beauties of rough sets and the rough set philosophy is that it tends to complement and reinforce research in many traditional research areas and applications. This is the main reason that many international conferences are now including rough sets into their lists of topics.

The papers contributed to this volume reflect advances in rough sets as well as complementary research efforts in the following areas:

- Rough set theory and applications
- Bioinformatics
- Computing with words
- Decision support systems
- Fuzzy set theory
- Hybrid intelligent systems
- Integrated intelligent systems
- Intelligent information systems
- Multi-agent systems
- Neural networks
- Pattern recognition
- Soft computing
- Statistical inference
- Web intelligence
- Approximate reasoning
- Computational intelligence
- Data mining
- Evolutionary computing
- Granular computing
- Image processing
- Intelligent decision support systems
- Machine learning
- Multi-criteria decision analysis
- Non-classical logic
- Petri nets and concurrency
- Spatial reasoning
- Uncertainty

It is our great pleasure to dedicate this volume to Professor Zdzisław Pawlak, who created rough set theory about a quarter of a century ago. The growth of rough sets and applications owes a great deal to Professor Pawlak's vibrant enthusiasm and wit as well as his great generosity towards others. His energetic style has stimulated and encouraged researchers, including the beginners in rough sets, for the last 25 years.

The depth, breadth, and richness of current rough set research directly originated from Professor Pawlak's inventiveness and the richness of his many insights and ideas concerning almost all areas of computer science. Actually, all four PC chairs were led to rough set theory by his diligent research, including his talks and lectures. Readers of this volume will be aware of the enthusiasm of all the authors for rough sets and related areas.

We wish to express our gratitude to Professors Zdzisław Pawlak and Lotfi A. Zadeh, who accepted our invitation to serve as honorary chairs and to present keynote papers for this conference. We also wish to thank Professors Lech Polkowski, Masahiro Inuiguchi, and Hiroki Arimura for accepting our invitation to be plenary speakers at RSCTC 2004.

We wish to express our thanks to all the PC members, each of whom reviewed more than ten papers in only one month. Without their contributions, we could not have selected high-quality papers with confidence.

We also want to thank all the authors who submitted valuable papers to RSCTC 2004 and all conference attendees.

All the submissions and reviews were made through the Cyberchair system (URL: http://www.cyberchair.org/). We wish to thank the staff of Cyberchair system development team. Without this system, we could not have edited this volume in such a speedy way.

Our special thanks go to Dr. Shoji Hirano, who launched the Cyberchair system for RSCTC 2004 and contributed to editing this volume, and Ms. Hiroko Ishimaru, who helped to compile all the manuscripts. Our gratitude also goes to Ms. Ulla Conti and her colleagues at Akademikonferens whose professionalism in organizing scientific meetings helped make it such an attractive conference. We also wish to acknowledge the help of Mr. Vladimir Yankovski for his design and maintenance of the conference Web pages and his ever cheerful approach to dealing with the daily chores created by such a big event.

Finally, we wish to express our thanks to Alfred Hofmann at Springer-Verlag for his support and cooperation.

June 2004

Shusaku Tsumoto
Roman Słowiński
Jan Komorowski
Jerzy W. Grzymala-Busse

RSCTC 2004 Conference Committee

Organizing Chair: Jan Komorowski

Honorary Chairs: Zdzisław Pawlak
Lotfi A. Zadeh

Organizing Committee: Jan Komorowski
Shusaku Tsumoto

Program Committee Chairs: Shusaku Tsumoto
Roman Słowiński
Jan Komorowski
Jerzy W. Grzymala-Busse

Program Committee

James Alpigini
Peter Apostoli
Malcolm Beynon
Hans Dieter Burkhard
Cory Butz
Nick Cercone
Chien-Chung Chan
Andrzej Czyżewski
Jitender S. Deogun
Didier Dubois
Ivo Duentsch
Salvatore Greco
Jerzy W. Grzymala-Busse
Shoji Hirano
Xiaohua (Tony) Hu
Masahiro Inuiguchi
Jouni Järvinen
Janusz Kacprzyk
Karl Henning Kalland
Daijin Kim
Jan Komorowski
Jacek Koronacki
Bożena Kostek
Vladik Kreinovich
Marzena Kryszkiewicz
Churn-Jung Liau
T.Y. Lin
Chunnian Liu
Qing Liu
Pawan Lingras
Astrid Lagreid
Benedetto Matarazzo
Lawrence J. Mazlack
Ernestina Menasalvas
Nakata Michinori
Sadaaki Miyamoto
Mikhail Moshkov
Tetsuya Murai
Sestuo Ohsuga
Ewa Orłowska
Sankar Pal
Witold Pedrycz
James Peters
Lech Polkowski
Sheela Ramanna
Vijay V. Raghavan
Zbigniew.W. Raś
Andrzej Skowron
Dominik Ślęzak
Roman Słowiński
Nguyen Hung Son
Jerzy Stefanowski
Jarosłav Stepaniuk
Zbigniew Suraj
Roman Świniarski
Andrzej Szałas
Marcin Szczuka
Jesper Tegner
Shusaku Tsumoto
Gwo-Hshiung Tzeng
Alicja Wakulicz-Deja
Guoyin Wang
Anita Wasilewska
Michael Wong
Jakub Wroblewski
JingTao Yao
Takahira Yamaguchi
Yiyu Yao
Ning Zhong
Wojciech Ziarko

Table of Contents

Plenary Papers

Theory

Logic and Rough Sets

Granular Computing

Rough and Fuzzy Relations

Foundations of Data Mining

Incomplete Information Systems

Interestingness

Multiagents and Information Systems

Fuzzy Logic and Modeling

Rough Classification

Rough Sets and Probabilities

Variable Precision Rough Set Model

Spatial Reasoning

Reduction

Rule Induction

Rough Sets and Neural Network

Clustering

Data Mining

Image and Signal Recognition

Information Retrieval

Decision Support

Adaptive and Opminization Methods

Bioinformatics

Medical Applications

Bibliography Project of International Rough Set Society

Decision Networks

Zdzisław Pawlak[1,2]

[1] Institute for Theoretical and Applied Informatics
Polish Academy of Sciences
ul. Bałtycka 5, 44-100 Gliwice, Poland
[2] Warsaw School of Information Technology
ul. Newelska 6, 01-447 Warsaw, Poland
zpw@ii.pw.edu.pl

Abstract. A decision network is a finite, directed acyclic graph, nodes of which represent logical formulas, whereas branches - are interpreted as decision rules. Every path in the graph represents a chain of decision rules, which describe compound decision.
Some properties of decision networks will be given and a simple example will illustrate the presented ideas and show possible applications.

Keywords: decision rules, decision algorithms, decision networks

1 Introduction

The main problem in data mining consists in discovering patterns in data. The patterns are usually expressed in form of decision rules, which are logical expressions in the form "*if* Φ *then* Ψ", where Φ and Ψ are logical formulas (propositional functions) used to express properties of objects of interest. Any set of decision rules is called a *decision algorithm.* Thus knowledge discovery from data consists in representing hidden relationships between data in a form of decision algorithms. However, for some applications, it is not enough to give only set of decision rules describing relationships in the database. Sometimes also knowledge of relationship between decision rules is necessary in order to understand better data structures. To this end we propose to employ a decision algorithm in which also relationship between decision rules is pointed out, called a *decision network.*

The decision network is a finite, directed acyclic graph, nodes of which represent logical formulas, whereas branches – are interpreted as decision rules. Thus every path in the graph represents a chain of decisions rules, which will be used to describe compound decisions.

Some properties of decision networks will be given and a simple example will be used to illustrate the presented ideas and show possible applications.

2 Decision Networks and Decision Rules

Let U be a non empty finite set, called the *universe* and let Φ , Ψ be logical formulas. The meaning of Φ in U, denoted by $|\Phi|$, is the set of all elements

S. Tsumoto et al. (Eds.): RSCTC 2004, LNAI 3066, pp. 1–7, 2004.

of U, that satisfies Φ in U. The truth value of Φ denoted $val(\Phi)$ is defined as $card|\Phi|/card(U)$, where $card(X)$ denotes cardinaity of X.

By *decision network* over $S = (U, \mathcal{F})$ we mean a pair $N = (\mathcal{F}, \mathcal{R})$, where $\mathcal{R} \subseteq \mathcal{F} \times \mathcal{F}$ is a binary relation, called a *consequence relation* and $\mathcal{F}$ is a set of logical formulas.

Any pair $(\Phi, \Psi) \in \mathcal{R}, \Phi \neq \Psi$ is referred to as a decision rule (in N).

We assume that S is known and we will not refer to it in what follows.

A *decision rule* (Φ, Ψ) will be also presented as an expression $\Phi \rightarrow \Psi$, read *if* Φ *then* Ψ, where Φ and Ψ are referred to as *predesessor* (*conditions*) and *successor* (*decisions*) of the rule, respectively.

The number $supp(\Phi, \Psi) = card(|\Phi \wedge \Psi|)$ will be called a *support* of the rule $\Phi \rightarrow \Psi$. We will consider nonvoid decision rules only, i.e., rules such that $supp(\Phi, \Psi) \neq 0$.

With every decision rule $\Phi \rightarrow \Psi$ we associate its *strength* defined as

$$str(\Phi, \Psi) = \frac{supp(\Phi, \Psi)}{card(U)}. \tag{1}$$

Moreover, with every decision rule $\Phi \rightarrow \Psi$ we associate the *certainty factor* defined as

$$cer(\Phi, \Psi) = \frac{str(\Phi, \Psi)}{val(\Phi)} \tag{2}$$

and the *coverage factor* of $\Phi \rightarrow \Psi$

$$cov(\Phi, \Psi) = \frac{str(\Phi, \Psi)}{val(\Psi)}, \tag{3}$$

where $val(\Phi) \neq 0$ and $val(\Psi) \neq 0$.

The coefficients can be computed from data or can be a subjective assessment.

We assume that

$$val(\Phi) = \sum_{\Psi \in Suc(\Phi)} str(\Phi, \Psi) \tag{4}$$

and

$$val(\Psi) = \sum_{\Phi \in Pre(\Psi)} str(\Phi, \Psi), \tag{5}$$

where $Suc(\Phi)$ and $Pre(\Psi)$ are sets of all succesors and predecessors of the corresponding formulas, respectively.

Consequently we have

$$\sum_{Suc(\Phi)} cer(\phi, \Psi) = \sum_{Pre(\Psi)} cov(\Phi, \Psi) = 1. \tag{6}$$

If a decision rule $\Phi \rightarrow \Psi$ uniquely determines decisions in terms of conditions, i.e., if $cer(\Phi, \Psi) = 1$, then the rule is *certain*, otherwise the rule is *uncertain*.

If a decision rule $\Phi \rightarrow \Psi$ covers all decisions, i.e., if $cov(\Phi, \Psi) = 1$ then the decision rule is *total*, otherwise the decision rule is *partial*.

Immediate consequences of (2) and (3) are:

$$cer(\Phi, \Psi) = \frac{cov(\Phi, \Psi)val(\Psi)}{val(\Psi)}, \tag{7}$$

$$cov(\Phi, \Psi) = \frac{cer(\Phi, \Psi)val(\Phi)}{val(\Psi)}. \tag{8}$$

Note, that (7) and (8) are Bayes' formulas. This relationship first was observed by Łukasiewicz [1].

Any sequence of formulas $\Phi_1, \ldots, \Phi_n$, $\Phi_i \in \mathcal{F}$ and for every i, $1 \le i \le n-1$, $(\Phi_i, \Phi_{i+1}) \in \mathcal{R}$ will be called a *path* from Φ_1 to Φ_n and will be denoted by $[\Phi_1 \ldots \Phi_n]$.

We define

$$cer[\Phi_1 \ldots \Phi_n] = \prod_{i=1}^{n-1} cer[\Phi_i, \Phi_{i+1}], \tag{9}$$

$$cov[\Phi_1 \ldots \Phi_n] = \prod_{i=1}^{n-1} cov[\Phi_i, \Phi_{i+1}], \tag{10}$$

$$str[\Phi_1 \ldots \Phi_n] = val(\Phi_1)cer[\Phi_1 \ldots \Phi_n] = val(\Phi_n)cov[\Phi_1 \ldots \Phi_n]. \tag{11}$$

The set of all paths form Φ to Ψ, denoted $< \Phi, \Psi >$, will be called a *connection* from Φ to Ψ.

For connection we have

$$cer < \Phi, \Psi >= \sum_{[\Phi \ldots \Psi] \in < \Phi, \Psi >} cer[\Phi \ldots \Psi], \tag{12}$$

$$cov < \Phi, \Psi >= \sum_{[\Phi \ldots \Psi] \in < \Phi, \Psi >} cov[\Phi \ldots \Psi], \tag{13}$$

$$\begin{aligned} str < \Phi, \Psi > &= \sum_{[\Phi \ldots \Psi] \in < \Phi, \Psi >} str[\Phi \ldots \Psi] = \\ &= val(\Phi)cer < \Phi, \Psi >= val(\Psi)cov < \Phi, \Psi > . \end{aligned} \tag{14}$$

With every decision network we can associate a flow graph [2, 3]. Formulas of the network are interpreted as nodes of the graph, and decision rules – as directed branches of the flow graph, whereas strength of a decision rule is interpreted as flow of the corresponding branch.

3 Independence of Formulas

Independency of logical formulas considered in this section first was proposed by Łukasiewicz [1].

Let $\Phi \rightarrow \Psi$ be a decision rule. Formulas Φ and Ψ are *independent* on each other if

$$str(\Phi, \Psi) = val(\Phi)val(\Psi). \tag{15}$$

Consequently

$$\frac{str(\Phi, \Psi)}{val(\Phi)} = cer(\Phi, \Psi) = val(\Psi) \tag{16}$$

and

$$\frac{str(\Phi, \Psi)}{val(\Psi)} = cov(\Phi, \Psi) = val(\Phi). \tag{17}$$

If

$$cer(\Phi, \Psi) > val(\Psi) \tag{18}$$

or

$$cov(\Phi, \Psi) > val(\Phi), \tag{19}$$

then Φ and Ψ *depend positively* on each other. Similarly, if

$$cer(\Phi, \Psi) < val(\Psi) \tag{20}$$

or

$$cov(\Phi, \Psi) < val(\Phi), \tag{21}$$

then Φ and Ψ *depend negatively* on each other.

Let us observe that relations of independency and dependency are symmetric ones, and are analogous to that used in statistics.

For every decision rule $\Phi \rightarrow \Psi$ we define a *dependency factor* $\eta(\Phi, \Psi)$ defined as

$$\eta(\Phi, \Psi) = \frac{cer(\Phi, \Psi) - val(\Psi)}{cer(\Phi, \Psi) + val(\Psi)} = \frac{cov(\Phi, \Psi) - val(\Phi)}{cov(\Phi, \Psi) + val(\Phi)}. \tag{22}$$

It is easy to check that if $\eta(\Phi, \Psi) = 0$, then Φ and Ψ are independent on each other, if $-1 < \eta(\Phi, \Psi) < 0$, then Φ and Ψ are negatively dependent and if $0 < \eta(\Phi, \Psi) < 1$ then Φ and Ψ are positively dependent on each other. Thus the dependency factor expresses a degree of dependency, and can be seen as a counterpart of correlation coefficient used in statistics.

Another dependency factor has been proposed in [4].

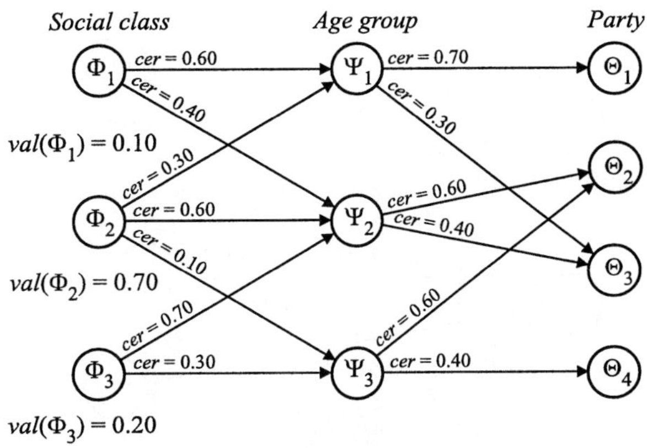

Fig. 1. Initial votes distribution.

4 An Example

Consider three disjoint age groups of voters Ψ_1 (*old*), Ψ_2 (*middle aged*) and Ψ_3 (*young*) – belonging to three social classes Φ_1 (*high*), Φ_2 (*middle*) and Φ_3 (*low*). The voters voted for four political parties Θ_1 (*Conservatives*), Θ_2 (*Labor*), Θ_3 (*Liberal Democrats*) and Θ_4 (*others*).

Social class and age group votes distribution is shown in Fig. 1.

First, we compute, employing formula (2), strength of each branch joining *Social class* and *Age group*. Having done this we can compute coverage factors for each *Age group* and using formula (5) we compute $val(\Psi_i)$.Repeating this procedure for *Age group* and *Party* we get results shown in Fig.2.

From the decision network presented in Fig. 2 we can see that, e.g., party Θ_1 obtained 19% of total votes, all of them from age group Ψ_1; party Θ_2 – 44% votes, which 82% are from age group Ψ_2 and 18% – from age group Ψ_3, etc.

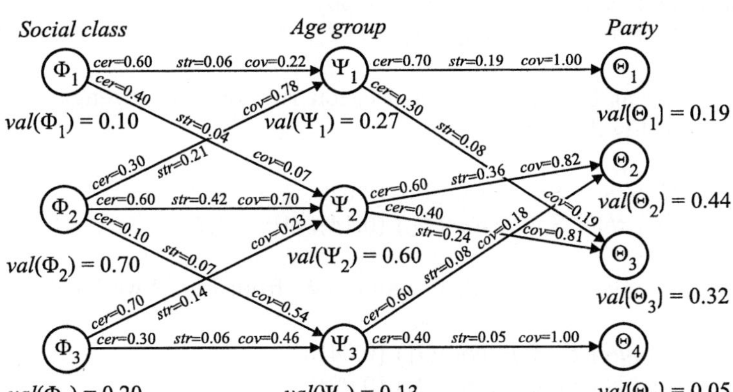

Fig. 2. Final votes distribution.

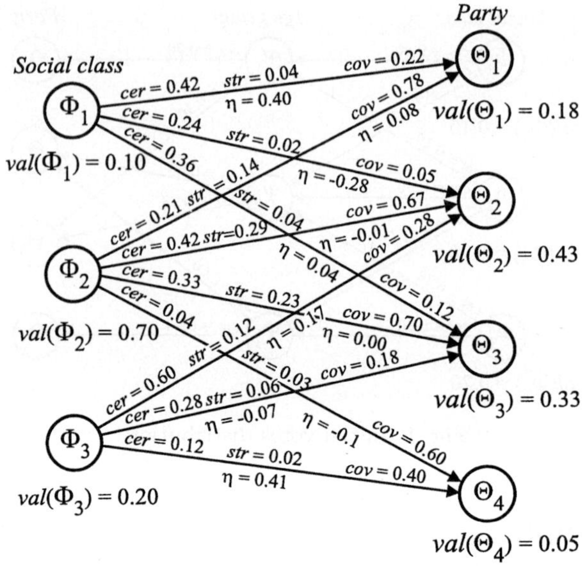

Fig. 3. Simplified decision network.

If we want to know how votes are distributed between parties with respects to social classes we have to eliminate age groups from the decision network. Employing formulas (9),...,(14) we get results shown in Fig. 3.

From the decision network presented in Fig. 3 we can see that party Θ_1 obtained 22% votes from social class Φ_1 and 78% from social class Φ_2, etc.

We can also present the obtained results employing decision algorithms. For simplicity we present only some decision rules of the decision algorithm. For example, from Fig.2 we obtain decision rules:

If Party (Θ_1) *then Age group* (Ψ_1) (0.19)
If Party (Θ_2) *then Age group* (Ψ_2) (0.36)
If Party (Θ_2) *then Age group* (Ψ_3) (0.08), etc.

The number at the end of each decision rule denotes strength of the rule. Similarly, from Fig.3 we get:

If Party (Θ_1) *then Soc. class* (Φ_1) (0.04)
If Party (Θ_1) *then Soc. class* (Φ_2) (0.14), etc.

We can also invert decision rules and, e.g., from Fig. 3 we have:

If Soc. class (Φ_1) *then Party* (Θ_1) (0.04)
If Soc. class (Φ_1) *then Party* (Θ_2) (0.02)
If Soc. class (Φ_1) *then Party* (Θ_3) (0.04), etc

In Fig. 3 values of dependency factors are also shown. It can be seen from the diagram that e.g., Φ_1 and Θ_1 are positively dependent ($\eta = 0.40$), whereas Φ_3 and Θ_3 are negatively dependent ($\eta = -0.07$). That means that there is relatively strong positive dependency between high social class and Conservatives, whereas there is very low negative dependency between low social class and Liberal Democrats.

5 Conclusion

In this paper a concept of decision network is introduced and examined. Basic properties of decision networks are given and their application to decision analysis is shown. Simple tutorial example at the end of the paper shows the possible application of the introduced ideas.

References

1. Łukasiewicz, J.: Die logishen Grundlagen der Wahrscheinilchkeitsrechnung. Kraków (1913), in: L. Borkowski (ed.), Jan Łukasiewicz – Selected Works, North Holland Publishing Company, Amsterdam, London, Polish Scientific Publishers, Warsaw (1970) 16-63
2. Pawlak, Z.: Probability, Truth and Flow Graphs, in: RSKD – International Workshop and Soft Computing, ETAPS 2003, A. Skowron, M. Szczuka (eds.), Warsaw (2003) 1-9
3. Pawlak, Z.: Flow graphs and decision algorithms, in: G. Wang, Q. Liu, Y. Y. Yao, A. Skowron (eds.), Proceedings of the Ninth International Conference on Rough Sets, Fuzzy Sets, Data Mining and Granular Computing RSFDGrC'2003), Chongqing, China, May 26-29, 2003, LNAI 2639, Springer-Verlag, Berlin, Heidelberg, New York, 1-11
4. Słowiński, R., Greco, S.: A note on dependency factor (manuscript).

Toward Rough Set Foundations. Mereological Approach

Lech Polkowski

Polish–Japanese Institute of Information Technology
Koszykowa 86, 02008 Warsaw, Poland
Department of Mathematics and Computer Science
University of Warmia and Mazury, Żołnierska 14a, 10561 Olsztyn, Poland
{Lech.Polkowski,polkow}@pjwstk.edu.pl

Abstract. In this semi–plenary lecture, we would like to discuss rough inclusions defined in Rough Mereology, a joint idea with Andrzej Skowron, as a basis for models for rough set theory. We demonstrate that mereological theory of rough sets extends and generalizes rough set theory written down in naive set theory framework.

Keywords: rough set theory, rough mereology, rough inclusions, granulation, granular rough set theory.

1 Introduction: Rough Set Principles

An information system (Pawlak, see [14]) is a well–known way of presenting data; it is symbolically represented as a pair $\mathbf{A}=(U, A)$. The symbol U denotes a set of *objects*, and the symbol A denotes the set of *attributes*. Each pair *(attribute, object)* is uniquely assigned a *value*: given $a \in A, u \in U$, the value $a(u)$ is an element of the *value set* V.

1.1 Information Sets

In this setting, the problem of ambiguity of description arises, that is approached by rough set theory (Pawlak , see [15]). Each object $u \in U$ is represented in the information system $\mathbf{A}$ by its *information set* $Inf_A(u) = \{(a, a(u)) : a \in A\}$, that corresponds to the row u–th of the data table $\mathbf{A}$.

Two objects, u, w, may have the same information set: $Inf(u) = Inf(w)$, in which case they are said to be *A–indiscernible* (Pawlak, see [14], [15]); the relation $IND(A) = \{(u, w) : Inf_A(u) = Inf_A(w)\}$ is said to be the *A–indiscernibility* relation. It is an equivalence relation. The symbol $[u]_A$ denotes the equivalence class of the relation $IND(A)$ containing u.

Attributes in the set A define in the universe U *concepts*; a concept $X \subseteq U$ is defined by A (is *A–definable*) whenever for each $u \in U$, either $[u]_A \subseteq X$ or $[u]_A \subseteq U \setminus X$. It follows that a concept X is A–definable if and only if X is a union of equivalence classes: $X = \bigcup\{[u]_A : u \in X\}$.

S. Tsumoto et al. (Eds.): RSCTC 2004, LNAI 3066, pp. 8–25, 2004.

A–definable sets have regular properties: their unions, intersections and complements in set–theoretical sense are also A–definable, i.e., A–definable sets form a *field of sets.*

In terms of definable sets other important ideas may be expressed.

1.2 Indiscernibility

First, it may be observed that the notion of indiscernibility may be defined with respect to any set $B \subseteq A$ of attributes, i. e., a *B–information set* $Inf_B(u) = \{(a, a(u)) : a \in B\}$ is defined and then the relation of *B–indiscernibility*,

$IND(B) = \{(u, w) : Inf_B(u) = Inf_B(w)\}$

is introduced, classes of which form *B–definable sets.*

Minimal with respect to inclusion subsets of the set A that preserve A–definable sets are called *A–reducts.* In analogy, any minimal subset $C \subseteq B \subseteq A$ with the property that $IND(C) = IND(B)$ is said to be a *B–reduct.*

In terms of indiscernibility relations, important relationships between sets of attributes can be expressed: the containment $IND(B) \subseteq IND(C)$ means that $[u]_B \subseteq [u]_C$ for each $u \in U$, and hence, $Inf_C(u)$ is uniquely defined for $Inf_B(u)$ witnessing to the *functional dependence* $\phi_{B,C} : INF(B) \to INF(C)$, where $INF(B) = \{Inf_B(u) : u \in U\}$, written down in the form of the symbol $B \Rightarrow C$.

1.3 Rough Sets

Given a set B of attributes, and a concept $X \subseteq U$, that is not B–definable, there exists $u \in U$ with neither $[u]_B \subseteq X$ nor $[u]_B \subseteq U \setminus X$. Thus, B–definable sets,

$B_{LOW}X = \{u \in U : [u]_B \subseteq X\}$ and $B^{UPP}X = \{u \in U : [u]_B \cap X \neq \emptyset\}$

are distinct, and $B_{LOW}X \subseteq X \subseteq B^{UPP}X$. The set $B_{LOW}X$ is the *lower B–approximation* to X whereas $B^{UPP}X$ is the *upper B–approximation* to X. The concept X is said to be *B–rough.*

1.4 Decision Systems

A particular case of information systems, *decision systems* are triples of the form $\mathbf{A}^d = (U, A, d)$ with (U, A) an information system, and d a *decision attribute,* $d : U \to V_d$, $d \notin A$. Relationships between the *conditional attributes* A, and the decision attribute d, may be of the form of functional dependence $A \Rightarrow \{d\}$ (in case $IND(A) \subseteq IND(\{d\})$) but it may be the case that $IND(A) \subseteq IND(\{d\})$ does not hold. In the latter case, a solution (Novotný and Pawlak, see [11]) is to restrict the set of objects to the set $POS_A^d = \{u \in U : [u]_A \subseteq [u]_d\}$, over which the functional dependence $A \Rightarrow \{d\}$ takes place.

1.5 Measures of Containment

In cases of a rough concept, or non–functional dependence, some measures of departure from exactness, or functionality have been proposed. In the former case of a B–rough set, the *approximation quality* (Pawlak, see [14]) $\gamma = \frac{|B_{LOW}X|}{|B^{UPP}X|}$ measures by means of the quotient of cardinalities of approximations the degree to which X is exact. Clearly, degree 1 indicates an exact set. The degree to which the dependence $A \Rightarrow \{d\}$ is functional is measured (Novotný and Pawlak, see [11])by the fraction $\beta = \frac{|POS_A(d)|}{|U|}$. Again, $\beta = 1$ means the functional dependence.

Measures like γ, β above may be traced back to the idea of Jan Łukasiewicz, see [10], of assigning fractional truth values to unary predicative implications of the form $\chi(u) \Rightarrow \xi(u)$ where u runs over a finite set U. The degree of truth of the implication was defined in [10] as the value of $\frac{|\{u \in U: \chi(u) \wedge \xi(u)|}{|\{u \in U: \chi(u)\}|}$.

1.6 Rough Sets and Rough Membership

The idea of a measure of degree of roughness was implemented by means of a *rough membership function* (Pawlak and Skowron, see [16]). Given a concept X, and a set of attributes B, the rough membership function $\mu_B^X : U \to [0,1]$ is defined by letting for $u \in U$,

$$\mu_B^X(u) = \frac{|[u]_B \cap X|}{|[u]_B|}. \tag{1}$$

One may observe that $\mu_B^X(u) = 1$ means that $[u]_B \subseteq X$ i.e., $u \in B_{LOW}X$, whereas $\mu_B^X(u) = 0$ means that $u \in U \setminus B^{UPP}X$. Thus, X is an exact concept if and only if $\mu_B^X : U \to \{0,1\}$. The value of $\mu_B^X(u)$ can be regarded as an estimate of the probability that a random object from the B–class of u is in X based on the information contained in B.

A B–rough concept X is characterized by the existence of an object u with $0 < \mu_B^X(u) < 1$.

2 A Set Theory for Rough Sets

On the basis of discussion of exact and rough sets in sects. 1.2, 1.3, it seems plausible to introduce a notion of an element relative to an information system $\mathbf{A}$=(U, A), and a set of attributes $B \subseteq A$, denoted $el_B^{\mathbf{A}}$ and defined by letting,

$$u el_B^{\mathbf{A}} X \Leftrightarrow [u]_B \subseteq X. \tag{2}$$

This notion of an element satisfies the basic property of the element notion, i.e.,

$$u el_B^{\mathbf{A}} X \wedge X \subseteq Y \Rightarrow u el_B^{\mathbf{A}} Y. \tag{3}$$

It is obvious that properties of this notion with respect to operations in a field of sets over U are in correspondence with the well–known properties of lower approximations.

We introduce a property of concepts,

(P(X)) for each $u \in U$, it is true that $uel^{\mathbf{A}}_{B}X \vee uel^{\mathbf{A}}_{B}U \setminus X$,

and we observe that,

a concept $T \subseteq U$ is B–exact if and only if $P(T)$ holds,
and,
a concept $T \subseteq U$ is B–rough if and only if $P(T)$ does not hold.

2.1 Mereology

We have seen that a formal rendering of duality exact/rough by means of the notion of an element in a set theory requires the notion of an element based on containment (subset) relation in naive set theory. By adopting this approach, we are entering the realm of set theories based on the notion of containment between objects, i.e., mereological set theories.

3 Mereology

From among mereological theories of sets, we choose the chronologically first, and conceptually most elegant, viz., the mereology proposed by Leśniewski (1916), see [7]. In what follows, we outline the basics of mereology, guided by a model of mereology provided by a field of sets with the relation of a subset. This, we hope, will clarify the notions introduced and will set a link between mereology and naive set theory.

We assume when discussing mereology that all objects considered are non–vacuous.

3.1 Parts

The notion of a part is basic for the Leśniewski mereology. The relation of being a part, denoted π, satisfies the requirements,

(P1) $x\pi y \wedge y\pi z \Rightarrow x\pi z.$
(P2) $x\pi y \Rightarrow \neg(y\pi x).$

It follows that $x\pi x$ holds for no x.

The relation of proper containment $\subset$ in a field of sets satisfies (P1), (P2).

The notion of a π*–element* (mereological element), $el(\pi)$, is defined as follows,

(El) $xel(\pi)y \Leftrightarrow x\pi y \vee x = y.$

By (El) and (P1-2), the notion of $el(\pi)$ has the following properties,

(El1) $xel(\pi)x$.
(El2) $xel(\pi)y \wedge yel(\pi)x \Rightarrow x = y$.
(El3) $xel(\pi)y \wedge yel(\pi)z \Rightarrow xel(\pi)z$,

i.e., $el(\pi)$ is a partial ordering on the mereological universe.

It follows by (El) that $el(\subset) = \subseteq$ is the mereological element relation in any field of sets.

3.2 Class Operator

In mereology due to Leśniewski, the relation of a part is defined for individual objects, not for collections of objects (in our presentation here this aspect is not highlighted because we omit the ontology scheme that in Leśniewski's theory precedes mereology), and this operator allows to make collections of objects into an object.

The definition of the class operator is based on the notion of element $el(\pi)$; we denote this operator with the symbol Cls_π. Given a non–empty collection M of objects, the class of M, denoted $Cls_\pi M$, is the object that satisfies the following requirements,

(Cls1) if $x \in M$ then $xel(\pi)Cls_\pi M$.
(Cls2) if $xel(\pi)Cls_\pi M$ then there exist objects y, z with the properties that $yel(\pi)x$, $yel(\pi)z$, and $z \in M$.
(Cls3) for each non–empty collection M, the class $Cls_\pi M$ exists and it is unique.

The requirement (Cls1) responds to the demand that each object in M be an element of the individual $Cls_\pi M$, and (Cls2) states that each element (viz., x) of $Cls_\pi M$ must have an element in common (viz., y) with an object (viz., z) in M, assuring that no superfluous object falls into the class of M.

The reader has certainly observed that the object $Cls_\subset M$ in case of a collection M of sets in a field of sets, is the union set $\bigcup M$.

From (Cls1-3), a rule follows, that is useful later in our discussion,

(INF) for given x, y, if for every z such that $zel_\pi x$ there exists t such that $zel_\pi t$ and $tel_\pi y$, then $xel_\pi y$.

We may conclude that mereology, a set theory based on the notion of a part, is a feasible vehicle for a non–standard set theory that renders intuitions fundamental to rough set theory, and commonly expressed in the language of naive set theory at the cost of operating with collections of objects, not objects themselves.

Following this line of analysis, we may define a more general version of rough set theory that does encompass the classical rough set theory as defined in (Pawlak, see op.cit., op.cit.).

3.3 Generalized Rough Set Theory (GRST)

An object of GRST will be a tuple $< (U, A), \mathcal{M}, \pi >$, where (U, A) is an information system, $\mathcal{M}$ is a collection of concepts (i.e., subsets of the universe U), and π is the relation of a part on the collection of (non–empty) concepts.

In this setting, we define *generalized exact sets* as classes of (non–empty) sub–families of $\mathcal{M}$. Denoting the class of generalized exact sets by $\mathcal{E}$, we have,

(E) $X \in \mathcal{E}$ if an only if either $X = \emptyset$ or $X = Cls_{\pi}\mathcal{N}$ for some non–empty sub–collection $\mathcal{N}$ of $\mathcal{M}$.

Letting π to be $\subset$ and $\mathcal{M}_{IND}$ to be the collection $\{[u]_A : u \in u\}$ for an information system (U, A), we obtain as $\mathcal{E}$ the class of A–definable sets.

We may, in the context of an information system (U, A), introduce a notion of part based on the lower approximation; to this end, we define a part relation π_{LOW} as follows: $X \pi_{LOW} Y$ if and only if $A_{LOW}X \subseteq A_{LOW}Y \wedge X \subset Y$ (rough lower part). The class construction yields then as the class $Cls_{\pi_{LOW}}\mathcal{M}_{IND}$ the class of A–definable sets, again.

Analogous construct in this mereological framework may be performed for the case of upper approximations (rough upper part) and in the case of rough equality (rough part) (see (Novotný and Pawlak [12]).

A problem arises of identifying useful in the application context part relations. Other possibility is to relax the notion of a part and to consider its graded variants.

4 Rough Mereology

We have seen in sect. 2.1 that mereology–based theory of sets is a proper theory of sets for rough set theory. In order to accomodate variants of rough set theory like Variable Precision Rough Sets (Ziarko, see [26]), and to account for modern paradigms like granular computing (Zadeh, see [6], [8], [22]), or computing with words (Zadeh, [25], see also [13]), it is suitable to extend the mereology based rough set theory by considering a more general relation of a part to a degree.

4.1 Set Partial Inclusions

As a starting point, we can consider the rough membership function of sect. 1.6. From the formula defining μ_B^X, a more general formula may be derived, viz., given two concepts X, Y, with X non–empty, we may form the quotient $\frac{|X \cap Y|}{|X|}$ as a measure of a degree to which X is Y. This measure, that we denote with the symbol μ satisfies the following,

(SI1) $\mu(X, X) = 1$.
(SI2) $\mu(X, Y) = 1$ if and only if $X \subseteq Y$.
(SI3) if $\mu(X, Y) = 1$ then $\mu(Z, X) \leq \mu(Z, Y)$ for each non–empty set Z.

We will call *set partial inclusions* functions defined on pairs of non–empty sets and satisfying (SI1-3).

Assuming that X, Y are subsets of a fixed finite universe U, and considering predicates $X(u), Y(u)$ defined as $X(u) : u \in X, Y(u) : u \in Y$, we see that $\mu(X,Y)$ is the degree to which the formula $X(u) \Rightarrow Y(u)$ is true, according to Łukasiewicz [10].

Clearly, μ has also probabilistic flavor as the conditional probability of X with respect to Y.

Measures based on μ are frequently met, e.g., in rough membership functions (Pawlak and Skowron, op.cit.), accuracy and coverage coefficients for decision rules (Tsumoto, [20]), association rules (Agrawal et al., [1]), variable precision rough sets (Ziarko, [26]), approximation spaces (Skowron and Stepaniuk, [19]). It seems therefore imperative to study the general context of such measures.

4.2 Rough Inclusions

We consider a universe U of non–empty objects along with a mereological relation π of a part, inducing the mereological element relation el_π.

A *rough inclusion* (Polkowski and Skowron, see [18])), is a relation $\mu \subseteq U \times U \times [0,1]$ that satisfies the following requirements,

(RI1) $\mu_\pi(x, x, 1)$ for each $x \in U$.
(RI2) $\mu_\pi(x, y, 1)$ if and only if $x el_\pi y$ for each pair x, y of elements of U.
(RI3) if $\mu_\pi(x, y, 1)$ then for each $z \in U$, and each $r \in [0,1]$, the implication holds: if $\mu_\pi(z, x, r)$ then $\mu_\pi(z, y, r)$.
(RI4) if $\mu_\pi(x, y, r)$ and $s < r$ then $\mu_\pi(x, y, s)$.

Clearly, letting, U to be the collection of non–empty subsets of a given non–empty finite set Ω, π the relation $\subset$, and el_π the relation $\subseteq$, we obtain a rough inclusion $\mu_\subset(X, Y, r)$ with $\mu_\subset(X, Y, r)$ true if $\frac{|X \cap Y|}{|X|} \geq r$. Clearly, there may be many μ's satisfying (RI1-4) with $\subseteq$ as the mereological element in (RI2), e.g, for any increasing strictly function $\phi : [0,1] \to [0,1]$ with $\phi(1) = 1$, the relation $\mu_\subset(X, Y, r)$ if and only if $\phi(\frac{|X \cap Y|}{|X|}) \geq r$; our purpose here is only to observe that the formula used in definitions of rough membership functions, accuracy and coverage coefficients, variable precision rough set models, etc., etc., can be used to define a rough inclusion on any collection of non–empty finite sets.

It seems that (RI1-4) is a collection of general properties of rough inclusions that sums up properties of partial containment. Neither symmetry nor transitivity hold in general for rough inclusions, as borne out by simple examples.

However, we recall a form of transitivity property as well as a form of symmetry of rough inclusions.

4.3 Transitivity and Symmetry of Rough Inclusions

Transitivity of rough inclusions was addressed in (Polkowski and Skowron, op.cit.) where a result was proved,

Proposition 1. *Given a rough inclusion* μ*, and a t–norm* T*, the relation* ν *defined by the statement:* $\nu(x, y, r)$ *if and only if for each object* z *there exist* $s_z, t_z \in [0, 1]$ *such that* $\mu(z, x, s_z), \mu(z, y, t_z)$ *hold and* $min_z \overline{T}(s_z, t_z) \geq r$*, where* $\overline{T}$ *is the residuated implication induced by* T [1] *is a rough inclusion that satisfies the* T*–transitivity rule* $\frac{\nu(x,y,r),\nu(y,z,s)}{\nu(x,z,T(r,s))}$.

Symmetric rough inclusions may be obtained from rough inclusions in a natural way: given a rough inclusion μ, we let $\mu_S(x, y, r)$ to hold if and only if $\mu(x, y, r)$ and $\mu(y, x, r)$ hold. Then μ_S is a rough inclusion.

In the next section, we address the problem of rough inclusions in information systems, where objects considered will be elements of the universe as well as certain concepts. We adopt a different approach than that of Proposition 1 as the latter leads to very small values and thus is of solely theoretical importance.

4.4 Rough Inclusions in Information Systems

We would like to begin with single elements of the universe U of an information system (U, A), on which to define rough inclusions.

First, we want to address the problem of transitive rough inclusions in the sense of sect. 4.2.

We recall that a t–norm T is *archimedean* if in addition to already stated properties (see footnote 1), it is continuous and $T(x, x) < x$ for each $x \in (0, 1)$. It is well known (Ling, see [9], cf. [17]) that any archimedean t–norm T, can be represented in the form,

$$T(x, y) = g(f(x) + f(y)), \tag{4}$$

where $f : [0, 1] \to [0, 1]$ is continuous decreasing and g is the pseudo–inverse to f[2].

We will consider the quotient set $U_{IND} = U/IND(A)$, and we define attributes on U_{IND} by means of the formula, $a([u]_{IND(A)}) = a(u)$.

For each pair x, y of elements of U_{IND}, we define the *discernibility set*,

$$DIS(x, y) = \{a \in A : a(x) \neq a(y)\} \subseteq A.$$

For an archimedean t–norm, T, we define a relation μ_T by letting,

$$\mu_T(x, y, r) \text{holds if and only if } g(\frac{|DIS(x, y)|}{|A|}) \geq r. \tag{5}$$

[1] For reading convenience, we recall that a t–norm, T, is a function from $[0, 1]^2$ into $[0, 1]$ that is symmetric, increasing in each coordinate, associative, and such that $T(1, x) = x, T(0, 0) = 0$ for each $x \in [0, 1]$. The residuated implication $\overline{T}$ is defined by the condition $z \leq \overline{T}(x, y) \Leftrightarrow T(z, x) \leq y$.

[2] This means that $g(x) = 1$ for $x \in [0, f(1)]$, $g(x) = 0$ for $x \in [f(0), 1]$, and $g(x) = f^{-1}(x)$ for $x \in [f(1), f(0)]$.

Proposition 2. *μ_T is a rough inclusion that satisfies the transitivity rule:*

if $\mu_T(x, y, r)$ and $\mu_T(y, z, s)$ then $\mu_T(x, z, T(r, s))$.

Proof. We have $\mu_T(x, x, 1)$ as $DIS(x, x) = \emptyset$ and $g(0) = 1$. Further, $\mu_T(x, y, 1)$ implies $DIS(x, y) = \emptyset$ hence $x = y$. This implies (RI3), and (RI4) clearly is satisfied by definition.
Concerning the transitivity rule, let us observe that,

$DIS(x, z) \subseteq DIS(x, y) \cup DIS(y, z)$,

so $\frac{|DIS(x,z)|}{|A|} \leq \frac{|DIS(x,y)|}{|A|} + \frac{|DIS(y,z)|}{|A|}$;
let
$g(\frac{|DIS(x,y)|}{|A|}) = r_1$, $g(\frac{|DIS(y,z)|}{|A|}) = s_1$, $g(\frac{|DIS(x,z)|}{|A|}) = t$.
Hence,
$\frac{|DIS(x,y)|}{|A|} = f(r_1)$, $\frac{|DIS(y,z)|}{|A|} = f(s_1)$,$\frac{|DIS(x,z)|}{|A|} = f(t)$,
and,
$f(t) \leq f(r_1) + f(s_1)$, hence, $t = g(f(t)) \geq g(f(r_1) + f(s_1)) = T(r_1, s_1) \geq T(r, s)$, witness to $\mu_T(x, z, T(r, s))$.

Proposition 2 paves the way to rough inclusions satisfying transitivity rules with archimedean t–norms.

Example 1. Particular examples of rough inclusions are the *Menger rough inclusion,* (MRI, in short) and the Łukasiewicz rough inclusion (LRI, in short), corresponding, respectively, to the Menger (product) t–norm $T_M(x, y) = x \cdot y$, and the Łukasiewicz product t–norm $T_L(x, y) = max\{0, x + y - 1\}$.

The Menger Rough Inclusion. For the t–norm T_M, the *generating function* $f(x) = -lnx$ whereas $g(y) = e^{-y}$ is the pseudo–inverse to f. According to Proposition 2, the rough inclusion μ_{T_M} is given by the formula,

$$\mu_{T_M}(x, y, r) \text{if and only if } e^{-\frac{|DIS(x,y)|}{|A|}} \geq r. \tag{6}$$

The Łukasiewicz Rough Inclusion. For t–norm T_L, the generating function $f(x) = 1 - x$ and $g = f$ is the pseudo–inverse to f. Therefore,

$$\mu_{T_L}(x, y, r) \text{if and only if} 1 - \frac{|DIS(x, y)|}{|A|} \geq r. \tag{7}$$

Expanding the function $e^{-\frac{|DIS(x,y)|}{|A|}} = 1 - -\frac{|DIS(x,y)|}{|A|} + \frac{1}{2!} \cdot (\frac{|DIS(x,y)|}{|A|})^2 - \ldots.$. and assuming that the expected value of $|DIS(x, y)| = \frac{|A|}{2}$, we obtain μ_{T_L} as a fair approximation to μ_{T_M} with expected error about 0.1. In the sequel, our examples will make use of μ_{T_L}.

In case of non–archimedean t–norms, the above approach does not work directly, as it is well-known that,e.g., in any representation (4) the function f is neither continuous nor decreasing (see, e.g., [9]). We leave this case for now open.

Let us observe that rough inclusions based on sets DIS are necessarily symmetric.

Let us show a simple example.

Example 2. Information system $\mathcal{A}$

Table 1. The information system $\mathcal{A}$

U	a_1	a_2	a_3	a_4
x_1	1	1	1	2
x_2	1	0	1	0
x_3	2	0	1	1
x_4	3	2	1	0
x_5	3	1	1	0
x_6	3	2	1	2
x_7	1	2	0	1
x_8	2	0	0	2

For the information system $\mathcal{A}$, we calculate values of LRI, shown in Table 2; as μ_{T_L} is symmetric, we show only the upper triangle of values.

Example 3. Values of μ_{T_L} for the universe of Table 1

Table 2. μ_{T_L} for Table 1

U	x_1	x_2	x_3	x_4	x_5	x_6	x_7	x_8
x_1	1	0.5	0.25	0.25	0.5	0.5	0.25	0.25
x_2	-	1	0.5	0.5	0.5	0.25	0.25	0.25
x_3	-	-	1	0.25	0.25	0.25	0.25	0.5
x_4	-	-	-	1	0.75	0.75	0.25	0
x_5	-	-	-	-	1	0.5	0	0
x_6	-	-	-	-	-	1	0.25	0.25
x_7	-	-	-	-	-	-	1	0.25
x_8	-	-	-	-	-	-	-	1

Rough Inclusions over Relational Information Systems. In some applications, a need may arise, to stratify objects more subtly than it is secured by sets DIS. A particular answer to this need can be provided by a relational information system by which we mean a system (U, A, R), where $R = \{R_a : a \in A\}$ with $R_a \subseteq V_a \times V_a$ a relation in the value set V_a.

A modified set $DIS^R(x,y) = \{a \in A : R_a(a(x), a(y))\}$. Then, for any archimedean t–norm T, and non–reflexive, non–symmetric, transitive, and linear, relation R, we define the rough inclusion μ_T^R by the modified formula, $\mu_T^R(x,y,r)$ if and only if $g(\frac{|DIS^R(x,y)|}{|A|} \geq r$,
where g is the pseudo–inverse to f in the representation (4); clearly, the notion of a part is: $x\pi^R y$ if and only if $x \neq y$ and $R_a(a(y), a(x))$ for each $a \in A$.

Particularly important is the case of preference relations (Greco, Słowiński et al., see [4]), where $R_a =<_a$ is a linear order on V_a for each $a \in A$.

Let us look at values of $\mu_{T_L}^{<}$ for the information system in Table 2 with value sets ordered linearly as a subset of real numbers.

Example 4. Values of $\mu_{T_L}^{<}$ for the universe of Table 1

Table 3. $\mu^{<}T_L$ for Table 1

U	x_1	x_2	x_3	x_4	x_5	x_6	x_7	x_8
x_1	1	1	0.75	0.5	0.5	0.5	0.75	0.75
x_2	0.5	1	0.5	0.5	0.5	0.25	0.5	0.5
x_3	0.5	1	1	0.5	0.5	0.25	0.75	0.75
x_4	0.75	1	0.75	1	1	0.75	0.75	0.75
x_5	0.75	1	0.75	0.75	1	0.5	0.5	0.75
x_6	1	1	1	1	1	1	1	1
x_7	0.5	0.75	0.5	0.5	0.5	0.25	1	0.5
x_8	0.5	0.75	0.75	0.25	0.25	0.25	0.75	1

As expected, the modified rough inclusion is non–symmetric and takes larger values; moreover, granules are R–hereditary: each granule $g_r(x)$ contains as elements all y with $R_a(a(y), a(x))$ for each $a \in A$. We now discuss problems of granulation of knowledge, showing an approach to them by means of rough inclusions.

5 Rough Mereological Granulation

We assume a rough inclusion μ on a mereological universe (U, el_π) with a part relation π. For given $r < 1$ and $x \in U$, we let,

$$g_r(x) = Cls(\Psi_r), \tag{8}$$

where

$$\Psi_r(y) \Leftrightarrow y\mu_r x. \tag{9}$$

The class $g_r(x)$ collects all atomic objects satisfying the class definition with the concept Ψ_r.

We will call the class $g_r(x)$ the *r–granule* about x; it may be interpreted as a neighborhood of x of radius r. We may also regard the formula $y\mu_r x$ as stating *similarity* of y to x (to degree r). We do not discuss here the problem of representation of granules; in general, one may apply sets or lists as the underlying representation structure.

Proposition 3. *The following are general properties of the granule operator g_r induced by a rough inclusion μ.*

1. *if $\mu(y,x,r)$ then $y el_\pi g_r(x)$.*
2. *if $\mu(x,y,r) \wedge y el_\pi z$ then $x el_\pi g_r(z)$.*
3. *$\forall z.[z el_\pi y \Rightarrow \exists w,q.(w el_\pi z \wedge w el_\pi q \wedge \mu(q,x,r)] \Rightarrow y el_\pi g_r(x)$.*
4. *if $y el_\pi g_r(x) \wedge z el_\pi y$ then $z el_\pi g_r(x)$.*
5. *if $s \leq r$ then $g_r(x) el_\pi g_s(x)$.*

Proof. Property 1 follows by definition of g_r and class definition (Cls1-3). Property 2 is implied by (RI3) and property 1. Property 3 follows by the inference rule (INF). Property 4 follows by transitivity of el_π. Property 5 is a consequence of (RI4).

By Proposition 3, the system $\{g_r(x) : x \in U, r \in [0,1]\}$ is a neighborhood system for a weak topology on the universe U.

5.1 Granulation via Archimedean t–Norm Based Rough Inclusions

For an archimedean t–norm T — induced rough inclusion μ_T, we have a more detailed result, viz.,

Proposition 4. *The following property holds for granules defined in terms of the rough inclusion μ_T:*
6. for each $x, y \in U_{IND}$, the equivalence: $x el_\pi g_r(y)$ if and only if $\mu_T(x,y,r)$.

Proof. Consider x, y, r as in claim 6. As $x el_\pi g_r(y)$, there exist by class definition, $u, w \in U_{IND}$ with properties, $u el_\pi x$, $u el_\pi q$, and $\mu_T(q,y,r)$.

By transitivity property, we have $\mu_T(u,y,T(1,r))$, i.e., $\mu_T(u,y,r)$; $\mu_T(u,x,1)$, by symmetry of μ_T, implies $\mu_T(x,u,1)$, hence, by transitivity property again, $\mu_T(x,y,T(1,r)$, i.e., $\mu_T(x,y,r)$.

The converse implication is Proposition 3. 1.

In particular, Proposition 4 holds for MRI and LRI.

Example 5. We consider the information system of Table 2 along with values of rough inclusions $\mu_{T_L}, \mu^{<}_{T_L}$ given, respectively, in Tables 2, 3. Admitting $r = .5$, we list below granules of radii .5 about objects $x_1 - x_8$ in both cases. We denote with the symbol $g_i, g_i^{<}$, respectively, the granule $g_{0.5}(x_i)$ defined by $\mu_{T_L}, \mu^{<}_{T_L}$, respectively, presenting them as sets.

We have,

1. $g_1 = \{x_1, x_2, x_5, x_6\}$,
2. $g_2 = \{x_1, x_2, x_3, x_4, x_5\}$,
3. $g_3 = \{x_2, x_3, x_8\}$,

4. $g_4 = \{x_2, x_4, x_5, x_6\}$,
5. $g_5 = \{x_1, x_2, x_4, x_5, x_6\}$,
6. $g_6 = \{x_1, x_4, x_5, x_6\}$,
7. $g_7 = \{x_7\}$,
8. $g_8 = \{x_3, x_8\}$,

what provides an intricate relationship among granules: $g_1, g_4, g_6 \subseteq g_5$, $g_8 \subseteq g_2$, g_2, g_5 incomparable by inclusion, g_7 isolated. We may contrast this picture with that for $\mu^{\leq}_{T_L}$.

1. $g_1^{\leq} = g_4^{\leq} = g_5^{\leq} = g_6^{\leq} = U$,
2. $g_2^{\leq} = g_3^{\leq} = g_7^{\leq} = U \setminus \{x_6\}$,
3. $g_8^{\leq} = \{x_1, x_2, x_3, x_7, x_8\}$,

providing a nested sequence of three distinct granules.

5.2 Extending Rough Inclusions to Granules

We now extend μ over pairs of the form x, g, where $x \in U_{IND}$, g a granule. We define μ in this case as follows,

$$\mu(x, g, r) \text{if and only if for some } y \in U_{IND}, y el_\pi g \text{ and } \mu(x, y, r). \tag{10}$$

The notion of element el_π on pairs x, g follows by treating g as a class of elements under element relation el_π, i.e., we admit that,

$x el \pi g$ if and only if for each element z of x, there exist elements w, t such that $w el_\pi z$, $w el_\pi q$, and $g(q)$.

By $g(q)$ true, we mean that q has the property defining g. Clearly, the extended relation el_π is transitive.

Proposition 5. *The relation μ on pairs x, y or x, g, where $x, y \in U_{IND}$, and g a concept, is a rough inclusion.*

Proof. Indeed, (RI1) and (RI4) are obviously satisfied. For (RI2), $\mu(x, g, 1)$ implies that there exists y with $y el_\pi g$ and $\mu(x, y, 1)$, hence, $x el_\pi y$ and finally $x el_\pi g$ by transitivity of el_π.

Concerning (RI3), assume that $\mu(x, g, 1)$ and $\mu(z, x, r)$, hence, for some $y el_\pi g$, we have $\mu(x, y, 1)$, hence, $\mu(z, y, r)$ by (RI3) for elements.

Finally, we define μ on pairs of the form g, h, of granules by means of,

$\mu(g, h, r)$ if and only if for each $x el_\pi g$ there exists y such that $y el_\pi h$, and $\mu(x, y, r)$.

The corresponding notion of element extended to pairs of concepts g, h will be defined as follows,

$gel_\pi h$ if and only if for each element $xel_\pi g$ there exist elements w, y with $wel_\pi x$, $wel_\pi y$ and $yel_\pi h$.

This notion of element is based on the inference rule; it is transitive as well.

Proposition 6. *The extended most general form of μ is a rough inclusion.*

Proof. (RI1, RI4) hold obviously; proof of (RI2) is as follows. For granules g, h, we have $\mu(g, h, 1)$ if and only if for each $xel_\pi g$, there is $yel_\pi h$ such that $\mu(x, y, 1)$, i.e., $xel_\pi y$, therefore, $gel_\pi h$.

Concerning (RI3), given $\mu(g, h, 1)$ and $\mu(k, g, r)$, for any $xel_\pi k$, there exists $yel_\pi g$ with $\mu(x, y, r)$; similarly, for y, we find $wel_\pi h$ with $\mu(y, w, 1)$. It follows by (RI3) for elements that $\mu(x, w, r)$ hence $\mu(x, h, r)$ and thus, x being arbitrary, $\mu(k, h, r)$.

Extended Archimedean Rough Inclusions. For a rough inclusion μ_T based on an archimedean t–norm T, the extended rough inclusion satisfies the generalized transitivity rule,

if $\mu_T(k, g, r)$ and $\mu_T(g, h, s)$ then $\mu_T(k, h, T(r, s))$.

Proof of the rule follows on lines of proofs given above for Propositions 5, 6.

We also notice a property of granules based on μ_T,

Proposition 7. *If $xel_\pi g_r(y)$ then $g_s(x)el_\pi g_{T(r,s)}(y)$.*

Proof. $xel_\pi g_r(y)$ and $zel_\pi g_s(x)$ imply by Proposition 4 that $\mu_T(x, y, r)$ and $\mu_T(z, x, s)$, hence, by transitivity, $\mu(z, y, T(r, s)$, again Proposition 4 implies that $zel_\pi g_{T(r,s)}(y)$.

5.3 Approximations by Granules

Given a granule g, and $r, s \in (0, 1)$, we can define, by means of the class operator, approximations to g by granules as follows, subject to the restriction that classes in question are non–empty.

The μ, r*–lower approximation* to g by a collection $H = \{h\}$ of granules is the class,

$$Cls_{LOW}(\mu, H, r) = Cls\Psi(\mu, g, r, H),$$

where $\Psi(\mu, g, r, H)(h)$ holds if and only if $\mu(h, g, r)$ and $h \in H$ hold.

Similarly, the μ, s*–upper approximation* to g by a collection H of granules is the class,

$$Cls^{UPP}(\mu, H, r) = Cls\Phi(\mu, g, r, H),$$

where $\Phi(\mu, g, r, H)(h)$ holds if and only if $\mu(h, g, t) \rightarrow t \leq s$ and $h \in H$ hold.

Taking set inclusion μ in the above definitions, we obtain approximations in the variable precision rough set model (Ziarko, op.cit.).

6 Rough Inclusions as Link to Fuzzy Sets

Because $y\mu_1 x$ is equivalent to y *el* x, we may interpret $\mu(y, x, r)$ as a statement of fuzzy membership; we will write $\mu_x(y) = r$ to stress this interpretation.

Clearly, by its definition, a rough inclusion is a relation, or, it may be regarded as a generalized fuzzy membership function, that takes intervals of the form $[0, w]$ as its values, leading to a higher–level fuzzy set. That follows from (RI4). Hence, inequalities like $a \leq \tau(x, y)$ are interpreted as follows: the value of a belongs in the interval = the value of $\tau(x, y)$. We should also bear in mind that rough inclusions reflect information content of the underlying information system, in particular they are determined relative to a chosen strategy by the system.

Thus, we may say, that rough inclusions induce globally a family of fuzzy sets $\{x : x \in U_{IND}\}$ with fuzzy membership functions $\{\mu_x : x \in U_{IND}\}$, in the above sense.

We assume additionally that the considered rough inclusion is μ_T for an archimedean t–norm T, relational or not (hence, possibly, not symmetric). Let us consider a relation τ on U_{IND} defined as follows,

$\tau(x, y, r)$ if and only if $\mu(x, y, r)$ and $\mu(y, x, r)$.

hence, $\tau(.,.,r)$ is for each r a *tolerance relation*. The following properties hold,

(T1) $\tau(x, x, 1)$.
(T2) $\tau(x, y, r)$ if and only if $\tau(y, x, r)$.
(T3) if $\tau(x, y, r)$ and $\tau(y, z, s)$ then $\tau(x, z, T(r, s))$.

We write $\tau(x, y)$ instead of $\chi_{x,\tau}(y)$ in cases when we treat τ as a fuzzy set, except for cases when the latter notation is necessary.

We may paraphrase (T1–3) in terms of the new notation,

(FS1) $\tau(x, x) = 1$.
(FS2) $\tau(x, y) = \tau(y, x)$.
(FS3) $\tau(x, z) \geq T(\tau(x, y), \tau(y, z))$.

Thus, τ is by (FS1–3), a *T-fuzzy similarity* (in the sense of [24]).

Following [24], we may define *similarity classes* $[x]_\tau$ as fuzzy sets satisfying,

$$\chi_{[x]_\tau}(y) = \tau(x, y). \tag{11}$$

Proposition 8. *The following are true,*
(SC1) $\chi_{[x]_\tau}(x) = 1$,
(SC2) $T(\chi_{[x]_\tau}(y), \tau(y,z)) \leq \chi_{[x]_\tau}(z)$,
(SC3) $T(\chi_{[x]_\tau}(y), \chi_{[x]_\tau}(z)) \leq \tau(y,z)$.

Proof. (SC1–3) follow by corresponding properties of τ given by (FS1–3).

Finally,

Proposition 9. *The family* $\{[x]_\tau : x \subseteq U\}$ *does satisfy the requirements to be a* fuzzy partition *[3], [5], [21], [24], viz.,*

(FP1) $\forall x \exists y. \chi_{[x]_\tau}(y) = 1$.
(FP2) $[x]_\tau \neq [z]_\tau \Rightarrow \ max_y\{min\{\chi_{[x]_\tau}(y), \chi_{[z]_\tau}(y)\}\} < 1$.
(FP3) $\bigcup_x [x]_\tau \times_T [x]_\tau = \tau$,

where $A \times_T B$ *denotes the fuzzy set defined as,*

$$\chi_{A \times_T B}(u,v) = T(\chi_A(u), \chi_B(v)),$$

and $\bigcup_x$ *denotes the supremum over all values of* x.

Proof. Indeed, (FP1–3) follow directly from properties of τ. For instance, (FP2) is justified as follows: if there was y with $\tau(x,y) = 1 = \tau(z,y)$, we would have $\tau(x,z), \tau(z,x) \geq T(1,1) = 1$ hence $x = z$.

For (FP3), on one hand, given x, y, z, we have,

$$T(\tau(x,y), \tau(x,z)) = T(\tau(y,x), \tau(x,z)) \leq \tau(y,z),$$

by (FS3), hence, $\bigcup_x [x]_\tau \times_T [x]_\tau(y,z) \leq \tau(y,z)$.

On the other hand, letting $x = y$, we have, $[x]_\tau \times_T [x]_\tau(y,z)= [y]_\tau \times_T [y]_\tau(y,z)=T(\tau(y,y), \tau(y,z))=T(1, \tau(y,z)=\tau(y,z)$ by (FS1) and $T(1,u) = u$, so $\bigcup_x [x]_\tau \times_T [x]_\tau(y,z) \leq \tau(y,z)$, which gives (FP3).

7 Conclusions

We have presented basic elements of mereological approach to rough set foundations. Not only mereological approach allows to render basic constructions of rough set theory, but also it provides a uniform description on the element level of all constructs. It also provides new constructs from methodological point of view, as the notion of a granule $g_r(x)$ involves a selection of attributes in a new way, related to mutual relationships among objects and attributes, and not as a block of attributes.

For the research in the nearest future, the general mereological granular rough set theory remains. We mean by this,

1. Granular information systems as pairs of the form (U_g, A_g) where U_g is a universe of granules and A_g is a set of derived attributes on granules.

2. Granular approximations as indicated above, with granular exact/rough sets.
3. Granular partitions and coverings as indicated above.
4. Granular reducts as attribute sets preserving (approximately) granular constructs.
5. Granular dependence and decision rules.

This approach should lead to knowledge compression and complexity reduction of algorithms.

References

1. R. Agrawal, H. Mannila, R. Srikant, H. Toivonen, and A. I. Verkamo. Fast discovery of association rules. In U.M. Fayyad, G. Piatetsky–Shapiro, P. Smyth, and R. Uthurusamy Eds. *Advances in Knowledge Discovery and Data Mining*: 307–328. AAAI Press, 1996.
2. L. Borkowski Ed. *Jan Łukasiewicz. Selected Works.* North Holland – Polish Sci. Publ., Amsterdam – Warsaw, 1970.
3. D. Dubois and H. Prade. Putting rough sets and fuzzy sets together. In: R. Słowiński Ed. *Intelligent Decision Support. Handbook of Applications and Advances of the Rough Sets Theory*: 203–232. Kluwer, 1992.
4. S. Greco, B. Matarazzo, and R. Słowiński. Rough approximation of a preference relation in a pairwise comparison table. In L. Polkowski and A. Skowron, Eds. *Rough Sets in Knowledge Discovery 2. Applications, Case Studies and Software Systems*: 13–36. Physica, Heidelberg, 1998.
5. U. Hoehle. Quotients with respect to similarity relations. *Fuzzy Sets Syst.*, 27: 31–44, 1988.
6. M. Inuiguchi, S. Hirano, and S. Tsumoto Eds. *Rough Set Theory and Granular Computing.* Physica, Heidelberg, 2003.
7. S. Leśniewski. On the foundations of mathematics. *Topoi*, 2: 7–52, 1982.
8. T. Y. Lin, Y. Y. Yao, and L. A. Zadeh, Eds. *Rough Sets, Granular Computing and Data Mining.* Physica, Heidelberg, 2001.
9. C.-H. Ling. Representation of associative functions. *Publ. Math. Debrecen*, 12: 189–212, 1965.
10. J. Łukasiewicz. *Die Logischen Grundlagen der Wahrscheinlichtkeitsrechnung.* Kraków, 1913. Eng. transl. In [2].
11. M. Novotný and Z. Pawlak. Partial dependency of attributes. *Bull. Polish Acad. Sci. Math.*, 36: 453–458, 1989.
12. M. Novotný and Z. Pawlak. On rough equalities. *Bull. Polish Acad. Sci. Math.*, 33: 99–104, 1985.
13. S.K. Pal, L. Polkowski, and A. Skowron, Eds. *Rough–Neural Computing. Techniques for Computing with Words.* Springer, Berlin, 2004.
14. Z. Pawlak. *Rough Sets: Theoretical Aspects of Reasoning about Data.* Kluwer, Dordrecht, 1992.
15. Z. Pawlak. Rough sets. *Intern. J. Comp. Inf. Sci.*, 11:341–356, 1982.
16. Z. Pawlak and A. Skowron. Rough membership functions. In R. R. Yager, M. Fedrizzi, and J. Kacprzyk, Eds. *Advances in the Dempster–Schafer Theory of Evidence*:251–271. Wiley, New York, 1994.
17. L. Polkowski. *Rough Sets. Mathematical Foundations.* Physica, Heidelberg, 2002.

18. L. Polkowski, A. Skowron. Rough mereology: a new paradigm for approximate reasoning. *International Journal of Approximate Reasoning*, 15(4): 333–365, 1997.
19. A. Skowron and J. Stepaniuk. Information granules: Towards foundations of granular computing. *International Journal for Intelligent Systems*, 16: 57–85, 2001.
20. S. Tsumoto. Automated induction of medical system expert rules from clinical databases based on rough set theory. *Information Sciences*, 112: 67–84, 1998.
21. L. Valverde. On the structure of F–indistinguishability operators. *Fuzzy Sets Syst.*, 17: 313–328, 1985.
22. Y. Y. Yao. Information granulation and approximation. In [13].
23. L. A. Zadeh. Fuzzy sets. *Information and Control*, 8: 338–353, 1965.
24. L. A. Zadeh. Similarity relations and fuzzy orderings. *Information Sciences*, 3: 177–200, 1971.
25. L. A. Zadeh and J. Kacprzyk (eds.). *Computing with Words in Information/Intelligent Systems 1*. Physica, Heidelberg, 1999.
26. W. Ziarko. Variable precision rough set model. *J. Computer and System Sciences*, 46 (1993), 39–59.

Generalizations of Rough Sets: From Crisp to Fuzzy Cases

Masahiro Inuiguchi

Department of Systems Innovation
Graduate School of Engineering Science, Osaka University
1-3, Machikaneyama, Toyonaka, Osaka 560-8531, Japan
inuiguti@sys.es.osaka-u.ac.jp
http://www-inulab.sys.es.osaka-u.ac.jp

Abstract. Rough sets can be interpreted in two ways: classification of objects and approximation of a set. In this paper, we discuss the differences and similarities of generalized rough sets based on those two different interpretations. We describe the relations between generalized rough sets and types of extracted decision rules. Moreover, we extend the discussion to fuzzy rough sets. Through this paper, the relations among generalized crisp rough sets and fuzzy rough sets are clarified and two different directions of applications in rule extraction are suggested.

1 Introduction

The usefulness and availability of rough sets in analyses of data, information, decision and conflict have been demonstrated in the literatures [1, 9, 13, 15]. Rough set approaches have been developed mainly under equivalence relations. In order to enhance the ability of the analysis, as well as from the mathematical interests, rough sets have been generalized by many researchers (for example, [2–6, 10, 11, 14, 16–19]). Among listed references, Ziarko [19] generalized rough sets by parameterizing the accuracy while the others generalized rough sets by extending the equivalence relation of approximation space. In this paper, we concentrate on the latter generalizations.

The equivalence relation implies that attributes are all nominal. Because of this weak assumption, unreasonable results for human intuition have been exemplified when some attributes are ordinal [6]. To overcome the unreasonableness caused by the ordinal property, the dominance-based rough set approach has been proposed by Greco et al. [6]. On the other hand, the generalization of rough sets is an interesting topic not only in mathematical point of view but also in practical point of view. Along this direction, rough sets have been generalized under similarity relations [10, 14], covers [2, 10] and general relations [18, 16, 17]. Those results demonstrate a diversity of generalizations. Moreover, fuzzy generalizations have been discussed in [3–5, 11]. Those studies exposed three different definitions of fuzzy rough sets.

Considering applications of rough sets in the generalized setting, the interpretation of rough sets plays an important role. This is because any mathematical

S. Tsumoto et al. (Eds.): RSCTC 2004, LNAI 3066, pp. 26–37, 2004.

model cannot be properly applied without its interpretation. Two interpretations have been implicitly considered in classical rough sets. One is rough set as classification of objects into positive, negative and boundary regions of a given concept. The other is rough set as approximation of a set by means of elementary sets. Those different interpretations are found in names 'positive region' (resp. 'possible region') and 'lower approximation' (resp. 'upper approximation') in classical rough sets. The former rough sets are called *classification-oriented* while the latter rough sets are called *approximation-oriented*. In this paper, we describe the differences and similarities of classification- and approximation-oriented rough sets.

In Section 2, we define classification- and approximation-oriented rough sets and show the fundamental properties and relationships. The correspondence of classification- and approximation-oriented rough sets with types of decision rules are described in Section 3. In Section 4, we extend the classification- and approximation-oriented rough sets to fuzzy environment. Finally, we give the concluding remarks in Section 5.

2 Crisp Rough Sets

2.1 Classification-Oriented Generalization

In this generalization, we assume that there exists a relation $P \subseteq U \times U$ such that $P(x) = \{y \in U \mid (y, x) \in P\}$ means a set of objects we intuitively identify as members of $X \subseteq U$ from the fact $x \in X$. Then if $P(x) \subseteq X$ for an object $x \in X$ then there is no objection against $x \in X$. In this case, $x \in X$ is consistent with the intuitive knowledge based on the relation P. Such an object $x \in X$ can be considered as a positive member of X. Hence the positive region of X can be defined as

$$P_*(X) = \{x \in X \mid P(x) \subseteq X\}. \tag{1}$$

On the other hand, by the intuition from the relation P, an object $y \in P(x)$ for $x \in X$ can be a member of X. Namely, such an object $y \in U$ is a possible member of X. Moreover, every object $x \in X$ is evidently a possible member of X. Hence the possible region of X can be defined as

$$P^*(X) = X \cup \bigcup \{P(x) \mid x \in X\}. \tag{2}$$

Using the positive region $P_*(X)$ and the possible region $P^*(X)$, we can define a rough set of X as a pair $(P_*(X), P^*(X))$. We call such rough sets as *classification-oriented rough sets under a positively extensive relation* P *of* X (for short *CP-rough sets*).

Since the relation P depends on the meaning of a set X, to define a CP-rough set of $U - X$, we should introduce another relation $Q \subseteq U \times U$ such that $Q(x) = \{y \in U \mid (y, x) \in Q\}$ means a set of objects we intuitively identify as members of $U - X$ from the fact $x \in U - X$. Using Q we have positive and possible regions of $U - X$ by

$$Q_*(U - X) = \{x \in U - X \mid Q(x) \subseteq U - X\}, \tag{3}$$

$$Q^*(U - X) = (U - X) \cup \bigcup\{Q(x) \mid x \in U - X\}. \tag{4}$$

Using $Q_*(X)$ and $Q^*(X)$, we can define certain and conceivable regions of X by

$$\bar{Q}_*(X) = U - Q^*(U - X) = X \cap \left(U - \bigcup\{Q(x) \mid x \in U - X\}\right), \tag{5}$$

$$\bar{Q}^*(X) = U - Q_*(U - X) = U - \{x \in U - X \mid Q(x) \subseteq U - X\}. \tag{6}$$

We can define another rough set of X as a pair $(\bar{Q}_*(X), \bar{Q}^*(X))$ with the certain region $\bar{Q}_*(X)$ and the conceivable region $\bar{Q}^*(X)$. We call this type of rough sets as *classification-oriented rough sets under a negatively extensive relation* Q of X (for short *CN-rough sets*).

Similar definitions to CP- and CN-rough sets can be found in [6, 10, 14, 16–18]. The definitions are not completely same. CP- and CN-rough sets are different from [16–18] in the facts that we take intersection and union with X. Moreover, CP- and CN-rough sets are different from [6, 10, 14] in the fact that we do not assume the reflexivity in P. However, the strong similarity can be found in the following fact: if we define $\hat{P} = P \cup \{(x, x) \mid x \in X\}$, we have $P_*(X) = \{x \in X \mid \hat{P}(x) \subseteq X\}$ and $P^*(X) = \bigcup\{\hat{P}(x) \mid x \in X\}$, i.e., $P_*(X)$ and $P^*(X)$ are the same as lower and upper approximations with respect to $\hat{P}$ in [6]. From the similarity to the definitions in [18], we understand that CP- and CN-rough sets are related to modal operators, i.e., necessity and possibility operators.

The fundamental properties of CP- and CN-rough sets are discussed in [7]. Since CP- and CN-fuzzy rough sets are extensions of CP- and CN-rough sets, the most of properties can be also found in Table 2 described later.

2.2 Approximation-Oriented Generalization

In order to generalize classical rough sets under the interpretation of rough sets as approximation of a set by means of elementary sets, we introduce a family with a finite number of elementary sets on U, $\mathcal{F} = \{F_1, F_2, \ldots, F_p\}$. Each F_i is a group of objects collected according to some specific meaning.

There are two ways to define lower and upper approximations of a set X under a family $\mathcal{F}$: one way is to define approximations by means of the union of elementary sets F_i and the other is to define approximations by means of the intersection of complements of elementary sets $U - F_i$. Lower and upper approximations of a set X under $\mathcal{F}$ are defined in the following two ways:

$$\mathcal{F}_*^{\cup}(X) = \bigcup\{F_i \mid F_i \subseteq X,\ i = 0, 1, \ldots, p\}, \tag{7}$$

$$\mathcal{F}_*^{\cap}(X) = \bigcup\left\{\bigcap_{i \in I}(U - F_i) \,\middle|\, \bigcap_{i \in I}(U - F_i) \subseteq X,\ I \subseteq \{1, 2, \ldots, p+1\}\right\}, \tag{8}$$

$$\mathcal{F}_{\cup}^*(X) = \bigcap\left\{\bigcup_{i \in I} F_i \,\middle|\, \bigcup_{i \in I} F_i \supseteq X,\ I \subseteq \{1, 2, \ldots, p+1\}\right\}, \tag{9}$$

$$\mathcal{F}^*_{\cap}(X) = \bigcap\{U - F_i \mid U - F_i \supseteq X,\ i = 0, 1, \ldots, p\}, \tag{10}$$

where, for convenience, we define $F_0 = \emptyset$ and $F_{p+1} = U$. Because we do not assume $F_i \cap F_j \neq \emptyset$ for $i \neq j$, we do not always have a unique maximal intersection $\bigcap_{i \in I}(U - F_i)$ determining $\mathcal{F}^{\cap}_*(X)$. We usually have several maximal intersections $\mathcal{F}^{\cap}_j(X) = \bigcap_{i \in I_j}(U - F_i)$, $j = 1, 2, \ldots, t^{\cap}$ such that $\mathcal{F}^{\cap}_*(X) = \bigcup_{j=1,2,\ldots,t^{\cap}} \mathcal{F}^{\cap}_j(X)$. Similarly, $\mathcal{F}^*_{\cup}(X)$ is usually expressed by several minimal unions $\mathcal{F}^{\cup}_j(X)$, $j = 1, 2, \ldots, t^{\cup}$ as $\mathcal{F}^*_{\cup}(X) = \bigcap_{j=1,2,\ldots,t^{\cup}} \mathcal{F}^{\cup}_j(X)$. We call a pair $(\mathcal{F}^{\cup}_*(X), \mathcal{F}^*_{\cup}(X))$ an *approximation-oriented rough set by means of the union of elementary sets F_i* under a family $\mathcal{F}$ (for short, an *AU-rough set*) and a pair $(\mathcal{F}^{\cap}_*(X), \mathcal{F}^*_{\cap}(X))$ an *approximation-oriented rough set by means of the intersection of complements of elementary sets $U - F_i$* under a family $\mathcal{F}$ (for short, an *AI-rough set*).

Similar definitions to those can be found in [2, 10, 17]. In [2, 10], the family is assumed a cover. Moreover the definition of upper approximations of [2] is different from (9) and (10). In [17], there exists a corresponding elementary set F_i for each object $x \in U$ but in this paper, we do not assume such a correspondence. From the explanations by Yao [17], AU- and AI-rough sets are related to topological operators, i.e., interior and closure operators.

The fundamental properties of AU- and AI-rough sets can be found in [7]. As described later, ξ- and σ-fuzzy rough sets are closely related to AU- and AI-rough sets. Thus, many of properties can be also found in Table 3.

Given a relation P, we may define a family by $\mathcal{P} = \{P(x) \mid x \in U\}$. Therefore, under a positively extensive relation P, we obtain not only CP-rough sets but also AU- and AI-rough sets. This is the same for a negatively extensive relation Q. Namely, by a family $\mathcal{Q} = \{Q(x) \mid x \in U\}$, we obtain AU- and AI-rough sets. Under those settings, relations between CP-/CN-rough sets and AU/AI-rough sets are discussed in [7]. Most of them are generalized to relationships listed in Table 4 in fuzzy rough sets described later.

3 Types of Decision Rules

3.1 Decision Rules Corresponding to CP- and CN-Rough Sets

First, let us discuss the type of decision rule corresponding to positive and certain regions of CP- and CN-rough sets. Considering a converse relation $Q^{\mathrm{T}} = \{(x, y) \mid (y, x) \in Q\}$, a certain region $\bar{Q}_*(X)$ can be represented by $\bar{Q}_*(X) = \{x \in X \mid Q^{\mathrm{T}}(x) \subseteq X\}$. Therefore the type of extracted decision rules are same but the difference is only in P versus Q^{T}.

From the definition of positive region $P_*(X)$ of (1), any object $y \in U$ satisfying the condition of the decision rules should fulfill $y \in X$ and $P_C(y) \subseteq X$. Considering this requirement, we should explore suitable conditions of the decision rules. When we confirm $y = x$ for an object $x \in P_*(X)$, we may obviously conclude $y \in P_*(X)$. Therefore for $x \in P_*(X)$, we obtain a rule,

$$\text{if } y = x \text{ then } y \in X.$$

Let us call this type of the decision rule, an *identity if-then rule* (for short, *id-rule*). The difficulty of the id-rule is how we recognize y to be same as x. In a way, we identify y as x when all attribute values which characterize y and x are same and there is no other object z whose all attribute values are same as y.

Moreover, when the relation P is transitive, we may conclude $y \in P_*(X)$ from the fact that $(y,x) \in P$ and $x \in P_*(X)$. This is because we have $P(y) \subseteq P(x) \subseteq X$ and $y \in P(x) \subseteq X$ from transitivity and from the fact $x \in P_*(X)$. In this case, we may have the following type of decision rule for $x \in P_*(X)$,

$$\text{if } (y,x) \in P \text{ then } y \in X.$$

This type of if-then rule is called a *relational if-then rule* (for short, *R-rule*). When the relation P is reflexive and transitive, the R-rule includes the corresponding id-rule.

3.2 Decision Rules Corresponding to AU-Rough Sets

Let us discuss the type of decision rule corresponding to the lower approximation of AU-rough set (7). From the definition, any object $y \in U$ satisfying the condition of the decision rules should fulfill $y \in F_i$ and $F_i \subseteq X$. We should explore suitable conditions of the decision rules considering this requirement. When we confirm $y \in F_i$ for an elementary set $F_i \in \mathcal{F}$ such that $F_i \subseteq X$, we can obviously conclude $y \in X$. From this fact, when $F_i \subseteq X$ we have the following type of decision rule;

$$\text{if } y \in F_i \text{ then } y \in X.$$

This type of if-then rule is called a *block if-then rule* (for short, *B-rule*). From the lower approximations of AU-rough sets, B-rules can be extracted.

3.3 Decision Rules Corresponding to AI-Rough Sets

Consider the maximal intersections $\mathcal{F}_j^{\cap}(X)$, $j = 1, 2, \ldots, t^{\cap}$ such that $\mathcal{F}_*^{\cap}(X) = \bigcup_{j=1,2,\ldots,t^{\cap}} \mathcal{F}_j^{\cap}(X)$. By the same discussion as in the previous subsection, for each $y \in \mathcal{F}_j^{\cap}(X)$ with some $j \in \{1, 2, \ldots, t^{\cap}\}$, we can conclude $y \in X$. Let $\mathcal{F}_j^{\cap}(X) = \bigcap_{i=1,2,\ldots,s}(U - F_{j_i})$. Then we may have the following rule for each $\mathcal{F}_j^{\cap}$:

$$\text{if } y \notin F_{j_1} \text{ and } \cdots \text{ and } y \notin F_{j_s} \text{ then } y \in X.$$

This type of if-then rule is called a *reverse block if-then rule* (for short, *RB-rule*). From the lower approximations of AU-rough sets, RB-rules can be extracted.

3.4 Results

The correspondence between generalized rough sets and types of decision rules is assembled in Table 1. The conditions of id-rules tend to be stronger than the B- and RB-rules. The differences in decision rules extracted from the same

Table 1. Correspondence between generalized rough sets and types of decision rules

rough sets	definition	type of decision rules
CP-rough sets	$\{x \in X \mid P(x) \subseteq X\}$	if $x = \bar{x}$ then $x \in X$, if $(x, \bar{x}) \in P$ then $x \in X$ (if P is transitive).
CN-rough sets	$X \cap (U - \bigcup\{Q(x) \mid x \in U - X\})$	if $x = \bar{x}$ then $x \in X$, if $(\bar{x}, x) \in Q$ then $x \in X$ (if Q is transitive).
AU-rough sets	$\bigcup\{F_i \in \mathcal{F} \mid F_i \subseteq X\}$	if $x \in F_i$ then $x \in X$.
AI-rough sets	*	if $x \notin F_{j_1}$ and $\cdots$ and $x \notin F_{j_s}$ then $x \in X$.

* $\bigcup\{\bigcap_{i \in I}(U - F_i) \mid \bigcap_{i \in I}(U - F_i) \subseteq X, I \subseteq \{1, \ldots, p+1\}\}$

decision tables are examined in [10]. Whereas id-rules and R-rules (if they exist) are safer but passive, B- and RB-rules are active but more conflictive. Since the conditions of B-rules and RB-rules are often overlapped, we may use those rules for interpolative reasoning. On the other hand, because they are safer, id-rules and R-rules (if they exist) will be useful to analyze decision tables with uncertain values such as missing values, multiple possible values, and so forth.

4 Fuzzy Rough Sets

4.1 Classification-Oriented Generalization

Let us assume that there exists a fuzzy binary relation $P \subseteq U \times U$ such that $\mu_{P(x)}(y) = \mu_P(y, x)$ represents to what extent we intuitively identify an object y as a member of X from the fact x is a member of a fuzzy set X, where $\mu_P : U \times U \to [0, 1]$ is a membership function of a fuzzy relation P. Then, given an appropriate implication function I, objection-freeness against the fact that x is a member of X can be measured by $\inf_{y \in U} I(\mu_{P(x)}(y), \mu_X(y))$, where $\mu_X : U \to [0, 1]$ is a membership function of X and an implication function $I : [0, 1] \times [0, 1] \to [0, 1]$ satisfies $I(0, 0) = I(0, 1) = I(1, 1) = 1$, $I(1, 0) = 0$, $I(\cdot, a)$ is decreasing for any $a \in [0, 1]$ and $I(a, \cdot)$ is increasing for any $a \in [0, 1]$. Combining $\mu_X(x)$, the consistency of membership of x with respect to X with the intuitive knowledge based on the relation P can be evaluated by $\min\left(\mu_X(x), \inf_{y \in U} I(\mu_{P(x)}(y), \mu_X(y))\right)$. In other words, this can be seen as the degree to which x is a positive member of X. Therefore, the membership function of the positive region $P_*(X)$ of X can be defined by

$$\mu_{P_*(X)}(x) = \min\left(\mu_X(x), \inf_{y \in U} I(\mu_P(y, x), \mu_X(y))\right). \tag{11}$$

On the other hand, by the intuition from the assumed relation P, an object $x \in U$ is a possible member of X at least to a degree $T(\mu_{P(y)}(x), \mu_X(y))$ if an object $y \in U$ has a positive membership degree $\mu_X(y) > 0$, where a conjunction function $T : [0, 1] \times [0, 1] \to [0, 1]$ satisfies $T(1, 1) = 1$, $T(0, 0) = T(0, 1) = T(1, 0) = 0$ and T is increasing in both arguments. Considering all possible

$y \in U$ such that $\mu_X(y) > 0$, $x \in U$ is a possible member of X at least to a degree $\sup_{y\in U} T(\mu_{P(y)}(x), \mu_X(y))$. Hence the possible region $P^*(X)$ of X can be defined by a membership function

$$\mu_{P^*(X)}(x) = \max\left(\mu_X(x), \sup_{y\in U} T(\mu_P(x,y), \mu_X(y))\right). \tag{12}$$

Note that we do not assume the reflexivity of P, i.e., $\mu_P(x,x) = 1$, $\forall x \in U$ so that we take the minimum between μ_X and $\inf_{y\in U} I(\mu_{P(x)}(y), \mu_X(y))$ in (11) and the maximum between μ_X and $\sup_{y\in U} T(\mu_{P(y)}(x), \mu_X(y))$ in (12). When P is reflexive and $I(1,a) \le a$ and $T(1,a) \ge a$ for all $a \in [0,1]$, we have

$$\mu_{P_*(X)}(x) = \inf_{y\in U} I(\mu_{P(x)}(y), \mu_X(y)), \quad \mu_{P^*(X)}(x) = \sup_{y\in U} T(\mu_{P(y)}(x), \mu_X(y)). \tag{13}$$

Those definitions of lower and upper approximations have been proposed by Dubois and Prade [3, 4]. They assumed the reflexivity of P, $I(1,a) = T(1,a) = a$, for all $a \in [0,1]$.

Using the positive region $P_*(X)$ and the possible region $P^*(X)$, we can define a fuzzy rough set of X as a pair $(P_*(X), P^*(X))$. We call such fuzzy rough sets as *classification-oriented fuzzy rough sets under a positively extensive relation P of X* (for short *CP-fuzzy rough sets*).

Since the relation P depends on the meaning of a set X, to define a CP-rough set of $U - X$, we should introduce another fuzzy relation $Q \subseteq U \times U$ such that $\mu_{Q(x)}(y) = \mu_Q(y,x)$ represents to what extent we intuitively identify an object y as a member of $U - X$ from the fact x is a member of the complementary fuzzy set $U - X$, where $\mu_Q : U \times U \to [0,1]$ is a membership function of a fuzzy relation Q. Using Q we have positive and possible regions of $U - X$ by the following membership functions,

$$\mu_{Q_*(U-X)}(x) = \min\left(n(\mu_X(x)), \inf_{y\in U} I(\mu_Q(y,x), n(\mu_X(y)))\right), \tag{14}$$

$$\mu_{Q^*(U-X)}(x) = \max\left(n(\mu_X(x)), \sup_{y\in U} T(\mu_P(x,y), n(\mu_X(y)))\right), \tag{15}$$

where $U - X$ is defined by a membership function $n(\mu_X(\cdot))$ and $n : [0,1] \to [0,1]$ is a decreasing function such that $n(n(a)) = a$, $a \in [0,1]$ (involutive). The involution implies the continuity of n.

Using $Q_*(X)$ and $Q^*(X)$, we can define certain region $\bar{Q}_*(X)$ and conceivable region $\bar{Q}^*(X)$ of X by the following membership functions,

$$\mu_{\bar{Q}_*(X)}(x) = \min\left(\mu_X(x), \inf_{y\in U} n(T(\mu_Q(x,y), n(\mu_X(y))))\right), \tag{16}$$

$$\mu_{\bar{Q}^*(X)}(x) = \max\left(\mu_X(x), \sup_{y\in U} n(I(\mu_Q(y,x), n(\mu_X(y))))\right). \tag{17}$$

We can define another fuzzy rough set of X as a pair $(\bar{Q}_*(X), \bar{Q}^*(X))$ with the certain region $\bar{Q}_*(X)$ and the conceivable region $\bar{Q}^*(X)$. We call this type

Table 2. Fundamental properties of CP- and CN-fuzzy rough sets

(i) $P_*(X) \subseteq X \subseteq P^*(X)$, $\bar{Q}_*(X) \subseteq X \subseteq \bar{Q}^*(X)$.

(ii) $P_*(\emptyset) = P^*(\emptyset) = \emptyset$, $P_*(U) = P^*(U) = U$,
$\bar{Q}_*(\emptyset) = \bar{Q}^*(\emptyset) = \emptyset$, $\bar{Q}_*(U) = \bar{Q}^*(U) = U$.

(iii) $P_*(X \cap Y) = P_*(X) \cap P_*(Y)$, $P^*(X \cup Y) = P^*(X) \cup P^*(Y)$,
$\bar{Q}_*(X \cap Y) = \bar{Q}_*(X) \cap \bar{Q}_*(Y)$, $\bar{Q}^*(X \cup Y) = \bar{Q}^*(X) \cup \bar{Q}^*(Y)$.

(iv) $X \subseteq Y$ implies $P_*(X) \subseteq P_*(Y)$, $P^*(X) \subseteq P^*(Y)$,
$X \subseteq Y$ implies $\bar{Q}_*(X) \subseteq \bar{Q}_*(Y)$, $\bar{Q}^*(X) \subseteq \bar{Q}^*(Y)$.

(v) $P_*(X \cup Y) \supseteq P_*(X) \cup P_*(Y)$, $P^*(X \cap Y) \subseteq P^*(X) \cap P^*(Y)$,
$\bar{Q}_*(X \cup Y) \supseteq \bar{Q}_*(X) \cup \bar{Q}_*(Y)$, $\bar{Q}^*(X \cap Y) \subseteq \bar{Q}^*(X) \cap \bar{Q}^*(Y)$.

(vi) When $\forall a, b \in [0,1], I(a,b) = n(T(a, n(b)))$ and $\forall x, y \in U, \mu_Q(x,y) = \mu_P(y,x)$,
$P^*(X) = U - Q_*(U - X) = \bar{Q}^*(X)$, $P_*(X) = U - Q^*(U - X) = \bar{Q}_*(X)$.

(vii) When $\forall a, b \in [0,1], T(a, I(a,b)) \leq b$, $X \supseteq P^*(P_*(X))$, $X \subseteq \bar{Q}_*(\bar{Q}^*(X))$.
When $\forall a, b \in [0,1]$, $I(a, T(a,b)) \geq b$, $X \subseteq P_*(P^*(X))$, $X \supseteq \bar{Q}^*(\bar{Q}_*(X))$.
When P, Q are T'-transitive, I is upper semi-continuous and I satisfies
$\forall a, b, c \in [0,1], I(a, I(b,c)) = I(T'(b,a), c)$,
$P_*(P_*(X)) = P_*(X)$, $\bar{Q}^*(\bar{Q}^*(X)) = \bar{Q}^*(X)$.
When P, Q are T-transitive, $T = T'$ is lower semi-continuous and associative,
$P^*(P^*(X)) = P^*(X)$, $\bar{Q}_*(\bar{Q}_*(X)) = \bar{Q}_*(X)$.
When P and Q are reflexive and T-transitive, $\forall a \in [0,1]$, $I(a, \cdot)$ is upper semi-continuous, $I(1,a) \leq a$ and $T = \xi[I]$ is associative,
$P^*(P_*(X)) = P_*(X)$, $\bar{Q}_*(\bar{Q}^*(X)) = \bar{Q}^*(X)$,
When P and Q are reflexive and T-transitive, $\forall a, b \in [0,1], I(a,b) = n(\xi[I](a, n(b)))$, $I(a, \cdot)$ is upper semi-continuous, $I(1,a) \leq a$, and $T = \xi[I]$ is associative,
$P_*(P^*(X)) = P^*(X)$, $\bar{Q}^*(\bar{Q}_*(X)) = \bar{Q}_*(X)$.

of rough sets as *classification-oriented rough sets under a negatively extensive relation* Q of X (for short *CN-fuzzy rough sets*).

It is shown that CP- and CN-fuzzy rough sets have the fundamental properties listed in Table 2 (see [8]). In Table 2, the inclusion relation between two fuzzy sets A and B is defined by $\mu_A(x) \leq \mu_B(x)$, for all $x \in U$. The intersection $A \cap B$ and union $A \cup B$ are defined by $\mu_{A \cap B}(x) = \min(\mu_A(x), \mu_B(x))$ and $\mu_{A \cup B}(x) = \max(\mu_A(x), \mu_B(x))$. $\xi[I]$ is defined by $\xi[I](a,b) = \inf\{s \in [0,1] \mid I(a,s) \geq b\}$.

4.2 Approximation-Oriented Generalization

Based on the certainty-qualification of fuzzy sets, Inuiguchi and Tanino [11] proposed the upper and lower approximations of a fuzzy set X under a family $\mathcal{F}$ of fuzzy sets by the following membership functions:

$$\mu_{\mathcal{F}_*^\xi(X)}(x) = \sup_{F \in \mathcal{F}} \xi[I]\left(\mu_F(x), \inf_{y \in U} I(\mu_F(y), \mu_X(y))\right), \tag{18}$$

$$\mu_{\mathcal{F}_*^\sigma(X)}(x) = \sup_{\mathcal{T} \subseteq \mathcal{F}} n\left(\sigma[I]\left(\inf_{y \in U} I\left(n(\mu_X(y)), \sup_{F \in \mathcal{T}} \mu_F(y)\right), \sup_{F \in \mathcal{T}} \mu_F(x)\right)\right), \tag{19}$$

$$\mu_{\mathcal{F}_\xi^*(X)}(x) = \inf_{F \in \mathcal{F}} n\left(\xi[I]\left(\mu_F(x), \inf_{y \in U} I\left(\mu_F(y), n(\mu_X(y))\right)\right)\right), \tag{20}$$

$$\mu_{\mathcal{F}^*_\sigma(X)}(x) = \inf_{\mathcal{T}\subseteq\mathcal{F}} \sigma[I]\left(\inf_{y\in U} I\left(\mu_X(y), \sup_{F\in\mathcal{T}} \mu_F(y) \right), \sup_{F\in\mathcal{T}} \mu_F(x) \right), \tag{21}$$

where I is assumed to be upper semi-continuous for all $a \in [0,1]$. $\sigma[I]$ is defined by $\sigma[I](a,b) = \sup\{s \in [0,1] \mid I(s,b) \geq a\}$ for an implication function I. A fuzzy rough set can be defined as a pair of lower and upper approximations. Therefore four possible definitions are conceivable. Inuiguchi and Tanino [11] selected a pair $(\mathcal{F}^\xi_*(X), \mathcal{F}^*_\xi(X))$. However, as generalized rough sets in a crisp setting, AU- and AI-rough sets correspond to pairs $(\mathcal{F}^\xi_*(X), \mathcal{F}^*_\sigma(X))$ and $(\mathcal{F}^\sigma_*(X), \mathcal{F}^*_\xi(X))$, respectively. A pair $(\mathcal{F}^\xi_*(X), \mathcal{F}^*_\xi(X))$ is called a ξ-fuzzy rough set and a pair $(\mathcal{F}^\sigma_*(X), \mathcal{F}^*_\sigma(X))$ a σ-fuzzy rough set.

The correspondence to AU- and AI-rough sets are clarified by the following representations:

$$\mu_{\mathcal{F}^\xi_*(X)}(x) = \sup\{\xi[I](\mu_F(x), h) \mid F \in \mathcal{F}, h \in [0,1] \text{ such that } \xi[I](\mu_F(y), h) \leq \mu_X(y), \forall y \in U\}, \tag{22}$$

$$\mu_{\mathcal{F}^\sigma_*(X)}(x) = \sup\left\{ n\left(\sigma[I]\left(h, \sup_{F\in\mathcal{T}} \mu_F(x) \right) \right) \,\middle|\, \mathcal{T} \subseteq \mathcal{F}, h \in [0,1] \text{ such that } \sigma[I]\left(h, \sup_{F\in\mathcal{T}} \mu_F(y) \right) \geq n(\mu_X(y)), \forall y \in U \right\}, \tag{23}$$

$$\mu_{\mathcal{F}^*_\xi(X)}(x) = \inf\{n(\xi[I](\mu_F(x), h)) \mid F \in \mathcal{F}, h \in [0,1] \text{ such that } \xi[I](\mu_F(y), h) \leq n(\mu_X(y)), \forall y \in U\}, \tag{24}$$

$$\mu_{\mathcal{F}^*_\sigma(X)}(x) = \inf\left\{ \sigma[I]\left(h, \sup_{F\in\mathcal{T}} \mu_F(x) \right) \,\middle|\, \mathcal{T} \subseteq \mathcal{F}, h \in [0,1] \text{ such that } \sigma[I]\left(h, \sup_{F\in\mathcal{T}} \mu_F(y) \right) \geq \mu_X(y), \forall y \in U \right\}. \tag{25}$$

The fundamental properties of ξ- and σ-rough sets are listed in Table 3. The proofs are found in [8].

As another kind of fuzzy rough set has been proposed by Greco et al. [5] under decision tables. The idea of lower and upper approximations can be extended by the following equations:

$$\mu_{X^+_*}(x) = \sup_{F\in\mathcal{F}} \sup_{\varphi^+_F} \{\varphi^+_F(\mu_F(x)) \mid \varphi^+_F(\mu_F(y)) \leq \mu_X(y), \forall y \in U, \varphi^+_F \text{ is non-decreasing}\}, \tag{26}$$

$$\mu_{X^-_*}(x) = \sup_{F\in\mathcal{F}} \sup_{\varphi^-_F} \{\varphi^-_F(\mu_F(x)) \mid \varphi^-_F(\mu_F(y)) \leq \mu_X(y), \forall y \in U, \varphi^-_F \text{ is non-increasing}\}, \tag{27}$$

$$\mu_{X^*_+}(x) = \inf_{F\in\mathcal{F}} \inf_{\psi^+_F} \{\psi^+_F(\mu_F(x)) \mid \psi^+_F(\mu_F(y)) \geq \mu_X(y), \forall y \in U, \psi^+_F \text{ is non-decreasing}\}, \tag{28}$$

$$\mu_{X^*_-}(x) = \inf_{F\in\mathcal{F}} \inf_{\psi^-_F} \{\psi^-_F(\mu_F(x)) \mid \psi^-_F(\mu_F(y)) \geq \mu_X(y), \forall y \in U, \psi^-_F \text{ is non-increasing}\}. \tag{29}$$

Table 3. Fundamental properties of ξ- and σ-rough sets

(i) $\mathcal{F}_*^\xi(X) \subseteq X \subseteq \mathcal{F}_\xi^*(X)$, $\mathcal{F}_*^\sigma(X) \subseteq X \subseteq \mathcal{F}_\sigma^*(X)$.
(ii) $\mathcal{F}_*^\xi(\emptyset) = \mathcal{F}_*^\sigma(\emptyset) = \emptyset$, $\mathcal{F}_\xi^*(U) = \mathcal{F}_\sigma^*(U) = U$.
When $a > 0$, $b < 1$ imply $I(a,b) < 1$ and $\inf_{x\in U}\sup_{F\in\mathcal{F}}\mu_F(x) > 0$,
$\mathcal{F}_\xi^*(\emptyset) = \emptyset$, $\mathcal{F}_*^\xi(U) = U$.
When $b < 1$ implies $I(1,b) < 1$ and $\inf_{x\in U}\sup_{F\in\mathcal{F}}\mu_F(x) = 1$,
$\mathcal{F}_\xi^*(\emptyset) = \emptyset$, $\mathcal{F}_*^\xi(U) = U$.
When $a > 0$, $b < 1$ imply $I(a,b) < 1$ and $\forall x \in U$, $\exists F \in \mathcal{F}$ such that $\mu_F(x) < 1$,
$\mathcal{F}_\sigma^*(\emptyset) = \emptyset$, $\mathcal{F}_*^\sigma(U) = U$.
When $a > 0$ implies $I(a,0) < 1$ and $\forall x \in U$, $\exists F \in \mathcal{F}$ such that $\mu_F(x) = 0$,
$\mathcal{F}_\sigma^*(\emptyset) = \emptyset$, $\mathcal{F}_*^\sigma(U) = U$.
(iii) $\mathcal{F}_*^\sigma(X \cap Y) = \mathcal{F}_*^\sigma(X) \cap \mathcal{F}_*^\sigma(Y)$, $\mathcal{F}_\sigma^*(X \cup Y) = \mathcal{F}_\sigma^*(X) \cup \mathcal{F}_\sigma^*(Y)$.
When $\forall a \in [0,1]$, $I(a,a) = 1$ and $\forall F_i, F_j \in \mathcal{F}$, $F_i \neq F_j$, $F_i \cap F_j = \emptyset$,
$\mathcal{F}_*^\xi(X \cap Y) = \mathcal{F}_*^\xi(X) \cap \mathcal{F}_*^\xi(Y)$, $\mathcal{F}_\xi^*(X \cup Y) = \mathcal{F}_\xi^*(X) \cup \mathcal{F}_\xi^*(Y)$.
(iv) $X \subseteq Y$ implies $\mathcal{F}_*^\xi(X) \subseteq \mathcal{F}_*^\xi(Y)$, $\mathcal{F}_*^\sigma(X) \subseteq \mathcal{F}_*^\sigma(Y)$,
$X \subseteq Y$ implies $\mathcal{F}_\xi^*(X) \subseteq \mathcal{F}_\xi^*(Y)$, $\mathcal{F}_\sigma^*(X) \subseteq \mathcal{F}_\sigma^*(Y)$.
(v) $\mathcal{F}_*^\xi(X \cup Y) \supseteq \mathcal{F}_*^\xi(X) \cup \mathcal{F}_*^\xi(Y)$, $\mathcal{F}_*^\sigma(X \cup Y) \supseteq \mathcal{F}_*^\sigma(X) \cup \mathcal{F}_*^\sigma(Y)$,
$\mathcal{F}_\xi^*(X \cap Y) \subseteq \mathcal{F}_\xi^*(X) \cap \mathcal{F}_\xi^*(Y)$, $\mathcal{F}_\sigma^*(X \cap Y) \subseteq \mathcal{F}_\sigma^*(X) \cap \mathcal{F}_\sigma^*(Y)$.
(vi) $\mathcal{F}_*^\xi(U - X) = U - \mathcal{F}_\xi^*(X)$, $\mathcal{F}_*^\sigma(U - X) = U - \mathcal{F}_\sigma^*(X)$,
$\mathcal{F}_\xi^*(U - X) = U - \mathcal{F}_*^\xi(X)$, $\mathcal{F}_\sigma^*(U - X) = U - \mathcal{F}_*^\sigma(X)$.
(vii) $\mathcal{F}_*^\xi(\mathcal{F}_*^\xi(X)) = \mathcal{F}_*^\xi(X)$, $\mathcal{F}_*^\sigma(\mathcal{F}_*^\sigma(X)) = \mathcal{F}_*^\sigma(X)$,
$\mathcal{F}_\xi^*(\mathcal{F}_\xi^*(X)) = \mathcal{F}_\xi^*(X)$, $\mathcal{F}_\sigma^*(\mathcal{F}_\sigma^*(X)) = \mathcal{F}_\sigma^*(X)$.

where X_*^+ and X_*^- are lower approximations assuming the positive and negative correlations between each $F \in \mathcal{F}$ and X, respectively. Similarly, X_+^* and X_-^* are upper approximations assuming the positive and negative correlations between each $F \in \mathcal{F}$ and X, respectively. When we do not know the positiveness or negativeness in correlations between X or when the positiveness or negativeness depends on each $F \in \mathcal{F}$, we may define the lower and upper approximations by $X_*^+ \cup X_*^-$ and $X_+^* \cap X_-^*$, respectively. In any case, we assume the monotonous relation between each $F \in \mathcal{F}$ and X.

Since $\xi[I](\cdot, h)$ and $\sigma[I](h, \cdot)$ are non-decreasing functions, we have $\mathcal{F}_*^\xi(X) \subseteq X_*^+$, $\mathcal{F}_*^\sigma(X) \subseteq X_*^-$, $\mathcal{F}_\xi^*(X) \supseteq X_-^*$ and $\mathcal{F}_\sigma^*(X) \supseteq X_+^*$ when U and $\mathcal{F}$ are composed of finite members.

We call a pair (X_*^+, X_+^*) a *P-fuzzy rough set* of X and a pair (X_*^-, X_-^*) an *N-fuzzy rough set* of X. Almost all fundamental properties of classical rough sets are preserved in P- and N-fuzzy rough sets. Only the duality between lower and upper approximations of a fuzzy rough set does not hold but we have $X_*^+ = U - (U - X)_-^*$ and $X_+^* = U - (U - X)_*^-$, i.e., the duality holds between P- and N-fuzzy rough sets.

4.3 Relationships between Two Kinds of Fuzzy Rough Sets

While ξ- and σ-fuzzy sets are defined by using implication functions, P- and N-fuzzy rough sets are independent of logical connectives, i.e., conjunction and implication functions. Since CP- and CN-fuzzy rough sets are also defined by

Table 4. Relationships between CP/CN-fuzzy rough sets and ξ/σ-fuzzy rough sets

(a) When P and Q are reflexive and $\forall a \in [0,1], I(1,a) = a$, $P_*(X) \subseteq \mathcal{P}_*^\xi(X) \subseteq X$, $\mathcal{Q}_\xi^*(X) \subseteq \bar{Q}^*(X) \subseteq X$. When P and Q are reflexive, X is a crisp set, $a \leq b$ if and only if $I(a,b) = 1$ and $\forall a \in [0,1], T(a,1) = a$, $X \subseteq \mathcal{P}_\sigma^*(X) \subseteq P^*(X)$, $X \subseteq \bar{Q}_*(X) \subseteq \mathcal{Q}_*^\sigma(X)$.
(b) When P and Q are T-transitive and $T = \xi[I]$ is associative, $\mathcal{P}_*^\xi(X) \subseteq P_*(X) \subseteq X$, $\bar{Q}^*(X) \subseteq \mathcal{Q}_\xi^*(X) \subseteq X$. When P and Q are T-transitive, $T = \xi[\sigma[I]]$ and $\forall a,b,c \in [0,1], \sigma[I](a, \sigma[I](b,c)) = \sigma[I](b, \sigma[I](a,c))$, $X \subseteq P^*(X) \subseteq \mathcal{P}_\sigma^*(X)$, $X \subseteq \mathcal{Q}_*^\sigma(X) \subseteq \bar{Q}_*(X)$.

using conjunction and implication functions, we may be interested in the relationships between CP-, CN-fuzzy rough sets and ξ-, σ-fuzzy rough sets. In this subsection, we describe the relationships.

Under given fuzzy relations P and Q described in Section 2, we discuss the relationships between two kinds of fuzzy rough sets. Families of fuzzy sets are defined by $\mathcal{P} = \{P(x),\ x \in U\}$ and $\mathcal{Q} = \{Q(x),\ x \in U\}$. The relationships are shown in Table 4. The proofs of the relationships can found in [8].

5 Concluding Remarks

In this paper we discuss generalized crisp rough sets and fuzzy rough sets from two different interpretations: rough sets as classification of objects and rough sets as approximation of a set. In each interpretation, we have more than two definitions of rough sets. The fundamental properties and relationships are described. Moreover, we discussed the correspondences between types of extracted decision rules and generalized crisp rough sets.

Classification-oriented rough sets will be useful to analyze decision tables under uncertainty because the corresponding rules tend to be safer. On the other hand, application-oriented rough sets will be effective in utilization of the knowledge from decision tables to infer the results of new cases by interpolation. The interpolation ability can be also useful in treatment of continuous attributes. From this fact, Inuiguchi and Tanino [12] have examined the utilization of approximation-oriented rough sets to function approximation. In near future, we shall apply those generalized rough sets to real world problems and invesigate the advantages of each kind of generalized rough sets.

References

1. Alpigini, J. J., Peters, J. F., Skowron, A., Zhong, N.: *Rough Sets and Current Trends in Computing*, LNAI 2475, Springer Verlag, Berlin (2002).
2. Bonikowski, Z., Bryniarski, E., Wybraniec-Skardowska, U.: Extensions and Intensions in the Rough Set Theory. *Information Sciences* **107** (1998) 149–167

3. Dubois, D., Prade, H.: Rough Fuzzy Sets and Fuzzy Rough Sets. *Int. J. General Syst.* **17** (1990) 191–209.
4. Dubois, D., Prade, H.: Putting Rough Sets and Fuzzy Sets Together. in: R. Słowiński (Ed.) *Intelligent Decision Support*, Kluwer, Dordrecht (1992) 203–232.
5. Greco, S., Inuiguchi, M., Słowiński, R.: Rough Sets and Gradual Decision Rules. in: G. Wang et al.(Eds.) *Rough Sets, Fuzzy Sets, Data Mining, and Granular Computing*, Springer-Verlag, Berlin-Heidelberg (2003) 156–164.
6. Greco, S., Matarazzo, B., Słowiński, R.: The Use of Rough Sets and Fuzzy Sets in MCDM. in: Gal, T., Stewart, T. J., Hanne, T. (Eds.) *Multicriteria Decision Making: Advances in MCDM Models, Algorithms, Theory, and Applications*, Kluwer Academic Publishers, Boston, MA (1999) 14-1–14-59.
7. Inuiguchi, M.: Two Generalizations of Rough Sets and Their Fundamental Properties. *Proceedings of 6th Workshop on Uncertainty Processing*, September 24–27 Hejnice, Czech Republic (2003) 113–124.
8. Inuiguchi, M.: Classification- versus Approximation-oriented Fuzzy Rough Sets. *Proceedings of IPMU 2004*, July 4-9, Perugia, Italy (2004).
9. Inuiguchi, M., Hirano, S., Tsumoto, S.: *Rough Set Theory and Granular Computing*, Springer Verlag, Berlin (2003).
10. Inuiguchi, M., Tanino, T.: Two Directions toward Generalization of Rough Sets, in: M. Inuiguchi, S. Hirano, S. Tsumoto (Eds.) *Rough Set Theory and Granular Computing*, Springer Verlag, Berlin (2003) 47–57.
11. Inuiguchi, M., Tanino, T.: New Fuzzy Rough Sets Based on Certainty Qualification. in: K. Pal, L. Polkowski, A. Skowron (Eds.) *Rough-Neural Computing*, Springer-Verlag, Berlin-Heidelberg (2003) 278–296.
12. Inuiguchi, M., Tanino, T.: Function Approximation by Fuzzy Rough Sets. in: B. Bouchon-Meunier, L. Foulloy, R. R. Yager (Eds.) *Intelligent Systems for Information Processing: From Representation to Applications*, Elsevier, Amsterdam (2003) 93–104.
13. Pawlak, Z.: *Rough Sets: Theoretical Aspects of Reasoning About Data*, Kluwer Academic Publishers, Boston, MA (1991).
14. Słowiński, R., Vanderpooten, D.: A Generalized Definition of Rough Approximations Based on Similarity. *IEEE Transactions on Data and Knowledge Engineering* **12**(2) (2000) 331–336.
15. Wang, G., Liu, Q., Yao, Y., Skowron, A.: *Rough Sets, Fuzzy Sets, Data Mining, and Granular Computing*, LNAI 2639, Springer Verlag, Berlin (2003).
16. Yao, Y.Y.: Two Views of the Theory of Rough Sets in Finite Universes. *International Journal of Approximate Reasoning* **15** (1996) 291–317.
17. Yao, Y.Y.: Relational Interpretations of Neighborhood Operators and Rough Set Approximation Operators. *Information Sciences* **111** (1998) 239–259.
18. Yao, Y.Y., Lin, T.Y.: Generalization of Rough Sets Using Modal Logics. *Intelligent Automation and Soft Computing* **2**(2) (1996) 103–120.
19. Ziarko, W.: Variable Precision Rough Set Model. *J. Comput. Syst. Sci.* **46**(1) (1993) 39–59.

Investigation about Time Monotonicity of Similarity and Preclusive Rough Approximations in Incomplete Information Systems*

Gianpiero Cattaneo and Davide Ciucci

Dipartimento di Informatica, Sistemistica e Comunicazione
Università di Milano – Bicocca, via Bicocca degli Arcimboldi 8, 20126 Milano (Italia)
{cattang,ciucci}@disco.unimib.it

Abstract. Starting from an incomplete information system, we add some information in two different ways: by an increase in the number of known values and by an increase in the number of attributes. The behavior of the similarity and preclusive rough approximations are studied in both cases.

1 Introduction

When collecting information about a given topic in a certain moment in time, it may happen that we do not exactly know all the details of the issue in question. This lack of knowledge can be due to several reasons: we do not know all the characteristics of some object, we do not know all the objects of our universe, we have not considered all the possible aspects of the objects or a mix of all these. It is also natural to conjecture that as time increases also our knowledge increases, in one or more of the aspects outlined above. In the rough sets context there are several questions worthy to analyze in presence of an increase of information. In particular, we can ask if a rough approximation of a set of objects becomes better or not and if the number of exact sets increases or decreases. In our analysis we take into account the similarity and preclusive approach to rough approximation ([1–4]), as two paradigms able to cope with a lack of knowledge, and study their behavior in presence of an increase of information.

Definition 1.1. *An* Incomplete Information System *is a structure* $\mathcal{K}(X) = \langle X, Att(X), val(X), F\rangle$ *where* X *(called the* universe*) is a non empty set of* objects *(*situations, entities, states*);* $Att(X)$ *is a non empty set of* attributes, *which assume values for the objects belonging to the set* X*;* $val(X)$ *is the set of all* possible values *that can be observed for an attribute* a *from* $Att(X)$ *in the case of an object* x *from* X*;* F *(called the* information map*) is a mapping* $F : X \times Att(X) \to (val(X) \cup \{*\})$ *which associates to any pair, consisting of an object* $x \in X$ *and of an attribute* $a \in Att(X)$*, the value* $F(x, a) \in val(X)$ *assumed by* a *for the object* x*. The privileged* null value $*$ *denotes the fact that the value assumed by an object* x_i *with respect to the attribute* a_j *is unknown.*

* This work has been supported by MIUR\COFIN project "Formal Languages and Automata: Methods, Models and Applications".

S. Tsumoto et al. (Eds.): RSCTC 2004, LNAI 3066, pp. 38–48, 2004.

Example 1.1. As a concrete example, let us consider two observers, O_1 and O_2 collecting information about some flats at time t_0. Both the observers have a partial knowledge on the same set of flats, i.e., for some flat they do not know all its features, for instance because some information was missing on the advertisement. The resulting information systems are reported in Table 1.

Table 1. Flats incomplete information systems.

Observer O_1, time t_0				
Flat	Price	Rooms	Down-Town	Furniture
f_1	high	2	yes	*
f_2	high	*	yes	no
f_3	*	2	*	no
f_4	low	*	no	no
f_5	low	1	*	no
f_6	*	1	yes	*

Observer O_2, time t_0				
Flat	Price	Rooms	Down-Town	Furniture
f_1	high	2	yes	*
f_2	high	*	yes	no
f_3	*	2	yes	no
f_4	low	*	no	no
f_5	low	1	*	no
f_6	*	1	*	*

Thus, the two observers have a different information only about flats f_3, f_6.

The different ways to increase the knowledge sketched above can now be formalized in the following way.

Definition 1.2. *Let* $\mathcal{K}^{(t_1)}(X) = \langle X_1, Att(X_1), val(X_1), F^{t_1}\rangle$ *and* $\mathcal{K}^{(t_2)}(X)$, *with* $t_1, t_2 \in \mathbb{R}$, $t_1 \leq t_2$ *be two incomplete information systems. We will say that there is a* monotonic increase of information

- of type 1 *iff* $\mathcal{K}^{(t_2)}(X) = \langle X_1, Att(X_1), val(X_1), F^{t_2}\rangle$ *and* $F^{(t_1)}(x,a) \neq *$ *implies* $F^{(t_2)}(x,a) = F^{(t_1)}(x,a)$.
  In such a case, we will write $\mathcal{K}^{(t_1)}(X) \preceq_1 \mathcal{K}^{(t_2)}(X)$.
- of type 2 *iff* $\mathcal{K}^{(t_2)}(X) = \left\langle X_1, Att'(X_1), val'(X_1), F^{(t_2)}\right\rangle$ *where* $Att(X_1) \subseteq Att'(X_1)$, $val(X_1) \subseteq val'(X_1)$ *and* $\forall a \in Att(X_1)$, $\forall x \in X_1, F^{(t_2)}(x,a) = F^{(t_1)}(x,a)$. *In such a case, we will write* $\mathcal{K}^{(t_1)}(X) \preceq_2 \mathcal{K}^{(t_2)}(X)$.
- of type 3 *iff* $\mathcal{K}^{(t_2)}(X) = \left\langle X_2, Att(X_2), val(X_2), F^{(t_2)}\right\rangle$ *where* $X_1 \subseteq X_2$, $Att(X_1) = Att(X_2)$, $val(X_1) = val(X_2)$ *and* $\forall x \in X_1$, $F^{(t_2)}(x,a) = F^{(t_1)}(x,a)$.

In this paper we are dealing with the first two cases, and we reserve the third situation and a mix of them to a future analysis.

2 Similarity and Preclusive Spaces: The Static Description

Given an information system, the relationship among pairs of objects belonging to the universe X can be described through a binary relation $\mathcal{R}$. A classification and logical–algebraic characterization of such binary relations can be found in literature (for an overview see [5]). In our analysis, we are dealing with a *tolerance* (or *similarity*) relation, and its opposite, a *preclusive* relation.

Definition 2.1. *A* similarity space *is a structure* $\mathcal{S} = \langle X, \mathcal{R} \rangle$, *where* X *(the* universe *of the space) is a non empty set of objects and* $\mathcal{R}$ *(the* similarity *relation of the space) is a reflexive and symmetric binary relation defined on* X.

In the context of an incomplete information system $\mathcal{K}(X)$, for a fixed set of attributes $D \subseteq Att(X)$ a natural similarity relation is that two objects are similar if they possess the same values with respect to all known attributes inside D. In a more formal way:

$$\forall x, y \in X : \quad x\mathcal{R}_D y \quad \text{iff} \quad \forall a_i \in D \subseteq Att(X), \\ \text{either} \quad F(x, a_i) = F(y, a_i) \quad \text{or} \quad F(x, a_i) = * \quad \text{or} \quad F(y, a_i) = * \quad (1)$$

This is the approach introduced by Kryszkiewicz in [6] which has the advantage that the possibility of null values "corresponds to the idea that such values are just missing, but they do exist. In other words, it is our imperfect knowledge that obliges us to work with a partial information table"[7].

Given a similarity space $\langle X, \mathcal{R} \rangle$, the *similarity class* generated by the element $x \in X$ is the collection of all objects similar to x, i.e., $S(x) := \{y \in X : x\mathcal{R}y\}$ Thus, the similarity class generated by x consists of all the elements which are indiscernible from x with respect to the similarity relation $\mathcal{R}$. In this way this class constitute a *granule of similarity knowledge* about x and it is also called the *granule* generated by x. Further, any granule is nonempty and their collection is a covering (in general not a partition) of the universe X.

Using this notion of similarity class, it is possible to define in a natural way a rough approximation by similarity of any set of objects ([8, 1, 9, 10]).

Definition 2.2. *Given a similarity space* $\langle X, \mathcal{R} \rangle$, *and a set of objects* $A \subseteq X$, *the* rough approximation of A by similarity *is defined as the pair of* similarity lower *approximation and* similarity upper *approximation* $\langle \mathbf{l}_{\mathcal{R}}(A), \mathbf{u}_{\mathcal{R}}(A) \rangle$, *where*

$$\mathbf{l}_{\mathcal{R}}(A) := \{x \in X : S(x) \subseteq A\} = \{x \in X : \forall z\ (x\mathcal{R}z \Rightarrow z \in A)\} \quad (2a)$$

$$\mathbf{u}_{\mathcal{R}}(A) := \{x \in X : S(x) \cap A \neq \emptyset\} = \{x \in X : \exists z\ (x\mathcal{R}z \textit{ and } z \in A)\} \quad (2b)$$

It is easy to verify that the chain of inclusions $\mathbf{l}_{\mathcal{R}}(A) \subseteq A \subseteq \mathbf{u}_{\mathcal{R}}(A)$ *holds.*

As said before, the opposite of a similarity relation is a *preclusive* relation: two objects are in a preclusive relation iff it is possible to distinguish one from the other. Using such a relation it is possible to define a notion dual to the one of similarity space.

Definition 2.3. *A* preclusive space *is a structure* $\mathcal{S} = \langle X, \# \rangle$, *where* X *(called the* universe *of the space) is a non empty set and* $\#$ *(called the* preclusive *relation of the space) is an irreflexive and symmetric relation defined on* X.

Obviously, any similarity space $\langle X, \mathcal{R} \rangle$ determines a corresponding preclusive space $\langle X, \#_{\mathcal{R}} \rangle$ with $x \#_{\mathcal{R}} y$ iff $\neg(x\mathcal{R}y)$, and vice versa any preclusive space $\langle X, \# \rangle$ determines a similarity space $\langle X, \mathcal{R}_{\#} \rangle$ with $x\mathcal{R}_{\#}y$ iff $\neg(x\#y)$. In this case we will say that we have a pair of *correlated* similarity–preclusive relations.

Suppose now a preclusive space $\langle X, \# \rangle$. The preclusive relation $\#$ permits us to introduce for any $H \in \mathcal{P}(X)$ (where we denote by $\mathcal{P}(X)$ the power set of X) its *preclusive complement* defined as $H^{\#} := \{x \in X : \forall y \in H \ (x \# y)\}$. In other words, $H^{\#}$ contains all and only the elements of X that are distinguishable from all the elements of H. We remark that, in the context of modal analysis of rough approximation spaces, the operation $^{\#}$ is a *sufficiency* operator [11].

On the Boolean lattice based on the power set $\mathcal{P}(X)$, we now have two, generally different, complementations: the usual set theoretic complementation ^{c} and the preclusive complementation $^{\#}$. By their interaction, it is possible to define a closure and an interior operator on $\mathcal{P}(X)$.

Proposition 2.1. *Let $\langle \mathcal{P}(X), \cap, \cup, {}^{c}, {}^{\#}, \emptyset, X \rangle$ be the algebraic structure based on the power set of X and generated by the preclusive space $\langle X, \# \rangle$. Then the mapping $\mathbf{l}_{\#} : \mathcal{P}(X) \to \mathcal{P}(X)$, $H \to \mathbf{l}_{\#}(H) := H^{c\#\#c}$ is an* interior operator*:*

(I_0)	$X = \mathbf{l}_{\#}(X)$	*(normalized)*
(I_1)	$\mathbf{l}_{\#}(H) \subseteq H$	*(decreasing)*
(I_2)	$\mathbf{l}_{\#}(H) = \mathbf{l}_{\#}(\mathbf{l}_{\#}(H))$	*(idempotent)*
(I_3)	$H \subseteq K$ *implies* $\mathbf{L}_{\#}(H) \subseteq \mathbf{l}_{\#}(K)$	*(monotonicity)*

Further, the mapping $\mathbf{u}_{\#} : \mathcal{P}(X) \to \mathcal{P}(X)$, $H \to \mathbf{u}_{\#}(H) := H^{\#\#}$ is a closure operator*, i.e.,*

(C_0)	$\emptyset = \mathbf{u}_{\#}(\emptyset)$	*(normalized)*
(C_1)	$H \subseteq \mathbf{u}_{\#}(H)$	*(increasing)*
(C_2)	$\mathbf{u}_{\#}(H) = \mathbf{u}_{\#}(\mathbf{u}_{\#}(H))$	*(idempotent)*
(C_3)	$H \subseteq K$ *implies* $\mathbf{U}_{\#}(H) \subseteq \mathbf{u}_{\#}(K)$	*(monotonicity)*

From the fact that according to (I_1) in general one has that $\mathbf{l}_{\#}(H) \subseteq H$, it is possible to single out the collection of all $\#$*–open* sets defined as: $\mathbb{O}(X, \#) := \{A \subseteq X : A = \mathbf{l}_{\#}(A) = A^{c\#\#c}\}$. Dually, the collection of all $\#$*–closed* sets is defined as: $\mathbb{C}(X, \#) := \{B \subseteq X : B = \mathbf{u}_{\#}(B) = B^{\#\#}\}$. These sets are not empty since both the empty set $\emptyset$ and the whole universe X are $\#$–open and $\#$–closed sets. It is easy to see that A is $\#$–open iff A^{c} is $\#$–closed, and similarly B is $\#$–closed iff B^{c} is $\#$–open. If a set is both $\#$–open and $\#$–closed, it is said to be $\#$*–clopen*. So, the collection of all $\#$–clopen sets is defined as: $\mathbb{CO}(X, \#) = \mathbb{C}(X, \#) \cap \mathbb{O}(X, \#)$. Both the empty set $\emptyset$ and the whole universe X are $\#$–clopen. In the sequel, if there is no confusion, we simply say open, closed, and clopen sets instead of $\#$–open, $\#$–closed, and $\#$–clopen sets.

By the increasing property (C_1) of the closure operator and the decreasing property (I_1) of the interior operator, it holds the chain of inclusions: $\mathbf{l}_{\#}(H) \subseteq H \subseteq \mathbf{u}_{\#}(H)$. Therefore, the pair $\langle \mathbf{l}_{\#}(H), \mathbf{u}_{\#}(H) \rangle$ can be thought of as a *preclusive rough approximation* of the set H by a preclusive open–closed pair. Moreover, it is the best approximation by open–closed sets. That is, for every closed set B which is an upper approximation of H, $H \subseteq B$, we have by monotonicity that $\mathbf{u}_{\#}(H) \subseteq \mathbf{u}_{\#}(B) = B$, and dually, for every open set B which is a lower approximation of H, $B \subseteq H$, we have by monotonicity that $B = \mathbf{l}_{\#}(B) \subseteq \mathbf{l}_{\#}(H)$.

Let us note that the preclusive upper and lower approximation of a set H can also be expressed as:

$$\mathbf{u}_{\#}(H) = \cap\{B \in \mathbb{C}(X,\#) : H \subseteq B\} \quad \mathbf{l}_{\#}(H) = \cup\{B \in \mathbb{O}(X,\#) : B \subseteq H\}.$$

In the case of a closed set H one has that $H = \mathbf{u}_{\#}(H)$, i.e., the upper closed approximation of any closed set is the set itself. In this sense we can say that closed sets are *upper exact sets*. In the case of an open set H obviously $H = \mathbf{l}_{\#}(H)$, obtaining that open sets can be considered as *lower exact sets*. Finally, we have that clopen sets are both lower and upper exact sets, so, we simply call them *exact sets*.

Example 2.1. Making reference to the information systems described by Table 1, let us consider the preclusive rough approximation with respect to the preclusive relation obtained as logical negation of (1) induced by the set $\mathcal{D} = Att(X)$ of all involved attributes. Then, the collection of closed sets, with respect to observers O_1 and O_2, are respectively

$$\mathbb{C}_1^{(t_0)}(X) = \{\emptyset, \{1\}, \{4\}, \{5\}, \{6\}, \{1,2\}, \{1,3\}, \{4,5\}, \{5,6\}, \{1,3,4\}, \{1,2,3\}, \{1,2,6\}, \{4,5,6\}, X\}$$

$$\mathbb{C}_2^{(t_0)}(X) = \{\emptyset, \{1,3\}, \{4,5\}, \{1,2,3\}, \{4,5,6\}, X\}$$

The clopen sets coincide in both cases and their collection is $\mathbb{CO}_1^{(t_0)}(X) = \mathbb{CO}_2^{(t_0)}(X) = \{\emptyset, \{1,2,3\}, \{4,5,6\}, X\}$.

In Table 2 using the information relative to observer O_1, examples of similar and preclusive approximations with respect to some particular subsets H of the involved universe are reported.

Table 2. Examples of Approximations, case 1 at time t_0.

$\mathbf{l}_{\mathcal{R}}(H)$	$\mathbf{l}_{\#}(H)$	H	$\mathbf{u}_{\#}(H)$	$\mathbf{u}_{\mathcal{R}}(H)$
$\emptyset$	$\emptyset$	$\{f_2\}$	$\{f_1, f_2\}$	$\{f_1, f_2, f_3, f_6\}$
$\emptyset$	$\emptyset$	$\{f_4, f_5\}$	$\{f_4, f_5\}$	$\{f_3, f_4, f_5, f_6\}$
$\emptyset$	$\emptyset$	$\{f_1, f_2, f_4, f_5\}$	$\{f_1, f_2, f_3, f_4, f_5, f_6\}$	$\{f_1, f_2, f_3, f_4, f_5, f_6\}$
$\{f_6\}$	$\{f_2, f_5, f_6\}$	$\{f_1, f_2, f_5, f_6\}$	$\{f_1, f_2, f_3, f_4, f_5, f_6\}$	$\{f_1, f_2, f_3, f_4, f_5, f_6\}$

As can be seen, in all the particular cases of Table 2 the following chain of inclusions holds:

$$\mathbf{l}_{\mathcal{R}}(H) \subseteq \mathbf{l}_{\#}(H) \subseteq H \subseteq \mathbf{u}_{\#}(H) \subseteq \mathbf{u}_{\mathcal{R}}(H) \tag{3}$$

This is a general property, which holds for all subsets of the universe of a preclusive space, as it has been proved in [12].

3 Increasing the Number of Known Values: The Dynamical Description

Starting from an incomplete information system one can wonder what happens when the number of known values increases. One could expect that for a fixed set of attributes to more knowledge there corresponds more open and closed sets, producing in this way a preclusive rough approximation which is better than the previous one (if the information increases, then the approximation should be better and better). However, this is not always the case and, as we are going to show through examples, there is no correspondence between unknown values and exact (either open or closed or clopen) sets of the preclusive environment.

Example 3.1. Let us consider the two information systems of Table 1, relative to a knowledge situation of two observers O_1 and O_2 at time t_0. Let us suppose that at a following time t_1 (i.e., $t_0 < t_1$) the two observers acquire the same information as described in Table 3. That is, observer O_1 has a better knowledge about flat f_3 and observer O_2 about flat f_6.

Table 3. Only the information regarding flat f_3 and f_6 is different from the one of Tables 1 with a global increase in time of the knowledge for both observers.

Flat	Price	Rooms	Down-Town	Furniture
f_3	*	2	no	no
f_6	*	1	yes	*

The collection of closed and clopen sets in this case are respectively:

$$\mathbb{C}^{(t_1)}_{(1,2)}(X) = \{\emptyset, \{4\}, \{6\}, \{1,3\}, \{4,5\}, \{1,3,4\}, \{1,2,3\}, \{4,5,6\}, \{1,2,3,6\}, X\}$$
$$\mathbb{CO}^{(t_1)}_{(1,2)}(X) = \{\emptyset, \{4,5\}, \{1,2,3\}, \{4,5,6\}, \{1,2,3,6\}, X\}$$

Thus, there are two observers that initially (time t_0) have a different knowledge about the same collection of flats (described by Tables 1). During the time, both the observers increase their knowledge reaching the same result exposed in Table 3 at a subsequent time t_1. The final result is that relatively to the same set of all attributes $\mathcal{D} = Att(X)$ there is a decrease (resp., increase) in the number of closed, and so also of open, sets in the case of observer O_1 (resp., O_2) moving from the situation of Table 1 at time t_0 to the situation of Table 3 at time t_1.

When considering the clopen sets we observe that their number increases in the situation relative to Table 3 with respect to both case 1 and case 2 (resp., observers O_1 and O_2). Again we ask whether this is a general property: to a greater knowledge corresponds a higher number of clopen sets. Also in this case, the answer is negative. Let us suppose that, with respect to the original situation of Table 3 at time t_1, both the observers in a later time, say $t_2 > t_1$, increase their knowledge about flat 5 according to Table 4.

Table 4. Information system relative to observers O_1 and O_2 at time $t_2 > t_1$.

Flat	Price	Rooms	Down-Town	Furniture
f_5	low	1	no	no

In this case, however, the number of clopen sets decreases with respect to the knowledge at time t_1: $\mathbb{CO}^{(t_2)}_{(1,2)}(X) = \{\emptyset, \{4,5\}, \{1,2,3,6\}, X\}$.

When considering the closed sets, it happens that they are numerically less at time t_2 with respect to the ones at time t_1, but the set $\{1,3,4,5\}$ is closed at time t_2 and not at time t_1:

$$\mathbb{C}^{(t_2)}_{(1,2)}(X) = \{\emptyset, \{6\}, \{1,3\}, \{4,5\}, \{4,5,6\}, \{1,3,4,5\}, \{1,2,3,6\}, X\}$$

As regards to the quality of preclusive approximations, we have the same uncertainty as in the case of exact sets. However, we can select those situations in which to an increase of knowledge in time there corresponds an increase in the quality of the approximations.

Definition 3.1. *Let $\mathcal{K}^{(t_0)}(X)$ and $\mathcal{K}^{(t_1)}(X)$ with $t_0 < t_1$ be two incomplete information systems such that $\mathcal{K}^{(t_0)}(X) \preceq_i \mathcal{K}^{(t_1)}(X)$ ($i = 1,2$). We will say that there is a* monotonic increase of knowledge of type i *iff* $\mathbb{C}^{(t_0)}(X) \subseteq \mathbb{C}^{(t_1)}(X)$, *and in this case we write $\mathcal{K}^{(t_0)}(X) \sqsubseteq_i \mathcal{K}^{(t_1)}(X)$.*

Proposition 3.1. *Let $\mathcal{K}^{(t_0)}(X)$ and $\mathcal{K}^{(t_1)}(X)$ ($t_0 < t_1$) be two incomplete information systems such that $\mathcal{K}^{(t_0)}(X) \sqsubseteq_1 \mathcal{K}^{(t_1)}(X)$. Then, $\forall H \subseteq X$ $\mathbf{l}^{(t_0)}_{\#}(H) \subseteq \mathbf{l}^{(t_1)}_{\#}(H) \subseteq H \subseteq \mathbf{u}^{(t_1)}_{\#}(H) \subseteq \mathbf{u}^{(t_0)}_{\#}(H)$.*

This desirable behavior, which holds in the generic case of *monotonic increase of knowledge*, does not hold in the case of a *monotonic increase of information* as can be seen in the following example.

Example 3.2. Let us consider the information system at time t_1 of Table 3. If we compute the approximations of the same sets used in Table 2, we obtain the following results.

Table 5. Examples of Approximations at time t_1.

$\mathbf{l}_{\mathcal{R}}(H)$	$\mathbf{l}_{\#}(H)$	H	$\mathbf{u}_{\#}(H)$	$\mathbf{u}_{\mathcal{R}}(H)$
$\emptyset$	$\emptyset$	$\{f_2\}$	$\{f_1, f_2, f_3\}$	$\{f_1, f_2, f_3, f_6\}$
$\{f_4\}$	$\{f_4, f_5\}$	$\{f_4, f_5\}$	$\{f_4, f_5\}$	$\{f_4, f_5, f_6\}$
$\{f_4\}$	$\{f_4, f_5\}$	$\{f_1, f_2, f_4, f_5\}$	$\{f_1, f_2, f_3, f_4, f_5, f_6\}$	$\{f_1, f_2, f_3, f_4, f_5, f_6\}$
$\{f_6\}$	$\{f_2, f_5, f_6\}$	$\{f_1, f_2, f_5, f_6\}$	$\{f_1, f_2, f_3, f_4, f_5, f_6\}$	$\{f_1, f_2, f_3, f_4, f_5, f_6\}$

That is, going from a situation at time t_0 to a situation at time t_1, i.e., adding information to the information system in a monotonic way, we have that the time evolution of the preclusive rough approximation of a set H is unpredictable, i.e., the approximation becomes either worst (case $\{f_2\}$), or better (cases $\{f_4, f_5\}$, $\{f_1, f_2, f_4, f_5\}$), or remains the same (case $\{f_1, f_2, f_5, f_6\}$).

Differently from the preclusive rough approximation, if we consider the similarity rough approximation, we can see, comparing Table 2 with Table 5, that the quality of the approximation is monotonic with respect to the quantity of information. This is a general result, as shown in the following proposition.

Proposition 3.2. *Let $\mathcal{K}^{(t_0)}(X)$ and $\mathcal{K}^{(t_1)}(X)$ ($t_0 < t_1$) be two incomplete information systems such that $\mathcal{K}^{(t_0)}(X) \preceq_1 \mathcal{K}^{(t_1)}(X)$. Then, $\forall H \subseteq X$ $\mathbf{l}_{\mathcal{R}}^{(t_0)}(H) \subseteq \mathbf{l}_{\mathcal{R}}^{(t_1)}(H) \subseteq H \subseteq \mathbf{u}_{\mathcal{R}}^{(t_1)}(H) \subseteq \mathbf{u}_{\mathcal{R}}^{(t_0)}(H)$.*

Concluding, if we suppose an increase of the information of type 1, we have an *unpredictable* behavior of the preclusive approximation as can be seen in Example 3.2 and a *monotone* behavior of the similarity approximation with respect to the knowledge increase. But at any fixed time the preclusive approximation of a fixed set is always better then the correlated similarity approximation, i.e., the chain (3) holds for any set in this fixed time. From an intuitive point of view we can imagine a situation similar to the one drawn in Figure 1.

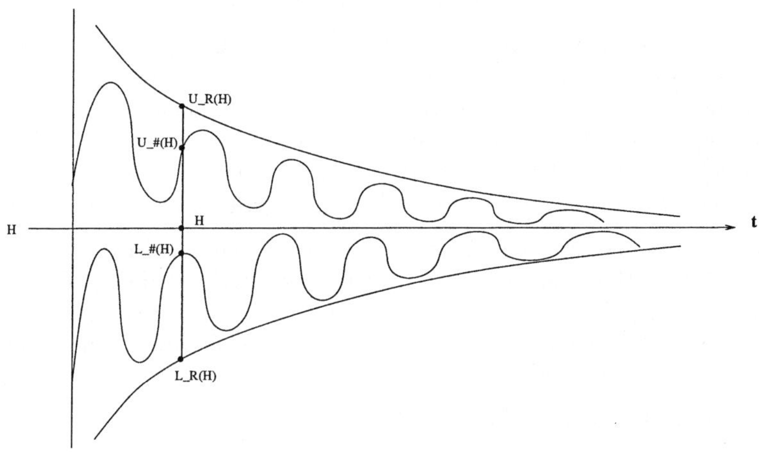

Fig. 1. An imaginary representation of the time evolution of the similarity and preclusive rough approximations.

All the examples considered until now are about incomplete information systems and the similarity relation given by Equation (1). However, the pathological behavior remarked about the monotonic increase of information holds also in other contexts. For instance in [12] we considered the binary relation, sometimes called *ϵ-indiscernibility* ([13]), induced by a pseudo–metric among objects of an information system with numerical set of possible values.

4 Increasing the Number of Attributes: Another Dynamics

The second situation we are taking into account, consists in an increase in time of the number of attributes of the information system. It can equivalently be interpreted as if we knew from the start all the attributes but at a first stage we use only a subset of them.

This case has been analyzed in literature in the case of classical (Pawlak) rough sets theory, which is based on an equivalence relation instead of a similarity one. For instance, Orlowska in [14] proves that if A, B are two sets of attributes such that $A \subseteq B$, then for any set of object X, the following relation holds:

$$\mathbf{l}_A(X) \subseteq \mathbf{l}_B(X) \subseteq X \subseteq \mathbf{l}_B(X) \subseteq \mathbf{l}_A(X)$$

That is, to an increase of information (consisting in an increase in the number of attributes of the information system) corresponds a better rough approximation. This result can be easily extended to similarity rough approximations.

Proposition 4.1. *Let $\mathcal{K}^{(t_0)}(X)$ and $\mathcal{K}^{(t_1)}(X)$ be two incomplete information systems such that $\mathcal{K}^{(t_0)}(X) \preceq_2 \mathcal{K}^{(t_1)}(X)$, i.e., there is a monotonic increase of information of type 2 between the two information systems as specified in Definition 1.2. Then, for all $H \in X$, $\mathbf{l}_{\mathcal{R}}^{t_0}(H) \subseteq \mathbf{l}_{\mathcal{R}}^{t_1}(H) \subseteq H \subseteq \mathbf{L}_{\mathcal{R}}^{t_1}(H) \subseteq \mathbf{l}_{\mathcal{R}}^{t_0}(H)$.*

On the other hand, if we consider the preclusive rough approximations we are in the same unpredictable situation of the previous section when evaluating the behavior of exact sets during time. In fact, as can be seen in the following counterexample, there is no relation between the exact sets, either closed (equivalently, open) or clopen, of two information systems linked by a monotonic increase of information of type 2 during the time transition $t_0 \to t_1$.

Example 4.1. Let us consider the information system of Table 4, relative to the knowledge of the observer O_1 (equivalently, O_2) at time t_2. Now, we set A={Price, Rooms, Furniture}, i.e., we suppose that at a previous time, say t_1, another observer O_3 did not know the attribute Down–Town. Then the clopen and closed sets are respectively:

$$\mathbb{CO}_3^{(t_1)}(X) = \{\emptyset, \{1,2,3\}, \{4,5,6\}, X\}$$

$$\mathbb{C}_3^{(t_1)}(X) = \{\emptyset, \{1\}, \{5\}, \{1,2\}, \{1,3\}, \{4,5\}, \{5,6\}, \{1,2,3\}, \{4,5,6\}, X\}$$

So with respect to the same observer O_3, there are sets, for instance $\{1,2,3\}$, which are clopen at time t_1 and not at time t_2 and vice versa, the set $\{1,2,3,6\}$ is clopen at time t_2 and not at time t_1. The same holds for the closed sets.

Also the preclusive approximations have the pathological behavior of the previous section: it is not possible to say if the approximation of the same set becomes better or worst at a subsequent time. However, it holds of course the general order chain among preclusive and similarity rough approximations: the first one is always better than the second one. So, also in the case of a monotonic increase of information of type 2, it is verified a phenomenon like the one of Figure 1.

Example 4.2. Let us consider the information system of Table 3 and compute the rough approximations of the same sets of Table 5 with respect to the set of attributes {Price, Down–Town, Furniture}. The results of this case are reported in Table 6.

Thus, with respect to the same observer, the preclusive approximation of the set $\{f_2\}$ becomes worst going from time t_0 where D={Price, Down-Town, Furniture}) to time t_1 where $D = Att(X)$. On the other hand the set $\{f_1, f_2, f_5, f_6\}$

Table 6. Examples of Approximations.

$\mathbf{l}_{\mathcal{R}}(H)$	$\mathbf{l}_{\#}(H)$	H	$\mathbf{u}_{\#}(H)$	$\mathbf{u}_{\mathcal{R}}(H)$
$\emptyset$	$\emptyset$	$\{f_2\}$	$\{f_1, f_2\}$	$\{f_1, f_2, f_3, f_6\}$
$\{f_4\}$	$\{f_4, f_5\}$	$\{f_4, f_5\}$	$\{f_4, f_5\}$	$\{f_3, f_4, f_5, f_6\}$
$\{f_4\}$	$\{f_4, f_5\}$	$\{f_1, f_2, f_4, f_5\}$	$\{f_1, f_2, f_3, f_4, f_5, f_6\}$	$\{f_1, f_2, f_3, f_4, f_5, f_6\}$
$\emptyset$	$\emptyset$	$\{f_1, f_2, f_5, f_6\}$	$\{f_1, f_2, f_3, f_4, f_5, f_6\}$	$\{f_1, f_2, f_3, f_4, f_5, f_6\}$

has a better approximation at time t_1 than t_0 and the approximation of the sets $\{f_4, f_5\}$ and $\{f_1, f_2, f_4, f_5\}$ is the same at time t_0 and t_1.

However, also in this case, it is possible to single out those situations which guarantee an increase in the quality of preclusive approximations.

Proposition 4.2. *Let $\mathcal{K}^{(t_0)}(X)$ and $\mathcal{K}^{(t_1)}(X)$ ($t_0 < t_1$) be two incomplete information systems such that $\mathcal{K}^{(t_0)}(X) \sqsubseteq_2 \mathcal{K}^{(t_1)}(X)$. Then, $\forall H \subseteq X$ $\mathbf{l}_{\#}^{(t_0)}(H) \subseteq \mathbf{l}_{\#}^{(t_1)}(H) \subseteq H \subseteq \mathbf{u}_{\#}^{(t_1)}(H) \subseteq \mathbf{u}_{\#}^{(t_0)}(H)$.*

As a future work, it would be interesting to understand which information systems give rise to a monotonic increase of knowledge, i.e., to condition $\mathbb{C}^{(t_0)}(X) \subseteq \mathbb{C}^{(t_1)}(X)$. Of course, we have no guarantee that such a characterization exists.

Moreover, type 1 and type 2 increase of information can be viewed as Dynamic Spaces of [15], so a study in this sense could give some further insight on the evolution in time of exact sets and rough approximations.

References

1. Skowron, A., Stepaniuk, J.: Tolerance approximation spaces. Fundamenta Informaticae **27** (1996) 245–253
2. Słowinski, R., Vanderpooten, D.: A generalized definition of rough approximations based on similarity. Transactions on Knowledge and Data Engineering **12** (2000) 331–336
3. Cattaneo, G.: Generalized rough sets (preclusivity fuzzy-intuitionistic BZ lattices). Studia Logica **58** (1997) 47–77
4. Cattaneo, G.: Abstract approximation spaces for rough theories. In Polkowski, L., Skowron, A., eds.: Rough Sets in Knowledge Discovery 1. Physica–Verlag, Heidelberg, New York (1998) 59–98
5. Orlowska, E.: Introduction: What you always wanted to know about rough sets. In Orlowska, E., ed.: Incomplete Information: Rough Set Analysis. Physica–Verlag, Heidelberg (1998) 1–20
6. Kryszkiewicz, M.: Rough set approach to incomplete information systems. Information Sciences **112** (1998) 39–49
7. Stefanowki, J., Tsoukiàs, A.: On the extension of rough sets under incomplete information. Volume 1711 of LNCS., Springer (1999) 73–81
8. Vakarelov, D.: A modal logic for similarity relations in Pawlak knowledge representation systems. Fundamenta Informaticae **XV** (1991) 61–79
9. Stepaniuk, J.: Approximation spaces in extensions of rough sets theory. Volume 1424 of LNCS., Springer (1998) 290–297

10. Stefanowski, J., Tsoukiàs, A.: Valued tolerance and decision rules. Volume 2005 of Lecture Notes in Artificial Intelligence., Berlin, Springer-Verlag (2001) 212–219
11. Düntsch, I., Orlowska, E.: Beyond modalities: Sufficiency and mixed algebras. In Orlowska, E., Szalas, A., eds.: Relational Methods for Computer Science Applications. Physica–Verlag, Heidelberg (2001) 277–299
12. Cattaneo, G., Ciucci, D.: Algebraic structures for rough sets. In Dubois, D., Polkowski, L., Gryzmala-Busse, J., eds.: Fuzzy Rough Sets. Springer Verlag (2003) In press.
13. Słowinski, R., Vanderpooten, D.: Similarity relation as a basis for rough approximations. In Wang, P., ed.: Advances in Machine Intelligence and Soft-Computing, vol.IV. Duke University Press, Durham, NC (1997) 17–33
14. Orlowska, E.: Kripke semantics for knowledge representation logics. Studia Logica **49** (1990) 255–272
15. Pagliani, P.: Pre–topologies and dynamic spaces. In: Proceedings of RSFDGrC03. Volume 2639 of LNCS., Heidelberg, Springer–Verlag (2003) 146–155
16. Greco, S., Matarazzo, B., Slowinski, R.: Dealing with missing data in rough set analysis of multi-attribute and multi-criteria decision problems. In Zanakis, S., Doukidis, G., Zopounidis, C., eds.: Decision Making: Recent Developments and Worldwide Applications. Kluwer Academic Publishers, Boston (2000) 295–316

The Ordered Set of Rough Sets

Jouni Järvinen

Turku Centre for Computer Science (TUCS)
Lemminkäisenkatu 14 A, FIN-20520 Turku, Finland
jjarvine@cs.utu.fi

Abstract. We study the ordered set of rough sets determined by relations which are not necessarily reflexive, symmetric, or transitive. We show that for tolerances and transitive binary relations the set of rough sets is not necessarily even a semilattice. We also prove that the set of rough sets determined by a symmetric and transitive binary relation forms a complete Stone lattice. Furthermore, for the ordered sets of rough sets that are not necessarily lattices we present some possible canonical completions.

1 Different Types of Indiscernibility Relations

The rough set theory introduced by Pawlak (1982) deals with situations in which the objects of a certain universe of discourse U can be identified only within the limits determined by the knowledge represented by a given indiscernibility relation. Based on such indiscernibility relation the lower and the upper approximation of subsets of U may be defined. The lower and the upper approximation of a subset X of U can be viewed as the sets of elements which certainly and possibly belong to X, respectively.

Usually it is presumed that indiscernibility relations are equivalences. However, some authors, for example, Järvinen (2001), Pomykała (2002), and Skowron and Stepaniuk (1996) have studied approximation operators which are defined by tolerances. Slowinski and Vanderpooten (2000) have studied approximation operators defined by reflexive binary relations, and Greco, Matarazzo, and Slowinski (2000) considered approximations based on reflexive and transitive relations. Yao and Lin (1996) have studied approximations determined by arbitrary binary relations, and in a recent survey Düntsch and Gediga (2003) explored various types of approximation operators based on binary relations. Furthermore, Cattaneo (1998) and Järvinen (2002), for instance, have studied approximation operations in a more general lattice-theoretical setting.

The structure of the ordered set of rough sets defined by equivalences was examined by Gehrke and Walker (1992), Iwiński (1987), and J. Pomykała and J.A. Pomykała (1988). In this work we study the structure of the ordered sets of rough sets based on indiscernibility relations which are not necessarily reflexive, symmetric, or transitive.

2 Lattices and Orders

Here we recall some basic notions of lattice theory which can be found, for example, in the books by Davey and Priestly (2002) and Grätzer (1998). A binary relation $\leq$ on a

S. Tsumoto et al. (Eds.): RSCTC 2004, LNAI 3066, pp. 49–58, 2004.

set P is called an *order*, if it is reflexive, antisymmetric, and transitive. An *ordered set* is a pair $\mathcal{P} = (P, \leq)$, with P being a set and $\leq$ an order on P.

Let $\mathcal{P} = (P, \leq)$ and $\mathcal{Q} = (Q, \leq)$ be two ordered sets. A map $\varphi \colon P \to Q$ is an *order-embedding*, if $a \leq b$ in $\mathcal{P}$ if and only if $\varphi(a) \leq \varphi(b)$ in $\mathcal{Q}$. An order-embedding φ onto Q is called an *order-isomorphism* between $\mathcal{P}$ and $\mathcal{Q}$. When there exists an order-isomorphism between $\mathcal{P}$ and $\mathcal{Q}$, we say that $\mathcal{P}$ and $\mathcal{Q}$ are *order-isomorphic* and write $\mathcal{P} \cong \mathcal{Q}$.

An ordered set $\mathcal{P} = (P, \leq)$ is a *lattice*, if for any two elements x and y in P, the *join* $x \vee y$ and the *meet* $x \wedge y$ always exist. The ordered set $\mathcal{P}$ is called a *complete lattice* if the *join* $\bigvee S$ and the *meet* $\bigwedge S$ exist for any subset S of P. The greatest element of $\mathcal{P}$, if it exists, is called the *unit* element and it is denoted by 1. Dually, the smallest element 0 is called the *zero* element. An ordered set is *bounded* if it has a zero and a unit.

A lattice $\mathcal{P} = (P, \leq)$ is *distributive* if it satisfies the conditions

$$x \wedge (y \vee z) = (x \wedge y) \vee (x \wedge z) \quad \text{and} \quad x \vee (y \wedge z) = (x \vee y) \wedge (x \vee z)$$

for all $x, y, z \in P$. Let $\mathcal{P} = (P, \leq)$ be a bounded lattice. An element $x' \in P$ is a *complement* of $x \in P$, if $x' \vee x = 1$ and $x' \wedge x = 0$. A bounded lattice is a *Boolean lattice* if it is complemented and distributive.

Example 1. If X is any set and $\mathcal{P} = (P, \leq)$ is an ordered set, we may order the set P^X of all maps from X to P by the *pointwise order*:

$$f \leq g \text{ in } P^X \overset{\text{def}}{\iff} (\forall x \in P)\ f(x) \leq g(x) \text{ in } P.$$

We denote by $\mathbf{2}$ and $\mathbf{3}$ the chains obtained by ordering the sets $\{0, 1\}$ and $\{0, u, 1\}$ so that $0 < 1$ and $0 < u < 1$, respectively.

Let us denote by $\wp(U)$ the set of all subsets of U. It is well-known that the ordered set $(\wp(U), \subseteq)$ is a complete Boolean lattice such that for all $\mathcal{H} \subseteq \wp(U)$,

$$\bigvee \mathcal{H} = \bigcup \mathcal{H} \text{ and } \bigwedge \mathcal{H} = \bigcap \mathcal{H}.$$

Each set $X \subseteq U$ has a complement $U - X$. Furthermore, $(\wp(U), \subseteq) \cong (\mathbf{2}^U, \leq)$.

Let $\mathcal{P} = (P, \leq)$ be a lattice with 0. An element x^* is a *pseudocomplement* of x if $x \wedge x^* = 0$ and $x \wedge a = 0$ implies $a \leq x^*$. A lattice is *pseudocomplemented* if every element has a pseudocomplement. If a lattice $\mathcal{P}$ with 0 is distributive, pseudocomplemented, and it satisfies the Stone identity $x^* \vee x^{**} = 1$ for any element $x \in P$, then $\mathcal{P}$ is a *Stone lattice*. It is obvious that every Boolean lattice is a Stone lattice and that every finite distributive lattice is pseudocomplemented.

3 Rough Sets Defined by Equivalences

This section is devoted to the structure of the ordered set of rough sets determined by equivalence relations. Let U be a set and let E be an equivalence relation on U. For any x, we denote by $[x]_E$ the *equivalence class* of x, that is,

$$[x]_E = \{y \in U \mid x\, E\, y\}.$$

For any set $X \subseteq U$, let

$$X^{\blacktriangledown} = \{x \in U \mid [x]_E \subseteq X\};$$
$$X^{\blacktriangle} = \{x \in U \mid [x]_E \cap X \neq \emptyset\}.$$

The sets $X^{\blacktriangledown}$ and $X^{\blacktriangle}$ are called the *lower* and the *upper approximation* of X, respectively. Two sets are said to be *roughly equivalent*, denoted by $X \equiv Y$, if $X^{\blacktriangledown} = Y^{\blacktriangledown}$ and $X^{\blacktriangle} = Y^{\blacktriangle}$. The equivalence classes of the relation $\equiv$ are called *rough sets*. The family of all rough sets is denoted by $\mathcal{R}$, that is,

$$\mathcal{R} = \{ [X]_{\equiv} \mid X \subseteq U\}.$$

Example 2. Let $U = \{a, b, c\}$ and let E be an equivalence on U such that

$$[a]_E = \{a, c\}, \quad [b]_E = \{b\}, \quad [c]_E = \{a, c\}.$$

The approximations are presented in Table 1. The rough sets are $\{\emptyset\}$, $\{\{a\}, \{c\}\}$, $\{\{b\}\}$, $\{\{a, b\}, \{b, c\}\}$, $\{\{a, c\}\}$, and $\{U\}$.

Table 1. Approximations of subsets

X	$X^{\blacktriangledown}$	$X^{\blacktriangle}$
$\emptyset$	$\emptyset$	$\emptyset$
$\{a\}$	$\emptyset$	$\{a, c\}$
$\{b\}$	$\{b\}$	$\{b\}$
$\{c\}$	$\emptyset$	$\{a, c\}$
$\{a, b\}$	$\{b\}$	U
$\{a, c\}$	$\{a, c\}$	$\{a, c\}$
$\{b, c\}$	$\{b\}$	U
U	U	U

Next we will briefly consider the structure of $\mathcal{R}$. The results presented here can be found in the works of Gehrke and Walker (1992), Iwiński (1987), and J. Pomykała and J.A. Pomykała (1988).

It is clear that rough sets can also be viewed as pairs of approximations $(X^{\blacktriangledown}, X^{\blacktriangle})$, since each approximation uniquely determines a rough set. The set of rough approximations can be ordered by

$$(3.1) \qquad (X^{\blacktriangledown}, X^{\blacktriangle}) \leq (Y^{\blacktriangledown}, Y^{\blacktriangle}) \overset{\text{def}}{\iff} X^{\blacktriangledown} \subseteq Y^{\blacktriangledown} \text{ and } X^{\blacktriangle} \subseteq Y^{\blacktriangle}.$$

It is known that $(\mathcal{R}, \leq)$ is a complete Stone lattice such that for any $\mathcal{H} \subseteq \wp(U)$,

$$\bigvee\{(X^{\blacktriangledown}, X^{\blacktriangle}) \mid X \in \mathcal{H}\} = (\bigcup\{X^{\blacktriangledown} \mid X \in \mathcal{H}\}, \bigcup\{X^{\blacktriangle} \mid X \in \mathcal{H}\});$$
$$\bigwedge\{(X^{\blacktriangledown}, X^{\blacktriangle}) \mid X \in \mathcal{H}\} = (\bigcap\{X^{\blacktriangledown} \mid X \in \mathcal{H}\}, \bigcap\{X^{\blacktriangle} \mid X \in \mathcal{H}\}).$$

Each element $(X^{\blacktriangledown}, X^{\blacktriangle})$ has a pseudocomplement $(U - X^{\blacktriangle}, U - X^{\blacktriangle})$. Furthermore,

$$(\mathcal{R}, \leq) \cong (\mathbf{2}^I \times \mathbf{3}^J, \leq),$$

where I is the set of the equivalence classes of E which have exactly one element, and J consists of E-classes having at least two members. Note that if all elements are pairwise discernible, that is, E is the identity relation $\{(x, x) \mid x \in U\}$, then $(\mathcal{R}, \leq) \cong (\mathbf{2}^U, \leq)$.

Example 3. The ordered set of rough sets of Example 2 is presented in Fig. 1.

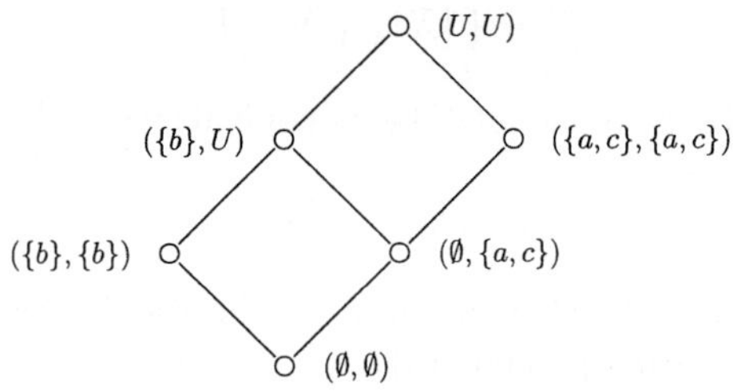

Fig. 1. Ordered set of rough sets

4 Structure of Generalized Rough Sets

Here we study ordered sets of rough sets defined by arbitrary binary relations. The motivation for this is that it is noted (see Järvinen (2002), for example) that neither reflexivity, symmetry, nor transitivity are necessary properties of indiscernibility relations, and we may present examples of indiscernibility relations that do not have these properties.

Let R be a binary relation on U. Let us denote

$$R(x) = \{y \in U \mid x \, R \, y\}.$$

We may now generalize the approximation operators by setting

$$X^{\blacktriangledown} = \{x \in U \mid R(x) \subseteq X\};$$
$$X^{\blacktriangle} = \{x \in U \mid R(x) \cap X \neq \emptyset\}$$

for all $X \subseteq U$. The relation $\equiv$ and the set $\mathcal{R}$ of rough sets may be defined as in Section 3. Furthermore, the order $\leq$ on $\mathcal{R}$ is now defined as in (3.1).

4.1 Tolerance Relations

First we consider the ordered set $(\mathcal{R}, \leq)$ in case of tolerance relations. As noted in the previous section, the ordered set of rough sets defined by equivalences is a complete Stone lattice. Surprisingly, if we omit the transitivity, the structure of rough sets changes quite dramatically. Let us consider a tolerance R on a set $U = \{a, b, c, d, e\}$ defined in Fig. 2 – the figure can be interpreted so that if $x \, R \, y$ holds, then there is an arrow from the point corresponding the element x to the point that corresponds y. Järvinen (2001) has shown that the ordered set of rough sets determined by the tolerance R is not even a $\vee$-semilattice nor a $\wedge$-semilattice. In that article one may also find the Hasse diagram of this ordered set.

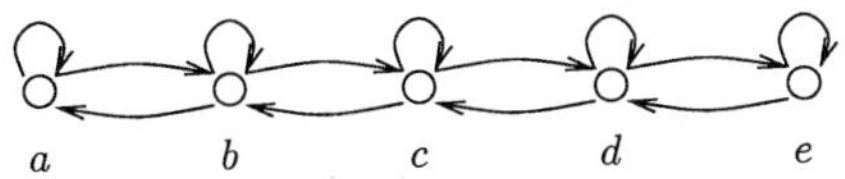

Fig. 2. Tolerance relation R

4.2 Transitive Relations

The removal of transitivity affects quite unexpectedly the structure of rough sets. Here we study rough sets determined by relations which are always at least transitive. We start by an example showing that the ordered sets of rough sets defined by merely transitive relations are not necessarily semilattices.

Example 4. Let $U = \{a, b, c, d, e, f, g, h, i, k\}$ and let R be the transitive relation on U depicted in Fig. 3. Note that since R is not reflexive, $X^{\blacktriangledown} \subseteq X^{\blacktriangle}$ does not hold.

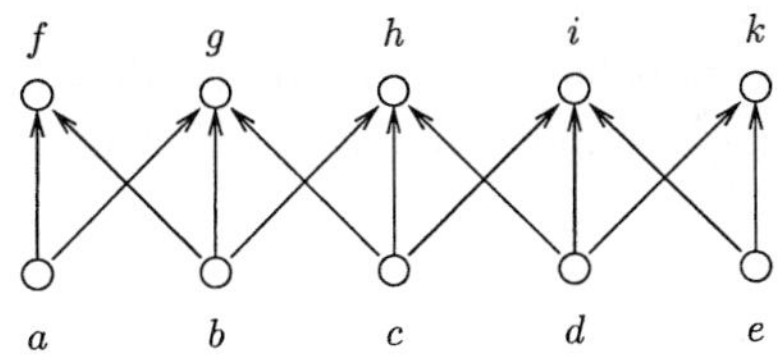

Fig. 3. Transitive relation R

For simplicity, let us denote the subsets of U which differ from $\emptyset$ and U by sequences of letters. For instance, $\{a, b, c\}$ is written as abc. The set of approximations determined by R is the 22-element set

$$\{(fghik, \emptyset), (fghik, ab), (fghik, abc), (fghik, bcd), (fghik, cde), (fghik, de), (afghik, abc), (fghik, abcd), (fghik, abcde), (fghik, abde), (fghik, bcde), (efghik, cde), (abfghik, abcd), (afghik, abcde), (cfghik, abcde), (defghik, bcde), (abcfghik, abcde), (abfghik, abcde), (aefghik, abcde), (defghik, abcde), (cdefghik, abcde), (abcdefghik, abcde)\}.$$

Now, for example, $(abfghik, abcd) \wedge (afghik, abcde)$ does not exist; the set of lower bounds of this pair is $\{(afghik, abc), (fghik, abcd), (fghik, abc), (fghik, ab), (fghik, bcd), (fghik, \emptyset)\}$, which does not have a greatest element. Similarly,

$(afghik, abc) \vee (fghik, abcd)$ does not exist because this pair of elements has two minimal upper bounds.

Hence, $(\mathcal{R}, \leq)$ is neither $\vee$-semilattice nor a $\wedge$-semilattice.

Our next proposition shows that the rough sets defined by a symmetric and transitive binary relation form a complete Stone lattice.

Proposition 5. *For a symmetric and transitive binary relation, the ordered set of rough sets $(\mathcal{R}, \leq)$ is a complete Stone lattice.*

Proof. Let R be a symmetric and transitive binary relation on a set U. Let us denote $U^* = \{x \in U \mid R(x) \neq \emptyset\}$. It is now obvious that $R \subseteq U^* \times U^*$. We start by showing that R is an equivalence on U^*. The relation R is symmetric and transitive by the definition. Suppose that $x \in U^*$. Then there exists a $y \in U^*$ such that $x \, R \, y$. Because R is symmetric, also $y \, R \, x$ holds. But this implies $x \, R \, x$ by the transitivity. Thus, R is an equivalence on U^*, and the resulting ordered set of rough sets on U^* is a complete Stone lattice.

Let us denote by $\mathcal{R}$ the set of rough sets on U, and by $\mathcal{R}^*$ the set of rough set on U^*. We show that $(\mathcal{R}^*, \leq) \cong (\mathcal{R}, \leq)$. Let $\Sigma = U - U^*$ and let us define a map

$$\varphi \colon \mathcal{R}^* \to \mathcal{R}, (X^{\blacktriangledown}, X^{\blacktriangle}) \mapsto (X^{\blacktriangledown} \cup \Sigma, X^{\blacktriangle}).$$

Assume that $x \in \Sigma$. Because $R(x) = \emptyset$, $R(x) \subseteq X$ and $R(x) \cap X = \emptyset$ hold for all $X \subseteq U$. By applying this it is easy to see that the map φ is an order-isomorphism, and hence $(\mathcal{R}, \leq)$ is a complete Stone lattice. □

Note that if R is symmetric and transitive, but not reflexive, the elements that are not related even to themselves behave quite absurdly: they belong to every lower approximation, but not in any upper approximation as shown in the previous proof.

5 Completions

We have shown that for tolerances and transitive binary relations, the set of rough sets is not necessarily even a semilattice. Further, it is not known whether $(\mathcal{R}, \leq)$ is always a lattice, when the underlying relation R is reflexive and transitive. We end this work by presenting some possible completions of $(\mathcal{R}, \leq)$. We will need the following definition. Let $\mathcal{P} = (P, \leq)$ be an ordered set and let $\mathcal{L} = (L, \leq)$ be a complete lattice. If there exists an order-embedding $\varphi \colon P \to L$, we say that $\mathcal{L}$ is a *completion* of $\mathcal{P}$.

5.1 Arbitrary Relations

Let us denote by $B^{\blacktriangledown}$ and by $B^{\blacktriangle}$ the sets of all lower and upper approximations of the subsets of U, respectively, that is, $B^{\blacktriangledown} = \{X^{\blacktriangledown} \mid X \subseteq U\}$ and $B^{\blacktriangle} = \{X^{\blacktriangle} \mid X \subseteq U\}$. It is shown by Järvinen (2002) that $(B^{\blacktriangledown}, \subseteq)$ and $(B^{\blacktriangle}, \subseteq)$ are complete lattices for an arbitrary relation R. This means that also $(B^{\blacktriangledown} \times B^{\blacktriangle}, \leq)$ is a complete lattice; the order $\leq$ is defined as in (3.1). Thus, $(B^{\blacktriangledown} \times B^{\blacktriangle}, \leq)$ is always a completion of $(\mathcal{R}, \leq)$ for any R.

5.2 Reflexive Relations

Let us now assume that R is reflexive. As we have noted, now $X^{\blacktriangledown} \subseteq X^{\blacktriangle}$ for any $X \subseteq U$. Let us denote

$$[B^{\blacktriangledown} \times B^{\blacktriangle}] = \{(X,Y) \in B^{\blacktriangledown} \times B^{\blacktriangle} \mid X \subseteq Y\}.$$

Obviously, $\mathcal{R} \subseteq [B^{\blacktriangledown} \times B^{\blacktriangle}]$. Because $[B^{\blacktriangledown} \times B^{\blacktriangle}]$ is a subset of $B^{\blacktriangledown} \times B^{\blacktriangle}$, we may order $[B^{\blacktriangledown} \times B^{\blacktriangle}]$ with the order inherited from $B^{\blacktriangledown} \times B^{\blacktriangle}$. It is also obvious that $([B^{\blacktriangledown} \times B^{\blacktriangle}], \leq)$ is a complete sublattice of $(B^{\blacktriangledown} \times B^{\blacktriangle}, \leq)$. Hence, we can write the following proposition.

Proposition 6. *If R is reflexive, then $([B^{\blacktriangledown} \times B^{\blacktriangle}], \leq)$ is a completion of $(\mathcal{R}, \leq)$.*

Next, we present another completion for $(\mathcal{R}, \leq)$ in case R is at least reflexive. As mentioned in Section 3, $(\mathcal{R}, \leq)$ is isomorphic to $(\mathbf{2}^I \times \mathbf{3}^J, \leq)$, where I is the set of the equivalence classes of E which have exactly one element, and J consists of E-classes having at least two members. Here we show that for reflexive relations this same ordered set can act as a completion. Note also for the proof of the next proposition that if R is reflexive, then $X^{\blacktriangledown} \subseteq X \subseteq X^{\blacktriangle}$ and $R(x) \in I$ implies $R(x) = \{x\}$.

Proposition 7. *If R is a reflexive relation, then $(\mathbf{2}^I \times \mathbf{3}^J, \leq)$ is a completion of $(\mathcal{R}, \leq)$, where $I = \{R(x) \mid |R(x)| = 1\}$ and $J = \{R(x) \mid |R(x)| > 1\}$.*

Proof. Let us define a map $\varphi\colon \mathcal{R} \to \mathbf{2}^I \times \mathbf{3}^J$ by setting $\varphi(X^{\blacktriangledown}, X^{\blacktriangle}) = (f, g)$, where the maps $f\colon I \to \mathbf{2}$ and $g\colon J \to \mathbf{3}$ are defined by

$$f(R(x)) = \begin{cases} 1 & \text{if } x \in X \\ 0 & \text{if } x \notin X \end{cases} \quad \text{and} \quad g(R(x)) = \begin{cases} 1 & \text{if } x \in X^{\blacktriangledown} \\ u & \text{if } x \in X^{\blacktriangle} - X^{\blacktriangledown} \\ 0 & \text{if } x \notin X^{\blacktriangle}. \end{cases}$$

Let us denote $\varphi(X^{\blacktriangledown}, X^{\blacktriangle}) = (f_1, g_1)$ and $\varphi(Y^{\blacktriangledown}, Y^{\blacktriangle}) = (f_2, g_2)$.

Assume that $(X^{\blacktriangledown}, X^{\blacktriangle}) \leq (Y^{\blacktriangledown}, Y^{\blacktriangle})$. We will show that $(f_1, g_1) \leq (f_2, g_2)$. If $f_1(R(x)) = 1$ for some $R(x) \in I$, then $x \in X$, and $R(x) = \{x\}$ implies $x \in X^{\blacktriangledown} \subseteq Y^{\blacktriangledown} \subseteq Y$. Thus, $f_2(R(x)) = 1$ and $f_1 \leq f_2$. If $g_1(R(x)) = 1$, then $x \in X^{\blacktriangledown} \subseteq Y^{\blacktriangledown}$ and $g_2(R(x)) = 1$. If $g_1(R(x)) = u$, then $x \in X^{\blacktriangle} \subseteq Y^{\blacktriangle}$, which implies $g_2(R(x)) \geq u$. Hence, also $g_1 \leq g_2$.

Conversely, assume that $(f_1, g_1) \leq (f_2, g_2)$. We will show that $(X^{\blacktriangledown}, X^{\blacktriangle}) \leq (Y^{\blacktriangledown}, Y^{\blacktriangle})$. Suppose that $x \in X^{\blacktriangledown}$. Then $1 = g_1(R(x)) \leq g_2(R(x))$ implies $x \in Y^{\blacktriangledown}$. If $x \in X^{\blacktriangle}$, then $u \leq g_1(R(x)) \leq g_2(R(x))$. This implies $x \in Y^{\blacktriangledown}$ or $x \in Y^{\blacktriangle} - Y^{\blacktriangledown}$, which obviously means that $x \in Y^{\blacktriangle}$ since $Y^{\blacktriangledown} \subseteq Y^{\blacktriangle}$. We have now proved that $X^{\blacktriangledown} \subseteq Y^{\blacktriangledown}$ and $X^{\blacktriangle} \subseteq Y^{\blacktriangledown}$. □

We end this section by presenting an example of the above-mentioned completions.

Example 8. Let us consider the relation R defined in Fig. 4. Obviously, R is reflexive, but not symmetric nor transitive.

Now the set of rough sets determined by the relation R is

$$\mathcal{R} = \{(\emptyset,\emptyset), (\emptyset,\{a,b\}), (\emptyset,\{a,c\}), (\emptyset,\{b,c\}), (\{a\},U), (\{b\},U), (\{c\},U), (U,U)\}.$$

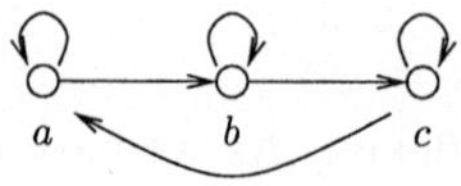

Fig. 4. Reflexive relation R

It is easy to observe that $(\mathcal{R}, \leq)$ is not a $\vee$-semilattice, because, for example, the elements $(\emptyset, \{a, b\})$ and $(\emptyset, \{a, c\})$ have the upper bounds $(\{a\}, U)$, $(\{b\}, U)$, $(\{c\}, U)$, and (U, U) – but they do not have a smallest lower bound. Similarly, $(\mathcal{R}, \leq)$ is not a $\wedge$-semilattice, because the elements $(\{a\}, U)$ and $(\{b\}, U)$ have the lower bounds $(\emptyset, \emptyset)$, $(\emptyset, \{a\})$, $(\emptyset, \{b\})$, and $(\emptyset, \{c\})$, but not a greatest lower bound. The Hasse diagram of $(\mathcal{R}, \leq)$ presented in Fig. 5.

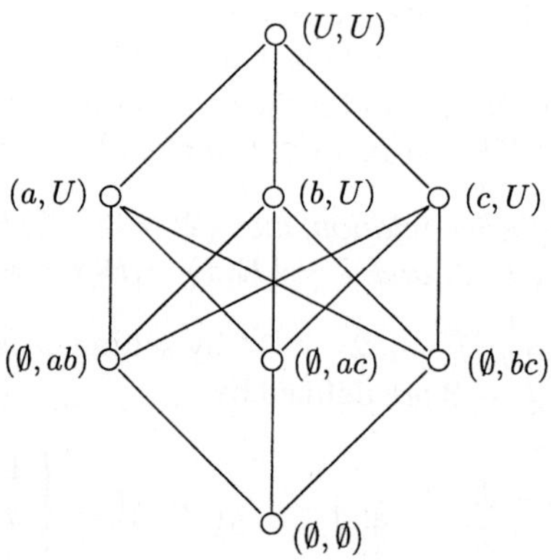

Fig. 5. Ordered set $(\mathcal{R}, \leq)$

The completions for $(\mathcal{R}, \leq)$ considered above are $(B^{\blacktriangledown} \times B^{\blacktriangle}, \leq)$, $([B^{\blacktriangledown} \times B^{\blacktriangle}], \leq)$, and $(\mathbf{2}^I \times \mathbf{3}^J, \leq)$, where $I = \emptyset$, $J = \{R(a), R(b), R(c)\}$, and $R(a) = \{a, b\}$, $R(b) = \{b, c\}$, $R(c) = \{a, c\}$. It is easy to notice that $B^{\blacktriangledown} \times B^{\blacktriangle}$ contains 25 elements, $[B^{\blacktriangledown} \times B^{\blacktriangle}]$ has 15 elements, and $\mathbf{2}^I \times \mathbf{3}^J$ consists of 27 elements.

Conclusions

In this paper we have considered rough sets determined by indiscernibility relations which are not necessarily reflexive, symmetric, or transitive. We have proved that if an indiscernibility relation is at least symmetric and closed, the the ordered set of rough sets is a complete Stone lattice. We have also shown that for tolerances and transitive binary relations, $(\mathcal{R}, \leq)$ is not necessarily even a semilattice. Additionally, it is not known whether the ordered set of rough sets $(\mathcal{R}, \leq)$ is a lattice, when the indiscernibility R is reflexive and transitive, but not symmetric. These observations are depicted in Fig. 6.

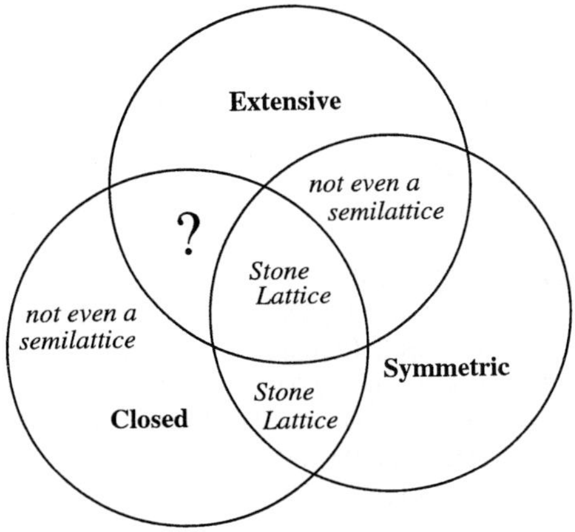

Fig. 6. Properties of ordered sets of rough sets

We also presented several possible and intuitive completions of $(\mathcal{R}, \leq)$. But as we saw in Example 8, the sizes of the completions are "too big". For example, we could made a completion of $(\mathcal{R}, \leq)$ of Example 8 just by adding the element $(\emptyset, U)$, and this completion has the size of only 9 elements, which much less than in the other completions presented. Therefore, we conclude this work by introducing the problem of determining the smallest completion of $(\mathcal{R}, \leq)$.

It would also interesting to study approximation operations which are defined as follows for any set $X \subseteq U$:

$$X^{\blacktriangledown} = X \cap \{x \in U \mid R(x) \subseteq X\};$$
$$X^{\blacktriangle} = X \cup \{x \in U \mid R(x) \cap X \neq \emptyset\}.$$

If the operations are defined as above, then

$$X^{\blacktriangledown} \subseteq X \subseteq X^{\blacktriangle}$$

for any relation R and for any set $X \subseteq U$. As we noticed in Example 4 and Proposition 5, for example, this does not generally hold.

Acknowledgements

Many thanks are due to Jari Kortelainen and Magnus Steinby for the careful reading of the manuscript and for their valuable comments and suggestions.

References

G. Cattaneo, Abstract Approximation Spaces for Rough Theories, in: L. Polkowski, A. Skowron (eds.), *Rough Sets in Knowledge Discovery I* (Physica, Heidelberg, 1998) 59–98.

B.A. Davey, H.A. Priestley, *Introduction to Lattices and Order. Second Edition* (Cambridge University Press, Cambridge, 2002).

I. Düntsch, G. Gediga, Approximation Operators in Qualitative Data Analysis, in: H. de Swart, E. Orlowska, G. Schmidt, M. Roubens (eds.), *Theory and Applications of Relational Structures as Knowledge Instruments: COST Action 274, TARSKI. Revised Papers*, Lecture Notes in Artificial Intelligence **2929** (Springer, Heidelberg, 2001) 214–230.

M. Gehrke, E. Walker, On the Structure of Rough Sets, *Bulletin of the Polish Academy of Sciences, Mathematics* **40** (1992) 235–245.

G. Grätzer, *General Lattice Theory. Second Edition* (Birkhäuser, Basel, 1998).

S. Greco, B. Matarazzo, R. Slowinski, Rough Set Approach to Decisions Under Risk, in: W. Ziarko, Y. Yao (eds.), *Proceedings of The Second International Conference on Rough Sets and Current Trends in Computing (RSCTC 2000)*, Lecture Notes in Artificial Intelligence **2005** (Springer, Heidelberg, 2001) 160–169.

T.B. Iwiński, Algebraic Approach to Rough Sets, *Bulletin of the Polish Academy of Sciences, Mathematics* **35** (1987) 673–683.

J. Järvinen, Approximations and Rough Sets Based on Tolerances, in: W. Ziarko, Y. Yao (eds.), *Proceedings of The Second International Conference on Rough Sets and Current Trends in Computing (RSCTC 2000)*, Lecture Notes in Artificial Intelligence **2005** (Springer, Heidelberg, 2001) 182–189.

J. Järvinen, On the Structure of Rough Approximations, *Fundamenta Informaticae* **50** (2002) 135–153.

Z. Pawlak, Rough Sets, *International Journal of Computer and Information Sciences* **5** (1982) 341–356.

J. Pomykała, J.A. Pomykała, The Stone Algebra of Rough Sets, *Bulletin of the Polish Academy of Sciences, Mathematics* **36** (1988) 495–512.

J.A Pomykała, About Tolerance and Similarity Relations in Information Systems, in: J.J. Alpigini, J.F. Peters, A. Skowron, N. Zhong (eds.), *Proceedings of The Third International Conference on Rough Sets and Current Trends in Computing (RSCTC 2002)*, Lecture Notes in Artificial Intelligence **2475** (Springer, Heidelberg, 2002) 175 – 182.

A. Skowron, J. Stepaniuk, Tolerance Approximation Spaces, *Fundamenta Informaticae* **27** (1996) 245–253.

R. Slowinski, D. Vanderpooten, A Generalized Definition of Rough Approximations Based on Similarity, *IEEE Transactions on Knowledge and Data Engineering* **12** (2000) 331–336.

Y.Y. Yao, T.Y. Lin, Generalization of Rough Sets using Modal Logics, *Intelligent Automation and Soft Computing. An International Journal* **2** (1996) 103–120.

A Comparative Study of Formal Concept Analysis and Rough Set Theory in Data Analysis

Yiyu Yao

Department of Computer Science, University of Regina
Regina, Saskatchewan, Canada S4S 0A2
yyao@cs.uregina.ca
http://www.cs.uregina.ca/~yyao

Abstract. The theory of rough sets and formal concept analysis are compared in a common framework based on formal contexts. Different concept lattices can be constructed. Formal concept analysis focuses on concepts that are definable by conjuctions of properties, rough set theory focuses on concepts that are definable by disjunctions of properties. They produce different types of rules summarizing knowledge embedded in data.

1 Introduction

Rough set theory and formal concept analysis offer related and complementary approaches for data analysis. Many efforts have been made to compare and combine the two theories [1, 4–8, 11, 13]. The results have improved our understanding of their similarities and differences. However, there is still a need for systematic and comparative studies of relationships and interconnections of the two theories. This paper presents new results and interpretations on the topic.

The theory of rough sets is traditionally formulated based on an equivalence relation on a set of objects called the universe [9, 10]. A pair of unary set-theoretic operators, called approximation operators, are defined [15]. A concept, represented by a subset of objects, is called a definable concept if its lower and upper approximations are the same as the set itself. An arbitrary concept is approximated from below and above by two definable concepts. The notion of approximation operators can be defined based on two universes linked by a binary relation [14, 18].

Formal concept analysis is formulated based on the notion of a formal context, which is a binary relation between a set of objects and a set of properties or attributes [3, 12]. The binary relation induces set-theoretic operators from sets of objects to sets of properties, and from sets of properties to sets of objects, respectively. A formal concept is defined as a pair of a set of objects and a set of properties connected by the two set-theoretic operators.

The notion of formal contexts provides a common framework for the study of rough set theory and formal concept analysis, if rough set theory is formulated based on two universes. Düntsch and Gediga pointed out that the set-theoretic

S. Tsumoto et al. (Eds.): RSCTC 2004, LNAI 3066, pp. 59–68, 2004.

operators used in the two theories have been considered in modal logics, and therefore referred to them as modal-style operators [1, 4, 5]. They have demonstrated that modal-style operators are useful in data analysis.

In this paper, we present a comparative study of rough set theory and formal concept analysis. The two theories aim at different goals and summarize different types of knowledge. Rough set theory is used for the goal of prediction, and formal concept analysis is used for the goal of description. Two new concept lattices are introduced in rough set theory. Rough set theory involves concepts described by disjunctions of properties, formal concept analysis deals with concepts described by conjunctions of properties.

2 Concept Lattices Induced by Formal Contexts

The notion of formal contexts is used to define two pairs of modal-style operators, one for formal concept analysis and the other for rough set theory [1, 4].

2.1 Binary Relations as Formal Contexts

Let U and V be two finite and nonempty sets. Elements of U are called objects, and elements of V are called properties or attributes. The relationships between objects and properties are described by a binary relation R between U and V, which is a subset of the Cartesian product $U \times V$. For a pair of elements $x \in U$ and $y \in V$, if $(x, y) \in R$, also written as xRy, we say that x has the property y, or the property y is possessed by object x.

An object $x \in U$ has the set of properties:

$$xR = \{y \in V \mid xRy\} \subseteq V. \tag{1}$$

A property y is possessed by the set of objects:

$$Ry = \{x \in U \mid xRy\} \subseteq U. \tag{2}$$

The complement of a binary relation is defined by:

$$R^c = U \times V - R = \{(x, y) \mid \neg(xRy)\}, \tag{3}$$

where ^{c} denotes the set complement. That is, xR^cy if and only if $\neg(xRy)$. An object $x \in U$ does not have the set of properties, $xR^c = \{y \in V \mid xR^cy\} = (xR)^c \subseteq V$. A property y is not possessed by the set of objects, $R^cy = \{x \in V \mid xR^cy\} = (Ry)^c \subseteq U$.

The triplet (U, V, R) is called a binary formal context. For simplicity, we only consider the binary formal context in the subsequent discussion.

2.2 Formal Concept Analysis

For a formal context (U, V, R), we define a set-theoretic operator $^* : 2^U \longrightarrow 2^V$:

$$\begin{aligned} X^* &= \{y \in V \mid \forall x \in U(x \in X \Longrightarrow xRy)\} \\ &= \{y \in V \mid X \subseteq Ry\} \\ &= \bigcap_{x \in X} xR. \end{aligned} \tag{4}$$

It associates a subset of properties X^* to the subset of objects X. Similarly, for any subset of properties $Y \subseteq V$, we can associate a subset of objects $Y^* \subseteq U$:

$$\begin{aligned} Y^* &= \{x \in U \mid \forall y \in V(y \in Y \Longrightarrow xRy)\} \\ &= \{x \in U \mid Y \subseteq xR\} \\ &= \bigcap_{y \in Y} Ry. \end{aligned} \tag{5}$$

They have the properties: for $X, X_1, X_2 \subseteq U$ and $Y, Y_1, Y_2 \subseteq V$,

$$\begin{array}{ll} (1) & X_1 \subseteq X_2 \Longrightarrow X_1^* \supseteq X_2^*, \qquad Y_1 \subseteq Y_2 \Longrightarrow Y_1^* \supseteq Y_2^*, \\ (2) & X \subseteq X^{**}, \quad Y \subseteq Y^{**}, \\ (3) & X^{***} = X^*, \quad Y^{***} = Y^*, \\ (4) & (X_1 \cup X_2)^* = X_1^* \cap X_2^*, \quad (Y_1 \cup Y_2)^* = Y_1^* \cap Y_2^*. \end{array}$$

A pair of mappings is called a Galois connection if it satisfies (1) and (2), and hence (3).

Consider now the dual operator of * defined by [1]:

$$\begin{aligned} X^{\#} &= X^{c*c} \\ &= \{y \in V \mid \exists x \in U(x \in X^c \wedge \neg(xRy))\} \\ &= \{y \in V \mid \neg(X^c \subseteq Ry)\} \\ &= \{y \in V \mid X^c \cap (Ry)^c \neq \emptyset\}. \end{aligned} \tag{6}$$

For a subset of properties $Y \subseteq V$, $Y^{\#}$ can be similarly defined. Properties of $^{\#}$ can be obtained from the properties of *. For example, we have $(X_1 \cap X_2)^{\#} = X_1^{\#} \cup X_2^{\#}$.

By definition, $\{x\}^* = xR$ is the set of properties possessed by x, and $\{y\}^* = Ry$ is the set of objects having property y. For a set of objects X, X^* is the *maximal* set of properties shared by *all* objects in X. Similarly, for a set of properties Y, Y^* is the *maximal* set of objects that have *all* properties in Y. For a subset $X \subseteq U$, a property in $X^{\#}$ is not possessed by at least one object not in X.

A pair (X, Y), $X \subseteq U, Y \subseteq V$, is called a formal concept if $X = Y^*$ and $Y = X^*$. The set of objects X is referred to as the extension of the concept, and the set of properties is referred to as the intension of the concept. Objects in X share all properties Y, and only properties Y are possessed by all objects in X. The set of all formal concepts forms a complete lattice called a concept lattice [3]. The meet and join of the lattice is given by:

$$\begin{aligned} (X_1, Y_1) \wedge (X_2, Y_2) &= (X_1 \cap X_2, (Y_1 \cup Y_2)^{**}), \\ (X_1, Y_1) \vee (X_2, Y_2) &= ((X_1 \cup X_2)^{**}, Y_1 \cap Y_2). \end{aligned} \tag{7}$$

By property (3), for any subset X of U, we have a formal concept (X^{**}, X^{*}), and for any subset Y of V, we have a formal concept (Y^{*}, Y^{**}).

2.3 Rough Sets

We consider a slightly different formulation of rough set theory based on a binary relation between two universes [4, 14, 18].

Given a formal context, we define a pair of dual approximation operators $^{\Box}, ^{\Diamond} : 2^U \longrightarrow 2^V$,

$$\begin{aligned} X^{\Box} &= \{y \in V \mid \forall x \in U(xRy \Longrightarrow x \in X)\} \\ &= \{y \in V \mid Ry \subseteq X\}, \quad (8) \\ X^{\Diamond} &= \{y \in V \mid \exists x \in U(xRy \wedge x \in X)\} \\ &= \{y \in V \mid Ry \cap X \neq \emptyset\} \\ &= \bigcup_{x \in X} xR. \quad (9) \end{aligned}$$

Similarly, we define another pair of approximation operators $^{\Box}, ^{\Diamond} : 2^V \longrightarrow 2^U$,

$$\begin{aligned} Y^{\Box} &= \{x \in U \mid \forall y \in V(xRy \Longrightarrow y \in Y)\} \\ &= \{x \in U \mid xR \subseteq Y\}, \quad (10) \\ Y^{\Diamond} &= \{x \in U \mid \exists y \in V(xRy \wedge y \in Y)\} \\ &= \{x \in U \mid xR \cap Y \neq \emptyset\} \\ &= \bigcup_{y \in Y} Ry. \quad (11) \end{aligned}$$

They have the properties: for $X, X_1, X_2 \subseteq U$ and $Y, Y_1, Y_2 \subseteq V$,

$$\begin{aligned} &\text{(i)} && X_1 \subseteq X_2 \Longrightarrow [X_1^{\Box} \subseteq X_2^{\Box}, X_1^{\Diamond} \subseteq X_2^{\Diamond}], \\ &&& Y_1 \subseteq Y_2 \Longrightarrow [Y_1^{\Box} \subseteq Y_2^{\Box}, Y_1^{\Diamond} \subseteq Y_2^{\Diamond}], \\ &\text{(ii)} && X^{\Box\Diamond} \subseteq X \subseteq X^{\Diamond\Box}, \quad Y^{\Box\Diamond} \subseteq Y \subseteq Y^{\Diamond\Box}, \\ &\text{(iii)} && X^{\Diamond\Box\Diamond} = X^{\Diamond}, \quad Y^{\Diamond\Box\Diamond} = Y^{\Diamond}, \\ &&& X^{\Box\Diamond\Box} = X^{\Box}, \quad Y^{\Box\Diamond\Box} = Y^{\Box}, \\ &\text{(iv)} && (X_1 \cap X_2)^{\Box} = X_1^{\Box} \cap X_2^{\Box}, \quad (X_1 \cup X_2)^{\Diamond} = X_1^{\Diamond} \cup X_2^{\Diamond}, \\ &&& (Y_1 \cap Y_2)^{\Box} = Y_1^{\Box} \cap Y_2^{\Box}, \quad (Y_1 \cup Y_2)^{\Diamond} = Y_1^{\Diamond} \cup Y_2^{\Diamond}. \end{aligned}$$

Based on the notion of approximation operators, we introduce two new concept lattices in rough set theory.

A pair (X, Y), $X \subseteq U, Y \subseteq V$, is called an object oriented formal concept if $X = Y^{\Diamond}$ and $Y = X^{\Box}$. If an object has a property in Y then the object belongs to X. Furthermore, only objects in X have properties in Y. The family of all object oriented formal concepts forms a lattice. Specifically, the meet $\wedge$ and join $\vee$ are defined by:

$$\begin{aligned} (X_1, Y_1) \wedge (X_2, Y_2) &= ((Y_1 \cap Y_2)^{\Diamond}, Y_1 \cap Y_2), \\ (X_1, Y_1) \vee (X_2, Y_2) &= (X_1 \cup X_2, (X_1 \cup X_2)^{\Box}). \quad (12) \end{aligned}$$

For a set of objects $X \subseteq U$, we have a formal concept $(X^{\Box\Diamond}, X^{\Box})$. For a set of properties $Y \subseteq V$, we have $(Y^{\Diamond}, Y^{\Diamond\Box})$.

A pair (X,Y), $X \subseteq U, Y \subseteq V$, is called a property oriented formal concept if $X = Y^{\Box}$ and $Y = X^{\Diamond}$. If a property is possessed by an object in X then the property must be in Y. Furthermore, only properties Y are possessed by objects in X. The family of all property oriented formal concepts forms a lattice with meet $\wedge$ and join $\vee$ defined by:

$$\begin{aligned}(X_1,Y_1) \wedge (X_2,Y_2) &= (X_1 \cap X_2, (X_1 \cap X_2)^{\Diamond}),\\ (X_1,Y_1) \vee (X_2,Y_2) &= ((Y_1 \cup Y_2)^{\Box}, Y_1 \cup Y_2).\end{aligned} \tag{13}$$

For a set of objects $X \subseteq U$, we can construct a property oriented formal concept $(X^{\Diamond\Box}, X^{\Diamond})$. For a set of properties $Y \subseteq V$, there is a property oriented formal concept $(Y^{\Box}, Y^{\Box\Diamond})$. The property oriented concept lattice was introduced by Düntsch and Gediga [4].

2.4 Relationships between Operators and Other Representations

Düntsch and Gediga referred to the four operators *, $^\#$, $^\Box$, and $^\Diamond$ as modal-style operators, called the sufficiency, dual sufficiency, necessity and possibility operators, respectively [1, 4].

The relationships between four modal-style operators can be stated as follows:

$$\begin{aligned}(X)^{\Box}_R &= \{y \in V \mid Ry \subseteq X\}\\ &= \{y \in V \mid X^c \subseteq (Ry)^c\}\\ &= \{y \in V \mid X^c \subseteq R^c y\}\\ &= (X^c)^*_{R^c};\end{aligned} \tag{14}$$

$$\begin{aligned}(X)^{\Diamond}_R &= \{y \in V \mid X \cap Ry \neq \emptyset\}\\ &= \{y \in V \mid X^{cc} \cap (Ry)^{cc} \neq \emptyset\}\\ &= (X^c)^{\#}_{R^c}.\end{aligned} \tag{15}$$

where the subscription R indicates that the operator $^\Box$ is defined with respect to the relation R. Conversely, we have $(X)^*_R = (X^c)^{\Box}_{R^c}$ and $(X)^{\#}_R = (X^c)^{\Diamond}_{R^c}$.

The relationships between binary relations and operators are summarized by: for $x \in U$, $y \in V$,

$$\begin{aligned}&xR = \{x\}^* = \{x\}^{\Diamond}, \qquad Ry = \{y\}^* = \{y\}^{\Diamond},\\ &xRy \Longleftrightarrow x \in \{y\}^* \Longleftrightarrow y \in \{x\}^*,\\ &xRy \Longleftrightarrow x \in \{y\}^{\Diamond} \Longleftrightarrow y \in \{x\}^{\Diamond}.\end{aligned} \tag{16}$$

From a binary relation R, we can define an equivalence relation E_U on U:

$$xE_Ux' \Longleftrightarrow xR = x'R. \tag{17}$$

Two objects are equivalent if they have exactly the same set of properties [11]. Similarly, we define an equivalence relation E_V on V:

$$yE_Vy' \Longleftrightarrow Ry = Ry'. \tag{18}$$

Two properties are equivalent if they are possessed by exactly the same set of objects [11].

Now we define a mapping, $j : 2^U \longrightarrow 2^V$, called the basic set assignment as follows:

$$j(X) = \{y \in V \mid Ry = X\}. \tag{19}$$

A property y is assigned to the set of objects that have the property. The following set:

$$\{j(X) \neq \emptyset \mid X \subseteq U\}, \tag{20}$$

is in fact the partition induced by the equivalence relation E_V. Similarly, a basic set assignment $j : 2^V \longrightarrow 2^U$ is given by:

$$j(Y) = \{x \in U \mid xR = Y\}. \tag{21}$$

The set:

$$\{j(Y) \neq \emptyset \mid Y \subseteq V\}, \tag{22}$$

is the partition induced by the equivalence relation E_V.

In terms of the basic set assignment, we can re-express operators *, $^\#$, $^\Box$ and $^\Diamond$ as:

$$\begin{aligned} X^* &= \bigcup_{X \subseteq F} j(F), & X^\# &= \bigcup_{X \cup F \neq U} j(F), \\ X^\Box &= \bigcup_{F \subseteq X} j(F), & X^\Diamond &= \bigcup_{F \cap X \neq \emptyset} j(F). \end{aligned} \tag{23}$$

It follows that $X^* \cap X^\Box = j(X)$.

3 Data Analysis Using Modal-Style Operators

Modal-style operators provide useful tools for data analysis [1, 4]. Different operators lead to different types of rules summarizing the knowledge embedded in a formal context. By the duality of operators, we only consider * and $^\Box$.

3.1 Rough Set Theory: Predicting the Membership of an Object Based on Its Properties

For a set of objects $X \subseteq U$, we can construct a set of properties $X^\Box$. It can be used to derive rules that determine whether an object is in X. If an object has a property in $X^\Box$, the object must be in X. That is,

$$\forall x \in U[\exists y \in V(y \in X^\Box \wedge xRy) \Longrightarrow x \in X].$$

It can be re-expressed as a rule: for $x \in U$,

$$\bigvee_{y \in X^\Box} xRy \Longrightarrow x \in X. \tag{24}$$

In general, the reverse implication does not hold.

In order to derive a reverse implication, we construct another set of objects $X^{\Box\Diamond} \subseteq X$. For the set of objects, we have a rule: for $x \in U$,

$$x \in X^{\Box\Diamond} \Longrightarrow \bigvee_{y \in X^{\Box}} xRy. \tag{25}$$

This can be shown as follows:

$$\begin{aligned} x \in X^{\Box\Diamond} &\Longrightarrow xR \cap X^{\Box} \neq \emptyset \\ &\Longrightarrow \exists y \in V(xRy \wedge y \in X^{\Box}) \\ &\Longrightarrow \bigvee_{y \in X^{\Box}} xRy. \end{aligned} \tag{26}$$

In general, X is not the same as $X^{\Box\Diamond}$, which suggests that one can not establish a double implication rule for an arbitrary set.

For a set of objects $X \subseteq U$, the pair $(X^{\Box\Diamond}, X^{\Box})$ is an object oriented formal concept. From the property $X^{\Box\Diamond\Box} = X^{\Box}$ and the rule (24), it follows:

$$\bigvee_{y \in X^{\Box}} xRy \Longrightarrow x \in X^{\Box\Diamond}. \tag{27}$$

By combining it with rule (25), we have a double implication rule:

$$x \in X^{\Box\Diamond} \Longleftrightarrow \bigvee_{y \in X^{\Box}} xRy. \tag{28}$$

The results can be extended to any object oriented formal concept. For $(X = Y^{\Diamond}, Y = X^{\Box})$, we have a rule:

$$x \in X \Longleftrightarrow \bigvee_{y \in Y} xRy. \tag{29}$$

That is, the set of objects X and the set of properties Y in (X, Y) uniquely determine each other.

3.2 Formal Concept Analysis: Summarizing the Common Properties of a Set of Objects

In formal concept analysis, we identify the properties shared by a set of objects, which provides a description of the objects. Through the operator *, one can infer the properties of an object based on its membership in a set X. More specifically, we have:

$$\forall y \in V \forall x \in U[(y \in X^* \wedge x \in X) \Longrightarrow xRy)].$$

This leads to a rule: for $x \in U$,

$$x \in X \Longrightarrow \bigwedge_{y \in X^*} xRy. \tag{30}$$

The rule suggests that an object in X must have all properties in X^*. The reverse implication does not hold in general.

For the construction of a reverse implication, we construct another set of objects $X^{**} \supseteq X$. In this case, we have:

$$\bigwedge_{y \in X^*} xRy \Longrightarrow x \in X^{**}. \tag{31}$$

An object having all properties in X^* must be in X^{**}. For an arbitrary set X, X may be only a subset of X^{**}. One therefore may not be able to establish a double implication rule for an arbitrary set of objects.

A set of objects X induces a formal concept (X^{**}, X^*). By property $X^{***} = X^*$ and rule (30), we have:

$$x \in X^{**} \Longrightarrow \bigwedge_{y \in X^*} xRy. \tag{32}$$

Combining it with rule (31) results in: for $x \in U$,

$$x \in X^{**} \Longleftrightarrow \bigwedge_{y \in X^*} xRy. \tag{33}$$

In general, for a formal concept $(X = Y^*, Y = X^*)$, we have:

$$x \in X \Longleftrightarrow \bigwedge_{y \in Y} xRy. \tag{34}$$

That is, the set of objects X and the set of properties Y determine each other.

3.3 Comparison

Rough set theory and formal concept analysis offer two different approaches for data analysis. A detailed comparison of the two methods may provide more insights into data analysis.

Fayyad *et al.* identified two high-level goals of data mining as prediction and description [2]. Prediction involves the use of some variables to predict the values of some other variables. Description focuses on patterns that describe the data. For a set of objects $X \subseteq U$, the operator $^{\Box}$ identifies a set of properties $X^{\Box}$ that can be used to predict the membership of an object x with respect to X. It attempts to achieve the goal of prediction. In contrast, the operator * identifies a set of properties X^* that are shared by all objects in X. In other words, it provides a method for description and summarization. In special cases, the tasks of prediction and description become the same one for certain sets of objects. In rough set theory, this happens for the family of object oriented formal concepts. In formal concept analysis, this happens for the family of formal concepts.

A property in $X^{\Box}$ is sufficient to decide that an object having the property is in X. The set $X^{\Box}$ consists of *sufficient* properties for an object to be in X. On the other hand, an object in X must have properties in X^*. The set X^* consists of *necessary* properties of an object in X. Therefore, rough set theory and formal concept analysis focus on two opposite directions of inference. The operator $^\square$ enables us to infer the membership of an object based on its properties. On the other hand, through the operator *, one can infer the properties of an object based on its membership in X. By combining the two types of knowledge, we obtain a more complete picture of the data.

By comparing the rules derived by rough set theory and formal concept analysis, we can conclude that the two theories focus on different types of concepts. Rough set theory involves concepts described by disjunctions of properties, formal concept analysis deals with concepts described by conjunctions of properties. They represent two extreme cases. In general, one may consider other types of concepts.

By definition, * and $^\diamond$ represent the two extremely cases in describing a set of objects based on their properties. Assume that $xR \neq \emptyset$ and $Ry \neq \emptyset$. Then we have the rules: for $x \in U$,

$$\begin{aligned} x \in X &\Longrightarrow \exists y \in V(y \in X^\diamond \wedge xRy), \\ x \in X &\Longrightarrow \forall y \in V(y \in X^* \Longrightarrow xRy). \end{aligned} \tag{35}$$

That is, an object has all properties in X^* and at least one property in $X^\diamond$. The pair $(X^*, X^\diamond)$ with $X^* \subseteq X^\diamond$ thus provides a characterization of X in terms of properties.

4 Conclusion

Both the theory of rough sets and formal concept analysis formalize in some meaningful way the notion of concepts. The two theories are compared in a common framework consisting of a formal context. Different types of concepts are considered in the two theories. They capture different aspects of concepts. Rough set theory involves concepts described by disjunctions of properties, formal concept analysis deals with concepts described by conjunctions of properties. One makes opposite directions of inferences using the two theories. The operator $^\square$ enables us to infer the membership of an object based on its properties, and the operator * enables us to infer the properties of an object based on its membership in X.

The combination of the two theories leads to a better understanding of knowledge embedded in data. One may combine modal-style operators to obtain new modal-style operators and analyze data using the new operators [1, 4, 5]. Further studies on the relationships between the two theories would lead to new results [16, 17].

References

1. Düntsch, I. and Gediga, G. Approximation operators in qualitative data analysis, in: *Theory and Application of Relational Structures as Knowledge Instruments*, de Swart, H., Orlowska, E., Schmidt, G. and Roubens, M. (Eds.), Springer, Heidelberg, 216-233, 2003.

2. Fayyad, U.M., Piatetsky-Shapiro, G. and Smyth, P. From data mining to knowledge discovery: an overview, in: *Advances in knowledge discovery and data mining*, Fayyad, U.M., Piatetsky-Shapiro, G., Smyth, P. and Uthurusamy, R. (Eds.), 1-34, AAAI/MIT Press, Menlo Park, California, 1996.
3. Ganter, B. and Wille, R. *Formal Concept Analysis, Mathematical Foundations*, Springer, Berlin, 1999.
4. Gediga, G. and Düntsch, I. Modal-style operators in qualitative data analysis, *Proceedings of the 2002 IEEE International Conference on Data Mining*, 155-162, 2002.
5. Gediga, G. and Düntsch, I. Skill set analysis in knowledge structures, to appear in *British Journal of Mathematical and Statistical Psychology.*
6. Hu, K., Sui, Y., Lu, Y., Wang, J. and Shi, C. Concept approximation in concept lattice, *Knowledge Discovery and Data Mining, Proceedings of the 5th Pacific-Asia Conference, PAKDD 2001, Lecture Notes in Computer Science 2035*, 167-173, 2001.
7. Kent, R.E. Rough concept analysis: a synthesis of rough sets and formal concept analysis, *Fundamenta Informaticae*, **27**, 169-181, 1996.
8. Pagliani, P. From concept lattices to approximation spaces: algebraic structures of some spaces of partial objects, *Fundamenta Informaticae*, **18**, 1-25, 1993.
9. Pawlak, Z. Rough sets, *International Journal of Computer and Information Sciences*, **11**, 341-356, 1982.
10. Pawlak, Z. *Rough Sets, Theoretical Aspects of Reasoning about Data*, Kluwer Academic Publishers, Dordrecht, 1991.
11. Saquer, J. and Deogun, J.S. Formal rough concept analysis, *New Directions in Rough Sets, Data Mining, and Granular-Soft Computing, 7th International Workshop, RSFDGrC '99, Lecture Notes in Computer Science 1711*, Springer, Berlin, 91-99, 1999.
12. Wille, R. Restructuring lattice theory: an approach based on hierarchies of concepts, in: *Ordered Sets*, Rival, I. (Ed.), Reidel, Dordrecht-Boston, 445-470, 1982.
13. Wolff, K.E. A conceptual view of knowledge bases in rough set theory, *Rough Sets and Current Trends in Computing, Second International Conference, RSCTC 2000, Lecture Notes in Computer Science 2005*, Springer, Berlin, 220-228, 2001.
14. Wong, S.K.M., Wang, L.S., and Yao, Y.Y. Interval structure: a framework for representing uncertain information, *Uncertainty in Artificial Intelligence: Proceedings of the 8th Conference*, Morgan Kaufmann Publishers, 336-343, 1992.
15. Yao, Y.Y. Two views of the theory of rough sets in finite universes, *International Journal of Approximation Reasoning*, **15**, 291-317, 1996.
16. Yao, Y.Y. Concept lattices in rough set theory, to appear in *Proceedings of 23rd International Meeting of the North American Fuzzy Information Processing Society*, 2004.
17. Yao, Y.Y. and Chen, Y.H. Rough set approximations in formal concept analysis, to appear in *Proceedings of 23rd International Meeting of the North American Fuzzy Information Processing Society*, 2004.
18. Yao, Y.Y., Wong, S.K.M. and Lin, T.Y. A review of rough set models, in: *Rough Sets and Data Mining: Analysis for Imprecise Data*, Lin, T.Y. and Cercone, N. (Eds.), Kluwer Academic Publishers, Boston, 47-75, 1997.

Structure of Rough Approximations Based on Molecular Lattices

Jian-Hua Dai

Institute of Artificial Intelligence
Zhejiang University, HangZhou 310027, P. R. China
jhdai@126.com

Abstract. Generalization of rough set model is one important aspect of rough set theory study, and it is very helpful to consummate rough set theory. Developing rough set theory using algebra systems has been paid great attention, and some researchers had reported significant developments. But the base algebra systems, on which approximation operators are defined, are confined to special Boolean algebras, including set algebra and atomic Boolean lattice. This paper introduces molecular lattices as base algebra system. Based on molecules of a molecular lattice, a mapping called meta-mapping is defined. Consequently, the approximation operators, which are more general and abstract compared with approximation operators reported in some papers, are defined based on the frame of molecular lattices. The properties of the approximations are also studied.

1 Introduction

The theory of rough sets deals with the approximation of an arbitrary subset of a universe by two definable or observable subsets called lower and upper approximations. In Pawlak rough set model [1], a subset of a universe is described by a pair of ordinary sets called the lower and upper approximations. It is clear that the approximations are two sets which are constructed based on an equivalence relation and the equivalence classes on it. The lower approximation of a given set is the union of all the equivalent classes which are subsets of the set, and the upper approximation is the union of all the equivalent classes which have a nonempty intersection with the set. Besides the set-oriented view of rough set theory, researchers also study rough set theory with operator-oriented view. Generalizing of approximation operators has caught many researchers' attentions. Lin and Liu [2] replaced equivalence relation with arbitrary binary relation, and the equivalence classes are replaced by neighborhood at the same time. By the two replacements, they define more general approximation operators. Yao [3] interpreted the rough set theory as an extension of set theory with two additional unary set-theoretic operators referred to as approximation operators. Such an interpretation is consistent with interpreting model logic as an extension of classical two-valued logic with two added unary operators. By introduc-

S. Tsumoto et al. (Eds.): RSCTC 2004, LNAI 3066, pp. 69–77, 2004.

ing approximation operators $\boldsymbol{L}$ and $\boldsymbol{H}$ into the base system $(2^U, \cap, \cup, \sim)$, $(2^U, \cap, \cup, \sim, \boldsymbol{L}, \boldsymbol{H})$ called rough set algebra is constructed. Based on atomic Boolean lattice, Jarvinen [4] proposed a more general framework for the study of approximation.

Wang [5,6] proposed theory of topological molecular lattices in the study of fuzzy-topology. With the development of theory of topological molecular lattices, the definition of molecular lattice had been relaxed to complete distributive lattice. Wang showed that every element in complete distributive lattice can be described as the union of $\vee$-irreducible element, which is called molecular.

This paper introduces molecular lattices as base algebra system on which a mapping φ, called meta-mapping, from molecular to general element is defined. Consequently, the lower approximation operator L_φ and upper approximation operator H_φ are defined using molecular and meta-mapping based on the frame of molecular lattice. The approximation operators are more general and abstract compared with approximation operators reported in some papers.

2 Preliminaries

In this section, we describe some preliminaries which are used in the following part of this paper. We assume that the reader is familiar with the usual lattice-theoretical notion and conventions.

Definition 1. Let $\boldsymbol{P}=(P,\leq)$ be an ordered set. A mapping $\varphi: P \rightarrow P$ is said to be

(a) order-preserving, if $x \leq y \Rightarrow \varphi(x) \leq \varphi(y)$, $\forall x, y \in P$;

(b) extensive, if $x \leq \varphi(y)$, $\forall x \in P$;

(c) symmetric, if $x \leq \varphi(y) \Rightarrow y \leq \varphi(x)$, $\forall x, y \in P$;

(d) constringent, if $\varphi(x) \leq x$, $\forall x \in P$.

Definition 2. Let $\boldsymbol{L}=(L, \leq)$ be a lattice. An element $a \in L$ is said to be a $\vee$-irreducible element, if $a = b \vee c \Rightarrow a = b$ or $a = c$, $\forall b, c \in L$.

Definition 3. Let $\boldsymbol{L}=(L, \leq)$ be a lattice. A nonzero $\vee$-irreducible element is called a molecule.

Lemma 1. Let $\boldsymbol{L}=(L, \leq)$ be a complete distributive lattice and let $L(M)$ be the set of molecules. Then every element in L can be described as the union of some molecules.

This lemma is taken from [6]. Based on this lemma, a complete distributive lattice is called a molecular lattice.

Lemma 2. Let $\boldsymbol{L}=(L, \leq)$ be a molecular lattice and let S,T be subsets of L. If $S \subseteq T$, then we have $\vee S \leq \vee T$ and $\wedge T \leq \wedge S$.

Proof. If $S=T$, it is easy to get this lemma. Else there exits an nonempty set Q satisfying $T = S \cup Q$ and $S \cup Q = \phi$. $\vee T = \bigvee_{x\in T} x = (\bigvee_{x \in S} x) \vee (\bigvee_{x \in Q} x) = (\vee S) \vee (\vee Q)$.

Since L is molecular lattice, $\vee T$, $\vee S$ and $\vee Q$ exist. Let $\vee T$, $\vee S$ and $\vee Q$ be t,s and q respectively. Then we have $t=s\vee q$. By the definition of $\vee$ in lattice, we get $s\leq s\vee q=t$ which implies $S\leq \vee T$.

$\wedge T \leq \wedge S$ can be proved similarly.

3 Generalizations of Approximations

In this section, we study properties of approximations in a more general setting of molecular lattices.

Let $L=(L, \leq)$ be a complete distributive lattice and let $L(M)$ be the set of molecules. We define a mapping $\varphi:L(M) \to L$ and we name this mapping as meta-mapping of molecular lattice L. To understand the mapping conveniently, we can specialize the molecular lattice to ordinary set algebra $(2^U, \subseteq)$. Let R be a binary relation on U. Note that every element in L can be described as the union of some molecules. The mapping can be viewed as $\varphi:U\to 2^U$, $x\mapsto [x]_R$ in the ordinary set algebra $(2^U, \subseteq)$.

Definition 4. Let $L=(L, \leq)$ be a molecular lattice and let $L(M)$ be the set of molecules.

$\varphi:L(M) \to L$ is an arbitrary meta-mapping in L. For $x\in L$, let

$$L_\varphi x=\vee \{m\in L(M)|\ \varphi(m)\leq x\},$$

$$H_\varphi x=\wedge \{m\in L(M)|\ x\leq \varphi(m)\}.$$

The elements $L_\varphi x$ and $H_\varphi x$ are the lower and the upper approximation of x with respect to φ respectively. Two elements x and y are equivalent if they have the same upper and the same lower approximations.

Theorem 1. Let $L=(L, \leq)$ be a molecular lattice with the least element 0 and the greatest element 1. Then we have:

(a) $H_\varphi 0=0$, $L_\varphi 1=1$;

(b) $x\leq y\Rightarrow L_\varphi x\leq L_\varphi y$, $H_\varphi x\leq H_\varphi y$;

(c) $S\subseteq L \Rightarrow \vee H_\varphi (S)= H_\varphi(\vee S)$, $\wedge L_\varphi (S)= L_\varphi(\wedge S)$.

Proof. (a)By definition 4, we have

$$L_\varphi 1=\vee \{m\in L(M)|\ \varphi(m)\leq 1\}=\vee \{ m \mid m\in L(M)\}$$

This implies $L_\varphi 1$ can be described as the union of all the molecules in L. From lemma 1 we know that the greatest element 1 can be described as the union of some molecules. Then we know $1\leq L_\varphi 1$. While 1 is the greatest element in L, hence we know $L_\varphi 1\leq 1$. So, we get $1=L_\varphi 1$. $H_\varphi 0=0$ can be proved similarly.

(b) we know the following by definition 4

$$L_\varphi x \vee L_\varphi y = (\vee\{m \in L(M) | \varphi(m) \in x\}) \vee (\vee\{m \in L(M) | \varphi(m) \leq y\}) \quad (1)$$

Since that $x \leq y$, we get $\varphi(m) \leq x \Rightarrow \varphi(m) \leq y$, then we have

$$\{m \in L(M) | \varphi(m) \leq x\} \subseteq \{m \in L(M) | \varphi(m) \leq y\}$$

By lemma 2, we know

$$\vee\{m \in L(M) | \varphi(m) \leq x\} \leq \vee\{m \in L(M) | \varphi(m) \leq y\} \quad (2)$$

From formula (1), (2) we know

$$L_\varphi x \vee L_\varphi y = \vee\{m \in L(M) | \varphi(m) \leq y\} = L_\varphi y$$

This means $L_\varphi x \leq L_\varphi y$. $H_\varphi x \leq H_\varphi y$ can be proved similarly.

(c) By (b) we know $\vee H_\varphi(S) \leq H_\varphi(\vee S)$. For $\forall x \in S$ satisfying $x \leq \varphi(m)$, we get

$$\varphi(m) \wedge (\bigvee_{x \in S} x) = \bigvee_{x \in S} (\varphi(m) \wedge x) = \bigvee_{x \in S} x = \vee S$$

This implies $\vee S \leq \varphi(m)$, and we know

$$\bigcup_{x \in S} \{m \in L(M) | x \leq \varphi(m)\} \subseteq \{m \in L(M) | \vee S \leq \varphi(m)\}$$

Since the formula above, together with lemma 2, we know

$$\begin{aligned} H_\varphi(\vee S) &= \wedge\{m \in L(M) | \vee S \leq \varphi(m)\} \\ &\leq \wedge(\bigcup_{x \in S} \{m \in L(M) | x \leq \varphi(m)\}) \\ &= \wedge\{\bigvee_{x \in S} \{m \in L(M) | x \leq \varphi(m)\}\} \\ &= \bigvee_{x \in S} \{\wedge\{m \in L(M) | x \leq \varphi(m)\}\} \\ &= \bigvee_{x \in S} \{H_\varphi x\} = \vee H_\varphi(S) \end{aligned}$$

So we have $\vee H_\varphi(S) = H_\varphi(\vee S)$. $\wedge L_\varphi(S) = L_\varphi(\wedge S)$ can be proved similarly.

Theorem 2. Let $L=(L,\leq)$ be a molecular lattice with the least element 0 and the greatest element 1. Then we have:

(a) $(H_\varphi(L), \leq)$ is a complete lattice with the least element 0 and the greatest element $H_\varphi 1$;

(b) $(L_\varphi(L), \leq)$ is a complete lattice with the least element $L_\varphi 0$ and the greatest element 1.

Proof. (a) For $(H_\varphi(L), \leq)$, suppose that $H_\varphi a, H_\varphi b \in H_\varphi(L)$. Since $a \leq a \vee b$, together with order-preserving property of H_φ, we have

$$H_\varphi a \leq H_\varphi(a \vee b), \quad H_\varphi b \leq H_\varphi(a \vee b) \quad (3)$$

For any $x \in H_\varphi(L)$ satisfying $H_\varphi a \leq x$, $H_\varphi b \leq x$, we get

$$x \vee H_\varphi(a \vee b) = x \vee (H_\varphi a \vee H_\varphi b) = (x \vee H_\varphi a) \vee H_\varphi b = x$$

This implies

$$H_\varphi(a \vee b) \leq x \tag{4}$$

By formula (3), we know $H_\varphi(a \vee b) = \sup\{H_\varphi a, H_\varphi b\}$. We can get $H_\varphi(a \wedge b) = \inf\{H_\varphi a, H_\varphi b\}$ in similar way. So $(H_\varphi(L), \leq)$ is a lattice.

Since formula (c) in theorem 1, we know that for any $H_\varphi(S) \subseteq H_\varphi(L)$, $\sup\{H_\varphi(S)\}$ exist and be $H_\varphi(S) \in H_\varphi(L)$. Similarly, $\inf\{H_\varphi(S)\}$ exist and be $L_\varphi(\wedge S) \in H_\varphi(L)$. Then we know $(H_\varphi(L), \leq)$ is a complete lattice.

(b) can be proved in similar way.

Theorem 3. Let $L=(L, \leq)$ be a molecular lattice. Let

$$L_\varphi R = \{\langle x, y\rangle \mid L_\varphi x = L_\varphi y\}$$

$$H_\varphi R = \{\langle x, y\rangle \mid H_\varphi x = H_\varphi y\}$$

Then we have:

(a) $L_\varphi R$ is congruence on the semi-lattice $(L, \wedge)$, and for any $x \in L$, $[x]_{L_\varphi R}$ has a least element;

(b) $H_\varphi R$ is congruence on the semi-lattice $(L, \vee)$, and for any $x \in L$, $[x]_{H_\varphi R}$ has a greatest element.

Proof. (a) It can be easily seen that $L_\varphi R$ is an equivalence relation. Suppose that x_1, x_2, y_1, $y_2 \in L$ and (x_1, x_2), $(y_1, y_2) \in L_\varphi R$, then we get

$$L_\varphi x_1 = L_\varphi y_1, \; L_\varphi x_2 = L_\varphi y_2 \tag{5}$$

By formula (c) in theorem 1, we have

$$L_\varphi(x_1 \wedge x_2) = L_\varphi x_1 \wedge L_\varphi x_2, \; L_\varphi(y_1 \wedge y_2) = L_\varphi y_1 \wedge L_\varphi y_2 \tag{6}$$

From formula (5) and (6), we know

$$L_\varphi(x_1 \wedge x_2) = L_\varphi(y_1 \wedge y_2)$$

It implies that $L_\varphi R$ is congruence on the semi-lattice $(L, \wedge)$.

In semi-lattice $(L, \wedge)$, suppose that $S \subseteq L$, then it easy to know that $\wedge S$ exist. So, we have $\wedge\{y \mid L_\varphi y = L_\varphi x\} \in L$. And because of

$$L_\varphi(\wedge\{y \mid L_\varphi y = L_\varphi x\}) = \wedge\{L_\varphi y \mid L_\varphi y = L_\varphi x\} = L_\varphi x$$

which implies that $\wedge\{y|\ L_\varphi y=L_\varphi x\}\in[x]_{L_\varphi R}$. It is obvious that $\wedge\{y|\ L_\varphi y=L_\varphi x\}$ is the least element of $[x]_{L_\varphi R}$.

(b) can be proved in similar way.

4 Approximations Respect to Classic Meta-mappings

In this section, we study the interesting properties of approximations more closely in cases when the meta-mapping φ is some classic mappings, including extensive, symmetric or constringent.

4.1 Extensive Meta-mapping

In this subsection we study the approximation operators L_φ and H_φ defined by an extensive mapping φ. We show that each element of molecular L is proved to be between its approximations.

Theorem 4. Let $\boldsymbol{L}=(L,\leq)$ be a molecular lattice and let $L(M)$ be the set of molecules. $\varphi:L(M)\rightarrow L$ is an extensive meta-mapping in $\boldsymbol{L}$. For any $x\in L$, $L_\varphi x\leq x\leq H_\varphi x$ holds.

Proof. Since φ is extensive, $x\leq\varphi(x)$ for all $x\in L$, and hence,

$$\{m\in L(M)|\ \varphi(m)\leq x\}\subseteq\{m\in L(M)|\ m\leq x\}$$

By lemma 2 and definition 3, we have

$$L_\varphi x=\vee\{m\in L(M)|\ \varphi(m)\leq x\}\leq\vee\{m\in L(M)|\ m\leq x\}=x$$

This means $L_\varphi x\leq x$. We can also prove $x\leq H_\varphi x$ in similar way.

Corollary 1. If $\varphi:L(M)\rightarrow L$ is an extensive meta-mapping in $\boldsymbol{L}$, then $L_\varphi 0=0$ and $H_\varphi 1=1$ hold.

4.2 Symmetric Meta-mapping

In this subsection, we study the properties of approximations when the meta-mapping φ is a symmetric mapping.

Theorem 5. Let $\boldsymbol{L}=(L,\leq)$ be a molecular lattice and let $L(M)$ be the set of molecules. $\varphi:L(M\rightarrow L$ is a symmetric meta-mapping in $\boldsymbol{L}$. For any $x\in L$, $H_\varphi L_\varphi x\leq x\leq L_\varphi H_\varphi x$ holds.

Proof. By definition 4, we have

$$H_\varphi L_\varphi x = \wedge \{m \in L(M) | \; L_\varphi x \leq \varphi(m)\}$$

Let $a \in L$ and $a \leq H_\varphi L_\varphi x$, then there exists $b \in L(M)$ satisfying

$$L_\varphi x \leq \varphi(b) \tag{7}$$

$$a \leq b \tag{8}$$

From definition 4, we know

$$L_\varphi x = \vee \{m \in L(M) | \; \varphi(m) \leq x\}$$

By formula (7), we know there exists $c \in L(M)$ satisfying $c \leq \varphi(b), \varphi(c) \leq x$. φ is an symmetric mapping, from definition 1 we get

$$b \leq \varphi(c) \tag{9}$$

$$\varphi(c) \leq x \tag{10}$$

Since formula (8), (9) and (10), we have $a \leq x$. This means that $a \leq x$ holds for any $a \in L$ satisfying $a \leq H_\varphi L_\varphi x$. Hence we know $H_\varphi L_\varphi x \leq x$ holds. $x \leq L_\varphi H_\varphi x$ can be proved in similar way.

Theorem 6. Let $\boldsymbol{L}=(L, \leq)$ be a molecular lattice and let $L(M)$ be the set of molecules. $\varphi : L(M) \rightarrow L$ is a symmetric meta-mapping in $\boldsymbol{L}$. Then we know:

(a) $L_\varphi H_\varphi$ is a closure operator;
(b) $H_\varphi L_\varphi$ is an interior operator.

Proof. By theorem 5, we have

$$x \leq L_\varphi H_\varphi x \tag{11}$$

Since H_φ is order-preserving, hence,

$$H_\varphi L_\varphi H_\varphi x \leq H_\varphi x \tag{12}$$

From theorem 5, we know $L_\varphi H_\varphi x \leq x$. By replacing $H_\varphi x$ with x, we get

$$H_\varphi x \leq H_\varphi L_\varphi H_\varphi x \tag{13}$$

By formula (11) and (12), we know $H_\varphi L_\varphi H_\varphi x = H_\varphi x$, and hence

$$L_\varphi H_\varphi (L_\varphi H_\varphi x) = L_\varphi H_\varphi x \tag{14}$$

Because of the order-preserving property of H_φ and L_φ, we know

$$x \leq y \Rightarrow H_\varphi x \leq H_\varphi y \Rightarrow L_\varphi H_\varphi x \leq L_\varphi H_\varphi y \tag{15}$$

By formula (10), (14) and (15), we know that operator $L_\varphi H_\varphi$ satisfies Kuratowski closure axioms. In other words, $L_\varphi H_\varphi$ is a closure operator.

(b) can be proved in the similar way.

Theorem 7. Let $\boldsymbol{L}=(L,\leq)$ be a molecular lattice. Let

$$L_\varphi \mathrm{R}=\{<x, y>|\ L_\varphi x=L_\varphi y\}$$

$$H_\varphi \mathrm{R}=\{<x, y>|\ H_\varphi x=H_\varphi y\}$$

Then we have:

(a) $L_\varphi H_\varphi x$ is the greatest element of $[x]_{L_\varphi \mathrm{R}}$;

(b) $H_\varphi L_\varphi x$ is the least element of $[x]_{H_\varphi \mathrm{R}}$.

Proof. (a) Since theorem 6, we get $H_\varphi L_\varphi H_\varphi x=H_\varphi x$ which implies

$$<x, L_\varphi H_\varphi x>\in H_\varphi \mathrm{R} \tag{16}$$

Suppose $y\in L$ and $<x, y>\in H_\varphi\mathrm{R}$, which means $H_\varphi y= H_\varphi x$, then we get $L_\varphi H_\varphi y= L_\varphi H_\varphi x$. From theorem 5 we know $y\leq L_\varphi H_\varphi y$. So, we get $y\leq L_\varphi H_\varphi x$. It implies

$$<x, y>\in H_\varphi \mathrm{R}\Rightarrow y\leq L_\varphi H_\varphi x \tag{17}$$

(b) can be proved in similar way.

4.3 Constringent Meta-mapping

We end our work by studying the case in which the meta-mapping φ is a constringent mapping.

Theorem 8. Let $\boldsymbol{L}=(L,\leq)$ be a molecular lattice and let $L(M)$ be the set of molecules. $\varphi:L(M)\rightarrow L$ is a constringent meta-mapping in $\boldsymbol{L}$. For any $x\in L$, $H_\varphi x\leq x\leq L_\varphi x$ holds.

Proof. Since φ is constringent, $x\leq \varphi(x)$ for all $x\in L$, and hence,

$$\{m\in L(M)|\ m\leq x\}\subseteq\{m\in L(M)|\ \varphi(m)\leq x\}$$

By lemma 2 and definition 4, we have

$$x=\vee\{m\in L(M)|\ m\leq x\}\leq\vee\{m\in L(M)|\ \varphi(m)\leq x\}=L_\varphi x$$

This means $x\leq L_\varphi x$. We can also prove $H_\varphi x\leq x$ in similar way.

Corollary 2. If $\varphi:L(M)\rightarrow L$ is a constringent meta-mapping in $\boldsymbol{L}$, then $H_\varphi 0= 0$ and $L_\varphi 1= 1$ hold.

Theorem 9. Let $\boldsymbol{L}=(L, \leq)$ be a molecular lattice and let $L(M)$ be the set of molecules. $\varphi: L(M) \rightarrow L$ is a symmetric meta-mapping in $\boldsymbol{L}$. For all $x \in L$, we know:

(a) $L_\varphi x \leq L_\varphi L_\varphi x$;

(b) $H_\varphi H_\varphi x \leq H_\varphi x$.

Proof. This theorem is easy to prove by theorem 8 and the order-preserving property of L_φ and H_φ.

5 Conclusion

This paper introduces molecular lattice as base algebra system on which a mapping, called meta-mapping, from molecular to general element is defined. Consequently, the lower approximation operator L_φ and upper approximation operator H_φ are defined using molecular and meta-mapping based on the frame of molecular lattice. We also study some interesting properties of approximations more closely in cases when the meta-mapping φ is some classic mappings, including extensive, symmetric or constringent. Jarvinen [4] studied approximations based on atomic Boolean lattice which provides a more general framework for the study of approximation than some other researchers' work. But atomic Boolean lattices can be viewed as a special kind of molecular lattices. Compared with atomic Boolean lattices, $a \wedge x \neq 0 \Leftrightarrow a \leq x$, is not necessary to hold in molecular lattices. Maybe we can say that this paper proposes a further general framework for the study of approximation.

References

1. Pawlak, Z., Rough Sets–Theoretical Aspects of Reasoning about Data. Kluwer Academic Publishers, Dordrecht (1991).
2. Lin, T.Y., Liu, Q., Rough approximate operators: Axiomatic rough set theory. In: Ziarko, W. P. (eds.): Rough Sets, Fuzzy Sets and Knowledge Discovery. London: Springer-Verlag (1994)256–260.
3. Yao, Y.Y., Constructive and algebraic methods of the theory of rough sets. Information Sciences, **109**(1-4) (1998)21–47.
4. Jarvinen, J., On the structure of rough approximations. In: Alpigini, J.J. et al. (eds.): Proceedings of 3rd International Conference on Rough Sets and Current Trends in Computing (RSCTC2002), Malvern, PA, USA (2002)123–230.
5. Wang, G.J., On construction of Fuzzy lattice. ACTA Mathematical SINICA(in Chinese), **29**(4) (1986) 539–543.
6. Wang, G.J., Theory of Topological Molecular Lattices. Fuzzy Sets and Systems **47** (1992) 351–376.

Rough Approximations under Level Fuzzy Sets

W.-N. Liu, JingTao Yao, and Yiyu Yao

Department of Computer Science, University of Regina
Regina, Saskatchewan, Canada S4S 0A2
{liuwe200,jtyao,yyao}@cs.uregina.ca

Abstract. The combination of fuzzy set and rough set theories lead to various models. Functional and set approaches are two categories based on different fuzzy representations. In this paper, we study rough approximations based on the notion of level fuzzy sets. Two rough approximation models, namely α-level rough set and β-level rough set, are proposed. It shows that β-level fuzzy rough set model can approximate a fuzzy set at different precisions.

1 Introduction

The distinct and complementary fuzzy set theory [15] and rough set theory [7] are generalizations of classical set theory. Attempts to combine these two theories lead to new notions [2, 10, 13]. The combination involves three types of approximations, i.e., approximation of fuzzy sets in crisp approximation spaces, approximation of crisp sets in fuzzy approximation spaces, and approximation of fuzzy sets in fuzzy approximation spaces [13].

The construction of fuzzy rough sets can be classified into two approaches, namely, functional approach and set approach. The first one formulates the lower and upper bounds with fuzzy membership functions. These formulas express the logical relations that lower and upper bounds must abide in approximation spaces [10].

The second approach [13] combines rough and fuzzy sets based on the cutting of fuzzy sets or fuzzy relations. When a fuzzy set is represented by a family of crisp subsets (α-level sets), these α-level sets can be approximated by equivalence relations in rough sets. A fuzzy relation can also be approximated by a family of equivalence relations (β-level sets). This family defines a family of approximation spaces. The new rough sets are based on these approximation spaces.

A third approach of the combination of fuzzy sets and rough sets can be considered by introducing the concept of level fuzzy sets. It has been argued that benefits do exist in the use of level fuzzy sets over level sets [1, 9, 11].

The present study examines some of the fundamental issues of the combination from the perspective of level fuzzy sets. The properties of α-level fuzzy sets and β-level fuzzy sets will be introduced in the next section. The models of α-level rough set and β-level rough set are studied. We discuss the properties of these models in Section 3.

S. Tsumoto et al. (Eds.): RSCTC 2004, LNAI 3066, pp. 78–83, 2004.

2 Fuzzy Rough Sets and Level Fuzzy Sets

We review the concept of fuzzy rough sets and level fuzzy sets. The properties of level fuzzy sets are also discussed.

2.1 Fuzzy Rough Sets

Many views of fuzzy rough sets exist. We adopt the notion of Radzikowska and Kerre [10], which absorbs some earlier studies [3, 4, 6] in the same direction. Let (U,R) be a fuzzy approximation space and $\tilde{P}(U)$ be the set of all fuzzy sets. For every $A \in \tilde{P}(U)$, $apr(A) = (\underline{apr}_R(A), \overline{apr}_R(A))$ where

$$\underline{apr}_R(A)(x) = \inf_{y \in U} I(R(x,y), A(y)) \tag{1}$$

$$\overline{apr}_R(A)(x) = \sup_{y \in U} T(R(x,y), A(y)). \tag{2}$$

$\underline{apr}_R(A)$ and $\overline{apr}_R(A))$ define the lower and upper approximations of a fuzzy set A respectively. They are constructed by means of an implicator I and a t-norm T. Equation 1 indicates that, for any $x \in U$, its membership degree is determined by looking at the elements resembling x, and by computing to what extent y is contained in a fuzzy set A. Equation 2 indicates that the membership degree of x is determined by the overlap between y and A.

2.2 Level Sets and Level Fuzzy Sets

Let A be a fuzzy set defined in universe U, and $\alpha \in (0, 1]$. The α-level set or α-cut of A is a crisp subset of U defined by

$$A_\alpha(x) = \begin{cases} 1 & \text{if } A(x) \geq \alpha \\ 0 & \text{otherwise} \end{cases};$$

the α-level fuzzy set or fuzzy α-cut of A is characterized by

$$\tilde{A}_\alpha(x) = \begin{cases} A(x) & \text{if } A(x) \geq \alpha \\ 0 & \text{otherwise} \end{cases}.$$

Based on above definitions, we can conclude that α-level fuzzy sets are obtained by reducing parts of fuzziness or information holding in the original fuzzy sets.

Let R be a fuzzy similarity relation on U, and $\beta \in (0, 1]$. The β-level set or β-cut of R is an equivalence relation on U defined by

$$R_\beta(x,y) = \begin{cases} 1 & \text{if } R(x,y) \geq \beta \\ 0 & \text{otherwise} \end{cases};$$

the β-level fuzzy set or fuzzy β-cut of R is characterized by

$$\tilde{R}_\beta(x,y) = \begin{cases} R(x,y) & \text{if } R(x,y) \geq \beta \\ 0 & \text{otherwise} \end{cases}.$$

Both α-level set and β-level set are called level sets; correspondingly, both α-level fuzzy set and β-level fuzzy set are called level fuzzy sets. The symmetry between level sets and level fuzzy sets indicates that the properties of level fuzzy sets are a fuzzy counterpart of the ones of level sets.

Property 1. $\forall\alpha \in [0,1]$, $\forall x \in U$, $\tilde{A}_\alpha \subseteq A$ and $supp\tilde{A}_\alpha \subseteq suppA$;
$\forall \alpha_1, \alpha_2 \in [0,1]$, $\alpha_2 \geq \alpha_1 \Rightarrow \tilde{A}_{\alpha_2} \subseteq \tilde{A}_{\alpha_1}$ and $supp\tilde{A}_{\alpha_2} \subseteq supp\tilde{A}_{\alpha_1}$.

Property 1 indicates that α-level fuzzy sets are monotonic with respect to fuzzy set inclusion. The supports of α-level fuzzy sets are monotonic with respect to set inclusion.

Property 2. For every $\beta \in [0,1]$, each $\tilde{R}_\beta$ of similarity relation R is a similarity relation on U, i.e. $\tilde{R}_\beta$ satisfies reflexive, symmetric and sup-min transitive conditions.

Proof.
It is only necessary to verify that $\tilde{R}_\beta$ satisfies the sup-min transitive condition.
when $R(x,y) \geq \beta$,
$\tilde{R}_\beta(x,y) \geq \sup_{z\in U}\{min\{R(x,z), R(z,y)\}\} \geq \sup_{z\in U}\{min\{\tilde{R}_\beta(x,z), \tilde{R}_\beta(z,y)\}\}$
when $R(x,y) < \beta$, $\tilde{R}_\beta(x,y) = 0$
$\beta > R(x,y) \geq \sup_{z\in U}\{min\{R(x,z), R(z,y)\}\}$
which means that $\forall z \in U$, $R(x,z) < \beta$ *or* $R(z,y) < \beta$ i.e.
$\forall z \in U$, $\tilde{R}_\beta(x,z) < \beta$ *or* $\tilde{R}_\beta(z,y) < \beta$ i.e.
$\forall z \in U$, $min\{\tilde{R}_\beta(x,z), \tilde{R}_\beta(z,y)\} = 0$
We still have the result: $\tilde{R}_\beta(x,y) \geq \sup_{z\in U}\{min\{\tilde{R}_\beta(x,z), \tilde{R}_\beta(z,y)\}\}$□

In fuzzy approximation space, basic granules of knowledge can be represented by similarity classes for each element in U [12]. The size of the support of every similarity class is used to measure the granularity of the class. More precisely, the similarity class for $x \in U$, denoted R_x, is a fuzzy set in U characterized by the membership function: $R_x(y) = R(x,y)$. The similarity class for $x \in U$ determined by $\tilde{R}_\beta$, denoted R_x^β, is characterized by the membership function: $R_x^\beta(y) = \tilde{R}_\beta(x,y)$.

Property 3. $\forall \beta, \beta_1, \beta_2 \in [0,1]$, $\forall x \in U$, $suppR_x^\beta \subseteq suppR_x$ and $\beta_2 \geq \beta_1 \Rightarrow R_x^{\beta_2} \subseteq R_x^{\beta_1}$.

Property 3 indicates that the β-level fuzzy sets of a similarity relation form a nested sequence of similarity relations. The bigger level β, the finer the similarity classes determined by $\tilde{R}_\beta$. Property 2 and 3 justify that β-level fuzzy sets are a fuzzy counterpart of β-level sets. The sequence of fuzzy relations coincides with the partition tree [5] constructed by β-level sets.

3 Level Fuzzy Sets Based Fuzzy Rough Sets

Any fuzzy set can be decomposed into a family of α-level sets and a family of α-level fuzzy sets. Any fuzzy relation can also be decomposed into a family of

β-level sets and a family of β-level fuzzy sets. In Section 3.1, the reference set A in $(\underline{apr}_R(A), \overline{apr}_R(A))$ is replaced with its α-level fuzzy set. In Section 3.2, fuzzy relation R in $(\underline{apr}_R(A), \overline{apr}_R(A))$ is substituted with its β-level fuzzy set. Two new fuzzy rough sets are obtained. We examine their properties and briefly demonstrate how level fuzzy sets simplify the computation of fuzzy rough sets.

3.1 α-Level Fuzzy Rough Set Model

Consider the approximation of an α-level fuzzy set of the reference set A, $\alpha \in (0,1]$, in the fuzzy approximation space (U,R). The fuzzy rough set $(\underline{apr}_R(\tilde{A}_\alpha), \overline{apr}_R(\tilde{A}_\alpha))$:

$$\underline{apr}_R(\tilde{A}_\alpha)(x) = \inf_{y \in U} I(R(x,y), \tilde{A}_\alpha(y)) \tag{3}$$

$$\overline{apr}_R(\tilde{A}_\alpha)(x) = \sup_{y \in U} T(R(x,y), \tilde{A}_\alpha(y)) \tag{4}$$

is called the α-level fuzzy rough sets of A. For the family of α-level fuzzy sets, we obtain a family of α-level fuzzy rough sets.

Property 4. If fuzzy implicator I is right monotonic, and implicator I and t-norm T are continuous, then $\forall \alpha, \alpha_1, \alpha_2 \in [0,1]$,
$\underline{apr}_R(A) \supseteq \underline{apr}_R(\tilde{A}_\alpha)$ and $\overline{apr}_R(A) \supseteq \overline{apr}_R(\tilde{A}_\alpha)$;

$\alpha_1 \le \alpha_2 \Rightarrow \underline{apr}_R(\tilde{A}_{\alpha_1}) \supseteq \underline{apr}_R(\tilde{A}_{\alpha_2})$ and $\overline{apr}_R(\tilde{A}_{\alpha_1}) \supseteq \overline{apr}_R(\tilde{A}_{\alpha_2})$.

Property 4 indicates that α-level fuzzy rough sets are monotonic with respect to fuzzy set inclusion. The property is similar to that of α-level rough sets. However, we have to concede that, unlike α-level rough sets [13], there is no guarantee that $\underline{apr}_R(\tilde{A}_\alpha)$ will be α-level fuzzy set of some fuzzy set. The conclusion is the same with $\overline{apr}_R(\tilde{A}_\alpha)$. We can not say that the family of $(\underline{apr}_R(\tilde{A}_\alpha), \overline{apr}_R(\tilde{A}_\alpha))$ define $(\underline{apr}_R(A), \overline{apr}_R(A))$.

Conversely, we notice that the computation of $(\underline{apr}(A), \overline{apr}(A))$ can be divided into the evaluation of implication I(R(x,y),A(y)), the evaluation of cojunction T(R(x,y),A(y)), and the evaluation of infimum and supremum. By the property of implicator I, if A(y)=0, the value of R(x,y) alone determines the value of I(R(x,y),A(y)) and $T(R(x,y),A(y)) \equiv 0$. There are less elements participating in the computation of $(\underline{apr}_R(A), \overline{apr}_R(A)$ by replacing the fuzzy set A with its α-level fuzzy set. From a practical view, α-level fuzzy sets simplify the computation of fuzzy rough sets. The total saved running time is in proposition to level α.

3.2 β-Level Fuzzy Rough Set Model

The family of β-level fuzzy sets of fuzzy relation R defines a family of approximation spaces: $(U, \tilde{R}_\beta)$, $\beta \in (0,1]$. For a $\beta \in (0,1]$, the fuzzy rough set

$(\underline{apr}_{\tilde{R}_\beta}(A), \overline{apr}_{\tilde{R}_\beta}(A))$:

$$\underline{apr}_{\tilde{R}_\beta}(A)(x) = \inf_{y \in U} I(\tilde{R}_\beta(x,y), A(y)) \tag{5}$$

$$\overline{apr}_{\tilde{R}_\beta}(A)(x) = \sup_{y \in U} T(\tilde{R}_\beta(x,y), A(y)) \tag{6}$$

are called the β-level fuzzy rough sets of A. With respect to a fuzzy approximation space, we obtain a family of β-level fuzzy rough sets. The following properties can be verified easily:

Property 5. If the fuzzy implicator I is a continuous R-implicator based on a continuous t-norm T, then $\forall A \in \tilde{P}(U)$, $\underline{apr}_{\tilde{R}_\beta}(A) \subseteq A \subseteq \overline{apr}_{\tilde{R}_\beta}(A)$.

Property 6. If fuzzy implicator I is left monotonic, and I and t-norm T are continuous, then
$\underline{apr}_R(A) \subseteq \underline{apr}_{\tilde{R}_\beta}(A)$ and $\overline{apr}_R(A) \supseteq \overline{apr}_{\tilde{R}_\beta}(A)$;
$\beta_1 \leq \beta_2 \Rightarrow \underline{apr}_{\tilde{R}_{\beta_1}}(A) \subseteq \underline{apr}_{\tilde{R}_{\beta_2}}(A)$ and $\overline{apr}_{\tilde{R}_{\beta_1}}(A) \supseteq \overline{apr}_{\tilde{R}_{\beta_2}}(A)$.

Property 6 indicates that β-level fuzzy rough sets are monotonic with respect to the refinement of fuzzy relations. Coarse similarity classes usually lead to a 'coarse' approximation with a great misclassification error, whereas smaller similarity classes usually lead to a 'fine' approximation with a less misclassification error. Property 5 and 6 also indicate that a nested sequence of β-level fuzzy sets can lead to hierarchical rough approximations. The approximating precision can be controlled by adjusting level β. However, unlike β-level rough sets, there is no guarantee that $(\underline{apr}_{\tilde{R}_\beta}(A), \overline{apr}_{\tilde{R}_\beta}(A))$ is a level fuzzy set of $(\underline{apr}(A), \overline{apr}(A))$.

Similar with α-level fuzzy rough sets, β-level fuzzy sets can eliminate part of the computation of lower approximation and upper approximation. The reason is that if R(x,y)=0, then $I(R(x,y), A(y)) \equiv 1$ and $T(R(x,y), A(y)) \equiv 0$. The total saved running time is in proposition to level β.

The β-level sets of similarity relations form a nested sequence of equivalence relations. Let $A \subseteq U$, for each β-level sets of R, R_β, a crisp β-level rough set $(\underline{apr}_{R_\beta}(A), \overline{apr}_{R_\beta}(A))$ satisfies all the properties of rough set.

Property 7. $\forall \beta_1, \beta_2 \in [0,1]$, $\beta_1 \leq \beta_2 \Rightarrow \underline{apr}_{R_{\beta_1}}(A) \subseteq \underline{apr}_{R_{\beta_2}}(A)$ and $\overline{apr}_{R_{\beta_1}}(A) \supseteq \overline{apr}_{R_{\beta_2}}(A)$.

4 Conclusions

We introduce a new approach to the combination of fuzzy sets and rough sets. The combination is based on level fuzzy sets. We propose both the α-level fuzzy rough set model and the β-level fuzzy rough set model. It provides a new perspective to the theories of fuzzy sets and rough sets. Similar to the α-level rough sets and the β-level rough sets, some useful properties are examined. The β-level fuzzy rough sets may approximate a fuzzy set at different precisions by choosing different β-level fuzzy sets of a similarity relation.

Level fuzzy sets may reduce the information that implication and cojunction have to work with. This may lead to a simple computation. The trade-offs between approximating precision and computational efficiency are under examination. Decision-theoretic Rough Set theory [14] may play an important role in selecting proper α and β level values.

References

1. Baets, B.D., Kerre, E., "The Cutting of Compositions", *Fuzzy Sets and Systems*, Vol.62, pp.295-309, 1994.
2. Cornelis, C., Cock, M.D. and Kerre, E.E., "Intuitionistic Fuzzy Rough Sets: At the Crossroads of Imperfect Knowledge", *Expert Systems*, Vol.20, No.5, pp.260-270, Nov., 2003.
3. Dubois, D. and Prade, H., "Putting rough sets and fuzzy sets together", *Intelligent Decision Support: Handbook of Applications and Advances of the Rough Sets Theory*, Slowinski, R., (Ed.), Kluwer Academic Publishers, Boston, pp.203-222, 1992.
4. Dubois, D. and Prade, H., "Rough Fuzzy Sets and Fuzzy Rough Sets", *International Journal of general systems*, 17, pp.191-209, 1990
5. Dubois, D., Prade, H., "Fuzzy Sets and Systems: Theory and Applications", Academic Press, New York, 1980.
6. Nakamura, A., "Fuzzy Rough Sets", *Notes on Multiple-Valued Logic in Japan*, 9, pp.1-8, 1988
7. Pawlak, Z., "Rough Sets: Theoretical Aspects of Reasoning About Data", Kluwer Academic Publishers, Dordrecht, 1991.
8. Radecki, T., "A Model of a Document Retrieval System based on the Concept of a Semantic Disjunctif Normal Form", *Kybernetes*, Vol.10, pp.35-42, 1981.
9. Radecki, T., "Level Fuzzy Sets", *J. Cybernet*, Vol.7, pp.189-198, 1977.
10. Radzikowska, A.M. and Kerre, E.E., "A Comparative Study of Fuzzy Rough Sets", *Fuzzy Sets and Systems*, Vol.126, pp.137-155, 2002.
11. Rembrand, B.R.B., Zenner and Rita M.M. DE Caluwe, "A New Approach to Information Retrieval Systems Using Fuzzy Expressions", *Fuzzy Sets and Systems*, Vol.17, pp.9-22, 1984.
12. Slowinski, R. and Vanderpooten, D., "A Generalized Definition of Rough Approximations Based on Similarity", *IEEE Transactions on Knowledge and data engineering*, Vol.12, No.2, pp.331-336, 2000.
13. Yao, Y.Y., "Combination of Rough and Fuzzy Sets Based on α-Level Sets", *Rough Sets and Data Mining: Analysis for Imprecise Data*, Lin, T.Y. and Cercone, N. (Ed.), Kluwer Academic, Boston, MA, pp.301-321, 1997.
14. Yao, Y.Y., Wong, S.K.M, "A Decision Theoretic Framework for Approximating Concepts", *International Journal of Man-machine Studies*, Vol.37, No.6, pp.793-809, 1992.
15. Zadeh, L., "Fuzzy Sets", *Information and Control*, Vol.8, pp.338-353, 1965.

Fuzzy-Rough Modus Ponens and Modus Tollens as a Basis for Approximate Reasoning

Masahiro Inuiguchi[1], Salvatore Greco[2], and Roman Słowiński[3,4]

[1] Graduate School of Engineering Science, Osaka University, 1-3 Machikaneyama Toyonaka, Osaka 560-8531, Japan
inuiguti@sys.es.osaka-u.ac.jp

[2] Faculty of Economics, University of Catania, Corso Italia, 55, 95129 Catania, Italy
salgreco@mbox.unict.it

[3] Institute of Computing Science, Poznań University of Technology, 60-965 Poznań, Poland
slowinsk@sol.put.poznan.pl

[4] Institute for Systems Research, Polish Academy of Sciences, 01-447 Warsaw, Poland

Abstract. We have proposed a fuzzy rough set approach without using any fuzzy logical connectives to extract gradual decision rules from decision tables. In this paper, we discuss the use of these gradual decision rules within modus ponens and modus tollens inference patterns. We discuss the difference and similarity between modus ponens and modus tollens and, moreover, we generalize them to formalize approximate reasoning based on the extracted gradual decision rules. We demonstrate that approximate reasoning can be performed by manipulation of modifier functions associated with the gradual decision rules.

1 Introduction

Rough set theory deals mainly with the ambiguity of information caused by granular description of objects, while fuzzy set theory treats mainly the uncertainty of concepts and linguistic categories. Because of the difference in the treatment of uncertainty, fuzzy set theory and rough set theory are complementary and their various combinations have been studied by many researchers (see for example [1], [3], [6], [7], [8], [9], [10], [12], [16], [17], [18]). Most of them involved some fuzzy logical connectives (t-norm, t-conorm, fuzzy implication) to define fuzzy set operations. It is known, however, that selection of the "right" fuzzy logical connectives is not an easy task and that the results of fuzzy rough set analysis are sensitive to this selection. The authors [4] have proposed fuzzy rough sets without using any fuzzy logical connectives to extract gradual decision rules from decision tables. Within this approach, lower and upper approximations, are defined using modifier functions following from a given decision table.

This paper presents results of a fundamental study concerning utilization of knowledge obtained by the fuzzy rough set approach proposed in [4]. Since the obtained knowledge is represented by gradual decision rules, we discuss inference pat-

S. Tsumoto et al. (Eds.): RSCTC 2004, LNAI 3066, pp. 84–94, 2004.

terns (modus ponens and modus tollens) for gradual decision rules. We discuss the difference and the similarity between modus ponens and modus tollens under some monotonicity conditions. Moreover, we discuss inference patterns of the generalized modus ponens and modus tollens as a basis for approximate reasoning. The results demonstrate that approximate reasoning can be performed by manipulation of modifier functions associated with the extracted gradual decision rules.

In the next section, we review gradual decision rules extracted from a decision table and underlying fuzzy rough sets. We describe fuzzy-rough modus ponens and modus tollens with respect to the extracted gradual decision rules in Section 3. We discuss the difference and the similarity between fuzzy-rough modus ponens and modus tollens. In Section 4, we generalize the modus ponens and modus tollens in order to make inference using different fuzzy sets in the gradual decision rules. We demonstrate that all inference can be done by manipulation of modifier functions. Finally, we give concluding remarks in Section 5.

2 Gradual Decision Rules Extracted from a Decision Table

In a given decision table, we may found some gradual decision rules of the following types [4]:

- *lower-approximation rules with positive relationship* (LP-rule): "if condition X has credibility $C(X)\geq\alpha$, then decision Y has credibility $C(Y)\geq f_{Y|X}^{+}(\alpha)$";
- *lower-approximation rules with negative relationship* (LN-rule): "if condition X has credibility $C(X)\leq\alpha$, then decision Y has credibility $C(Y)\geq f_{Y|X}^{-}(\alpha)$";
- *upper-approximation rule with positive relationship* (UP-rule): "if condition X has credibility $C(X)\leq\alpha$, then decision Y could have credibility $C(Y)\leq g_{Y|X}^{+}(\alpha)$";
- *upper-approximation rule with negative relationship* (UN-rule): "if condition X has credibility $C(X)\geq\alpha$, then decision Y could have credibility $C(Y)\leq g_{Y|X}^{-}(\alpha)$",

where X is a given condition (premise), Y is a given decision (conclusion) and $f_{Y|X}^{+}:[0,1]\rightarrow[0,1]$, $f_{Y|X}^{-}:[0,1]\rightarrow[0,1]$, $g_{Y|X}^{+}:[0,1]\rightarrow[0,1]$ and $g_{Y|X}^{-}:[0,1]\rightarrow[0,1]$ are functions relating the credibility of X with the credibility of Y in lower- and upper-approximation rules, respectively. Those functions can be seen as modifier functions (see, for example, [8]). An LP-rule can be regarded as a gradual decision rule [2]; it can be interpreted as: "the more object x is X, the more it is Y". In this case, the relationship between credibility of premise and conclusion is positive and certain. LN-rule can be interpreted in turn as: "the less object x is X, the more it is Y", so the relationship is negative and certain. On the other hand, the UP-rule can be interpreted as: "the more object x is X, the more it could be Y", so the relationship is positive and possible. Finally, UN-rule can be interpreted as: "the less object x is X, the more it could be Y", so the relationship is negative and possible.

Example 1. Let us consider a decision table about hypothetical car selection problem in which the mileage is used for evaluation of cars. We may define a fuzzy set X of *gas_saving_cars* by the following membership function:

$$\mu_{gas\_saving\_car}(x)=\begin{cases}0 & \text{if } mileage(x)<9\\ (mileage(x)-9)/6 & \text{if } 9\le mileage(x)<15\\ 1 & \text{if } mileage(x)\ge 15\end{cases}.$$

Table 1. A decision maker's evaluation of sample cars.

Car:	A	B	C	D	E	F	G	H	I	J
mileage (km/l)	12	12	13	14	15	9	11	8	14	13
$\mu_{gas\_saving\_car}$	0.5	0.5	0.67	0.83	1	0	0.33	0	0.83	0.67
acceptability	0.6	0.5	0.6	0.8	0.9	0.3	0.5	0.3	0.8	0.6

From Table 1, we may find the following gradual decision rules over $x\in\{A,B,\ldots,J\}$:

- LP-rule: "if x is gas_saving_car with credibility $\mu_{gas\_saving\_car}(\text{mileage}(x))\ge\alpha$, then x is acceptable_car with credibility $\mu_{acceptable\_car}(x)\ge f_{Y|X}^{+}(\alpha)$";
- UP-rule: "if x is gas_saving_car with credibility $\mu_{gas\_saving\_car}(\text{mileage}(x))\le\alpha$, then x is acceptable_car with credibility $\mu_{acceptable\_car}(x)\le g_{Y|X}^{+}(\alpha)$",

where $f_{Y|X}^{+}$ and $g_{Y|X}^{+}$are defined by

$$f_{Y|X}^{+}(\alpha)=\begin{cases}0.3 & \text{if } 0\le\alpha<0.33\\ 0.5 & \text{if } 0.33\le\alpha<0.67\\ 0.6 & \text{if } 0.67\le\alpha<0.83\\ 0.8 & \text{if } 0.83\le\alpha<1\\ 0.9 & \text{if } \alpha=1\end{cases} \quad\text{and}\quad g_{Y|X}^{+}(\alpha)=\begin{cases}0.3 & \text{if } \alpha=0\\ 0.5 & \text{if } 0<\alpha\le 0.33\\ 0.6 & \text{if } 0.33<\alpha\le 0.67\\ 0.8 & \text{if } 0.67<\alpha\le 0.83\\ 0.9 & \text{if } 0.83<\alpha\le 1\end{cases}.$$

In Example 1, we consider a fuzzy set of gas saving cars as condition of rules but if we would consider a fuzzy set of gas guzzler cars as condition of rules, we would obtain LN- and UN-rules. As illustrated in this example, the condition X and decision Y can be represented by fuzzy sets.

The functions $f_{Y|X}^{+}(\cdot)$, $f_{Y|X}^{-}(\cdot)$, $g_{Y|X}^{+}(\cdot)$ and $g_{Y|X}^{-}(\cdot)$ are related to specific definitions of lower and upper approximations considered within rough set theory [11]. Suppose that we want to approximate knowledge contained in Y using knowledge about X over a set U of all objects in a given decision table. Let us also adopt the hypothesis that X is positively related to Y. Then, we can define the lower approximation $\underline{App}^{+}(X,Y)$, and upper approximation $\overline{App}^{+}(X,Y)$ of Y by the following membership functions:

$$\mu[\underline{App}^{+}(X,Y),x]=\inf_{z\in U:\mu_X(z)\ge\mu_X(x)}\{\mu_Y(z)\},$$

$$\mu[\overline{App}^{+}(X,Y),x]=\sup_{z\in U:\mu_X(z)\le\mu_X(x)}\{\mu_Y(z)\}.$$

Similarly, if we adopt the hypothesis that X is negatively related to Y, then we can define the lower approximation $\underline{App}^{-}(X,Y)$, and upper approximation $\overline{App}^{-}(X,Y)$ of Y by the following membership functions:

$$\mu[\underline{App}^{-}(X,Y),x] = \inf_{z\in U:\mu_X(z)\le\mu_X(x)} \{\mu_Y(z)\},$$

$$\mu[\overline{App}^{-}(X,Y),x] = \sup_{z\in U:\mu_X(z)\ge\mu_X(x)} \{\mu_Y(z)\}.$$

The lower and upper approximations defined above can serve to induce certain and approximate decision rules over all possible objects $\hat{U} \supseteq U$ in the following way. Let us remark that inferring lower and upper credibility rules is equivalent to finding modifiers $f_{Y|X}{}^{+}(\cdot)$, $f_{Y|X}{}^{-}(\cdot)$, $g_{Y|X}{}^{+}(\cdot)$ and $g_{Y|X}{}^{-}(\cdot)$. These functions can be defined as follows: for each $\alpha\in[0,1]$

$$f_{Y|X}{}^{+}(\alpha)=\begin{cases}\sup\limits_{x\in U:\mu_X(x)\le\alpha} \mu[\underline{App}^{+}(X,Y),x] & \text{if } \alpha>0 \text{ and } \exists x\in U, \mu_X(x)\le\alpha \\ 0 & \text{otherwise}\end{cases},$$

$$f_{Y|X}{}^{-}(\alpha)=\begin{cases}\sup\limits_{x\in U:\mu_X(x)\ge\alpha} \mu[\underline{App}^{-}(X,Y),x] & \text{if } \alpha<1 \text{ and } \exists x\in U, \mu_X(x)\ge\alpha \\ 0 & \text{otherwise}\end{cases},$$

$$g_{Y|X}{}^{+}(\alpha)=\begin{cases}\inf\limits_{z\in U:\mu_X(x)\ge\alpha} \mu[\overline{App}^{+}(X,Y),x] & \text{if } \alpha<1 \text{ and } \exists x\in U, \mu_X(x)\ge\alpha \\ 1 & \text{otherwise}\end{cases},$$

$$g_{Y|X}{}^{-}(\alpha)=\begin{cases}\inf\limits_{z\in U:\mu_X(x)\le\alpha} \mu[\overline{App}^{-}(X,Y),x] & \text{if } \alpha>0 \text{ and } \exists x\in U, \mu_X(x)\le\alpha \\ 1 & \text{otherwise}\end{cases}.$$

Note that $\mu[\underline{App}^{+}(X,Y),x]=f_{Y|X}{}^{+}(\mu_X(x))$, $\mu[\overline{App}^{-}(X,Y),x]=g_{Y|X}{}^{-}(\mu_X(x))$ hold for $x\in U$ such that $\mu_X(x)>0$ and $\mu[\underline{App}^{-}(X,Y],x] = f_{Y|X}{}^{-}(\mu_X(x))$, $\mu[\overline{App}^{+}(X,Y),x]=g_{Y|X}{}^{+}(\mu_X(x))$ hold for $x\in U$ such that $\mu_X(x)<1$. We assume that data given in decision table are only a part of the whole but correct. Therefore we define $f_{Y|X}{}^{+}(0)=f_{Y|X}{}^{-}(1)=0$ and $g_{Y|X}{}^{+}(1) = g_{Y|X}{}^{-}(0)=1$ considering the possible existence of objects y, $z\in\hat{U}$ such that $\mu_X(y)=0$, $\mu_X(z)=1$, $\mu_Y(y)<\inf\{\mu_Y(x)|\ \mu_X(x)=0, x\in U\}$ and $\mu_Y(z)>\sup\{\mu_Y(x)|\ \mu_X(x)=1, x\in U\}$.

3 Fuzzy-Rough Modus Ponens and Modus Tollens

Given a decision table, we may induce gradual decision rules from X to Y expressed by functions $f_{Y|X}{}^{+}(\cdot)$ and $g_{Y|X}{}^{+}(\cdot)$ or by functions $f_{Y|X}{}^{-}(\cdot)$ and $g_{Y|X}{}^{-}(\cdot)$. Remark that we may also induce gradual decision rules from Y to X in the same way. For example, when we have a rule "if the speed of a truck is high, then its damage in a crash is big", we may obtain a rule "if the damage of a truck is big, then its speed had been high before the crash" at the same time.

Such invertibility often occurs when X and Y strongly coincide each other; in other words, Y can be explained by X almost completely. In order to clarify the differences between gradual decision rules from X to Y and from Y to X, we are using the following notation. By $f_{Y|X}{}^{+}(\cdot)$, $f_{Y|X}{}^{-}(\cdot)$, $g_{Y|X}{}^{+}(\cdot)$ and $g_{Y|X}{}^{-}(\cdot)$, we denote modifier functions corresponding to gradual decision rules from X to Y. Analogously, by $f_{X|Y}^{+}(\cdot)$, $f_{X|Y}^{-}(\cdot)$, $g_{X|Y}^{+}(\cdot)$ and $g_{X|Y}^{-}(\cdot)$, we denote modifier functions corresponding to gradual decision rules from Y to X. The first four modifiers are defined on the basis of rough approximations $\underline{App}^{+}(X,Y)$, $\overline{App}^{+}(X,Y)$, $\underline{App}^{-}(X,Y)$ and $\overline{App}^{-}(X,Y)$, respectively, while the last four modifiers are defined analogously on the basis of rough approximations $\underline{App}^{+}(Y,X)$, $\overline{App}^{+}(Y,X)$, $\underline{App}^{-}(Y,X)$ and $\overline{App}^{-}(Y,X)$.

While the previous sections concentrated on the issues of representation, rough approximation and gradual decision rule extraction, this section is devoted to inference with a generalized *modus ponens* (*MP*) and a generalized *modus tollens* (*MT*). The generalized *MP* described in this paper is not related to a probabilistic logic but a fuzzy logic while Rough *MP* is related to a probabilistic logic [12].

Classically, *MP* has the following form,

$$\begin{array}{lcl} \text{if} & X \rightarrow Y & \text{is true} \\ \text{and} & X & \text{is true} \\ \hline \text{then} & Y & \text{is true} \end{array}$$

MP has the following interpretation: assuming an implication $X \rightarrow Y$ (true decision rule) and a fact X (premise), we obtain another fact Y (conclusion). If we replace the classical decision rule above by our four kinds of gradual decision rules, then we obtain the following four fuzzy-rough *MP*:

$$(LP\text{-}MP)\ \begin{array}{ll} \text{if} & \mu_X(x)\geq\alpha \rightarrow \mu_Y(x)\geq f_{Y|X}^{+}(\alpha) \\ \text{and} & \mu_X(x)\geq\alpha' \\ \hline \text{then} & \mu_Y(x)\geq f_{Y|X}^{+}(\alpha') \end{array} \qquad (LN\text{-}MP)\ \begin{array}{ll} \text{if} & \mu_X(x)\leq\alpha \rightarrow \mu_Y(x)\geq f_{Y|X}^{-}(\alpha) \\ \text{and} & \mu_X(x)\leq\alpha' \\ \hline \text{then} & \mu_Y(x)\geq f_{Y|X}^{-}(\alpha') \end{array}$$

$$(UP\text{-}MP)\ \begin{array}{ll} \text{if} & \mu_X(x)\leq\alpha \rightarrow \mu_Y(x)\leq g_{Y|X}^{+}(\alpha) \\ \text{and} & \mu_X(x)\leq\alpha' \\ \hline \text{then} & \mu_Y(x)\leq g_{Y|X}^{+}(\alpha') \end{array} \qquad (UN\text{-}MP)\ \begin{array}{ll} \text{if} & \mu_X(x)\geq\alpha \rightarrow \mu_Y(x)\leq g_{Y|X}^{-}(\alpha) \\ \text{and} & \mu_X(x)\geq\alpha' \\ \hline \text{then} & \mu_Y(x)\leq g_{Y|X}^{-}(\alpha') \end{array}$$

In the classical *MP*, the inference pattern is applicable only when the given fact X is same as the premise X of the rule $X \rightarrow Y$, in fuzzy-rough *MP*, however, the inference pattern is applicable when the given fact has the same form of the inequality relation as the premise of the rule. Moreover, in the real world, we may apply these inference patterns to get the information about $\mu_Y(x)$ of a new object x due to rules we obtained from a given decision table and due to an observed value of $\mu_X(x)$. This means that the above reasoning is a kind of extrapolation. Therefore, we assume $x\in \hat{U}$ and $\hat{U} \supseteq U$.

On the other hand, the classical *MT* has the following form,

$$\begin{array}{lcl} \text{if} & X \rightarrow Y & \text{is true} \\ \text{and} & Y & \text{is false} \\ \hline \text{then} & X & \text{is false} \end{array}$$

In the same way as we did in fuzzy-rough *MP*, we would like to obtain fuzzy-rough *MT* such as

$$\begin{array}{lll} (LP\text{-}MT) & \text{if} & \mu_X(x)\geq\alpha\rightarrow\mu_Y(x)\geq f_{Y|X}{}^{+}(\alpha) \\ & \text{and} & \mu_Y(x)<\beta \\ \hline & \text{then} & \mu_X(x)<\varphi(\beta) \end{array} \tag{1}$$

We should find a proper function $\varphi:[0,1]\rightarrow[0,1]$ which validates (1). Let us define the following functions involving an infinitely small positive number ε:

$$(f_{Y|X}{}^{+})_\varepsilon{}^{-1}(\beta)=\begin{cases}\inf\{\alpha\in[0,1]\mid f^{+}_{Y|X}(\alpha)\geq\beta\}, & \text{if } \{\alpha\in[0,1]\mid f^{+}_{Y|X}(\alpha)\geq\beta\}\neq\phi,\\ 1+\varepsilon, & \text{otherwise,}\end{cases}$$

$$(f_{Y|X}{}^{-})_\varepsilon{}^{-1}(\beta)=\begin{cases}\sup\{\alpha\in[0,1]\mid f^{-}_{Y|X}(\alpha)\geq\beta\}, & \text{if } \{\alpha\in[0,1]\mid f^{-}_{Y|X}(\alpha)\geq\beta\}\neq\phi,\\ 0-\varepsilon, & \text{otherwise,}\end{cases}$$

$$(g_{Y|X}{}^{+})_\varepsilon{}^{-1}(\beta)=\begin{cases}\sup\{\alpha\in[0,1]\mid g^{+}_{Y|X}(\alpha)\leq\beta\}, & \text{if } \{\alpha\in[0,1]\mid g^{+}_{Y|X}(\alpha)\leq\beta\}\neq\phi,\\ 0-\varepsilon, & \text{otherwise,}\end{cases}$$

$$(g_{Y|X}{}^{-})_\varepsilon{}^{-1}(\beta)=\begin{cases}\inf\{\alpha\in[0,1]\mid g^{-}_{Y|X}(\alpha)\leq\beta\}, & \text{if } \{\alpha\in[0,1]\mid g^{-}_{Y|X}(\alpha)\leq\beta\}\neq\phi,\\ 1+\varepsilon, & \text{otherwise.}\end{cases}$$

The following theorem gives answers to this problem.

Theorem. The following assertions are true:

1) Knowing rule $\mu_X(x)\geq\alpha\rightarrow\mu_Y(x)\geq f_{Y|X}{}^{+}(\alpha)$ and $\mu_Y(x)<\beta$, we get $\mu_X(x)<(f_{Y|X}{}^{+})_\varepsilon{}^{-1}(\beta)$.
2) Knowing rule $\mu_X(x)\leq\alpha\rightarrow\mu_Y(x)\geq f_{Y|X}{}^{-}(\alpha)$ and $\mu_Y(x)<\beta$, we get $\mu_X(x)>(f_{Y|X}{}^{-})_\varepsilon{}^{-1}(\beta)$.
3) Knowing rule $\mu_X(x)\leq\alpha\rightarrow\mu_Y(x)\leq g_{Y|X}{}^{+}(\alpha)$ and $\mu_Y(x)>\beta$, we get $\mu_X(x)>(g_{Y|X}{}^{+})_\varepsilon{}^{-1}(\beta)$.
4) Knowing rule $\mu_X(x)\geq\alpha\rightarrow\mu_Y(x)\leq g_{Y|X}{}^{-}(\alpha)$ and $\mu_Y(x)>\beta$, we get $\mu_X(x)<(g_{Y|X}{}^{-})_\varepsilon{}^{-1}(\beta)$.
5) Knowing rule $\mu_X(x)\geq\alpha\rightarrow\mu_Y(x)\geq f_{Y|X}{}^{+}(\alpha)$ and $\mu_Y(x)<\beta$ such that there exists $\alpha\in[0,1]$, $f_{Y|X}{}^{+}(\alpha)\geq\beta$, we get $\mu_X(x)<g_{X|Y}{}^{+}(\beta)$, if and only if $\mu_X(x)>\mu_X(y)$ implies $\mu_Y(x)\geq\mu_Y(y)$, for any $x,y\in U$ such that there exists $z\in U$ satisfying $\inf\limits_{w\in U,\,\mu_X(w)\geq\mu_X(z)}\mu_Y(w)>\mu_Y(y)$.
6) Knowing rule $\mu_X(x)\leq\alpha\rightarrow\mu_Y(x)\geq f_{Y|X}{}^{-}(\alpha)$ and $\mu_Y(x)<\beta$ such that there exists $\alpha\in[0,1]$, $f_{Y|X}{}^{-}(\alpha)\geq\beta$, we get $\mu_X(x)>f_{X|Y}{}^{-}(\beta)$, if and only if $\mu_X(x)<\mu_X(y)$ implies $\mu_Y(x)\geq\mu_Y(y)$, for any $x,y\in U$ such that there exists $z\in U$ satisfying $\inf\limits_{w\in U,\,\mu_X(w)\leq\mu_X(z)}\mu_Y(w)>\mu_Y(y)$.
7) Knowing rule $\mu_X(x)\leq\alpha\rightarrow\mu_Y(x)\leq g_{Y|X}{}^{+}(\alpha)$ and $\mu_Y(x)>\beta$ such that there exists $\alpha\in[0,1]$, $g_{Y|X}{}^{+}(\alpha)\leq\beta$, we get $\mu_X(x)>f_{X|Y}{}^{+}(\beta)$, if and only if $\mu_X(x)>\mu_X(y)$ implies $\mu_Y(x)\geq\mu_Y(y)$, for any $x,y\in U$ such that there exists $z\in U$ satisfying $\sup\limits_{w\in U,\,\mu_X(w)\leq\mu_X(z)}\mu_Y(w)<\mu_Y(x)$.
8) Knowing rule $\mu_X(x)\geq\alpha\rightarrow\mu_Y(x)\leq g_{Y|X}{}^{-}(\alpha)$ and $\mu_Y(x)>\beta$ such that there exists $\alpha\in[0,1]$, $g_{Y|X}{}^{-}(\alpha)\leq\beta$, we get $\mu_X(x)<g_{X|Y}{}^{-}(\beta)$, if and only if $\mu_X(x)<\mu_X(y)$ implies $\mu_Y(x)\geq\mu_Y(y)$, for any $x,y\in U$ such that there exists $z\in U$ satisfying $\sup\limits_{w\in U,\,\mu_X(w)\geq\mu_X(z)}\mu_Y(w)<\mu_Y(x)$.

Assertions 1) to 4) of the Theorem imply the following four fuzzy-rough *MT*:

$$\begin{array}{lll} (LP\text{-}MT) & \text{if} & \mu_X(x)\geq\alpha\rightarrow\mu_Y(x)\geq f_{Y|X}{}^{+}(\alpha) \\ & \text{and} & \mu_Y(x)<\beta \\ \hline & \text{then} & \mu_X(x)<(f_{Y|X}{}^{+})_\varepsilon{}^{-1}(\beta) \end{array}$$

$$\begin{array}{lll} (LN\text{-}MT) & \text{if} & \mu_X(x)\leq\alpha\rightarrow\mu_Y(x)\geq f_{Y|X}{}^{-}(\alpha) \\ & \text{and} & \mu_Y(x)<\beta \\ \hline & \text{then} & \mu_X(x)>(f_{Y|X}{}^{-})_\varepsilon{}^{-1}(\beta) \end{array}$$

(*UP-MT*) if $\mu_X(x)\leq\alpha \rightarrow \mu_Y(x)\leq g_{Y|X}{}^{+}(\alpha)$
and $\mu_Y(x)>\beta$

then $\mu_X(x)> (g_{Y|X}{}^{+})_{\varepsilon}{}^{-1}(\beta)$

(*UN-MT*) if $\mu_X(x)\geq\alpha \rightarrow \mu_Y(x)\leq g_{Y|X}{}^{-}(\alpha)$
and $\mu_Y(x)>\beta$

then $\mu_X(x)< (g_{Y|X}{}^{-})_{\varepsilon}{}^{-1}(\beta)$

Thus, for (*LP-MT*) in (1), we have $\varphi(\beta)=(f_{Y|X}{}^{+})_{\varepsilon}{}^{-1}(\beta)$. As shown in Assertion 5), we can find that $|(f_{Y|X}{}^{+})_{\varepsilon}{}^{-1}(\beta)-g_{X|Y}{}^{+}(\beta)|\leq\varepsilon$ for each $\beta\in[0,1]$ when $\mu_Y(\cdot)$ is non-decreasing with respect to $\mu_X(\cdot)$. Moreover, as far as the largest $\mu_Y(\cdot)$ is achieved at the largest $\mu_X(\cdot)$, $(f_{Y|X}{}^{+})_{\varepsilon}{}^{-1}(\cdot)$ is significantly different from $g_{X|Y}{}^{+}(\cdot)$ only when $\mu_Y(\cdot)$ is not non-decreasing with respect to $\mu_X(\cdot)$. Therefore, we may use a distance between functions $(f_{Y|X}{}^{+})_{\varepsilon}{}^{-1}(\cdot)$ and $g_{X|Y}{}^{+}(\cdot)$ as a measure of monotonicity of the relation between $\mu_X(\cdot)$ and $\mu_Y(\cdot)$. For other modus tollens, we can conclude similarly. Because of the difference between fuzzy-rough modus ponens and modus tollens, a pair $(f_{Y|X}{}^{+}(\cdot), g_{Y|X}{}^{+}(\cdot))$ is not sufficient for inference between X and Y but a quadruple $(f_{Y|X}{}^{+}(\cdot), g_{Y|X}{}^{+}(\cdot), f_{X|Y}{}^{+}(\cdot), g_{X|Y}{}^{+}(\cdot))$ is necessary in the case of positive relationship.

4 Generalized Fuzzy-Rough Modus Ponens and Modus Tollens

Generalized modus ponens is formalized as

if	$X \rightarrow Y$	is true
and	X'	is true
then	Y'	is true

Namely, the fact X' is not always the same as the premise X of rule $X \rightarrow Y$. Such an inference we might often apply in the real life. For example, we may infer "the tomato is very ripe" from a fact "the tomato is very red", using our knowledge represented by the rule "if a tomato is red then it is ripe". Such an inference has been treated in fuzzy reasoning [19]. In this section, we propose to formalize this generalization using our fuzzy-rough *MP* and *MT*. First we discuss the generalized fuzzy-rough *MP*. (*LP-MP*) can be generalized as follows:

(*LP-LP-MP*) if $\mu_X(x)\geq\alpha \rightarrow \mu_Y(x)\geq f_{Y|X}{}^{+}(\alpha)$
and $\mu_{X'}(x)\geq\alpha'$

then $\mu_{Y'}(x)\geq f_{Y|X}{}^{+}(\alpha')$

(*LP-LP-MP*) generalizes (*LP-MP*) by replacing X and Y with X' and Y', respectively. Remark that Y' is not given here, but X' is. Therefore, our problem is to get to know Y'. Since it is often difficult to get an explicit answer, we consider the following alternative inference patterns:

(*LP-LP-MPw*) if $\mu_X(x)\geq\alpha \rightarrow \mu_Y(x)\geq f_{Y|X}{}^{+}(\alpha)$
and $\mu_{X'}(x)\geq\alpha'$

then $\mu_Y(x)\geq \psi(\alpha')$

We assume that there is a relation between X and X'. Moreover, we suppose that this relation is known at least to some extent. For example, we may have another decision table with object set $U' \subseteq \hat{U}$ which gives a relation between X and X'. We may then represent the relation between X and X' by gradual decision rules using functions $f_{X|X'}^{+}(\cdot)$, $f_{X|X'}^{-}(\cdot)$, $g_{X|X'}^{+}(\cdot)$ and $g_{X|X'}^{-}(\cdot)$ derived from the decision table with object set $U' \subseteq \hat{U}$. For example, consider the "red tomato" example. Assume that we collected a set U' of tomatoes with different shades of red. Then, to each tomato we may assign a degree of membership to fuzzy set of "red tomatoes" and a degree of membership to fuzzy set of "very red tomatoes". Arranging that information into a table, we obtain a decision table with a decision attribute specifying "the degree of very red" and a condition attribute specifying "the degree of red". Applying our rough-fuzzy approach to this table, we obtain the modifier functions $f_{X|X'}^{+}(\cdot)$, $f_{X|X'}^{-}(\cdot)$, $g_{X|X'}^{+}(\cdot)$ and $g_{X|X'}^{-}(\cdot)$.

To infer Y, we should obtain information of the type $\mu_X(x) \geq \alpha$" from $\mu_{X'}(x) \geq \alpha'$. This can be done through the following (*LP-MP*) with respect to X' and X:

$$\begin{array}{ll} \text{if} & \mu_{X'}(x) \geq \alpha \rightarrow \mu_X(x) \geq f_{X|X'}^{+}(\alpha) \\ \text{and} & \mu_{X'}(x) \geq \alpha' \\ \hline \text{then} & \mu_X(x) \geq f_{X|X'}^{+}(\alpha') \end{array}$$

Applying (*LP-MP*) with respect to X and Y to the inference result $\mu_X(x) \geq f_{X|X'}^{+}(\alpha')$, we obtain $\mu_Y(x) \geq f_{Y|X}^{+}(f_{X|X'}^{+}(\alpha'))$. Thus, we get $\psi(\alpha') = f_{Y|X}^{+}(f_{X|X'}^{+}(\alpha'))$ in (*LP-LP-MPw*), i.e.,

$$(LP\text{-}LP\text{-}MPw) \quad \begin{array}{ll} \text{if} & \mu_X(x) \geq \alpha \rightarrow \mu_Y(x) \geq f_{Y|X}^{+}(\alpha) \\ \text{and} & \mu_{X'}(x) \geq \alpha' \\ \hline \text{then} & \mu_Y(x) \geq f_{Y|X}^{+}(f_{X|X'}^{+}(\alpha')). \end{array}$$

The conclusion of this inference pattern is discussed below. When X and Y are defined through attribute values $a(x)$ and $b(x)$, namely, $\mu_X(x) = \mu_{(X)}(a(x))$ and $\mu_Y(x) = \mu_{(Y)}(b(x))$, this inference pattern is useful to know the possible range of attribute value $b(x)$ from the information about attribute value $a(x)$, as $\mu_{(X)}(a(x)) \geq \alpha'$. Actually, the possible range can be obtained as $\{b(x) \mid \mu_{(Y)}(b(x)) \geq f_{Y|X}^{+}(f_{X|X'}^{+}(\alpha'))\}$.

To have inference pattern (*LP-LP-MP*), we should utilize the following equivalence:

$$\alpha \geq f_{Y|X}^{+}(\beta) \text{ if and only if } \hat{g}_{X|Y}^{+}(\alpha) = \sup\{\mu_X(x) \mid \mu_Y(x) \leq \alpha\} \geq \beta \text{ and } \exists y \in U,\ \mu_X(y) = \beta. \quad (2)$$

This equivalence is valid not only for relation between Y and X but also for relation between X and X'. The conclusion is the same for two given facts $\mu_{X'}(x) \geq \alpha'$ and $\mu_{X'}(x) \geq h_{X'}(\alpha') = \sup\{\mu_{X'}(z) \mid \mu_{X'}(z) \leq \alpha',\ z \in U\}$, since we have $f_{X|X'}^{+}(\alpha') = f_{X|X'}^{+}(h_{X'}(\alpha'))$. Moreover, $\beta \geq h_{X'}(\alpha')$ implies $\bar{k}_{X'}(\beta) = \inf\{\mu_{X'}(z) \mid \mu_{X'}(z) > \beta,\ z \in U\} > \alpha'$. Therefore, we can draw the following chain of inferences: $\mu_Y(x) \geq f_{Y|X}^{+}(f_{X|X'}^{+}(\alpha'))$ if and only if $\hat{g}_{X|Y}^{+}(\mu_Y(x)) \geq f_{X|X'}^{+}(\alpha')$. $\hat{g}_{X|Y}^{+}(\mu_Y(x)) \geq f_{X|X'}^{+}(\alpha')$ is equivalent to $\hat{g}_{X|Y}^{+}(\mu_Y(x)) \geq f_{X|X'}^{+}(h_{X'}(\alpha'))$. $\hat{g}_{X|Y}^{+}(\mu_Y(x)) \geq f_{X|X'}^{+}(h_{X'}(\alpha'))$ if and only if $\hat{g}_{X'|X}(\hat{g}_{X|Y}^{+}(\mu_Y(x))) \geq h_{X'}(\alpha')$. Finally, $\hat{g}_{X'|X}(\hat{g}_{X|Y}^{+}(\mu_Y(x))) \geq h_{X'}(\alpha')$ implies $\bar{k}_{X'}(\hat{g}_{X'|X}(\hat{g}_{X|Y}^{+}(\mu_Y(x)))) > \alpha'$.

Since $f_{Y|X}^{+}(\cdot)$ is non-decreasing, we have $f_{Y|X}^{+}(\bar{k}_{X'}(\hat{g}_{X'|X}(\hat{g}_{X|Y}^{+}(\mu_Y(x))))) \ge f_{Y|X}^{+}(\alpha')$. Hence, we obtain $\mu_{Y'}(x) = f_{Y|X}^{+}(\hat{g}_{X'|X}(\hat{g}_{X|Y}^{+}(\mu_Y(x))))$, i.e.,

(*LP-LP-MP*) if $\mu_X(x)\ge\alpha \rightarrow \mu_Y(x)\ge f_{Y|X}^{+}(\alpha)$
and $\mu_{X'}(x)\ge\alpha'$

then $f_{Y|X}^{+}(\bar{k}_{X'}(\hat{g}_{X'|X}(\hat{g}_{X|Y}^{+}(\mu_Y(x))))) \ge f_{Y|X}^{+}(\alpha')$.

The conclusion of this inference pattern is more ambiguous than that of (*LP-LP-MPw*) because the relation between $\beta\ge h_{X'}(\alpha')$ and $\bar{k}_{X'}(\beta)>\alpha'$ is a one-way implication and we applied $f_{Y|X}^{+}(\cdot)$ which is not strictly increasing. However, the inference pattern may be useful to know approximately how a conclusion fuzzy set *Y* is modified when a premise fuzzy set *X* is modified to *X'*.

When deriving (*LP-LP-MP*), we obtained another inference pattern as follows:

(*LP-LP-MPm*) if $\mu_X(x)\ge\alpha \rightarrow \mu_Y(x)\ge f_{Y|X}^{+}(\alpha)$
and $\mu_{X'}(x)\ge\alpha'$

then $\bar{k}_{X'}(\hat{g}_{X'|X}(\hat{g}_{X|Y}^{+}(\mu_Y(x))))>\alpha'$
(which implies $\bar{k}_{X'}(\hat{g}_{X'|X}(\hat{g}_{X|Y}^{+}(\mu_Y(x))))\ge\alpha'$).

The conclusion of this inference pattern is more ambiguous than that of (*LP-LP-MPw*) but it is more specific than that of (*LP-LP-MP*). This inference pattern is useful when we would like to know the image of a fuzzy set *X'* through the rule $\mu_X(x)\ge\alpha \rightarrow \mu_Y(x)\ge f_{Y|X}^{+}(\alpha)$, given fuzzy sets *X* and *Y*.

Now, let us move to a discussion on the generalized fuzzy-rough modus tollens. We assume that a relation between *Y* and *Y''* is known. In the same way as (*LP-LP-MPw*), we obtain the following inference pattern:

(*LP-LP-MTw*) if $\mu_X(x)\ge\alpha \rightarrow \mu_Y(x)\ge f_{Y|X}^{+}(\alpha)$
and $\mu_{Y''}(x)<\alpha'$

then $\mu_X(x)<(f_{Y|X}^{+})_{\varepsilon}^{-1}((f_{Y''|Y}^{+})_{\varepsilon}^{-1}(\alpha'))$.

Similarly to (2), we obtain

$$\text{for any } \alpha\in[0,1],\ \alpha<(f_{Y|X}^{+})_{\varepsilon}^{-1}(\beta) \text{ if and only if } f_{Y|X}^{+}(\alpha)<\beta. \tag{3}$$

Equivalence (3) is much simpler than (2). Applying (3), we also obtain the following inference patterns:

(*LP-LP-MT'*) if $\mu_X(x)\ge\alpha \rightarrow \mu_Y(x)\ge f_{Y|X}^{+}(\alpha)$
and $\mu_{Y''}(x)<\alpha'$

then $(f_{Y|X}^{+})_{\varepsilon}^{-1}(f_{Y''|Y}^{+}(f_{Y|X}^{+}(\mu_X(x))))\le(f_{Y|X}^{+})_{\varepsilon}^{-1}(\alpha')$,

(*LP-LP-MTm'*) if $\mu_X(x)\ge\alpha \rightarrow \mu_Y(x)\ge f_{Y|X}^{+}(\alpha)$
and $\mu_{Y''}(x)<\alpha'$

then $f_{Y''|Y}^{+}(f_{Y|X}^{+}(\mu_X(x)))<\alpha'$

Those inference patterns correspond to (*LP-LP-MP'*) and (*LP-LP-MPm*), respectively. We cannot obtain a strict inequality in the conclusion of (*LP-LP-MT'*) because of non-strict monotonicity of $(f_{Y|X}^{+})_{\varepsilon}^{-1}(\cdot)$.

5 Conclusions and Further Research Directions

In this paper we discussed fuzzy-rough inference patterns with gradual decision rules extracted from a decision table. We discussed differences and similarities between modus ponens and modus tollens. We showed that all inference can be done by proper manipulations of modifier functions. If in the premise of the gradual decision rule fuzzy set X is defined with multiple attributes, the inference by manipulations of modifier functions are much easier than the direct inference method which requires manipulations of multidimensional fuzzy sets. Therefore, we plan to apply fuzzy-rough inference also to gradual decision rules defined with multiple attributes [5]. Moreover, we can apply the proposed fuzzy-rough inference to case based reasoning problems. On the other hand, the proposed fuzzy-rough inference may have some relations to deduction rules based on rough inclusion [14] as well as productions [15]. These would be the topics of our future studies.

Acknowledgements

The research of the second author has been supported by the Italian Ministry of Education, University and Scientific Research (MIUR). The third author wishes to acknowledge financial support from the State Committee for Scientific Research and from the Foundation for Polish Science.

References

1. Cattaneo, G.: Fuzzy Extension of Rough Sets Theory. In: L. Polkowski, A. Skowron (eds.), *Rough Sets and Current Trends in Computing*, LNAI 1424, Springer, Berlin (1998) 275-282
2. Dubois, D., Prade, H.: Gradual Inference Rules in Approximate Reasoning. *Information Sciences*, 61 (1992) 103-122
3. Dubois, D., Prade, H.: Putting Rough Sets and Fuzzy Sets Together. In: R. Słowiński (ed.): *Intelligent Decision Support: Handbook of Applications and Advances of the Sets Theory*, Kluwer, Dordrecht (1992) 203-232
4. Greco, S., Inuiguchi, M., Słowiński, R.: Rough Sets and Gradual Decision Rules. In: G. Wang, Q. Liu, Y. Yao, A. Skowron (eds.): *Rough Sets, Fuzzy Sets, Data Minig, and Granular Computing*, LNAI 2639, Springer-Verlag, Berlin (2003) 156-164
5. Greco, S., Inuiguchi, M., Słowiński, R.: Fuzzy Rough Sets and Multiple Premise Gradual Decision Rules. In: V. Di Gesù, F. Masulli, A. Petrosino (eds.): *Proceedings of WILF 2003 International Workshop on Fuzzy Logic and Applications*, Napoli, Italy (2003)
6. Greco, S., Matarazzo, B., Słowiński R.: The Use of Rough Sets and Fuzzy Sets in MCDM. In: T. Gal, T. Stewart, T. Hanne (eds.): *Advances in Multiple Criteria Decision Making*, Kluwer Academic Publishers, Boston (1999) 14.1-14.59
7. Greco, S., Matarazzo, B., Słowiński, R.: Rough Set Processing of Vague Information Using Fuzzy Similarity Relations. In: C.S. Calude and G. Paun (eds.): *Finite Versus Infinite – Contributions to an Eternal Dilemma*, Springer-Verlag, London (2000) 149-173

8. Inuiguchi, M., Greco, S., Słowiński, R., Tanino, T.: Possibility and Necessity Measure Specification Using Modifiers for Decision Making under Fuzziness. *Fuzzy Sets and Systems*, **137** (2003) 151-175
9. Inuiguchi, M., Tanino, T.: New Fuzzy Rough Sets Based on Certainty Qualification. In: S. K. Pal, L. Polkowski and A. Skowron (eds.): *Rough-Neural Computing: Techniques for Computing with Words*, Springer-Verlag, Berlin (2003) 278-296
10. Nakamura, A., Gao, J. M.: A Logic for Fuzzy Data Analysis, *Fuzzy Sets and Systems*, 39 (1991) 127-132
11. Pawlak, Z.: *Rough Sets*. Kluwer, Dordrecht (1991)
12. Pawlak, Z.: Reasoning about Data – A Rough Set Perspective. In: L. Polkowski and A. Skowron (eds.): *Rough Sets and Current Trends in Computing*, LNAI 1424 (1998) 25-34
13. Polkowski, L.: *Rough Sets: Mathematical Foundations*, Physica-Verlag, Heidelberg (2002)
14. Polkowski, L., Skowron, A.: Rough Mereology: A New Paradigm for Approximate Reasoning. *Int. Journal of Approximate Reasoning*, 15(4) (1996) 333-365
15. Skowron, A., Stepaniuk, J.: Information Granules and Rough-Neural Computing. In: S. K. Pal, L. Polkowski and A. Skowron (eds.): *Rough-Neural Computing: Techniques for Computing with Words*, Springer-Verlag, Berlin (2003) 43-84
16. Słowiński R.: Rough Set Processing of Fuzzy Information, In: T. Y. Lin, A. Wildberger (eds.): *Soft Computing: Rough Sets, Fuzzy Logic, Neural Networks, Uncertainty Management, Knowledge Discovery*, Simulation Councils, Inc., San Diego, CA (1995) 142-145
17. Słowiński, R., Stefanowski, J.: Rough Set Reasoning about Uncertain Data. *Fundamenta Informaticae* 27 (1996) 229-243
18. Yao, Y. Y.: Combination of Rough and Fuzzy Sets Based on α-level Sets. In: T.Y. Lin and N. Cercone (eds.): *Rough Sets and Data Mining: Analysis for Imprecise Data*, Kluwer, Boston (1997) 301-321
19. Zadeh, L. A.: Outline of a New Approach to the Analysis of Complex Systems and Decision Processes, *IEEE Trans. Systems Man Cybernet.*, 3 (1973) 28-44

Rough Truth, Consequence, Consistency and Belief Revision

Mohua Banerjee*

Department of Mathematics, Indian Institute of Technology, Kanpur 208 016, India
mohua@iitk.ac.in

Abstract. The article aims at re-visiting the notion of *rough truth* proposed by Pawlak in 1987 [11] and investigating some of its 'logical' consequences. We focus on the formal deductive apparatus $\mathcal{L}_{\mathcal{R}}$ [12], that is sound and complete with respect to a semantics based on rough truth (extended to rough validity). The notion of *rough consequence* [4] is used in a modified form to formulate $\mathcal{L}_{\mathcal{R}}$. The system has some desirable features of 'rough' reasoning – e.g. roughly true propositions can be derived from roughly true premisses in an information system. Further, *rough consistency* [4] is used to prove completeness. These properties of $\mathcal{L}_{\mathcal{R}}$ motivate us to use it for a proposal of *rough belief change*. During change, the operative constraints on a system of beliefs are that of *rough* consistency preservation and deductive closure with respect to $\mathcal{L}_{\mathcal{R}}$. Following the AGM [1] line, postulates for defining revision and contraction functions are presented. Interrelationships of these functions are also proved.

1 Introduction

Rough sets were introduced in 1982 by Z. Pawlak [10]. Approximate reasoning via rough concept formation and rough decision making were, clearly, major motivations. Rough logics emerged, one significant paper by Pawlak himself [11] paving the way. A good survey of other notable work can be found in [8]. However, the notion of rough truth as introduced in [11] and subsequently developed in [4, 2], has so far escaped proper attention. This article intends to reopen related issues and investigate some 'logical' implications of the notion.

It has generally been accepted that the propositional aspects of rough set theory are adequately expressed by the modal system S_5. An S_5(Kripke) model (X, R, π) (cf. e.g. [7]) is essentially an *approximation space* [10] $(X, R)(X \neq \emptyset)$, with the function π interpreting every well-formed formula (wff) of S_5 as a rough set in (X, R). If L, M denote the necessity and possibility connectives respectively, a modal wff $L\alpha$ $(M\alpha)$, representing 'definitely' ('possibly') α, is interpreted by π as the lower (upper) approximation $\underline{\pi(\alpha)}$ $(\overline{\pi(\alpha)})$ of the set $\pi(\alpha)$.

In this context, a wff α is said to be *roughly true* in $\mathcal{M}$, if $\overline{\pi(\alpha)} = X$. Most of everyday reasoning is indeed carried out even if a model of just the possible

* Research supported by Project No. BS/YSP/29/2477 of the Indian National Science Academy. Thanks are due to the referees for their comments and suggestions.

S. Tsumoto et al. (Eds.): RSCTC 2004, LNAI 3066, pp. 95–102, 2004.

versions of our beliefs is available. Rough truth reflects this trait. In [4, 2] we extended rough truth to *rough validity*, and also introduced the notions of *rough consequence*, *rough (in)consistency*. These were further considered in the context of predicate logic in [3]. The rationale behind the introduction of the concepts was as follows.

From the reasoning point of view, there seem to be desirable features of rough reasoning that S_5 fails to handle, e.g. derivability of roughly true propositions/beliefs from roughly true premisses (in the same information system). In particular, there is no interderivability of propositions that are both roughly true and logically equivalent in possibility. It was also felt that the notion of (in)consistency needs to be relaxed. In the face of an incomplete description of a concept p, one may not always think that p and 'not' p represent conflicting situations. There could be two options to define consistency here – according as 'possibly' p is satisfied, and 'necessarily' p is satisfied. It is thus that we have the two notions of rough consistency and rough inconsistency. The former also (indirectly) compliments rough truth, as will be apparent from the results given in the sequel.

In this paper, we focus on these features of rough reasoning again, and present (in Section 2) the syntactic counterpart $\mathcal{L}_{\mathcal{R}}$ [12] of a semantics based on rough truth, extended to rough validity. $\mathcal{L}_{\mathcal{R}}$ is built over S_5, and is a modified version of the rough consequence logic of [4]. Most of the results are stated without proof.

Research on belief change has seen a lot of development through the years. A pioneering work, undoubtedly, has been by AGM, authors of [1]. The formalisation propounded by AGM consists of three main kinds of belief change: *expansion, revision, and contraction.* In the first kind, a belief is inserted into a system S (say), irrespective of whether S becomes 'inconsistent' as a result. Revision and contraction represent, respectively, insertion and deletion of beliefs maintaining ('integrity' constraints of) consistency of the system, deductive closure and minimal information loss. (AGM) 'Rationality' postulates for revision and contraction functions were formulated in [1]. A to-and-fro passage between contraction and revision is established through the *Levi* and *Harper identities.* But the postulates have since been questioned, modified, and alternatives like algorithms for computing the functions, proposed (cf. [5, 14, 13, 15]). For instance, the AGM approach assumes representation of belief states by 'belief sets' – sets deductively closed relative to a (Tarskian) logic and so, usually, infinite. The agents are idealized, with unlimited memory and capacity of inference. Modification in defining belief change has been attempted (e.g.) by use of 'belief bases' (cf. [5, 13]), disbeliefs along with beliefs [6], non-Tarskian logics for the modelling of less idealized (more realistic) agents [16] or for the modelling of intuitive properties of epistemic states that the AGM approach fails to cover [9].

Rough set theory and in particular, the notion of rough truth seem appropriate for creating a 'non-classical' belief change framework. In order to make a beginning, we follow the AGM line of thought, and propose the basic postulates (cf. Section 3) for defining *rough belief change* functions. Agents, for us, are interested in situations where the rough truth of propositions/observations/beliefs matters. Beliefs are represented by the wffs of $\mathcal{L}_\mathcal{R}$; deduction is done through the apparatus provided by $\mathcal{L}_\mathcal{R}$, as it captures 'precisely' the semantics of rough truth. During revision/contraction of beliefs, we seek the preservation of *rough* consistency and deductive closure with respect to $\mathcal{L}_\mathcal{R}$. Interrelationships of the two kinds of functions, resulting from the use of the Levi and Harper identities, are proved. Some directions for further work are indicated in the last section.

2 The System $\mathcal{L}_\mathcal{R}$

The language of $\mathcal{L}_\mathcal{R}$, as mentioned in the Introduction, is that of S_5. In the following, Γ is any set of wffs, α, β any wffs, and $\vdash$ denotes derivation in S_5. There are two rules of inference:

$$R1. \quad \frac{\alpha}{\beta} \quad \textit{where} \vdash M\alpha \rightarrow M\beta \qquad R2. \quad \frac{M\alpha \quad M\beta}{M\alpha \wedge M\beta}$$

2.1 Rough Consequence

Definition 1. *α is a* rough consequence *of Γ (denoted $\Gamma \mid\!\sim \alpha$) if and only if there is a sequence $\alpha_1, ..., \alpha_n (\equiv \alpha)$ such that each $\alpha_i (i = 1, ..., n)$ is either (i) a theorem of S_5, or (ii) a member of Γ, or (iii) derived from some of $\alpha_1, ..., \alpha_{i-1}$ by R1 or R2.*
If Γ is empty, α is said to be a rough theorem, *written $\mid\!\sim \alpha$.*

It must be noted here that in [2, 4] a different, but equivalent version of $R1$ was considered, along with a second rule which can be derived in $\mathcal{L}_\mathcal{R}$. $R2$ was not considered there, but now appears essential for proving completeness.

The system is then strictly enhanced, in the sense that the set of rough theorems properly contains that of S_5-theorems – e.g. $\mid\!\sim \alpha \rightarrow L\alpha$, but $\not\vdash \alpha \rightarrow L\alpha$.

Some derived rules of inference:

$$DR1. \quad \frac{\alpha \quad \vdash \alpha \rightarrow \beta}{\beta} \qquad DR2. \quad \frac{(M\alpha)L\alpha \rightarrow \beta \quad (M\alpha)L\alpha}{\beta}$$

$$DR3. \quad \frac{M\alpha \quad \neg M\alpha}{\beta} \qquad DR4. \quad \frac{\alpha \rightarrow M\beta \quad \alpha \rightarrow \neg M\beta}{\neg\alpha}$$

One of the first major results is

Theorem 1. *(Deduction) For any Γ, α, β, if $\Gamma \cup \{\alpha\} \mid\!\sim \beta$ then $\Gamma \mid\!\sim \alpha \rightarrow \beta$.*

2.2 A Semantics of Rough Truth

Definition 2. *A model* $\mathcal{M} \equiv (X, R, \pi)$ *is a* rough model *of* Γ, *if and only if every member* γ *of* Γ *is roughly true in* $\mathcal{M}$, *i.e.* $\overline{\pi(\gamma)} = X$.

Definition 3. α *is a* rough semantic consequence *of* Γ *(denoted* $\Gamma \approx\!\!\!\models \alpha$*) if and only if every rough model of* Γ *is a rough model of* α. *If* Γ *is empty,* α *is said to be* roughly valid, *written* $\approx\!\!\!\models \alpha$.

Theorem 2. *(Soundness) If* $\Gamma \mid\!\sim \alpha$ *then* $\Gamma \approx\!\!\!\models \alpha$.

Observation 1. *The soundness result establishes the following.*

(a) The classical rules of Modus Ponens and Necessitation fail to be sound with respect to the rough truth semantics above. The rule $\{\alpha, \beta\} \mid\!\sim \alpha \wedge \beta$ *is not sound either, but R2 is sound and suffices for our purpose.*

(b) Interestingly, the converse of the deduction theorem is not true – e.g. $\mid\!\sim p \rightarrow Lp$, *but* $\{p\} \not\mid\!\sim Lp$, *with p any propositional variable. Thus* $\mathcal{L}_{\mathcal{R}}$ *differentiates between the object and meta level implications* $\rightarrow, \mid\!\sim$.

2.3 Rough Consistency

Definition 4. *A set* Γ *of wffs is* roughly consistent *if and only if the set* $M\Gamma \equiv \{M\gamma : \gamma \in \Gamma\}$ *is* (S_5)*-consistent.* Γ *is* roughly inconsistent *if and only if* $L\Gamma \equiv \{L\gamma : \gamma \in \Gamma\}$ *is* (S_5)*-inconsistent.*

It follows that a set can be simultaneously roughly consistent and inconsistent, a welcome feature in the vague context.

Observation 2.

(a) Inconsistency implies rough inconsistency, not conversely; consistency implies rough consistency, not conversely.

(b) Γ *is roughly consistent if and only if it has a rough model.*

Theorem 3. *If* Γ *is not roughly consistent then* $\Gamma \mid\!\sim \alpha$ *for every wff* α.

Therefore, $\mathcal{L}_{\mathcal{R}}$ is not 'paraconsistent' (cf. e.g. [5]) as far as rough consistency is concerned – it behaves classically. One may also remark that the proof of Theorem 3 uses the rule of inference $R2$ (in fact, $DR3$).

Theorem 4. *If* $\Gamma \cup \{\neg M\alpha\} \mid\!\sim \beta$ *for every wff* β, *then* $\Gamma \mid\!\sim \alpha$.

Theorem 5. *(Completeness) If* $\Gamma \approx\!\!\!\models \alpha$ *then* $\Gamma \mid\!\sim \alpha$.

Proof. We suppose that $\Gamma \not\mid\!\sim \alpha$. By Theorem 4 there is β such that $\Gamma \cup \{\neg M\alpha\} \not\mid\!\sim \beta$. Thus $\Gamma \cup \{\neg M\alpha\}$ is roughly consistent, using Theorem 3. By Observation 2(b), $\Gamma \cup \{\neg M\alpha\}$ has a rough model, which yields $\Gamma \not\approx\!\!\!\models \alpha$. □

3 Rough Belief Revision

In classical belief revision, the base language is assumed (cf. [5]) to be closed under the Boolean operators of negation, conjunction, disjunction and implication. The underlying consequence relation is supraclassical (includes classical consequence) and satisfies cut, deduction theorem, monotonicity and compactness.

In contrast, we consider the modal language of $\mathcal{L}_{\mathcal{R}}$ as the base. Due to Observation 1(a), the corresponding consequence relation C_R is *not* supraclassical, though it satisfies the other properties mentioned above. We follow the classical line for the rest of the definitions. A *belief set* is a set Γ of wffs such that $C_R(\Gamma) = \Gamma$. For a pair (Γ, α), there is a unique belief set $\Gamma^*_r\alpha$ ($\Gamma -_r \alpha$) representing *rough revision (contraction)* of Γ with respect to α. The new belief set is defined through postulates (that follow). The *expansion* $\Gamma +_r \alpha$ of Γ by the wff α is the belief set $C_R(\Gamma \cup \{\alpha\})$.

The major consideration is to preserve rough consistency during belief change. The idea, naturally, is that if $\Gamma +_r \alpha$ is roughly consistent, it could itself serve as $\Gamma^*_r\alpha$. Similarly, if Γ is roughly consistent, $\Gamma -_r \alpha$ may just be $C_R(\Gamma \setminus \{\alpha\})$ (in case $\alpha \in \Gamma$). Let us notice the difference with the classical scenario: suppose $\Gamma \equiv C_R(\{p\})$, p any propositional variable. Then $\Gamma +_r \neg p$ is roughly consistent, and so it is $\Gamma^*_r\neg p$ itself. But, classically, $\Gamma^*\neg p \subset \Gamma + \neg p$. Since we also have the notion of rough inconsistency, there is the option of avoiding such inconsistency during belief change. It is thus that there are two versions of postulates involving consistency preservation. The controversial *recovery* postulate in [1] is admitted here, only in the case of contraction with a *definable/describable* [10] belief, i.e. α such that $\vdash \alpha \leftrightarrow L\alpha$. Further, rough contraction/revision by two roughly equal beliefs is expected to lead to identical belief sets. To express this, we make use of the *rough equality connective* $\approx$ [2] in S_5: $\alpha \approx \beta \equiv (L\alpha \leftrightarrow L\beta) \wedge (M\alpha \leftrightarrow M\beta)$.

The postulates for rough revision

R_r1 For any wff α and belief set Γ, $\Gamma^*_r\alpha$ is a belief set.
R_r2 $\alpha \in \Gamma^*_r\alpha$.
R_r3 $\Gamma^*_r\alpha \subseteq \Gamma +_r \alpha$.
R_r4 If $\neg\alpha \notin \Gamma$, then $\Gamma +_r \alpha \subseteq \Gamma^*_r\alpha$.
R_r5 If $\Gamma^*_r\alpha$ is not roughly consistent, then $\mid\!\sim \neg\alpha$.
R_r5' If $\Gamma^*_r\alpha$ is roughly inconsistent, then $\mid\!\sim \neg\alpha$.
R_r6 If $\mid\!\sim \alpha \approx \beta$, then $\Gamma^*_r\alpha = \Gamma^*_r\beta$.

The postulates for rough contraction

C_r1 For any wff α and belief set Γ, $\Gamma -_r \alpha$ is a belief set.
C_r2 $\Gamma -_r \alpha \subseteq \Gamma$.
C_r3 If $\alpha \notin \Gamma$, then $\Gamma -_r \alpha = \Gamma$.
C_r4 If $\alpha \in \Gamma -_r \alpha$, then $\mid\!\sim \alpha$.
C_r4' If $L\alpha \in \Gamma -_r \alpha$, then $\mid\!\sim \alpha$.
C_r5 $\Gamma \subseteq (\Gamma -_r \alpha) +_r \alpha$, if α is of the form $L\beta$ or $M\beta$ for some wff β.
C_r6 If $\mid\!\sim \alpha \approx \beta$, then $\Gamma -_r \alpha = \Gamma -_r \beta$.

R_r1 and C_r1 express the constraint of deductive closure. $R_r2,3$ and $C_r2,3$ are self-explanatory. $\neg\alpha \notin \Gamma$ implies consistency and hence rough consistency of $\Gamma +_r \alpha$, so that, in view of the earlier remarks, R_r4 is justifiable in the rough context. In R_r5, we stipulate that $\Gamma^*_r\alpha$ is generally roughly consistent, except in the case when $\neg\alpha$ is roughly valid, i.e. in no situation 'definitely' α holds (though 'possibly' α may hold). C_r4 again stipulates that, in general, $\alpha \notin \Gamma -_r \alpha$, except when α 'is possible' in all situations. C_r4' could appear more relevant: 'definitely' α may follow from our beliefs despite contraction by α only if α is, in every situation, possible.

Observation 3. *R_r5 implies R_r5' and C_r4 implies C_r4'.*

The following interrelationships between rough contraction and revision are then observed, if the *Levi* and *Harper identities* [5] are used.

Theorem 6. *Let the Levi identity give $*_r$, i.e. $\Gamma^*_r\alpha \equiv (\Gamma -_r \neg\alpha) +_r \alpha$, where the contraction function $-_r$ satisfies C_r1-4 and C_r6. Then $*_r$ satisfies R_r1-6.*

Proof. R_r1-4 follow easily. R_r5 can be proved thus: suppose $\Gamma^*_r\alpha$ is not roughly consistent. By Theorem 3, $\Gamma^*_r\alpha {\mid\!\sim} \beta$, for any wff β in $\mathcal{L}_\mathcal{R}$. In particular, $\Gamma^*_r\alpha (\equiv C_\mathcal{R}((\Gamma -_r \neg\alpha) \cup \{\alpha\}) {\mid\!\sim} M\beta$, and $\Gamma^*_r\alpha {\mid\!\sim} \neg M\beta$, for any wff β. By using deduction theorem and *DR*4, $\Gamma -_r \neg\alpha {\mid\!\sim} \neg\alpha$. Hence by $C_r1,4$, ${\mid\!\sim} \neg\alpha$. R_r6 can be proved by observing that ${\mid\!\sim} \alpha \approx \beta$ if and only if ${\mid\!\sim} \neg\alpha \approx \neg\beta$, and by using C_r6. □

Theorem 7. *Let $-_r$ be given by the Harper identity, i.e. $\Gamma -_r \alpha \equiv \Gamma \cap \Gamma^*_r \neg\alpha$.*
(a) If the revision function $*_r$ satisfies R_r1-4, R_r5' and R_r6, then $-_r$ satisfies C_r1-6.
(b) If the revision function $*_r$ satisfies R_r1-6, then $-_r$ satisfies C_r1-3, C_r4' and $C_r5,6$.

Proof. Again $C_r1-3,6$ follow easily. For C_r5, let α be $L\beta$, for some wff β. If $\gamma \in \Gamma$, it can be shown that $\alpha \to \gamma \in \Gamma \cap \Gamma^*_r \neg\alpha$. By *DR*2, $\gamma \in (\Gamma -_r \alpha) +_r \alpha$.
(a) C_r4: As $\neg\alpha \in \Gamma^*_r \neg\alpha$ (by R_r2) as well as $\alpha \in \Gamma^*_r \neg\alpha$ (assumption), $\Gamma^*_r \neg\alpha$ is inconsistent, and hence roughly so. Thus by R_r5', ${\mid\!\sim} \neg\neg\alpha$. It follows that ${\mid\!\sim} \alpha$.
(b) C_r4': $L\alpha, \neg\alpha \in \Gamma^*_r \neg\alpha$, by assumption and R_r2. So, using S_5 properties, $M\Gamma^*_r \neg\alpha \vdash L\alpha$ as well as $M\Gamma^*_r \neg\alpha \vdash \neg L\alpha$, implying that $\Gamma^*_r \neg\alpha$ is not roughly consistent. By R_r5, ${\mid\!\sim} \neg\neg\alpha$. Thus ${\mid\!\sim} \alpha$. □

Observation 4.

(a) Let $\mathbf{R}(-_r)$, $\mathbf{C}(*_r)$ denote respectively, the revision and contraction functions obtained by using the Levi and Harper identities. Then $\mathbf{R}(\mathbf{C}(*_r)) = *_r$. However, in general, $\mathbf{C}(\mathbf{R}(-_r)) \neq -_r$.

(b) Rough belief revision and contraction coincide with the corresponding classical notions if $\vdash \alpha \leftrightarrow L\alpha$ for every wff α, i.e. all beliefs are definable/describable (S_5 collapses into classical propositional logic).

4 Conclusions

Some demands of 'rough' reasoning seem to be met by the rough consequence logic $\mathcal{L}_{\mathcal{R}}$. In particular, roughly consistent sets of premisses find rough models, and roughly true propositions can be derived from roughly true premisses. This offers grounds for the use of $\mathcal{L}_{\mathcal{R}}$ in a proposal of 'rough belief change'. Beliefs are propositions in $\mathcal{L}_{\mathcal{R}}$. The postulates defining revision and contraction express the constraints imposed on a set of beliefs during change – in particular, rough consistency is preserved, as is deductive closure with respect to $\mathcal{L}_{\mathcal{R}}$. We obtain expected consequences. (i) Classical belief change is a special case of rough belief change (cf. Observation 4(b)). (ii) Unlike the classical case, the definitions are not completely interchangeable (cf. Theorems 6,7 and Observation 4(a)).

One of the integrity constraints in [1] postulates minimal information loss during belief change. This was accounted for by proposing *epistemic entrenchment* (cf. [5]) – that sets a 'priority' amongst the beliefs of the system. So during contraction/revision, the less entrenched (important) beliefs may be disposed of to get the new belief set. Entrenchment is connected with the revision and contraction functions via representation theorems. With the proposed set of postulates of rough belief change in hand, one can attempt to define an appropriate notion of entrenchment. It could then be checked for instance, if such a notion leads to a class of methods for rough belief change that is computationally tractable as well.

References

1. Alchourrón, C., Gärdenfors, P., Makinson, D.: On the logic of theory change: partial meet functions for contraction and revision. *J. Symb. Logic* **50** (1985) 510–530.
2. Banerjee, M., Chakraborty, M.K.: Rough consequence and rough algebra. In: W.P. Ziarko, editor, *Rough Sets, Fuzzy Sets and Knowledge Discovery, Proc. Int. Workshop on Rough Sets and Knowledge Discovery (RSKD'93)*, pages 196–207. Springer-Verlag, 1994.
3. Banerjee, M., Chakraborty, M.K.: Rough logics: a survey with further directions. In: E. Orłowska, editor, *Incomplete Information: Rough Set Analysis*, pages 579–600. Springer-Verlag, 1998.
4. Chakraborty, M.K., Banerjee, M.: Rough consequence. *Bull. Polish Acad. Sc. (Math.)* **41(4)** (1993) 299–304.
5. Gärdenfors, P., Rott, H.: Belief revision. In: D.M. Gabbay, C.J. Hogger and J.A. Robinson, editors, *Handbook of Logic in AI and Logic Programming, Vol.4: Epistemic and Temporal Reasoning*, pages 35–132. Clarendon, 1995.
6. Gomolinska, A., Pearce, D.: Disbelief change. In: *Spinning Ideas: Electronic Festschrift in Honour of P. Gärdenfors.* N-E. Sahlin, editor, http://www.lucs.lu.se/spinning/, 2000.
7. Hughes, G.E., Cresswell, M.J.: *A New Introduction to Modal Logic.* Routledge, 1996.
8. Komorowski, J., Pawlak, Z., Polkowski, L., Skowron, A.: Rough sets: a tutorial. In: S.K. Pal and A. Skowron, editors, *Rough Fuzzy Hybridization: A New Trend in Decision-Making*, pages 3–98. Springer-Verlag, 1999.

9. Lepage, F., Lapierre, S.: Partial logic and the dynamics of epistemic states. In: *Spinning Ideas: Electronic Festschrift in Honour of P. Gärdenfors*. N-E. Sahlin, editor, http://www.lucs.lu.se/spinning/, 2000.
10. Pawlak, Z.: Rough sets. *Int. J. Comp. Inf. Sci.* **11** (1982) 341–356.
11. Pawlak, Z.: Rough logic. *Bull. Polish Acad. Sc. (Tech. Sc.)* **35(5-6)** (1987) 253–258.
12. Pawlak, Z., Banerjee, M.: A logic for rough truth. Preprint, 2004.
13. Rott, H.: *Change, Choice and Inference: A Study of Belief Revision and Nonmonotonic Reasoning*. Clarendon, 2001.
14. *Spinning Ideas: Electronic Festschrift in Honour of P. Gärdenfors*. N-E. Sahlin, editor, http://www.lucs.lu.se/spinning/, 2000.
15. *Studia Logica, Special Issue on Belief Revision*, **73**, 2003.
16. Wassermann, R.: Generalized change and the meaning of rationality postulates. *Studia Logica* **73** (2003) 299–319.

A Note on Ziarko's Variable Precision Rough Set Model and Nonmonotonic Reasoning

Tetsuya Murai[1], Masayuki Sanada[1], Y. Kudo[2], and Mineichi Kudo[1]

[1] Graduate School of Engineering, Hokkaido Univ., Sapporo 060-8628, Japan
{murahiko,m-sana,mine}@main.eng.hokudai.ac.jp

[2] Muroran Institute of Technology, Muroran 050-8585, Japan
kudo@csse.muroran-it.ac.jp

Abstract. Granular reasoning is a way of reasoning using granularized possible worlds and lower approximation in rough set theory. However, it can deal only with monotonicity. Then, the extended lower approximation in Ziarko's variable precision rough set model is introduced to describe nonmonotonic reasoning.

Keywords: Granular reasoning, Variable precision rough set model, Nonmonotonicity.

1 Introduction

Pawlak's rough set theory[7, 8] as well as granular computing[2, 9] are now one of the most remarkable theories in computer sciences. Further Ziarko[10]'s variable precision rough set model (VPRM, for short) is a useful tool of dealing with inconsistent information tables. The authors[3–6] have recently proposed a way of granular reasoning based on granularized possible worlds and lower approximation in rough set theory. However, it can deal only with monotonic reasoning. In this paper, we present a new formulation of nonmonotonic granular reasoning with the extended lower approximation in VPRM. The basic idea is that the class of exceptional elements is also classified in the β-lower approximation in VPRM without more detailed pieces of information.

2 Ziarko's Variable Precision Rough Set Model

Let U is a finite set and R is an equivalence relation on U. In Ziarko's VPRM[10], two approximations are extended in the following way: for $X \subseteq U$,

$$\underline{R}_\beta(X) \stackrel{\text{df}}{=} \bigcup\{E \in U/R \mid c(E, X) \leq \beta\},$$
$$\overline{R}_\beta(X) \stackrel{\text{df}}{=} \bigcup\{E \in U/R \mid c(E, X) < 1 - \beta\},$$

where U/R is the quotient set of U with respect to R and

$$c(E, X) = \begin{cases} 1 - \frac{|E \cap X|}{|E|}, & \text{if } E \neq \emptyset \\ 0, & \text{otherwise.} \end{cases}$$

S. Tsumoto et al. (Eds.): RSCTC 2004, LNAI 3066, pp. 103–108, 2004.

Using this measure c, Ziarko[10] defined the following extended inclusion by

$$E \overset{\beta}{\subseteq} X \overset{\text{df}}{\Longleftrightarrow} c(X,Y) \leq \beta,$$

then the above definition of extended lower approximation is rewritten as

$$\underline{R}_\beta(X) = \bigcup\{E \in U/R \mid E \overset{\beta}{\subseteq} X\}.$$

Then we have $\underline{R}_\beta(X) \subseteq \overline{R}_\beta(X) \Longleftrightarrow 0 \leq \beta < 0.5$,which means that β should be restricted in $[0, 0.5)$ in order to keep the meaning of the 'upper' and 'lower' approximations.

3 Nonmonotonicity in Granular Reasoning Using VPRM

3.1 Granularized Models and Zooming In and Out

Let us consider a possible-worlds model $\mathcal{M} = \langle U, \cdots, v\rangle$, where U is a set of possible worlds and v is a binary valuation: $v : \mathcal{P} \times U \to \{0,1\}$. When we need modal operators, the ellipsis '$\cdots$' in the model should be replaced either by some accessibility relation in case of well-known Kripke models or by some neighborhood system in case of Scott-Montague models.

Let $\mathcal{P}$ be a set pf atomic sentences and $\mathcal{L}_\mathcal{P}$ is the propositional language generated from $\mathcal{P}$ using a standard kind of set of connectives including modal operators in a usual way. Also let Γ be a subset of $\mathcal{L}_\mathcal{P}$ and let $\mathcal{P}_\Gamma$ be the set of atomic sentences which appears in each sentence in Γ. Then, we can define an equivalence relation R_Γ on U by

$$x R_\Gamma\, y \overset{\text{df}}{\Longleftrightarrow} v(\mathrm{p}, x) = v(\mathrm{p}, y), \text{ for any } \mathrm{p} \in \mathcal{P}_\Gamma,$$

which is called an *agreement relation*[1] in [1]. We regard the quotient set U/R_Γ as a set of *granularized possible worlds* with respect to Γ, denoted $\tilde{U}_\Gamma$, as

$$\tilde{U}_\Gamma \overset{\text{df}}{=} U/R_\Gamma = \{[x]_{R_\Gamma} \mid x \in U\}.$$

Thus we have a granularization of a set of possible worlds. We also make granularization of a valuation. In general, we cannot make a binary granularization but a three-valued one: $\tilde{v}_\Gamma : \mathcal{P} \times \tilde{U}_\Gamma \to 2^{\{0,1\}} \setminus \{\emptyset\}$. Actually it is defined by

$$\tilde{v}_\Gamma(\mathrm{p}, \tilde{w}) = \begin{cases} \{1\}, & \text{if } v(\mathrm{p}, w) = 1 \text{ for any } w \in \tilde{w}, \\ \{0\}, & \text{if } v(\mathrm{p}, w) = 0 \text{ for any } w \in \tilde{w}, \\ \{1,0\}, & \text{otherwise.} \end{cases}$$

In what follows, we abbreviate the two singletons $\{1\}$ and $\{0\}$ as simply 1 and 0, respectively.

[1] This is not an accessibility relation.

Now we have a granularized model $\tilde{\mathcal{M}}_\Gamma \stackrel{\mathrm{df}}{=} \langle \tilde{U}_\Gamma, \cdots, \tilde{v}_\Gamma \rangle$ of $\mathcal{M}$ with respect to Γ. Consult [1] when we need to construct a relation or neighborhood system in the granularized model. Based on this valuation, we can define the following *partially* defined relationship $\tilde{\mathcal{M}}, \tilde{w} \models p$ in the usual way.

For two finite subsets Γ, Γ' such that $\Gamma' \subseteq \Gamma \subseteq \mathcal{L}_\mathcal{P}$, we have $R_\Gamma \subseteq R_{\Gamma'}$, so U_Γ is a *refinement* of $U_{\Gamma'}$. Then we call a mapping $I_\Gamma^{\Gamma'} : \tilde{\mathcal{M}}_{\Gamma'} \to \tilde{\mathcal{M}}_\Gamma$ a *zooming in* from Γ' to Γ, and also call a mapping $O_{\Gamma'}^{\Gamma} : \tilde{\mathcal{M}}_\Gamma \to \tilde{\mathcal{M}}_{\Gamma'}$ a *zooming out* from Γ to Γ'. For, example, let $\{\mathrm{p}\} = \Gamma' \subseteq \Gamma = \{\mathrm{p}, \mathrm{q}\}$, then we can make the following zooming in and out:

$\tilde{U}_{\{\mathrm{p},\mathrm{q}\}}$	p	q
$\lVert\mathrm{p}\rVert^\mathcal{M} \cap \lVert\mathrm{q}\rVert^\mathcal{M}$	1	1
$\lVert\mathrm{p}\rVert^\mathcal{M} \cap (\lVert\mathrm{q}\rVert^\mathcal{M})^\mathrm{C}$	1	0
$(\lVert\mathrm{p}\rVert^\mathcal{M})^\mathrm{C} \cap \lVert\mathrm{q}\rVert^\mathcal{M}$	0	1
$(\lVert\mathrm{p}\rVert^\mathcal{M})^\mathrm{C} \cap (\lVert\mathrm{q}\rVert^\mathcal{M})^\mathrm{C}$	0	0

Zooming out $\longrightarrow$

Zooming in $\longleftarrow$

$\tilde{U}_{\{\mathrm{p}\}}$	p	q
$\lVert\mathrm{p}\rVert^\mathcal{M}$	1	$\{1,0\}$
$(\lVert\mathrm{p}\rVert^\mathcal{M})^\mathrm{C}$	0	$\{1,0\}$

3.2 Granular Reasoning

Let us consider the following classical inference (hypothetical syllogism)

$$a \text{ is p, p is q } / \ a \text{ is p.}$$

In rough theory, the first premise is often translated into '$\mathcal{M}, a \models \mathrm{p}$' in possible-worlds semantics. In a similar way, we can translate the second premise by using granularized models. When 'p is q' holds, we have $\lVert\mathrm{p}\rVert^\mathcal{M} \cap (\lVert\mathrm{q}\rVert^\mathcal{M})^\mathrm{C} = \emptyset$ and $\lVert\mathrm{p}\rVert^\mathcal{M} \cap \lVert\mathrm{q}\rVert^\mathcal{M} = \lVert\mathrm{p}\rVert^\mathcal{M}$. Thus we can make the following set of three granularized worlds and valuation:

$\tilde{U}_{\{\mathrm{p},\mathrm{q}\}}$	p	q
$\lVert\mathrm{p}\rVert^\mathcal{M}$	1	1
$(\lVert\mathrm{p}\rVert^\mathcal{M})^\mathrm{C} \cap \lVert\mathrm{q}\rVert^\mathcal{M}$	0	1
$(\lVert\mathrm{p}\rVert^\mathcal{M})^\mathrm{C} \cap (\lVert\mathrm{q}\rVert^\mathcal{M})^\mathrm{C}$	0	0

and, at the first granularized world, we have the following expression

$$\tilde{\mathcal{M}}_\Gamma, \lVert\mathrm{p}\rVert^\mathcal{M} \models \mathrm{q},$$

which means that, for every $x \in \lVert\mathrm{p}\rVert^\mathcal{M}$, $\mathcal{M}, x \models \mathrm{q}$. Thus, in particular, we have $\mathcal{M}, a \models \mathrm{q}$, which is the conclusion. The final process can be regarded as the result of 'zooming in' $I_\mathcal{P}^\Gamma$.

Here we make two remarks. Firstly, let us make further 'zooming out' in the following way:

$\tilde{U}_{\{\mathrm{p}\}}$	p	q
$\lVert\mathrm{p}\rVert^\mathcal{M}$	1	1
$(\lVert\mathrm{p}\rVert^\mathcal{M})^\mathrm{C}$	0	$\{1,0\}$

From this table, we can find

$$\|\mathrm{p}\|^{\mathcal{M}} \subseteq \underline{R_{\{\mathrm{p}\}}}(\|\mathrm{q}\|^{\mathcal{M}}) \subseteq \|\mathrm{q}\|^{\mathcal{M}}. \tag{1}$$

Hence we have

$$\tilde{\mathcal{M}}, \|\mathrm{p}\|^{\mathcal{M}} \models \mathrm{q} \Longleftrightarrow \|\mathrm{p}\|^{\mathcal{M}} \subseteq \underline{R_{\{\mathrm{p}\}}}(\|\mathrm{q}\|^{\mathcal{M}}). \tag{2}$$

Thus the lower approximation plays an essential role in the inference.

Secondly, the operation of zooming in from Γ' to Γ, where $\Gamma' \subseteq \Gamma$, increases the amount of information, and we can easily prove

$$\Gamma' \subseteq \Gamma \Longrightarrow (\tilde{\mathcal{M}}_{\Gamma'} \models \mathrm{p} \Longrightarrow \tilde{\mathcal{M}}_{\Gamma} \models \mathrm{p}),$$

which shows *monotonicity* of reasoning using the lower approximation.

Example 1. Let $\Gamma = \{\text{human}, \text{mortal}\}$ and Socrates $\in U$, then

Socrates is human.	$\Leftrightarrow$ Socrates $\in \|\text{human}\|^{\mathcal{M}}$	$\Leftrightarrow \mathcal{M}$, Socrates $\models$ human
human is mortal.	$\Leftrightarrow \|\text{human}\|^{\mathcal{M}} \subseteq \underline{R_{\{\text{human}\}}}(\|\text{mortal}\|^{\mathcal{M}})$	$\Leftrightarrow \tilde{\mathcal{M}}_{\Gamma}, \|\text{human}\|^{\mathcal{M}} \models$ mortal
Socrates is mortal.	$\Leftrightarrow$ Socrates $\in \|\text{mortal}\|^{\mathcal{M}}$	$\Leftrightarrow \mathcal{M}$, Socrates $\models$ mortal

3.3 Nonmonotonicity and Granular Reasoning

In this section, let us consider nonmonotonic reasoning like

Tweety is a bird .		Tweety is a penguin .
(Most) birds fly.	but	Penguin s do not fly.
(Maybe) Tweety flies.		Tweety does not fly.

in the framework of granular reasoning. Assume U is finite in this subsection and let $\Gamma' = \{\mathrm{p}, \mathrm{q}\}$. First we consider the former part:

$$a \text{ is p, (Most) p is q } / \text{ (Maybe) } a \text{ is p.}$$

The second premise, unfortunately, does not mean inclusion $\|\mathrm{p}\|^{\mathcal{M}} \subseteq \|\mathrm{q}\|^{\mathcal{M}}$. So we can make the following valuation:

$\tilde{U}_{\Gamma'}$	p q
$\|\mathrm{p}\|^{\mathcal{M}} \cap \|\mathrm{q}\|^{\mathcal{M}}$	1 1
$\|\mathrm{p}\|^{\mathcal{M}} \cap (\|\mathrm{q}\|^{\mathcal{M}})^{\mathrm{C}}$	1 0
$(\|\mathrm{p}\|^{\mathcal{M}})^{\mathrm{C}} \cap \|\mathrm{q}\|^{\mathcal{M}}$	0 1
$(\|\mathrm{p}\|^{\mathcal{M}})^{\mathrm{C}} \cap (\|\mathrm{q}\|^{\mathcal{M}})^{\mathrm{C}}$	0 0

That is, in general, $\|\mathrm{p}\|^{\mathcal{M}} \cap \|\mathrm{q}\|^{\mathcal{M}} \neq \emptyset$ and $\|\mathrm{p}\|^{\mathcal{M}} \cap (\|\mathrm{q}\|^{\mathcal{M}})^{\mathrm{C}} \neq \emptyset$. However, we have $|\, \|\mathrm{p}\|^{\mathcal{M}} \cap \|\mathrm{q}\|^{\mathcal{M}}| \gg |\, \|\mathrm{p}\|^{\mathcal{M}} \cap (\|\mathrm{q}\|^{\mathcal{M}})^{\mathrm{C}}|$, where $|X|$ is the cardinality of set X. Thus, at least, we have $\frac{|\,\|\mathrm{p}\|^{\mathcal{M}} \cap \|\mathrm{q}\|^{\mathcal{M}}|}{|\,\|\mathrm{p}\|^{\mathcal{M}}|} > \frac{1}{2}$. Then, using Ziarko's notion of inclusion, for some β $(0 \leq \beta < \frac{1}{2})$, $\|\mathrm{p}\|^{\mathcal{M}} \overset{\beta}{\subseteq} \|\mathrm{q}\|^{\mathcal{M}}$. Using this result, we can have the following inclusion similar to (1):

$$\|\mathrm{p}\|^{\mathcal{M}} \subseteq \underline{R}^{\beta}_{\{\mathrm{p}\}}(\|\mathrm{q}\|^{\mathcal{M}}). \tag{3}$$

Then we can extend $\models$ in the following way:

$$\tilde{\mathcal{M}}_{\Gamma'}, \|\mathrm{p}\|^{\mathcal{M}} \models_{\beta} \mathrm{q} \overset{\mathrm{df}}{\Longleftrightarrow} \|\mathrm{p}\|^{\mathcal{M}} \subseteq \underline{R}^{\beta}_{\{\mathrm{p}\}}(\|\mathrm{q}\|^{\mathcal{M}}),$$
$$\mathcal{M}, a \models_{\beta} \mathrm{q} \overset{\mathrm{df}}{\Longleftrightarrow} \tilde{\mathcal{M}}, \|\mathrm{p}\|^{\mathcal{M}} \models_{\beta} \mathrm{q} \quad (a \in \|\mathrm{p}\|^{\mathcal{M}})$$

The last formula is the tentative conclusion of nonmonotonic reasoning.

Note that when using the upper approximation like $\tilde{\mathcal{M}}, \|\mathrm{p}\|^{\mathcal{M}} \overline{\models}\, \mathrm{q} \Longleftrightarrow \|\mathrm{p}\|^{\mathcal{M}} \subseteq \overline{R_{\{\mathrm{p}\}}}(\|\mathrm{q}\|^{\mathcal{M}})$ instead of the Ziarko lower approximation, we have, in general, contradiction: $\tilde{\mathcal{M}}, \|\mathrm{p}\|^{\mathcal{M}} \overline{\models}\, \mathrm{q} \wedge \neg \mathrm{q}$.

Next we consider the latter part:

$$a \text{ is r, r is } \neg\mathrm{q} \ \ / \ \ a \text{ is } \neg\mathrm{q}.$$

Let $\Gamma = \{\mathrm{p}, \mathrm{r}\}$. Consider the composition of zooming in from Γ' to $\{\mathrm{p}, \mathrm{q}, \mathrm{r}\}$ and zooming out from $\{\mathrm{p}, \mathrm{q}, \mathrm{r}\}$ to Γ. Then we have the following set of granularized worlds $\tilde{U}_{\Gamma} = \{\|\mathrm{r}\|^{\mathcal{M}}, \|\mathrm{p}\|^{\mathcal{M}} \cap (\|\mathrm{r}\|^{\mathcal{M}})^{\mathrm{C}}, (\|\mathrm{p}\|^{\mathcal{M}})^{\mathrm{C}} \cap (\|\mathrm{r}\|^{\mathcal{M}})^{\mathrm{C}}\}$, where note that $\|\mathrm{p}\|^{\mathcal{M}} \cap \|\mathrm{r}\|^{\mathcal{M}} = \|\mathrm{r}\|^{\mathcal{M}}$, $(\|\mathrm{p}\|^{\mathcal{M}})^{\mathrm{C}} \cap \|\mathrm{r}\|^{\mathcal{M}} = \emptyset$. $\tilde{v}_{\Gamma}$ is given by

$\tilde{U}_{\{\mathrm{p},\mathrm{r}\}}$	p	r	q
$\|\mathrm{r}\|^{\mathcal{M}}$	1	1	0
$\|\mathrm{p}\|^{\mathcal{M}} \cap (\|\mathrm{r}\|^{\mathcal{M}})^{\mathrm{C}}$	1	0	1
$(\|\mathrm{p}\|^{\mathcal{M}})^{\mathrm{C}} \cap (\|\mathrm{r}\|^{\mathcal{M}})^{\mathrm{C}}$	0	0	$\{0,1\}$

Thus now we can use the usual classical reasoning. That is,

$$\tilde{\mathcal{M}}_{\Gamma}, \|\mathrm{r}\|^{\mathcal{M}} \models \neg\mathrm{q} \Longleftrightarrow \|\mathrm{r}\|^{\mathcal{M}} \cap \|\mathrm{q}\|^{\mathcal{M}} = \emptyset,$$

the right-hand side of which corresponds the second premise. Then we have $a \in (\|\mathrm{q}\|^{\mathcal{M}})^{\mathrm{C}}$, by which we have $\mathcal{M}, a \models \neg\mathrm{q}$, which is the conclusion of the second reasoning.

Example 2. Let $\{\mathrm{bird}, \mathrm{fly}\} = \Gamma' \subseteq \Gamma = \{\mathrm{bird}, \mathrm{fly}, \mathrm{penguin}\}$, Tweety$\in U$, then,

Tweety is bird.	$\Leftrightarrow$ Tweety $\in \|\mathrm{bird}\|^{\mathcal{M}}$	$\Leftrightarrow \mathcal{M}, \mathrm{Tweety} \models \mathrm{bird}$
(Most) Birds Fly.	$\Leftrightarrow \|\mathrm{bird}\|^{\mathcal{M}} \subseteq \underline{R}^{\beta}_{\{\mathrm{bird}\}}(\|\mathrm{fly}\|^{\mathcal{M}})$	$\Leftrightarrow \tilde{\mathcal{M}}_{\Gamma}, \|\mathrm{bird}\|^{\mathcal{M}} \models_{\beta} \mathrm{fly}$
(Maybe) Tweety Flies.	$\Leftrightarrow$ Tweety $\in \underline{R}^{\beta}_{\{\mathrm{bird}\}}(\|\mathrm{fly}\|^{\mathcal{M}})$	$\Leftrightarrow \mathcal{M}, \mathrm{Tweety} \models_{\beta} \mathrm{fly}$
but		
Tweety is penguin.	$\Leftrightarrow$ Tweety $\in \|\mathrm{penguin}\|^{\mathcal{M}}$	$\Leftrightarrow \mathcal{M}, \mathrm{Tweety} \models \mathrm{penguin}$
Penguins do not fly.	$\Leftrightarrow \|\mathrm{penguin}\|^{\mathcal{M}} \subseteq \underline{R_{\{\mathrm{penguin}\}}} \|\neg\mathrm{fly}\|^{\mathcal{M}}$	$\Leftrightarrow \tilde{\mathcal{M}}_{\Gamma}, \|\mathrm{penguin}\|^{\mathcal{M}} \models \neg\mathrm{fly}$
Tweety does not fly.	$\Leftrightarrow$ Tweety $\in \|\neg\mathrm{fly}\|^{\mathcal{M}}$	$\Leftrightarrow \mathcal{M}, \mathrm{Tweety} \models \neg\mathrm{fly}$

4 Concluding Remarks

In this paper, we described nonmonotonicity in granular reasoning using Ziarko's VPRM. That shows the model is very useful to describe human ordinary reasoning processes.

Acknowledgments

This work was partly supported by Grant-in-Aid No.14380171 for Scientific Research(B) of the Japan Society for the Promotion of Science, and by the Ministry of Public Management, Home Affairs, Posts and Telecommunications of Japan under grant Strategic Information and Communications R&D Promotion Program (SCOPE-S).

References

1. B.F.Chellas (1980): *Modal Logic: An Introduction*, Cambridge University Press.
2. T.Y.Lin (1998): Granular Computing on Binary Relation I: Data Mining and Neighborhood Systems, II: Rough Set Representations and Belief Functions. In L.Polkowski and A.Skowron (eds.), *Rough Sets in Knowledge Discovery 1: Methodology and Applications.* Physica-Verlag, 107–121, 122–140.
3. T.Murai, M.Nakata, Y.Sato (2001): A Note on Filtration and Granular Reasoning. *T.Terano et al.(eds.), New Frontiers in Artificial Intelligence, LNAI 2253*, Springer, 385-389.
4. T.Murai, G.Resconi, M.Nakata, Y.Sato (2002): Operations of Zooming In and Out on Possible Worlds for Semantic Fields. *E.Damiani et al.(eds.), Knowledge-Based Intelligent Information Engineering Systems and Allied Technologies*, IOS Press, 1083-1087.
5. T.Murai, G.Resconi, M.Nakata, Y.Sato (2003): Granular Reasoning Using Zooming In & Out: Part 2. Aristotle's Categorical Syllogism. *Electronical Notices in Theoretical Computer Science*, Elsevier, Vol.82, No.4.
6. T.Murai, G.Resconi, M.Nakata, Y.Sato (2003): Granular Reasoning Using Zooming In & Out: Part 1. Propositional Reasoning. *Proceedings of International Conference on Rough Sets, Fuzzy Sets, Data Mining, and Granular Computing*, LNAI, Springer, to appear.
7. Z.Pawlak (1982): Rough Sets. *International Journal of Computer and Information Sciences*, Vol. 11, 341–356.
8. Z.Pawlak (1991): *Rough Sets: Theoretical Aspects of Reasoning about Data.* Kluwer.
9. A.Skowron (2001): Toward Intelligent Systems: Calculi of Information Granules. *T.Terano et al.(eds.), New Frontiers in Artificial Intelligence, LNAI 2253*, Springer, 251-260, 2001.
10. W.Ziarko (1993): Variable Precision Rough Set Model. *Journal of Computer and System Sciences*, Vol.11, pp.39-59.

Fuzzy Reasoning Based on Propositional Modal Logic*

Zaiyue Zhang[1], Yuefei Sui[2], and Cungen Cao[2]

[1] Joint Laboratory of Intelligent Computing, Department of Computer Science
East China Shipbuilding Institute, Zhenjiang 212003, P.R.China
njzzy@yzcn.net
[2] Key Laboratory of Intelligent Information Processing
Institute of Computing Technology, Chinese Academy of Sciences
Beijing 100080, P.R. China
suiyyff@hotmail.com

Abstract. In order to deal with some vague assertions more efficiently, fuzzy modal logics have been discussed by many researchers. This paper introduces the notation of fuzzy assertion based on propositional modal logic. As an extension of the traditional semantics about the modal logics, the fuzzy Kripke semantics are considered and the formal system of the fuzzy reasoning based on propositional modal logic is established and the properties about the satisfiability of the reasoning system are discussed.

Keywords: propositional modal logic, fuzzy assertion, fuzzy reasoning

1 Introduction

Modal logic [1] is an important logic branch developed firstly in the category of nonclassical logics, and has been now widely used as a formalism for knowledge representation in artificial intelligence and an analysis tool in computer science [2],[3]. Along with the study of the modal logics, it has been found that the modal logic has a close relationship with many other knowledge representation theories. The most well-known result is the connection of the possible world semantics for the modal epistemic logic S_5 with the approximation space in rough set theory [4], where the system S_5 has been shown to be useful in the analysis of knowledge in various areas [5]. Typically, modal logics can be viewed as an extension of the classical first order logic and are limited to deal with crisp assertions, as its possible world semantics are crisp. That is, assertions about whether a formal proposition holds is a yes-no question. More often than not, the assertions encountered in the real world are not precise and thus cannot be treated simply by using yes or no. Fuzzy logic directly deals with the notion of

* The project was partially supported by the National NSF of China under the grant number 60310213 and the National 973 Project of China under the grant number G1999032701. The second author was partially supported by the National Laboratory of Software Development Environment.

S. Tsumoto et al. (Eds.): RSCTC 2004, LNAI 3066, pp. 109–115, 2004.

vagueness and imprecision. Therefore, it offers appealing foundation for generalization of modal logics in order to deal with some vague assertions. Combining fuzzy logic with modal logics, fuzzy modal logics come into our view. Hájek [6] provides a complete axiomatization of fuzzy S_5 system where the accessibility relation is the universal relation, and Godo and Rodríguez give a complete axiomatic system for the extension of Hájec's logic with another modality corresponding to a fuzzy similarity relation. In the paper, we shall consider the fuzzy reasoning based on propositional modal logic. We introduce the notation of fuzzy assertion based on propositional modal logic, establish a formal system of fuzzy reasoning based on propositional modal and discuss the satisfiability of the system.

2 Fuzzy Propositional Modal Logic $\mathcal{FPML}$

In general, propositional modal logic ($\mathcal{PML}$) will have its alphabet of symbols: a set of propositional symbols, denoted by $PV = \{p_1, p_2, ...\}$; the logical symbols, $\sim$ (negation), $\wedge$ (and), $\vee$ (or), $\rightarrow$ (material implication); the modal operator symbols $\Box$ (necessity operator) and $\Diamond$ (possibility operator). The set of *wffs*.of $\mathcal{PML}$ is the smallest set satisfying the following conditions: p is a *wff*., for each $p \in PV$; if φ is a *wff*. then $\sim \varphi$, $\Box\varphi$, $\Diamond\varphi$ are *wffs*.; if φ and ψ are *wffs*., then $\varphi \wedge \psi$, $\varphi \vee \psi$, $\varphi \rightarrow \psi$ are *wffs*..

A Kripke model for $\mathcal{PML}$ is a triple $M = \langle W, R, V\rangle$, where W is a set of possible worlds, R is a binary relation on W, called an accessibility relation, and $V : W \times PV \rightarrow \{0, 1\}$ is a truth assignment evaluating the truth value of each propositional symbol in each possible world. The function V can be extended to all *wffs*. recursively in the following way:

(2.1) $V(w, \sim \varphi) = 1 - V(w, \varphi)$,
(2.2) $V(w, \varphi \wedge \psi) = \min\{V(w, \varphi), V(w, \psi)\}$,
(2.3) $V(w, \varphi \vee \psi) = \max\{V(w, \varphi), V(w, \psi)\}$,
(2.4) $V(w, \varphi \rightarrow \psi) = \max\{1 - V(w, \varphi), V(w, \psi)\}$,
(2.5) $V(w, \Box\varphi) = \inf\{V(u, \varphi) : \langle u, w\rangle \in R\}$,
(2.6) $V(w, \Diamond\varphi) = \sup\{V(u, \varphi) : \langle u, w\rangle \in R\}$.

Any φ in $\mathcal{PML}$ can be viewed as a proposition. A proposition φ is either true or false in a possible world. However, in a vague system, we can not simply say that a proposition φ is true or false. Hence from a vague point of view, we attach for each proposition $\varphi \in \mathcal{PML}$ a number $n \in [0, 1]$ such that n expresses the believable degree of φ. Thus the basic expression, or *fuzzy assertions*, dealed with in fuzzy $\mathcal{PML}$ is a pair $\langle \varphi, n\rangle$, where $\varphi \in \mathcal{PML}$ is a proposition and $n \in [0, 1]$.

To built the semantics of $\mathcal{FPML}$, we shall follow Kripke's semantics for $\mathcal{PML}$. Let $\mathcal{M} = \langle \mathcal{W}, \mathcal{R}, \mathcal{V}\rangle$ be a triple, where $\mathcal{W}$ is a set of possible worlds, $\mathcal{R}$ is a binary relation on $\mathcal{W}$, called an accessibility relation, and now $\mathcal{V}$ turns to be a function $\mathcal{V} : \mathcal{W} \times PV \rightarrow [0, 1]$, called a *believable degree function*, such that for each $p \in PV$ and $n \in [0, 1]$, $\mathcal{V}(w, p) = n$, or abbreviated by $w(p) = n$, means that *the possible world* w *considers that the believable degree of proposition* p *is* n. The function $\mathcal{V}$ can also be extended to all *wffs*.of $\mathcal{PML}$ recursively. Let $w \in \mathcal{W}$ be a possible world and $\langle \varphi, n \rangle$ be a fuzzy assertion in $\mathcal{FPML}$. We say that w *satisfies* $\langle \varphi, n \rangle$, denoted by $Sat(w, \langle \varphi, n \rangle)$, if $w(\varphi) \geq n$.

Proposition 2.1. Let $\mathcal{M} = \langle \mathcal{W}, \mathcal{R}, \mathcal{V} \rangle$ be a Kripke semantic for $\mathcal{FPML}$, $w \in \mathcal{W}$ be a possible world, φ, ψ are wffs of $\mathcal{PML}$ and $n \in [0, 1]$. Then

(a) $Sat(w, \langle \sim \varphi, n \rangle)$ iff $w(\varphi) \leq 1 - n$;
(b) $Sat(w, \langle \varphi \wedge \psi, n \rangle)$ iff $Sat(w, \langle \varphi, n \rangle)$ and $Sat(w, \langle \psi, n \rangle)$;
(c) $Sat(w, \langle \varphi \vee \psi, n \rangle)$ iff $Sat(w, \langle \varphi, n \rangle)$ or $Sat(w, \langle \psi, n \rangle)$;
(d) $Sat(w, \langle \varphi \rightarrow \psi, n \rangle)$ iff $Sat(w, \langle \sim \varphi, n \rangle)$ or $Sat(w, \langle \psi, n \rangle)$;
(e) $Sat(w, \langle \Box\varphi, n \rangle)$ iff $Sat(u, \langle \varphi, n \rangle)$ for all $u \in \mathcal{W}$ such that $\langle u, w \rangle \in \mathcal{R}$;
(f) $Sat(w, \langle \Diamond\varphi, n \rangle)$ iff $Sat(u, \langle \varphi, n \rangle)$ for some $u \in \mathcal{W}$ such that $\langle u, w \rangle \in \mathcal{R}$.□

Let $\mathcal{M} = \langle \mathcal{W}, \mathcal{R}, \mathcal{V} \rangle$ be a model defined as above, and $\mathcal{A}$ be a set of fuzzy assertions. If there exists a $w \in \mathcal{W}$ such that $Sat(w, \gamma)$ for all $\gamma \in \mathcal{A}$ then $\mathcal{A}$ is said to be *satisfiable* in $\mathcal{M}$, and is denoted by $\mathcal{M} \approx_w \mathcal{A}$. If for all possible worlds $w \in \mathcal{W}$, $\mathcal{M} \approx_w \mathcal{A}$ then $\mathcal{A}$ is said to be *valid* in $\mathcal{M}$, and is denoted by $\mathcal{M} \approx \mathcal{A}$.

There are various types of propositional modal logic systems such as K-system, D-system, T-system, S4-system, S5-system and so on. If $M = \langle W, R, V \rangle$ is model such that R is an equivalent relation on W then M can be viewed as a semantics of S5-system. In order to lay a stress on the key points, we shall limit our discussing on those semantics model $\mathcal{M} = \langle \mathcal{W}, \mathcal{R}, \mathcal{V} \rangle$ such that the relation $\mathcal{R}$ is an equivalent relation on $\mathcal{W}$. As usual, we shall use $\sim$ and $\rightarrow$ as the basic connection words and $\Box$ as the basic modal operator symbol. Hence, the propositional modal logic system S5 contains following axioms and inference rules:

- Axioms:

A_p1 $(\varphi \rightarrow (\psi \rightarrow \varphi))$;
A_p2 $((\varphi \rightarrow (\psi \rightarrow \gamma)) \rightarrow ((\varphi \rightarrow \psi) \rightarrow (\varphi \rightarrow \gamma)))$
A_p3 $((\sim \varphi \rightarrow \sim \psi) \rightarrow (\psi \rightarrow \varphi))$;
$\mathbf{K}(\Box(\varphi \rightarrow \psi) \rightarrow (\Box\varphi \rightarrow \Box\psi))$;
$\mathbf{T}(\Box\varphi \rightarrow \varphi)$;
$\mathbf{E}(\Diamond\varphi \rightarrow \Box\Diamond\varphi)$.

- Inference rules: N(necessity rule) if $\vdash \varphi$ then $\vdash \Box\varphi$;
  MP (modus ponens) if $\vdash \varphi \rightarrow \psi$ and $\vdash \varphi$ then $\vdash \psi$

Propositional modal logic is based on proposition. If the believable degrees of the propositions are considered then we have firstly the following propositions.

Proposition 2.2. For any semantics model $\mathcal{M}$ of $\mathcal{FPML}$, following properties hold: (a) $\mathcal{M} \approx \langle A_p1, 0.5 \rangle$, (b) $\mathcal{M} \approx \langle A_p2, 0.5 \rangle$, (c) $\mathcal{M} \approx \langle A_p3, 0.5 \rangle$, (d) $\mathcal{M} \approx \langle \mathbf{K}, 0.5 \rangle$, (e) $\mathcal{M} \approx \langle \mathbf{T}, 0.5 \rangle$, (f) $\mathcal{M} \approx \langle \mathbf{E}, 0.5 \rangle$. □

Proposition 2.3. If $\mathcal{M} \approx \langle \varphi, n \rangle$ then $\mathcal{M} \approx \langle \Box\varphi, n \rangle$. □

Proposition 2.4. If $\mathcal{M} \approx \langle \varphi \rightarrow \psi, n \rangle$ and $\mathcal{M} \approx \langle \varphi, m \rangle$ then $\mathcal{M} \approx \langle \psi, n \rangle$, where $n, m \in [0, 1]$ such that $n > 1 - m$. □

3 Fuzzy Reasoning Based on $\mathcal{PML}$

Let Σ be a set of *wffs*.of $\mathcal{PML}$. A *wff*.φ is said to be a conclusion of Σ, denoted by $\Sigma \models \varphi$, if every model of Σ is also a model of φ. In $\mathcal{FPML}$, a set of basic fuzzy assertions is called a *fuzzy knowledge base.* Let $\widetilde{\Sigma}$ be a fuzzy knowledge base and $\langle\varphi, n\rangle$ be any fuzzy assertion. If any model of $\widetilde{\Sigma}$ is also a model of $\langle\varphi, n\rangle$ then we say that assertion $\langle\varphi, n\rangle$ is a conclusion of $\widetilde{\Sigma}$, which is denoted by $\widetilde{\Sigma} \approx \langle\varphi, n\rangle$.

If $\widetilde{\Sigma}$ is a fuzzy knowledge base then the crisp knowledge base with respect to $\widetilde{\Sigma}$ will be defined by $\Sigma = \{\varphi : \langle\varphi, n\rangle \in \widetilde{\Sigma}\}$. The following theorems give out some relations between $\models$ and $\approx$.

Theorem 3.1. Let $\widetilde{\Sigma}$ be a fuzzy knowledge base and Σ is a crisp one w.s.t. $\widetilde{\Sigma}$. For any φ and any $n > 0$, if $\widetilde{\Sigma} \approx \langle\varphi, n\rangle$ then $\Sigma \models \varphi$.

Proof: Let M be a model of Σ and w be any possible world. Then for any $\psi \in \Sigma$, $w(\psi) = 1$, hence for any $\langle\psi, m\rangle \in \widetilde{\Sigma}$, where $m \in [0,1]$, we have $Sat(w, \psi)$, thus M is also a model of $\widetilde{\Sigma}$, which implies $w(\varphi) \geq n > 0$. Notice that w is crisp, so it must be the case that $w(\varphi) = 1$. Therefor, M is a model of φ. □

The converse of Theorem 3.1 is not true in the general case. A closer relationship holds whenever we consider normalized fuzzy knowledge bases. A fuzzy assertion $\langle\varphi, n\rangle$ is said to be *normalized* if $n > 0.5$. A fuzzy knowledge base is normalized if every fuzzy assertion in it is. Let $\mathcal{M} = \langle\mathcal{W}, \mathcal{R}, \mathcal{V}\rangle$ be a fuzzy Kripke model and $\widetilde{w}$ is a possible world in $\mathcal{W}$. The crisp possible world with respect to $\widetilde{w}$, denoted by $Cri(\widetilde{w})$, is defined by $Cri(\widetilde{w})(p_i) = 1$ iff $\widetilde{w}(p_i) > 0.5$ for all $p_i \in PV$.

Lemma 3.2. Let $\mathcal{M} = \langle\mathcal{W}, \mathcal{R}, \mathcal{V}\rangle$ be a fuzzy Kripke model and $\widetilde{w} \in \mathcal{W}$. For any φ of $\mathcal{PML}$. If $\widetilde{w}(\varphi) > 0.5$ then $Cri(\widetilde{w})(\varphi) = 1$, and there exists a crisp Kripke model $M = \langle W, R, V\rangle$ such that $Cri(\widetilde{w}) \in W$ and $M \models \varphi$; If $\widetilde{w}(\varphi) < 0.5$ then $Cri(\widetilde{w})(\varphi) = 0$, and there exists a crisp Kripke model $M = \langle W, R, V\rangle$ such that $Cri(\widetilde{w}) \in W$ and $M \models \sim \varphi$.

Proof: It can be proved by induction on the connectives and modal words in φ. □

Theorem 3.3. If $\widetilde{\Sigma}$ is normalized then there is an $n \geq 0.5$ such that $\widetilde{\Sigma} \approx \langle\varphi, n\rangle$ iff $\Sigma \models \varphi$.

Proof: By Theorem 3.1, it is sufficient to show that there is an $n \geq 0.5$ such that if $\Sigma \models \varphi$ then $\widetilde{\Sigma} \approx \langle\varphi, n\rangle$. If not the case, then there exists a model $\mathcal{M}$ of $\widetilde{\Sigma}$ and a possible world $\widetilde{w} \in \mathcal{W}$ such that for all $\psi \in \Sigma$, $\widetilde{w}(\psi) > 0.5$ and $\widetilde{w}(\varphi) < 0.5$ i.e., $\widetilde{w}(\sim \varphi) > 0.5$. Assume that $\Sigma = \{\psi_1, \cdots, \psi_k\}$. Let $\Phi = (\bigwedge_{i=1}^{k} \psi_i) \wedge (\sim \varphi)$ and $n_0 = \min\{\widetilde{w}(\sim \varphi), \widetilde{w}(\psi_1), \cdots, \widetilde{w}(\psi_k)\}$. It is obvious that $\widetilde{w}(\Phi) > 0.5$. By Lemma 3.2, there exists a crisp model M such that M is a model of Σ but is not a model of φ, which contradicts that $\Sigma \models \varphi$. □

4 Satisfiability of Fuzzy Reasoning

The process of deciding whether $\widetilde{\Sigma} \models_{\approx} \gamma$ is called a fuzzy reasoning procedure based on $\mathcal{PML}$. We shall develop a reasoning system about fuzzy assertions in this section and study the satisfiability of the reasoning. The ideal is formed by combining the constraint propagation method introduced in [7] with the semantics chart method presented in [8], the former is usually proposed in the context of description logics [9], and the latter is used to solve the decidability problem of modal propositional calculus [10].

The alphabet of our fuzzy reasoning system contains the symbols used in $\mathcal{PML}$, a set of possible worlds symbols $\mathbf{w_1}, \mathbf{w_2}, \ldots$, a set of relation symbols $\{<, \leq, >, \geq\}$ and a special symbol $\mathcal{R}$. An expression in the fuzzy reasoning system is called a *fuzzy constraint* if it is in the form of $\langle \mathbf{w} : \varphi \; rel \; n \rangle$ or $\langle \langle \mathbf{w}, \mathbf{w}' \rangle : \mathcal{R} \geq 1 \rangle$, where $\varphi \in \mathcal{PML}$, $n \in [0,1]$ and $rel \in \{<, \leq, >, \geq\}$. The following are reasoning rulers:

- *The reasoning rules about* $\mathcal{R}$:
  (R_r) $\emptyset \Longrightarrow \langle \langle \mathbf{w}, \mathbf{w} \rangle : \mathcal{R} \geq 1 \rangle$;
  (R_s) $\langle \langle \mathbf{w}, \mathbf{w}' \rangle : \mathcal{R} \geq 1 \rangle \Longrightarrow \langle \langle \mathbf{w}', \mathbf{w} \rangle : \mathcal{R} \geq 1 \rangle$;
  (R_t) $\langle \langle \mathbf{w}, \mathbf{w}' \rangle : \mathcal{R} \geq 1 \rangle, \langle \langle \mathbf{w}', \mathbf{w}'' \rangle : \mathcal{R} \geq 1 \rangle \Longrightarrow \langle \langle \mathbf{w}, \mathbf{w}'' \rangle : \mathcal{R} \geq 1 \rangle$.
- *The general reasoning rules*:
  $(\sim_{\geq})$ $\langle \mathbf{w} : \sim \varphi \geq n \rangle \Longrightarrow \langle \mathbf{w} : \varphi \leq 1 - n \rangle$;
  $(\sim_{\leq})$ $\langle \mathbf{w} : \sim \varphi \leq n \rangle \Longrightarrow \langle \mathbf{w} : \varphi \geq 1 - n \rangle$;
  $(\rightarrow_{\geq})$ $\langle \mathbf{w} : \varphi \rightarrow \psi \geq n \rangle \Longrightarrow \langle \mathbf{w} : \varphi \leq 1 - n \rangle \mid \langle \mathbf{w} : \psi \geq n \rangle$;
  $(\rightarrow_{\leq})$ $\langle \mathbf{w} : \varphi \rightarrow \psi \leq n \rangle \Longrightarrow \langle \mathbf{w} : \varphi \geq 1 - n \rangle \, , \, \langle \mathbf{w} : \psi \geq n \rangle$;
  $(\Box_{\geq})$ $\langle \mathbf{w} : \Box\varphi \geq n \rangle \, , \, \langle \langle \mathbf{w}', \mathbf{w} \rangle : \mathcal{R} \geq 1 \rangle \Longrightarrow \langle \mathbf{w}' : \varphi \geq n \rangle$;
  $(\Box_{\leq})$ $\langle \mathbf{w} : \Box\varphi \leq n \rangle \Longrightarrow \langle \langle \mathbf{w}', \mathbf{w} \rangle : \mathcal{R} \geq 1 \rangle \, , \, \langle \mathbf{w}' : \varphi \leq n \rangle$.

The rules for the case $<$ and $>$ are quite similar.

Definition 4.1. An interpretation $\mathcal{I}$ of the system contains a interpretation domain $\mathcal{W}$ such that for any $\mathbf{w}$, its interpretation $\mathbf{w}^{\mathcal{I}} \in \mathcal{W}$ is a mapping from PV into $[0,1]$, and the interpretation $\mathcal{R}^{\mathcal{I}}$ is a relation on $\mathcal{W}$. An interpretation $\mathcal{I}$ satisfies a fuzzy constraint $\langle \mathbf{w} : \varphi \; rel \; n \rangle$ (resp.$\langle \langle \mathbf{w}, \mathbf{w}' \rangle : \mathcal{R} \geq 1 \rangle$) if and only if $\mathbf{w}^{\mathcal{I}}(\varphi) \; rel \; n$ (resp.$\langle \mathbf{w}^{\mathcal{I}}, \mathbf{w}'^{\mathcal{I}} \rangle \in \mathcal{R}^{\mathcal{I}}$). $\mathcal{I}$ satisfies a set S of fuzzy constraints iff $\mathcal{I}$ satisfies every element of it. A set S of fuzzy constraints is said to be satisfiable if there is an interpretation $\mathcal{I}$ such that $\mathcal{I}$ satisfies S.

Proposition 4.2. Let S be a set of fuzzy constraints. If S is satisfiable and $\langle \mathbf{w} : \Box\varphi \geq n \rangle \in S$ and $\langle \langle \mathbf{w}', \mathbf{w} \rangle : \mathcal{R} \geq 1 \rangle \in S$, then $S \cup \{\langle \mathbf{w}' : \varphi \geq n \rangle\}$ is satisfiable.

Proof: Let $\mathcal{I}$ be the interpretation satisfies S. Then we have that $\mathbf{w}^{\mathcal{I}}(\Box\varphi) \geq n$ and $\langle \mathbf{w}'^{\mathcal{I}}, \mathbf{w}^{\mathcal{I}} \rangle \in \mathcal{R}^{\mathcal{I}}$, which, by Proposition 2.1(e), implies that $\mathbf{w}'^{\mathcal{I}}(\varphi) \geq n$. The Proposition also holds if $\geq$ is replaced by $>$. □

Proposition 4.3. Let S be a set of fuzzy constraints. If S is satisfiable and $\langle \mathbf{w} :\sim \varphi \geq n\rangle \in S$ (resp. $\langle \mathbf{w} :\sim \varphi \leq n\rangle \in S, \langle \mathbf{w} :\sim \varphi > n\rangle \in S, \langle \mathbf{w} :\sim \varphi < n\rangle \in S$), then $S \cup \{\langle \mathbf{w} : \varphi \leq 1-n\rangle\}$ (resp. $S \cup \{\langle \mathbf{w} : \varphi \geq 1-n\rangle\}, S \cup \{\langle \mathbf{w} : \varphi < 1-n\rangle\}, S \cup \{\langle \mathbf{w} : \varphi > 1-n\rangle\}$) is satisfiable.

Proof: If interpretation $\mathcal{I}$ satisfies S, then, by Proposition 2.1(a), $\mathbf{w}^{\mathcal{I}}(\sim \varphi) \geq n$ iff $\mathbf{w}^{\mathcal{I}}(\varphi) \leq 1-n$, thus $\mathcal{I}$ also satisfies $S \cup \{\langle \mathbf{w} : \varphi \leq 1-n\rangle\}$. □

Proposition 4.4. If S is satisfiable and $\langle \mathbf{w} : \varphi \to \psi \leq n\rangle \in S$, then $S \cup \{\langle \mathbf{w} : \varphi \geq 1-n\rangle, \langle \mathbf{w} : \psi \leq n\rangle\}$ is satisfiable.

Proof: The Proposition can be easily proved by the fact that $\mathbf{w}^{\mathcal{I}}(\varphi \to \psi) \leq n$ iff $\mathbf{w}^{\mathcal{I}}(\varphi) \geq 1-n$ and $\mathbf{w}^{\mathcal{I}}(\psi) \leq n$. The Proposition also holds if $\geq$ and $\leq$ are replaced by $>$ and $<$ respectively. □

Proposition 4.5. If S is satisfiable and $\langle \mathbf{w} : \varphi \to \psi \geq n\rangle \in S$, then at least one of $S \cup \{\langle \mathbf{w} : \varphi \leq 1-n\rangle\}$ and $S \cup \{\langle \mathbf{w} : \psi \geq n\rangle\}$ is satisfiable.

Proof: This is simply because that if $\mathbf{w}^{\mathcal{I}}(\varphi \to \psi) \geq n$ then we have that either $\mathbf{w}^{\mathcal{I}}(\varphi \leq 1-n)$ or $\mathbf{w}^{\mathcal{I}}(\psi) \geq n$. The Proposition also holds if the relation symbols $\geq$ and $\leq$ are replaced by $>$ and $<$ respectively. □

Proposition 4.6. If S is satisfiable and $\langle \mathbf{w} : \Box\varphi \leq n\rangle \in S$, then $S \cup \{\langle\langle \mathbf{w}', \mathbf{w}\rangle : \boldsymbol{\mathcal{R}} \geq 1\rangle, \langle \mathbf{w}' : \varphi \leq n\rangle\}$ is satisfiable, where $\mathbf{w}'$ is a possible world symbol dose not appear in S.

Proof: Let $\mathcal{I}$ be the interpretation satisfies S. Then we have that $\mathbf{w}^{\mathcal{I}}(\Box\varphi) \leq n$, thus there exits a possible world $w' \in \mathcal{W}$ such that $\langle w', w\rangle \in \mathcal{R}$ and $w'(\varphi) \leq n$, where $w = \mathbf{w}^{\mathcal{I}}$ and $\mathcal{R} = \boldsymbol{\mathcal{R}}^{\mathcal{I}}$. We define an interpretation $\mathcal{I}'$ such that $\mathbf{w}'^{\mathcal{I}'} = w'$, $\boldsymbol{\mathcal{R}}^{\mathcal{I}'} = \boldsymbol{\mathcal{R}}^{\mathcal{I}} = \mathcal{R}$ and $\mathbf{w}''^{\mathcal{I}'} = \mathbf{w}''^{\mathcal{I}}$ for any $\mathbf{w}''$ appeared in S such that $\mathbf{w}'' \neq \mathbf{w}'$. Then it can be easily implied that $\mathcal{I}'$ satisfies S by the fact that the restriction of $\mathcal{I}'$ on S is equal to that of $\mathcal{I}$'s. Moreover, since $\langle w', w\rangle \in \mathcal{R}$ and $w'(\varphi) \leq n$, we have that $\langle \mathbf{w}'^{\mathcal{I}'}, \mathbf{w}^{\mathcal{I}'}\rangle \in \boldsymbol{\mathcal{R}}^{\mathcal{I}'}$ and $\mathbf{w}'^{\mathcal{I}'}(\varphi) \leq n$. Thus $S \cup \{\langle\langle \mathbf{w}', \mathbf{w}\rangle : \boldsymbol{\mathcal{R}} \geq 1\rangle, \langle \mathbf{w}' : \varphi \leq n\rangle\}$ is satisfied by $\mathcal{I}'$. The Proposition also holds if the relation symbols $\leq$ is replaced by $<$. □

5 Conclusion

We have established a formal fuzzy reasoning system based on propositional modal logic and study the satisfiability of reasoning procedure. Let $S_{\widetilde{\Sigma}} = \{\langle \mathbf{w} : \psi \geq n\rangle : \langle \psi, n\rangle \in \widetilde{\Sigma}\}$ and $S = S_{\widetilde{\Sigma}} \cup \{\langle \mathbf{w} : \varphi < n\rangle\}$, the problem of deciding whether $\widetilde{\Sigma} \models\!\approx \langle \varphi, n\rangle$ seems to have a close relationship with the satisfiability of S. Our further work is to build an efficient reasoning mechanism to decide whether a fuzzy assertion is a conclusion of some existing assertions, and analyze the soundness and completeness of the reasoning.

References

1. Chellas B.F. Modal Logic: An Introduction. Cambridge University Press, 1980.
2. Gabbay D.M, Hogger C.J, and Robinson J.A, editors. *Handbook of Logic in Artificial Intelligence and Logic Programming*, Vol. 1–4. Clarendon Press–Oxford, 1994.
3. Abramsky S, Gabbay D.M, and Maibaum T.S.E, editors. *Handbook of Logic in Computer Science*, Vol. 1–3. Clarendon Press–Oxford, 1992.
4. Pawlak Z. Rough sets. *International Journal of Computer and Information Science*, 1982, 11: 341-356.
5. Fagin R.F, Halpern J.Y, Moses Y, and Vardi M.Y. *Reasoning about Knowledge*. MIT press, 1996.
6. Hájek P, Harmancová D. A many-valued modal logics. In *Proceedings of IPMU'96*, 1996, 1021-1024.
7. Straccia U. A fuzzy description logic. In *Proceedings of AAAI'98, 15th National Conference on Artificial Intelligence*, Madison, Wisconsin, 1998.
8. Beihai Z. An introduction to modal logic. Beijing: Beijing University Press, 1991, 141-165.(In Chinese)
9. Buchheit M, Donini F M, and Scharerf A. Decidable reasoning in terminological knowledge representation systems. In *Proc. of the 13th Int. Joint Conf. on Artificial Intelligence (IJCAI'93)*, 1993, 704-709.
10. Kripke S A. Semantical analysis of modal logic II. In Addsion J W, *et al*(eds.), *The Theory of Models*, North-Holland, Amsterdam, 1965, 206-220.

Approximation Spaces and Information Granulation

Andrzej Skowron[1], Roman Swiniarski[2,3], and Piotr Synak[4]

[1] Institute of Mathematics, Warsaw University
Banacha 2, 02-097 Warsaw, Poland
skowron@mimuw.edu.pl
[2] Institute of Computer Science, Polish Academy of Sciences
Ordona 21, 01-237 Warsaw, Poland
[3] Department of Mathematical and Computer Sciences
San Diego State University
5500 Campanile Drive San Diego, CA 92182, USA
rswiniar@sciences.sdsu.edu
[4] Polish-Japanese Institute of Information Technology
Koszykowa 86, 02-008 Warsaw, Poland
synak@pjwstk.edu.pl

Abstract. We discuss approximation spaces in the granular computing framework. Such approximation spaces generalise the approaches to concept approximation existing in rough set theory. Approximation spaces are constructed as higher level information granules and are obtained as the result of complex modelling. We present illustrative examples of modelling approximation spaces including approximation spaces for function approximation, inducing concept approximation, and some other information granule approximations. In modelling of such approximation spaces we use an important assumption that not only objects but also more complex information granules involved in approximations are perceived using only partial information about them.

1 Introduction

The rough set approach is based on the approximation space concept. Approximation spaces for information systems [1] are defined by partitions or coverings defined by attributes of pattern space. One can distinguish two basic components in approximation spaces: uncertainty function and inclusion function [2]. This approach has been generalised to the rough mereological approach (see, e.g., [3–5]). The existing approaches are based on observation that the objects are perceived by information about them and due to the incomplete information they can be indiscernible. Hence, with each object one can associate an indiscernibility class, called also (indiscernibility) neighbourhood [6]. In the consequence, testing if given object belongs to a set is substituted by checking a degree to which its neighbourhood is included into the set. Such an approach covers several generalizations of set approximations like these based on tolerance relation or variable precision rough set model [7].

In real-life applications approximation spaces are complex information granules that are not given directly with data but they should be discovered from available data and domain knowledge by some searching strategies (see, e.g., [5, 8]). In the paper we

S. Tsumoto et al. (Eds.): RSCTC 2004, LNAI 3066, pp. 116–126, 2004.

present a general approach to approximation spaces based on granular computing. We show that the existing approaches to approximations in rough sets are particular cases of our approach. Illustrative examples include approximation spaces with complex neighbourhoods, approximation spaces for function approximation and for inducing concept approximations. Some other aspects of information granule construction, relevant for approximation spaces, are also presented. Furthermore, we discuss one more aspect of approximation spaces based on the observation that the definition of approximations does not depend only on perception of partial information about objects but also on perception of more complex information granules.

The presented approach can be interpreted in multi-agent setting [9, 5]. Each agent is equipped with its own relational structure and approximation spaces located in input ports. The approximation spaces are used for filtering (approximating) information granules sent by other agents. Such agents are performing operations on approximated information granules and sending the results to other agents, checking relationships between approximated information granules, or using such granules in negotiations with other agents. Parameters of approximation spaces are analogous to weights in classical neuron models. Agents are performing operations on information granules rather than on numbers. This analogy has been used as a starting point for the rough-neural computing paradigm [10] of computing with words [11].

2 Granule Approximation Spaces

Using the granular computing approach (see, e.g., [5]) one can generalise the approximation operations for sets of objects, known in rough set theory, to arbitrary information granules. The basic concept is the rough inclusion function ν [3–5].

First, let us recall the definition of information granule system [5].

Definition 1. *An* information granule system *is any tuple* $GS = (E, O, G, \nu)$ *where* E *is a set of elements called* elementary information granules, O *is a set of (partial)* operations *on information granules,* G *is a set of information granules constructed from* E *using operations from* O*, and* $\nu : G \times G \longrightarrow [0,1]$ *is a (partial) function called* rough inclusion.

The main interpretation of rough inclusion is to measure the inclusion degree of one granule in another. In the paper we use the following notation: $\nu_p(g, g')$ denotes that $\nu(g, g') \geq p$ holds; $Gran(GS) = G$; $\mathcal{G}$ denotes a given family of granule systems. $P(X)$ denotes the set of all subsets of X, $P^1(X) = P(X), P^{k+1}(X) = P(P^k(X))$ for $k \geq 1$.

We begin with the general definition of approximation space in the context of a family of information granule systems.

Definition 2. *Let* $\mathcal{G}$ *be a family of information granule systems. A* granule approximation space *with respect to* $\mathcal{G}$ *is any tuple*

$$\mathcal{AS}_{\mathcal{G}} = (GS, G, Tr), \tag{1}$$

where GS *is a selected (initial) granule system from* $\mathcal{G}$*;* $G \subseteq Gran(GS)$ *is some collection of granules; transition relation* Tr *is a binary relation on information granule systems from* $\mathcal{G}$*, i.e.,* $Tr \subseteq \mathcal{G} \times \mathcal{G}$.

Let $GS \in \mathcal{G}$. By $Tr[GS]$ we denote the set of all information granule systems reachable from GS:

$$Tr[GS] = \{GS' \in \mathcal{G} : GS\, Tr^*\, GS'\}, \tag{2}$$

where Tr^* is the reflexive and transitive closure of the relation Tr. By $Tr[GS, G]$ we denote the set of all Tr-terminal granule systems reachable from GS that consist of information granules from G:

$$Tr[GS, G] = \{GS' : (GS, GS') \in Tr^*, G \subseteq Gran(GS'), \text{ and } Tr[GS'] = \{GS'\}\}. \tag{3}$$

The elements of $Tr[GS, G]$ are called the candidate granule systems for approximation of information granules from G, generated by Tr from GS (G-candidates, for short). For any system $GS^* \in Tr[GS, G]$ we define approximations of granules from G by information granules from $Gran(GS^*) \setminus G$. Searching for granule systems from $Tr[GS, G]$ that are relevant for approximation of given information granules is one of the most important tasks in granular computing.

By using granule approximation space $\mathcal{AS}_{\mathcal{G}} = (GS, G, Tr)$, for a family of granule systems $\mathcal{G}$, we can define approximation of a given granule $g \in G$ in terms of its lower and upper approximations[1]. We assume that there is additionally given "make granule" operation $\oplus : P(G^*) \longrightarrow G^*$, where $G^* = Gran(GS^*)$, for any $GS^* \in Tr(GS, G)$, that constructs a single granule from a set of granules. A typical example of $\oplus$ is set theoretical union, however, it can be also realised by a complex classifier. The granule approximation is thus defined as follows:

Definition 3. *Let* $0 \le p < q \le 1$, $\mathcal{AS} = (GS, G, Tr)$ *be a granule approximation space, and* $GS^* \in Tr[GS, G]$. *The* $(\mathcal{AS}, GS^*, \oplus, q)$-lower approximation *of* $g \in G$ *is defined by*

$$LOW(\mathcal{AS}, GS^*, \oplus, q)(g) = \oplus(\{g' \in Gran(GS^*) \setminus G : \nu^*(g', g) \ge q\}) \tag{4}$$

where ν^* *denotes the rough inclusion of* GS^*. *The* $(\mathcal{AS}, GS^*, \oplus, p)$-upper approximation *of* g *is defined by*

$$UPP(\mathcal{AS}, GS^*, \oplus, p)(g) = \oplus(\{g' \in Gran(GS^*) \setminus G : \nu^*(g', g) > p\}) \tag{5}$$

where ν^* *denotes the rough inclusion of* GS^*.

The numbers p, q can be interpreted as inclusion degrees that make it possible to control the size of the lower and upper approximations. In case when $p = 0$ and $q = 1$ we have the case of full inclusion (lower approximation) and any non-zero inclusion (upper approximation).

One can search for optimal approximations of granules from G defined by $GS^* \in Tr[GS, G]$ using some optimisation criteria or one can search for relevant fusion of approximations of granules from G defined by $GS^* \in Tr[GS, G]$ [2].

In the following sections we discuss illustrative examples showing that the above scheme generalises several approaches to approximation spaces and set approximations. In particular, we include examples of information granules G and their structures, the rough inclusion ν as well as the operation $\oplus$.

[1] If there is no contradiction we use $\mathcal{AS}$ instead of $\mathcal{AS}_{\mathcal{G}}$.

[2] This problem will be investigated elsewhere.

3 Approximation Spaces

Let us recall the definition of an approximation space from [2, 1]. For simplicity of reasoning we omit parameters that label components of approximation spaces.

Definition 4. *An approximation space is a system $AS = (U, I, \nu)$, where*

- *U is a non-empty finite set of objects,*
- *$I : U \rightarrow P(U)$ is an uncertainty function, such that $x \in I(x)$ for any $x \in U$,*
- *$\nu : P(U) \times P(U) \rightarrow [0, 1]$ is a rough inclusion function.*

A set $X \subseteq U$ is *definable in AS* if and only if it is a union of some values of the uncertainty function. The standard rough inclusion function ν_{SRI} defines the degree of inclusion between two subsets of U by

$$\nu_{SRI}(X, Y) = \begin{cases} \frac{card(X \cap Y)}{card(X)} & \text{if } X \neq \emptyset \\ 1 & \text{if } X = \emptyset. \end{cases} \tag{6}$$

The lower and the upper approximations of subsets of U are defined as follows.

Definition 5. *For any approximation space $AS = (U, I, \nu)$, $0 \leq p < q \leq 1$, and any subset $X \subseteq U$ the q-*lower *and the p-*upper approximation *of X in AS is defined, respectively, by*

$$LOW_q(AS, X) = \{x \in U : \nu(I(x), X) \geq q\}, \tag{7}$$

$$UPP_p(AS, X) = \{x \in U : \nu(I(x), X) > p\}. \tag{8}$$

Approximation spaces can be constructed directly from information systems or information systems enriched by some similarity relations on attribute value vectors. The above definition generalises several approaches existing in the literature like these based on equivalence or tolerance indiscernibility relation as well as those based on exact inclusion of indiscernibility classes into concepts [1, 7].

Let us observe that the above definition of approximations is a special case of Definition 3. The granule approximation space $\mathcal{AS} = (GS, G, Tr)$ corresponding to $AS = (U, I, \nu)$ can be defined by

1. GS consisting of information granules being subsets of U (in particular, containing neighbourhoods that are values of the uncertainty function I) and of rough inclusion $\nu = \nu_{SRI}$.
2. $G = P(U)$.
3. $Tr[GS, G]$ consisting of exactly two systems: GS and GS^* such that
   - $Gran(GS^*) = G \cup \{(x, I(x)) : x \in U\}$;
   - the rough inclusion ν is extended by $\nu((x, I(x)), X) = \nu(I(x), X)$ for $x \in U$ and $X \subseteq U$.

Suppose the "make granule" operation $\oplus$ is defined by

$$\oplus(\{(x,\cdot) : x \in Z\}) = Z \text{ for any } Z \subseteq U.$$

Then for the approximation space AS and granule approximation space $\mathcal{AS}$ we have the following:

Proposition 1. *Let* $0 \leq p < q \leq 1$. *For any* $X \in P(U)$ *we have:*

$$LOW_q(AS, X) = LOW(\mathcal{AS}, GS^*, \oplus, q)(X), \tag{9}$$
$$UPP_p(AS, X) = UPP(\mathcal{AS}, GS^*, \oplus, p)(X). \tag{10}$$

4 Approximation Spaces with Complex Neighbourhoods

In this section we present approximation spaces that have more complex uncertainty functions. Such functions define complex neighbourhoods of objects, e.g., families of sets. This aspect is very important from the point of view of complex concepts approximation. A special case of complex uncertainty functions is such with values in $P^2(U)$, i.e., $I : U \longrightarrow P^2(U)$. Such uncertainty functions appear, e.g., in case of the similarity based rough set approach. One can define $I(x)$ to be a family of all maximal cliques defined by the similarity relation which x belongs to (see Section 7).

We obtain the following definition of approximation space:

Definition 6. *A k-th order approximation space is any tuple* $AS = (U, I^k, \nu)$, *where*

- U *is a non-empty finite set of objects,*
- $I^k : U \to P^k(U)$ *is an uncertainty function,*
- $\nu : P(U) \times P(U) \to [0, 1]$ *is a rough inclusion function.*

Let us note that up to the above definition there can be given different uncertainty functions for different levels of granulation. The inclusion function can be also defined in this way, however, in most cases we induce it recursively from ν. For example, in case of set approximation by means of given approximation space $AS = (U, I^k, \nu)$ we are interested in inclusion function $\nu^k : P^k(U) \times P(U) \to [0, 1]$, defined recursively by the corresponding relation ν_p^k, for $X \subseteq U$ and $\mathcal{Y} \subseteq P^k(U)$, as follows

- $\nu_p^k(\mathcal{Y}, X)$ iff $\exists Y \in \mathcal{Y}\ \nu_p^{k-1}(Y, X)$,
- $\nu_p^1(Y, X)$ iff $\nu_p(Y, X)$.

The definition of set approximations for the k-th order approximation spaces depends on the way the values of uncertainty function are perceived. To illustrate this point of view we consider the following two examples: the complete perception of neighbourhoods and the perception defined by the intersection of the family $I(x)$. In the former case we consider a new definition of set approximations.

Definition 7. *Let* $0 \leq p < q \leq 1$. *For any k-th order approximation space* $AS = (U, I^k, \nu)$, ν^k *induced from* ν, *and any subset* $X \subseteq U$ *the* q-lower *and the* p-upper approximation *of* X *in* AS *is defined, respectively, by*

$$LOW_q(AS, X) = \left\{x \in U : \nu^k\left(I^k(x), X\right) \geq q\right\}, \tag{11}$$

$$UPP_p(AS, X) = \left\{x \in U : \nu^k\left(I^k(x), X\right) > p\right\}. \tag{12}$$

We can observe that the approximation operations for these two cases are, in general, different.

Proposition 2. *Let us denote by $AS^\cap = (U, I^\cap, \nu)$ the approximation space obtained from the second order approximation space $AS = \left(U, I^2, \nu\right)$ assuming $I^\cap(x) = \cap I^2(x)$ for $x \in U$. We also assume that $x \in Y$ for any $Y \in I^2(x)$ and $x \in U$. Then, for $X \subseteq U$ we have*

$$LOW(AS, X) \subseteq LOW(AS^\cap, X) \subseteq X \subseteq UPP(AS^\cap, X) \subseteq UPP(AS, X). \tag{13}$$

One can check (in an analogous way as in Section 3) that the above definition of approximations is a special case of Definition 3.

5 Relation and Function Approximation

One can directly apply the definition of set approximation to relations. For simplicity, but without loss of generality, we consider binary relations only. Let $R \subseteq U \times U$ be a binary relation. We can consider approximation of R by an approximation space $AS = (U \times U, I, \nu)$ in an analogous way as in Definition 5:

$$LOW_q(AS, R) = \{(x, y) \in U \times U : \nu(I(x, y)), X) \geq q\}, \tag{14}$$

$$UPP_p(AS, R) = \{(x, y) \in U \times U : \nu(I(x, y), X) > p\}, \tag{15}$$

for $0 \leq p < q \leq 1$. This definition can be also easily extended to the case of complex uncertainty function as in Definition 7. However, the main problem is how to construct relevant approximation spaces, i.e., how to define uncertainty and inclusion functions. One can consider, e.g., uncertainty function $I(x, y) = I(x) \times I(y)$ (assuming that one dimensional uncertainty function is given) and the standard inclusion, i.e., $\nu = \nu_{SRI}$.

Now, let us consider an approximation space $AS = (U, I, \nu)$ and a function $f : Dom \longrightarrow U$, where $Dom \subseteq U$. By $Graph(f)$ we denote the set $\{(x, f(x)) : x \in Dom\}$. We can easily see that if we apply the above definition of relation approximation to f (it is a special case of relation) then the lower approximation is almost always empty. Thus, we have to construct the relevant approximation space $AS^* = (U \times U, I^*, \nu^*)$ in different way, e.g., by extending the uncertainty function as well as the inclusion function on subsets of $U \times U$. We assume that the value $I^*(x, y)$ of the uncertainty function, called the neighbourhood (or the window) of (x, y), for $(x, y) \in U \times U$, is defined by

$$I^*(x, y) = I(x) \times I(y). \tag{16}$$

Next, we should decide how to define values of the inclusion function on pairs $(I^*(x, y), Graph(f))$, i.e., how to define the degree r to which the intersection $I^*(x, y) \cap Graph(f)$ is included into $Graph(f)$.

One can consider a ratio

$$r = \frac{card(\{x \in I(x) \cap Dom : f(x) \in I(y)\})}{card(I(x))}, \tag{17}$$

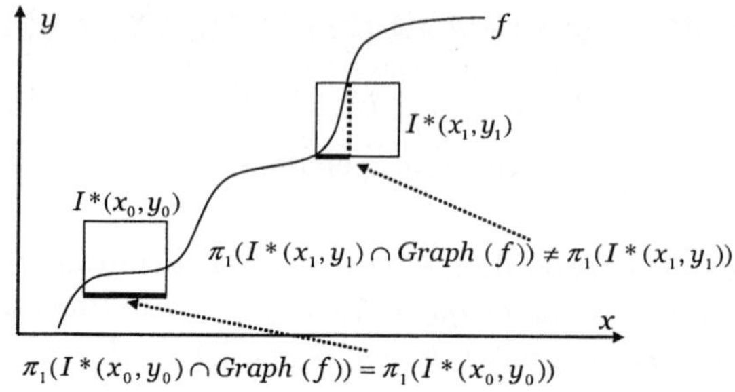

Fig. 1. Function approximation

i.e., the ratio of the number of all objects from $I(x) \cap Dom$ (if any) on which f takes a value from $I(y)$ to the number of objects in $I(x)$.

If $r = 1$ then (x, y) defining the window $I^*(x, y)$ is in the lower approximation of $Graph(f)$; if $0 < r \leq 1$ then (x, y) defining the window $I^*(x, y)$ is in the upper approximation of $Graph(f)$.

Using the above intuition, we assume that the inclusion holds to degree one if the domain of $Graph(f)$ restricted to $I(x)$ is equal to $I(x)$. This can be formally defined by the following condition:

$$\pi_1(I^*(x,y) \cap Graph(f)) = \pi_1(I^*(x,y)), \tag{18}$$

where π_1 denotes the projection on the first coordinate. It is equivalent to

$$\forall x' \in I(x)\ f(x') \in I(y). \tag{19}$$

Thus, the inclusion function ν^* for subsets $X, Y \subseteq U \times U$ is defined by

$$\nu^*(X,Y) = \begin{cases} \frac{card(\pi_1(X \cap Y))}{card(\pi_1(X))} & \text{if } \pi_1(X) \neq \emptyset \\ 1 & \text{if } \pi_1(X) = \emptyset. \end{cases} \tag{20}$$

Hence, the relevant inclusion function in approximation spaces for function approximations is such a function that does not measure the degree of inclusion of its arguments but their perceptions, represented in the above example by projections of corresponding sets. One can choose another definition, e.g., based on the density of pixels (in case of images) in a window that are matched by the function graph.

Proposition 3. *Let $AS^* = (U \times U, I^*, \nu^*)$ be an approximation space with I^*, ν^* defined by (16), (20), respectively, and let $f : Dom \longrightarrow U$ where $Dom \subseteq U$. Then*

1. $(x, y) \in LOW_1(AS^*, Graph(f))$ iff $\forall x' \in I(x)\ f(x') \in I(y)$.
2. $(x, y) \in UPP_0(AS^*, Graph(f))$ iff $\exists x' \in I(x)\ f(x') \in I(y)$.

In case of arbitrary parameters p, q satisfying $0 \leq p < q \leq 1$ we have

Proposition 4. *Let $AS^* = (U \times U, I^*, \nu^*)$ be an approximation space with I^*, ν^* defined by* (16), (20), *respectively, and let $f : Dom \longrightarrow U$ where $Dom \subseteq U$. Then*

1. $(x,y) \in LOW_q(AS^*, Graph(f))$ iff $card(\{x' \in I(x) : f(x') \in I(y)\}) \geq q \cdot card(I(x))$.
2. $(x,y) \in UPP_p(AS^*, Graph(f))$ iff $card(\{x' \in I(x) : f(x') \in I(y)\}) > p \cdot card(I(x))$.

In our example we define the inclusion degree between two subsets of Cartesian product using, in a sense, the inclusion degree between their projections. Hence, subsets of Cartesian products are perceived by projections.

Again, one can consider the definition of approximation space for function approximation as a special case of the granule approximation space introduced in Definition 2 with the non standard rough inclusion introduced in this section.

6 Concept Approximation

In this section we consider the problem of approximation of concepts over a universe U^∞ (concepts that are subsets of U^∞). We assume that the concepts are perceived only through some subsets of U^∞, called samples. This is a typical situation in the machine learning, pattern recognition, or data mining approaches [12]. In this section we explain the rough set approach to induction of concept approximations.

Let $U \subseteq U^\infty$ be a finite sample. By Π_U we denote a perception function from $P(U^\infty)$ into $P(U)$ defined by $\Pi_U(C) = C \cap U$ for any concept $C \subseteq U^\infty$. Let $AS = (U, I, \nu)$ be an approximation space over the sample U.[3] The problem we consider is how to extend the approximations of $\Pi_U(C)$ defined by AS to approximation of C over U^∞. We show that the problem can be described as searching for an extension $AS_C = (U^\infty, I_C, \nu_C)$ of the approximation space AS, relevant for approximation of C. This requires to show how to extend the inclusion function ν from U to relevant subsets of U^∞ that are suitable for the approximation of C. Observe (cf. Definition 5) that for the approximation of C it is enough to induce the necessary values of the inclusion function ν_C without knowing the exact value of $I_C(x) \subseteq U^\infty$ for $x \in U^\infty$.

Let AS be a given approximation space for $\Pi_U(C)$ and let us consider a language L in which the neighbourhood $I(x) \subseteq U$ is expressible by a formula $patt(x)$, for any $x \in U$. It means that $I(x) = \|patt(x)\|_U \subseteq U$, where $\|patt(x)\|_U$ denotes the meaning of $patt(x)$ restricted to the sample U. In case of rule based classifiers patterns of the form $patt(x)$ are defined by feature value vectors.

We assume that for any new object $x \in U^\infty \setminus U$ we can obtain (e.g., as a result of sensor measurement) a pattern $patt(x) \in L$ with semantics $\|patt(x)\|_{U^\infty} \subseteq U^\infty$. However, the relationships between information granules over U^∞ like sets: $\|patt(x)\|_{U^\infty}$ and $\|patt(y)\|_{U^\infty}$, for different $x, y \in U^\infty$ (or between $\|patt(x)\|_{U^\infty}$ and $y \in U^\infty$), are, in general, known only if they can be expressed by relationships between the restrictions of these sets to the sample U, i.e., between sets $\Pi_U(\|patt(x)\|_{U^\infty})$ and $\Pi_U(\|patt(y)\|_{U^\infty})$.

The set of patterns $\{patt(x) : x \in U\}$ is usually not relevant for approximation of the concept $C \subseteq U^\infty$. Such patterns are too specific or not enough general, and directly can be applied only to a very limited number of new objects. However, by using some generalisation strategies, one can search, in a family of patterns definable from $\{patt(x) : x \in U\}$ in L, for such new patterns that are relevant for approximation of concepts over U^∞. Let us consider a subset $PATTERNS(AS, L, C) \subseteq L$ chosen as a set of pattern candidates for relevant approximation of a given concept C. For example,

---

[3] For simplicity of reasoning, in this section we use standard definition of approximation spaces (Definition 4).

in case of rule based classifier one can search for such candidate patterns among sets definable by subsequences of feature value vectors corresponding to objects from the sample U. The set $PATTERNS(AS, L, C)$ can be selected by using some quality measures checked on meanings (semantics) of its elements restricted to the sample U (like the number of examples from the concept $\Pi_U(C)$ and its complement that support a given pattern). Then, on the basis of properties of sets definable by these patterns over U we induce approximate values of the inclusion function ν_C on subsets of U^∞ definable by any of such patterns and the concept C.

Next, we induce the value of ν_C on pairs (X, Y) where $X \subseteq U^\infty$ is definable by a pattern from $\{patt(x) : x \in U^\infty\}$ and $Y \subseteq U^\infty$ is definable by a pattern from $PATTERNS(AS, L, C)$.

Finally, for any object $x \in U^\infty \setminus U$ we induce the approximation of the degree $\nu_C(\|patt(x)\|_{U^\infty}, C)$ applying a conflict resolution strategy $Conflict\_res$ (a voting strategy, in case of rule based classifiers) to two families of degrees:

$$\{\nu_C(\|patt(x)\|_{U^\infty}, \|patt\|_{U^\infty}) : patt \in PATTERNS(AS, L, C)\}, \tag{21}$$

$$\{\nu_C(\|patt\|_{U^\infty}, C) : patt \in PATTERNS(AS, L, C)\}. \tag{22}$$

Values of the inclusion function for the remaining subsets of U^∞ can be chosen in any way – they do not have any impact on the approximations of C. Moreover, observe that for the approximation of C we do not need to know the exact values of uncertainty function I_C – it is enough to induce the values of the inclusion function ν_C. Observe that the defined extension ν_C of ν to some subsets of U^∞ makes it possible to define an approximation of the concept C in a new approximation space AS_C by using Definition 5.

In this way, the rough set approach to induction of concept approximations can be explained as a process of inducing a relevant approximation space.

The granule approximation space $\mathcal{AS} = (GS, G, Tr)$ modelling the described process of concept approximations under fixed: U^∞, $C \subseteq U^\infty$, sets of formulas (patterns) $\{patt(x) : x \in U\}$, $PATTERNS(AS, L, C)$, and their semantics $\| \cdot \|_{U^\infty}$ can be defined by

1. GS consisting of the following granules: $C \in P(U^\infty)$, the sample $U \subseteq U^\infty$, $C \cap U$, $U \setminus C$, sets $\|patt(x)\|_U$, defined by $patt(x)$ for any $x \in U$, and the rough inclusion $\nu = \nu_{SRI}$.
2. $G = \{C\}$.
3. The transition relation Tr extending GS to GS' and GS' to GS^*. $Gran(GS')$ is extended from $Gran(GS)$ by the following information granules: sets $\|patt(x)\|_{U^\infty}$, defined by $patt(x)$ for any $x \in U^\infty$, $\|patt\|_{U^\infty}$, for $patt \in PATTERNS(AS, L, C)$. The rough inclusion is extended using estimations described above. GS^* is constructed as follows:
   - $Gran(GS^*) = G \cup$ $\cup\{(x, \|patt(x)\|_{U^\infty}, \|patt\|_{U^\infty}) : x \in U^\infty \text{and} patt \in PATTERNS(AS, L, C)\}$
   - The rough inclusion ν is extended by:
   $$\nu((x, X, Y), C) = Conflict\_res(\{\nu_C(X, Y) : Y \in \mathcal{Y}\}, \{\nu_C(Y, C) : Y \in \mathcal{Y}\}) \tag{23}$$
   where $X, Y \subseteq U^\infty$, $\mathcal{Y} \subseteq P(U^\infty)$ are sets and the family of sets on which values of ν_C have been estimated in (21) and (22);

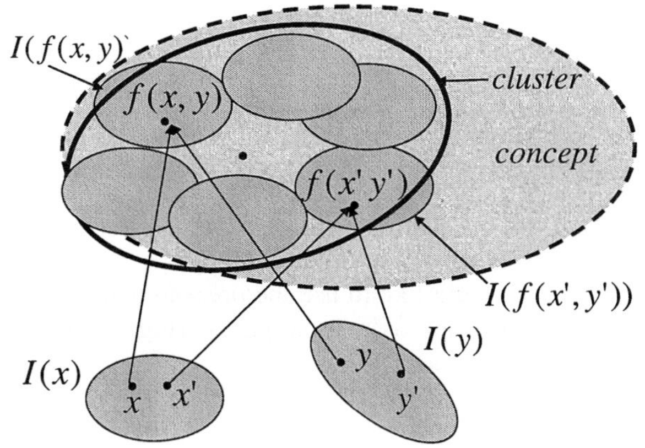

Fig. 2. Relational structure granulation

– The “make granule" operation $\oplus$ satisfies the following constraint:

$$\oplus\{(x, \cdot, \cdot) : x \in Z\} = Z \text{ for any } Z \subseteq C^{\infty}.$$

7 Relational Structure Granulation

In this section we discuss an important role that the relational structure granulation [5], [8] plays in searching for relevant patterns in approximate reasoning, e.g., in searching for relevant approximation patterns (see Section 6 and Figure 2). For any object there is defined a neighbourhood specified by the value of uncertainty function from an approximation space (see Definition 4). From these neighbourhoods some other, more relevant ones (e.g., for the considered concept approximation), should be found. Such neighbourhoods can be extracted by searching the space of neighbourhoods generated from values of uncertainty function by applying some operations to them like generalisation operations, set theoretical operations (union, intersection), clustering and operations on neighbourhoods defined by functions and relations in an underlying relational structure[4]. Figure 2 illustrates an exemplary scheme of searching for neighbourhoods (patterns, clusters) relevant for concept approximation. In the example f denotes a function with two arguments from the underlying relational structure. Due to the uncertainty, we cannot perceive objects exactly but only by using available neighbourhoods defined by the uncertainty function from an approximation space. Hence, instead of the value $f(x, y)$ for a given pair of objects (x, y) one should consider a family of neighbourhoods $\mathcal{F} = \{I(f(x', y')) : (x', y') \in I(x) \times I(y)\}$. From this family $\mathcal{F}$ a subfamily of neighbourhoods, $\mathcal{F}'$, can be chosen that consists of neighbourhoods with some properties relevant for approximation. Next, such subfamily $\mathcal{F}'$ can be generalised to clusters that are relevant for concept approximation, i.e., clusters sufficiently included into the approximated concept (see Figure 2). The inclusion degrees can be measured by granulation of the inclusion function from the relational structure.

[4] Relations from such structure may define relations between objects or their parts.

8 Conclusions

We have discussed problems of approximation space modelling for concept approximation. We also presented consequences for concept approximation of the assumption that information granules involved in concept approximations are perceived by partial information about them. Illustrative examples of approximation spaces were included. We also emphasised the role of relational structure granulation in searching for relevant approximation spaces for concept approximations.

In our further work we would like to use the presented approach for modelling of searching processes for relevant approximation spaces using data and domain knowledge represented, e.g., in natural language.

Acknowledgements

The research has been supported by the grant 3T11C00226 from Ministry of Scientific Research and Information Technology of the Republic of Poland.

References

1. Pawlak, Z.: Rough Sets: Theoretical Aspects of Reasoning about Data. Volume 9 of System Theory, Knowledge Engineering and Problem Solving. Kluwer Academic Publishers, Dordrecht, The Netherlands (1991)
2. Skowron, A., Stepaniuk, J.: Tolerance approximation spaces. Fundamenta Informaticae **27** (1996) 245–253
3. Polkowski, L., Skowron, A.: Rough mereology: A new paradigm for approximate reasoning. International Journal of Approximate Reasoning **15** (1996) 333–365
4. Polkowski, L., Skowron, A.: Towards adaptive calculus of granules. In Zadeh, L.A., Kacprzyk, J., eds.: Computing with Words in Information/Intelligent Systems, Heidelberg, Germany, Physica-Verlag (1999) 201–227
5. Skowron, A., Stepaniuk, J.: Information granules and rough-neural computing. In [10] 43–84
6. Lin, T.Y.: The discovery, analysis and representation of data dependencies in databases. In Polkowski, L., Skowron, A., eds.: Rough Sets in Knowledge Discovery 1: Methodology and Applications. Volume 18 of Studies in Fuzziness and Soft Computing. Physica-Verlag, Heidelberg, Germany (1998) 107–121
7. Ziarko, W.: Variable precision rough set model. Journal of Computer and System Sciences **46** (1993) 39–59
8. Peters, J.F., Skowron, A., Synak, P., Ramanna, S.: Rough sets and information granulation. In Bilgic, T., Baets, D., Kaynak, O., eds.: Tenth International Fuzzy Systems Association World Congress IFSA, Istanbul, Turkey, June 30-July 2. Volume 2715 of Lecture Notes in Artificial Intelligence. Springer-Verlag, Heidelberg, Germany (2003) 370–377
9. Skowron, A.: Toward intelligent systems: Calculi of information granules. Bulletin of the International Rough Set Society **5** (2001) 9–30
10. Pal, S.K., Polkowski, L., Skowron, A., eds.: Rough-Neural Computing: Techniques for Computing with Words. Cognitive Technologies. Springer-Verlag, Heidelberg, Germany (2003)
11. Zadeh, L.A.: A new direction in AI: Toward a computational theory of perceptions. AI Magazine **22** (2001) 73–84
12. Kloesgen, W., Żytkow, J., eds.: Handbook of Knowledge Discovery and Data Mining. Oxford University Press, Oxford (2002)

Granular Language and Its Applications in Problem Solving

Qing Liu

Department of Computer Science, Nanchang University
Nanchang 330029, China

Abstract. Problem solving in AI points out that a global problem is decomposed into several locals, until into elementary sub-problems solved directly. Subsequently, the solutions of various sub-problems are amalgamated into an answer of the global problem. The solving problem in practice is represented by a logical formula, and then the formula is decomposed into several sub-formulas, until into propositions or predicates. The solutions of these sub-formulas are amalgamated into an answer of the global formula. If the formula is described as a granulation, then it will be collapsed into several sub-granules. So, the collapsing algorithm and rules of amalgamating will be defined. In order to realizing the idea in above, a granular language and its calculus will be discussed.

Keywords: Decompose, Amalgamation, Granules, Problem solving, Granular Language.

1 Introduction

In 1985,Professor Hobbs in Stanford university published a paper with the title "Granularity" [1] at the International Joint conference on Artificial Intelligence, Los Angeles in USA. At present, information granules are defined by partial relation or partial lattice in many literatures. Such as, different granularities are defined by different partial relation and different partial lattice. Hobbs introduces the decomposing of granulation and amalgamating of granules [1]. The concepts will be applied in problem solving of AI. Hence, we propose a granular language, and construct its calculus laws.

2 Granular Language

Let $IS = (U, A)$ be an information system [2],where U is a set of all objects; A is a set of attributes. (a, v) or a_v is defined as a description on IS,where $a \in A$ is an attribute, v is a value of attribute a with respect to object $x \in U$. That is, $a(x) = v$, thus (a, v) or a_v is thought as an atomic formula in Rough Logic. The meaning set of a_v is defined as follows:

$$m(a_v) = \{x \in U : x \mid\approx_{IS} a_v\}$$

Order binary pair $(a_v, m(a_v))$ is called an elementary granule [3].

S. Tsumoto et al. (Eds.): RSCTC 2004, LNAI 3066, pp. 127–132, 2004.

If φ is the combination of form a_v or (a, v) with respect to the usual logical connectives: $\sim$ (negative), $\vee$ (disjunctive), $\wedge$(conjunctive), $\rightarrow$ (implication) and $\leftrightarrow$ (equivalent), then $(\varphi, m(\varphi))$ is the logical combination of form $(a_v, m(a_v))$ with respect to granular connectives$\sim$(negative), $\oplus$(disjunctive), $\otimes$(conjunctive), $\uplus$(implication) and $\odot$(equivalent). Hence, $(\varphi, m(\varphi))$ is called a combination granulation of granules.

Definition 1 (syntax). Let us define the granular language consisted of elementary granules on IS, their syntax is defined as follows [4]:
(1) The descriptor of form (a, v) or a_v is an atom in rough logic, thus $((a, v), m((a, v)))$ is defined as an atom formula in granular language;
(2) $B \subseteq A$ is a subset of attributes. The structure of form $(\varphi, m(\varphi))$ is a formula in the granular language, where φ is the logical combination of form (a, v) or a_v, $a \in B$;
(3) If $(\varphi, m(\varphi))$ and $(\psi, m(\psi))$ are formulas in the granular language, then $((\sim \varphi, m(\sim \varphi)), (\varphi \vee \psi, m(\varphi \vee \psi))), (\varphi \wedge \psi, m(\varphi \wedge \psi))$ are also granular formulas in the language;
(4) The formulas defined via finite quotation (1)-(3) are considered in the granular language.

Truth value of a formula in GL (Granular Language) is defined by the means of model and valuation symbols. So, satisfiability of G-formula expresses that the formula taking true or rough true in the model.

Definition 2 (semantics). The semantics of G-formula is to assign values to the constants, variables, functions and predicates occurring in G-formula [5]:
(1) Each constant symbol in formula $G - \varphi$, c is interpreted as an entity e on U. That is, $e \in U$, having $T_{I_G u_G}(G - \varphi) = I_G(c) = e$;
(2) Each individual variable in $G - \varphi$, x is assigned an entity e' on U. That is, $e' \in U$, having $T_{I_G u_G}(G - \varphi) = u_G(x) = e'$;
(3) Each n-tuple function symbol in $G - \varphi$, f is interpreted as a mapping in IS, f: $U^n \rightarrow U$;
(4) Each n-tuple predicate symbol in $G - \varphi$, p is interpreted as an attribute a on A, it is a relation R: $U^n \rightarrow [\xi_*, \xi^*] \subseteq [0, 1]$, where ξ_* and ξ^* is the qualities of lower and upper approximations of domain defined $B \subseteq A$ with respect to R respectively.

Where I_G is a G-interpretation on IS, u_G is an evaluation to variable in I_G, $T_{I_G u_G}(G - \varphi)$ is a united assignment symbol. Let the model of satisfiability for G-formula in GL_{IS} be a five-tuple:

$$M = (U, A, I_G, VAL, m).$$

Where U, A is same as above. The attribute subset $B \subseteq A$ is an indiscernibility relation on U; $I_G = \{I_G^1, \ldots I_G^h\}$ is the set of all interpretation on U; $VAL = \{u_G^1, \ldots, u_G^t\}$ is the set of all evaluation symbols on U; u_G is to assign an entity on U to individual variable; m assigns a subset on U to G-formula φ or sub-formulas of φ or clause of φ. It is lower satisfiable, upper satisfiable and satisfiable for interpretation $I_G \in IG$ and evaluation $u_G \in VAL$, denoted by $M, u_G \models_{IS-L\varphi} (\varphi, m(\varphi))$, $M, u_G \models_{IS-H\varphi} (\varphi, m(\varphi))$ and $M, u_G \models_{IS-m(\varphi)} (\varphi, m(\varphi))$ respectively.

For convenience, L and H is the rough lower (B_*) and upper(B^*) approximate operators of indiscernibility relation $B \subseteq A$ respectively [6].

Proposition 1 (satisfibilities)
(1) $M, u_G \models_{IS-L_{a_v}} (a_v, m(a_v))$ iff $m(a_v) = \{x \in U : u_G(x) \in L_{a_v} \wedge x \models_{IS} a_v\} \neq \emptyset$;
$M, u_G \models_{IS-H_{a_v}} (a_v, m(a_v))$ iff $m(a_v) = \{x \in U : u_G(x) \in H_{a_v} \wedge x \models_{IS} a_v\} \neq \emptyset$;
$M, u_G \models_{IS-m(a_v)} (a_v, m(a_v))$ iff $m(a_v) = \{x \in U : u_G(x) \in (m(a_v)) \wedge x \models_{IS} a_v\} \neq \emptyset$;
where $v \in V$ is the values of attributes on IS;
(2) $M, u_G \models_{IS-L_\varphi} (\varphi, m(\varphi))$ iff $m(\varphi) \neq \emptyset$ on L_φ;
$M, u_G \models_{IS-H_\varphi} (\varphi, m(\varphi))$ iff $m(\varphi) \neq \emptyset$ on H_φ;
$M, u_G \models_{IS-m(\varphi)} (\varphi, m(\varphi))$ iff $m(\varphi) \neq \emptyset$;
(3) $M, u_G \models_{IS-L_{\varphi\wedge\psi}} (\varphi \wedge \psi, m(\varphi \wedge \psi))$ iff $m(\varphi \wedge \psi) \neq \emptyset$ on $L_{\varphi\wedge\psi}$;
$M, u_G \models_{IS-H_{\varphi\wedge\psi}} (\varphi \wedge \psi, m(\varphi \wedge \psi))$ iff $m(\varphi \wedge \psi) \neq \emptyset$ on $H_{\varphi\wedge\psi}$;
$M, u_G \models_{IS-m(\varphi\wedge\psi)} (\varphi \wedge \psi, m(\varphi \wedge \psi))$ iff $m(\varphi \wedge \psi) \neq \emptyset$;
(4) $M, u_G \models_{IS-L_{\varphi\vee\psi}} (\varphi \vee \psi, m(\varphi \vee \psi))$ iff $m(\varphi \vee \psi) \neq \emptyset$ on $L_{\varphi\vee\psi}$;
$M, u_G \models_{IS-H_{\varphi\vee\psi}} (\varphi \vee \psi, m(\varphi \vee \psi))$ iff $m(\varphi \vee \psi) \neq \emptyset$ on $H_{\varphi\vee\psi}$;
$M, u_G \models_{IS-m(\varphi\vee\psi)} (\varphi \vee \psi, m(\varphi \vee \psi))$ iff $m(\varphi \vee \psi) \neq \emptyset$;
(5) $M, u_G \models_{IS-L_{\sim\varphi}} (\sim \varphi, \sim m(\varphi))$ iff $\sim m(\varphi) \neq \emptyset$ on $L_{\sim\varphi}$;
$M, u_G \models_{IS-H_{\sim\varphi}} (\sim \varphi, \sim m(\varphi))$ iff $\sim m(\varphi) \neq \emptyset$ on $H_{\sim\varphi}$;
$M, u_G \models_{IS-m(\sim\varphi)} (\sim \varphi, \sim m(\varphi))$ iff $\sim m(\varphi) \neq \emptyset$;
(6) $M, u_G \models_{IS-L_\varphi} ((\forall x)\varphi(x), m(\varphi))$ iff $\forall x \in VAR = \{x_1, \ldots, x_n, \ldots\}$, the set of variables, having entity $e \in U$, that $u_G(x) = e$ and $\models_{IS-L_{\varphi(e)}\varphi(e)}$;
$M, u_G \models_{IS-H_\varphi} ((\forall x)\varphi(x), m(\varphi))$ iff $\forall x \in VAR$, having $e \in U$, that $u_G(x) = e$ and $\models_{IS-H_{\varphi(e)}} \varphi(e)$;
$M, u_G \models_{IS-m(\varphi)} ((\forall x)\varphi(x), m(\varphi))$ iff $\forall x \in VAR$, having $e \in U$, that $u_G(x) = e$ and $\models_{IS-m(\varphi(e))} \varphi(e)$;
Hence the meaning of (6) is that $\varphi(e)$ is satisfiable for each entity e. Generally, U on $IS = (U, A)$ is required to be a non-empty and finite set. So, meaning of (6) may be written by following (6').
(6') $M, u_G \models_{IS-L_\varphi} ((\forall x)\varphi(x), m(\varphi))$ iff $m(\varphi(e_1) \wedge \ldots \wedge \varphi(e_n)) \neq \emptyset$ on L_φ, for each $e_i \in U$, and having $u_G(x_i) = e_i \in L_\varphi$ for each interpretation $I_G \in IG$ and evaluation $u_G \in VAL$;
$M, u_G \models_{IS-H_\varphi} ((\forall x)\varphi(x), m(\varphi))$ iff $m(\varphi(e_1) \wedge \ldots \wedge \varphi(e_n)) \neq \emptyset$ on H_φ, for each $e_i \in U$, and having $u_G(x_i) = e_i \in H_\varphi$ for each interpretation $I_G \in IG$ and evaluation $u_G \in VAL$;
$M, u_G \models_{IS-m(\varphi)} ((\forall x)\varphi(x), m(\varphi))$ iff $m(\varphi(e_1) \wedge \ldots \wedge \varphi(e_n)) \neq \emptyset$, for each $e_i \in U$, and having $u_G(x_i) = e_i \in m(\varphi)$ for each interpretation $I_G \in IG$, $u_G \in VAL$.

Definition 3 (Truth). For $\forall \varphi \in RL_{IS}$, $T_{I_G u_G}(\varphi, m(\varphi)) = Card(m(\varphi))/Card(U)$ denotes the ratio for number of elements on U satisfied φ to total of objects on U, the ratio is called truth value of G-formula in granular language.

Proposition 2 (Properties of Granular Language)
(1) $|\sim (\varphi \to \psi, m(\varphi \to \psi))$ is derivable iff $|\sim \varphi \to \psi$ is derivable and $m(\varphi) \subseteq m(\psi)$ is held;
(2) $\forall \varphi, \psi \in RL_{IS}$, then
a) $m(a_v) = \{x \in U : a(x) = v \in V\}$, where V is the set of attribute values, m is a functional symbol of G-formula semantics or interpretation domain function of common logical formulas;
b) $(\sim \varphi, m(\sim \varphi)) = (\sim \varphi, U - (\varphi, m(\varphi))$;
c) $(\varphi \vee \psi, m(\varphi \vee \psi)) = (\varphi, m(\varphi)) \oplus (\psi, m(\psi))$;
d) $(\varphi \wedge \psi, m(\varphi \wedge \psi)) = (\varphi, m(\varphi)) \otimes (\psi, m(\psi))$;
e) $((\forall x)\varphi(x), m(\varphi)) = (\varphi(e_1) \wedge \ldots \wedge \varphi(e_n), m(\varphi(e_1) \wedge \ldots \wedge \varphi(e_n)))$
$= (\varphi(e_1), m(\varphi(e_1))) \otimes \ldots \otimes (\varphi(e_n), m(\varphi(e_n)))$.
Assuming here that universe U of all objects is finite. That is, for $\forall x \in VAR$, $u_G \in VAL$, there exists an entity $e_i \in U$, such that $u_G(x) = e_i$, $i = 1, \ldots, n$.
(3) Let $G = ((\varphi, m(\varphi)), (\psi, m(\psi)))$ and $G' = ((\varphi', m(\varphi')), (\psi', m(\psi')))$ be two granulations. They are close in degree at least p on IS, written by $Cl_p(G, G')$, then having
a) $Cl_p(m(\varphi), m(\varphi'))$;
b) $Cl_p(m(\psi) - m(\varphi), m(\psi') - m(\varphi'))$;
c) $Cl_p(U - m(\varphi), U - m(\varphi'))$.
(4) If $G = ((\varphi, m(\varphi)), (\psi, m(\psi)))$ and $G' = ((\varphi', m(\varphi')), (\psi', m(\psi')))$ are the granulations defined by decision rules, and $Cl_p((\varphi, m(\varphi)), (\varphi', m(\varphi')))$, then having $Cl_p((\psi, m(\psi)), (\psi', m(\psi')))$.

3 Applications of Granules for Solving-Problem in AI

The problem solving in AI is an idea of collapsing more complex ones into simple sub-problems, the steps for problem solving based on granular computing is defined as follows:

(1) Gather a group data connecting with the goal of solving problem from situation;
(2) The group data is constructed into a rough logical formula φ, and then the global granulation $(\varphi, m(\varphi))$ corresponding with φ is constructed;
(3) Rough logical formula φ is equivalently transformed into following Skolem clause form CNF:
$$C_1 \wedge C_2 \wedge \ldots \wedge C_n$$
Where each $C_i = L_{i_1} \vee \ldots \vee L_{i_m}$ is a disjunction of literals L_{i_j}.
(4) Granule of C_i is defined as $(C_i, m(C_i))$, where
$$m(C_i) = \{x \in U : x \mid\approx C_i\}$$
The symbol $|\approx$ is the satisfiability for rough logical formulas.
(5) The granulation corresponding to clause form $C_1 \wedge C_2 \wedge \ldots \wedge C_n$ is written by $(C_1 \wedge C_2 \wedge \ldots \wedge C_n, m(C_1) \cap m(C_2) \ldots \cap m(C_n))$
(6) It may prove that following equivalent form is true:
$$(\varphi, m(\varphi)) \equiv \textstyle\prod_{i=1}^{n}(C_i, m(C_i)) \equiv$$
$$(C_1 \wedge C_2 \wedge \ldots \wedge C_n, m(C_1) \cap m(C_2) \ldots \cap m(C_n))$$

Table 1. Decision Table 1 $DT = (U, A \cup \{d\})$

N \ A	a	b	c	d
1	n(5)	n(4)	n(0)	n(1)
2	n(3)	n(4)	n(0)	n(0)
3	n(3)	n(4)	n(0)	n(2)
4	n(0)	n(2)	n(0)	n(1)
5	n(3)	n(2)	n(1)	n(2)
6	n(5)	n(2)	n(0)	n(1)

Example 1. Let $a_{n(3)} \to c_{n(0)} \vee c_{n(1)}$ be a rough logical formula on information system IS in above. Granular formula corresponding with the formula is thought to be $(a_{n(3)} \to c_{n(0)} \vee c_{n(1)}, m(a_{n(3)} \to c_{n(0)} \vee c_{n(1)}))$. We may compute the truth value of the G-formula by the means of decomposing granulation and amalgamating granules.

Computing: The clause form of the formula, $\sim a_{n(3)} \vee c_{n(0)} \vee c_{n(1)}$ is computed. The meaning set of the clause, $m(\sim a_{n(3)}) \cup m(c_{n(0)}) \cup m(c_{n(1)}) = \{1,4,5\} \cup \{1,2,3,4,6\} \cup \{5\} = \{1,2,3,4,5,6\}$. So, The truth value of the G-formula,

$$T_{IGUG}(a_{n(3)} \to c_{n(0)} \vee c_{n(1)}, m(a_{n(3)} \to c_{n(0)} \vee c_{n(1)})) = Card(m(a_{n(3)} \to c_{n(0)} \vee c_{n(1)}))/m(U) = 1.$$

Hence, the G-formula is true in the information system IS.

Example 2. Let $IS = (U, A)$ be our developing systems of diagnosis and treating in medicine. Where U is a set of the patients; A is a set of symptoms (attributes) for the patients. The systems possess the functions testing blood viscosity concentration for patients [7,8]. Now the data set gathered in clinic for the patient, denoted by $P = \{Wang, Male, 65, 3.5\}$, where Wang is name, Male is sex, 65 is age, and 3.5 is blood viscosity concentration of testing a patient via testing instrument.

We represent the solving problem for waiting by rough logical formula $\varphi = name_{Wang} \wedge Sex_{male} \wedge Age_{65} \wedge TV_{3.5}$. Now we collapse this formula into several sub-formulas or predicates and to solve these sub-formulas or predicates according to the algorithm given in the system [8],that is, solving the predicates $P_1 = name_{Wang}$, $P_2 = Sex_{male}$, $P_3 = Age_{65}$ and $P_4 = TV_{3.5}$. The granules corresponding with the predicates are constructed respectively. Namely, the granules are $G_1 = (P_1, m(P_1))$, $G_2 = (P_2, m(P_2))$, $G_3 = (P_3, m(P_3))$ and $G_4 = (P_4, m(P_4))$. The global granulation corresponding to φ is $G = (\varphi, m(\varphi))$. So $G = G_1 \otimes G_2 \otimes G_3 \otimes G_4$. The steps of solving procedure are listed [7,8]. Finally, the patient is diagnosticated as Level=-5, that is, the level of blood viscosity concentration is -5. To belong to blood lower viscosity syndrome (BLVS), this is an answer of the global granulation $G = (\varphi, m(\varphi))$ corresponding to φ [7,8].

4 Conclusion

This paper proposes a granular language, in brief written by GL. The language formulas are an ordered binary pair; The language is defined on information system $IS = (U, A)$. So the assignment to individual variables in the formulas is an entity on U. The study of GL opens a new path for applications of classical logic. Which provides also a new idea for problem solving in AI. GL is a new generalization of Rough Logic. Truth concept and its operations of the language are different from classical logic and the non-standard logic. Further research will be to study temporal granular language, which may be used to describe the irregular knowledge. The results of the research will pioneer a new path for wider applications of classical logic.

Acknowledgement

This study is supported by the Natural Science Foundation of China (NSFC-#60173054) and the Natural Science Foundation of Jiangxi province (JXPNSF-0311101) in China.

References

1. J.R. Hobbs, Granularity, Proc.of IJCAI, Los Angeles, 1985.
2. Z. Pawlak, Rough Set-Theoretical Aspects of Reasoning about Data, Kluwer Academic Publishers, Dordrecht, 1991.
3. A. Skowron, J. Stepaniuk. and James. F. Peters, Extracting Patterns Using Information Granules, Proceedings of RSTGC2001,Bulletin of International Rough Set Society Vol.5, No.1/2, May 20-22,2001.
4. Qing Liu and Qun Liu, Approximate Reasoning Based on Granular Computing in Granular Logic, The Proceedings of ICMLS2002, Nov. 4-6, 2002, by IEEE.
5. Q. Liu and Z.H. Huang, G-Logic and its Resolution Reasoning, Chinese Journal of Computer (in Chinese), accepted.
6. T.Y. Lin and Q. Liu, First order Rough Logic I: Approximate Reasoning via Rough Sets, Fundamenta Informaticae, Vol.27,No.2-3, August 1996.
7. Q. Liu, F. Jiang and D.Y. Deng, Design and Implement for the Diagnosis Software of Blood Viscosity Syndrome Based on Hemorheology Based on GrC., LNAI 2639, The Proceedings of 9th RSFDGrC2003, Oct.17-22, 2003, by Springer.
8. Q. Liu, Granules and Reasoning Based on Granular Computing, LNAI 2718, Proceedings of 16th IEA/AIE 2003, Uk, June 2003, by Springer.

Belief Reasoning, Revision and Fusion by Matrix Algebra

Churn-Jung Liau

Institute of Information Science
Academia Sinica, Taipei, Taiwan
liaucj@iis.sinica.edu.tw

Abstract. Representation of belief states is an important issue for knowledge based systems. In this paper, we develop a matrix representation for ordered belief states and show that belief reasoning, revision and fusion can all be interpreted as operations of matrix algebra. Thus, the matrix representation can serve as the basis of algebraic semantics for belief logic.

Keywords: Belief states, matrix algebra, belief reasoning, belief revision, belief fusion, multi-agent systems.

1 Introduction

Knowledge representation is crucially important to knowledge-based applications. While we expect proper knowledge to be true, the term "knowledge" used in knowledge-based systems usually refers to information and belief in a broad sense. Therefore, knowledge can be fallible information in such applications. Consequently, the representation of belief states plays a key role in knowledge-based systems.

In many domains, such as epistemic reasoning[10, 11], belief revision[1, 14, 15] and belief fusion[2, 6, 16, 18–21, 23, 27], a knowledge base or a belief base consists of a set of sentences in a logical language. Since a belief base can be identified with the set of models satisfying it, an agent's belief state is usually represented as a subset of possible worlds.

However, some more finely tuned representations have been proposed, such as total pre-orders over the set of possible worlds [4, 7, 17, 24], ordinal conditional functions [5, 26, 28], possibility distributions[3, 8, 9], belief functions[25], and pedigreed belief states[12, 13]. One of the most popular representation formalisms is an ordering over the set of possible worlds.

A natural representation of an ordering can be achieved by using a Boolean matrix, if the set of possible worlds is finite. In this paper, we adopt such a representation and show that belief reasoning, revision and fusion can be interpreted in matrix algebra. Thus, the matrix representation can serve as the basis of algebraic semantics for belief logic.

S. Tsumoto et al. (Eds.): RSCTC 2004, LNAI 3066, pp. 133–142, 2004.

2 Matrix Representation of Belief States

In this paper, A, B and$M$ (possibly with subscripts) denote real-valued matrices. If M is a $n \times m$ matrix, then for $0 \le i \le n-1$ and $0 \le j \le m-1$, $M(i,j), M(i,\cdot)$ and $M(\cdot,j)$ denote the element in the (i,j) entry, the i-th row vector and the j-th column vector of the matrix respectively. Usually, we also write $M(i)$ and $M(j)$ for the row vector and the column vector if they are clear from the context. A *Boolean matrix* is a real-valued matrix whose elements all belong to the set $\{0,1\}$. Also, let I, $\mathbf{1}$ and $\mathbf{0}$ denote the unit square matrix, complete matrix and zero matrix respectively. In other words,I, $\mathbf{1}$ and $\mathbf{0}$ are Boolean matrices such that $I(i,j) = 1$ iff $i = j$, $\mathbf{1}(i,j) = 1$ and $\mathbf{0}(i,j) = 0$ for all i and j. The dimensions (i.e., numbers of rows and columns) of I, $\mathbf{1}$ and $\mathbf{0}$ depend on the context. If necessary, we will write $I_{n\times m}$, $\mathbf{1}_{n\times m}$, or $\mathbf{0}_{n\times m}$ to indicate their dimensions. Furthermore, we will identify a 1×1 matrix with its element.

The following operations of matrix algebra are extensively used in this paper.

Definition 1. *Let A and B be two matrices and r is a real number. The following binary operations can be defined when A and B have the same dimensions:*

1. *Max:* $(A \vee B)(i,j) = \max(A(i,j), B(i,j))$,
2. *Min:* $(A \wedge B)(i,j) = \min(A(i,j), B(i,j))$,
3. *Sum:* $(A + B)(i,j) = A(i,j) + B(i,j)$,
4. *Difference:* $(A - B)(i,j) = A(i,j) - B(i,j)$,
5. *Scalar product:* $(r \cdot A)(i,j) = r \cdot A(i,j)$.

When the column number of A is equal to the row number of B, another binary operation, the (Boolean) product, can be defined as:

$$(A \cdot B)(i,j) = \max_{0 \le k \le n-1} \min(A(i,k), B(k,j))$$

where n is the column number of A. Let $m \ge 0$, then A^m is inductively defined as $A^{m-1} \cdot A$ where $A^0 = I$. Furthermore, there are also several unary operations:

1. *Transposition:* $A^t(i,j) = A(j,i)$,
2. *Transitive closure:* $A^+ = \bigvee_{m \ge 1} A^m$
3. *Indicator:* $A^d(i,j) = \begin{cases} 1, \text{ if } A(i,j) > 0 \text{ and } A(i,j) \ge A(j,i), \\ 0, \text{ otherwise.} \end{cases}$

■

If $\Phi_0 = \{p, q, \cdots\}$ is a finite set of atomic propositions and $\mathcal{L}$ is the propositional language based on Φ_0, then a possible world is a truth assignment $w : \Phi_0 \to \{0,1\}$. As usual, the domain of w can be extended to the set of all well-formed formulas (wffs) in $\mathcal{L}$. If $\mathcal{W} = \{w_0, w_1, \cdots, w_{n-1}\}$ denotes the set of all possible worlds, then a *belief state* is defined as an $n \times n$ Boolean matrix B. Intuitively, a belief state B defines an associated ordering relation $\prec_B$ over $\mathcal{W}$ such that $B(i,j) = 1$ iff $w_j \prec_B w_i$. For each wff φ, the *characteristic matrix* of φ is the $n \times n$ Boolean matrix M_φ defined by

$$M_\varphi(i,j) = \begin{cases} 1, \text{ if } i = j \text{ and } w_i(\varphi) = 1, \\ 0, \text{ otherwise.} \end{cases}$$

Note that by this definition, we have the equations:

$$M_{\varphi\vee\psi} = M_\varphi \vee M_\psi$$

$$M_{\varphi\wedge\psi} = M_\varphi \wedge M_\psi$$

$$M_{\neg\varphi} = I - M_\varphi$$

where I is the $n \times n$ unit matrix.

3 Belief Reasoning, Revision and Fusion

Given the matrix representation of belief states and wffs, we can implement the tasks of belief reasoning, revision and fusion using matrix algebra.

3.1 Belief Reasoning

Definition 2. *Given a belief state B and two wffs φ and ψ, we say that φ preferentially implies ψ under B, denoted by $\varphi \models_B \psi$, iff*

$$(\mathbf{1}_{1\times n} - \mathbf{1}_{1\times n} \cdot M_\psi) \cdot [\mathbf{1}_{n\times 1} - (M_\varphi \cdot B \cdot M_\varphi \vee M_{\neg\varphi}) \cdot \mathbf{1}_{n\times 1}] = 0,$$

where we assume $\cdot$ has precedence over other binary operations. ■

The intuition of the above definition can be seen by interpreting a belief state as an ordering over possible worlds. Let $\prec$ be a binary relation over $\mathcal{W}$ and $X \subseteq \mathcal{W}$, then the *choice set*[12] of X with respect to $\prec$ is

$$C(X, \prec) = \{w \in X : \nexists w' \in X, w' \prec w\}.$$

Let the *truth set* of a wff φ be defined as $|\varphi| = \{w \in \mathcal{W} : w(\varphi) = 1\}$, then the set of minimal models of φ with respect to $\prec$, denoted by $Min(\varphi, \prec)$, is equal to $C(|\varphi|, \prec)$. The following proposition states the relationship between the preferential implication and minimal model belief reasoning.

Proposition 1. *Let B be a belief state and $\prec_B$ be its associated ordering, then for any wffs φ and ψ*

$$\varphi \models_B \psi \text{ iff } Min(\varphi, \prec_B) \subseteq |\psi|.$$

Proof: Let

$$A_1 = M_\varphi \cdot B \cdot M_\varphi \vee M_{\neg\varphi},$$

$$A_2 = \mathbf{1}_{n\times 1} - A_1 \cdot \mathbf{1}_{n\times 1},$$

$$A_3 = \mathbf{1}_{1\times n} - \mathbf{1}_{1\times n} \cdot M_\psi$$

then $A_1(i, j) = 1$ iff one of the following two conditions holds:

(i) $w_i \models \varphi$, $w_j \models \varphi$ and $w_j \prec_B w_i$, or
(ii)$i = j$ and $w_i \not\models \varphi$.

Thus, $\max_{0 \leq j \leq n-1} A(i,j) = 1$ iff $w_i \notin Min(\varphi, \prec_B)$. This results in $A_2(i,0) = 1$ iff $w_i \in Min(\varphi, \prec_B)$. On the other hand, $A_3(0,i) = 1$ iff $w_i \not\models \psi$. Therefore,

$$\begin{aligned} & Min(\varphi, \prec_B) \subseteq |\psi| \\ \Leftrightarrow & \nexists 0 \leq i \leq n-1,\ w_i \in Min(\varphi, \prec_B) \text{ and } w_i \not\models \psi \\ \Leftrightarrow & A_3 \cdot A_2 = \max_{0 \leq i \leq n-1} \min(A_3(1,i), A_2(i,1)) = 0 \\ \Leftrightarrow & \varphi \models_B \psi. \end{aligned}$$

■

Note that we do not impose any restriction on the matrix representation of belief states, so minimal models of a wff φ may not exist. Some reasonable restrictions have been proposed, such as transitivity and modularity[12]. However, our definition can still be used in the more restricted form of belief states.

3.2 Belief Revision

Definition 3. *Let B be a belief state and φ be a wff, then the revised state of B by φ is defined as*

$$B^\circ\varphi = [B \vee (M_{\neg\varphi} \cdot \mathbf{1} \wedge \mathbf{1} \cdot M_\varphi)] \wedge (M_{\neg\varphi} \cdot \mathbf{1} \vee \mathbf{1} \cdot M_\varphi),$$

where the dimension of $\mathbf{1}$ *is* $n \times n$. ■

This definition corresponds to a natural approach to revise an ordering over possible worlds with a wff. Let $\prec$ be an ordering relation over $\mathcal{W}$, then revising $\prec$ with a wff φ results in a new ordering $\prec' = Rev(\prec, \varphi)$ defined by

$$\begin{aligned} w \prec' w' \Leftrightarrow & \ w(\varphi) = 1 \text{ and } w'(\varphi) = 0, \text{ or} \\ & \ w(\varphi) = w'(\varphi) \text{ and } w \prec w'. \end{aligned}$$

According to this definition, after the revision, all possible worlds satisfying φ are preferred over those that do not, whereas the ordering between other worlds is kept intact. The following proposition shows the equivalence between these two definitions.

Proposition 2. *Let B be a belief state and φ be a wff, then*

$$Rev(\prec_B, \varphi) = \prec_{B^\circ\varphi}$$

where $\prec_B$ and $\prec_{B^\circ\varphi}$ are, respectively, the associated ordering of B and $B^\circ\varphi$.

Proof: First, we note that for all $0 \leq i \leq n-1$, $(M_{\neg\varphi} \cdot \mathbf{1})(i,j) = 1$ iff $w_j(\varphi) = 0$ and for all $0 \leq j \leq n-1$, $(\mathbf{1} \cdot M_{\neg\varphi})(i,j) = 1$ iff $w_i(\varphi) = 1$. Let $A_1 = B \vee (M_{\neg\varphi} \cdot \mathbf{1} \wedge \mathbf{1} \cdot M_\varphi)$ and $A_2 = M_{\neg\varphi} \cdot \mathbf{1} \vee \mathbf{1} \cdot M_\varphi$, then

$$A_1(i,j) = 1 \Leftrightarrow B(i,j) = 1 \vee (w_i(\varphi) = 0 \wedge w_j(\varphi) = 1)$$

and

$$A_2(i,j) = 1 \Leftrightarrow w_i(\varphi) = 0 \vee w_j(\varphi) = 1$$
$$\Leftrightarrow w_i(\varphi) = w_j(\varphi) \vee (w_i(\varphi) = 0 \wedge w_j(\varphi) = 1).$$

Therefore,

$$B^\circ\varphi(i,j) = 1 \Leftrightarrow A_1(i,j) = 1 \wedge A_2(i,j) = 1$$
$$\Leftrightarrow (w_i(\varphi) = 0 \wedge w_j(\varphi) = 1) \vee (w_i(\varphi) = w_j(\varphi) \wedge B(i,j) = 1).$$

This is equivalent to

$$w_j \prec_{B^\circ\varphi} w_i \Leftrightarrow (w_i(\varphi) = 0 \wedge w_j(\varphi) = 1) \vee (w_i(\varphi) = w_j(\varphi) \wedge w_j \prec_B w_i),$$

so we have $\prec_{B^\circ\varphi} = Rev(\prec_B, \varphi)$.

■

An alternative revision strategy, called *natural revision*, has been proposed in [4]. In that operator, only minimal possible worlds satisfying φ in the original belief state are preferred over others. Consequently, more possible worlds remain intact in natural revision. Formally, a natural revision of $\prec$ with a wff φ results in a new ordering $\prec' = NRev(\prec, \varphi)$ defined by[1]

1. if $w \in Min(\varphi, \prec)$, then $w \prec' v$ for any $v \notin Min(\varphi, \prec)$ and
2. if $v, w \notin Min(\varphi, \prec)$, then $w \prec' v$ iff $w \prec v$.

The natural revision operator can be modelled in the matrix representation by the following definition.

Definition 4. *Let B be a belief state and φ be a wff. Define the column vector (i.e. $n \times 1$ matrices)* $\mathbf{a}$ *and the row vector(i.e. $1 \times n$ matrices)* $\mathbf{b}$ *as follows:*

$$\mathbf{a} = (M_\varphi \cdot B \cdot M_\varphi \vee M_{\neg\varphi}) \cdot \mathbf{1}_{n\times 1}$$

$$\mathbf{b} = (\mathbf{1}_{n\times 1} - \mathbf{a})^t.$$

Then, the naturally revised state of B by φ is defined as

$$B^*\varphi = [B \vee (\mathbf{1}_{n\times 1} \cdot \mathbf{b})] \wedge (\mathbf{a} \cdot \mathbf{1}_{1\times n}).$$

■

Proposition 3. *Let B be a belief state and φ be a wff, then*

$$NRev(\prec_B, \varphi) = \prec_{B^*\varphi}$$

where $\prec_B$ and $\prec_{B*\alpha\varphi}$ are respectively the associated ordering of B and $B^*\varphi$.

[1] In [4], natural revision operator is only applied to belief states represented by total pre-orders, so the definition here is a slight generalization of that given in [4].

Proof: Let $A = M_\varphi \cdot B \cdot M_\varphi \vee M_{\neg\varphi}$, then

$$A(i,j) = 1 \Leftrightarrow w_i(\varphi) = w_j(\varphi) = 1 \text{ and } w_j \prec_B w_i, \text{ or} \\ i = j \text{ and } w_i(\varphi) = 0.$$

Thus, $\mathbf{a}(i,0) = \max_{0 \le j \le n-1} A(i,j) = 1$ iff $w_i \notin Min(\varphi, \prec_B)$ and $\mathbf{b}(0,j) = 1$ iff $w_j \in Min(\varphi, \prec_B)$. Therefore, $B^*\varphi(i,j) = 1$ iff the following two conditions are simultaneously satisfied:

1. $w_j \prec_B w_i$ or $w_j \in Min(\varphi, \prec_B)$;
2. $w_i \notin Min(\varphi, \prec_B)$.

Consequently, we have

$$w_j \prec_{B^*\varphi} w_i \Leftrightarrow w_j \in Min(\varphi, \prec_B) \text{ and } w_i \notin Min(\varphi, \prec_B) \text{ or} \\ w_j \prec_B w_i \text{ and } w_i, w_j \notin Min(\varphi, \prec_B),$$

so $NRev(\prec_B, \varphi) = \prec_{B^*\varphi}$ by the definition.
■

3.3 Belief Fusion

In belief fusion, the notion of pedigreed belief states proposed in [12, 13] is a very general one. The advantage of the pedigreed belief state representation is that it can keep track of information about the credibility of sources. By the matrix notation, we can easily represent a pedigreed belief state and the belief state induced from it. Let Ω be a set of information sources, then it is assumed that for each source $s \in \Omega$, there is a belief state B_s associated with it. It is also assumed that the credibility of information sources is determined by a ranking function $rank : \Omega \to \mathcal{N}$, where $\mathcal{N}$ is the set of positive integers.

Definition 5. *Let Ω be a set of information sources and $rank : \Omega \to \mathcal{N}$ be its ranking function, then*

1. *the pedigreed belief state of qualitatively fusing Ω is*
$$PB_q(\Omega) = \bigvee_{s \in \Omega} rank(s) \cdot B_s,$$
2. *the pedigreed belief state of arithmetically fusing Ω is*
$$PB_a(\Omega) = \sum_{s \in \Omega} rank(s) \cdot B_s,$$
3. *the pedigreed belief state of exponentially fusing Ω is*
$$PB_e(\Omega) = \sum_{s \in \Omega} \alpha^{rank(s)-1} \cdot B_s,$$
where $\alpha \ge |\Omega|$ is a real number,

4. *the belief state of fusing* Ω *(qualitatively, arithmetically, or exponentially) is*

$$\oplus_x(\Omega) = (PB_x(\Omega))^d$$

where $x = q, a,$ *or* e. ■

The definition of qualitative fusion is taken from [12]. In that work, a *generalized belief state* is defined as a modular and transitive relation over $\mathcal{W}$. A relation $\prec$ over $\mathcal{W}$ is transitive if $w_1 \prec w_2$ and $w_2 \prec w_3$ imply $w_1 \prec w_3$ and modular if $w_1 \prec w_2$ implies that for any $w \in \mathcal{W}$, $w \prec w_2$ or $w_1 \prec w$. Therefore, each information source s is associated with a generalized belief state $\prec^s$ and an aggregation operator $AGRRf$ is defined for a set of information sources S as

$$AGRRf(S) = \{(w, v) \mid \exists s \in S.\ w \prec^s v \wedge (\forall s' \sqsupset s \in S.\ w \approx^{s'} v)\}$$

where $s' \sqsupset s$ means that $rank(s') > rank(s)$ and $w \approx^{s'} v$ means that $\neg(w \prec^{s'} v) \wedge \neg(v \prec^{s'} w)$. The pedigreed belief state for a set of information sources S is then defined as a pair $(\prec, l)$, where $\prec = AGRRf(S)$ and $l : \prec \to \mathcal{N}$ such that

$$l((w, v)) = \max\{rank(s) \mid w \prec^s v, s \in S\}.$$

Note that in our definition, each information source is associated with a belief state in matrix form, whereas in [12], it is associated with a generalized belief state in the form of a modular and transitive relation. Let Ω denote a set of information sources in our definition such that each $\prec_{B_s}$ is transitive and modular. Then, we can define S_Ω as the corresponding set of information sources in the sense of [12], so that each $s \in S_\Omega$ is associated with the ordering $\prec_{B_s}$.

Proposition 4. *Let* Ω *be a set of information sources in our definition, then*

$$AGRRf(S_\Omega) = \prec_{\oplus_q(\Omega)}$$

and for each $0 \leq i, j \leq n-1$ *such that* $\oplus_q(\Omega)(i, j) = 1$,

$$l((w_j, w_i)) = PB_q(\Omega)(i, j).$$

Proof:

1. On the one hand, using the definition of indicator operation, for all $0 \leq i, j \leq n-1$, $w_j \prec_{\oplus_q(\Omega)} w_j$ iff $PB_q(\Omega)(i, j) > 0$ and $PB_q(\Omega)(i, j) \geq PB_q(\Omega)(j, i)$. Since $PB_q(\Omega)(i, j) = \max_{s \in \Omega} rank(s) \cdot B_s(i, j)$, $PB_q(\Omega)(i, j) > 0$ implies $\exists s \in S,\ B_s(i, j) = 1$, i.e. $\exists s \in S, w_j \prec_{B_s} w_i$. Let s_0 denote such an information source such that $rank(s_0) = PB_q(\Omega)(i, j)$, then $PB_q(\Omega)(i, j) \geq PB_q(\Omega)(j, i)$ implies $\forall s \sqsupset s_0$, $B_s(i, j) = B_s(j, i) = 0$, i.e. $\forall s \sqsupset s_0$, $w_j \approx^s w_i$. Therefore, $w_j \prec_{\oplus_q(\Omega)} w_j$ implies $(w_j, w_i) \in AGRRf(S_\Omega)$. On the other hand, if $(w_j, w_i) \in AGRRf(S_\Omega)$, then there exists $s \in \Omega$ such that $B_s(i, j) = 1$ and for all s' such that $rank(s') > rank(s)$, $B_{s'}(j, i) = B_{s'}(i, j) = 0$. Therefore, $PB_q(\Omega)(i, j) > 0$ and $PB_q(\Omega)(i, j) \geq PB_q(\Omega)(j, i)$ hold. This in turn implies $w_j \prec_{\oplus_q(\Omega)} w_j$.
2. $PB_q(\Omega)(i, j) = \max_{s \in \Omega} rank(s) \cdot B_s(i, j) = \max\{rank(s) \mid w_j \prec_{B_s} w_i, s \in \Omega\} = l((w_j, w_i))$

■

While the operator $AGRRf(S)$ preserves the modularity of the generalized belief states associated with sources in S, it does not preserve the transitivity. The resultant belief state for the fusion is, in fact, the transitive closure of $AGRRf(S)$. Therefore, the definition of qualitative fusion is for a very general notion of belief states according to the matrix representation. If some additional properties (such as modularity and transitivity) are imposed on the definition of belief states, some further operations (such as transitive closure) are required for implementation of the belief fusion operator.

In [12], it is suggested that aggregation of sources based on a general framework of voting is also possible. While qualitative fusion accounts for the ranking of sources supporting or disagreeing with an opinion, it does not count the percentage of sources in each camp. The definition of arithmetic fusion implements the idea in a straightforward way by algebraic operations. When all sources are equally credible, this corresponds to merging by majority in the spirit of [22].

However, if the credibility of the sources are highly variant, it is possible that many sources of low credibility will outweigh one of high credibility. To circumvent this problem, we can use the exponential fusion. Since the base of the exponential terms is not less than the number of sources, it is guaranteed that the opinion of higher ranks will dominate all opinions of lower ranks.

4 Conclusion

In this paper, we show that matrix algebra can be applied to belief reasoning, revision and fusion in knowledge-based systems. By employing a Boolean matrix representation of belief states, the main tasks for belief or knowledge management in such systems can be reduced to algebraic operations in matrix algebra. This enables a uniform treatment of these reasoning tasks.

To make our approach general, we do not impose any restrictions on the matrix representation of belief states. However, in real applications, belief states are usually assumed to have some special structures, such as modularity and transitivity. In such cases, the closure of an algebraic operation with respect to these additional properties will become very important. In the further work, we will investigate how the closure property may influence the representation of belief states and the choice of algebraic operations.

Furthermore, the dimensions of matrices used in the representation of belief states are, in general, exponential with respect to the number of propositional variables. Since the dimensions of these matrices may be very large, it is impractical to implement reasoning tasks of belief logic directly via the semantic representation. Instead, a proof theory for belief logic should be developed and the matrix representation proposed in this paper can serve as the basis of an algebraic semantics for such logic.

Acknowledgements

I would like to thank three anonymous referees for their valuable remarks.

References

1. C.E. Alchourrón, Gärdenfors, and D. Makinson. "On the logic of theory change: Partial meet contraction and revision functions". *Journal of Symbolic Logic*, 50:510–530, 1985.
2. C. Baral, S. Kraus, J. Minker, and V. S. Subrahmanian. "Combining knowledge bases consisting of first-order theories". *Computational Intelligence*, 8(1):45–71, 1992.
3. S. Benferhat, D. Dubois, and H. Prade. "From semantic to syntactic approaches to information combination in possibilistic logic". In B. Bouchon-Meunier, editor, *Aggregation and Fusion of Imperfect Information*, pages 141–161. Physica-Verlag, 1997.
4. C. Boutilier. "Revision sequences and nested conditionals". In *Proceedings of the 13th International Joint Conference on Artificial Intelligence*, pages 519–525, 1993.
5. C. Boutilier. "Generalized update: Belief change in dynamic settings". In *Proceedings of the 14th International Joint Conference on Artificial Intelligence*, pages 1550–1556, 1995.
6. L. Cholvy. "A logiccal approach to multi-souces reasoning". In M. Masuch and L. Pólos, editors, *Knowledge Representation and Reasoning under Uncertainty*, LNCS 808, pages 183–196. Springer-Verlag, 1994.
7. A. Darwiche and J. Pearl. "On the logic of iterated belief revision". *Artificial Intelligence*, 89(1):1–29, 1997.
8. D. Dubois and H. Prade. "Belief change and possibility theory". In P. Gärdenfors, editor, *Belief Revision*, pages 142–182. Cambridge University Press, 1992.
9. D. Dubois and H. Prade. "Possibility theory in information fusion". In *Proc. of the Third International Conference on Information Fusion*, pages TuA–1, 2000.
10. R. Fagin, J.Y. Halpern, Y. Moses, and M.Y. Vardi. *Reasoning about Knowledge.* MIT Press, 1996.
11. J.Y. Halpern and Y. Moses. "A guide to completeness and complexity for modal logics of knowledge and belief". *Artificial Intelligence*, 54:311–379, 1992.
12. P. Maynard-Reid II and D. Lehmann. "Representing and aggregating conflicting beliefs". In *Proceedings of the 7th International Conference on Principles of Knowledge Representation and Reasoning*, pages 153–164, 2000.
13. P. Maynard-Reid II and Y. Shoham. "Belief fusion: Aggregating pedigreed belief states". *Journal of Logic, Language and Information*, 10(2):183–209, 2001.
14. H. Katsuno and A. Medelzon. "On the difference between updating a knowledge base and revising it". In *Proceedings of the Second International Conference on Principles of Knowledge Representation and Reasoning (KR'91)*, pages 387–394. Morgan Kaufmann Publisher, 1991.
15. H. Katsuno and A. Medelzon. "Propositional knowledge base revision and minimal change". *Artificial Intelligence*, 52:263–294, 1991.
16. S. Konieczny. "On the difference between merging knowledge bases and combining them". In *Proceedings of the Seventh International Conference on Principles of Knowledge Representation and Reasoning (KR'00).*, pages 135–144. Morgan Kaufmann Publisher, 2000.
17. D. Lehmann. "Belief revision, revised". In *Proceedings of the 14th International Joint Conference on Artificial Intelligence*, pages 1534–1540, 1995.
18. C.J. Liau. "A conservative approach to distributed belief fusion". In *Proc. of the Third International Conference on Information Fusion*, pages MoD4–1, 2000.

19. C.J. Liau. "Epistemic logics for information fusion". In T.D. Nielsen and N.L. Zhang, editors, *Proc of the 7th European Conference on Symbolic and Quantitative Approaches to Reasoning with Uncertainty*, LNAI 2711, pages 489–501. Springer-Verlag, 2003.
20. C.J. Liau. "A modal logic framework for multi-agent belief fusion". *ACM Transactions on Computational Logic*, 2004.
21. J. Lin. "Information sharing and knowledge merging in cooperative information systems". In *Proceedings of the Fourth Workshop on Information Technologies and Systems*, pages 58–66, 1994.
22. J. Lin and A.O. Mendelzon. "Knowledge base merging by majority". In R. Pareschi and B. Fronhoefer, editors, *Dynamic Worlds: From the Frame Problem to Knowledge Management.* Kluwer Academic Publisher, 1999.
23. S. Pradhan, J. Minker, and V. Subrahmanian. "Combining databases with prioritized information". *Journal of Intelligent Information Systems*, 4(3):231–260, 1995.
24. K. Segerberg. "Belief revision from the point of view of doxastic logic". *Bull. of the IGPL*, 3(4):535–553, 1995.
25. P. Smets. " Data fusion in the transferable belief model". In *Proc. of the Third International Conference on Information Fusion*, pages WeA–1, 2000.
26. W. Spohn. "Ordinal conditional functions: a dynamic theory of epistemic states". In W.L. Harper and B. Skyrms, editors, *Causation in Decision, Belief Change, and Statistics, II*, pages 105–134. Kluwer Academic Publishers, 1988.
27. V.S. Subrahmanian. "Amalgamating knowledge bases". *ACM Transactions on Database Systems*, 19(2):291–331, 1994.
28. M.A. Williams. "Transmutations of knowledge systems". In J. Doyle, E. Sandewall, and P. Torasso, editors, *Proceedings of the 4th International Conference on Principle of Knowledge Representation and Reasoning*, pages 619–629. Morgan Kaufmann Publishers, 1994.

On the Correspondence between Approximations and Similarity

Patrick Doherty[1] and Andrzej Szałas[1,2]

[1] Dept. of Computer and Information Science
Linköping University
SE-581 83 Linköping, Sweden
patdo@ida.liu.se

[2] The College of Economics and Computer Science
Olsztyn, Poland
andsz@ida.liu.se

Abstract. This paper focuses on the use and interpretation of approximate databases where both rough sets and indiscernibility partitions are generalized and replaced by approximate relations and similarity spaces. Similarity spaces are used to define neighborhoods around individuals and these in turn are used to define approximate sets and relations. There is a wide spectrum of choice as to what properties the similarity relation should have and how this affects the properties of approximate relations in the database. In order to make this interaction precise, we propose a technique which permits specification of both approximation and similarity constraints on approximate databases and automatic translation between them. This technique provides great insight into the relation between similarity and approximation and is similar to that used in modal correspondence theory. In order to automate the translations, quantifier elimination techniques are used.

1 Introduction

There is a natural generalization of relational databases where one uses intuitions from rough set theory [14] and rather than storing and querying crisp relations, one stores and queries rough relations consisting of an upper and lower approximation of the implicit crisp relation whose definition one tries to approximate [4]. There is also a natural generalization of an indiscernibility relation used in rough set theory, where rather than partitioning the universe of discourse U into indiscernibility classes, one can consider a covering of U by similarity-based neighborhoods (see, e.g., [8]) with lower and upper approximations of relations defined via the neighborhoods. To mark the difference, we will use the terms approximate relations and approximate databases instead of rough relations and rough databases. Approximate databases and tolerance spaces have been shown to be quite versatile in many applications areas requiring the use of approximate knowledge structures [5, 7].

When taking this step and generalizing to approximate relations and databases, there are many choices that can be made as regards the constraints one

S. Tsumoto et al. (Eds.): RSCTC 2004, LNAI 3066, pp. 143–152, 2004.

might want to place on the similarity relation used to define upper and lower approximations. For example, we would not want the relation to have the property of transitivity since similar things don't naturally chain in a transitive manner. Many of these issues are discussed in the context of rough sets (see, e.g., [15–17]). Whatever choices are made, one wants to ensure that these constraints are enforced while querying an approximate database. In a similar manner, there are many constraints that are more naturally expressed in terms of upper and lower approximations which must remain consistent with the properties one assumes for the underlying similarity relation and which also have to be enforced while querying the approximate database. For example, for any relation in an approximate database, we would like to ensure that the lower approximation is a subset of the upper approximation. There are even constraints we might like to enforce that refer to the crisp relation of which we implicitly represent in terms of an upper and lower approximation. For example the lower approximation should be a subset of this crisp relation.

The goal of this paper is to study the interaction between constraints stated in terms of a language of approximate relations and constraints stated in terms of the underlying similarity relation which is used to define neighborhoods. To do this, we first define a language of set theoretical terms which permit us to represent boolean constraints on upper and lower approximations. We then introduce a first-order language and translation function which translates constraints in the set theoretical language into first-order formulas. These first-order formulas are then quantified over various relations in the formulas because we are interested in universal constraints. We then use quantifier elimination techniques to generate logically equivalent formulas in a first-order language but in this case, the resulting output only refers to the similarity relation if the elimination is successful.

This technique is analogous to techniques used in modal correspondence theory [19] where one studies the nature and expressiveness of modal axioms by viewing them as expressing constraints on the possible worlds alternative relation in the underlying Kripke frames. These constraints are represented as 1st- or higher-order logical formulas and correspondence theory is the study of the generation and relations between these correspondences. We approach the topic of the relation between approximate relation axioms and the formulas expressing constraints on the underlying similarity relation in a similar manner. In this case though, we can often automatically generate the resulting correspondence through the use of quantifier eliminations techniques [6] developed by the authors in another context.

The correspondences considered in this paper are not surprising in the view of [19] as well as results more directly oriented towards rough set theory (for an overview of results see, e.g., [11]). However, the novelty of our approach is that we show a uniform, principled way to compute appropriate correspondences and focus on similarity spaces rather then Kripke structures.

2 Preliminaries

The starting point for our approach are tolerance spaces, as introduced in [8]. Technically, they allow us to classify a universe of individuals into indiscernibility or tolerance neighborhoods based on a parameterized tolerance relation. This is a generalization on the indiscernibility partitions used in rough set theory where instead of partitions, the neighborhoods provide a covering of the universe. In fact, tolerance functions are required to induce reflexive and symmetric neighborhood relations, while rough neighborhood relations are additionally transitive.

Tolerance spaces can still be generalized to represent even weaker notions of similarity in a universe of individuals. Consequently, we consider similarity spaces, where the definition of a similarity function has no initial constraints.

Definition 1. *By a* similarity function *on a set U we mean any function* $\tau : U \times U \longrightarrow [0, 1]$.

For $p \in [0, 1]$ by a similarity relation to a degree at least p, induced by τ, *we mean the relation* $\sigma^p \stackrel{\text{def}}{=} \{\langle x, y\rangle \mid \tau(x, y) \geq p\}$. □

In what follows, we assume p is given and use $\sigma(x, y)$ to denote the characteristic function of σ^p.

Similarity relations are used to construct similarity neighborhoods.

Definition 2. *By a* neighborhood function wrt σ^p *we mean a function given by* $n^{\sigma^p}(u) \stackrel{\text{def}}{=} \{u' \in U \mid \sigma^p(u, u') \text{ holds}\}$. *By a* neighborhood *of u wrt σ^p we mean the value* $n^{\sigma^p}(u)$. □

Definition 3. *A* similarity space *is defined as the tuple $S = \langle U, \tau, p\rangle$, consisting of a nonempty set U, called the* domain *of S, a* similarity function τ, *and a* similarity threshold $p \in [0, 1]$.

Let $A \subseteq U$. The lower and upper approximation of A wrt S, *denoted respectively by A_{S^+} and $A_{S^\oplus}$, are defined by* $A_{S^+} = \{u \in U : n^{\sigma^p}(u) \subseteq A\}$, $A_{S^\oplus} = \{u \in U : n^{\sigma^p}(u) \cap A \neq \emptyset\}$. □

We shall often provide similarity spaces as pairs $\langle U, \sigma\rangle$, where σ is a similarity relation induced by a given similarity function and threshold. This simplifies the presentation and is sufficient for the purposes of the current paper.

The following proposition provides us with an alternative way to define upper and lower approximations and will be used throughout the paper.

Proposition 1. *Let $S = \langle U, \sigma\rangle$ be a similarity space and let $A \subseteq U$. Then* $A_{S^+} = \{a \in A \mid \forall b\, [\sigma(a, b) \to b \in A]\}$ *and* $A_{S^\oplus} = \{a \in A \mid \exists b\, [\sigma(a, b) \wedge b \in A]\}$. □

As a basis for doing quantifier elimination, we will use the following lemma due to Ackermann [1] (see also, e.g., [6, 18]), where $\Psi\left[P(\overline{\alpha}) \leftarrow [\Phi]^{\overline{x}}_{\overline{\alpha}}\right]$ means that every occurrence of P in Ψ is to be replaced by Φ where the actual arguments $\overline{\alpha}$ of P, replaces the variables of $\overline{x}$ in Φ (and the bound variables are renamed if necessary).

Lemma 1. *Let P be a predicate variable and let Φ and $\Psi(P)$ be first–order formulae such that $\Psi(P)$ is positive w.r.t. P and Φ contains no occurrences of P at all. Then* $\exists P\,\forall\bar{x}\,(P(\bar{x}) \rightarrow \Phi(\bar{x},\bar{y})) \wedge \Psi(P) \equiv \Psi\left[P(\overline{\alpha}) \leftarrow [\Phi]^{\bar{x}}_{\overline{\alpha}}\right]$ *and similarly if the sign of P is switched and Ψ is negative w.r.t. P.* □

3 Languages for Expressing Similarity and Approximation Constraints

In order to specify constraints on approximate relations and similarity relations and to show correspondences between them, we will introduce a number of languages and translations between them. We begin by defining a language for approximation constraints.

Definition 4. *Let U be a set, $\bar{A}$ be a tuple of set symbols*[1] *(respective sets are assumed to be included in U) and let $S = \langle U, \sigma \rangle$ be a similarity space.* Set-theoretical terms over vocabulary $\bar{A} \cup \{S\}$ *are defined as follows:*

- *for $A \in \bar{A}$, A is a set-theoretical term*
- *if α is a set-theoretical term then $-\alpha, \alpha_{S^+}, \alpha_{S^\oplus}$ are set-theoretical terms*
- *if α, β are set-theoretical terms then $\alpha \cup \beta$ is also a set-theoretical term.*

If α and β are set-theoretical terms over $\bar{A} \cup \{S\}$ then $\alpha \subseteq \beta$ is an atomic set-theoretical formula over $\bar{A} \cup \{S\}$. *The set of* set-theoretical formulas *is the least set which contains all atomic set-theoretical formulas and is closed under the classical propositional connectives.* □

We also define $(\alpha \cap \beta) \stackrel{\text{def}}{=} -(-\alpha \cup -\beta)$ and $(\alpha = \beta) \stackrel{\text{def}}{\equiv} (\alpha \subseteq \beta \wedge \beta \subseteq \alpha)$.

Given approximation constraints in the language above, we would like to translate such constraints into formulas in a first-order language as follows.

Definition 5. *Let $U, \bar{A}, S$ be as in Definition 4. Let α be a set-theoretical term over $\bar{A} \cup \{S\}$ and x be a variable over U. Then the* translation $Tr(\alpha, x)$ of set-theoretical terms *into first-order formulas is defined inductively as follows:*

- $Tr(A, x) \stackrel{\text{def}}{=} A'(x)$, *where $A \in \bar{A}$ and A' is a fresh unary relation symbol*
- $Tr(-\alpha, x) \stackrel{\text{def}}{=} \neg Tr(\alpha, x)$
- $Tr(\alpha_{S^+}, x) \stackrel{\text{def}}{=} \forall y\,[\sigma(x,y) \rightarrow Tr(\alpha, y)]$, *where y is a fresh variable*
- $Tr(\alpha_{S^\oplus}, x) \stackrel{\text{def}}{=} \exists y\,[\sigma(x,y) \wedge Tr(\alpha, y)]$, *where y is a fresh variable*
- $Tr(\alpha \cup \beta, x) \stackrel{\text{def}}{=} Tr(\alpha, x) \vee Tr(\beta, x)$.

The translation $Tr(\gamma, x)$ of set-theoretical formulas *into first-order formulas is defined to satisfy* $Tr(\alpha \subseteq \beta, x) \stackrel{\text{def}}{=} \forall x\,(Tr(\alpha, x) \rightarrow Tr(\beta, x))$ *and to preserve the classical propositional connectives.* □

Example 1. Let a vocabulary consist of sets A,B,C and similarity space S. Then:

$$Tr((A \cup B)_{S^+} \subseteq C_{S^\oplus}, x) =$$
$$= \forall x\,[\forall y\,(\sigma(x,y) \rightarrow (A(y) \vee B(y))) \rightarrow \exists z\,(\sigma(x,z) \wedge C(z))].$$ □

[1] Later on we will use the same symbols to denote sets and corresponding characteristic relations.

4 Computing Correspondences between Approximations and Similarity

For the purposes of this section, we will fix a similarity space $S = \langle U, \sigma \rangle$ and a tuple of sets $\bar{A}$, where all sets in $\bar{A}$ are included in U.

4.1 The General Technique

The general techniques used to compute correspondences between similarity constraints and approximation constraints are those described in [18] in the context of modal logics, but rather than working with the alternative relation on possible worlds, we will work with the similarity space S. The steps are as follows:

1. express the required property of approximations as a set-theoretical formula $\gamma(\bar{A})$ over vocabulary $\bar{A} \cup \{S\}$
2. compute the translation $Tr(\gamma(\bar{A}), x)$ of the formula obtained in step 1 according to Definition 5
3. consider the formula $\forall \bar{A}\, [Tr(\gamma(\bar{A}), x)]$ and eliminate second-order variables $\bar{A}$, if possible.

If the second-order quantifier elimination is successful then the resulting formula uses only the non-logical symbols σ and $=$ and is logically equivalent to the initial logical translation of the set-theoretical property. The quantifier elimination step can be automated using the algorithm given in [18] or its generalization known as the DLS algorithm of [6]. There are also other applicable methods which may be used (for an overview of known techniques see [12]).

In the remainder of this section, we will select a number of approximation constraints for analysis and show their correspondence with similarity constraints.

4.2 The Meaning of Inclusion $A_{S^+} \subseteq A_{S^\oplus}$

Consider the very basic requirement in rough set theory that the lower approximation of a set should be contained in its upper approximation, i.e., for any set A we have $A_{S^+} \subseteq A_{S^\oplus}$. The translation of this approximation constraint results in the following first-order formula:

$$\begin{aligned} Tr(A_{S^+} \subseteq A_{S^\oplus}, x) &= \forall x\, [Tr(A_{S^+}, x) \rightarrow Tr(A_{S^\oplus}, x)] \\ &= \forall x\, [\forall y\, (\sigma(x,y) \rightarrow A(y)) \rightarrow \exists z\, (\sigma(x,z) \wedge A(z))]. \end{aligned}$$

We universalize over all relations A and get the following second-order formula:

$$\forall A\, \forall x\, [\forall y\, (\sigma(x,y) \rightarrow A(y)) \rightarrow \exists z\, (\sigma(x,z) \wedge A(z))].$$

To apply Ackermann's lemma, a number of syntactic transformations on the original formula are required. In this case, we first negate this formula and switch the order of initial existential quantifiers:

$$\exists x\, \exists A\, [\forall y\, (\sigma(x,y) \rightarrow A(y)) \wedge \forall z\, (\neg\sigma(x,z) \vee \neg A(z))].$$

Ackermann's lemma is then applied resulting in a logically equivalent first-order formula representing the following similarity constraint:

$$\exists x\, [\forall z\, (\neg\sigma(x, z) \lor \neg\sigma(x, z))].$$

After simplifying and negating again we find that the initial requirement is equivalent to $\forall x\, \exists z\, \sigma(x, z)$, i.e., to the seriality of σ.[2] Upon analysis, this leads to an interesting observation:

Proposition 2. *The condition that for any set A, the approximation constraint $A_{S^+} \subseteq A_{S^\oplus}$ holds, is equivalent to the seriality of σ, i.e., to $\forall x\, \exists z\, \sigma(x, z)$.* □

Seriality is a weaker requirement on σ than reflexivity, since reflexivity implies seriality. Assuming this is the only constraint placed on σ, what might this mean intuitively. In an epistemic context, one use of such a weak notion of similarity might be to represent a type of self-awareness, or lack of self-awareness in this case. Here is an example:

Example 2. Consider a society of (at least two) similar robots equipped with cameras and image processing software that allows a robot to recognize similar objects. Assume that because of its camera placement each robot can observe the whole environment except for itself. Assume any robot knows that it is similar to other robots. Based only on such knowledge no robot can verify that it is similar to itself. Here similarity is serial, but not reflexive. □

The following example shows another situation where similarity could be interpreted as serial, but not reflexive.

Example 3. On a daily basis, humans often use many different relations of similarity concurrently. In commonsense reasoning these relations are generally kept apart, because this would lead to invalid conclusions. For example, assume we consider a similarity between parents and children in the sense that a child is similar to it's parent. Suppose further that we do not want to mix this notion of similarity with other similarities, e.g. those of persons to themselves. More formally we can say that $\sigma(x, y)$ holds if x is a child of y. Since everybody has a parent, σ is serial. Obviously it is not reflexive, since no one is its own child. In this case it would not be symmetric or transitive. □

4.3 The Meaning of Inclusion $A_{S^+} \subseteq A$

The properties we consider in this section and the next two sections are well-known topological properties if one considers the lower approximation to be the interior operation and the upper approximation to be the closure operation. From a modal logic perspective, the lower and upper approximations can be considered analogous to modal necessity and possibility, respectively.

[2] This property reflects the axiom D of modal logics. The properties considered in consecutive subsections reflect modal axioms T, B and 4, respectively.

We first translate the approximation constraint $Tr(A_{S^+} \subseteq A, x)$ into:

$$\forall x\, [\forall y\, (\sigma(x,y) \rightarrow A(y)) \rightarrow A(x)].$$

A straightforward calculation, similar to one used for modal logics in [18] shows that the universal requirement

$$\forall A\, \forall x\, [\forall y\, (\sigma(x,y) \rightarrow A(y)) \rightarrow A(x)]$$

is equivalent to the similarity constraint $\forall x\, \sigma(x,x)$, i.e., to the reflexivity of σ.

Proposition 3. *The condition that for any set A, $A_{\sigma^+} \subseteq A$ holds is equivalent to the reflexivity of σ, i.e., to the requirement that $\forall x\, \sigma(x,x)$ holds.* □

4.4 The Meaning of Inclusion $A \subseteq (A_{S^\oplus})_{S^+}$

We first translate the approximation constraint $Tr(A \subseteq (A_{S^\oplus})_{S^+}, x)$ into a first-order formula:

$$\forall x\, [A(x) \rightarrow \forall y\, (\sigma(x,y) \rightarrow \exists z\, (\sigma(y,z) \wedge A(z)))].$$

A straightforward calculation, similar to one used for modal logics in [18] shows that the universal requirement

$$\forall A \forall x\, [\forall y\, (\sigma(x,y) \rightarrow A(y)) \rightarrow A(x)]$$

is equivalent to the similarity constraint $\forall x, y\, [\sigma(x,y) \rightarrow \sigma(y,x)]$, i.e., to the symmetry of σ.

Proposition 4. *The condition that for any set A, $A \subseteq (A_{S^\oplus})_{S^+}$ holds is equivalent to the symmetry of σ, i.e., to the requirement that $\forall x, y\, [\sigma(x,y) \rightarrow \sigma(y,x)]$ holds.* □

4.5 The Meaning of Inclusion $A_{S^+} \subseteq (A_{S^+})_{S^+}$

We first translate the approximation constraint $Tr(A_{S^+} \subseteq (A_{S^+})_{S^+}, x)$ into:

$$\forall x\, [\forall y(\sigma(x,y) \rightarrow A(y)) \rightarrow \forall z(\sigma(x,z) \rightarrow \forall u\, (\sigma(z,u) \rightarrow A(u)))].$$

A straightforward calculation, similar to one used for modal logics in [18] shows that the universal requirement

$$\forall A \forall x\, [\forall y(\sigma(x,y) \rightarrow A(y)) \rightarrow \forall z(\sigma(x,z) \rightarrow \forall u\, (\sigma(z,u) \rightarrow A(u)))]$$

is equivalent to the similarity constraint $\forall x, z, u\, [(\sigma(x,z) \wedge \sigma(z,u)) \rightarrow \sigma(x,u)]$, i.e., to the transitivity of σ.

Proposition 5. *The condition that for any set A, $A_{S^+} \subseteq (A_{S^+})_{S^+}$ holds is equivalent to the transitivity of σ, i.e., to $\forall x, z, u\, [(\sigma(x,z) \wedge \sigma(z,u)) \rightarrow \sigma(x,u)]$.* □

5 Approximate Database Considerations

Based on the results above, when working with approximate databases, it is important that the use of the database is consistent with the approximation and similarity constraints envisioned by the database engineer and required by the particular application. In some respects, the approximate and similarity constraints have the role of integrity constraints in standard database theory. Yet, enforcing these constraints is not as straightforward. We now consider this issue.

Definition 6. *By a* (relational, crisp) database *we understand a tuple*

$$D = \langle U, \{R^j \mid j \in J\} \rangle,$$

where U is a finite set, called the domain *of D and $\{R^j \mid j \in J\}$ is a finite collection of relations over U. By an* approximate database *we understand a tuple*

$$D = \left\langle U, \left\{ R^j \mid R^j = \left\langle R^j_+, R^j_\oplus \right\rangle \text{ and } j \in J \right\} \right\rangle,$$

where R^j_+s and $R^j_\oplus$s are crisp relations of the same arity, satisfying $R^j_+ \subseteq R^j_\oplus$. □

Let R be a relation[3] with it's approximations R_{S^+} and $R_{S^\oplus}$ represented in an approximate database D. Note that R is available only through its approximations and is not itself stored in D.

We assume a similarity space $S = \langle U, \sigma \rangle$ and the ability to verify whether $\sigma(x, y)$ holds for tuples x and y which are stored in D.

Consider first a simpler case of constraints referring to approximations only. Such constraints can be directly represented in the database since approximations are represented as database relations. The requirements $R_{S^+} \subseteq R_{S^\oplus}$ and $R_{S^+} \subseteq (R_{S^+})_{S^+}$ are examples of such constraints. In this case, both the lower and upper approximations, R_{S^+} and $R_{S^\oplus}$ can be computed according to Proposition 1, since we assume that σ can be verified on elements which are stored in D.

A more complicated case arises when an approximation constraint refers to R, the crisp relation being approximated, since R is not stored in D. In such cases, one will often need to enforce meta-constraints, i.e., constraints that have to be ensured by database designers, and which cannot explicitly be represented or computed in an approximate database.

Let us start with the requirement that $R_{S^+} \subseteq R$ holds. In order to preserve its meaning in D, one has to ensure the following meta-constraint:

> the lower approximation $R_{S^+} \subseteq R$ can only contain those tuples which are known to satisfy R.

The requirement $R \subseteq (R_{S^\oplus})_{S^+}$ is more problematic. In some cases it can be replaced by a constraint that does not refer to R directly. For example, using

[3] Of course, any relation is a set of tuples, so our previous considerations apply here, too.

our analogy to modal logic ($R \to \Box\Diamond R$), it is well known that in the presence of reflexivity and transitivity, this axiom can be replaced by the property called 5.

The corresponding similarity relation for 5 is known to be Euclidean, i.e., it satisfies $\forall x, y, z[(\sigma(x,y) \wedge \sigma(x,z)) \to \sigma(y,z)]$ (see, e.g., [2, 3, 9]). In the language of approximate constraints, this would be expressed as $R_{S^\oplus} \subseteq (R_{S^\oplus})_{S^+}$, which refers to R via approximations only. In fact, in the presence of this property, transitivity is no longer required, since any Euclidean and reflexive relation is also both symmetric and transitive[4].

In order to preserve the symmetry requirement on σ, one has to ensure that the following meta-constraint is preserved:

> all tuples satisfying R are to be included in the lower approximation of the upper approximation $R_{S^\oplus}$.

In general, it is difficult to ensure this meta-constraint. One alternative to the meta-constraint would be to store, for any relation R, R_{S^+} together with $(-R)_{S^+}$. For any database update adding to or deleting a tuple of type compatible with tuples in R from the database, one would then have to check whether the approximations still satisfy the conditions of Proposition 1.

This technique is tractable, but expensive, as any database update might cause an integrity check. One could also apply techniques based on the static verification of database transactions which, in many cases, would result in much more efficient solutions to this problem. A technique which can be applied in this context was developed in [10].

6 Conclusions

Assuming the use of approximate databases as our starting point which appeal to a generalization of indiscernibility relations to tolerance or similarity spaces, we have proposed a set of techniques which permit the expression of approximation constraints and similarity constraints. We provide a method to automatically translate between the two and show how intuitions from modal logic and modal correspondence theory can be put to good use, not only in acquiring insight as to the interaction between similarity and approximation, but in providing more efficient means of enforcing such constraints in approximate databases.

References

1. W. Ackermann. Untersuchungen über das eliminationsproblem der mathematischen logik. *Mathematische Annalen*, 110:390–413, 1935.
2. R. A. Bull and K. Segerberg. Basic modal logic. In D. Gabbay and F. Guenthner, editors, *Handbook of Philosophical Logic*, volume 2, pages 1–88. D. Reidel Pub. Co., 20198402.

[4] This easily follows from the well-known fact that modal logic $KT5$ characterized with a reflexive and Euclidean accessibility relation is the same as $S5$, where the accessibility relation is reflexive, symmetric and transitive - see, e.g., [3].

3. B. F. Chellas. *Modal Logic - an Introduction.* Cambridge University Press, 1980.
4. P. Doherty, J. Kachniarz, and A. Szałas. Using contextually closed queries for local closed-world reasoning in rough knowledge databases. In *[13]*, 2003.
5. P. Doherty, W. Łukaszewicz, A. Skowron, and A. Szałas. Approximation transducers and trees: A technique for combining rough and crisp knowledge. In S. K. Pal, L. Polkowski, and A. Skowron, editors, *Rough-Neuro Computing: Techniques for Computing with Words*, Heidelberg, 2003. Springer–Verlag.
6. P. Doherty, W. Łukaszewicz, and A. Szałas. Computing circumscription revisited. *Journal of Automated Reasoning*, 18(3):297–336, 1997.
7. P. Doherty, W. Łukaszewicz, and A Szałas. Information granules for intelligent knowledge structures. In *Proc. 9th International Conference on rough sets, fuzzy sets, data mining and granular computing*, LNCS. Springer-Verlag, 2003.
8. P. Doherty, W. Łukaszewicz, and A Szałas. Tolerance spaces and approximative representational structures. In *Proceedings of 26th German Conference on Artificial Intelligence.* Springer-Verlag, 2003.
9. G. E. Hughes and M. J. Cresswell. *An Introduction to Modal Logic.* Methuen and Co. Ltd., London, New York, 1968.
10. J. Kachniarz and A. Szałas. On a static approach to verification of integrity constraints in relational databases. In E. Orłowska and A. Szałas, editors, *Relational Methods for Computer Science Applications*, pages 97–109. Springer Physica-Verlag, 2001.
11. C-J Liau. An overview of rough set semantics for modal and quantifier logics. *Int. Journal of Uncertainty, Fuzziness and Knowledge-Based Systems*, 8(1):93–118, 2000.
12. A. Nonnengart, H.J. Ohlbach, and A. Szałas. Elimination of predicate quantifiers. In H.J. Ohlbach and U. Reyle, editors, *Logic, Language and Reasoning. Essays in Honor of Dov Gabbay, Part I*, pages 159–181. Kluwer, 1999.
13. S. K. Pal, L. Polkowski, and A. Skowron, editors. *Rough-Neuro Computing: Techniques for Computing with Words.* Springer–Verlag, Heidelberg, 2003.
14. Z. Pawlak. *Rough Sets. Theoretical Aspects of Reasoning about Data.* Kluwer Academic Publishers, Dordrecht, 1991.
15. A. Skowron and J. Stepaniuk. Tolerance approximation spaces. *Fundamenta Informaticae*, 27:245–253, 1996.
16. R. Słowiński and D. Vanderpooten. Similarity relation as a basis for rough approximations. In P. Wang, editor, *Advances in Machine Intelligence & Soft Computing*, pages 17–33, Raleigh NC, 1997. Bookwrights.
17. R. Słowiński and D. Vanderpooten. A generalized definition of rough approximations based on similarity. *IEEE Trans. on Data and Knowledge Engineering*, 12(2):331–336, 2000.
18. A. Szałas. On the correspondence between modal and classical logic: An automated approach. *Journal of Logic and Computation*, 3:605–620, 1993.
19. J. Van Benthem. Correspondence theory. In D. Gabbay and F. Guenthner, editors, *Handbook of Philosophical Logic*, volume 2, pages 167–247. D. Reidel Pub. Co., 1984.

Toward Rough Knowledge Bases with Quantitative Measures

Aida Vitória[1], Carlos Viegas Damásio[2], and Jan Małuszyński[3]

[1] Dept. of Science and Technology, Linköping University, S 601 74 Norrköping, Sweden
aidvi@itn.liu.se

[2] Centro de Inteligência Artificial (CENTRIA), Dept. Informática, Faculdade de Ciências e Tecnologia, Universidade Nova de Lisboa, 2829-516 Caparica, Portugal
cd@di.fct.unl.pt

[3] Dept. of Computer and Information Science, Linköping University, S 581 83 Linköping, Sweden
janma@ida.liu.se

Abstract. We present a language for defining new rough relations from given decision tables and we show how to query relations defined in this way. The language provides a uniform formalism for expressing rough data together with background knowledge, and for capturing well-known techniques such as the variable precision rough set model. Its essential feature is the use of quantitative measures, such as support, strength and accuracy.

1 Introduction

Existing rough set techniques [1] do not provide natural support for incorporation of background knowledge. Addressing this problem, we have recently proposed a language [2, 3] that caters for implicit definition of rough sets from given ones. Our language seems to address similar problems as the system **CAKE** [4]. For comparison and discussion of some important differences see [3].

This paper extends our language of [2, 3] with quantitative measures, such as support, strength, accuracy, and coverage, which play an essential role in applications. The extension is very expressive since new rough sets can now be defined using conditions with quantitative measures. For example, we show that the variable precision rough set model [5] can be naturally expressed in this language. Another important add-on of the language is that clauses defining new rough sets are parameterized by weighted functions combining the supports of indiscernibility classes of given rough sets into the supports of the defined ones. We claim that this parameterization allows to define rough sets better tailored to specific applications. The rough sets defined in our language and their related quantitative measures can be queried, as discussed in Section 3. The practical application of Section 4 illustrates the usefulness of the language.

For space reasons, a formal declarative semantics and the operational semantics of the language are not discussed in this paper.

S. Tsumoto et al. (Eds.): RSCTC 2004, LNAI 3066, pp. 153–158, 2004.

2 Rough Sets

We extend the notion of rough set used in our previous work [2, 3] to take into account quantitative measures. Individuals of a universe of discourse U are in many cases classified on the basis of some associated information, such as values of certain chosen attributes. Formally, an attribute a is a total function $a : U \to V_a$. Every object is associated with a tuple of attributes and this tuple is the only way of referring to the object. Hence, different individuals with same attribute values are indiscernible.

Definition 1. *Given a set of attributes* $A = \{a_1, \ldots, a_n\}$, *a* rough set *(or* rough relation*)* S *is a pair of sets* $(\overline{S}, \overline{\neg S})$ *satisfying conditions (i) and (ii).*

(i) The elements of sets $\overline{S}$ *and* $\overline{\neg S}$ *are expressions of the form* $\langle t_1, \ldots, t_n \rangle : k$, *where* $\langle t_1, \ldots, t_n \rangle \in \prod_{a_i \in A} V_{a_i}$ *and* k *is an integer larger than zero.*

(ii) $(\langle t_1, \ldots, t_n \rangle : k \in \overline{S} \Rightarrow \forall k' \neq k (\langle t_1, \ldots, t_n \rangle : k' \notin \overline{S}))$ *and* $(\langle t_1, \ldots, t_n \rangle : k \in \overline{\neg S} \Rightarrow \forall k' \neq k (\langle t_1, \ldots, t_n \rangle : k' \notin \overline{\neg S}))$.

The rough complement *of a rough set* $S = (\overline{S}, \overline{\neg S})$ *is the rough set* $\neg S = (\overline{\neg S}, \overline{S})$.

For simplicity, we write t to designate a general tuple $\langle t_1, \ldots, t_n \rangle$ and $[t]$ represents the indiscernibility class described by tuple t. Intuitively, an element $t : k \in \overline{S}$ ($t : k \in \overline{\neg S}$) indicates that the indiscernibility class $[t]$ belongs to the upper approximation of rough set S ($\neg S$) and that this class contains $k > 0$ individuals that are positive examples of the concept described by S ($\neg S$). *Lower approximation* of rough set S, represented by $\underline{S}$, is defined as $\underline{S} = \{t : k_1 \in \overline{S} \mid \forall k_2 > 0 \, (t : k_2 \notin \overline{\neg S})\}$. The *boundary region*, represented by $\underline{\overline{S}}$, is defined as $\underline{\overline{S}} = \{t : k_1 : k_2 \mid \exists k_1, k_2 > 0 \, (t : k_1 \in \overline{S} \text{ and } t : k_2 \in \overline{\neg S})\}$.

Obviously, a decision table can be seen as an alternative representation of a rough set $D = (\overline{D}, \overline{\neg D})$. The fact that we consider only binary decision attributes is not a restriction in practice, as shown in [3] (see example 4.4).

Quantitative Measures. Let a tuple t be the description of an indiscernibility class $[t]$ of a decision table $\mathcal{D} = (U, A, \mathsf{d})$. Assume also that $|d|$ ($|\neg d|$) is the number of individuals (or lines of the table) that have positive (negative) outcome for the decision attribute d. The following quantitative measures are used.

- The *support* of $d(t)$, represented by $\mathtt{supp}(d(t))$, corresponds to the number of individuals in the indiscernibility class $[t]$ that are positive examples. Thus, if $t : k \in \overline{D}$ then $\mathtt{supp}(d(t)) = k$.
- The *strength* of $d(t)$, represented by $\mathtt{strength}(d(t))$, indicates how often individuals in the indiscernibility class $[t]$ have positive outcome for the decision attribute d. Thus, if $t : k \in \overline{D}$ then $\mathtt{strength}(d(t)) = \frac{k}{|d| + |\neg d|}$.
- The *accuracy* of $d(t)$, represented by $\mathtt{acc}(d(t))$, corresponds to the conditional probability $Pr(d(i) = \mathtt{yes} \mid i \in [t])$. Thus, if $t : k_1 \in \overline{D}$ and $t : k_2 \in \overline{\neg D}$ then, $\mathtt{acc}(d(t)) = \frac{k_1}{k_1 + k_2}$.

These definitions extend naturally to $\neg d(t)$. The implementation of the language will allow introduction of other quantitative measures in addition to those discussed above.

3 A Language for Defining Rough Relations

In this section, we extend the language for defining rough relations, presented in [2, 3], with quantitative measures. We restrict the definition of new rough relations to be non recursive.

A *quantitative measure expression* is a condition involving quantitative measures. For instance, $\texttt{acc}(p(c_1, c_2)) > \texttt{acc}(\neg q(c_1, c_2))$ is a quantitative measure expression stating that the accuracy of the indiscernibility class $[\langle c_1, c_2\rangle]$ of rough relation P is larger than the accuracy of the indiscernibility class $[\langle c_1, c_2\rangle]$ of rough relation $\neg Q$.

A *rough program* is a set of *rough facts* and *rough clauses*. Rough facts encode rough relations defined explicitly by a decision table, while rough clauses are used to define implicitly new rough relations obtained by combining different regions (e.g. lower approximation, upper approximation, and boundary) of other rough relations. Rough facts are expressions of either the form $\overline{r}(c_1, \dots, c_n) : k_1.$ or $\overline{\neg r}(c_1, \dots, c_n) : k_2.$, where each c_i is a constant. These facts state that $\langle c_1, \dots, c_n\rangle : k_1 \in \overline{R}$ and $\langle c_1, \dots, c_n\rangle : k_2 \in \overline{\neg R}$, respectively, where R is the rough relation denoted by r. A *rough literal* is an expression of either the form $\overline{r}(t_1, \dots, t_n)$, or $\underline{r}(t_1, \dots, t_n)$, or $\overline{\underline{r}}(t_1, \dots, t_n)$, or $\overline{\neg r}(t_1, \dots, t_n)$, or $\underline{\neg r}(t_1, \dots, t_n)$, or $\overline{\underline{\neg r}}(t_1, \dots, t_n)$. A rough clause has the form *head* :-$[\alpha, F]$ *body*. where the *head* is a rough literal not referring to the boundary region and the *body* is a sequence (representing conjunction) of rough literals and quantitative measure expressions. Moreover, α should be a rational number between 0 and 1 and F should be an associative and commutative binary function.

An example of a rough clause is $\overline{p}(X_1, X_2)$:-[1,min] $\underline{q}(X_1, X_2), \overline{\neg r}(X_1, X_2)$, where symbols like p, q, and r denote some rough relations P, Q, and R, respectively. The expression $\underline{q}(X_1, X_2)$ can be seen as representing an indiscernibility class belonging to the lower approximation of rough relation Q. Note that X_1 and X_2 are variables that can be thought as representing any attribute value. Informally, this rough clause states that, given a tuple $\langle c_1, c_2\rangle$ describing an indiscernibility class, if $\langle c_1, c_2\rangle : k_2 \in \underline{Q}$ and $\langle c_1, c_2\rangle : k_3 \in \overline{\neg R}$ then $\langle c_1, c_2\rangle : k_1 \in \overline{P}$, where $\texttt{supp}(p(c_1, c_2)) = k_1 \geq \lfloor 1 \times \texttt{min}(k_2, k_3)\rfloor$. Hence, function $F = \texttt{min}$ is used to combine $\texttt{supp}(q(c_1, c_2))$ with the $\texttt{supp}(\neg r(c_1, c_2))$. Note that the support k_1 should be computed by taking into account all clauses of a rough program.

In a rough clause, the user-defined parameters α and F make it possible to tune the definition to a particular application and data. For example, a rough clause like $\underline{p}(X, c)$:-[0.8,_] $\underline{q}(X, c)$. could be used if the user strongly doubts of the reliability of the information carried by 20% of the examples, belonging to any indiscernibility class only with positive examples of Q and for which the second attribute has value c. To represent that the choice of function F is irrelevant, we use the symbol '_'.

Also the problem of how to combine the support information, obtained from the expressions in the body strongly depends on the application. For instance, in a clause describing join of two decision tables, F should be the multiplication. In other applications, different functions (e.g. the minimum) might be more appropriate.

Variable Precision Rough Relations. We discuss next how quantitative measure expressions in the body of rough clauses can be used to build more generalized rough approximations of a relation, in the same spirit of the *variable precision rough set model* (VPRSM) [5]. This section also illustrates an important application of our language, since the VPRSM is the rough set model most used in practical applications.

Let $Pr(q)$ be the prior probability of an individual to be a positive example of rough relation Q denoted by a predicate q. Thus, $Pr(q) = \frac{|q|}{|q|+|\neg q|}$. Moreover, assume that l and u are two *precision control parameters* such that $0 \leq l < Pr(q) < u \leq 1$. Generalization of lower (upper) approximation and boundary region of a rough relation can be obtained as follows. The lower approximation of Q $(\neg Q)$is obtained from those indiscernibility classes $[t]$ such that $\mathtt{acc}(q(t)) \geq u$ $(\mathtt{acc}(q(t)) \leq l)$. Those indiscernibility classes $[t]$ such that $l < \mathtt{acc}(q(t)) < u$ are considered to belong to the boundary region $\overline{\underline{Q}}$. This technique can also be seen as a way to "thin" the boundary region and make the approximations obtained less sensitive to possible noise contained in the data.

Example 1. Let q denote a rough relation Q (possibly obtained directly from a decision table and encoded as a set of facts in our language), l and u be two precision control parameters. We define then a new rough relation Q_1 according to the ideas discussed above. Note that the use of $\overline{q}(X_1, X_2), \overline{\neg q}(X_1, X_2)$ in the body of the third and fourth rough clauses captures those indiscernibility classes $[t]$ in the boundary of Q. Moreover, it is worth to note the use of function `sum` to combine $\mathtt{supp}(q(t))$ with $\mathtt{supp}(\neg q(t))$, since $\mathtt{supp}(q(t)) + \mathtt{supp}(\neg q(t))$ gives the total number of individuals in the indiscernibility class $[t]$.

$\overline{q_1}(X_1, X_2)$:-[1,_] $\underline{q}(X_1, X_2)$.
$\overline{\neg q_1}(X_1, X_2)$:-[1,_] $\underline{\neg q}(X_1, X_2)$.
% Any indiscernibility class t in the boundary s.t. $acc(q(t)) \geq u$
% is considered to be in $[t] \in \underline{Q}$
$\underline{q_1}(X_1, X_2)$:-[1, sum] $\overline{q}(X_1, X_2), \overline{\neg q}(X_1, X_2), \mathtt{acc}(q(X_1, X_2)) \geq u$.
% Any indiscernibility class t in the boundary s.t. $acc(q(t)) \leq l$
% is considered to be in $\underline{\neg Q}$
$\underline{\neg q_1}(X_1, X_2)$:-[1, sum] $\overline{q}(X_1, X_2), \overline{\neg q}(X_1, X_2), \mathtt{acc}(q(X_1, X_2)) \leq l$.
% Any indiscernibility class t in the boundary s.t. $l < acc(q(t)) < u$
% remains in the boundary
$\overline{q_1}(X_1, X_2)$:-[1,_] $\overline{q}(X_1, X_2), \mathtt{acc}(q(X_1, X_2)) > l, \mathtt{acc}(q(X_1, X_2)) < u$.
$\overline{\neg q_1}(X_1, X_2)$:-[1,_] $\overline{\neg q}(X_1, X_2), \mathtt{acc}(q(X_1, X_2)) > l, \mathtt{acc}(q(X_1, X_2)) < u$.

Query Language is designed to identify subsets of the rough relations described by a given program and to classify new individuals. Due to the space limitations we can only provide an informal idea. A basic query has the form of rough literal. The answer identifies a subset of the respective rough relation. A query of the form $K = m(r(t))$ binds the variable K with the quantitative measure m of the indiscernibility class $[t]$ of rough relation R. A sequence of the above discussed queries is interpreted as conjunction. For instance, the rough query $(\overline{p}(X_1, b), K = \texttt{acc}(p(X_1, b))\ ,\ \mathcal{P})$ requests the description of all indiscernibility classes in the upper approximation of P such that the second attribute has value b. Moreover, it is also requests information about the accuracy of each of these indiscernibility classes.

We turn now our attention to classifier queries. These queries are of the form $(\texttt{classify}(d(t))\ ,\ \mathcal{P})$. For example, each tuple $t = \langle c_1, c_2, c_3 \rangle$ describing an indiscernibility class of a rough relation D can be seen as a decision rule. Assume that rough relation D corresponds (implicitly) to the decision table $\mathcal{D} = (U, \{a_1, a_2, a_3\}, \mathtt{d})$. If $t \in \overline{D}$ then it induces the decision rule $(a_1 = c_1 \wedge a_2 = c_2 \wedge a_3 = c_3) \rightarrow \mathtt{d} = \texttt{yes}$. If $t \in \overline{\neg D}$ then it induces the decision rule $(a_1 = c_1 \wedge a_2 = c_2 \wedge a_3 = c_3) \rightarrow \mathtt{d} = \texttt{no}$.

The query $(\texttt{classify}(d(c_1, X, c_3)), \mathcal{P})$ requests a prediction for the decision class to which a new individual i described by $(a_1 = c_1 \wedge a_3 = c_3)$ may belong. To answer this query a standard strategy is followed: each rule that match the description of i casts a number of votes corresponding to its support and the decision class is decided by majority of votes. The answer to the rough query is either the pair $(\mathtt{d} = \texttt{yes}, C_F)$, or $(\mathtt{d} = \texttt{no}, C_F)$, or $(\mathtt{d} = \texttt{unknown}, 0)$, where C_F represents a certainty factor. The last case corresponds to the situation where no decision rule is fired.

4 An Application Example

Given a rough relation representing implicity a decision table $\mathcal{D}_A = (U, A, \mathtt{d})$, it may be useful to evaluate how removal of some attributes from A affects the ability of making a decision. In other words, given a subset of attributes $B \subset A$, we may wish to identify those individuals i for which the knowledge about attributes B is absolutely necessary for making a decision, i.e. for determining $d(i)$. A similar problem has been studied in [6]. The set of those individuals i can be defined as $M = (\overline{D}_{A \setminus B} \cap \underline{D}_A) \cup (\overline{D}_{A \setminus B} \cap \underline{\neg D}_A)$. Although this definition looks different from the one used in [6], they are both equivalent. However, the formulation presented here is more suitable in the context of our framework. The set of individuals for which knowledge about attributes B is not strictly needed can then be defined as $\neg M = \underline{\neg D}_{A \setminus B} \cup \underline{D}_{A \setminus B} \cup \overline{\underline{D}}_A$.

Example 2. Consider a decision table $\mathcal{H}\mathrm{p} = (U, \{\mathtt{Age}, \mathtt{A}_1, \mathtt{A}_2\}, \mathtt{Hp})$ encoded as a set of rough facts, where U is a set of patients examined for heart problems (decision attribute Hp). Assume that the conditional attributes $\mathtt{A}_1$ and $\mathtt{A}_2$ represent two medical tests and that $\mathtt{A}_2$ is usually considered as being desirable to avoid. The following rough clauses monitor the impact in the boundary region of Hp of not considering test $\mathtt{A}_2$. Rough clauses (3) and (4) encode the set M. Rough clauses (5), (6), and (7) capture the set $\neg M$.

(1) $\overline{\mathtt{d}}$(Age, A1) :-[1,_] $\overline{\mathtt{hp}}$(Age, A1, A2).
(2) $\overline{\neg\mathtt{d}}$(Age, A1) :-[1,_] $\overline{\neg\mathtt{hp}}$(Age, A1, A2).
(3) $\overline{\mathtt{m}}$(Age, A1) :-[1,min] $\overline{\underline{\mathtt{d}}}$(Age, A1), $\underline{\mathtt{hp}}$(Age, A1, A2).

(4) $\overline{\mathtt{m}}$`(Age, A1) :-[1,min]` $\underline{\mathtt{d}}$`(Age, A1),` $\underline{\neg\mathtt{hp}}$`(Age, A1, A2).`
(5) $\overline{\neg\mathtt{m}}$`(Age, A1) :-[1,_]` $\underline{\neg\mathtt{d}}$`(Age, A1).`
(6) $\overline{\neg\mathtt{m}}$`(Age, A1) :-[1,_]` $\underline{\mathtt{d}}$`(Age, A1).`
(7) $\overline{\neg\mathtt{m}}$`(Age, A1) :-[1,sum]` $\overline{\mathtt{hp}}$`(Age, A1, A2),` $\overline{\neg\mathtt{hp}}$`(Age, A1, A2).`

We give now an example of a useful query. Assume that rough program $\mathcal{P}$ contains all facts encoding the decision table and the rough clauses (1) – (7).

- *"For which patients it may be useful to request the expensive test A_2? And what is the expected gain if only those patients undergo test A_2?"*
  Rough query: $(\overline{\mathtt{m}}(Age, A1), K_1 = \mathtt{strength}(\mathtt{m}(Age, A1)),$ $K_2 = \mathtt{strength}(\neg\mathtt{m}(Age, A1))$, $\mathcal{P})$.
  Notice that $\sum_{[t]\in\overline{M}}(\mathtt{strength}(\mathtt{m}(t)) + \mathtt{strength}(\neg\mathtt{m}(t)))$ gives an indication of the expected gain.

5 Future Work

The implementation based on compilation of rough programs into Prolog is under way. It will be made available through a Web page and will be accompanied by an extended report. We are studying the possibility of integrating it with the **Rosetta** system [7]. In this way, we could use the algorithms already available in **Rosetta** to compute reducts. On the other hand, **Rosetta** could profit from the fact that the VPRSM is easily definable in our language.

As future work, we plan to support several classification algorithms and other quantitative measures. One possibility to achieve this is by a predefined library of classification algorithms and quantitative measures. Another possibility is to extend the language with primitives for specification of classification algorithms and quantitative measures.

References

1. Pawlak, Z.: Rough sets. International Journal of Information and Computer Science **11** (1982) 341–356
2. Vitória, A., Damásio, C.V., Małuszyński, J.: Query answering for rough knowledge bases. In Wang, G., Liu, Q., Yao, Y., Skowron, A., eds.: Proc. of the 9th International Conference on Rough Sets, Fuzzy Sets, Data Mining, and Granular Computing, RSFDGrC'03. Volume 2639 of LNCS/LNAI., (Springer) 197–204
3. Vitória, A., Damásio, C.V., Małuszyński, J.: From rough sets to rough knowledge bases. Fundamenta Informaticae **57** (2003) 215–246
4. Doherty, P., Lukaszewicz, W., Szalas, A.: CAKE: A Computer Aided Knowledge Engineering Technique. In: Proc. of the 15th European Conference on Artificial Intelligence, (ECAI'02), Amsterdam, IOS Press (2002) 220–224
5. Ziarko, W.: Variable precision rough set model. Journal of Computer and Systems Science **46** (1993) 39–59
6. Komorowski, J., Øhrn, A.: Modelling prognostic power of cardiac tests using rough sets. Journal of Artificial Intelligence in Medicine **15** (1999) 167–191
7. Øhrn, A., Komorowski, J.: ROSETTA: A rough set toolkit for analysis of data. In: Proc. of Fifth International Workshop on Rough Sets and Soft Computing (RSSC'97). Volume 3. (1997) 403–407

Considering Semantic Ambiguity and Indistinguishability for Values of Membership Attribute in Possibility-Based Fuzzy Relational Models

Michinori Nakata

Faculty of Management and Information Science,
Josai International University
1 Gumyo, Togane, Chiba, 283-8555, Japan

Abstract. A possibility-based fuzzy relational model is proposed under considering semantic ambiguity and indistinguishability for values of membership attribute. In order to eliminate the semantic ambiguity, a membership attribute is attached to every attribute. This clarifies where each value of membership attributes comes from. What the values of membership attributes mean depends on the property of those attributes. In order to eliminate the indistinguishability for values of membership attribute, these values are expressed by possibility distributions on the interval [0,1]. This clarifies what effects an imprecise data value allowed for an attribute has on its value of membership attribute. Therefore, there is no semantic ambiguity and no indistinguishability for the values of membership attributes in the possibility-based fuzzy relational model.

1 Introduction

Several possibility-based fuzzy relational models dealing with imperfection are proposed by using fuzzy sets and possibility theory[9, 10, 12, 16]. These possibility-based fuzzy relational models have the advantage that they can flexibly deal with imperfect information in Codd's framework[3]. However, the possibility-based fuzzy relational models are accompanied by generating new types of imperfection. Extended relational models handling imperfection must not generate any new types of imperfection. Thus, first we consider semantic ambiguity in possibility-based fuzzy relational models, which was pointed out by Tanaka et al[11]. For example, suppose that the following tuple t exists in a relation $SUPPLIES$ ($SUPPLIER$, $STATUS$, $CITY$, μ) where the primary key is $SUPPLIER$ and μ is a membership attribute:

$$t = (Jones, 20, Uppsala, 0.8)$$

We can interpret this tuple as either of the following:

S. Tsumoto et al. (Eds.): RSCTC 2004, LNAI 3066, pp. 159–168, 2004.

- With the degree 0.8, the supplier is Jones;
- With the degree 0.8, Jones's status is 20;
- With the degree 0.8, the city where Jones is located is Uppsala;
- With the degree 0.8, the supplier is Jones and Jones' status is 20;
- With the degree 0.8, the supplier is Jones and the city where Jones is located is Uppsala;
- With the degree 0.8, Jones' status is 20 and the city where Jones is located is Uppsala;
- With the degree 0.8, the supplier is Jones, Jones' status is 20, and the city where Jones is located is Uppsala.

Such semantic ambiguity is generated from not clarifying with which attributes the membership attribute value is related.

Second, we consider indistinguishability for values of membership attribute, which was pointed out by Chiang et al. [2][1]. In conventional possibility-based fuzzy relational models a value of membership attribute is a single value or a pair of values contained in the interval [0,1]. This value denotes to what degree a tuple value is compatible with imposed restrictions on a relation and is calculated with using a possibility measure and/or a necessity measure. Suppose that an attribute value $t[A_i]$ in a tuple t is expressed in a normal possibility distribution $\pi_{t[A_i]}$ and a restriction c imposed on the attribute is expressed in a normal membership function μ_c. Then, compatibility degrees $Com(c \mid t[A_i])_N$ and $Com(c \mid t[A_i])_\Pi$ obtained from using necessity measure and possibility measure are, respectively,

$$Com(c \mid t[A_i])_N = \min_u \max(1 - \pi_{t[A_i]}(u), \mu_c(u)),$$
$$Com(c \mid t[A_i])_\Pi = \max_u \min(\pi_{t[A_i]}(u), \mu_c(u)).$$

These often give the same value of membership attribute to different imprecise values expressed in normal possibility distributions. For example, suppose that the relation $SUPPLIES$ has the following two tuples:

$$t_1 = (Adams, 20, 1/Uppsala + 0.8/Stockholm + 1/Västeras, 1),$$
$$t_2 = (Jones, 30, 1/Uppsala + 0.2/Stockholm + 1/Norrkoping, 1).$$

When we apply a restriction "$CITY = 1/Uppsala + 0.9/Stockholm$" to the relation $SUPPLIES$, we calculate a compatibility degree of each tuple value with the restriction in order to obtain membership attribute values. Calculation by using a possibility measure gives the same value 1 for these two tuples; even if a necessity measure is used, the same value 0 is obtained[2], although the two tuples have different degrees 0.8 and 0.2 for $Stockholm$ in imprecise values of attribute $CITY$. This comes from that both calculations by possibility and necessity measures reduce the compatibility of the imprecise value to

[1] Chiang et al address the case where a possibility measure is used.

[2] The measure that Chiang et al[2] proposed is equal to α - $Com(c \mid t[A_i])_\Pi$ if a compatibility degree $Com(c \mid t[A_i])_\Pi$ in possibility is less than a threshold α otherwise 0. Thus, their measure also gives the same degree 0 to the above two tuples.

the restriction to a numerical value on the interval $[0, 1]$. Strictly speaking, as is shown in the above formula, these calculations give one numerical value by mixing membership values of a possibility distribution expressing an imprecise value and of a membership function expressing a restriction under using min and max operations. Consequently, only a part of membership values contributes to an obtained compatibility degree and the information for the parts that do not contribute is lost. This leads to indistinguishability for the compatibility degree. This indistinguishability should be eliminated to utilize imperfect information selectively. In order to consider the above mentioned two new types of imperfection, we propose a new possibility-based fuzzy relational model. First, we attach a membership attribute to each conventional attribute in place of a membership attribute attached to the universal set of the conventional attributes in a relation. Thus, any database scheme is constructed from a set of pairs of an attribute and its membership attribute in this model. This is a generalization of fuzzy relation scheme[5, 8]. Furthermore, every value of membership attribute is expressed in a possibility distribution on the interval [0,1]. This is a generalized expression for values of membership attribute[13].

In section 2, we formally define a possibility-based fuzzy relational model freed from semantic ambiguity and indistinguishability for values of membership attribute. In section 3, we show how to calculate a value of membership attribute attached to each attribute in a tuple. And then we address an interpretation for the value of membership attribute attached to each attribute in a tuple. In section 4, we show ranking of values of membership attribute. In section 5, we mention criterions of acceptable and unacceptable tuples. The last section presents some conclusions.

2 Framework

Possibility-based fuzzy relational models are regarded as ones extended conventional relational models[3] by using fuzzy sets[14] and possibility theory[4, 15]. To consider semantic ambiguity in possibility-based fuzzy relational models, we introduce membership attributes attached to individual attributes in place of a membership attribute attached to the universal set of conventional attributes composing a fuzzy relation scheme[8].

Definition 2.1
A fuzzy relation scheme R consists of a set of a conventional attribute A_i and its membership attribute μ_{A_i}; namely, the fuzzy relation scheme with arity n is written as

$$R(A_1, \mu_{A_1}, A_2, \mu_{A_2}, \ldots, A_n, \mu_{A_n}).$$

Definition 2.2
A value $t[A_i]$ of an attribute A_i in a tuple t is expressed in a normal possibility distribution $\pi_{t[A_i]}$.

$$t[A_i] = \sum_{u \in D_i} \pi_{t[A_i]}(u)/u, \ \sup_{u \in D_i} \pi_{t[A_i]}(u) = 1,$$

where each domain D_i is a crisp set and consists of normal elements and an extraneous one that is the "property inapplicable" type of null. So far, the values of membership attribute have been expressed by a single numerical value or a pair of values. These values are calculated by using possibility and necessity measures. Values obtained from using possibility measure are apt to be the same compatibility degree 1 with a restriction, whereas values from necessity measure are to be the same degree 0. Thus, we cannot strictly compare imprecise values in what extent they are compatible with a restriction. In order to utilize imprecise values selectively, we should consider detailed effects of imprecise values and restrictions on obtained compatibility degrees. Thus, we express a value of membership attribute in a normal possibility distribution on the interval [0,1], as is done by Umano and Fukami[13].

Definition 2.3
A value $t[\mu_{A_i}]$[3] of membership attribute μ_{A_i} attached to an attribute A_i in a tuple t is expressed in a normal possibility distribution on the interval [0,1].

$$t[\mu_{A_i}] = \sum_{u \in [0,1]} \pi_{\mu_{A_i}}(u)/(u), \quad \sup_u \pi_{\mu_{A_i}}(u) = 1.$$

Consequently, all the values of attributes and membership attributes are expressed in normal possibility distributions in our model. Thus, our model can be called a generalized possibility-distribution-fuzzy-relational model.

3 Values of Membership Attribute

In possibility-based fuzzy relational models having a membership attribute value attached to a tuple value, the membership attribute value is a compatibility degree of the tuple value with imposed restrictions[6]. In our model this is expressed as follows:

Definition 3.1
A value of membership attribute attached to an attribute in a tuple of a relation is a compatibility degree of that tuple value with related parts with the attribute among imposed restrictions on that relation.

This value denotes to what extent that attribute value is compatible with imposed restrictions on that relation.

When imposed restrictions on a relation r are a set of restrictions $\{c_1, \ldots, c_n\}$, we calculate a compatibility degree with $C = \wedge_p c_p$. Each restriction c_p can be expressed in conjunctive normal form of restriction elements; namely, $c_p = \wedge_{p_j} c_{p_j}$, where each element c_{p_j} can contain logical operators $\vee(or)$ and $\sim(not)$. Let C_{A_i} be the part of C that consists of what A_i appears among the restriction

[3] If necessary, we can easily obtain a value $t[\mu](= \wedge_i t[\mu_{A_i}])$ of membership for a tuple value from $t[\mu_{A_i}]$.

elements; namely, $C_{A_i} = \wedge_{i_j} c_{i_j}$, where c_{i_j} is an element that A_i appears. A value of membership attribute attached to an attribute A_i is:

$$t[\mu_{A_i}] = Com(C_{A_i} \mid t[\mathcal{A}]).$$

$Com(C_{A_i} \mid t[\mathcal{A}])$ is equal to $Com(C_{A_i} \mid t[A_i])$ if C_{A_i} does not contain any attribute except A_i. If each element c_{i_j} is noninteractive,

$$Com(C_{A_i} \mid t[\mathcal{A}]) = \wedge_{i_j} Com(c_{i_j} \mid t[\mathcal{A}]),$$

where $\mathcal{A} = (A_1, \ldots, A_n)$ and $Com(c_{i_j} \mid \mathcal{A})$ is a compatibility degree of a tuple value $t[\mathcal{A}]$ with a restriction element c_{i_j}. This method shows that the value of membership attribute is determined by all the restriction elements containing that attribute.

Subsequently, we show how to evaluate $Com(c|t[\mathcal{A}])$ for a restriction element c. Suppose that the restriction element c contains the only attribute A_i; for example, c is $A_i = a$. A compatibility degree of an attribute value $t[\mathcal{A}]$ with c is:

$$Com(c|t[\mathcal{A}]) = Com(A_i = a|t[A_i]) = \sum_u \pi_{t[A_i]}(u)/\mu_a(u),$$

where μ_a is a membership function expressing a. This formula is derived from the satisfaction degree $\mu_a(u)$ of a possible value u of $t[A_i]$ with a and the degree $\pi_{t[A_i]}(u)$ in possibility that $t[A_i]$ can take u. Two different types of degrees separate; namely, both effects of imprecise values and restrictions on the compatibility degree do not mix in this formula. We can separately know detailed effects of imprecise values and restrictions on the compatibility degree. Thus, the distinguishability, created from mixing membership values of an imprecise value and restrictions under using min and max operations, disappears for calculated compatibility degrees[4].

When a restriction element c contains a logical operator $\sim$ that denotes negation; for example, $\sim (A_i = a)$,

$$Com(\sim (A_i = a)|t[\mathcal{A}]) = \sum_u \pi_{t[A_i]}(u)/\mu_{\bar{a}}(u),$$

where $\mu_{\bar{a}}(u) = 1 - \mu_a(u)$.

When c contain a logical operator $\vee$ that denotes disjunction; for example, c is $A_i = a \vee A_j = b$ where $i \neq j$,

$$\begin{aligned} Com(c|t[\mathcal{A}]) &= Com(A_i = a \vee A_j = b|t[\mathcal{A}]) \\ &= Com(A_i = a|t[\mathcal{A}]) \vee Com(A_j = b|t[\mathcal{A}]) \\ &= \sum_{u,v} \min(\pi_{t[A_i]}(u), \pi_{t[A_j]}(v))/\max(\mu_a(u), \mu_b(v)). \end{aligned}$$

[4] Indeed, different degrees $Com(c|t_1[CITY]) = 1/1 + 0.8/0.9 + 1/0$ and $Com(c|t_2[CITY]) = 1/1 + 0.2/0.9 + 1/0$ are obtained for two tuples t_1 and t_2 in section 1.

If $i = j$,

$$Com(c|t[\mathcal{A}]) = Com(A_i = a \vee b|t[\mathcal{A}]) = \sum_u \pi_{t[A_i]}(u)/\max(\mu_a(u), \mu_b(u)).$$

For conjunction $\wedge$ of two restriction elements c_i and c_j ; for example, c_i is $A_i = a$ and c_j is $A_j = b$ where $i \neq j$,

$$\begin{aligned} Com(c_i \wedge c_j|t[\mathcal{A}]) &= Com(c_i|t[\mathcal{A}]) \wedge Com(c_j|t[\mathcal{A}]) \\ &= \sum_{u,v} \min(\pi_{t[A_i]}(u), \pi_{t[A_j]}(v))/\min(\mu_a(u), \mu_b(v)). \end{aligned}$$

If $i = j$,

$$Com(c_i \wedge c_j|t[\mathcal{A}]) = Com(A_i = a \wedge b|t[\mathcal{A}]) = \sum_u \pi_{t[A_i]}(u)/\min(\mu_a(u), \mu_b(u)).$$

Example 3.2
Suppose that the only imposed restriction on relation $scs1$ is "*If SUPPLIER is* $1/a$+$1/b$, *then STATUS is about* 20 *and CITY is* $1/x$+$1/y$". This restriction is reformulated in conjunctive normal form as follows:

$$\begin{aligned} C &= \sim (S\# = 1/a + 1/b) \vee ((ST = \textit{about } 20) \wedge (CT = 1/x + 1/y)), \\ &= (\sim (S\# = 1/a + 1/b) \vee (ST = \textit{about } 20)) \wedge \\ &\quad (\sim (S\# = 1/a + 1/b) \vee (CT = 1/x + 1/y)), \end{aligned}$$

where $S\#$, CT, and ST are abbreviations of $SUPPLIER$, $CITY$, and $STATUS$, respectively.

Thus, parts related with each attribute are as follows:

$$\begin{aligned} C_{S\#} &= C, \\ C_{CT} &= \sim (S\# = 1/a + 1/b) \vee (CT = 1/x + 1/y), \\ C_{ST} &= \sim (S\# = 1/a + 1/b) \vee (ST = \textit{about } 20), \end{aligned}$$

When *about* x is $0.3/(x-3) + 0.8/(x-2) + 1/(x-1) + 1/x + 1/(x+1) + 0.8/(x+2) + 0.3/(x+3)$, each value of membership attributes attached to attributes is as follows:

*scs*1

$S\#$	$\mu_{S\#}$	CT	μ_{CT}	ST	μ_{ST}
$1/a$	1/0+1/.3	$1/x$	1/1	1/16+1/17	1/0+1/.3
$1/b$	1/.8+1/1	$1/y$	1/1	1/21+1/22	1/.8+1/1
$1/c$	1/1	$1/x$	1/1	1/23	1/1

Any relation in relational models has a set X of attributes corresponding to the primary key by whose value every tuple can be uniquely distinguished. When Y is a collection of attributes not contained in X, a functional dependency $X \to Y$ holds in the relation. Under these circumstances it is natural that an interpretation of values of membership attributes attached to attributes in X is different from one to attributes in Y. Suppose that a value of an attribute A_i is v in a tuple t. If the attribute is contained in the primary key X, the value $t[\mu_{A_i}]$ of membership attribute is the degree with which the value of A_i is v; otherwise, it is the degree with which the value $t[X]$ of the primary key has the property that the value of A_i is v.

Example 3.3
Suppose that the primary key is $SUPPLIER$ in relation $scs1$. We interpret each value of membership attributes of the second tuple in Example 3.2 as follows:
The degree that a supplier is b is $1/0.8 + 1/1$;
The degree that the city where b is located is y is $1/1$;
The degree that the status of b is $1/21 + 1/22$ is $1/0.8 + 1/1$.

4 Ranking of Values of Membership Attribute

We are often required to sort tuples in ascending order or descending order for values of membership attribute. We can rank values of membership attribute in order for the following cases:

Ranking of Values of Membership Attribute
Suppose that two values $t_1[\mu_{A_i}]$ and $t_2[\mu_{A_i}]$ of membership attribute are obtained. If $t_1[\mu_{A_i}] \vee t_2[\mu_{A_i}] = t_2[\mu_{A_i}]$ or $t_1[\mu_{A_i}] \wedge t_2[\mu_{A_i}] = t_1[\mu_{A_i}]$, then $t_1[\mu_{A_i}] \leq t_2[\mu_{A_i}]$.

Unfortunately, we cannot always rank values of membership attribute in order by using this way, because two values of membership attribute do not always satisfy the above relationship. Thus, we rank values of membership attribute in order in another way, when we cannot rank two values of membership attribute in order by using the above way. Every value of membership attribute, a calculated value, is a compatibility degree of a tuple value with a part of restrictions. From this value we can obtain compatibility degrees in necessity and in possibility; namely, values of membership attribute obtained by using necessity and possibility measures as follows:

Suppose that a value $t[\mu_{A_i}]$ of membership attribute μ_{A_i} attached to an attribute A_i in a tuple t is $\sum_{u \in [0,1]} \pi_{\mu_{A_i}}(u)/u$.

$$t_N[\mu_{A_i}] = \min_u \max(1 - \pi_{\mu_{A_i}}(u), u),$$
$$t_\Pi[\mu_{A_i}] = \max_u \min(\pi_{\mu_{A_i}}(u), u),$$

where $t_N[\mu_{A_i}]$ and $t_\Pi[\mu_{A_i}]$ are values of membership attribute in necessity and in possibility. By using these values we rank values of membership attribute in ascending order or in descending order as follows:

Definition 4.1
Suppose that we obtain $(t_{N,1}[\mu_{A_i}], t_{\Pi,1}[\mu_{A_i}])$ and $(t_{N,2}[\mu_{A_i}], t_{\Pi,2}[\mu_{A_i}])$ from $t_1[\mu_{A_i}]$ and $t_2[\mu_{A_i}]$, respectively.

$$\begin{aligned}&\text{If } t_{N,1}[\mu_{A_i}] < t_{N,2}[\mu_{A_i}], \text{then } t_1[\mu_{A_i}] \prec t_2[\mu_{A_i}];\\ &\text{if } t_{N,1}[\mu_{A_i}] = t_{N,2}[\mu_{A_i}] \text{ and } t_{\Pi,1}[\mu_{A_i}] < t_{\Pi,2}[\mu_{A_i}], \text{then } t_1[\mu_{A_i}] \prec t_2[\mu_{A_i}];\\ &\text{if } t_{N,1}[\mu_{A_i}] = t_{N,2}[\mu_{A_i}] \text{ and } t_{\Pi,1}[\mu_{A_i}] = t_{\Pi,2}[\mu_{A_i}], \text{then } t_1[\mu_{A_i}] \approx t_2[\mu_{A_i}];\\ &\quad\text{otherwise} \quad t_1[\mu_{A_i}] \succ t_2[\mu_{A_i}],\end{aligned}$$

where $\prec$, $\succ$, and $\approx$ denote order by using necessity and possibility measures.

Proposition 4.2
If $t_1[\mu_{A_i}] \leq t_2[\mu_{A_i}]$, then $t_1[\mu_{A_i}] \preceq t_2[\mu_{A_i}]$, where $\preceq$ denotes $\prec$ or $\approx$.

5 Acceptable Tuples

It is known that unacceptable components appear in possibility-based fuzzy relational models having a membership attribute attached to the universal set of attributes[1, 7]. This is also true for our model, because an imprecise value is allowed for any attribute value. Each attribute value has possible attribute values. For a possible attribute value its compatibility degree with imposed restrictions is greater than or equal to its incompatibility degree, whereas for another possible attribute value it does not so. The former possible attribute value is called acceptable and the latter unacceptable. For an attribute value we have three cases as follows:

1. All possible attribute values are acceptable.
2. Some possible attribute values are acceptable, whereas the others are unacceptable.
3. All possible attribute values are unacceptable.

Under these circumstances the criterion of acceptable tuples in our model is as follows:

Criterion of Acceptable Tuples
A tuple is acceptable to a relation if for all the attributes of that tuple there exists at least one possible value whose compatibility degree with imposed restrictions is greater than or equal to its incompatibility degree.

This criterion corresponds to the cases 1 and 2. On the other hand, the criterion of unacceptable tuples is as follows:

Criterion of Unacceptable Tuples
A tuple is unacceptable to a relation if for all the possible values of at least one attribute in that tuple the compatibility degree with imposed restrictions is less than the incompatibility degree.

This criterion corresponds to the case 3 and is formulated as follows:

$$\exists A_i \;\; u < 0.5 \;\; for \;\; all \;\; u \;\; with \;\; \mu_{t[A_i]}(u) > 0.$$

Tuples that satisfy the criterion are called unacceptable tuples. Even if a tuple is an unacceptable one in a relation, it remains in the relation. This assures us that correct results are obtained in query processing[5]. However, acceptable tuples should be separated from unacceptable ones, because users take an interest in the acceptable tuples, but not the unacceptable ones in query processing. Hence, only acceptable tuples should be shown to users from derived relations in query processing, although unacceptable tuples have to remain in order to obtain correct results.

Example 5.1
By the criterion of unacceptable tuples, the first tuple in relation *scs*1 of Example 3.2 is unacceptable.

6 Conclusions

We have proposed a new possibility-based fuzzy relational model where semantic ambiguity and indistinguishability for values of membership attribute do not appear. First, every attribute is accompanied by its membership attribute. This extension clarifies where each value of membership attributes comes from. The value of membership attribute attached to an attribute in a relation denotes to what extent that attribute value is compatible with imposed restrictions on that relation. And also the interpretation of values of membership attributes clarifies by this extension. The meaning of a value of membership attribute attached to an attribute depends on whether that attribute is contained in the primary key. Thus, there is no semantic ambiguity for the values of membership attributes. Second, values of membership attributes are expressed in normal possibility distributions on the interval [0, 1]. This clarifies what effects imprecise values have on values of membership attributes. We can more selectively use the information that imprecise values have than in the conventional possibility-based fuzzy relational models. Thus, there is no indistinguishability for the values of membership attributes in our possibility-based fuzzy relational model.

We have strictly dealt with imperfect information in Codd's framework in order to free possibility-based fuzzy relational models from semantic ambiguity and indistinguishability for values of membership attribute. This is particularly significant in order to utilize imperfect information without loss of information. On the other hand, some features that are cumbersome for users appear: values of membership attribute have representational complexity, unacceptable tuples remain in relations, a compatibility degree of a tuple value with the whole restrictions is not explicitly shown, and so on. To lighten burdens of users from these features and to flexibly respond to a variety of queries from users, some interfaces would be required in databases strictly handling imperfection.

[5] For example, we cannot obtain correct results for difference operations without considering unacceptable tuples.

Acknowledgement

The author wishes to thank the anonymous reviewers for their valuable comments. This research has partially been supported by the Grant-in-Aid for Scientific Research (B), Japan Society for the Promotion of Science, No. 14380171.

References

1. Bosc, P. and Pivert, O. [2003] On the Impact of Regular Functional Dependencies When Moving to a Possibilistic Database Framework, Fuzzy Sets and Systems, **171**, 207-227.
2. Chiang, D. A., Lin, N. P., and Shis, C. C. [1998]Matching Strengths of Answers in Fuzzy Relational Databases, IEEE Transactions on Systems, Man, and Cybernetics, Part C: Applications and Reviews, **28**:3, 476-481.
3. Codd, E. F. [1970] A Relational Model of Data for Large Shared Banks, Communications of ACM, **13**, 377-387.
4. Dubois, D. and Prade, H. with the Collaboration of H. Farreny, R. Martin-Clouaire and C. Testemale [1988] Possibility Theory: An Approach to Computerized Processing of Uncertainty, Plenum Publishing Co. 1988.
5. Medina, J. M., Pons, O., and Vila, M. A. [1994] GEFRED: A Generalized Model of Fuzzy Relational Databases, Information Sciences, **76**, 87-109.
6. Nakata, M. [1993] Integrity Constraints in Fuzzy Databases, in Proceedings of the first Asian Fuzzy System Symposium, (Singapore, November 23-26, 1993).
7. Nakata, M. [1996] Unacceptable Components in Fuzzy Relational Databases, International Journal of Intelligent Systems, **11**:9, pp.633-648.
8. Nakata, M. [1999] A Semantic-Ambiguity-Free Relational Model for Handling Imperfect Information, Journal of Advanced Computational Intelligence, **3**, 3-12.
9. Prade, H. [1984] Lipski's Approach to Incomplete Information Data Bases Restated and Generalized in the Setting of Zadeh's Possibility Theory, Information Systems 9:1, 27-42.
10. Prade, H. and Testemale, C. [1984] Generalizing Database Relational Algebra for the Treatment of Incomplete or Uncertain Information and Vague Queries, Information Science, **34**, 115-143.
11. Tanaka, K., Kobayashi, S., and Sakanoue, T. [1991] Uncertainty Management in Object-Oriented Database Systems, Proceedings of Database and Expert Systems Applications, DEXA '91, D. Karagiannis, Ed., Springer-Verlag, pp. 251-256.
12. Umano, M. [1982] FREEDOM-O: A Fuzzy Database System, Fuzzy Information and Decision Processes, M. M. Gupta and E. Sanchez, eds., North-Holland, Amsterdam, pp. 339-347.
13. Umano, M. and Fukami, S. [1994] Fuzzy Relational Algebra for Possibility-Distribution-Fuzzy-Relational Model of Fuzzy Data, Journal of Intelligent Information Systems, **3**, 7-27.
14. Zadeh, L. A. [1965] Fuzzy Sets, Information and Control, **12**, 338-353.
15. Zadeh, L. A. [1978] Fuzzy Sets as a Basis for a Theory of Possibility, Fuzzy Sets and Systems, **1**, 3-28.
16. Zemankova, M. and Kandel, A. [1984] Fuzzy Relational Databases – Key to Expert Systems, Verlag TÜV Rheinland, Cologne, 1984.

Research on Integrating Ordbms and Rough Set Theory

HuiQin Sun, Zhang Xiong, and Ye Wang

Bei Hang University 601#, XueYuan Road 37#
HaiDian District, Beijing, China 100083
Sunhuiqin2000@yahoo.com.cn

Abstract. It is a new application area that integrating rough set theory and ORDBMS to implement data mining in ORDBMS. A suitable rough set algebra must be designed to implement the tight coupling between rough set and ORDBMS. Equivalence matrices algebra doesn't meet this requirement and must be extended. We extend the equivalence matrices algebra to define the low and upper approximation, relative core and reduction. A prototype system has been designed and implemented in our research, called RSORDMS, adding data mining capabilities to ORDBMS while preserving its traditional power. In the prototype system, a technique is adopted which combines rough set with SQL to make data cleaning and core computation very fast, which can be proved by experiments. The whole prototype system has a good performance.

1 Introduction

With the development of data mining, on the one hand improving the methods' performance should be still on research. On the other hand its architecture should be emphasized which is the basis of data mining applied in practice. There are several advantages of tight coupling [1] between data mining and the mature database. Firstly, database is mature after development of many years. Data mining system, which needn't to be designed from start as the current system, can be smoothly integrated with all kinds of applications. Secondly, the research work of data mining is more successive. The knowledge of data mining can be defined and queried by the common query languages. Good query optimization relating to the improvement of data mining can be embedded into database as standard library functions.

In 1997, ORACLE published ORACLE8 providing the feature of object and relation. From then on, the ORDBMS(Object Relation Database Management System) based on object and relation model becomes mainstream. ORDBMS supports abstract data types and user defined functions which extend the system [2].

Rough set has the ability of classification and rule extraction which has the wider application areas. Integrating rough set theory with the architecture of database will unify the advantages of rough set with that of database and drive the development of both rapidly.

S. Tsumoto et al. (Eds.): RSCTC 2004, LNAI 3066, pp. 169–175, 2004.

2 Difficulties and Strategies

There are several difficulties in implementing tight coupling between rough set and ORDBMS. Firstly, traditional rough set algebra is based on set operations, for example, deciding if one set is the subset of another set. Traditional ORDBMS can't provide these operations. This paper solves this problem by adopting the method of translating traditional rough set algebra to equivalence matrix algebra. Secondly, how to improve the performance of the system? Such techniques are adopted as combining rough set with SQL to make data cleaning and core computation very fast. The method of core computation will be presented in the following section. A method of data cleaning is introduced as follows to eliminate the inconsistent and reduplicate data before data mining which is faster and easier than that of literature [9]:

(1) Eliminate the reduplicate objects. If the values of all attributes of two objects are same, they are reduplicate and just one of those objects should be remained. Suppose table a is composed of condition attributes (b and c) and decision attributes (d) in ORACLE. The following SQL statement implements this function:
delete from a where a.rowid!=(select max(rowid) from a b
where a.b=b.b and a.c=b.c and a.d=b.d)

(2) Eliminate the inconsistent objects. Two objects u_i and u_j are inconsistent means that the values of all condition attributes of those two objects are the same but the values of their decision attributes are different. The following SQL statement implements this function to table a in (1):
delete from a where a.rowid!=(select max(rowid) from a b
where a.b=b.b and a.c=b.c)

3 The Algebra Based on Rough Set Theory

The current equivalence matrix algebra is incomplete because it only defines the absolute reduction without the definition of relative reduction and core. This paper extends equivalence matrix algebra of rough set.

3.1 Basic Extension of Algebra

Definition 1 [3]: Let S = <U, A, V, f> be a information system, $X_i, X_j \in U$, $C \subseteq A$. Binary n×n equivalence matrix Mc = [a_{ij}] is defined as follows:

$$a_{ij} = \begin{cases} 1, & x_i E_c x_j \\ 0 & else \end{cases}$$, i,j=1,2,…,n; where Ec is an equivalence relation defined as follows: $xE_c y \Leftrightarrow (\forall c \in C), f(x,c) = f(y,c)$

Equivalence relation is an important concept in rough set theory. Literature [3] proves the isomorphism between equivalence matrices and relations.

Definition 2 [3]: Let $M_1 = [r_{ij}]$, $M_2 = [r_{ij}']$ be two binary nxn matrices. The intersection $M_1 \cap M_2$ of M_1 and M_2 is defined as follows: $M_1 \cap M_2 = [s_{ij}]$, $s_{ij} = r_{ij} \cap r_{ij}' = \min(r_{ij}, r_{ij}')$.

Definition 3: Definition of decision array , "$\leqslant$" and "$\cap$"operator.

Let S = <U,A,V,f> be an information system, X is a set, which is corresponding to an array x[length], where length is the number of elements in U. If $u_i \in X$ then x[i]=1 else x[i] = 0. Sx and Sy are two arrays. If every element in Sx is less than that of Sy, then Sx $\leqslant$ Sy. Sx $\cap$ Sy = Sz , If Sx[i] = 1 and Sy[i] = 1 then Sz[i] = 1 else Sz[i] = 0.

We can get the conclusion: x and y are two sets. The corresponding arrays are Sx and Sy. If $x \subseteq y$ then Sx $\leqslant$ Sy; If Sx $\leqslant$ Sy then $x \subseteq y$.

Theorem 1: The "$\leqslant$" operation of decision arrays elements is isomorphic to the "$\subseteq$" operation of sets. The "$\cap$" operation of array elements is isomorphic to the "$\cap$" operation of sets.

Proof: Suppose that Sx and Sy are two decision arrays corresponding to sets of x and y. $\forall$ Sx, Sy, Sx $\leqslant$ Sy if and only if $x \subseteq y$. And $\forall$ Sx, it is only corresponding to set x and vice versa.

On the one hand, $\forall$ Sx, Sy, Sx $\cap$ Sy = Sz , Sz[i] = 1 If and only if Sx[i] = 1 and Sy[i] = 1. On the other hand, $x \cap y = z$, ui$\in$ z if and only if ui$\in$ x and ui$\in$ y; i.e., Sz[i] = 1 If and only if Sx[i] = 1 and Sy[i] = 1. □

After the definition of equivalence matrices and decision arrays, it is simple to get the low and upper approximation. The algorithm proposed by this paper is as follows:

Algorithm 1: The low and upper approximation of set X

1) Form the equivalence matrix Mc and the array of the set X, Sx.
2) For i = 1 to n
3) Compute if the i'th row of Mc is the subset of Sx. If i'th row of Mc is"$\leqslant$"Sx and j'th element of i'th row of Mc is "1", set the j'th element of Su to be "1". Compute the intersection the i'th row of Mc and the array Sx. If the k'th element of the result is "1", set the k'th element of Sv to be "1".
4) For j = 1 to n If $a_{ij} \in$ Mc is not "1", next j; Otherwise set the elements of j'th row of Mc to be zeros. next j
5) Next i

Su is the array of the low approximation of X. Sv is the array of the upper approximation of X. The corresponding objects of Su and Sv are the low and upper approximations of set X. Su is also called the positive region of the set X.

Definition 4: Array Sx , Sy. If Sx $\leqslant$ Sy, then Sy $\leqslant$ Sx is equal to the difference operation in math. If Sy[i] = 1 and Sx[i] = 1, the result is zero. If Sy[i] = 0 and Sx[i] = 0, the result is zero. If Sy[i] =1 and Sx[i] = 0, the result is "1".

Algorithm 2: The negative and boundary region of set
Suppose that Su and Sv is the array of the low approximation and upper approximation of X, all element of Sy are “1”. The negative region is Sy–Su. The boundary region is Sv–Su.

Algorithm 3: the positive region of the whole information system S = <U,A,V,f>
In algorithm 3, the decision sets are multi-sets and the decision arrays are multi-arrays. So we need to compare multi-arrays, not just an array as algorithm 1.

1) Form equivalence matrix and multi decision arrays: S_{d1}, S_{d2},…, S_{dk}.
2) Array Sx := S_{d1}
3) Repeat the steps of algorithm 1.
4) Set Sx to be the next decision array. If the next decision array is not NULL, Go to 3). Otherwise, the whole algorithm ends. Su is the positive region of the whole information system.

3.2 Advanced Extension of Algebra

We will introduce the definitions and algorithms of relative core and reduction based on equivalence matrices and SQL statement.

Definition 5 [3]: Let X be a non-empty subset of A: $\Phi \subset X \subseteq A$. Given an attribute $x \in X$, we say that x is significant in X if $M_X < M_{X-\{x\}}$; and that x is not significant or nonsignificant in X if $M_X = M_{X-\{x\}}$.

In Literature [3], the core is composed of all significant elements, which can be also seen as the absolute core of information system.

The relative core and reduction are more common in practice. The following part will give the definitions and algorithms of relative core and reduction based on equivalence matrices.

Definition 6: Let S = <U,A,V,f> be an information system. Condition attributes set corresponding to matrix M_c is C. Decision attributes set is D corresponding to decision arrays S_{d1}, S_{d2}, …, S_{dk}. The positive region is $POS_C(D)$ according to algorithm 3.

Definition 7: Suppose the symbols are same as definition 6. For every attribute $x \in C$, positive region of $POS_C(D)$ and $POS_{(C-\{x\})}(D)$ are gotten according to algorithm 3. x is significant in C relative to D if $POS_C(D) <> POS_{(C-\{x\})}(D)$, and x is not significant or nonsignificant in C relative to D if $POS_C(D) = POS_{(C-\{x\})}(D)$. The set of all significant attributes in C relative to D is called relative core, expressed by C_X.

Definition 8: Suppose the symbols are same as definition 6. If (1) $POS_C(D) = POS_{C0}(D)$,(2) C_0 is independent, that is, $POS_{C0}(D) < > POS_P(D)$ for every $P \subset C_0$, then C_0 is the relative reduction of D.

Core, one of the most important rough set's concepts. It can be used as a basis to compute a reduct. The paper computes the core according to several algorithms.

Algorithm 4: Method 1 of relative core based on equivalence matrix
This method is based on definition 7. For every condition attribute x, If $POS_C(D)$ <> $POS_{C-\{x\}}(D)$, then x belongs to relative core. The core is composed of all such x.

Algorithm 5: Method 2 of relative core based on equivalence matrices
Suppose that Condition attributes set is C. Decision attributes set D is corresponding to equivalence matrix M_D. For each $x \in C$ corresponding to equivalence matrix M_x and $M_{C-\{x\}}$. Suppose that the value between i'th object and j'th object is zero in M_D, which is zero in M_x and "1" in $M_{C-\{x\}}$. Then x belongs to the core of C relative to D.

Proof: From literature [5] a discernibility matrix M ={m_{ij}} is defined as follows:

$$m_{ij} = \begin{cases} \{x \in C : F(u_i,x) \neq F(u_j,x)\}, if F(u_i,D) \neq F(u_j,D) \\ \phi \quad else \end{cases} \quad i,j=1,2,\ldots,n;$$

Where C is the set of condition attributes, x is a condition attribute, D is the set of decision attributes, u_i and u_j are two objects. $F(u_i,D) \neq F(u_j,D)$ means the decision attributes vaules of D between u_i and u_j are different. $F(u_i,x) \neq F(u_j,x)$ means the condition attribute values of x between u_i and u_j are different.

The following conclusion is given [5]: in a consistent and complete information system, if and only if m_{ij} is a single condition attribute, it belongs to the relative core.

Suppose the conditions of the above algorithm are satisfied. We analyze these conditions that if the value between i'th object and j'th object is zero in M_D, then the decision attributes values between u_i and u_j are different. For each attribute $x \in X$, the value between i'th object and j'th object is zero in M_x which is "1" in $M_{X-\{x\}}$, that is, the values of all condition attributes except x are same. Because x is a single attribute, x belongs to the core from literature [5]. Because the matrix is symmetrical, we only search the element of the upper triangle or low triangle.

Algorithm 6 (The method 3 for relative core with SQL statement in consistent information system): The SQL statements in ORACLE run very fast even with a large amount of data. The following relative core is computed from a simple and feasible algorithm with SQL language. Designing the corresponding SQL language is based on the principle of literature [5]. In a consistent and complete information system, for two objects u_i and u_j, the values of their decision attribute are different but the values of all except one condition attributes are the same. This single condition attribute belongs to the relative core of the decision table. Suppose that table a includes: condition attributes a1, a2, a3, a4 and decision attributes d. The PL/SQL program deciding if a1 is significant to table a is listed as follows:

```
procedure ComputeCore;
    TYPE t_cursor IS REF CURSOR;
    v_a  integer;  v_cursor t_cursor;
  begin
    OPEN v_cursor FOR
```

```
    select count(*) from a ,a  b
    where a.a2=b.a2 and a.a3=b.a3 and a.a4=b.a4
          and a.a1<>b.a1 and a.d<>b.d;
    FETCH v_cursor into v_a;
    IF v_a=0 THEN
      DBMS_OUTPUT.PUT_LINE('a1 is nonsignificant');
    ELSE DBMS_OUTPUT.PUT_LINE('a1 is significant');
    END IF;
    CLOSE v_cursor;
  end.
```

Some experiments have been done with a large amount of data. Data comes from UCI. The results of experiments is listed as follows:

Table 1. The results of experiments.

Database	m	N	Algorithm 5(seconds)	Algorithm 6(seconds)
Table 1	14	4	0.087	0.001
	70	7	0.12	0.006
vote	435	16	2.3	0.045
Chess	3196	36	116.8	0.58
Mushroom	8124	22	230.6	1.23

Where m is the number of objects and N is the number of condition attributes.

From the results of experiments, we know the algorithm 6 is feasible with high performance, which adapts to the large data sets.

Algorithm 7 (The method 1 for relative core with SQL statement in inconsistent information system): Under the condition of inconsistent data, SQL language for relative core is also designed which is based on the principle of literature [10] and [11]. Firstly a temporary table is created according to definition 7 in literature [11]. Secondly, the SQL statements similar to algorithm 6 which are built on the temporary table are created deciding if each condition attribute is significant.

4 Conclusion

Although the unique advantages of rough set theory have been paid more attention to, application of rough set theory has no obvious effects in industries as Ziarko said in the literature [6]. In order to promote rough set theory to be used in wider practical areas, extending ORDBMS to integrate rough set is of bright application prospect.

This paper extends the algebra of integrating rough set theory and ORDBMS. A prototype system has been designed and implemented, called RSORDMS (Rough Set-Object Relation Data Mining System). RSORDMS keeps the power of the object relation systems while adding data mining capabilities. The result of experiments shows the system runs effectively with good performance. We are faced with several difficulties: (1) How to make our system adapt to vast amount of data? (2) The design of query language of rough set theory. These are what we will further research.

References

1. Jia Wei Han. *Data Mining*. Beijing: Higher Education Press, 2001.
2. Patrick O'Neil. Database: principles, programming and performance. China Machine Press, 2002.
3. J.W. Guan, D.A.Bell, Z.Guan. Matrix computation for information systems. *Information sciences*, 2001, January, Vol.131. Issue: 1-4:129-156.
4. Wang guoyin. *Rough set theory and knowledge acquisition.* Press of Xi'an Jiao Tong University. 2001.
5. Hu XiaoHua, Cercone N. Learning in relational databases: a rough set approach. *Computational Intelligence*, 11(2),1995, 338 – 347.
6. Ziarko W. Rough sets: Trends, challenges, and prospect. In: Ziarko W, Yao Y Y ed. *Rough Sets and current Trends in computing*, Berlin : Springer Verlag, 2001,1 ~ 7.
7. Liu Shao-hui, Shi zhong-zhi. Research on efficient algorithms for rough set methods. *Chinese Journal of Computers*, 26(5), 2003, 524~529.
8. Scott Urman. *ORACLE8i Advanced PL/SQL Programming*. China Machine Press, 2001.
9. Tian-Le Tan,Zhi-Huan Song, Ping Li. Matrix computation for data cleaning and rule extraction in information system. *Proceedings of the First International Conference on Machine Learning and Cybernetics*, Beijing, 2002, 116-120.
10. Ye Dong-yi, Chen Zhao-jiong. A new discernibility matrix and the computation of a core. *ACTA electronic SINICA*, 30(7), 2002,1086-1088.
11. Zheng Zheng, Guo yin Wang. Yu Wu. Objects' Combination Based Simple Computation of Attribute Core. *Proceedings of the 2002 IEEE International Symposium on Intelligent Control*, Canada, 2002,513-519.

Feature Subset Selection Based on Relative Dependency between Attributes

Jianchao Han[1], Xiaohua Hu[2], and Tsao Young Lin[3]

[1] Dept. of Computer Science, California State University Dominguez Hills
1000 E. Victoria St., Carson, CA 90747, USA
[2] College of Information Science and Technology, Drexel University
3141 Chestnut St., Philadelphia, PA 19104, USA
[3] Dept. of Computer Science, San Jose State University
One Washington Square, San Jose, CA 94403, USA

Abstract. Feature subset selection is an importent component of knowledge discovery and data mining systems to help reduce the data dimensionality. Rough sets theory provides a mechanism of selecting feature subsets. In the rough set community, most feature subset selection algorithms are attributes reduct-oriented; that is, finding minimum reducts of the conditional attributes of a decision table. Two main approaches to finding attribute reducts are categorized as discernibility functions-based and attribute dependency-based. These algorithms, however, suffer from intensive computations of either discernibility functions for the former or positive regions for the latter. In this paper, we propose a new concept, called *relative attribute dependency*, and present a sufficient and necessary condition of the minimum conditional attributes reduct of a decision table represented with the relative attribute dependency. The relative attribute dependency can be calculated by counting the distinct rows of the sub-decision table, instead of generating discernibility functions or positive regions. Thus the computation efficiency of minimum reducts are highly improved. We develop two algorithms for finding minimum reducts of the conditional attributes, one brute-force algorithm and the other heuristic algorithm using attribute entropy as the heuristic function. We also show the results of these algorithms by an illustrative example.

Keywords: Feature subset selection, Data reduction, Rough set theory

1 Introduction

Feature subset selection is a process we employ to choose a subset of attributes from the original attributes set. Feature subset selection has been studied intensively in the past decades [3, 4, 6–8, 14]. The purpose of feature selection is to identify the significant features, eliminate the irrelevant or dispensable features to the learning task, and build a good learning model. The benefits of feature selection are twofold: it considerably decreases the running time of the induction algorithm, and increases the accuracy of the resulting model.

S. Tsumoto et al. (Eds.): RSCTC 2004, LNAI 3066, pp. 176–185, 2004.

Two kinds of attributes are generally perceived as being unnecessary: attributes that are irrelevant to the target concept such as student ID, and attributes that are redundant given other attributes. These two kinds of unnecessary attributes may exist simultaneously but redundant attributes are more difficult to eliminate because of the interactions between attributes. Moreover, noise attributes may mislead learning algorithms into incorrect learning results.

All existing feature subset selection algorithms fall into two categories [3, 6]: (1) the filter approach and (2) the wrapper approach. In the filter approach, the feature subset selection is performed as a preprocessing step to induction algorithms. Some of the well-known filter feature subset selection algorithms are RELIEF [4] and PRESET [7]. The filter approach is ineffective in dealing with the feature redundancy. In the wrapper approach [3], the feature subset selection is "wrapped around" an induction algorithm, so that the bias of the operators that define the search and that of the induction algorithm interact mutually. Though the wrapper approach suffers less from feature interaction, nonetheless, its running time would make the wrapper approach infeasible in practice, especially if there are many features, because the wrapper approach keeps running the induction algorithm on different subsets from the entire attributes set until a desirable subset is identified.

In the rough set community, most feature subset selection algorithms are attributes reduct-oriented; that is, finding minimum reducts of the conditional attributes of a decision table. Two main approaches to finding attribute reducts are recognized as discernibility functions-based [2, 4, 14] and attribute dependency-based [12, 13, 15]. These algorithms, however, suffer from intensive computations of either discernibility functions for the former or positive regions for the latter, although some computation efficiency improvement have been made in some new developments [1, 4, 5, 8, 10].

In this paper, we propose a new definition of attribute dependency, called *relative attribute dependency*, and present a sufficient and necessary condition of the minimum reduct of conditional attributes of a decision table, represented with the relative attribute dependency. The relative attribute dependency degree can be calculated by counting the distinct rows of the sub-table of the decision table, instead of generating discernibility functions or positive regions. Thus the computation efficiency of finding minimum reducts is highly improved.

The rest of the paper is organized as follows: Traditional rough set attribute reduction based on attribute dependency is reviewed in Section 2; in Section 3, the concept of relative attribute dependency is defined and its properties are discussed, and, importantly, the sufficient and necessary condition of a minimum reduct of conditional attributes set of a decision table is built and represented with the relative attribute dependency; With this relative attribute dependency, in Section 4, we develop two algorithms for finding minimum reducts of the conditional attributes, one brute-force algorithm and the other heuristic algorithm using attribute entropy as the heuristic function; We also show the results of these algorithms by an illustrative example in Section 5; finally, Section 6 is the conclusion and our future work.

2 Rough Set-Based Attribute Reduction

Rough set-based attribute reduction techniques are based on the rough set theory proposed in [9]. In rough sets theory, the data is collected in a table, called decision table. Rows of the decision table correspond to objects, and columns correspond to attributes. In the data set, we assume we are given a set of examples with a class label to indicate the class to which each example belongs. We call the class label the decision attribute, the rest of the attributes the condition attributes. U is used to denote the decision table, C the condition attributes set, D the decision attributes set, where $C \cap D = \Phi$, and t denotes a row of the decision table. The value of attribute $q \in C \cup D$ in the row t is written as a mapping function $f_q(t) : U \to Dom(q)$, where $Dom(q)$ is the set of all possible values of q. For the given attribute $q \in C \cup D$, the mapping function $f_q(t)$ defines an equivalence relationship over U, and partitions U into a set of pairwise subsets, denoted as U/q:

$$U/q = \{[q_i] | \forall\, q_i \in Dom(q)\},$$

where $[q_i] = \{t | f_q(t) = q_i, t \in U\}$.

Assume Q is a subset of $C \cup D$. Two rows t and s in U are indiscernible with respect to Q, if and only if $f_q(s) = f_q(t), \forall q \in Q$. The indiscernibility relation with respect to $Q \subseteq C \cup D$ is denoted as $IND(Q)$, which is also an equivalence relationship over U. The $IND(Q)$ partitions U into a set of pairwise disjoint subsets, denoted as $U/IND(Q)$, which can be calculated as $U/IND(Q) = \oplus\{U/q | q \in Q\}$, where $X \oplus Y = \{A \cap B | \forall\, A \in X, \forall\, B \in Y, A \cap B \neq \emptyset\}$.

A subset X of U, $X \subseteq U$, can be approximated by a pair of sets, named the *lower* and *upper approximation* with respect to an attribute subset $Q \subseteq C \cup D$. The *lower approximation* of X w.r.t. Q, denoted $\underline{Q}X$, is defined as $\underline{Q}X = \cup\{Y | Y \in U/IND(Q), Y \subseteq X\}$, and the *upper approximation* of X w.r.t. Q, denoted $\overline{Q}X$, is defined as $\overline{Q}X = \cup\{Y | Y \in U/IND(Q), Y \cap X \neq \emptyset\}$, respectively.

Definition 1. *(Positive region) Assume $P \subseteq C \cup D$ and $Q \subseteq C \cup D$, the positive region of Q w.r.t. P, denoted $POS_P(Q)$, is defined as*

$$POS_P(Q) =_{def} \bigcup_{X \in U/IND(Q)} \underline{P}X. \tag{1}$$

Definition 2. *(Degree of Attribute Dependency) $\forall\, P \subseteq C \cup D, \forall\, Q \subseteq C \cup D$, the degree of dependency of Q from P, denoted $\gamma_P(Q)$, is defined as*

$$\gamma_P(Q) =_{def} \frac{|POS_P(Q)|}{|U|}. \tag{2}$$

where $|X|$ denotes the cardinality of the set X.

The degree of attribute dependency provides a measure how an attributes subset is dependent on another attributes subset [9]. $\gamma_P(Q) = 1$ means that Q totally depends on P, $\gamma_P(Q) = 0$ indicates that Q is totally independent from P, while $0 < \gamma_P(Q) < 1$ denotes a partially dependency of Q from P. Particularly, assume $P \subset C$, then $\gamma_P(D)$ can be used to measure the dependency of the decision attributes from a conditional attributes subset.

Definition 3. *(Significance of Attributes)* $\forall\ P \subseteq C \cup D, \forall\ Q \subseteq C \cup D$, *and* $\forall\ p \in P$, *the significance of* p *to* P *w.r.t.* Q, *denoted* $\sigma_P(p|Q)$, *is defined as*

$$\sigma_P(p|Q) =_{def} \gamma_{P\cup\{p\}}(Q) - \gamma_P(Q). \tag{3}$$

The task of rough set attribute reduction is to find a subset of the conditional attributes set, which functions as the original conditional attributes set without loss of classification capability. This subset of the conditional attributes set is called *reduct*, and defined as follows.

Definition 4. *(Reduct and Minimum Reduct) A subset* R *of* C *is called a reduct of* C*, if and only if*

$$POS_R(D) = POS_C(D), \text{ or equivalently}, \gamma_R(D) = \gamma_C(D). \tag{4}$$

A reduct R *of* C *is called a minimum reduct of* C *if* $\forall\ Q \subset R, Q$ *is not a reduct of* C*. In the following, the terminology reduct indicates minimum reduct unless specified.*

A decision table may have more than one reduct. Anyone of them can be used to replace the original conditional attributes set. Finding all the reducts from a decision table is NP-Hard [14]. Fortunately, in many real applications, it is usually not necessary to find all of them. One is sufficient. A natural question is which reduct is the best if there exist more than one reduct. The selection depends on the optimality criterion associated with the attributes. If it is possible to assign a cost function to attributes, then the selection can be naturally based on the combined minimum cost criteria. In the absence of an attribute cost function, the only source of information to select the reduct is the contents of the data table [7]. For example, the number of attributes can be used as the criteria and the best reduct is the one with the smallest number of attributes. However, finding the reduct with the smallest number of attributes is also NP-hard [14]. Some heuristic approaches to finding a "good" enough reduct have been proposed. One of these approaches utilizes the significance of attributes w.r.t. the decision attributes as the heuristic function and the degree of attribute dependency as the measure [7, 12, 13, 15]. A recent algorithm, called QuickReduct, was developed in [12]. QuickReduct is a forward searching hill climber and a filter approach of feature selection. The algorithm initializes the candidate reduct R as an empty set, and attributes are added to R incrementally using the following heuristic: the next attribute to be added to the candidate reduct is the one that has the highest significance to the candidate reduct w.r.t. the decision attributes. Formally, the next attribute to be added to R is

$$\arg \max_{p\in C-R} \sigma_R(p|D) = \arg \max_{p\in C-R}[\gamma_{R\cup\{p\}}(D) - \gamma_R(D)] = \arg \max_{p\in C-R} \gamma_{R\cup\{p\}}(D). \tag{5}$$

R is increased until $\gamma_R(D) = \gamma_C(D)$ when R is a reduct of C. The basic idea behind this algorithm is that the degree of attribute dependency is monotonically increasing. Actually, one can easily verify, $\forall\ p \in C - R, \gamma_R(D) \leq \gamma_{R\cup\{p\}}(D)$. This monotonicity ensures that QuickReduct finds a minimum reduct, although it is not guaranteed to yield the best reduct with the smallest number of attributes. A variant of QuickReduct is called QuickReduct II and was shown in [13]. QuickReduct II is also a filter algorithm, but performs the backward elimination using the same heuristic.

3 Relative Dependency between Attributes

Most existing rough set-based attribute reduction algorithms suffer from intensive computation of either discernibility functions or positive regions. In the QuickReduct family of algorithms, in order to choose the next attribute to be added to the candidate reduct, one must compute the degree of dependency of all remaining conditional attributes from the decision attributes, meaning that the positive regions $POS_{R\cup\{p\}}(D), \forall\ p \in C - R$, must be computed. To improve the efficiency of the attribute reduction algorithms, in this section, we will define a new concept, called the degree of relative attribute dependency. For this purpose, we assume that the decision table is consistent, that is, $\forall\ t, s \in U$, if $f_D(t) \neq f_D(s)$, then $\exists q \in C$ such that $f_q(t) \neq f_q(s)$. This assumption is not realistic in most real-life applications. Fortunately, any decision table can be uniquely decomposed into two decision tables, with one being consistent and the other the boundary area [9], and our method could be performed on the consistent one.

Definition 5. *(Projection) Let $P \subseteq C \cup D$. The projection of U on P, denoted $\Pi_P(U)$, is a sub table of U and constructed as follows:*

1) eliminate attributes $C \cup D - P$; and
2) merge all indiscernible tuples (rows).

Definition 6. *(Degree of Relative Dependency) Let $Q \subseteq C$. The degree of relative dependency, denoted $\kappa_Q(D)$, of Q on D over U is defined as*

$$\kappa_Q(D) = \frac{|\Pi_Q(U)|}{|\Pi_{Q\cup D}(U)|}, \tag{6}$$

where $|\Pi_X(U)|$ is actually the number of equivalence classes in $U/IND(X)$.

One can easily see that $\Pi_Q(U)$ is also a projection of $\Pi_{Q\cup D}(U)$ on P. The relative attributes dependency is the proportion of the projection of the decision table on a condition attributes subset to the projection of the decision table on the union of the condition attributes subset and the decision attributes set, while the regular attributes dependency defined in Definition 2 is the proportion of the positive region of one attributes subset w.r.t. to another attributes subset to the decision table.

Lemma 7. *$\forall\, Q \subseteq C$, $\Pi_{Q \cup D}(U)$ is consistent if and only if $|\Pi_Q(U)| = |\Pi_{Q \cup D}(U)|$.*

Lemma 8. *If U is consistent, then $\forall\, Q \subset C, |\Pi_Q(U)| \leq |\Pi_{Q \cup D}(U)|$.*

Lemma 9. *Assume U is consistent, then $\forall\, Q \subset C, 0 < \kappa_Q(D) \leq 1$, and $\kappa_C(D) = 1$.*

Proof. By Lemma 8 and Definition 6, one can infer $\kappa_Q(D) \leq 1$. By Lemma 7, one can infer $\kappa_C(D) = 1$.

Lemma 10. *If U is consistent, then $\forall\, Q \subset C, POS_C(D) = POS_Q(D)$ if and only if $|\Pi_Q(U)| = |\Pi_{Q \cup D}(U)|$.*

Proof. That U is consistent indicates that $POS_C(D) = U$ [9], and that $|\Pi_Q(U)| = |\Pi_{Q \cup D}(U)|$ means that $\Pi_{Q \cup D}(U)$ is consistent by Lemma 7. It can be easily inferred that $\Pi_{Q \cup D}(U)$ is consistent if and only if $POS_Q(D) = U$.

Theorem 11. *Assume U is consistent. $R \subseteq C$ is a reduct of C w.r.t. D if and only if $\kappa_R(D) = \kappa_C(D)$, and $\forall\, Q \subset R, \kappa_Q(D) \neq \kappa_C(D)$.*

Proof. $\kappa_R(D) = \kappa_C(D)$ if and only if, by Lemma 9, $\kappa_R(D) = 1$ if and only if, by Definition 6, $|\Pi_R(U)| = |\Pi_{R \cup D}(U)|$ if and only if, by Lemma 10, $POS_R(D) = POS_C(D)$. Similarly, $\forall\, Q \subset R, \kappa_Q(D) \neq \kappa_C(D)$ if and only if $POS_Q(D) \neq POS_C(D)$. By Definition 4, one can see that the theorem holds.

4 Algorithms for Finding Minimum Reducts Based on Relative Dependency

The degree of relative attribute dependency provides a mechanism of finding a minimum reduct of the conditional attributes set of a decision table. In this section, we introduce two algorithms to implement this mechanics. The first algorithm is based on the brute-force backward elimination and the other is heuristic backward elimination based on attribute entropy.

Algorithm 1 (*Brute-force Elimination*):
Input: A consistent decision table U with conditional attributes set C and decision attributes set D
Output: R – a minimum reduct of conditional attributes set C w.r.t. D in U

$R \leftarrow C$
For each attribute $q \in C$
  If $\kappa_{R-\{q\}}(D) = 1$ **Then**
    $R \leftarrow R - \{q\}$
Return R

Lemma 12. *Assume U is consistent. $\forall\, P \subseteq Q \subseteq C$, if $\kappa_Q(D) < 1$, then $\kappa_P(D) < 1$.*

Proof. Since $\kappa_Q(D) < 1$, by Definition 6, we have $|\Pi_Q(U)| < |\Pi_{Q \cup D}(U)|$. By Lemma 7, $\Pi_Q(U)$ is inconsistent, and thus $\Pi_P(U)$ is inconsistent. Therefore, $|\Pi_Q(U)| < |\Pi_{Q \cup D}(U)|$, and hence $\kappa_P(D) < 1$.

Theorem 13. *The outcome of Algorithm 1 is a minimum reduct of C w.r.t. D in U, and its time complexity is $O(|C||U|)$.*

Proof. Assume the output of Algorithm 1 is R. From the algorithm it can be easily observed that $\kappa_R(D) = 1$, and $\forall\ q \in R, \kappa_{R-\{a\}}(D) < 1$. By Lemma 12, one can see $\forall\ B \subset R, \kappa_B(D) < 1$. Therefore, by Theorem 11, we conclude that R is a minimum reduct of C w.r.t. D in U.

Since $\forall\ Q \subseteq C, \kappa_Q(D)$ can be computed in $O(|U|)$ time by counting the number of rows in $\Pi_Q(U)$, the running time of *Algorithm 1* is $O(|C||U|)$.

One may note that the outcome of *Algorithm 1* is an arbitrary reduct of the condition attributes set C, if C has more than one reduct. Which reduct is generated depends on the order of attributes that are checked for dispensibility in Step 2 of the algorithm. Some authors propose algorithms for constructing the *best* reduct, but what is the best depends on how to define the criteria, such as the number of attributes in the reduct, the number of possible values of attributes, etc. In the absence of criteria, the only source of information to select the reduct is the contents of the data table [7]. A common metric of data content is information entropy contained in the data items. The following *Algorithm 2* utilizes the information entropy conveyed in the attributes as a heuristic of selecting attributes to be eliminated.

Information entropy has been used in many feature subset selection and classification algorithms. In C4.5 [11], information entropy and information gain are used to select attributes to be split during the construction of a decision tree.

Given the partition by D, $U/IND(D)$, of U, the entropy, or expected information based on the partition by $q \in C$, U/q, of U, is given by

$$E(q) = \sum_{Y \in U/q} \frac{|Y|}{|U|} I(q|Y), \textit{ where } I(q|Y) = - \sum_{X \in U/IND(D)} \frac{|Y \cap X|}{|Y|} \log_2 \left(\frac{|Y \cap X|}{|Y|}\right). \tag{7}$$

Thus, the entropy $E(q)$ can be represented as

$$E(q) = -\frac{1}{|U|} \sum_{X \in U/IND(D)} \sum_{Y \in U/q} |X \cap Y| \log_2 \frac{|X \cap Y|}{|Y|} \tag{8}$$

Algorithm 2 tests the conditional attributes for elimination in the descending order of the attribute entropy. The reason is that the higher attribute entropy means the more expected information is needed using the attribute to classify the objects [11].

Algorithm 2 (*Entropy-based Elimination*):
Input: A consistent decision table U with conditional attributes set C and decision attributes set D

Output: R – a minimum reduct of conditional attributes set C w.r.t. D in U

$R \leftarrow C$, $Q \leftarrow \emptyset$
For each attribute $q \in C$
  Compute $E(q)$, $Q \leftarrow Q \cup \{< q, E(q) >\}$
While $Q \neq \emptyset$
  $q \leftarrow \arg\max\{E(p) | < p, E(p) > \in Q\}$
  $Q \leftarrow Q - \{< q, E(q) >\}$
  If $\kappa_{R-\{q\}}(D) = 1$ **Then**
    $R \leftarrow R - \{q\}$
Return R

Theorem 14. *The outcome of Algorithm 2 is a reduct of C w.r.t. D in U, and its time complexity is $O(|C||U|\log|U|)$.*

Proof. The difference between it Algorithm 1 and *Algorithm 2* is in selecting the next attribute to be eliminated, thus *Algorithm 2* is a special case of *Algorithm 1*. Therefore Theorem 13 ensures that the output of *Algorithm 2* is a minimum reduct of C w.r.t. D in U.

One can verify that, by sorting the decision table by the values of D and q [8], $E(q)$ can be calculated in $O(|U|\log|U|)$ time. Thus *Algorithm 2* can be performed in $O(|C|(|C| + |U|\log|U|))$ time. Since $|C| \ll |U|$ in most real-life applications, this time complexity is reduced to $O(|C||U|\log|U|)$.

5 An Illustrative Example

We illustrate the two algorithms presented in the previous section by an artificial data set in this section. The consistent decision table U is shown in Table 1, consisting of conditional attributes set $C = \{a, b, c, d\}$ and the decision attribute set $D = \{d\}$, where *Id* is only used to identify the rows. One can verify that C has two reducts w.r.t. D, one is $\{a, c\}$ and the other $\{a, d\}$.

Table 1. A consistent decision table

Id	a	b	c	d	e
t_1	1	1	2	1	2
t_2	1	2	1	2	1
t_3	2	2	2	1	2
t_4	3	1	2	2	1
t_5	3	2	2	1	1
t_6	1	2	2	1	2
t_7	3	2	1	2	1
t_8	1	1	1	2	1

With *Algorithm 1*, the initial candidate reduct $R = C = \{a, b, c, d\}$. Assume the conditional attributes are tested for elimination in the natural order of a, b, c, and d.

Testing a, $\kappa_{R-\{a\}}(D) = \frac{|\Pi_{\{b,c,d\}}(U)|}{|\Pi_{\{b,c,d,e\}}(U)|} = \frac{5}{6} < 1$, thus, R is kept unchanged.

Testing b, $\kappa_{R-\{b\}}(D) = \frac{|\Pi_{\{a,c,d\}}(U)|}{|\Pi_{\{a,c,d,e\}}(U)|} = \frac{8}{8} = 1$, therefore, b is eliminated from R and $R = \{a, c, d\}$.

Testing c, $\kappa_{R-\{c\}}(D) = \frac{|\Pi_{\{a,d\}}(U)|}{|\Pi_{\{a,d,e\}}(U)|} = \frac{6}{6} = 1$, hence, c is eliminated from R and $R = \{a, d\}$.

Testing d, $\kappa_{R-\{d\}}(D) = \frac{|\Pi_{\{a\}}(U)|}{|\Pi_{\{a,e\}}(U)|} = \frac{3}{4} < 1$, so, d is kept in R.

The outcome of *Algorithm 1* with this attribute testing order is $R = \{a, d\}$. If d is tested before c, however, the outcome will be $R = \{a, c\}$.

With *Algorithm 2*, the entropy of each attribute $q \in C$ is calculated as follows.

$$\begin{aligned} U/IND(D) = U/e &= \{\{t_1, t_3, t_6\}, \{t_2, t_4, t_5, t_7, t_8\}\} \\ U/a &= \{\{t_1, t_2, t_6, t_8\}, \{t_4, t_5, t_7\}, \{t_3\}\} \\ U/b &= \{\{t_1, t_4, t_8\}, \{t_2, t_3, t_5, t_6, t_7\}\} \\ U/c &= \{\{t_1, t_3, t_4, t_5, t_6\}, \{t_2, t_7, t_8\}\} \\ U/d &= \{\{t_1, t_3, t_5, t_6\}, \{t_2, t_4, t_7, t_8\}\} \end{aligned}$$

$$\begin{aligned} E(a) &= -\tfrac{1}{|U|} \textstyle\sum_{X \in U/e} \sum_{Y \in U/a} |X \cap Y| \log_2 \frac{|X \cap Y|}{|Y|} = 0.5 \\ E(b) &= -\tfrac{1}{|U|} \textstyle\sum_{X \in U/e} \sum_{Y \in U/b} |X \cap Y| \log_2 \frac{|X \cap Y|}{|Y|} = 0.8262 \\ E(c) &= -\tfrac{1}{|U|} \textstyle\sum_{X \in U/e} \sum_{Y \in U/c} |X \cap Y| \log_2 \frac{|X \cap Y|}{|Y|} = 0.6069 \\ E(d) &= -\tfrac{1}{|U|} \textstyle\sum_{X \in U/e} \sum_{Y \in U/d} |X \cap Y| \log_2 \frac{|X \cap Y|}{|Y|} = 0.8113 \end{aligned}$$

Thus, the conditional attributes will be tested for elimination in the order of b, d, c, and a, which leads the outcome of *Algorithm 2* to the minimum reduct $R = \{c, a\}$ of C w.r.t. $D = \{e\}$.

6 Conclusion

The degree of attribute dependency has been used as a metric in the rough set community to select conditional attributes for attribute reduction. The computation of the dependency degree requires the computation of positive regions of attributes subset w.r.t. others. This is usually time-consuming.

In this paper, we proposed a new concept of attribute dependency, called *relative attribute dependency*, and defined the degree of relative attribute dependency, which can be calculated by counting the distinct rows of the sub-table of the decision table, or the cardinality of a projection of the decision table. A sufficient and necessary condition of the minimum reduct of conditional attributes of a decision table is proposed with the representation of the degree of the relative attribute dependency for a consistent decision table. Two attribute reduction algorithms for finding minimum reducts were presented based on the degree of relative attribute dependency. The correctness of these algorithms was proved and their time complexity was analyzed. Because of the simplicity of computing the relative attribute dependency degree, the time efficiency of finding minimum reducts is highly improved.

Our future work will focus on the following aspects: apply these algorithms to the medical data classification, find out the criteria of the best reducts for this application, and then improve the algorithms to search for the best or approximately best reducts.

References

1. Bazan, J., Nguyen, H., Nguyen, S., Synak, P., Wroblewski, J., Rough set algorithms in classification problems, *Rough Set Methods and Applications: New Developments in Knowledge Discovery in Information Systems*, L. Polkowski, T. Y. Lin, and S. Tsumoto (eds), 49-88, Physica-Verlag, Heidelberg, Germany, 2000
2. Cercone N., Ziarko W., Hu X., Rule Discovery from Databases: A Decision Matrix Approach, *Proc. of ISMIS*, Zakopane, Poland, 653-662, 1996
3. John,G., Kohavi, R., Pfleger,K., Irrelevant Features and the Subset Selection Problem, *Proc. ICML*, 121-129, 1994
4. Kira,K., Rendell,L.A. The feature Selection Problem: Traditional Methods and a New Algorithm, *Proc. AAAI*, MIT Press, 129-134, 1992
5. Kumar A., New Techniques for Data Reduction in Database Systems for Knowledge Discovery Applications, *Journal of Intelligent Information Systems*, 10(1), 31-48, 1998
6. Liu, H., Motoda., H. (eds), Feature Extraction Construction and Selection: A Data Mining Perspective. Kluwer Academic Publisher, 1998
7. Modrzejewski, M., Feature Selection Using Rough Sets Theory, *Proc. ECML*, 213-226, 1993
8. Nguyen, H., Nguyen, S., Some efficient algorithms for rough set methods, *Proc. IPMU* Granada, Spain, 1451-1456, 1996
9. Pawlak Z., Rough Sets: Theoretical Aspects of Reasoning about Data, Kluwer Academic Publishers, 1992
10. Polkowski, L., Skowron, A., Rough mereology: A new paradigm for approximate reasoning, *J. of Approximate Reasoning*, 15(4):333-365, 1996
11. Quinlan, J. R., C4.5: Programs for Machine Learning, San Mateo, CA: Morgan Kaufmann, 1993
12. Shen, Q., Chouchoulas, A., A modular approach to generalizing fuzzy rules with reduced attributes for the monitoring of complex systems, *Enginnering Applications of Artificial Intelligence*, 13(3):263-278, Pergamon, 2000
13. Shen, Q., Chouchoulas, A., A rough-fuzzy approach for generating classification rules, *Pattern Recognition*, 35:2425-2438, Pergamon, 2002
14. Skowron, A., Rauszer C., The Discernibility Matrices and Functions in Information Systems, *Intelligent Decision Support - Handbook of Applications and Advances of the Rough Sets Theory*, K. Slowinski (ed), Kluwer, Dordrecht, 331-362, 1992
15. Ziarko, W., The Discovery, analysis and representation of data dependencys in databases, *Knoweldge Discovery in Databases*, G. Patesky-Shapiro and W. J. Frawley (eds), MIT Press, 1991.

Granular Computing on Extensional Functional Dependencies for Information System

Qiusheng An[1] and Junyi Shen[2]

[1] Department of Mathematics and Computer
Shanxi Normal University, Linfen 041004, China
[2] School of Electronics and Information Engineering
Xi'an Jiaotong University ,Xi'an 710049, China
aaqqss@sina.com

Abstract. In this paper, a new approach to discover extensional functional dependencies for information systems is presented based on information granules using their bit representations. The principle of information granules, granular computing and the machine oriented model for data mining are investigated firstly. In addition, the approach to identify the classical functional dependencies, identity dependencies and partial dependencies is discussed and some conclusions on extensional functional dependencies are obtained. The information granules are represented with bit, then the data format can be closed to the inner representations of the computer, hence, the patterns contained in the information system can be directly mined.

1 Introduction

As we known, fuzzy set theory was originally proposed by Lotfi A.Zadeh in 1965, and information granularity were introduced in his paper [1] in 1979. The label "granular computing" was suggested by professor T.Y.Lin [2]; Andrzej Skowron and Jaroslaw Stepaniuk introduced the discovery of information granules, information granule in distributed environment, rough mereological and the calculus of information granules [3],[4],[5],[6],[7]; Lotfi A.Zadeh presented fuzzy information granulation and its centrality in human reasoning and fuzzy logic in [8]; Y.Y.Yao illuminated granular computing on modeling data mining, stratified rough sets and granular computing in [9],[10]. Specially, T.Y.Lin introduced data mining, rough sets and granular computing, modeling the real world for data mining and the machine oriented model for data mining in his paper [11],[12], and the new method and some conclusions are very important in improving the efficiency of data mining.

In this paper, based on the machine oriented model for data mining, we report the study on extensional functional dependencies with granular computing.

2 Preliminaries

Definition 1. An information system I is a system $<U, A>$,where $U=\{u_1,u_2,\dots u_{|U|}\}$ is a finite non-empty set, called a universe or an object space, elements of U are called

S. Tsumoto et al. (Eds.): RSCTC 2004, LNAI 3066, pp. 186–191, 2004.

objects; $A=\{a_1,a_2,...a_{|A|}\}$ is also a finite non-empty set; elements of A are called attributes; for every $a\in A$ there is a mapping a from U into some space, i.e. $a:U\rightarrow a(U)$, and $a(U)=\{a(u)|u\in U\}$ is called the domain of attribute a.

Definition 2. Information granules are viewed as linked collections of objects (data points, in particular) drawn together by the criteria of indistinguishability, similarity or functionality. For an information system $I=<U, A>$, elementary granule is defined by $EF_K(u)$, where $EF_K(u)$ is a conjunction of selectors of the form $A_i=A_i(u)$, $||EF_K(u)||_I= ||\wedge_{A_i\in K} A_i=A_i(u)||_I$, $K\subseteq A$, $u\in U$, $||.||$ is a function from Φ into power set 2^U.[7],[8]

Definition 3. A binary relation B^i is the subset $B^i\subseteq V\times U$, it defines a set, called binary (or elementary) neighborhood at $p\in V$. $B^i_p=\{u|u\ B^i\ p\}$.The map $\beta^i: p\rightarrow B^i_p$ is called a binary granulation, and the set $\{ B^i_p \}$ is a binary neighborhood system[11].

Definition 4. A binary granular structure consists of 4-tuple (V,U,B,C),where V is called the object space ,U is the data space, $B=\{B^i,i=1,2,...,n\}$ is a finite set of crisp/fuzzy binary relation, and C is a finite set of concept spaces, each of which consists of all the names (attribute values) of the elementary neighborhood, $B^i_p=\{u|u\ B^i\ p\}$.When $V=U$ and the binary relations are equivalence relations, i.e.$B=E$, then the triple (U,E,C) is called rough granular structure, where C, in this case, consists of the names(attributes and attribute values) of equivalence relations and equivalence classes of E. [11]

Definition 5. Binary relation B induces a binary granulation, $B: U\rightarrow 2^U: p\rightarrow B_p$.This map induces a partition by the inverse map B^{-1}, the induced equivalence class $B^{-1}(B_p)$ is called the center of elementary granules B_p. [11]

3 Machine Oriented Models for Data Mining (MOMDM)

3.1 The Concept of MOMDM

In fact, the concept of information system is a generalization of the concept of a relation in database, unlike relations in database, an information system may consist of duplicate rows (tuples), namely different objects may have identical values. Relational database theory is interested in attribute values, while information system is interested in both objects and attribute values. In general, relational database is human oriented processing of massive data according to their semantics, e.g., attribute values are its primary processing units. On the other hand, data mining is machine derivations of hidden semantics, called patterns, from the mathematical structure of stored data, its primary processing unit is elementary granule, so a relation use granules (bit patterns) as attribute values is a model using entities as primitives, it is called a machine oriented model [11].

3.2 Bit Representations of Information Granules

In an information system, let θ_1,θ_2 are two equivalence relations on U, for an equivalence relation θ, denote the corresponding classification by U/θ.

Lemma 1. Let <*U, A*> be an information system ,then for *X, Y*$\subseteq$*A*, we have $\theta_X \cap \theta_Y = \theta_{X\cup Y}$. [14]

Definition 6. Let *BIT* be a mapping function, $BIT: M \rightarrow bin_1 bin_2 \ldots bin_i \ldots bin_{|U|}$, where $M=\{\ldots, v_i, \ldots, v_j, \ldots\}$ is the center of elementary granules, $bin_i=1$ if $v_i \in M$, $bin_i=0$ if $v_i \notin M$.

An information table of suppliers and its rough granular structure are listed in Table 1 and Table 2, respectively [12].

In Table 1, it is consists of attribute values Twenty, Ten and Thirty for attribute status, we have NAME(Twenty)=$\{v_1,v_4\}$, where NAME is the canonical name of Twenty, its bit representation is 10010 and denotes BIT(Twenty)=10010. Furthermore, its bit representation is BIT(Ten)=01100 for NAME(Ten)=$\{v_2,v_3\}$ and its bit representation is BIT(Thirty)=00001 for NAME(Thirty)=$\{v_5\}$. Obviously, Twenty, Ten, Thirty form a partition {10010,01100,00001} of *U*.

Table 1. Information table of suppliers.

U	S#	Sname	Status	City
V_1	S_1	Smith	Twenty	C_1
V_2	S_2	Jones	Ten	C_2
V_3	S_3	Blake	Ten	C_2
V_4	S_4	Clark	Twenty	C_1
V_5	S_5	Adams	Thirty	C_3

Table 2. Rough granular structure.

Attribute value	Granule center	Bit representation
Twenty	v_1,v_4	10010
Ten	v_2,v_3	01100
Thirty	v_5	00001
C_1	v_1,v_4	10010
C_2	v_2,v_3	01100
C_3	v_5	00001

Proposition 1. For an information system, every attribute is equivalent to an equivalence relation and an attribute value is equivalent to an equivalence granule.

Proposition 2. Let {*BIT(1),…,BIT(K)*} be a partition of *U*, then $BIT(1) \vee \ldots \vee BIT(K) = \underbrace{11\ldots1}_{|U|}$ holds, where $|U|$ is the cardinality of objects.

Proposition 3. Let $\{BIT_s(1),\ldots,BIT_s(K)\}$, $\{BIT_t(1),\ldots,BIT_t(L)\}$ are two partitions of U, then $\{BIT_s(1) \vee \ldots \vee BIT_s(K)\} \wedge \{BIT_t(1) \vee \ldots \vee BIT_t(L)\} = \underbrace{11\ldots1}_{|U|}$ holds.

Proposition 4. Let $\{BIT_1(A_i(x_1)),\ldots, BIT_{|\theta_{A_i}|}(A_i(x_{|\theta_{A_i}|}))\}$ be a partition of U, then we have $\{BIT_1(A_1(x_1)) \vee \ldots \vee BIT_{|\theta_{A_1}|}(A_1(x_{|\theta_{A_1}|}))\} \wedge \ldots \wedge \{BIT_1(A_m(x_1)) \vee \ldots \vee BIT_{|\theta_{A_m}|}(A_m(x_{|\theta_{A_m}|}))\} = \underbrace{11\ldots1}_{|U|}$ holds.

Definition 7. Two attribute A_j^k, A_j^l are isomorphic, denoted by $A_j^k \approx A_j^l$, iff there is a one to one map $s{:}Dom(A_j^k) \rightarrow Dom(A_j^l)$ such that $A_j^k(u)=s(A_j^l)$ for all $u\in U$. [12]

4 Granular Computing on Extensional Functional Dependencies

4.1 Granular Computing on Classical Functional Dependencies

Definition 8 EFD: $X\rightarrow Y$ is a extensional functional dependency if for every X-value there is a uniquely determined Y-value in the relation instance R. [13]

Lemma 2. A classical functional dependency $X\rightarrow Y$ can be defined as $\theta_X \subseteq \theta_Y$, i.e. $\bigcap_{a\in X} \theta_a \subseteq \bigcap_{a\in Y} \theta_a$, Where θ_X, θ_Y are two equivalence relations of U. [14]

From the point of view of information granules, for $X, Y \subseteq A$, θ_X can be defined as $\{A^{-1}_X(p)|\ A^{-1}_X(p) \in BIT(2^U)\}$, θ_Y can be defined as $\{A^{-1}_Y(p)|\ A^{-1}_Y(p) \in BIT(2^U)\}$, where $A^{-1}_X(p)$, $A^{-1}_Y(p)$ are bit representations of attribute values or sub-tuples, $BIT(2^U)$ is the set of bit representations of power set of U.

Proposition 5. Extensional Functional dependency must be hold between two isomorphic attributes or attribute subsets.

Theorem 1. Let X, Y $\subseteq$ A, extensional functional dependency X$\rightarrow$Y holds iff for every $BIT(v_i(X)) \in \{A^{-1}_X(p)|\ A^{-1}_X(p) \in BIT(2^U)\}$, must have a $BIT(v_j(Y)) \in \{A^{-1}_Y(p)|\ A^{-1}_Y(p) \in BIT(2^U)\}$, which satisfies $BIT(v_i(X)) \wedge BIT(v_j(Y)) = BIT(v_i(X))$.

Table 3. Skull Information System.

U	A_1	A_2	A_3	A_4	A_5	A_6
V_1	4	1	K	X	8.36	M
V_2	5	2	J	Y	5.14	M
V_3	4	1	L	X	8.38	M
V_4	3	1	K	X	8.29	F
V_5	4	2	J	Y	5.27	M

For example, Table 3 is revised from [13]: for attributes A_1 and A_6, we have $\theta_{A_1} = \{4, 5, 3\} = \{10101, 01000, 00010\}$, $\theta_{A_6} = \{M, F\} = \{11101, 00010\}$, where $BIT(4) \wedge BIT(M) = 10101 \wedge 11101 = 10101 = BIT(4)$, $BIT(5) \wedge BIT(M) = 01000 \wedge 11101 = 01000 = BIT(5)$, $BIT(3) \wedge BIT(F) = 00010 \wedge 00010 = 00010 = BIT(3)$, so $A_1 \rightarrow A_6$ holds, similarly, $A_2 \rightarrow A_4$ holds.

4.2 Granular Computing for Identity Functional Dependencies

Definition 9 An identity dependency between two subsets X, Y of attributes for an information system I=<U, A> is a statement, denoted by $X \leftrightarrow Y$, which holds in the information system I, if and only if both $X\rightarrow Y$ and $Y\rightarrow X$ hold [13],[14].

An identity dependency $X \leftrightarrow Y$ can be defined as $\theta_X = \theta_Y$, i.e., $\bigcap_{a\in X} \theta_a = \bigcap_{a\in Y} \theta_a$.

Theorem 2. Let $X, Y \subseteq A$, an identity functional dependency $X \leftrightarrow Y$ holds if and only if for every $BIT(p_1) \in \{A^{-1}_X(p) | A^{-1}_X(p) \in BIT(2^U)\}$, exists a $BIT(p_2) \in \{A^{-1}_Y(p) | A^{-1}_Y(p) \in BIT(2^U)\}$, satisfies $BIT(p_2)=BIT(p_1)$.

An identity dependency implies that the bit representations are equal between corresponding attribute values.

Proposition 6. An identity functional dependency must be hold between two isomorphic attributes or attribute subsets.

For example in Table 3, for attributes A_2, A_4, the bit representation of attribute value *1* is same as *X*, the bit representation of attribute value 2 is same as *Y*, so we have $A_2 \leftrightarrow A_4$ holds.

Obviously, an identity functional dependency is the special case of classical functional dependency.

4.3 Granular Computing for Partial Functional Dependencies

Definition 10. Let $I=<U, A>$ be an information system, $P, Q \subseteq A$ are attribute subsets of *A*, we say that *Q* depends in a degree K $(0 \leq K \leq 1)$ on *P* is $K=\gamma_P(Q)=card(pos_p(Q))/card(U)$, where $POS_p(Q)$ is the *P* positive discourse of *Q*, if $K=1$, we say that *Q* depends totally on *P*, if $0<k<1$, we say that *Q* depends partially (to a degree k) on *P* and if $K=0$ we say that *Q* is totally independent on *P*. [15],[16]

Theorem 3. Let $X, Y \subseteq A$, partial functional dependency $X \xrightarrow{p} Y$ holds if exist some $BIT(p_1) \in \{A^{-1}_X(p) | A^{-1}_X(p) \in BIT(2^U)\}$, there have a $BIT(p_2) \in \{A^{-1}_Y(p) | A^{-1}_Y(p) \in BIT(2^U)\}$, which satisfies $BIT(p_1) \wedge BIT(p_2)= BIT(p_1)$.

5 Conclusion

Granular computing is a new soft computing method related to fuzzy set theory and rough set theory. In this paper, we report a method using granular computing to discover extensional functional dependencies based on information granules using bit representations for information system, at the same time, several examples are provided to validate our results.

References

1. L.A. Zadeh: Fuzzy Sets and Information Granularity. In: M. Gupta, R, Ragade, R. Yager (eds.): Advances in Fuzzy Set Theory and Applications. North-Holland, Amsterdam(1979)3-18
2. L.A. Zadeh: Some Reflections on Information Granulation and its Centrality in Granular Computing, Computing with Words, the Computational Theory of Perceptions and Precisiated Natural Language. In: T.Y. Lin, Y.Y. Yao, L.A. Zadeh (eds.): Data Mining, Rough Sets and Granular Computing (2002) 1-17
3. Skowron A, Stepaniuk J.: Towards discovery of information granules. 3rd European Conference on principles and Practice of Knowledge Discovery in Databases, September 15-18, 1999, Prague. Czech Republic, Lecture Notes in Artificial Intelligence 1704. Springer-Verlag (1999) 542-547

4. Skowron A, Stepaniuk J.: Information Granules in Distributed Environment. New Directions in Rough Sets, Data Mining, and Granular-Soft Computing. Yamaguchi, Japan November 9-11, Lecture notes in Artificial Intelligence 1711. Springer-Verlag (1999)357-365
5. Polkowski L., Skowron A.: Rough mereology: A new paradigm for approximate reasoning. International Journal of Approximate Reasoning ,15(4)(1996)333-365
6. Polkowski L. Skowron A.: Towards Adaptive Calculus of Granules. In: Zadeh L.A, Kacprzyk J. (eds.) :Computing with words in information/intelligence systems 1. Foundations. Heidelberg: Physica-Verlag(1999)
7. Skowron A., Stepaniuk J.: Information Granules:Towards Foundations of Granular Computing International Journal of Intelligent Systems, Vol. 16 (2001) 57-85
8. Lotfi A. Zadeh,: Toward a theory of fuzzy information granulation and its certainty in human reasoning and fuzzy logic. Fuzzy Sets and Systems, Vol. 90, no.2 (1997) 111-127
9. Y.Y. Yao: On Modeling Data Mining with Granular Computing. Proceedings of the 25th Annual International Computer Software and Applications Conference (COMPSAC 2001), Chicago, USA, October 8-12, 2001, IEEE Computer Society, Los Alamitos, California,638-643
10. Y.Y. Yao: Stratified Rough Sets and Granular Computing. In: Dave, R.N., Sudkamp.T. (eds.): Proceedings of the 18th International Conference of the North American Fuzzy Information Processing Society, New York, USA, June 10-12, 1999, IEEE Press, 800-804
11. T.Y. Lin:Association Rules in Semantically Rich Relations.Granular Computing approach. Proceedings of International Workshop on Rough Set Theory and Granular Computing, Bulletin of International Rough Set Society, Matsue, Shimane, Japan May 20-22, 2001. Vol 5. No.1/2, 143-149
12. T.Y. Lin:Data Modeling for Data Mining.In:Belur V.Dasarathy(eds):Data Mining and Knowledge Discovery:Theory, Tools and Technology IV. Proceedings of SPIE, Vol.4730(2002)138-145
13. T.Y. Lin:Granular Computing in Data Mining. In: T.Y. Lin, Y.Y. Yao. L.A. Zadeh (eds): Data Mining, Rough Sets and Granular Computing (2002) 21-42
14. J. W. Guan, D.A. BELL: Rough computational methods for information systems. Artificial Intelligence, 105 (1998) 77-103
15. Wang G Y, Liu F.: The Inconsistency in Rough Set Based Rule Generation. The Second International Conference on Rough Sets and Current Trends in Computing(2000)332-339
16. Wang G Y.: Rough Set theory and knowledge acquisition. The publisher of Xi'an Jiaotong university(2001)

Greedy Algorithm for Decision Tree Construction in Context of Knowledge Discovery Problems

Mikhail Ju. Moshkov[1,2]

[1] Faculty of Computing Mathematics and Cybernetics
Nizhny Novgorod State University
23, Gagarina Ave., Nizhny Novgorod, 603950, Russia
moshkov@unn.ac.ru

[2] Institute of Computer Science, University of Silesia
39, Będzińska St., Sosnowiec, 41-200, Poland

Abstract. In the paper a greedy algorithm for minimization of decision tree depth is considered and bounds on the algorithm precision are discussed. Under some natural assumptions on the class NP and on the class of considered tables, this algorithm is, apparently, close to best approximate polynomial algorithms for minimization of decision tree depth. Unfortunately, the performance ratio of this algorithm grows almost as natural logarithm on the number of rows in the table. Except usual greedy algorithm we study greedy algorithm with threshold which constructs approximate decision trees. Such approach is fully admissible if we see on decision trees as on a way for knowledge representation. We obtain upper bounds on the depth of decision trees, constructed by this algorithms, which are independent of the number of rows in the table.

Keywords: data table, knowledge discovery, greedy algorithm, approximate decision tree

1 Introduction

Decision trees are widely used in different applications as algorithms for task solving. Another possibility (which will be studied in this paper) is to use decision trees as a way for knowledge representation. We will try to minimize decision tree depth since trees with smaller depth can be interpreted more easily.

First, we consider approximate algorithm for decision tree depth minimization which can be applicable to real data tables with both discrete and continuous variables having missing values [4]. At the beginning, we transform given data table into a decision table, possibly, with many-valued decisions (i.e. pass to the model which is usual for rough set theory [5, 6]). Later, we apply to this table a greedy algorithm which is similar to algorithms for decision tables with one-valued decisions [3], but uses more complicated uncertainty measure.

We discuss bounds on precision of this algorithm. From these bounds and from results of [2] follows that under some natural assumptions on the class

S. Tsumoto et al. (Eds.): RSCTC 2004, LNAI 3066, pp. 192–197, 2004.

NP and on the class of considered tables, the algorithm is, apparently, close to best approximate polynomial algorithms for minimization of decision tree depth. Unfortunately, the performance ratio of this algorithm grows almost as natural logarithm on the number of rows in the decision table.

Except usual greedy algorithm we study greedy algorithm with threshold. This algorithm constructs an approximate decision tree for which in each terminal node the uncertainty is at most fixed part (for example, 5%) of initial uncertainty. We prove that the depth of constructed decision tree is bounded from above by a linear function on the minimal depth $h(T)$ of exact decision tree for decision table T. In the case of 5%-inaccuracy, for example, in the capacity of such function we can take the function $3 \cdot h(T) + 1$. Note that the obtained bound does not depend on the number of rows in the decision table.

Such approach is justified in the case, when we see on decision tree as on a way of knowledge representation. If a given data table contains a noise, then the construction of an exact decision tree may be excessive. On the other hand, if we will try to discover a knowledge based on obtained tree, it will be more convenient for us to work with tree having smaller depth.

2 Data Tables and Attributes

A data table D is a rectangular table with t columns which correspond to variables $x_1, \ldots, x_t$. The rows of D are t-tuples of variable $x_1, \ldots, x_t$ values. Values of some variables in some rows can be missed. The table D can contain equal rows. The variables are separated into discrete and continuous. A discrete variable x_i takes values from an unordered finite set A_i. A continuous variable x_j takes values from the set of real numbers. Each row r of the table D is labelled by an element $y(r)$ from a finite set C. One can interpret these elements as values of a new variable y. The problem connected with the table D is to predict the value of y using variables $x_1, \ldots, x_t$. To this end we will not use values of $x_1, \ldots, x_t$ directly. We will use values of some attributes depending on variables from the set $\{x_1, \ldots, x_t\}$.

An attribute is a function f depending on variables $x_{i_1}, \ldots, x_{i_m} \in \{x_1, \ldots, x_t\}$ and taking values from the set $E = \{0, 1, *\}$. Let r be a row of D. If values of all variables $x_{i_1}, \ldots, x_{i_m}$ are definite in r then for this row the value of $f(x_{i_1}, \ldots, x_{i_m})$ belongs to the set $\{0, 1\}$. If value of at least one of variables $x_{i_1}, \ldots, x_{i_m}$ is missed in r then for this row the value of $f(x_{i_1}, \ldots, x_{i_m})$ is equal to $*$.

Consider some examples of attributes. In the system CART [1] the attributes are considered (in the main) each of which depends on one variable x_i. Let x_i be a continuous variable, and a be a real number. Then the considered attribute takes value 0 if $x_i < a$, takes value 1 if $x_i \geq a$, and takes value $*$ if the value of x_i is missed. Let x_i be a discrete variable, which takes values from the set A_i, and B be a subset of A_i. Then the considered attribute takes value 0 if $x_i \notin B$, takes value 1 if $x_i \in B$, and takes value $*$ if the value of x_i is missed. It is possible to consider attributes depending on many variables. For example, let φ be a polynomial depending on continuous variables $x_{i_1}, \ldots, x_{i_m}$. Then the considered attribute takes value 0 if $\varphi(x_{i_1}, \ldots, x_{i_m}) < 0$, takes value 1 if $\varphi(x_{i_1}, \ldots, x_{i_m}) \geq 0$, and takes value $*$ if the value of at least one of variables $x_{i_1}, \ldots, x_{i_m}$ is missed.

Let $F = \{f_1, ..., f_k\}$ be a set of attributes which will be used for prediction of the variable y value. We will say that two rows r_1 and r_2 are equivalent relatively F if each attribute f_i from F takes the same value on r_1 and r_2. The considered equivalence relation divides the set of rows of the table D into equivalence classes $S_1, \ldots, S_q$. Let $j \in \{1, \ldots, q\}$. The rows from the equivalence class S_j are indiscernible from the point of view of values of attributes from F. So when we will predict the value y using only attributes from F we will give the same answer (element from C) for any row from S_j. Denote by $C(S_j)$ the set of elements d from C such that

$$|\{r : r \in S_j, y(r) = d\}| = \max_{c \in C} |\{r : r \in S_j, y(r) = c\}| \ .$$

It is clear that only answers from the set $C(S_j)$ minimize the number of mistakes for rows from the class S_j. For any $r \in S_j$ denote $C(r) = C(S_j)$.

Now we can formulate exactly the problem $\text{Pred}(D, F)$ of prediction of the variable y value: for a given row r of the data table D we must find a number from the set $C(r)$ using values of attributes from F.

3 Decision Tables with Many-Valued Decisions

We will assume that the information about the problem $\text{Pred}(D, F)$ is represented in the form of a decision table $T = T(D, F)$. The table T has k columns corresponding to the attributes $f_1, \ldots, f_k$ and q rows corresponding to the equivalence classes $S_1, \ldots, S_q$. We will denote these rows $S_1, \ldots, S_q$ as the corresponding equivalence classes. The value $f_j(S_i) = f_j(r_i)$ is on the intersection of a row S_i and a column f_j, where r_i is an arbitrary row from the equivalence class S_i. For $i = 1, \ldots, q$ the row S_i of the table T is labelled by the subset $C(S_i)$ of the set C.

For the decision table T the problem $\text{Pred}(D, F)$ can be formulated as follows: for a given row S_i of the decision table T we must find a number from the set $C(S_i)$ using values of attributes from F.

We will consider sub-tables of the table T which can be obtained from T by removal of some rows. Let T' be a sub-table of T.

Denote by $\text{Row}(T')$ the set of rows of the table T'. The table T' will be called degenerate if $\text{Row}(T') = \emptyset$ or $\bigcap_{S_i \in \text{Row}(T')} C(S_i) \neq \emptyset$.

A nonempty subset B of the set $\text{Row}(T')$ will be called boundary set if $\bigcap_{S_i \in B} C(S_i) = \emptyset$ and $\bigcap_{S_i \in B'} C(S_i) \neq \emptyset$ for any nonempty subset B' of the set B such that $B' \neq B$. We denote by $R(T')$ the number of boundary subsets of the set $\text{Row}(T')$. It is clear that $R(T') = 0$ if and only if T' is a degenerate table. Later we will interpret the value $R(T')$ as the uncertainty of the table T'.

If we want to solve the problem $\text{Pred}(D, F)$ exactly then for a given row S_i of the table T we must localize it in a sub-table T' of the table T such that

$R(T') = 0$. If we want to solve the problem Pred(D,F) approximately then for a given row S_i of the table T we must localize it in a sub-table T' of the table T such that $R(T')$ is at most some threshold. For example, $R(T') \le \alpha R(T)$ where α is a rational number such that $0 < \alpha < 1$.

Let $i_1,\ldots,i_m \in \{1,\ldots,k\}$ and $\delta_1,\ldots,\delta_m \in E = \{0,1,*\}$. We denote by $T'(i_1,\delta_1)\ldots(i_m,\delta_m)$ the sub-table of the table T' that consists of rows each of which on the intersections with columns $f_{i_1},\ldots,f_{i_m}$ has elements $\delta_1,\ldots,\delta_m$ respectively.

4 Decision Trees

As algorithms for exact and approximate solving of the problem Pred(D,F) we will consider decision trees with attributes from the set F. Such decision tree is finite directed tree with the root in which each terminal node is not labelled, each non-terminal node is labelled by an attribute from the set F. Three edges start in each non-terminal node. These edges are labelled by 0, 1 and $*$ respectively.

Let Γ be a decision tree with attributes from F and v be a terminal node of Γ. We correspond to v a subtable $T(v)$ of the decision table $T = T(D,F)$. If v is the root of Γ then $T(v) = T$. Let v be not the root. Let in the directed path from the root to the node v non-terminal nodes be labelled by attributes $f_{i_1},\ldots,f_{i_m}$ and edges be labelled by elements $\delta_1,\ldots,\delta_m$ from the set E. Then $T(v) = T(i_1,\delta_1)\ldots(i_m,\delta_m)$.

Let α be a rational number such that $0 \le \alpha < 1$. We will say that Γ solves the problem Pred(D,F) with the inaccuracy α if $R(T(v)) \le \alpha R(T)$ for any terminal node v of the decision tree Γ.

The depth of a decision tree is the maximal length of a path from the root to a terminal node of the tree. We denote by $h(\Gamma)$ the depth of a decision tree Γ. By $h(T) = h(D,F)$ we denote the minimal depth of a decision tree with attributes from F which solves the problem Pred(D,F) with the inaccuracy 0.

5 Greedy Algorithm with Threshold

Let α be a rational number such that $0 \le \alpha < 1$. Describe an algorithm U_α which for decision table $T = T(D,F)$ constructs a decision tree $U_\alpha(T)$ solving the problem Pred(D,F) with the inaccuracy α.

1-*st step.* Construct a tree consisting of a single node w. If $R(T) \le \alpha R(T)$ then proceed to the second step. If $R(T) > \alpha R(T)$ then mark the node w by the table T and proceed to the second step.

Suppose $t \ge 1$ steps have already been made. The tree obtained in the step t will be denoted by G.

$(t+1)$-*st step.* If no one node of the tree G is labelled by a table then we denote by $U_\alpha(T)$ the tree G. The work of the algorithm U_α is completed.

Otherwise we choose certain node v in the tree G which is labelled by a sub-table of the table T. Let the node v be labelled by the table T'. If $R(T') \le \alpha R(T)$ then we remove the table T' and proceed to the $(t+2)$-step. Let $R(T') > \alpha R(T)$.

For $i = 1, \ldots, k$ we compute the value $Q_i = \max\{R(T'(i, \delta)) : \delta \in E\}$. We mark the node v by the attribute f_{i_0} where i_0 is the minimal i for which Q_i has minimal value. For each $\delta \in E$ we add to the tree G the node $v(\delta)$, mark this node by the table $T'(i_0, \delta)$, draw the edge from v to $v(\delta)$, and mark this edge by the element δ. Proceed to the $(t + 2)$-step.

6 Bounds on Algorithm U_0 Precision

If T is a degenerate table then the decision tree $U_0(T)$ consists of one node. The depth of this tree is equal to 0. Consider now the case when T is a non-degenerate table.

Theorem 1. ([4]) *Let the decision table $T = T(D, F)$ be non-degenerate. Then*

$$h(U_0(T)) \leq h(T) \ln R(T) + 1 \ .$$

Let t be a natural number. Denote by $\text{Tab}(t)$ the set of decision tables T such that $|C(S_i)| \leq t$ for any row $S_i \in \text{Row}(T)$. Let $T \in \text{Tab}(t)$. One can show that each boundary subset of the set $\text{Row}(T)$ has at most $t + 1$ rows. Using this fact it is not difficult to show that the algorithm U_α, $0 \leq \alpha < 1$, has polynomial time complexity on the set $\text{Tab}(t)$.

Using results from [2] on precision of approximate polynomial algorithms for set covering problem it is possible to prove that if $NP \not\subseteq DTIME(n^{O(\log \log n)})$ then for any ε, $0 < \varepsilon < 1$, there is no polynomial algorithm which for a given decision table $T = T(D, F)$ from $\text{Tab}(t)$ constructs a decision tree Γ such that Γ solves the problem $\text{Pred}(D, F)$ with the inaccuracy 0 and $h(\Gamma) \leq (1 - \varepsilon) h(T) \ln R(T)$.

Using Theorem 1 we conclude that if $NP \not\subseteq DTIME(n^{O(\log \log n)})$ then the algorithm U_0 is, apparently, close to best (from the point of view of precision) approximate polynomial algorithms for minimization of decision tree depth for decision tables from $\text{Tab}(t)$ (at least for small values of t). Unfortunately, the performance ratio of this algorithm grows almost as natural logarithm on the number of rows in decision table.

7 Bounds for Algorithm U_α, $\alpha > 0$

If T is a degenerate table then the decision tree $U_\alpha(T)$ consists of one node. The depth of this tree is equal to 0. Consider now the case when T is a non-degenerate table.

Theorem 2. *Let α be a rational number such that $0 < \alpha < 1$, and the decision table $T = T(D, F)$ be non-degenerate. Then*

$$h(U_\alpha(T)) \leq h(T) \ln \alpha^{-1} + 1 \ .$$

Let t be a natural number. As it was mentioned above, the algorithm U_α has polynomial time complexity on the set $\mathrm{Tab}(t)$.

Note that bound from Theorem 2 does not depend on the number of rows in the decision table T, and the value $\ln \alpha^{-1}$ grows relatively slowly with the decrease of α. For example, if $\alpha = 0.1$ then $\ln \alpha^{-1} < 2.31$, if $\alpha = 0.01$ then $\ln \alpha^{-1} < 4.61$, if $\alpha = 0.001$ then $\ln \alpha^{-1} < 6.91$.

8 Conclusion

A greedy algorithm with threshold for construction of approximate decision trees is described. This algorithm is applicable to real data tables, which are transformed into decision tables.

The algorithm possesses two peculiarities which may be helpful if we will see on the constructed decision tree as on a way for representation of knowledge about data table.

The structure of the algorithm is so simple that it is possible to obtain upper bounds on depth of constructed decision trees. These bounds are independent of the number of rows in data table.

The second peculiarity of the algorithm is the way of the work with missing values: if we compute the value of an attribute $f(x_{i_1}, \ldots, x_{i_m})$, and the value of at least one of variables $x_{i_1}, \ldots, x_{i_m}$ is missed then the computation will go along the special edge labelled by $*$.

Acknowledgments

This work was partially supported by Russian Foundation for Basic Research (project 02-01-00543).

References

1. Breiman, L., Friedman, J.H., Olshen, R.A., Stone, C.J.: Classification and Regression Trees. Wadsworth & Brooks, 1984
2. Feige, U.: A threshold of $\ln n$ for approximating set cover (Preliminary version). Proceedings of 28th Annual ACM Symposium on the Theory of Computing (1996) 314–318
3. Moshkov, M.Ju.: Conditional tests. Problems of Cybernetics **40**, Edited by S.V. Yablonskii. Nauka Publishers, Moscow (1983) 131–170 (in Russian)
4. Moshkov, M.Ju.: Greedy algorithm of decision tree construction for real data tables. LNCS Transactions on Rough Sets, Springer-Verlag (submitted)
5. Pawlak, Z.: Rough Sets - Theoretical Aspects of Reasoning about Data. Kluwer Academic Publishers, Dordrecht, Boston, London, 1991
6. Skowron, A., Rauszer, C.: The discernibility matrices and functions in information systems. Intelligent Decision Support. Handbook of Applications and Advances of the Rough Set Theory. Edited by R. Slowinski. Kluwer Academic Publishers, Dordrecht, Boston, London (1992) 331–362

GAMInG – A Framework for Generalization of Association Mining via Information Granulation

Ying Xie and Vijay V. Raghavan

The Center for Advanced Computer Studies
University of Louisiana at Lafayette
Lafayette, LA 70504-4330, USA
{yxx2098,raghavan}@cacs.louisiana.edu

Abstract. Rather than finding new association-mining types one at a time, in this paper, we propose a framework, which is called Generalization of Association Mining via Information Granulation (GAMInG), based on which new association-mining types capable of discovering new patterns hidden in data can be systematically defined.

1 Introduction

Rather than finding new association-mining types one at a time, in this paper, we propose a framework based on which new association-mining types capable of discovering new patterns hidden in data can be systematically defined. The proposed framework, which is called Generalization of Association Mining via Information Granulation (GAMInG), is based on the observation that, given an information table, not only there is likelihood of association to exist among values within an individual object (or tuple), but also among values of individual attribute(s) appearing within a granule that is a clump of objects, which are drawn together by indistinguishability, similarity, proximity or functionality [3]. The various ways to granulate objects suggest the possible existence of various association types among data. The most important contribution of this framework lies in its potential to extend the capability of association mining itself.

2 Generalization of Association Mining

In this section, we will give a formal definition of the proposed GAMInG framework. Let a 5-tuple $\mathcal{A} = (U, A, \{V_a \mid a \in A\}, \{S_a \mid a \in A\}, \{I_a \mid a \in A\})$ denote an information table, where U is a finite nonempty set of tuples, A is a finite nonempty set of attributes (including interesting derived attributes), V_a is a finite nonempty set of values for attribute $a \in A$, $S_a = \phi$ or $S_a = < V_a, \leq >$, which is the order on V_a, $I_a : U \rightarrow V_a$ is an information function. The proposed GAMInG Framework defines a knowledge discovery process based on an information table $\mathcal{A}$, which consists of the following steps: Step1: Granulation; Step2: Marking the *bag-defining attribute* values for each granule; Step3: Constructing *granulated information table*; Step4: Finding frequent patterns from the granulated information table; Step5: Generating rules from frequent patterns.

S. Tsumoto et al. (Eds.): RSCTC 2004, LNAI 3066, pp. 198–203, 2004.

STEP 1. Granulation: This step is used to granulate tuples in a specific way. Choose subset $B \subset A$. Each attribute in B is called a ***granule-defining attribute (granule attribute)***; while each attribute in A – B is called ***bag-defining attribute (bag attribute)***. For each granule attribute $b \in B$, define a binary relation r_b on V_b. Let $R_B = \{r_b \mid b \in B\}$ denote the set of all the relations defined on granule attributes. R_B determines a set called binary neighborhood for each tuple $t \in U$:

$$t_{R_B} = \{u \in U \mid \underset{r_b \in R_B}{\wedge} (I_b(t), I_b(u)) \in r_b\}$$

The family of non-empty t_{R_B} decides the set of granules on U: $G = \{t_{R_B} \neq \Phi \mid t \in U\}$. Each element $G_i \in G$ is called a ***granule*** of U, which is a set of tuples.

STEP 2. Marking the bag attribute values for each granule: The marking of the bag attribute values by this step is used to interpret the association rules we may get.

Let the set of granule attributes $B = \{b1, b2, \ldots, bk\}$.
for each granule $G_i \in G$,
for each granule attribute $b \in B$,
let $V_{bi} = \{ I_b(t_{ij}) \mid t_{ij} \in G_i\}$ be the set of values on attribute b of the tuples in G_i, where t_{ij} is the *jth* tuple in G_i, then we define ***marking function*** $f_{bi}: V_{bi} \rightarrow M_{bi}$, where
$M_{bi} = \{m_{bij} \mid m_{bij}$ *is the marking symbol of the value of tuple* t_{ij} *on attribute b, where* $t_{ij} \in G_i\}$.
for each bag attribute $c \in A - B$,
for each tuple $t_{ij} \in G_i$,
let $v_{cij} = I_c(t_{ij})$ be the value of tuple t_{ij} on bag attribute c. We mark v_{cij} as v_{cij}^m, where

$$v_{cij}^m = v_{cij}[f_{(b1)i}(I_{(b1)}(t_{ij}))f_{(b2)i}(I_{(b2)}(t_{ij}))\ldots f_{(bk)i}(I_{(bk)}(t_{ij}))]$$

Let the bag $v_{ci}^m = \{v_{cij}^m \mid t_{ij} \in G_i\}$, which is the value of granule G_i on the bag attribute c.

Let the bag $v_i^m = \bigcup_{c \in A-B} v_{ci}^m$.

STEP 3 Constructing Granular Information Table: An example of granular information table is shown in table 2. (Table 1 is the original information table; granular attribute is *d; binary relation defined on d is* $r_d = \{(v_i, v_j) \mid v_i, v_j \in V_d \wedge v_i \leq v_j \leq v_i + 2\}$; marking function is defined as $f_{d1}(v) = v - v_{\min}$). This example also shows that inter-transaction association mining [2] is a special case of the GAMInG framework.

Table 1. Stock Information Table For Company A and B.

Tuples	(Company A) a	(Company B) b	(Days) d
t1	**Up$_a$**	Down$_b$	1
t2	Same$_a$	**Down$_b$**	2
t3	Down$_a$	**Up$_b$**	3
t4	**Up$_a$**	Up$_b$	4
t5	Down$_a$	**Down$_b$**	5
t6	Same$_a$	**Up$_b$**	6
t7	Down$_a$	Down$_b$	7
t8	Down$_a$	Same$_b$	8
t9	Up$_a$	Same$_b$	9
t10	**Up$_a$**	Same$_b$	10
t11	Same$_a$	**Down$_b$**	11
t12	Same$_a$	**Up$_b$**	12

Table 2. An Granular Information Table Constructed from Table 1.

G_i	v_i^m (Bag)
G$_1$	**Up$_a$[0]**,Same$_a$[1],Down$_a$[2],Down$_b$[0],**Down$_b$[1],Up$_b$[2]**
G$_2$	Same$_a$[0],Down$_a$[1],Up$_a$[2], Down$_b$[0],Up$_b$[1],Up$_b$[2]
G$_3$	Down$_a$[0],Up$_a$[1],Down$_a$[2], Up$_b$[0],Up$_b$[1],Down$_b$[2]
G$_4$	**Up$_a$[0]**,Down$_a$[1],Same$_a$[2], Up$_b$[0],**Down$_b$[1],Up$_b$[2]**
G$_5$	Down$_a$[0],Same$_a$[1],Down$_a$[2], Down$_b$[0],Up$_b$[1],Down$_b$[2]
G$_6$	Same$_a$[0],Down$_a$[1],down$_a$[2], Up$_b$[0],Down$_b$[1],Same$_b$[2]
G$_7$	Down$_a$[0],Down$_a$[1],Up$_a$[2], Down$_b$[0],Same$_b$[1],Same$_b$[2]
G$_8$	Down$_a$[0],Up$_a$[1],Up$_a$[2], Same$_b$[0],Same$_b$[1],Same$_b$[2]
G$_9$	Up$_a$[0],Up$_a$[1],Same$_a$[2], Same$_b$[0],Same$_b$[1],Down$_b$[2]
G$_{10}$	**Up$_a$[0]**, Same$_a$[1],Same$_a$[2] , Same$_b$[0],**Down$_b$[1],Up$_b$[2]**
G$_{11}$	Same$_a$[0],Same$_a$[1], Down$_b$[0],Up$_b$[1]
G$_{12}$	Same$_a$[0], Up$_b$[0]

STEP 4 Finding frequent patterns from the granulated information table: For the granulated information table, each granule G_i can be viewed as a transaction; each marked value can be viewed as an item, based on which the algorithm such as apriori can be run in order to find the frequent pattern.

3 Finding Different Association Patterns by Exploring Different Binary Relations

The most important step of the GAMInG framework is Granulation. By defining different relations on different granule attributes, we can granulate tuples in different ways such that different association patterns will be exposed. In this section, we will explore several useful relations that can be applied to customize the step of Granulation in order to discover new frequent patterns.

3.1 Binary Relation Based on Interval Number

An interval number $[\underline{a}, \overline{a}]$ with $\underline{a} \leq \overline{a}$ is the set of real numbers defined by: $[\underline{a}, \overline{a}] = \{x \mid \underline{a} \leq x \leq \overline{a}\}$. Interval number can be applied to define binary neighborhood on an attribute with continuous real values by defining binary relation *r*, where $r = \{(v_1, v_2) \mid \underline{a} \leq \mid v_1 - v_2 \mid \leq \overline{a}\}$. This relation is quite useful in granulating tuples in a GIS (Geometric Information System) database. For example, table 3 shows a snippet of GIS. We choose the *location* as the granule attribute, based on which the relation mentioned above is defined, and then we may get a rule like: *"Within half mile of*

McDonald, there is a Burger King". Furthermore, by combining the above relation defined on attribute "Location" with the relation defined on attribute "Open Date", we may get the rule like: *"After McDonald and Burger King open branches, KFC will likely open a branch within two months and less than one mile away".*

Table 3. A snippet of GIS.

Tuples	Company	Open Date	Sales	Advertising Expense	Location
	McDonald				(32.4, 54,3)
	Burger King				(60.3, 21.6)
	McDonald				(62.0, 21.8)
	Burger King				(33.5, 54.0)
	...				...

3.2 Binary Relation Based on Conditional Probability Relation

If tuples are granulated according to a group of homogeneous attributes, such as the attributes *a, b, c* and *d* shown in table 4, one may find some new interesting patterns. For example, if we granulate the tuples in table 4 based on attributes *a, b, c, d,* the following rule, which can be used for prediction, will be discovered, as long as it exists in data: *"The behavior of these stocks in January is always similar to that in May".* In order to granulate tuples based on a group of homogeneous attributes in the step of Granulation, we first need to derive an attribute called *set attribute* from them, and then define a special binary relation on the *set attribute* based on *conditional probability relation.*

- **Set Attribute:** Given a information table $\mathcal{A} =(U, A, \{V_a \mid a\in A\}, \{S_a \mid a\in A\}, \{I_a \mid a \in A\})$, we call attribute $a\in A$ is a *set attribute,* if $I_a(t) = \{s_1, s_2,..., s_k\}$ is a set of k elements for any tuple $t\in U$.

- **Conditional Probability Relation:** A conditional probability relation is a mapping, $R: U \times U \to [0,1]$, such that for $x, y \in U$,

$$R(x,y) = P(x \mid y) = P(y \to x) = \frac{|x \cap y|}{y}.$$

- **Binary Relation based on Conditional Probability Relation:** Now, one can define the binary relation r_s on V_s based on conditional probability relation, such that

$$r_s = \{(x,y) \mid R(x,y) \geq \alpha, x, y \in V_s\}, \text{ where } \alpha \in [0,1].$$

When the tuples are granulated by this relation on the *set attribute s*, the type of pattern mentioned above can be discovered.

Table 4. A snippet of Stock Information Table.

Tuples	(Stock A) a	(Stock B) b	(Stock C) c	(Stock D) d	Months
t1	$High_a$	$High_b$	Low_c	Low_d	1
t2	$High_a$	Low_b	Low_c	Low_d	2
t3	Low_a	Low_b	$High_c$	Low_d	3
...					...

3.3 Fuzzy Binary Relation

More than often, user may prefer linguistic terms, which is more natural and flexible than using crisp numbers in rules, such as: *"**Around** McDonald's, there is a Burger King"*. For the example shown in table 4, similarly, instead of using crisp sets to describe the price of each stock, one may prefer fuzzy version of concepts *high, low,* which is able to avoid the unreasonable sharp transition between inclusion and exclusion of them. Therefore, it is always necessary to introduce or derive *fuzzy attributes* in an information table. In order to granulate tuples on fuzzy attributes, fuzzy relation needs to be defined and employed. In this subsection, we first discuss fuzzy attribute, and then a fuzzy binary relation based on *fuzzy conditional probability* will be explored.

• **Fuzzy Attribute:** Given an information table $\mathcal{A} = (U, A, \{V_a \mid a \in A\}, \{S_a \mid a \in A\}, \{I_a \mid a \in A\})$, we call attribute $a \in A$ is a *fuzzy attribute*, if $I_a(t) = (\mu_1, \mu_2, \ldots \mu_k)$ is an ordinal set, where $\mu_i \in [0,1]$, and $\sum_{1 \le i \le k} \mu_i = 1$ for any tuple $t \in U$.

There are two ways to derive fuzzy attribute from numeric attribute. The first one is unsupervised, by running fuzzy clustering algorithm such as 3M algorithm [8] on numeric attribute to obtain the natural fuzzy cluster structure of it. The second one is called supervised, by predefining the linguistic terms and their corresponding membership functions.

• **Fuzzy Binary Relation Based on Fuzzy Conditional Probability Relation:** Given an information table $\mathcal{A} = (U, A, \{V_a \mid a \in A\}, \{S_a \mid a \in A\}, \{I_a \mid a \in A\})$, let $a \in A$ is a fuzzy attribute, on which *fuzzy conditional probability relation is defined* as a mapping $R: V_a \times V_a \to [0,1]$, such that for any two values $u, v \in V_a$, assuming $u = (\mu_{u1}, \mu_{u2}, \ldots \mu_{uk})$, $v = (\mu_{v1}, \mu_{v2}, \ldots \mu_{vk})$, we have:

$$R(u,v) = \frac{\sum_{1 \le i \le k} \min(\mu_{ui}, \mu_{vi})}{\sum_{1 \le i \le k} \mu_{vi}} = \sum_{1 \le i \le k} \min(\mu_{ui}, \mu_{vi}),$$

Based on fuzzy conditional probability relation, a fuzzy binary relation r_a can be defined on fuzzy attribute a: $r_a = \{<(x,y), \mu> \mid x, y \in V_a \wedge \mu = R(x,y)\}$. Now, let $R_B = \{r_a \mid a \in A \text{ and } a \text{ is fuzzy attribute}\}$ denote the set of all the relations defined on fuzzy attributes. R_B defines a set called fuzzy binary neighborhood for each tuple $t \in U$:

$$t_{R_B} = \{<u, \mu> \mid u \in U \wedge \mu = \min_{r_a \in R_B} (\mu_{r_a}(I_a(t), I_a(u)))\}.$$

Fuzzy binary neighborhood determines fuzzy granule on U. For efficiency, we apply λ^*-level [6] fuzzy binary neighborhood for each $t \in U$, such that:

$$t_{R_B}(\lambda^*) = \{<u, \mu> \mid u \in U \wedge \mu \ge \lambda\}, \text{ where } \lambda \in [0,1]$$

• **Association within Fuzzy Granule:** Assuming $G_i = \{<t1, 0.8>, <t2, 0.9>, <t3, 0.7>\}$ is a λ^*-level fuzzy granule, and the bag attribute value of *t1, t2, t3* is *a, b, c* respectively. The marking of these bag attribute values by the membership value of *t1, t2* and *t3* in granule G_i will be: *a[0.8], b[0.9], c[0.7]*. Then the support of association (a, b, c) by granule G_i is *min(0.8, 0.9, 0.7)=0.7*. The final support of (a, b, c) is the sum of supports provided by all the granules.

3.4 Arbitrary Binary Relation

In fact, arbitrary binary relation can be defined on one or more attributes, as long as it is meaningful to users. This mechanism will be expected to greatly enhance the applicability and flexibility of association mining.

4 Conclusions

Due to the observation that association patterns always exist within granules rather than just being embedded in tuples, we propose a framework called Generalization of Association Mining via Information Granulation (GAMInG), based on which different association patterns can be discovered by granulating information in different ways. Because of the multiplicity of the binary relations one can define, our framework has the potential to greatly extend the applicability of association mining.

References

1. R. Agrawal, T. Imielinski and A. Swami, "Mining association rules between sets of items in large databases", Proc. ACM-SIGMOD Int. Conf. on Management of Data, Washington, DC., 1993.
2. H. Lu, L. Feng and J. Han, "Beyond intra-transaction association analysis: Mining multidimensional inter-transaction association rules", ACM Trans. on Information Systems, Vol.18, No.4, 2000.

Mining Un-interpreted Generalized Association Rules by Linear Inequalities
Descriptive/Deductive Data Mining Approach

Tsau Young Lin

Department of Computer Science
San Jose State University, San Jose, California 95192
tylin@cs.sjsu.edu

Abstract. Taking the spirit of descriptive statistic methods data mining is viewed as a deductive science, no inductive generalizations or predicative assertions. We call this approach descriptive/deductive data mining (DDM) to stress spirit of descriptive statistic methods and the role of mathematical deductions.
Such a seemingly restrictive methodology, somewhat surprisingly, turns out to be quite far reaching. Previously, we have observed in ICDM02 that (1) Isomorphic relations have isomorphic patterns (classical association rules). This observation implies, from data mining prospect, that relations and patterns are syntactic in nature. We also have reported that (2) attributes or features (including un-interpreted ones) of a given relation can be enumerated mathematically, though, in intractable time. In this paper, we proved (3) generalized association rules (including un-interpreted rules) can be discovered by solving a finite set of integral linear inequalities within polynomial time.

Keywords: association rules, attribute, feature, bitmap indexes, granular data model, data mining

1 Introduction

The following two quotes should explain what and why we take this approach. "By descriptive statistic methods we shall understand any treatments of numerical data which does not involve inductive generalizations" ([5], pp 5). "The. . . (theoretical) error appears the very moment that we use partial information and derive general conclusion." ([5], pp.123) To avoid the theoretical error, we adopt the descriptive statistic methods. The goal is to formalize association rules mining. In essence, data mining is viewed as a deductive science, no inductive generalizations or predicative assertions. Data are the "axioms" and patterns are the "theorems." This approach will be called descriptive or deductive data mining (DDM); the name reflects the spirit of descriptive statistic methods, or the role of mathematical deductions.

S. Tsumoto et al. (Eds.): RSCTC 2004, LNAI 3066, pp. 204–212, 2004.

1.1 A Complete Cycles of Information Flows

To understand data mining fully, we need to understand the cycle of information flows:

1. Slice of real world $\Longrightarrow$ Data: A slice of real world is (knowledge) represented by a relational table of symbols; we will refer to this table as data. These symbols, called semantics primitives in AI, are used to represent some primitive concepts or facts of the slice of real world. Here, we should stress that the real world semantics of these symbols are not implemented.
2. Data $\Longrightarrow$ Patterns: From the relational table of symbols, patterns are extracted by deductions, e.g., counting. This step is essentially "theorem" proving.
3. Patterns $\Longrightarrow$ Real world phenomena. Mathematically, patterns are (algebraic, logic and etc) expressions of these symbols. In terms of the original interpretations of symbols (semantics primitives), patterns are high level hidden phenomena

Unfortunately, human interpretations are not automat-able. Many patterns are uninterpretable.

1.2 Some Reflection

Perhaps, one may criticize taking such a restrictive view on data mining is almost like burying our heads in the sands. Indeed, we are! On the other hands, we would like to avoid theoretical error, which may leads misconception and etc., in the following quote: "The . . error appears the very moment that we use partial information and derive general conclusion." ([5], pp.123) The main goal of our research is to examine the mathematical foundation and through the new understanding to develop new direction of data mining applications. In fact, up to now, we have far reaching observations and discoveries; see initial accomplishments.

1.3 Some Twists in Finite World

It is important to note that under the view of DDM, many traditional database notions, such as, attributes (features), discovered patterns all have some twists. In database theory, we define various notions from human's prospect. In DDM, we have to rely on data to describe them. So first of all we should realize there are only finitely many data are given, and hence there could only have finitely many distinct "things" that can be described by data under DDM view.

2 Data and Patterns in DDM

In this section, we will examine closely the notion of relational tables (the raw data) from DDM point of view. There are two notions associated any data in DDM.

1. Formula: A primitive symbol (undefined notion in the system) or an (algebraic or logical) expression of primitive symbols.
2. Interpretations (without implementation): To human, each primitive symbol represents a piece of real world fact or concept. Each expression, to human, denotes some higher level fact or concept of real world, however, we should stress such a denotation is not implemented in the system (hence it can not be processed by automated data mining procedures).

2.1 Raw Data – An Information Table of Symbols

As usual let V be a set V of entities that denote a slice of real world, called the universe. Let $A = \{A^1, A^2, \dots, A^n\}$ be a set of attributes. The set of actual values that have occurred in the Representation is denoted by $Dom(A^j)$.

Let the map

$$K : V \longrightarrow Dom(A) = Dom(A^1) \times \dots Dom(A^n)$$

be the knowledge representation. In traditional database theory, the *image* of the *map* K, is the relational table. We will consider the *graph* $(v, K(v))$, and call it information table. Throughout the whole paper, by abuse of notation,

K may mean
(1) the knowledge representation $K : V \longrightarrow Dom(A)$
(2) the information table $(v, K(v))$
(3) the classical relation $R = ImK$, the image of K, which is a set of tuples (actually should be a bag).
(4) Since A and V determines K and vice versa, we may use (V, A) and K interchangeably.

Let us stress again in DDM, the table K is an algebraic expression of undefined primitive symbols that, to human, do denote some real world facts or concepts (at the same time such denotations are no implemented)

2.2 Patterns – Association Rules

Association rule mining originated from on the market basket data [1]. However, in many software systems, the data mining tools are added to general DBMS. So we will be interested in data mining on general relations. For definitions, we have the following translations: an item is an attribute value, a q-itemset is a subtuple of length q, a large q-itemset is a high frequency q-pattern. In other words,

– A subtuple of length q is a high frequency q-pattern, or simply a q-pattern, if its occurrences are greater than or equal to a given threshold. When q is understood, we will drop the q.

2.3 Properties of Data in DDM – Syntactic in Nature

We take this section from [10] almost verbatim. Attributes A^i and A^j are isomorphic iff there is a one-to-one and onto map, $s : Dom(A^i) \longrightarrow Dom(A^j)$ such that $A^j(v) = s(A^i(v)) \; \forall \, v \in V$. The map s is called an isomorphism. Intuitively, two attributes (columns) are isomorphic iff one column turns into another one by properly renaming its attribute values.

Let $K = (V, A)$ and $H = (V, B)$ be two information tables, where $A = \{A^1, \ldots A^n\}$ and $B = \{B^1, \ldots B^m\}$. Then, K and H are said to be isomorphic if every A^i is isomorphic to some B^j, and vice versa. By our assumption (all attributes are distinct), K and H have the same degree (number of attributes), that is, $n = m$; See more general version in [10]. The following theorem should be obvious.

Theorem 2.3.1. Isomorphic relations have isomorphic patterns.

Corollary 2.3.2. The notion of patterns is a property of isomorphic class.

3 Granular Data Model(GDM)

We take this section almost verbatim from [10].

We have observed that (Section 2) each A^j is a map, hence its inverse images aturally defines an equivalence relation on V. We denote this equivalence relation by Q^j. The set V/Q^j, which consists of all elementary granules (equivalence classes), is called the quotient set. The equivalence class of the given attribute(equivalence relation) is called an *elementary granule.* The intersection of elementary granules is called a granule; it is an equivalence class of the intersection (of equivalence relations). The map $P^j : V \longrightarrow V/Q^j : v \longrightarrow [v]$ is called the natural projection, where [v] is the granule containing v. It should be clear (a standard mathematical fact) that V/Q^j is mapped on-to-one onto $Dom(A^j)$. We call the latter map naming map or interpretation; the element of $Dom(A^j)$ could be considered a meaningful name (to a human) of the granule; note that, however, to a system it is merely another symbol.

A relation K, as a map, can be factored through the natural projection $C_K : V \longrightarrow V/Q^1 \times \ldots \times V/Q^n$ and the naming map $NAME : V/Q^1 \times \ldots \times V/Q^n \longrightarrow C^1 \times \ldots \times C^n$. Note $NAME$ is the product of $NAME^j$ and is often referred to as the interpretation. Table 1 illustrates how K is factored. *Theorem* 3.1. Patterns of GDM are isomorphic (via interpretation) to the patterns of K.

This is a corollary of Theorem 2.3.1. To find all patterns of K, we only need to find the patterns on C_K (and vice versa).

The GDM C_K is uniquely determined by its universe V, and the family Q of equivalence relations, so we also denote it by (V, Q). From the prospect of first order logic, (V, Q) is a model of some rather simple kind of first order logic.

1. GDM C_K is a table format of (V, Q).
2. Granules of Q^j are called *elementary* granules.

Table 1. GDM C_K at left-hand-side is isomorphic to K at right- hand-side

GDM C_K						Relation K		
V		$(Q^0$	Q^2	$Q^3)$		$(S\#$	$STATUS$	$CITY)$
v_1		$(\{v_1\}$	$\{v_1, v_7\}$	$\{v_1\})$		$(S_1$	$TWENTY$	NY)
v_2		$(\{v_2\}$	$\{v_2, v_3, v_4, v_5, v_6\}$	$\{v_2, v_3, v_4, v_5, v_6\})$		$(S_2$	TEN	SJ)
v_3		$(\{v_3\}$	$\{v_2, v_3, v_4, v_5, v_6\}$	$\{v_2, v_3, v_4, v_5, v_6\})$	NAME	$(S_3$	TEN	SJ)
v_4	$\longrightarrow$	$(\{v_4\}$	$\{v_2, v_3, v_4, v_5, v_6\}$	$\{v_2, v_3, v_4, v_5, v_6\})$	$\longrightarrow$	$(S_4$	TEN	SJ)
v_5		$(\{v_5\}$	$\{v_2, v_3, v_4, v_5, v_6\}$	$\{v_2, v_3, v_4, v_5, v_6\})$		$(S_5$	TEN	SJ)
v_6		$(\{v_6\}$	$\{v_2, v_3, v_4, v_5, v_6\}$	$\{v_2, v_3, v_4, v_5, v_6\})$		$(S_6$	TEN	SJ)
v_7		$(\{v_7\}$	$\{v_1, v_7\}$	$\{v_7, v_8, v_9\})$		$(S_7$	$TWENTY$	LA)
v_8		$(\{v_8\}$	$\{v_8, v_9\}$	$\{v_7, v_8, v_9\})$		$(S_8$	$THIRTY$	LA)
v_9		$(\{v_9\}$	$\{v_8, v_9\}$	$\{v_7, v_8, v_9\})$		$(S_9$	$THIRTY$	LA)

3. A q-tuple of C_K corresponds to an intersection of elementary granules in (V, Q); the intersection is called q-granule.
4. High frequency patterns of (V, Q) are q-granules whose cardinality is greater than the given threshold.

Definition 3.2. The pair (V, Q) is called the *granular data model*; it is a special case of granular structure [14].

4 Theory of Un-interpreted Features

4.1 Partition Lattices Are (Un-)Interpretable Features

An attribute is also called a feature. In AI, they have been used interchangeably. In database theory, an attribute is a representation of property, characteristic, and etc. [17],[15],[16]. However, from DDM prospect, an attribute is merely a named equivalence relation on the universe. So the study of attributes (features) is reduced to that of equivalence relations. Let $\Delta(V)$ be the set of all equivalence relations (partitions) on V. Recall that an attribute, by forgetting its interpretation, induces a partition, so we have

Proposition 4.1. There is a map

$$\theta : 2^A \longrightarrow \Delta(V),$$

that respects the meet, but not the join, operations. Lee called the image, $Im\theta$, the relation lattice, which is un-interpreted version of 2^A. Lee also observe that [7]

1. The join in $Im\theta$ is different from that of $\Delta(V)$.
2. So $Im\theta$ is a subset, but not a sublattice, of $\Delta(V)$.

Such an embedding is an unnatural one, but Lee focused his efforts on it. However, we will, instead, take a natural embedding

Definition 4.3. The smallest lattice generated by $Im\theta$, by abuse of language, is called the (Lin's) relation lattice, denoted by L(Q) which is un-interpreted closure of 2^A (by intersection and union). Some of the closure are uninterpretable in terms of A.

This definition will not cause confusion, since we will not use Lee's notion at all. The difference between $L(Q)$ and $Im\theta$ is that former contains all the joins of distinct attributes.

The pair $(V, L(Q))$ is the GDM of the (Lin's) relation lattice.

4.2 Feature Completion and Complete Relation Lattice

The smallest lattice, denoted by $L^*(Q)$, that consists of all coarsenings of $L(Q)$ is called the *complete relation lattice.*

Main Theorem 4.1. $L^*(Q)$ is the set of all derived attributes of the canonical model.

Definition 4.2. The pair $U_K = (V, L^*(Q))$ is the completion of $C_K = (V, Q)$ and is called the universal model of K.

A relation K can be uniquely factored into C_K and $NAME$, so K can be regarded as a pair $(C_K, NAME)$. If in addition there is a given concept hierarchy [4], that is, an extension $E(NAME)$ of the interpretation $NAME$ is defined on a subset $E(Q)$ of $L^*(Q)$. This additional information is called background knowledge

Data mining with this additional background knowledge $E(Q)$ is called data mining on derived attributes. Basically, it is data mining on an extended table. The extended table has the granular data model $(V, E(Q))$. If $E(Q)$ covers the attributes that support the "invisible patterns," We can mine the invisible patterns. Since $L^*(Q)$ is finite, in theory we can always find it. The bound is the Bell number [3] of the cardinal number of the smallest partition in $L^*(Q)$.

5 Associations and Generalized Associations

We will illustrate the idea by examples. Two standard measures called support and confidence are used for mining associations. In this paper we will focus on support only, we call the sub-tuples *associations*, if they meet the support requirement; it is one form of high frequency patterns. The *Corollary* 3.3 in Section 4 tells us that associations can be expressed by granules. We will illustrate the idea using the canonical model in Table 1 (support: ≥ 3). The association can be expressed as granules:

1. Associations of length one:
   (a) TEN $= \{v_2, v_3, v_4, v_5, v_6\}$
   (b) SJ $= \{v_2, v_3, v_4, v_5, v_6\}$
   (c) LA $=\{v_7, v_8, v_9\}$

Table 2. The Universal Model U_K of C_K, partially displayed; it should have 15 (= B_4) columns

Universal Model; attribute vales are names of granules						
V		Q^0	Q^2	Q^3	$Q^2 \cap Q^3 = G$	...
v_1		$\{v_1\}$	$\{v_1, v_7\}$ =TWENTY	$\{v_1\}$=NY	$\{v_1\}$= TWENTY ∩ NY	...
v_2		$\{v_2\}$	$\{v_2, v_3, v_4, v_5, v_6\}$= TEN	$\{v_2, v_3, v_4, v_5, v_6\}$= SJ	$\{v_2, v_3, v_4, v_5, v_6\}$ =TEN ∩ SJ	...
v_3		$\{v_3\}$	$\{v_2, v_3, v_4, v_5, v_6\}$= TEN	$\{v_2, v_3, v_4, v_5, v_6\}$ = SJ	$\{v_2, v_3, v_4, v_5, v_6\}$= TEN ∩ SJ	...
v_4	$\longrightarrow$	$\{v_4\}$	$\{v_2, v_3, v_4, v_5, v_6\}$= TEN	$\{v_2, v_3, v_4, v_5, v_6\}$ =SJ	$\{v_2, v_3, v_4, v_5, v_6\}$ =TEN ∩ SJ	...
v_5		$\{v_5\}$	$\{v_2, v_3, v_4, v_5, v_6\}$= TEN	$\{v_2, v_3, v_4, v_5, v_6\}$ =SJ	$\{v_2, v_3, v_4, v_5, v_6\}$ =TEN ∩ SJ	...
v_6		$\{v_6\}$	$\{v_2, v_3, v_4, v_5, v_6\}$= TEN	$\{v_2, v_3, v_4, v_5, v_6\}$=SJ	$\{v_2, v_3, v_4, v_5, v_6\}$ =TEN ∩ SJ	...
v_7		$\{v_7\}$	$\{v_1, v_7\}$=TWENTY	$\{v_7, v_8, v_9\}$ =LA	$\{v_7\}$ =TWENTY ∩ LA	...
v_8		$\{v_8\}$	$\{v_8, v_9\}$=THIRTY	$\{v_7, v_8, v_9\}$ =LA	$\{v_8, v_9\}$ =THIRTY ∩ LA	...
v_9		$\{v_9\}$	$\{v_8, v_9\}$=THIRTY	$\{v_7, v_8, v_9\}$=LA	$\{v_8, v_9\}$= THIRTY ∩ LA	...

2. Associations of length two:
   (a) (TEN, SJ) = TEN ∩ SJ= $\{v_2, v_3, v_4, v_5, v_6\}$
3. No associations of length $q \leq 3$.

Now let us examine the universal model in Table 2. The column G in Table 2 is the smallest element in the complete relation lattice $L^*(Q)$. So every element of $L^*(Q)$ is a coarsening of G. In other words, every granule in $L^*(Q)$ is a union of some granules from the partition G (by the expression *"a granule in $L^*(Q)$" we mean a granule belonging to one of its partitions.* In this example, the granules in G are { TWENTY ∩ NY, TEN ∩ SJ, TWENTY ∩ LA, THIRTY ∩ LA }. Let $|\bullet|$ be the cardinality of $\bullet$. The following expression represents the cardinality of granules in $L^*(Q)$, which is a union of some granules from the partition G.

$$|\text{TWENTY} \cap \text{NY}| * x_1 + |\text{TEN} \cap \text{SJ}| * x_2 + |\text{TWENTY} \cap \text{LA}| * x_3 + |\text{THIRTY} \cap \text{LA}| * x_4 \geq 3.$$

By taking the actual value of the cardinalities of the granules, we have,

$$1 * x_1 + 5 * x_2 + 1 * x_3 + 2 * x_4 \geq 3.$$

We will express the solutions in vector form, (x_1, x_2, x_3, x_4). It is an "integral convex set" in 4-dimensional space:
The "boundary solutions" are:

1 (0, 1, 0, 0); this solution means $TEN \cap SJ$'s cardinality by itself already meets the threshold (≥ 3).

2 (0, 0, 1, 1); this solution means we need the union of two granules, TWENTY ∩ LA and THIRTY ∩ LA, to meet the threshold. In other words, we need a generalized concept that covers both the subtuple (TWENTY, LA)= TWENTY ∩ LA and (THIRTY, LA)= THIRTY ∩ LA. For this particular case, since LA = (TWENTY, LA) ∪ (THIRTY, LA), hence LA is the desirable generalized concept.

3 (1, 0, 0, 1); this solution means we need the union of two granules, TWENTY∩NY ∪ THIRTY∩LA, as a single generalized concept.

"Internal points" are

4 (1, 1, 0, 0); we skip the interpretations.
5 (0, 1, 1, 0)
6 (0, 1, 0, 1)
7 (0, 1, 1, 1)
8 (1, 1, 1, 0)
9 (1, 1, 0, 1)
10 (1, 0, 1, 1)
11 (1, 1, 1, 1)

We re-express these formulas in granular form and simplify them into disjoint normal forms.

1 TEN∩SJ = TEN = SJ
2 TWENTY∩LA ∪ THIRTY∩LA =LA
3 TWENTY∩NY ∪ THIRTY∩LA
4 TWENTY∩NY ∪ TEN∩SJ = ¬ LA
5 TEN∩SJ ∪ TWENTY∩LA = TEN ∪ TWENTY∩LA = SJ ∪ T WENTY∩LA
6 TEN∩SJ ∪ THIRTY∩LA = ¬ TWENTY
7 TEN∩SJ ∪ TWENTY ∩ LA ∪ THIRTY ∩ LA = TEN ∪ LA = SJ ∪ LA
8 TWENTY∩NY ∪ TEN∩SJ ∪ TWENTY∩ LA = TEN ∪ TWENTY = ¬ THIRTY
9 TWENTY∩NY ∪ TEN∩SJ ∪ THIRTY∩ LA = ¬ (TWENTY ∩ LA)
10 TWENTY∩NY ∪ TWENTY∩LA ∪ THIRTY∩LA = ¬ SJ
11 TWENTY∩NY ∪ TEN∩SJ ∪ TWENTY∩ LA ∪ THIRTY∩LA = all

If the simplified expression is a single clause (in the original symbols), it is the (non-generalized) associations. We have the following associations

1. TEN (= SJ = TEN∩SJ)
2. SJ
3. TEN∩SJ
4. LA (=TWENTY∩LA ∪ THIRTY∩LA))

6 Conclusions

From DDM point of view, we ha e

1. Associations are the properties of the isomorphic class, in other words, isomorphic relations have isomorphic associations.
2. The probability theory based on item counting is a property of the isomorphic class.
3. Un-interpreted attributes (features)are partitions; they can be enumerated.
4. Generalized associations can be found by solving integral linear inequalities.

Some items in the above table seem indicate that relations with some additional semantics need to be explored; some initial results have been reported, more work are needed, [11], [13].

References

1. R. Agrawal, T. Imielinski, and A. Swami, "Mining Association Rules Between Sets of Items in Large Databases," in Proceeding of ACM-SIGMOD international Conference on Management of Data, pp. 207-216, Washington, DC, June, 1993
2. G. Birkhoff and S. MacLane, A Survey of Modern Algebra, Macmillan, 1977
3. Richard A. Brualdi, Introductory Combinatorics, Prentice Hall, 1992.
4. Y.D. Cai, N. Cercone, and J. Han. Attribute-oriented induction in relational databases. In Knowledge Discovery in Databases, pages 213–228. AAAI/MIT Press, Cambridge, MA, 1991.
5. John E. Freund, Modern Elementary Statistics, Prentice Hall, 1952
6. A. Barr and E.A. Feigenbaum, The handbook of Artificial Intelligence, William Kaufmann 1981
7. T. T. Lee, "Algebraic Theory of Relational Databases," The Bell System Technical Journal Vol 62, No 10, December, 1983, pp.3159-3204.
8. T. Y. Lin, "Database Mining on Derived Attributes," Spring-Verlag Lecture Notes on AI #2475, 2002, pp.14-32.
9. T. Y. Lin, "Mathematical Foundation of Association Rules - Mining Generalized Associations by Integral Linear Inequalities," in: the Proceedings of Foundation of Data Mining and Discovery Workshop (which is part of IEEE international Conference on Data Mining), Maebashi, Japan, Dec 9-12, 2002, pp. 81-88.
10. T. Y. Lin, "Attribute (Feature) Completion – The Theory of Attributes from Data Mining Prospect," in: Proceeding of IEEE international Conference on Data Mining, Maebashi, Japan, Dec 9-12, 2002, pp. pp.282-289
11. T. Y. Lin, "Data Mining and Machine Oriented Modeling: A Granular Computing Approach," Journal of Applied Intelligence, Kluwer, Vol. 13, No 2, September/October,2000, pp.113-124.
12. T. Y. Lin, "Attribute Transformations on Numerical Databases," Lecture Notes in Artificial Intelligence 1805, Terano, Liu, Chen (eds), PAKDD2000, Kyoto, Japan, April 18-20, 2000, 181-192.
13. T. Y. Lin, "Data Mining: Granular Computing Approach." In: Methodologies for Knowledge Discovery and Data Mining, Lecture Notes in Artificial Intelligence 1574, Third Pacific-Asia Conference, Beijing, April 26–28, 1999, 24-33.
14. T. Y. Lin, "Granular Computing on Binary Relations I: Data Mining and Neighborhood Systems." In: Rough Sets In Knowledge Discovery, A. Skoworn and L. Polkowski (eds), Springer-Verlag, 1998, 107-121.
15. H. Liu and H. Motoda, "Feature Transformaion and Subset Selection," IEEE Intelligent Systems, Vol. 13, No. 2, March/April, pp.26-28 (1998)
16. H. Liu and H. Motoda (eds), Feature Extraction, Construction and Selection – A Data Mining Perspective, Kluwer Academic Pubihsers (1998).
17. Hiroshi Motoda and Huan Liu "Feature Selection, Extraction and Construction," Communication of IICM (Institute of Information and Computing Machinery, Taiwan) Vol 5, No. 2, May 2002, pp. 67-72. (proceeding for the workshop "Toward the Foundation on Data Mining" in PAKDD2002, May 6, 2002.

A Graded Applicability of Rules

Anna Gomolińska*

University of Białystok, Department of Mathematics
Akademicka 2, 15267 Białystok, Poland
anna.gom@math.uwb.edu.pl

Abstract. We address the problem of rough applicability of rules within the framework of approximation spaces. The graded applicability of a rule for an object of an approximation space, introduced here, is viewed as a fundamental form of rough applicability. It is based on the graded meaning of a set of formulas, defined in our previous works. The notion of graded applicability enjoys a number of interesting properties and it is useful – in our opinion – in modeling of rule-based complex systems like multi-agent systems.

1 Introduction

When thinking of the problem of application of a rule, one can distinguish, among others, three more specific questions: applicability, results of application, and quality of a rule. The first question concerns the premises, the second – the conclusion(s), and the last one – the relationship between the premises and the conclusion of a rule. In this article, applicability of rules is addressed within the framework of approximation spaces. We introduce a notion of graded applicability of a rule for an object, based on the graded meaning of formulas and their sets [2, 3]. The graded applicability of rules, presented here, is viewed as a fundamental form of rough applicability to be further extended and refined.

The concept of graded applicability is interesting not merely for its theoretical properties. In our opinion, it may be useful in modeling of rule-based complex systems like systems of social agents, where rules are often followed in a flexible way. By means of this notion and its extensions, varied aspects concerning applicability of rules may be investigated and explained in theoretical terms. Another area in which one can use appropriate soft concepts of applicability of rules, based on the notion proposed here, is multi-criterial classification and, in particular, decision making. Graded forms of applicability cope with some cases of missing values of attributes and contribute to the greater effectiveness in classifying objects.

Throughout the paper, for a set x and $n > 0$, $\#x$ denotes its cardinality, $\wp x$ – the power set, and x^n – the Cartesian product of x taken n times. Let

* Many thanks to Andrzej Skowron, Marcin Wolski, and the anonymous referees for valuable remarks. The research has been partially supported by the grant 3T11C00226 from Ministry of Scientific Research and Information Technology of the Republic of Poland.

S. Tsumoto et al. (Eds.): RSCTC 2004, LNAI 3066, pp. 213–218, 2004.

$i = 1, \ldots, n$, $(x_i, \leq_i)$ be partially ordered sets, and $s, t \in x_1 \times \ldots \times x_n$. Then, $\pi_i(t)$ denotes the i-th element of t. By $\geq_i$ we denote the converse relation of $\leq_i$, whereas by $<_i, >_i$ – the strict versions of $\leq_i, \geq_i$, respectively. $\preceq$ is a partial ordering such that $s \preceq t$ iff $\forall i = 1, \ldots, n. \pi_i(s) \leq_i \pi_i(t)$. Degrees of applicability of rules are constructed from numbers of $[0,1]$ and a constant c, denoting "crisp" as opposite to "vague". By assumption $c \leq c$, where $\leq$ extends the natural ordering on $[0,1]$ to the set $T \stackrel{\text{def}}{=} [0,1] \cup \{c\}$. Additionally, let $T_1 \stackrel{\text{def}}{=} T \times [0,1]$. Parentheses and c will be dropped in formulas if no confusion results.

Section 2 is devoted to the notion of an approximation space. In Sect. 3, the concepts of graded satisfiability and graded meaning of formulas and their sets are recalled. The notion of graded applicability of rules is presented in Sect. 4. In the next section, we give an illustrative example. Section 6 contains a concise summary.

2 Approximation Spaces

By an *approximation space* (AS) we understand a triple $\mathcal{M} = (U, \Gamma, \kappa)$, where U is a non-empty set, $\Gamma : U \mapsto \wp U$ is an *uncertainty mapping*, and $\kappa : (\wp U)^2 \mapsto [0,1]$ is a *rough inclusion function* (RIF) [6][1]. The ASs, studied initially, were those induced by the *Pawlak information systems* [4].

Elements of U, referred to as objects and denoted by u, v with subscripts if needed, are known by their properties only. Some objects may seem to be similar from an observer's perspective. Objects enjoying the same properties are similar in a peculiar way: They are indiscernible. It is assumed that every object is necessarily similar to itself. Thus, the universe U is covered by a family of clusters of objects, called granules of information. In $\mathcal{M}$, the mapping Γ assigns to every object u, an elementary granule $\Gamma(u)$ of objects similar to u. By assumption, $u \in \Gamma(u)$.

The most popular RIFs, called *standard*, are based on the frequency count. For a finite U and $x, y \subseteq U$, the standard RIF κ^{st} is defined by $\kappa^{st}(x,y) = \begin{cases} \frac{\#(x \cap y)}{\#x} & \text{if } x \neq \emptyset \\ 1 & \text{otherwise.} \end{cases}$ A RIF is *quasi-standard* if it is defined as the standard one for finite first arguments. In general, a RIF assigns to every pair (x, y) of subsets of U, a number of the unit interval $[0,1]$, expressing the degree of inclusion of x in y. Polkowski and Skowron proposed *Rough Mereology*, a formal theory of being-a-part-in-degree, axiomatically characterizing a general notion of RIF [5]. In our approach, every RIF $\kappa : (\wp U)^2 \mapsto [0,1]$ is supposed to satisfy (A1)–(A3) for any $x, y, z \subseteq U$:

(A1) $\kappa(x,y) = 1$ iff $x \subseteq y$.

(A2) If $x \neq \emptyset$, then $\kappa(x,y) = 0$ iff $x \cap y = \emptyset$.

(A3) If $y \subseteq z$, then $\kappa(x,y) \leq \kappa(x,z)$.

[1] Originally, Γ and κ were equipped with lists of tuning parameters, dropped for simplicity here. Such ASs were referred to as *parameterized*.

The essense of ASs is that sets of objects of the universe are approximated by means of uncertainty mappings and RIFs. There are many alternative ways of approximation (see, e.g., [1] for a discussion and references).

3 The Graded Meaning of Formulas

In this section, we briefly recall the notions of graded satisfiability and graded meaning of formulas, studied in [2, 3]. Suppose a language L is given, expressing properties of $\mathcal{M}$. Formulas of L, denoted by α, β, γ with subscripts if needed, form the set FOR. Assume that a commutative conjunction ($\wedge$) occurs in L. Then, the conjunction of all elements of a non-empty finite set of formulas X is denoted by $\bigwedge X$.

Given a relation of (crisp) satisfiability of formulas for objects of U, $\models_c$, where $u \models_c \alpha$ reads as "α is *c-satisfied* for u", the *c-meaning* of α is understood along the standard lines as the set $||\alpha||_c = \{u \mid u \models_c \alpha\}$. These notions are refined by introducing degrees $t \in [0,1]$:

$$u \models_t \alpha \text{ iff } \kappa(\Gamma(u), ||\alpha||) \geq t \text{ and } ||\alpha||_t = \{u \mid u \models_t \alpha\}. \tag{1}$$

$u \models_t \alpha$ reads as "α is t-satisfied for u", and $||\alpha||_t$ is called the *t-meaning* of α. Where $t \in T$, the set of all formulas, t-satisfied for an object u, is denoted by $|u|_t$:

$$|u|_t = \{\alpha \mid u \models_t \alpha\}. \tag{2}$$

Along the standard lines, a set of formulas X is *c-satisfied* for u, $u \models_c X$, iff $\forall \alpha \in X.u \models_c \alpha$. The (crisp) meaning of X is the set $||X||_c = \{u \mid u \models_c X\}$. Next, let $\kappa^* : (\wp\text{FOR})^2 \mapsto [0,1]$ be a RIF and $t \in T_1$. Then,

$$u \models_t X \text{ iff } \kappa^*(X, |u|_{\pi_1(t)}) \geq \pi_2(t) \text{ and } ||X||_t = \{u \mid u \models_t X\}. \tag{3}$$

$u \models_t X$ reads as "X is *t-satisfied* for u", and $||X||_t$ is the *t-meaning* of X.

4 A Graded Form of Applicability of Rules

Rules over L, denoted by r with sub/superscripts if needed, are to describe dependencies and properties of objects of U and their sets in $\mathcal{M}$, and they consist of two components: finitely many premises and conclusion(s), all being formulas of L. From our standpoint it is of minor importance whether or not a rule may have one or more conclusions; we omit this question for the time being. The set of premises of r is denoted by $P(r)$ and the set of all rules over L by RUL. In $\mathcal{M}$, a rule r is *applicable* for an object u iff $P(r)$ is satisfied for u, or in other words, $u \in ||P(r)||$.[2] This concept is refined in two ways: by replacing the crisp satisfiability of premises by its graded counterpart and

[2] Equivalently, r is applicable for u iff all premises of r are satisfied for u, i.e., $\forall \alpha \in P(r).u \in ||\alpha||$.

by weakening the condition that all premises be satisfied. Where $t \in T_1$, $\mathrm{apl}_t(u)$ denotes the set of all rules t-applicable for u. Intuitively, r is *t-applicable* for u [3] if u satisfies a sufficiently large part of $P(r)$ in a sufficient degree, where sufficiency is determined by t; otherwise r is *t-inapplicable* for u. Formally,

$$r \in \mathrm{apl}_t(u) \overset{\mathrm{def}}{\leftrightarrow} \kappa^*(P(r), |u|_{\pi_1(t)}) \geq \pi_2(t), \text{i.e., iff } u \in ||P(r)||_t. \qquad (4)$$

Theorem 1. *For any objects u, v, formulas α, β, a set of formulas X, a finite set of formulas Y, rules r, r_1, r_2, a finite non-empty set of rules $\{r_i\}_{i \in I}$, $s_1 \in [0,1]$, $s \in T$, $t, t_1, t_2 \in T_1$, and assuming that κ^* is quasi-standard in (j), we have:*

(*a*) If $\Gamma(u) = \Gamma(v)$, then $\mathrm{apl}_t(u) = \mathrm{apl}_t(v)$.

(*b*) $r \in \mathrm{apl}_{(s,1)}(u)$ iff $P(r) \subseteq |u|_s$ iff $u \in \bigcap\{||\alpha||_s \mid \alpha \in P(r)\}$.

(*c*) $\mathrm{apl}_{(s,0)}(u) = \mathrm{RUL}$.

(*d*) If $P(r) = \{\alpha\}$ and $\pi_2(t) > 0$, then $r \in \mathrm{apl}_t(u)$ iff $u \in ||\alpha||_{\pi_1(t)}$.

(*e*) If $t_1 \preceq t_2$, then $\mathrm{apl}_{t_2}(u) \subseteq \mathrm{apl}_{t_1}(u)$.

(*f*) $\mathrm{apl}_{(1,s_1)}(u) \subseteq \mathrm{apl}_{(s,s_1)}(u) \subseteq \mathrm{apl}_{(0,s_1)}(u) = \mathrm{RUL}$.

(*g*) $\bigcap\{\mathrm{apl}_t(u) \mid u \in U \wedge t \in T_1\} = \{r \in \mathrm{RUL} \mid ||P(r)|| = U\}$.

(*h*) If $P(r_1) \subseteq P(r_2)$ and $r_2 \in \mathrm{apl}_{(s,1)}(u)$, then $r_1 \in \mathrm{apl}_{(s,1)}(u)$.

(*i*) If $\exists \alpha \in P(r).||\alpha||_s = \emptyset$, then $\forall u.r \notin \mathrm{apl}_{(s,1)}(u)$.

(*j*) If $P(r_2) = P(r_1) - Y$ and $||Y||_{(\pi_1(t),1)} = U$, then $r_2 \in \mathrm{apl}_t(u)$ implies $r_1 \in \mathrm{apl}_t(u)$.

(*k*) If $P(r_2) \neq \emptyset$, $P(r_1) = \{\bigwedge P(r_2)\}$, and $\pi_2(t) > 0$, then $r_1 \in \mathrm{apl}_t(u)$ implies $r_2 \in \mathrm{apl}_t(u)$.

(*l*) If $P(r) = \bigcup_{i \in I} P(r_i)$ and $\pi_2(t) = 1$, then $r \in \mathrm{apl}_t(u)$ iff $\{r_i\}_{i \in I} \subseteq \mathrm{apl}_t(u)$.

(*m*) If $P(r_2) = P(r_1) - X$, $\pi_2(t) = 1$, and $||P(r_1) \cap X||_t = U$, then $r_1 \in \mathrm{apl}_t(u)$ iff $r_2 \in \mathrm{apl}_t(u)$.

(*n*) If $P(r_2) = P(r_1) \cup X$, $\pi_2(t) = 1$, and $||X - P(r_1)||_t = U$, then $r_1 \in \mathrm{apl}_t(u)$ iff $r_2 \in \mathrm{apl}_t(u)$.

To give a few comments, observe that t-applicability of rules is determined up to granulation by (a). Next, the partial order on the family of parameterized operators of applicability apl_t reverses the order on parameters by (e), (f). $\mathrm{apl}_{(1,1)}$ is the least element and $\mathrm{apl}_{(0,0)}$ – the greatest one. Finally, axiomatic rules, i.e., rules without premises are t-applicable for all $u \in U$ and $t \in T_1$ in virtue of (g).

5 An Illustrative Example

Consider a Pawlak information system $\mathcal{A} = (U, A)$, where $U = \{2, \ldots, 12\}$ and $a_1, a_2, a_3 \in A$. Any attribute $a \in A$ assigns to each object $u \in U$, a value

[3] In other words, r is *applicable* for u *in degree* t.

$a(u) \in V_a$. Values of attributes are denoted by b with subscripts if needed. Let $b_1 \in V_{a_1}$, $b_2, b_3 \in V_{a_2}$, $b_4 \in V_{a_3}$, and $*$ represent other values. A simple logical language, interpreted in $\mathcal{A}$, is defined. Constant symbols are elements of A and $\bigcup_{a \in A} V_a$. Propositional connectives are the classical ones. Atomic formulas have the form (a_i, b). Formulas are obtained from the atomic formulas along the standard lines. For any formulas $(a_i, b), \alpha, \beta$, satisfiability for an object u is defined as follows: $u \models (a_i, b)$ iff $a_i(u) = b$; $u \models \alpha \wedge \beta$ iff $u \models \alpha$ and $u \models \beta$; $u \models \neg\alpha$ iff $u \not\models \alpha$. Let $\alpha = ((a_1, b_1) \wedge (a_2, b_2)) \vee (a_3, b_4)$, $\beta = \neg(a_2, b_2) \wedge \neg(a_2, b_3)$, and $\gamma = \neg\alpha \vee \beta$. Then, $||\alpha|| = \{2, 4, 6, 8, 11, 12\}$, $||\beta|| = \{4, 5, 11\}$, and $||\gamma|| = \{3, 4, 5, 7, 9, 10, 11\}$. Table 1 shows a fragment of $\mathcal{A}$. According to the mapping Γ, objects 2, 6 are similar to 2, i.e., $\Gamma(2) = \{2, 6\}$. Subsequently, $\Gamma(3) = \{3, 5, 9\}$, $\Gamma(4) = \{4, 11\}$, $\Gamma(5) = \{4, 5\}$, $\Gamma(6) = \{2, 6, 12\}$, $\Gamma(7) = \{4, 7, 8\}$, $\Gamma(8) = \{3, 8\}$, $\Gamma(9) = \{9, 10\}$, $\Gamma(10) = \{3, 9, 10\}$, $\Gamma(11) = \{2, 11\}$, and $\Gamma(12) = \{6, 12\}$. It is assumed that the RIFs considered are quasi-standard. Consider a rule r with premises α, γ (i.e., $P(r) = \{\alpha, \gamma\}$) and with one conclusion β.[4] For $t = (t_1, t_2) \in T_1$, the t-meaning of $P(r)$ is given in Table 2 and the conditions for t-applicability of r for objects of U in Table 3.

Table 1. A fragment of the information system $\mathcal{A}$.

$a \backslash u$	2	3	4	5	6	7	8	9	10	11	12
a_1	b_1	b_1	$*$	$*$	b_1	$*$	b_1	$*$	$*$	$*$	b_1
a_2	b_2	b_3	$*$	$*$	b_2	b_2	b_3	b_3	b_3	$*$	b_2
a_3	b_4	$*$	b_4	$*$	$*$	$*$	b_4	$*$	$*$	b_4	$*$

Table 2. The t-meaning of $P(r)$.

$t_2 \backslash t_1$	0	$(0, \frac{1}{3}]$	$(\frac{1}{3}, \frac{1}{2}]$	$(\frac{1}{2}, \frac{2}{3}]$	$(\frac{2}{3}, 1]$	c
0	U	U	U	U	U	U
$(0, \frac{1}{2}]$	U	U	U	$U - \{8\}$	$U - \{7, 8\}$	U
$(\frac{1}{2}, 1]$	U	$\{4, 5, 7, 8, 11\}$	$\{4, 5, 8, 11\}$	$\{4\}$	$\{4\}$	$\{4, 11\}$

Table 3. The conditions for t-applicability of r.

u	Condition
2, 3, 6, 9, 10, 12	$t_1 = 0 \vee t_2 \leq \frac{1}{2}$
4	$t \in T_1$
5	$t_1 \leq \frac{1}{2} \vee t_2 \leq \frac{1}{2}$
7	$t_1 \leq \frac{1}{3} \vee t_2 = 0 \vee ((t_1 \leq \frac{2}{3} \vee t_1 = c) \wedge t_2 \leq \frac{1}{2})$
8	$t_1 \leq \frac{1}{2} \vee t_2 = 0 \vee (t_1 = c \wedge t_2 \leq \frac{1}{2})$
11	$t_1 \leq \frac{1}{2} \vee t_1 = c \vee t_2 \leq \frac{1}{2}$

[4] Actually, r is an instance of the resolution rule.

Thus, r is applicable, i.e., $(c, 1)$-applicable for 4 and 11. Let $t_2 = 1$. r may also be applied for 5 and 8 if $\frac{1}{3} < t_1 \leq \frac{1}{2}$. On the other hand, t-applicability is more restrictive than the crisp one for $t_1 > \frac{1}{2}$. In this case, r is t-applicable for 4 only.

6 Summary

In the paper, intended as an introduction to a larger study of the problem of soft application of rules, we started with a fundamental concept of graded applicability of a rule for an object of an AS. In our opinion, both this notion as well as some of its extensions and refinements may prove useful in modeling of rule-based complex systems, e.g., systems of social agents, where rules are often applied in a soft, flexible way. For scarce space, the illustration has been limited to one example. For the same reason, we had to omit many interesting references to the literature and the proof of the theorem. Also, only a few short comments on the properties of graded applicability are included.

References

1. Gomolińska, A.: A comparative study of some generalized rough approximations. Fundamenta Informaticae **51(1–2)** (2002) 103–119
2. Gomolińska, A.: A graded meaning of formulas and their sets in generalized approximation spaces. In Czaja, L. (ed.) Proc. Int. Workshop on Concurrency, Specification and Programming CS&P'2003, Czarna, Poland, Warsaw University Publ. ISBN 83-88374-71-0 (2003) 157–170
3. Gomolińska, A.: A graded meaning of formulas in approximation spaces. Fundamenta Informaticae (to appear)
4. Pawlak, Z.: Rough Sets. Theoretical Aspects of Reasoning about Data. Kluwer Acad. Publ. Dordrecht (1991)
5. Polkowski, L., Skowron, A.: Rough mereology: A new paradigm for approximate reasoning. Int. J. Approximated Reasoning **15(4)** (1996) 333–365
6. Skowron, A., Stepaniuk, J.: Tolerance approximation spaces. Fundamenta Informaticae **27** (1996) 245–253

On the Degree of Independence of a Contingency Matrix

Shoji Hirano and Shusaku Tsumoto

Department of Medical Informatics
Shimane University, School of Medicine
Enya-cho Izumo City, Shimane 693-8501 Japan
hirano@ieee.org, tsumoto@computer.org

Abstract. A contingency table summarizes the conditional frequencies of two attributes and shows how these two attributes are dependent on each other. Thus, this table is a fundamental tool for pattern discovery with conditional probabilities, such as rule discovery. In this paper, a contingency table is interpreted from the viewpoint of statistical independence and granular computing. The first important observation is that a contingency table compares two attributes with respect to the number of equivalence classes. For example, a $n \times n$ table compares two attributes with the same granularity, while a $m \times n (m \geq n)$ table compares two attributes with different granularities. The second important observation is that matrix algebra is a key point of analysis of this table. Especially, the degree of independence, rank plays a very important role in evaluating the degree of statistical independence. Relations between rank and the degree of dependence are also investigated.

1 Introduction

Independence (dependence) is a very important concept in data mining, especially for feature selection. In rough sets[1], if two attribute-value pairs, say $[c = 0]$ and $[d = 0]$ are independent, their supporting sets, denoted by C and D do not have a overlapping region ($C \cap D = \phi$), which means that one attribute independent to a given target concept may not appear in the classification rule for the concept. This idea is also frequently used in other rule discovery methods: let us consider deterministic rules, described as *if-then* rules, which can be viewed as classic propositions ($C \rightarrow D$). From the set-theoretical point of view, a set of examples supporting the conditional part of a deterministic rule, denoted by C, is a subset of a set whose examples belong to the consequence part, denoted by D. That is, the relation $C \subseteq D$ holds and deterministic rules are supported only by positive examples in a dataset[2].

When such a subset relation is not satisfied, indeterministic rules can be defined as if-then rules with probabilistic information[3]. From the set-theoretical point of view, C is not a subset, but closely overlapped with D. That is, the relations $C \cap D \neq \phi$ and $|C \cap D|/|C| \geq \delta$ will hold in this case[1]. Thus, probabilistic

[1] The threshold δ is the degree of the closeness of overlapping sets, which will be given by domain experts. For more information, please refer to Section 3.

S. Tsumoto et al. (Eds.): RSCTC 2004, LNAI 3066, pp. 219–228, 2004.

rules are supported by a large number of positive examples and a small number of negative examples.

On the other hand, in a probabilistic context, independence of two attributes means that one attribute (a_1) will not influence the occurrence of the other attribute (a_2), which is formulated as $p(a_2|a_1) = p(a_2)$.

Although independence is a very important concept, it has not been fully and formally investigated as a relation between two attributes. Tsumoto introduces linear algebra into formal analysis of a contigency table [4]. The results give the following interesting results. First, a contingency table can be viewed as comparison between two attributes with respect to information granularity. Second, algebra is a key point of analysis of this table. A contingency table can be viewed as a matrix and several operations and ideas of matrix theory are introduced into the analysis of the contingency table. Especially, The degree of independence, rank plays a very important role in extracting a probabilistic model from a given contingency table.

This paper gives a further investigation on the degree of independence of contingency matrix. The paper is organized as follows: Section 2 shows preliminaries. Section 3 discusses the former results. Section 4 gives the relations between rank and submatrices of a matrix. Finally, Section 6 concludes this paper.

2 Contingency Table from Rough Sets

2.1 Notations

In the subsequent sections, the following notations is adopted, which is introduced in [5]. Let U denote a nonempty, finite set called the universe and A denote a nonempty, finite set of attributes, i.e., $a : U \to V_a$ for $a \in A$, where V_a is called the domain of a, respectively. Then, a decision table is defined as an information system, $A = (U, A \cup \{\mathcal{D}\})$, where $\{\mathcal{D}\}$ is a set of given decision attributes. The atomic formulas over $B \subseteq A \cup \{\mathcal{D}\}$ and V are expressions of the form $[a = v]$, called descriptors over B, where $a \in B$ and $v \in V_a$. The set $F(B, V)$ of formulas over B is the least set containing all atomic formulas over B and closed with respect to disjunction, conjunction and negation. For each $f \in F(B, V)$, f_A denote the meaning of f in A, i.e., the set of all objects in U with property f, defined inductively as follows.

1. If f is of the form $[a = v]$ then, $f_A = \{s \in U | a(s) = v\}$
2. $(f \wedge g)_A = f_A \cap g_A$; $(f \vee g)_A = f_A \vee g_A$; $(\neg f)_A = U - f_a$

2.2 Multi-way Contingency Table

Two-way contingency table can be extended into a contingency table for multinominal attributes.

Definition 1. *Let R_1 and R_2 denote multinominal attributes in an attribute space A which have m and n values. A contingency tables is a table of a set* *of the meaning of the following formulas:* $|[R_1 = A_j]_A|$, $|[R_2 = B_i]_A|$, $|[R_1 = A_j \wedge R_2 = B_i]_A|$, $|[R_1 = A_1 \wedge R_1 = A_2 \wedge \cdots \wedge R_1 = A_m]_A|$, $|[R_2 = B_1 \wedge R_2 = A_2 \wedge \cdots \wedge R_2 = A_n]_A|$ *and* $|U|$ $(i = 1, 2, 3, \cdots, n$ *and* $j = 1, 2, 3, \cdots, m)$. *This table is arranged into the form shown in Table 1, where:* $|[R_1 = A_j]_A| = \sum_{i=1}^{m} x_{1i} = x_{\cdot j}$, $|[R_2 = B_i]_A| = \sum_{j=1}^{n} x_{ji} = x_{i\cdot}$, $|[R_1 = A_j \wedge R_2 = B_i]_A| = x_{ij}$, $|U| = N = x_{\cdot\cdot}$ $(i = 1, 2, 3, \cdots, n$ *and* $j = 1, 2, 3, \cdots, m)$.

Table 1. Contingency Table $(n \times m)$

	A_1	A_2	$\cdots$	A_n	Sum
B_1	x_{11}	x_{12}	$\cdots$	x_{1n}	$x_{1\cdot}$
B_2	x_{21}	x_{22}	$\cdots$	x_{2n}	$x_{2\cdot}$
$\cdots$	$\cdots$	$\cdots$	$\cdots$	$\cdots$	$\cdots$
B_m	x_{m1}	x_{m2}	$\cdots$	x_{mn}	$x_{m\cdot}$
Sum	$x_{\cdot 1}$	$x_{\cdot 2}$	$\cdots$	$x_{\cdot n}$	$x_{\cdot\cdot} = \lvert U\rvert = N$

For example, let us consider an information table shown in Table 2. The relationship between b and e can be examined by using the corresponding contingency table as follows. First, the frequencies of four elementary relations are counted, called *marginal distributions*: $[b = 0]$, $[b = 1]$, $[e = 0]$, and $[e = 1]$. Then, the frequencies of four kinds of conjunction are counted: $[b = 0] \wedge [e = 0]$, $[b = 0] \wedge [e = 1]$, $[b = 1] \wedge [e = 0]$, and $[b = 1] \wedge [e = 1]$. Then, the following contingency table is obtained (Table 1).

One of the important observations from granular computing is that a contingency table shows the relations between two attributes with respect to intersection of their supporting sets. For example, in Table 3, both b and e have two different partitions of the universe and the table gives the relation between b and e with respect to the intersection of supporting sets.

3 Rank of Contingency Table (Two-Way)

3.1 Preliminaries

Definition 2. *A corresponding matrix* $C_{T_{a,b}}$ *is defined as a matrix the element of which are equal to the value of the corresponding contingency table* $T_{a,b}$ *of two attributes* a *and* b*, except for marginal values.*

Definition 3. *The rank of a table is defined as the rank of its corresponding matrix. The maximum value of the rank is equal to the size of (square) matrix, denoted by* r.

Let the table given in Table 3 be defined as $T_{b,e}$. Then, $C_{T_{b,e}}$ is:

$$\begin{pmatrix} 1 & 1 \\ 2 & 1 \end{pmatrix}$$

Table 2. A Small Dataset

a	b	c	d	e
1	0	0	0	1
0	0	1	1	1
0	1	2	2	0
1	1	1	2	1
0	0	2	1	0

Table 3. Corresponding Contingency Table

	b=0	b=1	
e=0	1	1	2
e=1	2	1	3
	3	2	5

Since the determinant of $C_{T_{b,e}}$ $det(C_{T_{b,e}})$ is not equal to 0, the rank of $C_{T_{b,e}}$ is equal to 2. It is the maximum value ($r = 2$), so b and e are statistically dependent.

3.2 Independence when the Table Is Two-Way

From the results in linear algebra, several results are obtained. (The proofs is omitted.) First, it is assumed that a contingency table is given as two-way $m = 2$, $n = 2$ in Table 1. Then the corresponding matrix ($C_{T_{R_1,R_2}}$) is given as:

$$\begin{pmatrix} x_{11} & x_{12} \\ x_{21} & x_{22} \end{pmatrix},$$

Proposition 1. *The determinant of $det(C_{T_{R_1,R_2}})$ is equal to $|x_{11}x_{22} - x_{12}x_{21}|$.*

Proposition 2. *The rank will be:*

$$rank = \begin{cases} 2, & if\ det(C_{T_{R_1,R_2}}) \neq 0 \\ 1, & if\ det(C_{T_{R_1,R_2}}) = 0 \end{cases}$$

If the rank of $det(C_{T_{b,e}})$ is equal to 1, according to the theorems of the linear algebra, it is obtained that one row or column will be represented by the other column. That is,

Proposition 3. *Let r_1 and r_2 denote the rows of the corresponding matrix of a given two-way table, $C_{T_{b,e}}$. That is,*

$$r_1 = (x_{11}, x_{12}), r_2 = (x_{21}, x_{22})$$

Then, r_1 can be represented by r_2: $r_1 = kr_2$, where k is given as:

$$k = \frac{x_{11}}{x_{21}} = \frac{x_{12}}{x_{22}} = \frac{x_{1\cdot}}{x_{2\cdot}}$$

From this proposition, the following theorem is obtained.

Theorem 1. *If the rank of the corresponding matrix is 1, then two attributes in a given contingency table are statistically independent. Thus,*

$$rank = \begin{cases} 2, & dependent \\ 1, & statistical\ independent \end{cases}$$

Table 4. Contingency Table for c and d

	c=0	c=1	c=2	
d=0	1	0	0	1
d=1	0	1	1	2
d=2	0	1	1	2
	1	2	2	5

Table 5. Contingency Table for a and c

	a=0	a=1	
c=0	0	1	1
c=1	1	1	2
c=2	2	0	2
	3	2	5

4 Rank of Contingency Table (Multi-way)

In the case of a general square matrix, the results in the two-way contingency table can be extended. Especially, it is very important to observe that conventional statistical independence is only supported when the rank of the corresponding is equal to 1. Let us consider the contingency table of c and d in Table 2, which is obtained as follows. Thus, the corresponding matrix of this table is:

$$\begin{pmatrix} 1 & 0 & 0 \\ 0 & 1 & 1 \\ 0 & 1 & 1 \end{pmatrix},$$

whose determinant is equal to 0. It is clear that its rank is 2. It is interesting to see that if the case of $[d = 0]$ is removed, then the rank of the corresponding matrix is equal to 1 and two rows are equal. Thus, if the value space of d into $\{1, 2\}$ is restricted, then c and d are statistically independent. This relation is called *contextual independence* [6], which is related with conditional independence.

However, another type of weak independence is observed: let us consider the contingency table of a and c. The table is obtained as Table 5:
Its corresponding matrix is:

$$\begin{pmatrix} 0 & 1 \\ 1 & 1 \\ 2 & 0 \end{pmatrix},$$

Since the corresponding matrix is not square, the determinant is not defined. But it is easy to see that the rank of this matrix is two. In this case, even any attribute-value pair removed from the table will not generate statistical independence.

However, interesting relations can be found. Let r_1, r_2 and r_3 denote the first, second and third row, respectively. That is, $r_1 = (0, 1)$, $r_2 = (1, 1)$ and $r_3 = (2, 0)$.

Then, it is easy to see that $r_3 = 2(r_2 - r_1)$, which can be viewed as:

$$p([c = 2]) = 2(p([c = 1]) - p([c = 0])),$$

which gives a probabilistic model between attribute-value pairs. According to linear algebra, when we have a $m \times n (m \geq n)$ or $n \times m$ corresponding matrix, the rank of the corresponding matrix is less than n. Thus:

Theorem 2. *If the corresponding matrix of a given contingency table is not square and of the form $m \times n (m \geq n)$, then its rank is less than n. Especially, the row $r_{n+1}, r_{n+2}, \cdots, r_m$ can be represented by:*

$$r_k = \sum_{i=1}^{r} k_i r_i (n+1 \leq k \leq m),$$

where k_i and r denote the constant and the rank of the corresponding matrix, respectively. This can be interpreted as:

$$p([R_1 = A_k]) = \sum_{i=1}^{r} k_i p([R_1 = A_i])$$

Finally, the relation between rank and independence in a multi-way contingency table is obtained.

Theorem 3. *Let the corresponding matrix of a given contingency table be a square $n \times n$ matrix. If the rank of the corresponding matrix is 1, then two attributes in a given contingency table are statistically independent. If the rank of the corresponding matrix is n, then two attributes in a given contingency table are dependent. Otherwise, two attributes are contextual dependent, which means that several conditional probabilities can be represented by a linear combination of conditional probabilities. Thus,*

$$rank = \begin{cases} n & \textit{dependent} \\ 2, \cdots, n-1 & \textit{contextual independent} \\ 1 & \textit{statistical independent} \end{cases}$$

□

5 Rank and Degree of Dependence

5.1 Submatrix and Subdeterminant

The next interest is the structure of a corresponding matrix with $1 \leq rank \leq n-1$. First, let us define a submatrix (a subtable) and subdeterminant.

Definition 4. *Let A denote a corresponding matrix of a given contigency table $(m \times n)$. A corresponding submatrix $A^{i_1 i_2 \cdots i_r}_{j_1 j_2 \cdots j_s}$ is defined as a matrix which is given by an intersection of r rows and s columns of A $(i_1 < i_2 < \cdots < i_r, j_1 < j_2 < \cdots < j_r)$.*

Definition 5. *A subdeterminant of A is defined as a determinant of a submatrix $A^{i_1 i_2 \cdots i_r}_{j_1 j_2 \cdots j_s}$, which is denoted by $det(A^{i_1 i_2 \cdots i_r}_{j_1 j_2 \cdots j_s})$.*

Let us consider the contingency table given as Table 1. Then, a subtable for $A^{i_1 i_2 \cdots i_r}_{j_1 j_2 \cdots j_s}$ is given as Table 6.

Table 6. A subtable ($r \times s$)

	A_{j1}	A_{j2}	$\cdots$	A_{j_r}	Sum
B_{i_1}	$x_{i_1j_1}$	$x_{i_1j_2}$	$\cdots$	$x_{i_1j_r}$	$x_{i_1\cdot}$
B_{i_2}	$x_{i_2j_1}$	$x_{i_2j_2}$	$\cdots$	$x_{i_2j_r}$	$x_{i_2\cdot}$
$\cdots$	$\cdots$	$\cdots$	$\cdots$	$\cdots$	$\cdots$
B_{i_r}	$x_{i_rj_1}$	$x_{i_rj_2}$	$\cdots$	$x_{i_rj_n}$	$x_{i_r\cdot}$
Sum	$x_{\cdot 1}$	$x_{\cdot 2}$	$\cdots$	$x_{\cdot n}$	$x_{\cdot\cdot} = \lvert U \rvert = N$

5.2 Rank and Subdeterminant

Let δ_{ij} denote a co-factor of a_{ij} in a square corresponding matrix of A. Then,

$$\Delta_{ij} = (-1)^{i+j} det(A^{1,2,\cdots,i-1,i+1,\cdots,n}_{1,2,\cdots,j-1,j+1,\cdots,n}).$$

It is notable that a co-factor is a special type of submatrix, where only ith-row and j-column are removed from a original matrix. By the use of co-factors, the determinant of A is defined as:

$$det(A) = \sum_{j=1}^{n} a_{ij}\Delta_{ij},$$

which is called *Laplace expansion.*

From this representation, if $det(A)$ is not equal to 0, then $\Delta_{ij} \neq 0$ for $\{a_{i1}, a_{i2}, \cdots, a_{in}\}$ which are not equal to 0. Thus, the following proposition is obtained.

Proposition 4. *If $det(A)$ is not equal to 0 if at least one co-factor of $a_{ij}(\neq 0)$, Δ_{ij} is not equal to 0.*

It is notable that the above definition of a determinant gives the relation between a original matrix A and submatrices (co-factors). Since cofactors gives a square matrix of size $n-1$, the above proposition gives the relation between a matrix of size n and submatrices of size $n-1$. In the same way, we can discuss the relation between a corresponding matrix of size n and submatrices of size $r(1 \leq r < n-1)$.

5.3 Rank and Submatrix

Let us assume that corresponding matrix and submatrix are square ($n \times n$ and $r \times r$, respectively).

Theorem 4. *If the rank of a corresponding matrix of size $n \times n$ is equal to r, at least the determinant of one submatrix of size $r \times r$ is not equal to 0. That is, there exists a submatrix $A^{i_1i_2\cdots i_r}_{j_1j_2\cdots j_r}$, which satisfies $det(A^{i_1i_2\cdots i_r}_{j_1j_2\cdots j_r}) \neq 0$*

Corollary 1. *If the rank of a corresponding matrix of size $n \times n$ is equal to r, all the determinants of the submatrices whose number of columns and rows are larger than $r+1(\leq n)$ are equal to 0.*

Example. Let us consider the following corresponding matrix:

$$A = \begin{pmatrix} 1 & 2 & 3 \\ 4 & 5 & 6 \\ 7 & 8 & 9 \end{pmatrix}.$$

The determinant of A is:

$$det(A) = 1 \times (-1)^{1+1} det \begin{pmatrix} 5 & 6 \\ 8 & 9 \end{pmatrix} + 2 \times (-1)^{1+2} det \begin{pmatrix} 4 & 6 \\ 7 & 9 \end{pmatrix}$$
$$+3 \times (-1)^{1+3} det \begin{pmatrix} 4 & 5 \\ 7 & 8 \end{pmatrix} = 0$$

Thus, the rank of A is smaller than 2.

All the subdeterminants of A are:

$$det \begin{pmatrix} 5 & 6 \\ 8 & 9 \end{pmatrix} = -3,\ det \begin{pmatrix} 4 & 6 \\ 7 & 9 \end{pmatrix} = -6,\ det \begin{pmatrix} 4 & 5 \\ 7 & 8 \end{pmatrix} = -3,$$
$$det \begin{pmatrix} 1 & 2 \\ 7 & 8 \end{pmatrix} = -6,\ det \begin{pmatrix} 1 & 3 \\ 7 & 9 \end{pmatrix} = -12,\ det \begin{pmatrix} 2 & 3 \\ 8 & 9 \end{pmatrix} = -6,$$
$$det \begin{pmatrix} 1 & 2 \\ 4 & 5 \end{pmatrix} = -3,\ det \begin{pmatrix} 1 & 3 \\ 4 & 6 \end{pmatrix} = -6,\ det \begin{pmatrix} 2 & 3 \\ 5 & 6 \end{pmatrix} = -3.$$

Since all the subdeterminants of A are not equal to 0, the rank of A is equal to 2. Actually, since

$$(4\ 5\ 6) = \frac{1}{2}\{(1\ 2\ 3) + (7\ 8\ 9)\},$$

and $(7 \quad 8 \quad 9)$ cannot be represented by $k(1 \quad 2 \quad 3)(k : integer)$, the rank of this matrix is equal to 2.

Thus, one attribute-value pair is statistically dependent on other two pairs, statistically independent of the other attribute. In other words, if two pairs are fixed, the remaining one attribute-value pair will be statistically independently determined.

5.4 Determinantal Divisors

From the subdeterminants of all the submatrices of size 2, all the subdeterminants of a corresponding matrix has the greatest common divisor, equal to 3.

From the recursive definition of the determinants, it is show that the subdeterminants of size $r+1$ will have the greatest common divisor of the subdeterminants of size r as a divisor. Thus,

Theorem 5. *Let $d_k(A)$ denote the greatest common divisor of all the subdeterminants of size k, $det(A^{i_1 i_2 \cdots i_k}_{j_1 j_2 \cdots j_r})$. $d_1(A), d_2(A), \cdots, d_n(A)$ are called determinantal divisors. From the definition of Laplace expansion,*

$$d_k(A) | d_{k+1}(A).$$

□

In the example of the above subsection, $d_1(A) = 1$, $d_2(A) = 3$ and $d_3(A) = 0$.

Example. Let us consider the following corresponding matrix:

$$B = \begin{pmatrix} 1 & 2 & 3 \\ 4 & 5 & 6 \\ 7 & \mathbf{11} & 9 \end{pmatrix}.$$

Calculation gives: $d_1(B) = 1$, $d_2(B) = 3$ and $d_3(B) = 42$.

It is notable that a simple change of a corresponding matrix gives a significant change to the determinant, which suggests a change of structure in dependence/independence.

The relation between $d_k(A)$ gives a interesting constraint.

Proposition 5. *Since $d_k(A)|d_{k+1}(A)$, the sequence of the devisiors is monotonically increasing one:*

$$d_1(A) \leq d_2(A) \cdots d_r(A),$$

where r denotes the rank of A.

The sequence of B illustrates this: $1 < 3 < 42$.

5.5 Divisors and Degree of Dependence

Since the determinant can be viewed as the degree of dependence, this result is very important. If values of all the subdeterminants (size r) are very small (nearly equal to 0) and $d_r(A) \simeq 1$, then the values of the subdeterminants (size $r+1$) are very small. This property may hold until the r reaches the rank of the corresponding matrix. Thus, the sequence of the divisiors of a corresponding matrix gives a hidden structure of a contingency table.

Also, this results show that $d_1(A)$ and $d_2(A)$ are very important to estimate the rank of a corresponding matrix. Since $d_1(A)$ is only given by the greatest common divisor of all the elements of A, $d_2(A)$ are much more important components. This also intuitively suggests that the subdeterminants of A with size 2 are principal components of a corresponding matrix from the viewpoint of statistical dependence.

Recall that statistical independence of two attributes is equivalent to a corresponding matrix with rank being 1. A matrix with rank being 2 gives a context-dependent independence, which means three values of two attributes are independent, but two values of two attributes are dependent.

The more results concerning determinantal divisors will be reported in the near future.

5.6 Subdeterminants and Degree of Dependence

Since the determinants give the degree of dependence, the degree of dependence can be evaluted by the values of subdeterminants.

For the above examples (A), since

$$det \begin{pmatrix} 1 & 3 \\ 7 & 9 \end{pmatrix} = -12$$

gives the maximum value, the first and the third attribute-value pairs for two attributes are dependent each other.

On the other hand, concerning B, since

$$det \begin{pmatrix} 2 & 3 \\ 11 & 9 \end{pmatrix} = -15$$

gives the maximum value, the second and the third attribute-value pairs for two attributes are dependent each other.

6 Conclusion

In this paper, a contingency table is interpreted from the viewpoint of granular computing and statistical independence. From the correspondence between contingency table and matrix, the following observations are obtained: in the case of statistical independence, the rank of the corresponding matrix of a given contingency table is equal to 1. That is, all the rows of contingency table can be described by one row with the coefficient given by a marginal distribution. If the rank is maximum, then two attributes are dependent. Otherwise, some probabilistic structure can be found within attribute -value pairs in a given attribute. Thus, matrix algebra is a key point of the analysis of a contingency table and the degree of independence, rank plays a very important role in extracting a probabilistic model.

References

1. Pawlak, Z.: Rough Sets. Kluwer Academic Publishers, Dordrecht (1991)
2. Tsumoto, S.: Knowledge discovery in clinical databases and evaluation of discovered knowledge in outpatient clinic. Information Sciences (2000) 125–137
3. Tsumoto, S., Tanaka, H.: Automated discovery of medical expert system rules from clinical databases based on rough sets. In: Proceedings of the Second International Conference on Knowledge Discovery and Data Mining 96, Palo Alto, AAAI Press (1996) 63–69
4. Tsumoto, S.: Statistical independence as linear independence. In Skowron, A., Szczuka, M., eds.: Electronic Notes in Theoretical Computer Science. Volume 82., Elsevier (2003)
5. Skowron, A., Grzymala-Busse, J.: From rough set theory to evidence theory. In Yager, R., Fedrizzi, M., Kacprzyk, J., eds.: Advances in the Dempster-Shafer Theory of Evidence. John Wiley & Sons, New York (1994) 193–236
6. Butz, C.: Exploiting contextual independencies in web search and user profiling. In: Proceedings of World Congress on Computational Intelligence (WCCI'2002) (CD-ROM). (2002)

K Nearest Neighbor Classification with Local Induction of the Simple Value Difference Metric

Andrzej Skowron and Arkadiusz Wojna

Faculty of Mathematics, Informatics and Mechanics
Warsaw University
ul. Banacha 2, 02-097 Warsaw, Poland
{skowron,wojna}@mimuw.edu.pl

Abstract. The classical k nearest neighbor (k-nn) classification assumes that a fixed global metric is defined and searching for nearest neighbors is always based on this global metric. In the paper we present a model with local induction of a metric. Any test object induces a local metric from the neighborhood of this object and selects k nearest neighbors according to this locally induced metric. To induce both the global and the local metric we use the weighted Simple Value Difference Metric (SVDM). The experimental results show that the proposed classification model with local induction of a metric reduces classification error up to several times in comparison to the classical k-nn method.

1 Introduction

The classical machine learning methods [1, 2] induce a mathematical model of data from training data and apply this model to reason about test objects. The induced model remains invariant while reasoning about different test objects. For many real-life data it is not possible to induce relevant global models. This fact has been recently observed by researches from different areas like data mining, statistics, multiagent systems [3–5]. The main reason is that phenomena described by real-life data are often too complex and we do not have enough knowledge to induce global models or a parameterized class of such models together with searching methods for the relevant global model in such a class. We propose a step toward development of methods dealing with such a real-life data. For any test object x first we use some heuristics (in our example based on distances) that make it possible to eliminate objects not relevant for classifying x. From the remaining (rather of small size) neighborhood of x a local model (in our case a distance function) is induced that is relevant for classifying the test object x. Hence, our idea is based on extracting for a given test object x its local model that is dependent on x and next using this model for classifying x.

To apply this idea we extend the k nearest neighbor (k-nn) method [6, 7] with one additional intermediate step (see Figure 1). First it induces a global metric like in the classical k-nn. Then for each test object x the extended algorithm selects a neighborhood of x and it induces a local metric based only on the selected neighborhood. After that the k nearest neighbors of the test object x

S. Tsumoto et al. (Eds.): RSCTC 2004, LNAI 3066, pp. 229–234, 2004.

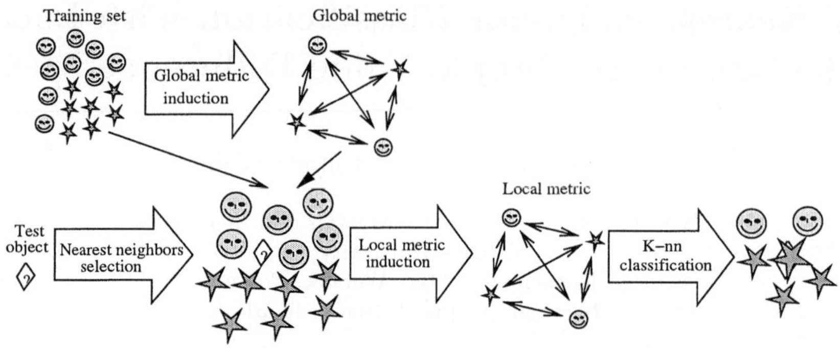

Fig. 1. K-nn classification with local metric

are selected according to the locally induced metric. Local metric induction is a step towards building a model that depends locally on properties of a test object. In both definitions of metrics: local and global, we use the weighted version of the Simple Value Difference Metric [8] defined for data with nominal attributes.

We have tested three data sets each with several thousand of training objects, and the model with local metric induction has reduced the classification error of the classical k-nn from 30% up to several times depending on the tested set.

2 Related Work

The classical nearest neighbor method was introduced by Cover and Hart [6] and the extension of 1-nn to k-nn was described by Duda and Hart [7]. Local adaptation of a metric in the k-nn method was considered only in the context of a multidimensional space with real value attributes.

Friedman proposed a method that combines k-nn with recursive partitioning used in decision trees [9]. For each test object the method starts with the whole training set and it constructs a sequence of partitions. Each partition eliminates a number of training objects. In this way after the last partition a small set of k objects remains to be used for classification. To make a single partition the direction with the greatest decision discernibility is selected.

The algorithm proposed by Hastie and Tibshirani [10] starts with the Euclidean metric and for each test object it iteratively changes the weights of attributes. At each iteration it selects a neighborhood of a test object and it applies local discriminant analysis to shrink the distance in the direction parallel to the boundary between decision classes. Finally it selects k nearest neighbors according to the locally transformed metric.

Domeniconi and Gunopulos use a similar idea but they use support vector machines instead of local discriminant analysis to determine class boundaries and to shrink the distance [11]. Support vectors can be computed during the learning phase what makes this approach much more efficient in comparision to local discriminant analysis.

3 K Nearest Neighbors with the Global SVDM Metric

We assume that a training set $\mathbb{U}$ is provided and each object $x \in \mathbb{U}$ is labeled with a decision $dec(x)$ from a finite set V_d. The task is to learn from a training set $\mathbb{U}$ how to induce the correct decision for new unlabeled data objects.

K-nn is a widely used classification model assuming that data objects are given from a pseudometric space $\mathbb{X}$ with a distance function $\rho : \mathbb{X}^2 \to \mathbb{R}$. The distance function ρ is induced from a training set $\mathbb{U}$ during the learning phase. Then for each data object x to be classified the set $S(x,k)$ of the k nearest neighbors of x is selected from $\mathbb{U}$ according to a distance function ρ and a decision is inferred from the decisions of the nearest neighbors in $S(x,k)$.

In the paper we use one of the most popular procedures to determine a decision for a test object x. For each decision value $v \in V_d$ the *Strength* measure counts the number of the nearest neighbors from $S(x,k)$ with the decision v:

$$Strength(x,v) = |\{y \in S(x,k) : dec(y) = v\}|$$

As a decision for a test object x the algorithm assigns the most frequent decision in the set of the k nearest neighbors $S(x,k)$:

$$dec_{k-nn}(x) = \arg\max_{v \in V_d} Strength(x,v)$$

As a distance function ρ we use the weighted version of the Simple Value Difference Metric (SVDM) [12]. It assumes that data objects are represented as vectors of nominal values $x = (x_1, \ldots, x_n)$. The distance between two data objects $x = (x_1, \ldots, x_n)$ and $y = (y_1, \ldots, y_n)$ is defined by

$$\rho(x,y) = \sum_{i=1}^{n} w_i \cdot \rho_i(x_i, y_i)$$

where $\rho_i(\cdot,\cdot)$ is a measure of similarity between two attribute values and w_i are weights computed in the second phase of the metric induction process. Two nominal values x_i, y_i are considered to be similar if they imply similar decision distribution, i.e., if they correlate similarly with the decision on the training set $\mathbb{U}$:

$$\rho_i(x_i, y_i) = \sum_{v \in V_d} |P(dec = v|x_i) - P(dec = v|y_i)|$$

As an attribute weighting procedure we use a procedure described in [8].

4 *K* Nearest Neighbors with Local Metrics

In this section we describe an extension of the k-nn method with local metric induction. The learning phase of the extended method is analogical to the classical k-nn. It induces a global metric ρ from a training set $\mathbb{U}$.

Algorithm 1 presents the classification of a single query object x by the extended method. First the algorithm selects the n nearest neighbors $N(x,n)$

Algorithm 1 K nearest neighbors with local metric

```
ρ - the weighted SVDM metric induced from the whole training set 𝕌
x - a query object to be classified

N(x,n) := the set of n nearest neighbors of x from 𝕌 according to ρ
ρ^x := local weighted SVDM metric induced from the neighborhood N(x,n)
S(x,k) := the set of k nearest neighbors of x from N(x,n)
          according to ρ^x  (k ≤ n)
dec_{local-knn}(x) := arg max_{v∈V_d} |{y ∈ S(x,k) : dec(x) = v}|
```

of x from $\mathbb{U}$ according to the global metric ρ. Next it induces a local metric ρ^x using only the selected neighborhood $N(x,n)$. After that the algorithm selects the nearest neighbors of x again but only the k nearest neighbors and only from the neighborhood set $N(x,n)$. The selected set $S(x,k)$ is then used to compute the majority decision $dec_{local-knn}(x)$ that is returned as the final result for the query object x. Both for the global and for the local metric definition the algorithm uses the weighted version of the SVDM metric described in Section 4.

To improve classification accuracy the neighborhood size n should be large, at least several hundred. To accelerate selection of a large number of nearest neighbors from a training set we use the advanced hierarchical indexing [8].

The optimal value k can be estimated from a training set. We use the procedure analogical to the estimation procedure proposed for the classical k-nn [13].

The classical k-nn is called a lazy method: it induced a global metric and it performs the rest of computation at the moment of classification. The described algorithm extends this idea: it repeats metric induction at the moment of classification. The proposed extension allows to use the local properties of data topology in the neighborhood of a query object and to adjust the metric definition to these local properties.

5 Experimental Results

We have performed experiments for 3 large benchmark data sets with nominal attributes from the UCI repository [14] (in parenthesis the number of attributes, the training set and the test set size): *chess* (36, 2131, 1065), *nursery* (8, 8640, 4320) and *DNA-splice* (60, 2000, 1186). The data sets provided as a single file (*chess, nursery*) have been randomly split into a training and a test part with the ratio 2 to 1. The data set *splice* have been tested with the original partition.

Each data set has been tested with the classical k-nn and with the extended k-nn with three different values of the neighborhood size n: 100, 200 and 500. To make the results comparable all four classification models have been tested with the same partition of a data set and with the same global metric. Each method estimated the optimal value k from a training set in the range $1 \leq k \leq n$ and it used this value during classification of a test set. Each test has been repeated 3 times for each data set and the average classification error has been calculated.

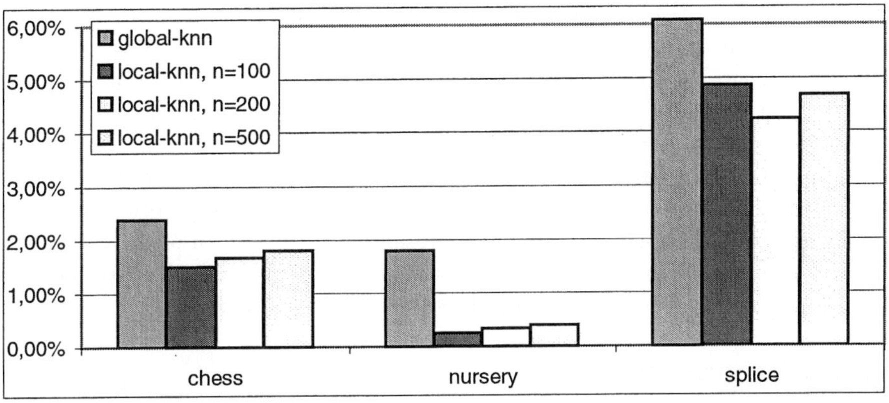

Fig. 2. Classification error of the classical k-nn and the extended k-nn with three different neighborhood sizes: 100, 200 and 500

Figure 2 presents the comparision of the average classification errors obtained from the experiments. The graph shows that for all data sets the k-nn model with local metric induction reduces the classification error significantly in comparision to the classical k-nn based on a global metric. In case of the data sets *chess* and *splice* the reduction is between 20% and 40% depending on the neighborhood size and in case of the data set *nursery* the reduction is severel times (over 7 times in the best case). The presented results prove that a large profit can be obtained if one applies a local approach to data instead of the global one.

The difference between the results for *nursery* and for two other data sets seems to correlate with the data set size. It implies that the larger data set is the more profitable it is to include local metric induction as an intermediate step.

The interesting issue is the dependence between the classification error and the neighborhood size n used to induce a local metric. The best error reduction was obtained for $n = 100$ in case of two data sets and for $n = 200$ in case of the data set *splice*. In particular, the optimal neighborhood size is larger in case of the data set *splice* than in case of *nursery* although the latter data set is about 4 times larger than the former one. It indicates that the optimal neighborhood size depends strongly on the properties of a data set and an advanced technique is necessary to estimate this optimal size.

6 Conclusions

In the paper we proposed a new classification model that is an extension of the classical k-nn and we compared the accuracy of the new and the original method. The classical k-nn assumes that a fixed distance function is defined for the whole data space. The extended model induces a different distance function for each object to be classified and it uses only local information around the object to induce this distance function. This approach allowed us to adapt the metric depending on the local properties of data topology.

We have applied the new method to the classification problem for data with nominal attributes. The experimental results show that the presented approach has an adventage over the original k-nn method. The extended method reduces the classification error from several tens percent up to several times.

The k-nn model with a local metric corresponds to the idea of transductive reasoning [5]. The transductive approach assumes that a classification model should depend on the objects to be classified and it should be adapted according to the properties of these objects. The presented extension of k-nn implements transduction: local metric induction adapts the metric defintion to the local topology in the neighborhood of an object to be classifed.

Acknowledgments

This work was supported by the grants 4 T11C 040 24 and 3 T11C 002 26 from Ministry of Scientific Research and Information Technology of the Republic of Poland.

References

1. Mitchell, T.M.: Machine Learning. McGraw-Hill, Portland (1997)
2. Pawlak, Z.: Rough Sets - Theoretical Aspects of Reasoning about Data. Kluwer Academic Publishers, Dordrecht (1991)
3. Breiman, L.: Statistical modeling - the two cultures. Statistical Science **16** (2001) 199–231
4. Skowron, A., Stepaniuk, J.: Information granules and rough-neural computing. In: Rough-Neural Computing: Techniques for Computing with Words. Cognitive Technologies. Springer-Verlag, Heidelberg, Germany (2003) 43–84
5. Vapnik, V.: Statistical Learning Theory. Wiley, Chichester, GB (1998)
6. Cover, T.M., Hart, P.E.: Nearest neighbor pattern classification. IEEE Transactions on Information Theory **13** (1967) 21–27
7. Duda, R.O., Hart, P.E.: Pattern Classification and Scene Analysis. Wiley, New York, NY (1973)
8. Wojna, A.G.: Center-based indexing in vector and metric spaces. Fundamenta Informaticae **56** (2003) 285–310
9. Friedman, J.: Flexible metric nearest neighbor classification. Technical Report 113, Department of Statistics, Stanford University, CA (1994)
10. Hastie, T., Tibshirani, R.: Discriminant adaptive nearest neighbor classification. IEEE Transactions on Pattern Analysis and Machine Intelligence **18** (1996) 607–616
11. Domeniconi, C., Gunopulos, D.: Efficient local flexible nearest neighbor classification. In: Proceedings of the Second SIAM International Conference on Data Mining. (2002)
12. Domingos, P.: Unifying instance-based and rule-based induction. Machine Learning **24** (1996) 141–168
13. Góra, G., Wojna, A.G.: RIONA: a new classification system combining rule induction and instance-based learning. Fundamenta Informaticae **51** (2002) 369–390
14. Blake, C.L., Merz, C.J.: UCI repository of machine learning databases. http://www.ics.uci.edu/~mlearn/MLRepository.html, Department of Information and Computer Science, University of California, Irvine, CA (1998)

A Note on the Regularization Algorithm*

Wojciech Jaworski

Faculty of Mathematics, Computer Science and Mechanics
Warsaw University, Banacha 2, 02-07 Warsaw, Poland
wj189182@students.mimuw.edu.pl

Abstract. Regularization Algorithm (also called Regularization Network) is a technique for solving problems of learning from examples – in particular, the problem of approximating a multivariate function from sparse data. We analyze behavior of Regularization Algorithm for regularizator parameter equal to zero. We propose an approximative version of algorithm in order to overcome the computational cost for large data sets. We give proof of convergence and estimation for error of approximation.

Keywords: computational learning theory, regularization algorithm, approximate regularization algorithm

1 Introduction

The purpose of this paper is to analyze properties of Regularization Algorithm (RA, for short) and present its approximate version, which is more useful for data analysis than standard version because it has the lower computational complexity.

This paper is based on concepts introduced by Smale and Poggio [1],[2],[4],[8].

RA is used to solve problems of learning from examples, in particular problems of approximating a multivariate function from sparse data. The algorithm is searching for a function that minimizes a functional

$$\mathcal{E}_{\gamma,\mathbf{z}}(f) = \frac{1}{m}\sum_{i=1}^{m}(f(x_i) - y_i)^2 + \gamma\|f\|_K^2,$$

where $\mathbf{z} = ((x_1, y_1), \ldots, (x_m, y_m))$ is a sample of the length m, $x_i \in \mathbb{R}^n$ are examples and $y_i \in \mathbb{R}$ are decisions, $\|\cdot\|_K$ is the norm in the reproductive kernel Hilbert space. The function $f_{\gamma,\mathbf{z}}$ minimizing $\mathcal{E}_{\gamma,\mathbf{z}}$ is given by

$$f_{\gamma,\mathbf{z}}(x) = \sum_{i=1}^{m} a_i K(x, x_i),$$

where $\mathbf{a} = (a_1, \ldots, a_m)$ is a solution of a system of linear equations in $\mathbb{R}^m$:

$$(\gamma m I + K[\mathbf{x}])\mathbf{a} = \mathbf{y}.$$

* This paper consists of a part of my Master Thesis supervised by A. Skowron.

S. Tsumoto et al. (Eds.): RSCTC 2004, LNAI 3066, pp. 235–243, 2004.

Derivation of the above formula is included in Section 2.

The main results of the paper concern of the RA behavior for parameter γ equal to zero and derivation of the approximate algorithm that not requires solving the above linear equation system.

In Section 3 we show that if examples in a sample are pairwise different and $\gamma = 0$ then $f_{\gamma,\mathbf{z}}$ exists, $\mathcal{E}_{\gamma,\mathbf{z}}(f_{\gamma,\mathbf{z}}) = 0$, and $f_{\gamma,\mathbf{z}}$ minimizes the norm on the set of functions for which $\mathcal{E}_{\gamma,\mathbf{z}}$ has value 0. Next, the transformation that allow us to extend this result to all sets of examples is given.

In Section 4 an approximate regularization algorithm is derived. It is grounded on the expansion idea of inverse operator into geometric series and getting the first N terms of that series. Iterative formula that makes it possible to execute approximate algorithm by means of N multiplications of matrix by a vector is presented. Moreover the estimation of error of such an approximation if found.

In Conclusions, we also outline some further research directions.

2 Regularization Algorithm

In the first place we'll define a slightly more general version of RA.

Theorem 2.1. *Let ρ be a probabilistic measure over $\mathbf{z}$, $\rho_i = \rho(z_i) > 0$. Let*

$$\mathcal{E}_{\rho,\gamma,\mathbf{z}}(f) = \frac{1}{m}\sum_{i=1}^{m}(f(x_i) - y_i)^2\rho_i + \gamma\|f\|_K^2,$$

and $\gamma > 0$. Then a function $f_{\rho,\gamma,\mathbf{z}}$ that minimizes $\mathcal{E}_{\rho,\gamma,\mathbf{z}}$ can be expressed by

$$f_{\rho,\gamma,\mathbf{z}}(x) = \sum_{i=1}^{m} a_i K(x, x_i),$$

where $\mathbf{a} = (a_1, \ldots, a_m)$ is the unique solution of well-posed linear system in $\mathbb{R}^m$:

$$(\gamma R^{-1} + K[\mathbf{x}])\mathbf{a} = \mathbf{y},$$

where R is a diagonal matrix with the value ρ_i on the i-th entry of diagonal.

Proof. $\gamma > 0$, so $\gamma\|f\|_K < \infty$ iff $f \in \mathcal{H}_K$. Hence may assume that $f \in \mathcal{H}_K$ and $f = \sum c_k\phi_k$. Then $\|f\|_K^2 = \sum \frac{c_k^2}{\lambda_k}$. Let

$$H(f) = \sum_{i=1}^{m}(y_i - f(x_i))^2\rho_i + \gamma\sum_k \frac{c_k^2}{\lambda_k}.$$

For every $k \geq 1$

$$\frac{\partial H(f)}{\partial c_k} = \sum_{i=1}^{m} 2(y_i - f(x_i))(-\phi_k(x_i))\rho_i + 2\gamma\frac{c_k}{\lambda_k}.$$

If f is minimum of H, then $\frac{\partial H(f)}{\partial c_k} = 0$ for all k.
So, we obtain $c_k = \frac{\lambda_k}{\gamma} \sum_{i=1}^{m} (y_i - f(x_i))\phi_k(x_i)\rho_i$.

Let $a_i = \frac{y_i - f(x_i)}{\gamma}\rho_i$. Then $c_k = \lambda_k \sum_i a_i \phi_k(x_i)$ and

$$f(x) = \sum_{k=1}^{\infty} c_k \phi_k(x) = \sum_{k=1}^{\infty} (\lambda_k \sum_{i=1}^{m} a_i \phi_k(x_i))\phi_k(x) =$$

$$= \sum_{i=1}^{m} a_i \sum_{k=1}^{\infty} \lambda_k \phi_k(x_i)\phi_k(x) = \sum_{i=1}^{m} a_i K(x_i, x).$$

In definition of a_i we replace $f(x_i)$ with $\sum_{i=1}^{m} a_i K(x_i, x)$ and we obtain:

$$a_i = \frac{y_i - \sum_{k=1}^{m} a_i K(x_k, x_i)}{\gamma} \rho_i.$$

Hence

$$R^{-1}\mathbf{a} = \frac{\mathbf{y} - K[\mathbf{x}]\mathbf{a}}{\gamma}.$$

Corollary 2.2. *Function $f_{\gamma,\mathbf{z}}$ minimizing $\mathcal{E}_{\gamma,\mathbf{z}}$ may be expressed by*

$$f_{\gamma,\mathbf{z}}(x) = \sum_{i=1}^{m} a_i K(x, x_i),$$

where $\mathbf{a} = (a_1, \ldots, a_m)$ is the solution of linear system in $\mathbb{R}^m$:

$$(\gamma m I + K[\mathbf{x}])\mathbf{a} = \mathbf{y}.$$

Proof. Proof follows immediately from the above theorem for $\rho_i = \frac{1}{m}$.

3 Regularization Algorithm for $\gamma = 0$

K is positive definite so $K[\mathbf{x}]$ is positive, if only components of $\mathbf{x}$ are pairwise different. On the other hand, when in $\mathbf{x}$ are two identical components then $K[\mathbf{x}]$ has two identical rows, so 0 is its eigenvalue.

Regularization algorithm is executable if only $\gamma m I + K[\mathbf{x}]$ is invertible. So, if the sequence of examples $\mathbf{x}$ doesn't have any repetition then the algorithm may be executed for $\gamma = 0$.

Algorithm can be extended over all sequences of examples through cumulating identical examples: Let $\mathbf{z}' = \{(x'_1, y'_1), \ldots, (x'_{m'}, y'_{m'})\}$ be a sample such that $x'_i \neq x'_j$ for $i = 1, \ldots, m'$, and ρ a probabilistic measure defined as follows: Assume that for each $x \in \mathbf{x}$ exists $x' \in \mathbf{x}'$ such that $x = x'$. Let $A_i = \{j \in 1, \ldots, m : x'_i = x_j\}$. Then $y'_i = \frac{1}{|A_i|} \sum_{j \in A_i} y_i$, $\rho_i = \frac{|A_i|}{m}$. $\mathbf{z}'$ depends on $\mathbf{z}$ in following way:

Proposition 3.1.

$$\forall_{f\in\mathcal{H}_K}\ \mathcal{E}_{\gamma,\mathbf{z}}(f)=\mathcal{E}_{\rho,\gamma,\mathbf{z}'}(f)+C,$$

where C is a constant independent from f and γ.

Proof.

$$\mathcal{E}_{\gamma,\mathbf{z}}(f)=\frac{1}{m}\sum_{i=1}^{m}(f(x_i)-y_i)^2+\gamma\|f\|_K^2=\sum_{i=1}^{|\mathbf{z}'|}\sum_{j\in A_i}\frac{1}{m}(f(x_j)-y_j)^2+\gamma\|f\|_K^2$$

$$\sum_{j\in A_i}\frac{1}{m}(f(x_j)-y_j)^2=\frac{1}{m}\sum_{j\in A_i}(f(x_i')-y_j)^2=$$

$$=\frac{1}{m}(|A_i|f(x_i')^2-2\sum_{j\in A_i}f(x_i')y_j+\sum_{j\in A_i}y_j^2)=$$

$$=\frac{1}{m}(|A_i|(f(x_i')-\sum_{j\in A_i}y_j)^2-|A_i|(\sum_{j\in A_i}y_j)^2+\sum_{j\in A_i}y_j^2)=\rho_i(f(x_i')-y_i')^2+c_i.$$

It follows from the above, that it is enough to consider samples without repetitions of examples.

Then our algorithm has the following properties:

Proposition 3.2.

$$\mathcal{E}_{\mathbf{z}}(f_{\rho,0,\mathbf{z}})=\mathcal{E}_{\rho,0,\mathbf{z}}(f_{\rho,0,\mathbf{z}})=0.$$

Proof. We will show that $f_{\rho,0,\mathbf{z}}(x_j)=y_j$. We have

$$f_{\rho,0,\mathbf{z}}(x_j)=\sum_{i=1}^{m}a_iK(x_j,x_i).$$

Since $\gamma=0$, we have $K[\mathbf{x}]\mathbf{a}=\mathbf{y}$. Hence $\sum_{i=1}^{m}a_iK(x_j,x_i)=y_j$.

Theorem 3.3.

$$\|f_{\rho,0,\mathbf{z}}\|_K=\inf_{f:\mathcal{E}_{\mathbf{z}}(f)=0}\|f\|_K$$

and $f_{\rho,0,\mathbf{z}}$ is the only function for which infimum is reached.

Proof. $\mathcal{E}_{\rho,\gamma,\mathbf{z}}(f)$ is continuous with respect to $f\in\mathcal{H}_K$ and $\gamma\in\mathbb{R}$. Let $F(\gamma):(0,+\infty)\to\mathcal{H}_K$, $F(\gamma)=f_{\rho,\gamma,\mathbf{z}}$. $F(\gamma)$ is a function for which $\inf_f\mathcal{E}_{\rho,\gamma,\mathbf{z}}(f)$ is reached. Now, observe that F is continuous because of continuity of regularization algorithm and

$$\lim_{\gamma\to 0}F(\gamma)=f_{\rho,0,\mathbf{z}},\quad \lim_{\gamma\to\infty}F(\gamma)=f_0,\quad f_0\equiv 0.$$

Let

$$S_\alpha=\{f\in\mathcal{H}_K:\mathcal{E}_{\rho,0,\mathbf{z}}(f)=\alpha\},\alpha\in[0,\mathcal{E}_{\rho,0,\mathbf{z}}(f_0)).$$

From Proposition 3.2 follows, that $f_{\rho,0,\mathbf{z}} \in S_0$, and from continuity of F, that for each other S_α belongs value of F. Thus, for every α, S_α is non-empty.

Assume that $F(\gamma_\alpha) \in S_\alpha$. Than, $F(\gamma_\alpha)$ minimizes $\|\cdot\|_K$ on S_α, because if not $F(\gamma_\alpha)$ wouldn't be the only infimum $\mathcal{E}_{\rho,\gamma_\alpha,\mathbf{z}}$. It also follows, that there is exactly one value of F in S_α.

Let $g \in S_0$, and let $G : (0,\varepsilon) \to \mathcal{H}_K$, be continuous and let $G(\alpha) \in S_\alpha$ and $\lim_{\alpha\to 0} G(\alpha) = g$. Then, for each $\alpha \in (0,\varepsilon)$, we have $\|F(\gamma_\alpha)\|_K \leq \|G(\alpha)\|_K$, so

$$\|f_{\rho,0,\mathbf{z}}\|_K = \lim_{\alpha\to 0} \|F(\gamma_\alpha)\|_K \leq \lim_{\alpha\to 0} \|G(\alpha)\|_K = \|g\|_K.$$

Hence, we obtain $\|f_{\rho,0,\mathbf{z}}\|_K = \inf_{f\in S_0} \|f\|_K$.

The only thing left, is to show that $f_{\rho,0,\mathbf{z}}$ is the only function for which infimum is reached. Let $f \in S_0 - f_{\rho,0,\mathbf{z}}$. Then, $f + f_{\rho,0,\mathbf{z}} \in S_0$, and

$$0 = \mathcal{E}_{\rho,0,\mathbf{z}}(f + f_{\rho,0,\mathbf{z}}) = \sum_{i=1}^{m} (f(x_i) + f_{\rho,0,\mathbf{z}}(x_i) - y_i)^2 \rho_i = \sum_{i=1}^{m} f(x_i)^2 \rho_i.$$

Consequently, $f(x_i) = 0$, and $S_0 - f_{\rho,0,\mathbf{z}}$ is a subspace of $\mathcal{H}_K$. $S_0 - f_{\rho,0,\mathbf{z}}$ is closed because it has a finite co-dimension. S_0 is a closed affine subspace of $\mathcal{H}_K$, so there is one and only one point in S_0 that minimizes the norm.

4 Approximate Regularization Algorithm

The RA defined above requires solving of system of m linear equations. This is computationally expensive for large m. Instead of solving such linear system exactly, approximate solution can be found. The idea of an approximate algorithm is based on expanding the operator $(\gamma R^{-1} + K[\mathbf{x}])^{-1}$ into series and taking some first terms of this series.

We will use the standard formula for geometric series:

Lemma 4.1. *For $\lambda \in (0,2)$ the following formulas are true:*

$$\sum_{i=0}^{\infty} (1-\lambda)^i = \frac{1}{\lambda}, \quad \sum_{i=0}^{N} (I-\lambda)^i = (I - (I-\lambda)^{N+1})\lambda^{-1}.$$

The formulas are also true for positive operators:

Lemma 4.2. *Let A be positive on a finite dimensional linear space such that all its eigenvalues are in $(0,2)$. Then*

$$\sum_{i=0}^{\infty} (I-A)^i = A^{-1}, \quad \sum_{i=0}^{N} (I-A)^i = (I - (I-A)^{N+1})A^{-1}.$$

Now, we use the formula for operator $\gamma R^{-1} + K[\mathbf{x}]$. Let $\lambda_{\max}$ and $\lambda_{\min}$ be the greatest and smallest eigenvalues of $K[\mathbf{x}]$. Let $\rho_{\max}$ i $\rho_{\min}$ be the greatest and smallest eigenvalues of R.

Theorem 4.3. *Let* $\mu > \frac{1}{2}(\lambda_{\max} + \gamma\frac{1}{\rho_{\min}})$. *Then*

$$(\gamma R^{-1} + K[\mathbf{x}])^{-1} = \frac{1}{\mu}\sum_{i=0}^{\infty}(I - \frac{1}{\mu}(\gamma R^{-1} + K[\mathbf{x}]))^i.$$

Let $K_{\mu,N}$ be a partial sum of series:

$$K_{\mu,N} = \frac{1}{\mu}\sum_{i=0}^{N}(I - \frac{1}{\mu}(\gamma R^{-1} + K[\mathbf{x}]))^i =$$

$$= (I - (I - \frac{1}{\mu}(\gamma R^{-1} + K[\mathbf{x}]))^{N+1})(\gamma R^{-1} + K[\mathbf{x}])^{-1}.$$

We will find the error of approximation after getting partial sum of series. We will assume about μ only that $\mu > 0$. The condition $\mu > \frac{1}{2}(\lambda_{\max} + \gamma\frac{1}{\rho_{\min}})$ is not needed for $K_{\mu,N}$ to be well defined.

Theorem 4.4. *Let* $h(\lambda) = \frac{(1-\frac{\lambda}{\mu})^{N+1}}{\lambda}$, *then*

$$\|(\gamma R^{-1} + K[\mathbf{x}])^{-1} - K_{\mu,N}\|_2 \leq \max(|h(\lambda_{\min} + \gamma\frac{1}{\rho_{\max}})|, |h(\lambda_{\max} + \gamma\frac{1}{\rho_{\min}})|).$$

Proof.

$$(\gamma R^{-1} + K[\mathbf{x}])^{-1} - K_{\mu,N} = (I - \frac{1}{\mu}(\gamma R^{-1} + K[\mathbf{x}]))^{N+1}(\gamma R^{-1} + K[\mathbf{x}])^{-1}.$$

Let Λ be the set of eigenvalues of $\gamma R^{-1} + K[\mathbf{x}]$. Then

$$\|(I - \frac{1}{\mu}(\gamma R^{-1} + K[\mathbf{x}]))^{N+1}(\gamma R^{-1} + K[\mathbf{x}])^{-1}\| = \max_{\lambda\in\Lambda}|(1 - \frac{1}{\mu}\lambda)^{N+1}\lambda^{-1}|.$$

We find the extrema of function h. We have

$$h'(\lambda) = \frac{-(N+1)\frac{\lambda}{\mu}(1 - \frac{\lambda}{\mu})^N - (1 - \frac{\lambda}{\mu})^{N+1}}{\lambda^2},$$

$h'(\lambda) = 0$ iff $1 - \frac{\lambda}{\mu} = 0$ or $-(N+1)\frac{\lambda}{\mu} - (1 - \frac{\lambda}{\mu}) = 0$. The second equation is identical to $N\frac{\lambda}{\mu} = -1$. Hence, $\lambda < 0$ so it is unimportant to us. The only case left is $1 - \frac{\lambda}{\mu} = 0$, i.e., $\mu = \lambda$.

The function $|h(\lambda)|$ is equal to 0 for $\mu = \lambda$ and is monotonic on intervals $(0, \mu)$ and (μ, ∞). Thus

$$\max_{\lambda\in\Lambda}|h(\lambda)| = \max(|h(\min\lambda \in \Lambda\lambda)|, |h(\max\lambda \in \Lambda\lambda)|) \leq$$

$$\leq \max(|h(\lambda_{\min} + \gamma\frac{1}{\rho_{\max}})|, |h(\lambda_{\max} + \gamma\frac{1}{\rho_{\min}})|).$$

Now, we can find the μ that minimizes the error. Let

$$c = \frac{\lambda_{\max} + \gamma\frac{1}{\rho_{\min}}}{\lambda_{\min} + \gamma\frac{1}{\rho_{\max}}}.$$

The coefficient c is called the *condition* of operator $\gamma R^{-1} + K[\mathbf{x}]$.

Theorem 4.5. *The error is minimized by*

$$\mu = (\lambda_{\min} + \gamma\frac{1}{\rho_{\max}})\frac{\sqrt[N+1]{c}}{\sqrt[N+1]{c}+1},$$

and is equal to

$$\frac{1}{\lambda_{\min} + \gamma\frac{1}{\rho_{\max}}}(\frac{c-1}{c+\sqrt[N+1]{c}})^{N+1}.$$

Proof. Let $\lambda_1 = \lambda_{\min} + \gamma\frac{1}{\rho_{\max}}$ and $\lambda_2 = \lambda_{\max} + \gamma\frac{1}{\rho_{\min}}$.
From the shape of function $|h|$ and the error formula in the above theorem it follows that we seek for μ satisfying the following conditions:

$$\lambda_1 < \mu < \lambda_2 \text{ and } |h(\lambda_1)| = |h(\lambda_2)|.$$

From the definition of h we obtain

$$|h(\lambda)| = |\frac{(1-\frac{\lambda}{\mu})^{N+1}}{\lambda}| = (\frac{|1-\frac{\lambda}{\mu}|}{\sqrt[N+1]{\lambda}})^{N+1}.$$

So, we look for μ such that:

$$\frac{|1-\frac{\lambda_1}{\mu}|}{\sqrt[N+1]{\lambda_1}} = \frac{|1-\frac{\lambda_2}{\mu}|}{\sqrt[N+1]{\lambda_2}},$$

$$(\mu - \lambda_1)\sqrt[N+1]{c} = \lambda_2 - \mu,$$

$$\mu(\sqrt[N+1]{c}+1) = \lambda_2 + \lambda_1\sqrt[N+1]{c} = \lambda_1(c+\sqrt[N+1]{c}).$$

From this we obtain μ and the error can be simply calculated:

$$\frac{(1-\frac{\lambda_1}{\mu})^{N+1}}{\lambda_1} = \frac{1}{\lambda_1}(1-\frac{\sqrt[N+1]{c}+1}{c+\sqrt[N+1]{c}})^{N+1} = \frac{1}{\lambda_1}(\frac{c-1}{c+\sqrt[N+1]{c}})^{N+1}.$$

Now, we define the iterative algorithm that calculates $K_{\mu,N}\mathbf{y}$ by means of N multiplications of $K[\mathbf{x}]$ by a vector. Let

$$\mathbf{y}_0 = \mathbf{y},$$

$$\mathbf{y}_{N+1} = \frac{1}{\mu}\mathbf{y} + (I - \frac{1}{\mu}(\gamma R^{-1} + K[\mathbf{x}]))\mathbf{y}_N.$$

Theorem 4.6.

$$\mathbf{y}_N = K_{\mu,N}\mathbf{y}.$$

Proof. Let

$$K_{\mu,0} = I,$$

$$K_{\mu,N+1} = \frac{1}{\mu}\sum_{i=0}^{N+1}(I - \frac{1}{\mu}(\gamma R^{-1} + K[\mathbf{x}]))^i = \frac{1}{\mu}I + (I - \frac{1}{\mu}(\gamma R^{-1} + K[\mathbf{x}]))K_{\mu,N}.$$

So

$$\mathbf{y}_0 = K_{\mu,0}\mathbf{y},$$

$$\mathbf{y}_{N+1} = \frac{1}{\mu}I\mathbf{y} + (I - \frac{1}{\mu}(\gamma R^{-1} + K[\mathbf{x}]))K_{\mu,N}\mathbf{y} = K_{\mu,N+1}\mathbf{y}.$$

5 Conclusions

There are many algorithms for solving of the learning-approximation problem [5], [9]. The algorithms differ in properties, complexity, hypothesis spaces. Yet it is impossible to judge which one is the best. The properties distinguishing the Regularization Algorithm make it possible to create approximation that preserve the values for known samples and is smooth at the same time. The other advantage is the firm mathematical theory that allows a deep analysis of the algorithm behavior.

That's why the good applications for regularization algorithm seems to be the ones in which samples have low error rate and the details are important.

The meaning of the condition of the $K[\mathbf{x}]$ matrix remains an open question. The condition plays crucial role for the error value of the approximate RA. It also seems to be related to the dimension of the example space and might be an important statistics for determining such a dimension.

We plan to use the RA algorithm for inducing local models for each classified new object. For any new object first the set of objects relevant for such object is extracted from data (e.g., using knn strategy [5]) and next the RA algorithm can be applied to the extracted data. Such an approach seems to follow the main idea outlined in Epilog of [9]

In our future study we also would like to develop a "discrete" version of the RA algorithm assuming that objects can be indiscernible, i.e., assuming that reasoning is performed under granularity of knowledge [6], [7].

Acknowledgements

The research has been supported by the grant 3T11C00226 from Ministry of Scientific Research and Information Technology of the Republic of Poland.

References

1. F. Cucker and S. Smale , *On the mathematical foundations of learning*, Bulletin of AMS, 39:1-49, 2001.

2. F. Cucker and S. Smale, *Best choices for regularization parameters in learning theory*, Foundations of computational Mathematics, 2(4):413-428, 2002.
3. T. Dodd, R. Harrison, *Iterative Solution to Approximation in Reproducing Kernel Hilbert Spaces*, 15th IFAC World Congress: b'02 (CDROM).
4. T. Evgeniou, M. Pontil and T. Poggio, *Regularization Networks and Support Vector Machines*, Advances in Computational Mathematics 13 (2000) 1-50.
5. J. H. Friedman, T. Hastie, R. Tibshirani, *Statistical Learning: Data Mining, Inference, and Prediction*, Springer-Verlag, Heidelberg, 2001
6. S. K. Pal, L. Polkowski, A. Skowron (Eds.), *Rough-Neural Computing: Techniques for Computing with Words*, Cognitive Technologies. Springer-Verlag, 2004.
7. Z. Pawlak, *Rough Sets: Theoretical Aspects of Reasoning about Data*, Kluwer Academic Publishers, Dordrecht, 1991.
8. T. Poggio and S. Smale, *The Mathematics of Learning: dealing with Data*, Notices of the AMS, 50(5):537-544, 2003.
9. V. N. Vapnik, *Statistical Learning Theory*, Wiley, New York, 1998.

Characteristic Relations for Incomplete Data: A Generalization of the Indiscernibility Relation

Jerzy W. Grzymała-Busse[1,2]

[1] Department of Electrical Engineering and Computer Science, University of Kansas
Lawrence, KS 66045, USA
Jerzy@ku.edu
http://lightning.eecs.ku.edu/index.html

[2] Institute of Computer Science, Polish Academy of Sciences, 01-237 Warsaw, Poland

Abstract. This paper shows that attribute-value pair blocks, used for many years in rule induction, may be used as well for computing indiscernibility relations for completely specified decision tables. Much more importantly, for incompletely specified decision tables, i.e., for data with missing attribute values, the same idea of attribute-value pair blocks is a convenient tool to compute characteristic sets, a generalization of equivalence classes of the indiscernibility relation, and also characteristic relations, a generalization of the indiscernibility relation. For incompletely specified decision tables there are three different ways lower and upper approximations may be defined: singleton, subset and concept. Finally, it is shown that, for a given incomplete data set, the set of all characteristic relations for the set of all congruent decision tables is a lattice.

1 Introduction

An idea of an attribute-value pair block, used for many years in rule induction algorithms such as LEM2 [3], may be applied not only for computing indiscernibility relations for completely specified decision tables but also for computing characteristic relations for incompletely specified decision tables. A characteristic relation is a generalization of the indiscernibility relation.

Using attribute-value pair blocks for completely specified decision tables, equivalence classes of the indiscernibility relation are computed first, then the indiscernibility relation is defined from such equivalence classes. Similarly, for incompletely specified decision tables, attribute-value pair blocks, defined in a slightly modified way, are used to compute characteristic sets, then characteristic relations are computed from these sets.

Decision tables are incomplete mainly for two reasons. First, an attribute value is lost, i.e., it was recorded but currently is unavailable. Second, the original value was irrelevant and as such not recorded and the case was classified on the basis of remaining attribute values. Such missing attribute values will be called "do not care" conditions.

Initially, decision tables with all missing attribute values that are lost were studied, within rough set theory, in [6], where two algorithms for rule induction

S. Tsumoto et al. (Eds.): RSCTC 2004, LNAI 3066, pp. 244–253, 2004.

from such data were presented. This approach was studied later, see, e.g., [10],[11] where the indiscernibility relation was generalized to describe such incompletely specified decision tables.

The first attempt to study "do not care" conditions using rough set theory was presented in [2], where a method for rule induction was introduced in which missing attribute values were replaced by all values from the domain of the attribute. "Do not care" conditions were also studied later, see, e.g., [7], [8], where the indiscernibility relation was again generalized, this time to describe incomplete decision tables with "do not care" conditions.

In this paper we will assume that the same incomplete decision table may have missing attribute values of both types – lost attribute values and "do not care" conditions.

For a given completely specified decision table and concept, the lower and upper approximations of the concept are unique, though they may be defined in a few different ways [9]. For an incomplete decision table, lower and upper approximations of the concept may be defined in a few different ways, but – in general – the approximations of different types differ. In this paper we will discuss three different lower and upper approximations, called singleton, subset, and concept approximations [4]. Singleton lower and upper approximations were studied in [7], [8], [10], [11]. As it was observed in [4], concept lower and upper approximations should be used for data mining. Note that similar three definitions of lower and upper approximations, though not for incomplete decision tables, were studied in [12].

The last topic of the paper is studying the class of congruent incomplete decision tables, i.e., tables with the same set of all cases, the same attribute set, the same decision, and the same corresponding specified attribute values. Two congruent decision tables may differ only by missing attribute values (some of them are lost attribute values the others are "do not care" conditions). A new idea of a signature, a vector of all missing attribute values, is introduced. There is a one-to-one correspondence between signatures and congruent decision tables. The paper includes also the Homomorphism Theorem showing that the defined operation on characteristic relations is again a characteristic relation for some congruent decision table. For a given incomplete decision table, the set of all characteristic relations for the set of all congruent decision tables is a lattice.

2 Blocks of Attribute-Value Pairs, Characteristic Sets, and Characteristic Relations

An example of a decision table is presented in Table 1. Rows of the decision table represent *cases*, while columns represent *variables*. The set of all cases is denoted by U. In Table 1, $U = \{1, 2, ..., 7\}$. Independent variables are called *attributes* and a dependent variable is called a *decision* and is denoted by d. The set of all attributes will be denoted by A. In Table 1, $A = \{Age, Hypertension, Complications\}$. Any decision table defines a function ρ that maps the direct product of U and A into the set of all values. For example, in Table 1, $\rho(1, Age)$

Table 1. A complete decision table

	Attributes			Decision
Case	Age	Hypertension	Complications	Delivery
1	20..29	no	none	fullterm
2	20..29	yes	obesity	preterm
3	20..29	yes	none	preterm
4	20..29	no	none	fullterm
5	30..39	yes	none	fullterm
6	30..39	yes	alcoholism	preterm
7	40..50	no	none	fullterm

= 20..29. Function ρ describing Table 1 is completely specified (total). A decision table with completely specified function ρ will be called *completely specified*, or, simpler, *complete.*

Rough set theory [9] is based on the idea of an indiscernibility relation, defined for complete decision tables. Let B be a nonempty subset of the set A of all attributes. The indiscernibility relation $IND(B)$ is a relation on U defined for $x, y \in U$ as follows

$$(x, y) \in IND(B) \;\; if \; and \; only \; if \;\; \rho(x, a) = \rho(y, a) \;\; for \; all \; a \in B.$$

The indiscernibility relation $IND(B)$ is an equivalence relation. Equivalence classes of $IND(B)$ are called *elementary sets* of B and are denoted by $[x]_B$. For example, for Table 1, elementary sets of $IND(A)$ are {1, 4}, {2}, {3}, {5}, {6}, {7}. The indiscernibility relation $IND(B)$ may be computed using the idea of blocks of attribute-value pairs. Let a be an attribute, i.e., $a \in A$ and let v be a value of a for some case. For complete decision tables if $t = (a, v)$ is an attribute-value pair then a *block* of t, denoted $[t]$, is a set of all cases from U that for attribute a have value v. For Table 1,

[(Age, 20..29)] = {1, 2, 3, 4},
[(Age, 30..39)] = {5, 6},
[(Age, 40..50)] = {7},
[(Hypertension, no)] = {2, 3, 5, 6},
[(Hypertension, yes)] = {1, 4, 7},
[(Complications, none)] = {1, 3, 4, 5, 7},
[(Complications, obesity)] = {2}, and
[(Complications, alcoholism)] = {6}.

The indiscernibility relation $IND(B)$ is known when all elementary sets of $IND(B)$ are known. Such elementary sets of B are intersections of the corresponding attribute-value pairs, i.e., for any case $x \in U$,

$$[x]_B = \cap\{[(a, v)] | a \in B, \rho(x, a) = v\}.$$

We will illustrate the idea how to compute elementary sets of B for Table 1 where $B = A$:

$[1]_A = [4]_A = [(Age, 20..29)] \cap [(Hypertension, no)] \cap [(Complications, none)] = \{1, 4\}$,
$[2]_A = [(Age, 20..29)] \cap [(Hypertension, yes)] \cap [(Complications, obesity)] = \{2\}$,
$[3]_A = [(Age, 20..29)] \cap [(Hypertension, yes)] \cap [(Complications, none)] = \{3\}$,
$[5]_A = [(Age, 30..39)] \cap [(Hypertension, yes)] \cap [(Complications, none)] = \{5\}$,
$[6]_A = [(Age, 30..39)] \cap [(Hypertension, yes)] \cap [(Complications, alcohol)] = \{6\}$,
and
$[7]_A = [(Age, 40..50)] \cap [(Hypertension, no)] \cap [(Complications, none)] = \{7\}$.

A decision table with an incompletely specified (partial) function ρ will be called *incompletely specified*, or *incomplete*. For the rest of the paper we will assume that all decision values are specified, i.e., they are not missing. Also, we will assume that all missing attribute values are denoted either by "?" or by "*", lost values will be denoted by "?", "do not care" conditions will be denoted by "*". Additionally, we will assume that for each case at least one attribute value is specified. Incomplete decision tables are described by characteristic relations instead of indiscernibility relations. Also, elementary sets are replaced by characteristic sets. An example of an incomplete table is presented in Table 2.

Table 2. An incomplete decision table

	Attributes			Decision
Case	Age	Hypertension	Complications	Delivery
1	?	*	none	fullterm
2	20..29	yes	obesity	preterm
3	20..29	yes	none	preterm
4	20..29	no	none	fullterm
5	30..39	yes	?	fullterm
6	*	yes	alcoholism	preterm
7	40..50	no	?	fullterm

For incomplete decision tables the definition of a block of an attribute-value pair must be modified. If for an attribute a there exists a case x such that $\rho(x, a) =?$, i.e., the corresponding value is lost, then the case x should not be included in any block $[(a, v)]$ for all values v of attribute a. If for an attribute a there exists a case x such that the corresponding value is a "do not care" condition, i.e., $\rho(x, a) = *$, then the corresponding case x should be included in all blocks $[(a, v)]$ for every possible value v of attribute a. This modification of the definition of the block of attribute-value pair is consistent with the interpretation of missing attribute values, lost and "do not care" condition. Thus, for Table 2

[(Age, 20..29)] = {2, 3, 4, 6},
[(Age, 30..39)] = {5, 6},
[(Age, 40..50)] = {6, 7},
[(Hypertension, no)] = {1, 4, 7},
[(Hypertension, yes)] = {1, 2, 3, 5, 6},

[(Complications, none)] = {1, 3, 4},
[(Complications, obesity)] = {2},
[(Complications, alcoholism)] = {6}.

We define a *characteristic set* $KB(x)$ as the intersection of blocks of attribute-value pairs (a, v) for all attributes a from B for which $\rho(x, a)$ is specified and $\rho(x, a) = v$. For Table 2 and $B = A$,

$K_A(1) = \{1, 3, 4\}$,
$K_A(2) = \{2, 3, 4, 6\} \cap \{1, 2, 3, 5, 6\} \cap \{2\} = \{2\}$,
$K_A(3) = \{2, 3, 4, 6\} \cap \{1, 2, 3, 5, 6\} \cap \{1, 3, 4\} = \{3\}$,
$K_A(4) = \{2, 3, 4, 6\} \cap \{1, 4, 7\} \cap \{1, 3, 4\} = \{4\}$,
$K_A(5) = \{5, 6\} \cap \{1, 2, 3, 5, 6\} = \{5, 6\}$,
$K_A(6) = \{1, 2, 3, 5, 6\} \cap \{6\} = \{6\}$, and
$K_A(7) = \{6, 7\} \cap \{1, 4, 7\} = \{7\}$.

The characteristic set $K_B(x)$ may be interpreted as the smallest set of cases that are indistinguishable from x using all attributes from B and using a given interpretation of missing attribute values. Thus, $K_A(x)$ is the set of all cases that cannot be distinguished from x using all attributes. The *characteristic relation* $R(B)$ is a relation on U defined for $x, y \in U$ as follows:

$$(x, y) \in R(B) \; if \; and \; only \; if \; y \in K_B(x).$$

We say that $R(B)$ is *implied* by its characteristic sets $K_B(x)$, $x \in U$. The characteristic relation $R(B)$ is reflexive but – in general – does not need to be symmetric or transitive. Also, the characteristic relation $R(B)$ is known if we know characteristic sets $K(x)$ for all $x \in U$. In our example, $R(A)$ = {(1, 1), (1, 3), (1, 4), (2, 2), (3, 3), (4, 4), (5, 5), (5, 6), (6, 6), (7, 7)}. The most convenient way to define the characteristic relation is through the characteristic sets.

3 Lower and Upper Approximations

For completely specified decision tables lower and upper approximations are defined on the basis of the indiscernibility relation. Any finite union of elementary sets, associated with B, will be called a *B-definable set.* Let X be any subset of the set U of all cases. The set X is called a *concept* and is usually defined as the set of all cases defined by a specific value of the decision. In general, X is not a B-definable set. However, set X may be approximated by two B-definable sets, the first one is called a *B-lower approximation* of X, denoted by $\underline{B}X$ and defined as follows

$$\{x \in U | [x]_B \subseteq X\}.$$

The second set is called a B-upper approximation of X, denoted by $\overline{B}X$ and defined as follows

$$\{x \in U | [x]_B \cap X \neq \emptyset.$$

The above shown way of computing lower and upper approximations, by constructing these approximations from singletons x, will be called the *first method.*

The B-lower approximation of X is the greatest B-definable set, contained in X. The B-upper approximation of X is the smallest B-definable set containing X.

As it was observed in [9], for complete decision tables we may use a *second method* to define the B-lower approximation of X, by the following formula

$$\cup\{[x]_B | x \in U, [x]_B \subseteq X\},$$

and the B-upper approximation of x may de defined, using the second method, by

$$\cup\{[x]_B | x \in U, [x]_B \cap X \neq \emptyset).$$

For incompletely specified decision tables lower and upper approximations may be defined in a few different ways. First, the definition of definability should be modified. Any finite union of characteristic sets of B is called a *B-definable* set. In this paper we suggest three different definitions of lower and upper approximations. Again, let X be a concept, let B be a subset of the set A of all attributes, and let $R(B)$ be the characteristic relation of the incomplete decision table with characteristic sets $K(x)$, where $x \in U$. Our first definition uses a similar idea as in the previous articles on incompletely specified decision tables [7], [8], [10], [11] i.e., lower and upper approximations are sets of singletons from the universe U satisfying some properties. Thus, lower and upper approximations are defined by analogy with the above first method, by constructing both sets from singletons. We will call these approximations *singleton*. A singleton B-lower approximation of X is defined as follows:

$$\underline{B}X = \{x \in U | K_B(x) \subseteq X\}.$$

A singleton B-upper approximation of X is

$$\overline{B}X = \{x \in U | K_B(x) \cap X \neq \emptyset\}.$$

In our example of the decision table presented in Table 2 let us say that $B = A$. Then the singleton A-lower and A-upper approximations of the two concepts: {1, 4, 5, 7} and {2, 3, 6} are:

$$\underline{A}\{1,4,5,7\} = \{4,7\},$$

$$\underline{A}\{2,3,6\} = \{2,3,6\},$$

$$\overline{A}\{1,4,5,7\} = \{1,4,5,7\},$$

$$\overline{A}\{2,3,6\} = \{1,2,3,5,6\}.$$

Note that the set $\overline{A}\{1,4,5,7\} = \{1,4,5,7\}$ is not A-definable (this set cannot be presented as a union of intersections of attribute-value pair blocks). Therefore singleton approximations are not useful. The second method of defining lower and upper approximations for complete decision tables uses another idea: lower and upper approximations are unions of elementary sets, subsets of U. Therefore we may define lower and upper approximations for incomplete decision tables by analogy with the second method, using characteristic sets instead of elementary sets. There are two ways to do this. Using the first way, a *subset* B-lower approximation of X is defined as follows:

$$\underline{B}X = \cup\{K_B(x)|x \in U, K_B(x) \subseteq X\}.$$

A *subset* B-upper approximation of X is

$$\overline{B}X = \cup\{K_B(x)|x \in U, KB(x) \cap X \neq \emptyset\}.$$

Since any characteristic relation $R(B)$ is reflexive, for any concept X, singleton B-lower and B-upper approximations of X are subsets of the subset B-lower and B-upper approximations of X, respectively. For the same decision table, presented in Table 2, the subset A-lower and A-upper approximations are

$$\underline{A}\{1,4,5,7\} = \{4,7\},$$

$$\underline{A}\{2,3,6\} = \{2,3,6\},$$

$$\overline{A}\{1,4,5,7\} = \{1,3,4,5,6,7\},$$

$$\overline{A}\{2,3,6\} = \{1,2,3,4,5,6\}.$$

The second possibility is to modify the subset definition of lower and upper approximation by replacing the universe U from the subset definition by a concept X. A *concept* B-lower approximation of the concept X is defined as follows:

$$\underline{B}X = \cup\{K_B(x)|x \in X, K_B(x) \subseteq X\}.$$

Obviously, the subset B-lower approximation of X is the same set as the concept B-lower approximation of X. A concept B-upper approximation of the concept X is defined as follows:

$$\overline{B}X = \cup\{K_B(x)|x \in X, KB(x) \cap X \neq \emptyset\} = \cup\{K_B(x)|x \in X\}.$$

The concept B-upper approximation of X is a subset of the subset B-upper approximation of X. Besides, the concept B-upper approximations are truly the smallest B-definable sets containing X. For the decision presented in Table 2, the concept A-lower and A-upper approximations are

$$\underline{A}\{1,4,5,7\} = \{4,7\},$$

$$\underline{A}\{2,3,6\} = \{2,3,6\},$$

$$\overline{A}\{1,4,5,7\} = \{1,3,4,5,6,7\},$$

$$\overline{A}\{2,3,6\} = \{2,3,6\}.$$

Note that for complete decision tables, all three definitions of lower approximations, singleton, subset and concept, coalesce to the same definition. Also, for complete decision tables, all three definitions of upper approximations coalesce to the same definition. This is not true for incomplete decision tables, as our example shows.

4 Congruent Decision Tables

In this section, for simplicity, all characteristic relations will be defined for the entire set A of attributes instead of its subset B. In addition, and the characteristic relation will be denoted by R instead of $R(A)$. Finally, in characteristic sets $K_A(x)$, the subscript A will be omitted.

Two decision tables with the same set U of all cases, the same attribute set A, the same decision d, and the same specified attribute values will be called *congruent*. Thus, two congruent decision tables may differ only by missing attribute values * and ?. Obviously, there is $2n$ congruent decision tables, where n is the total number of all missing attribute values in a decision table.

To every incomplete decision table we will assign a *signature* of missing attribute values, a vector $(p_1, p_2, ..., p_n)$, where p_i is equal to either ? or *, the value taken from the incomplete decision table; $i = 1, 2, ..., n$, by scanning the decision table, row after row, starting from the top row, from left to right. Thus every consecutive missing attribute value should be placed as a component of the signature, where p_1 is the first missing attribute value, identified during scanning, and p_n is the last one. For Table 2, the signature is (?, *, ?, *, ?). In the set of all congruent decision tables, a signature uniquely identifies the table and vice versa. On the other hand, congruent decision tables with different signatures may have the same characteristic relations. For example, tables congruent with Table 2, with signatures (?, *, *, *, *) and (*, ?, *, *, *), have the same characteristic relations. Two congruent decision tables that have the same characteristic relations will be called *indistinguishable*.

Let D_1 and D_2 be two congruent decision tables, let R_1 and R_2 be their characteristic relations, and let $K_1(x)$ and $K_2(x)$ be their characteristic sets for some $x \in U$, respectively. We say that $R_1 \leq R_2$ if and only if $K_1(x) \subseteq K_2(x)$ for all $x \in U$. For two congruent decision tables D_1 and D_2 we define a characteristic relation $R = R_1 \cdot R_2$ as implied by characteristic sets $K_1(x) \cap K_2(x)$. For two signatures p and q, $p \cdot q$ is defined as a signature r with $r_i(x) = *$ if and only if $p_i(x) = *$ and $q_i(x) = *$, otherwise $r_i(x) = ?$, $i = 1, 2, ..., n$.

Let $A = \{a_1, a_2, ..., a_k\}$. Additionally, let us define, for $x \in U$ and $a \in A$, the set $[(a, \rho(x, a))]^+$ in the following way: $[(a, \rho(x, a))]^+ = [(a, \rho(x, a))]$ if $\rho(x, a) \neq *$ and $\rho(x, a) \neq ?$ and $[(a, \rho(x, a))]^+ = U$ otherwise.

Proofs of the following results are not included because of a space limit.

Lemma. For $x \in U$, the characteristic set $K(x) = \cap_{i=1}^{k}[(a_i, \rho(x, a_i))]^+$.

Let D be an incomplete decision table and let p be the signature of D. Let ψ be a function that maps a signature p into a characteristic relation R of D.

Homomorphism Theorem. Let p and q be two signatures of congruent decision tables. Then $\psi(p \cdot q) = \psi(p) \cdot \psi(q)$, i.e., ψ is a homomorphism.

Thus, $\psi(p) \cdot \psi(q)$ is the characteristic relation of a congruent decision table with the signature $p \cdot q$. For the set L of all characteristic relations for the set of all congruent decision tables, the operation $\cdot$ on relations is idempotent, commutative, and associative, therefore, L is a semilattice [1], p. 9. Moreover,

L has a universal upper bound $\psi(*, *, ..., *)$ and its length is finite, so L is a lattice, see [1], p. 23. The second lattice operation, resembling addition, is defined directly from the diagram of a semilattice.

Let us define subset E of the set of all congruent decision tables as the set of tables with exactly one missing attribute value "?" and all remaining attribute values equal to "*". Let G be the set of all characteristic relations associated with the set E. The lattice L can be generated by G, i.e., every element of L can be expressed as $\psi(*, *, ...*)$ or as a product of some elements from G.

5 Conclusions

An attribute-value pair block is a very useful tool not only for dealing with completely specified decision tables but, much more importantly, also for incompletely specified decision tables. For completely specified decision tables attribute-value pair blocks provide for easy computation of equivalence classes of the indiscernibility relation. Similarly, for incompletely specified decision tables, attribute-value pair blocks make possible, by equally simple computations, determining characteristic sets and then, if necessary, characteristic relations.

For a given concept of the incompletely specified decision table, lower and upper approximations can be easily computed from characteristic sets – knowledge of characteristic relations is not required. Note that for incomplete decision tables there are three different approximations possible: singleton, subset and concept. The concept approximations are the best fit for the intuitive expectations for lower and upper approximations. Our last observation is that for a given incomplete decision table, the set of all characteristic relations for the set of all congruent decision tables is a lattice.

References

1. Birkhoff, G.: Lattice Theory. American Mathematical Society, Providence, RI (1940).
2. Grzymala-Busse, J.W.: On the unknown attribute values in learning from examples. Proc. of the ISMIS-91, 6th International Symposium on Methodologies for Intelligent Systems, Charlotte, North Carolina, October 16–19, 1991. Lecture Notes in Artificial Intelligence, vol. 542, Springer-Verlag, Berlin, Heidelberg, New York (1991) 368–377.
3. Grzymala-Busse, J.W.: LERS – A system for learning from examples based on rough sets. In Intelligent Decision Support. Handbook of Applications and Advances of the Rough Sets Theory, ed. by R. Slowinski, Kluwer Academic Publishers, Dordrecht, Boston, London (1992) 3–18.
4. Grzymala-Busse, J.W.: Rough set strategies to data with missing attribute values. Workshop Notes, Foundations and New Directions of Data Mining, the 3-rd International Conference on Data Mining, Melbourne, FL, USA, November 19–22, 2003, 56–63.

5. Grzymala-Busse, J.W. and Hu, M.: A comparison of several approaches to missing attribute values in data mining. Proceedings of the Second International Conference on Rough Sets and Current Trends in Computing RSCTC'2000, Banff, Canada, October 16–19, 2000, 340–347.
6. Grzymala-Busse, J.W. and A. Y. Wang A.Y.: Modified algorithms LEM1 and LEM2 for rule induction from data with missing attribute values. Proc. of the Fifth International Workshop on Rough Sets and Soft Computing (RSSC'97) at the Third Joint Conference on Information Sciences (JCIS'97), Research Triangle Park, NC, March 2–5, 1997, 69–72.
7. Kryszkiewicz, M.: Rough set approach to incomplete information systems. Proceedings of the Second Annual Joint Conference on Information Sciences, Wrightsville Beach, NC, September 28–October 1, 1995, 194–197.
8. Kryszkiewicz, M.: Rules in incomplete information systems. *Information Sciences* **113** (1999) 271–292.
9. Pawlak, Z.: Rough Sets. Theoretical Aspects of Reasoning about Data. Kluwer Academic Publishers, Dordrecht, Boston, London (1991).
10. Stefanowski, J. and Tsoukias, A.: On the extension of rough sets under incomplete information. Proceedings of the 7th International Workshop on New Directions in Rough Sets, Data Mining, and Granular-Soft Computing, RSFDGrC'1999, Ube, Yamaguchi, Japan, November 8–10, 1999, 73–81.
11. Stefanowski, J. and Tsoukias, A.: Incomplete information tables and rough classification. *Computational Intelligence* **17** (2001) 545–566.
12. Yao, Y.Y.: Two views of the theory of rough sets in finite universes. *International J. of Approximate Reasoning* **15** (1996) 291–317.

Data Decomposition and Decision Rule Joining for Classification of Data with Missing Values

Rafał Latkowski[1] and Michał Mikołajczyk[2]

[1] Warsaw University, Institute of Computer Science,
ul. Banacha 2, 02-097 Warszawa, Poland,
R.Latkowski@mimuw.edu.pl

[2] Warsaw University, Institute of Mathematics,
ul. Banacha 2, 02-097 Warszawa, Poland,
M.Mikolajczyk@mimuw.edu.pl

Abstract. In this paper we present a new approach to handling incomplete information and classifier complexity reduction. We describe a method, called D^3RJ, that performs data decomposition and decision rule joining to avoid the necessity of reasoning with missing attribute values. In the consequence more complex reasoning process is needed than in the case of known algorithms for induction of decision rules. The original incomplete data table is decomposed into sub-tables without missing values. Next, methods for induction of decision rules are applied to these sets. Finally, an algorithm for decision rule joining is used to obtain the final rule set from partial rule sets. Using D^{3}RJ method it is possible to obtain smaller set of rules and next better classification accuracy than standard decision rule induction methods. We provide an empirical evaluation of the D^{3}RJ method accuracy and model size on data with missing values of natural origin.

1 Introduction

Rough Set theory, proposed by Pawlak in 1982, creates a framework for handling the imprecise and incomplete data in information systems. However, in standard formalization it is not addressed to the problem of missing attribute values. Some methods for reasoning with missing attribute values were proposed by Grzymała-Busse, Stefanowski, Skowron, Słowiński, Kryszkiewicz and many others. Current findings on Granular Computing, Approximated Reasoning Schemes and Rough-Mereology (see, e.g., [9]) inspired research on new methods for handling incomplete information as well as better understanding of classifier and knowledge description complexity. In this paper we describe two of issues: reasoning under missing attribute values and reduction of induced concept description. A concatenation of solutions for problems related to these issues results in high quality classifier induction method, called D^{3}RJ.

The D^3RJ method is based on data decomposition and decision rule joining. The aim of this method is to avoid the necessity of reasoning with missing attribute values and to achieve better classification accuracy at the reduced

S. Tsumoto et al. (Eds.): RSCTC 2004, LNAI 3066, pp. 254–263, 2004.

classification time. The D³RJ method is based on more complex reasoning process, comparing the case of typical algorithms for induction of decision rules. The original incomplete data table is decomposed into data sub-tables without missing values. This is done using total templates that represent information granules describing the resulting data subset. Next, methods for induction of decision rules are applied to these sets. The standard decision rule induction methods are used here. In this way the knowledge hidden in data is extracted and synthesized in form of decision rules, that can also be perceived as information granules. Finally, an algorithm for decision rule joining is used to obtain classifier consisting of generalized rules built from previously induced decision rules. This final phase realizes an additional step of knowledge synthesization and can be perceived as transformation of simpler granules into the more complex ones. The D³RJ method makes is possible to obtain smaller set of rules and to achieve better classification accuracy than standard decision rule induction methods known from literature.

In the following section we introduce some necessary formal concepts. In Section 3 overview of the D³RJ method is provided. Section 4 describes the data decomposition phase. Next, the description of rule induction is provided. Section 6 describes the decision rule joining. Section 7 contain the empirical evaluation of the D³RJ method. The final section presents some conclusions and remarks.

2 Preliminaries

2.1 Decision Tables

For the classification and the concept approximation problems we consider data represented in *information systems* called also *information tables* due to its natural tabular representation (see, e.g., [10, 3]). A *decision system* (*decision table*) is an information system with a distinguished attribute called decision (see, e.g., [10, 3]). The standard definition assumes that all objects have a complete description. In a real world data, however, frequently not all attribute values are known. To be able to deal with missing attribute values we have to extend the definition of a decision table.

Definition 1. *A decision table with missing attribute values* $\mathbb{A} = (U, A, \{d\})$ *is a pair, where* U *is a non-empty finite set of objects called the universe and* A *is a non-empty set of attributes such that* $a_i \in A$, $a_i : U \to V_i^*$, *where* $V_i^* = V_i \cup \{*\}$ *and* $* \notin V_i$, *are conditional attributes and* $d : U \to V_d$ *is a special attribute called decision.*

The special symbol "$*$" denotes absence of the regular attribute value and if $a_i(x) = *$ we say that a_i is not defined on x. If all attribute values are known, the definition of the decision table with missing attribute values is equivalent to the definition of the decision table. From now on we will call decision tables with missing attribute values just decision tables, for short.

2.2 Total Templates

To discover knowledge hidden in data we should search for patterns of regularities in decision tables. A standard tool for describing a data regularities are *templates* (cf. [7, 8]). The concept of template requires some modifications to be applicable in the incomplete decision table decomposition.

Definition 2. *Let* $\mathbb{A} = (U, A, \{d\})$ *be a decision table and let* $a_i \neq *$ *be a* total descriptor. *An object* $u \in U$ *satisfies a total descriptor* $a_i \neq *$, *if the value of the attribute* $a_i \in A$ *on this object* u *is not missing in* $\mathbb{A}$, *otherwise the object* u *does not satisfy total descriptor.*

Definition 3. *Let* $\mathbb{A} = (U, A, \{d\})$ *be a decision table. Any conjunction of total descriptors* $(a_{k_1} \neq *) \wedge \ldots \wedge (a_{k_n} \neq *)$ *is called a* total template. *An object* $u \in U$ *satisfies total template* $(a_{k_1} \neq *) \wedge \ldots \wedge (a_{k_n} \neq *)$ *if the values of attributes* $a_{k_1}, \ldots, a_{k_n} \in A$ *on the object* u *are not missing in* $\mathbb{A}$.

Total templates are used to discover regular areas in data without missing values. On the basis of the total templates we can create a granule system in following way. We consider decision sub-tables $\mathbb{B} = (U_{\mathbb{B}}, B, \{d\})$ of the decision table $\mathbb{A}$, where $U_{\mathbb{B}} \subseteq U$ and $B \subseteq A$. A template t uniquely determines a granule $\mathcal{G}_t = \{\mathbb{B} = (U_{\mathbb{B}}, B, \{d\})\}$ consisting of such data tables $\mathbb{B}$ that all objects from $U_{\mathbb{B}}$ satisfies template t and all attributes $b \in B$ occur in descriptors of template t. In granule $\mathcal{G}_t$ exists the maximal decision table $\mathbb{B}_t = (U_{\mathbb{B}_t}, B_t, \{d\})$, such that for all $\mathbb{B}' = (U_{\mathbb{B}'}, B', \{d\}) \in \mathcal{G}_t$ the condition $U_{\mathbb{B}'} \subseteq U_{\mathbb{B}_t} \wedge B' \subseteq B_t$ is satisfied. Such maximal decision table has all attributes that occur in descriptors of template t and all objects from U that satisfy template t. We will use this fact later to present the data decomposition process in a formal and suitable for implementation way.

2.3 Decision Rules

Decision rules and methods for decision rule induction from decision data table without missing attribute values are well known in rough-sets (see, e.g., [10, 3]).

Definition 4. *Let* $\mathbb{A} = (U, A, \{d\})$ *be a decision table. The decision rule is a function* $\mathbb{R}\colon U \to V_d \cup \{?\}$, *where* $? \notin V_d$. *The decision rule consist of condition* α *and value of decision* $d^{\mathbb{R}} \in V_d$ *and can be also denoted in form of logical formula* $\alpha \Rightarrow d^{\mathbb{R}}$. *If the condition* α *is satisfied for an object* $x \in U$, *then the rule classifies* x *to the decision class* $d^{\mathbb{R}}$ $(\mathbb{R}(x) = d^{\mathbb{R}})$. *Otherwise, rule* $\mathbb{R}$ *for* x *is not applicable, which is expressed by the answer* $? \notin V_d$.

In above definition one decision rule describes a part of exactly one decision class (in mereological sense [9]). If several rules are satisfied for a given object, than voting methods have to be used to solve potential conflicts. The simplest approach assigns each rule exactly one vote. In more advanced approach the weights are assigned to decision rules to measure their strength in voting (e.g. using their quality).

Decision rule induction algorithms produce rules with conjunction of descriptors in the rule predecessor:

$$(a_{i_1}(x) \in r^{a_{i_1}} \wedge \cdots \wedge a_{i_n}(x) \in r^{a_{i_n}}) \Rightarrow d^{\mathbb{R}},$$

where $x \in U$, $a_{i_1}, \ldots, a_{i_n} \in A$, $r^{a_{i_j}} \subseteq V_{i_j}$. The classic algorithms induce decision rules with only one value in each descriptor, for example:

$$\mathbb{R}_1 : (a_1(x) = 1 \wedge a_3(x) = 4 \wedge a_7(x) = 2) \Rightarrow d^{\mathbb{R}}.$$

The D³RJ method produces more general rules, where each descriptor can enclose subset of values. We call such rules the *generalized decision rules* (cf. [7, 13]).

The conditional part of a decision rule can be represented by ordered sequence of attribute value subsets $\{r^a\}_{a \in A}$ for any chosen liner order on A. For example, the decision rule $\mathbb{R}_1$, can be represented by:

$$\mathbb{R}_1 : (\{1\}, \emptyset, \{4\}, \emptyset, \emptyset, \emptyset, \{2\}) \Rightarrow d^{\mathbb{R}}.$$

The empty set denotes absence of condition for that attribute.

Definition 5. *Let* $\mathbb{A} = (U, A, \{d\})$ *be a decision table and let* $\mathbb{R}_1$, $\mathbb{R}_2$ *be generalized rules calculated from the decision table* $\mathbb{A}$. *Then we can define the distance function:*

$$\mathrm{dist}(\mathbb{R}_1, \mathbb{R}_2) = \begin{cases} \mathrm{card}(A)^2 & \text{when } d^{\mathbb{R}_1} \neq d^{\mathbb{R}_2} \\ \sum_{a \in A} d_a(r_1^a, r_2^a) & \text{otherwise} \end{cases}$$

where:

$$d_a(X, Y) = \begin{cases} \mathrm{card}(A) & \text{when } X = \emptyset \wedge Y \neq \emptyset \text{ or } X \neq \emptyset \wedge Y = \emptyset \\ \frac{\mathrm{card}((X-Y) \cup (Y-X))}{\mathrm{card}(V_i)} & \text{otherwise} \end{cases}.$$

The presented above distance function is used in D³RJ method for comparison of decision rules logical structure and for estimation of their similarity.

3 D³RJ

The D³RJ method is developed in the frameworks of Granular Computing and Rough-Mereology [9]. The processing consists of four phases called the data decomposition, decision rule induction, decision rule shortening and decision rule joining.

In the first phase the data that describe the whole investigated phenomenon is decomposed — partitioned into a number of subsets that describe, in a sense, parts of investigated phenomenon. Such procedure creates an overlapped, but non-exhaustive covering that consists of elements similar to the covered data. These elements are data subsets and parts in the mereological sense of the whole, i.e., the original data. The data decomposition method is aiming to avoid the problem of reasoning from data with incomplete object descriptions.

In the second phase information contained in parts, i.e., data subsets is transformed using inductive learning, to a set of decision rules. As it is explained later, we can apply any method of decision rule induction, including such ones that cannot deal with missing values. Often methods that make it possible to properly induce decision rules from data with missing values lead to inefficient algorithms or algorithms with low quality of classification. With help of a data decomposition all of them are applied to a data without missing values to take an advantage of their lower computational complexity and more precise decision rules.

Third phase is the rule shortening. It is very useful because it reduces complexity of rule set and improves classifier resistance to noise and data disturbations.

In the fourth phase the set of rule granules is converted to the smaller set of simplified but more powerful representation of decision rules. In this phase decision rules are clustered and joined to a coherent classifier. The constructed generalized rules can be treated as the higher level granules that represent knowledge extracted from several decision rules. The main objectives of the decision rule joining are reduction of classifier complexity and simplification of knowledge representation.

The D^{3}RJ method returns a classifier that can be applied to a data with missing attribute values in both, learning and classifying.

4 Data Decomposition

The data decomposition should be done in accordance to regularities in a real-world interest domain. We expect the decomposition to reveal patterns of missing attribute values with a similar meaning for the investigated real-world problem.

With the help of introduced concept of total template it is possible to express the goal of the data decomposition phase in terms of total templates. The finite set of templates $S = \{t_1, \ldots, t_n\}$ determines uniquely a finite decomposition $D = \{B_{t_1}, \ldots, B_{t_n}\}$ of the decision table $\mathbb{A}$, where $B_{t_i} \in \mathcal{G}_{t_i}$ is a maximal decision sub-table related to template t_i. Such a transformation reduces problem of data decomposition to the problem of covering decision table with templates, which is frequently investigated (see e.g. [7, 8]) and we can use an advantage of broad experience in this area. In almost all approaches a greedy heuristic to this problem is employed. The greedy algorithm generates the best template for a decision table with respect to a defined criterion and removes all objects that are covered by generated template. In subsequent iterations the decision table is reduced in size by objects that are already covered and the generation of the next best template is repeated. The algorithm continues until all objects are covered, i.e., all objects were removed in previous iterations.

The problem of selecting the optimal criterion for defining the best template with respect to the data decomposition with total templates was already investigated (cf. [4]). There were proposed some template evaluation functions that perform efficiently at reasonable computational cost. The simplest template evaluation function is based only on size of maximal decision table related to this total template.

$$q_1(t) = w(t) \cdot h(t) \tag{1}$$

The $w(t)$ in above formula is the number of attributes in maximal decision table related to template t (width), thus the number of attributes that appear in descriptors of template t. The $h(t)$ is the number of objects in maximal decision table related to template t (height). A more complex template evaluation function incorporates also a heuristical template evaluation:

$$q_2(t) = w(t) \cdot h(t) \cdot G(t)^{\beta}, \tag{2}$$

where parameter β controls the importance factor of an rough-set heuristical evaluation function and

$$G(t) = \sum_{i=1}^{K} \frac{\max_{c \in V_d} \text{card}(\{y \in [x^i]_{\text{IND}_t} : d(y) = c\})}{\text{card}([x^i]_{\text{IND}_t})}. \tag{3}$$

In above formula K is the number of indiscernibility classes (classes of abstraction of the indiscernibility relation IND_t) and $[x^i]_{\text{IND}_t}$ denotes the i-th indiscernibility class. The indiscernibility relation IND_t is based on the maximal complete decision sub-table related to the template t.

5 Decision Rule Induction

The data decomposition phase delivers a number of data tables free from missing values. Such data tables enable us to apply any classifier induction method. In particular, the methods for inducing decision rules, that frequently suffer from lack of possibility to induce rules from data with missing values can be used. On each data table returned from the decomposition phase we apply an algorithm for decision rule induction.

In D^3RJ we use a method inducing all possible consistent decision rules, called also optimal decision rules. This method induces decision rules based on indiscernibility matrix (see e.g. [3, 12, 11]).

When the rules are too detailed, they are difficult to join and joining problem become to very time consuming. We can overcome this problem using shortening algorithm for decision rules (see, e.g., [6, 14]).

In the obtained set of all decision rules one object is usually covered by many rules. In D^3RJ method the problem of redundant decision rules is solved by rule joining. Such a proceeding delivers even less decision rules than without using the data decomposition and provide stable and accurate classifier with a compact concept description.

6 Decision Rule Joining

In the decision rule joining we allow to join only rules from the same decision class. It is possible to join two rules that have different decisions but it will make our system more complicated.

First, let us consider an example of simple rule joining. Rules to be joined:

$$\mathbb{R}_1 : (\{1\}, \{3\}, \emptyset, \{1\}, \{2\}, \emptyset, \{2\}) \Rightarrow d,$$
$$\mathbb{R}_2 : (\{2\}, \{3\}, \emptyset, \{2\}, \{2\}, \emptyset, \{3\}) \Rightarrow d.$$

After joining we obtain a generalized decision rule:

$$\mathbb{R} : (\{1, 2\}, \{3\}, \{\emptyset\}, \{1, 2\}, \{2\}, \{\emptyset\}, \{2, 3\}) \Rightarrow d.$$

Moreover, we can join the generalized rules exactly in the same way as classical ones. Formally speaking a new rule obtained from $\mathbb{R}_m$ and $\mathbb{R}_n$ have a form $\{r^a_{\mathbb{R}_m+\mathbb{R}_n}\}_{a\in A} \Rightarrow d$, where $r^a_{\mathbb{R}_m+\mathbb{R}_n} := r^a_m \cup r^a_n$. The D^{3}RJ method utilizes a decision rule joining algorithm as described in following points.

1. Let $X^{\mathbb{R}}$ be a set of all induced rules. We can assume that it is a set of generalized rules, because every classical rule can be interpreted as a generalized rule.
2. Let $\mathbb{R}_m \in X^{\mathbb{R}}$ and $\mathbb{R}_n \in X^{\mathbb{R}}$ be such, that $d^{\mathbb{R}_m} = d^{\mathbb{R}_n}$ and
$$\mathrm{dist}(\mathbb{R}_m, \mathbb{R}_n) = \min_{i,j}\{\mathrm{dist}(\mathbb{R}_i, \mathbb{R}_j) : \mathbb{R}_i, \mathbb{R}_j \in X^{\mathbb{R}} \wedge d^{\mathbb{R}_i} = d^{\mathbb{R}_j}\}.$$
3. If there exist $\mathbb{R}_m$ and $\mathbb{R}_n$ in $X^{\mathbb{R}}$ such that $\mathrm{dist}(\mathbb{R}_m, \mathbb{R}_n) < \varepsilon$ then the set of rules $X^{\mathbb{R}}$ is modified as follows:
$$X^{\mathbb{R}} := X^{\mathbb{R}} - \{\mathbb{R}_m, \mathbb{R}_n\},$$
$$X^{\mathbb{R}} := X^{\mathbb{R}} \cup \{\mathbb{R}_{\mathbb{R}_m+\mathbb{R}_n}\},$$
where $\mathbb{R}_{\mathbb{R}_m+\mathbb{R}_n}$ is a new rule obtained by joining $\mathbb{R}_m$ and $\mathbb{R}_n$.
4. If the set $X^{\mathbb{R}}$ has been changed then we go back to step 2, otherwise the algorithm is finished.

We can assume that, for example, $\varepsilon = 1$. The algorithm ends when in the set $X^{\mathbb{R}}$ are no two rules from the same decision class that are close enough.

Presented method called Linear Rule Joining (LRJ) is very simple and efficient in time.

7 Empirical Evaluation

There were carried out some experiments in order to evaluate the D^{3}RJ method. Results were obtained using the ten-fold Cross-Validation (CV10) evaluation. The experiments were performed with different decomposition approaches as well as without using decomposition method at all. In experiments we used following data tables: att, ech, edu, hco, head, hep, hur2, hyp, inf2, pid2 and smo2. All data tables used in evaluation of the decomposition method were taken from *Recursive-Partitioning.com* [5] and contain from 10.5% up to 100% cases with missing values of natural origin. In presented results the exhaustive rule induction method was used to induce classifiers from the decision subtables. This

Table 1. Classification accuracy of the classical exhaustive decision rule induction and the D^{3}RJ method. Results are averaged using ten fold cross-validation over 11 data tables used in experiments and α is the rule shortening factor.

α	No decomposition	$w \cdot h$	$w{\cdot}h{\cdot}G$	$w{\cdot}h{\cdot}G^8$
1.0	70.15%	69.60%	70.57%	69.57%
0.9	71.66%	69.83%	70.42%	70.20%
0.8	71.36%	69.74%	70.13%	69.45%
0.7	71.87%	68.44%	69.57%	70.12%
0.6	69.72%	67.78%	69.07%	68.91%
0.5	67.93%	68.32%	69.39%	69.38%
0.4	66.81%	67.88%	68.60%	68.62%
0.3	68.28%	68.30%	68.78%	68.83%
0.2	66.47%	69.31%	69.46%	69.79%
0.1	66.14%	69.77%	69.15%	68.97%

Table 2. Number of decision rules using the classical exhaustive decision rule induction and the D^{3}RJ method.

α	No decomposition	$w \cdot h$	$w{\cdot}h{\cdot}G$	$w{\cdot}h{\cdot}G^8$
1.0	9970.54	1101.51	979.35	841.60
0.9	8835.55	1029.09	912.40	795.65
0.8	6672.00	893.29	798.13	701.93
0.7	4945.65	759.05	679.10	601.71
0.6	3114.22	564.05	510.35	460.64
0.5	1682.63	372.40	377.78	369.90
0.4	1158.45	253.72	246.65	236.31
0.3	661.78	146.45	147.34	144.81
0.2	366.80	75.36	84.64	87.41
0.1	227.59	40.12	45.45	45.11

method is implemented in the *RSES-Lib* software (see [2]). The data decomposition was done with the help of a genetic algorithm for best template generation.

Table 1 presents a general comparison of the classification accuracy using the exhaustive decision rule induction with the D^{3}RJ method using various decomposition criteria and shortening factor values. Table contains the classification accuracy averaged over 11 tested data sets. In the Table 2 the similar comparison is presented with respect to the number of decision rules. The detailed results are presented in next tables. From averages presented in Table 1 one can see that in general the classification accuracy of the D^{3}RJ method is slightly worse than standard decision rules at the top of the table, but slightly better at the bottom of it, where the shortening factor is lower. Table 2 that present number of decision rules, shows that the D^{3}RJ method requires 5–10 times less decision rules than the standard exhaustive decision rules, called also optimal decision rule. Thus, the reduction of the classification abilities is not as high as the reduction of the model size.

Table 3. The detailed empirical evaluation of the D^{3}RJ method using the shortening factor $\alpha = 1.00$, and template evaluation function $q = w{\cdot}h{\cdot}G$.

Table	Before joining		After joining		Profit	
	Accuracy	# Rules	Accuracy	# Rules	Com-pres-sion	Imp-rove-ment
att	56.09 ±3.23	2924.0 ±698.65	53.39 ±3.24	408.0 ±9.35	5.58	-2.70
ech	61.89 ±8.24	317.3 ±56.14	63.61 ±9.55	45.4 ±6.30	3.46	1.72
edu	46.22 ±5.28	4146.0 ±52.83	53.22 ±3.93	716.3 ±14.51	5.70	7.00
hco	79.90 ±8.25	2313.7 ±702.85	78.79 ±5.39	496.5 ±63.07	4.28	-1.11
head	64.20 ±3.59	703.4 ±18.29	67.31 ±6.06	224.2 ±7.30	2.63	3.11
hep	82.40 ±5.59	2496.1 ±148.23	80.08 ±6.16	579.7 ±154.07	1.31	-2.32
hur2	79.57 ±7.76	322.3 ±59.52	78.02 ±7.56	19.8 ±4.47	3.90	-1.55
hyp	97.63 ±1.06	1381.8 ±113.04	97.82 ±0.96	166.1 ±10.79	3.39	0.19
inf2	64.10 ±9.98	5003.7 ±237.77	65.24 ±9.74	4769.8 ±481.91	1.02	1.14
pid2	70.71 ±4.64	4056.0 ±226.20	72.39 ±2.35	109.3 ±5.18	17.87	1.68
smo2	53.03 ±2.17	8252.7 ±51.57	66.41 ±2.55	1217.1 ±17.11	6.49	13.38
avg	68.70 ±5.44	2901.55 ±215.01	70.57 ±5.23	979.35 ±67.96	2.96	1.87

Table 3 presents detailed experimental results of D^{3}RJ method with use of template evaluation function $q = w{\cdot}h{\cdot}G$ and shortening factor α in range $[0.1, 1.0]$. The results are presented for the standard decomposition method without the decision rule joining as well as with the decision rule joining. The decomposition method without the decision rule joining uses the standard voting over all decision rules induced from sub-tables. The compression ratio presented in this table is the ratio of the number of decision rules without the decision rule joining to the number of decision rules with the decision rule joining. The improvement is the difference of the classification accuracy between classification without and with decision rule joining. As we can see the decision rule joining not only reduces the number of decision rules, but also improves the classification accuracy.

8 Conclusions

The presented method consists of two main steps. The first one, called the decomposition step, makes it possible to split decision table with missing attribute values into more tables without missing values. In the second step one classifier (decision system) is induced from decision tables returned from the first step by joining some smaller subsystems of decision rules.

In the consequence we obtained a simple strategy for building decision systems for data tables with missing attribute values. Moreover, we can use in this task a parallel computing because created subsystems are independent. It seems that in this way it is possible to solve many hard classification problems in relatively short time. The obtained results showed that the presented method is very promising for classification problems with missing attribute values in data sets.

Acknowledgments

The authors would like to thank professor Andrzej Skowron for his support while writing this paper. The research has been supported by the grant 3T11C00226 from Ministry of Scientific Research and Information Technology of the Republic of Poland.

References

1. Alpigini, J.J., Peters, J.F., Skowron, A., Zhong, N., eds.: Rough Sets and Current Trends in Computing, Third International Conference, RSCTC 2002, Malvern, PA, USA, October 14–16, 2002, Proceedings. LNCS 2475, Springer (2002)
2. Bazan, J.G., Szczuka, M.S., Wróblewski, J.: A new version of rough set exploration system. [1] 397–404
3. Komorowski, J., Pawlak, Z., Polkowski, L., Skowron, A.: Rough sets: A tutorial. In Pal, S.K., Skowron, A., eds.: Rough Fuzzy Hybridization. A New Trend in Decision Making, Singapore, Springer (1999) 3–98
4. Latkowski, R.: On decomposition for incomplete data. Fundamenta Informaticae **54** (2003) 1–16
5. Lim, T.: Missing covariate values and classification trees. http://www.recursive-partitioning.com/mv.shtml, Recursive-Partitioning.com (2000)
6. Møllestad, T., Skowron, A.: A rough set framework for data mining of propositional default rules. In Raś, Z.W., Michalewicz, M., eds.: Foundations of Intelligent Systems — ISMIS 1996. LNCS 1079, Springer (1996) 448–457
7. Nguyen, S.H.: Regularity Analysis and its Application in Data Mining. PhD thesis, Warsaw University, Faculty of Mathematics, Computer Science and Mechanics (1999)
8. Nguyen, S.H., Skowron, A., Synak, P.: Discovery of data patterns with applications to decomposition and classification problems. In Polkowski, L., Skowron, A., eds.: Rough Sets in Knowledge Discovery 2: Applications, Case Studies and Software Systems, Physica-Verlag (1998) 55–97
9. Pal, S.K., Polkowski, L., Skowron, A., eds.: Rough-Neural Computing: Techniques for Computing with Words. Springer (2004)
10. Pawlak, Z.: Rough sets: Theoretical aspects of reasoning about data. Kluwer, Dordrecht (1991)
11. Skowron, A.: Boolean reasoning for decision rules generation. In Komorowski, H.J., Raś, Z.W., eds.: Methodologies for Intelligent Systems — ISMIS 1993. LNCS 689, Springer (1993) 295–305
12. Skowron, A., Rauszer, C.: The discernibility matrices and functions in information systems. In Słowiński, R., ed.: Intelligent Decision Support. Handbook of Applications and Advances in Rough Sets Theory, Dordrecht, Kluwer (1992) 331–362
13. Wang, H., Düntsh, I., Gediga, G., Skowron, A.: Hyperrelations in version space. Journal of Approximate Reasoning (to appear, 2004)
14. Ziarko, W.: Variable precision rough sets model. Journal of Computer and System Sciences **46** (1993) 39–59

Bayesian Confirmation Measures within Rough Set Approach

Salvatore Greco[1], Zdzisław Pawlak[2,3], and Roman Słowiński[4,5]

[1] Faculty of Economics, University of Catania, Corso Italia, 55, 95129 Catania, Italy
salgreco@mbox.unict.it
[2] Institute of Theoretical and Applied Informatics, Polish Academy of Sciences
44-100 Gliwice, Poland
[3] Warsaw School of Information Technology, 01-447 Warsaw, Poland
zpw@ii.pw.edu.pl
[4] Institute of Computing Science, Poznań University of Technology, 60-965 Poznań, Poland
[5] Institute for Systems Research, Polish Academy of Sciences, 01-447 Warsaw, Poland
slowinsk@sol.put.poznan.pl

Abstract. Bayesian confirmation theory considers a variety of non-equivalent confirmation measures quantifying the degree to which a piece of evidence supports a hypothesis. In this paper, we apply some of the most relevant confirmation measures within the rough set approach. Moreover, we discuss interesting properties of these confirmation measures and we propose a new property of monotonicity that is particularly relevant within rough set approach. The main result of this paper states which one of the confirmation measures considered in the literature have the desirable properties from the viewpoint of the rough set approach.

1 Introduction

Reasoning from data is the domain of inductive reasoning. Contrary to deductive reasoning, where axioms expressing some universal truths constitute a starting point of reasoning, inductive reasoning uses data about a sample of a larger reality to start inference.

Rough set theory (Pawlak 1982, 1991) is a mathematical approach to data analysis. Rough-set-based data analysis starts from a data table, called *information table*. The information table contains data about objects of interest, characterized by a finite set of attributes. Among the attributes, *condition attributes C* and *decision attributes D* are distinguished, in order to analyze how values of attributes *C* associate with values of attributes *D*. An information table where condition attributes and decision attributes are distinguished is called *decision table*. From a decision table one can induce some relationships (patterns) in form of "*if* ... *then* ..." decision rules. More exactly, the decision rules say that if some condition attributes have given values, then some decision attributes have other given values. With every decision rule induced from a decision table, three coefficients are traditionally associated: the strength, the certainty and the coverage factors of the rule. They are useful to show that discovering patterns in data can be represented in terms of Bayes' theorem (Pawlak 2002; Greco,

S. Tsumoto et al. (Eds.): RSCTC 2004, LNAI 3066, pp. 264–273, 2004.

Pawlak, Słowiński 2002) in a different way from that offered by standard Bayesian inference techniques, without referring to prior and posterior probabilities, inherently associated with Bayesian inference methodology.

Within inductive reasoning, classical Bayesian theory considers a variety of non-equivalent confirmation measures (see (Fitelson 2001) for a survey) which quantify the degree to which a piece of evidence E provides, "evidence for or against" or "support for or against" a hypothesis H. In this paper, we take into account some of the most relevant of these confirmation measures and apply them within rough set approach to data analysis. Moreover, we discuss some interesting properties of these confirmation measures, which are particularly relevant within rough set approach.

Our research is strongly related to the rich discussion about the interestingness measure for decision rules in data mining (see, for example, (Hilderman and Hamilton 2002) and (Yao and Zhong 1999) for exhaustive reviews of the subject). Moreover, some confirmation measures considered in this paper may remember statistical independence tests of a contingency table. Indeed, some interestingness measures of decision rules, which are based on these statistical tests, have been proposed in the specialized literature (see, for example, (Flach and Lachiche 2001), (Tsumoto 2002), (Zembowicz and Zytkow 1996)). It is worth stressing that the confirmation measures take a different perspective than the statistical approach. First, observe that the independence (dependence) measures are symmetric while decision rules, for which these measures are conceived, are not symmetric. Even if some authors tried to generalize classical statistical analysis of a contingency table in order to handle typical asymmetries of rule induction (Flach and Lachiche 2001), our approach is different in nature because we are interested in some desirable properties of confirmation measures rather than in their statistical properties.

We think that our research, besides operational impact, can also be interesting for philosophical research about confirmation. In fact, quantitative confirmation theory is strongly based on probability functions, however, there is a great and well-known controversy relative to interpretation, origin and status of probability. Conclusively, in this paper, we use the theory of quantitative confirmation theory which, instead, is based on observed data, without any consideration of probability functions.

Let us also remark that the concept of confirmation we are interested in is related to the concept of independence of logical formulas (propositions), as presented by Łukasiewicz (1913). In brief, his definition of independence between two propositions Φ and Ψ amounts to say that the credibility of Ψ given Φ is the same as the credibility of Ψ given $\neg\Phi$. Thus, independence means that the credibility of Φ does not influence the credibility of Ψ. For this definition Łukasiewicz proved the law of multiplication which says that if propositions Φ and Ψ are independent, then the credibility of Ψ given Φ is equal to the product of the individual credibilities of Φ and Ψ. From this law, Pawlak (2003) derived a dependency factor for flows in decision networks and then he applied this formula to decision rules (Pawlak 2004). The dependency factors derived from the concept of Łukasiewicz and the measures of confirmation studied in this paper are based, however, on different desiderata.

The article is organized as follows. Section 2 introduces confirmation measures and recalls some desirable properties of symmetry and asymmetry proposed by Eells and Fitelson. Section 3 gives some basic notions concerning decision rules and decision algorithms within rough set approach. Section 4 introduces rough set confirmation measures. In section 5, we introduce a specific monotonicity property of rough set confirmation measures. Section 6 investigates which one among the considered rough set confirmation measures satisfies the monotonicity property. Final section draws conclusions and some directions of future research. Proofs of theorems and many interesting extensions can be found in (Greco, Pawlak, Słowiński 2004).

2 Confirmation Measures

According to Fitelson (2001), measures of confirmation quantify the degree to which a piece of evidence E provides, "evidence for or against" or "support for or against" a hypothesis H. Fitelson remarks, moreover, that measures of confirmation are supposed to capture the impact rather than the final result of the "absorption" of a piece of evidence.

Bayesian confirmation assume the existence of a probability Pr. In the following, given a proposition X, $Pr(X)$ is the probability of X. Given X and Y, $Pr(X|Y)$ represents the probability of X given Y, i.e.

$$Pr(X|Y) = Pr(X \wedge Y)/Pr(Y).$$

In this context, a measure of confirmation of a piece of evidence E with respect to a hypothesis H is denoted by $c(E,H)$. $c(E,H)$ is required to satisfy the following minimal property:

$$c(E,H) = \begin{cases} >0 & \text{if } Pr(H|E) > Pr(H) \\ =0 & \text{if } Pr(H|E) = Pr(H) \\ <0 & \text{if } Pr(H|E) < Pr(H) \end{cases}$$

The most well known confirmation measures proposed in the literature are the following:

$$d(E,H) = Pr(H|E) - Pr(H), \quad r(E,H) = log\left[Pr(H|E)/Pr(H)\right]$$

$$l(E,H) = log\left[Pr(E|H)/Pr(E|\neg H)\right], \quad f(E,H) = \frac{Pr(E|H) - Pr(E|\neg H)}{Pr(E|H) + Pr(E|\neg H)}$$

$$s(E,H) = Pr(H|E) - Pr(H|\neg E), \quad b(E,H) = Pr(H \wedge E) - Pr(H)\,Pr(E)$$

Measure $d(E,H)$ has been supported by Earman (1992), Eells (1982), Gillies (1986), Jeffrey (1992) and Rosenkrantz (1994). Measure $r(E,H)$ has been defended by Horwich (1982), Keynes (1921), Mackie (1969), Milne (1995, 1996), Schlesinger (1995) and Pollard (1999). Measure $l(E,H)$ and $f(E,H)$ have been supported by Kemeny and Oppenheim (1952), Good (1984), Heckerman (1988), Pearl (1988), Schumm (1994). Fitelson (2001) has advocated for measure $f(E,H)$. Measure $s(E,H)$ has been proposed by Christensen (1999) and Joyce (1999). Measure $b(E,H)$ has been introduced by Carnap (1962).

Many authors have considered, moreover, some more or less desirable properties of confirmation measures. Fitelson (2001) makes a comprehensive survey of these considerations. At the end of his retrospective, Fitelson concludes that the most convincing confirmation measures are $l(E,H)$ and $f(E,H)$. He also proves that $l(E,H)$ and $f(E,H)$ are ordinally equivalent, i.e. for all E,H and E', H',

$$l(E,H) \geq l(E',H') \text{ if and only if } f(E,H) \geq f(E',H').$$

Among the properties of confirmation measures reviewed by Fitelson (2001), there are properties of symmetry introduced by Carnap (1962) and investigated recently by Eells and Fitelson (2000). For all E and H, one can have:

- Evidence Symmetry (ES): $c(E,H) = -c(\neg E,H)$
- Commutativity Symmetry (CS): $c(E,H) = c(H,E)$
- Hypothesis Symmetry (HS): $c(E,H) = -c(E,\neg H)$
- Total Symmetry (TS): $c(E,H) = c(\neg E,\neg H)$

Eells and Fitelson (2000) remarked that, given (CS), (ES) and (HS) are equivalent, and that (TS) follows from the conjunction of (ES) and (HS). Moreover, they advocate in favor of (HS) and against (ES), (CS) and (TS). The reason in favor of (HS) is that the significance of E with respect to H should be of the same strength, but of opposite sign, as the significance of E with respect to $\neg H$.

Eells and Fitelson (2000) prove that

1) s and b satisfy (ES), while d,r,l and f do not satisfy (ES),
2) d,s,b,f and l satisfy (HS), while r does not satisfy (HS),
3) r and b satisfy (CS), while d,s,f and l do not satisfy (CS),
4) s and b satisfy (TS), while d,r,f and l do not satisfy (CS).

Thus, assuming that (HS) is a desirable property, while (ES), (CS) and (TS) are not, Eells and Fitelson (2000) conclude that with respect to the property of symmetry, d, f and l are satisfying confirmation measures while s, r and b are not satisfying confirmation measures.

3 Decision Rules and Decision Algorithm

Let $S = (U, A)$ be an information table, where U and A are finite, non-empty sets called the *universe* and the set of *attributes*, respectively. If in set A two disjoint subsets of *condition* and *decision attributes* are distinguished (C and D, respectively), then the system is called *decision table* and is denoted by $S = (U, C, D)$. With every subset of attributes, one can associate a formal language of logical formulas $\boldsymbol{L}$ defined in a standard way and called the *decision language*. Formulas for a subset $B \subseteq A$ are build up from attribute-value pairs (a, v), where $a \in B$ and $v \in V_a$ (set V_a is a domain of a), by means of logical connectives $\wedge$ (*and*), $\vee$ (*or*), $\neg$ (*not*). We assume that the set of all formula sets in $\boldsymbol{L}$ is partitioned into two classes, called *condition* and *decision formulas*, respectively.

A *decision rule* induced from S and expressed in $\boldsymbol{L}$ is presented as $\Phi \to \Psi$, read "*if* Φ, *then* Ψ", where Φ and Ψ are condition and decision formulas in $\boldsymbol{L}$, called *premise* and *conclusion*, respectively. A decision rule $\Phi \to \Psi$ is also seen as a binary relation between premise and conclusion, called *consequence relation* (see critical discussion about interpretation of decision rules as logical implications in (Greco, Pawlak, Słowiński 2004)).

Let $\|\Phi\|$ denote the set of all objects from universe U, having the property Φ in S.

If $\Phi \to \Psi$ is a decision rule, then $supp_S(\Phi,\Psi) = card(\|\Phi \wedge \Psi\|)$ will be called the *support* of the decision rule and $\sigma_S(\Phi,\Psi) = supp_S(\Phi,\Psi)/card(U)$ will be referred to as the *strength* of the decision rule.

With every decision rule $\Phi \to \Psi$ we associate a *certainty factor* $cer_S(\Phi,\Psi) = supp_S(\Phi,\Psi)/card(\|\Phi\|)$ and a *coverage factor* $cov_S(\Phi,\Psi) = supp_S(\Phi,\Psi)/card(\|\Psi\|)$.

If $cer_S(\Phi,\Psi)=1$, then the decision rule $\Phi \to \Psi$ is called *certain*, otherwise the decision rule is referred to as *uncertain*. A set of decision rules supported in total by the universe U creates a *decision algorithm* in S.

4 Confirmation Measures and Decision Algorithms

Given a decision rule $\Phi \to \Psi$, the confirmation measure we want to introduce should give the credibility of the proposition: **Ψ is satisfied more frequently when Φ is satisfied rather than when Φ is not satisfied.**

Differently from Bayesian confirmation, however, we start from a decision table rather than from a probability measure. In this context, the probability Pr of Φ is substituted by the relative frequency Fr in the considered data table S, i.e.

$$Fr_S(\Phi) = card(\|\Phi\|)/card(U).$$

Analogously, given Φ and Ψ, $Pr(\Psi|\Phi)$ – the probability of Ψ given Φ – is substituted by the certainty factor $cer_S(\Phi,\Psi)$ of the decision rule $\Phi \to \Psi$.

Therefore, a measure of confirmation of property Ψ by property Φ, denoted by $c(\Phi,\Psi)$, where Φ is a condition formula in $\boldsymbol{L}$ and Ψ is a decision formula in $\boldsymbol{L}$, is required to satisfy the following minimal property

$$c(\Phi,\Psi) = \begin{cases} >0 & if\ cer_S(\Phi,\Psi) > Fr_S(\Psi) \\ =0 & if\ cer_S(\Phi,\Psi) = Fr_S(\Psi) \\ <0 & if\ cer_S(\Phi,\Psi) < Fr_S(\Psi) \end{cases} \tag{i}$$

(i) can be interpreted as follow:

- $c(\Phi,\Psi)>0$ means that property Ψ is satisfied more frequently when Φ is satisfied (then, this frequency is $cer_S(\Phi,\Psi)$), rather than generically in the whole decision table (where this frequency is $Fr_S(\Psi)$),
- $c(\Phi,\Psi)=0$ means that property Ψ is satisfied with the same frequency when Φ is satisfied and generically in the whole decision table,
- $c(\Phi,\Psi)<0$ means that property Ψ is satisfied less frequently when Φ is satisfied, rather than generically in the whole decision table.

The specific confirmation measures recalled in section 2 can be rewritten in this context as follows:

$$d(\Phi,\Psi) = cer_S(\Phi,\Psi) - Fr_S(\Psi), \quad r(\Phi,\Psi) = log\left[\frac{cer_S(\Phi,\Psi)}{Fr_S(\Psi)}\right]$$

$$l(\Phi,\Psi) = log\left[\frac{cer_S(\Psi,\Phi)}{cer_S(\neg\Psi,\Phi)}\right], \quad f(\Phi,\Psi) = \frac{cer_S(\Psi,\Phi) - cer_S(\neg\Psi,\Phi)}{cer_S(\Psi,\Phi) + cer_S(\neg\Psi,\Phi)}$$

$$s(\Phi,\Psi) = cer_S(\Phi,\Psi) - cer_S(\neg\Phi,\Psi), \quad b(\Phi,\Psi) = cer_S(\Phi,\Psi) - Fr_S(\Phi)\, Fr_S(\Psi)$$

Clearly, all the results about confirmation measures obtained within Bayesian confirmation theory are valid for the confirmation measures defined in the context of decision algorithms considered within rough set theory. Therefore, according to Fitelson's conclusions reminded in section 2, we believe that $l(\Phi,\Psi)$ and $f(\Phi,\Psi)$ are the most convincing confirmation measures, which continue to be ordinally equivalent in this new context. Below, we call the confirmation measures presented in the above language of decision algorithms, the *rough set confirmation measures*.

5 Desirable Properties for Rough Set Confirmation Measures

Even if all the formal properties of the Bayesian confirmation measures hold also for the corresponding rough set confirmation measures, we think that there is a new property which would be desirable for the latter measures.

To introduce this new property, let us remark that for each formula Φ, Ψ in $\boldsymbol{L}$, one can express the rough set confirmation measures in terms of the following four values:

- $a=supp_S(\Phi,\Psi)$ - number of objects in U for which Φ and Ψ hold together,
- $b=supp_S(\neg\Phi,\Psi)$ - number of objects in U for which Φ doesn't hold while Ψ holds,
- $c=supp_S(\Phi,\neg\Psi)$ - number of objects in U for which Φ holds while Ψ doesn't hold,
- $d=supp_S(\neg\Phi,\neg\Psi)$ - number of objects in U for which both Φ and Ψ don't hold.

Therefore, the rough set confirmation measures can be expressed as follows:

$$d(\Phi,\Psi)=\frac{ad-bc}{(a+c)(a+b+c+d)},\quad r(\Phi,\Psi)=log\left[\left(\frac{a}{a+c}\right)\Big/\left(\frac{a+b}{a+b+c+d}\right)\right]$$

$$l(\Phi,\Psi)=log\left[\left(\frac{a}{a+b}\right)\Big/\left(\frac{c}{c+d}\right)\right],\quad f(\Phi,\Psi)=\frac{ad-bc}{ad+bc+2ac}$$

$$s(\Phi,\Psi)=\frac{ad-bc}{(a+c)(b+d)},\quad b(\Phi,\Psi)=\frac{ad-bc}{(a+b+c+d)^2}$$

In this context, we propose the following property of monotonicity:

(M) $c(\Phi,\Psi) = F[supp_S(\Phi,\Psi),\ supp_S(\neg\Phi,\Psi),\ supp_S(\Phi,\neg\Psi),\ supp_S(\neg\Phi,\neg\Psi)]$ is a function non-decreasing with respect to $supp_S(\Phi,\Psi)$ and $supp_S(\neg\Phi,\neg\Psi)$ and non-increasing with respect to $supp_S(\neg\Phi,\Psi)$ and $supp_S(\Phi,\neg\Psi)$.

The monotonicity property (M) has the following interpretation. Monotonicity of $c(\Phi,\Psi)$ with respect to $supp_S(\Phi,\Psi)$ means that any evidence in which Φ and Ψ hold together increases (or at least does not decrease) the credibility of the decision rule $\Phi\rightarrow\Psi$. Monotonicity of $c(\Phi,\Psi)$ with respect to $supp_S(\Phi,\neg\Psi)$ means that any evidence in which Φ holds and Ψ does not hold decreases (or at least does not increase) the credibility of the decision rule $\Phi\rightarrow\Psi$. Analogously, with respect to $supp_S(\neg\Phi,\Psi)$, any evidence in which Φ does not hold and Ψ holds decreases (or at least does not increase) the credibility of the decision rule $\Phi\rightarrow\Psi$, and with respect to $supp_S(\neg\Phi,\neg\Psi)$, any evidence in which both Φ and Ψ do not hold increases (or at least does not decrease) the credibility of the decision rule $\Phi\rightarrow\Psi$.

Let us remark that the monotonicity with respect to $supp_S(\Phi,\Psi)$ and $supp_S(\Phi,\neg\Psi)$ is rather intuitive. In the context of automated analysis of data, Hajek and Havranek

(1978) suggest the same monotonicity property M, however, not for a confirmation measure of rule $\Phi \rightarrow \Psi$ (for which they suggest the increasing monotonicity with respect to $supp_S(\Phi,\Psi)$ and the decreasing monotonicity with respect to $supp_S(\Phi,\neg\Psi)$ only), but for a more specific association measure.

We can explain the monotonicity with respect to $supp_S(\neg\Phi,\Psi)$ and $supp_S(\neg\Phi,\neg\Psi)$, considering our interpretation of property (i) from section 4: a positive value of a confirmation measure $c(\Phi,\Psi)$ means that property Ψ is satisfied more frequently when property Φ is satisfied rather than when Φ is not satisfied. From this viewpoint, an evidence in which Φ is not satisfied and Ψ is satisfied (objects $\|\neg\Phi\wedge\Psi\|$) increases the frequency of Ψ in the situations where Φ is not satisfied and thus it should decrease the value of the confirmation. Analogously, an evidence in which both Φ and Ψ are not satisfied (objects $\|\neg\Phi\wedge\neg\Psi\|$) decreases the frequency of Ψ in the situations where Φ is not satisfied and thus it should increase the value of the confirmation.

We want to give also a more formal justification to the monotonicty of confirmation measures with respect to $supp_S(\neg\Phi,\Psi)$ and $supp_S(\neg\Phi,\neg\Psi)$. Let us consider the following definition of confirmation: property Φ confirms property Ψ if

$$cer_S(\Phi,\Psi) > Fr_S(\Psi). \qquad \text{(iii)}$$

Let us remark that definition (iii) corresponds to the definition of *incremental confirmation* introduced by Carnap (1962, new preface) under the name of "*confirmation as increase in firmness*" in the following form: evidence Φ confirms hypothesis Ψ if $Pr(\Psi|\Phi) > Pr(\Psi)$.

The confirmation measures $d(\Phi,\Psi)$, $r(\Phi,\Psi)$, $l(\Phi,\Psi)$, $f(\Phi,\Psi)$, $s(\Phi,\Psi)$ and $b(\Phi,\Psi)$ can be seen as quantitative generalizations of the qualitative incremental confirmation (Fitelson 2001).

Redefining (iii) in terms of $a=supp_S(\Phi,\Psi)$, $b=supp_S(\neg\Phi,\Psi)$, $c=supp_S(\Phi,\neg\Psi)$ and $d=supp_S(\neg\Phi,\neg\Psi)$, we get:

$$a/(a+c) > (a+b)/(a+b+c+d). \qquad \text{(iii')}$$

The following theorem is useful for justifying the property of monotonicity.

Theorem 1. Let us consider case α in which

$$a=supp_S(\Phi,\Psi),\quad b=supp_S(\neg\Phi,\Psi),\quad c=supp_S(\Phi,\neg\Psi),\quad d=supp_S(\neg\Phi,\neg\Psi),$$

and case α' in which

$$a'=supp_S(\Phi',\Psi'),\quad b'=supp_S(\neg\Phi',\Psi'),\quad c'=supp_S(\Phi',\neg\Psi'),\quad d'=supp_S(\neg\Phi',\neg\Psi').$$

Let us suppose, moreover, that

$$cer_S(\Phi,\Psi) < Fr_S(\Psi), \quad \text{while} \quad cer_S(\Phi',\Psi') > Fr_S(\Psi').$$

The following implications are satisfied:

1) if $a'=a+\Delta$, $b'=b$, $c'=c$ and $d'=d$, then $\Delta>0$,
2) if $a'=a$, $b'=b+\Delta$, $c'=c$ and $d'=d$, then $\Delta<0$,
3) if $a'=a$, $b'=b$, $c'=c+\Delta$ and $d'=d$, then $\Delta<0$,
4) if $a'=a$, $b'=b$, $c'=c$ and $d'=d+\Delta$, then $\Delta>0$.

Theorem 1 has the following interpretation. Passing from case α to case α', we pass from a situation in which property Φ does not confirm property Ψ, to a situation in which property Φ' confirms property Ψ'. Theorem 1 says that this passage from non-confirmation to confirmation is permitted by an increase of $supp_S(\Phi,\Psi)$ or $supp_S(\neg\Phi,\neg\Psi)$, or by a decrease of $supp_S(\neg\Phi,\Psi)$ or $supp_S(\Phi,\neg\Psi)$. Thus, the theorem supports the claim that confirmation given by property Φ to property Ψ is positively related to $supp_S(\Phi,\Psi)$ and $supp_S(\neg\Phi,\neg\Psi)$, and negatively related to $supp_S(\neg\Phi,\Psi)$ and $supp_S(\Phi,\neg\Psi)$.

In fact, Theorem 1 supports the monotonicity property (M) because, if the passage from a situation of non-confirmation to a situation of confirmation implies a specific sign of modifications of the four values $supp_S(\Phi,\Psi)$, $supp_S(\neg\Phi,\neg\Psi)$, $supp_S(\neg\Phi,\Psi)$ and $supp_S(\Phi,\neg\Psi)$, it is natural to expect that confirmation measures will react analogously to modifications of the above values.

6 Rough Set Confirmation Measures Satisfying Monotonicity

Theorem 2. $l(\Phi,\Psi)$, $f(\Phi,\Psi)$ and $s(\Phi,\Psi)$ satisfy monotonicity property (M), while $d(\Phi,\Psi)$, $r(\Phi,\Psi)$ and $b(\Phi,\Psi)$ do not satisfy (M).

The content of Theorem 2 is quite clear and immediate, however, a more detailed comment may be useful. From our viewpoint, the most important discovery coming from Theorem 2 is that the confirmation measure $d(\Phi,\Psi)$ does not satisfy the monotonicity property. The importance of this result is threefold:

1) $d(\Phi,\Psi)$ is a very simple rough set confirmation measure, coherent with the definition of incremental confirmation; it is rather counterintuitive that $d(\Phi,\Psi)$ does not satisfy monotonicity, while other confirmation measures having as complex formulation as $l(\Phi,\Psi)$ and $f(\Phi,\Psi)$ do;
2) $d(\Phi,\Psi)$ does not satisfy monotonicity with respect to $supp_S(\Phi,\Psi)$; in this case the monotonicity property is indeed an uncontestable principle;
3) $d(\Phi,\Psi)$ is not ruled out by the symmetry/asymmetry test performed by Eells and Fitelson (2000); this means that the contribution of monotonicity property (M) in reducing the field of "coherent" confirmation measures is very relevant; in fact, the only confirmation measures which satisfy both symmetry/asymmetry properties of Eells and Fitelson and monotonicity property (M) are the two ordinally equivalent confirmation measures $l(\Phi,\Psi)$ and $f(\Phi,\Psi)$.

7 Conclusions

The main result of this paper states that, from among the confirmation measures considered in the literature and recalled in section 2, the only confirmation measures satisfying the desirable properties of symmetry/asymmetry of Eells and Fitelson (2000), as well as our monotonicity property (M) are the two ordinally equivalent measures $l(\Phi,\Psi)$ and $f(\Phi,\Psi)$. In particular, our property (M) rules out $d(\Phi,\Psi)$. Let us remark that using the symmetry/asymmetry properties, it is not possible to discard $d(\Phi,\Psi)$, while using our monotonicity property, it is not possible to discard $s(\Phi,\Psi)$. This can be interpreted in the sense that the symmetry/asymmetry properties together with our monotonicity property (M) can be considered as complementary basic principles on which a sound theory of confirmation measures can be founded. A special attention merits, moreover, the violation of the monotonicity property by confirmation measure $b(\Phi,\Psi)$ which is the corroboration measure proposed by Carnap (1962). From our point of view, the violation of the monotonicity property by this confirmation measure is more troubling than its violation of the symmetry/asymmetry property proposed by Eells and Fitelson. In fact Carnap (1962) liked that his corroboration measure b satisfies all four symmetry properties ES, HS, CS and TS, because he was interested in representing quantitatively a completely symmetric relevance relation.

We think that the quite theoretical results presented in this paper can be the basis for important operational development within rough set theory and, in general, within data analysis. Only to give some idea of interesting issues for future researches consider the use of measures $l(\Phi,\Psi)$ and $f(\Phi,\Psi)$ for assessing the interest of decision rules induced from a data table, as well as classification with these rules. Considering the huge number of decision rules which can be induced from a data set, and the necessity of presenting only the most interesting rules to the users, this is a problem of primary importance for data analysis. We believe that the contribution of rough set confirmation measures to solving this problem is very important.

Acknowledgements

The research of the first author has been supported by the Italian Ministry of Education, University and Scientific Research. The third author wishes to acknowledge financial support from the State Committee for Scientific Research and from the Foundation for Polish Science.

References

Carnap, R. (1962), *Logical Foundations of Probability.* (2nd ed.) University of Chicago Press.

Christensen, D. (1999), Measuring Confirmation. *Journal of Philosophy* XCVI, 437–61.

Earman, J. (1992), *Bayes or Bust: A Critical Examination of Bayesian Confirmation Theory.* MIT Press, Cambridge.

Eells, E. (1982), *Rational Decision and Causality.* Cambridge University Press.

Eells, E., Fitelson, B. (2000), Measuring confirmation and evidence. *Journal of Philosophy* 97, 663–672.

Fitelson, B. (2001), *Studies in Bayesian Confirmation Theory.* Ph.D. thesis, University of Wisconsin – Madison.

Flach, P.A., Lachiche, N. (2001), Confirmation-guided discovery of first-order rules with tertius. *Machine Learning* 42, 61–95.

Gillies, D. (1986), In defense of the Popper-Miller argument. *Philosophy of Science* 53, 110–113.

Good, I. (1984), The best explicatum for weight of evidence. *Journal of Statistical Computation and Simulation* 19, 294–299.

Greco, S., Pawlak, Z., Słowiński, R. (2002), Generalized decision algorithms, rough inference rules, and flow graphs. [In]: J.J.Alpigini, J.F.Peters, A.Skowron, N.Zhong (eds.), *Rough Sets and Current Trends in Computing*. LNAI 2475, Springer, Berlin, pp. 93–104.

Greco, S., Pawlak, Z., Słowiński, R. (2004), Can Bayesian confirmation measures be useful for rough set decision rules? Submitted.

Hajek, P., Havranek, T. (1978), *Mechanising Hypothesis Formulation: Mathematical Foundation for a General Theory*. Springer-Verlag, Berlin.

Heckerman, D. (1988), An axiomatic framework for belief updates. [In]: L.Kanal & J. Lemmer (eds.), *Uncertainty in Artificial Intelligence* (2). Elsevier, New York, pp.11–22.

Hilderman, R.J., Hamilton, H.J. (2002), *Knowledge Discovery and Measures of Interest* , Kluwer, Boston.

Horwich, P.(1982), *Probability and Evidence*. Cambridge University Press.

Horvitz, E. and Heckerman, D. (1986), The inconsistent use of certainty measures in artificial intelligence research. In L. Kanal and J. Lemmer (eds.), *Uncertainty in Artificial Intelligence* (1). Elsevier, New York, pp. 137–151.

Jeffrey, R. (1992), *Probability and the Art of Judgment.* Cambridge University Press.

Joyce, J. (1999), *The Foundations of Causal Decision Theory*. Cambridge University Press.

Kyburg, H. (1983), Recent work in inductive logic. [In]: Lucey and Tabor (eds.), *Recent Work in Philosophy*. Rowman and Allanfield, Totowa, N.J., pp. 89–150.

Keynes, J.(1921), *A Treatise on Probability*. Macmillan, London.

Łukasiewicz, J. (1913), *Die Logische Grundlagen der Wahrscheinlichkeitsrechnung*, Cracow; English translation in: L. Borkowski (ed.), *Jan Łukasiewicz – Selected Works*, North Holland & Polish Scientific Publishers, Amsterdam-Warsaw, 1970.

Mackie, J. L. (1963), The paradox of confirmation. *The British Journal for the Philosophy of Science* 13, 265–277.

Mackie, J. (1969), The relevance criterion of confirmation. *The British Journal for the Philosophy of Science* 20, 27–40.

Milne, P. (1995), A Bayesian defence of Popperian science? *Analysis* 55, 213–215.

Milne, P. (1996), Log [P(h|e)/P(h|b)] is the one true measure of confirmation. *Philosophy of Science* 63, 21–26.

Pawlak, Z. (1982), Rough Sets. *Int. J. of Computer and Information Sciences* 11, 341–356.

Pawlak, Z. (1991), *Rough Sets – Theoretical Aspects of Reasoning about Data.* Kluwer Academic Publishers, Boston.

Pawlak, Z. (2002), Rough Sets, decision algorithms and Bayes' Theorem. *European Journal of Operational Research* 136, 181–189.

Pawlak, Z. (2003), Flow graphs and decision algorithms. [In]: G. Wang, Q. Liu, Y.Y. Yao, A. Skowron (eds.), *Rough Sets, Fuzzy Sets, Data Mining and Granular Computing.* LNAI 22639, Springer, Berlin, pp. 1–11.

Pawlak, Z. (2004), Decision networks. [In]: J.W. Grzymala-Busse, J. Komorowski, R. Słowiński, S. Tsumoto (eds.), *Rough Sets and Current Trends in Computing*. LNAI, Springer-Verlag, Berlin, in this volume.

Pearl, J. (1988), *Probabilistic Reasoning in Intelligent Systems: Networks of Plausible Inference.* Morgan Kaufman, San Francisco.

Pollard, S. (1999), Milne's measure of confirmation. *Analysis* 59, 335–337.

Schlesinger, G. (1995), Measuring degrees of confirmation. *Analysis* 55, 208–212.

Rosenkrantz, R. (1994), Bayesian confirmation: paradise regained. *The British Journal for the Philosophy of Science* 45, 467–476.

Schum, D. (1994), *The Evidential Foundations of Probabilistic Reasoning*. Wiley, New York.

Tsumoto, S. (2002), Statistical test for rough set approximation based on Fisher's exact test. [In]: J. J. Alpigini, J. F. Peters, A. Skowron, N. Zhong (eds.), *Rough Sets and Current Trends in Computing.* LNAI 2475, Springer, Berlin, 2002, pp. 381-388.

Yao, Y.Y., and Zhong, N. (1999), An analysis of quantitative measures associated with rules. [In]: N. Zhong and L. Zhou (eds.), *Methodologies for Knowledge Discovery and Data Mining.* LNAI 1574, Springer, Berlin, pp. 479-488.

Zembowicz, R., Zytkow, J. (1996), From contingency tables to various forms of knowledge in databases. [In]: U. M. Fayyad, G. Piatetsky-Shapiro, P. Smyth, R. Uthurusamy, (eds.), *Advances in Knowledge Discovery and Data Mining*, AAAI Press & The MIT Press, Menlo Park and Cambridge, pp. 329-349.

Discovering Maximal Potentially Useful Association Rules Based on Probability Logic*

Jitender Deogun, Liying Jiang, and Vijay V. Raghavan

Department of Computer Science and Engineering
University of Nebraska — Lincoln
Lincoln, NE 68588-0115
{ljiang,deogun}@cse.unl.edu

Abstract. *Apriori-like* algorithms are widely used for mining *support-based* association rules. In such applications, the underlying assumption is that rules of frequent itemsets are useful or interesting to the users. However, in many applications, infrequent events may be of interest or frequency of events may have no relationship to their *interestingness* to the user. *Apriori-like* algorithms do not present efficient methods for discovering interesting infrequent itemsets. In this paper, We present a new model of Knowledge Discovery in Databases (KDD) based on probability logic and develop a new notion of Maximal Potentially UseFul (MaxPUF) patterns, leading to a new class of association rules called maximal potentially useful (MaxPUF) association rules, which is a set of high-confidence rules that are most informational and potentially useful. MaxPUF association rules are defined independent of support constraint, and therefore are suitable for applications in which both frequent and infrequent itemsets maybe of interest. We develop an efficient algorithm to discover MaxPUF association rules. The efficiency and effectiveness of our approach is validated by experimemts based on weather data collected at the Clay Center, Nebraska, USA from 1959 to 1999.

1 Introduction

In data mining, an association rule is of the form $X \Rightarrow Y$, where X is antecedent, Y is consequent, and $X \cap Y \neq \emptyset$. The *support* of a rule $sup(X \Rightarrow Y)$, indicating the percentage of transations in dataset that contain both X and Y. The *confidence* of $X \Rightarrow Y$ denotes the probability that a transaction contains Y given that it contains X, $conf(X \Rightarrow Y) = sup(X \Rightarrow Y)/sup(X)$. Many algorithms have been proposed for discovering association rules. Among these, *Apriori* algorithm [1] is the most useful. The main idea of *Apriori* algorithm is using support metric to filter infrequent itemsets, and rules are constructed using only frequent itemsets. However, in many applications, infrequent events may be also of interest or frequency of events may have no relationship to their *interestingness* to the

* This research was supported in part by NSF Digital Government Grant No. EIA-0091530, USDA RMA Grant NO. 02IE08310228, and NSF EPSCOR, Grant No. EPS-0091900.

S. Tsumoto et al. (Eds.): RSCTC 2004, LNAI 3066, pp. 274–284, 2004.

user. For example, an event of earthquake in climate databases is infrequent, and thus all the itemsets including earthquake are also infrequent. However, it certainly would be of interest to discover rules that reflect the associations between earthquake and other events.

Apriori-like algorithms use *support* as the main constraint and are based on the paradigm that usefulness of rules is related to the frequency of itemsets. In this paper, we develop a new logic framework for KDD based on probability logic, and we define the notion of usefulness of association rules that is independent of support constraint based on the new KDD model. In this model, important notions of KDD such as concept, pattern, potentially and useful patterns are logically formulated. We introduce a new notion Maximal Potentially UseFul (MaxPUF) patterns, and define a new class of association rules — Maximal Potentially UseFul association rules. MaxPUF association rules are those association rules that are most informational and potentially useful to the user. MaxPUF association rules are constructed independent of the support threshold and thus are suitable for applications that both frequent and infrequent itemsets are of interest. We develop a new algorithm for M discovering MaxPUF association rules and analyze the experimental results.

The rest of the paper is organized as follows. In Section 2, we introduce a new KDD model based on probability logic. MaxPUF patterns and MaxPUF association rules are defined in Section 3. We present the algorithm for discovering MaxPUF association rules in Section 4. Experimental results and analysis are presented in Section 5, and concluding remarks are given in Section 6.

2 Logic KDD Model Based on Probability Logic

Table 1. Students DB

Student	Hair-color			Eye-color		
	red	black	blond	brown	blue	green
N_1	X			X		
N_2	X				X	
N_3	X					X
N_4		X		X		

Discovering interesting patterns has been an area of active research in KDD. To facilitate interesting pattern discovery, we have been working on developing new logic models of KDD that integrate *formal concept analysis* (FCA) [4] and *probability logic* [5]. The basic notions of FCA are those of a formal context and a formal concept. A *formal context* is a triple $(\mathcal{G}, \mathcal{M}, \mathcal{I})$ where $\mathcal{G}$ is a set of objects, $\mathcal{M}$ is a set of attributes, and I is a binary relation from $\mathcal{G}$ to $\mathcal{M}$. For a set of objects $A \subseteq \mathcal{G}$, $\beta(A)$ is defined as the maximum set of attributes shared by all the objects in A. And for $B \subseteq \mathcal{M}$, $\alpha(B)$ is the maximum set of objects that posses all the attributes in B. *A formal concept* in the context $(\mathcal{G}, \mathcal{M}, \mathcal{I})$ is a pair (A, B) such that $\beta(A) = B$ and $\alpha(B) = A$. The set A is called the *extent* of the concept and B is called the *intent* of the concept. E.g, Table 1 is a formal context derived from student database, and (N_2,*H-red*$\wedge$*E-blue*) is a formal concept.

Probability logic [5] extends first-order logic [2] with probability expression capability. It defines a language that includes predicate symbols, object variables, statistical probability operation "[ ]". Predicate symbols represent conjunctions of attributes, and thus denote possible *intent* of formal concepts. Object variables define the domain of a set of objects of interest, and thus represent possible *extent* of formal concepts. "[ ]" computes the probability of propositions represented by predicate symbol over a set of objects, e.g, in the database of Table 1, (*H-red*) and (*H-red*)$\wedge$(*E-blue*) are two predicate symbols. If x represents all the students, then $[H\text{-}red]_x = \frac{3}{4}$. Now, we define *concept* and *pattern* in probability logic.

Definition 1. Concept. *if P is a predicate symbol and x is an object variable, then P_x is a concept, we simply denote it as concept P if the domain of objects is clear from the context. moreover if P_1,...,P_j are concepts with the same domain, then $P = P_1 \wedge P_2 ... \wedge P_j$ is a concept.*

If $P = \bigwedge_{i=1}^{n} P_i$, we say P is a *superconcept* of P_i and P_i is a *subconcept* of P, $1 \leq i \leq n$. There are two special concepts: ϕ and $\dashv$. ϕ is null predicate whose intent is null and $\dashv$ is all predicate whose extent is null. we call all the superconcepts and subconcepts of a concept Q as *relative concepts* of Q. It is easy to see ϕ and $\dashv$ are relative concepts of all the concepts.

Definition 2. Pattern. *If P is a concept, then $[P] = r$ $(0 \leq r \leq 1)$ is an* elementary pattern. *If P, Q are concepts and $Q \neq \phi$, then $[P|Q] = r$ is a* conditional pattern. *P is called* con<u>S</u>equent <u>C</u>oncept (SC), *and Q is* con<u>D</u>ition <u>C</u>oncept (DC) *of the pattern. Probability r is called* confidence *of the pattern.*

Elementary patterns denotes the statistical probability of concepts, which is the frequency of concepts in databases. *Conditional patterns* denote the conditional probability of *SC* given that *DC* occurrs. Using model of *pattern*, we can logically formulate *<u>A</u>ssociation <u>R</u>ules (AR)* as a conditional pattern. *DC* of conditional pattern represents *antecedent* of *AR* and *SC* of conditional pattern represents *consequent* of *AR*. *Probability* of conditional pattern denotes *confidence* of *AR*. *Support* of antecedent and consequent is equal to the *probability* of elementary patterns of them.

<u>P</u>otentially <u>U</u>seful <u>P</u>atterns (PUPs) are defined based on *direct inference mechanism* [5], intuitively, if we have the knowledge that the probability over a narrower reference class is significantly different from the wider reference class, the narrower reference class should be chosen as the proper reference class. E.g., three concepts A, B and $B \wedge C$, respectively represent a disease, population of an area, and a sub-population of this area. Suppose we deduct two patterns: [A|B]=35% and [A|B$\wedge$C]=45%. We say pattern [A|B$\wedge$C]=45% is potentially useful since it reflects the important information that the sub-population of the area have the disease at a rate higher than average, and we notice $(B \wedge C)$ is a narrower class than B.

Definition 3. PUP. *Let C, P be any concepts except ϕ, and $P_1, .., P_n$ be all subconcepts of P. Pattern $[C|P] = r$ is a potentially useful pattern if $r - \max_{1 \leq i \leq n}([C|P_i]) > s$. s is called significance controller.*

PUPs define usefulness by reflecting the sharp relative change of conditional probability (confidence) of certain consequent concept with a narrower condition concept (*DC* with more items). They imply that unusual cases occurr from the statistical point of view.

3 Maximal Potentially Useful Patterns and Rules

3.1 Maximal Potentially Useful Patterns

While PUPs focus on the relative change of confidence among patterns when different condition concepts are applied, there exist a set of interesting patterns that classify usefulness and uselessness directly by the threshold of confidence, which we define as *Maximal Potential Useful (MaxPUF) patterns.*

Definition 4. MaxPUF pattern. *Given confidence threshold* θ*, if pattern* $[B|A] = r \geq \theta$*, and there is no pattern* $[B|A'] \geq \theta$ *where* $A' \subset A$*, then* $[B|A] = r$ *is a MaxPUF pattern of consequent concept* B *among all the relative concepts of condition concept* A*.*

The meaning of MaxPUF pattern is that among high-confidence patterns of a certain consequent concept, we try to find those patterns whose condition concepts have smallest number of items. A is called a *valid DC* of consequent concept B if $[B|A] = r$ is a MaxPUF pattern.

Lemma 1. *For a given consequent concept, its MaxPUF patterns are most informational among all the high-confidence patterns of this consequent concept.*

To understand the lemma, we examine an example. Suppose confidence threshold is θ, two patterns $[SC|1] < \theta$ and $[SC|1,4] \geq \theta$, we claim there is no need to explore pattern $[SC|1,3,4]$. Because if $[SC|1,3,4] < \theta$, then it is useless; if $[SC|1,3,4] \geq \theta$,it is not as useful as $[SC|1,4]$, since (1,4) is sufficient condition so that *SC* occur frequently, and (1,3,4) only adds redundant condition constraints. All the possible *DC*s constitute a lattice. *DC* of MaxPUF pattern is the point of articulation in the lattice. Below this point, no high-confidence pattern can be constructed with the relative concepts of the valid *DC*. *Valid DC* is the most informational condition concept, because it is the minimal condition concept to make the given *SC* occurs at high frequency.

Lemma 2. *Given threshold* θ*, if* $[B|A] < \theta$*, then* $[B'|A] < \theta$ *where* $B \subseteq B'$*.*

Lemma 2 states that under identical condition, if the pattern of a consequent concept does not have high enough confidence, then neither does that of any of its superconcepts. For brevity, proofs are omitted.

3.2 Maximal Potentially Useful Association Rules

Based on MaxPUF patterns, we define a special class of association rules – *Maximal Potentially Useful (MaxPUF)* association rules. Generally speaking, the association rules derived from MaxPUF patterns are MaxPUF association rules. MaxPUF association rules have two fold advantage over conventional association rules. On one hand, conventional association rules often suffer the problem that too many rules are discovered, of which many are not interesting. However, the number of MaxPUF association rules is much smaller, and at the same time, these are the most informational rules. On the other hand, conventional association rules depend on the support constraint and only reflect associations among frequent itemsets; while MaxPUF association rules are defined by the potential usefulness that is more related to the confidence of a rule, and independent of support constraint, and thus are suitable for applications that both frequent and infrequent itemsets are of interest.

4 Algorithm of Discovering MaxPUF Association Rules

We formulate the problem of discovering MaxPUF association rules as a process of discovering MaxPUF patterns. From MaxPUF patterns, we can directly construct MaxPUF association rules. Input: 1) Transaction database $T = \{T_1, T_2, ..., T_k\}$; 2) each item in transaction database is formulated as a concept, and all the items are divided into two categories based on their functions: consequent concept set $IS = \{IS_1, IS_2, ...IS_n\}$ and condition concept set $ID = \{ID_1, ID_2, ...ID_m\}$; and 3) confidence threshold θ. Output: All MaxPUF patterns.

To find MaxPUF patterns, the idea is to first construct possible candidate patterns, then validate the candidates. As each MaxPUF pattern include *condition concept (DC)* and *consequent concept (SC)*, to construct candidate patterns, we expand *DC* and *SC* from 1-item to m-item or n-item concepts. The process starts with fixing an *SC*, then use *DC-expansion* to explore its *valid DCs* by checking *DCs* of 1-item to n-item. *SC-expansion* generates *SCs* of 1-item to n-item. All *DCs* and *SCs* constitute *DC-lattice* and *SC-lattice*, and the *expansions* are processes to traverse these two lattices. Algorithm 1 shows the overall framework of the process. Line 3 is *DC-expansion*, and the *while loop* begin from Line 1 deal with *SC-expansion.*

Algorithm 1: Discover MaxPUF Pattern

```
1) while (There are unexplored consequent concept)
2)     Generate an unexplored consequent concept B;
3)     Traversal DC lattice to discover all valid DCs of B;
4)     Oupput consequent concept B and all of its valid DCs;
5) end while
```

In this algorithm, *SC-expansion* forms 2^n *SCs* and hence has time complexity of $O(2^n)$. Similarly, *DC-expansion* has time complexity of $O(2^m)$. Therefore Algorithm 1 has complexity of $O(2^{n+m})$. If $n + m$ is big, the computations will be very expensive. Thus, the question is how to efficiently prune unlikely candidates. In the following, we use the properties of MaxPUF pattern to prune *SC* and *DC* candidates.

4.1 Intersection Operation

To compute the *confidence* of a pattern, we need to compute the *support* of DC and $DC\&SC$. Vertical database layout is proven to be efficient in computing support [6, 7]. It consists of a list of items, with each item followed by its *Transaction id (Tid)* list.

Using verticle layout, we represent each *concepts* as a pair (I, T). $I = (a_1, ..., a_m)$ is the set of items that are ordered increasingly by item *id*, and $T = (t_1, ..., t_n)$ is *Tid* list. An important operation *intersection* ($\wedge$) is defined as follows: given two concepts, A=(I_a, T_a) and B=(I_b, T_b), define $A \wedge B$=(I_c, T_c), where $I_c = I_a \cup I_b$ and $T_c = T_a \cap T_b$.

4.2 Consequent Concept Expansion

SC-expansion generates consequent concepts and try to avoid generating those that do not possibly have *valid DCs*. From Lemma 2 of Section 3, we have the following two corollaries.

Corollary 1. *For consequent concepts B and B', if $B \subset B'$, then only* valid DCs *of B and their superconcepts are possible* valid DCs *of B'.*

Prove: Let S be the set of all *valid DCs* of B, and superconcepts thereof, confidence threshold is θ. $A \notin S \Rightarrow [B|A] = \frac{sup(AB)}{sup(A)} < \theta$. Since $[B'|A] = \frac{sup(AB')}{sup(A)}$ and $sup(AB') < sup(AB) \Rightarrow [B'|A] < \theta$, A is not *valid DCs* of B'.

Corollary 2. *For consequent concepts B and B', $B \subset B'$, if B has no* valid DC*, then neither does B'.*

We omit the proof of this corollary as it is strait-forward. Corollary 1 states that in *SC-expansion*, if B is generated earlier than B', then we can take advantage of *valid DCs* of B to prune DC candidates when looking for *valid DCs* of B'. According to Corollary 2, if an SC has no *valid DC*, its superconcepts need not to be generated since no MaxPUF pattern of them will exist. According to these, the order of generating consequent concepts have great effect on the performance of prunning DC and SC candidates.

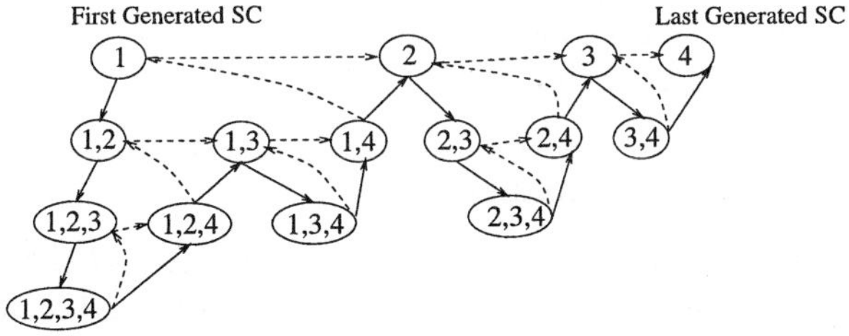

Fig. 1. Order of Generating Consequent Concepts in Depth-first Order

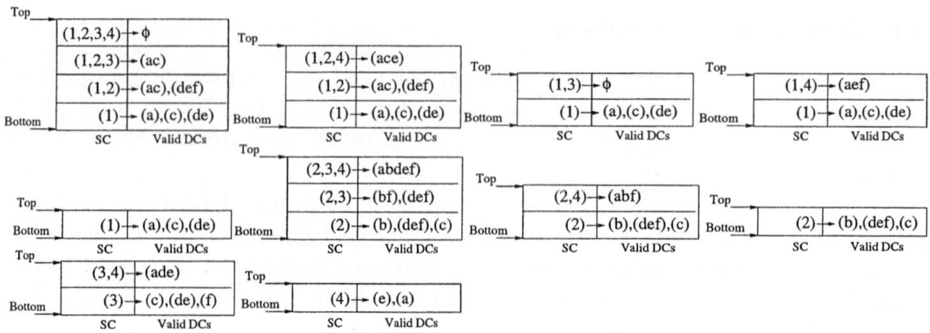

Fig. 2. Dynamic Stack Changes

We generate consequent concepts using, depth-first search order. It first generates one 1-item *SC* and then its superconcepts. After all of the superconcepts have been generated, the method generates the next 1-item *SC* and repeats the process, until all the possible *SC*s have been generated. A k-item *SC* is generated by expanding a $(k-1)$-item *SC* with one additional item. We push an *SC* and its *valid DC*s into the stack after it is generated and pop them after all of its superconcepts have been generated. If a k-item *SC* has no *valid DC*s, according to Corollary 2, we don't need to generate any of its superconcepts, that means we can pop this concept immediately from the stack.

Figures 1 and 2 show an example of *SC-expansion*. In this example, $IS = \{1,2,3,4\}$. The first *SC* candidate is (1), push (1) and its *valid DC*s into the stack. Next generate *SC*=(1,2). Repeat the processes, until $(1,2,3,4)$ has been generated. $(1,2,3,4)$ is on the top of the stack and it has no ungenerated superconcept, thus pop it from the stack, and similiarly pop $(1,2,3)$. Then generate *SC*=$(1,2,4)$, a superconcept of $(1,2)$ that is on the top of the stack now. Repeat these processes, until (4) is generated, and *SC-expansion* finishes.

In this method, at any time, memory only stores a small number of *SC*s from the *SC* lattice and their *valid DC*s, that is, those *SC*s on the path in *SC lattice* from a 1-item *SC* to the newly generated concept. Moreover, when exploring the *valid DC*s of a k-item *SC* $(k > 1)$, only one of its subconcept and its *valid DC*s are stored in the stack, which is the $(k-1)$-item concept on top of the stack. *Valid DC*s of this $(k-1)$-item concept and their superconcepts are possible *valid DC*s of the newly generated k-item *SC*.

4.3 Condition Concept Expansion

Once a consequent concept is generated, we use *DC-expansion* to discover *valid DC*s by checking all possible condition concepts. We prune *DC* candidates in two ways. On one hand, we can take advange of the stack information built by *SC-expansion*, on the other hand, we will use the Apriori property of *DC-expansion*.

Stack information is used at the begining of *DC-expansion* to prune *DC* candidates. There are two cases: (1) discover *valid DC*s of 1-item *SC*s, and (2) discover *valid DCs* of k-item *SCs* ($k > 1$). For Case (1) the stack is empty and no pruning can be applied, and thus *DC-expansion* checks the concepts begining from 1-item *DCs* until m-item *DCs* ($m = |ID|$). For Case (2), a subconcept (B') of the newly generated $SC\,(B)$ is on the top of the stack. Since only the valid *DCs* of B' and their superconcepts are possible *DC* candidates of B, therefore, *DC-expansion* begins from those *valid DCs* and continue with their superconcepts.

Corollary 3. Apriori property of *DC-expansion. For a given consequent concept, if a k-item condition concept is valid, then none of its (k-1)-item subconcepts are valid.*

Apriori property is derived from the definition of MaxPUF pattern. Using this property, we generate a k-item *DC* candidate only if none of its $(k-1)$-item subconcepts are valid. In implementing *DC-expansion*, the data structure include three sets: (1) CC^k: k-item *DC* candidates set; (2) VC^k: k-item valid *DC* set; (3) CE^k: those k-item *DCs* used to generate $(k+1)$-item *DC* candidates. It is easy to see $CE^k = CC^k - VC^k$, since once a *DC* is valid, then none of its superconcepts could be valid and thus should not be candidates.

5 Experiments and Analysis

Experiments are designed to find MaxPUF association rules from weather related databases, and discover relationships between weather events and environmental indices. Datasets are collected at the weather station in Clay Center, NE, from 1950-1999. These are: 1) Standardized Precipitation Index (SPI) data from the National Drought Mitigation Center, 2) Palmer Drought Severity Index (PDSI) from the National Climatic Data Center, 3) North Atlantic Oscillation Index (NAO) from the Climatic Research Unit at the University of East Anglia, UK, 4) Pacific Ocean Southern Oscillation Index (SOI) and Multivariate ENSO Index (MEI) available from NOAA's Climate Prediction Center, and 5) Pacific/North American (PNA) Index and Pacific Decadal Oscillation (PDO) Index available from the Joint Institute for the Study of the Atmosphere and Ocean.

After normalizing and discretizing each dataset [8], we performed experiments to use the proposed algorithm to find MaxPUF association rules with different confidence threshold. We use the global climatic indices (SOI, MEI, NAO, PDO, PNA) as condition data sets, and the local precipitation indices (SPI3, SPI6, SPI9, SPI12, PDSI) as consequent data sets. The first experiments consider nine indices without PDSI, the second experiments consider all ten indices. The experiments were run on a Pentium 1.0GHz PC with 256 MB main memory. Algorithms are coded in C++. The experimental results are showed in Figure 3 and 4.

From the experimental results, we observe that as confidence threshold decreases, the execution time increases. And at the same time, more consequent concepts are generated. This is because more *SCs* have *valid DCs* with lower confidence threshold. An interesting observation is that the total number of *valid DCs* does not necessarily increases as confidence decreases, which means

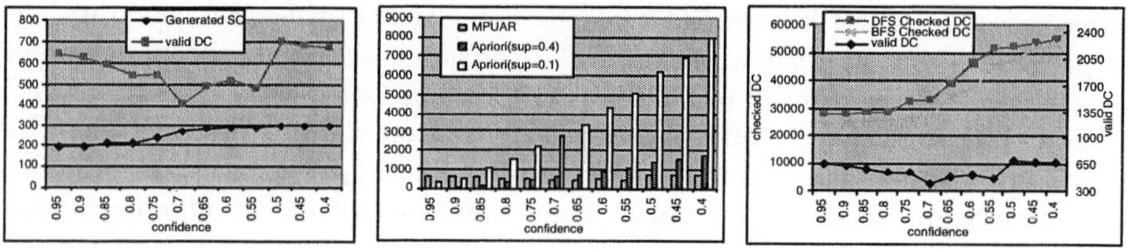

Fig. 3. 9-indices Performance Study

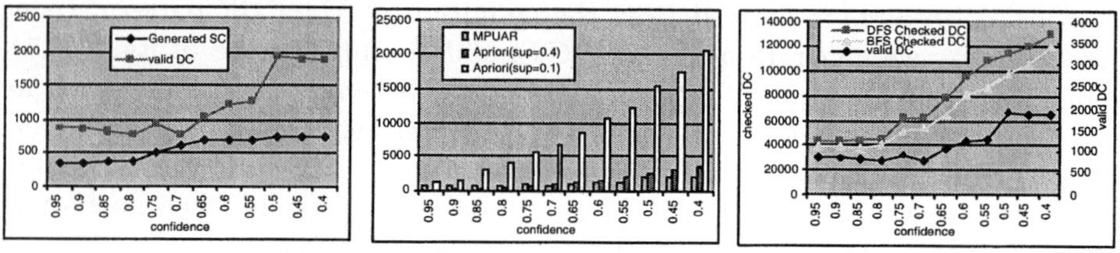

Fig. 4. 10-indices Performance Study

the number of MaxPUF association rules is not proportional to the confidence threshold. To explain this, we need to consider two aspects that affect the number of MaxPUF association rules: the number of *SC*s that have *valid DC*s and the number *valid DC*s each *SC* has. As confidence threshold decreases, since more consequent concepts have *valid DC*s, usually, the total number of *valid DC*s should increase correspondingly. But on the other side, let us consider that the total number of *valid DC*s each *SC* has. Usually, most *valid DC* has items less than $\frac{2}{N}$ (N is the total number of items); and if $n < \lceil \frac{2}{N} \rceil$, total number of n-item *DC*s is much less than $(n+i)$-item *DC*s $(1 \leq i \leq \frac{2}{N})$; if an n-item *DC* is not valid, then it is very possible that many $(n+i)$-item *DC*s are valid; comparing to the case that if the n-item *DC* is valid, then there is only one *valid DC*. So we could say the earlier the *valid DC* appears, the more possible that a *SC* has less *valid DC*s. As confidence threshold decreases, the *valid DC* will usually appear earlier, and thus each *SC* has a smaller number of *valid DC*s. If the tendency that *SC*s to have a smaller number of *valid DC*s prevails over the tendency that more *SC*s have *valid DC*s, then the total number of *valid DC*s will decrease instead of increasing as confidence decreases.

Comparing MaxPUF association rules and association rules found by Apriori algorithm, we find MaxPUF association rules are more informational. With high-confidence support, MaxPUF association rules find some useful rules about infrequent items which Apriori cannot discover. As confidence threshold decreases, the number of rules given by Apriori increases very quickly, and many of the rules generated are trivial or uninteresting. In contrast, MaxPUF association rules give a relatively stable rule set, which also demonstrates that MaxPUF association rules are most informational rule set; they reveal most useful information while ignore less critical ones.

In *DC-expansion*, the sooner the *valid DC* appears among all the relative concepts, the fewer *DC* candidates will be generated, since no superconcepts of the *valid DC* need to be checked. It is more possible that a small number of *DC*s is valid at lower confidence threshold. So *DC-expansion* favors smaller confidence threshold. For *SC-expansion*, the worst case is when all *SC*s have *valid DC*s, in which *SC-expansion* will generate all the *SC*s and make its complexity $O(2^n)$. But usually, it is not possible. The more *SC*s that have no *valid DC*s appear, the fewer *SC*s are generated, since all the superconcepts of such *SC*s need not to be generated. In general, *SC-expansion* favors larger confidence threshold, as it is more possible that an *SC* has no *valid DC* at larger confidence threshold. Figures 3 and 4 show that the number of *SC*s generated decreases as confidence threshold increases, and the total number of generated *SC*s is not very large.

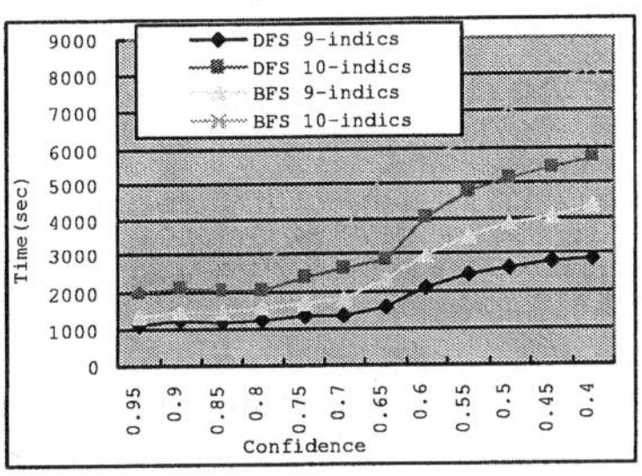

Fig. 5. *Execution time*

Although *SC-expansion* and *DC-expansion* behave differently with respect to confidence threshold, from our experiments, we see the process use less time with larger confidence threshold. To explain this, consider the overall process, *DC-expansion* is included in *SC-expansion*. If an *SC* is not generated, then *DC-expansion* is not executed at all. Thus, the number of *SC*s generated has greater affect on the whole process, i.e, the algorithm overall favors larger confidence threshold. Figure 5 shows that as confidence decreasses, execution time increases. The increasing trend is slower at higher confidence threshold but becomes faster with lower confidence.

6 Conclusions

In this paper, we extend the KDD model of probability logic developped in [3] with the notion of *maximal potentially useful pattern*. Similar to *potentially useful pattern*, MaxPUF pattern defines usefulness of a pattern as associated with proper narrower condition concepts. PUPs seek the sharp relative change of confidence when narrower condition is applied, while MaxPUF patterns use confidence threshold to seek articulation points which points high-confidence patterns to non-high-confidence patterns. PUPs are difficult to discover, as it is a process of complete exploration of patterns. MaxPUF patterns are simpler but very useful, as in real applicationsfinding high-confidence patterns are the often main goal and MaxPUF patterns are most informational pattern. We define a new class of association rules — MaxPUF association rules based on MaxPUF patterns. MaxPUF association rules are a compact set of rules that are most informational and potentially interesting to the users, and they overcomes the problem of conventional association rule that too many rules including trivial rules are discovered along with useful rules. Our experimental results show the number of MaxPUF association rules is much smaller than the that found by Apriori. Moreover, MaxPUF association rules are not restricted by support parameter, which makes MaxPUF association rules suitable for applications that both infrequent and frequent events are of interest. Our experimental results show that the proposed algorithm yield very good performances in discovering MaxPUF association rules.

References

1. R. Agrawal, T. Imielinski and A. Swami, Mining Association Rules between Sets of Items in Large Databases, Proceedings of the ACM SIGMOD International Conference on Management of Data, 1993.
2. C. H. Papadimitriou, computational complexity, MIT, 87-91, 1993.
3. J. Deogun, L. Jiang, Y. Xie and V. Raghavan, Probability Logic Modeling of Knowledge Discovery in Databases, The 14th International Symposium on Methodologies for Intelligent Systems, 2003.
4. B. Ganter and R. Wille, 1999, Formal Concept Analsis: Mathematical Foundations, Berlin.
5. F. Bacchus, Representing and Reasoning With Probabilistic Knowledge, MIT Press, Cambridge, Massachusetts, London, England, 1990.
6. M. Zaki, S. Parthasarathy, M. Ogihara, and W. Li, New algorithms for fast discovery of association rules. Proceedings of the Third International Conference on Knowledge Discovery and Data Mining (KDD-97), 1997.
7. M. Zaki, S. Parthasarathy, and W. Li, A localized algorithm for parallel association mining, In 9th ACM Symp. Parallel Algorithms and Architectures, 1997.
8. S. Harms, J. Deogun, J. Saquer and T. Tadesse, Discovering Representative Episodal Association Rules from Event SequencesUsing Frequent Closed Episode Sets and Event, Proceedings of the IEEE International Conf. on Data Mining, 2001.

Semantics and Syntactic Patterns in Data

Eric Louie[1] and Tsau Young Lin[2]

[1] IBM Almaden Research Center
650 Harry Road,San Jose, CA 95120
ewlouie@almaden.ibm.com
[2] Department of Computer Science
San Jose State University, San Jose, California 95192
tylin@cs.sjsu.edu

Abstract. This paper examines the semantics and syntactic views of classical association rule mining. A relational table is considered as a (knowledge) representation of a universe (= the set of real world entities). A pattern is said to be realizable, if there is a real world phenomenon corresponding to it. The central two issues are: Why do unrealizable data patterns appear? How could they be pruned away? For this purpose, the semantics of the original schema are considered. In additions, semantic is included into the knowledge representation of the universe. Based on model theory, two new relational structures, functions and binary relations, are added to represent some additional semantics of the given universe. Association rule mining based on such additional semantics are considered

Keywords: Data mining, interesting-ness, isomorphism, semantics, undirected association rules.

1 Introduction

Data mining has been defined as a non-trivial process of identifying valid, novel, potentially useful, and ultimately understandable patterns from data [2]. Essentially, this "definition" addresses two important points

– Patterns are derived from raw data, and
– Patterns should be realizable in the sense it corresponds to a real world phenomena (therefore "valid" and "useful")

We should comment here that in [4], we have speak about interpretability; it is about the interpretability in terms of the primitive symbols, so it is an intermediate step between the data patterns and real world patterns.

Majority of data mining researches have been devoted to first bullet, namely, searching new algorithms to transform the data to patterns. In this paper, we focus on the second bullet:

S. Tsumoto et al. (Eds.): RSCTC 2004, LNAI 3066, pp. 285–294, 2004.

- Why do unrealizable data patterns appear?
- What constraints should we impose on data so that data patterns are closer to the patterns of real world?

See [10], [14], [9], [5] for some initial works.

1.1 Patterns – Undirected Association Rules

Two standard measures, support and confidence, are often used in association rule mining. Between these two measures, support is the important and essential one; we will focus on it, and define the pattern as follows.

- *A sub-tuple in a given relational table is called a (undirected) association rules or simply a data pattern, if the support of the subtuple exceeds the threshold*

In other words, if a piece of (sub)data repeats itself sufficiently many times, then it is a pattern.

1.2 Raw Data for Data Mining – Relational Tables

Let us recall some mathematical notations. Let X and Y be sets and $f : X \longrightarrow Y$ be a map (a single valued function). In college mathematics, X is called the domain of f, the set of $\{y \mid y \in Y \text{ and } y = f(x)\}$ is called the image under f, and the set $\{(x, f(x))|x \in X\}$ is called the graph. The main objects of our study are relations (since we do allow repeated rows, so a more appropriate name are bag relations [3]). A relation is a bag of tuples that represent real world entities by lists (sets) of attribute values. So a relation is, in fact, a map,

$$K : V \longrightarrow R$$

from the set V of entities onto the bag R of tuples. The traditional database theory focus only on R, the image of the map K, and call it a relation. In such representation the "independent variable V" plays no explicit role. For data mining, it is more convenient to have independent variables in the formulation. So we will use the graph $\{(v, K(v)) \mid v \in V\}$ and call it the information table or simply table. However, throughout the whole, by abuse of language:

K may mean
(1) the knowledge representation $K : V \longrightarrow Dom(A^1) \times \ldots Dom(A^n)$
(2) the information table $(v, K(v))$
(3) the classical relation $R = ImK$, the image of K, which is a bag of tuples.
(4) Since A and V determines K and vice versa, we may use (V, A) and K interchangeably.

2 Classical Association Rules – Syntactic Phenomena

2.1 The Isomorphism of Relational Tables

This section is taken from [5] almost in verbatim. We need some notations: Let $K = (V, A)$ and $H = (V, B)$ be two information tables, where $A = \{A^1, \ldots A^n\}$ and $B = \{B^1, \ldots B^m\}$. Let C^i, C^j be two attributes from either A or B. Attributes C^i and C^j are isomorphic iff there is a one-to-one and onto map, $s : Dom(C^i) \longrightarrow Dom(C^j)$ such that $C^j(v) = s(C^i(v)) \; \forall \; v \in V$; here $Dom(\bullet)$ denote the set of current attribute values in $\bullet$. The map s is called an isomorphism. Intuitively, two attributes (columns) are isomorphic iff one column turns into another one by properly renaming its attribute values. Relations, K and H are said to be isomorphic if every A^i is isomorphic to some B^j, and vice versa. We will assume *all attributes are distinct*,and hence the two relations K and H have the same degree (number of attributes), that is, $n = m$; See [5] for more general version. The following theorem should be obvious.

Theorem 2.1.1. Isomorphic relations have isomorphic patterns.

The impacts of this simple theorem are surprisingly far reaching. It essentially declares that patterns are syntactic in nature. They are patterns of the whole isomorphic class, even though many of the isomorphic relations may have very different semantics; see next Section.

Theorem 2.1.2. Any "interesting-ness" of patterns defined by item counting or its probability theory is a property of the isomorphic class.

2.2 The Isomorphism of Patterns

The two relations, Table 1 and 2, are isomorphic, but their semantics are completely different, one table is about (hardware) parts, the other is about suppliers (sales persons). Yet these two relations have isomorphic patterns;

1. Length one:

   (a) TEN, TWENTY, MAR, SJ, LA in Table 1
   (b) 10, 20, SCREW, BRASS, ALLOY in Table 2

Table 1. Relational Table K

V	K	($S\#$	Business Amount (in m.)	Birth Month	CITY)
v_1	$\longrightarrow$	(S_1	TWENTY	MAR	NY)
v_2	$\longrightarrow$	(S_2	TEN	MAR	SJ)
v_3	$\longrightarrow$	(S_3	TEN	FEB	NY)
v_4	$\longrightarrow$	(S_4	TEN	FEB	LA)
v_5	$\longrightarrow$	(S_5	TWENTY	MAR	SJ)
v_6	$\longrightarrow$	(S_6	TWENTY	MAR	SJ)
v_7	$\longrightarrow$	(S_7	TWENTY	APR	SJ)
v_8	$\longrightarrow$	(S_8	THIRTY	JAN	LA)
v_9	$\longrightarrow$	(S_9	THIRTY	JAN	LA)

Table 2. Relational Table K'

V	K	($S\#$	Weight	Part Name	Material
v_1	$\longrightarrow$	(P_1	20	SCREW	STEEL)
v_2	$\longrightarrow$	(P_2	10	SCREW	BRASS)
v_3	$\longrightarrow$	(P_3	10	NAIL	STEEL)
v_4	$\longrightarrow$	(P_4	10	NAIL	ALLOY)
v_5	$\longrightarrow$	(P_5	20	SCREW	BRASS)
v_6	$\longrightarrow$	(P_6	20	SCREW	BRASS)
v_7	$\longrightarrow$	(P_7	20	PIN	BRASS)
v_8	$\longrightarrow$	(P_8	30	HAMMER	ALLOY)
v_9	$\longrightarrow$	(P_9	30	HAMMER	ALLOY)

2. Length two: :

   (a) (TWENTY, MAR), (MAR, SJ), (TWENTY, SJ) in Table 1,
   (b) (20, SCREW), (SCREW, BRASS), (20, BRASS), in Table 2

2.3 Non-isomorphism of Realizability – Addressing the Semantics

However, the realizablility is non-isomorphic:

Assumption: Support $\geq$ 3

1 Table 1: (TWENTY, SJ) is an interesting rule; it means the amount of business in San Jose is likely to be 20 million.

1' Table 2: (20, BRASS) is a junk pattern; this rule is not meaningful at all. Material, such as BRASS has no specific weight. Examine the schema, we see 20 refers to PIN, not BRASS.

2' Table 2: (SCREW, BRASS) is an interesting rule; it says screws are most likely made from BRASS.

2 Table 1: (MAR, SJ) is a junk pattern; this rule is not meaningful, because MAR refers to a supplier, not to a city. Examine the schema, we find there is no association between the two columns (attributes) that contain these two values.

3' Table 2: (20, SCREW) is an interesting rule; it says screws are most likely weighing 20.

3 Table 1: (TWENTY, MARCH) is a junk pattern; TWENTY refers to supplier, not March.

The discussions above are summarized in Table 3 Let us assume that there is an ideal algorithm that can extract exactly the real-world-patterns. Using this algorithm, we should have extracted only the rule (TWENTY, SJ) from Table 1. So the question is

Why do junk patterns, (TWENTY, MARCH) and (20, BRASS), show up in Table 1?

Table 3. (Undirected) Association Rules of Length Two

Meaningful Patterns	Realizable?	Junk Patterns	Realizable?
(TWENTY, MARCH)	No	(20, SCREW)	Yes
(MARCH, SJ)	No	(SCREW, BRASS)	Yes
(TWENTY, SJ)	Yes	(20, BRASS)	No

The reason is that the current notion of association rule mining is based on counting, which is syntactic in nature. Association rules are isomorphic to each other within the isomorphic class. are So the answer to previous question is

> The junk patterns appear in Table 1, because they isomorphic to real world patterns,(20, SCREW) and and(TWENTY, SJ) in other table,i.e., Table 2.

So we offer the following conjecture to conclude this section:

Conjecture: *The set of (undirected) association rules is the union of all isomorphic copies of real world patterns in other tables within the isomorphic class*

These observations explain why there are so many association rules. This clearly shows that in order the association rules to be really useful, we must model and capture the semantics of the raw data.

3 Capturing the Semantics

Here we will consider the modeling of "real world" (the set of entities) that is represented by a relation. We will start with the classical world model that is represented by a classical relation. Then we add some relational structures into this classical world model.

3.1 Additional Semantics

The analysis above indicates that real world modeling may be important in data mining, if we do want mining patterns that have real world meaning (realizable). Unfortunately, the relational data model is an over simplified model; it is based on Cantor sets and "forget" the interactions among members of real world objects. So its semantic strength is very limited. For deeper semantics, additional modeling is needed.

What would be the "correct" mathematical structure to capture the semantics of real world objects? This is a question that has many ad hoc answers; we decide to consult the history. First order logic and its model theory probably are the most comprehensive theory for modeling the real world. Moreover, relational theory is rested on the first order logic. So logic or its model theory is a natural candidates [15], [13],[14].

1. Model theory uses relations and functions to capture the real world structure;
2. Logic uses predicates and function symbols to describe the structure of real world.

We choose model theory. Previously we have explored the simplest structure, namely, to each attribute domain one binary relation is added [14], [11]. In [7], we consider one additional real valued function for each domain. In this paper, we integrate these into one framework.

4 The Semantics of Tuples, Schema and Patterns

The semantic interactions and associations among attribute values of a tuple

1. may extend to associations of columns, and
2. will inherit to patterns.

We need to exploit the extensions and inheritance. Though the semantic information at individual tuple level is impossible, but at column level, namely, the schema such information is available. The known semantic information of columns are, e.g., functional, multi-valued and join dependencies; these are often spell out in database design, and readily available to us.

Unfortunately, there are no known algebraic structure can encode the complete information. To prune away many unrealizable associations, we need to rely on users' input.

Table 4. A Table K_c

V	K	$(S\#$	Business amount(in m.)	Birth Day	CITY)
v_1	$\longrightarrow$	$(S_1$	20	MAR	$C_1)$
v_2	$\longrightarrow$	$(S_2$	10	MAR	$C_2)$
v_3	$\longrightarrow$	$(S_3$	10	FEB	$C_1)$
v_4	$\longrightarrow$	$(S_4$	10	FEB	$C_3)$
v_5	$\longrightarrow$	$(S_5$	20	MAR	$C_2)$
v_6	$\longrightarrow$	$(S_6$	20	MAR	$C_2)$
v_7	$\longrightarrow$	$(S_7$	20	APR	$C_2)$
v_8	$\longrightarrow$	$(S_8$	30	JAN	$C_3)$
v_9	$\longrightarrow$	$(S_9$	30	JAN	$C_3)$

5 Adding a Binary Relation to a Domain

We will express them in terms of "near" and "Inequality" binary granulations; a binary granulation and a binary relation are equivalent notion.

Table 5. A Binary Relation of "near"

CITY	CITY
C_1	C_1
C_1	C_2
C_2	C_1
C_2	C_2
C_2	C_3
C_3	C_2
C_3	C_3

1. "near" -binary granules
   $"near"_{C_1} = \{C_1, C_2\}, "near"_{C_2} = \{C_1, C_2, C_3\}, "near"_{C_3} = \{C_2, C_3\}$.
   NEIGH(C_1) is used to denote the granule, when the binary relation is not explicitly given.
2. "Inequality" -binary granules
   $Inequality_{10} = \{10\}, Inequality_{20} = \{10, 20\}, Inequality_{30} = \{10, 20, 30\}$,

5.1 The Impact of Binary Relations to Data Mining

In mining such a data model, first concern is the cost in checking the added structure. However, the cost is well compensated by the saving. It does have cost in checking the continuity of association rules. However, the pruning of non-continuous rules save the time in computing the long rules. An association rule, say ab, is continuous, if every $x \in$ NEIGH(a) is associated with some $y \in$ NEIGH(b); see [14],[10]. One beauty of continuity is that the compositions of continuous rules are also continuous, so the only cost is at the length 2. From experiments on artificial data, it shows that the adding of a binary relation to domain is a promising approach.

6 Functions Added Data Model

This section is adopt from from [7] for convenience. The function f^j may be associated with intuitive interpretations such as profits or cost. Intuitively it is natural to compute profit additively, namely, $f(A) = \sum_{i \in A} f(i)$ for an itemset in association rule mining. In general, this may not be accurate. For example, in security, the security level of an itemset (set of objects) is often computed by $f(A) = Max_{i \in A} f(i)$, and integrity by $f(A) = Min_{i \in A} f(i)$.

We will use the semantic neutral term and call f a valued-added function (security value, integrity value or cost). In [7], we focus on the functions only, in this paper, we take slightly different view: Each attribute consists of two columns, the original column and a new added column which consists of the function value. So if each item set has two values, one is attribute value, the other is the function value.

Definition 1. Large value itemsets (LVA-itemsets), *by abuse of language, we may refer to it as (undirected)* **value added association rules**. *Let B be a subset of the attributes A, f a real-valued function that assigns a value to each itemset, and s_q be a given threshold value for q-itemset, $q = 1, 2, \ldots$.*

1. *Sum-version: A granule $b = (b_1 \cap b_2 \cap \ldots \cap b_q)$, namely, a sub-tuple $b = (b_1, b_2, \ldots, b_q)$, is a large value q-VA- itemset*
   a *b is a high frequent itemset, and*
   b *if $Sum(b) \geq s_q$, where*

$$Sum(b) = \sum_j x_o^j * p(x_o^j) = \sum_{j=1}^{q} f^j(b_j) * |b|/|U|, \tag{1}$$

   where $x_o^j = f^j(b_j)$.
   The same considerations for rest of items.
2. *Min-version: A granule $b = (b_1 \cap b_2 \cap \ldots \cap b_q)$ is a large value q-VA-itemset if $Min(b) \geq s_q$, where*

$$Min(b) = Min_j x_o^j * p(x_o^j) = Min_{j=1}^{q} f^j(b_j) * |b|/|U|. \tag{2}$$

3. *Max-version: A granule $b = (b_1 \cap b_2 \cap \ldots \cap b_q)$ is a large value q-VA-itemset if $Max(b) \geq s_q$, where*

$$Max(b) = Max_j x_o^j * p(x_o^j) = Max_{i=1}^{q}(f(b_i) * |b|). \tag{3}$$

4. *Mean version: It captures the mean trends of the data. Two attributesA^{j_1}, A^{j_2} is mean associated, if $|E(X^{j_1}) - E(X^{j_2})| \leq s_q$, where $E(\cdot)$ is the expected value, $|\cdot|$ is the absolute value.*

6.1 The Impact of Added Structure to Data Mining

The difference between this and last sections is that the values of the function do participate in computing. For example, the existing of real valued function implies the existing of a neighborhood system on an attribute domain D (which has a neighborhood system). However, the imposed constraints are imposed more than on the structure of D, we use the real values. To compute VA-association is quite expensive, if we use values alone.

7 Structures Preserving Association Rules

7.1 Algorithms for Sum-Version

An immediate thought would be to mimic the classical theory. Unfortunately, "apriori" may not always be applicable. Note that counting plays a major role in classical association rules. However, in the value added case, the function values are the main concerns. So in [7], we only concern with function values so the thresholds are compared only against the sum, max, min, and average of the function values. However, in this paper, we consider both, therefore, even though the function part is still the same, but we have another criteria, so the computation is not as bad.

Consider the case $q = 2$. Assume $s_1 = s_2$ and f is not the constant 1. Let $b = b_1 \cap b_2$ be a 2-large granule. We have,

$$Sum(b_1) = f(b_1) * |b_1|/|U|, Sum(b_2) = f(b_2) * |b_2|/|U|, \tag{4}$$

$$Sum(b) = Sum(b_1) + Sum(b_2) \geq s_2. \tag{5}$$

In classical case, $|b| \leq |b_i|, i = 1, 2$; and the apriori exploits this relationship. In the function case, such a relationship is not there; apriori criteria are not useful. So the remarks on function part made in [7] is still valid: Algorithm for finding value added association rules is a brutal exhaustive search.

7.2 Algorithms for Max- and Min-versions

As above, the key question is: Could we conclude any relationship among $M(b_1)$, $M(b_2)$, and $M(b)$, where M = Max and Min? Nothing for Max, but for Min, we do have:

$$Min(f(b_1), f(b_2)) \leq Min(b_i), i = 1, 2, \tag{6}$$

Hence we have apriori algorithms for Min-version.

8 Conclusions

Our analysis shows that the association rules found by high frequency seem carry very little semantics of the given relation. In this paper, we enrich the relation by

1. the added relational structures to domain along the line of model theory; the added structure are
   (a) binary relational structures, and
   (b) some functions along the lines of model theory
2. a pattern will be pruned away, if it does not inherit the semantics of the original schema.

Such considerations enrich the semantics and improved the pruning of unnecessary realizable association rules.

References

1. R. Agrawal, T. Imielinski, and A. Swami, "Mining Association Rules Between Sets of Items in Large Databases," in Proceeding of ACM-SIGMOD international Conference on Management of Data, pp. 207-216, Washington, DC, June, 1993

2. Fayad, U. M., Piatetsky-Sjapiro, G. Smyth, P. From Data Mining to Knowledge Discovery: An overview. In Fayard, Piatetsky-Sjapiro, Smyth, and Uthurusamy eds., Knowledge Discovery in Databases, AAAI/MIT Press, 1996.
3. H Gracia-Molina, J. Ullman. & J. Windin, J, Database Systems The Complete Book, Prentice Hall, 2002.
4. T. Y. Lin "Mining Un-interpreted Generalized Association Rules by Linear Inequalities:Deductive Data Mining Approach," in: the proceeding of RSCTC2004, this volume.
5. T. Y. Lin, "Attribute (Feature) Completion– The Theory of Attributes from Data Mining Prospect," in: the Proceedings of International Conference on Data Mining, Maebashi, Japan, Dec 9-12, 2002, pp.282-289
6. T. Y. Lin and Eric Louie, "Semantics Oriented Association Rules," In: 2002 World Congress of Computational Intelligence, Honolulu, Hawaii, May 12-17, 2002, 956-961 (paper # 5754)
7. T. Y. Lin, Y. Y. Yao, and E. Louie, "Value Added Association Rules, "6th Pacific-Asia Conference(PAKDD2002), Taipei, Taiwan, May 6-8, 2002, pp. 328-333, Lecture Notes on Artificial Intelligent series# 2336
8. T. Y. Lin, Y. Y. Yao, and E. Louie, "Value Added Association Rules, "6th Pacific-Asia Conference, Taipei, Taiwan, May 6-8, 2002
9. T.Y. Lin, Eric Louie, "Modeling the Real World for Data Mining: Granular Computing Approach" Joint 9th IFSA World Congress and 20th NAFIPS Conference, July 25-28, Vancouver, Canada, 2001
10. T. Y. Lin, "Data Mining: Granular Computing Approach." In: Methodologies for Knowledge Discovery and Data Mining, Lecture Notes in Artificial Intelligence 1574, Third Pacific-Asia Conference, Beijing, April 26-28, 1999, 24-33.
11. T. Y. Lin, "Granular Computing on Binary Relations I: Data Mining and Neighborhood Systems." In: Rough Sets In Knowledge Discovery, A. Skoworn and L. Polkowski (eds), Springer-Verlag, 1998, 107-121.
12. Tsau Young Lin, Database Mining on Derived Attributes–Granular and Rough Computing Approach, In : Rough sets and Current Trends in Computing, Alpigini, Peters Skowron, Zhong (eds), Lecture Notes on Artificial Intelligence, 2002, pp 14-32.
13. T.Y. Lin, Eric Louie, "Association Rules in Semantically Rich Relations." In: Exploring New Frontiers on Artificial Intelligence, Lecture Notes on Artificial Intelligent series # 2253, pp 380-384. 2002
14. "Data Mining and Machine Oriented Modeling: A Granular Computing Approach," Journal of Applied Intelligence, Kluwer, Vol. 13, No 2, September/October,2000, pp.113-124.
15. Pei, J. Han, and L. V. S. Lakshmanan, "Mining Frequent Itemsets with Convertible Constraints", Proc. 2001 Int. Conf. on Data Engineering (ICDE'01), Heidelberg, Germany, April 2001.

Dialogue in Rough Context

Mihir K. Chakraborty[1] and Mohua Banerjee[2,*]

[1] Department of Pure Mathematics, University of Calcutta
35, Ballygunge Circular Road, Kolkata 700 019, India
mihirc99@cal3.vsnl.net.in

[2] Department of Mathematics, Indian Institute of Technology
Kanpur 208 016, India
mohua@iitk.ac.in

Abstract. Two agents Ag_1 and Ag_2 confront each other with their own perspectives represented by approximation spaces (U, R_1) and (U, R_2) [3]. They enter into a *dialogue* (negotiation) over either the extension of the same 'concept' or over two pieces of information or beliefs, A and B, the first for Ag_1 and the second for Ag_2 respectively, which are subsets of U. A combined approximation space (U, R) emerges out of the superimposition of the equivalence classes due to R_1 and R_2.
Each agent performs some specified *operations* one at a time. After an operation by an agent the turn comes to the co-agent. *Rounds* and *effects* of rounds are then defined. A *dialogue* is a sequence of rounds.
There are certain *rules* of the game that depend on the three approximation spaces.
The *result* of a dialogue after n rounds starting with the initial sets A, B is a pair (A_n, B_n), A_n, B_n being supersets of A and B respectively. A dialogue is characterised depending on the various kinds of overlap of the sets A_n and B_n and their lower and upper approximations. It is *satisfactory* if the sets A_n and B_n turn out to be roughly equal with respect to the approximation space (U, R). Dialogues of lower satisfaction are not altogether rejected. This latter type generalizes the notion of Belief-Merging [2].
Some preliminary observations are made and future directions of work are indicated.

1 Introduction

The basic premise is that two subjects generally have two different perceptions about the universe of discourse. Viewed from the angle of Rough Set theory [3], these perceptions (or contexts) are represented by indiscernibility relations (which are being taken as equivalences) giving rise to two partitions of the universe. The universe is hence split into granules, small or large (the equivalence classes) according to the perceptions of the subjects. Now, any concept is given by a subset of the universe – the extension of the concept – but because of the

* Research supported by Project No. BS/YSP/29/2477 of the Indian National Science Academy.

S. Tsumoto et al. (Eds.): RSCTC 2004, LNAI 3066, pp. 295–299, 2004.

granularity of the universe, the concept is 'understood' only in a rough way – by the subset's lower and upper approximations [3]. The two agents may now converse for a consensus and each one may like to revise (extend, in this study) the initial extensions (subsets). Even if an extension acceptable by both the subjects does not emerge, a reasonable amount of overlap may come out. In this paper, we have attempted to give a first formal account of the idea. A method is suggested for carrying out the 'conversation'.

So there are

- ▷ two agents Ag_1 and Ag_2,
- ▷ a universe of discourse U,
- ▷ two equivalence relations R_1 and R_2 representing the perceptions (or contexts) of the two agents respectively, giving rise to two approximation spaces (U, R_1) and (U, R_2).

A third approximation space (U, R) arises out of R_1 and R_2 by superimposing the two partitions framed by them. It is, in fact, a refinement of (U, R_1) and (U, R_2).

Two initial subsets A, B of U are also given, corresponding to Ag_1 and Ag_2 respectively, called the *starting sets* of the two agents. Interpretations of these sets may vary – some are presented later in the paper.

Given any subset S of U, the lower (upper) approximations are denoted by $lo_1(S), lo_2(S), lo(S)$ $(up_1(S), up_2(S), up(S))$ in the spaces $(U, R_1), (U, R_2), (U, R)$ respectively. Let a, $b \in U$.

Definition 1. *Each of the agents can perform any of the following* operations.
o_1 : *a is proposed*
o_2 : *a is accepted*
o_3 : *a is not accepted*
o_4 : *a is conditionally accepted and simultaneously b is proposed*

Note 1. o_4 means that an agent accepts a conditionally, *only if* b is accepted by the other agent.

Let $o_i(a)$, $i = 1, 2, 3$ and $o_4(a, b)$ denote that the respective operation has been performed on the element a (and b). After an operation by an agent Ag the turn comes to the co-agent *co-Ag*.

Definition 2. *A* round *is a sequence of operations (performed in the given order), and can be of four types.*
RD_1 : $o_1(a)$ *by Ag*, $o_2(a)$ *by co-Ag*
RD_2 : $o_1(a)$ *by Ag*, $o_3(a)$ *by co-Ag*
RD_3 : $o_1(a)$ *by Ag*, $o_4(a, b)$ *by co-Ag*, $o_2(b)$ *by Ag*
RD_4 : $o_1(a)$ *by Ag*, $o_4(a, b)$ *by co-Ag*, $o_3(b)$ *by Ag*

Definition 3. *A* dialogue *is a sequence of rounds such that, except the first one, each round begins at the agent where the previous round ends.*

Definition 4. *If the agents are at a stage with sets P, Q associated with the agent and co-agent respectively, and if a round begins at the agent holding P, then the* effect *of the round on (P, Q) is defined according to the type of the round.*

E_1 *(for RD_1) is the pair* $(P \cup \{a\}, Q \cup \{a\})$
E_2 *(for RD_2) is the pair* $(P \cup \{a\}, Q)$ *or* (P, Q)
E_3 *(for RD_3) is the pair* $(P \cup \{a, b\}, Q \cup \{a, b\})$
E_4 *(for RD_4) is the pair* (P, Q) *or* $(P \cup \{a\}, Q \cup \{b\})$

Remark 1. The effects may be interpreted as follows.
E_1: *Ag* proposes a, *co-Ag* accepts. So both P and Q are augmented by a.
E_2: *Ag* proposes a, *co-Ag* does not accept. So, there are two possibilities, viz. *Ag* includes her proposed object, and *Ag* does not do so.
E_3: *Ag* proposes a, and *co-Ag* conditionally accepts it provided *Ag* accepts b. *Ag* agrees. So, both the agents incorporate a and b in their extensions.
E_4: *Ag* proposes a, and *co-Ag* conditionally accepts it provided *Ag* accepts b. *Ag* does not agree. Then one option is that both a and b are given up by both the agents. The other option is interesting. Since *Ag* proposes a, she feels an obligation to include it, while *co-Ag* thinks that b should be included since she has preferred it over a (that *Ag* has proposed). This operation is not reducible to E_1 or E_2.

Definition 5. *Let a dialogue start with the pair* (A_0, B_0). *The* result *of such a dialogue after n rounds is the pair* (A_n, B_n), *obtained through a sequence of pairs* $(A_1, B_1), (A_2, B_2), ..., (A_n, B_n)$, *where* (A_i, B_i), $i = 1, 2, ..., n$ *is the effect on* (A_{i-1}, B_{i-1}) *of the* ith *round.*

There are certain *rules* of the game that depend on the three approximation spaces.

1. At any stage (A_i, B_i) of a dialogue starting with the pair (A_0, B_0), the agent Ag_1 (Ag_2) may propose, under operation o_1, an element a in A_i (B_i) or a in $up_2(B_i)$ ($up_1(A_i)$).
   Note 2. This means that a is proposed by an agent, only if a is within her 'region' or a is within her co-agent's 'possible region'. The idea is that an agent, being doubtful about the whole of her possible region (specifically, the boundary [3]), keeps it open for the co-agent's scrutiny. That is why she does not offer a candidate from her own possible region but chooses one from the possibility zone of her co-agent.
2. There may be some specific objects (within the permissible domain as mentioned in 1) that an agent may not like to propose.
3. If an agent Ag_k, $k = 1, 2$ applies operation o_4 by using the objects a and b, then aR_kb must hold, i.e. a and b must be indiscernible with respect to the agent Ag_k.
4. If a round starts, it must be completed. For instance, if an agent proposes an object, the co-agent must either accept or not accept it (she must react). Similar rule applies to the other operations also.
5. A dialogue ends at the nth round if, either the agent who is to start the $n+1$th round does not intend to propose any object, or A_n and B_n are roughly equal whereas, for $i = 1, 2, ..., n-1$, A_i, B_i are not so.

There is no condition on acceptability of objects – we allow uncertainty and subjectivity here.

Now the result of a dialogue may be of any of the following categories.
(a) $up(A_n) \cap up(B_n) = \emptyset$.
(b) $up(A_n) \cap up(B_n) \neq \emptyset$, $A_n \cap B_n = \emptyset$.
(c) $A_n \cap B_n \neq \emptyset$, $lo(A_n) \cap lo(B_n) = \emptyset$.
(d) $lo(A_n) \cap lo(B_n) \neq \emptyset$.

The categories may have further subcategories. For instance,
Subcategories of category (b):
(b_1) $A_n \cap up(B_n) \neq \emptyset$
(b_2) $up(A_n) \cap B_n \neq \emptyset$
(b_3) $up(A_n) \subseteq up(B_n)$
(b_4) $up(B_n) \subseteq up(A_n)$
Subcategories of category (c):
(c_1) $A_n \cap lo(B_n) \neq \emptyset$
(c_2) $lo(A_n) \cap B_n \neq \emptyset$
Subcategories of category (d):
(d_1) $lo(A_n) \subseteq lo(B_n)$
(d_2) $lo(B_n) \subseteq lo(A_n)$

A special category:
- ▷ $lo(A_n) \subseteq lo(B_n)$ and $up(A_n) \subseteq up(B_n)$
- ▷ $lo(B_n) \subseteq lo(A_n)$ and $up(B_n) \subseteq up(A_n)$
- ▷ $lo(A_n) = lo(B_n)$ and $up(A_n) = up(B_n)$

Note 3. The lower and upper approximations referred to in these (sub)categories are all with respect to the approximation space (U, R).

A dialogue is *satisfactory* if the sets A_n and B_n turn out to be roughly equal with respect to the approximation space (U, R).

Example 1. Let $U = \{a, b, c, d, e, f, g, h\}$;
partition by R_1: $\{a, c\}, \{b, d, h, e\}, \{f, g\}$;
partition by R_2: $\{a, b, d\}, \{c, e\}, \{f, g, h\}$.
The (superimposed) partition by R: $\{a\}, \{b, d\}, \{c\}, \{e\}, \{f, g\}, \{h\}$.
Let $A = \{c, b\}$, $B = \{d, c, f\}$.
Rounds –

▷ r_1 (of type RD_4):
$o_1(g)$ by Ag_1, $o_4(g, f)$ by Ag_2, $o_3(f)$ by Ag_1
Effect: (A_1, B_1), where $A_1 = \{c, b, g\}$, $B_1 = \{d, c, f\}$.

▷ r_2 (of type RD_2):
$o_1(e)$ by Ag_1, $o_3(e)$ by Ag_2
Effect: (A_2, B_2), where $A_2 = A_1$, $B_2 = B_1$.

▷ r_3 (of type RD_1):
$o_1(d)$ by Ag_2, $o_2(d)$ by Ag_1
Effect: (A_3, B_3), where $A_3 = \{c, b, g, d\}$, $B_3 = B_2$.

▷ r_4 (of type RD_3):
$o_1(b)$ by Ag_1, $o_4(b, a)$ by Ag_2, $o_2(a)$ by Ag_1
Effect: (A_4, B_4), where $A_4 = \{c, b, g, d, a\}$, $B_4 = \{d, c, f, b, a\}$.

The *result* of the dialogue (r_1, r_2, r_3, r_4) is the pair (A_4, B_4), and A_4, B_4 are roughly equal with respect to the superimposed partition. So the dialogue ends at the 4th round, and is satisfactory.

Observation 1.

(a) Since the relation R is a refinement of both R_1 and R_2, $lo_1(A) \subseteq lo(A) \subseteq lo(A_i)$. Also, $up(A) \subseteq up_1(A)$. Similar results hold for B and B_i.

(b) Suppose we impose an extra rule: at any stage $i+1$, any proposed object should be within $up_1(A_i) \cap up_2(B_i)$. Then we have the following.

1. *A dialogue cannot start unless $up_1(A) \cap up_2(B)$ is non-empty.*
2. *At each stage, the upper approximations remain the same, but the lower approximations may be extended.*
3. *Objects outside the union of $up_1(A)$ and $up_2(B)$ never enter the scene.*
4. *If $lo(A_i) = lo(B_i)$ then $A \subseteq up_2(B)$, $B \subseteq up_1(A)$, and $lo_1(A), lo_2(B) \subseteq lo(A_i \cap B_i)$.*

2 Possible Interpretations and Queries

Given the preceding framework, there could be the following interpretations.

I (A, B) are two pieces of information/beliefs of two agents. The problem is to 'merge' these into a single one (if possible) and if not, to ask the agents to perform reasonable revisions (in this case by enlargements) so that a 'common ground' is reached, i.e. until a stage when the intersection of some enlargements A_i, B_i becomes non-empty [2].

II Two agents are trying to come to a consensus on the *extension* of a concept. But their perspectives (approximation spaces) are different. Yet they are tolerant enough to give serious hearing to each other's view and willing to give some concessions. So they enter a dialogue or negotiation [4, 5].

A natural mathematical query could now be the following: to find (necessary and) sufficient conditions, in terms of the relationship between the equivalences R_1 and R_2, and/or the conditions of acceptability (that have been left open), so that various categories of *results* are obtained. Further, suitable objects/morphisms could be defined to represent the dialogue set-up in a category-theoretic framework. In this context, connections with the category of rough sets in [1] could be explored.

References

1. Banerjee, M., Chakraborty, M.K.: A category for rough sets. *Foundations of Computing and Decision Sciences* **18(3-4)** (1993) 167–180.
2. Booth, R.: A negotiation style framework for non-prioritized revision. Preprint, University of Leipzig, 2003.
3. Pawlak, Z.: Rough sets. *Int. J. Comp. Inf. Sci.* **11** (1982) 341–356.
4. Walton, D.N., Krabbe, E.C.W.: *Commitment in Dialogue: Basic Concepts of Interpersonal Reasoning*, SUNY Press, Albany, 1995.
5. Wooldridge, H.J., Parsons, S.: Languages for negotiation. In: *Proc. 14th European Conf. on AI, ECAI 2000*, 2000.

Constrained Sums of Information Systems

Andrzej Skowron[1] and Jarosław Stepaniuk[2]

[1] Institute of Mathematics
Warsaw University
Banacha 2, 02-097 Warsaw, Poland
skowron@mimuw.edu.pl

[2] Department of Computer Science
Białystok University of Technology
Wiejska 45a, 15-351 Białystok, Poland
jstepan@ii.pb.bialystok.pl

Abstract. We study properties of infomorphisms between information systems. In particular, we interpret infomorphisms between information systems in terms of sums with constraints (constrained sums, for short) that are some operations on information systems. Applications of approximation spaces, used in rough set theory, to study properties of infomorphisms are included.

1 Introduction

One of the main task in granular computing is to develop calculi of information granules [7], [13], [9], [10]. Information systems used in rough set theory are particular kinds of information granules. In the paper we introduce and study operations on such information granules basic for reasoning in distributed systems of information granules. The operations are called constrained sums. They are developed by interpreting infomorphisms between classifications [1]. In [11] we have shown that classifications [1] and information systems [5] are, in a sense, equivalent. We also extend the results included in [11] on applications of approximation spaces to study properties of infomorphisms. Operations, called constrained sums, seem to be very important in searching for patterns in data mining [3] (e.g., in spatio-temporal reasoning) or in more general sense in generating relevant granules for approximate reasoning using calculi on information granules [7], [11].

The paper is organized as follows. In Section 2 we present basic concepts. In Section 3 we introduce sums of information systems and approximation spaces. In Section 4 we discuss constrained sums of information systems and hierarchical information systems.

2 Approximation Spaces and Infomorphisms

In this section we recall basic notions for our considerations.

S. Tsumoto et al. (Eds.): RSCTC 2004, LNAI 3066, pp. 300–309, 2004.

2.1 Approximation Spaces

We recall a general definition of an approximation space. Several known approaches to concept approximations can be covered using such spaces, e.g., the tolerance based rough set model or the variable precision rough set model.

For every non-empty set U, let $P(U)$ denote the set of all subsets of U.

Definition 1. *[8],[12] A parameterized approximation space is a system* $AS_{\#,\$} = (U, I_{\#}, \nu_{\$})$, *where*

- U *is a non-empty set of objects,*
- $I_{\#} : U \to P(U)$ *is an uncertainty function,*
- $\nu_{\$} : P(U) \times P(U) \to [0,1]$ *is a rough inclusion function,*

and $\#, \$$ *are denoting vectors of parameters.*

The uncertainty function defines for every object x a set of similarly described objects.

A set $X \subseteq U$ is *definable in* $AS_{\#,\$}$ if and only if it is a union of some values of the uncertainty function.

The rough inclusion function defines the degree of inclusion between two subsets of U (see, e.g., [8], [12]):

$$\nu_{SRI}(X,Y) = \begin{cases} \frac{card(X \cap Y)}{card(X)} & \text{if } X \neq \emptyset \\ 1 & \text{if } X = \emptyset. \end{cases}$$

This measure is widely used by data mining and rough set communities. However, Jan Łukasiewicz [4] was first who used this idea to estimate the probability of implications.

The lower and the upper approximations of subsets of U are defined as follows.

Definition 2. *For an approximation space* $AS_{\#,\$} = (U, I_{\#}, \nu_{\$})$ *and any subset* $X \subseteq U$ *the lower and the upper approximations are defined by*

$LOW(AS_{\#,\$}, X) = \{x \in U : \nu_{\$}(I_{\#}(x), X) = 1\}$,

$UPP(AS_{\#,\$}, X) = \{x \in U : \nu_{\$}(I_{\#}(x), X) > 0\}$, *respectively.*

2.2 Infomorphisms

In this section we recall the definition of infomorphism for two information systems [11]. We also present some new properties of infomorphisms. The infomorphisms for classifications are introduced and studied in [1].

We denote by $\Sigma(IS)$ the set of Boolean combinations of descriptors over IS and by $\|\alpha\|_{IS} \subseteq U$ is denoted the semantics of α in IS.

For all formulas $\alpha \in \Sigma(IS)$ and for all objects $x \in U$ we will denote $x \models_{IS} \alpha$ if and only if $x \in \|\alpha\|_{IS}$.

Definition 3. *[1, 11] If $IS_1 = (U_1, A_1)$ and $IS_2 = (U_2, A_2)$ are information systems then an infomorphism between IS_1 and IS_2 is a pair $(f^\wedge, f^\vee)$ of functions $f^\wedge : \Sigma(IS_1) \to \Sigma(IS_2)$, $f^\vee : U_2 \to U_1$, satisfying the following equivalence*

$$f^\vee(x) \models_{IS_1} \alpha \text{ if and only if } x \models_{IS_2} f^\wedge(\alpha), \tag{1}$$

for all objects $x \in U_2$ and for all formulas $\alpha \in \Sigma(IS_1)$.

The infomorphism will be denoted shortly by $(f^\wedge, f^\vee) : IS_1 \rightleftarrows IS_2$.

Proposition 1. *[11] For any infomorphism $(f^\wedge, f^\vee) : IS_1 \rightleftarrows IS_2$ we obtain the following equality*

$$(f^\vee)^{-1}(\|\alpha\|_{IS_1}) = \|f^\wedge(\alpha)\|_{IS_2} \text{ for any } \alpha \in \Sigma(IS_1). \tag{2}$$

Definition 4. *Let $(f^\wedge, f^\vee)$ be an infomorphism between IS_1 and IS_2. We define two binary relations $\sim_{f^\wedge} \subseteq \Sigma(IS_1) \times \Sigma(IS_1)$ and $\approx_{f^\vee} \subseteq U_2 \times U_2$ as follows*

1. *$\alpha \sim_{f^\wedge} \beta$ if and only if $f^\wedge(\alpha) = f^\wedge(\beta)$ for any $\alpha, \beta \in \Sigma(IS_1)$,*
2. *$x \approx_{f^\vee} y$ if and only if $f^\vee(x) = f^\vee(y)$ for any $x, y \in U_2$.*

We obtain the following proposition:

Proposition 2. *For any infomorphism $(f^\wedge, f^\vee) : IS_1 \rightleftarrows IS_2$ between IS_1 and IS_2 the following properties hold:*

1. *The relations $\sim_{f^\wedge}$ and $\approx_{f^\vee}$ are equivalence relations;*
2. *$\alpha \sim_{f^\wedge} \beta$ if and only if*
$$\|\alpha\|_{IS_1} \cap f^\vee(U_2) = \|\beta\|_{IS_1} \cap f^\vee(U_2)$$
for any $\alpha, \beta \in \Sigma(IS_1)$,
3. *$x \approx_{f^\vee} y$ if and only if*
$$(x \in \|f^\wedge(\alpha)\|_{IS_2} \text{ if and only if } y \in \|f^\wedge(\alpha)\|_{IS_2}) \text{ for any } \alpha \in \Sigma(IS_1)$$
where $x, y \in U_2$,
4. *either $[x]_{\approx_{f^\vee}} \subseteq \|f^\wedge(\alpha)\|_{IS_2}$ or $[x]_{\approx_{f^\vee}} \cap \|f^\wedge(\alpha)\|_{IS_2} = \emptyset$ for any $\alpha \in \Sigma(IS_1)$ and $x \in U_2$,*
5. *any formula $\alpha \in f^\wedge(\Sigma(IS_1))$ is crisp (definable) in $U_2/\approx_{f^\vee}$, i.e., $\|\alpha\|_{IS_2}$ is a union of some equivalence classes from $U_2/\approx_{f^\vee}$.*

Let us recall that formulas from $\Sigma(IS_2) - f^\wedge(\Sigma(IS_1))$ can be defined approximately in $U_2/\approx_{f^\vee}$ (see [11]).

Proposition 2 gives a characterization of infomorphisms.

Definition 5. *Let $(f^\wedge, f^\vee) : IS_1 \rightleftarrows IS_2$ be an infomorphism between IS_1 and IS_2. We define two information systems:*

$$IS_1' = (f^\vee(U_2), \Sigma(IS_1')) \text{ and } IS_2' = (U_2', \Sigma(IS_2'))$$

where

– *$\Sigma(IS_1')$ is a subset of $\Sigma(IS_1)$ consisting of exactly one element from each equivalence class from $\Sigma(IS_1)/\sim_{f^\wedge}$ and*
– *U_2' is a subset of U_2 consisting of exactly one element from each equivalence class from $U_2/\approx_{f^\vee}$ and $\Sigma(IS_2') = f^\wedge(\Sigma(IS_1))$.*

Proposition 3. *Let $(f^\wedge, f^\vee) : IS_1 \rightleftarrows IS_2$ be an infomorphism between IS_1 and IS_2. Then $(g^\wedge, g^\vee) : IS_1' \rightleftarrows IS_2'$ is an infomorphism where $(g^\wedge, g^\vee)$ is a pair of bijections defined by $g^\wedge(\alpha) = f^\wedge(\alpha)$ and $g^\vee(x) = f^\vee(x)$ for any $\alpha \in \Sigma(IS_1')$ and any $x \in U_2'$.*

In Proposition 3 we assume that $\|\alpha\|_{IS_2'} = \|\alpha\|_{IS_2} \cap U_2'$ for $\alpha \in \Sigma(IS_2')$. This proposition expresses that on domains accessible in communication (between two agents represented by information systems) established by a given infomorphism, the infomorphism is defined by selection functions on equivalence classes of formulas and objects, respectively. Such functions are bijections. From this fact it follows that, roughly speaking, infomorphisms of information systems can be realized by operations which we call constrained sums. The details are presented in the following sections.

However, observe that the communication established by infomorpshims do not assure the complete knowledge between communicating agents (information systems). In particular, formulas (concepts) from $\Sigma(IS_2) - f^\wedge(\Sigma(IS_1))$ are not in general definable in IS_1, only their approximations are known for IS_1 [11].

3 Sum of Information Systems and Approximation Spaces

3.1 Sum of Information Systems

In this section we introduce a sum of two information systems.

Definition 6. *Let $IS_1 = (U_1, A_1)$ and $IS_2 = (U_2, A_2)$ be information systems. These information systems can be combined into a single information system, denoted by $+(IS_1, IS_2)$, with the following properties:*

– *The objects of $+(IS_1, IS_2)$ consist of pairs (x_1, x_2) of objects from IS_1 and IS_2 i.e. $U = U_1 \times U_2$*
– *The attributes of $+(IS_1, IS_2)$ consist of the attributes of IS_1 and IS_2, except that if there are any attributes in common, then we make distinct copies, so as not to confuse them.*

Proposition 4. *There are infomorphisms $(f_k^\wedge, f_k^\vee) : IS_k \rightleftarrows +(IS_1, IS_2)$ for $k = 1, 2$ defined as follows:*

– *$f_k^\wedge(\alpha) = \alpha_{IS_k}$ (the IS_k-copy of α) for each $\alpha \in \Sigma(IS_k)$*
– *for each pair $(x_1, x_2) \in U$, $f_k^\vee((x_1, x_2)) = x_k$*

Given any information system IS_3 and infomorphisms $(f_{k,3}^\wedge, f_{k,3}^\vee) : IS_k \rightleftarrows IS_3$, there is a unique infomorphism $(f_{1+2,3}^\wedge, f_{1+2,3}^\vee) : +(IS_1, IS_2) \rightleftarrows IS_3$ such that in Figure 1 one can go either way around the triangles and get the same result.

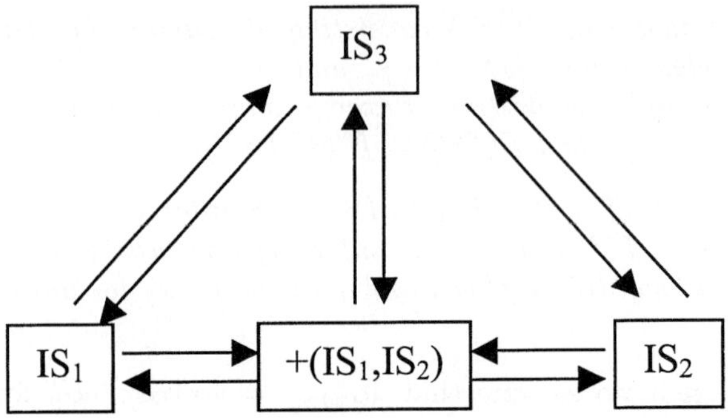

Fig. 1. Sum of Information Systems IS_1 and IS_2

Example 1. Let us consider a diagnostic agent testing failures of the space robotic arm. Such an agent should observe the arm and detect a failure if, e.g., some of its parts are in abnormal relative position. Assume, in our simple example that projections of some parts on a plane are observed and a failure is detected if projection of some parts that are triangles or rectangles are in some relation, e.g., the triangle is not included sufficiently inside of the rectangle. Hence, any considered object consists of parts: a triangle and a rectangle. Objects are perceived by some attributes expressing properties of parts and a relation (constraint) between them.

First, we construct an information system, called the sum of given information systems. Such system represents objects composed from parts without any constraint. It means that we consider as the universe of objects the Cartesian product of the universes of parts (Tables 1-3).

Let us consider three information systems $IS_{rectangle} = (U_{rectangle}, A_{rectangle})$, $IS_{triangle} = (U_{triangle}, A_{triangle})$, and $+(IS_{rectangle}, IS_{triangle}) = (U_{rectangle} \times U_{triangle}, \{(a,1),(b,1),(c,2)\})$ presented in Tables 1-3, respectively. Let $U_{rectangle}$ be a set of rectangles and $A_{rectangle} = \{a, b\}$, $V_a = [0, 300]$ and $V_b = \{yes, no\}$, where the value of a means a length in millimeters of horizontal side of rectangle and for any object $x \in U_{rectangle}$ $b(x) = yes$ if and only if x is a square.

Let $U_{triangle}$ be a set of triangles and $A_{triangle} = \{c\}$ and $V_c = \{t_1, t_2\}$, where $c(x) = t_1$ if and only if x is an acute–angled triangle and $c(x) = t_2$ if and only if x is a right–angled triangle.

We assume all values of attributes are made on a given projection plane. The results of measurements are represented in information systems. Tables 1-2 include only illustrative examples of the results of such measurements.

We assume that $(a,1)((x_i,y_j)) = a(x_i)$, $(b,1)((x_i,y_j)) = b(x_i)$ and $(c,2)((x_i,y_j)) = c(y_j)$, where $i = 1,\ldots,6$ and $j = 1,2$.

3.2 Sum of Approximation Spaces

In this section we present a simple construction of approximation space for the sum of given approximation spaces.

Table 1. Information System $IS_{rectangle}$ with Uncertainty Functions

$U_{rectangle}$	a	b	$I_a(\cdot)$	$I_b(\cdot)$	$I_{A_1}(\cdot)$
x_1	165	*yes*	$\{x_1, x_3, x_5, x_6\}$	$\{x_1, x_3\}$	$\{x_1, x_3\}$
x_2	175	*no*	$\{x_2, x_4, x_6\}$	$\{x_2, x_4, x_5, x_6\}$	$\{x_2, x_4, x_6\}$
x_3	160	*yes*	$\{x_1, x_3, x_5\}$	$\{x_1, x_3\}$	$\{x_1, x_3\}$
x_4	180	*no*	$\{x_2, x_4\}$	$\{x_2, x_4, x_5, x_6\}$	$\{x_2, x_4\}$
x_5	160	*no*	$\{x_1, x_3, x_5\}$	$\{x_2, x_4, x_5, x_6\}$	$\{x_5\}$
x_6	170	*no*	$\{x_1, x_2, x_6\}$	$\{x_2, x_4, x_5, x_6\}$	$\{x_2, x_6\}$

Table 2. Information System $IS_{triangle}$ with Uncertainty Function I_{A_2}

$U_{triangle}$	c	$I_{A_2}(\cdot)$
y_1	t_1	$\{y_1, y_3\}$
y_2	t_2	$\{y_2\}$
y_3	t_1	$\{y_1, y_3\}$

Let $AS_{\#_k} = (U_k, I_{\#_k}, \nu_{SRI})$ be an approximation space for information system IS_k, where $k = 1, 2$. We define an approximation space $+(AS_{\#_1}, AS_{\#_2})$ for information system $+(IS_1, IS_2)$ as follows:

1. the universe is equal to $U_1 \times U_2$,
2. $I_{\#_1,\#_2}((x_1, x_2)) = I_{\#_1}(x_1) \times I_{\#_2}(x_2)$,
3. the inclusion relation ν_{SRI} in $+(AS_{\#_1}, AS_{\#_2})$ is the standard inclusion function.

Proposition 5. *Let $X \subseteq U_1$ and $Y \subseteq U_2$. We have the following properties of approximations:*

$$LOW(+(AS_{\#_1}, AS_{\#_2}), X \times Y) = LOW(AS_{\#_1}, X) \times LOW(AS_{\#_2}, Y), \quad (3)$$
$$UPP(+(AS_{\#_1}, AS_{\#_2}), X \times Y) = UPP(AS_{\#_1}, X) \times UPP(AS_{\#_2}, Y). \quad (4)$$

Proof. We have $I_{\#_1,\#_2}((x_1, x_2)) \subseteq X \times Y$ iff $I_{\#_1}(x_1) \subseteq X$ and $I_{\#_2}(x_2) \subseteq Y$. Moreover, $I_{\#_1,\#_2}((x_1, x_2)) \cap (X \times Y) \neq \emptyset$ iff $I_{\#_1}(x_1) \cap X \neq \emptyset$ and $I_{\#_2}(x_2) \cap Y \neq \emptyset$.

Example 2. For information system $IS_{rectangle}$ we define an approximation space $AS_{A_1} = (U_{rectangle}, I_{A_1}, \nu_{SRI})$ such that $y \in I_a^5(x)$ if and only if $|a(x) - a(y)| \leq 5$. This means that rectangles x and y are similar with respect to the length of horizontal sides if and only if the difference of lengths is not greater than 5 millimeters. Let $y \in I_b(x)$ if and only if $b(x) = b(y)$ and $y \in I_{A_1}(x)$ if and only if $\forall_{c \in A_1} y \in I_c(x)$. Thus, we obtain uncertainty functions represented in the last three columns of Table 1. For information system $IS_{triangle}$ we define an approximation space as follows: $y \in I_{A_2}(x)$ if and only if $c(x) = c(y)$ (see the last column of Table 2). For $+(IS_{rectangle}, IS_{triangle})$ we obtain $I_{A_1,A_2}((x, y)) = I_{A_1}(x) \times I_{A_2}(y)$ (see the last column of Table 3).

Table 3. An Information System $+(IS_{rectangle}, IS_{triangle})$ with Uncertainty Function I_{A_1,A_2}

$U_{rectangle} \times U_{triangle}$	$(a,1)$	$(b,1)$	$(c,2)$	$I_{A_1,A_2}((\cdot,\cdot))$
(x_1, y_1)	165	*yes*	t_1	$\{x_1, x_3\} \times \{y_1, y_3\}$
(x_1, y_2)	165	*yes*	t_2	$\{x_1, x_3\} \times \{y_2\}$
(x_1, y_3)	165	*yes*	t_1	$\{x_1, x_3\} \times \{y_1, y_3\}$
(x_2, y_1)	175	*no*	t_1	$\{x_2, x_4, x_6\} \times \{y_1, y_3\}$
(x_2, y_2)	175	*no*	t_2	$\{x_2, x_4, x_6\} \times \{y_2\}$
(x_2, y_3)	175	*no*	t_1	$\{x_2, x_4, x_6\} \times \{y_1, y_3\}$
(x_3, y_1)	160	*yes*	t_1	$\{x_1, x_3\} \times \{y_1, y_3\}$
(x_3, y_2)	160	*yes*	t_2	$\{x_1, x_3\} \times \{y_2\}$
(x_3, y_3)	160	*yes*	t_1	$\{x_1, x_3\} \times \{y_1, y_3\}$
(x_4, y_1)	180	*no*	t_1	$\{x_2, x_4\} \times \{y_1, y_3\}$
(x_4, y_2)	180	*no*	t_2	$\{x_2, x_4\} \times \{y_2\}$
(x_4, y_3)	180	*no*	t_1	$\{x_2, x_4\} \times \{y_1, y_3\}$
(x_5, y_1)	160	*no*	t_1	$\{x_5\} \times \{y_1, y_3\}$
(x_5, y_2)	160	*no*	t_2	$\{x_5\} \times \{y_2\}$
(x_5, y_3)	160	*no*	t_1	$\{x_5\} \times \{y_1, y_3\}$
(x_6, y_1)	170	*no*	t_1	$\{x_2, x_6\} \times \{y_1, y_3\}$
(x_6, y_2)	170	*no*	t_2	$\{x_2, x_6\} \times \{y_2\}$
(x_6, y_3)	170	*no*	t_1	$\{x_2, x_6\} \times \{y_1, y_3\}$

4 Constrained Sums

In this section we consider operations on information systems that can be used in searching for hierarchical patterns. The operations are parameterized by constraints. Hence, in searching for relevant patterns one can search for relevant constraints and elementary information systems used to construct hierarchical patterns represented by constructed information systems.

4.1 Constrained Sums of Information Systems

In this section we consider a new operation on information systems often used in searching, e.g., for relevant patterns. This operation is more general than theta join operation used in databases [2]. We start from the definition in which the constraints are given explicitly.

Definition 7. *Let $IS_i = (U_i, A_i)$ for $i = 1, \ldots, k$ be information systems and let R be a k-ary constraint relation in $U_1 \times \ldots \times U_k$, i.e., $R \subseteq U_1 \times \ldots \times U_k$. These information systems can be combined into a single information system relatively to R, denoted by $+_R(IS_1, \ldots, IS_k)$, with the following properties:*

- *The objects of $+_R(IS_1, \ldots, IS_k)$ consist of k-tuples $(x_1, \ldots, x_k)$ of objects from R, i.e., all objects from $U_1 \times \ldots \times U_k$ satisfying the constraint R.*
- *The attributes of $+_R(IS_1, \ldots, IS_k)$ consist of the attributes of $IS_1, \ldots, IS_k$, except that if there are any attributes in common, then we make distinct copies, so as not to confuse them.*

Usually the constraints are defined by conditions expressed by Boolean combination of descriptors of attributes (see Section 2.2). It means that the constraints are built from expressions a *in* V, where a is an attribute and $V \subseteq V_a$, using propositional connectives $\wedge$, $\vee$, $\neg$. Observe, that in the constraint definition we use not only attributes of parts (i.e., from information systems $IS_1, \ldots, IS_k$) but also some other attributes specifying relation between parts. In our example (see Table 4), the constraint R_1 is defined as follows: *the triangle is sufficiently included in the rectangle.* Any row of this table represents an object (x_i, y_j) composed of the triangle y_j included sufficiently into the rectangle x_i.

Let us also note that constraints are defined using primitive (measurable) attributes different than those from information systems describing parts. This makes the constrained sum different from the theta join [2]. On the other hand one can consider that the constraints are defined in two steps. In the first step we extend the attributes for parts and in the second step we define the constraints using some relations on these new attributes.

Let us observe that the information system $+_R(IS_1, \ldots, IS_k)$ can be also described using an extension of the sum $+(IS_1, \ldots, IS_k)$ by adding a new binary attribute that is the characteristic function of the relation R and by taking a subsystem of the received system consisting of all objects having value one for this new attribute.

The constraints used to define the sum (with constraints) can be often specified by information systems. The objects of such systems are tuples consisting of objects of information systems that are arguments of the sum. The attributes describe relations between elements of tuples. One of the attribute is a characteristic function of the constraint relation (restricted to the universe of the information system). In this way we obtain a decision system with the decision attribute defined by the characteristic function of the constraint and conditional attributes are the remaining attributes of this system. From such decision table one can induce classifier for the constraint relation. Next, such classifier can be used to select tuples in the construction of constrained sum.

Example 3. Let us consider three information systems $IS_{rectangle} = (U_{rectangle}, A_{rectangle})$, $IS_{triangle} = (U_{triangle}, A_{triangle})$, $+_{R_1}(IS_{rectangle}, IS_{triangle})$, presented in Table 1, Table 2 and Table 4, respectively. We assume that $R_1 = \{(x_i, y_j) \in U_{rectangle} \times U_{triangle} : i = 1, \ldots, 6 \quad j = 1, 2\}$. We also assume that $a'((x_i, y_j)) = a(x_i)$, $b'((x_i, y_j)) = b(x_i)$ and $c'((x_i, y_j)) = c(y_j)$, where $i = 1, \ldots, 6$ and $j = 1, 2$.

The above examples are illustrating an idea of specifying constraints by examples. Table 4 can be used to construct a decision table partially specifying characteristic functions of the constraint. Such a decision table should be extended by adding relevant attributes related to the object parts making it possible to induce the high quality classifiers for the constraint relation. The classifier can be next used to filter composed pairs of objects that satisfy the constraint. This is important construction because the constraint specification usually cannot be defined directly in terms of measurable attributes. It can be specified, e.g., in

Table 4. Information System $+_{R_1}(IS_{rectangle}, IS_{triangle})$

$(U_{rectangle} \times U_{triangle}) \cap R_1$	a'	b'	c'
(x_1, y_1)	165	*yes*	t_1
(x_1, y_2)	165	*yes*	t_2
(x_2, y_1)	175	*no*	t_1
(x_2, y_2)	175	*no*	t_2
(x_3, y_1)	160	*yes*	t_1
(x_3, y_2)	160	*yes*	t_2
(x_4, y_1)	180	*no*	t_1
(x_4, y_2)	180	*no*	t_2
(x_5, y_1)	160	*no*	t_1
(x_5, y_2)	160	*no*	t_2
(x_6, y_1)	170	*no*	t_1
(x_6, y_2)	170	*no*	t_2

natural language. This is the reason that the process of inducing of the relevant classifiers for constraints can require hierarchical classifier construction [6].

The constructed constrained sum of information systems can consists of some incorrect objects. This is due to not proper filtering of objects by the classifier for constraints induced from data (with accuracy usually less than 100%). One should take this issue into account in constructing nets of information systems.

4.2 Constrained Sum of Approximation Spaces

Let $AS_{\#_i} = (U_i, I_{\#_i}, \nu_{SRI})$ be an approximation space for information system IS_i, where $i = 1, \ldots, k$ and let $R \subseteq U_1 \times \ldots \times U_k$ be a constraint relation. We define an approximation space $+_R(AS_{\#_1}, \ldots, AS_{\#_k})$ for $+_R(IS_1, \ldots, IS_k)$ as follows:

1. the universe is equal to R,
2. $I_{\#_1,\ldots,\#_k}((x_1, \ldots, x_k)) = (I_{\#_1}(x_1) \times \ldots \times I_{\#_k}(x_k)) \cap R$,
3. the inclusion relation ν_{SRI} in $+_R(AS_{\#_1}, \ldots, AS_{\#_k})$ is the standard inclusion function.

Proposition 6. *Let $X_i \subseteq U_i$ for $i = 1, \ldots, k$. We obtain the following properties of approximations:*

$$LOW(+_R(AS_{\#_1}, \ldots, AS_{\#_k}), X_1 \times \ldots \times X_k) = R \cap (LOW(AS_{\#_1}, X_1) \times \ldots \times LOW(AS_{\#_k}, X_k)) \quad (5)$$

$$UPP(+_R(AS_{\#_1}, \ldots, AS_{\#_k}), X_1 \times \ldots \times X_k) = R \cap (UPP(AS_{\#_1}, X_1) \times \ldots \times UPP(AS_{\#_k}, X_k)). \quad (6)$$

Conclusions

In many cases the constraint relations are soft relations. Hence, they can be defined as fuzzy or rough relations. Properties of sums of information systems constructed relatively to soft constraints will be the subject of our further study. Moreover, hierarchical construction of patterns and classifier based on the introduced foundations is another interesting topic to study toward approximate reasoning in distributed or multiagent systems.

Acknowledgements

The research has been supported by the grants 3 T11C 002 26 and 4 T11C 014 25 from Ministry of Scientific Research and Information Technology of the Republic of Poland.

References

1. Barwise, J., Seligman, J.: Information Flow: The Logic of Distributed Systems, Cambridge University Press Tracts in Theoretical Computer Science 44, 1997.
2. Garcia-Molina, H., Ullman, J.D., Widom, J.D.: Database Systems: The Complete Book, Prentice Hall, Upper Saddle River, New Jersey, 2002.
3. Kloesgen, W., Żytkow, J. (eds.): Handbook of Knowledge Discovery and Data Mining, Oxford University Press, Oxford, 2002.
4. Łukasiewicz, J.: Die logischen grundlagen der wahrscheinilchkeitsrechnung, Kraków 1913. In Borkowski, L., ed.: Jan Łukasiewicz - Selected Works. North Holland Publishing Company, Amstardam, London, Polish Scientific Publishers, Warsaw, 1970.
5. Pawlak, Z.: Rough Sets. Theoretical Aspects of Reasoning about Data, Kluwer Academic Publishers, Dordrecht, 1991.
6. Pal, S.K., Polkowski, L., Skowron, A. (Eds.): Rough-Neural Computing: Techniques for Computing with Words. Springer-Verlag, Berlin, 2004.
7. Polkowski, L., Skowron, A.: Towards adaptive calculus of granules. In: [14], 201–227.
8. Skowron, A., Stepaniuk, J.: Tolerance Approximation Spaces, Fundamenta Informaticae **27**, 1996, 245–253.
9. Skowron, A., Stepaniuk, J.: Information Granules: Towards Foundations of Granular Computing, International Journal of Intelligent Systems **16**(1), 2001, 57–86.
10. Skowron, A., Stepaniuk, J.: Information Granules and Rough-Neuro Computing. in [6], 43–84.
11. Skowron, A., Stepaniuk, J., Peters, J.F.: Rough Sets and Infomorphisms: Towards Approximation of Relations in Distributed Environments, Fundamenta Informaticae, **54**(1-2), 2003, 263–277.
12. Stepaniuk, J.: Knowledge Discovery by Application of Rough Set Models, (Eds.) L. Polkowski, S. Tsumoto, T.Y. Lin, Rough Set Methods and Applications. New Developments in Knowledge Discovery in Information Systems, Physica–Verlag, Heidelberg, 2000, 137–233.
13. Zadeh, L.A.: Toward a theory of fuzzy information granulation and its certainty in human reasoning and fuzzy logic. *Fuzzy Sets and Systems* **90** (1997) 111–127.
14. Zadeh, L.A., Kacprzyk, J. (eds.): *Computing with Words in Information/Intelligent Systems* **1-2**, Physica-Verlag, Heidelberg, 1999.
15. Zadeh, L.A.: A new direction in AI: Toward a computational theory of perceptions. *AI Magazine* **22**(1), 2001, 73–84.

Defeasible Deontic Control for Discrete Events Based on EVALPSN

Kazumi Nakamatsu[1], Hayato Komaba[2], Atsuyuki Suzuki[2], Chung-Lun Lie[3], and Sheng-Luen Chung[3]

[1] School of S.H.S.E., University of Hyogo, Himeji 670-0092 Japan
nakamatu@shse.u-hyogo.ac.jp
[2] Dept. Information, Shizuoka University, Hamamatsu 432-8011 Japan
{cs0038,suzuki}@cs.inf.shizuoka.ac.jp
[3] Dept. Electric and Electronics, NTUST, Taipei, 106 Taiwan
{M9007207,slchung}@mail.ntust.edu.tw

Abstract. We have developed an annotated logic program called an EVALPSN(Extended Vector Annotated Logic Program with Strong Negation), which can deal with defeasible deontic reasoning and some kinds of contradiction, and applied EVALPSN to automatic safety verification, traffic signal control, robot action control, etc.. Generally, discrete event control can be represented as deontic rules such as it is forbidden for both the cat and mouse to occupy the same room simultaneously, and must deal with contradiction to avoid unexpected system states. We show that such discrete event control can be easily formalized in EVALPSN. In this paper, we introduce the application of EVALPSN to discrete event control with taking a famous example Cat and Mouse.

Keywords: annotated logic program, paraconsistent logic, discrete event systems, defeasible deontic reasoning, EVALPSN.

1 Introduction

We have developed an annotated logic program called an EVALPSN in order to deal with not only deontic notion such as obligation, forbiddance and permission but also conflict or contradiction in a framework of paraconsistent logic programming, and shown that EVALPSN can deal with defeasible deontic reasoning in [2, 3]. EVALPSN has a feature to be able to deal with various kinds of contradiction such as contradiction between forbiddance and permission as knowledge, and make a decision by defeasible reasoning, although usual paraconsistent logic programs cannot deal with such deontic contradiction and decision-making. The feature has been applied to automated safety verification [5], and some kinds of control such as robot action and traffic signal controls [4, 6].

In this paper, we introduce that EVALPSN can be easily applied to the control of discrete event systems [9] with taking a discrete event contol example called *Cat and Mouse*, and show how to formalize the Cat and Mouse control in EVALPSN. In addition, we have shown that EVALPSN can be implemented

S. Tsumoto et al. (Eds.): RSCTC 2004, LNAI 3066, pp. 310–315, 2004.

on a microchip as electronic circuits, which proves that EVALPSN defeasible deontic control is suitable for real-time control [7].

This paper is organized as follows : first, we introduce the basic ideas of EVALPSN defeasible deontic control; next, we take the Cat and Mouse example for discrete event control and describe how to formalize its control in EVALPSN in details; last, we show some examples for the Cat and Mouse EVALPSN control.

2 EVALPSN Control for Cat and Mouse

Basically, EVALPSN action control is performed in logic programming with deontic notions, and its outline can be described as the following three steps :

1 norms such as policies, regulations, properties etc. for system control are formalized in EVALPSN;
2 the environment information such as sensor values of the object system to be controlled is input to the EVALPSN control; then, forbiddance or permission for system actions or events are derived;
3 actions that must be performed at the next step are derived based on the defeasible reasoning between permission and forbiddance derived in the present step.

Cat and Mouse Example [9]. A cat and a mouse are placed in the maze shown in **Fig. 1**. Each doorway in the maze is either for the exclusive use of the cat, or for the exclusive use of the mouse, and must be traversed in the direction indicated. the cat and mouse are somewhat whimsical but could represent, for example, autonomous vehicles in an automated factory. It is assumed that each doorway, with the exception of c_7, can be opened or closed as required in order to control the movement of the cat and the mouse. The objective is to find the control schema which permits the cat and the mouse the greatest possible freedom of movement but which also guarantees that

a) the cat and the mouse never occupy the same room simultaneously, and
b) it is always possible for the cat and the mouse to return to the initial state, i.e., the state in which the cat is in room 2, and the mouse in the room 4.

In order to formalize the control for the Cat and Mouse in EVALPSN, we consider two control rules corresponding to the constrained properties **a)** and **b)**. Suppose that there are three rooms i, j and k, and doorways $d_n (1 \leq n \leq 4)$ in **Fig. 2**. Then, the properties **a)** and **b)** can be interpreted as the following general control **Rules 1** and **2**.

Rule 1: if an animal *ani* is in the room i and its enemy animal *eani* is in the room j at the time t, then both the animals *ani* and its enemy animal *eani* are strictly forbidden to move into each enemy's room.

Rule 2: if an animal *ani* is in the room i and its enemy animal *eani* is in the room k at the time t; if the animal *ani* moves into the room j and a deadlocked state occurs, the animal *ani* is forbidden to move into the room j; on the other hand, if the animal *eani* does so, the animal *eani* is also forbidden from that.

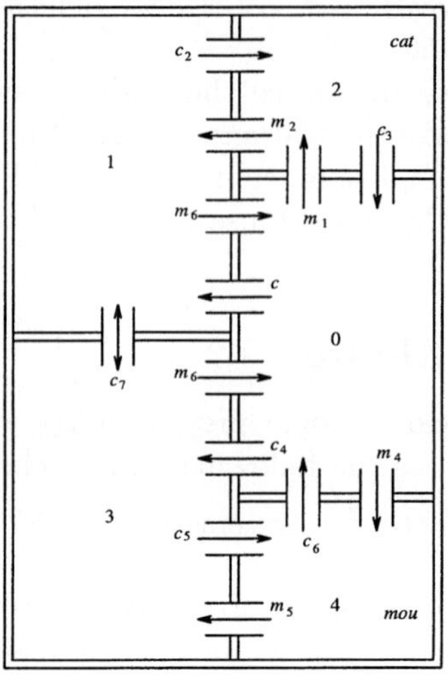

Fig. 1. Cat and Mouse Maze

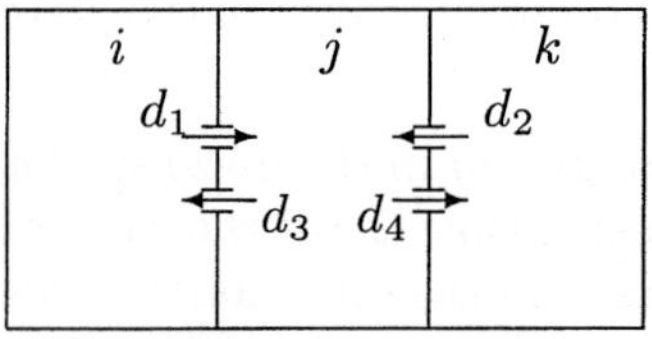

Fig. 2. Rooms

These general rules can be easily translated into EVALPSN, however, we have to consider the deadlock state of the example and avoid it. Suppose that the cat is in the room 0 and the mouse is in the room 3. As the doorway c_7 for the cat cannot be controlled, all the doorways c_1,c_4, and m_6 must be closed according to the property **a)**. Then, there is no available doorway for both the cat and the mouse to return back to their initial rooms, and the property **b)** cannot be kept. In order to avoid such a deadlocked state, we apply the EVALPSN defeasible deontic reasoning to the control. Roughly speaking, defeasible reasoning is a reasoning based on defeasible rules and superiority relations between them [8]. We formalize the Cat and Mouse control to avoid the deadlock state by the following two defeasible rules and the superiority relation, d-rule 1 > d-rule 2. The d-rule 1 represents that if the cat is in the room 0, it is defeasibly allowed to enter the room 3, and the d-rule 2 represents that if the mouse is in the room 4, it is also defeasibly allowed to enter the room 3. The superiority relation, d-rule 1 > d-rule 2 means that if both the antecedents of the d-

$$\text{d-rule 1} \quad occupy(cat, 0, t) \Rightarrow \neg \bigcirc \neg occupy(cat, 3, t),$$

$$\text{d-rule 2} \quad occupy(mou, 4, t) \Rightarrow \neg \bigcirc \neg occupy(mou, 3, t).$$

rules 1 and 2 are satisfied, only the consequent of the d-rule 1 can be derived, and if only the antecedent of the d-rule 2 is satisfied, the consequent of the d-rule 2 can be derived.

In order to formalize the Cat and Mouse control in EVALPSN, we introduce some predicates and some sets of annotations, then the rules 1 and 2 are translated into EVALPSN.

$occu(i,t)$ represents that the room i is occupied by an animal at the time t, and the cat and the mouse are represented by conflicting annotations `cat` and `mou` for the predicate $occu(i,t)$, respectively; therefore, we have an EVALPSN literal $occu(i,t):[\mathtt{ani},\mu]$, providing $\mathtt{ani} \in \{\mathtt{cat},\mathtt{mou}\}$ and $\mu \in \{\alpha,\beta,\gamma\}$;

$door(d_m,t)$ represents that the doorway d_m is controlled to be in a state at the time t, and the states "opened" and "closed" of doorways are also represented by conflicting annotations `op` and `cl` for the predicate $door(d_m,t)$, respectively; therefore, we have an EVALPSN literal $door(d_m,t):[\mathtt{state},\mu]$, providing $\mathtt{state} \in \{\mathtt{op},\mathtt{cl}\}$ and $\mu \in \{\alpha,\beta,\gamma\}$.

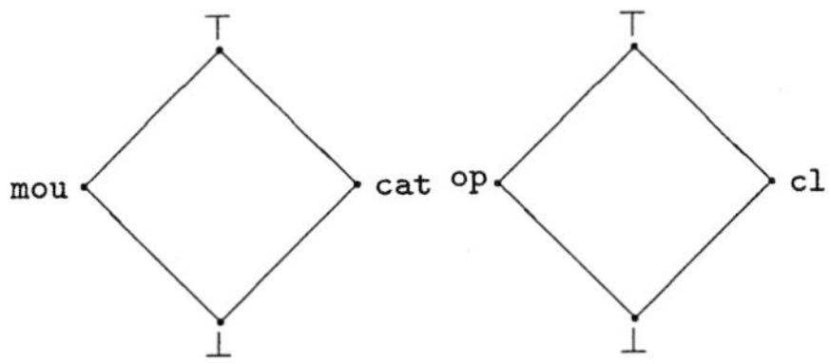

Fig. 3. Lattices for Cat and Mouse

In EVALPSN control for the Cat and Mouse, we use the complete lattices $\mathcal{T}_v = \{\bot, \mathtt{cat}, \mathtt{mou}, \top\}$ or $\mathcal{T}_v = \{\bot, \mathtt{op}, \mathtt{cl}, \top\}$ of annotations, which are shown in **Fig. 3**, and the epistemic negation $\neg_1$ for the sets of annotations is defined as : $\neg_1[\mathtt{cat}, \mu] = [\mathtt{mou}, \mu]$, $\neg_1[\mathtt{mou}, \mu] = [\mathtt{cat}, \mu]$, $\neg_1[\mathtt{op}, \mu] = [\mathtt{cl}, \mu]$, $\neg_1[\mathtt{cl}, \mu] = [\mathtt{op}, \mu]$. For example, an literal $occu(i,t) : [\mathtt{cat}, \beta]$ represents both the obligation for the cat to occupy the room i and the forbiddance for the mouse ($\neg_1\mathtt{cat}$) from occupying the room i. Then the **Rule 1** can be formalized in the following two EVALPSN clauses in conflict :

$$occu(i,t):[\mathtt{ani},\alpha] \wedge occu(j,t):[\neg_1\mathtt{ani},\alpha] \rightarrow occu(j,t):[\neg_1\mathtt{ani},\beta],$$
$$occu(i,t):[\mathtt{ani},\alpha] \wedge occu(j,t):[\neg_1\mathtt{ani},\alpha] \rightarrow occu(i,t):[\mathtt{ani},\beta].$$

where $\mathtt{ani} \in \{\mathtt{cat}, \mathtt{mou}\}$. Here, we take the exceptional doorway control such that the doorway c_7 cannot be controlled into account, i.e., the rooms 1 and 3 can be viewed as the same room for the cat. Therefore, for example, if the cat is in the room 1, the mouse is forbidden to move into the room 3. In addition, unreachable states such that the cat is in the room 2 and the mouse is in the room 1, and deadlocked states such that the cat is in the room 0 and the mouse is in the room 3 do not have to be considered. Then we have :

$$occu(2,t):[\mathtt{cat},\alpha] \wedge occu(0,t):[\mathtt{mou},\alpha] \rightarrow occu(0,t):[\mathtt{mou},\beta], \quad (1)$$
$$occu(2,t):[\mathtt{cat},\alpha] \wedge occu(0,t):[\mathtt{mou},\alpha] \rightarrow occu(2,t):[\mathtt{cat},\beta], \quad (2)$$
$$occu(1,t):[\mathtt{cat},\alpha] \wedge occu(4,t):[\mathtt{mou},\alpha] \rightarrow occu(3,t):[\mathtt{cat},\beta], \quad (3)$$
$$occu(3,t):[\mathtt{cat},\alpha] \wedge occu(4,t):[\mathtt{mou},\alpha] \rightarrow occu(4,t):[\mathtt{mou},\beta], \quad (4)$$
$$occu(3,t):[\mathtt{cat},\alpha] \wedge occu(4,t):[\mathtt{mou},\alpha] \rightarrow occu(3,t):[\mathtt{cat},\beta]. \quad (5)$$

On the other hands, if the state such that an animal *ani* is in the room i and its enemy animal *eani* is in the room j is a deadlocked state, the **Rule 2** can be formalized as :

$$occu(i,t):[\mathtt{ani},\alpha] \wedge occu(k,t):[\neg_1\mathtt{ani},\alpha] \rightarrow occu(j,t):[\mathtt{ani},\beta],$$

where $\mathtt{ani} \in \{\mathtt{cat}, \mathtt{mou}\}$. Therefore, we have two EVALPSN clauses :

$$occu(2,t):[\mathtt{cat},\alpha] \wedge occu(3,t):[\mathtt{mou},\alpha] \rightarrow occu(0,t):[\mathtt{mou},\beta], \quad (6)$$
$$occu(0,t):[\mathtt{cat},\alpha] \wedge occu(4,t):[\mathtt{mou},\alpha] \rightarrow occu(3,t):[\mathtt{cat},\beta]. \quad (7)$$

Although some EVALPSN clauses to derive forbiddance have already been provided, we need some more EVALPSN clauses to control the doorways' states ("opened" or "closed") directly according to the previously derived forbiddance as follows : if there is forbiddance from an animal occupying a room at the time t, the corresponding doorways must be closed, otherwise, they must be opened at the time $t+1$ (the next step). Therefore, the following EVALPSN clauses to control the doorways' states are needed.

$$occu(0,t):[\texttt{mou},\beta] \rightarrow door(c_3,t+1):[\texttt{cl},\beta], \tag{8}$$
$$occu(2,t):[\texttt{cat},\beta] \rightarrow door(m_1,t+1):[\texttt{cl},\beta], \tag{9}$$
$$occu(3,t):[\texttt{cat},\beta] \rightarrow door(m_5,t+1):[\texttt{cl},\beta], \tag{10}$$
$$occu(4,t):[\texttt{mou},\beta] \rightarrow door(c_5,t+1):[\texttt{cl},\beta], \tag{11}$$
$$\sim occu(0,t):[\texttt{mou},\beta] \rightarrow door(c_3,t+1):[\texttt{op},\beta], \tag{12}$$
$$\sim occu(2,t):[\texttt{cat},\beta] \rightarrow door(m_1,t+1):[\texttt{op},\beta], \tag{13}$$
$$\sim occu(3,t):[\texttt{cat},\beta] \rightarrow door(m_5,t+1):[\texttt{op},\beta], \tag{14}$$
$$\sim occu(4,t):[\texttt{mou},\beta] \rightarrow door(c_5,t+1):[\texttt{op},\beta]. \tag{15}$$

EVALPSN Control Examples

Suppose that the cat is in the room 2 and the mouse is in the room 4, and all the doorways are opened initially. Then, each doorway's state is controlled by the EVALPSN as follows :

1. if the cat moves first from its initial room 2 into the room 0; we have the forbiddance from the mouse moving into the room 3, only the doorway m_5 must be controlled to be closed by the clause (7), and all the other doorways c_3, m_1 and c_5 must be controlled to be opened by the clauses (12), (13) and (15); then, the mouse is isolated in the room 4;
2. if the cat moves from the room 0 into the room 3; we have the forbiddance from both the cat moving into the room 4 and the mouse moving into the room 3 by the clauses (4) and (5), both the doorways c_5 and m_5 must be controlled to be closed by the clauses (10) and (11), and the doorways c_3 and m_1 must be controlled to be opened by the clauses (12) and (13); then the mouse is still isolated in the room 4;
3. if the cat moves from the room 3 into the room 1; we have the forbiddance from the mouse moving into the room 3 by the clause (3), only the doorway m_5 must be controlled to be closed by the clause (10), and all the other doorways c_3, m_1 and c_5 must be controlled to be opened by the clauses (12), (13) and (14); then the mouse is still isolated in the room 4;
4. if the cat returns from the room 1 to the room 2; since we have forbiddance from neither the cat moving into the room 0 nor the mouse moving into the room 3, all the doorways c_3, m_1, m_5 and c_5 must be controlled to be opened by the clauses (12), (13), (14) and (15); then both the cat and the mouse are free to move;
5. on the other hand, if the mouse moves first from the room 4 into the room 3; we have the forbiddance from the cat moving into the room 0 by the clause (6), the doorway c_3 must be controlled to be closed by the clause (8), and all the other doorways m_1, m_5 and c_5 must be controlled to be opened by the clauses (13), (14) and (15); then the cat is isolated in the room 2;
6. if the mouse moves from room 3 into the room 0; we have the forbiddance from the cat moving into the room 0 by the clause (1), we also have the

forbiddance from the mouse moving into the room 2 by the clause (2), the doorways c_3 and m_1 must be controlled to be closed by the clauses (8) and (9), and both the doorways m_5 and c_5 must be controlled to be opened by the clauses (14) and (15); then, the cat is still isolated in the room 2;

3 Conclusion and Future Work

In this paper, we have introduced that EVALPSN defeasible deontic control can be applied to discrete event control by taking the Cat and Mouse as an example. Generally, discrete event control such as pipeline control in chemical plants is required to have temporal reasoning ability. EVALPSN can be easily extended to be able to deal with temporal reasoning by extending its annotations.

References

1. Nakamatsu, K., Abe, J.M., and Suzuki, A., "Defeasible Reasoning Between Conflicting Agents Based on VALPSN", *Proc. AAAI Workshop Agents' Conflicts*, pp.20–27. AAAI Press, 1999.
2. Nakamatsu, K., Abe, J.M., and Suzuki, A., "A Defeasible Deontic Reasoning System Based on Annotated Logic Programming", *Computing Anticipatory Systems, CASYS2000*, AIP Conference Proceedings Vol.573, pp.609–620. American Institute of Physics, 2001.
3. Nakamatsu, K., Abe, J.M., and Suzuki, A., "Annotated Semantics for Defeasible Deontic Reasoning", *Proc. the 2nd RSCTC*, LNAI Vol.2005, pp.432–440, Springer-Verlag, 2001.
4. Nakamatsu, K., Abe, J.M., and Suzuki, A., "Defeasible Deontic Robot Control Based on Extended Vector Annotated Logic Programming", *Computing Anticipatory Systems, CASYS2001*, AIP Conference Proceedings Vol.627, pp.490–500, American Institute of Physics, 2002.
5. Nakamatsu, K., Abe, J.M., and Suzuki, A., "A Railway Interlocking Safety Verification System Based on Abductive Paraconsistent Logic Programming", *Soft Computing Systems*, Frontiers in AI Applications, Vol.87, pp.775–784, IOS Press, 2002.
6. Nakamatsu, K., Seno, T., Abe, J.M., and Suzuki, A., "Intelligent Real-time Traffic Signal Control Based on a Paraconsistent Logic Program EVALP", *Proc. RSFDGrC2003*, LNCS Vol.2639, pp.719–723. Springer-Verlag, 2003.
7. Nakamatsu, K., Mita, Y., Shibata, T., and Abe, J.M., "Defeasible Deontic Action Control Based on Paraconsistent Logic Program and its Hardware Implementation". *Proc. CIMCA2003* (CD-ROM), 2003.
8. Nute, D.(ed.) *Defeasible Deontic Reasoning*, Synthese Library, Vol.263, Kluwer Academic Publishers, 1997.
9. Ramadge, J.G.P. and Wonham, W.M., "The Control of Discrete Event Systems", Proc. IEEE, Vol.77, No.1, pp.81-98, 1989.

Rough Set Based Fuzzy Modeling by Occupancy Degree and Optimal Partition of Projection

Chang-Woo Park[1], Young-Wan Cho[2], Jun-Hyuk Choi[1], and Ha-Gyeong Sung[1]

[1] Precision Machinery Research Center, Korea Electronics Technology Institute
203-103 B/D 192,Yakdae-Dong, Wonmi-Gu, Puchon-Si, Kyunggi-Do, 420-140, Korea
drcwpark@keti.re.kr

[2] Dept. of Electrical and Electronic Eng., Yonsei Univ.
ywcho@yeics.yonsei.ac.kr

Abstract. The rough set theory suggested by Pawlak has a property that it can represent the degree of consistency between condition and decision attributes of data pairs which don't have linguistic information. In this paper, by using this ability of rough set theory, we define a measure called occupancy degree which can represent a consistency degree of premise and consequent variables in fuzzy rules describing experimental data pairs. We also propose a method by which we partition the projected data on input space and find an optimal fuzzy rule table and membership functions of input and output variables from data without preliminary linguistic information.

1 Introduction

Up to now, a number of studies on fuzzy modeling have been proposed during last decades. These are approaches using fuzzy clustering method [1][2], TSK model approaches in which output variables of each rule, that is, fuzzy partitioned subspace are expressed by linear combination of input variables [3][4], optimal parameter searching approaches using learning ability of Neural Network and/or solution searching ability of Genetic Algorithm [5][6]. Approaches using pattern recognition are sensitive to clustering algorithm. TSK model has its merit in describing a slight nonlinear system but it has difficulties in that its identification algorithm becomes very complex and its performance is deteriorated for heavy nonlinear system.

The rough set theory proposed by Pawlak [7][8] has a property that it can express the consistency between condition and decision attributes of data by numerical value. Some techniques of rough set theory are suitable for quantifying the consistency of assigned informations when data are described in terms of condition and decision attributes. In this paper, we define a measure to represent the consistency of linguistic expressions in fuzzy rules describing given data pairs. And we propose a method to generate optimal fuzzy rules and to determine membership functions of linguistic variables by partitioning the projection of classified output into input space. The validity of proposed method is examined by modeling input-output data generated by arbitrary defined membership functions and fuzzy rules.

S. Tsumoto et al. (Eds.): RSCTC 2004, LNAI 3066, pp. 316–326, 2004.

2 Rough Set [7]

The rough set theory proposed by Pawlak [8] is a mathematical theory dealing with uncertainty in data. Rough sets relies on the notion of lower and upper approximation of a set and it is applied to rough fuzzy control, modeling, system identification and discovery of discussion rules from experimental data.

2.1 The Lower Approximation and Upper Approximation

The rough set theory is founded on the assumption that with every object of the universe of discourse we associate some information set. When data are given as information table like table1, objects(data) of the first column are expressed in terms of informations of the first low called attributes to the extent of entry called attribute-values. Suppose that we are given the universe set U containing all objects, set of attributes A and attribute-values V_a associated with each attribute $a \in A$. A binary relation $I(B)$ on U called an indiscernibility relation is defined for all subset B of A as follows:

$xI(B)y$ if and only if $a(x) = a(y)$ for every $a \in B$, where $a(x)$ denotes the value V_a of attribute a for element x.

The indiscernibility relation $I(B)$ partition the universe set U into equivalence classes, which contain all objects that are indiscernible in terms of attributes set B. The family of all equivalence classes is denoted by $U / I(B)$ or U / B and an equivalence class containing x is denoted by $B(x)$. If x and y are element of $I(B)$, it is said that x and y are B - indiscernible, which imply that x and y are indiscernible in terms of attributes B. The B -lower and B -upper approximation is defined for any subset X of the universe U in order to express the set X with attribute set B.

$B_*(X)$ and $B^*(X)$ which are defined by following two operations for any subset X of the universe U are called B - lower and B -upper approximation of X, respectively.

$$B_*(X) = \{x \in U / B(x) \subseteq X\}$$
$$B^*(X) = \{x \in U / B(x) \cap X \neq \phi\}$$

The set $BR_B(X) = B^*(X) - B_*(X)$ is referred to as the B -boundary region of X. This boundary region imply how exactly the set X is represented with respect to attribute set B. Thus, if $BR_B(X) = \phi$, then X is said to be crisp with respect to B and if $BR_B(X) \neq \phi$, then X is said to be rough. As we know by above definition, it is necessary to note that the definition of rough set is not only about X itself but also related with attribute set B.

2.2 Partial Dependency and Consistency Measure

It is important in data analysis to find out dependency between attributes. We have to discover dependency between premise and consequent attributes of data in order to generate fuzzy rules. Using a measure k called partial dependency, we can express the dependency of consequent attributes on premise attributes.

Table 1. Information table expressed with linguistic variables.

Attribute object	error	Error derivative	output	attribute object	error	error derivative	output
d1	NB	NB	PB	d11	NB	NB	PS
d2	NS	NB	PB	d12	NS	NB	PB
d3	NS	NS	PS	d13	NB	ZE	ZE
d4	NB	NS	PS	d14	ZE	ZE	ZE
d5	NB	NB	PB	d15	ZE	PS	NS
d6	NB	NS	PB	d16	PS	ZE	NS
d7	NS	ZE	PS	d17	ZE	PB	NS
d8	NB	ZE	PS	d18	ZE	PS	NS
d9	NS	ZE	PS	d19	PS	PS	NB
d10	NS	NS	PS	d20	PB	PB	NB

NB : Negative Big, NS : Negative Small, ZE : Zero, PS : Positive Small, PB : Positive Big

Let D and C be subsets of A. We say that D depends in degree k on C, if $k = \frac{|POS_C(D)|}{|U|}$, where $POS_C(D) = \underset{X \in U/I(D)}{U} C_*(X)$

The expression $POS_C(D)$, called a positive region of the partition $U/I(D)$ with respect to C, is the set of all element of U that can be uniquely classified to blocks of the partition $U/I(D)$, by means of C. Thus the coefficient k express the ratio of all elements of the universe, which can be properly classified to blocks of the partition $U/I(D)$, employing attributes C. Since the partial dependency k represents the certainty that if an object of U satisfies the attributes C, then the object satisfies the attribute D, it is properly used to represent the consistency between premise and consequent variables of fuzzy rules.

In the table1, error and error derivative correspond to condition attribute C and output corresponds to decision attribute D. Each row of the table shows the relation between input and output linguistic variables. In the rows corresponding to data d2, d12, same premise (NS, NB) determines same consequent PB, whereas d1, d5, d11 have same premise (NB, NB) but different consequent value. The former correspondences are said to be consistent and the latter are said to be inconsistent. In order to deal with the consistency of information values, consistency measure $\gamma(C,D)$ is defined as follows: $\gamma(C,D) = \frac{|POS_C(D)|}{|U|}$, where C is a set of condition attributes and D is a set of decision attributes. As we know in the above definition, the consistency measure represents the number of consistent objects, in terms of describing informations, to all objects in a decision table.

3 Generation of Fuzzy Rules and Membership Functions

To obtain a fuzzy model describing given data, we have to go through the process of defining linguistic variables and making a rule table with defined linguistic variables. The rule table have to consist with the relation between input and output values of given data. As we know in the table1, the fact that same premise (NB, NB) have different consequent value (PB, PS) implies the inconsistency of assigned linguistic variables. Thus, in order to increase consistency in fuzzy rules, we have to modify linguistic variables and/or fuzzy rules.

In this paper, we define and use a modified consistency measure called occupancy degree, which represents the consistency of generated rules. We also propose a method by which fuzzy rules are generated and membership functions are defined so as to increase the occupancy degree. Suppose that input space(condition attributes) $X \times Y$ is partitioned into crisp rectangular segments as eq.(1) and eq.(2). The output space(decision attribute) Z is also divided by same manner as input space.

$$X_i \cap X_j = \phi, \qquad i \neq j \tag{1-1}$$

$$X_1 \cup X_2 \cup \cdots \cup X_l = X \tag{1-2}$$

$$X_i = \{x / x_{i-1} \leq x < x_i\}, \quad (i = 1,2,,\cdots,l, \quad x_0 = x_{\min}, \quad x_l = x_{\max}) \tag{1-3}$$

$$Y_i \cap Y_j = \phi, \qquad i \neq j \tag{2-1}$$

$$Y_1 \cup Y_2 \cup \cdots \cup Y_m = Y \tag{2-2}$$

$$Y_j = \{y / y_{j-1} \leq y < y_j\}, \quad (j = 1,2,,\cdots,m, \quad y_0 = y_{\min}, \quad y_m = y_{\max}) \tag{2-3}$$

where, $x_{\min}$, $y_{\min}$, $x_{\max}$, $y_{\max}$ are minimum and maximum value of x, y, respectively.

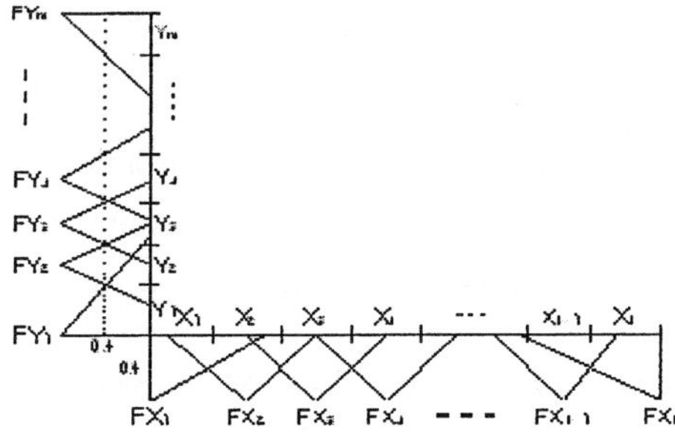

Fig. 1. Fuzzy partition of input variable.

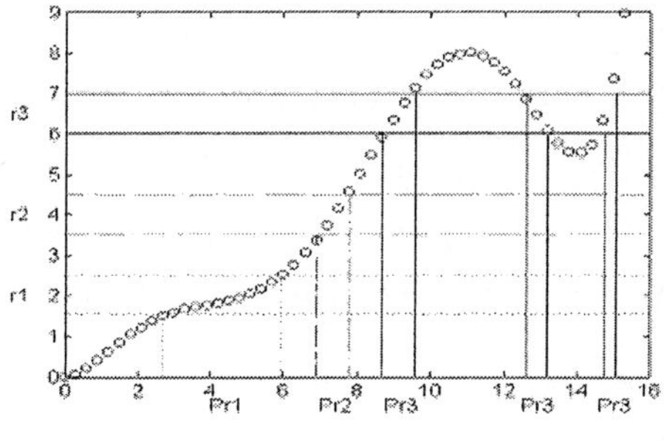

Fig. 2. Variation of data distribution with respect to output variable.

We use triangle type membership functions defined by eq.(3) for fuzzy sets FX_i, FY_j, FZ_k, which correspond to crisp set X_i, Y_j, Z_k, respectively.

$$\mu_{FX_i}(\frac{x_{i-1}+x_i}{2})=1, \qquad \mu_{FX_i}(x_{i-1})=\mu_{FX_i}(x_i)=0.4 \tag{3-1}$$

$$\mu_{FY_j}(\frac{y_{j-1}+y_j}{2})=1, \qquad \mu_{FY_j}(y_{j-1})=\mu_{FY_j}(y_j)=0.4 \tag{3-2}$$

$$\mu_{FZ_k}(\frac{z_{k-1}+z_k}{2})=1, \qquad \mu_{FZ_k}(z_{k-1})=\mu_{FZ_k}(z_k)=0.4 \tag{3-3}$$

If input and output space have been fuzzy partitioned, generating fuzzy rules is the same meaning as determining a following mapping f.

$$f: FX \times FY \rightarrow FZ$$

where,

$$FX=\{FX_1, FX_2, \cdots, FX_l\} \tag{4}$$
$$FY=\{FY_1, FY_2, \cdots, FY_m\}$$
$$FZ=\{FZ_1, FZ_2, \cdots, FZ_n\}$$

When we determine the mapping f, we should note the fact that it is not desirable that determined mapping conflicts with the expression of data by linguistic variable pairs assigned to the data. For example, in table1, if the $NB \times NB$ is mapped into PS, it means that " *If error is NB and error derivative is NB, then output is PS* ". This rule conflicts with objects d1, d5, because their output attribute values are " PB ". Thus, in order to consider the consistency of mapping f with linguistic variable pairs assigned to data, we define occupancy degree of decision(consequent) attribute Z_k with respect to condition(premise) attributes pair $X_i \times Y_j$ as follows:

$$O_{X_i \times Y_j}(Z_k)=\frac{|Z_k \cap X_i \times Y_j|}{|X_i \times Y_j|} \tag{5}$$

where, Z_k is an equivalence class divided by consequent attribute Z, i.e., $Z_k \in U/I(Z)$. $|X_i \times Y_j|$ denotes the number of data included in the subspace $X_i \times Y_j$ and $|X|$ denotes the cardinality of set X. As we know in eq.(5), the occupancy degree expresses the ratio of objects which have consequent variable Z_k, to all objects included in the premise subspace $X_i \times Y_j$. In the table1, for example, if $X_i = NB$, $Y_j = NB$ and $Z_k = PB$, the occupancy degree of PB with respect to $NB \times NB$ is $O_{NB \times NB}(PB)=\frac{2}{3}$, and that of PS is $O_{NB \times NB}(PB)=\frac{1}{3}$. More examples such as $O_{NB \times NB}(PB)=1$, $O_{NB \times NB}(PB)=\frac{1}{2}$ explain that the occupancy degree has meaning of how consistently data, which have same premise variables, are corresponded to consequent variables.

The optimal fuzzy rule table can be obtained by determination of optimal mapping f in eq.(4). We construct the mapping with eq.(6), which has the meaning that each partitioned subspace of premise variables is assigned to a consequent variable that has maximum occupancy degree.

$$f(X_i, Y_j) = Z_k \tag{6}$$

where, $\overset{\max}{Z_d \in U/I(D)}\ occup_{X_i \times Y_j}(Z_d) = Z_k$

This mapping f is varied with partition of input space, which is determined by $x_i, y_j\ (i = 0,1,\cdots,l,\quad j = 0,1,\cdots,m)$ in eq.(1-3) and eq.(2-3). We propose an optimal partition method to divide input space into product subspaces so that the consistency of correspondence between premise and consequent variables is maximized.

A fuzzy model is determined by organic combination of linguistic variables and describing rules. The membership functions of linguistic variables are obtained by fuzzy partition of input and output variables. Since fuzzy partition of input and output variables means formation of basic units of modeling space, it is desirable that we perform the partition by such a way that given data are distributed evenly in each partitioned space. Clustering methods as fuzzy C means algorithm have been used for a way of partitioning. But, since these methods use only distance between data, they have difficulties in grasping the structure of data distribution. As the TSK model approaches [7][8], in which input space is divided by considering the linearity of model, the fuzzy partition of input and output space is desirable to be obtained so that we can easily identify the model corresponding to divided subspace, by grasping the structure of data distribution. Since fuzzy partition of input variables is dependent on that of output variable, it is also desirable that fuzzy partition of input space, that is, identification of premise structure in a fuzzy model is obtained simultaneously together with that of output space. Unfortunately, there is no reasonable method to identify the premise and consequent structure simultaneously as far as we know. In this paper, we propose a method to divide the consequent variable by considering the relation with premise variables. If given data are assumed to be uniformly distributed in the input space, we can know from fig.2 that the number of data having consequent values included in increment Δz has implicit informations about data distribution. That is, the smaller number of data exist in the region(r2) where output varies drastically with respect to input, than in the region(r1) of slowly variation. Also, a large number of heavy nonlinear system have such characteristic that input regions(Pr3) of data having similar output values(r3) lie scattered. In order to reflect these facts, we consider the variation of data distribution with respect to output variable by eq.(7) and eq.(8), and we accomplish fuzzy partition of output variable based on these variations in this paper. Fig.5 shows the results of eq.(7) and eq.(8) for data given in fig.4.

$$s(z) = | I_z | \tag{7}$$

where, I_z is set of data pairs (x_i , y_i , z_i) which have output values included in the region $z_{\min} \le z_i \le z$ and $| I_z |$ denotes the cardinality of set I_z .

$$d(z)=\frac{1}{n}\sum_{i=1}^{n}\{(x_i-\bar{x})^2+(y_i-\bar{y})^2\}^{\frac{1}{2}} \tag{8}$$

where, $\bar{x}=\frac{1}{n}\sum_{i=1}^{n}x_i$, $\bar{y}=\frac{1}{n}\sum_{i=1}^{n}y_i$, $n=|I_z|$ and x_i , y_i are input variable values of data $(x_i, y_i, z_i)\in I_z$.

We can know from the fig.5 that sudden change of variation (e.g. at point -0.8, -0.1, 0.9) in graph(a) means that increasing or decreasing tendency of data distribution changes abruptly or some changes in data distribution formation are happened at these points. And sudden change in graph(b)(e.g. -0.8, -0.1, 0.4, 0.6, 0.9) means that data having same output value start to be scattered in input space. Thus, we can accomplish fuzzy partition of consequent variable by considering variations in graph(a) and (b). After classifying data with respect to already partitioned consequent variables, we project the classified data on input space as fig.3. Then, we can detect a skeleton of global data distribution in the input space from classified projection. In order to obtain a fuzzy model for given data pairs from the classified projection, we determine premise fuzzy variables by partitioning input variables and make each product space of premise fuzzy variables correspond into a consequent fuzzy variable.

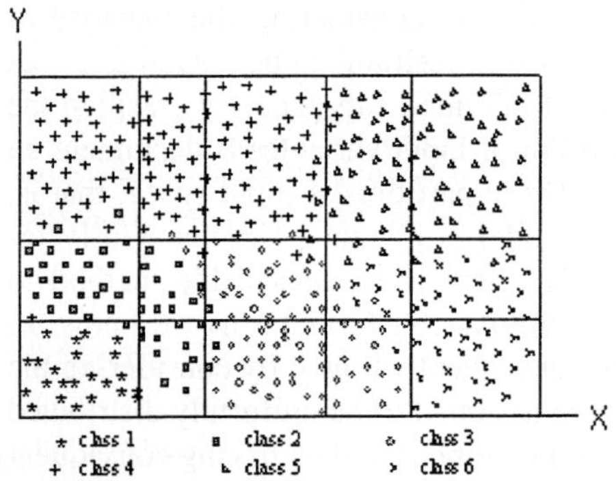

Fig. 3. Partition of classified projection.

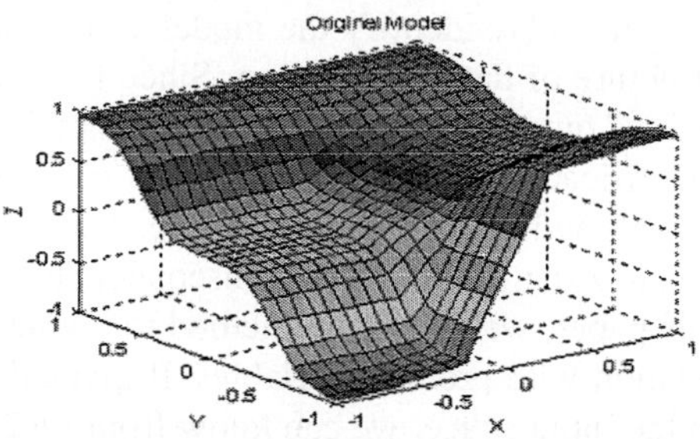

Fig. 4. Distribution of data to be modeled.

The partition is so obtained that as possible as same kind of class, that is, data having same consequent fuzzy variable exist in each input product subspace constituted with partitioned variables. We find out optimal division line, by which input space is partitioned, so that the partition maximize the $\prod_{i=1}^{l}\prod_{j=1}^{m} O_{X_i\times Y_j}(Z_k)$ for all product subspace $X_i \times Y_j$, using optimal solution searching algorithm such as Neural Network or Genetic Algorithm. Since the partition determine not only membership functions of premise variables but also mapping f , i.e., fuzzy rules between premise and consequent variables, we can accomplish fuzzy model by obtaining optimal partition. The procedure of model identification using occupancy degree and optimal division of projection is abstracted as following:

• Procedure of Model Identification

▹ STEP1 : Divide consequent variable into several segments which have boundaries at break points of graphs of eq.(7) and eq.(8). These break points imply sudden changes of data distribution formation with respect to consequent variable.

▹ STEP2 : Classify given experimental data by consequent variables divided in STEP1 and then project the classified data on input space.

▹ STEP3 : Divide input space so that objective function $\prod_{i=1}^{l} \prod_{j=1}^{m} O_{X_i \times Y_j}(Z_k)$ is maximized for divided subspaces.

▹ STEP4 : Define membership function for each crisp segment divided in STEP1 and STEP3 using eq.(3).

▹ STEP5 : Determine consequent linguistic variable corresponded to each input subspace obtained in STEP3 by way of eq.(6) and then construct fuzzy rule table.

4 Modeling and Results

To verify the validity of modeling using occupancy degree and optimal partition of projection proposed in this paper, we sampled 25×25 pairs of data from arbitrary 2-input 1-output fuzzy system. The sampled data is distributed as in fig.4.

As the first step of modeling procedure, we make partition of output variables. As explained in the previous section, the partition of output variable is achieved at sudden changing points of functions represented by eq.(7) and eq.(8). The graph (a) and (b) in fig.5 show variations of the number of data included in set I_z of eq.(7) and mean distance of eq.(8) with respect to output variable z , respectively. Membership functions of fuzzy sets corresponding to consequent crisp divisions are defined by eq.(3-3) and showed in fig.6. After classifying given data into several classes which are discriminated by crisply divided consequent variables, and then projecting classified classes on input space $X \times Y$, we get fig.7. In order to obtain premise membership functions and to construct optimal fuzzy rules, we divide input space so that objective function $\prod_{i=1}^{l} \prod_{j=1}^{m} occup_{X_i \times Y_j}(Z_k)$ is maximized. In this paper, we use Genetic Algorithm for finding out optimal division line. The divided input subspace and corresponding consequent variable form a fuzzy rule.

We can define fuzzy membership function for each crisply divided input variable using eq. (3-1), (3-2), and the results are shown in fig.8. Each input subspace generated by optimal division, which is obtained in the process to determine premise membership functions, is used as a premise product space of fuzzy rule. As a consequent variable corresponded to a input subspace, the one which has maximum occupancy degree for the subspace is chosen.

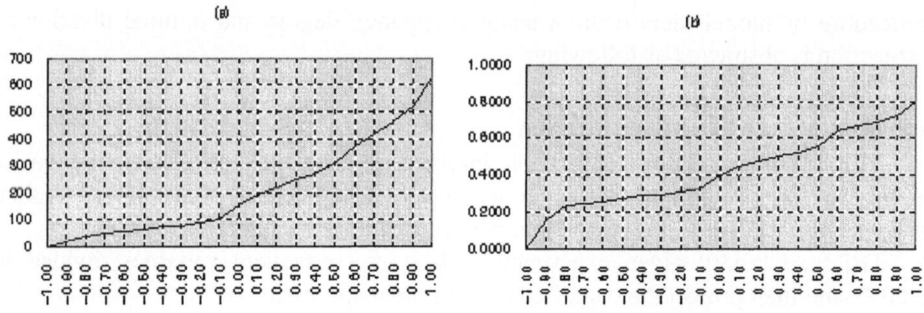

Fig. 5. Variation of the number of data(a), mean distance(b) for output variable z.

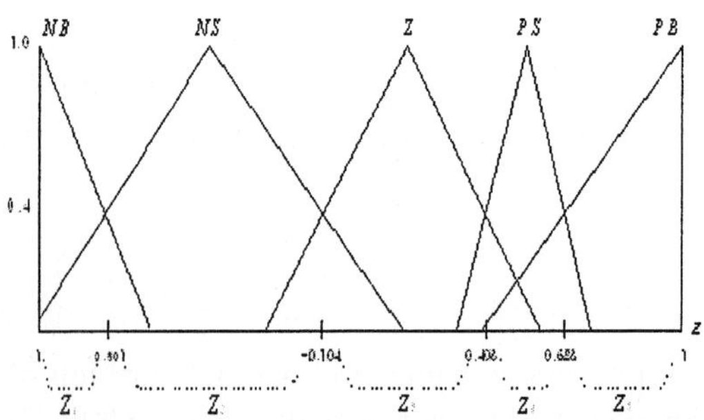

Fig. 6. Crisp and fuzzy partition of output variable.

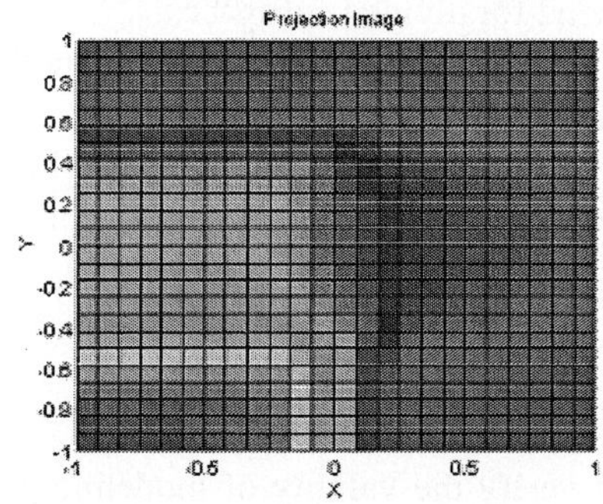

Fig. 7. Projection of output classes into input space.

The table2 is fuzzy rule table so obtained. Fig.9 shows the result of initial model constructed with fuzzy sets in fig.6 and fig.8 and fuzzy rules in table2, and fig.10 shows modeling error. We can know from fig.4, fig.9 and fig.10 that though algorithm of the proposed modeling method is simple, it can generate initial membership functions and fuzzy rules which describe given original data very approximately.

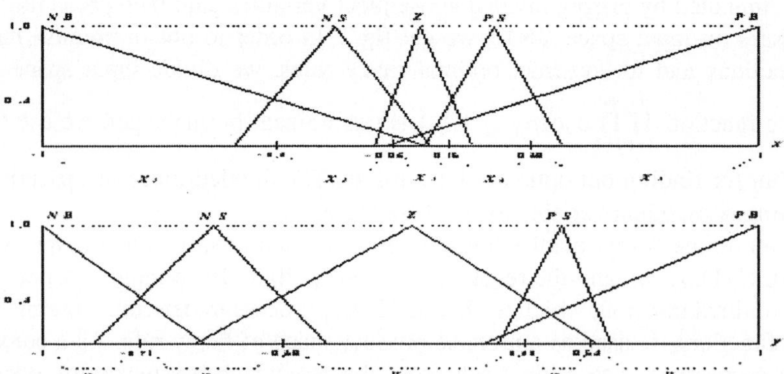

Fig. 8. Crisp and fuzzy partition of input variables.

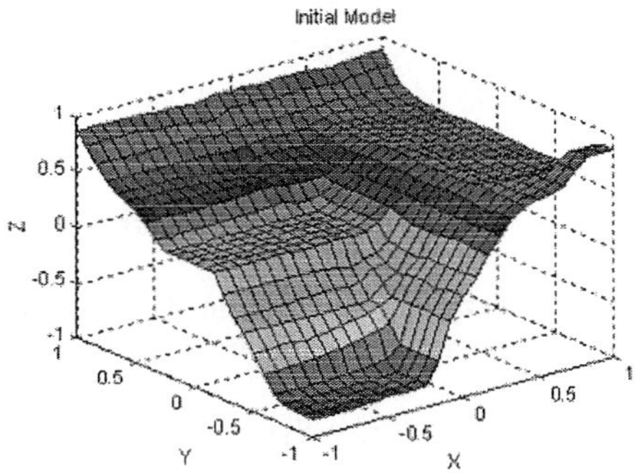

Fig. 9. Result of initial modeling.

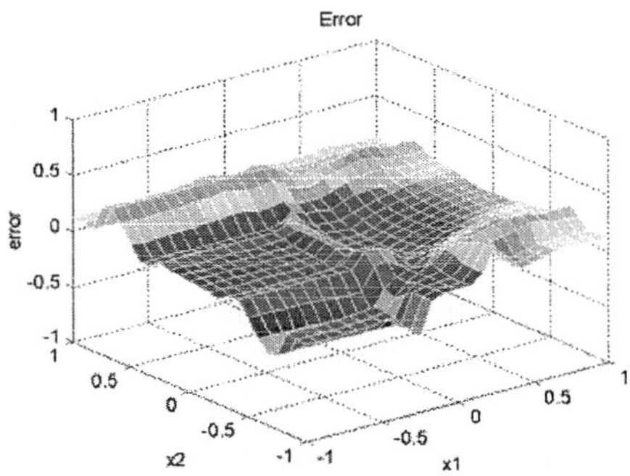

Fig. 10. Error of initial model.

Table 2. Generated rule table.

Y \ X	NB	NS	Z	PS	PB
NB	NB	NS	Z	PS	PB
NS	NS	NS	Z	PS	PB
Z	PS	PS	PS	PS	PS
PS	PB	PS	PS	PS	PB
PB	PB	PB	PS	PB	PB

5 Conclusion

In this paper, using a rough set measure which represents the degree of consistency between condition and decision attribute values of data pairs, we define a modified consistency measure called occupancy degree to represent the consistency of premise and consequent values in terms of generated linguistic variables. We also propose an optimal partition of projection method by which membership functions are defined and fuzzy rules are generated from given experimental data pairs without preliminary explicit linguistic information. We applied the proposed method to identify an arbitrary defined fuzzy system in order to verify the validity.

References

1. J. C. Bezdek,: Some Recent Applications of Fuzzy C-means in Pattern Recognition and Image Processing, IEEE Workshop on Lang. Autom., pp. 247-252 (1983)
2. M. Delgano, A.F.Gomez-Skarmeta, and F. Martin,: A Fuzzy Clustering-Based Rapid Prototyping for Fuzzy Rule-Based Modeling, IEEE Trans. on Fuzzy Systems, Vol.5, no.2, May (1997)

3. T. Takagi, M. Sugeno,: Fuzzy Identification of Systems and its Application to Modeling and Control, IEEE Trans. Systems, Man, Cybernetics 15(1), pp. 116-132 (1985)
4. M. Sugeno, G. T. Kang,: Structure Identification of Fuzzy Model, Fuzzy Sets and Systems 28, pp. 15-33 (1988)
5. S. Horikawa, T. Furuhashi, and Y. Uchikawa,: On Fuzzy modeling using fuzzy neural networks with the back-propagation algorithm, IEEE Trans. on Neural Networks, vol.3, pp.801-806, May (1992)
6. H. Inoue, K. Kamei, K. Inoue,: Auto-Generation of Fuzzy Production Rules Using Hyper Elliptic Cone Membership Function by Genetic Algorithm, Proc. of Intern. Conf. on Soft Computing, Japan, pp. 82-85 (1996)
7. Z. Pawlak,: Why Rough Sets?, Proc. of IEEE Int. Conf. Fuzzy Systems, pp. 738-743 (1996)
8. Z. Pawlak,: Rough Sets, Int. J. of Computer and Information Sciences, 11, pp. 341-356 (1982)

A Novel High Performance Fuzzy Controller Applied to Traffic Control of ATM Networks

Mahdi Jalili-Kharaajoo

Young Researchers Club, Islamic Azad University, Tehran, Iran
mahdijalili@ece.ut.ac.ir

Abstract. In this paper, we will design a fuzzy logic based intelligent high performance traffic controller for Asynchronous Transfer Mode (ATM) networks. In the proposed fuzzy traffic controller, the actual mean cell rate of traffic source is estimated and the traffic controller is adjusted so its loss load is equal to generated excessive load. Simulation results show that the proposed fuzzy traffic controller can outperform the traditional Usage Parameter Control (UPC) mechanisms.

1 Introduction

Asynchronous Transfer Mode (ATM) is a new technology to support wide variety of services including Constant Bit Rate (CBR), Variable Bit Rate (VBR), Unspecified Bit Rate (UBR) and Available Bit Rate (ABR). The traffic control includes traffic parameters and the requested QoS. Traffic parameters such as peak cell rate, maximum burst size and minimum cell rate are used to describe the inherent characteristics of a traffic source. At the network side, Connection Admission Control (CAC) [1-4] is responsible to describe the acceptance or rejection of the new requested connection. When congestion happens, the number of input cells to the network increases, because of cell loss in intermediate nodes, the number of delivered cells to the destination wick decrease and the network performance will be degraded. So, in order to protect network resources from any misbehavior of traffic source, the input traffic stream must be monitored by a proper policing algorithm. This policing function is performed by UPC at the edge of network. A UPC mechanism must avoid inappropriate control actions on a traffic steam generated by well behavior sources. An ideal UPC mechanism must be capable to detect any illegal traffic situation (high selectivity) in real time (high responsiveness). Some of the most popular UPC mechanisms can be found in [5-8].

During the past years, the fuzzy control has found many applications in telecommunications networks [9-12]. A survey of recent advances in fuzzy logic in telecommunication applications including queuing, buffer management, distributed access control, load management, routing, call acceptance, policing, congestion mitigation, bandwidth allocation, channel assignment, network management and quantitative performance evaluation in networks is presented in [13]. In this work, a high performance Fuzzy Traffic Controller (FTC) for ATM networks is presented. In the proposed FTC, the excessive load of traffic source is estimated and the traffic controller is adjusted so that its loss load is equal to the generated excessive load. The proposed FTC uses a network congestion indicator to decide passing, marking or discarding the input cell.

S. Tsumoto et al. (Eds.): RSCTC 2004, LNAI 3066, pp. 327–333, 2004.

2 Fuzzy Traffic Controller (FTC)

In this section, the proposed FTC is described. Fig. 1 shows an ATM multiplexer where a number of incoming cells are directed towards the same output link. Before entering the network, every source is forced by the proposed FTC. The basic block diagram of FTC is shown in Fig. 2. The proposed FTC consists of two fuzzy controllers, an excessive load estimator and a loss load estimator. The Fuzzy Controller 1 (FC1) monitors the input traffic steam to detect any possible violation from traffic contract. The output of FC1, V, demonstrates the violation rate of traffic source. The Fuzzy controller 2 (FC2) is responsible to decide to accept, market or discard the input cells. The FC2 is a two-input-single-output fuzzy controller with the following inputs:

- The number of cells in the multiplexer buffer, K.
- The violation rate of traffic source (the output of FC1).

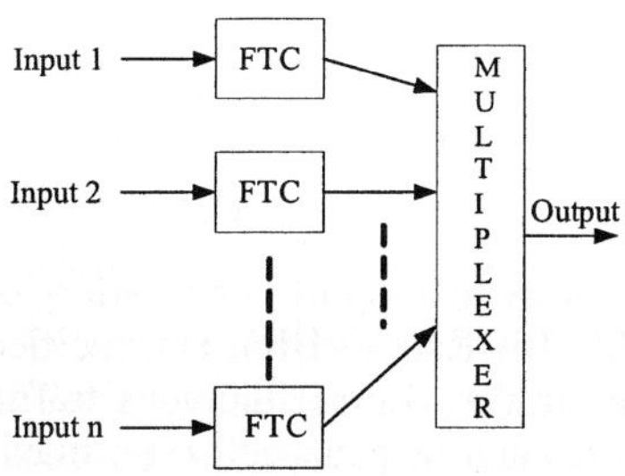

Fig. 1. An ATM multiplexer.

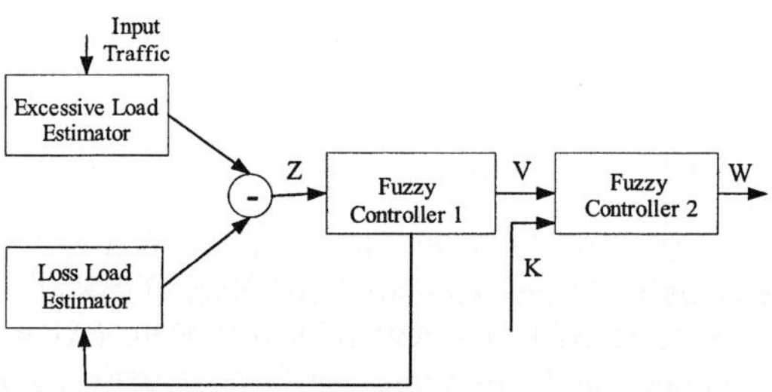

Fig. 2. Basic block diagram of the proposed FTC.

2.1 Mean Cell Rate Estimation

Two methods are proposed to estimate the normalized actual mean cell rate σ of the traffic source. In the first method, the number of input cells in a constant time window T_o is counted. The new time window starts immediately at the end of preceding window. If N_k represents the number of input cells in the kth time window, then the normalized actual mean cell rate, σ_k, is calculated by the following recursive formula

$$\hat{\sigma}_k = \frac{k-1}{k}\hat{\sigma}_{k-1} + \frac{N_k}{kT_o m_o}$$

where m_o is the negotiated mean cell rate.

In the second method, in each burst/silence period, the number of input cells in the burst phase and also the length of silence are measured. The number of input cells in the kth burst and the length of kth silence are represented by two random variables X_k and S_k, respectively. By using the Maximum Likelihood Estimation (MLE) method and assuming the geometric distribution for mean number of input cells in the burst phase and also experimental distribution for silence phase, the mean number of cells in the bust phase, $E(X_k)$, and the mean silence length, $E(S_k)$, are estimated by the following formula

$$E(X_k) = \frac{\sum_{i=1}^{k} X_k}{k}, E(S_k) = \frac{\sum_{i=1}^{k} S_k}{k}$$

At the end of kth burst/silence period, the normalized actual mean cell rate of traffic source is determined as

$$\hat{\sigma}_k = \frac{E(X_k).\Delta.b_o}{\left(E(X_k).\Delta + E(S_k)\right)m_o}$$

where Δ, m_o are the cell inter-arrival time during a burst and the peak cell rate of traffic source, respectively.

2.2 Fuzzy Controller 1 (FC1)

An ideal UPC mechanism has a zero detection probability up to the negotiated parameter and a detection probability corresponding to the percentage of excess cells beyond the negotiation parameter point. So, the detection probability P_d of an ideal UPC mechanism can be calculated as $P_d = (\sigma - 1)/\sigma$. If the traffic source violates from its traffic descriptor, then σ will be greater than one and the source has generated an excessive load equal to $\sigma - 1$. The loss load ρ of an ideal UPC mechanism must be equal to the generated excessive load of traffic source. We define a random variable Z as $Z = \hat{\sigma} - \hat{\rho} - 1$, where $\hat{\sigma}$ and $\hat{\rho}$ are the estimated values of σ and ρ, respectively. The main responsibility of FC1 is to control the random variable Z near zero. The fuzzy conditional rules corresponding to the membership functions depicted in Fig. 3 are as follows.

1. IF Z is Negative, then V is Zero.
2. IF Z is Zero, then V is Low.
3. IF Z is Positive, then V is High.

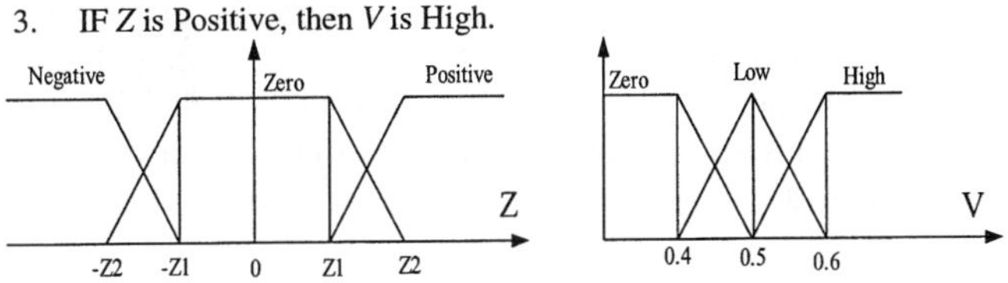

Fig. 3. The membership functions of FC1.

2.3 Fuzzy Controller 2 (FC2)

One of the most important problems of the traditional UPC is that the input cells may be discarded even if the output multiplexer link is underutilized. To remove this problem, the FC2 uses a feedback via the multiplexer buffer to improve the channel utilization. The FC2 in a two-input single-output fuzzy controller, which uses the state of multiplexer buffer and the violation rate of traffic source (the output of FC1), as two linguistic inputs. By using the knowledge stored in the rule base and according to the values of linguistic inputs, the FC2 decides to pass, mark or discard the input cells. The fuzzy conditional rules according to the membership functions showed in Fig. 4 are as follows

1. If *V* is Low and *K* is Low, then *W* is Pass.
2. If *V* is Low and *K* is Medium, then *W* is Pass.
3. If *V* is Low and *K* is High, then *W* is Mark.
4. If *V* is High and *K* is Low, then *W* is Pass.
5. If *V* is High and *K* is Medium, then *W* is Mark.
6. If *V* is High and *K* is High, then *W* is Discard.

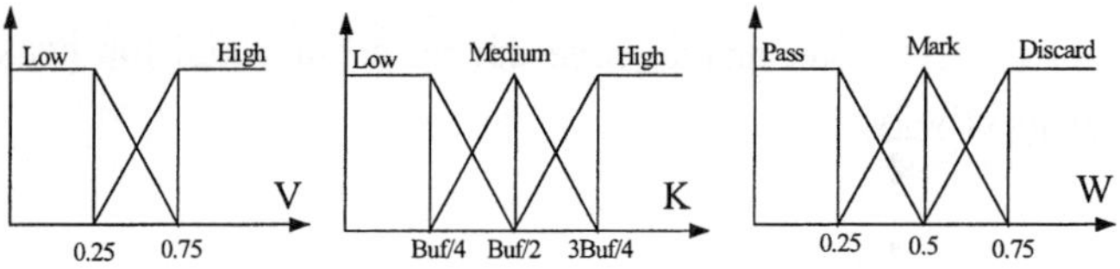

Fig. 4. The membership functions of FC2.

3 Performance Evaluation of the Proposed FTC

In this section, the performance of the proposed FTC is evaluated and compared with that of traditional UPC mechanisms including LB, JW and EWMA. Two voice traffic sources, with traffic characteristics shown in the Table, are used to derive the system. The number of cells per burst has a geometric distribution with a mean of *E[x]* and the silence phase has an exponential distribution with a mean of *E[s]*. The traffic parameters are based on ADPCM with a 64 bytes information fields [14]. In both the FC1 and the FC2, the mamdani's interface method and center of gravity difuzzification technique are used [15]. An ATM multiplexer with N independent ON/OFF input voice sources is simulated. The multiplexer is modeled as a finite queue served by a single server with First-In First-Out (FIFO) service discipline. The output link of multiplexer is a T1 (1.544 Mbps) pipe. As mentioned above, the actual mean cell rate of traffic source is estimated by two methods. For each method 1 and 2, the corresponding FTC is called Fuzzy1 and Fuzzy2, respectively. All UPC mechanisms are dimensioned to achieve a detection probability less than 10^{-6} at the nominal cell arrival rate. The time window T_o is set to 10Δ. The flexibility factor of EWMA mechanism, γ, is selected as $\gamma = 0.91$. For the traffic source 1, the values of parameters are selected as follows

$$C_{LB} = 1.2, C_{JW} = 1.77, C_{EWMA} = 1.2, N = 1100, Z1 = 0.12(0.06), Z2 = 0.5(0.5).$$

where *N* and *C* represent the counter size and the over-dimensioning factor of UPC mechanism, respectively.

For the traffic source 2, the values of parameters are selected as

$$C_{LB} = 1.45, C_{JW} = 2.5, C_{EWMA} = 1.3, N = 670, Z1 = 0.112(0.07), Z2 = 0.6(0.5).$$

The values of Z_1 and Z_2 shown in the parenthesis are the corresponding values for Fuzzy2. The selectively curves of the proposed FTC and the other traditional mechanisms for two traffic sources 1 and 2 are shown in Figs. 5 and 6, respectively. As it can be seen, the proposed FTC has a detection probability which is very close to the ideal controller specially Fuzzy2. For example, when traffic source1 generates 10% excessive load, the violation probability of Fuzzy2 is improved about 3.2,2 and 1.5 order of magnitude in comparison with JB, LB and EWMA, respectively.

Table 1. Traffic characteristics of two voice sources.

Traffic characteristics			
Source	**b_o(bps)**	**m_o(bps)**	**E(X)**
1	32000	11200	22
2	64000	22000	58

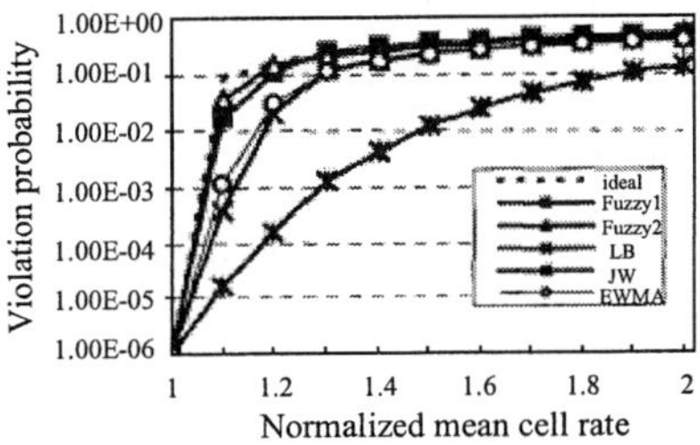

Fig. 5. Selectivity curve of FC2 for traffic source 1.

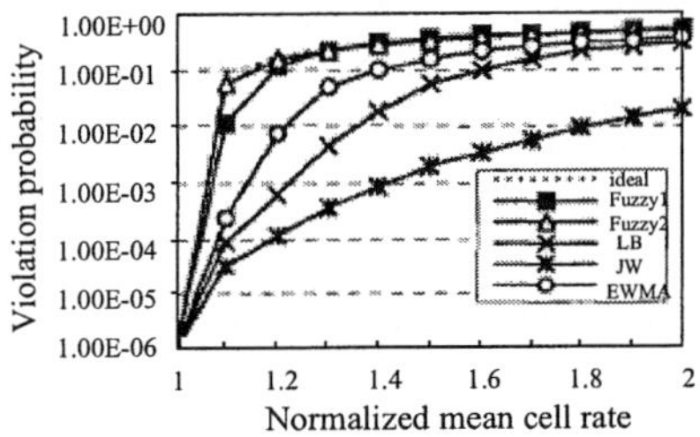

Fig. 6. Selectivity curve of FC2 for traffic source 2.

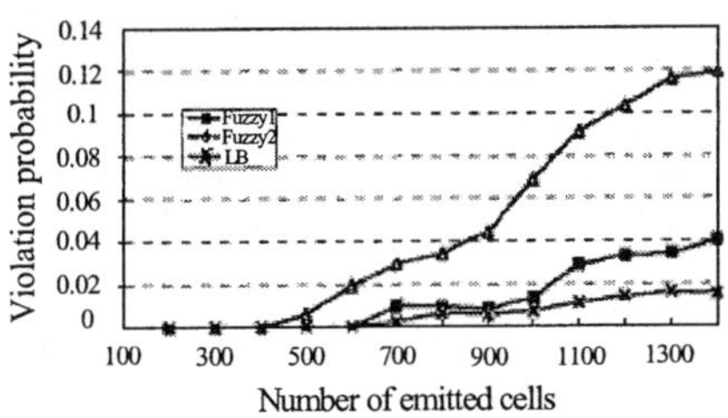

Fig. 7. Dynamic behavior of FTC and LB.

In Fig. 7, the dynamic behavior of FTC is compared with that of LB. In this case, the traffic source 2 generates 50% overload by increasing the mean number of cells during the burst phase. In order to improve the dynamic behavior of LB, the bucket size is set to 300. as shown in Fig. 7, the proposed Fuzzy2 starts detecting violation after only 500 and its violation probability grows very fast so that after emitting 1500 cells the violation probability grows slowly.

For the FC2, the fixed threshold A and B are set to 0.3 and 0.7, respectively, in Fig. 8, the system cell loss of the proposed FTC is compared with that of LB and EWMA mechanisms. In this case, 40 voice sources (64 kbps) with an actual mean cell rate 50% higher than the negotiated one, have been connected to the inputs of multiplexer. This figure shows the both the Fuzzy1 and Fuzzy2 have a lower system cell loss probability than the LB and EWMA mechanisms. Fig. 9 shows the link utilization versus the number of connected sources. The multiplexer buffer size is set to 35 cells. As shown in this figure, both the Fuzzy1 and Fuzzy2 achieve better system utilization

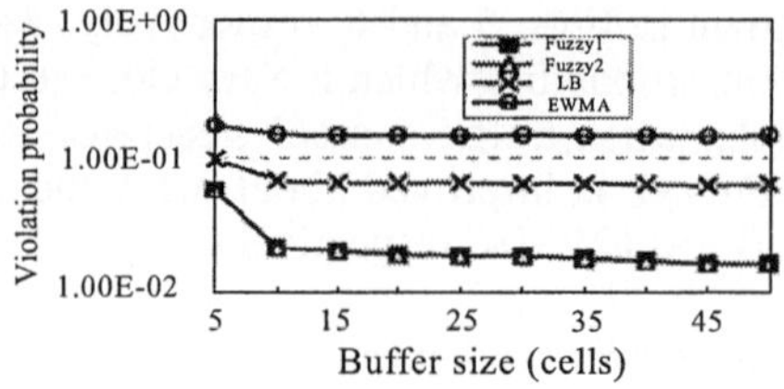

Fig. 8. Cell loss probability versus buffer size.

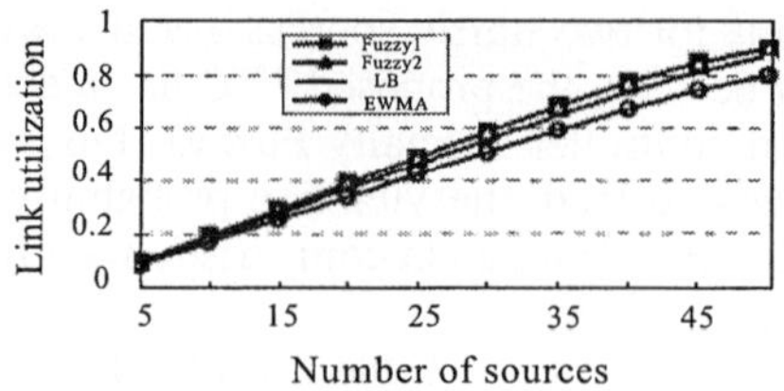

Fig. 9. Link utilization versus number of sources.

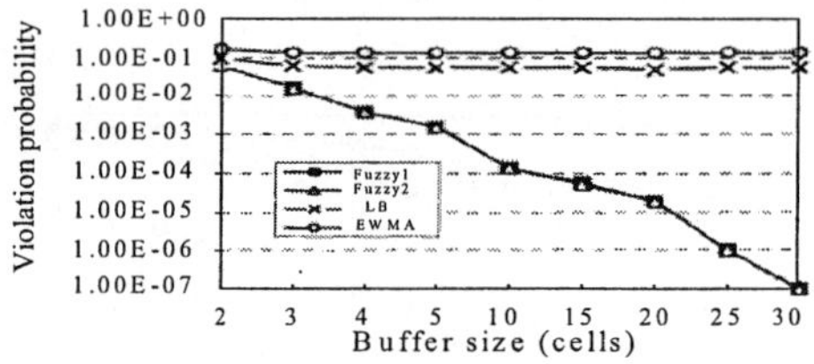

Fig. 10. Cell loss probability versus buffer size.

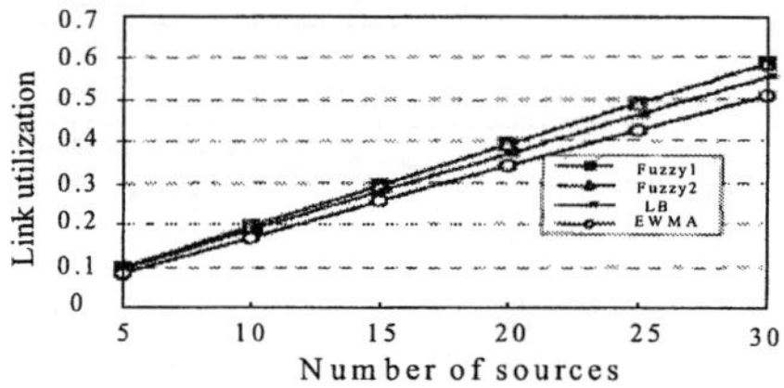

Fig. 11. Link utilization versus number of sources.

than LB and EWMA mechanisms. It is found that for a multiplexer with 50 connected sources, the system utilization is effectively improved by 3% and 10% in comparison with LB and EWMA mechanisms, respectively.

In order to observe the efficiency of the proposed controller, the number of input sources of multiplexer is reduced to 2.5. In this case, the output link of multiplexer is always underutilized. Figs. 10 and 11 show the system cell loss probability and the link utilization, respectively. As it can be seen from Fig. 10, the system cell loss probably of both Fuzzy1 and Fuzzy2 is less than traditional UPC mechanisms. Fig. 11 shows that for a multiplexer with 30 connected sources and a buffer size equal to 25 cells, the system utilization is effectively improved by 3% and 8% in comparison with LB and EWMA mechanisms, respectively.

4 Conclusion

In the paper, a high performance fuzzy traffic controller for ATM networks was proposed. The fuzzy traffic controller was adjusted in such a manner that its loss load is equal to excessive load generated by the traffic source. Simulation results showed that the proposed fuzzy traffic controller demonstrates much better selectivity and effectiveness than the other conventional UPC mechanisms.

References

1. Wei, H. Lisheng, S. Huihe, Flow control based on Dahlin control algorithm in ATM networks, in Proc. American Control Conference, pp.2449-2454, 2002.
2. S. Jaganattan, J. Talluri, Adaptive predictive congestion control of high speed ATM networks, IEEE Trans. Brodcasting, 48(2), pp.129-130, 2002.

3. S. Tarbonriech, C.T. Abdallah, M. Ariola, Bounded control of multiple-delay systems with application to ATM networks, in Proc 40th IEEE CDC, pp.2315-2320, 2001.
4. S. Jaganattan, A. Tohmaz, congestion control of ATM networks using a learning methodology, in Proc. IEEE Conf. Control Application, Mexico, pp. 135-140, 2001.
5. J.S. Turner, New directions in communications (or which way in the information age?), in Proc. Int. Zurich Sym. Digit. Communication, Zurich, Switzerland, pp.25-32-1986.
6. E.P. Rathgeb, Modeling and performance comparison of policing mechanisms for ATM networks, IEEE JSAC, 9(3), pp.325-334, 1991.
7. M. Buto, E. Cavallero, Effectiveness of the leaky bucket policing mechanism in ATM networks, IEEE JSAC, 9(3), pp.335-342, 1991.
8. N. Yamanaka, Y. Sato, K Sato, Performance limitation of leaky bucket algorithm for usage parameter control and bandwidth allocation method, IEICE Trans. Comm., E-75-B, pp.82-86, 1992.
9. V. Catania, G. Ficilini, S. Palaazo, D. Panno, A comparative analysis of Fuzzy versus Conventional policing mechanisms for ATM networks, IEEE/ACM Trans. Networking, 4, pp.449-459, 1996.
10. Bensaou, S.T.C. Chu, D. H.K., Tsang, Estimation of the cell loss ratio in ATM networks with a fuzzy system and application to measured-based call admission control, IEEE/ACM Trans. Networking, 5(4), pp.572-584, 1997.
11. Douligeris, G. Develekos, A fuzzy logic approach to congestion control in ATM networks, in Proc. IEEE Int. Conf. Communication, WA, USA, pp.1969-1973, 1995.
12. Pitsillidies, Y.A. Sekercioglu, Fuzzy logic control of cell flow in ATM, in Proc. Australian Telecommunication Network application Conference, pp.249-254, 1994.
13. S. Ghosh, Q. Rezouqi, H.J. Schumacher, A. Celmins, A survey of recent advances in fuzzy logic in telecommunication networks and new challenges, IEEE Trans. Fuzzy Sys., 6(3), pp.443-447, 1998.
14. H. Heffes, D. Lucantoni, a markov modulated characterization of packetized voice and data traffic and related statistical multiplexer performance, IEEE JSAC, 6, pp.856-868, 1986.
15. C.C. Lee, Fuzzy logic in control systems: Fuzzy logic controller, part II, IEEE Trans. Systems, Man, Cybernetics, 20(2), pp.419-432, 1990.

Design of a Speed Drive Based on Fuzzy Logic for a Dual Three-Phase Induction Motor

Mahdi Jalili-Kharaajoo

Young Researchers Club, Azad University, Tehran, Iran
mahdijalili@ece.ut.ac.ir

Abstract. The main objective of this paper is devoted to a fuzzy speed controller for a multiphase induction machine. In the proposed approach of this paper, using a simple and flexible structure of a fuzzy controller, worthy results such as, high accuracy in regulating speed for any conditions, fast reaction to the variation with minimum offset, minimum pulsation in the output torque, and minimum distortion in the phase current are obtained.

1 Introduction

The main goals to bring up multiphase machines are access to high power range (due to the lack of power semiconductors in this range) beside more reliability [1,2]. The concept of reliability in such structures means that the loss of one phase doesn't prevent the machine from starting and running [3].

Lipo [3], is referred to as vector space decomposition. The analytical modeling and control of the machine are accomplished in three two-dimensional orthogonal subspace (d-q-z1-z2-o1-o2) and excited via the six-phase voltage source inverter (VSI). In general, VSI has a total of 64 switching modes that with the proposed transformation matrix, the 64 voltage vectors corresponding to the switching modes are projected on these three planes and a SVPWM control strategy covers the applied volt-seconds of the machine in all three planes. This, in addition to complicating the choice of the switching vectors, greatly increased the computation time required for the implementation of Lipo's scheme such that, operation of a machine with a frequency and sampling frequency above 15HZ and 2KHZ respectively, was not practical. Bakhshai in [4], using the similarity between the voltage pattern of three and six-phase systems, and based on three-phase SVPWM obtained better results.

In this paper, first the machine model used for the control process is discussed. Then, the structure of fuzzy controller is considered and finally, the simulation results for demonstrating the performance of proposed controller is presented.

2 Model of the Motor

The machine model used in this paper is a simple two-axis (d-q) model that was presented by Singh in [5]. The reason for selecting this simple model is that, a fuzzy controller doesn't need a precise and complicated six dimensional model such as the one used by Lipo in [3] for the SVPWM controller. The dual three-phase induction motor configuration is achieved by splitting the phase belt of a conventional three-

S. Tsumoto et al. (Eds.): RSCTC 2004, LNAI 3066, pp. 334–339, 2004.

phase motor into two equal halves with a phase separation of 30o electrical between the two. Since the three-phase winding has been split into two halves, it is clear that if the voltage of the machine is to remain the same, the windings must be replaced with coils of double the number of turns and half the cross section.

Fig. 1-a. shows the schematic diagram of magnetic axes for the stator and rotor windings for a two-pole six phase induction machine. The stator phases are normally divided into two star connected three-phase sets, labeled "ABC" and "abc" with their magnetic axes displaced from each other by 30° (electrical). The windings of each three-phase set are uniformly distributed and have axes that are displaced 120° apart. The three-phase rotor windings a_r, b_r, c_r are sinusoidally distributed and have the axes that are 120° displaced from each other. The defining equations for such a machine are

$$V_{q1} = R_1 I_{q1} + \omega\lambda_{d1} + P\lambda_{q1}\,,\; V_{d1} = R_1 I_{d1} - \omega\lambda_{q1} + P\lambda_{d1}$$
$$V_{q2} = R_2 I_{q2} + \omega\lambda_{d2} + P\lambda_{q2}\,,\; V_{d2} = R_2 I_{d2} - \omega\lambda_{q2} + P\lambda_{d2} \quad (1)$$
$$V'_{qr} = R'_r I'_{qr} + (\omega-\omega_r)\lambda'_{dr} + P\lambda'_{dr}\,,\; V'_{dr} = R'_r I'_{dr} - (\omega-\omega_r)\lambda'_{qr} + P\lambda'_{qr}$$

where

$$\lambda_{q1} = L_{11} I_{q1} + \frac{3}{2} L_{ms}(I_{q1} + I_{q2} + I'_{qr})\,,\; \lambda_{d1} = L_{11} I_{d1} + \frac{3}{2} L_{ms}(I_{d1} + I_{d2} + I'_{dr})$$
$$\lambda_{q2} = L_{11} I_{q2} + \frac{3}{2} L_{ms}(I_{q1} + I_{q2} + I'_{qr})\,,\; \lambda_{d2} = L_{11} I_{d2} + \frac{3}{2} L_{ms}(I_{d1} + I_{d2} + I'_{dr}) \quad (2)$$
$$\lambda'_{qr} = L'_{lr} I_{qr} + \frac{3}{2} L_{ms}(I_{q1} + I_{q2} + I'_{qr})\,,\; \lambda'_{dr} = L'_{lr} I_{dr} + \frac{3}{2} L_{ms}(I_{d1} + I_{d2} + I'_{dr})$$

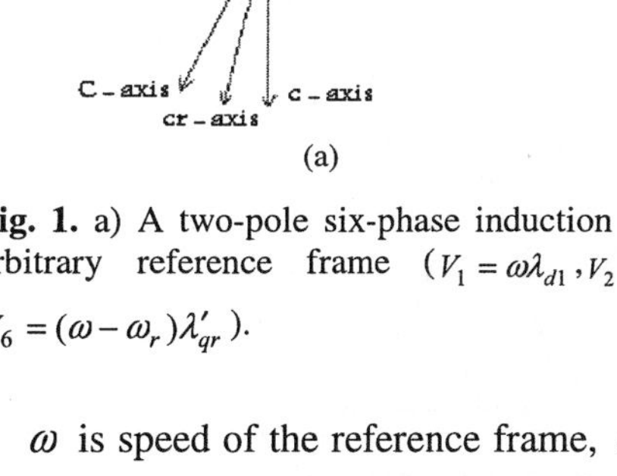

(a)

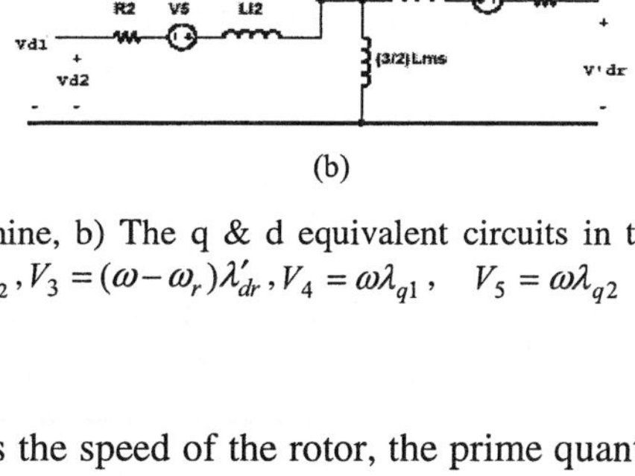

(b)

Fig. 1. a) A two-pole six-phase induction machine, b) The q & d equivalent circuits in the arbitrary reference frame ($V_1 = \omega\lambda_{d1}, V_2 = \omega\lambda_{d2}, V_3 = (\omega-\omega_r)\lambda'_{dr}, V_4 = \omega\lambda_{q1}$, $V_5 = \omega\lambda_{q2}$, $V_6 = (\omega-\omega_r)\lambda'_{qr}$).

ω is speed of the reference frame, ω_r is the speed of the rotor, the prime quantities in rotor equations are the ones referred to stator, and the equivalent circuits for the above equations in (d-q) frame are shown in Fig. 1-b. The parameters of the machine are the same as in [5].

3 Fuzzy Logic Controller

In the past decade, impressive changes in the field of fuzzy logic in industry applications, and especially in three-phase electrical drive systems were observed. The main reasons for popularity of a fuzzy controller can be summarized as follows:

- There is no need for accurate modeling and analysis of the controlled systems; and therefore, it can be applied to highly nonlinear systems.
- The experience of experts can be used.
- Because of parallel processing characteristics as well as its simple structure, the calculation time will not be high, even with many system parameters & variables.

The fuzzy controller used in this paper, is a direct fuzzy controller (DFC). The most significant input variables to the fuzzy regulator are selected as the speed error and its time variation as in the following:

$$e(k) = \omega_r^*(k) - \omega_r(k) \qquad \text{Speed Error} \tag{3}$$

$$\Delta e(k) = e(k) - e(k-1) \qquad \text{Variation Error} \tag{4}$$

where, k is the sampling time. The variation of the modulation index $\Delta M(k)$ is chosen as the regulator output (that send to the both of three-phase inverters) and hence, the command signal is calculated from:

$$M(k) = M(k-1) + \Delta M(k) \tag{5}$$

A change in this variable causes a change in the output rms voltage of each inverter, which is proportional to the flux linkage and speed. Note that, there is a 30° phase displacement between SPWM signals of the inverters.

The range of each input and output is portioned into seven membership functions, each corresponding to a linguistic variable. The controller treats each measurement as a fuzzy singleton and fuzzifies it using the fuzzy sets shown in Fig. 2. Triangular shapes were chosen as the membership function because they simplified the controller's computations due to the linear equations in evaluation of membership functions. A 50% overlap in the membership functions of all fuzzy sets was used so the control-

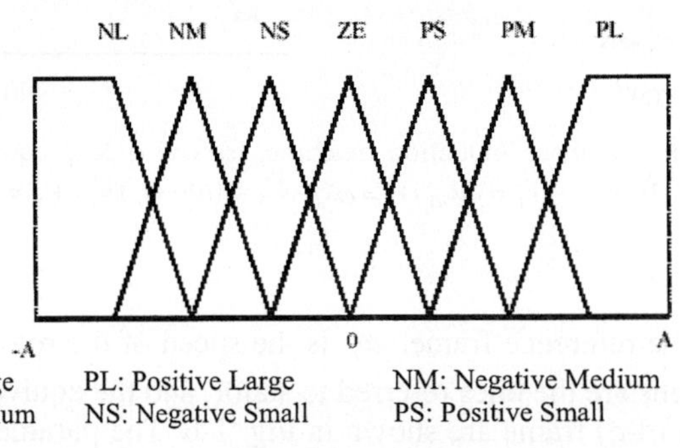

NL: Negative Large PL: Positive Large NM: Negative Medium
PM: Positive Medium NS: Negative Small PS: Positive Small ZE: Zero Equal

Fig. 2. Partitions & membership function of inputs & output of the controller (for speed error A=0.08, for error variation A=0.1 and for modulation index A=0.02).

Table 1. Results of the fuzzy controller.

Change of Error (columns); Error (rows)

	NL	NM	NS	ZE	PS	PM	PL
NL	*NL*	*NL*	*NL*	*NL*	*NM*	*NS*	*ZE*
NM	*NL*	*NL*	*NL*	*NM*	*NS*	*ZE*	*PS*
NS	*NL*	*NL*	*NM*	*NS*	*ZE*	*PS*	*PM*
ZE	*NL*	*NM*	*NS*	*ZE*	*PS*	*PM*	*PL*
PS	*NM*	*NS*	*ZE*	*PS*	*PM*	*PL*	*PL*
PM	*NS*	*ZE*	*PS*	*PM*	*PL*	*PL*	*PL*
PL	*ZE*	*PS*	*PM*	*PL*	*PL*	*PL*	*PL*

ler would produce smooth control action. Since the fuzzy sets are seven for each of the speed error and its variation, thus a total of $7 \times 7 = 49$ combinations take place. Every combination is associated to a conditional instruction as follows:

If e is NL and e is PL, then M is ZE.

The rule sets for the proper modulation index based on $e(k)$ and $\Delta e(k)$ are presented in Table.

The equivalent control surface for the rules in Table 1 is shown in Fig. 3. This figure illustrates the flexibility of the fuzzy controller in covering any condition. In opposite, PI controller has a solidly smooth surface such that, any change in its structure causes a change in the whole of surface and therefore, its adjustment is complicated. For convenience, the step-by-step procedure for calculations at every sampling interval is summarized, as follows [3]:

- Evaluation and normalization of error $e(k)$ and its variation $\Delta e(k)$.
- Determination of the membership degree for each of the fuzzy sets $\mu_{ei}(e)$ and $\mu_{\Delta ei}(\Delta e)$.
- Calculation of the membership degree $\mu_{R_{ij}}$ associated with every relation using the *MIN* operator: $\mu_{R_{ij}} = MIN(\mu_{ei}(e), \mu_{\Delta ei}(\Delta e))$.
- Defuzzification and de-normalization of $\Delta M(k)$.
- Calculation of the command modulation index by the following iterative procedure: $M(k) = M(k-1) + \Delta M(k)$.

4 Simulation Results

The simulation phase is achieved by the FUZZY and SIMULINK toolboxes of the MATLAB software. The switching frequency of each inverter is 4KHZ, except in the last figure set which is 2KHZ. The sampling time for the decision making of the fuzzy controller is 2msec. The ability of the controller in regulating the speed of machine in an acceptable range for any loading condition is shown in Fig. 4. While the speed reference is set to 0.4 p.u. and the machine is initially operating with a load of 0.5 p.u., a sudden torque pulse of 0.5 p.u. is superimposed on the load as shown in Fig. 3-a. Some significant points that are deduced from this figure are as in the following:

- Speed offset against load change is limited to less than 0.005 p.u. as shown in Fig. 3-b.
- Speed error at steady state and at any load condition is approximately limited to 0.001 p.u.
- The steady state peak-to-peak torque oscillations are limited to 0.025 p.u. and 0.05 p.u. for load of 0.5 p. and 1 p.u., respectively as shown in Fig. 3-a. Also, the transient offset due to 1 p.u. step load demand is 0.2 p.u.

In Fig. 4-a. the ability of the fuzzy controller in tracking the reference speed is illustrated. A series of 0.2 p. speed command steps superimposed on each other respectively are applied as shown in Fig. 4-a. Relative these changes, 0.02 p.u. torque steps are applied to get good damping factors at higher speeds as shown Fig. 4-b. From these figures, the following points are observed:

- Smooth and fast tracking of the actual speed with the reference speed in the whole of the operational range without any overshoot or additional oscillation .In other words the system has a critical damped behavior.
- Low torque offsets associated with these speed variations and thus low absorbing phase current.

In both of the above simulations (Fig. 3-c and Fig. 4-c) a linear relation between the modulation index and torque can be seen. This feature can be utilized in direct torque control (DTC) schemes as a simpler and more effective control variable instead of the use of the flux linkage.

In order to compare the results of the current approach with the previous works, the results of [3] for the phase current is used. This comparison is shown in Fig. 5. In [3], Lipo has compared the phase current for the following three different control strategies:

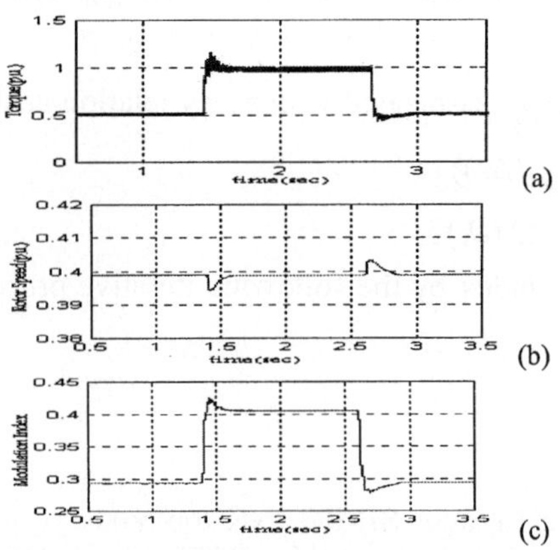

Fig. 3. Simulation result due to a torque pulse of 0.5 p.u. a) Electromagnetic torque, b) Speed of machine , c) Modulation index.

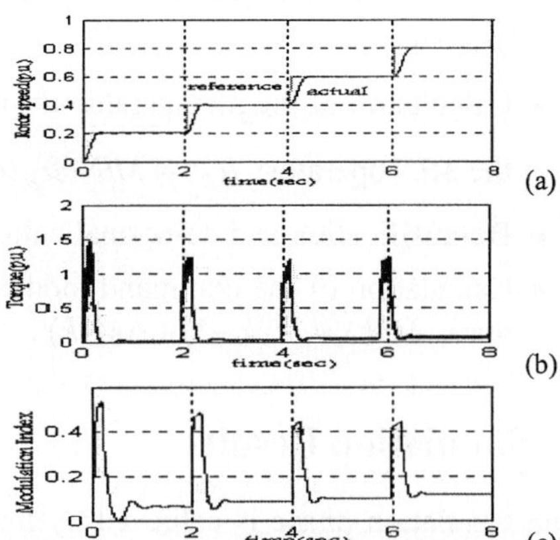

Fig. 4. Simulation results due to a step change in reference speed: a) Reference & Actual speeds, b) Electromagnetic torque, c) Modulation index.

- Vector space decomposition in a six dimensional space (d-q-z1-z2-o1-o2).
- Conventional space vector PWM in a two dimensional space (d-q).
- Sine-Triangular PWM in a two dimensional space (d-q).

From comparison of the results, it is clear that the fuzzy controller phase current has the most sinusoidal shape with the least distortion with respect to the previous works. The switching frequency in all of the schemes is equal to 2KHZ. Of course, in this comparison the main goal is to compare the current shape quality and not quantity.

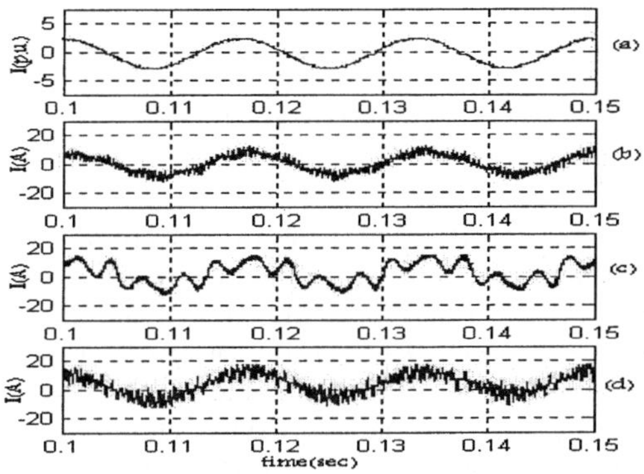

Fig. 5. Simulation results for the comparison of phase currents due to different schemes: a) Using the proposed scheme based on fuzzy logic with a load of 1 p.u. & Speed of 0.4 p.u. b) Using vector space decomposition scheme. c) Using conventional space vector PWM scheme. d) Using sine-triangular PWM scheme.

5 Conclusion

From the above results it is clear that, the proposed controller despite of its simple structure, has all of the features of a high precision speed controller for operating in the whole of speed range and for any loading and environmental conditions. This structure with some changes in fuzzy rules can be easily used in speed control of such machines under unbalanced conditions such as loss of one or two phases.

References

1. T.M. Jahns, Improved Reliability in Solid-State ac Drives by Means of Multiple Independent Phase-Drive Units, IEEE Trans. IA, 16(3), pp.321-331, 1980.
2. A.R. Bakhshai, G. Boos and H. Jin, Space Vector PWM Control of a Split-Phase Induction Machine Using the Vector Classification Technique, in Proc. IEEE Applied Power Electronics Conference and Exposition, pp. 802-808, 1998.
3. Y. Zhao T.A. Lipo, Space Vector PWM Control of Dual Three-Phase Induction Machine Using Space Vector Decomposition, IEEE Trans. IA, 31(5), pp 1100-1109, 1995.
4. G.K. Singh, High Horse Power Rating in ac Drives by Means of Phase Redundancy Technique-Some Experimental Investigation, in Proc. IEEE TENCON, India, 1998.
5. V. Pant, G.K. Singh and S.N. Singh, Modeling of a Multi-Phase Induction Machine Under Fault Condition, in Proc. IEEE Int. Conf. PEDS'99, Hong Kong, 1999.

Rough Set Theory Analysis on Decision Subdivision

Jiucheng Xu[1], Junyi Shen[1], and Guoyin Wang[2]

[1] School of Electronic and Information Engineering, Xi'an Jiaotong University
Xi'an, 710049, P.R. China
xjch3701@mailst.xjtu.edu.cn

[2] Institute of Computer Science and Technology
Chongqing University of Posts and Telecommunications
Chongqing 400065, P.R. China
wanggy@cqupt.edu.cn

Abstract. The degree of subdivision of the decision attribute value influences upon the accuracy of approximation classification, the approximation quality of rules, the core attributes and the information entropy in decision systems based on rough set theory. The finer the decision attribute discretization of a decision table is, the less the accuracy of approximation classification, the approximation quality of rules, and information entropy are on any condition attribute set. Meanwhile, if the attribute values of decision attributes are divided into finer values, then the core attributes set obtained from the finer decision table must include the core attributes set obtained from the previous decision table. These conclusions are proved theoretically. So the discrete degree of decision attributes should be chosen properly. The research is helpful to attribute reduction and enhancing confidences of decision rules.

1 Introduction

Decision system (DS) includes generally a great deal of data objects in a field. Vagueness of decision values probably result in conflicted decisions to the unseen objects in the decision table (i.e. DS) although those rules obtained from the decision table don't conflict[1]. Thus the confidences of decision rules are reduced, and the applied ranges of decision rules become relatively narrow. Obviously, it is necessary to discuss subdivision question of decision values.

Before we analyze the data of decision tables with rough set theory, these data is often required to translate into discrete data. Discrete algorithms of data are discussed in [2∼5]. In this paper, based on rough set theory, we mainly discuss subdivision questions of decision attribute values in DS. At the same time, the relations between the decision subdivision and every one of the accuracy of approximation classification, the approximation quality of rules, core attribute and information entropy are proved theoretically. In a decision table, we find that the degree of subdivision of decision attribute values has direct influence upon attribute reduction and confidences of decision rules. The research is significant to further data mining and decision subdivisions.

S. Tsumoto et al. (Eds.): RSCTC 2004, LNAI 3066, pp. 340–345, 2004.

2 Some Methods of Rough Set Theory Analysis

A decision system can be denoted by $S =< U, A >$, where universe U is a finite set of objects, $U = \{1, 2, \cdots, n\}$, n is the number of objects; $A = C \cup D$ is a set of attributes, subsets C and D are the condition attribute set and the decision attribute set respectively. $C = \{a_1, a_2, \cdots, a_m\}$, m is the number of condition attributes. The set D includes generally a attribute, let $D = \{d\}$, d is a decision attribute. Given an attribute subset $B \in A$,

$$IND(B) = \{(x, y) \in U \times U | \forall a \in B, a(x) = a(y)\}. \quad (1)$$

Clearly, $IND(B)$ is an indiscernible relation. The number of the equivalence classes in the partition $U/IND(B)$ is denoted by $|U/IND(B)|$. For the other relevant concepts of rough set, readers could refer to [7,8].

Definition 1. [7] *Suppose that $F = \{F_1, F_2, \cdots, F_m\}$ is a partition on universe U, B is an attribute subset, the accuracy of approximation classification of F by B is defined as*

$$d_B(F) = (\sum_{i=1}^{m} |B_-(X_i)|) / \sum_{i=1}^{m} |B^-(X_i)|. \quad (2)$$

Definition 2. [6, 9] *For $Q \subseteq C$, the approximation quality $\gamma(Q \to d)$ of the rule $Q \to d$ is defined as*

$$\gamma(Q \to d) = (\sum |\{Q_-(X) : X \in U/IND(d)\}|)/|U|. \quad (3)$$

Definition 3. *Suppose that decision table $S =< U, A >$, $A = C \cup D$, $F = \{F_1, F_2, \cdots, F_m\}$ is a partition on D. The information entropy of the partition F is defined as*

$$E(F) = (\sum_{i=1}^{m} |F_i| log |F_i|)/|U|. \quad (4)$$

3 The Relation between Decision Subdivision and Rough Set Theory

In decision tables, various causes often result in decision values of objects inexact and vague [1]. For example, the influenza value of every object in Table 1 is either "yes" or "no", without further description to the degree of influenza. The influenza value is rough. Data mining prediction methods of decision values can deal with the problem of decision value subdivision through the fine quantization, meanwhile can also correct the inexactness and fault of decision etc. [5,10]. Table 2 is a subdivision of decision attribute values of Table 1. Obviously, Table 2 is more exact than Table 1 in decision diagnosis.

Suppose that in decision table $S =< U, A >$, decision attribute set $D = \{d\}$, d is a decision attribute, the number of discrete values of attribute d is $t (t \geq 2)$, the domain of attribute values of d is $\{0, 1, \cdots, t-1\}$, then the decision

Table 1. Influenza diagnosis decision table

object ID	headache	muscle-aches	temperature	influenza
1	yes	yes	normal	no
2	yes	yes	high	yes
3	yes	yes	higher	yes
4	no	yes	normal	no
5	no	no	high	no
6	no	yes	higher	yes

Table 2. The decision values subdivision of Table 1

object ID	headache	muscle-aches	temperature	influenza
1	yes	yes	normal	no
2	yes	yes	high	light
3	yes	yes	higher	serious
4	no	yes	normal	no
5	no	no	high	no
6	no	yes	higher	relative serious

attribute d determines a partition $F = \{X_0, X_1, \cdots, X_{t-1}\}$ of universe U, where $X_i = \{x | \forall x \in U, d(x) = i\}, i = 0, 1, 2, \cdots, t-1$. For $X_i \in F$, if X_i is further subdivided into X_{i1} and X_{i2}, $X_i = X_{i1} \cup X_{i2}$ and $X_{i1} \cap X_{i2} = \emptyset$ [6], then we obtain a new decision table S' by subdivided S. Let $F' = \{X_0, X_1, \cdots, X_{i-1}$ $, X_{i_1}, X_{i2}, X_{i+1}, \cdots, X_{t-1}\}$ be a partition of universe U obtained according to decision attribute d' in decision table S' (in order to distinguish, denoted d in S' by d'). Then there are some following properties between decision table S and S'.

Theorem 1. *Suppose that S' is a decision table obtained by further subdividing a decision attribute value in decision table S into two values, the other decision attribute values in S' are the same as the ones in S. If $Q \to d$ is a decision rule of decision table S, $Q \to d'$ is a decision rule of decision table S', $Q \subseteq C$, then, $\gamma(Q \to d') \leq \gamma(Q \to d)$.*

Proof. As above mentioned, $F = \{X_0, X_1, \cdots, X_{t-1}\}$ and $F' = \{X_0, X_1, \cdots,$ $X_{i-1}, X_{i1}, X_{i2}, X_{i+1}, \cdots, X_{t-1}\}$ are partitions of decision table S and S' respectively, where $X_i = X_{i1} \cup X_{i2}$ and $X_{i1} \cap X_{i2} = \emptyset$. Then we have $Q_-(X_i) = Q_-(X_{i1} \cup X_{i2})$, $Q_-(X_{i1} \cup X_{i2}) \geq Q_-(X_{i1}) \cup Q_-(X_{i2})$, namely $Q_-(X_i) \geq Q_-(X_{i1})$ $\cup Q_-(X_{i2})$. By Definition 2, $\gamma(Q \to d') \leq \gamma(Q \to d)$. □

Corollary 1. *Suppose that $F = \{X_0, X_1, \cdots, X_{t-1}\}$ is a partition of universe U obtained according to decision attribute d in decision table $S(t \geq 3)$. If some two approximation decision equivalence class X_j and X_{j+1}, whose decision attribute values are adjacent in decision table, are merged to $X_j \cup X_{j+1}$, then form a new decision table SS, and we define $X_{j'} = X_j \cup X_{j+1}$, i.e., $X_{j'} = \{x | \forall x \in U,$*

$d(x) = j$ or $d(x) = j+1\}$. The new partition $F' = \{X_0, X_1, \cdots, X_{j-1}, X_{j'}, X_{j+2}, \cdots, X_{t-1}\}$ of universe U is obtained by the decision attribute dd in SS (in order to distinguish, denote d in SS by dd), $0 \le j < t-2$. Then, $\gamma(Q \to d) \le \gamma(Q \to dd)$.

Theorem 2. *Suppose that S' is a decision table, and the decision table is obtained by further subdividing a decision attribute value in decision table S into two values. The other decision values in S' are the same as ones in S. If the decision attribute d determines a partition F of universe U in the decision table S, the decision attribute d' determines a partition F' of universe U in the decision table S', and F' is a subdivision of F. Let B be a condition attribute subset, then $d_B(F') \le d_B(F)$.*

The proof of Theorem 2 is similar to Theorem 1, so it is omitted here.

Theorem 3. *If $S =< U, A >$ is a consistent decision table, P is a condition attribute reduction corresponding to decision attribute $D = d$, $P \subseteq Q$, $Q \subseteq C$, $F = \{X_0, X_1, \cdots, X_{t-1}\}$ is a partition obtained according to attribute d on universe U. Then*

(1) $\gamma(Q \to d) = 1$;

(2) $d_Q(F) = 1$.

Proof. Since S is a consistent decision table, and P is a condition attribute reduction corresponding to decision attribute $D = \{d\}$, $F = \{X_0, X_1, \cdots, X_{t-1}\}$, we have that $POS_C(F) = POS_P(F) = U$, where $POS_C(F) = \bigcup_{X_i \in F} C_-(X_i)$ and $POS_P(F) = \bigcup_{X_i \in F} P_-(X_i)$.

By virtue of $P \subseteq Q$, $Q \subseteq C$, we have that $POS_Q(F) = U$.

Furthermore, $F = \{X_0, X_1, \cdots, X_{t-1}\}$ is a partition with respect to attribute d on universe U, $POS_Q(F) = \bigcup_{X_i \in F} Q_-(X_i)$, hence $Q_-(X_i) = X_i$, $i = 0, 1, 2, \cdots, t-1$.

Since $X_i \cap X_j = \emptyset$, $i \neq j$, $i, j = 0, 1, 2, \cdots, t-1$, so $Q^-(X_i) = X_i$.

By Definitions 1 and 2, we have that $\gamma(Q \to d) = 1$ and $d_Q(F) = 1$. □

Theorem 4. *Suppose that S is completely consistent decision table, S' is a decision table which is obtained by further subdividing a decision attribute value in S into two values, the other decision values in S' are the same as ones in S. If $a_i \in C$ is a core attribute of S, then a_i must be a core attribute of S'.*

Proof. If $F = \{X_0, X_1, \cdots, X_{t-1}\}$ is a partition of universe U according to decision attribute d in decision table S, $a_i \in C$ is a core attribute of S , $P = C \setminus \{a_i\}$, then $POS_P(F) \neq POS_C(F)$, here $POS_P(F) = \bigcup_{X_i \in F} P_-(X_i)$ and $POS_C(F) = \bigcup_{X_i \in F} C_-(X_i)$.

Since $POS_P(F) = \bigcup_{X_i \in F} P_-(X_i)$, $POS_C(F) = \bigcup_{X_i \in F} C_-(X_i)$, and for any $X_i \in F$, we have $P_-(X_i) \subseteq C_-(X_i)$, then $POS_P(F) \subset POS_C(F)$.

If X_i is subdivide into X_{i1} and $X_{i2} (X_i \subset F)$, then we form a new decision table S', and $X_i = X_{i1} \cup X_{i2}$, $X_{i1} \cap X_{i2} = \emptyset$.

Let $F1 = \{X_0, X_1, \cdots, X_{i-1}, X_{i1}, X_{i2}, X_{i+1}, \cdots, X_{t-1}\}$ be a partition of U obtained according to decision attribute d' in decision table S' (in order to distinguish, denote d in S' by d'), then

$$POS_P(F1) = A \cup P_-(X_{i1}) \cup P_-(X_{i2}) \cup B,$$

where $A = P_-(X_0) \cup P_-(X_1) \cup \cdots \cup P_-(X_{i-1})$, $B = P_-(X_{i+1}) \cup \cdots \cup P_-(X_{t-1})$.
Since

$$POS_P(F) = A \cup P_-(X_i) \cup B = A \cup P_-(X_{i1} \cup X_{i2}) \cup B,$$
$$P_-(X_{i1} \cup X_{i2}) \supseteq P_-(X_{i1}) \cup P_-(X_{i2}),$$

then $POS_P(F1) \subseteq POS_P(F)$.
As above mentioned, we know that $POS_P(F) \subset POS_C(F)$.
So $POS_P(F1) \subset POS_C(F)$, i.e., $POS_P(F1) \neq POS_C(F)$.
Since decision table S is completely consistent, then S' is also completely consistent. Namely, $POS_C(F) = POS_C(F1) = U$,
thus $POS_P(F1) \neq POS_C(F1)$, i.e., a_i is a core attribute of S'. □

Theorem 5. *Suppose that P and Q are two partitions of universe U with respect to decision attribute d, $P = \{P_1, P_2, \cdots, P_m\}$, $Q = \{Q_1, Q_2, \cdots, Q_n\}$, and $P \neq Q$. If $\forall P_i \in P$, $\exists Q_j \in Q$ with $P_i \subseteq Q_j$, then $E(P) < E(Q)$.*

Proof. Clearly $m > n$, and we can find a partition $B = \{B_1, B_2, \cdots, B_n\}$ of $\{1, 2, \cdots, m\}$ such that $Q_j = \cup_{i \in B_j} P_i$, $j = 1, 2, \cdots, n$. Hence, by Definition 3,

$$E(Q) = (\textstyle\sum_{j=1}^{n} |Q_j| \log |Q_j|)/|U| = (\sum_{j=1}^{n} |\bigcup_{i \in B_j} P_i| \log |\bigcup_{i \in B_j} P_i|)/|U|$$
$$= (\textstyle\sum_{j=1}^{n} (\sum_{i \in B_j} |P_i|) \log (\sum_{i \in B_j} |P_i|))/|U|.$$

Since $(\sum_{i \in B_j} |P_i|) \log (\sum_{i \in B_j} |P_i|) \geq \sum_{i \in B_j} |P_i| \log |P_i|$, and $m > n$,
then we can find at least one $B_{j0} \in B$ such that $|B_{j0}| > 1$.
Thus, $(\sum_{i \in B_{j0}} |P_i|) \log (\sum_{i \in B_{j0}} |P_i|) > \sum_{i \in B_{j0}} |P_i| \log |P_i|$. Hence,

$$E(Q) > (\sum_{j=1}^{n} (\sum_{i \in B_j} |P_i|) \log |P_i|))/|U| = (\sum_{j=1}^{m} |P_i| \log |P_i|)/|U| = E(P),$$

namely, $E(P) < E(Q)$. □

By the above theorems, we obtain a conclusion that the finer the decision attribute discretization of decision table is, the less the approximation quality γ of a rule, the accuracy d of approximation classification and information entropy are on any condition attribute set [9,11]. Meanwhile, if the attribute values of decision attributes are divided into finer values, then the core attributes set obtained from the finer decision table must include the core attributes set obtained from previous decision table. So the discrete degree of decision attributes should be chosen properly. About correlative study of incomplete decision tables, we should discuss it in next paper.

4 Conclusion

Based on rough set theory, we study the subdivision question of decision values in decision systems. Then we mainly research the relationship between decision subdivision and every one of the accuracy of approximation classification, the approximation quality of decision rules, core attributes and information entropy. The degree of subdivision of decision attribute value has direct influence upon the attribute reduction and confidences of decision rules in decision tables. Meanwhile, the ideas and techniques of this paper are very important to data mining and system decision in these fields, such as medicine, meteorology and chemical industry.

References

1. Pawlak, Z., Slowinski, R.: Rough set approach to multi-attribute decision analysis. Institute of Computer Science, Warsaw University of Technology, Tech Report: **36** (1993)
2. Nguyen, H.S., Skowron, A.: Quantization of real values attributes, rough set and boolean reasoning approaches. In: Proc. of the Second Joint Annual Conference on Information Science. Wrightsville Beach, NC (1995) 34-37
3. Nguyen, S.H., Nguyen, H S.: Some Efficient Algorithms for Rough Set Methods. In: Proc. of the Conference of Information Processing and Management of Uncertainty in Knowledge-Based Systems. Granada, Spain (1996) 1451-1456
4. Knowledge Systems Group.: Rosetta Technical Reference Manual (1999)
5. Zhang Yingshan: Theory of Multilateral Matrix. Chinese Statistic Press, Peking (In Chinese) (1993)
6. Ivo Duntsch, Gunther Gediga.: Simple data filtering in rough set systems. International Journal of Approximate Reasoning **18**(1998) 93-106
7. Pawlak, Z.: Rough Sets. Norwell: Kluwer Academic Punlishers (1991)
8. Pawlak, Z.: Rough sets. International Journal of Information and Computer Science **11(5)**(1982) 341-356
9. Ivo Duntsch, Gunther Gediga: Uncertainty measures of rough set prediction. Artificial Intelligence **106**(1998) 109-137
10. Lee, T.L., Tsai, C.P., Jeng, D.S.: Neural network for the prediction and supplement of tidal record in Taichung Harbor, Taiwan. Advances in Engineering Software **33**(2002) 329-338
11. Theresa Beaubouef, Frederick E.Petry: Information-theoretic measures of uncertainty for rough sets and rough relational databases. Journal of Information Sciences **109** (1998)185-195

Rough Set Methods in Approximation of Hierarchical Concepts

Jan G. Bazan[1], Sinh Hoa Nguyen[2], Hung Son Nguyen[3], and Andrzej Skowron[3]

[1] Institute of Mathematics,University of Rzeszów
Rejtana 16A, 35-959 Rzeszów, Poland
[2] Japanese-Polish Institute of Information Technology
Koszykowa 86, 02-008, Warsaw, Poland
[3] Institute of Mathematics, Warsaw University
Banacha 2, 02-097 Warsaw, Poland
{bazan,hoa,son,skowron}@mimuw.edu.pl

Abstract. Many learning methods ignore domain knowledge in synthesis of concept approximation. We propose to use hierarchical schemes for learning approximations of complex concepts from experimental data using inference diagrams based on domain knowledge. Our solution is based on the rough set and rough mereological approaches. The effectiveness of the proposed approach is performed and evaluated on artificial data sets generated by a traffic road simulator.

1 Introduction

Many problems in machine learning, pattern recognition or data mining can be formulated as searching related to concept approximation [5]. A typical concept approximation process uses a given information about objects from a finite subset of universe, called training set or sample, to induce the description of the approximation. In many learning tasks, e.g., identification of dangerous situations on the road by unmanned vehicle aircraft (UAV), the target concept is too complex and it can not be approximated directly from feature value vectors. If the target concept is a composition of some simpler ones, the layered learning [17] is an alternative approach to concept approximation.

Assuming that a hierarchical concept decomposition is given, the main idea is to gradually synthesize a target concept from simpler ones. A learning process can be imagined as a treelike structure with the target concept located at the highest layer. At the lowest layer, basic concepts are approximated using feature values available from a data set. At the next layer more complex concepts are synthesized from the basic concepts. This process is repeated for successive layers.

The importance of hierarchical concept synthesis is now well recognized by researchers (see, e.g., [8, 11, 12]). An idea of hierarchical concept synthesis, in the rough mereological and granular computing frameworks has been developed (see, e.g., [8, 12, 13]) and problems of compound concept approximation are discussed, e.g., in [3, 8, 14, 16].

S. Tsumoto et al. (Eds.): RSCTC 2004, LNAI 3066, pp. 346–355, 2004.

In this paper we deal with concepts that are specified by decision classes in decision systems [9]. The crucial for inducing concept approximations is to create the description of concepts in such a way that makes it possible to maintain the acceptable level of imprecision along all the way from the basic attributes to the final decision. We discuss some strategies for concept composing founded on the rough set approach. We also examine effectiveness of layered learning approach by comparison with the standard rule-based learning approach. Quality of the new approach is verified with respect to the robustness of concept approximation, preciseness of concept approximation, computation time required for concept induction, and concept description length. Experiments are carried out on artificial data sets generated by a traffic road simulator.

2 Rough Set Approach to Concept Approximation

Formally, the concept approximation problem can be formulated as follows: given an universe $\mathcal{U}$ of objects (cases, states, patients, observations, etc.), and a concept X which can be interpreted as a subset of $\mathcal{U}$, the problem is to find a description of X, that can be expressed in a predefined descriptive language $\mathcal{L}$. We assume that $\mathcal{L}$ consists of such formulas that are interpretable as subsets of $\mathcal{U}$.

There are many reasons that force as to find some approximated rather than exact description of a given concept. Let us recall some of them: (i) not satisfactory expressive power of language $\mathcal{L}$ in the universe $\mathcal{U}$: in many learning tasks, the concept X is already defined in some language $\mathcal{L}^*$, (e.g., natural language), but we have to describe X in another, usually poorer language $\mathcal{L}$ (e.g., consisting of boolean formulae defined by some features); (ii) a given concept X is specified partially: in inductive learning approach, values of characteristic function of X are given only for objects from a *training set* $U \subseteq \mathcal{U}$ of objects.

Rough set theory offers an interesting idea to describe a concept in such situations. In the following section, we recall the rough set approach to concept approximation problem. Let us fix some notation used in next sections.

Usually, we assume that the input data for concept approximation problem is given by a decision table, i.e., a tuple $\mathbb{S} = (U, A, dec)$, where U is a non-empty, finite set of *training objects*, A is a non-empty, finite set, of *attributes* and $dec \notin A$ is a distinguished attribute called *decision*. Each attribute $a \in A$ is a function $a : U \to V_a$ called *evaluation function*, where V_a is called the *domain* of a. For any non-empty set of attributes $B \subseteq A$ and any object $x \in U$, we define the *B-signature* of x by: $inf_B(x) = \{(a, a(x)) : a \in B\}$. The set $INF_B(\mathbb{S}) = \{inf_B(x) : x \in U\}$ is called the *B-signature* of $\mathbb{S}$.

Without loss of generality, we assume that the domain of the decision *dec* is equal to $V_{dec} = \{1, \ldots, d\}$. For any $k \in V_{dec}$, the set $CLASS_k = \{x \in U : dec(x) = k\}$ is called the kth *decision class of* $\mathbb{S}$. The decision *dec* determines a partition of U into decision classes, i.e., $U = CLASS_1 \cup \ldots \cup CLASS_d$. Rough set methodology for concept approximation can be described as follows.

Definition 1. *Let $X \subseteq \mathcal{U}$ be a concept and let $U \subseteq \mathcal{U}$ be a finite sample of $\mathcal{U}$. Assume that for any $x \in U$ there is given information if $x \in X \cap U$ or*

$x \in \mathcal{U} - X$. An approximation (induced from sample U) of the concept X is any pair $\mathbb{P} = (\mathbf{L}, \mathbf{U})$ satisfying the following conditions:

1. $\mathbf{L} \subseteq \mathbf{U} \subseteq \mathcal{U}$;
2. $\mathbf{L}, \mathbf{U}$ *are subsets of* $\mathcal{U}$ *expressible in the language* $\mathcal{L}$;
3. $\mathbf{L} \cap U \subseteq X \cap U \subseteq \mathbf{U} \cap U$;
4. *the set* $\mathbf{L}$ ($\mathbf{U}$) *is maximal (minimal) in the family of sets definable in* $\mathcal{L}$ *satisfying (3).*

The sets $\mathbf{L}$ and $\mathbf{U}$ are called the *lower approximation* and the *upper approximation* of the concept $X \subseteq \mathcal{U}$, respectively. The set $\mathbf{BN} = \mathbf{U} \setminus \mathbf{L}$ is called the *boundary region of approximation* of X. The set X is called *rough* with respect to its approximations $(\mathbf{L}, \mathbf{U})$ if $\mathbf{L} \neq \mathbf{U}$, otherwise X is called *crisp* in $\mathcal{U}$. The pair $(\mathbf{L}, \mathbf{U})$ is also called the *rough set* (for the concept X). The condition (4) in the above list can be substituted by inclusion to a degree to make it possible to induce approximations of higher quality of the concept on the whole universe $\mathcal{U}$. In practical applications the last condition in the above definition can be hard to satisfy. Hence, by using some heuristics we construct sub-optimal instead of maximal or minimal sets. The rough approximation of concept can be also defined by means of rough membership function.

Definition 2. *Let $X \subseteq \mathcal{U}$ be a concept and let decision table $\mathbb{S} = (U, A, dec)$ describe the set of training objects $U \subseteq \mathcal{U}$. A function $f : \mathcal{U} \to [0,1]$ is called a rough membership function of the concept $X \subseteq \mathcal{U}$ if, and only if $(\mathbf{L}_f, \mathbf{U}_f)$ is a rough approximation of X (induced from sample U), where $\mathbf{L}_f = \{x \in \mathcal{U} : f(x) = 1\}$ and $\mathbf{U}_f = \{x \in \mathcal{U} : f(x) > 0\}$.*

Many methods of discovering rough approximations of concepts from data have been proposed, e.g., method based on reducts [9][10], on k-NN classifiers [3], or on decision rules [3]. In the next section we will use rough membership functions to construct the layered learning algorithm. Hence, let us recall now a construction of rough membership function for concept approximation. The construction is based on decision rules.

Searching for decision rules, which are *short, strong* and *having high confidence*, from a given decision table is a challenge for data mining. Many methods based on rough set theory have been proposed to deal with such problems (see, e.g., [2, 6]).

Given a decision table $\mathbb{S} = (U, A, dec)$. Let us assume that $\mathbf{RULES}(\mathbb{S})$ is a set of decision rules induced by some rule extraction method. For any object $x \in \mathcal{U}$, let $MatchRules(\mathbb{S}, x)$ be the set of rules from $\mathbf{RULES}(\mathbb{S})$ supported by x. One can define the rough membership function $\mu_{CLASS_k} : \mathcal{U} \to [0,1]$ for the concept determined by $CLASS_k$ as follows:

1. Let $\mathbf{R}_{yes}$ be the set of all decision rules from $MatchRules(\mathbb{S}, x)$ for k^{th} class and let $\mathbf{R}_{no} \subset MatchRules(\mathbb{S}, x)$ be the set of decision rules for other classes.
2. We define two real values w_{yes}, w_{no}, called "for" and "against" weights for the object x by

$$w_{yes} = \sum_{\mathbf{r} \in \mathbf{R}_{yes}} strength(\mathbf{r}) \qquad w_{no} = \sum_{\mathbf{r} \in \mathbf{R}_{no}} strength(\mathbf{r}) \tag{1}$$

where $strength(\mathbf{r})$ is a normalized function depending on $length$, $support$, $confidence$ of $\mathbf{r}$ and some global information about the decision table $\mathbb{S}$ like table size, class distribution (see [2]).

3. One can define the value of $\mu_{CLASS_k}(x)$ by

$$\mu_{CLASS_k}(x) = \begin{cases} \text{undetermined} & \text{if } \max(w_{yes}, w_{no}) < \omega \\ 0 & \text{if } w_{no} - w_{yes} \geq \theta \text{ and } w_{no} > \omega \\ 1 & \text{if } w_{yes} - w_{no} \geq \theta \text{ and } w_{yes} > \omega \\ \frac{\theta + (w_{yes} - w_{no})}{2\theta} & \text{in other cases} \end{cases}$$

where ω, θ are parameters set by user. These parameters make it possible in a flexible way to control the size of boundary region for the approximations established according to Definition 2.

3 Layered Learning Approach Based on Rough Set Theory

In this section we discuss a composing strategy for concepts from already existing ones. Such strategy realizes a crucial step in concept synthesis. We discuss a method that makes it possible to control the level of approximation quality along all the way from basic concepts to the target concept.

We assume that a concept hierarchy H is given. The concept hierarchy should contain either inference diagram or dependence diagram that connect the target concept with input attributes through intermediate concepts. A training set is represented by decision table $\mathbb{S}_S = (U, A, D)$, where D is a set of decision attributes corresponding to all intermediate concepts and to the target concept. Decision values indicate if an object belong to basic concepts and to the target concept, respectively.

Using information available from a concept hierarchy for each basic concept C_b one can create a training decision system $\mathbb{S}_{C_b} = (U, A_{C_b}, dec_{C_b})$, where $A_{C_b} \subseteq A$, and $dec_{C_b} \in D$. To approximate the concept C_b one can apply any classical method (e.g., k-NN, supervised clustering, or rule-based approach [7]) to the table $\mathbb{S}_{C_b}$. In further discussion we assume that basic concepts are approximated by rule based classifiers (see Section 2) derived from relevant decision tables.

To avoid overly complicated notation let us limit ourselves to the case of constructing compound concept approximation on the basis of two simpler concept approximations. Assume we have two concepts C_1 and C_2 that are given to us in the form of rule-based approximations derived from decision systems $\mathbb{S}_{C_1} = (U, A_{C_1}, dec_{C_1})$ and $\mathbb{S}_{C_1} = (U, A_{C_1}, dec_{C_1})$. Henceforth we are given two rough membership functions $\mu_{C_1}(x)$, $\mu_{C_2}(x)$. These functions are determined with use of parameter sets $\{w_{yes}^{C_1}, w_{no}^{C_1}, \omega^{C_1}, \theta^{C_1}\}$ and $\{w_{yes}^{C_2}, w_{no}^{C_2}, \omega^{C_2}, \theta^{C_2}\}$, respectively. We want to establish similar set of parameters $\{w_{yes}^{C}, w_{no}^{C}, \omega^{C}, \theta^{C}\}$ for the target concept C, which we want to describe with use of rough membership function μ_C. As previously, the parameters ω, θ controlling of the boundary region are user-configurable. But, we need to derive $\{w_{yes}^{C}, w_{no}^{C}\}$ from the data.

The issue is to define a decision system from which rules used to define approximations can be derived. To this end we concentrate on this matter.

We assume that both simpler concepts C_1, C_2 and the target concept C are defined over the same universe of objects $\mathcal{U}$. Moreover, all of them are given on the same sample $U \subset \mathcal{U}$. To complete the construction of the decision system $\mathbb{S}_C = (U, A_C, dec_C)$ we need to specify the conditional attributes from A_C and the decision attribute dec_C. The decision attribute value $dec_C(x)$ is given for any object $x \in U$. For conditional attributes, we assume that they are either rough membership functions for simpler concepts (i.e., $A_C = \{\mu_{C_1}(x), \mu_{C_2}(x)\}$) or weights for simpler concepts (i.e., $A_C = \{w_{yes}^{C_1}, w_{no}^{C_1}, w_{yes}^{C_2}, w_{no}^{C_2}\}$). The output set O_i for each concept C_i, where $i = 1, 2$, consists of either one attribute which is a rough membership function μ_{C_i} (in the first case) or two attributes $w_{yes}^{C_i}, w_{no}^{C_i}$ which describe fitting degrees of objects to the concept C_i and its complement, respectively.

By extracting rules from $\mathbb{S}_C$ rule-based approximations of the concept C are created. Algorithm 1 is the layered learning algorithm used in our experiments.

Algorithm 1 Layered learning algorithm

Input: Decision system $\mathbb{S} = (U, A, d)$, concept hierarchy H;
Output: Schema for concept composition

for $l := 0$ to *max_level* **do**
  for (any concept C_k at the level l in H) **do**
    if $l = 0$ **then**
      $\mathbb{S}_{C_k} := (U, A_k, dec_{C_k})$; $\{A_k \subset A$ is a set of attributes relevant to $C_k\}$
    else
      $A_k := \bigcup O_{k_i}$; {where the sum is taken for all sub-concepts C_{k_i} of C_k}
      $\mathbb{S}_{C_k} := (U, A_k, dec_{C_k})$;
    end if
    generate a rule set determining of the concept C_k approximation;
    generate the output vector $O_k = \{w_{yes}^{C_k}, w_{no}^{C_k}\}$, where $w_{yes}^{C_k}(x)$ and $w_{no}^{C_k}(x)$ are the fitting degree of object x to the concept C_k and its complement.
  end for
end for

It is important to observe that such rules describing C use attributes that are in fact classifiers themselves. Therefore, in order to have more readable and intuitively understandable description as well as more control over quality of approximation (especially for new cases) it pays to stratify and interpret attribute domains for attributes in A_C. Instead of using just a value of membership function or weight we would prefer to use linguistic statements such as *"the likeliness of the occurrence of* C_1 *is low"*. In order to do that we have to map the attribute value sets onto some limited family of subsets. Such subsets are then identified with notions such us *"certain"*, *"low"*, *"high"* etc. It is quite natural, especially in case of attributes being membership functions, to introduce linearly ordered subsets of attribute ranges, e.g., $\{negative, low, medium, high, positive\}$. That yields fuzzy-like layout, or linguistic variables, of attribute values. One may (and in some cases should) consider also the case when these subsets overlap.

Stratification of attribute values and introduction of linguistic variable attached to inference hierarchy serves multiple purposes. First, it provides a way for representing knowledge in more human-readable format since if we have a new situation (new object $x^* \in \mathcal{U} \setminus U$) to be classified (checked against compliance with concept C) we may use rules like: ***If*** *compliance of* x^* *with* C_1 *is* *high or medium* ***and*** *compliance of* x^* *with* C_2 *is* *high* ***then*** $x^* \in C$.

Another advantage of imposing the division of attribute value sets lays in extended control over flexibility and validity of system constructed in this way. As we may define the linguistic variables and corresponding intervals, we gain the ability of making system more stable and inductively correct. In this way we control the general layout of boundary regions for simpler concepts that contribute to construction of the target concept. The process of setting the intervals for attribute values may be performed by hand, especially when additional background information about the nature of the described problem is available. One may also rely on some automated methods for such interval construction, such as, e.g., clustering, template analysis and discretization. Some extended discussion on foundations of this approach, which is related to rough-neural computing [8] and computing with words can be found in [15, 16].

4 Experimental Results

To verify a quality of hierarchical classifiers we performed some experiments with the road simulator system.

4.1 Road Simulator

Learning to recognize and predict traffic situations on the road is the main issue in many unmanned vehicle aircraft (UVA) projects. It is a good example for the hierarchical concept approximation problem. We demonstrate the proposed layered learning approach on our own simulation system.

ROAD SIMULATOR is a computer tool generating data sets consisting of recording vehicle movements on the roads and at the crossroads. Such data sets are next used to learn and test complex concept classifiers working on information coming from different devices (sensors) monitoring the situation on the road. Let us present some important features of this system.

During the simulation the system registers a series of parameters of the local simulations, that is simulations related to each vehicle separately, as well as two global parameters of the simulation that is parameters specifying driving conditions during the simulation. The local parameters are related to driver's profile, which is randomly determined, when a new vehicle appears on the board, and may not be changed until it disappears from the board. The global parameters like visibility, weather conditions are set randomly according to some scenario. We associate the simulation parameters with the readouts of different measuring devices or technical equipment placed inside the vehicle or in the outside environment (e.g., by the road, in a police car, etc.). Apart from those sensors, the simulator registers a few more attributes, whose values are determined by the sensor's values in a way specified by an expert. In Figure 1 we present an example of a hierarchical diagram for the some exemplary concepts. During the simulation data may be generated and stored in a text file in a form of a rectangle table (information system). Each row of this table depicts the situation of a single vehicle, e.g., the values of sensors and concepts values. Within each simulation step descriptions of situations of all the vehicles are stored into a file.

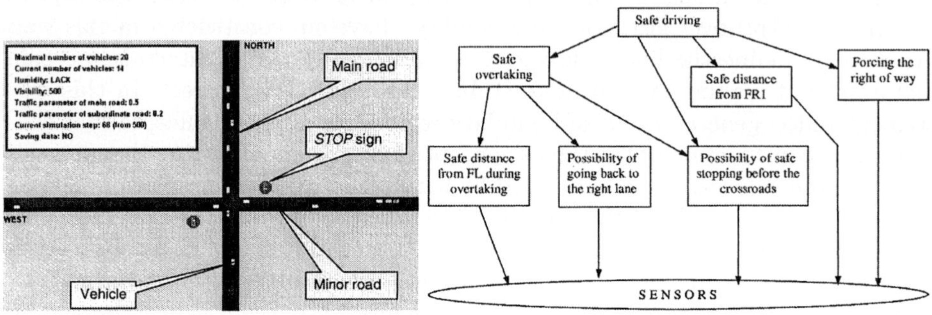

Fig. 1. The board of simulation and the relationship diagram of exemplary concepts

4.2 Experiment Setup

We have generated 6 training data sets: *c10_s100, c10_s200, c10_s300, c10_s400, c10_s500, c20_s500* and 6 corresponding testing data sets named by *c10_s100N, c10_s200N, c10_s300N, c10_s400N, c10_s500N, c20_s500N.* All data sets consists of 100 attributes. The smallest data set consists of above 700 situations (100 simulation units) and the largest data set consists of above 8000 situations (500 simulation units).

We compare the accuracy of two classifiers, i.e., **RS:** the standard classifier induced by the rule set method, and **RS-L:** the hierarchical classifier induced by the RS-layered learning method. In the first approach, we employed the RSES system [4] to generate the set of minimal decision rules. We use the simple voting strategy for conflict resolution in new situation classification.

In the RS-layered learning approach, from training table we create five subtables to learn five basic concepts (see Figure 1): C_1: "*safe distance from FL during overtaking,*" C_2: "*possibility of safe stopping before crossroads,*" C_3: "*possibility of going back to the right lane,*" C_4: "*safe distance from FR1,*" C_5: "*forcing the right of way.*" A concept C_6: "*safe_overtaking*" is located in the next level. To approximate concept C_6, we create a table with three conditional attributes. These attributes describe fitting degrees of objects to concepts C_1, C_2, C_3, respectively. The target concept C_7: "*safe_driving*" is located in the third level of the concept decomposition hierarchy. To approximate C_7 we also create a decision table with three attributes, representing fitting degrees of objects to the concepts C_4, C_5, C_6, respectively.

Classification Accuracy: Similarly to real life situations, the decision class "safe_driving = YES" is dominating. The decision class "safe_driving = NO"

takes only 4% - 9% of training sets. Searching for approximation of "safe_driving = NO" class with the high precision and generality is a challenge of leaning algorithms. Let us concentrate on approximation quality of the "NO" class. In Table 1 we present the classification accuracy of RS and RS-L classifiers. One can observe, the accuracy of "YES" class of both standard and hierarchical classifiers is high. Whereas accuracy of "NO" class is very poor, particularly in case of the standard classifier. The hierarchical classifier showed to be much better than the standard classifier for this class. Accuracy of "NO" class of the hierarchical classifier is quite high when the size of training sets is sufficiently large.

Table 1. Classification accuracy of standard and hierarchical classifiers

Accuracy	Total		Class YES		Class of NO	
	RS	**RS-L**	**RS**	**RS-L**	**RS**	**RS-L**
$c10\_s100N$	0.94	0.97	1	1	0	0
$c10\_s200N$	0.99	0.96	1	0.98	0.75	0.60
$c10\_s300N$	0.99	0.98	1	0.98	0	0.78
$c10\_s400N$	0.96	0.77	0.96	0.77	0.57	0.64
$c10\_s500N$	0.96	0.89	0.99	0.90	0.30	0.80
$c20\_s500N$	0.99	0.89	0.99	0.88	0.44	0.93
Average	0.97	0.91	0.99	0.92	**0.34**	**0.63**

Robustness and Coverage Rate: Robustness and coverage rate of classifiers are evaluated by their recognition ability for unseen situations. The recognition rate of situations belonging to "NO" class is very poor in the case of the standard classifier. One can see in Table 2 the improvement on coverage degree of "YES" class and "NO" class of the hierarchical classifier.

Table 2. Coverage rate of standard and hierarchical classifiers

Covering rate	Total		Class YES		Class NO	
	RS	**RS-L**	**RS**	**RS-L**	**RS**	**RS-L**
$c10\_s100N$	0.44	0.72	0.44	0.74	0.50	0.38
$c10\_s200N$	0.72	0.73	0.73	0.74	0.50	0.63
$c10\_s300N$	0.47	0.68	0.49	0.69	0.10	0.44
$c10\_s400N$	0.74	0.90	0.76	0.93	0.23	0.35
$c10\_s500N$	0.72	0.86	0.74	0.88	0.40	0.69
$c20\_s500N$	0.62	0.89	0.65	0.89	0.17	0.86
Average	0.62	0.79	0.64	0.81	**0.32**	**0.55**

Computing Speed: With respect to time the layered learning approach shows a tremendous advantage in comparison with the standard learning approach. In the case of the standard classifier, computational time is measured as a time required for computing a rule set used to decision class approximation. In the case of hierarchical classifier computational time is the total time required for

Table 3. Time for standard and hierarchical classifier generation (experiments were performed on computer with processor AMD Athlon 1.4GHz., 256MB RAM)

Table names	**RS**	**RS-L**	**Speed up ratio**
c10_s100	94 s	2.3 s	40
c10_s200	714 s	6.7 s	106
c10_s300	1450 s	10.6 s	136
c10_s400	2103 s	34.4 s	60
c10_s500	3586 s	38.9 s	92
c20_s500	10209 s	98.0s	104
Average			**90**

all sub-concepts and target concept approximation. One can see in Table 3 that the speed up ratio of the layered learning approach to the standard one is from 40 to 130.

5 Conclusions

We presented a new method for concept synthesis. It is based on the layered learning approach. Unlike traditional approach, in the layered learning approach the concept approximations are induced not only from accessed data sets but also from expert's domain knowledge. In the paper, we assume that knowledge is represented by concept dependency hierarchy. The layered learning approach showed to be promising for the complex concept synthesis. Experimental results with road traffic simulation are showing advantages of this new approach in comparison to the standard approach. The concept approximation by composition of sub-concepts is the main problem in the layered learning approach. In future we plan to investigate more advanced approaches for concept composition.

One interesting possibility is to use patterns defined by rough approximations of concepts defined by different kinds of classifiers in synthesis of compound concepts. We also would like to develop methods for rough-fuzzy classifier's synthesis (see Section 3). In particular, the mentioned in Section 3 method based on rough-fuzzy classifiers introduces more flexibility for such composing because a richer class of patterns introduced by different layers of rough-fuzzy classifiers can lead to improving of classifier quality [8].

We also plan to apply layered learning approach to real-life problems, especially when domain knowledge is specified in natural language. This can make further links with the computing with words paradigm [8, 18]. This is in particular linked with the rough mereological approach (see, e.g., [12]) and with the rough set approach for approximate reasoning in distributed environments [13, 15], in particular with methods of information system composition [1, 15].

Acknowledgements

The research has been partially supported by the grant 3 T11C 002 26 from Ministry of Scientific Research and Information Technology of the Republic of Poland.

References

1. Barwise, J., Seligman, J., eds.: Information Flow: The Logic of Distributed Systems. Cambridge University Press, Cambridge, UK (1997)
2. Bazan, J.G.: A comparison of dynamic and non-dynamic rough set methods for extracting laws from decision tables. In Polkowski, L., Skowron, A., eds.: Rough Sets in Knowledge Discovery 1: Methodology and Applications. Physica-Verlag, Heidelberg (1998) 321–365
3. Bazan, J., Nguyen, H.S., Skowron, A., Szczuka, M.: A view on rough set concept approximation. LNAI **2639**, Heidelberg, Springer-Verlag (2003) 181–188
4. Bazan, J.G., Szczuka, M.: RSES and RSESlib - a collection of tools for rough set computations. LNAI **2005** , Springer-Verlag, Heidelberg (2001) 106–113
5. Kloesgen, W., Żytkow, J., eds.: Handbook of Knowledge Discovery and Data Mining. Oxford University Press, Oxford (2002)
6. Komorowski, J., Pawlak, Z., Polkowski, L., Skowron, A.: Rough sets: a tutorial. In Pal, S.K., Skowron, A., eds.: Rough Fuzzy Hybridization: A New Trend in Decision-Making. Springer-Verlag, Singapore (1999) 3–98
7. Mitchell, T.: Machine Learning. Mc Graw Hill (1998)
8. Pal, S.K., Polkowski, L., Skowron, A., eds.: Rough-Neural Computing: Techniques for Computing with Words. Springer-Verlag, Heidelberg (2003)
9. Pawlak, Z.: Rough Sets: Theoretical Aspects of Reasoning about Data. Volume 9 of System Theory, Knowledge Engineering and Problem Solving. Kluwer Academic Publishers, Dordrecht (1991)
10. Pawlak, Z., Skowron, A.: A rough set approach for decision rules generation. In: Thirteenth International Joint Conference on Artificial Intelligence IJCAI, Chambéry, France, Morgan Kaufmann (1993) 114–119
11. Poggio, T., Smale, S.: The mathematics of learning: Dealing with data. Notices of the AMS **50** (2003) 537–544
12. Polkowski, L., Skowron, A.: Rough mereology: A new paradigm for approximate reasoning. International Journal of Approximate Reasoning **15** (1996) 333–365
13. Skowron, A.: Approximate reasoning by agents in distributed environments. In Zhong, N., Liu, J., Ohsuga, S., Bradshaw, J., eds.: Intelligent Agent Technology Research and Development: Proceedings of IAT01, Maebashi, Japan, October 23-26. World Scientific, Singapore (2001) 28–39
14. Skowron, A.: Approximation spaces in rough neurocomputing. In Inuiguchi, M., Tsumoto, S., Hirano, S., eds.: Rough Set Theory and Granular Computing. Springer-Verlag, Heidelberg (2003) 13–22
15. Skowron, A., Stepaniuk, J.: Information granule decomposition. Fundamenta Informaticae **47(3-4)** (2001) 337–350
16. Skowron, A., Szczuka, M.: Approximate reasoning schemes: Classifiers for computing with words. In: Proceedings of SMPS 2002. Advances in Soft Computing, Heidelberg, Canada, Springer-Verlag (2002) 338–345
17. Stone, P.: Layered Learning in Multi-Agent Systems: A Winning Approach to Robotic Soccer. The MIT Press, Cambridge, MA (2000)
18. Zadeh, L.A.: A new direction in AI: Toward a computational theory of perceptions. AI Magazine **22** (2001) 73–84

Classifiers Based on Two-Layered Learning

Jan G. Bazan

Institute of Mathematics, University of Rzeszów
Rejtana 16A, 35-959 Rzeszów, Poland
bazan@univ.rzeszow.pl

Abstract. In this paper we present an exemplary classifier (classification algorithm) based on two-layered learning. In the first layer of learning a collection of classifiers is induced from a part of original training data set. In the second layer classifiers are induced using patterns extracted from already constructed classifiers on the basis of their performance on the remaining part of training data. We report results of experiments performed on the following data sets, well known from literature: diabetes, heart disease, australian credit (see [5]) and lymphography (see [4]). We compare the standard rough set method used to induce classifiers (see [1] for more details), based on minimal consistent decision rules (see [6]), with the classifier based on two-layered learning.

1 Introduction

A *classifier* (*classification algorithm*) is an algorithm that permits us to repeatedly make a forecast on the basis of accumulated knowledge in new situations. Classifiers are induced from training data and next they are used to classify new, unseen cases. Each new object is assigned to a class belonging to a predefined set of classes on the basis of observed values of suitably chosen attributes (features).

There have been proposed many approaches for classifier construction like classical and modern statistical techniques, neural networks, decision trees, decision rules and inductive logic programming (see, e.g., [3, 5] for more details).

One of the most popular method for inducing of classifiers is based on learning rules from examples. The standard rough set methods based on calculation of all (or some) reducts make it possible to compute, for a given data, the descriptions of concepts by means of minimal consistent decision rules (see, e.g., [6], [2]).

In the majority of rough set applications the computation of decision rules is done only at some initial stage of inductive learning. Next, the decision rules are used to built a classifier that can be applied to any tested object.

Another approach can be based on a two-layered learning strategy. In the first layer of learning a collection of classifiers is induced from a part of original training data set. Whereas in the second layer classifiers are induced using patterns extracted from already constructed classifiers on the basis of their performance on the remaining part of training data (called validation table).

The aim of the paper is to compare the performance of classifiers based on calculation of all minimal consistent decision rules with methods based on

S. Tsumoto et al. (Eds.): RSCTC 2004, LNAI 3066, pp. 356–361, 2004.

two-layered learning presented in Section 2. We report experiments supporting our hypothesis that classifiers induced using the two-layered strategy show better performance on unseen objects than the traditional classifiers (see Section 3), especially if the misclassification cost is very high (e.g., some medical data, market data etc.). For comparison we use several data sets, in particular: lymphography (see, e.g., [4]) and StatLog's data (see [5]).

2 Classifiers Based on Two-Layered Learning

Many decision rule generation methods have been developed using rough set theory (see, e.g., [1, 4, 8]). We assume that the reader is familiar with basic notions of the rough set theory. One of the most interesting approaches to the decision rule generation is related to *minimal consistent decision rules* (i.e. decision rule with minimal number of descriptors in premise) (see [6, 1]). The classifier based on all minimal consistent decision rules we will be denoted by Algorithm 1.

The standard rough set methods based on calculation of all minimal consistent decision rules are not always relevant for inducing classifiers. This happens, e.g., when the number of examples supporting the decision rule is relatively small. Then, instead of minimal consistent decision rules, we use approximate decision rules to eliminate this drawback. Different methods are now widely used to generate approximate decision rules (see [1] for more details). In our method for computing of approximate rules, we begin with generation of minimal consistent decision rules from a given decision table. Next, we compute approximate rules from already calculated decision rules. Our method is based on the notion of consistency of decision rule. The original optimal rule is reduced (by descriptor dropping) to an approximate rule with confidence exceeding a fixed threshold (see, e.g., [1] for more details).

In the majority of rough set applications the computation of decision rules is done only at some initial stage of inductive learning. Therefore, if we use algorithm based on approximate rules, the threshold of confidence for approximate rules computation has to be chosen at the moment of rules computation and next we can use approximate rules computed by this threshold for any tested object. The choice of threshold can be optimized for a given data set in the following way. The original training table is divided into a *training table* and *validation table.* Approximate decision rules are computed for the training table for any selected confidence threshold from a fixed set of thresholds. An optimization of the confidence threshold is performed using the validation table. The set of rules with the lowest classification error rate for validation table is chosen.

However, for the vast majority of data sets, we cannot find one, optimal confidence threshold that is relevant for all approximate rules (in classifying of any tested object). For example, we can have several thresholds of confidence obtained for a given data. Some of them can be optimal for some part of data set, the others can be optimal for some other parts. In the classical method, (mentioned above) a threshold relevant for the largest part of data set is chosen.

Another approach can be based on classifier construction using all approximate rule sets computed for a family of confidence thresholds. Such classifiers are used to classify new objects using a special decision table. Such table is constructed on the basis of classification results of objects from the validation table using decision rule sets computed for the training table. Decision rules computed for this special table can resolve conflicts between decision rule sets computed for training table. Therefore this special table will be called a *conflict table.* The calculation of rules for the training table is called a *learning on the first layer.* Whereas, the calculation of rules for the conflict table is called a *learning on the second layer.*

The structure of any classifier constructed on the first layer of learning allows us to identify the classifier with an algorithm for membership function derivation (see [2]). We can define it as a parameterised function μ_{CLASS_k} of the form:

IF $\max(w_{yes}, w_{no}) < \omega$ **THEN** $\mu_{CLASS_k}(u) = 0$
OTHERWISE

$$\mu_{CLASS_k}(u) = \begin{cases} 1 & \text{if } w_{yes} - w_{no} \geq \theta \\ \frac{\theta + (w_{yes} - w_{no})}{2\theta} & \text{if } |w_{yes} - w_{no}| < \theta \\ 0 & \text{if } w_{yes} - w_{no} \leq -\theta \end{cases}$$

where u is any tested object, $CLASS_k$ is the k-th decision class from the given decision table, real values w_{yes}, w_{no} called "for" and "against" weights to the object u are a normalised functions depending on properties of rules which have been computed for the training table (see [2], [1]) and ω, θ are parameters set by the user. These parameters allow us to search for new relevant features (attributes) based on attributes from the given decision table. We use these parameters to define new attributes on the second layer of complex classifier. Hence, condition attribute values of the conflict table are computed using function μ_{CLASS_k} for any decision class $CLASS_k$, where $1 \leq k \leq d$ (d is a number of decision classes) and for any θ from a fixed set (see [2]). Whereas, the decision attribute of the conflict table is the same as in the validation table.

We have mentioned before that in the vast majority of data sets it is not possible to find the optimal confidence threshold that is universally optimal (i.e., guaranteeing the high classification quality tested objects) for all approximate rules computed using such threshold. Hence, building the conflict table, we cannot classify objects from validation table using all approximate rule sets. Therefore for any set of approximate rules we construct a special table, called an *initial classifying table.* The structure of this table is the same as the structure of validation table, apart from the decision attribute that is replaced by another attribute computed using the result of classification test performed on the validation table by decision rules computed from the training table. Any object from the validation table is classified by rules computed from the training table and if the result of classification is correct, a value of decision attribute in the initial classifying table is equal 1. If the result of classification is incorrect or tested object isn't recognized, a value of decision attribute in the initial classifying table is equal 0. Hence, decision rules computed from the initial classifying table can classify any tested object to the decision class 1 or 0. If the result of classification is equal 1, than original object from validation table (or more extended table) can be classified by rules generated from the original training table, values of function μ_{CLASS_k} (for any decision class) can be computed and inserted to the conflict table. Otherwise, the value MISSING (does not concern) is inserted to the conflict table instead of values of function μ_{CLASS_k}.

The experimental data sets usually consist of numerical attributes with large numbers of values. Therefore, if we want to calculate decision rules of the high quality, we have to use some discretization method. In this paper we use discretization methods based on the rough set techniques (see [7, 1] for details).

We present an algorithm based on the two-layered learning more formally.

Algorithm 2. *The classifier based on the two-layered learning*
Step 1. Split randomly a given table T into two subtables: the training table $T1$ and the validation table $T2$ (e.g., $T1$ is 50% of T).
Step 2. Generate discretization cuts for the table T and store them using a set variable C.
Step 3. Discretize the tables T, $T1$ and $T2$ using cuts from the set C (tables after discretization will by represented by TS, $TS1$ and $TS2$).
Step 4. For all selected confidence thresholds p perform the following operations:
a) calculate all rules for the table $TS1$ and store them using a variable $R(p)$,
b) shorten rules from set $R(p)$ to an approximate rules with threshold p
c) construct table $T2(p)$ in the following way:
(i) condition attributes of table $T2(p)$ are the same as in the table $T2$;
(ii) decision attribute of table $T2(p)$ is obtained by classifying table $TS2$ using rules from set $R(p)$:
- if object u from table $TS2$ is properly classified by rules from $R(p)$ then set value 1 as the decision value for u in the table $T2(p)$
- otherwise set value 0 as the decision value for u in the table $T2(p)$,
d) generate discretization cuts for table $T2(p)$ and store cuts to set $C2(p)$,
e) discretize table $T2(p)$ using cuts from set $C2(p)$ (table after discretization will by represented as $TS2(p)$),
f) calculate all rules for table $TS2(p)$ and store them in the set $RR(p)$.
Step 5. Create empty table TC.
Step 6. For all selected thresholds p do
a) For all selected θ insert attributes to the table TC computed in the following way:
(1) discretize object u using $C2(p)$,
(2) classify object u by rules from set $RR(p)$,
(3) if u is classified to the class with label 1 then
- discretize object u using C,
- classify object u by rules from set $R(p)$,
- compute values $\mu_{CLASS_1}(u)$, ..., $\mu_{CLASS_d}(u)$,
- insert values $\mu_{CLASS_1}(u)$, ..., $\mu_{CLASS_d}(u)$ to the table TC as value of attributes determined by $R(p)$ and θ;
otherwise insert value MISSING to the table TC instead of values $\mu_{CLASS_1}(u)$, ..., $\mu_{CLASS_d}(u)$
b) Copy the decision attribute from table $T2$ to table TC.
Step 7. Calculate all rules for table TC and store them using a set variable RC.

Table 1. Results of experiments with data sets

Data	Algorithm	Error rate	Coverage	Real error rate
Diabetes	A1	0.288	1.0	0.288
Diabetes	A2	0.241	0.747	0.435
Heart disease	A1	0.199	1.0	0.199
Heart disease	A2	0.161	0.868	0.272
Australian credit	A1	0.151	1.0	0.151
Australian credit	A2	0.141	0.962	0.174
Lymphography	A1	0.241	1.0	0.241
Lymphography	A2	0.218	0.835	0.348

Algorithm 2 can be used to classify any tested object u as follows. For a given object u we construct object uc analogously to the case of objects from the table TC (see Step 6 of Algorithm 2). Next, the object uc is classified using rules from RC, but if uc isn't recognized by rules from RC or it is classified to the boundary region or classification on u described by the decision attribute from the original data is inconsistent (table TC can be inconsistent) then the object uc is not classified.

Our hypothesis is that the performance of the classifier presented above is better than the classifier constructed using Algorithm 1. In the next section we will test this hypothesis using different data sets.

3 Experiments with Data

We present the results of experiments performed on the following four data sets, well known from literature: diabetes, heart disease, australian credit (see "StatLog" project - [5]) and lymphography (see, e.g., [4]).

The results of experiments were obtained by: 12, 9, 10 and 10-fold cross validation for the diabetes, heart disease, australian credit and lymphography data respectively.

Algorithms presented in this paper are implemented in object-oriented programming library: "RSES-lib 2.1", creating the computational kernel of the system "RSES 2.1" (see [8]).

We compare the results of Algorithm 2, presented in this paper, with those obtained by Algorithm 1 (see Section 2). Table 1 shows the results of the considered classification algorithms for the data sets mentioned before. In case of the cross-validation method we present the average (from all folds) values of error rate and coverage.

One can see that error rate of Algorithm 2 (on the covered region of objects) is lower than error rate obtained by Algorithm 1 for analyzed data sets. Therefore we conclude, that results of Algorithm 2 is better than results of Algorithm 1 for recognized objects by these algorithms.

In the algorithm presented above we use an algorithm for calculation of all reducts. Hence, the complexity of Algorithm 2 is very high. Therefore we plan to develop heuristics to obtain some knowledge about the reduct set instead calculation of all reducts (see [8]).

4 Summary

We have presented classifiers based on two-layered learning. The experiments show that the classification quality of such classifiers on covered regions of objects are better than results of the classifier based on the whole set of decision rules. In case the object misclassification cost is high (e.g., some medical data, market data etc.) one can prefer to have a classifier (Algorithm 2) returning answer *I don't know* if there is a high risk that the generated decision by classifier is false.

Acknowledgements

I wish to thank professor Andrzej Skowron for inspiration, stimulating discussions and great support while writing this paper.

The research has been supported by the grant 3T11C00226 from Ministry of Scientific Research and Information Technology of the Republic of Poland.

References

1. Bazan J.: A comparison of dynamic non-dynamic rough set methods for extracting laws from decision tables. In: [7], pp. 321–365.
2. Bazan, J., Nguyen, H.S., Skowron, A., Szczuka, M.: A view on rough set concept approximation. In Wang, G., Liu, Q., Yao, Y., Skowron, A., eds.: Proceedings of the Ninth International Conference on Rough Sets, Fuzzy Sets, Data Mining and Granular Computing (RSFDGrC'2003), Chongqing, China. Volume 2639 of Lecture Notes in Artificial Intelligence, Heidelberg, Germany, Springer-Verlag (2003) 181-188.
3. Friedman, J.H. and Hastie, T., and Tibshirani, R.: The elements of statistical learning: Data mining, inference, and prediction. Springer-Verlag, Heidelberg (2001).
4. Grzymała-Busse J., A New Version of the Rule Induction System LERS Fundamenta Informaticae, Vol. 31(1), 1997, pp. 27–39
5. Michie, D., Spiegelhalter, D., J., Taylor, C., C.: Machine learning, neural and statistical classification. Ellis Horwood, New York (1994)
6. Pawlak Z., Rough sets: Theoretical aspects of reasoning about data, Kluwer Dordrecht, 1991.
7. Polkowski L., Skowron A. (eds.), Rough Sets in Knowledge Discovery vol. 1–2, Physica-Verlag, Heidelberg, 1998
8. The RSES Homepage – `logic.mimuw.edu.pl/~rses`

Rough Fuzzy Integrals for Information Fusion and Classification

Tao Guan and Boqin Feng

School of Electronics and Information Engineering, Xi'an Jiaotong University
Xi'an, 710049, China

Abstract. This paper presents two extended fuzzy integrals under rough uncertainty, i.e. rough upper fuzzy and lower fuzzy integrals, and extended properties are also given. Furthermore, these two integrals are applied here in information fusion and classification processes for rough features, and the corresponding extended models are also proposed. These types of integrals generalize fuzzy integrals and enlarge their domains of applications in fusion and classification under rough uncertainty. Examples show that they fuse or classify objects with rough features with fairly good effects while the existed methods based on reals can not solve.

1 Introduction

Since fuzzy integrals are proposed by Sugeno [1], they have been deeply investigated and widely applied in decision making, information fusion, pattern recognition. Fuzzy integrals are based on fuzzy measures that measure fuzzy sets in fuzzy measure spaces, of which $\{g_\lambda | \lambda > -1\}$ is an important collection.

As another theory of measuring uncertain information, rough set theory [2] explains the indiscernibility between objects in terms of finite features, while fuzzy sets measure the fuzziness of boundaries between sets [3]. Recently two new extended set theories emerge by putting fuzzy sets and rough sets together, i.e. fuzzy rough sets and rough fuzzy sets [3–5], which have some special characteristics and applications. Rough fuzzy set theory is a new tool to approximate fuzzy concepts in approximation space by associating fuzzy set with rough set theories.

This paper presents the rough fuzzy integrals and their properties. This kind of approximations are similar to Darboux sums [5]. They are useful in information fusion and classification of objects with rough features.

2 Fuzzy Measures and Fuzzy Integrals

The concepts of fuzzy measures and fuzzy integrals are introduced by Sugeno in 1972 [1]. Given fuzzy measure space $(U, \mathcal{B}, g)$ where $\mathcal{B}$ is the Borel field of U and g is a fuzzy measure defined on $\mathcal{B}$, the basic definitions of fuzzy measures and fuzzy integrals [1] are described by Sugeno as

S. Tsumoto et al. (Eds.): RSCTC 2004, LNAI 3066, pp. 362–367, 2004.

Definition 1. *A set function defined on $\mathcal{B}$ which has the following properties is called a fuzzy measure.*

$\diamond$ $g(\emptyset) = 0,\ g(U) = 1$;

$\diamond$ *If* $A, B \in \mathcal{B}$ *and* $A \subset B$, *then* $g(A) \leq g(B)$;

$\diamond$ *If* $F_n \in \mathcal{B}$ *for* $1 \leq n < \infty$ *and a sequence* $\{F_n\}$ *is monotone(in the sense of inclusion), then* $lim_{n \to \infty} g(F_n) = g(lim_{n \to \infty} F_n)$.

Definition 2. *Let* $h : U \mapsto [0, 1]$ *be a* $\mathcal{B}$*-measurable function. A fuzzy integral over* $A \in \mathcal{B}$ *of a function* $\mu(x)$ *with respect to* g *is defined as follows:*

$\int_A \mu(x) \circ g(\cdot) = \sup_{\alpha \in [0,1]} [\alpha \wedge g(A \cap H_\alpha)]$, *where* $H_\alpha = \{x \in U | \mu(x) \geq \alpha\}$.

Further discussions on fuzzy integrals appear in [1].

3 Rough Fuzzy Integrals and Properties

3.1 Rough Approximations of a Fuzzy Set

Rough fuzzy sets present roughness of fuzzy sets and are explicated by Dibois in [5]. For fuzzy set μ, its rough membership functions are $\underline{R}\mu$ and $\overline{R}\mu$ where R is an indiscernibility relation on U, which are introduced again as

$$\underline{R}\mu(x) = inf\{\mu(y) | y \in [x]_R\}, \quad \overline{R}\mu(x) = sup\{\mu(y) | y \in [x]_R\},$$

Obviously they constitute rough approximations of $\mu(x)$. The approximations are obviously associating with R.

3.2 Rough Fuzzy Integrals

Let $\mathcal{F} = (U, \mathcal{S}, g)$ be a fuzzy measure space [6, 7] and R is an indiscernibility relation on U, $|U| < \infty$, then the following definitions firstly are given.

Definition 3. *[6] The simple functions in* $(U, \mathcal{B}, m)$ *are functions that have the form* $f = \sum_{i=1}^{n} \alpha_i \chi_{C_i}$ *where* $\alpha_i \neq 0$, C_i *is the* $\mathcal{B}$*-measurable set and* m *is Lebegue measure. The simple functions are Lebegue integrable in* $(U, \mathcal{B}, m)$ *if* $m(C_i) < \infty$ *for every index* i .

Definition 4. *The simple functions in* $\mathcal{F}$ *are expressed as* $\mu = \sum_{i=1}^{n} \alpha_i \chi_{C_i}$, *where* $\{C_i | i \leq r\}$ *is a collection of crisp subsets of* U *and* $\alpha_i s$ *are constants in* $[0, 1]$.

Example 1. In the fuzzy objective information system (U, A, V, f) where $|U| < \infty$, we have $C_i \in \frac{U}{R_B}$, $i = 1, 2, \cdots, n$, where R_B is an indiscernibility relation derived from attribute subset B of A.

Moreover, α_i could be explained as M_i or m_i in D.Dubois's paper[3] which could be expressed as

$$m_i = inf\{\mu(x) | x \in C_i\}, \quad M_i = sup\{\mu(x) | x \in C_i\}. \tag{1}$$

Theorem 1. *Assumed that* μ *is a simple function in* $\mathcal{F}$, *then it is integrable if* $g(C_i) < 1$ *for every index* i *for which* $\alpha_i \neq 0$ *and* $C_i \in \frac{U}{R}$.

Proof. $\int_A \mu \circ g(\cdot) = sup_{\alpha\in[0,1]}[\alpha \wedge g(A \cap H_\alpha)] = \max_{1\le i\le n}[\alpha_i \wedge g(A \cap H_{\alpha_i})] < 1$, where $H_{\alpha_i} = \cup_j\{C_j|\forall x \in C_j, \mu(x) \ge \alpha_i\}$.

Theorem 2. *Let μ be a fuzzy subset of U, then $\underline{R}\mu$ and $\overline{R}\mu$ are simple functions in $\mathcal{F}$ that derived from (U, R).*

Proof. Because of $|U| < \infty$, then $\underline{R}\mu$, $\overline{R}\mu$ are expressed as according to (1):
$\underline{R}\mu = \sum_{i=1}^n m_i\chi_{C_i}$, $\overline{R}\mu = \sum_{i=1}^n M_i\chi_{C_i}$, where $C_i \in \frac{U}{R}$ and $|\frac{U}{R}| = n$.

Theorem 3. *Let $\mu : U \mapsto [0,1]$ be a fuzzy subset of $\mathcal{F}$, then $\underline{R}\mu$ and $\overline{R}\mu$ are integrable in $\mathcal{F}$.*

Proof. Because $\underline{R}\mu$ and $\overline{R}\mu$ are simple functions in $\mathcal{F}$, then they are integrable.

Theorem 4. *Let $\mu : U \mapsto [0,1]$ is a $\mathcal{F}$-measurable function, then the rough upper and lower fuzzy integrals over $A \in \mathcal{F}$ of μ with respect to g are defined as*
$\int_A \underline{R}\mu\circ g(\cdot) = \max_{1\le i\le n}[m_i\wedge g(A\cap\underline{H}_{m_i})]$, $\int_A \overline{R}\mu\circ g(\cdot) = \max_{1\le i\le n}[M_i\wedge g(A\cap\overline{H}_{M_i})]$,
where $\underline{H}_{m_i} = \cup_j\{C_j|\underline{R}\mu(C_j) \ge m_i\}$, $\overline{H}_{M_i} = \cup_j\{C_j|\overline{R}\mu(C_j) \ge M_i\}$. Especially when $A = C_i, 1 \le i \le n$, we get
$\int_{C_i} \underline{R}\mu \circ g(\cdot) = m_i \wedge g(C_i)$, $\int_{C_i} \overline{R}\mu \circ g(\cdot) = M_i \wedge g(C_i)$.

Property 1. For $A, B \subset U$. Let μ_1, μ_2 be two fuzzy subsets of U and R be an indiscernibility relation on U, then
(a) $\int_A \underline{R}\mu \circ g(\cdot) \ge 0$ and $\int_A \overline{R}\mu \circ g(\cdot) \ge 0$;
(b) If $\mu = c$, then $\int_A \underline{R}\mu \circ g(\cdot) = \int_A \overline{R}\mu \circ g(\cdot) = \int_A \mu \circ g(\cdot) = max(c, g(A))$;
(c) If $A \subset B$, then $\int_A \underline{R}\mu\circ g(\cdot) \le \int_B \underline{R}\mu\circ g(\cdot)$, and $\int_A \overline{R}\mu\circ g(\cdot) \le \int_B \overline{R}\mu\circ g(\cdot)$;
(d) If $\mu_1 \le \mu_2$, then $\int_A \underline{R}\mu_1 \circ g(\cdot) \le \int_A \underline{R}\mu_2 \circ g(\cdot)$, and $\int_A \overline{R}\mu_1 \circ g(\cdot) \le \int_A \overline{R}\mu_2 \circ g(\cdot)$;
(e) $\int_A \overline{R}\underline{R}\mu \circ g(\cdot) = \int_A \underline{R}\underline{R}\mu \circ g(\cdot) = \int_A \underline{R}\mu \circ g(\cdot)$;
(f) $\int_A \overline{R}\overline{R}\mu \circ g(\cdot) = \int_A \underline{R}\overline{R}\mu \circ g(\cdot) = \int_A \overline{R}\mu \circ g(\cdot)$;
(g) $\int_A \underline{R}\mu \circ g(\cdot) \le \int_A \mu \circ g(\cdot) \le \int_A \overline{R}\mu \circ g(\cdot)$;
(h) $\int_{C_i} \underline{R}\mu \circ g(\cdot) \le \int_{C_i} \overline{R}\mu \circ g(\cdot)$.

Proof is finished by monotonicity principle of fuzzy integrals [1] and rough logic [8].

Definition 5. *Let μ_1, μ_2 be two fuzzy subsets of $\mathcal{F}$, we call them rough upper or lower integration equality on U if they separately satisfy*
$\int_{C_i} \underline{R}\mu_1\circ g(\cdot) = \int_{C_i} \underline{R}\mu_2\circ g(\cdot)$, *or* $\int_{C_i} \overline{R}\mu_1\circ g(\cdot) = \int_{C_i} \overline{R}\mu_2\circ g(\cdot)$, *for* $1 \le i \le n$, *which separately denoted as "$=^\sim$" and "$=_\sim$" for brevity.*

Theorem 5. *Suppose that two convex fuzzy sets μ_1, μ_2 satisfy $\mu_1 \le \mu_2$, then $\int_A \underline{R}\mu_1 \circ g(\cdot) \le \int_A \underline{R}\mu_2 \circ g(\cdot)$ and $\int_A \overline{R}\mu_1 \circ g(\cdot) \le \int_A \overline{R}\mu_2 \circ g(\cdot)$ for $A \subset U$.*
Proof is obtained by using property (d).

Theorem 6. *Suppose that two convex fuzzy sets μ_1, μ_2 satisfy $\mu_1 \le \mu_2$, $\mu_1 =^\sim \mu_2$ and $\mu_1 =_\sim \mu_2$ for $\forall C_i, i \le n$, then $\mu_1 = \mu_2$.*

Proof. By Definition 5, Theorem 5, proof can be easily obtained.

4 Applications to Information Fusion and Classification

Information fusion and classification by fuzzy integrals has been investigated by Keller et al [9–11], and their applications include handwritten word classifiers [10], computer vision [11]. The fusion and classification models proposed in [9] base on fuzzy integrals which use and produce reals. However, in some situations such as interval values, their models are not suitable to classify patterns or objects. One of extended types of classifiers based on rough fuzzy integrals is presented here for patterns or objects with rough interval values. The following definitions are firstly present.

Definition 6. *A feature f is called a rough feature if it satisfies $f : U \to I[0,1]$, where U denotes the object set and $I[0,1]$ denotes the collection of crisp subsets of U. Moreover, $f(x)$ is called rough feature value of x.*

Table 1 shows an information table with rough features and rough feature values.

Definition 7. *$(U, \mathcal{F}, \nu)$ is a rough feature space, where*
◇ U is the object set $\{x_i : i \leq n\}$;
◇ $\mathcal{F}$ is the set of rough features, $\mathcal{F} = \{f_i : i \leq m\}$, $f_i : U \to I[0,1]$;
◇ ν is the inclusion measure, $\nu : I[0,1] \times I[0,1] \to [0,1]$, for $\forall x, y \in U$.

In $(U, \mathcal{F}, \nu)$ we define the rough fuzzy integral operator T with rough relation R, such that $T : U \times \mathcal{F} \to I[0,1]$, i.e. $T : U \times \mathcal{F} \to [\int \underline{R}f_i \cdot g(\cdot), \int \overline{R}f_i \cdot g(\cdot)]$. Here $[\int \underline{R}f_i \cdot g(\cdot), \int \overline{R}f_i \cdot g(\cdot)]$ is called the confidence interval to some class, where $g(\cdot)$ can be computed by fuzzy densities g^i. Additionally, R can be constructed from data of features.

Definition 8. *Given operator T and classes $c_i, i \leq k$, we define the following formula as the membership degree of x_j to c_i.*

$$\gamma_{ij} = \begin{cases} \frac{|T(x_j,\mu_{x_j}) \cap c_i|}{|c_i|} & \text{if } T(x_j, \mu_{x_j}) - c_i \neq \emptyset, \\ 1 & \text{otherwise} \end{cases}$$

If $\gamma_i = max_q\{\gamma_q | q \leq k\}$, then we say $x \in c_i$. Furthermore, the precision of x_j to c_i is defined as

$$\delta_{ij} = \begin{cases} \frac{|T(x_j,\mu_{x_j}) \cap c_i|}{|T(x_j,\mu_{x_j})|} & \text{if } T(x_j, \mu_{x_j}) - c_i \neq \emptyset, \\ 1 & \text{otherwise} \end{cases},$$

where μ_{x_j} denotes the fuzzy function of x about $\mathcal{F}$, and $|\cdot|$ means cardinality.

Fig.1 presents the fusion model by using rough fuzzy integrals. It preprocesses the object data by using some commonly used methods, such as moving average for missing data. Then rough features are extracted with possible forms, such as $[0.1, 0.4]$ or $\{0.1, 0.4\}$. μ_i is the rough fuzzy function of x_i defined by above rough feature functions. The simple way to specifying R is to let each feature be an equivalence class, as shown in Fig.2. Furthermore, in the classification model as Fig.3, there exist several fusion nodes for different classes. For given fuzzy densities g^i, the fusion or classification results are expressed as rough values, with which their confidences in some class can be calculated.

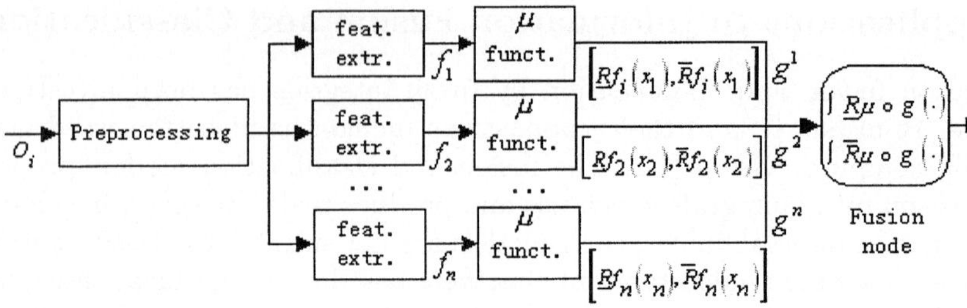

Fig. 1. The fusion model by using rough fuzzy integrals

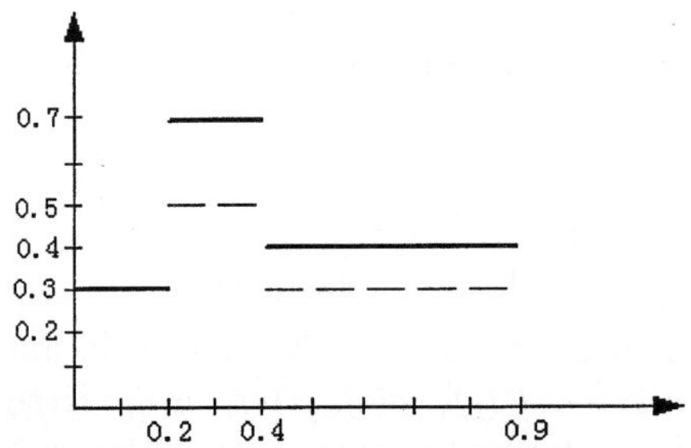

Fig. 2. The rough fuzzy function of object 1 in Table 1

Table 1. An information table with rough features where $\overline{\mu}$ and $\underline{\mu}$ are expressed by f_1, f_2, f_3

Object	f_1	f_2	f_3
1	[0.3,0.3]	[0.5,0.7]	[0.3,0.4]
2	[0.4,0.5]	{0.6, 0.7}	[0.1,0.5]
3	{0.2, 0.3}	[0.4,0.6]	[0.4,0.4]
4	[0.1,0.1]	[0.3,0.5]	{0.3, 0.5}
5	[0.1,0.3]	[0.5,0.6]	[0.4,0.6]
6	[0.1,0.4]	[0.4,0.6]	[0.2,0.3]
7	[0.3,0.5]	{0.3, 0.5}	[0.1,0.2]
8	{0.1, 0.2}	[0.4,0.5]	[0.4,0.5]

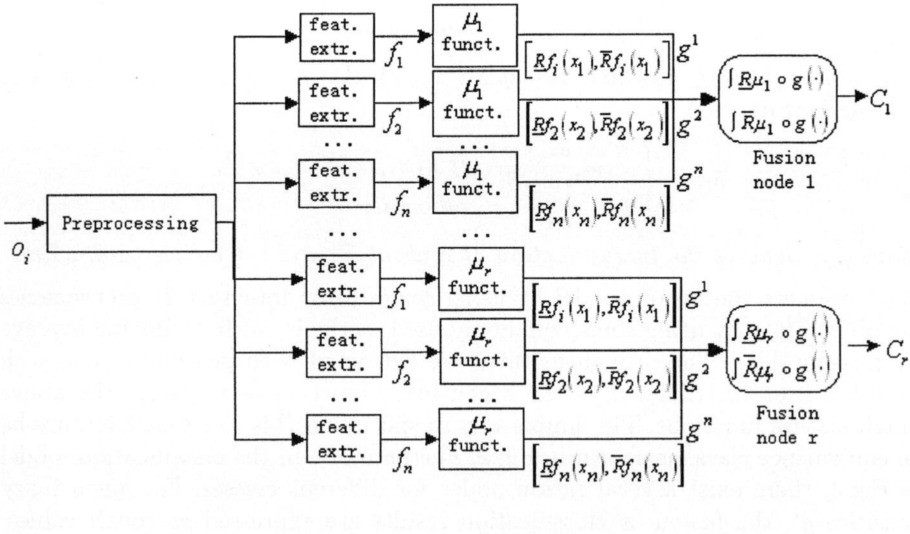

Fig. 3. The fusion model by using rough fuzzy integrals

Example 2. We consider the information table shown as Table 1. The first object is illustrated in Fig.2. Suppose $g^1 = 0.2$, $g^2 = 0.2$ and $g^3 = 0.5$, two class $c_1 = [0.3, 0.4]$, $c_2 = [0.4, 0.5]$, then we obtain $\lambda = 0.4$ with $\lambda + 1 = \prod_{i=1}^{3}(1 + \lambda g^i), \lambda > -1$, and $T(x_1, \mu_{x_1}) = [0.3, 0.4]$, $T(x_2, \mu_{x_2}) = [0.4, 0.5]$, and $\gamma_{11} = 1$,$\gamma_{12} = 0$,$\gamma_{21} = 0$,$\gamma_{22} = 1$, and $\delta_{11} = 1$, $\delta_{12} = 0$, $\delta_{21} = 0$, $\delta_{22} = 1$, so $x_1 \in c_1$ and $x_2 \in c_2$ with certainty, where γ_{ij} and δ_{ij} denote the membership degree and precision of x_j to c_i respectively.

5 Conclusions

Rough extensions of fuzzy integrals in this paper are efficient in information fusion and classification of objects or patterns with rough features and enlarge application fields of fuzzy integrals in information fusion and classification.

References

1. M. Sugeno: Fuzzy measures and fuzzy integrals. Trans. S.I.C.E. 8, No.2 (1972)
2. Z. Pawlak: Rough sets. International Journal of Computer and Information Sciences 11(1982) 341-356
3. Y.Y.Yao: A comparative study of fuzzy sets and rough sets. Journal of Information Sciences 109(1998) 227-242
4. Anna Maria Radzikowska, Etienne E. Kerre: A comparative study of fuzzy rough sets. Fuzzy Sets and Systems 126(2002) 137-155
5. D. Dubois, H. Prade: Rough fuzzy sets and fuzzy rough sets. Int. J. General Systems. 17(2-3),pp.191-209,1990
6. Paul R. Halmos: Measure theory. Graduate Texts in Mathematics 18, Spring-Verlag, 1974
7. Z. Wang, G. J. Klir: Fuzzy measure theory. Plenum Press, New York, 1992
8. T.Y. Lin, Qing Liu, Xiaoling Zou: Models for first order rough logic applications to data mining. 'Soft Computing in Intelligent Systems and Information Processing', Proceedings of the 1996 Asian Fuzzy Systems Symposium. 11-14 Dec. 1996, pp.152-157
9. James M. Keller, Jeffrey Osborn: Training the fuzzy integral. International Journal of Approximation Reasoning 1996:15, 1-24
10. Paul D. Gader, Magdi A. Mohamed, James M. Keller: Fusion of handwritten word classifiers. Pattern Recognition Letters 17(1996), pp.577-584
11. Hossein Tahani, James M. Keller: Information fusion in computer vision using the fuzzy integral. IEEE Trans. On Systems, Man, and Cybernetics, Vol.20, No.3, May/June 1990

Towards Jointree Propagation with Conditional Probability Distributions

Cory J. Butz, Hong Yao, and Howard J. Hamilton

Department of Computer Science, University of Regina
Regina, Saskatchewan, Canada S4S 0A2
{butz,yao2hong,hamilton}@cs.uregina.ca

Abstract. In this paper, we suggest a novel approach to jointree computation. Unlike all previous jointree methods, we propose that jointree computation should use conditional probability distributions rather than potentials. One salient feature of this approach is that the exact form of the messages to be transmitted throughout the network can be identified a priori. Consequently, irrelevant messages can be ignored, while relevant messages can be computed more efficiently. We discuss four advantages of our jointree propagation method.

1 Introduction

Probabilistic expert systems have been successfully applied in practice to a wide variety of problems involving uncertainty [4, 5]. This success is due in large part to the development of efficient algorithms for propagating probabilities in a jointree [2, 5]. In these methods, each node in the jointree has an associated probability table, called a *potential*. Jointree propagation typically involves two phases; an inward phase from the leaf nodes to the root node, and an outward phase from the root node to the leaf nodes. During the inward pass, each node sends an unknown message (a probability table) that the receiving node multiplies with its potential. After the outward pass, the probability table for each node is the desired marginal distribution. These jointree algorithms, however, perform unnecessary computation, since they do not know the form of the messages being passed between nodes in the jointree.

In this paper, we suggest a method for determining the exact conditional probability distributions that will be sent between nodes during jointree propagation. This method is built upon a simple graphical representation of the conditional probability distributions originally assigned to each jointree node. Knowing the exact form of the messages to be sent has several advantages. Most importantly, *unnecessary* computation can be avoided. The traditional jointree methods [5] will propagate empty messages, i.e., tables consisting entirely of all ones. Since absorbing a message of all ones does not change the potential for the receiving node, the message does not need to be computed, transmitted, and absorbed during propagation. Secondly, the amount of *parallelism* can be increased. Since the messages to be sent are known in advance, we explicitly demonstrate

S. Tsumoto et al. (Eds.): RSCTC 2004, LNAI 3066, pp. 368–377, 2004.

that a non-leaf node may have enough information to send a message before hearing from the leaf nodes. Thirdly, our method suggests a *hierarchical* representation of a Bayesian network, which has been the focus of several recent investigations such as [3]. This hierarchical representation is based on the fact that when our jointree propagation method finishes, the conditional probability tables at each jointree node define a local Bayesian network. Finally, our work here on probabilistic inference in a jointree extends research on inference in a Bayesian network [9].

This paper is organized as follows. Section 2 reviews background information. Traditional jointree propagation is discussed in Section 3. In Section 4, critical remarks on these works are given. We present our method for jointree propagation with conditionals in Section 5. In Section 6, advantages of our approach are provided. The conclusion is presented in Section 7.

2 Background Knowledge

In this section, we review the notions of Bayesian networks and jointrees [5].

Let U be a finite set of discrete variables, each with a finite domain. Let V be the Cartesian product of the variable domains. A *joint probability distribution* is a function p on V such that $0 \leq p(v) \leq 1$ for each configuration $v \in V$ and $\sum_{v \in V} p(v) = 1.0$. Henceforth, we may say p is on U with the frame V understood. The *marginal distribution* $p(X)$ for $X \subseteq U$ is defined as $\sum_{U-X} p(U)$. If $p(X) > 0$, then the *conditional probability distribution* $p(Y|X)$ is defined as $p(YX)/p(X)$. A *potential* is a function ϕ on V such that $\phi(v)$ is a nonnegative real number and $\sum_{v \in V} \phi(v)$ is positive, i.e., at least one $\phi(v) > 0$.

A *Bayesian network* [4] is a directed acyclic graph (DAG) D together with a conditional probability distribution $p(a_i|P_i)$ for each variable a_i in D, where P_i denotes the parent set of variable a_i in D.

Example 1. Let $U = \{a, b, c, d, e, f, g, h, i, j, k\}$ be a set of binary variables. Consider the DAG $\{(a, b), (b, g), (c, d), (c, e), (c, h), (d, f), (e, f), (f, g), (g, j), (g, k), (h, i), (h, j), (i, j)\}$. Corresponding conditionals are given in Figure 1.

In Example 1, the *conditional independencies* [6] encoded in the DAG indicate that the product of the conditionals in Figure 1 is a unique joint distribution $p(U)$, namely,

$$p(U) = p(a) \cdot p(b|a) \cdot p(c) \cdot p(d|c) \cdot p(e|c) \cdot p(f|d, e) \cdot p(g|b, f) \cdot p(h|c) \\ \cdot p(i|h) \cdot p(j|g, h, i) \cdot p(k|g).$$

The important point is that Bayesian networks provide a semantic modeling tool which greatly facilitate the acquisition of probabilistic knowledge. Specifying $p(U)$ directly would require 2047 prior probabilities ($2^{11} - 1$ for eleven binary variables), while the Bayesian network conditionals can be specified using only 30 conditional probabilities. Probabilistic inference, on the other hand, is typically carried out on a jointree (a chordal undirected graph).

a	$p(a)$
1	0.496

a b	$p(b\|a)$
0 1	0.052
1 1	0.358

c e	$p(e\|c)$
0 1	0.383
1 1	0.286

c	$p(c)$
1	0.577

c d	$p(d\|c)$
0 1	0.714
1 1	0.627

c h	$p(h\|c)$
0 1	0.214
1 1	0.651

d e f	$p(f\|d,e)$
0 0 1	0.710
0 1 1	0.193
1 0 1	0.485
1 1 1	0.602

h i	$p(i\|h)$
0 0	0.104
1 1	0.369

b f g	$p(g\|b,f)$
0 0 1	0.027
0 1 1	0.123
1 0 1	0.898
1 1 1	0.405

g k	$p(k\|g)$
0 1	0.593
1 1	0.416

g h i j	$p(j\|g,h,i)$
0 0 0 1	0.178
0 0 1 1	0.565
0 1 0 1	0.446
0 1 1 1	0.729
1 0 0 1	0.931
1 0 1 1	0.582
1 1 0 1	0.403
1 1 1 1	0.222

Fig. 1. *Conditionals* for the Bayesian network in Example 1.

Probabilistic inference means computing the probability values of a particular set of variables given that other variables take on certain values. There are several efficient methods for probabilistic inference in jointrees [5].

The DAG is converted into a chordal undirected graph by applying the moralization and triangulation procedures. The *moralization* [4] D^m of a DAG D on set U of variables is the unique undirected graph defined as $D^m = \{(a,b) | a, b \in F_i$ for at least one variable $a_i \in U\}$, where F_i is the family set $\{a_i\} \cup P_i$ of a_i. If necessary, undirected edges are added to the moralization D^m to create a chordal graph D^t. An undirected graph is *chordal* (or *triangulated*) if each cycle of length four or more possesses an edge (a,b) between two nonadjacent nodes a and b in the cycle. Each maximal clique in the chordal graph is represented by a node in a jointree, defined as follows.

Definition 1. [5] A *jointree* is a tree with the property that any variable in two nodes is also in every *separating set* on the path between the two.

Example 2. One possible jointree for the Bayesian network in Example 1 is depicted in Figure 2. We label the nodes of this jointree as ab, bfg, $cdefgh$, $ghij$, and gk. The separating sets are $\{b\}$, $\{f,g\}$, $\{g,h\}$, and $\{g\}$.

3 Conventional Jointree Propagation

We will refer to the method in [1] as the *Aalborg* jointree propagation method which is regarded as the best jointree propagation algorithm [5].

The objective of jointree propagation is to compute a marginal distribution $p(X)$ for each jointree node X. The first step is to construct an initial potential $\phi(X)$ for each node X in the jointree. For each configuration x of X, set $\phi(x) = 1.0$. Next, assign each conditional $p(a_i|P_i)$ in the Bayesian network to precisely one node X containing $\{a_i\} \cup P_i$ and set $\phi(X) = \phi(X) \cdot p(a_i|P_i)$.

Example 3. Recall the conditionals in Figure 1 and the constructed jointree in Figure 2. First, we set $\phi_1(a,b) = 1.0$, $\phi_2(b,f,g) = 1.0$, $\phi_3(c,d,e,f,g,h) = 1.0$,

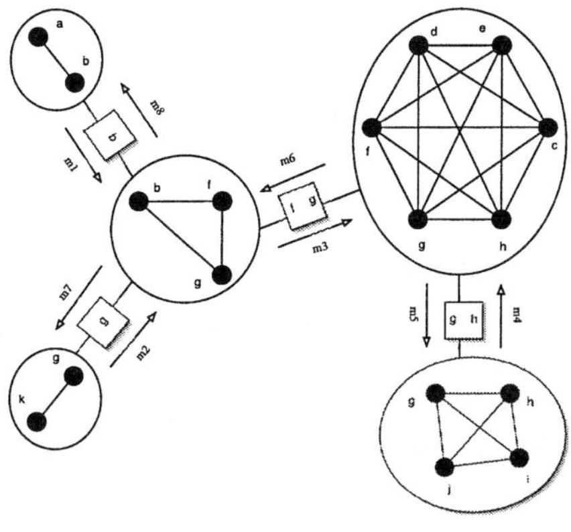

Fig. 2. Traditionally, eight *unknown* messages $m1, m2, \ldots, m8$ are propagated in the jointree $\{ab, bfg, cdefgh, ghij, gk\}$.

$\phi_4(g,h,i,j) = 1.0$, and $\phi_5(g,k) = 1.0$. Second, we can multiply the given conditionals in Figure 1 to the jointree potentials as follows:

$$\begin{aligned}
\phi_1(a,b) &= \phi_1(a,b) \cdot p(a) \cdot p(b|a), \\
\phi_2(b,f,g) &= \phi_2(b,f,g) \cdot p(g|b,f), \\
\phi_3(c,d,e,f,g,h) &= \phi_3(c,d,e,f,g,h) \cdot p(c) \cdot p(d|c) \cdot p(e|c) \cdot p(f|d,e) \cdot p(h|c), \\
\phi_4(g,h,i,j) &= \phi_4(g,h,i,j) \cdot p(i|h) \cdot p(j|g,h,i), \\
\phi_5(g,k) &= \phi_5(g,k) \cdot p(k|g).
\end{aligned}$$

The Aalborg jointree propagation method works as follows [5]. One node is chosen as the root node. Each separator S also has a potential $\phi(S)$ initialized to all ones.

Rule 1. Each nonroot node waits to send its message to a given neighbour until it has received messages from all its other neighbours.

Rule 2. The root node waits to send messages to its neighbours until it has received messages from all of them.

Rule 3. When a node is ready to send its message to a particular neighbour, it computes the message by marginalizing its current table to its intersection with this neighbour, and then sends the message to the separator between it and the neighbour.

Rule 4. When a separator receives a message ψ from one of its two nodes, it divides the message ψ by its current table ϕ, sends the quotient ψ/ϕ on to the other node, and then replaces ϕ with ψ.

Rule 5. When a node receives a message, it replaces its current table with the product of that table and the message.

Rules 1 and 2 force the propagation to move in to the root and then back out to the leaves. At the end of the inward pass, the table at the root r is $p(r)$. At the end of the outward pass, the tables on all of the nodes are marginals.

The next example shows how the eight messages in Figure 2 are computed, where node $cdefgh$ is chosen as the root.

Example 4. Node ab computes message $m1$ as $m1(b) = \sum_a \phi_1(a, b)$. Node bfg absorbs message $m1$ as $\phi_2'(b, f, g) = \phi_2(b, f, g) \cdot m1(b)$. Similarly, node gk computes message $m2(g) = \sum_k \phi_5(g, k)$, which node bfg absorbs giving $\phi_2''(b, f, g) = \phi_2'(b, f, g) \cdot m2(g)$ as shown in Figure 3. Node bfg next computes message $m3 = \sum_b \phi_2''(b, f, g)$, as depicted in Figure 3, and sends it to node $cdefgh$. The rest of the propagation follows in a similar fashion.

b	f	g	$\phi_2''(b, f, g)$
0	0	0	0.507
0	0	1	0.287
0	1	0	0.313
0	1	1	0.481
1	0	0	0.156
1	0	1	0.050
1	1	0	0.028
1	1	1	0.178

$m3 =$

f	g	$\phi_2''(f, g)$
0	0	0.663
0	1	0.337
1	0	0.341
1	1	0.659

Fig. 3. The potential $\phi_2''(b, f, g)$ at jointree node bfg in Figure 2 after bfg receives message $m1$ from node ab and message $m2$ from node gk. The subsequent message $m3$ from bfg to its neighbour node $cdefgh$.

4 Critical Remarks on Jointree Propagation

The Aalborg method [1] performs unnecessary computation because it lumps conditionals into potentials. This lumping process also blurs useful information.

Example 5. Potential $\phi_1(a, b)$ in Example 3 is *not* an arbitrary table:

$$\phi_1(a, b) = p(a) \cdot p(b|a) \;\; = \;\; p(a, b).$$

It is already the desired marginal distribution $p(a, b)$.

Example 6. Whereas the Aalborg approach views message $m1$ as a *potential*, it follows from Example 5 that $m1$ is in fact the marginal distribution $p(b)$.

Example 7. Message $m2 = \phi_5(g)$ consists entirely of ones:

$$\phi_5(g) = \sum_k \phi_5(g, k) \;\; = \;\; \sum_k p(k|g) \;\; = \;\; 1.0.$$

Example 8. Message $m4 = \phi_4(g, h)$ consists entirely of ones:

$$\phi_4(g,h) = \sum_{i,j} \phi_4(g,h,i,j) = \sum_{i,j} p(i|h) \cdot p(j|g,h,i) = \sum_i p(i|h) \cdot \sum_j p(j|g,h,i)$$
$$= \sum_i p(i|h) \cdot 1.0 = \sum_i p(i|h) = 1.0.$$

Example 9. Message $m8$ consists of all ones. Recall that $p(a, b) = \phi_1(a, b) \cdot m8$. As shown in Example 5, $\phi_1(a, b) = p(a) \cdot p(b|a) = p(a, b)$. By substitution, $p(a, b) = p(a, b) \cdot m8$. Thus, $m8 = 1.0$.

Example 10. Node bfg receives $m1 = p(b)$ from node ab and message $m2 = 1.0$ from gk. Consider the message $\phi_2''(f, g)$ it sends out. Since $I(b, \emptyset, f)$ holds in the Bayesian network in Example 1, $p(b, f) = p(b) \cdot p(f)$. Hence,

$$\phi_2''(f,g) = \sum_b \phi_2(b,f,g) \cdot m1 \cdot m2 = \sum_b p(g|b,f) \cdot p(b) \cdot 1.0 = \sum_b \frac{p(g,b,f)}{p(b,f)} \cdot p(b)$$
$$= \sum_b \frac{p(g,b,f)}{p(b) \cdot p(f)} \cdot p(b) = \sum_b \frac{p(g,b,f)}{p(f)} = \frac{p(g,f)}{p(f)} = p(g|f).$$

Closer inspection of Figure 3 reveals that the seemingly random message $m3 = \phi_2''(f, g)$ is really the conditional $p(g|f)$.

Whereas the Aalborg method [1] views messages propagated in a jointree as *potentials*, Examples 6 - 10 clearly indicate that these messages are instead *conditionals*. While [2] is able to identify the empty messages of all ones in the Aalborg approach, in the next section we seek to identify the exact form of *all* messages.

5 Jointree Propagation with Conditionals

We now present a method for jointree propagation with conditional probability distributions instead of potentials.

Our first task is to graphically depict conditionals. A conditional $p(a_i|P_i)$ is represented as a DAG with nodes $\{a_i\} \cup P_i$ and directed edges from the parent set P_i to a_i, i.e,. $\{(b, a_i)|b \in P_i\}$. However, we use a *black* node to indicate the child a_i and *white* nodes for the parents P_i.

In Example 3, the conditionals assigned to each jointree node can be depicted as in Figure 4. For instance, jointree node ab has conditionals $p(a)$ and $p(b|a)$, while node $ghij$ has conditionals $p(i|h)$ and $p(j|g, h, i)$.

We now turn our attention to identifying the message form a priori. To do so, we introduce a graphical method for eliminating variables, or more precisely, eliminating *black* variables. Before presenting the elimination method, we introduce some notation for simplified discussion. If the directionality of an edge between two variables a and b is immaterial, then we denote the edge as $[a, b]$. Thus, $[a, b]$ means either (a, b) or (b, a).

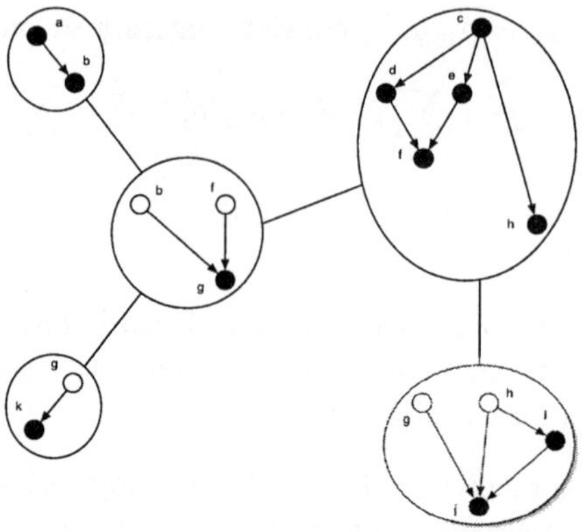

Fig. 4. The conditionals assigned to each jointree node are not lumped into potentials.

Consider a DAG with nodes N and edges E. Fix a topological ordering $\prec$ of the nodes in the DAG. The black variable $b \in N$ is eliminated by applying the following three simple steps:

(e1) $E = E \cup \{(a,c) | [a,b] \in E, (b,c) \in E \text{ and } a \prec c\}$,
(e2) $E = E - \{[a,b] | [a,b] \in E\}$,
(e3) $N = N - \{b\}$.

The messages to be propagated in the jointree can be identified a priori by eliminating black variables.

Example 11. Jointree node ab will send message $p(b)$ to node bfg. This is easily verified by eliminating black variable a from ab.

Example 12. After node bfg receives its conditional from ab, it can send a conditional on fg to its neighbour $cdefgh$ by eliminating black variable b.

The other messages in Figure 5 can be identified in a similar fashion. These messages are computed as follows.
Message $p(b)$ in node ab.

$$p(b) = \sum_a p(a) \cdot p(b|a) \quad \text{(4 mults., 2 additions)}$$

Messages $p(f)$, $p(g)$ and $p(h|g)$ in node $cdefgh$.

$$p(f|c,e) = \sum_d p(d|c) \cdot p(f|d,e) \quad \text{(16 mults., 8 adds.)}$$

$$p(f|c) = \sum_e p(e|c) \cdot p(f|c,e) \quad \text{(16 mults., 4 additions)}$$

$$p(c,f) = p(c) \cdot p(f|c) \quad \text{(4 multiplications)}$$

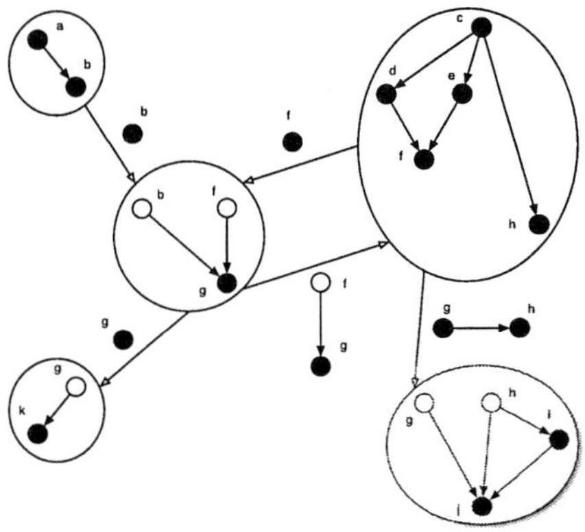

Fig. 5. Unlike Figure 2, the exact form of the messages is known a priori.

$$p(f) = \sum_c p(c, f) \quad \text{(2 additions)}$$

$$p(f, h) = \sum_c p(c, f) \cdot p(h|c) \quad \text{(8 mults., 4 additions)}$$

$$p(g, h) = \sum_f p(f, h) \cdot p(g|f) \quad \text{(8 mults., 4 additions)}$$

$$p(g) = \sum_h p(g, h) \quad \text{(2 additions)}$$

$$p(h|g) = p(g, h)/p(g) \quad \text{(4 divisions)}.$$

Messages $p(g|f)$ and $p(g)$ in node bfg.

$$p(g|f) = \sum_b p(b) \cdot p(g|b, f) \quad \text{(8 mults., 4 additions)}$$

$$p(g) = \sum_f p(f) \cdot p(g|f) \quad \text{(4 mults., 2 additions)}.$$

Hence, jointree computation using conditionals only requires 32 additions, 68 multiplications, and 4 divisions.

6 Advantages of Our Approach

In this section, we highlight four advantages of our approach, namely, efficiency, increased parallelism, hierarchical representation of Bayesian networks, and probabilistic inference in Bayesian networks.

It can be verified that the Aalborg approach [1] computes the desired marginals from the respective potentials using 152 additions, 176 multiplications and 24 divisions. The initial potentials for the jointree can be computed using 176 multiplications. Therefore, the total Aalborg method required 152 additions, 352 multiplications, and 24 divisions to compute the marginals $p(a,b)$, $p(b,f,g)$, $p(c,d,e,f,g,h)$, $p(g,h,i,j)$, and $p(g,k)$ from the Bayesian network in Example 1. On the contrary, in our approach we keep the conditionals in tack. This allows the determination of the exact form of the messages to be propagated throughout the network. This saves computation as irrelevant messages are ignored and relevant messages can be computed efficiently. Below are the total number of computations required for the Aalborg method, including the initial construction of the potentials, and those needed for our method of jointree propagation using conditionals.

Jointree Propagation	+	×	÷
With potentials	152	352	24
With conditionals	32	68	4

Clearly, our method shows great promise. Future work will include comparisons with [2] made on data sets of large, real-world Bayesian networks.

Our method allows for increased parallel computation. As previously mentioned, Rule 1 of the Aalborg method forces the propagation to start with the leaf nodes. Propagation using conditionals allows both nonleaf and leaf nodes to start sending messages *concurrently*. For example, leaf node ab and nonleaf node $cdefgh$ can *simultaneously* send messages $p(b)$ and $p(f)$ to node bfg. On the contrary, in the Aalborg approach, nonleaf node $cdefgh$ is forced to wait to hear from leaf node $ghij$ before sending its message to bfg.

Our method reveals a hierarchical representation of Bayesian networks. When the Aalborg method terminates, the probability table at each jointree node is a marginal distribution. Similarly, when our jointree propagation finishes, the conditional probability tables at each node define the desired marginal distributions. In our example,

$$\begin{aligned}
p(a,b) &= p(a)\cdot p(b|a),\\
p(b,f,g) &= p(b)\cdot p(f)\cdot p(g|b,f),\\
p(c,d,e,f,g,h) &= p(c)\cdot p(d|c)\cdot p(e|c)\cdot p(f|d,e)\cdot p(g|f)\cdot p(h|c),\\
p(g,h,i,j) &= p(g)\cdot p(h|g)\cdot p(i|h)\cdot p(j|g,h,i),\\
p(g,k) &= p(g)\cdot p(k|g).
\end{aligned}$$

More importantly, by definition, they define a local Bayesian network on these variables. We believe this local DAG structure was the one sought in [3], where the internal structure of the jointree nodes is muddled by undirected graphs.

Our last advantage pertains to probabilistic inference in Bayesian networks. Some researchers [9] have argued that it is better to perform probabilistic inference in a DAG rather than in a jointree. Nevertheless, Zhang and Poole [9] admit that precomputation of some conditionals can be very useful, although they explicitly state it is not clear which conditionals should be precomputed.

After our propagation finishes, each jointree node has a local DAG complete with computed conditionals. Hence, the inference method in [9] could be applied to each local DAG instead of the entire homogeneous DAG. This warrants future attention as Xiang [8] found that queries in practice tend to involve variables in close proximity to each other.

7 Conclusion

To the best of our knowledge, this is the first study to ever suggest jointree propagation using conditionals instead of potentials. Our original objective was to find a way to determine the messages to be propagated in advance. Knowing the exact message a priori allows irrelevant messages (tables of all ones such as $m2$, $m8$ and $m4$) to be ignored, while relevant messages can be computed more efficiently. The experimental results in Section 6 explicitly demonstrate the effectiveness of our approach. In addition, our method allows for increased parallel computation in the jointree. Finally, the work presented here is also very relevant to the studies on hierarchical representation of Bayesian networks [3] and probabilistic inference in Bayesian networks [9].

References

1. F.V. Jensen, S.L. Lauritzen and K.G. Olesen. Bayesian updating in causal probabilistic networks by local computations. *Computational Statistics Quarterly*, 4, 269–282, 1990.
2. A.L. Madsen and F.V. Jensen. Lazy propagation: a junction tree inference algorithm based on lazy evaluation. *Artificial Intelligence* 113(1-2): 203-245, 1999.
3. K.G. Olesen and A.L. Madsen. Maximal prime subgraph decomposition of Bayesian networks. *IEEE Transactions on Systems, Man, and Cybernetics*, B, 32(1):21-31, 2002.
4. J. Pearl. *Probabilistic Reasoning in Intelligent Systems: Networks of Plausible Inference*, Morgan Kaufmann, 1988.
5. G. Shafer. *Probabilistic Expert Systems*, Society for Industrial and Applied Mathematics, 1996.
6. S.K.M. Wong, C.J. Butz and Wu, D. On the implication problem for probabilistic conditional independency, *IEEE Transactions on Systems, Man, and Cybernetics*, A, 30(6): 785–805, 2000.
7. S.K.M. Wong and C.J. Butz. Constructing the dependency structure of a multiagent probabilistic network, *IEEE Transactions on Knowledge and Data Engineering*, 13(3):395–415, 2001.
8. Y. Xiang. *Probabilistic Reasoning in Multiagent Systems*, Cambridge, 2002.
9. N.L. Zhang and D. Poole. Exploiting causal independence in Bayesian network inference. *Journal of Artificial Intelligence Research*, 5, 301–328, 1996.

Condition Class Classification Stability in RST due to Continuous Value Discretisation

Malcolm J. Beynon

Cardiff Business School, Cardiff University
Colum Drive, Cardiff, CF10 3EU, Wales, UK
BeynonMJ@cardiff.ac.uk

Abstract. Rough Set Theory (RST) is a nascent technique for object classification, where each object in an information system is characterised and classified by a number of condition and decision attributes respectively. A level of continuous value discretisation (CVD) is often employed to reduce the possible large granularity of the information system. This paper considers the effect of CVD on the association between condition and decision classes in RST. Moreover, the stability of the classification of the objects in the condition classes is investigated. Novel measures are introduced to describe the association of objects (condition classes) to the different decision classes.

1 Introduction

Rough Set Theory (RST) introduced in [5] is a technique for object classification. One RST issue relates to the granularity of the information system, which affects the number and specificity of the decision rules constructed. To allow more opportunity for interpretability a level of continuous value discretisation (CVD) is often employed to reduce the associated granularity [3]. Beynon [1] introduced a stability measure to quantify the effectiveness of the CVD of continuous attributes.

In this paper these stability measures are used to investigate the classification of objects in condition classes associated with RST. Moreover, for a condition class of objects a set of probability values are constructed to elucidate the level of clustering of condition classes which are associated with the same decision outcome.

2 Fundamentals of RST

The domain of an RST analysis is the information system, made up of a set of objects (U), characterised by a set of condition attributes (C) and classified by a set of decision attributes (D). From C and D equivalence classes (condition - $E(C)$ and decision - $E(D)$) are constructed through an indiscernibility relation. RST allows the association of the objects in U to a decision outcome $Y_j \in E(D)$ based on $P \subseteq C$ to be described in terms of a pair of sets; lower approximation $\underline{P}Y_j$ and upper approximation $\overline{P}Y_j$, more formally defined by:

S. Tsumoto et al. (Eds.): RSCTC 2004, LNAI 3066, pp. 378–383, 2004.

$$\underline{PY_j} = \{o_i \in U \mid o_i \in X_p \in E(P) \text{ and } X_p \subseteq Y_j\},$$
$$\overline{PY_j} = \{o_i \in U \mid o_i \in X_p \in E(P) \text{ and } X_p \cap Y_j \neq \varnothing\}.$$

From their definition the objects in a $\underline{PY_j}$ have a definite classification to the respective decision outcome. A measure denoting the quality of classification $\gamma(P, D)$ is considered, defined by $\gamma(P, D) = \sum_{j=1}^{|E(D)|} |\underline{PY_j}| \Big/ |U|$. This measure aids the identification of subsets of condition attributes P which have the same (or near same) level of classification as C, defined reducts [5, 6].

Throughout this paper we consider the case of when there are q condition attributes $c_1, c_2, \ldots, c_q$ (sets of continuous values), which have been intervalised by some CVD process. The jth interval of the nth condition attribute $c_n (1 \leq n \leq q)$ is defined I_j^n, $\mathrm{rgt}(\mathrm{I}_j^n)$ and $\mathrm{lft}(\mathrm{I}_j^n)$ denote its right and left boundary points. Given c_n has been discretised into k_n intervals, then the proportion of the distribution constructed from the data in the jth interval actually in the rth interval is given by (from [1]):

$$S_{n,j,r} = \int_{\mathrm{lft}(\mathrm{I}_r^n)}^{\mathrm{rgt}(\mathrm{I}_r^n)} \frac{1}{\sqrt{2m_{n,j}\pi}} \sum_{i=1}^{m_{n,j}} \frac{1}{\mathrm{rgt}(\mathrm{I}_j^n) - \mathrm{lft}(\mathrm{I}_j^n)} \exp\left[-\frac{1}{2}\left(\frac{x - x_i}{\mathrm{rgt}(\mathrm{I}_j^n) - \mathrm{lft}(\mathrm{I}_j^n)}\right)^2\right] \mathrm{d}x ,$$

where $m_{n,j}$ is the number of values in the I_j^n interval. It is necessary for $\sum_{r=1}^{k_n} S_{n,j,r} = 1$, but this may not be attainable, hence the $S_{n,j,r}$ values should be normalised. Subsequently, $S_{n,j,r}$ is the probability of an object's value from the nth condition attribute categorised as in the jth interval, could be categorised to the rth interval.

3 Classification Stability of a Condition Class

Each condition class $X_p^{r_g}$ ($p = 1, \ldots, |X^{r_g}|$) associated with a reduct r_g made up of the condition attributes $c_h^{r_g}$ ($h = 1, \ldots, |r_g|$) is defined by a distinct series of condition attribute descriptor values, defined $[\delta_{p,1}^{r_g}, \delta_{p,2}^{r_g}, \ldots, \delta_{p,|r_g|}^{r_g}]$. A $\delta_{p,h}^{r_g}$ ($h = 1, \ldots, |r_g|$) denotes the descriptor value of the hth condition attribute for an object in the pth condition class in the r_g reduct.

For o_i its set of descriptor values associates it with a condition class, say $X_q^{r_g} = [\delta_{q,1}^{r_g}, \delta_{q,2}^{r_g}, \ldots, \delta_{q,|r_g|}^{r_g}]$. In the presence of CVD there exists levels of probability to which descriptor value an object value may be associated with. Given $o_i \in X_q^{r_g}$, the individual component probability values which describe it and all objects in the condition class $X_q^{r_g}$ as possibly being in another condition class, say $X_p^{r_g}$ is given by $[S_{c_1^{r_g}, \delta_{q,1}^{r_g}, \delta_{p,1}^{r_g}}, S_{c_2^{r_g}, \delta_{q,2}^{r_g}, \delta_{p,2}^{r_g}}, \ldots, S_{c_{|r_g|}^{r_g}, \delta_{q,|r_g|}^{r_g}, \delta_{p,|r_g|}^{r_g}}]$.

The $S_{c_h^{r_g}, \delta_{q,h}^{r_g}, \delta_{p,h}^{r_g}}$ are component probabilities which need to be aggregated together to describe the $X_q^{r_g}$ condition class's transference of classification to the condition class $X_p^{r_g}$. Since the membership of an object to a condition class is a conjunction based on the associated descriptive values, a geometric mean (aggregation) value is utilised. It follows, the probability that an object contained in the condition class $X_q^{r_g}$ should be in $X_p^{r_g}$ is defined $\mathrm{CT}_{q,p}^{r_g}$ and given by $\mathrm{CT}_{q,p}^{r_g} = \left(\prod_{h=1}^{|r_g|} S_{c_h^{r_g}, \delta_{q,h}^{r_g}, \delta_{p,h}^{r_g}} \right)^{1/|r_g|}$, $1 \le q$, $p \le |r_g|$.

The containment probabilities $\mathrm{CT}_{q,p}^{r_g}$ $1 \le q, p \le |r_g|$ are on objects in all the condition classes associated with a reduct r_g. With RST, only condition classes which each contain objects classified to a single decision class are further considered. A measure $w\mathrm{DT}_{q,i}^{r_g}$ is presented for this which is weighted by the number of objects in each condition class (further considered), and given by:

$$w\mathrm{DT}_{q,i}^{r_g} = \frac{\sum\limits_{X_p^{r_g} \subseteq Y_i} \left(\ln |X_p^{r_g}| \, \mathrm{CT}_{q,p}^{r_g} \right)}{\sum\limits_{j=1}^{|E(D)|} \left(\sum\limits_{X_p^{r_g} \subseteq Y_j} \left(\ln |X_p^{r_g}| \, \mathrm{CT}_{q,p}^{r_g} \right) \right)} = \frac{\sum\limits_{X_p^{r_g} \subseteq Y_i} \left(\ln |X_p^{r_g}| \left(\prod\limits_{h=1}^{|r_g|} S_{c_h^{r_g}, \delta_{q,h}^{r_g}, \delta_{p,h}^{r_g}} \right)^{1/|r_g|} \right)}{\sum\limits_{j=1}^{|E(D)|} \left(\sum\limits_{X_p^{r_g} \subseteq Y_j} \left(\ln |X_p^{r_g}| \left(\prod\limits_{h=1}^{|r_g|} S_{c_h^{r_g}, \delta_{q,h}^{r_g}, \delta_{p,h}^{r_g}} \right)^{1/|r_g|} \right) \right)}.$$

The $\ln|X_p^{r_g}|$ value is a level of grouping of the objects in a condition class. A series of these values can be constructed $w\mathrm{DT}_{q,1}^{r_g}$, $w\mathrm{DT}_{q,2}^{r_g}$, …, $w\mathrm{DT}_{q,|E(D)|}^{r_g}$, where $w\mathrm{DT}_{q,i}^{r_g}$ is the probability that a condition class $X_q^{r_g}$ found from the reduct r_g should be associated with a decision class $Y_i \in E(D)$.

4 Application of Class Stability Analysis to the Iris Data Set

The Iris data set is made up of 3 classes of 50 plants each, where a decision class (decision outcome) refers to a particular type of Iris plant (i.e., Iris Setosa, Iris Versicolour and Iris Virginica). Four continuous condition attributes (Sepal length (c_1), Sepal width (c_2), Petal length (c_3) and Petal width (c_4)) describe each plant. The paper of Browne et al. [2], includes a level of CVD on the Iris data set to reduce the overall granularity of the associated information system. In Table 1, the interval boundary values defining the CVD of each condition attribute are reported and the number of original values in each interval (in brackets).

Table 1. Intervalisation of the condition attributes in the Iris data set (Browne et al., 1998).

	Very small (1)	Small (2)	Large(3)	Very Large (4)
c_1	$x < 50$: (22)	$50 \leq x < 60$: (61)	$60 \leq x < 70$: (54)	$70 \leq x$: (13)
c_2	$x < 24$: (8)	$24 \leq x < 31$: (75)	$31 \leq x < 38$: (55)	$38 \leq x$: (12)
c_3	$x < 30$: (50)	$30 \leq x < 40$: (11)	$40 \leq x < 55$: (61)	$55 \leq x$: (28)
c_4	$x < 10$: (50)	$10 \leq x < 14$: (28)	$14 \leq x < 21$: (49)	$21 \leq x$: (23)

Following [1], a series of estimated distributions can be constructed for each set of objects (plants) in the constructed intervals. This uses the method of Parzen windows [4], their functional form included in the expression for $S_{n,j,r}$, see Fig. 1.

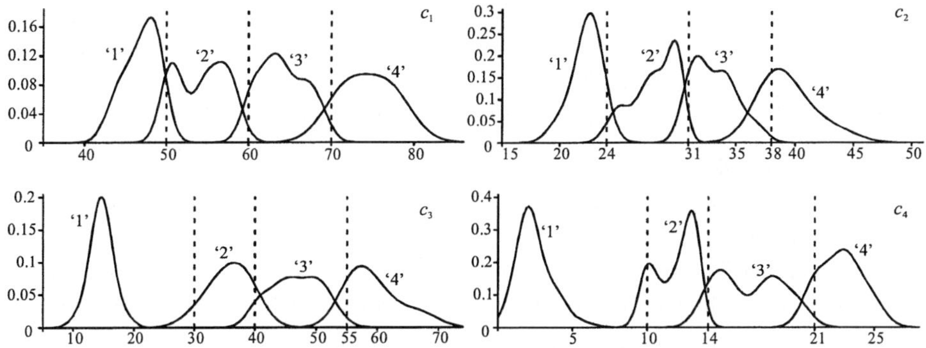

Fig. 1. Estimated distributions of attribute values in each constructed interval.

In Fig. 1 the graphs of each constructed estimated distribution are presented, also included are vertical dashed lines defining the boundaries between intervals. An initial inspection of the graphs show a level of overlap in the distributions, this is due to their domains each being over $(-\infty, \infty)$ but highlights possible indecisiveness in the boundaries constructed. To illustrate, the boundary between intervals '3' and '4' of the c_2 attribute are further considered. The estimated distribution of the '4' interval spreads considerably into the domain of the '3' interval, a consequence of a majority of the values in the '4' interval being close to the (left) boundary value. From [1], this indecisiveness can be quantified, with the $S_{n,j,r}$ values associated with each attribute evaluated, see Table 2.

In Table 2, the $S_{n,j,j}$ values in bold represent the stability (probability) that an object's original value is in the correct interval described by the correct descriptor value. The lowest of these is associated with the '4' interval of the c_2 attribute ($S_{2,4,4}$ = 0.6883), previously discussed. The other values are the probability that an object's original value could be in a neighbouring interval. Understandably these other probability values are largest in the immediate neighbour intervals of the $S_{n,j,j}$ values.

Using these constructed intervals with all condition attributes C (= $\{c_1, c_2, c_3, c_4\}$) there exist 34 condition classes. Of these, 30 include objects described to the same decision outcomes within the individual condition class.

Table 2. $S_{n,j,r}$ values for the different intervals describing condition attributes.

$S_{n,j,r}$		Intervals '1'	'2'	'3'	'4'	$S_{n,j,r}$		Intervals '1'	'2'	'3'	'4'
	'1'	**0.9082**	0.0918	0.0000	0.0000		'1'	**1.0000**	0.0000	0.0000	0.0000
c_1	'2'	0.1182	**0.8630**	0.0188	0.0000	c_3	'2'	0.0872	**0.7552**	0.1576	0.0000
	'3'	0.0000	0.0890	**0.8878**	0.0232		'3'	0.0000	0.0694	**0.9111**	0.0195
	'4'	0.0000	0.0000	0.1282	**0.8718**		'4'	0.0000	0.0000	0.1751	**0.8249**
	'1'	**0.8503**	0.1497	0.0000	0.0000		'1'	**1.0000**	0.0000	0.0000	0.0000
c_2	'2'	0.0320	**0.9297**	0.0384	0.0000	c_4	'2'	0.1357	**0.8204**	0.0439	0.0000
	'3'	0.0000	0.1453	**0.8458**	0.0089		'3'	0.0001	0.1224	**0.8555**	0.0221
	'4'	0.0000	0.0000	0.3117	**0.6883**		'4'	0.0000	0.0000	0.1484	**0.8516**

The associated quality of classification is $\gamma(C, D) = 0.7733$, indicating 116 out of the 150 plants are assigned a definite classification. No proper subset ($P \subset C$) offers the same level of quality of classification as C. In the spirit of [6], consideration is given to subsets of condition attributes which offer a similar level of quality of classification. Investigation showed $\{c_1, c_3, c_4\}$ is a 'near' reduct (defined r_1), with $\gamma(\{c_1, c_3, c_4\}, D) = 0.7667$ (one less plant given a definite classification as with C). This reduct has 17 condition classes of which 15 include objects each described to the same decision outcome within their individual condition classes. For these condition classes the descriptor values which define it (and number of objects) are presented along with the $w\mathrm{DT}^{r_g}_{q,i}$ ($q = 1, \ldots, 15$ and $r = 1, \ldots, 3$) values, see Table 3.

Table 3. Stability details on condition classes $X^{r_1}_q$, $q = 1, .. 15$.

q	$X^{r_1}_q : \lvert X^{r_1}_q \rvert$	$w\mathrm{DT}^{r_1}_{q,i}$, $i = 1, \ldots, 3$	q	$X^{r_1}_q : \lvert X^{r_1}_q \rvert$	$w\mathrm{DT}^{r_1}_{q,i}$, $i = 1, \ldots, 3$
1	[1, 1, 1]: 20	**0.9999**, 0.0001, 0.0000	9	[3, 3, 2]: 7	0.0005, **0.9393**, 0.0603
2	[1, 2, 2]: 1	0.4206, **0.5794**, 0.0000	10	[3, 3, 4]: 5	0.0000, 0.0000, **1.0000**
3	[1, 3, 3]: 1	0.0002, **0.9998**, 0.0000	11	[3, 4, 3]: 5	0.0000, 0.2250, **0.7750**
4	[2, 1, 1]: 30	**0.9998**, 0.0002, 0.0000	12	[3, 4, 4]: 11	0.0000, 0.0000, **1.0000**
5	[2, 2, 2]: 9	0.2511, **0.7488**, 0.0001	13	[4, 3, 3]: 1	0.0000, **0.3131**, 0.6869
6	[2, 2, 3]: 1	0.0201, **0.9430**, 0.0369	14	[4, 4, 3]: 6	0.0000, 0.0824, **0.9176**
7	[2, 3, 2]: 11	0.0014, **0.9866**, 0.0120	15	[4, 4, 4]: 6	0.0000, 0.0000, **1.0000**
8	[2, 3, 4]: 1	0.0000, 0.0001, **0.9999**			

In Table 3, each of the 15 condition classes is defined based on its set of descriptor values, also the number of objects contained therein (ranges from 1 to 30). The sets of $w\mathrm{DT}^{r_1}_{q,i}$ values are also presented for each condition class. The actual decision outcome each condition class is associated with is given in bold, the largest value is underlined. For $X^{r_1}_{13}$, different $w\mathrm{DT}^{r_1}_{q,i}$ values are in bold and underlined. A set of $w\mathrm{DT}^{r_1}_{q,i}$ values can be represented as a coordinate in a simplex plot, see Fig. 2.

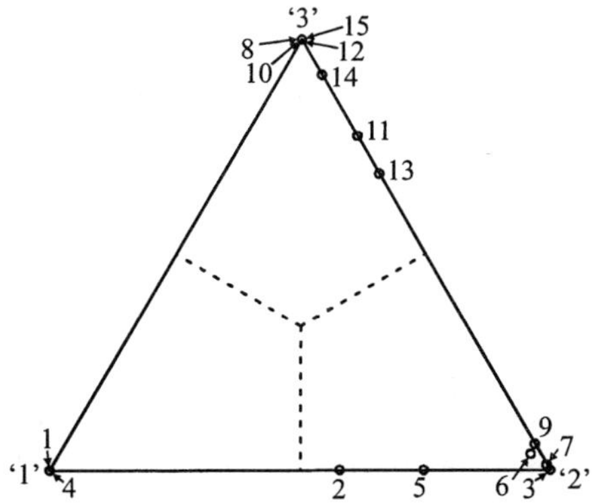

Fig. 2. Simplex plot representation of the classification stability of each condition class.

The dashed lines present the boundaries between where in a simplex plot a single value in [$w\mathrm{DT}^{r_1}_{q,1}$, $w\mathrm{DT}^{r_1}_{q,2}$, $w\mathrm{DT}^{r_1}_{q,3}$] is the largest, the '1', '2' and '3' labels denoting the pth index of the decision outcomes Y_1, Y_2 and Y_3 respectively. The presented simplex plot elucidates a number of features associated with the sets of $w\mathrm{DT}^{r_1}_{q,i}$ values. One considers the notion of the condition classes in a 'condition class space'.

5 Conclusions

This paper has investigated the effect of continuous value discretisation (CVD) on the strength of the classification associated with a condition class. The definition of intervals describing the original object values approximate the information content of a condition attribute and hence the association of a condition class with a particular decision outcome. The introduction of a number of measures quantifies these levels of association.

References

1. Beynon, M. J.: Stability of Continuous Value Discretisation: An Application within Rough Set Theory, International Journal of Approximate Reasoning 35 (2004), 29–53.
2. Browne, C., Dünstch, L., Gediga, G.: IRIS revisited: A comparison of discriminant and enhanced rough set data analysis. in: L. Polkowski, A. Skowron, (Eds.), Rough sets in knowledge discovery 2: Applications, case studies and software systems, Physica-Verlag, New York, 1998, 345–368.
3. Nguyen, H.S.: Discretization problem for rough sets methods, in: L. Polkowski, A. Skowron, (Eds.) Rough Sets and Current Trends in Computing, Proceedings of the First International Conference RSCTC'98, Warsaw, Poland, 1998, 545–552.
4. Parzen, E.: On estimation of a probability density function mode. Annals of Mathematical Statistics 33 (1962), 1065–1076.
5. Pawlak, Z.: Rough sets. International Journal of Information and Computer Sciences 11 (5) (1982) 341–356.
6. Słowiński, K., Słowiński, R.: Sensitivity analysis of rough classification, International Journal of Man-Machine Studies 32 (1990), 693–705.

The Rough Bayesian Model for Distributed Decision Systems

Dominik Ślęzak[1,2]

[1] Department of Computer Science, University of Regina
Regina, SK, S4S 0A2, Canada
slezak@uregina.ca
[2] Polish-Japanese Institute of Information Technology
Koszykowa 86, 02-008 Warsaw, Poland

Abstract. The article presents a new approach to understanding the concepts of the theory of rough sets basing on the inversive probabilities derivable from distributed decision systems. The Rough Bayesian model – a novel probabilistic extension of rough sets related to Bayes' factor and Bayesian methods of the statistical hypothesis testing is proposed. Advantages of the Rough Bayesian model are illustrated by the examples.

Keywords: Rough Sets, Decision Systems, Inverse Probabilities, Bayesian Reasoning, Bayes' Factor.

1 Introduction

The theory of *rough sets* [3] is a methodology of dealing with uncertainty in data. The idea is to approximate the *target concepts* (*events*, *decisions*) using the classes of *indiscernible* objects. Every concept is assigned the *positive*, *negative*, and *boundary regions* of data, where it is *certain*, *impossible*, and *possible but not certain*, according to the data based information. Rough sets have been extended in various ways to deal with practical challenges. There are several extensions relying on the data based probabilities. The *Variable Precision Rough Set* (*VPRS*) model [8] softens the requirements for certainty and impossibility using the degrees concerning *posterior probabilities*. Research reported in [4, 6] points also at the connections between rough sets and *Bayesian reasoning* [7] by means of *prior* and *inverse probabilities*.

Posterior probabilities provide an intuitive framework for reasoning with inexact dependencies. It has been observed in logics [1], machine learning [2], as well as, e.g., in some rough set implementations [5]. However, posterior probabilities are not always derivable from data in a reliable way. In some cases the only information can be extracted from data by means of inverse probabilities corresponding to the belief in the observed evidence conditioned by the concepts we want to approximate. Then, we can still go back to posterior probabilities using the *Bayes' rule*, if we know prior probabilities of target concepts. We can also build the rough-set-like models based on parameterized comparison of prior and posterior probabilities [6]. The problem starts when we can neither estimate prior probabilities from data nor define them using background knowledge.

S. Tsumoto et al. (Eds.): RSCTC 2004, LNAI 3066, pp. 384–393, 2004.

We propose a new interpretation of rough sets based only on inverse probabilities. We also introduce a parameterized probabilistic extension of the original rough set model based on *Bayes' factor* [7]. We show that in the case of known prior probabilities our *Rough Bayesian* model works similarly to VPRS. However, it is much better applicable to the multi-decision data problems where prior probabilities are dynamically changing, remain unknown, or simply undefinable.

We define our model within the framework of *distributed decision systems*, where the objects supporting the target concepts corresponding to different *decision classes* are stored in separate data sets. In this way, we emphasize that the only probability estimates we can use are of inverse character, that is they are naturally conditioned by particular decisions. We discuss why such form of data storage seems to be more reliable than the original decision systems [3].

2 Data Representation

In [3] it was proposed to represent data as an *information system* $\mathbb{A} = (U, A)$, where U denotes the *universe* of *objects* and each *attribute* $a \in A$ is identified with function $a : U \to V_a$, for V_a denoting the set of values of a. Each subset $B \subseteq A$ induces a partition over U with classes defined by grouping together objects having identical values of B. We obtain the partition space U/B, which is often referred to as *B-indiscernibility relation* $IND_{\mathbb{A}}(B)$, and where elements $E \in U/B$ are called the *B-indiscernibility classes* of objects.

Elements of U/B correspond to *B-information vectors* $w \in V_B$ – collections of *descriptors* (a, v), $a \in B$, $v \in V_a$. They are obtained using *B-information function* $B : U \to V_B$ where $B(e) = \{(a, a(e)) : a \in B\}$. For instance, for $B = \{a_1, a_3\}$ and $\mathbb{A} = (U, A)$ in Fig. 1, B-information vector $\{(a_1, 2), (a_3, 2)\}$ corresponds to conjunction of conditions $a_1 = 2$ and $a_3 = 2$, which is satisfied by the elements of $E = \{e_3, e_6, e_8, e_9, e_{15}, e_{19}, e_{20}\}$.

Information provided by $\mathbb{A} = (U, A)$ can be applied to approximate the *target events* $X \subseteq U$ by means of the elements of U/B, $B \subseteq A$. We can express such

U	a_1	a_2	a_3	a_4	a_5	d
e_1	1	1	0	1	2	0
e_2	0	0	0	2	2	0
e_3	2	2	2	1	1	1
e_4	0	1	2	2	2	1
e_5	2	1	1	0	2	0
e_6	2	2	2	1	1	1
e_7	0	1	2	2	2	0
e_8	2	2	2	1	1	1
e_9	2	2	2	1	1	1
e_{10}	0	0	0	2	2	0

U	a_1	a_2	a_3	a_4	a_5	d
e_{11}	1	2	0	0	2	0
e_{12}	1	1	0	1	2	1
e_{13}	0	1	2	2	2	1
e_{14}	2	1	1	0	2	0
e_{15}	2	2	2	1	1	0
e_{16}	1	1	0	1	2	1
e_{17}	1	1	0	1	2	0
e_{18}	2	1	1	0	2	0
e_{19}	2	2	2	1	1	1
e_{20}	2	2	2	1	1	1

Fig. 1. Decision system $\mathbb{A} = (U, A \cup \{d\})$, $U = \{e_1, \ldots, e_{20}\}$, $A = \{a_1, \ldots, a_5\}$. Decision d induces decision classes $X_1 = \{e_3, e_4, e_6, e_8, e_9, e_{12}, e_{13}, e_{16}, e_{19}, e_{20}\}$ and $X_0 = U \backslash X_1$.

targets using a distinguished attribute $d \notin A$. Given $V_d = \{0, \ldots, r-1\}$, we define the sets $X_k = \{e \in U : d(e) = k\}$. We refer to such extended information system $\mathbb{A} = (U, A \cup \{d\})$ as to a *decision system*, where d is called the *decision attribute*, and the sets X_k are referred to as the *decision classes.*

3 Data Based Probabilities

Let us assume that the events X_k are labelled with prior probability $P(X_k)$. It is reasonable to assume that X_k is likely to occur and that its occurrence is not certain, that is that $0 < P(X_k) < 1$. Let us also assume that each class E is assigned posterior probability $P(X_k|E)$, which expresses belief that X_k will occur under the evidence corresponding to E. We can reconsider probabilities in terms of attribute-value conditions. For instance, if $k = 1$ and E groups the objects satisfying conditions $a_1 = 2$ and $a_3 = 2$, then we can write $P(d = 1)$ instead of $P(X_1)$, and $P(d = 1|a_1 = 2, a_3 = 2)$ instead of $P(X_1|E)$.

In machine learning [2], posterior probabilities correspond to the certainty (accuracy, precision) factors. In particular, one can compare prior and posterior knowledge to state whether a new evidence (satisfaction of conditions) increases or decreases belief in a given event (membership to a given decision class) [6]. The easiest way of the data based probability estimation is the following:

$$P(X_k|E) = \frac{|X_k \cap E|}{|E|} \quad \text{and} \quad P(X_k) = \frac{|X_k|}{|U|} \tag{1}$$

For instance, we get $P(d = 1|a_1 = 2, a_3 = 2) = 6/7$, which estimates our belief that an object satisfying $a_1 = 2$ and $a_3 = 2$ will belong to X_1. It seems to increase significantly our belief in X_1 with respect to $P(d = 1) = 1/2$.

One can also operate with inverse probabilities $P(E|X_k)$, which express a likelihood of the evidence E under the assumption about X_k [7]. Posterior probabilities are then derivable by using the Bayes' rule, e.g.:

$$P(X_1|E) = \frac{P(E|X_1)P(X_1)}{P(E|X_0)P(X_0) + P(E|X_1)P(X_1)} \tag{2}$$

If we use estimations of the form $P(E|X_k) = |X_k \cap E|/|X|$, then (2) provides us with the same value of $P(X_k|E)$ as in case of (1). For instance, we obtain

$$P(d = 1|a_1 = 2, a_3 = 2) = \frac{3/5 \cdot 1/2}{1/10 \cdot 1/2 + 3/5 \cdot 1/2} = 6/7$$

However, in some cases estimation (1) can provide us with invalid results. Then it is desirable to combine inverse probability estimates with prior probabilities expressing background knowledge, not necessarily derivable from the data [7]. For instance, let us suppose that X_1 corresponds to a rare but important target event like, e.g., some medical pathology. Then, we are going to collect the cases supporting this event very accurately. However, we are not going to collect information about all the "healthy" cases as X_0. In the medical data sets we can rather expect the 50:50 proportion between positive and negative examples. It does not mean, however, that $P(X_1)$ should be estimated as 1/2. Moreover, it is questionable whether posterior probabilities $P(X_1|E)$ should be derived from such data using estimation (1) – it is simply difficult to accept that $|E|$ can be calculated as the non-weighted sum of $|E \cap X_0|$ and $|E \cap X_1|$.

4 Distributed Decision Systems

The above example shows that sometimes the decision system is actually a collection of uncombinable data sets supporting particular events. Let us propose the following formal way of representing such situations:

Definition 1. *Let the set of r mutually exclusive target events be given. By a* distribute decision system $\mathcal{A}$ *we mean the collection of r information systems*

$$\mathcal{A} = \{\mathbb{A}_0 = (X_0, A), \ldots, \mathbb{A}_{r-1} = (X_{r-1}, A)\} \tag{3}$$

where X_k denotes the set of objects supporting the k-th event, $k = 0, \ldots, r-1$, and A is the set of attributes describing all the objects in $X_0, \ldots, X_{r-1}$.

Let us consider $\mathcal{A}$ consisting of two information systems illustrated in Fig. 2. Any information derivable from $\mathbb{A}_k$ is naturally conditioned by X_k, for $k = 0, 1$. Given B-information vector $w \in V_B$, $B \subseteq A$, we can set up

$$P_k(B = w) = \frac{|\{e \in X_k : B(e) = w\}|}{|X_k|} \tag{4}$$

as the probability that a given object will have the values described by w on B *conditioned* by its membership to X_k. For instance, $P_0(a_1 = 2, a_3 = 2) = 1/10$ and $P_1(a_1 = 2, a_3 = 2) = 3/5$ are estimates of probabilities that a given object will satisfy $a_1 = 2$ and $a_3 = 2$, if it supports the events X_0 and X_1, respectively.

One can see that if we use estimation

$$P(B = w|d = k) = P_k(B = w) \tag{5}$$

X_0	a_1	a_2	a_3	a_4	a_5
e_1	1	2	0	0	2
e_2	1	1	0	1	2
e_3	0	0	0	2	2
e_4	2	1	1	0	2
e_5	2	1	1	0	2
e_6	2	2	2	1	1
e_7	0	1	2	2	2
e_8	1	1	0	1	2
e_9	2	1	1	0	2
e_{10}	0	0	0	2	2

X_1	a_1	a_2	a_3	a_4	a_5
o_1	2	2	2	1	1
o_2	0	1	2	2	2
o_3	1	1	0	1	2
o_4	2	2	2	1	1
o_5	2	2	2	1	1

Fig. 2. Distribute decision system $\mathcal{A} = \{\mathbb{A}_0 = (X_0, A), \mathbb{A}_1 = (X_1, A)\}$, where $A = \{a_1, \ldots, a_5\}$, $X_0 = \{e_1, \ldots, e_{10}\}$, and $X_1 = \{o_1, \ldots, o_5\}$.

then inverse probabilities derivable from $\mathcal{A}$, Fig. 2, are identical with those derivable from $\mathbb{A}$, Fig. 1. Actually, we created Fig. 1 artificially by doubling the objects from $\mathbb{A}_1$ and merging them with $\mathbb{A}_0$ from Fig. 2. Therefore, if we assume that due to our knowledge we should put $P(X_1) = 1/2$, then Fig. 2 will provide also the same posterior probabilities as Fig. 1.

Distributed decision systems do not provide a means for calculation of posterior probabilities unless we know prior ones for particular decision classes. On the other hand, we get more flexibility with respect to the changes of prior probabilities, which can be easily combined with the estimates (5). For instance, let us go back to the case study from the previous section and assume that the objects in $\mathbb{A}_1 = (X_1, A)$ are very carefully chosen cases of a rare medical pathology while the elements of X_0 describe a representative sample of human beings not suffering from this pathology. Let us put $P(X_1) = 1/1000$. Then we get

$$P(d = 1|a_1 = 2, a_3 = 2) = \frac{3/5 \cdot 1/1000}{1/10 \cdot 999/1000 + 3/5 \cdot 1/1000} = 2/335$$

It shows how different posterior probabilities can be obtained from the same distributed decision system for various prior probability settings. Obviously, we could obtain identical results from appropriately created classical decision systems (like in case of the system in Fig. 1). However, such a way of data translation is unnecessary or even impossible, if prior probabilities are not specified.

From technical point of view, it does not matter whether we keep the data in the form of distributed or merged decision system, unless we do not use estimations (1). However, we find Definition 1 as a clearer way to emphasize the nature of the data based probabilities that we can really believe in. Indeed, inverse probabilities (5) are very often the only ones, which can be reasonably estimated from real-life data sets. This is because the process of the data acquisition is often performed in parallel for various decisions and, moreover, the experts can (and wish to) handle the issue of the information representativeness only at the level of separate decision classes.

5 Rough Set Model

In Section 2 we mentioned that information systems can be applied to approximate the target events by means of indiscernibility classes. A method of such data based approximation was proposed in [3], as the theory of *rough sets*. Given $\mathbb{A} = (U, A)$, $B \subseteq A$, and $X \subseteq U$, one can express its main idea in the following probabilistic way: the *B-positive*, *B-negative*, and *B-boundary rough set regions* (abbreviated as *RS-regions*) are defined as

$$\begin{aligned} \mathcal{POS}_B(X) &= \bigcup\{E \in U/B : P(X|E) = 1\} \\ \mathcal{NEG}_B(X) &= \bigcup\{E \in U/B : P(X|E) = 0\} \\ \mathcal{BND}_B(X) &= \bigcup\{E \in U/B : 0 < P(X|E) < 1\} \end{aligned} \tag{6}$$

$\mathcal{POS}_B(X)$ is an area of the universe where the occurrence of X is *certain*. $\mathcal{NEG}_B(X)$ covers an area where the occurrence of X is *impossible*. Finally,

$\mathcal{BND}_B(X)$ defines an area where the occurrence of X is *possible* but *uncertain.* The boundary area typically covers large portion of the universe, if not all. If $\mathcal{BND}_B(X)=\emptyset$, then X is *B-definable.* Otherwise, it is a *B-rough set.*

The RS-regions can be formulated for decision classes in any decision table. For example, for $\mathbb{A}=(U, A\cup\{d\})$ from Fig. 1 and $B=\{a_1,a_3\}$, we obtain

$$\begin{array}{c} \mathcal{POS}_B(X_1)=\emptyset \qquad \mathcal{NEG}_B(X_1)=\{e_2,e_5,e_{10},e_{14},e_{18}\} \\ \mathcal{BND}_B(X_1)=\{e_1,e_3,e_4,e_6,..,e_9,e_{11},..,e_{13},e_{15},..,e_{17},e_{19},e_{20}\} \end{array} \tag{7}$$

The RS-regions can be easily interpreted also by means of inverse probabilities:

Proposition 1. *Let $\mathbb{A}=(U,A\cup\{d\})$ and $B\subseteq A$ be given. Consider the k-th decision class $X_k\subseteq U$. For any $E\in U/B$ we obtain the following characteristics:*

$$\begin{array}{ll} E\subseteq \mathcal{POS}_B(X_k) & \Leftrightarrow P(E|X_k)>0\wedge \forall_{l:\, l\neq k}\left(P(E|X_l)=0\right) \\ E\subseteq \mathcal{NEG}_B(X_k) & \Leftrightarrow P(E|X_k)=0 \\ E\subseteq \mathcal{BND}_B(X_k) & \Leftrightarrow P(E|X_k)>0\wedge \exists_{l:\, l\neq k}\left(P(E|X_l)>0\right) \end{array} \tag{8}$$

The above result enables us to think about the rough set regions as follows:

1. Object e belongs to $\mathcal{POS}_B(X_k)$, if and only if the vector $B(e)\in V_B$ is *likely* to occur under the assumption that e supports the event X_k and *unlikely* to occur under the assumption that it supports any alternative event X_l, $l\neq k$.
2. Object e belongs to $\mathcal{NEG}_B(X_k)$, if and only if the vector $B(e)\in V_B$ is *unlikely* to occur under the assumption that e supports the event X_k.
3. Object e belongs to $\mathcal{BND}_B(X_k)$, if and only if the vector $B(e)\in V_B$ is *likely* to occur under the assumption that e supports X_k but this is also the case for some alternative events X_l, $l\neq k$.

As a conclusion, the rough set model can be formulated without using prior or posterior probabilities. It means that in case of rough sets we do not need any kind of background knowledge even if the only probabilities reasonably represented in data are inverse ones. The rough set regions are not influenced by the changes of prior probabilities. We do not even need the existence of those probabilities. The assumption that a given event is likely to occur and that its occurrence is not certain can be read as a requirement that it is supported by some objects and that some alternative events are supported as well.

Following the above argumentation, let us reconsider the original RS-regions for distribute data, without the need of merging them within one decision system.

Definition 2. *Let the system $\mathcal{A}=\{\mathbb{A}_0=(X_0,A),\ldots,\mathbb{A}_{r-1}=(X_{r-1},A)\}$ be given. For any X_k and $B\subseteq A$, we define the B-*positive, *B*-negative, *and B-*boundary distributed rough set regions *(abbreviated as* DRS-regions*) as follows:*

$$\begin{array}{ll} \mathcal{DPOS}_B(X_k) & =\{w\in V_B : P_k(B=w)>0\wedge \forall_{l:\, l\neq k}\left(P_l(B=w)=0\right)\} \\ \mathcal{DNEG}_B(X_k) & =\{w\in V_B : P_k(B=w)=0\} \\ \mathcal{DBND}_B(X_k) & =\{w\in V_B : P_k(B=w)>0\wedge \exists_{l:\, l\neq k}\left(P_l(B=w)>0\right)\} \end{array} \tag{9}$$

The difference between (9) and (6) is that the distributed rough set regions are expressed in terms of B-information vectors, regarded as the conditions satisfiable by the objects. Besides, both definitions work similarly if they refer to the same inverse probabilities. For instance, the DRS-regions obtained for $B = \{a_1, a_3\}$ from Fig. 2 look as follows:

$$\mathcal{DPOS}_B(X_1) = \emptyset \qquad \mathcal{DNEG}_B(X_1) = \{\{(a_1,0),(a_3,0)\},\{(a_1,2),(a_3,1)\}\}$$
$$\mathcal{DBND}_B(X_1) = \{\{(a_1,0),(a_3,2)\},\{(a_1,1),(a_3,0)\},\{(a_1,2),(a_3,2)\}\} \tag{10}$$

One can see that the supports of the above B-information vectors within the decision system from Fig. 1 sum up to the corresponding RS-regions in (7).

6 Probabilistic Extensions of Rough Sets

One can use the probabilities to soften the requirements for certainty and impossibility in the rough set model. It provides better applicability to practical problems, where even a slight increase or decrease of probabilities can be as important as expecting them to equal 1 or 0. The *Variable Precision Rough Set* (*VPRS*) model [8] is based on parameter-controlled grades of posterior probabilities in defining the approximation regions. It relies on the *lower* and *upper limit certainty thresholds* l and u, which satisfy the postulate $0 \le l < P(X) < u \le 1$. For $\mathbb{A} = (U, A)$ and $B \subseteq A$, the *B-positive*, *B-negative*, and *B-boundary VPRS-regions* of the event $X \subseteq U$ are defined as follows:

$$\begin{aligned} \mathcal{POS}_B^u(X) &= \bigcup\{E \in U/B : P(X|E) \ge u\} \\ \mathcal{NEG}_B^l(X) &= \bigcup\{E \in U/B : P(X|E) \le l\} \\ \mathcal{BND}_B^{l,u}(X) &= \bigcup\{E \in U/B : l < P(X|E) < u\} \end{aligned} \tag{11}$$

In the context of machine learning, the VPRS model's ability to flexibly control approximation regions' definitions allows for efficient capturing probabilistic relations existing in data. However, as we discussed before, the estimates of posterior probabilities are not always reliable. Obviously, we could use the Bayes' rule for rewriting VPRS in terms of distributed decision systems, just like we did in case of original RS-regions. However, this time it would require a permanent usage of prior probabilities, which is too often questionable.

In the next section we propose a completely novel extension of the theory of rough sets, which is based entirely on inverse probabilities and – in this way – relates directly to the *Bayesian* rough set characteristics constituted by Proposition 1. To prepare the background, let us first focus on non-distributed decision system $\mathbb{A} = (U, A \cup \{d\})$ with $V_d = \{0, 1\}$. Using statistical terminology, let us interpret the decision classes X_1 and X_0 as corresponding to the *positive* and *negative verification* of some *hypothesis*. Let us consider the *Bayes' factor*, which occurs in many statistical approaches [7]. For a given $B \subseteq A$ and $E \in U/B$, it can be written as $P(E|X_0)/P(E|X_1)$ and used for verifying X_1 against X_0.

Let us reconsider this way of the Bayesian hypothesis verification as condition

$$X_1 \text{ is verified positively, if and only if } P(E|X_0) \le \varepsilon P(E|X_1) \tag{12}$$

where $\varepsilon \in [0, 1)$. For lower values of ε, the positive hypothesis verification under the evidence $E \in U/B$ requires more significant advantage of $P(E|X_1)$ over $P(E|X_0)$. In particular, we obtain a new interpretation of the rough set model:

1. Indiscernibility class $E \in U/B$ is contained in the RS-region $\mathcal{POS}_B(X_1)$, if and only if X_1 can be *positively* verified under the evidence provided by E at the maximal level of statistical significance, expressed by (12) for $\varepsilon = 0$.
2. $E \in U/B$ is contained in $\mathcal{NEG}_B(X_1)$, if and only if X_1 can be *negatively* verified at the maximal level of significance (we replace X_0 and X_1 in (12)).
3. $E \in U/B$ is contained in $\mathcal{BND}_B(X_1)$, if and only if it is not sufficient to verify X_1 *neither positively nor negatively* at the maximal level of significance.

For higher values of ε, we soften the requirements for the positive/negative verification. Therefore, let us refer to $\varepsilon \in [0, 1)$ as to *the degree of the significance approximation.* For ε tending to 1, we can replace $P(E|X_0) \leq \varepsilon P(E|X_1)$ by $P(E|X_0) < P(E|X_1)$, which was studied in [6] as providing *any* increase of belief in X_1. Also, across the whole range of $\varepsilon \in [0, 1)$, we obtain the following:

Proposition 2. *Let $\varepsilon \in [0, 1)$, $\mathbb{A} = (U, A \cup \{d\})$ with $V_d = \{0, 1\}$, $B \subseteq A$, and $E \in U/B$ be given. Then we have*

$$\begin{array}{l} P(E|X_0) \leq \varepsilon P(E|X_1) \Leftrightarrow P(X_1|E) \geq u_\varepsilon > P(X_1) \\ P(E|X_1) \leq \varepsilon P(E|X_0) \Leftrightarrow P(X_1|E) \leq l_\varepsilon < P(X_1) \end{array} \tag{13}$$

where

$$l_\varepsilon = \frac{\varepsilon P(X_1)}{\varepsilon P(X_1) + P(X_0)} \quad \textit{and} \quad u_\varepsilon = \frac{P(X_1)}{P(X_1) + \varepsilon P(X_0)} \tag{14}$$

In this way, the Bayes' factor test (12) refers to the VPRS idea of comparing posterior and prior probabilities. However, it does not need their explicit specification. This advantage can be explained using the following identity:

$$\frac{P(E|X_0)}{P(E|X_1)} = \frac{P(X_0|E)\,/\,P(X_0)}{P(X_1|E)\,/\,P(X_1)} \tag{15}$$

It shows that by using condition (12) we actually require that the increase of belief in X_0 given E, expressed by $P(X_0|E)/P(X_0)$, should be *ε-negligibly small* with respect to the increase of belief in X_1, that is that $P(X_0|E)/P(X_0) \leq \varepsilon P(X_1|E)/P(X_1)$. Identity (15) also shows that we do not need neither $P(X_k|E)$ nor $P(X_k)$ while comparing these belief changes for $k = 0, 1$. Obviously, the interpretation based on (15) would work also for (distributed) decision systems with more than two decision classes.

7 Rough Bayesian Model

Basing on the above discussion, we are ready to formalize the new rough set extension related to inverse probabilities. We will refer to it as to the *Rough Bayesian* model because of its relationship to Bayes' factor and Bayesian reasoning in general. We provide the definition for the distributed decision systems to emphasize that the Rough Bayesian model does not need to assume *anything* about prior or posterior probabilities. We believe that in this form our idea is possibly closest to the practical applications.

Definition 3. *Let* $\mathcal{A} = \{\mathbb{A}_0 = (X_0, A), \ldots, \mathbb{A}_{r-1} = (X_{r-1}, A)\}$ *be given. For any* $\varepsilon \in [0,1)$, X_k, $B \subseteq A$, *we define the* ε-approximate B-positive, B-negative, *and* B-boundary rough Bayesian regions *(abbreviated as* RB-regions*) as follows:*

$$\begin{aligned} \mathcal{BPOS}_B^{\varepsilon}(X_k) &= \{w \in V_B : \forall_{l:\, l \neq k}\, (P_l(B=w) \leq \varepsilon P_k(B=w))\} \\ \mathcal{BNEG}_B^{\varepsilon}(X_k) &= \{w \in V_B : \exists_{l:\, l \neq k}\, (P_k(B=w) \leq \varepsilon P_l(B=w))\} \\ \mathcal{BBND}_B^{\varepsilon}(X_k) &= \{w \in V_B : \exists_{l:\, l \neq k}\, (P_l(B=w) > \varepsilon P_k(B=w)) \\ &\qquad \wedge \forall_{l:\, l \neq k}\, (P_k(B=w) > \varepsilon P_l(B=w))\} \end{aligned} \tag{16}$$

The meaning of RB-regions can be interpreted in various ways, for instance by basing on (15) and comparing the increase of beliefs in the target events or by extending the Bayesian rough set interpretation following Proposition 1 onto the case of positive levels of significance approximation. Below we provide yet another, probably the simplest way of understanding the above RB-regions.

1. $w \in V_B$ belongs to $\mathcal{BPOS}_B^{\varepsilon}(X_k)$, if and only if it is *significantly* (up to ε) *more likely* to occur under X_k than under any other hypothesis X_l, $l \neq k$.
2. $w \in V_B$ belongs to $\mathcal{BNEG}_B^{\varepsilon}(X_k)$, if and only if there is an alternative hypothesis X_l, $l \neq k$, which makes w *significantly more likely* than X_k does.
3. $w \in V_B$ belongs to $\mathcal{BBND}_B^{\varepsilon}(X_k)$, if and only if it is not *significantly more likely* under X_k than under all other X_l, $l \neq k$, but there is also no alternative hypothesis, which makes w *significantly more likely* than X_k does.

The Rough Bayesian model enables us to test the target events directly against each other by comparing the likelihoods. It is especially profitable for multi-decision problems. The advantages, however, can be observed in any cases when prior and posterior probabilities are not reliable enough.

Let us conclude with the example concerning Fig. 2. For $\varepsilon = 0.2$, we obtain the following RB-regions for $B = \{a_1, a_3\}$:

$$\begin{aligned} \mathcal{BPOS}_B^{0.2}(X_1) &= \{\{(a_1,2),(a_3,2)\}\} \\ \mathcal{BNEG}_B^{0.2}(X_1) &= \{\{(a_1,0),(a_3,0)\},\{(a_1,2),(a_3,1)\}\} \\ \mathcal{BBND}_B^{0.2}(X_1) &= \{\{(a_1,0),(a_3,2)\},\{(a_1,1),(a_3,0)\}\} \end{aligned}$$

In comparison to (10), the case of $a_1 = 2$ and $a_3 = 2$ starts to support the B-positive RB-region of X_1. If we can assume that $P(X_1) = 1/2$, then we obtain analogous result in terms of VPRS-regions calculated from Fig. 1 for

$$l = \frac{1/5 \cdot 1/2}{1/5 \cdot 1/2 + (1 - 1/2)} = \frac{1}{6} \qquad u = \frac{1/2}{1/2 + 1/5(1 - 1/2)} = \frac{5}{6}$$

In particular, for $E = \{e \in U : a_1(e) = 2 \wedge a_3(e) = 2\}$, we get $P(X_1|E) \geq 5/6$. Now, if we assume $P(X_1) = 1/1000$, then there is no sense to keep the upper limit $u = 5/6$ any more. However, there is no change required if we rely on the RB-regions. With the same $\varepsilon = 0.2$ we simply get different interpretation in terms of posterior probabilities. Namely, we recalculate the VPRS degrees as

$$l = \frac{1/5 \cdot 1/1000}{1/5 \cdot 1/1000 + (1 - 1/1000)} \approx \frac{1}{5000} \quad u = \frac{1/1000}{1/1000 + 1/5(1 - 1/1000)} \approx \frac{1}{200}$$

As a result, we obtain a convenient method of defining the rough-set-like regions based on inverse probabilities, which – if necessary – can be translated onto the parameters related to more commonly used posterior probabilities. However, our Rough Bayesian model can be applied also in case that such translation is impossible, that is when prior probabilities are unknown or even undefinable.

8 Final Remarks

We discussed a new interpretation of rough sets based on inverse probabilities. We introduced the Rough Bayesian model as a parameterized probabilistic extension based on Bayes' factor, which is used in many statistical approaches to the hypothesis testing. We proposed distributed decision systems as a new way of storing data, providing estimations of inverse probabilities.

We believe that the framework based on the Rough Bayesian model for distributed decision systems is well applicable to the practical data analysis problems. In our opinion, the presented results are also helpful in stating theoretical foundations for correspondence between rough sets and Bayesian reasoning.

Acknowledgments

Supported by the grant awarded from the Faculty of Science at the University of Regina, as well as by the internal research grant of PJIIT, partially financed by Polish National Committee for Scientific Research.

References

1. Łukasiewicz, J.: Die logischen Grundlagen der Wahrscheinchkeitsrechnung. Kraków (1913). In: L. Borkowski (ed.), Jan Łukasiewicz – Selected Works. North Holland Publishing Company; PWN (1970).
2. Mitchell, T.: Machine Learning. Mc Graw Hill (1998).
3. Pawlak, Z.: Rough sets – Theoretical aspects of reasoning about data. Kluwer Academic Publishers (1991).
4. Pawlak, Z.: New Look on Bayes' Theorem – The Rough Set Outlook. In: Proc. of JSAI RSTGC'2001, pp. 1–8.
5. Polkowski, L., Tsumoto, S., Lin, T.Y. (eds): Rough Set Methods and Applications. Physica Verlag (2000).
6. Ślęzak, D., Ziarko, W.: Attribute Reduction in the Bayesian Version of Variable Precision Rough Set Model. In: Proc. of RSKD'2003. Elsevier, ENTCS 82/4 (2003).
7. Swinburne, R. (ed.): Bayes's Theorem. Proc. of the British Academy 113 (2003).
8. Ziarko, W.: Variable precision rough sets model. Journal of Computer and Systems Sciences, 46/1 (1993) pp. 39–59.

On Learnability of Decision Tables

Wojciech Ziarko

Department of Computer Science, University of Regina
Regina, SK, S4S 0A2, Canada

Abstract. The article is exploring the learnabilty issues of decision tables acquired from data within the frameworks of rough set and of variable precision rough set models. Measures of learning problem complexity and of learned table domain coverage are proposed. Several methods for enhancing the learnabilty of decision tables are discussed, including a new technique based on value reducts.

1 Introduction

Decision Tables are specifications of mutually disjoint sets of decision rules. In typical applications, the decision tables are designed manually, based on the prior knowledge of possible input vectors and associated decisions. In some application areas, for example in complex control systems, this kind of knowledge is not available, or even worse, the relation between inputs and decisions is not functional. This problem was initially addressed by Pawlak in his idea of decision tables in the context of rough set theory [9]. In this approach, the experimental data, rather than human knowledge, are used as a basis for decision table derivation or *learning*. Pawlak's approach was subsequently extended in [3, 4, 5] to make use of probabilistic information in the decision table-based decisions, leading to the introduction of *probabilistic decision tables* [5] in the context of the variable precision rough set model (VPRS) [4]. One of the key issues to be addressed when deriving decision tables from data, is the *learnability* issue. The learnability issue implies questions such as, for example, how to evaluate the degree of coverage of the universe, how to maximize the degree coverage, how to validate the correctness of the mapping specified by the tables or how to detect insufficient coverage. In the following sections, an attempt is made to answer some of these questions within the frameworks of rough set and VPRS models. Measures of learning problem complexity and of learned table domain coverage are proposed. Several methods for enhancing the learnabilty of decision tables are also discussed, including a new technique based on value reducts. Some related research was published in [9, 11].

2 Rough Decision Tables

The universe of interest is a set of objects U about which observations are acquired by sampling sensor readings or by some other means. The observations

S. Tsumoto et al. (Eds.): RSCTC 2004, LNAI 3066, pp. 394–401, 2004.

are expressed through values of a finite set of functions $C \cup D$ on U, referred to as *attributes.* The functions belonging to the set C are called *condition attributes*, whereas functions in D are referred to as *decision attributes.* We can assume, without loss of generality, that there is only one decision attribute, that is $D = \{d\}$. Each attribute a belonging to $C \cup D$ is a mapping $a : U \rightarrow V_a$, where V_a is a finite set of values called the *domain* of the attribute a. In many applications, condition attributes are functions obtained by discretizing values of variables representing values of measurements and the decision attribute is a function obtained by discretizing values of one of the variables representing decision or prediction target. The set of condition attributes C defines a joint mapping denoted as $\mathbf{C} : U \rightarrow \mathbf{C}(U) \subseteq \otimes_{a \in C} V_a$, where $\otimes$ denotes Cartesian product operator of all attribute domains of attributes in C. Both condition attributes and the decision attributes jointly define a mapping denoted as $\mathbf{C} \cup \mathbf{D} : U \rightarrow \mathbf{C} \cup \mathbf{D}(U) \subseteq \otimes_{a \in C \cup D} V_a$. The mapping $\mathbf{C} \cup \mathbf{D}$ can be represented by an *information table* composed of *information vectors.* The investigation of information tables is a significant part of rough set theory.

For each combination of condition attribute values $x \in \mathbf{C}(U)$, the set $E_x = \mathbf{C}^{-1}(x) = \{e \in U : \mathbf{C}(e) = x\}$ is called a *C-elementary set.* Each C-elementary set is a collection of objects with identical values of the attributes belonging to the set C. Similarly, the subsets of the universe corresponding to the information vectors are called *(C,D)-elementary sets.* In general, any subset z of values of attributes $B \subseteq C \cup D$ of an information vector x corresponds to a set of objects $\mathbf{B}^{-1}(z)$ matching these values, where $\mathbf{B}^{-1}(z) = \{e \in U : \mathbf{B}(e) = z\}$. The collection of all elementary sets forms a partition of the universe U, denoted as $U/C = \{E_x\}_{x \in \mathbf{C}(U)}$. In practice, the partition U/C is a representation of the limits of our ability to distinguish individual objects of the universe. The pair $\mathbb{A} = (U, U/C)$ is called an *approximation space.* Similar to condition attributes, the decision attribute induces a partition of U consisting of *decision classes* (*D*-elementary sets) $U/D = \{F_1, F_2, \ldots F_k\}$, $k \geq 2$, corresponding to different values of the attribute $d \in D$. That is, if the domain of d is $V_d = \{v_1^d, v_2^d, \ldots, v_k^d\}$, then $F_i = \{e \in U : d(e) = v_i^d\}$, $1 \leq i \leq k$. Our interest here is in the analysis of the relation $Inf(C, D)$ between condition and decision attributes, in particular, to find out whether this relation is functional, or if not, which part of it is not functional. For that purpose, the *rough approximation regions* of the decision classes are defined as follows.

The *positive region* $POS^{C,D}(i)$ of the class F_i, $1 \leq i \leq k$ in the approximation space $\mathbb{A}$ is defined as $POS^{C,D}(i) = \cup\{E \in U/C : E \subseteq F_i)\}$. The *negative region* $NEG^{C,D}(i)$ of the class F_i is defined as $NEG^{C,D}(i) = \cup\{E \in U/C : E \subseteq (U - F_i)\}$. The complement of the positive regions of all decision classes $BND^{C,D}(U) = U - \cup_i POS^{C,D}(i)$ is called the *boundary region* of the partition U/D in the approximation space $\mathbb{A}$.

We define a *rough decision table* $DT^{C,D}$ as a mapping derived from the information table, which is associating each combination of condition attribute values $x \in \mathbf{C}(U)$ with a unique designation of the rough approximation region the respective elementary set E_x belongs to, i.e.

$$DT^{C,D}(x) = \begin{cases} 0 \Leftrightarrow E_x \subseteq BND^{C,D}(U) \\ i \Leftrightarrow E_x \subseteq POS^{C,D}(i) \end{cases} \tag{1}$$

In general, the mapping produces one of $k+1$ values, with the value 0 representing the lack of definite decision. The rough decision table is *deterministic* if the boundary region is empty. Otherwise, it is *non-deterministic.* The rough decision table is an approximate representation of the relation between condition and decision attributes. It is most useful for decision making or prediction when the relation is deterministic (functional) or largely deterministic (partially functional).

We will treat the case of two-valued (binary) decision attributes separately, since the relation represented by the information table $Inf(C, D)$ can be expressed in a simplified form by decomposing it into a number relations with the same condition attributes and a re-defined binary decision attribute. With binary decision attribute, the decision classes will be denoted as $U/D = \{F_+, F_-\}$, corresponding to assumed values + and − of the decision attribute $d \in D$. That is, $F_+ = \{e \in U : d(e) = +\}$ and $F_- = \{e \in U : d(e) = -\}$. It is convenient to express the rough approximation regions in this case as follows.

The *positive region* $POS^{C,D}(U)$ of the class F_+ in the approximation space $\mathbb{A}$ is defined as $POS^{C,D}(+) = \cup\{E \in U/C : E \subseteq F_+)\}$. The *negative region* $NEG^{C,D}(+)$ of the class F_+ is defined as $NEG^{C,D}(+) = \cup\{E \in U/C : E \subseteq F_-)\}$ and the boundary region of the class F_+ and of the partition U/D is given by $BND^{C,D}(+) = U - (POS^{C,D}(+) \cup NEG^{C,D}(+))$.

For shortness, in what follows, when defining rough decision table $DT^{C,D}$, based on an information table with a binary decision attribute, we will use symbols $-, 0, +$ to designate negative, boundary and positive regions, respectively:

$$DT^{C,D}(x) = \begin{cases} - \Leftrightarrow E_x \subseteq NEG^{C,D}(+) \\ 0 \Leftrightarrow E_x \subseteq BND^{C,D}(+) \\ + \Leftrightarrow E_x \subseteq POS^{C,D}(+) \end{cases} \tag{2}$$

3 Probabilistic Decision Tables

When the relation between condition and decision attributes is mostly non-deterministic, the probabilistic decision tables [5] can be used to provide more accurate representation of the relation between condition and decision attributes. With the probabilistic decision tables, decisions or predictions can made with a controlled degree of certainty, usually significantly higher than the certainty of a random guess. In this sense, the probabilistic decision tables help in achieving a degree of *certainty gain* [2] in decisions or predictions rather than aiming at achieving totally certain decisions or predictions, which might be impossible. The probabilistic decision tables are defined for binary decision attributes only in the context of VPRS model.

In the VPRS approach, each elementary set E is assigned a conditional probability function value $P(F_+|E)$, denoted briefly as $P(+|E)$. In addition, we assume the existence of the prior probability function $P(F_+)$, denoted as

$P(+)$. We assume that both decision classes F_+ and F_- are likely to occur, that is $0 < P(+) < 1$. The values of conditional and prior probability functions are normally estimated from finite sample data $U' \subseteq U$ by calculating $P(+|E) = \frac{card(F_+ \cap E \cap U')}{card(E \cap U')}$ and $P(+) = \frac{card(F_+ \cap U')}{card(U')}$, where $card(*)$ denotes cardinality of a set.

The rough approximation regions of the VPRS are based on the values of significance threshold parameters, referred to as lower limit l and upper limit u, such that $0 \leq l < P(+) < u \leq 1$. The definition of the u-positive region $POS_u^{C,D}(+)$ of the class F_+ is dependent upon the upper limit parameter u, which reflects the least acceptable degree of conditional probability $P(+|E)$ to include elementary set E in $POS_u^{C,D}(+)$. That is, $POS_u^{C,D}(+) = \cup\{E \in U/C : P(+|E) \geq u\}$. Intuitively, u represents the desired level of improved prediction accuracy over the prior probability P(+) when predicting the occurrence of the class F_+, given that event E actually occurred.

The l-negative region $NEG_l^{C,D}(+)$ of the class F_+ is controlled by the lower limit parameter l, such that $0 \leq l < P(+)$ or, alternatively, such that $1 - P(+) = P(-) < 1 - l$. $NEG_l^{C,D}(+)$ is an area where the occurrence of the set F_+ is significantly less likely than random guess (prior) probability $P(+)$ or alternatively, where the occurrence of F_- is significantly more likely than $P(-)$. That is, $NEG_l^{C,D}(+) = \cup\{E \in U/C : P(+|E) \leq l\}$ or $NEG_l^{C,D}(+) = \cup\{E \in U/C : P(-|E) \geq 1 - l\} = POS_{1-l}^{C,D}(-)$.

The (l, u)-boundary region is an area where there is no sufficient probabilistic bias towards neither F_+ nor F_-. That is, $BND_{l,u}^{C,D}(+) = \cup\{E \in U/C : l < P(+|E) < u\}$ or $BND_{l,u}^{C,D}(+) = \cup\{E \in U/C : 1 - u < P(-|E) < 1 - l\} = BND_{1-u,1-l}^{C,D}(-)$.

The *probabilistic information table* $Inf(C, D, P)$ is an information table with an extra column in which each information vector $y \in Inf(C, D)$ is assigned its probability $P(y)$. The probability can be estimated from sample $U' \subseteq U$ in a standard way by calculating $P(y) = card(E_y \cap U')/card(U')$. Based on the probabilistic information table, the *probabilistic decision table* $DT_{l,u}^{C,D}$ can be defined as a mapping associating each combination of condition attribute values $x \in \mathbf{C}(U)$ with a pair of values representing (a) the unique designation of the rough approximation region the elementary set E_x belongs to and (b) the estimated value of the conditional probability function $P(+|E_x)$:

$$DT_{l,u}^{C,D}(x) = \begin{cases} (P(+|E_x), -) \Leftrightarrow E_x \subseteq NEG_l^{C,D}(+) \\ (P(+|E_x), 0) \Leftrightarrow E_x \subseteq BND_{l,u}^{C,D}(+) \\ (P(+|E_x), +) \Leftrightarrow E_x \subseteq POS_u^{C,D}(+) \end{cases} \tag{3}$$

The rough decision tables are special cases of probabilistic decision tables because the VPRS model reduces to the original model of rough sets when $l = 0$ and $u = 1$.

4 Completeness of Learned Tables

One of the key issues when applying both rough and probabilistic decision tables to new observations is their completeness. Because in practical applications information tables are usually derived based on a proper subset of the universe, they may not provide complete representation of the elementary sets or the relations existing in the universe. Consequently, any decision tables obtained from such information tables would also be incomplete. The information table is *complete* if all (C,D)-elementary sets of $U/C \cup D$ are represented in the table. In such a table, all "new cases" would be matched by some rows of the information table. We say that probabilistic information table is complete if all (C,D)-elementary sets and their probabilities are correctly represented in the table.

In many applications, it is impossible to determine if the information table is complete. However, we can devise a process of incremental learning which would result in a gradual "growth" of the information table and of the derived rough decision table, as more and more observations would become available, with the convergence to a stable state at some point of time [9, 10]. To assess the feasibility of such a learning process, it is essential to evaluate potential *learnability* of the information table and of the derived decision table by using appropriate measures. By learnability we mean the effective ability to converge to a stable state, i.e. within reasonable time and based on reasonably sized number of new observations. Although it is impossible to precisely determine the time and training data size limits to reach the convergence, it is relatively easy to identify information tables which are very unlikely to converge within reasonable time. It can be achieved by *learning complexity* estimation, which resembles analysis of computational complexity of algorithms. To evaluate the learnability limit of an information table, we introduce the notion of *theoretical complexity* of a table, $com(Inf(C,D))$, as a product of cardinalities of all its attribute domains: $com_T(Inf(C,D)) = \prod_{a \in C \cup D} card(V_a)$.

Clearly, the theoretical complexity grows exponentially with the number of attributes, making it impossible to learn tables even with relatively small number of multi-valued attributes.

The *actual complexity* $com_A(Inf(C,D))$ of an information table learning problem is equal to the number of elementary sets in the universe U: $com_A(Inf(C,D)) = card(U/C \cup D)$.

The *theoretical domain coverage* measure, $cov_{U'}(Inf(C,D))$, provides a crude estimate of the percentage coverage of the universe by the information table. It is given by the ratio of the number of the elementary sets represented by the table to its theoretical complexity: $cov_T^{U'}(Inf(C,D)) = card(U'/C \cup D)/com_T(Inf(C,D))$, where $U' \subseteq U$ is a sample set of objects.

The *actual domain coverage* measure, $cov_A^{U'}(Inf(C,D))$, can be defined as the ratio of the number of the (C,D)-elementary sets represented by an information table to actual number of elementary sets in the universe, i.e. $cov_A^{U'}(Inf(C,D)) = card(U'/C \cup D)/card(U/C \cup D)$. Since the actual domain coverage is normally unknown, the completeness level of the information table has to be judged based on the theoretical domain coverage. Low theoretical domain coverage is indicative of highly incomplete information table.

Similarly to information tables, completeness and coverage measures can be defined for decision tables. The actual domain coverage can be expressed as $cov_A^{U'}(DT^{C,D}) = card(U'/C)/card(U/C)$, i.e. as the ratio of the number of C-elementary sets represented by the decision table to actual number of C-elementary sets in U.

The theoretical domain coverage is given by $cov_T^{U'}(DT^{C,D}) = card(U'/C)/com_T(DT^{C,D})$ where $com_T(DT^{C,D})$ is a theoretical complexity of a decision table, defined by $com_T(DT^{C,D}) = \prod_{a \in C} card(V_a)$.

Producing decision tables, or structures of decision tables [6], which would have high domain coverage and sufficient accuracy is an optimization problem. Below, we review some new and existing techniques applicable to producing more learnable, lower complexity decision tables.

Replacing Multivalued Decision Attributes with Binary Attributes. When there are more than two, $k > 2$, values of the decision attribute, the information table $Inf(C, \{d\})$ can be replaced by k information tables with binary decision attributes while preserving essential relations. With the given domain $V_d = \{v_1^d, v_2^d, \ldots, v_k^d\}$ of the decision attribute d, an information table $Inf(C, d_j)$ would be created for each value v_j, $1 \leq j \leq k$ by defining a new decision attribute d_j such that, for all $e \in U$, $d_j(e) = +$ if $d(e) = v_j^d$ and $d_j(e) = -$ if $d(e) \neq v_j^d$. The modified tables $Inf(C, d_j)$ have the desired property of potentially higher domain coverage as demonstrated by the following proposition:

Proposition 1. $cov_T^{U'}(Inf(C, d_j)) \geq cov_T^{U'}(Inf(C, \{d\}))$.

Proof. The above property follows from the fact that according to the definition of function d_j, any decision attribute value $d(e) \neq v_j^d$ will be replaced by $-$. This will result in merging of all those information vectors of $Inf(C, \{d\})$ which have identical values of condition attributes. The merging will cause a drop in the number of information vectors by no more than the factor of $k/2$. The drop in theoretical complexity of the information table will be exactly by the factor of $k/2$, which completes the proof.

Reducing Attribute Domains. By grouping condition attribute values to define new, more general attributes, for example by using a positive and negative region-preserving discretization techniques, the theoretical complexity of both information table and of the decision table will be reduced. It will also lead to the reduction of the actual complexity of the learning problem since the universe U will be divided into smaller number of elementary classes obtained via merging elementary sets existing prior to the discretization. The theoretical domain coverage would not decrease, and most likely would grow, because the number of information vectors would drop, in the worst case, by the same factor as the drop of theoretical complexity.

Eliminating Redundant Attributes. Elimination of redundant attributes through computation of attribute *reduct* [9] is an important technique leading to reduction of theoretical complexity and to growth of theoretical coverage. The mechanism of this technique is essentially the same as of the reduction of attribute domains. It is causing merging of some of the information vectors leading to simpler and more learnable information tables and related decision tables.

Creating Hierarchies of Decision Tables. When dealing with rough or probabilistic decision tables, further complexity reduction can be achieved by forming a linear hierarchy of decision tables [6]. This method was developed for rough and probabilistic decision tables derived from information tables with binary decision attributes. In this approach, the number of condition attributes in a decision table is further reduced, beyond reduct of attributes to produce some relatively large boundary area and to retain some positive or negative region of the target decision class. The boundary area is then treated as a lower level universe by itself, for which next layer of decision table is produced, and so on. The process continues until desired accuracy classifier composed of linked decision tables is formed.

Using Suitably Selected Mappings of Attribute Values. The most general technique involves using suitably selected binary-valued mappings of one or more condition attributes to form new *composite attributes*. The mappings must be selected in such a way as to ensure that: (a1) some elementary sets belonging positive region would be given the same value, i.e. would merge according to the given mapping, or some elementary sets belonging to negative region would be given the same value; (b1) the collection of positive or negative region elementary sets given the same value by different mappings would cover both regions. The mappings should not be redundant, which can be assured by computing *reduct* of the composite attributes. As other techniques described here, this method would cause merging of elementary sets and consequently would lead to decision table domain coverage increase and actual learning complexity reduction. A promising approach to composite attribute creation, which was tested with good results, involves using *value reducts* [9]. Let $z \in \mathbf{B}(U)$ where $B \subseteq C$. The vector of attribute values z is a value reduct if (a2) $\mathbf{B}^{-1}(z) \subseteq POS_u(+) \cup NEG_l(+)$, and (b2) no proper subset of the vector z satisfies the condition (a2) above. Based on the value reduct, the desired composite mapping on U, referred to *value reduct attribute* $\mathbf{B}_z$, can be defined as $\mathbf{B}_z(e) = 1$ if $\mathbf{B}(e) = z$, and $\mathbf{B}_z(e) = 0$ if $\mathbf{B}(e) \neq z$. Since sets of objects matching value reducts cover both positive and negative regions then the requirement (b1) will be satisfied. The requirement (a1) is likely to be satisfied on a number of information vectors because, as experience with data sets indicates, value reducts typically cover more than one vector. Value reducts can be computed using existing algorithms for computation of minimal length rules for rough approximation regions [7].

5 Conclusions

The methods for increasing ability of decision tables to learn need to be applied together for best results. The true test of their effectiveness can be possible only when using large quantities of real world data for developing decision tables. It appears, that the issue of learnability of decision tables is a fundamental one with respect to assuring the success of a practical application of rough set approach to machine learning class of problems.

Acknowledgement

The reported research was supported by Natural Sciences and Engineering Research Council of Canada.

References

1. Pawlak, Z. Rough sets - Theoretical aspects of reasoning about data. Kluwer (1991).
2. Ślęzak, D. Ziarko, W. Attribute reduction in the Bayesian version of variable precision rough set model. Proc. of RSKD'2003. Elsevier, ENTCS 82/4 (2003).
3. Yao, Y.Y. Wong, S.K.M. A decision theoretic framework for approximating concepts. Intl. Journal of Man-Machine Studies, vol. 37, (1992) 793-809.
4. Ziarko, W. Variable precision rough sets model. Journal of Computer and Systems Sciences, vol. 46, no. 1, (1993) 39-59.
5. Ziarko, W. Probabilistic decision tables in the variable precision rough set model. Computational Intelligence, vol. 17, no 3, (2001) 593-603.
6. Ziarko, W. Acquisition of hierarchy-structured probabilistic decision tables and rules from data. Proc. of IEEE Intl. Conference on Fuzzy Systems, Honolulu, (2002) 779-784.
7. Grzymala-Busse, J. Ziarko. W. Data mining based on rough sets. Data Mining: Opportunities and Challenges. IDEA Group Publishing, (2003) 142-173.
8. Ziarko, W. Ning, S. Machine learning through data classification and reduction. Fundamenta Informaticae, vol. 30, (1997) 371-380.
9. Marek, W. Pawlak, Z. One dimension learning. Fundamenta Informaticae, vol. 8, no. 1, (1985) 83-88.
10. Tsumoto, S. Characteristics of accuracy and coverage in rule induction. Lecure Notes in AI 2639, Springer Verlag, (2003), 237-224.

Remarks on Approximation Quality in Variable Precision Fuzzy Rough Sets Model

Alicja Mieszkowicz-Rolka and Leszek Rolka

Department of Avionics and Control
Rzeszów University of Technology
ul. W. Pola 2, 35-959 Rzeszów, Poland
{alicjamr,leszekr}@prz.edu.pl

Abstract. In this paper some properties of the variable precision fuzzy rough sets model will be considered. A new way of determining the positive region of classification will be proposed, which is useful in evaluation of approximation quality in variable precision fuzzy or crisp rough sets applications. The notions of the fuzzy rough weighted mean u-lower and l-upper approximation will be discussed. Fuzzy rough approximations will be evaluated basing on selected R-implicators.

1 Introduction

The idea of merging the theories of fuzzy sets and rough sets for modelling uncertainty was introduced by Dubois and Prade [2], and Nakamura [13]. It was further developed and discussed in many papers e.g. [1, 3, 5, 8, 9, 15].

The goal of the present paper is to contribute to the fuzzy rough framework by taking into account issues that can arise in practical applications. To this end we continue our previous work, which was aimed at utilising the variable precision rough set (VPRS) model of Ziarko in analysis of fuzzy information systems [12].

The VPRS approach turned out to be helpful in analysing large, inconsistent decision tables with crisp attributes [10, 11]. This is because of alleviating the restrictive character of the original rough sets model by allowing a small degree of misclassification i.e. by including into the positive region of classification even those indiscernibility classes that would be normally rejected.

Similar idea of relaxation of principles was also proposed in the framework of Dominance-Based Rough Set Approach in [4].

The application of the fuzzy extension of rough sets given by Dubois and Prade leads to analogical problems to those observed in case of the original (crisp) rough set theory [12]. Even a relative small inclusion error of an similarity class results in rejection (membership value equal to zero) of that class from the lower approximation. Small inclusion errors can also lead to an excessive increase of the upper approximation. These facts justify the need for a generalisation of VPRS in the form of the variable precision fuzzy rough sets (VPFRS) model.

First, we discuss the issue of evaluating the approximation quality of classification basing on the crisp VPRS model. An alternative way of determining

S. Tsumoto et al. (Eds.): RSCTC 2004, LNAI 3066, pp. 402–411, 2004.

the positive region of classification will be presented. This helps to alleviate an excessive increase of the approximation quality due to the tolerance of the VPRS approach.

In the next section we discuss the details of our variable precision fuzzy rough sets approach. The considered VPFRS model is particulary based on the use of fuzzy R-implications. We extend the VPFRS concept by introducing the notions of fuzzy rough weighted mean u-lower and l-upper approximation. This is a refinement, which allows to determine the mean fuzzy rough approximations more accurate than in case of the ordinary average.

Finally, the modified definition of the positive region, given in the first section, will be adopted for evaluation of the generalised approximation quality in case of fuzzy information systems.

In the last section the presented VPFRS approach will be illustrated by an example.

2 Approximation Quality in VPRS Model

The starting-point of the VPRS model was a modified relation of (crisp) set inclusion introduced by Ziarko [16]. It is based on the notion of inclusion error $e(A, B)$ of a nonempty set A in a set B:

$$e(A, B) = 1 - \frac{\mathrm{card}(A \cap B)}{\mathrm{card}(A)} \; . \tag{1}$$

In the extended version of VPRS, proposed by Katzberg and Ziarko [6], a lower limit l and an upper limit u for the required inclusion grade are used, with

$$0 \leq l < u \leq 1 \; . \tag{2}$$

Basing on the limits l and u, one can define the u-lower and the l-upper approximation of any subset A of the universe X by an indiscernibility (equivalence) relation R.

The u-lower approximation of A by R, denoted as $\underline{R}_u A$ is a set

$$\underline{R}_u A = \{x \in X\colon\; e([x]_R, A) \leq 1 - u\} \tag{3}$$

where $[x]_R$ denotes an indiscernibility class of R containing the element x.

The l-upper approximation of A by R, denoted as $\overline{R}_l A$ is a set

$$\overline{R}_l A = \{x \in X\colon\; e([x]_R, A) < 1 - l\} \; . \tag{4}$$

Let $Y = \{Y_1, Y_2, \ldots, Y_n\}$ be a classification of the universe X. The u-positive classification region of Y by R is defined as follows:

$$\mathrm{Pos}_{R_u}(Y) = \bigcup_{i=1}^{n} \underline{R}_u(Y_i) \; . \tag{5}$$

By using (5) we express the u-approximation quality of Y by R as:

$$\gamma_{R_u}(Y) = \frac{\mathrm{card}(\mathrm{Pos}_{R_u}(Y))}{\mathrm{card}(X)} = \frac{\sum_{i=1}^{n} \mathrm{card}(\underline{R}_u(Y_i))}{\mathrm{card}(X)} \tag{6}$$

Usually, the classification Y is generated by indiscernibility relation R basing on a set of decision attributes D. The approximation of Y is performed by means of indiscernibility classes obtained for a set of condition attributes C. Hence, we get a measure of u-approximation quality, which we denote here by k_{WZ}:

$$k_{\mathrm{WZ}} = \frac{\mathrm{card}(\mathrm{Pos}_{C_u}(D^\star))}{\mathrm{card}(X)} = \frac{\sum_{i=1}^{m} \mathrm{card}(\underline{C}_u(D_i))}{\mathrm{card}(X)} \tag{7}$$

where $D^\star = \{D_1, D_2, \ldots, D_m\}$ is the family of indiscernibility classes obtained with respect to the decision attributes D.

Unfortunately, the measure (7) produces too "optmistic" results due to the tolerance of the VPRS model. In order to alleviate this property we proposed in [10, 11] a modified definition of the positive region of an approximated set A by rejecting all elements of the approximating classes, which are not included in A:

$$\mathrm{Pos}_{R_u}(A) = \{x \in X\colon\ x \in [x]_R \cap A \ \text{and}\ e([x]_R, A) \leq 1 - u\}\,. \tag{8}$$

This way we get a new measure of u-approximation quality, denoted by k_{AR}:

$$k_{\mathrm{AR}} = \frac{\mathrm{card}(\mathrm{Pos}_{C_u}(D^\star))}{\mathrm{card}(X)} = \frac{\sum_{i=1}^{n}\sum_{j=1}^{m} \delta_{ij}\mathrm{card}(C_i \cap D_j)}{\mathrm{card}(X)} \tag{9}$$

where

$$\delta_{ij} = \begin{cases} 1 & \text{if } e(C_i \cap D_j) \leq 1 - u \\ 0 & \text{otherwise} \end{cases}$$

n – number of equivalence classes for condition attributes C,
m – number of equivalence classes for decision attributes D.

3 Variable Precision Fuzzy Rough Sets

Our further considerations will be based on the use of fuzzy compatibility relation R, which is symmetric and reflexive. The compatibility relation R generates a partition of the universe X into fuzzy compatibility classes. We denote by X_i some compatibility class in X, where $i = 1 \ldots n$. Any fuzzy set F defined in the universe X can be approximated by the obtained compatibility classes.

The problem that should be considered is how to evaluate the inclusion grade of one fuzy set in another fuzzy set. Different measures of fuzzy sets inclusion were considered in the literature e.g. [1] and [9].

The starting-point of our approach is the definition of inclusion grade of a fuzzy set A in a fuzzy set B with respect to particular elements of A. Hence, we get a new fuzzy set called the fuzzy inclusion set of A in B and denoted by A^B. We apply in the definition an implication operator $\rightarrow$:

$$\mu_{A^B}(x) = \begin{cases} \mu_A(x) \rightarrow \mu_B(x) & \text{if } \mu_A(x) > 0 \\ 0 & \text{otherwise} \end{cases} \tag{10}$$

Furthermore, we assume that the grade of inclusion with respect to x should be equal to 1, if the inequality $\mu_A(x) \leq \mu_B(x)$ for that x is satisfied:

$$\mu_A(x) \rightarrow \mu_B(x) = 1, \quad \text{if } \mu_A(x) \leq \mu_B(x) \,. \tag{11}$$

The requirement (11) is always satisfied by residual implicators (R-implicators), which are defined using a t-norm operator $*$ as follows:

$$x \rightarrow y = \sup\{\lambda \in [0,1] : \; x * \lambda \leq y\} \,. \tag{12}$$

In the following, two popular R-implicators will be applied:

- the Gaines implicator: $x \rightarrow y = 1$ if $x \leq y$ and y/x otherwise,
- the Łukasiewicz implicator: $x \rightarrow y = \min(1, 1 - x + y)$.

The idea of Ziarko will be extended on fuzzy sets by introducing a generalised measure of inclusion error. We should express the error that would be made, when the "worst" elements of approximating set, in the sense of their membership in the fuzzy inclusion set A^B, were omitted. This can be done by utilising the notion of α-cut [7], which is defined for any fuzzy set A and $\alpha \in [0,1]$ as follows:

$$A_\alpha = \{x \in X : \; \mu_A(x) \geq \alpha\} \tag{13}$$

We define a measure called the α-inclusion error $e_\alpha(A, B)$ of any nonempty fuzzy set A in a fuzzy set B:

$$e_\alpha(A, B) = 1 - \frac{\text{power}(A \cap A^B_\alpha)}{\text{power}(A)} \,. \tag{14}$$

For crisp sets A and B, and for any value of $\alpha > 0$ the measure (14) is identical with the inclusion error (1) defined by Ziarko. The set A^B in that case is equal to the crisp intersection $A \cap B$.

Now, we define the u-lower approximation of a fuzzy set F by R as a fuzzy set of X/R with the membership function expressed as follows:

$$\mu_{\underline{R}_u F}(X_i) = \begin{cases} f_{i_u} & \text{if } \exists \alpha_u = \sup\{\alpha \in (0,1] : \; e_\alpha(X_i, F) \leq 1 - u\} \\ 0 & \text{otherwise} \end{cases} \tag{15}$$

where

$$f_{i_u} = \inf_{x \in S_{i_u}} \mu_{X_i}(x) \rightarrow \mu_F(x), \qquad S_{i_u} = \text{supp}(X_i \cap X^F_{i\alpha_u}) \,.$$

We can define in a similar manner the l-upper approximation of the set F by R as a fuzzy set of X/R with the membership function expressed by:

$$\mu_{\overline{R}_l F}(X_i) = \begin{cases} f_{i_l} & \text{if } \exists \alpha_l = \sup\{\alpha \in (0,1] : \; e'_\alpha(X_i, F) < 1 - l\} \\ 0 & \text{otherwise} \end{cases} \tag{16}$$

where

$$f_{i_l} = \sup_{x \in S_{i_l}} \mu_{X_i}(x) * \mu_F(x), \qquad S_{i_l} = \mathrm{supp}(X_i \cap (X_i \cap F)_{\alpha_l})$$

$$e'_\alpha(X_i, F) = 1 - \frac{\mathrm{power}(X_i \cap (X_i \cap F)_\alpha)}{\mathrm{power}(X_i)} .$$

However, the fuzzy rough approximations expressed by means of limit values of membership functions seem to be not always suitable for analysis of real data. We propose an alternative definition of fuzzy rough approximations, in which the mean value of membership (in the fuzzy inclusion set) for all used elements of the approximating class is utilised. This approach can be particulary justified in analysis of large universes. In such cases the obtained results should correspond to the statistical properties of information system, and not merely depend on a single value of membership function.

We define the mean u-lower approximation of the set F by R as a fuzzy set of X/R with the following membership function:

$$\mu_{\underline{R}_u F}(X_i) = \begin{cases} f_{i_u} & \text{if } \exists \alpha_u = \sup\{\alpha \in (0,1] : \ e_\alpha(X_i, F) \le 1 - u\} \\ 0 & \text{otherwise} \end{cases} \tag{17}$$

where

$$f_{i_u} = \frac{\mathrm{power}(X_i^F \cap X_{i_{\alpha_u}}^F)}{\mathrm{card}(X_{i_{\alpha_u}}^F)} . \tag{18}$$

The membership function of the mean l-upper approximation of the set F by R is defined as follows:

$$\mu_{\overline{R}_l F}(X_i) = \begin{cases} f_{i_l} & \text{if } \exists \alpha_l = \sup\{\alpha \in (0,1] : \ e_\alpha(X_i, F) < 1 - l\} \\ 0 & \text{otherwise} \end{cases} \tag{19}$$

where

$$f_{i_l} = \frac{\mathrm{power}(X_i^F \cap X_{i_{\alpha_l}}^F)}{\mathrm{card}(X_{i_{\alpha_l}}^F)} . \tag{20}$$

The quantities f_{i_u} and f_{i_l} express the mean value of inclusion grade of X_i in F, determined by using only those elements of X_i, which are included in F at least to a degree of α_u and α_l respectively.

Another problem that we should be aware of is different importance of particular elements in the approximating class. This is directly determined by the membership function of the class. Therefore, we propose to refine the above definitions by basing them on the weighted mean membership in the inclusion set.

The weighted mean u-lower approximation of the set F by R is a fuzzy set of X/R with the membership function expressed as in (17) and f_{i_u} redefined as follows:

$$f_{i_u} = \frac{\mathrm{power}((X_i^F \cap X_{i_{\alpha_u}}^F) \cdot X_i)}{\mathrm{card}(X_{i_{\alpha_u}}^F)} . \tag{21}$$

The weighted mean l-upper approximation of the set F by R is a fuzzy set of X/R with the membership function expressed as in (19) and f_{i_l} redefined as follows:

$$f_{i_l} = \frac{\text{power}((X_i^F \cap X_{i_{\alpha_l}}^F) \cdot X_i)}{\text{card}(X_{i_{\alpha_l}}^F)} \tag{22}$$

The operator $\cdot$ used in (21) and (22) denotes the product of fuzzy sets, obtained by multiplication of the respective values of membership functions.

4 Approximation Quality in VPFRS Model

The measure of u-approximation quality (6) can be generalised in order to deal with fuzzy sets and fuzzy relations [12].

For a family $\Phi = \{F_1, F_2, \ldots, F_n\}$ of fuzzy sets and a fuzzy compatibility relation R the u-approximation quality of Φ by R is defined as follows:

$$\gamma_{R_u}(\Phi) = \frac{\text{power}(\text{Pos}_{R_u}(\Phi))}{\text{card}(X)} \tag{23}$$

$$\text{Pos}_{R_u}(\Phi) = \bigcup_{F_i \in \Phi} \omega(\underline{R}_u F_i) \tag{24}$$

The fuzzy extension ω denotes here a mapping from the domain X/R into the domain of the universe X, which is expressed for any fuzzy set A by:

$$\mu_{\omega(A)}(x) = \mu_A(X_i), \quad \text{if } \mu_{X_i}(x) = 1 \, . \tag{25}$$

Similarly, we can generalise (7) for evaluating the u-approximation quality of compatibility classes obtained with respect to fuzzy decision attributes by compatibility classes obtained with respect to fuzzy condition attributes:

$$k_{\text{WZ}} = \frac{\text{power}(\text{Pos}_{C_u}(D^\star))}{\text{card}(X)} \tag{26}$$

where $D^\star = \{D_1, D_2, \ldots, D_m\}$ is the family of indiscernibility classes obtained with respect to the decision attributes D.

Next, we define the fuzzy counterpart of the restricted positive region of a fuzzy set F as follows:

$$\text{Pos}_{R_u}(F) = \omega(\underline{R}_u F) \cap F \tag{27}$$

Finally, we express the generalised u-approximation quality k_{AR} as:

$$k_{\text{AR}} = \frac{\text{power}(\text{Pos}_{C_u}(D^\star))}{\text{card}(X)} = \frac{\text{power}(\bigcup_{D_i \in D^\star} \omega(\underline{C}_u(D_i)) \cap D_i)}{\text{card}(X)} \tag{28}$$

5 Examples

We apply in the following example the variable precision fuzzy rough approximations to analysis of a decision table with fuzzy attributes (Table 1).

We use a compatibility relation R for comparing any elements $x, y \in X$ with fuzzy values of attributes, which is defined as follows [12]:

$$\mu_R(x,y) = \min_{q \in Q} \sup_{u \in U_q} \min(\mu_{V_q(x)}(u), \mu_{V_q(y)}(u)) \tag{29}$$

where $V_q(x), V_q(y)$ are fuzzy values of the attribute q for x and y respectively.

Table 1. Decision table with fuzzy attributes

x	c_1	c_2	c_3	d
x_1	$V_{c_{11}}$	$V_{c_{22}}$	$V_{c_{31}}$	$V_{d_{11}}$
x_2	$V_{c_{12}}$	$V_{c_{21}}$	$V_{c_{32}}$	$V_{d_{12}}$
x_3	$V_{c_{12}}$	$V_{c_{22}}$	$V_{c_{32}}$	$V_{d_{13}}$
x_4	$V_{c_{11}}$	$V_{c_{22}}$	$V_{c_{31}}$	$V_{d_{11}}$
x_5	$V_{c_{12}}$	$V_{c_{22}}$	$V_{c_{32}}$	$V_{d_{13}}$
x_6	$V_{c_{12}}$	$V_{c_{21}}$	$V_{c_{31}}$	$V_{d_{11}}$
x_7	$V_{c_{11}}$	$V_{c_{22}}$	$V_{c_{31}}$	$V_{d_{13}}$
x_8	$V_{c_{11}}$	$V_{c_{22}}$	$V_{c_{31}}$	$V_{d_{11}}$
x_9	$V_{c_{12}}$	$V_{c_{21}}$	$V_{c_{32}}$	$V_{d_{12}}$
x_{10}	$V_{c_{11}}$	$V_{c_{22}}$	$V_{c_{31}}$	$V_{d_{11}}$

The membership functions of fuzzy attributes have typical "triangular" form with intersection levels assumed as follows:

for $V_{c_{11}}$ and $V_{c_{12}}$: 0.25, for $V_{c_{21}}$ and $V_{c_{22}}$: 0.3, for $V_{c_{31}}$ and $V_{c_{32}}$: 0.35,
for $V_{d_{11}}$ and $V_{d_{12}}$: 0.3, for $V_{d_{12}}$ and $V_{d_{13}}$: 0.3,
otherwise : 0.

By using (29) we get a family $D^\star = \{D_1, D_2, D_3\}$ of compatibility classes with respect to the fuzzy decision attribute d:

$D_1 = \{$ 1.00/x_1, 0.30/x_2, 0.00/x_3, 1.00/x_4, 0.00/x_5, 1.00/x_6, 0.00/x_7, 1.00/x_8, 0.30/x_9, 1.00/x_{10} $\}$,
$D_2 = \{$ 0.30/x_1, 1.00/x_2, 0.30/x_3, 0.30/x_4, 0.30/x_5, 0.30/x_6, 0.30/x_7, 0.30/x_8, 1.00/x_9, 0.30/x_{10} $\}$,
$D_3 = \{$ 0.00/x_1, 0.30/x_2, 1.00/x_3, 0.00/x_4, 1.00/x_5, 0.00/x_6, 1.00/x_7, 0.00/x_8, 0.30/x_9, 0.00/x_{10} $\}$,

and a family $C^\star = \{C_1, C_2, C_3, C_4\}$ of compatibility classes with respect to the fuzzy condition attributes c_1, c_2, c_3:

$$C_1 = \{\ 1.00/x_1,\ 0.25/x_2,\ 0.25/x_3,\ 1.00/x_4,\ 0.25/x_5,\ 0.25/x_6,\ 1.00/x_7,\ 1.00/x_8,\ 0.25/x_9,\ 1.00/x_{10}\ \},$$
$$C_2 = \{\ 0.25/x_1,\ 1.00/x_2,\ 0.30/x_3,\ 0.25/x_4,\ 0.30/x_5,\ 0.35/x_6,\ 0.25/x_7,\ 0.25/x_8,\ 1.00/x_9,\ 0.25/x_{10}\ \},$$
$$C_3 = \{\ 0.25/x_1,\ 0.30/x_2,\ 1.00/x_3,\ 0.25/x_4,\ 1.00/x_5,\ 0.30/x_6,\ 0.25/x_7,\ 0.25/x_8,\ 0.30/x_9,\ 0.25/x_{10}\ \},$$
$$C_4 = \{\ 0.25/x_1,\ 0.35/x_2,\ 0.30/x_3,\ 0.25/x_4,\ 0.30/x_5,\ 1.00/x_6,\ 0.25/x_7,\ 0.25/x_8,\ 0.35/x_9,\ 0.25/x_{10}\ \}.$$

It is possible to use another methods for obtaining fuzzy similarity partitions e.g. [1]. Nevertheless, the proposed variable precision fuzzy rough approximations are also suitable for application in such cases.

Selected u-lower approximations of D_1, D_2 and D_3 by the elements of the family $C^\star$ are presented in the Table 2. The u-approximation quality k_{WZ} and k_{AR} for various values of the required inclusion grade is given in the Table 3.

If the intersection levels for all fuzzy values of attributes were equal to 0, then the Table 1 would be equivalent to a crisp decision table. In that case we would obtain $k_{\mathrm{WZ}} = k_{\mathrm{AR}} = 0.5$ for $u = 1$, and $k_{\mathrm{WZ}} = 1$, $k_{\mathrm{AR}} = 0.9$ for $u = 0.8$. Knowing this, we can easier interpret the final results given in the Table 3. In general, the measure k_{WZ} produces larger values since it uses all elements of approximating classes C_i for determining the positive region of classification of the family $D^\star$. The values obtained with k_{AR} are usually smaller and not so different from those generated for the crisp decision table mentioned above.

After analysis of many examples we can state that the measure k_{AR} based on the weighted mean u-lower approximation and on the Łukasiewicz R-implicator is the most suitable for determination of the u-approximation quality of classification in the VPFRS model. This is because the Łukasiewicz R-implicator turned out to be the most sensitive to changes of the upper limit u. Additionally the approximations based on the weighted mean membership do reflect different importance of particular elements in the approximating classes.

6 Conclusions

The proposed definition of the positive region of classification, which bases on the intersection the approximated set and the approximating class is useful in evaluation of approximation quality in variable precision fuzzy or crisp rough sets model. It leads to a new generalised measure of u-approximation quality k_{AR}, which is not so tolerant as the measure of u-approximation quality k_{WZ}. Alternatively, it would be possible to modify the definitions of the variable precision fuzzy rough approximations in the domain of the universe, in order to get the same results. This can be important, especially for investigations concerning the axiomatisation of the VPFRS model. The presented VPFRS approach is based on R-implicators. It would be interesting to consider an VPFRS model without using fuzzy logical connectives according to the idea given in [4].

Table 2. Selected u-lower approximations of D_1, D_2 and D_3

	u	Method					
		G-inf	G-mean	G-w.mean	Ł-inf	Ł-mean	Ł-w.mean
$\mu_{\underline{R}_u D_1}(C_1)$	1	0.00	0.00	0.00	0.00	0.00	0.00
	0.8	0.00	0.00	0.00	0.75	0.94	0.98
	0.75	1.00	1.00	1.00	1.00	1.00	1.00
$\mu_{\underline{R}_u D_1}(C_2)$	1	0.00	0.00	0.00	0.30	0.77	0.61
	0.8	0.00	0.00	0.00	0.30	0.77	0.61
	0.75	0.30	0.80	0.58	0.30	0.77	0.61
$\mu_{\underline{R}_u D_1}(C_4)$	1	0.00	0.00	0.00	0.70	0.91	0.92
	0.8	0.00	0.00	0.00	0.75	0.96	0.97
	0.75	0.86	0.96	0.96	0.95	0.99	0.99
$\mu_{\underline{R}_u D_2}(C_2)$	1	0.86	0.99	0.99	0.95	1.00	1.00
	0.8	1.00	1.00	1.00	1.00	1.00	1.00
	0.75	1.00	1.00	1.00	1.00	1.00	1.00
$\mu_{\underline{R}_u D_3}(C_3)$	1	0.00	0.00	0.00	0.70	0.87	0.92
	0.8	0.00	0.00	0.00	0.75	0.89	0.94
	0.75	0.00	0.00	0.00	0.75	0.89	0.94

Table 3. u-approximation quality for different values of required inclusion grade

Method	k_{WZ} $u = 1$	k_{AR} $u = 1$	k_{WZ} $u = 0.8$	k_{AR} $u = 0.8$	k_{WZ} $u = 0.75$	k_{AR} $u = 0.75$
G-inf	0.412	0.412	0.440	0.440	0.846	0.776
G-mean	0.788	0.438	0.790	0.440	0.968	0.786
G-w.mean	0.630	0.438	0.632	0.440	0.928	0.786
Ł-inf	0.550	0.550	0.800	0.755	0.945	0.875
Ł-mean	0.792	0.601	0.944	0.889	0.977	0.907
Ł-w.mean	0.696	0.592	0.975	0.907	0.987	0.917

References

1. Bodjanova, S.: Approximation of Fuzzy Concepts in Decision Making. Fuzzy Sets and Systems, Vol. 85 (1997) 23–29
2. Dubois, D., Prade, H.: Putting Rough Sets and Fuzzy Sets Together. In: Słowiński, R. (ed.): Intelligent Decision Support. Handbook of Applications and Advances of the Rough Sets. Kluwer Academic Publishers, Boston Dordrecht London (1992)
3. Greco, S., Matarazzo, B., Słowiński, R.: Rough Set Processing of Vague Information Using Fuzzy Similarity Relations. In: Calude, C.S., Paun, G. (eds.): Finite Versus Infinite – Contributions to an Eternal Dilemma. Springer-Verlag, Berlin Heidelberg New York (2000)

4. Greco, S., Matarazzo, B., Słowiński, R., Stefanowski, J.: Variable Consistency Model of Dominance-Based Rough Set Approach. In: Ziarko, W., Yao, Y. (eds.): Rough Sets and Current Trends in Computing. Lecture Notes in Artificial Intelligence, Vol. 2005. Springer-Verlag, Berlin Heidelberg New York (2001) 170–181
5. Greco, S., Inuiguchi, M., Slowinski, R.: Rough Sets and Gradual Decision Rules. In: Wang, G., Liu, Q., Yao, Y., Skowron, A. (eds.): Rough Sets, Fuzzy Sets, Data Mining, and Granular Computing. Lecture Notes in Computer Science, Vol. 2639. Springer-Verlag, Berlin Heidelberg New York (2003) 156–164
6. Katzberg, J.D., Ziarko, W.: Variable Precision Extension of Rough Sets. Fundamenta Informaticae, Vol. 27 (1996) 155–168
7. Klir, J., Folger, T. A.: Fuzzy Stets Unertainty and Information. Prentice Hall, Englewood, New Jersey (1988)
8. Lin, T.Y.: Topological and Fuzzy Rough Sets. In: Słowiński, R. (ed.): Intelligent Decision Support. Handbook of Applications and Advances of the Rough Sets. Kluwer Academic Publishers, Boston Dordrecht London (1992) 287–304
9. Lin, T.Y.: Coping with Imprecision Information – Fuzzy Logic. Downsizing Expo, Santa Clara Convention Center (1993)
10. Mieszkowicz-Rolka, A., Rolka, L.: Variable Precision Rough Sets in Analysis of Inconsistent Decision Tables. In: Rutkowski, L., Kacprzyk, J. (eds.): Advances in Soft Computing. Physica-Verlag, Heidelberg (2003)
11. Mieszkowicz-Rolka, A., Rolka, L.: Variable Precision Rough Sets. Evaluation of Human Operator's Decision Model. In: Sołdek, J., Drobiazgiewicz, L. (eds.): Artificial Intelligence and Security in Computing Systems. Kluwer Academic Publishers, Boston Dordrecht London (2003)
12. Mieszkowicz-Rolka, A., Rolka, L.: Fuziness in Information Systems. Electronic Notes in Theoretical Computer Science, Vol. 82, Issue No. 4. http://www.elsevier.nl/locate/entcs/volume82.html (2003)
13. Nakamura, A.: Application of Fuzzy-Rough Classifications to Logics. In: Słowiński, R. (ed.): Intelligent Decision Support. Handbook of Applications and Advances of the Rough Sets. Kluwer Academic Publishers, Boston Dordrecht London (1992)
14. Pawlak, Z.: Rough Sets. Theoretical Aspects of Reasoning about Data. Kluwer Academic Publishers, Boston Dordrecht London (1991)
15. Radzikowska, A.M., Kerre, E.E.: A Comparative Study of Fuzzy Rough Sets. Fuzzy Sets and Systems, Vol. 126 (2002) 137–155
16. Ziarko, W.: Variable Precision Rough Sets Model. Journal of Computer and System Sciences, Vol. 40 (1993) 39–59

The Elucidation of an Iterative Procedure to β-Reduct Selection in the Variable Precision Rough Sets Model

Malcolm J. Beynon

Cardiff Business School, Cardiff University
Colum Drive, Cardiff, CF10 3EU, Wales, UK
BeynonMJ@cardiff.ac.uk

Abstract. One area of study in rough set theory is the ability to select a subset of the condition attributes which adequately describe an information system. For the variable precision rough sets model (VPRS), its associated β-reduct selection process is compounded by a β value defining the VPRS related majority inclusion relation to object classification. This paper investigates the role of an iterative procedure in the necessary β-reduct selection process.

1 Introduction

One ongoing debate in Rough Set Theory (RST) [5], is with respect to the notion of reducts - subsets of condition attributes which may adequately describe the information system (IS) considered. For reduct selection, one approach has been the iterative removal of condition attributes [6], based on which of them offers the lowest incremental decrease in the associated quality of classification.

The Variable Precision Rough Sets model - VPRS [7], allows for a level of miss-classification of objects (based on a β value). The inclusion of the β value compounds their subsequent selection of a β-reduct (in VPRS). Beynon [2], considered the whole domain of the β value and the possible different levels of quality of classification within sub-domains (intervals) of β.

In this paper a further investigation of β-reduct selection within VPRS is undertaken, with an iterative procedure for β-reduct selection presented.

2 Fundamentals of VPRS

This section briefly presents the fundamentals of VPRS, see [2, 7]. The universe U refers to all the objects in an IS characterised by sets of the condition and decision attributes C and D, then with $Z \subseteq U$ and $P \subseteq C$, Z is partitioned into three regions:

$$POS_P^\beta(Z) = \bigcup_{\Pr(Z|X_i)\geq\beta} \{X_i \in E(P)\},\ NEG_P^\beta(Z) = \bigcup_{\Pr(Z|X_i)\leq 1-\beta} \{X_i \in E(P)\}$$
$$\text{and } BND_P^\beta(Z) = \bigcup_{1-\beta<\Pr(Z|X_i)<\beta} \{X_i \in E(P)\},$$

S. Tsumoto et al. (Eds.): RSCTC 2004, LNAI 3066, pp. 412–417, 2004.

where $E(\cdot)$ denotes a set of equivalence classes (in the above definitions, they are condition classes based on P). Ziarko [7] defines in VPRS the measure of *quality of classification* (*QoC*), defined by:

$$\gamma^{\beta}(P, D) = \frac{\text{card}\left(\bigcup_{\Pr(Z|X_i)\geq\beta}\{X_i \in E(P)\}\right)}{\text{card}(U)}, \text{ where } Z \in E(D) \text{ and } P \subseteq C,$$

for a specified value of β. The *QoC* is used operationally to define and extract *reducts*. In VPRS [7], referred to here as a β-reduct $RED^{\beta}(C, D)$, has the twin properties that; (1) $\gamma^{\beta}(C, D) = \gamma^{\beta}(RED^{\beta}(C, D), D)$, (2) No proper subset of $RED^{\beta}(C, D)$, can also give the same *QoC*. It is noted this definition is overly strict for VPRS, when compared with the view of [6] presented earlier.

3 Investigation of Iterative Procedure in β-Reduct Selection

As shown in [2] for a subset of condition attributes distinct β intervals over the β domain have different levels of *QoC*. The iterative procedure starts with the consideration of the difference in the *QoC* associated with a subset of condition attributes P and that from the whole set of attributes C over the whole β domain (or a sub-domain, as in [1]). Firstly, we consider the intervals of the β domain for which the associated levels of *QoC* are different based on C, defined β^{C} they are given by:

$$\beta^{C}: (\beta^{C}_{1,1}, \beta^{C}_{1,2}], (\beta^{C}_{2,1}, \beta^{C}_{2,2}], \ldots, (\beta^{C}_{i,1}, \beta^{C}_{i,2}], \ldots, (\beta^{C}_{|\beta^{C}|,1}, \beta^{C}_{|\beta^{C}|,2}].$$

For P, its β intervals over the β domain with different levels of *QoC* is defined β^{P}:

$$\beta^{P}: (\beta^{P}_{1,1}, \beta^{P}_{1,2}], (\beta^{P}_{2,1}, \beta^{P}_{2,2}], \ldots, (\beta^{P}_{i,1}, \beta^{P}_{i,2}], \ldots, (\beta^{P}_{|\beta^{P}|,1}, \beta^{P}_{|\beta^{P}|,2}].$$

Each of these β-intervals is distinct in their levels of *QoC*, defined $\gamma^{\frac{1}{2}(\beta^{C}_{i,1}+\beta^{C}_{i,2})}(C,D)$ $i = 1, \ldots, |\beta^{C}|$ and $\gamma^{\frac{1}{2}(\beta^{P}_{i,1}+\beta^{P}_{i,2})}(P,D)$, $i = 1, \ldots, |\beta^{P}|$ associated with P and C respectively. These intervals and concomitant *QoC* values are used to next define a nearness measure, described previously. To evaluate the difference between these levels of $\gamma^{\frac{1}{2}(\beta^{C}_{1,1}+\beta^{C}_{1,2})}(C,D)$ and $\gamma^{\frac{1}{2}(\beta^{P}_{i,1}+\beta^{P}_{i,2})}(P,D)$, the sets of intervals β^{C} and β^{P} are merged, defined $\beta^{P\cup C}$, and is denoted by:

$$\beta^{P\cup C}: (\beta^{P\cup C}_{1,1}, \beta^{P\cup C}_{1,2}], (\beta^{P\cup C}_{2,1}, \beta^{P\cup C}_{2,2}], \ldots, (\beta^{P\cup C}_{i,1}, \beta^{P\cup C}_{i,2}], \ldots, (\beta^{P\cup C}_{|\beta^{P\cup C}|,1}, \beta^{P\cup C}_{|\beta^{P\cup C}|,2}].$$

A weighted difference measure over $\beta^{P\cup C}$, defined $\Delta\gamma^{\beta}_{P\cup C}(P,D)$, is given by:

$$\Delta\gamma^{\beta}_{P\cup C}(P,D) = 2\sum_{i=1}^{|\beta^{P\cup C}|}(\beta^{P\cup C}_{i,2} - \beta^{P\cup C}_{i,1})\times|\gamma^{\frac{1}{2}(\beta^{P\cup C}_{i,1}+\beta^{P\cup C}_{i,2})}(P,D) - \gamma^{\frac{1}{2}(\beta^{P\cup C}_{i,1}+\beta^{P\cup C}_{i,2})}(C,D)|.$$

This stage of the approach is not identifying β-reducts, only those subsets of condition attributes with least $\Delta\gamma^{\beta}_{P\cup C}(P,D)$ values. That is, no specific mention of β

intervals where *QoC* with respect to *P* and *C* are equal (or near equal) is given. However, considering the smallest values of the measure $\Delta\gamma^{\beta}_{P\cup C}(P,D)$ is in the right direction with respect to the subsequent future β-reduct selection.

The iterative procedure proposed starts from no condition attribute (an empty set), for which a first condition attribute should be augmented (identified). The first condition attribute identified as being in a possible β-reduct is found from the $\{c_j\}$, j = 1, …, $|C|$ and is the one which has the smallest $\Delta\gamma^{\beta}_{P\cup C}(\{c_j\},D)$ value. Defining this identified single condition attribute $\{c_j\}$ as R_1, the augmentation of a second condition attribute is found by:

$$R_2 = R_1 \cup \{c_j\} \rightarrow \min(\Delta\gamma^{\beta}_{P\cup C}(R_1 \cup \{c_j\},D)\,,\, c_j \in C - R_1).$$

The augmentation of the $c_j \in C - R_1$ to R_1 is dependent on which not previously included condition attribute offers the smallest $\Delta\gamma^{\beta}_{P\cup C}(R_1 \cup \{c_j\},D)$ measure from $\Delta\gamma^{\beta}_{P\cup C}(R_1,D)$. Then the successive augmentation of condition attributes to a defined R_{i-1} (set of condition of attributes of size i – 1) is given by:

$$R_i = R_{i-1} \cup \{c_j\} \rightarrow \min(\Delta\gamma^{\beta}_{P\cup C}(R_{i-1} \cup \{c_j\},D)\,,\, c_j \in C - R_{i-1}).$$

It follows, each of these R_i, i = 1, …, N subsets of condition attributes, for its size is the nearest to C as described earlier in terms of the levels of quality of classification over the whole β domain. Since they are the nearest, the next stage is to identify if these R_i, i = 1, …, N can be considered β-reducts, if only over a sub domain of the β domain. Following [6], the philosophy of acceptable *QoC* is followed. That is, it is suggested here a level of non-equality between the *QoC* of *C* and *P* is acceptable (hence referral to possible β-reducts in the subsequent analysis).

4 Application of Iterative Procedure to Iris Data Set

The iris data set is 150 plants, three decision outcomes (plant types), and four continuous valued condition attributes (plant measurements), see [3]. To reduce the overall granularity of this IS a level of continuous valued discretisation (CVD) is undertaken. Here, the four characteristics were each dichotomised based on their respective mean values; c_1: 13.0 [65, 85], c_2: 13.0 [61, 89], c_3: 13.0 [94, 56] and c_4: 13.0 [89, 61] (for each condition attribute the 150 plants are partitioned into two intervals). To demonstrate the understanding and association of β intervals and concomitant levels of *QoC* for the whole set of condition attributes *C* over the β domain (0.5, 1], the respective β intervals are reported in Table 1 (four β intervals exist for which the associated levels of *QoC* are different).

Table 1. Levels of *QoC* over the β domain (0.5, 1).

QoC	150/150	108/150	64/150	48/150
β interval	(0.5000, 0.5714]	(0.5714, 0.6364]	(0.6364, 0.8125]	(0.8125, 1.0000]

Adopting the procedure described in section 3, the nearness of subsets of condition attributes in relation to levels of QoC compared to that for the whole set of condition attributes is considered. The first stage is to evaluate the nearness values $\Delta\gamma^{\beta}_{P\cup C}(\{c_j\},D)$, j = 1, …, $|C|$, see Table 2, where each $\{c_j\}$, j = 1, …, 4 is represented by β-intervals over the whole β domain, with their respective levels of QoC also given. The associated nearness value $\Delta\gamma^{\beta}_{P\cup C}(\{c_j\},D)$ for each condition attribute is also presented.

Table 2. $\Delta\gamma^{\beta}_{P\cup C}(\{c_j\},D)$ related measures on singleton subsets of condition attributes.

P			Intervals		$\Delta\gamma^{\beta}_{P\cup C}(\{c_j\},D)$
c_1	QoC	150/150	65/150	0/150	0.1957
	β interval	(0.5000, 0.5882]	(0.5882, 0.7692]	(0.7692, 1.0000]	
c_2	QoC	150/150	61/150	0/150	0.1758
	β interval	(0.5000, 0.5618]	(0.5618, 0.8197]	(0.8197, 1.0000]	
c_3	QoC	56/150	0/150		0.3733
	β interval	(0.5000, 0.6786]	(0.6786, 1.0000]		
c_4	QoC	150/150	61/150	0/150	0.2933
	β interval	[0.5000, 0.5618]	[0.5618, 0.6721]	[0.6721, 1.0000]	

In Table 2, the smallest of these nearness values is 0.1758, subsequently $R_1 = \{c_2\}$, and forms the basis for larger subsets of condition attributes to be identified (using the nearness measure). That is, $\{c_2\}$ is the first condition attribute from which successive condition attributes can be augmented to, subject to minimising the $\Delta\gamma^{\beta}_{P\cup C}(R_i,D)$ nearness measure in each iteration, see Table 3.

Table 3. Successive condition attributes with associated details.

i			Intervals	QoC	β interval	$\Delta\gamma^{\beta}_{P\cup C}(\cdot)$
2	c_1	150/150	67/150	8/150		0.1331
		[0.5000, 0.6024]	[0.6204, 0.8475]	[0.8475, 1.0000]		
3	c_3	150/150	85/150	64/150	46/150	0.0667
		[0.5000, 0.5692]	[0.5692, 0.5714]	[0.5714, 0.7222]	[0.7222, 1.0000]	

In Table 3, the successive augmentation of the next two condition attributes are shown with their associated details in the form of β intervals and levels of QoC. In each case the new (minimum) nearness value is also presented. Hence $R_2 = \{c_1, c_2\}$ etc., the details of the successive iterations of condition attributes constructing the R_3 and R_4, are presented in Fig. 1.

In Fig. 1, each graph is made up of bold horizontal lines (β intervals) with vertical dashed lines used to simply connect the β intervals. The fourth graph along (right to left) shows the augmentation of c_4 to $\{c_1, c_2, c_3\}$, this represents the details of the whole set of condition attributes C (see Table 2). A general inspection of the graphs shows a convergence from right to left, indicating as the number of condition attributes in a R_i increases so the β intervals and levels of QoC tend to those of C.

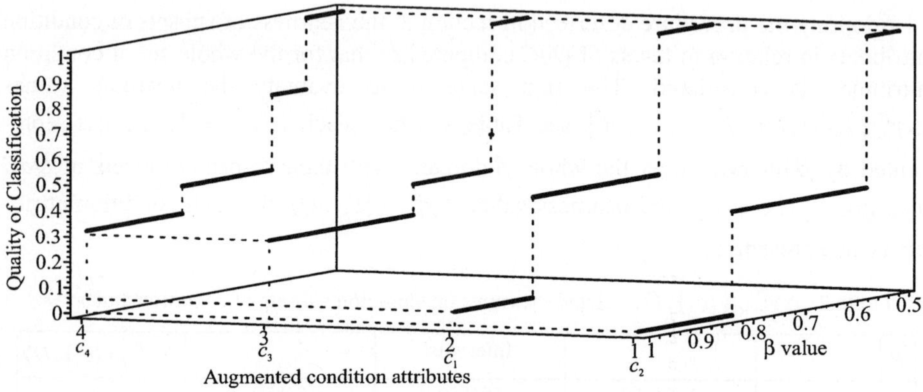

Fig. 1. Graphical representation of details from augmented condition attributes.

5 Application of Iterative Procedure to Wine Data Set

The wine data set [4] considers 178 wines categorised by three wine cultivators and characterised by 13 attributes. The granularity of this data set was lessened with a dichotomising of each condition attribute based on their mean value; c_1, 12.9300; c_2, 3.2700; c_3, 2.2950; c_4, 20.3000; c_5, 116.0000; c_6, 2.4300; c_7, 2.7100; c_8, 0.3950; c_9, 1.9950; c_{10}, 7.1400; c_{11}, 1.0950; c_{12}, 2.6350; c_{13}, 979.0000. To describe the results from the iterative procedure on this data set the condition attribute and concomitant nearness values for each iteration are presented in Table 4.

Table 4. Summary details of augmented condition attributes (for wine data set).

R_i		$\Delta\gamma^{\beta}_{P\cup C}(\{c_j\},D)$	R_i		$\Delta\gamma^{\beta}_{P\cup C}(\{c_j\},D)$	R_i		$\Delta\gamma^{\beta}_{P\cup C}(\{c_j\},D)$
1	c_1	0.6142	5	c_4	0.1164	9	c_{13}	0.0337
2	c_{12}	0.2966	6	c_{10}	0.0861	10	c_8	0.0225
3	c_{11}	0.2107	7	c_2	0.0674	11	c_5	0.0000
4	c_3	0.1605	8	c_6	0.0449			

In Table 4, c_1 with $\Delta\gamma^{\beta}_{P\cup C}(\{c_1\},D)$ = 0.6142 offers the optimum ‘nearness’ information. Interestingly, only 11 iterations are shown, since on the final iteration the nearness value is 0.0000. This indicates the condition attributes c_7 and c_9 are superfluous in the possible β-reduct selection process (based on the CVD utilised). The full details of each iteration can be presented graphically, see Fig. 2.

The results in Fig. 2 are analogous to those presented in Fig. 1 for the Iris data set. A noticeable facet in Fig. 2 is the convergence of the shapes of the graphs as the size of the R_i increases (right to left).

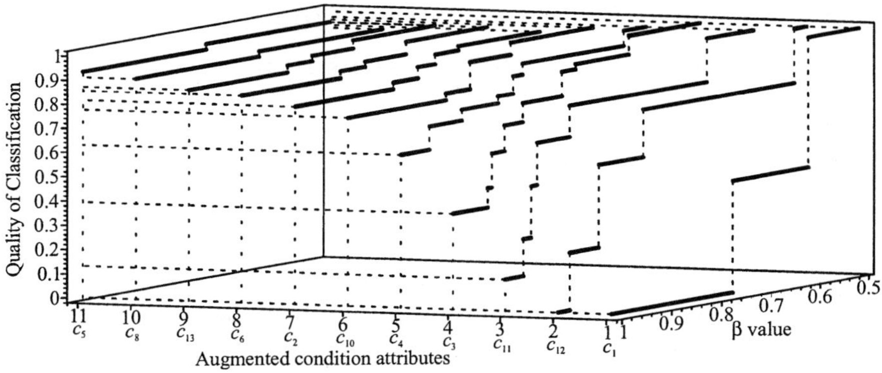

Fig. 2. Graphical representation of details from augmented condition attributes.

6 Conclusions

This paper has investigated the problem of β-reduct selection in the variable precision rough sets model (VPRS). Central to this study has been the relationship between β intervals and the levels of *QoC*. These factors have allowed an iterative procedure for the identification of possible β-reducts to be introduced. In this case, a nearness measure is constructed based on the absolute difference between the levels of *QoC* of a subset and the whole set of condition attributes and the size of the β interval associated with this difference.

The relevant analysis on two well known data sets highlights the effectiveness of this iterative procedure. The graphical results in particular show a notional/understandable convergence of the graphs increasing in number of condition attributes to that associated with the whole set of condition attributes.

References

1. An, A., Shan, N., Chan, C., Cercone, N., Ziarko, W.: Discovering rules for water demand prediction: An enhanced rough-set approach. Engineering Application and Artificial Intelligence 9 (1996) 645–653.
2. Beynon, M. Reducts within the Variable Precision Rough Set Model: A Further Investigation. European Journal of Operational Research 134 (2001) 592–605.
3. Browne, C., Dünstch, L., Gediga, G.: IRIS revisited: A comparison of discriminant and enhanced rough set data analysis. in: L. Polkowski, A. Skowron, (Eds.), Rough sets in knowledge discovery 2: Applications, case studies and software systems, Physica-Verlag, New York, 1998, 345–368.
4. Forina, M., Learadi, R., Armanino, C., Lanteri, S.: PARVUS: An Extendible Package of Programs for Data Exploration, Classification and Correlation. Elsevier Amsterdam, 1988.
5. Pawlak, Z.: Rough sets. International Journal of Information and Computer Sciences 11 (5) (1982) 341–356.
6. Słowiński, K. and Słowiński, R.: Sensitivity analysis of rough classification. International Journal of Man-Machine Studies 32 (1990) 693–705.
7. Ziarko, W.: Variable precision rough set model. Journal of Computer and System Sciences 46 (1993) 39–59.

A Logic-Based Framework for Qualitative Spatial Reasoning in Mobile GIS Environment

Mohammad Reza Malek[1,2]

[1] Institute for Geoinformation, Technical University Vienna
Gusshausstr. 27-29/127, 1040 Wien, Austria
malek@geoinfo.tuwien.ac.at

[2] Dept. of Surveying and Geomatic Eng., Eng. Faculty, University of Tehran, Tehran, Iran

Abstract. The mobile computing technology has been increasingly grown in the past decade; however there still exist some important constraints that complicate work with a mobile information system. The limited resources on the mobile computing would restrict some features that are available on the traditional computing technology. In this article we suggest an idea based on space and time partitioning in order to provide a paradigm that treats moving objects in mobile GIS environment. A logic-based framework for representing and reasoning about qualitative spatial relations over moving agents in space and time is proposed. We motivate the use of influenceability relation as primary relation and show how a logical calculus can be built up from this basic concept. We derive the connection relation as a basis of topological relation and a kind of time order as a basis of time from our suggested primary influenceability relation. This framework finds applications in intelligent transportation system (ITS), and any mobile autonomous navigation systems.

1 Introduction

Mobile agents and movement systems have been rapidly gaining momentum worldwide. Within the last few years, we were facing advances in wireless communication, computer networks, location-based engines, and on-board positioning sensors. Mobile GIS as an integrating system of mobile agent, wireless network, and some GIS capability has fostered a great interest in the GIS field [16]. Although the mobile computing has been increasingly grown in the past decade, however there exist still some important constraints which complicate the design of mobile information systems. The limited resources on the mobile computing would restrict some features that are available on the traditional computing. The resources include computational resources (e.g., processor speed, memory, etc.) user interfaces (e.g., display, pointing device, etc), bandwidth of mobile connectivity, and energy source [13, 24].

Though much work has been done concerning temporal and motion aspects of spatial objects [4, 17, 31], it is still an open area of research. Generally speaking, the lack of theory to tackle moving objects and able to support the behavioral view [19] can

S. Tsumoto et al. (Eds.): RSCTC 2004, LNAI 3066, pp. 418–426, 2004.

be seen easily [30]. The aforementioned deficiency is more highlighted in mobile GIS environment due to its resource constraints. Hence, it makes us to pay our attention to this topic.

One of most important characteristic of qualitative properties of spatial data and perhaps the most fundamental aspect of space is topology and topological relationship. Topological relations between spatial objects like meet and overlap are such relationships that are invariant with respect to specific transformations due to homeomorphism. The study of topological properties of spatial data is of great importance in a wide variety of application areas, including: Spatial and Geoinformation Systems (GIS), the semantics of spatial prepositions in natural languages, robotic, artificial intelligent , and computer vision [7, 14, 23].

In this paper, in order to provide a paradigm that treats with moving objects in mobile GIS environment, a logical framework is presented. In this framework the concept of spatial influenceability from relativistic physics, is combined with the partition and conquer idea from computer science. It means dividing the space and time into small parts; say space-time cell; and using influenceability concept presented in this article provides a theoretical framework of mobile agents in space-time. We provide convincing evidence of this theory, by demonstrating how it can provide models of RCC (the fruitfulness of region-based approaches in dynamic environment can be seen in [9])as well as time relations.

The remainder of the paper is structured as follows. Section 2 reviews related works. Section 3 shall present the fundamental concepts. Section 3 introduces our suggested model. In section 4 we discuss two examples of spatio-temporal relationships between two moving agents. Finally, we draw some conclusions.

2 Related Work

During recent years, topological relations have been much investigated in the static environments. Thirteen topological relations between two temporal intervals were identified by [1]. After 4-intersection model [10] the famous 9-intersection approach [11] was proposed for formalism of topological relations. This approach is based on point-set topological concepts. In 9-intersection method, a spatial object A is decomposed into three parts: an interior denoted by A^o, an exterior denoted by A^- , and a boundary denoted by ∂A. There are nine intersections between six parts of two objects. Some drawbacks of such point-based topological approach is reported in [20]. The other significant approach known as RCC (Region-Connection Calculus) has been provided by [7, 20]. RCC as a pointless topology is based upon a single primitive contact relation, called connection, between regions. In this logic-based approach the notion of a region as consisting of a set of points is not used at all. A similar method, so-called Mereotopology, is developed in [2, 33]. The main difference between last two t is that open and closed regions are not distinguishable in RCC whereas those in Asher and Vieu's theory are.

A number of researches have been focusing on spatio-temporal and 4-dimensional GIS. Research has been accomplished on different aspects of spatio-temporal modeling, representation, reasoning, computing, and database structure, see e.g., [17] and the extension of representation in GIS from two dimensions to three and four, can be found in [31] and [4]. Transportation modeling is an important key issue that impedes its full integration within GIS and forces the need for improvements in GIS [18].

A method for reducing the size of computation is computation slice[15, 29]. The computation slicing as an extension of program slicing is useful to narrow the size of the program. It can be used as a tool in program debugging, testing, and software maintenance. Unlike a partitioning in space and time, which always exists, a distributed computation slice may not always exist [15].

Among others, two works using divide and conquer idea, called honeycomb and space-time grid, are closer to our proposal. The honeycomb model [12] focuses on temporal evolution of subdivisions of the map, called spatial partitions, and give a formal semantics for them. This model develops to deal with map and temporal map only. In [5] the concept of space-time grid is introduced. Based upon the space-time grid, they developed a system to managing dynamically changing information. In the last work, they attempt to use the partitioning approach instead of an indexing one. This method can be used for storing and retrieving the future location of moving object.

In the previous work of the author [25, 26, 27] applications of partitioning in space-time and using influenceability in motion planning and finding a collision-free path was demonstrated. This article can be considered as a theoretical foundation of them.

3 Preliminaries

Causality is widely known and esteemed concept. There is much literature on causality, extending philosophy, physics, artificial intelligence, cognitive science and so on. In our view, influenceability stands for spatial causal relation, i.e. objects must come in contact with one another; cf. [3]. In the relativistic physics based on the postulate that the vacuum velocity of light $\boldsymbol{c}$ is constant and maximum velocity, the light cone can be defined as a portion of space-time containing all locations which light signals could reach from a particular location (Figure 1). With respect to a given event, its light cone separates space-time into three parts, inside and on the future light cone, inside and on the past light cone, and elsewhere. An event $\boldsymbol{A}$ can influence (influenced by) another event; $\boldsymbol{B}$; only when $\boldsymbol{B}$ ($\boldsymbol{A}$) lies in the light cone of $\boldsymbol{A}$ ($\boldsymbol{B}$). In a similar way, the aforementioned model can be applied for moving objects. Henceforth, a cone is describing an agent in mobile GIS environment for a fixed time interval.

The currently known laws of physics, which are the best available to the movement modeling, are expressed in differential equation defined over a 4-dimensional space-time continuum. The assumption of a 4-dimensional continuum implies the existence of 4-dimensional spatio-temporal parts. It is assumable to consider a continuous movement on a differential manifold $\boldsymbol{M}$ which represents such parts in space and time. That means every point of it has a neighborhood homeomorphic to an open set in $\boldsymbol{R}^n$. A path through $\boldsymbol{M}$ is the image of a continuous map from a real interval into

M. The homeomorphism at each point of *M* determines a Cartesian coordinate system (x_0, x_1, x_2, x_3) over the neighborhood. The coordinate x_0 is called time. In addition, we assume that the manifold *M* can be covered by a finite union of neighborhoods. Generally speaking, this axiom gives ability to extend coordinate system to the larger area. This area shall interpret as one cell or portion of space-time. The partitioning method is application dependent. The partitioning method is depended on application purposes [6, 34] on the one hand, and limitation of the processor speed, storage capacity, bandwidth, and size of display screen [35] on the other hand.

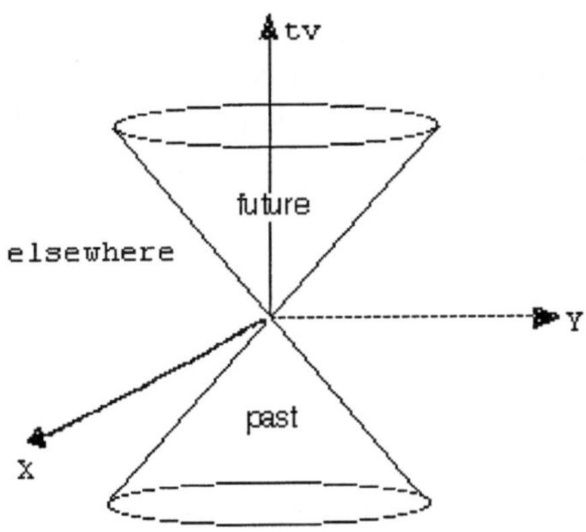

Fig. 1. A cone separates space-time into 3 zones, past, future, and elsewhere.

4 Algebraic and Topological Structure

As mentioned before, we suggest a framework based on partitioning space-time into small parts, solving the problem in those small cells and connect the results to each other to find the final result. The reasons behind are clear. Firstly, the problems can be solved easier and many things are predictable at a small part of space-time. Secondly, in the real world, multi vehicle (group of moving agents) modeling task has various kinds of problems. All of these problems can not be solved at once. There are successful experiments based upon this idea in the mathematics like dynamic programming and in computer science. Therefore it is natural to use similar concepts for handling spatial aspects of moving objects.

Hence, a moving agent is defined by a well-known acute cone model in space-time[21, 22]. This cone is formed of all possible locations that an individual could feasibly pass through or visit. The current location or apex vertex and speed of object is reported by navigational system or by prediction. The hyper surface of the cone becomes a base model for spatio-temporal relationships, and therefore enables analysis and further calculations in space-time. It also indicates fundamental topological and metric properties of space-time.

Let us take influenceability as an order relation (symbolized by $\prec$) be primitive relation. It is natural to postulate that influenceability is irreflexive, antisymmetric, but transitive, i.e.,

$$(A \prec B) \wedge (B \prec C) \Rightarrow A \prec C \tag{1}$$

Thus, it can play the role of 'after'.

Definition 1 (Temporal order): Let A and B be two moving objects with t_a and t_b corresponding temporal orders, respectively. Then,

$$(A \prec B) \Rightarrow (t_a < t_b) \tag{2}$$

The main reason of defining influenceability is the fact that this relation can play the role of any kind of accident and collision. It is well-known that the accident is the key parameter in most transportation systems. As an example the probability of collision defines the GPS navigation integrity requirement [32]. In addition, this model due to considering causal relation is closer to a naïve theory of motion [28]. Connection as a reflexive and symmetric relation [7]can be defined by influenceability as follows:

Definition 2 (Connect relation): Two moving objects are connected if the following equation holds;

$$(\forall xy)C(x,y) \overset{def}{=} [(x \prec y) \vee (y \prec x)] \wedge \{\neg(\exists a)[(x \prec a \prec y) \vee (y \prec a \prec x)]\} \tag{3}$$

Consequently, all other exhaustive and pairwise disjoint relations in region connected calculus (RCC), i.e., *disconnection* (DC), *proper part* (PP), *externally connection* (EC), *identity* (EQ), *partially overlap* (PO), *tangential proper part* (TPP), *nontangential proper part* (NTPP), and the inverses of last two TPPi and NTPPi, can be defined.

The acceptance of the unique framework defined by influenceability by other agents is consensus task from mobile computation terminology point of view. The leader agent, say *a*, can be elected by the following conditions:

$$\forall x \in \{The\ set\ of\ movingagents\} : a \prec x .$$

Furthermore, some other relations can be defined, such as which termed as *speed-connection* (see fig. 2):

$$SC(x,y) \overset{def}{=} \neg EQ(x,y) \wedge \{[C(x,y) \wedge (\forall ab)\ (C(x,a) \wedge (C(x,b) \wedge C(y,a) \wedge C(y,b)] \Rightarrow C(a,b)\} \tag{4}$$

5 Examples

What has been shown so far is that if we regard a moving agent in mobile GIS environment as a cone then we can express certain important relations over agents purely in terms of the influenceability. In this section we illustrate the expressive power of the theory by giving two examples.

Fig. 2. Speed-connection relation between two agents.

5.1 Example 1

Let A<B; say A is before B; and EC(A,B); say A is externally connected to B. The following relationships are distinguishable in our framework which other wise are not in 9-intersection. As it can be seen in figure 3, 3a is a speed-connection relation that is defined by (4). In the case 3c, for every D, if A is speed-connected to D and D is connected to B, then $B \prec D$. It means

$$\{\forall D \mid [SC(A,D) \wedge C(D,B)] \Rightarrow (B < D)\}.$$

There is no such condition in the 3b.

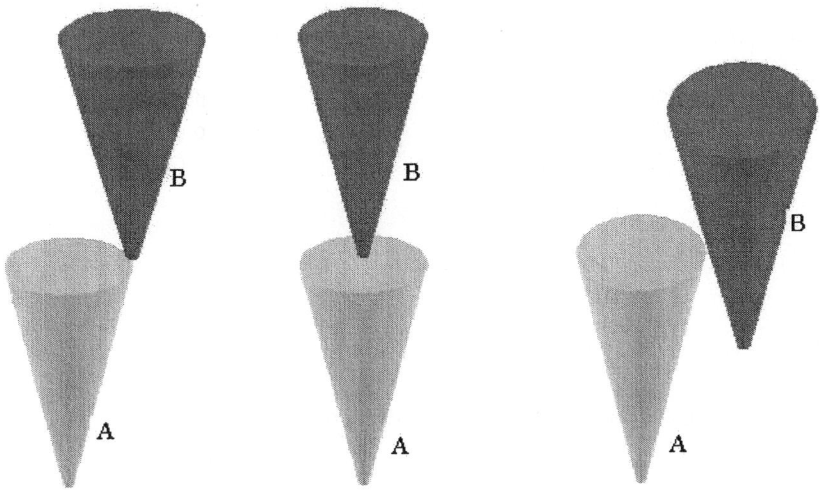

(a) (b) (c)

Fig. 3. Three distinguishable relations when A<B and EC(A,B).

5.2 Example 2

Let A<B and PO(A,B); say A partial overlaps B. The following relationships are distinguishable in our framework (see figure 4). 4a shows a general overlap. Let us first explain the 4d. The 4d is called time-proper overlap relation; indicated by TPO(A,B); and it can be used as a basis for defining collinearity in direction of time . TPO is introduced by

$$TPO(A,B) \overset{def}{=} \{\ \forall D \mid [SC(A,D) \Rightarrow PO(B,D)]\ \}$$

The 4c can be defined by TPO relation. For every D, if SC(A,D) implies to C(B,D) and the case is not TPO(A,B) then 4c is its outcome. That is:

$$\{\forall D \mid [\ (SC(A,D) \Rightarrow C(B,D)\ ) \wedge \neg TPO(A,B)\ ]\}$$

If there exists a D such that TPO(D,B) implies to case 4c between A and D then it results in 4b.

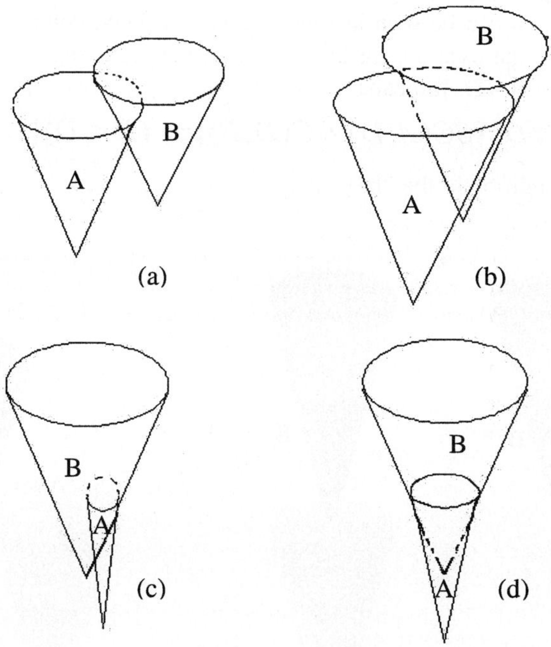

Fig. 4. Four distinguishable relations when A<B and PO(A,B).

6 Conclusion and Further Work

Today we are more mobile than anytime in the past. Although the mobile computing has been rapidly increased in the past decade, however there exists still shortcoming of a theoretical framework for qualitative spatial reasoning. This paper has demonstrated that concerns to mobile GIS theory can profitably be addressed in terms of the partition and conquer idea, and influenceability relation. Of particular significance is the fact that the RCC can be given in a way that a unique framework is prepared for moving agents. The expressive power of this idea is shown by some examples in section 4.

There are some possible directions for further work. In the future, it should be answered if it is possible to use a distributive lattice to describe influenceability. Then, using Birkhoff's Representation Theorem [8] has significant computational advantages.

Acknowledgement

The author is partially supported by Ministry of science, research, and technology of Iran under grant 805935. I would like to thank Prof. Dr. A. Frank (Technical University of Vienna) and Dr. M. Delavar (University of Tehran) for their valuable comments.

References

1. Allen, J.F., *Maintaining Knowledge about Temporal Intervals.* Communications of the ACM, (1983). 26(11): p. 832-843.
2. Asher, N. and L. Vieu. *Towards a geometry of common sense: a semantics and a complete axiomatisation of mereotopology.* in *IJCAI95*,.(1995).
3. Born, M., *Natural Philosophy of Cause and Chance*, New York, Dover Publications, (1949).
4. Breunig, M., *On the Way to Component-Based 3D/4D Geoinformation Systems.* Lecture Notes in Earth Sciences. Vol. 94, Berlin Heidelberg: Springer-Verlag, (2001).
5. Chon, H., D. Agrawal, and A.E. Abbadi. *Using Space-Time Grid for Efficient Management of Moving Objects.* in *MobiDE*, (2001).
6. Chon, H., D. Agrawal, and A.E. Abbadi. *Storage and Retrieval of Moving Objects.* in *International Conference on Mobile Data Management*,.(2001).
7. Cohn, A.G., et al., *RCC: a calculus for Region based Qualitative Spatial Reasoning.* Geoinformatica, (1997), 1: p. 275-316.
8. Davey, B.A. and H.A. priestley, *Introduction to lattices and Order*, Cambridge, UK: Cambridge University press, (1990).
9. Donnely, M. and B. Smith. *Layers: A New Approach to Locating Objects in Space.* in *COSIT 2003*, Kartause Ittingen, Swiss: Springer, (2003).
10. Egenhofer, M.J. and R.D. Franzosa, *Point-set topological spatial relations.* International Journal of Geographical Information Systems, (1991), 5(2): p. 161-174.
11. Egenhofer, M.J. and J.R. Herring, *Categorizing Binary Topological Relationships Between Regions, Lines, and Points in Geographic Databases*, Department of Surveying Engineering, University of Maine, Orono, (1991).
12. Erwig, M. and M. Schneider. *The Honeycomb Model of Spatio-temporal partitions.* in *Spatio-Temporal database management*, Edinburgh, Scotland: Springer,(1999).

13. Forman, G.H. and J. Zahorjan, *The Challenges of Mobile Computing.* IEEE Computer, (1994), 27(4): p. 38-47.
14. Freeman, J., *The modelling of spatial relations.* Computer Graphics and Image Processing, (1975), 4: p. 156-171.
15. Garg, V.K. and N. Mittal. *Computation Slicing: Techniques and Theory.* in *DISC 2001.* Lisbon, Portugal, (2001).
16. GIS-LOUNGE, *Mobile and Field GIS.* 2003, http://gislounge.com/ll/mobilegis.shtml: Accessed: November 2003.
17. Gittings, B., *Innovation in GIS.* Vol. 6. , Taylor & Francis, (1999).
18. Golledge, R.G. and M. Egenhofer, *GIS and disaggregate behavioral travel modeling.* Geographical Systems, (1998), (5): p. 1-7.
19. Goodchild, M., *GIS and Transportation: Status and Challenges.* GeoInformatica, (2000), 4(2): p. 127-139.
20. Gotts, N.M., J.M. Gooday, and A.G. Cohn, *A connection based approach to commonsense topological description and reasoning.* The Monist, (1995), 79(1).
21. Hendricks, M.D., M. Egenhofer, and K. Hornsby. *Structuring a wayfinder's Dynamic space-Time environment.* in *COSIT 2003*, Kartause Ittingen, Switzerland: Springer, (2003).
22. Hornsby, K. and M.J. Egenhofer. *Modeling Moving Objects over Multiple Granularities.* in *Annals of Mathematics and Artificial Intelligence*, (2000).
23. Laurini, R. and D. Thompson, *Fundamentals of Spatial Information Systems.* APIC Series, San Diego: Academic Press, (1992).
24. Li, L., C. Li, and Z. Lin. *Investigation On the Concept Model Of Mobile GIS.* in *Symposium on Geospatial theory, Processing and Applications*, Ottawa, (2002).
25. Malek, M.R. *Motion Modeling in GIS.* in *GEOMATIC 82*, Tehran, Iran: National Cartographic Center, (2003).
26. Malek, M.R. *Motion Modeling in GIS: A case study on collision-free path in space-time.* in *EURESCO (Modeling for wayfinding services)*, Bad Herrenalb, Germany: (Oral presentation), (2003).
27. Malek, M.R. and Delavar M.R., *A Mobile Computing Approach to Find An Optimal Collision-free Path.* (Under review).
28. McClosky, M., *Naive theories of motion*, in *Mental models*, D. Gentner and S. Stevens, Editors, Lawrence Erlbaum: Hillsdale, (1983).
29. Mittal, N., *Techniques for Analysing Distributed Copmputations*, in *Department of Computer Science*, The university of Texas: Austin, USA, (. 2002).
30. Muller, p. *A Qualitative Theory of Motion Based on Spatio-Temporal Primitives.* in *Sixth International Conference on Principles of Knowledge Representation and Reasoning (KR'98)*, Trento, Italy: Morgan Kaufmann, (1998).
31. Raper, J., *Multidimensional Geographic Information Science.* 2000: Taylor & Francis.
32. Sang, J., *Theory and Development of GPS Integrity Monitoring System*, in *Space Centre for Satellite Navigation.* 1996, Queesland University of Technology: Queesland.
33. Smith, B., *Mereotopology: A Theory of Parts and Boundaries.* Data and Knowledge Engineering, 1996, (1996): p. 287-303.
34. Wolfson, O., et al. *Databases for Tracking Mobile Units in Real Time.* in *Database Theory- ICDT'99, 7th International Conference, LNCS 1540*, (1998).
35. Zhao, Y., *Vehicle Location and Navigation Systems.* The Artech House ITS Series, Boston: Artech House, (1997).

Spatial Object Modeling in Intuitionistic Fuzzy Topological Spaces

Mohammad Reza Malek[1,2]

[1] Institute for Geoinformation, Technical University Vienna
Gusshausstr. 27-29/127, 1040 Wien, Austria
malek@geoinfo.tuwien.ac.at

[2] Dept. of Surveying and Geomatic Eng., Eng. Faculty, University of Tehran , Tehran, Iran

Abstract. In Geoinformation systems (GIS) there is need to model spatial region with indeterminate boundary and under uncertainties. Although fuzzy logic methods are of great interest in many GIS applications, however the traditional fuzzy logic has two important deficiencies: first, to apply the fuzzy logic, we need to assign, to every property and for every value, a crisp membership function and second, it does not distinguish between the situation in which there is no knowledge about a certain statement and a situation that the belief to the statement in favor and against is the same. In order to solve these problems, we motivate to use intuitionistic fuzzy logic. This paper gives fundamental concepts and properties of an intuitionistic fuzzy spatial region. We provide a theoretical framework for both dominant ontologies used in GIS; namely point-set topology and Region Connected calculus.

1 Introduction

The development of general theories of uncertainty modeling of spatial objects and spatial relations has recently found increased attention in Geoinformation system (GIS). Describing spatial phenomena suffers from uncertainty. Sources of uncertainty are the inexact or incomplete definition of objects, and the inability to observe precise and complete relevant data (see [4]). The description of objects-static or dynamic- is not only uncertain in the above mentioned sense, but also contradictory in different contexts[11].

Although fuzzy logic methods are of great interest in many GIS applications, however the traditional fuzzy logic has two important deficiencies: first, to apply the fuzzy logic, we need to assign, to every property and for every value, a crisp membership function and second, it does not distinguish between the situation in which there is no knowledge about a certain statement and a situation that the belief to the statement in favor and against is the same. Due to this fact, it is not recommended for problems with missing data and where grades of membership are hard to define [13]. Land use and land cover is one important example of using fuzzy logic in GIS, because most of which is obtained from the classification procedure over not precisely

S. Tsumoto et al. (Eds.): RSCTC 2004, LNAI 3066, pp. 427–434, 2004.

defined and indeterminate spatial objects like urban and rural or forest and grassland. In satellite images some pixels might remain unclassified due to clouds or absorption of the sensors signal. Missing data causes problems in the classification of pixels. Another major source of uncertainty in satellite images is age. Frequently there occurs the need to combine aged images with new data. The procedure will face cases in which arguments indicate that part of e.g. a grassland area did not change and some arguments against. In such situations using intuitionistic fuzzy logic would be reasonable.

One of most important characteristics of qualitative properties of spatial data and perhaps the most fundamental aspect of space is topology and topological relationship. Topological relations between spatial objects like meet and overlap are such relationships that are invariant with respect to specific transformations due to homeomorphism.

In this paper, fuzzy object and uncertainty modeling of spatial relationships are analyzed from the view point of intuitionistic fuzzy (IF) logic. We demonstrate how it can provide model for fuzzy region; i.e., regions with indeterminate boundaries; in Region Connected Calculus (RCC) and 9-intersection model as well. The remainder of this paper is structured as follows: Section 2 reviews the related works. Section 3 introduces necessary concepts. Section 4 proposes some novel concepts and their properties to define a simple intuitionistic fuzzy spatial region (IFSR). Then, section 5 briefly discusses how one can use IF logic in the RCC. Finally, we give concluding remarks.

2 Related Work

The famous 9-intersection approach [9] was proposed for formalism of topological relations. This approach is based on point-set topological concepts. In 9-intersection method, a spatial object A is decomposed into three parts: an interior denoted by A^o, an exterior denoted by A^E, and a boundary denoted by ∂A. There are nine intersections between six parts of two objects. The other significant approach known as RCC (Region-Connection Calculus) has been provided by Cohn et al. [7, 10]. RCC as a pointless topology is based upon a single primitive contact relation, called connection, between regions. In this logic-based approach the notion of a region as consisting of a set of points is not used at all.

During recent years, the topological relations have been extended into fuzzy domains. The intersection model is extended to vague regions by three main approaches: the work of Clementini and Di Felice [5] on regions with "broad boundary", the work of Zhan [16] who developed a method for approximately analyzing binary topological relations between geographic regions with indeterminate boundaries based on fuzzy sets, and Tang and Kainz [15] that provided a 3*3, a 4*4, and a 5*5 intersection matrix based on different topological parts of two fuzzy regions. The extension of the RCC schemes to accommodate vague region has been addressed by Lehmann and Cohn [12] and by Cohn and Gotts [6].

The notion of intuitionistic fuzzy sets (IFS) was introduced by Atanassov [1, 2, 3] as a generalization of fuzzy sets. Later the concept of intuitionistic fuzzy topology was introduced by Coker [8].

3 Preliminaries

First we shall present the fundamental concepts and definitions given by Atanassov.

Definition 3.1 (Atanassov [3]): Let X be a nonempty fixed set. An intuitionistic fuzzy set (IFS) *A* in *X* is an object having the following form

$$A := \{< x, \mu_A(x), \nu_A(x) > | \, x \in X\}$$

where the function $\mu_A : X \to [0,1]$ and $\nu_A : X \to [0,1]$ define the degree of membership and the degree of non-membership of the element $x \in X$, respectively. For every $x \in X$, μ_A and ν_A satisfy:

$$0 \leq \mu_A(x) + \nu_A(x) \leq 1 .$$

In contrary of traditional fuzzy, the addition of μ_A and ν_A does not necessarily have to be 1. This is particularly useful when system may lack complete information.

Definition 3.2 (Atanassov [3]): For every two IFSs A and B, the following operations can be defined:

$$A \subseteq B \textit{ iff } (\forall x \in X)(\mu_A(x) \leq \mu_B(x) \textit{ and } \nu_A(x) \geq \nu_B(x));$$

$$A = B \textit{ iff } (\forall x \in X)(\mu_A(x) = \mu_B(x) \textit{ and } \nu_A(x) = \nu_B(x));$$

$$A^c := \{< x, \nu_A(x), \mu_A(x) > | \, x \in X\};$$

$$A \cap B := \{< x, \min(\mu_A(x), \mu_B(x)), \max(\nu_A(x), \nu_B(x)) > | \, x \in X\};$$

$$A \cup B := \{< x, \max(\mu_A(x), \mu_B(x)), \min(\nu_A(x), \nu_B(x)) > | \, x \in X\};$$

$$\bigcup A_i := \{< x, \max(\mu_i), \min(\nu_i) > | \, x \in X\} \quad i \in I;$$

$$\bigcap A_i := \{< x, \min(\mu_i), \max(\nu_i) > | \, x \in X\} \quad i \in I;$$

$$[]A := \{< x, \mu_A(x), 1 - \mu_A(x) > | \, x \in X\} \; (\textit{Neccessity operator});$$

$$\langle\rangle A := \{< x, 1 - \nu_A(x), \nu_A(x) > | \, x \in X\} \; (\textit{Posibility operator}).$$

Definition 3.3 (Coker [8]):

We define $0_{\sim}$ and $1_{\sim}$ as follows:

$$0_{\sim} := \{< x, 0, 1 > | \, x \in X\} \qquad 1_{\sim} := \{< x, 1, 0 > | \, x \in X\}.$$

Consequently, an intuitionistic fuzzy topology (IFT for short) on a nonempty set X is a family T of IFSs in X satisfying the following axioms:

$$(T1)\ 0_{\sim}, 1_{\sim} \in T;$$

$$(T2)\ G_i \cap G_j \in T \ for\ any\ G_i, G_j \in T;$$

$$(T3)\ \bigcup G_i \in T \ for\ arbitrary\ family\ \{G_i \mid i \in I\} \subset T.$$

The pair (IFS(X),T) is called an intuitionistic fuzzy topological space (IFTS) and any IFS in T is known as an intuitionistic fuzzy open set (IFOS for short) in X. The complement A^c is called an intuitionistic fuzzy closed set (IFCS) in X.

4 Some Topological Notions of Fuzzy Region

After consideration of some definitions and theorems, a simple IF spatial region (IFSR) will be introduced.

__Definition 4.1__[8]: Let (X,T) be an IF topological space and $A = < x, \mu_A, \nu_A >$ be an IFS in X. Then the fuzzy interior and fuzzy closure are defined by:

$$A^- = \bigcap\{K : K \ is\ an\ IFCS\ in\ X\ and\ A \subseteq K\},$$

$$A^o = \bigcup\{G : G\ is\ an\ IFOS\ in\ X\ and\ G \subseteq A\}.$$

__Corollary 4.1__[8]:

$$A^o \cap B^o = (A \cap B)^o, A^- \cup B^- = (A \cup B)^-$$

$$A^o \subseteq A \subseteq A^-$$

$$A^{oc} = A^{c-}, A^{-c} = A^{co}.$$

Now, we add some further definitions and propositions.

__Definition 4.2__: We define a IF boundary (IFB) of an IFS $A = < x, \mu_A, \nu_A >$ by:

$$\partial A = A^- \cap A^{c-}.$$

The following theorem shows the intersection methods no longer guarantees a unique solution.

__Corollary 4.2__: $\partial A \cap A^o = 0_{\sim}$ iff A^o is crisp (i.e., $A^o = 0_{\sim}\ or\ A^o = 1_{\sim}$).

Proof. =>) If $A^o = \{< x, 0 < \mu_{A^o} < 1, 0 < \nu_{A^o} < 1 > | x \in X\}$, then $A^- = \{< x, 0 < \mu_{A^-} \le 1, 0 \le \nu_{A^-} < 1 > | x \in X\}$ and $A^{oc} = \{< x, 0 < \nu_{A^o} < 1, 0 < \mu_{A^o} < 1 > | x \in X\}$. Then, $\partial A \cap A^o = A^- \cap A^{c-} \cap A^o = A^- \cap A^{oc} \cap A^{c-} = \{x, 0 < \min(\mu_{A^o}, \mu_{A^-}, \nu_{A^-}) < 1,$ $0 < \max(\nu_{A^o}, \nu_{A^-}, \mu_{A^o}) < 1 \mid x \in X\}$.

Therefore, if $\partial A \cap A^o = 0_{\sim}$, then $A^o = 0_{\sim}$ or $A^o = 1_{\sim}$.

<=) If A^o is crisp, then $A^o = 0_{\sim}$ or $A^o = 1_{\sim}$. If $A^o = 1_{\sim}$ then $A^{oc} = 0_{\sim}$ and $A^- = 1_{\sim}$, then $\partial A \cap A^o = 0_{\sim}$. If $A^o = 0_{\sim}$ then it immediately results that $\partial A \cap A^o = 0_{\sim}$.

<u>Definition 4.3</u>: Let $A =< x, \mu_A, \nu_A >$ be an IFS in (*X,T*). Suppose that the family of IFOS's contained in A are indexed by the family $< x, \mu_{G_i}, \nu_{G_i} >: i \in I\}$ and the family of IFOS's containing A are indexed by the family $< x, \mu_{K_j}, \nu_{K_j} >: j \in J\}$. Then two interiors, closures, and boundaries are defined as following:

$$A^o_{[]} :=< x, \max(\mu_{G_i}), \min(1 - \mu_{G_i}) > \quad A^o_{\langle\rangle} :=< x, \max(1 - \nu_{G_i}), \min(\nu_{G_i}) >$$

$$A^-_{[]} :=< x, \min(\mu_{K_j}), \max(1 - \mu_{K_j}) > \quad A^-_{\langle\rangle} :=< x, \min(1 - \nu_{K_j}), \max(\nu_{K_j}) >$$

$$\partial A_{[]} := A^-_{[]} \cap A^{c-}_{[]} \qquad \partial A_{\langle\rangle} := A^-_{\langle\rangle} \cap A^{c-}_{\langle\rangle}.$$

<u>Proposition 4.1</u>:

(a) $A^o_{[]} \subseteq A^o \subseteq A^o_{\langle\rangle}$ (b) $A^-_{[]} \subseteq A^- \subseteq A^-_{\langle\rangle}$

(c) $A^o_{\{[],\langle\rangle\}} = \{[],\langle\rangle\} A^o \; and \; A^-_{\{[],\langle\rangle\}} = \{[],\langle\rangle\} A^-$

Proof. We shall only prove (c), and the others are obvious. $[]A^o =< x, \max(\mu_{G_i}), 1 - \max(\mu_{G_i}) >$. Based on knowing that $1 - \max(\mu_{G_i}) = \min(1 - \mu_{G_i})$, then $[]A^o =< x, \max(\mu_{G_i}), \min(1 - \mu_{G_i}) >= A^o_{[]}$. In a similar way the others can be proved.

<u>Definition 4.4</u>: Let $A =< x, \mu_A, \nu_A >$ be an IFS in (*X,T*). We define exterior of A as follows:

$$A^E = X \cap A^c.$$

The introduced concepts can be further demonstrated with the figure below. A traditional fuzzy region and an IFSR are shown in Figure 1.

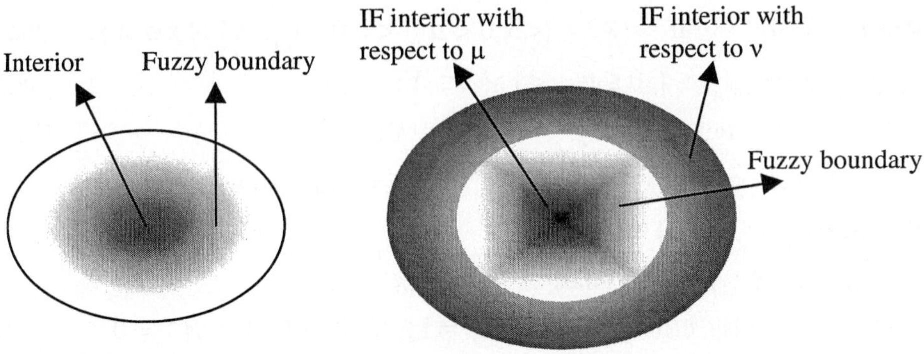

Fig. 1. A region in traditional and intuitionistic fuzzy viewpoints.

Definition 4.5:
An IFOS A is called *regular open* iff $A = A^{-o}$, and An IFCS A is called *regular closed* iff $A = A^{o-}$.

Now, we shall obtain a formal model for a simple spatial fuzzy region based on IF C_5-connectedness defined in [8].

Definition 4.6: An IFS A is called a simple fuzzy region in a C_5-connectedness IFTS, such that:
(1) $A^-, A^-_{[]}, and\ A^-_{\langle\rangle}$ are regular closed, (2) $A^o, A^o_{[]}, and\ A^o_{\langle\rangle}$ are regular open, and (3) $\partial A, \partial A_{[]}, and\ \partial A_{\langle\rangle}$ are C_5-connectedness.

Figure 2 illustrates a schematic view of an IF simple region.

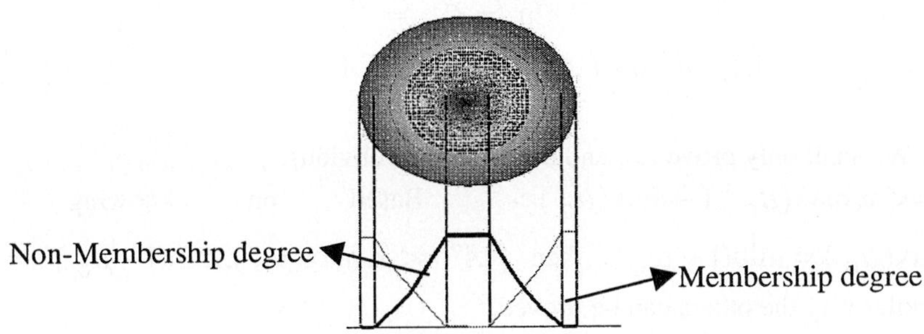

Fig. 2. The representation of a simple IF region.

Having $A^o, A^o_{[]}, A^o_{\langle\rangle}, A^E, \partial A, \partial A_{[]}$, and ∂A_ν for two regions, we enable to find spatial relationships between two IFRS.

5 An IF Version of RCC

As mentioned before, in RCC a connect relation, C(x,y), is taken as a primary relation and understood to mean that x is connected with y. Using the relation C, further eight jointly exhaustive and pairwise disjoint (JEPD) base relations can be defined[7]. The eight are: DC (Disconnected), EC (Externally Connected), PO (Partially Overlapping), TPP (Tangential Proper Part), NTPP (Non-Tangential Proper Part), EQ (Equal), TPPI (Tangential Proper Part Inverse), and NTPPI (Non-Tangential Proper Part Inverse). Much of the appeal of formalism like RCC is its closeness to human thinking. This is more preserved with an IF logic.

Let $X \times X$ be the Cartesian product X with itself as defined in [3]. Then, *C(x,y)* can be defined for every $x, y \in X$ as:

$$C(x,y) := \{< (x,y), \mu_C(x,y), \nu_C(x,y) > \mid (x,y) \in X \times X\}.$$

The table 1 shows the translation of some relations in RCC into IF. For the sake of simplicity, we shall use $\underset{\sim}{x}$, μ_R, and ν_R instead of (x,y), $\mu_R(x,y)$, $\nu_R(x,y)$, respectively.

Table 1. Some RCC relations, where $\neg$, $\wedge$, $\Rightarrow$ stand for negation, logical and, and implication, respectively.

Crisp Relation	*Intuitionistic Fuzzy relation*
$DC(\underset{\sim}{x}) = \neg C(\underset{\sim}{x})$	$DC(\underset{\sim}{x}) = \{< \underset{\sim}{x}, \nu_C, \mu_C > \mid \underset{\sim}{x} \in X \times X\}$
$P(\underset{\sim}{x}) = \forall z[C(z,x) \Rightarrow C(z,y)]$	$P(\underset{\sim}{x}) = \{< \underset{\sim}{x}, \min_{z \in X} (\max(\nu_z, \mu_x)), \max_{z \in X} (\min(\mu_z, \nu_y))) > \mid \underset{\sim}{x} \in X \times X\}$
$PP(\underset{\sim}{x}) = P(x,y) \wedge \neg P(y,x)$	$PP(\underset{\sim}{x}) = \{< \underset{\sim}{x}, \min(\mu_{p(x,y)}, \nu_{p(y,x)}), \max(\nu_{p(x,y)}, \mu_{p(y,x)}) > \mid \underset{\sim}{x} \in X \times X\}$
$EQ(\underset{\sim}{x}) = P(x,y) \wedge P(y,x)$	$EQ(\underset{\sim}{x}) = \{< \underset{\sim}{x}, \min(\mu_{p(x,y)}, \mu_{p(y,x)}), \max(\nu_{p(x,y)}, \nu_{p(y,x)}) > \mid \underset{\sim}{x} \in X \times X\}$

6 Conclusion and Future Work

In contrary of the traditional fuzzy logic, IF logic is well equipped to deal with missed data. By employing IFSs in spatial data models, we can express a hesitation concerning the object of interest. Because it distinguishes between the situation in which there is no knowledge about a certain statement and a situation that the belief to the statement in favor and against is the same. This article has gone a step forward in developing methods that can be used to define fuzzy spatial regions and their relationships.

The main contributions of the paper are defining some new operators to describe fuzzy objects, describing a simple fuzzy region, and translating the RCC terms to IF logic. This paper has demonstrated that fuzzy spatial object may profitably be addressed in terms of intuitionistic fuzzy logic.

We leave the finding spatial relationships and defining complex regions as well as other spatial objects as our future work.

References

1. Atanassov, K.T., Intuitionistic Fuzzy Sets. Fuzzy Sets and Systems, 1986. 20: p. 87-96.
2. Atanassov, K.T., More on Intuitionistic Fuzzy Sets. Fuzy sets and Systems, 1989. 33: p. 37-45.
3. Atanassov, K.T., Intuitionistic Fuzzy Logic: Theory and Application. Studies in Fuzziness and Soft Computing. 1999, Heidelberg: Physica-Verlag.
4. Burrough, P.A. and Frank, A.U., eds. Geographic Objects with Indeterminate Boundaries. GISDATA Series, ed. I. Masser and Salgé, F. Vol. II. 1996, Taylor & Francis: London.
5. Clementini, E. and Di Felice, P., An Algebraic Model for Spatial Objects with Indeterminate Boundaries, in Geographic Objects with Indeterminate Boundaries,European Science Foundation, P.A. Burrough and Frank, A.U., Editors. 1996, Taylor & Francis. p. 155-169.
6. Cohn, A.G. and Gotts, N.M., The 'egg-yolk' Representation of Regions with Indeterminate Boundaries, in Geographic Objects with Indeterminate Boundaries, P. Burrough and Frank, A.U., Editors. 1996, Taylor & Francis: London. p. 171-187.
7. Cohn, A.G., et al., RCC: a calculus for Region based Qualitative Spatial Reasoning. Geoinformatica, 1997. 1: p. 275-316.
8. Coker, D., An introduction to intuitionistic fuzzy topological space. Fuzzy sets and Systems, 1997. 88: p. 81-89.
9. Egenhofer, M.J. and Herring, J.R., Categorizing Binary Topological Relationships Between Regions, Lines, and Points in Geographic Databases. 1991, Department of Surveying Engineering, University of Maine, Orono, ME.
10. Gotts, N.M., Gooday, J.M., and Cohn, A.G., A connection based approach to commonsense topological description and reasoning. The Monist, 1995. 79(1).
11. Kokla, M. and Kavouras, M., Fusion of Top-level and Geographic Domain Omtologies based on Context Formation and Complementarity. International Journal of Geographical Information Science, 2001. 15(7): p. 679-687.
12. Lehmann, F. and Cohn, A.G. The EGG/YOLK reliability data integration using sorts with prototypes. in Infonmation Knowledge Management. 1994: ACM Press.
13. Roy, A.J., A Comparison of Rough Sets, Fuzzy sets and Non-monotonic Logic. 1999, University of Keele: Staffordshre.
14. Stell, J.G. and Worboys, M.F. The Algebraic Structure of Sets of Regions. in Spatial Information Theory (COSIT '97). 1997. Laurel Highlands, PA: Springer.
15. Tang, X. and Kainz, W. Analysis of Topological relations between Fuzzy Regions in a General Fuzzy Topological space. in Symposium on Geospatial Theory, Processing and Applications. 2002. Ottawa.
16. Zhan, F.B., Approximate analysis of binary topological relations between geographic regions with indeterminate boundaries. Soft Computing, 1998. 2: p. 28-34.

Rough Spatial Interpretation

Shuliang Wang[1,2], Hanning Yuan[3], Guoqing Chen[1], Deren Li[3], and Wenzhong Shi[4]

[1] School of Economics and Management, Tsinghua University, Beijing 100084, China
[2] International School of Software, Wuhan University, Wuhan 430072, China
[3] School of Remote Sensing Engineering, Wuhan University, Wuhan 430072, China
[4] Department of Land Surveying and Geo-Informatics
The Hong Kong Polytechnic University, Kowloon, Hong Kong
hnyuanslwang@yahoo.com

Abstract. Rough set is a new approach to uncertainties in spatial analysis. In this paper, we complete three works under the umbrella of rough space. First, a set of simplified rough symbols is extended on the basis of existing rough symbols. It is in terms of rough interpretation and specialized indication. Second, rough spatial entity is proposed to study the real world as it is, without forcing uncertainties to change into a crisp set. Third, rough spatial topological relationships are studied by using rough matrix and their figures. The relationships are divided into three types, crisp entity and crisp entity (CC), rough entity and crisp entity (RC) and rough entity and rough entity (RR). A universal intersected equation is further developed. Finally, rough membership function is further extended with the gray scale in our case study. And the maximum and minimum maps of river thematic classification are generated via the rough membership function and rough relationships.

1 Introduction

By using the geographical information system (GIS), people try to abstract, generalize and analyze a spatial entity in a computerized information system. And it is fundamental to determine whether or not a spatial element (e.g., pixel) belongs to a predefined entity, which is performed according to the accessible values. As the real spatial entity is often complex but not crisp, people have to select its most important aspects. First the exact object model is used in GIS [1]. But the procedure may lose details in one or more dimensions, and some attribute values of the spatial entity are further inaccessible, inexact or vague, which make it indiscernible to associate the spatial element to a given entity. In order to improve the exact object model, some theories and techniques, for example, continuous field model, error band, epsilon band, "S" band, fuzzy set, evidence theory, cloud theory, have been further put forward and applied. Each of them can deal with some aspects of the uncertainty, for example, characterizing indeterminate phenomena via mathematical syntax and semantics. As an extension of set theory for the study of spatial entity characterized by incomplete and inexact information [2], rough set is further developed on spatial interpretation in this paper.

S. Tsumoto et al. (Eds.): RSCTC 2004, LNAI 3066, pp. 435–444, 2004.

Rough set specifies a spatial entity by giving an upper and a lower approximation. The lower approximation is the set of spatial elements that surely belong to the spatial entity, while the upper approximation is the set of spatial elements that possibly belong to it. Since it was introduced, rough set has been applied in medicine system, language processing, pattern recognition, etc. Recently, rough set has also been applied in GIS. Stell and Worboys used rough set to handle imprecision due to finite spatial or semantic resolution. Ahlqvist et al. thought that rough set was a feasible alternative to GIS via rough classification and accuracy assessment [3-6]. However, in the process of rough set applications and developments, various descriptive symbols came into being, and it has been proved to be difficult to study rough set further [2-6]. Simultaneously, the lower approximation is the subset of the upper approximation in rough set, and it is always computed twice. This wastes a great deal of resource since the certain lower approximation occupies the most part of a spatial entity.

2 Trial to Standardize Rough Set Symbols

Pawlak [2] originally considered a rough set as a family of sets with the same lower and upper approximations. As an extension to the crisp set, rough set focuses on the uncertainties caused by incomplete, insufficient or inaccessible information. Compared with other methods, rough set can close describe the spatial entities as they are in the real world, including both certainties and uncertainties. Based on Pawlak's work, Iwinski [3] regarded a rough set as a pair of composed sets. Then Pawlak [3] gave another way to describe a rough set by rough membership function. Based on whether statistical information is used or not, the existing rough set models may be grouped into two major classes: algebraic and probabilistic models [4]. The probabilistic rough set can be defined with a rough membership function $\mu_X(x) \in [0, 1]$ [2] (Eq.1).

$$\mu_X(x) = \frac{R_{card}(X \cap [x]_R)}{R_{card}([x]_R)} = \begin{cases} 1 & x \in Pos(x) \\ (0,\ 1) & x \in Bnd(x) \\ 0 & x \in Neg(x) \\ 1-\mu_{\sim X}(x) & x \in \sim X \end{cases} \tag{1}$$

There exist various rough set models to be unified. With the applications of the rough set, different types of symbols on the rough set concepts are developed due to different fields and intents. Even if the rough set inventor, Zdzisław Pawlak, often gave different symbols in his papers [2-6]. In order to understand a paper, readers have to compare the new symbols with old ones. Thus it is difficult to further communicate with each other in different application fields of the rough set. The more widely rough set is applied, the worse this situation will be. In the sequel, the further development of the rough set will be impeded. "In view of many generalizations and extensions of rough set theory, some kind of unification of the basic theory seems to be badly needed." [3]. So it becomes very necessary to standardize various symbols. As a trial to unify rough set symbols, a set of simplified genetic rough symbols is proposed on the basis of the existing different rough symbols [2-6], mainly Pawlak symbols. The new symbols are in terms of rough interpretation and specialized indication (Table 1). For example, "*Lr*", "*X*" of "*Lr*(*X*)" respectively denote "*L*ower approximation in *r*ough set", "spatial entity *X*" in GIS.

Table 1. List of rough symbols and their definitions.

Proposed symbols	Existing symbols	Presentations
U	U	Discourse universe that is a finite and non-empty set.
R	R	Equivalence relation on U, $R \subseteq U \times U$. (U, R) formalizes an approximate space.
X	X	Arbitrary set $X \subseteq U$
$\sim X$	$-X$, $\sim X$	The complement set of X, $X \cup (\sim X) = U$
$\frac{U}{R}$	$\frac{U}{R}$	Equivalence class set composed of disjoint subsets of U partitioned by R.
$[x]_R$	$[x]_{IND(R)}$, $[x]_R$, $R(x)$, $r(x)$	Equivalence class of R including element x. It may also interpreted as all rough-related elements of x, or a neighborhood of x.
$Lr(X)$	$\underline{APR}(X)$, $\underline{A}(X)$, $\underline{A}X$, $\underline{X}$, $Int(X)$, $R\_(X)$, R^*	Lower approximation (interior set) of X on U. $Lr(X) = \{x \in U \mid [x]_R \subseteq X\}$
$Ur(X)$	$\overline{APR}(X)$, $\bar{A}(X)$, $\bar{A}X$, $\overline{X}$, $Cl(X)$, $R^-(X)$, R_*	Upper approximation (closure set) of X on U. $Ur(X) = \{x \in U \mid [x]_R \cap X \neq \Phi\}$
$Pos(X)$	$POS(X)$	Positive region. $Pos(X) = Lr(X)$
$Neg(X)$	$NEG(X)$	Negative region. $Neg(X) = U - Ur(X)$
$Bnd(X)$	$BND(X)$, $Bn(X)$, $Bd(X)$, $Boundary(X)$	Boundary region. $Bnd(X) = Ur(X) - Lr(X)$

In Table 1 context, rough set characterizes both certainties and uncertainties. $Lr(X)$ is certain "Yes", $Neg(X)$ is sure "No", while both $Ur(X)$ and $Bnd(X)$ are uncertain "Yes or no". That is to say, with respect to an element $x \in$ U, it is sure that $x \in Pos(X)$ belongs to X in terms of its features, but $x \in Neg(X)$ does not belong to X; while $x \in Bnd(X)$ cannot be ensured by means of available information whether it belongs to X or not. So it can be seen that $Lr(X) \subseteq X \subseteq Ur(X) \subseteq U$, $U = Pos(X) \cup Bnd(X) \cup Neg(X)$, and $Ur(X) = Pos(X) \cup Bnd(X)$. X is defined iif $Lr(X) = Ur(X)$, while X is rough with respect to $Bnd(X)$ iif $Lr(X) \neq Ur(X)$. A subset $X \subseteq U$ defined with the lower approximation and upper approximation is called rough set. Rough degree is $R_d(X) = R_{card}(Ur(X) - Lr(X)) / R_{card}(X) \times 100\%$. Where, $R_{card}(X)$ denotes the cardinality of set X. X is crisp when $R_d(X) = 0$. For instance, regard U as an image, the rectangle becomes a pixel.

3 Rough Spatial Entity

Both spatial entities and spatial relationships formalize an approximate space. A spatial entity may be interpreted as spatial phenomena, natural objects with geometric feature of point, line, area, volume, cases, states, processes, observations and so on. As an alternative, rough set is proposed to characterize spatial entities in GIS. U is composed of spatial entities with attributes (features, variables, etc.), and R is the spatial relationship among the spatial entities. Both of them formalize an approximate space (U, R). Point, line and area in vector space, pixel and grid in raster space, unit cube in a multi-dimensional space are considered as equivalence class of rough spatial entity. In rough set context, point, line, area and volume have size and shape. Attributes and a pair of approximations describe a point, and a series of such points linked together are lines. The lines called boundaries bound areas, and volumes are bounded by smooth area.

A pair of upper approximation and lower approximation specifies a rough spatial entity. Given a spatial entity $X \subseteq U$, X may not be represented precisely for the available information is insufficient. The observed value of an attribute is usually unequal to its true value. When an attribute has been observed for many times, the observed values may formalize an uncertain observed zone around the true value, namely a pair of approximations. As to a spatial element $x \in U$, lower approximation $Lr(X)$ is the set of x that surly belongs to the true X, while upper approximation $Ur(X)$ is the set of x that possibly belongs to X. And uncertain region of X is $Bnd(X)$ (Fig.1).

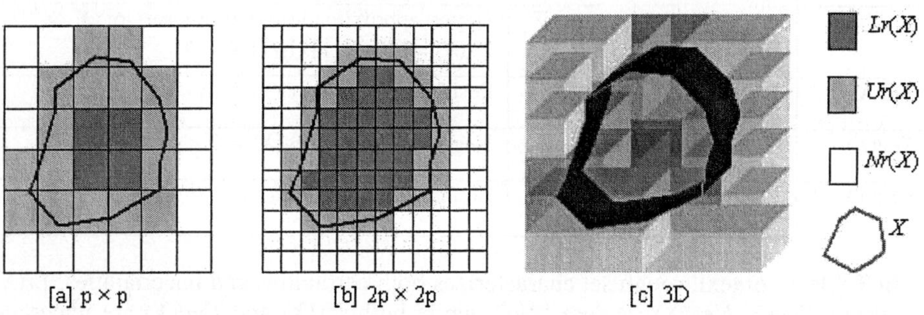

Fig. 1. Rough spatial entity and its illustrations of low resolution, high resolution and 3D.

Thus, during the spatial analysis based on GIS, rough set can more totally propagate the spatial entity properties (both certain and uncertain) for most spatial true values are not known exactly. As an alternative mathematical interpretation in the sense of rough set, object model is $Lr(X) = Ur(X)$, field model , error band, epsilon band, and "S" band are $Lr(X) \neq Ur(X)$. And for rough degree R_d (X), field model > error band > epsilon band > "S" band. Each of them may be taken as the special condition of rough space. Since vector data and raster data are main original data in GIS, rough vector space and rough raster space will be mainly studied in this section.

[1] Rough Vector Space. The object model represents spatial entities via crisply delineated point, line, area and volume in a defined absolute reference system. Their attributes that characterize the space at the points, along the lines, within the area or volumes, are assumed to be constant over the whole object extent. It is implemented by GIS vector structure. For example, lines are linked by a defined topology to form networks, which, if opened, can represent rivers, or if closed, the abstract or defined boundaries of polygons in turn represent land parcels, soil units or administrative areas. The object model is assumed $Lr(X) = Ur(X)$ without roughness. In fact, $Lr(X) \neq Ur(X)$ when reality is described by the object model in a computerized GIS. Spatial vector objects often have an extension around them for errors and uncertainties due to unavailable information (Fig.2 [a], [b]). Given uncertain positive parameters δ_1, δ_2 in rough set context, X can be represented $X = Lr(X) + \delta_1$ or $X = Ur(X) - \delta_2$. In the sense of δ_1 and δ_2, $Bnd(X) = \delta_1 + \delta_2$, $\sim X = U - X = U - Lr(X) + \delta_1 = U - Ur(X) + \delta_2$. Error ellipse may be used as their depicted mathematical model. Burrough (1996) argued that the object model was suitable for a spatial entity that could be mapped on external features of the landscape, while the field model adapted to a spatial entity when its single quantitative attributes were measured and mapped.

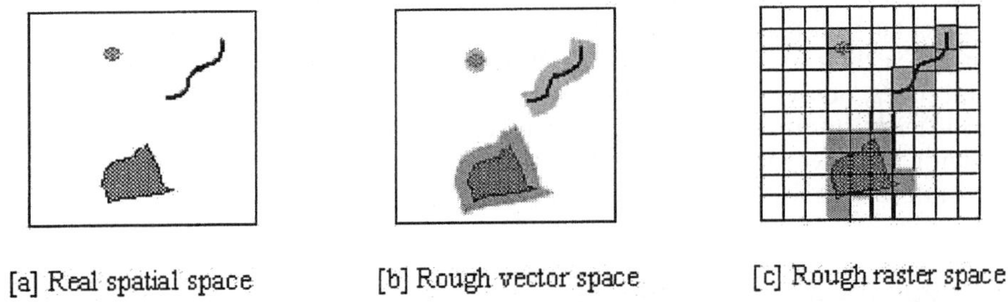

Fig. 2. Rough spatial point, line and area.

[2] Rough Raster Space. Rough raster space brings approximations into the shapes and forms of a spatial entity. Raster data is for the field model opposed to the object model. Rough spatial point, line and area in the raster space are essential when the real world is put into a computerized GIS. They are illustrated in Fig.2 [a], [c]. As Fig.2 revealed, $Lr(X)$ of the point and line are both empty. $Lr(X)$ of the area has only two equivalence classes. All $Ur(X)$ are relatively bigger than X and $Lr(X)$. So spatial uncertainties (positional and attribute uncertainties) in GIS really exists. Cartographic generalization is a changeable processing of the lower approximation of spatial objects and their upper approximation. However, the pair of approximations of various spatial entities changes in different directions. One becomes bigger, while the other smaller.

Rough set gives a new interpretation on image resolution. Spatial raster data become important for many images are raster. A raster is regarded as a spatial equivalence class in the rough raster space. The spatial entities are defined with the raster data approximately, e.g. boundaries. And a piece of spatial image is discretized to a regular grid, i.e. an image pixel at a predetermined resolution. The image resolution decides the pixel size. The higher the image resolution is, the less rough degree $R_d(X)$ of the spatial raster entity X is. When the resolution is high enough, or the raster is small enough, the pair of lower and lower approximations of an entity are equal, $Lr(X) = Ur(X)$, namely, the entity is not rough. However, bigger computation storage is also demanded. Therefore, rough set gives another new interpretation on remote sensing image changing with resolution.

[3] Rough Multi-dimensional Space. It is composed of a series of unit spatial cubic objects. Spatial object is composed of many blocks. It seems a spatial object like building is built up with toy's blocks. Blocks belonging to the lower approximation are included in the spatial object, while the skin of the objects crosses blocks belonging to the upper approximation but not belonging to the lower approximation. In other words, two "balls" with the same center represent a spatial entity in the multi-dimensional rough raster space. One with a smaller radius is composed of the lower approximation, while the other with a bigger radius is the upper approximation.

[4] Study Objects as They Are. Mathematically, point has no size, line has length but no size, and area no thickness. The attributes of a spatial entity are assumed to very continuously and smoothly, and they can be described with a smooth mathematical function. However, this model is so abstract that it is not as well as the real world. Thus, uncertainties are unavoidable when an abstract mathematical object is used to study the complex real object. It is ideal to study a spatial entity as it is. Rough set tries its best to maintain the original characters of the real world via a pair of lower and upper approximations. True value is the lower approximation, while the observed extension is the upper approximation. When a spatial entity has been observed for several times, observed values formalize an extension around the true value because of insufficient information. Rough set can keep and propagate the uncertain information until final decisions. We argue that superfluous information is better than removal information before a decision is determined.

4 Rough Spatial Relationships

Rough spatial topological relationship *R* is essential in a rough space (*U*, *R*). Before rough topology is advanced, it is necessary to briefly review the development of topological relationships. Munkres defined the meaning of standard topology. Original spatial topological relationships were for simple point (0-dimensional), line (1-dimensional) and area (2-dimensional), with 4-intersection model on interior X^0 and boundary ∂X. When their limitations appeared, it was extended to 9-intersection model on interior, boundary and exterior X^-. Then Clementini and Felice introduced areas with broad boundaries composed of an inner boundary and an outer boundary, and reduce the 2^9 topological matrices to the 44 matrices with 0 and 1 values. Chen et al. proposed a Voronoi-based 9-intersection model via replacing the exterior X^- of an entity with its Voronoi region X^v with *o* (empty) and Ø (none-empty) values [5-6]. However, it is difficult to ensure their interior X^0, exterior X^-, or X^v exactly because of insufficient information. In the sequel, boundary ∂X is also unsure. It is a true case that uncertainties exist, and is unavoidable in GIS. As an alternative, we propose rough topology via respectively replacing the interior, boundary and exterior with positive region, boundary region and negative region as Eq.2.

$$R_{r9}(A,B) = \begin{pmatrix} Pos(A)\cap Pos(B) & Pos(A)\cap Bnd(B) & Pos(A)\cap Neg(B) \\ Bnd(A)\cap Pos(B) & Bnd(A)\cap Bnd(B) & Bnd(A)\cap Neg(B) \\ Neg(A)\cap Pos(B) & Neg(A)\cap Bnd(B) & Neg(A)\cap Neg(B) \end{pmatrix} \tag{2}$$

Eq.2 is surely able to tell and propagate certainties (*Pos*(*X*), *Neg*(*X*)) and uncertainties (*Bnd*(*X*)). 1 (none-empty) and 0 (empty) values are employed for GIS is computerized. Note that *Neg(X)* is different from ~*X*, the complement of *X* for *Neg(X)* = *U* - *Ur(X)*, while ~*X* = *U* – *X* = *U* - *Ur(X)* + δ_2. So rough spatial relationships give richer information that includes certain and uncertain data, and this may improve the quality of image interpretation. In this sense, Eq.2 is universal whenever different thematic maps are overlapped. In the rough space of the same image map, it is sure that *Pos(A)* ∩ *Pos(B)* = 0.

The rough relationships may be divided into three kinds, i.e., CC (rough relationships between crisp entities and crisp entities), RC (Rough relationships between rough entities and crisp entities) and RR (rough relationships between rough entities and rough entities). Here, rough area-area topological relationships in 2-dimensional space are proposed mainly. Because area is from line, and line is from point, area is studied as a case. The topologies of point-point, point-line, point-area, line-line and line-area may be regarded as the special cases of area-area. Fig.3 illustrates the intersection relationships between two rough spatial entities. Where, *Lr(A), Lr(B)* are respectively the lower approximations of rough entities *A*, *B*; *Ur(A)*, *Ur(A)* are respectively the upper approximations; *Bnd(AB)* is a rough region between *A* and *B*, which is the most uncertain part. Because the indeterminate region often happens in the boundary, it is unable for an uncertainty to take place between the lower approximation *A* and *B*. So the meet relationship often exists at the indeterminate transition zone in image classification, which is composed of two neighboring upper approximations. In the rough space, the set of topological relationships are {disjoint, touch/meet, overlap, equal, covers, covered by, contains, contained by / inside} which are studied by using rough matrices and their figures (Fig.3). Excluding spatial entities that contain roughness, there are also crisp spatial entities (e.g. administrative boundary) in rough space. According to the abovementioned, a crisp spatial entity *X* is a special rough entity where *Lr(X)* = *Ur(X)*. So rough spatial relationships in the same rough space are divided into three types, CC (Fig.3 [a]), RC (Fig.3 [b]) and RR (Fig.3 [c]).

Moreover, a universal equation can be deduced from Eq.2 to represent the intersected rough regions. When more than two rough spatial entities are intersected, rough regions among them are proposed to describe with $Bnd(A_1, \ldots, A_i, \ldots, A_n)$ (Eq.3).

$$R_{r9}(A_1,\ldots,A_i,\ldots,A_n)=\begin{pmatrix} R_{r9}(A_1,A_1) & \ldots & R_{r9}(A_1,A_i) & \ldots & R_{r9}(A_1,A_n) \\ \ldots & \ldots & \ldots & \ldots & \ldots \\ R_{r9}(A_i,A_1) & \ldots & R_{r9}(A_i,A_i) & \ldots & R_{r9}(A_i,A_n) \\ \ldots & \ldots & \ldots & \ldots & \ldots \\ R_{r9}(A_n,A_1) & \ldots & R_{r9}(A_n,A_i) & \ldots & R_{r9}(A_n,A_n) \end{pmatrix} \quad (3)$$

Here, we take n = 3 as an example to interpret the equation. Supposed there are three rough spatial entities *A*, *B* and *C*, which intersect with each other. Besides the two intersected regions, *Bnd(A,B)*, *Bnd(A,C)* and *Bnd(B,C)*, a new rough region *Bnd(ABC)* also appears.

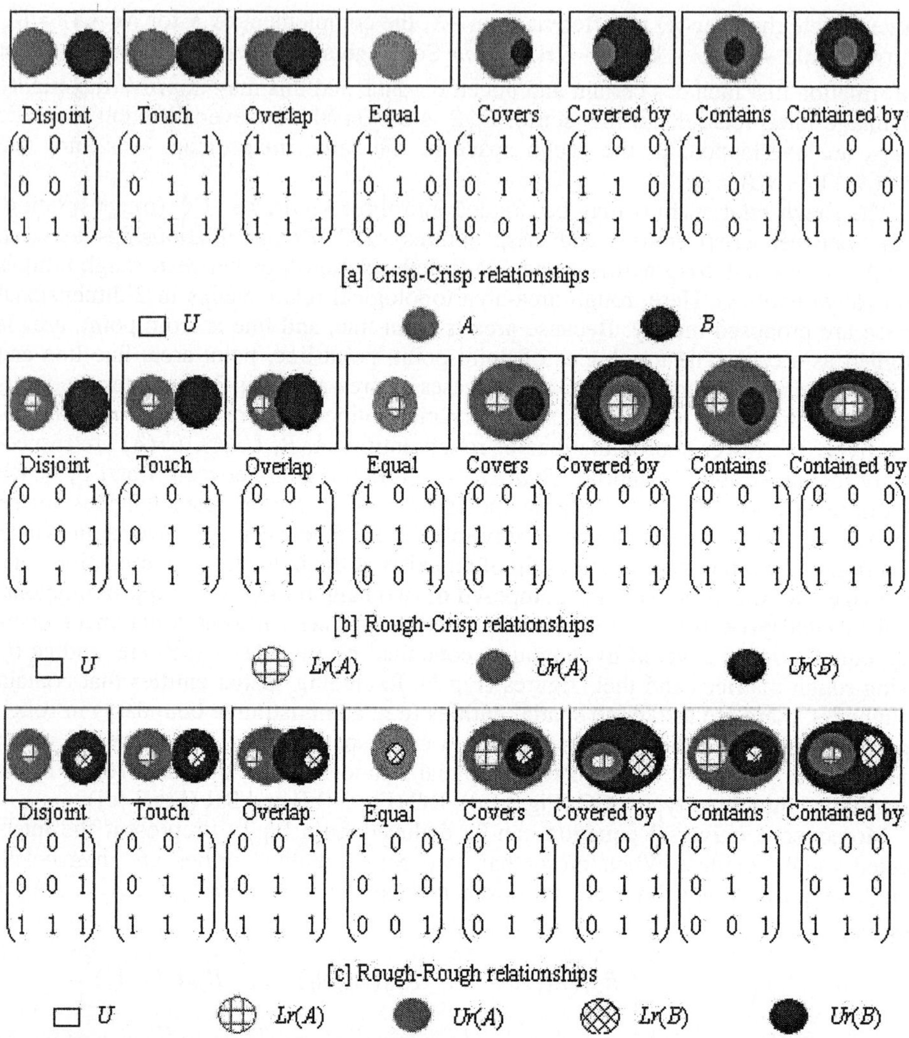

Fig. 3. Rough spatial topological relationships and their corresponding rough matrices.

5 Case Study

As a case study, the method of rough spatial description -based rough classification is proposed and is used to extract river information from a remote sensing image. Based on a pair of lower and upper approximations, maximum and minimum maps of river thematic classification are generated via integrating the reduction of superfluous attributes, rough membership function and rough relationships. The original image (Fig.4 [a]) is a piece of remote sensing TM image.

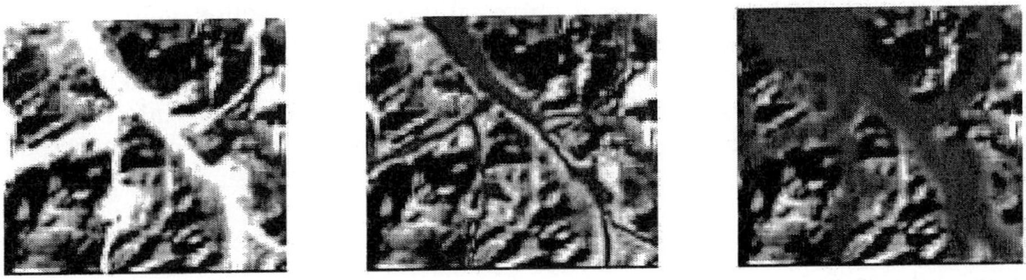

Fig. 4. Rough water thematic maps (continuums).

There are many conditional attributes affecting the decisional attributes, i.e., image classification. The conditional attributes include image gray scale, the satellite parameters, air refraction and so on. After other conditional attributes are reduced, gray scale is selected to extract the river classification from the image. Let G_x be the gray scale of a pixel x and G_X is the gray scale of river pixel. Then the rough membership function (Eq.4) can be extended from Eq.1.

$$\mu_X(x) = \frac{G_x}{G_X} = \begin{cases} 1 & x \in Lr(X) \\ (0,\ 1] & x \in Ur(X) \\ 0 & x \in Neg(X) \end{cases} \tag{4}$$

As Fig.4 (b)(c) revealed, the lower approximation *Lr*(*X*) is the minimum water map with certainties, while the upper approximation *Ur*(*X*) is the maximum water map with uncertainties. Here, $R_d(X) = R_{card}(Ur(X) - Lr(X)) / R_{card}(X) \times 100\% = 10.37\%$. Compared with the crisp classification with only one result, the rough classification not only includes both certainties and uncertainties, but also tells the certainties from the uncertainties.

Furthermore, the results are compared with those from the maximum likelihood classification and the fuzzy classification, which indicates that the rough classification based on rough set contains more information and with high precision. We get the maximum possible river, minimum certain river, rough confidence degree, possible error, etc. The maximum possible river approaches the river in floodtime, while the minimum certain river comes near the river in low water. Moreover, the precision is improved 7% than the maximum likelihood classification or 2% than fuzzy classification.

6 Conclusions

We have proposed a set of rough set symbols in terms of rough interpretation and specialized indication. In rough set context, we also proposed rough spatial entities and their topological relationships. A universal intersected equation and rough membership function with gray scale are further developed. Three kinds of rough spatial topological relationships, i.e., CC, RC and RR, were studied by using rough matrices and their figures. The result of the case study not only included more information but also was confidential and practical. This has indicated the method of rough spatial description is a valuable approach to geomatics.

Acknowledgements

This study is supported by the funds from National Natural Science Foundation of China (Grant No.70231010), and National High Technology R&D Program (863) (Grant No.2003AA132080).

References

1. Burrough P. A., Frank A. U. (1996) *Geographic Objects with Indeterminate Boundaries* (London: Taylor & Francis).
2. Pawlak Z.(1991) *Rough sets: theoretical aspects of reasoning about data* (London: Kluwer Academic Publishers).
3. Polkowski L., Skowron A.(1998) *Rough Sets in Knowledge Discovery* 1*: Methodologies and Applications*.Heidelberg: Physica-Verlag.
4. Polkowski L, Skowron, A. (1998) *Rough Sets in Knowledge Discovery* 2*: Applications, Case Studies and Software Systems*. Heidelberg: Physica-Verlag.
5. Wang S.L.,et al (2002) Theory and application of Geo-rough space. *Geomatics and Information Science of Wuhan University*, 27(3): 274-282, (in Chinese).
6. Polkowski L.,Tsumoto S., Lin T. Y. (2000) Rough Methods and Applications: New Developments in Knowledge Discovery in Information Systems, Berlin: Phisica-Verlag.

A Scalable Rough Set Knowledge Reduction Algorithm

Zhengren Qin, Guoyin Wang, Yu Wu, and Xiaorong Xue

Institute of Computer Science and Technology
Chongqing University of Posts and Telecommunications
Chongqing, 400065, P.R.China
Finalgas@sohu.com

Abstract. Knowledge reduction algorithms based on rough set play an important role in KDD because of its advantage in dealing with uncertain data. However, it is hard for classical rough set knowledge reduction algorithms to deal with huge data sets. A structure of Class Distribution List (CDL) is presented in this paper to express the distribution of all attribute values in the whole sample space. With database technology, a CDL can be generated through classifying the original data sets. Then, a group of rough-set-based knowledge reduction algorithms are revised using CDL. This method can process huge data sets directly. As a framework, CDL method can also be used in other rough set algorithms to improve their scalability without decreasing their accuracy. Efficiency of our algorithms is proved by simulation experiments.

1 Introduction

The problem of processing huge data sets has been studied for many years. Random sampling [1] was developed by Carlett to solve this problem in 1991, but it cannot work when the number of samples is over 32,000. Philip K. Chan considered partitioning the data into subsets that fit in memory and then developing a classifier on each subset in parallel, but the accuracy is less than those processing the data sets as a whole [2]. SLIQ [3] and SPRINT [4], developed by IBM Almaden Research Center in 1996, are two important algorithms with the ability to deal with disk-resident data directly. Their performance is equivalent to that of classical decision tree algorithms. Many other improved algorithms, such as CLOUDS [5] and ScalParc [6], are developed later. RainForest [7] is a framework for fast decision tree construction for large datasets. Its speed and effect are better than SPRINT in some cases. L. A. Ren, Q. He and Z. Z. Shi used hyper surface separation and HSC classification method to classify huge data sets with good performance [8, 9].

Rough set is a mathematic tool developed to deal with uncertain information in recent years. It is a good method in processing uncertain data and incomplete data. However, there are two disadvantages in classical rough set algorithms. One is their weak ability in dealing with huge data sets, so rough set algorithms are facing the challenge of massive data sets now [10]. The second disadvantage is that these algorithms did not take the advantage of database technology. In classical knowledge

S. Tsumoto et al. (Eds.): RSCTC 2004, LNAI 3066, pp. 445–454, 2004.

acquisition algorithms comparison among all samples is needed. Consequently, the whole data sets always lives in memory to keep the efficiency. It is usually better than original algorithms to combine database technology with classification algorithms [11, 12]. In fact, it is not necessary for all data to be loaded and processed once. Only part of the whole data is useful each time.

A structure of Class Distribution List (CDL) is presented in this paper to express the distribution of condition attribute values in the whole sample space. With the help of database technology, we can classify the original data sets and generate a CDL efficiently. A group of rough-set-based knowledge reduction algorithms including discretization, attribute reduction and value reduction is revised with CDL. Since a CDL could be generated in multi-steps, there is no restriction of memory size for the new revised algorithms. Moreover, our method could be used in other rough set algorithms to improve their scalability without loss of accuracy.

The rest of this paper is organized as follows. The next section describes CDL and our scalable strategy based on database technology. Section 3 discusses revised knowledge reduction algorithms. Section 4 proves the efficiency of our algorithms with simulation experiments. The last section concludes the paper.

2 Scalable Strategy Based on Database Technology

2.1 Basic Concepts of Rough Set Used in This Paper

For the convenience of illustration, some basic notions are introduced at first.

Definition 1. U is a finite set of objects. P and Q are equivalence clusters defined on U. *The P positive region of Q* is defined as

$$\mathrm{POS}_P(Q) = \bigcup_{X \in U/Q} \mathrm{P}_-(X) \cdot$$

Definition 2. A decision table is defined as $<U, C \cup D, V, f>$, where U is a finite set of objects. C is its condition attribute set and D is its decision attribute set. Let $U/P=\{X_1, X_2, \dots, X_n\}$ and $U/D=\{Y_1, Y_2, \dots, Y_m\}$, where $P(P \subseteq C)$ is a subset of condition attributes. Then *the conditional information entropy of D with reference to P* is defined as

$$H(D \mid P) = -\sum_{i=1}^{n} p(X_i) \sum_{j=1}^{m} p(Y_j \mid X_i) \log(p(Y_j \mid X_i)) ,$$

where $p(Y_j \mid X_i)=|Y_j \cap X_i|/ X_i$, $i=1,2, \dots ,n, j=1,2, \dots ,m$.

More specific descriptions about rough set are available in [13].

2.2 Class Distribution List (CDL)

A structure of list CDL(P) is developed to express the information of $\mathrm{POS}_P(D)$ and U/P in this section. In CDL, two neighbor samples are linked with symbol '&', '@' or '#' according to the following 3 conditions.

- The two samples with different condition attribute values are linked with '#'.
- The two samples with the same condition attribute values and different decision attribute values are linked with '@'.
- The two samples with the same condition and decision attribute values are linked with '&'.

All condition classes are divided by '#'. That is, each part between two successive '#' symbols is a condition class.

A decision table is shown in Table 1. We can get a class distribution list CDL({*Salary*})=#1@3&5#2&7#4@6#8# from it. We can find from CDL({*Salary*}) that sample 1, 3 and 5 have the same attribute value on *salary*, but the decision value of sample 3 and 5 is different from the decision value of sample 1. Sample 4 and 6 have the same *salary* value but different *Class* value. There are collisions between sample 4 and 6. In this decision table, we can also find directly that $U/\{Class\} = \{\{1,2,4,7\},\{3,5,6,8\}\}$ and $U/\{Salary\} = \{\{1,3,5\},\{2,7\},\{4,6\},\{8\}\}$, therefore, $POS_{\{Salary\}}(\{Class\}) = \{2,7\} \cup \{8\}$. Thus, we can find that CDL({*Salary*}) could represent directly the information of $U/\{Salary\}$ and $POS_{\{Salary\}}(\{Class\})$.

A CDL can be divided into two parts: Inconsistent Class Distribution List (ICDL) and Consistent Class Distribution List (CCDL). CCDL can be further divided into two parts according to the number of samples in each condition class. One is Single Sample Consistent Distribution List (SSCDL) and the other is Multi Sample Consistent Distribution List (MSCDL). SSCDL includes the condition classes covering only one sample. MSCDL includes all consistent condition classes containing more than one sample. ICDL includes all inconsistent condition classes. For example, the former CDL({*Salary*}) can be divided into 3 parts: ICDL({*Salary*})=#1@3&5#4@6#, SSCDL({*Salary*})=#8# and MSCDL({*Salary*})=#2&7#.

Table 1. A decision table.

Index	Salary	Age	Class
1	H	30	B
2	L	23	B
3	H	40	G
4	M	55	B
5	H	55	G
6	M	45	G
7	L	60	B
8	VH	35	G

Table 2. A decision table.

Index	Salary	Age	Class
1	H	(*,35]	B
2	L	(*,35)	B
3	H	(35,45]	G
4	M	(45, *)	B
5	H	(45, *)	G
6	M	(35, 45]	G
7	L	(45, *)	B
8	VH	(*, 35]	G

CDL shows the distribution of condition attribute values in the whole sample space. It has all information needed for knowledge reduction. SSCDL and MSCDL can be easily obtained and processed by executing SQL Query language without generating actual CDL. ICDL reflects the inconsistent part of a decision table. We will discuss the method of generating ICDL using database technology in the next section since it is the base of knowledge reduction. ICDL should be memory-resident to improve the efficiency of our algorithms. A big ICDL can also be divided into several parts and generated in multi-steps in order to save memory.

2.3 ICDL Generation Algorithm

The technology for ICDL generation is discussed in this section. Many feasible methods could be adopted. The simplest way may be sorting the original data sets at first and then comparing all samples one by one. However, this method is not efficient especially in processing huge data sets since all data must be loaded into memory step by step for comparison. A fast and efficient way is developed to generate ICDL in algorithm 1.

Algorithm 1: ICDL Generation Algorithm
Input: a decision table (*DT*), the number of samples the computer memory can hold (*Msamples*), a subset of condition attributes (*SCA*).
Output: ICDL (*SCA*).
/* Note: *DA* – the decision attribute, *Index* – the sample ID. */

1. Execute SQL Query " select *SCA* into *DT2* from *DT* group by *SCA* having count (*)>1 and count (distinct *DA*)>1"; /* Put the condition attribute values of attributes *SCA* of all inconsistent samples into *DT2*. */
2. ICDL=null; Insert symbol '#' into ICDL;
3. For each condition attribute value $VSCA_i$ in *DT2*
4. {Execute Query "select distinct (*DA*) into *DT3* from *DT* where $SCA=VSCA_i$"; /* Put the decision attribute values of the samples S_t into *DT3*, where S_t $(SCA)=VSCA_i$. */
5. For each decision attribute value VDA_j in *DT3*
6. {Execute Query "select *Index* into *DT4* from *DT* where $SCA=VSCA_i$ and $DA=VDA_j$";/*Put all the samples S_t into *DT4*, where S_t $(SCA)=VSCA_i$ and S_t $(DA)=VDA_j$. */
7. For each sample S_k in *DT4*
8. {If (The number of samples of ICDL > *Msamples*) then
9. {Insert symbol '#' at the end of ICDL; Return ICDL; ICDL=null;}
10. Insert sample S_k and symbol '&' at the end of ICDL;}
11. Change the last symbol of ICDL from '&' to '@';}
12. Change the last symbol of ICDL from '@' to '#';}

The complexity of this algorithm is $O(dmn^2)$, where m is the number of condition attributes considered, n is the number of samples and d is the number of decision values. CDL can also be generated in multi-steps, and therefore the new algorithms can deal with huge data sets.

3 Revised Knowledge Reduction Algorithm

Many classical knowledge reduction algorithms based on rough set could be revised using ICDL. The revised version of algorithms are always more scalable and better to deal with huge data sets than the original algorithms. In this section, a group of revised algorithms will be presented.

3.1 Revised Discretization Algorithm

Discretization is very important in rough-set-based knowledge acquisition. In this section, the discretization algorithm based on attribute importance [13] is modified to deal with huge data sets with CDL.

3.1.1 Information Entropy Computation Using CDL

It is fast to compute the information entropy of a subset of condition attributes using CDL. The information entropy of SSCDL and MSCDL is 0. We need to consider ICDL only in information entropy calculation. It is necessary to scan an ICDL to calculate its entropy. A temp-list is generated dynamically while scanning each condition class, and then the temp-entropy is computed using the temp-list. The total-entropy is the sum of all temp-entropy. There are two parts in a temp-list: the top-part that contains the number of samples in the condition class and the bottom-part that expresses the distribution of its samples. A new column is added in the bottom-part while meeting '@'. The top-part is marked as '?' until meeting '#'. Figure 1 shows an example of computing the information entropy of ICDL({*Salary*}) of Table 1.

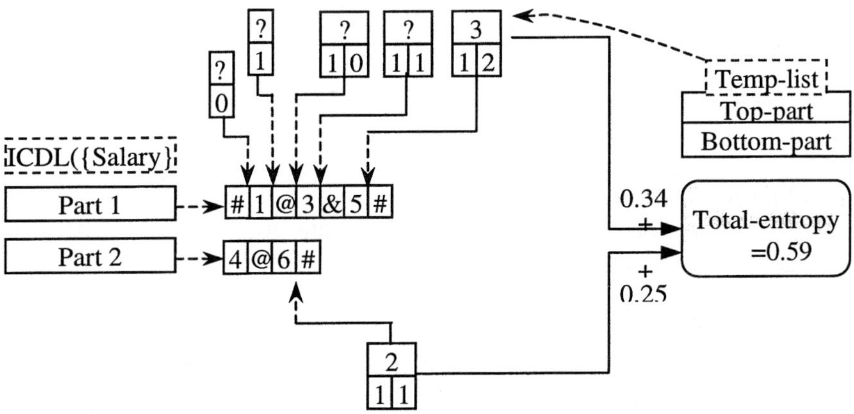

Fig. 1. An example of information entropy calculation.

3.1.2 Revised Discretization Algorithm

Algorithm 2: Discretization (*DT*)
Input: a complete decision table *DT*.
Output: a discretized decision table *DT*.

1. For each real condition attribute a_i
2. {Compute the information entropy of a_i using ICDL($\{a_i\}$);}
3. Sort all real condition attributes in descending of their information entropy;
4. For each real condition attribute a_i
5. {Generate ICDL($C\backslash\{a_i\}$);
6. S_{zone}=null; /*S_{zone} is a set of condition attribute values of the attribute a_i,*/

7. For each cut-point (S_a, S_b) /*S_a and S_b are two successive values of the condition attribute a_i. */
8. {S_{zone}+=S_a;
9. For each sample SV_j in DT having SV_j (a_i)=S_h, where $S_h \in S_{zone}$
10. {For each sample SV_k in DT having SV_k (a_i)=S_b
11. {If (Both of SV_j and SV_k are in the same condition class of ICDL(C\{a_i }) and there is '@' between SV_j and SV_k) then
12. {Choose the cut-point (S_a, S_b); S_{zone}=null;}}}}}

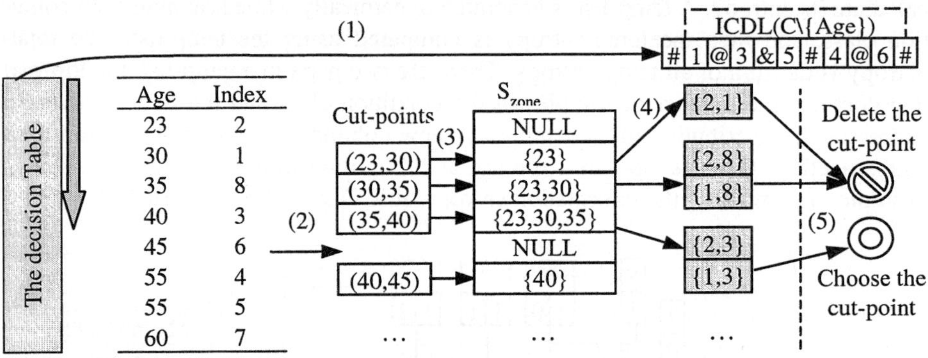

Fig. 2. An example of discretization.

3.1.3 A Sample of Discretization

Figure 2 shows the process of discretizing the attribute 'Age' of Table 1. All steps of Figure 2 are described in the following.

(1) Generate ICDL(C\{Age}).
(2) Generate all possible cut-points of the attribute 'Age'.
(3) Insert the small one of the two condition attribute values of each cut-point into S_{zone}, where S_{zone} is a set of condition attribute values of the attribute 'Age'. For example, we insert 30 into S_{zone} for cut-point (30,35), and then S_{zone} ={23,30}.
(4) Generate two corresponding samples SV_1 and SV_2 for each cut-point (S_a, S_b), where SV_1(Age)=S_b, SV_2 (Age)$\in S_{zone}$, and S_{zone}={S_1, S_2, ..., S_m, S_a}. For example, we can generate {2,8} and {1,8} for cut-point (23,30).
(5) Choose or delete the current cut-point. From Figure 2, the two corresponding samples 1 and 3 are in the same condition class of ICDL(C\{Age}) and there is '@' between them. Thus, the cut-point (35,40) is chosen.

The discretized decision table is shown in Table 2.

3.2 Revised Attribute Reduction Algorithm

The attribute reduction algorithm CEBARKNC [14] is used here. It is fast to compute the information entropy of a subset of condition attributes using CDL. CEBARKNC can also be modified using ICDL to improve its scalability. The only difference of the revised one and the original algorithm CEBARKNC is the method of entropy computation, so the description of this algorithm is omitted here.

3.3 Revised Value Reduction Algorithm

The heuristic value reduction algorithm [15] is used in this section to generate rules. The algorithm tries to find the best reduction using value core. CDL is also used to improve its scalability. At the first step of the original algorithm, all columns of the decision table are processed one by one and then they are refreshed and marked by the results. In our method, all columns are also considered in turn.

- The condition attributes of samples in SSCDL are marked as '?'.
- The condition attributes of samples in MSCDL are marked as '*'.
- The condition attributes of samples in ICDL need not to be changed.

SQL Query will be generated and executed directly while processing SSCDL and MSCDL. The revised algorithm is described in the following.

Algorithm 3: Value Reduction (*DT*)
Input: a complete discrete decision table *DT*.
Output: rules table *RT*.
/*Note: *DA* – decision attribute, *Index* – Sample ID, C- the condition attribute set. */

1. Execute SQL Query "Select * into *RT* from *DT*"; /*
2. For each condition attribute a_i
3. {Execute Query "update *RT* set a_i ='?' where *index* in (Select min (*index*) as *index* from *DT* group by C\ a_i having count (*)=1)"; /* Mark the condition attributes of samples in SSCDL as '?'. */
4. Execute Query "select *C*\ a_i into *DT2* from *DT* group by *C*\ a_i having count (*)>1 and count (distinct *DA*)=1"; /* Put all samples in MSCDL into *DT2*. */
5. Execute Query "update *RT* set *RT*. a_i ='*' where *RT.index* in (select A.*index* from *DT* A, *DT2* B where A. *C*\ a_i =B. *C*\ a_i)"; /* Mark the condition attributes of samples in MSCDL as '*'. */
   /* The other samples in ICDL need not to be changed. */}
6. The remained operations are the same as that of the original heuristic value reduction algorithm [15].

4 Experiment Results

4.1 Accuracy Test

In order to test the validity and accuracy of the revised algorithms with CDL, the revised algorithms are implemented and compared with the original classical algorithms upon 8 data sets from UCI. The original algorithms are from RIDAS [16], which is developed by the Chongqing Univ. of Posts and Telecommunications, China. The following hardware and software are used in our experiments.

- Hardware: CPU-PIV 1.7G, Memory-256M
- OS: Windows Advance Server 2000
- Developing tools for RIDAS: Visual C++ 6.0
- Developing tools for revised algorithms: SQL Server 2000 & Visual C++ 6.0

Table 3 shows the experiment results. A conclusion can be drawn that the new algorithms have almost the same accuracy and recognition rate as the original ones.

Table 3. Comparison of accuracy and recognition rate.

Data set	NTrain	NAttr	Ntest	Revised algorithms		Original algorithms	
				Accuracy (%)	Recognition rate (%)	Accuracy (%)	Recognition rate (%)
CAR	1300	7	428	92.29%	100%	92.99%	100%
KPKOPT	20000	7	8056	72.38%	95.26%	73.13%	96.75%
NURSERY	11000	9	1960	98.33%	100%	97.11%	100%
TIC	800	10	158	91.77%	100%	92.04%	96.20%
LIVER	900	7	360	97.78%	100%	96.39%	100%
TITANIC	1600	4	601	79.53%	100%	78.54%	100%
LETTER	14000	17	6000	78.71%	90.27%	77.83%	91.17%
RINGNORM	5200	21	2200	64.92%	74.50%	65.06%	75.05%
Mean				84.46%	95%	84.13%	94.89%

Note: NTrain is the number of samples of each training data set. NAttr is the number of attributes of each training data set. NTest is the number of samples of each testing data set.

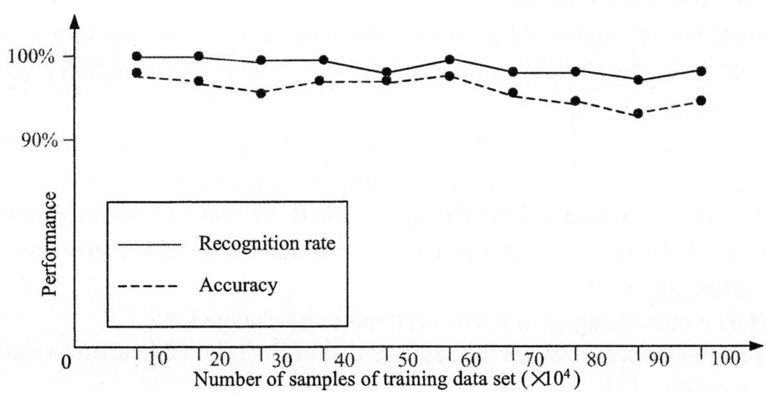

Fig. 3. Comparison of accuracy and recognition rate.

4.2 Scalability Test

In this section all huge data sets are generated using the Quest Synthetic Data Generation Code [17] provided by IBM Almaden Research Center. There are 9 condition attributes and 1 decision attribute in each data set. The number of samples of each training data set increases from 100,000 to 1,000,000. The number of samples of each testing data set is 30% of its corresponding training data set.

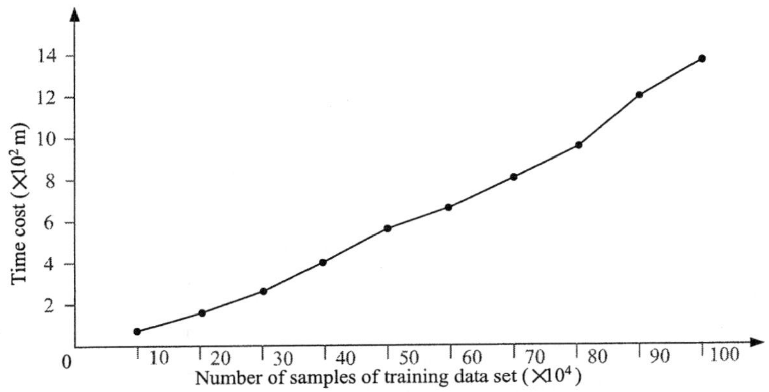

Fig. 4. Comparison of learning time.

Figure 3 shows the curve of accuracy and recognition rate. Figure 4 shows the curve of time cost in knowledge acquisition. It is noticeable that the RIDAS system using rough-set-based classical knowledge reduction algorithms could not process such large data sets. From Figure 3 and 4, we can find that our revised algorithms improve the scalability of the original algorithms without decreasing their accuracy.

5 Conclusion

Processing huge data sets effectively is always a problem in Data Mining and Machine Learning. The same problem lies also in theories based on rough set. This paper develops a structure of CDL to express the distribution of condition attribute values in the whole sample space and the positive region of the attribute set with reference to the decision attribute. A group of knowledge reduction algorithms is revised using CDL. The method of generating a CDL in multi-steps has not the restriction of memory size, so the revised algorithms can deal with huge data sets directly. Moreover, this method could be used in other rough-set-based algorithms to improve their scalability without loss of accuracy. Finding an optimal method to improve the efficiency and speed of dealing with huge data sets will be our future work.

Acknowledgements

This paper is partially supported by National Natural Science Foundation of P. R. China (No.60373111), PD Program of P. R. China, Application Science Foundation of Chongqing, and Science & Technology Research Program of the Municipal Education Committee of Chongqing of China.

References

1. Catlett, J., Megainduction: Machine Learning on Very Large Databases, PhD thesis, Basser Department of Computer Science, University of Sydney, Sydney, Australia, 1991
2. Chan, P., An Extensible Meta-learning Approach for Scalable and Accurate Inductive Learning, PhD thesis, Columbia University, New York, USA, 1996
3. Mehta, M., Agrawal, R., Rissanen, J., SLIQ: A fast scalable classifier for data mining, In: Proceedings of 5th International Conference on Extending Database Technology (EDBT), Avignon, France, pp.18-32, 1996
4. Shafer, J., Agrawal, R., Mehta, M., SPRINT: A scalable parallel classifier for data mining. In: Proceedings of 22nd International Conference on Very Large Databases (VLDB), Morgan Kaufmann, USA, pp.544-555, 1996
5. Alsabti, K., Ranka, S., Singh, V., CLOUDS: A Decision Tree Classifier for Large Datasets, In: Proceedings of the Fourth International Conference on Knowledge Discovery and Data Mining (KDD'98), New York, USA, pp.2-8, 1998
6. Joshi, M., Karypis, G., Kumar, V., ScalParC: A new scalable and efficient parallel classification algorithm for mining large datasets, In: Proceedings of the 12th International Parallel Processing Symposium (IPPS/SPDP'98), Orlando, Florida, USA, pp.573-580, 1998
7. Gehrke, J., Ramakrishnan, R., Ganti, V., RainForest: A Framework for Fast Decision Tree Constructionof Large Datasets. In: Proceedings of the 24th International Conference on Very Large Databases (VLDB), New York, USA, pp.416-427, 1998
8. Ren, L. A., He, Q., Shi, Z. Z., A Novel Classification Method in Large Data, Computer Engineering and Applications, China, 38(14), pp.58-60, 2002
9. Ren, L. A., He, Q., Shi, Z. Z., HSC Classification Method and Its Applications in Massive Data Classifying, Chinese Journal of Electronics, China, 30(12), pp.1870-1872, 2002
10. Shi, Z. Z., Knowledge Discovery, Beijing: Tsinghua University Press, China, 2002
11. Sattler, K., Dunemann, O., SQL Database Primitives for Decision Tree Classifiers, In: Proceedings of the 10th ACM CIKM International Conference on Information and Knowledge Management, Atlanta, Georgia, USA, 2001
12. Liu, H. Y., Lu, H. J., Chen, J., A Scalable Classification Algorithm Exploring Database Technology, Journal of Software, China, 13(06), pp.1075-1081, 2002
13. Wang, G. Y., Rough Set Theory and Knowledge Acquisition, Xi'an: Xi'an Jiaotong University Press, 2001
14. Wang, G. Y., Yu, H., Yang, D. C., Decision Table Reduction based on Conditional Information Entropy, Chinese J.Computes, China, 25(7), pp.759-766, 2002
15. Chang, L. Y., Wang, G. Y., Wu, Y., An Approach for Attribute Reduction and Rule Generation Based on Rough Set Theory, Journal of Software, China, 10(11), pp.1206-1211, 1999
16. Wang, G. Y., Zheng, Z., Zhang, Y., RIDAS-A Rough Set Based Intelligent Data Analysis System, In: Proceedings of 1st International Conference On Machine Learning and Cybernetics (ICMLC 2002), Beijing, China, pp. 646-649, 2002
17. IBM Almaden Research Center,Quest Synthetic Data Generation Code for Classification, Available as http://www.almaden.ibm.com/software/quest/Resources/datasets/syndata.html

Tree-Like Parallelization of Reduct and Construct Computation

Robert Susmaga

Institute of Computing Science, Poznan University of Technology
Piotrowo 3a, 60–965 Poznan, Poland
Robert.Susmaga@CS.PUT.Poznan.PL

Abstract. The paper addresses the problem of parallel computing in reduct/construct generation. The reducts are subsets of attributes that may be successfully applied in information/decision table analysis. Constructs, defined in a similar way, represent a notion that is a kind of generalization of the reduct. They ensure both discernibility between pairs of objects belonging to different classes (in which they follow the reducts) as well as similarity between pairs of objects belonging to the same class (which is not the case with reducts). Unfortunately, exhaustive sets of minimal constructs, similarly to sets of minimal reducts, are NP-hard to generate. To speed up the computations, decomposing the original task into multiple subtasks and executing these in parallel is employed. The paper presents a so-called constrained tree-like model of parallelization of this task and illustrates practical behaviour of this algorithm in a computational experiment.

1 Introduction

This paper addresses the problem of generating sets of exact reducts and constructs in information systems. The reduct is a notion that has been given much attention in numerous papers, especially within the Rough Sets community [2, 5, 8, 9, 10, 14]. The idea of reducts, constructs and attribute reduction in information tables is, in general, related to a more general problem of feature selection, which has been the focus of many papers in the area of Machine Learning [3].

From the computational point of view the most challenging problem related to reducts and constructs is that of generating full sets of exact reducts/constructs. The problem of generating reducts of minimal cardinality has been proved to be NP-hard in [8]. As a result, the reduct generating algorithms may be classified into exact (exponential) and approximate (polynomial) algorithms. The approximate algorithms are much quicker than their exact counterparts, but they generate either single solutions or small samples of solutions. Additionally, the solutions generated by them need not be exact reducts/constructs.

This paper addresses the computational aspects of reducts/construct generation, which is especially important when generating sets of all possible reducts/constructs. The main technique designed to improve the overall computing time of the reduct generating procedure is parallelization. It was first introduced in [10], where the idea

S. Tsumoto et al. (Eds.): RSCTC 2004, LNAI 3066, pp. 455–464, 2004.

and a method of decomposing a reduct generating task into a number of subtasks (a flat parallelization model) have been presented. This paper introduces a method in which the parallel computations are performed in a tree-like manner and which is therefore referred to as the tree-like parallelization model.

The actual reduct generating algorithm being parallelized is an algorithm introduced in [11]. This algorithm is a successor of a family of algorithms [9, 11, 13] based on the notion of discernibility matrix [8]. The computational experiments reported in this paper show that the presented tree-like parallelization of the algorithm is a good alternative to the older flat parallelization scheme.

2 Terminology and Definitions

The main data set considered in this paper is a *decision table*, which is a special case of an *information table* [7]. Formally, the decision table is defined as a 4-tuple $DT=\langle U,Q,V,\delta\rangle$, where:

- U is a non-empty, finite set of objects under consideration,
- Q is a non-empty, finite set of condition ($C \neq \varnothing$) and decision ($D \neq \varnothing$) attributes, such that $C \cup D = Q$ and $C \cap D = \varnothing$; here it will be further assumed that $D = \{d\}$,
- V is a non-empty, finite set of attribute values,
- δ is an information function, $\delta\colon U \times Q \rightarrow V$.

Let $IND(P) \in U \times U$ denote an *indiscernibility relation*, defined for a non-empty set of attributes $P \subseteq Q$ as:

$$IND(P) = \{(x,y) \in U \times U\colon \forall_{q \in P}\ \delta(x,q) = \delta(y,q)\}.$$

If a pair of objects belongs to $IND(P)$ then these two objects are indiscernible from each other (cannot be distinguished) on all attributes from the set P. The relation $IND(P)$ is reflexive, symmetric and transitive (it is an equivalence relation).

By $DIS(P) \in U \times U$, the *discernibility relation*, we shall denote the opposite relation, defined as:

$$DIS(P) = \{(x,y) \in U \times U\colon (x,y) \notin IND(P)\}.$$

If a pair of objects belongs to $DIS(P)$ then these two objects differ on at least one attribute from the set P. The relation $DIS(P)$ is not reflexive and not transitive, but it is symmetric.

Finally, let $SIM(P) \in U \times U$ denote a *similarity relation*, defined for a set of attributes $P \subseteq Q$ as:

$$SIM(P) = \{(x,y) \in U \times U\colon \exists_{q \in P}\ \delta(x,q)=\delta(y,q)\}.$$

If a pair of objects belongs to $SIM(P)$ then these two objects are indiscernible on at least one attribute from the set P. In other words $(x,y) \in SIM(P)$ when $\exists_{\varnothing \neq P' \subseteq P}\ (x,y) \in IND(P')$. The relation $SIM(P)$ is reflexive and symmetric, but it is not transitive (it is a tolerance relation).

Given a $P \subseteq Q$, the relation $IND(P)$ induces a partition of objects from U into disjoint subsets. In particular, $IND(\{d\})$ partitions the objects into subsets referred to as classes. Thus if $(x,y) \in IND(\{d\})$ then the objects x and y are said to belong to the same class; otherwise they are said to belong to different classes.

According to its classic definition, the idea of a *relative reduct* is its ability to distinguish objects belonging to different classes. A relative reduct R ($R \subseteq C$) is a subset of attributes satisfying:

$$\forall_{p \in U \times U} \{[p \in DIS(D) \wedge p \in DIS(C)] \rightarrow p \in DIS(R)\} \quad (1)$$

$$\forall_{q \in R} \exists_{p \in U \times U} \{p \in DIS(D) \wedge p \in DIS(R) \wedge p \notin DIS(R - \{q\})\} \quad (2)$$

Formula (1) ensures that the reduct has not lower ability to distinguish objects belonging to different classes than the whole set of attributes (this feature may be referred to as *consistency*). Formula (2) requires that the reduct is minimal with regard to inclusion, i. e. it does not contain redundant attributes or, in other words, it does not include other reducts (further referred to as *minimality*). Since subsets that simply distinguish objects can have poor properties this definition can be augmented to require both discernibility and similarity between objects from different classes as well as similarity between objects from the same class.

A subset of condition attributes R ($R \subseteq C$) is a *construct* iff:

$$\forall_{p \in U \times U} \{[p \in DIS(D) \wedge p \in DIS(C)] \Rightarrow p \in DIS(R)\} \quad (3)$$

$$\forall_{p \in U \times U} \{[p \in SIM(D) \wedge p \in SIM(C)] \Rightarrow p \in SIM(R)\} \quad (4)$$

$$\forall_{q \in R} \begin{cases} \exists_{p \in U \times U} \{p \in DIS(D) \wedge p \in DIS(R) \wedge p \notin DIS(R - \{q\})\} \\ \quad or \\ \exists_{p \in U \times U} \{p \in SIM(D) \wedge p \in SIM(R) \wedge p \notin SIM(R - \{q\})\} \end{cases} \quad (5)$$

So, a construct is a subset of attributes that retains the discernibility of objects belonging to different classes as well as the similarity of objects belonging to the same class (formulae (3) and (4)). Alike reduct, the construct R is minimal (formula (5)), so removing its attribute would invalidate any (or both) of the conditions (3) and (4).

3 The Constrained Tree-Like Parallelization Model

Owing to the inescapable resemblance between constructs and reducts, the constructs can be generated using a straightforward modification of the algorithm for generating reducts (the Fast Reduct Generating Algorithm, FRGA, [11]).

This algorithm naturally decomposes into two phases: (I) generating, absorbing and sorting the pairwise-comparison list (PCL), and (II) searching for the minimal subsets (reducts or constructs). When generating reducts PCL is created to contain all subsets of condition attributes that provide discernibility between objects belonging to different classes. Finding a subset of attributes that has a non-empty intersection with each element of this list ensures that this subset will distinguish all objects belonging to different classes. If such a subset is minimal (with regard to inclusion) then it constitutes a reduct. So, the process of searching for all reducts resolves itself to generating all minimal (wrt inclusion) subsets of condition attributes that have common parts with all elements of PCL. In case of constructs the only difference is that PCL should contain both subsets of attributes that provide discernibility between objects belonging to other classes and subsets of attributes that provide similarity between objects belonging to the same class.

Formally, to generate reducts the elements of PCL should be defined as follows:

$$C_{ij} := \{q \in C : \delta(x,q) \neq \delta(y,q)\} \text{ for all } (x,y) \notin IND(\{d\}) \tag{6}$$

while to generate constructs – as follows:

$$C_{ij} := \begin{cases} \{q \in C : \delta(x,q) \neq \delta(y,q) \ \ if\ (x,y) \notin IND(\{d\}) \\ \{q \in C : \delta(x,q) = \delta(y,q) \ \ if\ (x,y) \in IND(\{d\}) \end{cases} \text{ for all } (x,y) \in U \times U. \tag{7}$$

It is important to stress that whether the algorithm is used for generating reducts or constructs does not influence its main computational 'mechanisms' (phase II). In particular it has no influence whatsoever on the parallelization issues.

The algorithm is presented in Fig. 1. This figure illustrates in particular the main iteration of phase II, which processes one PCL element at a time. All minimal subsets of attributes found in each iteration are accumulated in the set Red_i, which becomes the set of reducts/constructs after completing the last iteration. Because the elements of Red_i have no influence on one another, after each iteration the set can be partitioned into subsets that can be processed in parallel [1] by independent subtasks.

The presented constrained tree-like parallelization model is basically controlled by three parameters:

- Branching Factor (*BF*), specifying the computational load of a given computing task, which (when reached) allows the task to be split into new subtasks,
- Subtask Count (*SC*), controlling the number of subtasks to be created at split-time,
- Maximum Subtasks (*MS*), the constraint on the total number of tasks allowed.

The constrained model is a development of the previous, unconstrained, tree-like model [12], which implemented no control on the total number of tasks allowed and which, in turn, is a development of the flat model [29].

In the flat model there was only one split of the initial task into a predefined number of subtasks. The model was controlled by two parameters: *BF* and *SC*. As soon as the cardinality of Red_i exceeded *BF* the initial task was split into *SC* subtasks, and these continued their computation in parallel. This ensured full control over the total number of subtasks, but was hardly effective, since the proper value of *SC* was hard to assess. Additionally, the particular subtasks usually turned out unbalanced, which

Input: A set of objects U ($|U|=N$). ***Output:*** The set K of all reducts/constructs.
Params: Branching Factor (BF), Subtask Count (SC), Maximum Subtasks (MS).

PHASE I – creation of the Sorted Absorbed PCL ($SAPCL$)

Step 1
Create the absorbed comparison list $APCL$ by eliminating non-minimal elements:

$APCL:=\{C_{ij}: C_{ij}\neq\varnothing$ and for no $C_{kl}\in APCL: C_{kl}\subset C_{ij}\}$,
where C_{ij} is defined according to formula (6) or (7).

The resulting absorbed discernibility list contains elements $(C_1, C_2, \ldots, C_d)$,
where $d\in[1, N(N-1)/2]$. Usually $d<<N(N-1)/2$.

Step 2
Sort the $APCL$ in ascending order of the cardinality of its elements (to create $SAPCL$).

PHASE II Search for reducts/constructs.

Step 1
$Red_0:=\{\varnothing\}$.

Step 2
$K:=$ *Cons-RecursiveSearch* (1, R_0, MS)

Procedure *Cons-RecursiveSearch* (*InitialIdx*, *PreviousSolution*, *Branches*)

Step 1
$Red_{\text{InitialIdx-1}}:=PreviousSolution$.

Step 2
For $i:=InitialIdx..d$ do:

$S_i:=\{R\in Red_{i-1} : R\cap C_i\neq\varnothing\}$.

$$T_i:=\bigcup_{q\in Ci}\ \bigcup_{R\in Ri-1:R\cap Ci\neq\varnothing}\{R\cup\{q\}\}$$

$MIN_i:=\{R\in T_i: Minimial(R)=true\}$.
$Red_i:=S_i\cup MIN_i$.
If ($|Red_i|\geq BF$) and ($Branches>1$) and ($i<d$) then
  $N:=\min\{Branches, SC\}$
  Divide the value of *Branches* into values $B^1, B^2, \ldots, B^N$ such that:
  - $B^1+B^2+\ldots+B^N=Branches$.
  - $|B^m-B^n|\leq 1$, for each $m\neq n$, $m,n\in[1,\ldots,N]$,

  Partition the set Red_i into subsets $Red_i^1, Red_i^2, \ldots, Red_i^N$, such that:
  - $Red_i^1\cup Red_i^2\cup\ldots\cup Red_i^N=Red_i$,
  - $Red_i^m\cap Red_i^n=\varnothing$, for each $m\neq n$, $m,n\in[1,\ldots,N]$,
  - $|Red_i^j|$ is as close to B^j as possible.

  For $j=1..N$ do:
    $K^j:=Cons\text{-}RecursiveSearch\ (\ i+1, Red_i^j, B^j\ )$
  EndFor
  Return $K^1\cup\ldots\cup K^2\cup K^N$ as the result of the procedure
EndIf
EndFor

Fig. 1. The constrained tree-like parallelization of reduct/construct generating algorithm.

means that some of them finished relatively early (as they produced only few reducts/constructs) while others finished very late (since they had to generate very many reducts/constructs). This differentiated considerably the computing times of the subtasks and decreased the benefits of parallelization.

The problem of unbalance could relatively easily be solved by introducing a hierarchical (or tree-like) splitting scheme. In such (unconstrained) model every (and not only the initial) subtask can be split after the cardinality of its Red_i exceeds BF. Such a multiple-splitting scheme balances the loads of the subtasks, but may lead to uncontrolled proliferation of subtasks. Thus the flat parallelization model restrains the total number of subtasks while the unconstrained tree-like parallelization model properly balances these subtasks.

The constrained tree-like parallelization model is an attempt to control both the total number of subtasks as well as the balance between these subtasks. It retains the tree-like splitting scheme, but limits the total number of splits and tries to keep the subtasks well-balanced at the same time.

4 Experimental Evaluation of the Constrained Algorithm

The following subsections present the computational experiments with two data sets: 'Election' [6]) and 'Forestry' [4]. They are shortly characterized in Table 1. The table contains also the number of generated reducts and constructs as well as the computing times T_0 in case of both 'Election' and 'Forestry' (sequential approach). The parallel computing times will be then denoted as T_i, for i=1, 2, ...

Table 1. Basic characteristics of the data sets used in the experiments.

Data Set	*Election*	*Forestry*
# Cond. Attr.	26	37
# Objects	444	63
# Classes	2	5
# Reducts	355971	90045
# Constructs	0	324076
Reduct computing time	2.09E+02 s	1.88E+00 s
Construct computing time	1.00E–03 s	1.16E+01 s

Two indices will be basically used when presenting the computational characteristics of the different parallelization models:

- nominal speed-up, defined as $nS=T_0/(max\ T_i)$,
- per-processor speed-up, defined as $ppS=nS/P$, where P is the number of processors engaged in the task (equal to the number of subtasks started).

The experiments were carried out in batches in which different values of the parameters were applied and examined. The results are, however, only presented for the most prominent combinations of parameter values, usually for SC=5, 10 (or MS=5, 10) and for BF=1000, 10000 and 100000.

Table 2 shows the nominal speed-ups computed for a batch of parallel experiments in which reducts were generated for 'Election' and constructs for 'Forestry' with *SC*=5, 10 and *BF*=1000, 10000 and 100000.

Table 2. Nominal speed-ups *nS* in flat parallelization model.

	Election (reducts)		*Forestry (constructs)*	
	SC=5	*SC*=10	*SC*=5	*SC*=10
BF=1000	2.6	4.7	2.9	5.8
BF=10000	3.3	7.6	2.8	5.7
BF=100000	3.1	6.1	2.2	3.3

Generally, the nominal speed-ups improve with growing *BF*, although disproportionately large values of *BF* will decrease the speed-up for obvious reasons (excessively delayed start of the parallel subtasks). This is also clearly the case of 'Election'. Increasing *BF* delays the moment of partitioning Red_i and thus provides the resulting subtasks with more numerous parts of Red_i (in the case of 'Forestry' this is not at all evident – the data set proved a much poorer illustrator of speed-up development in this experiment). In result the subtasks tend to be more balanced, which has a great positive influence on the nominal speed-up.

Obviously, the increase of the nominal speed-up will always turn into a decrease for excessively large *BF* values (as is the case for *BF*=100000 in Table 2). Because the number of reducts/constructs to be generated for these two particular data sets is about 320000÷350000, then *BF*=100000 allows the parallel subtasks to be initiated and started only after the cardinality of Red_i (see Fig. 1) reaches 100000, which is rather late. And strongly delayed initiation of parallel subtasks, regardless of their balance or imbalance level, cannot lead to good speed-ups.

Table 3. Per-processor speed-ups *ppS* in flat parallelization model.

	Election (reducts)		*Forestry (constructs)*	
	SC=5	*SC*=10	*SC*=5	*SC*=10
BF=1000	0.52	0.47	0.58	0.58
BF=10000	0.66	0.76	0.56	0.57
BF=100000	0.62	0.61	0.22	0.33

The corresponding per-processor speed-ups achieved in this experiment are presented in Table 3. In the flat parallelization model *ppS=nS/SC*.

Table 4 presents the speed-ups achieved for a batch of computations in the unconstrained tree-like parallelization model. Notice that Table 4 specifies no *SC* column, since *SC* was equal 2 in all the unconstrained experiments. This is because in the tree-like model this parameter has an interpretation that is different from that in the flat model. In the flat model the split of the single initial task into *SC* subtasks takes place only once, so the parameter *SC* simultaneously determines the final number of subtasks (and thus the number of processors engaged). In case of the tree-like model the split can occur many times, so the total number of subtasks initiated is hard to assess in advance.

Table 4. Nominal speed-ups *nS* in unconstrained tree-like parallelization.

	Election (reducts)	*Forestry (constructs)*
BF=1000	611.3	191.3
BF=10000	63.1	20.8
BF=100000	3.7	2.1

The general remark regarding the unconstrained tree-like computations is that it can achieve very high speed-ups indeed. This is, however, achieved at the cost of engaging very many (potentially too many) processors to the job.

The corresponding per-processor speed-ups are presented in Table 5.

Table 5. Per-processor speed-ups *ppS* in unconstrained tree-like parallelization.

	Election (reducts)	*Forestry (constructs)*
BF=1000	0.94	0.35
BF=10000	0.99	0.39
BF=100000	0.93	0.53

Also here the results for 'Election' proved much clearer than those for 'Forestry'. This may be because 'Forestry' turns out to be computationally much less demanding than 'Election' (see Table 1, which shows the sequential computing times for these sets). Despite similar numbers of results generated (355971 for 'Election' and 324076 for 'Forestry') the computing times differ considerably (209 s and 11.6 s, respectively).

The nominal speed-ups for the constrained tree-like model are presented in Table 6.

Table 6. Nominal speed-ups *nS* in constrained tree-like parallelization.

	Election (reducts)		*Forestry (constructs)*	
	MS=5	*MS*=10	*MS*=5	*MS*=10
BF=1000	4.2	11.5	3.7	7.8
BF=10000	5.3	12.2	4.1	8.6
BF=100000	4.7	4.2	2.2	2.0

The average *nS* of the constrained model is unfortunately smaller than that of the unconstrained model, but this is hardly avoidable in situations where the number of processors to be engaged in the computing task is limited (and this is the case with the constrained tree-like model).

Table 7. Per-processor speed-ups *ppS* in constrained tree-like parallelization.

	Election (reducts)		*Forestry (constructs)*	
	MS=5	*MS*=10	*MS*=5	*MS*=10
BF=1000	0.84	1.15	0.75	0.78
BF=10000	1.06	1.22	0.81	0.86
BF=100000	0.93	0.71	0.44	0.51

The per-processor speed-ups of the constrained model are presented in Table 7.

As it can be observed, for *BF*=1000, 10000 the *ppS* is simply equal to *nS*/*MS*, which is the direct result of the fact that the maximum number of processors was actually employed in the computations. This is not the case, however, for *BF*=100000 (at *MS*=10), where fewer processors were actually engaged (6 for 'Election' and 4 for 'Forestry'). Therefore the actual values of *ppS* are higher than *nS*/*MS*.

It should be also clear that the constrained tree-like model would have been proved even better if less computationally demanding tasks had been reported here. Example of such task is the computation of constructs for 'Election'. Because the number of resulting constructs is 0, the computation is best done with one processor (no subdivisions of the initial task is required). This would be promptly 'discovered' by the tree-like model, which (because of the small workload of the initial task) would never subdivide this task and finally engage only one processor. The flat model, however, would split into its usual number of subtasks, thus unnecessarily engaging a bigger number of processors.

5 Conclusions

The main purpose of the research reported in this paper has been the introduction and practical evaluation of a constrained tree-like parallel algorithm for reduct/construct generation. The main objective of parallelization is the utilization of spare computing power (in the form of multiple processors) to speed-up the computations.

The results of experiments confirm the high utility of the constrained parallelization. First of all, the parallel approach to reduct/construct generation adequately matches the computing power of the algorithm to the specific needs of the given data set. Additionally, the flat parallelization model ensures control over the total number of processors engaged in the computation while the hierarchical split of tasks into subtasks in the tree-like models helps balancing the computational load of different subtasks. In result, the constrained tree-like approach turns out to be a good merger of both solutions.

Acknowledgements

Substantial parts of the presented experiments were conducted at the Supercomputing and Networking Centre of Pozna , Poland. The paper has been supported by the Polish State Committee for Scientific Research, research grant no. 4T11F–002–22.

References

1. Akl S. G.: *The Design and Analysis of Parallel Algorithms*, Prentice Hall International, Inc, Eaglewood Cliffs, New Jersey (1989).
2. Bazan J., Skowron A., Synak P.: 'Dynamic Reducts as a Tool for Extracting Laws from Decision Tables', In: *Methodologies for Intelligent Systems. Proceedings of the 8th International Symposium ISMIS'94*, Charlotte, NG, *LNAI* Vol. 869, Springer-Verlag (1994), 346–355.
3. Dash M., Liu H.: 'Feature Selection for Classification', *Intelligent Data Analysis* (on-line journal), **1** no. 3 (1997), http://www-east.elsevier.com/ida.
4. M. Flinkman, W. Michalowski, S. Nilsson, R. Słowiński, R. Susmaga, S. Wilk , 'Use of rough sets analysis to classify Siberian forest ecosystem according to net primary production of phytomass', *INFOR*, **38** (3) 2000, 145–161.
5. Kohavi R., Frasca B.: 'Useful Feature Subsets and Rough Set Reducts', In: *Proceedings of the Third International Workshop on Rough Sets and Soft Computing*, San Jose State University, San Jose, California (1994).
6. Murphy P.M., Aha D.W.: 'UCI Repository of Machine Learning Databases', University of California, Department of Information and Computer Science, Irvine, CA (1992), WWW page: http://www.ics.uci.edu/~mlearn, e-mail: ml-repository@ics.uci.edu.
7. Pawlak Z. *Rough Sets. Theoretical Aspects of Reasoning About Data*, Kluwer Academic Publishers, Dordrecht, (1991).
8. Skowron A., Rauszer C.: 'The Discernibility Functions Matrices and Functions in Information Systems', In: Slowinski R., (ed.), *Intelligent Decision Support. Handbook of Applications and Advances of the Rough Set Theory*, Kluwer Academic Publishers, Dordrecht (1992), 331–362.
9. Susmaga R.: 'Experiments in Incremental Computation of Reducts', In: Skowron A., Polkowski L., (eds), *Rough Sets in Data Mining and Knowledge Discovery*, Springer-Verlag, Berlin (1998).
10. Susmaga R.: 'Parallel Computation of Reducts', In: Polkowski L., Skowron A., (eds), *Proceedings of the First International Conference on Rough Sets and Current Trends in Computing*, Warsaw 1998, Springer-Verlag, Berlin (1998), 450–457.
11. Susmaga R.: 'Effective Tests for Inclusion Minimality in Reduct Generation', *Foundations of Computing and Decision Sciences*, **23** (4) (1998), 219–240.
12. R. Susmaga, 'Tree-Like Parallelization of Reduct and Construct Computation', *Research Report RA-009/03*, Poznań University of Technology, Poznań, 2003.
13. Tannhäuser M.: *Efficient Reduct Computation* (in Polish), M. Sc. Thesis, Institute of Mathematics, Warsaw University, Warsaw (1994).
14. Wroblewski J.: 'Covering with Reducts – A Fast Algorithm for Rule Generation', In: Polkowski L., Skowron A., (eds), *Proceedings of the First International Conference on Rough Sets and Current Trends in Computing*, Warsaw 1998, Springer-Verlag, Berlin (1998), 402–407.

Heuristically Fast Finding of the Shortest Reducts

Tsau Young Lin and Ping Yin

Department of Computer Science
San Jose State University, San Jose, California 95192
tylin@cs.sjsu.edu

Abstract. It is well known that finding the shortest reduct is NP hard. In this paper, we present an heuristic fast way of finding shortest relative reducts by exploring the specific nature of the input data. As a byproduct, we can show that the shortest relative reducts can be found in polynomial time, *provided that we do know apriori that the lengths of the shortest reducts is bounded by a constant*, that is, independent of the column size n. It should be noted that there are heuristic factors in the algorithm ("speeds" are not guaranteed) but the results, namely, the founded shortest reducts, are the precise answers.

Keywords: Data mining, rough set, reduct, granular computing, bitmap.

1 Introduction

In this paper, we re-visit one of the key notions in rough set theory - relative reduct of a decision table. Mathematically, a decision table is a classical relation instance, in which attributes are divided into to two classes, conditional and decision attributes. A tuple, (c1, c2, . . .d1,d2, . . .) is interpreted as an if-then-rule: If "a patience has symptoms," (c1, c2, . . .), then "he has infected with diseases," (d1, d2, . . .).

A reduct is, then, a minimal set of "simplest" rules that is extracted from a given decision table in such a way that the minimal set still maintains the original decision power; here "simplest" means the minimal rule length. However, to find the best reduct (the shortest one) is an NP hard problem [11]. It is an extension version (vs intension) of the more familiar NP hard problem, the candidate key problem in relational databases [12].

As many data analysis problems are NP-hard, so we need to have some strategies to handle this type of problems. We believe, one of the "correct" strategies is to exploit the nice-ness of the input data, so even a general NP-hard problem can be convergent swiftly on some non-worst cases. This paper is one of such efforts.

The theory developed here is based on the machine oriented modeling [3], that formalizes the bitmap indexes, a common notion in databases [1].

S. Tsumoto et al. (Eds.): RSCTC 2004, LNAI 3066, pp. 465–470, 2004.

2 Main Ideas

Even though finding reduct is NP-hard, for small tables the issue is not serious. If a database has more than 100 attributes (the number of subtables is one less 2^100 = power 10 of thousands) and over million records, it's impossible, within a reasonable time, to find the best reducts using the traditional algorithms. However, if, first, we can heuristically find a very short set, let's say, a set of length 5 for the given database, then to find the best one, we only need to check all combinations of 5 attributes. This paper is an extended abstract of [8].

The main strategy consists of two sub-tasks: the first one is to find a short condition attributes set heuristically, which gives an upper bound on the total problem; the second one is to find the best reduct based on such a bound.

A Subproblem – A Heuristic Shortest Reduct. We propose an algorithm that finds a heuristic "best" reduct. The idea is derived from such an intuitive observation: the more distinct values does an attribute has the more likely this attribute will determine the others [8]. Formally, we have the following:

Proposition. A lower cardinality attribute cannot functionally determine a higher cardinality attributes. :

The proof follows immediate from observing that an extensional functional dependence is a single valued function, that is, it assigns the distinct values of an attribute, say A, onto another one, say B. So several values of A are mapped onto a single value of B, that is, the cardinality of A is greater than or equal to that of B. So if we sort the attributes by their cardinality, and collect one attribute at time, we can reach the reduct very "quickly."

The Main Problem – Best Reducts. Let K denote the given relational table, S the "heuristic shortest" reduct found above (Section 4), and B one of the best reducts (the "real" shortest reducts).

First, we observe that the size $|B|$ of the best reducts (could be more than one shortest reduct) is less than or equal to the size $|S|$ of heuristic shortest, where $|\bullet|$ denotes the number of attributes in $\bullet$. So in the main algorithm, we may consider the reduct problem of each sub-table; each is NP-hard on its small degree $s = |S|$. We have two cases:

Case I: $|S| = |K|$: In this case, the heuristic reduct is the original table; this is an worst case.

Case II: $s = |S|$ is "substantially small"(or if we do know $|S|$ of each input data is independent of $|K|$, e.g., it only depends on the row numbers): then the best reduct is reduced to find the shortest reducts of all the sub-tables. In this case, each sub-problem is bounded by a small *constant* or independent of $|K|$). Then the real cost is on the enumerating all sub-tables; there are $\{^k_s\}$ many sub-tables. So to find the best reduct we only needs a polynomial time (of degree $\{^k_s\}$)$\times$ (*a constant*); note if $s = 0.5k$, it is not "substantially small," in fact, a worst case.

3 Finding the Best Reducts Based on Heuristic Results

In this part, we will find the best reduct of condition attributes based on the heuristic results in Section 4.

1. Sharpen the result: Using any "standard" method, we find the shortest reduct from *HeuristicReduct* that is founded in Section 4. It is a "very small" NP-hard problem; its cost is small and does not cause worry. We denote the shorest reduct by *BestHeuristicReduct*. For simplicity, we write $S = BestHeuristicReduct$.
2. Check all possible $s = |S|$-subtables of the whole database. There are $\{^k_s\}$ combinations. Here a s-subtable means a sub-table whose conditional attributes have size s. In other words, it is a decision table with conditional attribute of size s plus the decision attributes of original table.

Remark 1: The *usual method* in the Section 3, Item 1)is referring, e.g., the one in [7]. There are few small things worth noting: in usual method, we remove systematically the redundant attributes. Note that while we are so doing, we observe that we only need to consider the case in which the number of columns is lying inclusively between two and the size of *HeuristicReduct*; this is because we have already checked each single attribute within the set. This observation could be a small saving.

Continue with the Example given below (Section 4.1, Table 1), the condition attribute set we got is $\{A_1, A_2, A_3\}$. So, by the remark above, we only need to check the cases whose size satisfies, $2 \leq \ size \ < 3$. By checking $\{A_1, A_2\}$, $\{A_1, A_3\}$ and $\{A_2, A_3\}$, we found that the set $\{A_1, A_2, A_3\}$ can be shrank to $\{A_1, A_2\}$, which is the S.

To check all possible s-subtables, first we note that s likely is very small, and by chances, S could be the best reduct of the whole database.

Remark 2: we would like to add that in check each small subtables, we observed that if it has the size less than the size of decision attribute, it can not be a reduct (by the proposition).

From Remark 2, we only need to check the combination of one, that are A_4 and A_5. But A_4 and A_5 both have size less than decision attribute. Hence, the final answer, the best reduct is $\{A_1, A_2\}$.

This completes the example.

4 Heuristic Shortest Reduct

This section is based on the heuristic idea that we have explained above. In other words, higher cardinality attributes are most likely to be an indispensable attribute. So we can inductively increase the candidate set according to the cardinality of an attribute. By this approach, even though we may not get the best one, hopefully, a very good approximation.

Table 1. Original table for finding condition attributes

Patient	A_1	A_2	A_3	A_4	A_5	A_6
R_1	1	1	2	1	2	2
R_2	1	2	3	1	3	3
R_3	2	3	1	2	3	3
R_4	2	2	3	2	3	4
R_5	3	4	4	2	2	4
R_6	3	5	4	2	2	2
# of distinct values	3	5	4	2	2	3

4.1 An Example

The idea will be illustrated by the following Table 1, where attribute A_6 is the decision attribute.

- First, attribute A_2 is selected into the candidate set. Since A_2 has largest cardinality. But A_2 cannot determine A_6 since R_2 and R_4 are inconsistent.
- So A_3, which has 4 values, is added . A_3, by itself cannot decideA_6 since R_2 and R_4 are inconsistent. Combine A_2 and A_3 together, they still cannot decide A_6 since R_2 and R_4 remain inconsistent.
- Third, the next largest value set A_1, which has 3 values, is added. Though A_1 by itself cannot decide A_6, but combined attributes set does.

So, write $HeuristicReduct = \{A_2, A_3, A_1\}$, which is the "shortest" condition attribute set we found for now; we sharpen the result in Section 3.

5 Some Technical Notes on Granular Data Model

First, we refer the readers to [2] in this volume for the notion of granular data model(GDM).

5.1 Bitmaps

For large databases, proper management between the access to secondary storage and main memory is the essence. We note that bit based GDM.

1. greatly minimize the storage of database (of certain type).
2. greatly speed up the data processing time: In traditional operations, such as search, there may involve many string operations, which are slow. But for bitmaps, we use Boolean operation, which is much faster [3].
3. greatly increase the parallelism: Each bitmap can be divided into section and each section of bit data can be evaluated in parallel.

Our approach works well for Low Cardinality Attributes. If a database has many attributes that have high cardinality, then some kinds of compressions or list representations are needed see [1]. For data mining, we usually are interested in Low Cardinality Attributes; so this is good approach.

6 Conclusions

To avoid distraction, we did not explain many fundamental notions, such as data mining, granular computing, rough sets, computation theory, and many programming issues in experiments; we refer them to [4],[7],[5],[10],[9],[3],[6],[1]. The experiment shows that granular computing (bit manipulations) seems a powerful notion for database processing, especially in decision support systems [8]. Its bitmap representation is an effective way of storing and manipulation of very large dataset. It greatly reduces the time for communicating between memory and secondary storage, and maximizes the parallelism. Of course, there are limitations; it may need some additional techniques (e.g., compressions) when the distinct values is high [1]. However, for data mining, we often are not interested on this type of attributes. There are very little patterns when most of attribute values are distinct.

This paper may be considered as a new approach to NP types problems: Instead of dwelling on the worst cases, we explore the non-worst cases from their data structures. Due to the special nature of reduct, we use the cardinality of distinct values to "guess" a good short reduct quickly; this is the "NP" part. From this information, we can find the shortest reduct in polynomial time, provided the "guess" returned a good result.

References

1. Hector Garcia-Molina, Jeffrey D. Ullman. Jennifer Widom, Database Systems-The Complete Book, Prentice Hall, 2002
2. T. Y. Lin "Mining Un-interpreted Generalized Association Rules by Linear Inequalities: Deductive data mining approach," In: the proceedings of RSCTC 2004, June 1-5, Uppsala, Sweden, to appear.
3. T. Y. Lin, "Data Mining and Machine Oriented Modeling: A Granular Computing Approach," Journal of Applied Intelligence, Kluwer, Vol 13, No 2, 2000, 113-124.
4. T. Y. Lin, N Cercone, Rough Set And Data Mining, Analysis for Imprecise Data, Kluwer Academic Publisher,1997, 2nd print, 2000
5. T. Y. Lin and H. Cao, "Searching Decision Rules in Very Large Databases using Rough Set Theory." In : Rough sets and Current Trends in Computing, Ziarko & Yao (eds) Lecture Notes on Artificial Intelligence, 2000, 346-353, Also see, Hui Cao, Fast Data Mining Algorithms Using Rough Sets Theory, Thesis, San Jose State University , California, August 2000
6. T.Y. Lin. "An Overview of Rough Set Theory from the Point of View of Relational Databases," Bulletin of International Rough Set Society, Vol I, No1, March , 1997, 30-34.
7. Z. Pawlak, Rough sets. Theoretical Aspects of Reasoning about Data, Kluwer Academic Publishers, 1991
8. Ping Yin, " Data Mining on Rough Set Theory Using Bit Strings, Thesis, San Jose State University.
9. James L. Johnson, Database, Model, Languages, Design, Oxford University Press, 1997

10. H. Sever and V. V. Raghavan and T. D. Johnsten, "The Status of Research on Rough Sets for Knowledge Discovery in Databases," ICNPAA-98: Second Int'l Conf. On Nonlinear Problems in Aviation and Aerospace, 29 April - 1 May 1998, Daytona Beach, FL (http://cuadra.nwrc.gov/pubs/srj98.pdf)
11. A. Skowron abd C. Rauszer, "The discernibility matrices and functions in information systems," in: Decision Support by Experience - Application of the Rough Sets Theory, R. Slowinski (ed.), Kluwer Academic Publishers, 1992,331-362
12. D. Ullman, Database and Knowledge - Base Systems, Volume 1: Classical Database Systems, Computer Science Press, 1988

Study on Reduct and Core Computation in Incompatible Information Systems*

Tian-rui Li, Ke-yun Qing, Ning Yang, and Yang Xu

Department of Mathematics, School of Science,
Southwest Jiaotong University, Chengdu, Sichuan 610031, P.R. China
trli@swjtu.edu.cn

Abstract. Reduct and core computation is one of the key problems in rough set theory due to its applications in data mining extensively. Much attention presently has paid to it in compatible information system. However, in practice, many information systems are incompatible because of noise or incomplete data. In this paper, reduct and core computation for incompatible information systems is studied based on the algebraic view. A new method to construct discernibility matrix is proposed, which is a generalization of the methods presented by Hu(1995), Ye(2002) and Qing(2003). Moreover, the results are suitable for compatible information systems.

1 Introduction

The rough set theory, proposed by Pawlak in the early 1980s [1], can serve as a new mathematical tool to deal with vagueness and uncertainty. Since its introduction, this theory has generated a great deal of interest among researchers in many areas.

Reduct and core computation is one of the hot research topics of rough set due to their applications in data mining extensively [2,8,12,15]. Much study on this area had been reported and many useful results were obtained until now [3–7,9–16]. However, most work was based on compatible information systems. In practice, many information systems are incompatible because of noise or incomplete data. In order to obtain the succinct decision rules from them by using rough set method, knowledge reductions are needed. In [5], the problem of calculating the core attributes of a decision table is studied. Several errors and limitations in [12] are analyzed. Definitions of core attributes in the algebraic and information views are studied and the difference between these two views is discovered.

In addition, some other work investigated the above problem in different ways [14,15]. For example, in [14], a new concept of knowledge reduction, maximum distribution reduction, in inconsistent information systems was introduced.

* This work was partially supported by the National Natural Science Foundation of China (NSFC) under the grant No.60074014 and the Basic Science Foundation of Southwest Jiaotong University.

S. Tsumoto et al. (Eds.): RSCTC 2004, LNAI 3066, pp. 471–476, 2004.

It could eliminate the harsh requirements of the distribution reduction and overcome the drawback of the possible reduction that the derived decision rules may be in incompatible with the ones derived from the original system.

However, from the viewpoint of data mining, incompatible decision rules may be more interesting than compatible rules. Moreover, reducts of information systems in the algebraic and information views are different [5]. In this paper, reduct and core computation for incompatible information systems is studied based on the algebraic view. The original reduct concept can still be used without losing those incompatible decision rules which maybe be more useful in real applications. A new condition $T(x, y)$, a generalization of the method in [12, 13, 16], is proposed and then new discernibility matrix, which can be used to obtain decision rules, is constructed based on it. Only $T(x, y)$ is computed and positive regions do not need to be computed in the process of constructing discernibility matrix.

2 Preliminaries

This section recalls necessary rough set concepts used in the paper. Detail description of the theory can be found in [1-3].

Definition 1. *An information system is an ordered quadruple $S = (U, AT \cup D, V, f)$, where U is a non-empty finite set of objects, $AT \cup D$ is a non-empty finite set of attributes, AT denotes the set of condition attributes and D denotes the set of decision attributes, $AT \cap D = \phi$. V is the union of attribute domains, $f : U \times (AT \cup D) \to V$ is an information function which associates an unique value of each attribute with every object belonging to U. Let a is an attribute in A, x_i is an object in U, then $f(x_i, a)$ denotes the value of object x_i in attribute a.*

For an information system $S = (U, AT \cup D, V, f)$ and $A \subseteq AT$ derives an equivalence relation (indiscernibility relation), $ind(A)$, on U as $(x, y) \in ind(A)$ means for every $a \in A$, $f(x, a) = f(y, a)$. For every x of U, the equivalence class of x in relation $ind(A)$ is represented as $[x]_A$. Let ${}^U/_A$ represents the set of all this equivalence classes. Denote $\alpha(x, y) = \{a \,|a \in AT, (x, y) \notin ind(a)\}$.

Definition 2. *Let $A \subseteq AT, X \subseteq U$, the lower and upper approximations with respect to $ind(A)$ are defined as $\underline{A}(X) = \{x \in U \,|[x]_A \subseteq X\}$, $\overline{A}(X) = \{x \in U \,|[x]_A \cap X \neq \phi\}$, respectively.*

Definition 3. *Let $A \subseteq AT$, a positive region A in D, $pos_A(D)$, is defined as $pos_A(D) = \bigcup_{X \in {}^U/_D} \underline{A}(X)$.*

Definition 4. *For $A \subseteq AT$, $a \in A$, a is superfluous in A with respect to D if $pos_A(D) = pos_{A-\{a\}}(D)$; otherwise a is indispensable in A with respect to D. If every $a \in A$ is indispensable in A with respect to D, then A is orthogonal with respect to D.*

Definition 5. *$A \subseteq AT$ is defined as D-reduct of AT if $pos_A(D) = pos_{AT}(D)$ and A is orthogonal with respect to D.*

Denote $core_D(AT)$ as the set of all indispensable attributes of AT with respect to D, called as D-core, and $red_D(AT)$ as the set of D-reducts of AT. Then, $core_D(AT) = \cap red_D(AT)$ [12].

Definition 6. *For an information system $S = (U, AT \cup D, V, f)$, if $^U/_{AT} \subseteq {}^U/_D$, then this information system is compatible, otherwise, this information system is incompatible.*

3 Reduct and Core Computation in Incompatible Information Systems

Proposition 1. *Let $A \subseteq AT$, then $pos_{AT}(D) = pos_A(D) \Leftrightarrow$ for every $X \in {}^U/_D$, $\underline{AT}(X) = \underline{A}(X)$.*

Proof. It is similar to the proof of Proposition 2 in [16].

Proposition 2. *For every $A \subseteq AT$, $x \in U$, the following statements are equivalent.*

(1) $\left|{}^{[x]_A}/_D\right| = 1$;
(2) $[x]_A \subseteq [x]_D$;
(3) $x \in \underline{A}([x]_D)$;
(4) $x \in pos_A(D)$.

Proof. It is obvious.

Lemma 1. *For every $x, y \in U$, the following statements are equivalent.*

(1) $(x, y) \notin ind(D)$;
(2) $[x]_D \neq [y]_D$;
(3) $[x]_D \cap [y]_D = \phi$;
(4) $\left|{}^{([x]_{AT} \cup [y]_{AT})}/_D\right| > 1$.

Proof. It is obvious.

For every $x, y \in U$, let $T(x, y)$ represents the following two conditions like that in [16]:

(1) $\min\{\left|{}^{[x]_{AT}}/_D\right|, \left|{}^{[y]_{AT}}/_D\right|\} = 1$; (2) $\left|{}^{([x]_{AT} \cup [y]_{AT})}/_D\right| > 1$.

Proposition 3. *For every $x, y \in U$, suppose $T(x, y)$ holds, then $\alpha(x, y) \neq \phi$.*

Proof. It is similar to the proof of Proposition 4 in [16].

Lemma 2. *For every $A \subseteq AT$, $x \in U$, the following statements are equivalent.*

(1) $[x]_A \neq [y]_A$;
(2) $[x]_A \cap [y]_A = \phi$;
(3) $x \notin [y]_A$;
(4) *there exists $a \in A$, satisfy that $(x, y) \notin ind(a)$;*
(5) $A \cap \alpha(x, y) \neq \phi$.

Proof. It is obvious.

Corollary 1. *For every $x, y \in U$, if* $\min\{\left|{}^{[x]_{AT}}/_D\right|, \left|{}^{[y]_{AT}}/_D\right|\} = 1$, *then the following two statements are equivalent:*

(1) $\left|{}^{([x]_{AT} \cup [y]_{AT})}/_D\right| > 1$; (2) ${}^{[x]_{AT}}/_D \neq {}^{[y]_{AT}}/_D$.

Proposition 4. $pos_{AT}(D) = pos_A(D) \Leftrightarrow$ *For every $x, y \in U$, if $T(x, y)$ holds, then $A \cap \alpha(x, y) \neq \phi$.*

Proof. "$\Rightarrow$" Suppose $pos_{AT}(D) = pos_A(D)$, $x, y \in U$, and $T(x, y)$ holds. From Proposition 3, we have $\alpha(x, y) \neq \phi$, namely, there exists $a \in AT$, satisfy that $(x, y) \notin ind(a)$. Since $\min\{\left|{}^{[x]_{AT}}/_D\right|, \left|{}^{[y]_{AT}}/_D\right|\} = 1$, we suppose that $\left|{}^{[x]_{AT}}/_D\right| = 1$. Thus $x \in pos_{AT}(D) = pos_A(D)$. It follows that $[x]_A \subseteq [x]_D$ according to Proposition 2.

(1) If $\left|{}^{[y]_{AT}}/_D\right| = 1$, then $y \in pos_{AT}(D) = pos_A(D)$. According to Proposition 2, we have $[y]_A \subseteq [y]_D$. Since $\left|{}^{([x]_{AT} \cup [y]_{AT})}/_D\right| > 1$, we have $[x]_D \cap [y]_D = \phi$ according to Lemma 1 and hence $[x]_A \cap [y]_A = \phi$. Consequently, we have $A \cap \alpha(x, y) \neq \phi$ by Lemma 2.

(2) If $\left|{}^{[y]_{AT}}/_D\right| > 1$, then $y \notin pos_{AT}(D) = pos_A(D)$. According to Proposition 2, we have $[y]_A \not\subset [x]_D$ and therefore $[x]_A \neq [y]_A$. Consequently, we have $A \cap \alpha(x, y) \neq \phi$ by Lemma 2.

"$\Leftarrow$" It is only to proof that for every $x \in U$, $\underline{AT}([x]_D) = \underline{A}([x]_D)$. It is obvious that $\underline{AT}([x]_D) \supseteq \underline{A}([x]_D)$. If $y \in \underline{AT}([x]_D)$, then $[y]_{AT} \subseteq [x]_D$, namely $(x, y) \in ind(D)$ and $\left|{}^{[y]_{AT}}/_D\right| = 1$. For every $z \in [y]_A$, we have $A \cap \alpha(y, z) = \phi$ by lemma 2 and therefore $T(y, z)$ does not hold. Since $\left|{}^{[y]_{AT}}/_D\right| = 1$, then we have $\left|{}^{([y]_{AT} \cup [z]_{AT})}/_D\right| = 1$, namely, $(y, z) \in ind(D)$. It follows that $z \in [x]_D$. Therefore, we have $y \in \underline{A}([x]_D)$.

Proposition 5. *$A \subseteq AT$ is D-reduct of AT $\Leftrightarrow$ A is the minimal subset that satisfy: For every $x, y \in U$, if $T(x, y)$ holds, then $A \cap \alpha(x, y) \neq \phi$.*

Proof. "$\Rightarrow$" Let $A \subseteq AT$ be D-reduct of AT, then $pos_A(D) = pos_{AT}(D)$. It follows that A is the set that satisfy: For every $x, y \in U$, if $T(x, y)$ holds, then $A \cap \alpha(x, y) \neq \phi$. If $B \subset A$ also satisfy: For every $x, y \in U$, if $T(x, y)$ holds, then $B \cap \alpha(x, y) \neq \phi$. It follows that $pos_B(D) = pos_{AT}(D) = pos_A(D)$, which is a contradiction since A is orthogonal with respect to D.

"$\Leftarrow$" If A is the minimal subset that satisfy: For every $x, y \in U$, if $T(x, y)$ holds, then $A \cap \alpha(x, y) \neq \phi$. It follows that A is the minimal subset that satisfy $pos_A(D) = pos_{AT}(D)$, namely, A is D-reduct of AT.

Proposition 6. $core_D(AT) = \cup\{\alpha(x, y) \,|T(x, y)$ *holds and* $|\alpha(x, y)| = 1\}$.

Proof. Assume that $T(x, y)$ holds and $|\alpha(x, y)| = 1$. Then we suppose $\alpha(x, y) = \{a\}$. Let A be a D-reduct of AT. Since $A \cap \alpha(x, y) \neq \phi$, we have $a \in A$ and therefore $a \in \cap red_D(AT) = core_D(AT)$.

Conversely, if $a \in core_D(AT)$, then a is indispensable in AT with respect to D, namely, $pos_{AT}(D) \neq pos_{AT-\{a\}}(D)$. Since $pos_{AT}(D) \supseteq pos_{AT-\{a\}}(D)$, we have $pos_{AT}(D) \supset pos_{AT-\{a\}}(D)$. Therefore, there exists $x \in U$ satisfy that $x \in pos_{AT}(D)$ and $x \notin pos_{AT-\{a\}}(D)$. According to Proposition 2, we have $x \in \underline{AT}([x]_D)$ and $x \notin \underline{AT-\{a\}}([x]_D)$. Thus, by definition of lower approximation, we get $[x]_{AT-\{a\}} \not\subset [x]_D$. It follows that there exists $y \in [x]_{AT-\{a\}}$, satisfy that $y \notin [x]_D$. Then $\left|([x]_{AT} \cup [y]_{AT})/_D\right| > 1$. Since $x \in \underline{AT}([x]_D)$, we have $\left|[x]_{AT}/_D\right| = 1$, namely, $\min\{\left|[x]_{AT}/_D\right|, \left|[y]_{AT}/_D\right|\} = 1$. Therefore $T(x,y)$ holds. Since $y \in [x]_{AT-\{a\}}$, we obtain $(x,y) \in ind(AT-\{a\})$. Because $[x]_{AT} \subseteq [x]_D$, $y \notin [x]_D$, we have $y \notin [x]_{AT}$ and hence $(x,y) \notin ind(AT)$. Therefore $\alpha(x,y) = \{a\}$.

Corollary 2. *For a compatible information system, if $T(x,y)$ holds, then we have* $\left|([x]_{AT} \cup [y]_{AT})/_D\right| = 2$.

From this corollary, in compatible information systems, the above reduct method is equal to the method in [12]. In other words, our proposed method is a generalization of the method in [12]. Because in practice we do not know whether an information system is compatible or not in advance, our method is meaningful in order to obtain the decision information automatically and quickly by computer.

From Proposition 5 and condition $T(x,y)$, we can construct the discernibility matrix like in [12, 13, 16] as the following:

Let $x, y \in U$, the element $C_D(x,y)$ of discernibility matrix C_D is defined as :

$$C_D(x,y) = \begin{cases} \alpha(x,y), & if\ T(x,y)\ holds \\ \phi, & otherwise \end{cases}$$

From discernibility matrix, we can obtain all the D-reduct and D-core. Note that we need not compute the positive region of AT in D here.

4 Conclusion

Much work on reduct and core computation of compatible information system presently has been reported until now. However many information systems are incompatible in real applications. In order to obtain the succinct decision rules from incompatible information systems by using rough set method, knowledge reductions are needed. Therefore, it is meaningful to study the reduct and core computation in incompatible information systems. In this paper, reduct and core computation for incompatible information systems is studied based on the algebraic view. A new condition $T(x,y)$ is presented and then new discernibility matrix is constructed based on it. Only $T(x,y)$ is computed and positive regions do not need to be computed in the process of constructing discernibility matrix. The above results also show that our proposed method is suitable for compatible information systems. Our further study is to develop the algorithm to obtain succinct decision rules in incompatible information systems by using the proposed method.

References

1. Pawlak Z.: Rough sets: Theoretical aspects of reasoning about data, Kluwer, Dordrecht (1991)
2. Polkowski L., Skowron A.(eds.): Rough Sets in Knowledge Discovery, Physica-Verlag, Heidelberg (1998)
3. Skowron A , Rauszer C.: The Discernibility Matrixes and Functions in Information System. In : Slowinski R ed. Intelligent Decision Support Handbook of Applications and Advances of the Rough Sets Theory. Kluwer, Dordrecht (1992) 331-362
4. Wang J., Wang J.: Reduction Algorithm Based on Discernibility Matrix: The Ordered Attribute Method, Journal computer science and Technology 16(2001) 489-504
5. Wang G.Y.: Calculation Methods for Core Attributes of Decision Table, Chinese Journal of Computers 26(2003) 611-615
6. Miao D.Q., Hu G.R.: A Heuristic Algorithm for Reduction of Knowledge. (in Chinese) Journal of Computer Research and Development 36(1999) 681-684
7. Slezak, D.: Searching for dynamic reducts in inconsistent decision tables. In: Proceedings of IPMU'98. Paris, France, 2 (1998) 1362–1369
8. Li T.R., Xu Y.: A Generalized Rough Set Approach to Attribute Generalization in Data Mining, FLINS'00, Bruges, Belgium, World Scientific (2000) 126-133
9. Chang L.Y., Wang G.Y., Wu Y.: An Approach for Attribute Reduction and Rule Generation Based on Rough Set Theory(in Chinese), Journal of software 10(1999) 1206-1211
10. Liu Q., Liu S.H., Zheng F.: Rough Logic and its Applications in data Reduction (in Chinese). Journal of Software 12(2001) 415-419
11. Kryszkiewicz M.: Comparative Studies of Alternative Type of Knowledge Reduction in Inconsistent Systems. International Journal of Intelligent Systems 16(2001) 105-120
12. Hu X., Cercone N.: Learning in Relational Databases: a Rough Set Approach. J. Computational Intelligence, 2(1995) 323–337
13. Ye D.Y., Chen Z.J.: A New Discenibility Matrix and the Computation of a Core. Acta Electronica Sinica, 30(2002) 1086–1088
14. Zhang, W.X., Mi, J.S., Wu, W.Z.: Approaches to Knowledge Reducts in Inconsistent Systems. Chinese Journal of Computers 26 (2003) 12-18
15. Mi J.S., Wu W.Z., Zhang W.X.: Approaches to Approximation Reducts in Inconsistent Decision Tables, LNAI 2639(2003) 283–286
16. Qing K.Y. et al.: Reduction of Decision Table and Computation of Core, TR-03-16, Southwest Jiaotong University(2003) 1-8, submitted to Chinese Journal of Computer

The Part Reductions in Information Systems*

Chen Degang

Department of Mathematics, Bohai University, Jinzhou, 121000, P.R.China
Department of Automation, Tsinghua University, Beijing, 100084, P.R.China
chengdegang@263.net.cn

Abstract. In this paper the definition of part reduction is proposed in information systems to describe the minimal description of a definable set by attributes of the given information system. The part reduction can present more optimum description of single decision class than the existing reductions and relative reductions. It is proven that the core of reduction or relative reduction can be expressed as the union of the cores of part reductions. So a deep insight is presented to the classical reductions and relative reductions of information systems so that a unified framework of the reductions of information systems can be set up. The method of discernibility matrix for computing reductions is also generalized to compute the part reductions in information systems.

1 Introduction

The concept of rough set was originally proposed by Pawlak[1] as a formal tool for modeling and processing incomplete information in information systems. This theory evolved into a far-reaching methodology centering on analysis of incomplete information[2-7] and it also can be used for representation of uncertain or imprecise knowledge, identification and evaluation of data dependencies, reasoning with uncertainty, approximate pattern classification, knowledge analysis, etc.

The most important application of rough set theory is that of information-preserving attribute reduction in databases. Given a dataset with discretized attribute values, it is possible to find a subset of the original attributes that are the most informative. All the possible minimal subsets of attributes that lead to the same partitioning as the whole set form the collection of all the reductions.

In recent years, more attention has been paid to reductions in decision systems [8-14] and many types of knowledge reduction have been proposed, some of them are possible reduct, approximate reduct, generalized decision reduct, $\mu-$decision reduct, $\mu-$reduct , $\alpha-$reduct, local reduct and dynamic reduct. All of these reductions aim at a common requirement, i.e., keeping the description to the decision attributes for some information measures. Since these reductions are firstly defined for every object in the decision system then defined for the whole system, they can be viewed as

* This paper is supported by a grant of Tianyuan mathematical foundation of China(A0324613) and a grant of Liaoning Education committee (20161049) of China.

S. Tsumoto et al. (Eds.): RSCTC 2004, LNAI 3066, pp. 477–482, 2004.

global reductions. On the other hand, in many practical problems for a decision attributes, people always pay more attention on some special values of the decision attributes than others. For example, in the case of decision-making of medical diagnosis, people always pay more attention on the features lead to the disease than the ones may not lead to the disease. The global reductions need more features than a single decision result need, which means high prediction cost. On the other hand, from the theoretical viewpoint, every attribute in the reduction or the relative reduction may play different role, thus further study to the interior structure of the reduction can present more precise recognitions to the properties of reductions. So a deep research to the reductions for a single decision class is important and valuable either to the practical problems or to the rough sets theory itself, and this is the main purpose of this paper.

2 The Part Reductions in Information Systems

Some well-known notions in Pawlak rough set theory such as information system, set approximations and reduction we refer the readers to [1,4], we do not list them here in case of the length of this paper. We also omit the proofs of the theorems and propositions in this section for the same reason.

Suppose (U,A) is an information system, R_A is the indiscernibility relation determined by A. A subset $X \subseteq U$ is called definable if $\underline{R_A}X = \overline{R_A}X = X$, where $\underline{R_A}X$ and $\overline{R_A}X$ are the lower and upper approximation of X respectively, denote the collection of all the definable sets of (U,A) as $D(U,A)$, then $D(U,A)$ is a $\sigma-$algebra and its atomic set is $\{[x]_{R_A} : x \in U\}$, i.e., every element in $D(U,A)$ is the join of some elements in $\{[x]_{R_A} : x \in U\}$ while every element in $\{[x]_{R_A} : x \in U\}$ can not be the join of other elements. For any nonempty set $X \in D(U,A)$ and $a \in A$, if $X \in D(U, A-\{a\})$, then a is called superfluous in A for X, otherwise is indispensable in A for X. The set A is independent for X if all its attributes are indispensable for X in A. The subset $B \subseteq A$ is called a part reduction of A for X if B is independent for X, i.e., $X \in D(U,B)$ and for any $b \in B$, $X \notin D(U, B-\{b\})$. The part reduction of A for X is the minimal subset of A to ensure X as a definable set. If there exists $a \in A$ such that X is an equivalence class of R_a, then $\{a\}$ is a part reduction of A for X. Following we study the properties of the part reductions. Clearly for any information system (U,A) and every $X \in D(U,A)$, the part reduction for X exists and generally the part reduction is not unique. If we denote the collection of all the part reductions for X as $\{B_i : i \le l\}$, then $B = \bigcap_{i=1}^{l} B_i$ is the part core for X which is the collection of all the indispensable attributes in A for X. The part core for X will be denoted as $Core_X(A)$. If the part core is not empty, then every part reduction includes the part core. The following proposition is straightforward.

Proposition 1. For every $a \in A$, a is superfluous in A for X if and only if a is superfluous in A for X^c; a is indispensable in A for X if and only if a is indispensable in A for X^c; $B \subseteq A$ is a part reduction of A for X if and only if B is a part reduction of A for X^c.

Suppose $X, Y \in D(U, A)$ and $X \neq Y$, then $Core_{X \bigcup Y}(A) \subseteq Core_X(A) \bigcup Core_Y(A)$. The converse inclusion may not hold. The part reduction can also be defined for several definable sets $X_1, X_2, ..., X_N$, $X_i \bigcap X_j = \phi$, it just need to change X by $X_1, X_2, ..., X_N$ in the above definition of part reduction for X. The part reduction of A for $X_1, X_2, ..., X_N$ is the minimal subset of A to ensure every $X_1, X_2, ..., X_N$ (not $\bigcup_{i=1}^N X_i$) as a definable set. We have the following theorem.

Theorem 1. Suppose $\mathbf{X} = \{X_1, X_2, ..., X_N\} \subseteq D(U, A)$ and $X_i \bigcap X_j = \phi$. Then $Core_{\mathbf{X}}(A) = \bigcup_{i=1}^N Core_{X_i}(A)$.

By Theorem 1 we have the following two theorems.

Theorem 2. Suppose $\mathbf{X} = \{X_1, X_2, ..., X_N\} \subseteq D(U, A)$ and $X_i \bigcap X_j = \phi$. Then a is superfluous in A for $\{X_1, X_2, ..., X_N\}$ if and only if a is superfluous in A for every X_i.

Theorem 3. Suppose $S = (U, C \bigcup \{d\})$ is a decision system, then $Core_{\{d\}}(C) = \bigcup Core_{\underline{R_C} D_j}(C)$, here $\{D_1, D_2, ..., D_l\}$ is the partition induced by $\{d\}$.

In Theorem 3, if the decision system is consistent, then $\bigcup_{j=1}^l \underline{R_C} D_j = U$ holds, if it is inconsistent, then $\bigcup_{j=1}^l \underline{R_C} D_j \neq U$ holds. However, an information system can be regarded as a consistent decision system when R_A is seem as the equivalence relation corresponding to the decision attribute. Thus Theorem 3 implies that the relative core(core) of relative reduction(reduction) in decision systems(information systems) can be viewed as the union of some part cores, every attribute in the relative core plays different role, i.e., it is indispensable for some special decision classes and not for all decision classes. It is possible that the number of attributes in a part reduction is smaller than the number of attributes in a reduction or a relative reduction. So if more attention is paid on a single decision class than the totals, the attributes employed to describe this single decision class might be less than the ones described the wholes. This is the objective of part reductions. Following we study the computing of part reductions.

Definition 1. Suppose (U, A) is an information system, $U/R_A = \{M_1, M_2, ..., M_k\}$, $X \in D(U, A)$. The set

$$D_X(M_i,M_j)=\begin{cases}\{a\in A: a(M_i)\neq a(M_j)\}, M_i\cup M_j\not\subset X, (M_i\cup M_j)\cap X\neq\phi\\ A, \textit{otherwise}\end{cases}$$

is called the discernibility attributes set of M_i and M_j for X, $D_X=(D_X(M_i,M_j): i,j\leq k)$ is called the discernibility attributes matrix of (U,A) for X.

Theorem 4. The discernibility attributes matrix of (U,A) for X satisfies the following properties:'

(1) $D_X(M_i,M_j)=A$ if one of $M_i\cup M_j\subseteq X$ or $M_i\cup M_j\subseteq X^c$ holds. Specially $D_X(M_i,M_i)=A$ holds.

(2) $D_X(M_i,M_j)=D_X(M_j,M_i), i,j\leq l$.

(3) $D_X(M_i,M_j)\subseteq D_X(M_i,M_s)\cup D_X(M_s,M_j)$.

Theorem 5. Suppose (U,A) is an information system, $U/R_A=\{M_1,M_2,...,M_k\}$, $X\in D(U,A)$. Then we have:

(1) For any $B\subseteq A$, $B\cap D_X(M_i,M_j)\neq\phi$ holds for every $i,j\leq l$ if and only if $X\in D(U,B)$.

(2) For any $B\subseteq A$, $X\in D(U,B)$ if and only if for any $E\subseteq A$, $B\cap E=\phi$ implies $E\notin D_X$.

(3) If there exist M_i, M_j such that $D_X(M_i,M_j)=\{a\}$, then $a\in Core_X(A)$.

Theorem 6. Suppose (U,A) is an information system, $U/R_A=\{M_1,M_2,...,M_k\}$, $X\in D(U,A)$, $D_X=(D_X(M_i,M_j): i,j\leq k)$ is the discernibility attributes matrix of (U,A) for X. A discernibility function f_{UA} for (U,A) is a Boolean function defined by $f_{UA}=\wedge\{\vee D_X(M_i,M_j)\}$. If $f_{UA}=\bigvee_{t=1}^{p}(\bigwedge_{r=1}^{q_t} a_{i_r})$ satisfying every element in $B_t=\{a_{i_r}: r\leq q_t\}$ appears only one time in B_t, then the set $\{B_t: t\leq p\}$ is the collection of all the part reductions of A for X.

Remark 1. The definition of discernibility attributes matrix can also be defined for several definable sets $X_1,X_2,...,X_N$, $X_i\cap X_j=\phi$ as

$$D_X(M_i,M_j)=\begin{cases}\{a\in A: a(M_i)\neq a(M_j)\}, M_i\cup M_j\not\subset X_i, (M_i\cup M_j)\cap X_i\neq\phi, i=1,...,N\\ A, \textit{otherwise}\end{cases}$$

Similar conclusions as Theorem 4-6 can be obtained.

Following we employ an example to illustrate our idea.

Example 1. Suppose (U, A) is an information system, $U = \{x_1, x_2, \ldots, x_8\}$, $A = \{a_1, a_2, a_3\}$ be a set of attribute where R_1, R_2 and R_3 are equivalence relations corresponding to a_1, a_2 and a_3 respectively whose equivalence classes are defined by $U/R_1 = \{\{x_1, x_4, x_5\}, \{x_2, x_8\}, \{x_3\}, \{x_6, x_7\}\}$, $U/R_2 = \{\{x_1, x_3, x_5\}, \{x_6\}, \{x_2, x_4, x_7, x_8\}\}$ and $U/R_3 = \{\{x_1, x_5\}, \{x_6\}, \{x_2, x_7, x_8\}, \{x_3, x_4\}\}$. The equivalence classes of R_A are computed as $U/R_A = \{\{x_1, x_5\}, \{x_2, x_8\}, \{x_3\}, \{x_4\}, \{x_6\}, \{x_7\}\}$

It is easy to compute $\{a_1, a_2\}$ and $\{a_1, a_3\}$ are two reductions of A and $\{a_1\}$ is the core. Clearly $Core_{\{x_1,x_5\}}(A) = Core_{\{x_3\}}(A) = Core_{\{x_4\}}(A) = Core_{\{x_6\}}(A) = \phi$, and $Core_{\{x_2,x_8\}}(A) = Core_{\{x_7\}}(A) = \{a_1\}$, so the core of A is the union of all the part cores for the equivalence classes of R_A. Further more, $\mathrm{Red}_{\{x_1,x_5\}}(A) = \{\{a_1, a_2\}, \{a_3\}\}$, other part reductions with respect to elements in U/R_A can be computed similarly.

If we add a decision attribute $\{d\}$ where D is the equivalence relation whose equivalence classes are defined as $U/D = \{\{x_1, x_3, x_5\}, \{x_2, x_8\}, \{x_4, x_6, x_7\}\}$, then $(U, A \cup \{d\})$ is a consistent decision system. Then the discernibility attributes matrix of (U, A) for $\{x_1, x_3, x_5\}$ is

$$D_{\{x_1,x_3,x_5\}}(M_i, M_j) = \begin{pmatrix} A & & & & & \\ A & A & & & & \\ A & A & A & & & \\ \{a_2, a_3\} & A & \{a_1, a_2\} & A & & \\ A & A & A & A & A & \\ A & A & A & A & A & A \end{pmatrix}$$

The corresponding discernibility function f_{UA} is $f_{UA} = (a_2 \vee a_3) \wedge (a_1 \vee a_2)$ $= a_2 \vee (a_1 \wedge a_3)$, so the part reduction of A for $\{x_1, x_3, x_5\}$ is $\{\{a_2\}, \{a_1, a_3\}\}$. Similarly $\mathrm{Re}\,d_{\{x_2,x_8\}}(A) = \{\{a_1\}\}$ and $\mathrm{Re}\,d_{\{x_4,x_6,x_7\}}(A) = \{\{a_1, a_2\}, \{a_1, a_3\}\}$, so $Core_D(A) = \{a_1\}$ and $\mathrm{Re}\,d_D(A) = \{\{a_1, a_2\}, \{a_1, a_3\}\}$. If we pay more attention on $\{x_1, x_3, x_5\}$, then only one attribute $\{a_2\}$ is enough while only $\{a_1\}$ is enough for $\{x_2, x_8\}$.

References

1. Pawlak, Z.: Rough Sets. Internat. J. Comput. Inform. Sci. vol. 11, 5(1982)341-356
2. Jagielska, I., Matthews C., Whitfort T.: An investigation into the application of neural networks, fuzzy logic, genetic algorithms, and rough sets to automated knowledge acquisition for classification problems. Neurocomputing 24(1999) 37-54

3. Kryszkiewicz M.: Rough set approach to incomplete information systems. Information Sciences 112(1998)39-49
4. Pawlak Z.: Rough sets: Theoretical Aspects of Reasoning about Data. Kluwer Academic Publishers, Boston(1991)
5. Tsumoto S.: Automated extraction of medical expert system rules from clinical databases based on rough set theory. Information Sciences 112 (1998)67-84
6. Skowron A., Polkowski L.: Rough sets in knowledge discovery. vols. 1,2, Springer, Berlin (1998)
7. Slowinski R. (Ed.): Intelligent decision support: Handbook of applications and advances of the rough sets theory. Kluwer Academic Publishers, Boston(1992)
8. Kryszkiewicz M.: Comparative study of alternative type of knowledge reduction in insistent systems. International Joural of intelligent systems 16(2001)105-120
9. Skowron A., Rauszer C.: The discernibility matrices and functions in information systems, In: R. Slowinski(Ed.). Intelligent decision support: Handbook of applications and advances of the rough sets theory. Kluwer Academic Publishers (1992)
10. Slezak D.: Searching for dynamic reducts in inconsistent decision tables. In: Proceedings of IPMU'98. Paris, France, Vol.2, (1998)1362-1369
11. Slezak D.: Approximate reducts in decision tables. In: Proceedings of IPMU'96, Vol.3. Granada, Spain(1996) 1159-1164
12. Bazan J.: A comparison of dynamic and non-dynamic rough set methods for extracting laws from decision system. In L. Polkowski, A. Skowron (Eds), Rough sets in knowledge discovery, vols. 1. Physica-Verlag, Heidelberg(1998)321-365
13. Bazan J., Skowron A., Synak P.: Dynamic reducts as a tool for extracting laws from decision tables. In Proceeding of the Symposium on Methodologies for Intelligent Systems. Charlotte, NC, LNAI869. Springer- Verlag, Berlin(1994) 346-355
14. Bazan J., Nguyen H.S.,.Nguyen S.H, Synak P., Wroblewski J.: Rough set algorithms in classification problem, in:[Polkowski-Tsumoto-Lin],(2000)49-88

Rules from Belief Networks: A Rough Set Approach

Teresa Mroczek[1], Jerzy W. Grzymała-Busse[1,2], and Zdzisław S. Hippe[1]

[1] University of Information Technology and Management
ul. Sucharskiego 2, 35-225 Rzeszów, Poland
{zhippe,tmroczek}@wenus.wsiz.rzeszow.pl
[2] Department of Electrical Engineering and Computer Science, University of Kansas
Lawrence KS 66045-7523, USA
jerzy@ku.edu

Abstract. A new version of the ***Belief*SEEKER** software that incorporates some aspects of rough set theory is discussed in this paper. The new version is capable of generating certain belief networks (for consistent data) and possible belief networks (for inconsistent data). Then, both types of networks can be readily converted onto respective sets of production rules, which includes both certain and/or possible rules. The new version or broadly speaking - methodology, was tested in mining the melanoma database for the best descriptive attributes of skin illness. It was found, that both types of knowledge representation, can be readily used for classification of melanocytic skin lesions.

Keywords: classification of skin lesions, Bayesian belief networks, belief rules

1 Introduction

Our previous investigations devoted to computer-assisted classification of melanocytic lesions on the skin [1] were based on supervised machine learning within a model of consistent and inconsistent knowledge, using **LERS** [2] and a suite of in-house developed machine learning programs [3]. It was found that particularly promising results of classification of skin lesions were obtained using the program ***Belief*SEEKER**, capable of generating *certain* belief networks (for consistent data) and *possible* belief networks (for inconsistent data, the case frequently met in medical diagnoses). In the present research, the application of belief networks to solve the problem of correct classification of four concepts hidden in our melanoma data (*Benign nevus, Blue nevus, Suspicious nevus* and *Melanoma malignant*) is dealt with anew. However, a novel approach based on the conception of development of production rules from belief networks, was currently investigated. Therefore, a new version of the program ***Belief*SEEKER** was elaborated and applied. In comparison to previous version, described in [4], the new release generates *certain* and *possible* belief networks (applying some elements of rough sets theory [5]), and additionally can generate sets of IF..THEN

S. Tsumoto et al. (Eds.): RSCTC 2004, LNAI 3066, pp. 483–487, 2004.

production rules, also of both categories (i.e. *certain* rules and *possible* rules, referred to as *belief rules*).

2 Selected Features of *Belief*SEEKER

For the sake of keeping the size of article in recommended bounds, only some basic functions of the ***Belief*SEEKER** system are described here. The first step in producing belief networks is to load a decision table into the system. During the loading process, the system executes very extensive searching for erroneous and missing values, and additionally informs the user about the number of inconsistent, redundant and/or correct cases in the file. Then the **one** belief network with arbitrarily selected Dirichlet parameter [4] can be generated, or a **set** of belief networks are developed in the incremental change of this factor. Some of the networks are retained and applied in the classification process of unseen cases. Simultaneously, for each network various sets of production rules can be generated, using various levels of a specific parameter, called tentatively by us *certainty factor*, **CF** (lower **CF** generates more rules for a given network). It was found that the optimum **CF** value for prevailing number of investigated belief networks was in the range 0.6 - 0.4. An extensive search throughout available literature pointed out, that the conversion of production rules into belief networks has been already mentioned (see [6]), whereas the approach developed by us (i.e. conversion: belief networks $\Rightarrow$ production rules) seems to be less known.

3 Description of the Investigated Dataset. Experiments

The investigated dataset is a collection of cases describing melanoma data of 410 anonymous patients. The detailed description of this set and attributes used is given in a paper submitted for this conference [7]. From the source dataset, 26 cases were randomly extracted and stored in a separated file. In this way, two working sets were created: the first was used in all experiments for learning (**E384144.TAB**; **384** cases, **14** attributes, **4** concepts), and the second file was used for testing of belief networks and belief rules developed (**E026144.TAB**; **26** cases, **14** attributes, **4** concepts). However, some number of contradictory cases was intentionally inserted into the learning set in order to check the capability of ***Belief*SEEKER** in applying rough sets approach to process inconsistent data. But in the further text we focused our attention on belief networks and belief rules, belonging only to the category *certain*.
Belief networks generated for Dirichlet's parameter α = 1, 10, 50 and 100 are shown in Fig. 1. It was found that for the first network (α=1) two descriptive attributes (**TDS**, and *color blue*) were most important. Then, for the second network (α=10) an additional attribute asymmetry was recognized, whereas the third network (α=50) did select branched streaks as the subsequent important attribute. Finally, the last network (α=100) enumerates the following five descriptive attributes: **TDS**, *asymmetry*, *color blue*, *color dark brown*, *branched streaks* and *structureless areas* as the most important symptoms, influencing

categorization of investigated skin lesions. All networks have chosen the **TDS** parameter so it seems to be the most important attribute in diagnosing of the illness. These results fully confirm our previous findings, that **TDS** - contrary to other sources [8] - plays very important role, significantly increasing melanoma diagnosis accuracy.

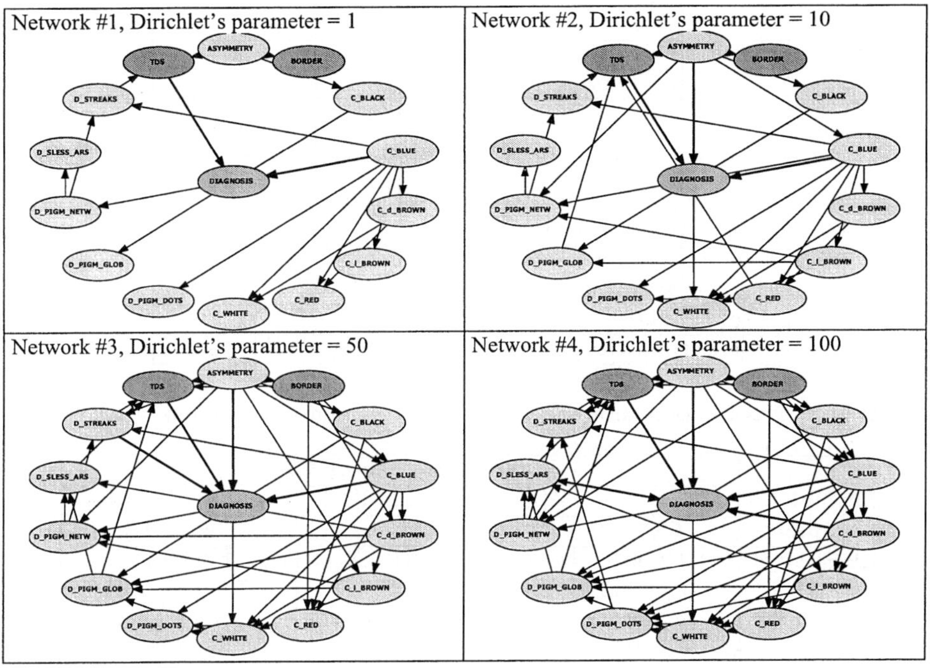

Fig. 1. Belief networks developed for the learning set with various levels of Dirichlet's parameter

As a next step in our research the classification accuracy was tested separately for belief networks (Table 1) and belief rules (Table 2). Data shown in Table 1 points out that for Dirichlet's parameter $\alpha = 1$, 10 and 50 the error rate is the same, whereas for α =100 it rose significantly. On the other hand, the accuracy of belief rules (generated for each network, Table 2) is related to the certainty factor in a rather complicated way. For **CF** = 0.9, four different sets of belief rules were obtained (containing 5, 7, 9 and 10 rules, respectively), capable to errorless diagnosing of roughly 69% of unseen cases. However, it should be stressed, that over 30of the unseen cases were not "touched" by any of the set of rules developed. Quite interesting result were obtained for **CF** = 0.5. Here all unseen cases were covered by three different rule sets (developed for $\alpha = 1$, 10 and 50), and classificated with satisfactory accuracy (error rate only 7.7%).

Due to page restrictions, only results gained for the network **#2** ($\alpha = 10$) are discussed here. This network seemed to be optimal; it enumerates symptoms

Table 1. Classification accuracy of belief networks, developed for the training set with different α

Descriptive attributes		**Dirichlet's parameter**			
		α=1	α=10	α=50	α=100
	asymmetry		+	+	+
	border				
Color	*black*				
	blue	+	+	+	+
	dark brown				+
	light brown				
	red				
	white				
Diversity of structure	*pigment dots*				
	pigment globules				
	pigment network				
	structureless areas				+
	branched streaks			+	
	TDS	+	+	+	+
Error rate [%]		**7.7%**	**7.7%**	**7.7%**	**15.3%**

Table 2. Classification accuracy of belief rules, obtained for various α and **CF**

Dirichlet's parameter	**Certainty factor CF** **Error rate [%] / Unclassified[%] / Number of rules** **CF = 0.9**	**CF = 0.7**	**CF = 0.5**
α=1	0 / 30.8 / 5	0 / 30.8 / 6	7.7 / 0 / 8
α=**10**	**0 / 38.5 / 7**	**0 / 30.8 / 13**	**7.7 / 0 / 14**
α=50	0 / 38.5 / 9	3.8 / 11.5 / 19	7.7 / 0 / 21
α=100	0 / 38.5 / 10	3.8 / 30.8 / 23	11.5 / 3. 8 / 31

most widely used by medical doctors in diagnosing of skin lesion. Additionally, belief rules generated for it (see Fig. 2), in comparison to sets of rules created for other networks are very concise, succinct, and easily accepted in "manual" diagnosing.

The approach presented in the paper allows one to generate feasible solutions in diagnosing melanocytic skin lesions; it is based on the development of Bayesian belief networks and then belief rules. It can be assumed that both types of knowledge representations can be readily used for classification and/or identification of other types of illnesses.

For belief networks **#2** and **#3** (α = 10 and 50, respectively), the developed sets of rules display the same accuracy, but are less concise. It seems that belief rules, generated in addition to belief networks, will provide better insight into the problem being solved, and should allow for natural and easy understandable interpretation of the meaning of the descriptive attributes used. In broader sense, the elaborated methodology can be applied for classification of various objects (concepts, ideas, processes, etc.), described by means of attributional logic.

RULE 1	IF TDS >= 1.000 AND TDS <= 2.925 AND C_BLUE IS absent THEN DIAGNOSIS IS Benign nevus
RULE 2	IF TDS > 2.925 AND TDS <= 4.850 AND C_BLUE IS absent THEN DIAGNOSIS IS Benign nevus
RULE 3	IF TDS >= 1.000 AND TDS <= 2.925 AND C_BLUE IS present THEN DIAGNOSIS IS Blue nevus
RULE 4	IF TDS > 2.925 AND TDS <= 4.850 AND C_BLUE IS present THEN DIAGNOSIS IS Blue nevus
RULE 5	IF TDS > 6.775 AND TDS <= 8.700 AND C_BLUE IS absent THEN DIAGNOSIS IS Melanoma malignant
RULE 6	IF TDS > 4.850 AND TDS <= 6.775 AND C_BLUE IS present THEN DIAGNOSIS IS Melanoma malignant
RULE 7	IF TDS > 6.775 AND TDS <= 8.700 AND C_BLUE IS present THEN DIAGNOSIS IS Melanoma malignant
RULE 8	IF TDS > 4.850 AND TDS <= 6.775 AND C_BLUE IS absent THEN DIAGNOSIS IS Suspicious nevus

Fig. 2. Concise set of belief rules produced for the network **#1** ($\mu = 1$, certainty factor (**CF**) = 0.5)

References

1. J.W. Grzymała-Busse, Z.S. Hippe: A Search for the Best Data Mining Method to Predict Melanoma. **In**: J.J. Alpigini, J.F. Peters, A. Skowron, N. Zhong (Eds.) Rough Sets and Current Trends in Computing, Springer-Verlag, Heidelberg 2002, pp. 538-545.
2. M.R. Chmielewski, J.W. Grzymała-Busse, Neil W. Peterson, S. Than: The Rule Induc-tion System LERS - A Version for Personal Computers. **Foundations of Computing and Dec. Sciences 1993** (18, No 3-4) pp. 181-211.
3. P. Błajdo, J.W. Grzymała-Busse, Z.S. Hippe, M. Knap, T. Marek, T. Mroczek, M. Wrzesień: A suite of machine learning tools for knowledge extraction from data. **In**: R. Tadeusiewicz, A. Ligęza, M. Szymkat (Eds.), Computer Methods and Systems in Scientific Research, Edition of "Oprogr. Naukowe", Cracow 2003, s. 479-484 (in Polish).
4. Z.S. Hippe, T. Mroczek: Melanoma classification and prediction using belief networks, **In**: M. Kurzynski, E. Puchała, M. Wozniak (Eds.) Computer Recognition Systems, Wrocław University of Technology Edit. Office, Wrocław 2003, pp. 337-342.
5. Z. Pawlak: Rough Sets. Theoretical Aspects of Reasoning about Data. Kluwer Academic Publishers, Dordercht-Boston-London, 1991.
6. G.F. Cooper, E. Herskovits: A Byesian method for the induction of probabilistic networks from data. **Machine Learning 1992**(9)309-347.
7. R. Andrews, S. Bajcar, J.W. Grzymała-Busse, Z.S. Hippe, C. Whiteley: Optimization of the ABCD Formula for Melanoma Diagnosis Using C4.5, a Data Mining System. (Submitted for Fourth International Conference on Rough Sets and Current Trends in Computing, RSCTC'2004, Uppsala (Sweden) 01-05.06.2004).
8. H. Lorentzen, K. Weissman, L. Secher, C. S. Peterson, F. G. Larsen: The dermatoscopic ABCD rule does not improve diagnostic accuracy of malignant melanoma. **Acta Derm. Venereol. 79** (1999) 469-472.

The Bagging and n^2-Classifiers Based on Rules Induced by MODLEM

Jerzy Stefanowski

Institute of Computing Science
Poznań University of Technology, 60-965, Poznań, Poland
Jerzy.Stefanowski@cs.put.poznan.pl

Abstract. An application of the rule induction algorithm MODLEM to construct multiple classifiers is studied. Two different such classifiers are considered: the bagging approach, where classifiers are generated from different samples of the learning set, and the n^2-classifier, which is specialized for solving multiple class learning problems. This paper reports results of an experimental comparison of these multiple classifiers and the single, MODLEM based, classifier performed on several data sets.

1 Introduction

Classification is one of common tasks performed in knowledge discovery and machine learning. It includes assigning a decision class label to a set of unclassified objects described by a fixed set of attributes. Different learning algorithms can be applied to induce various forms of classification knowledge from provided learning examples. This knowledge can be successively used to classify new objects. In this sense learning process results in creating *classification system* – shortly called *classifier*. Typical measure used to evaluate such systems is a *classification accuracy*, i.e. a percentage of correctly classified testing examples.

Recently, there has been observed a growing interest in increasing classification accuracy by integrating different classifiers into one composed classification system. In proper circumstances such a composed system could better classify new (or testing) examples than its component classifiers used independently. Experimental evaluations have confirmed that the use of multiple classifiers leads to improving classification accuracy in many problems. The author and his cooperators have also carried research within this framework, e.g. introducing the architecture of the n^2-classifier [10], examining the influence of the choice of learning algorithms or attribute selection on the performance of the composed classification system [10, 11, 15].

In this paper we consider classifiers based on *rules induced from examples*. A number of various algorithms have already been developed to induce such rules, for a review see, e.g., [15, 17]. Although different rule based classifiers have been proved to be efficient for several learning problems, they may not led to satisfactory high classification accuracy for some other, more difficult, data sets. Therefore, it is interesting to check how the performance of rule based classifiers could be improved by using the framework of multiple classifiers.

S. Tsumoto et al. (Eds.): RSCTC 2004, LNAI 3066, pp. 488–497, 2004.

The main aim of this paper is to examine the application of the rule induction algorithm, called MODLEM, in two different multiple classifiers: the bagging approach and the n^2-classifier. The bagging is an approach that combines homogeneous classifiers generated from different distributions of learning examples. The n^2-classifier is a more specialized approach to solve multiple class learning problems by using a set of binary classifiers, which are responsible for distinguishing between pairs of classes. The rule induction algorithm MODLEM has been previously introduced by the author in [13].

In this study we want to check experimentally how much both multiple classifiers could improve the classification accuracy compared against the single rule classifier. Moreover, we will evaluate the computational costs of creating these combined classifiers. Finally, we would like to discuss properties of learning problems which could be essential for an efficient usage of both multiple classifiers.

2 Multiple Classifiers – General Issues

The combined classification system (multiple classifier) is a set of single classifiers whose individual predictions are combined in some way to classify new objects. Combining identical classifiers is useless. The member classifier should have a substantial level of disagreement, i.e. they make error independently with respect to one another [4]. As to combining classification predictions from single classifiers, generally, there are either *group* or *specialized decision making* [6]. In the first method all base classifiers are consulted to classify a new object while the other method chooses only these classifiers whose are expertised for this object. *Voting* is the most common method used to combine single classifiers. The vote of each classifier may be weighted, e.g., by the posterior probability referring to its performance on the training data.

The integration of single classifiers into one composed system has been approached in many ways, for some review see, e.g. [4, 6, 14, 15]. In general, one can distinguish two categories: using either *homogeneous* or *heterogeneous classifiers*. In the first category, the same learning algorithm is used over different samples of the data set. Particular attention has been put to *bagging* and *boosting* approaches that manipulate the training data in order to generate diversified classifiers. In a case of heterogeneous classifiers, one can apply a set of different learning algorithms to the same data set and their predictions could be combined, e.g., by *stacked generalization* or *meta-learning*.

3 The Bagging Approach

The *Bagging* approach (**B**ootstrap **agg**regat**ing**) was introduced by Breiman [2]. It aggregates by voting classifiers generated from different bootstrap samples. The *bootstrap sample* is obtained by uniformly sampling with replacement objects from the training set. Each sample has the same size as the original set, however, some examples do not appear in it, while others may appear more than once. For a training set with m examples, the probability of an example being selected at least once is $1-(1-1/m)^m$. For a large m, this is about 1 - $1/e$. Each bootstrap sample contains, on the average, 63.2% unique examples from the training set.

Given the parameter T which is the number of repetitions, T bootstrap samples $S_1, S_2, \ldots, S_T$ are generated. From each sample S_i a classifier C_i is induced by the same learning algorithm and the final classifier C^* is formed by aggregating T classifiers. A final classification of object x is built by a uniform voting scheme on $C_1, C_2, \ldots, C_T$, i.e. is assigned to the class predicted most often by these sub-classifiers, with ties broken arbitrarily. The approach is presented briefly below. For more details see [2].

(**input** LS learning set; T number of bootstrap samples; LA learning algorithm
output C^* classifier)
begin
  for $i = 1$ **to** T **do**
  begin
    $S_i :=$ bootstrap sample from LS; {sample with replacement}
    $C_i := LA(S_i)$; {generate a sub-classifier}
  end; {end for}
  $C^*(x) = \arg\max_{y \in K_j} \sum_{i=1}^{T} (C_i(x) = y)$ {the most often predicted class}
end

Experimental results presented in [2, 3, 12] show a significant improvement of classification accuracy while using decision tree classifiers. For more theoretical discussion on the justification of bagging the reader is referred to [2].

4 The n^2-Classifier

This kind of multiple classifier is a specialized approach to solve *multiple class learning problems*. Although the standard way to solve multi-class learning problems includes the direct use of the multiple class learning algorithm such as, e.g. algorithm for inducing decision trees, there exist more specialized methods dedicated to this problem, e.g., one-per-class method, distributed output codes classification schemes, error-correcting techniques and they can outperform the direct use of the single multiclass learning algorithms, see e.g. discusions [10, 14].

The n^2-classifier is composed of $(n^2 - n)/2$ base binary classifiers (where n is a number of decision classes; $n > 2$). The main idea is to discriminate each pair of the classes: (i, j), $i, j \in [1..n], i \neq j$, by an independent binary classifier C_{ij}. Each base binary classifier C_{ij} corresponds to a pair of two classes i and j only. Therefore, the specificity of the training of each base classifier C_{ij} consists in presenting to it a subset of the entire learning set that contains only examples coming from classes i and j. The classifier C_{ij} yields a binary classification indicating whether a new example $\mathbf{x}$ belongs to class i or to class j. Let us denote by $C_{ij}(\mathbf{x})$ the classification of an example $\mathbf{x}$ by the base classifier C_{ij}.

The complementary classifiers: C_{ij} and C_{ji} (where $i, j \in <1 \ldots n>$; $i \neq j$) solve the same classification problem – a discrimination between class i-th and

j-th. So, they are equivalent ($C_{ij} \equiv C_{ji}$) and it is sufficient to use only $(n^2 - n)/2$ classifiers $C_{ij}(i < j)$, which correspond to all combination of pairs of n classes.

An algorithm providing final classification assumes that a new example $\mathbf{x}$ is applied to all base classifiers C_{ij}. As a result, their binary predictions $C_{ij}(\mathbf{x})$ are computed. The final classification should be obtained by a proper aggregation of these predictions. The simplest aggregation rule is based on finding a class that wins the most pairwise comparisons. The more sophisticated approach, considered in this paper, includes a *weighted* majority voting rules, where the vote of each classifier is modified by its credibility, which is calculated as its classification performance during learning phase; more details in [10].

The quite similar approach was independently introduced by Friedman [5]. Then it was extended and experimentally studied by Hastie and Tibshirani [9], which called it *classification by pairwise coupling.* The experimental studies, e.g. [5, 9, 10], have shown that such multiple classifiers perform usually better than the standard classifiers. Previously the author and J.Jelonek have also examined how the choice of a learning algorithm influences the classification performance of the n^2-classifier [10]. Additionally, they have considered different approaches of attribute selection for each pairwise binary classifier [11].

5 The Rule Induction by the MODLEM Algorithm

The rule induction algorithm, called MODLEM, has been introduced by Stefanowski in [13], see also its more precise description in [15] or [8]. Due to the size of this paper we skip the formal presentation of this algorithm and we only discuss its main idea. It is based on the scheme of a *sequential covering* and it heuristically generates a *minimal set* of decision rules for every decision concept (decision class or its rough approximation in case of inconsistent examples). Such a set of rules attempts to cover all (or the most significant) *positive examples* of the given concept and not to cover any *negative examples* (or as little as possible of them). The main procedure for rule induction scheme starts from creating a first rule by choosing sequentially the 'best' elementary conditions according to chosen criteria (i.e., the first candidate for the condition part is one elementary condition; If it does not fulfill the requirement to be accepted as a rule, then the next - currently best evaluated - elementary condition is added to the candidate condition part, etc.; This specialization is performed until the rule could be accepted). When the rule is stored, all learning positive examples that match this rule are removed from consideration. The process is iteratively repeated while some significant positive examples of the decision concept remain still uncovered. Then, the procedure is sequentially repeated for each set of examples from a succeeding decision concept. In the basic version of the MODLEM algorithm elementary conditions are evaluated by using one of two measures either *class entropy* or *Laplace accuracy* [13, 15]. It is also possible to consider a lexicographic order of two criteria measuring the rule positive cover and then its conditional probability (originally considered by Grzymala in his LEM2 algorithm or its last, quite interesting modification called MLEM2).

The extra specificity of the MODLEM algorithm is handling directly numerical attributes during rule induction while elementary conditions of rules are created, without any preliminary discretization phase [8]. In MODLEM elementary conditions are represented as either $(a < v_a)$ or $(a \geq v_a)$, where a denotes an attribute and v_a is its value. If the same attribute is chosen twice while building a single rule, one may also obtain the condition $(a = [v_1, v_2))$ that results from an intersection of two conditions $(a < v_2)$ and $(a \geq v_1)$ such that $v_1 < v_2$. For nominal attributes, these conditions are $(a = v_a)$. For more details about the function finding best elementary conditions see, e.g., [8, 13].

Finally, the unordered set of induced rules is applied to classify examples using the classification strategy introduced by Grzymala in LERS system [7], which takes into account strength of all rules completely matched and also allows partially matches if no rule fits the description of the tested example.

6 Experiments

The first aim of experiments is to check how much two different techniques discussed in this paper, could increase a classification accuracy of the rule classifier induced by the MODLEM algorithm. Although we can expect such an improvement, we want to evaluate its amount and compare both approaches. Thus, on several benchmark data sets the use of the single rule based classifier is compared against the bagging classifier and the n^2 classifier, which include sub-classifiers also trained in an appropriated way by MODLEM. The second aim of this experiment is to evaluate the computational time of creating these multiple classifiers. We would like to verify whether the potential classification improvement is not burden with too high costs.

The MODLEM algorithm is used with the entropy measure to choose elementary conditions. All experiments are performed on the benchmark data sets, which are coming either from Machine Learning Repository at the University of California at Irvine [1] or from author's case studies, see [15]. Due to the paper size we skip their detailed characteristics . The classification accuracy is estimated by a *stratified* version of 10-*fold cross-validation technique*, i.e. the training examples are partitioned into 10 equal-sized blocks with similar class distributions as in the original set.

In this paper we partly summarize some results already obtained by the author in his preliminary studies (bagging [16] and n^2 [15]). However, we extend them by new data sets. Furthermore, we add new elements concerning evaluation of computational costs. Let us remarks the due to the specifies of each multiple classifier the sets of data are not identical for each of them. The bagging is a more universal approach to create an efficient classifier. Therefore, we used a few "easier" data sets (e.g., *iris*, *bank* or *buses*), where standard, single classifiers are expected to be sufficient and a larger number of more difficult data sets (having different characteristics – the choice was done according to the number of objects and characteristics of attributes). We also took into account some multiple-class learning problem, to compare with another multiple classifiers.

For the n^2-classifier - which is a specialized approach for multiple-class learning problems - we considered a set of multiple-class data; Here the choice is inspired by our earlier experiments with this kind of classifier [10, 11].

Table 1. Comparison of classification accuracies [%] obtained by the single MODLEM based classifier and the bagging approach

Name of dataset	Single MODLEM	Bagging - with different T 3	5	7	10
bank	93.81 ± 0.94	95.05 ± 0.91	94.95 ± 0.84	95.22 ± 1.02	93.95* ± 0.94
buses	97.20 ± 0.94	98.05* ± 0.97	99.54 ± 1.09	97.02* ± 1.15	97.45* ± 1.13
zoo	94.64 ± 0.67	93.82* ± 0.68	93.89* ± 0.71	93.47 ± 0.73	93.68 ± 0.70
hepatitis	78.62 ± 0.93	82.00 ± 1.14	84.05 ± 1.1	81.05 ± 0.97	84.0 ± 0.49
iris	94.93 ± 0.5	95.13* ± 0.46	94.86* ± 0.54	95.06* ± 0.53	94.33* ± 0.59
automobile	85.23 ± 1.1	82. 98 ± 0.86	83.0 ±0.99	82.74 ±0.9	81.39 ± 0.84
segmentation	85.71 ± 0.71	86.19* ± 0.82	87.62 ± 0.55	87.61 ± 0.46	87.14 ± 0.9
glass	72.41 ± 1.23	68.5 ± 1.15	74.81 ± 0.94	74.25 ± 0.89	76.09 ± 0.68
bricks	90.32* ± 0.82	90.3 * ± 0.54	89.84* ± 0.65	91.21* ± 0.48	90.77* ± 0.72
vote	92.67 ± 0.38	93.33* ± 0.5	94.34 ± 0.34	95.01 ± 0.44	96.01 ± 0.29
bupa	65.77 ± 0.6	64.98* ± 0.76	76.28 ± 0.44	70.74 ± 0.96	75.69 ± 0.7
election	88.96 ± 0.54	90.3 ± 0.36	91.2 ± 0.47	91.66 ± 0.34	90.75 ± 0.55
urology	63.80 ± 0.73	64.8 ± 0.83	65.0 ± 0.43	67.40 ± 0.46	67.0 ± 0.67
german	72.16 ± 0.27	73.07* ± 0.39	76.2 ± 0.34	75.62 ± 0.34	75.75 ± 0.35
crx	84.64 ± 0.35	84.74* ± 0.38	86.24 ± 0.39	87.1 ± 0.46	89.42 ± 0.44
pima	73.57 ± 0.67	75.78* ± 0.6	74.35* ± 0.64	74.88 ± 0.44	77.87 ± 0.39

While creating the bagging classifier, we have to tune the parameter T being the number of bootstrap samples and sub-classifiers. We have decided to check it experimentally, as the literature review has not given clear conclusions. Inspired by good results obtained by Quinlan for small numbers of T (for decision trees [12]), we examined the following values of T: 3, 5, 7 and 10. The results of these experiments are given in Table 1. For each dataset, the first column shows the classification accuracy obtained by a single classifier over the 10 cross-validations. Standard deviation is also given. The next columns contain results for the bagging classifiers with changing the number of sub-classifiers. An asterisk indicates that difference for these compared classifiers and a given data set are not statistically significant (according to two-paired t-Student test).

The experiments with the n^2-classifier were performed on 11 data sets, all concerning multiple-class learning problems. The number of classes varies from 3 up to 14. The MODLEM algorithm was again used to create sub-classifiers from subsets of learning examples coming from each pair of classes. Classification accuracies are presented in Table 2 - the second and third columns (presented in a similar way as in Table 1).

Then, let us move to the discussion of computation costs for each multiple classifier. An extra computation time for the bagging is easy to evaluate. If T

Table 2. Comparison of classification accuracies [%] and computation times [s] for the single MODLEM based classifier and the n^2-classifier also based on decision rules induced by MODLEM algorithm

Name of data set	Accuracy of single MODLEM (%)	Accuracy of n^2_{MODLEM} (%)	Time of comput. MODLEM	Time of comput. n^2_{MODLEM}
automobile	85.25 ± 1.3	87.96 ± 1.5	15.88 ± 0.4	5.22 ± 0.3
cooc	55.57 ± 2.0	59.30 ± 1.4	4148,7 ± 48.8	431.51 ± 1.6
ecoli	79.63 ± 0.8	81.34 ± 1.7	27.53 ± 0.5	11.25 ± 0.7
glass	72.07 ± 1.2	74.82 ± 1.4	45.29 ± 1.1	13.88 ± 0.4
hist	69.36 ± 1.1	73.10 ± 1.4	3563.79 ± 116.1	333.96 ± 0.8
meta-data	47.2 ± 1.3	49.83 ± 1.9	252.59 ± 78.9	276.71 ± 5.21
iris	94.2 ± 0.6	95.53* ± 1.2	0.71 ± 0.04	0.39 ± 0.04
soybean-large	91.09 ± 0.9	91.99* ± 0.8	26.38 ± 0.3	107.5 ± 5.7
vowel	81.81 ± 0.5	83.79 ± 1.2	3750.57 ± 30.4	250.63 ± 0.7
yeast	54.12 ± 0.7	55.74 ± 0.9	1544.3 ± 13.2	673.82 ± 9.4
zoo	94.64 ± 0.5	94.46* ± 0.8	0.30 ± 0.02	0.34 ± 0.12

classifiers are generated, than the approach requires approximately T times the computational effort of learning the single classifier by the MODLEM algorithm. The construction of the n^2-classifier is a more interesting case. In our previous works [10, 11] we noticed that the increase of classification accuracy (for other learning algorithms than MODLEM) is burden with increasing the computational costs (sometimes quite high). Here, for using MODLEM, the results are just opposite. Table 2 (two last columns) contains results of computation times (average value over 10 folds with standard deviations). Let us remark that all calculations have been performed on the same PC machine.

7 Discussion of Results and Final Remarks

First, let us discuss results of the experiments for each multiple classifier.

The bagging classifier significantly outperformed the single classifier on 11 of 16 data. The differences between compared classifiers were non-significant for 3 data sets (*buses*, *iris* and *bricks*) and the single classifier won only for *zoo* and *automobile*. We could comments that the worse performance of the bagging classifier occurred for rather "easier" data (characterized by a linear class separation). However, the bagging was a winner for more difficult problems. One can also notice the slightly worse performance of the bagging for quite small data (e.g. *buses*, *zoo* - which seemed to be too small for sampling), while it much improved for data sets containing the higher number of examples. Considering the number of sub-classifier T, it seems to be difficult to determine the best one value. For majority of data sets, the highest accuracy was obtained for T equal to 7 or 10. For few data set we have performed additional experiments with increasing T up to 20 [16]. However, we have not observed an improvement, except *glass* and *pima*.

The results obtained for the n^2-classifier indicate a significant improvement of the classification accuracy for the majority of multiple-class learning problems (7 of 11). Again, the multiple classifier was not useful for easier problems (e.g. *iris*). The differencies between compared classifiers were not significant for smaller number of examples. Moreover, similarly for using the bagging, the data set *zoo* was "too diffcult" - it was the only data, where the single classifier was slightly better than the n^2-classifier. Coming back to our previous results for the n^2-classifier [10] we can remark that the comparable classification improvements were observed for the case of using decision trees.

Comparing results of both multiple classifier should be very cautious as we had a quite limited number of common data sets. It seems that the n^2-classifier, which is in fact a specialized approach to learning multiple classes, is slightly better – compare results for *auto*, *glass* and even *zoo*. However, we should perform more experiments on a larger number of data sets.

The analysis of computation costs leads us to quite intriguing observation on using the MODLEM algorithm within the n^2-classifier. Generally, using it does not increase the computation time. What is even more astonishing, for the majority data sets (8 of 11) constructing the n^2-classifier requires even less time (from 2 up to 10 times less) than training the standard single classifier. However one should not be puzzled about this observation. Let us first remind the idea behind pairwise classification. Friedman argues [5] that the general all classes learning methods are limited in that for each there are broad classes of ("complex", non-linear) decision concepts with which they have difficulty. Even for universal approximators the learning sample size may place such limits. However, each pairwise decisions is more likely to be a simpler function of input attributes. This is especially when each decision class is well separated from most of the others. So, pairwise decision boundaries between each pair of classes could be simpler and can be quite often aproximated with linear functions while for the standard multiple class approach the decision boundary could be more complicated and more difficult to learn, e.g. with non-linear approximators.

Here, let us remind that for each of n decision classes the MODLEM algorithm sequentially generates the set of rules discriminating positive examples of the given class from all negative examples belonging to *all* other (n - 1) classes. So, besides the more complex decision boundaries (as discussed above), the computation time of this algorithm may also increase with the higher number of examples and classes. In the case of n^2-classifier the task is simpler, as it is sufficient to find these elementary condition which discriminate *two* classes only. Intuitively, we could expect that much smaller number of attributes is sufficient to distinguish a pair of classes. Moreover, having a smaller number of examples from two classes, the number of different attribute values should also be smaller (therefore, a smaller number of conditions is tested while inducing rules). This hypothesis is somehow confirmed by a detailed analysis of the characteristics of rule sets induced by the single standard classifier and the n^2-classifier. For instance, for *ecoli* data the MODLEM algorithm (used as a standard multiple-class approach) induced 46 rules, which contain totally 171 elementary conditions (on average 3.7 per each rule); Each rule covers on average 9.3 examples. The n^2-classifier contains 118 rules (for all binary sub-classifier) using 217 conditions (on average 1.8 per rule); However each rule covers 26.5 examples! Similar observations have been made for the many of other data sets. It seems that in our experiments creating subspaces of attributes dedicated for discriminating pairs of classes has been more efficient than using the same set of attributes for distinguishing all decision classes at the same time.

The bagging classifier needs more computations and the additional costs depends on T - the number of sub-classifiers. Coming back to the expected improvement of classification accuracy, the bagging is more general approach than n^2 specialized for multiple-classes. Simiarly to the n^2-classifier, bagging also works better for more "complex/non-linear" decision concepts. We could expect it as according to Breiman the bagging should be constructed with *unstable* learning algorithms, i.e. ones whose output classifier undergoes major changes in response to small changes in learning data. Similar to decision tree inducers the algorithm MODLEM is the unstable algorithm in the sense of this postulate.

To sum up, the results of our experiments have shown that the MODLEM algorithm can be efficiently used within the framework of two considered multiple classifiers for data sets concerning more "complex" decision concepts. The n^2-classifier is particularly well suited for multiple class data where exist "simpler" pairwise decision boundaries between pairs of classes. However, the relative merits of these new approaches depends on the specifies of particular problems and a training sample size.

Let us notice that there is a disadvantage of the multiple classifiers - loosing a simple and easy interpretable structure of knowledge represented in a form decision rules. These are ensembles of diversified rule sets specialized for predictive aims not one set of rules in a form for a human inspection.

For future research, it could be interesting to consider yet another techniques for aggregating predictions from sub-classifier. In particular it concerns the n^2-classifier, whose sub-classifiers are trained to distinguish particular pairs of classes only. Therefore, they could be excluded (or weaken) from voting for examples likely coming from different classes.

References

1. Blake C., Koegh E., Mertz C.J.: Repository of Machine Learning, University of California at Irvine (1999).
2. Breiman L.: Bagging predictors. Machine Learning, 24 (2), (1996) 123–140.
3. Bauer E., Kohavi R.: An empirical comparison of voting classification algorithms: Bagging, boosting, and variants. Machine Learning, 36 (1/2), (1999) 105–139.
4. Dietrich T.G.: Ensemble methods in machine learning. In: Proc. of 1st Int. Workshop on Multiple Classifier Systems, (2000) 1–15.
5. Friedman J.: Another approach to polychotomous classification, Technical Report, Stanford University (1996).
6. Gama J.: Combining classification algorithms. Ph.D. Thesis, University of Porto (1999).

7. Grzymala-Busse J.W.: Managing uncertainty in machine learning from examples. In: Proc. 3rd Int. Symp. in Intelligent Systems, Wigry, Poland, IPI PAN Press, (1994) 70–84.
8. Grzymala-Busse J.W., Stefanowski J.: Three approaches to numerical attribute discretization for rule induction. International Journal of Intelligent Systems, 16 (1), (2001) 29–38.
9. Hastie T., Tibshirani R., Classification by pairwise coupling. In: Jordan M.I. (eds.) Advances in Neural Information Processing Systems: 10 (NIPS-97), MIT Press, (1998) 507-513.
10. Jelonek J., Stefanowski J.: Experiments on solving multiclass learning problems by the n^2-classifier. In: Proceedings of 10th European Conference on Machine Learning ECML 98, Springer LNAI no. 1398, (1998) 172–177.
11. Jelonek J., Stefanowski J.: Feature selection in the n^2-classifier applied for multiclass problems. In: Proceedings of the AI-METH 2002 Conference on Artificial Intelligence Methods, Gliwice, (2002) 297-301.
12. Quinlan J.R.: Bagging, boosting and C4.5. In: Proceedings of the 13th National Conference on Artificial Intelligence, (1996) 725–730.
13. Stefanowski J.: The rough set based rule induction technique for classification problems. In: Proceedings of 6th European Conference on Intelligent Techniques and Soft Computing EUFIT 98, Aachen 7-10 Sept., (1998) 109–113.
14. Stefanowski J.: Multiple and hybrid classifiers. In: Polkowski L. (ed.) Formal Methods and Intelligent Techniques in Control, Decision Making, Multimedia and Robotics, Post-Proceedings of 2nd Int. Conference, Warszawa, (2001) 174–188.
15. Stefanowski J.: Algorithims of rule induction for knowledge discovery. (In Polish), Habilitation Thesis published as Series Rozprawy no. 361, Poznan Univeristy of Technology Press, Poznan (2001).
16. Stefanowski J.: Bagging and induction of decision rules. In: Int. Symposium on Intelligent Systems; Post-Proceedings of the IIS'2002. Series: Advances of Soft Computing, Physica Verlag, Heidelberg, (2002) 121-130.
17. Klosgen W., Żytkow J.M. (eds.): Handbook of Data Mining and Knowledge Discovery, Oxford Press (2002).

A Parallel Approximate Rule Extracting Algorithm Based on the Improved Discernibility Matrix

Liu Yong, Xu Congfu, and Pan Yunhe

Institute of Artificial Intelligence, Zhejiang University
Hangzhou 310027, China
cckaffe@yahoo.com.cn, xucongfu@cs.zju.edu.cn

Abstract. A parallel rule-extracting algorithm based on the improved discernibility matrix [2] is proposed, by this way, a large amount of raw data can be divided into some small portions to be processed in parallel. The confidence factor is also introduced to the rule sets to obtain the uncertainty rules. The most important advantage of this algorithm is that it does not need to calculate the discernibility matrix corresponding to these overall data.

1 Introduction

Rough set (*RS*) theory is first proposed by Z.Pawlak [1] in 1982. It is a kind of very useful mathematical tool to deal with vagueness and uncertainty information. Recently, this theory attracts more attentions in the fields of data mining, knowledge discovery in database (KDD), pattern recognition, decision support systems (DSS) etc. The main idea of this theory is that it provides us with a kind of mechanism of extracting the classification rules by knowledge reduction, while keeping the satisfactory capacity of classification. There are many successful applications by using *RS* theory in the following areas such as machine learning, data mining, knowledge discovery, decision analysis, and knowledge acquisition etc.[3]. When we apply *RS* theory to solve practical problems, for example, to discover knowledge and rules from database, we usually have to face the following embarrassed situation: there are millions of data records in the database, and if the traditional rule-extracting algorithms based on *RS* theory are adopted, it will consume $O(G^2)$ (here G is the number of raw data records) time complexity to obtain the data discernibility relationship during the process of rule extracting. It is obvious that the above process will consume a huge amount of computational time and memory space when dealing with very large databases or data warehouses, and therefore the efficiency of these algorithms is very low. In fact, the aforesaid condition is very common in practice, so it is necessary to study the efficient rule-extracting algorithms based on *RS* theory. In practice, if the computational speed conflicts with its accuracy, and suppose that the result accuracy which is not less than a threshold can be accepted by the users, people usually pay more attention to the speed of rule extracting than the accuracy of

S. Tsumoto et al. (Eds.): RSCTC 2004, LNAI 3066, pp. 498–503, 2004.

rule set. Based on the above underlying hypothesis, in this paper, we propose a kind of parallel approximate rule-extracting algorithm based on improved discernibility matrix [2]. There are four aspects of distinguished advantages existing in our parallel algorithm: (1) It can extract uncertainty rules as well as certainty rules easily from huge data sets by adopting the confidence factor to control the process of the extraction of those uncertainty rules. (2) Its computational complexity is rather lower compared with other relative algorithms. (3) It is not only suitable for the problems of duality decision but also for those of multiple-decision. (4) The rule set extracted by our algorithm is a superset of the real rule set.

2 Related Works

Shan and *Ziakro* proposed an incremental *RS* learning algorithm [7], the main idea of this algorithm is as follows: firstly, calculate a decision matrix corresponding to each decision attribute, then extract rules from these generated decision matrixes. According to *Shan* and *Ziakro's* algorithm, it needs to calculate the decision matrix for every decision attribute respectively, so the number of decision matrixes is equal to that of the decision attributes. One of the main disadvantages of *Shan* and *Ziakro's* algorithm is that it does not support inconsistent data. To solve this problem, *Bian* [8] brought forward an improved algorithm based on *Shan* and *Ziakro's* algorithm. The algorithm presented in [8] uses an extended decision matrix to deal with those inconsistent data that cannot be solved by *Shan* and *Ziakro's* algorithm. However, there are also some other disadvantages existing in both of the above-mentioned algorithms: (1) Both of them need to calculate the decision matrix for each decision attribute, while the number of decision attributes is usually very large (e.g. in those information systems with huge of data). Because a large number of decision matrixes should be calculated respectively, so this process will consume much time and memory. (2) Both of them cannot obtain the uncertainty rules, which are also very important in the information systems, and they do not make full use of all the information existing in data systems. Therefore we propose a new rule-extracting algorithm based on the improved discernibility matrix [2], and our algorithm can solve the aforesaid disadvantages effectively.

3 Parallel Rule-Extracting Algorithm

3.1 Category of Incremental Data

Pawlak [4, 5] pointed out that there exist three kinds of conditions when a new item of information is added to the information system, and it is similar to the condition that a new rule is added to the original rule set. In this article, there may exist four kinds of categories of new rules, which are added to the original rule set. The definition of incremental rule is presented as follows:

Consider information system $S = (U, A)$, and suppose M is the rule set, there is a rule $\phi_i \rightarrow \varphi_i$, where i is an element in U, ϕ_i is the antecedent, and φ_i is the consequent. In this new category system, there exist four possible conditions when a new item of data is added to the information system S. They are defined respectively as follows:

Definition 1. *CS* **category** the new added datum x belongs to CS category, if and only if $\exists(\phi \rightarrow \varphi) \in M, \phi_x \rightarrow \phi$ and $\varphi_x = \varphi$.

Definition 2. *CN* **category** the new added datum x belongs to CN category, if and only if $\forall(\phi \rightarrow \varphi) \in M, \varphi_x \neq \varphi$.

Definition 3. *CC* **category** the new added datum x belongs to CC category, if and only if x does not belong to CN category, and $y \in U$ satisfies $\phi_x \equiv \phi_y$ and $\varphi_x \neq \varphi_y$.

Definition 4. *PC* **category** the new added datum x belongs to PC category, if and only if x does not belong to CN category, and $y \in U$ satisfies $\phi_x \neq \phi_y$.

Normally, when new data arrive at the information system, the category of these data needs to be determined firstly, then the discernibility matrix is updated, and finally the new rule sets can be obtained.

3.2 Parallel Rule-Extracting Algorithm

The parallel rule-extracting algorithm is composed of the following three parts: the first one is the raw data set division part, the second one is parallel normal rule-extracting part, and the third is multiple rule sets combination part. The data division part split the raw data into several individual data sets that can be calculated in parallel. The normal rule-extracting algorithm deals with the individual data set by using the improved discernibility matrix, and multiple rule sets combination algorithm deals with the incremental data set to generate a consistent rule set.

Data Division. Suppose there are G items in a raw data set, we divide this data set into N+1 portions, here $N = [\sqrt{G}]$, and $[G]$ means the integrity portion of G, the N+1 portions are notated as $S_1, S_2, S_3, ..., S_{N+1}$. When the number of raw data items is huge, the number of these portions satisfies the following formula:

$$|S_1| = |S_2| = |S_3| = ... = |S_N| = N >> |S_{N+1}|$$

Parallel Normal Rule-Extracting Algorithm. In this part, for each data portion divided by the above step, we have:

Step 1. Data preprocess. This step begins with the Decision Table, which contains the condition attribute set C and the decision attribute set D. Then an information system $S = (U, A)$ is obtained.

Step 2. Divide the condition attribute set C into the object equivalence class $E_i \in U/IND(C), i = 1, 2, ..., |U/IND(C)|$.

Step 3. Divide the decision attribute set D into the decision equivalence class $X_j \in U/IND(D), j = 1, 2, ..., |U/IND(D)|$.

Step 4. Calculate the improved discernibility matrix.

Step 5. Calculate the discernibility functions [6] $f(E_i)$ for each object equivalence class E_i.

Step 6. According to the discernibility function $f(E_i)$, calculate the comparative discernibility function $f(E_i, C)$ by using the following rules:

if $f(E_i) = 0$, then $f(E_i, C) = C$ else $f(E_i, C) = f(E_i)$

Step 7. Export the decision rules based on the $f(E_i, C)$:

if $E_i \subseteq X_j$, then the generated rule is a certainty rule;

if $E_i \not\subset X_j$ and $E_i \bigcap X_j \neq 0$, then the generated rule is an uncertainty rule, whose confidence factor is defined as:

$$\alpha = \frac{|E_i \bigcap X_j|}{E_i}$$

The above algorithm is executed in parallel to obtain the initial rule set M_i for each portion S_i.

Multiple Rule Set Combination Algorithm. After obtaining the individual rule set $\{M_1, M_2, M_3, ..., M_{N+1}\}$, we present an algorithm to combine multiple rule sets to generate the approximate rule set correspond to the raw data. Each rule in M_i is notated as $[R_i^k, \alpha_i^{R_i^k}, N_i]$, where R_i^k is the rule $(\phi \to \varphi)$, $\alpha_i^{R_i^k}$ is the confidence factor of R_i^k, and N_i is the number of items in M_i. The algorithm of combining multiple rule sets is given as follows,

For each rule in Mi, let $M = M_1 \bigoplus M_2 \bigoplus M_3 \bigoplus ... \bigoplus M_N \bigoplus M_{N+1}$, here M is the ultimate approximate rule set after combination. $M = \{[R_i^k, \alpha_i^{R_i^k}, N_i], k = 1, 2, 3, ...\}$, The $\bigoplus$ operation includes these following steps:

Step 1. Those rules in M which notated as $RS(M)$, are combined as

$$RS(M) = RS(M_1) \bigcup RS(M_2) \bigcup RS(M_3) \bigcup ... \bigcup RS(M_N) \bigcup RS(M_{N+1})$$

Step 2. The number of items is changed to the total number of items in the raw data.

$$G = N_1 + N_2 + N_3 + ... + N_N + N_{N+1}$$

Step 3. The confidence factor (α^{R^k}) for each rule in M is adjusted by the following formula:

$$\alpha^{R^k} = \frac{\sum_{i=1}^{N+1} N_i \alpha_i^{R_i^k}}{\sum_{i=1}^{N+1} N_i} \tag{1}$$

Note that in formula (1), if a rule does not exist in M_i, then $\alpha_i^{R_i^k} = 0$. According to the above process of data division, the formula (1) can be predigested to the following formula (2):

$$\alpha^{R^k} = \frac{N \sum_{i=1}^{N} \alpha_i^{R_i^k}}{G} + (1 - \frac{[\sqrt{G}]^2}{G}) \alpha_{N+1}^{R_{N+1}^k} \tag{2}$$

After re-calculating the confidence factor for each rule, then the approximate rule-extracting algorithm ends.

4 Performance Analysis

In this section, our parallel approximate algorithm is compared with the traditional rule-extracting algorithms according to time and spatial complexity. Before analyze the complexity of our parallel approximate algorithm, let's first have an overview on the traditional rule-extracting algorithms, which are similar to the parallel rule-extracting algorithm discussed in section 3.2.

The time complexity of traditional rule-extracting algorithms by using improved discernibility matrix is composed of the matrix computational complexity and the rule export complexity (including the complexity of computing discernibility functions). Suppose G is the number of items in the original raw data (there is no redundancy in these data) and T_{max} is the maximum time consumed by those basic operations, which include the computation of basic units of discernibility matrix and the computation of rule-extracting from this matrix. So the total consumed time and space are defined as formula (3) and (4):

$$T_{all} = T_{max} \times \sum_{i}^{G} i + T_{max} \times G \tag{3}$$

The discernibility matrix is a symmetry matrix, so only half of the matrix need to be calculated.

$$S_{all} = S_{max} \times \sum_{i}^{G} i \tag{4}$$

where S is the maximum spatial unit in computation operations. Then we can obtain the time and spatial complexity for the traditional algorithms.

$$T_{complexity} = O(G^2) \tag{5}$$

$$S_{complexity} = O(G^2) \tag{6}$$

As for our parallel rule-extracting algorithm, the terms are the same as the above formula. The consumed time and space are calculated by formula (7) and (8):

$$T_{all}^{'} = T_{max} \times \sum_{i}^{G} i + T_{max} \times N + T_{max} \times N \times N \tag{7}$$

here N is the number of data segment. And the total consumed time includes the time of unit data's discernibility matrix computation, rule-extracting and rule combination.

$$S_{all}^{'} = S \times N \times \sum_{i}^{G} i \tag{8}$$

So the complexity of our parallel algorithm can be defined as follows:

$$T'_{complexity} = O(N^2) = O(G) \tag{9}$$

$$S'_{complexity} = O(N^3) = O(G\sqrt{G}) \tag{10}$$

5 Conclusion

From the aforesaid analysis, our parallel rule-extracting algorithm is rational, since it can deal with those time-consuming computational problems with inconsistent information. This algorithm can obtain both the certainty rules and uncertainty rules, so it can make full use of the existing information in the system; the introduction of confidence factor can afford a more accruable description for the uncertainty rules. This algorithm is an approximate algorithm and its time complexity and spatial complexity are less than the traditional rule-extracting algorithms, it is very useful under those conditions that the number of data set is huge and the computational speed is more important than the computational accuracy.

Acknowledgements

This paper is supported by the projects of Zhejiang Provincial Natural Science Foundation of China (No. 602045, and No. 601110), and it is also supported by the advanced research project sponsored by China Defense Ministry.

References

1. Pawlak, Z. Rough sets. International Journal of Computer and Information Science, 11(5):341-356, 1982.
2. Bazan, J.G., Nguyen, H.S., Nguyen, S.H, Synak, P., Wroblewski, J.: Rough Set Algorithms in Classification Problem. In: Polkowski, L., Tsumoto, S., Lin, T.Y. (eds), Rough Set Methods and Applications, Physica-Verlag, 2000 pp. 49-88.
3. Pawlak, Z., Grzymala-Busse, J., Slowinski, R. Rough sets. Communications of the ACM, 8(11): 89- 95, 1995.
4. Pawlak, Z. Rough sets: theoretical aspects and reasoning about data. Kluwer Academic Publishers, 1991.
5. Pawlak, Z. On learning - a rough set approach. In: G. Goos, et al. (eds.), Proceedings of International Symposium on Computation Theory and Lecture Notes in Computer Science, Vol.208, pp.197-227, 1984.
6. Skowron A. The Rough sets theory and evidence theory. Fundamenta Informaticae 13: 245-262, 1990.
7. Shan, N., Ziarko, W. An incremental learning algorithm for constructing decision ruls. In: Kluwer. R. S. (eds.), Rough Sets, Fuzzy Sets and Knowledge Discovery, Springer-Verlag, pp.326-334,1994.
8. Bian, Xuehai. Certain rule learning of the inconsistent data. Journal of East China Shipbuilding Institute, 12(1):25-30, 1998 (*In Chinese*).

Decision Rules in Multivalued Decision Systems

Wojciech Rząsa[1], Artur Paluch[2], and Zbigniew Suraj[1,2]

[1] Institute of Mathematics, University of Rzeszow
Rejtana 16A, 35-310 Rzeszow, Poland
wrzasa@univ.rzeszow.pl
[2] The Chair of Computer Science Foundations
University of Information Technology and Management
H. Sucharskiego 2, 35-225 Rzeszow, Poland
{apaluch,zsuraj}@wenus.wsiz.rzeszow.pl

Abstract. The paper includes some notions from the area of decision systems analysis defined for systems with multifunctions as attributes. Apart from retuned notions of indiscernibiliy relation, reduct or decision rule which are natural generalization of respective classical notions there is described an algorithm of minimal decision rules generation in considered type of decision systems. Moreover we shortly compare the rules with the ones generated as for classical decision systems. An adapted confusion matrix is presented to show output of classification of new objects to respective decision classes. We also suggest as an example a kind of real life data that are suitable for being analyzed according to the presented algorithms.

1 Introduction

The article contains foundamental notion from the area of multivalued decision systems analysis. They are used to present a way of decision rules generation in mentioned type of decision systems. Although, as we show it is possible to treat decision systems with multifunctions as attributes like classical decision systems but it is not suitable depiction because it causes loss of information hidden in elements of each value of each attribute. Motivation for the paper were problems we had with analysis a concrete real life temporal data by means of available tools.

The article has the following structure. In section 2 there are given some basic notions like information indistinguishability relation for multivalued information systems that is used to define reduct, two types of inconsistent multivalued decision system and algorithm for recognizing them. Section 3 is dedicated to description of decision rules in multivalued decision systems. In section 4 we investigate some problems that occur during classification of new objects by means of decision rules generated as it is shown in section 3.

S. Tsumoto et al. (Eds.): RSCTC 2004, LNAI 3066, pp. 504–509, 2004.

2 Basic Definitions

A pair $S = (U, A)$ is called a *multivalued information system* if and only if S is an information system (cf. [4]) and every attribute $a \in A$ is a function $a : U \to Pow(Y_a)$ for some sets Y_a. Henceforth we will use the following notions and symbols for any multivalued information system $S = (U, A)$: $Y_a = \bigcup_{u \in U} a(u)$ for $a \in A$, and it is called a *set of elementary values of the attribute* a; $V_a = \bigcup_{u \in U} \{a(u)\}$ for $a \in A$, and it is called a *set of values of the attribute* a. There are known several semantics of multivalued information systems (cf. [1]). In the paper we assume conjunctive and non exhaustive interpretation: if u is an object and *language* is an attribute then the expression *language*(u) $= \{Eng, Pol\}$ denotes "u speaks English, Polish and possibly other languages". Let $S = (U, A)$ be a multivalued information system and let $B \subseteq A$. Relations $ING_S \subseteq U \times U$ and $DG_S \subseteq U \times U$ defined as follows $ING_S(B) = \{(u, v) \in U \times U | \forall a \in B[a(u) \subseteq a(v)]\}$, $DG_S(B) = U \times U - ING_S(B)$ are respectively examples of informational indistinguishability and distinguishability relations. (cf. [3]) In the following the relations will be denoted with omitting index S. For a given multivalued information system $S = (U, A)$ every minimal (with respect to inclusion) nonempty subset B of set A, together with minimal (with respect to inclusion) nonempty subsets Y'_a of sets Y_a for $a \in B$ is called a *reduct* of the system S if and only if $ING(B) = ING(A)$. Notions of *multivalued decision system, condition attributes* and *decision* are defined for multivalued information systems in analogous way as for classical ones. In the paper multivalued decision systems with one-element sets of decision only are consider and they are denoted as a pair $S = (U, A \cup \{d\})$. Moreover we assume that $d : U \to Pow(Y_d) - \{\emptyset\}$.

Example 1. Let us consider information system given in Table 1. The set $B = \{a', d\}$, where $a'(u) = a(u) - \{0\}$ for every $u \in U$, is a reduct of the information system.

Table 1. Multivalued decision system

$U \backslash A \cup \{d\}$	a	b	d
u_1	{0, 1}	{0, 1, 2}	{0, 1}
u_2	{0, 2}	{1, 2}	{1, 2, 3}
u_3	{1}	{0, 2}	{1, 2}
u_4	{1, 2}	{0, 1, 2}	{0}

Let $S = (U, A \cup \{d\})$ be a multivalued decision system. System S is called *consistent* if for all $u, v \in U$ $[uING(A)v \Rightarrow uING(\{d\})v]$. A multivalued decision system which is not consistent is called *inconsistent*. For every inconsistent multivalued decision system it is possible to define two types of inconsistency. The following algorithm is used to do it:

Algorithm 1
Input: Inconsistent multivalued decision system $S = (U, A \cup \{d\})$.
Output: Multivalued decision system $S' = (U, A \cup \{d'\})$.
begin
  repeat for every pair $(u, v) \in U \times U$, such that $uING(A)v$ and $uDG(\{d\})v$
    if $d(u) \cap d(v) \neq \emptyset$ **then** $d(u) := d(u) \cap d(v)$
    else break;
  repeat for every $u \in U$
    $d'(u) := d(u)$;
  if $S' = (U, A \cup \{d'\})$ is inconsistent **then** *isConsistent*:=**false**
  else *isConsistent*:=**true**;
end.

The outcome of the algorithm does not depend on the order of the pairs $(u, v) \in U \times U$ considered in the first loop of the algorithm. An inconsistent multivalued decision system S is called *partially inconsistent* if and only if Algorithm 1 transforms it into a multivalued consistent decision system S'; otherwise system S is called *entirely inconsistent.*

3 Decision Rules Generation

For multivalued decision systems we may construct the notion of a decision rule in the way similar as we do for the classical decision systems. (cf. [2]) But now, atomic formulae over sets $B \subseteq A \cup \{d\}$ and Y (where $Y = \bigcup_{a \in A} Y_a \cup Y_d$), that is so called descriptors, are expressions of the form $e \in a$, where $e \in Y_a$ and $a \in B$. Any expression of the form $\tau \Rightarrow e \in d$, where τ is a single descriptor $e \in a$ over B and Y (in that case $||\tau||_S = \{u \in U| \quad e \in a(u)\}$) or a conjuction of such descriptors (if $\tau = \tau_1 \wedge \tau_2$ and τ_1, τ_2 are descriptors then $||\tau||_S = ||\tau_1||_S \cap ||\tau_2||_S$) with constraints $||\tau||_S \neq \emptyset$ is called a *decision rule* for S. Decision rule $\tau \Rightarrow e \in d$ is true in S if and only if $||\tau||_S \subseteq ||e \in d||_S$. A decision rule true in S is minimal in S if and only if none of decision rules $\tau' \Rightarrow e \in d$ such that the set of descriptors of τ' is properly included in the set of descriptors from τ is true in S. In the same way we may define decision rules with descriptors over sets $B \subseteq A \cup \{d\}$ and $V = \bigcup_{a \in A} V_a \cup Vd$ of the form $v \subseteq a$, where $v \subseteq V_a$ and $a \in B$. Decision rule of the form $\tau \Rightarrow v \subseteq d$ is equivalent to the set of decision rules of the form $\{\tau_i \Rightarrow e_i \in d| \quad i = 1, .., p\}$ if and only if for all multivalued decision systems S if $\tau \Rightarrow v \subseteq d$ is a decision rule in it then each of the rules $\tau_i \Rightarrow e_i \in d$ for $i = 1, .., p$ is also a decision rule in it and vice versa, and the following conditions hold: $||\tau||_S = ||\tau_1 \wedge .. \wedge \tau_p||_S$ and $||v \subseteq d||_S = ||e_1 \in d \wedge .. \wedge e_p \in d||_S$.

Example 2. Rules $\{0, 2\} \subseteq a \Rightarrow \{2, 3\} \subseteq d$ and $\{0\} \subseteq a \Rightarrow \{1\} \subseteq d$ are equivalent respectively with two-element set of rules$\{0 \in a \wedge 2 \in a \Rightarrow 2 \in d, 0 \in a \wedge 2 \in a \Rightarrow 3 \in d\}$ and with rule $0 \in a \Rightarrow 1 \in d$ in every multivalued decision system where the above expressions are decision rules. All the rules are minimal in decision system given in Table 1.

Let us notice that for every multivalued decision system (with mentioned semantics) it is possible to generate decision rules as for the classical decision systems. It is enough to consider values of attributes as indivisible. Yet such rules seem to be more appropriate for systems with exhaustive semantics (where expression $language(u) = \{Eng, Pol\}$ means "u speaks English and Polish and non of other languages").

Algorithm 2
Input: Multivalued decision system $S = (U, A \cup \{d\})$ such that $|U| = n$.
Output: Set of all minimal decision rules for S with descriptors of the form $e \in a$.

```
begin
  generate discernibility matrix M_{n×n} = (m_ij), where
  m_ij = {e ∈ a|e ∈ [a(u_i) − a(u_j)] ∧ a ∈ A ∪ {d}};
  repeat for every row i of matrix M
    repeat for every descriptor e ∈ d that occurs in the considered row begin
      initialize discernibility function f_d := 1;
      isConsistency: = true;
      repeat for every cell m_ij of the matrix which contains descriptor e ∈ d
        if there are descriptors with condition attributes than
          f_d := f_d ∧ ∨(e_{n_k} ∈ a_k), where descriptors e_{n_k} ∈ a_k
          are in the considered cell and a_k ≠ d, for all k
        else begin
          isConsistency:=false;
          break;
        end if
      if isConsistency:= true then begin
        find prime implicants of function f_d;
        convert found prime implicants into predecessors of rules
          with successor e ∈ d;
      end if
      remove a decision rule if there is identical another one;
    end repeat
end.
```

For presenting the rules it is more comfortable to use descriptors of the form $v \subseteq a$ because of not bigger number of them in comparison with rules consisted of descriptors $e \in a$.

4 Classification

Now, let us consider the problem of classification of new objects on the base of prior knowledge. There are two problems associated with the classification: solving conflicts between families of decision rules that propose different values of decision for new object and computing the coefficient of the quality of the rules. Let us start with an example.

Example 3. Table 2 presents a multivalued decision system consisting of two objects. Let it be a test table for decision rules generated for the decision system given in Table 1.

Table 2. Test table

$U \backslash A \cup \{d\}$	a	b	d
u_5	{0}	{0, 1}	{0, 1, 2}
u_6	{0, 2}	{0}	{0, 1}

One can check that none of classical decision rules generated from data in Table 1 match object u_5. In opposite the following minimal rules generated according to Algorithm 2 match the object: $\{0\} \subseteq a \wedge \{0\} \subseteq b \Rightarrow \{0\} \subseteq d$; $\{0,1\} \subseteq b \Rightarrow \{0\} \subseteq d$; $\{0\} \subseteq a \Rightarrow \{1\} \subseteq d$. They propose the set {0, 1} to be included in the value of decision for object u_5. Object u_6 is matched by exactly one minimal classical rule $a = \{0,2\} \Rightarrow d = \{1,2,3\}$ and four determined according to Algorithm 2: $\{0\} \subseteq a \wedge \{0\} \subseteq b \Rightarrow \{0\} \subseteq d$; $\{0\} \subseteq a \Rightarrow \{1\} \subseteq d$; $\{0,2\} \subseteq a \Rightarrow \{2,3\} \subseteq d$; $\{2\} \subseteq a \wedge \{0\} \subseteq b \Rightarrow \{0\} \subseteq d$. They suggest each elementary value from set {0, 1, 2, 3} to belong to the value of d. But such set is not an element of V_d of the decision system given in Table 1 so we are willing to recognize this situation as a classification conflict. We suggest assuming the following definition: two or more classes of decision rules DR_i $(i \geq 2)$ generated according to Algorithm 2 are in conflict during classifying an object u if and only if all of the rules from DR_i match u and the set $V_{acc}d$ of acceptable values of decision does not include (consist of) all values proposed by the rules. The set $V_{acc}d$ may be defined in different ways. In generally $V_{acc}d \subseteq \{v | v \subseteq d(u), u \in U\}$, where U is universe of training table but strict definition of $V_{acc}d$ depends on context of applying. Let for need of Example 3 $V_{acc}d = \{v | v = d(u), u \in U\}$ and let the conflict in classifying objects u_6 be settled in advantage of value {0, 1}. Table 3 presents confusion matrix [5] for objects from Table 2 classified in the way described below by means of decision rules generated according to Algorithm 2. There are extra one (last) row and column where coefficients of partially correct classification are computed. They may be determined in several ways. For example, we can regard predicted value as partially correct if it is a part of actual value in a degree bigger than a fixed threshold or in accordance with the rule $(p \wedge q \Rightarrow p)$ if predicted value is a part (is included) of actual value. The coefficient presented in Table 3 is determined according to the last rule.

Table 3. Confusion matrix

A	Predicted				
c		{0, 1}	{0, 1, 2}		
t	{0, 1}	1	0	1	1
u	{0, 1, 2}	1	0	0	1
a		0.5	undefined	0.5	
l		1	undefined		1

Example 4. Let us assume a temporal information system is given (cf. [6]). The task is to discover sequence rules between temporal templates discovered from the system and test them for some new cases. The solution of the problem may be as follows. After finding a sequence of temporal templates with maximal length we encode by single symbols their descriptors instead of whole templates as it is proposed in [6]. Next we build a multivalued decision system (number of attributes denotes how many steps back we want to seek regularities between templates) [6] and find decision rules for the system as described in section 3. Let us say there is the following regularity: *if* $a_0 = 1 \wedge a_1 = 0$ in one moment *then* $a_1 = 1 \wedge a_3 = 2$ after 2 moments. If at least once happened that instead of actual template a longer one was found (for example because of accidentally distribution of unimportant attributes' values) then proper regularity will be discovered only by applying decision rules generated according to Algorithm 2 (cf. semantics of decision rules). For checking quality of generated rules one may follow our proposal from section 4.

5 Conclusions

In the paper boolean reasoning based algorithm for certain rules generation in multivalued decision systems with conjunctive and non exhaustive semantics is given. Apart from that, the notion of conflict between rules is redefined and a coefficient of partially correct classification is introduced. The example given at the end of the paper shows alternative way to given in [6] of temporal template analysis. As continuation of the paper experiments with real life data are going to be made to verify presented ideas as well as extension of described considerations including uncertain rules generation.

References

1. Düntsch, I., Gediga, G., Orłowska, E.: Relational Attribute Systems , in International Journal of Human - Computer Studies (2000) 1 – 17;
2. Komorowski, J., Pawlak, Z., Polkowski, L., Skowron, A.: Rough Set: A Tutorial, in S. K. Pal and A. Skowron (Eds.), Rough fuzzy Hybridization: A new Trend in decision-making, Springer-Verlag, Singapore, pp. 3–98
3. Orłowska, E.: Introduction: What You Always Wanted to Know about Rough Sets, in E. Orłowska (Ed.), Incomplete Information : Rough Set Analysis, Physica - Verlag, Heidelberg - New York, (1998), 1 – 20;
4. Orłowska, E., Pawlak, Z.: Representation of Nondeterministic Information, Theoretical Computer Science 29 (1984), 27 –39
5. The ROSETTA Homepage, http://www.idi.ntnu.no/~aleks/rosetta
6. Synak, P.: Temporal Templates and Analysis of Time Related Data, in: W. Ziarko and Y. Yao (Eds.), The Second International Conference, RSCTC 2000, Lectures Notes in Artificial Intelligence 2001, Springer-Verlag, Berlin (2001), 420–427.

Multicriteria Choice and Ranking Using Decision Rules Induced from Rough Approximation of Graded Preference Relations

Philippe Fortemps[1], Salvatore Greco[2], and Roman Słowiński [3]

[1] Department of Math & O.R, Faculty of Engineering, Mons, 7000 Mons, Belgium
Philippe.Fortemps@fpms.ac.be
[2] Faculty of Economics, University of Catania, 95129 Catania, Italy
salgreco@mbox.unict.it
[3] Institute of Computing Science, Poznan University of Technology, 60-965 Poznan, and Institute for Systems Research, Polish Academy of Sciences, 01-447 Warsaw, Poland
slowinsk@sol.put.poznan.pl

Abstract. The approach described in this paper can be applied to support multicriteria choice and ranking of actions when the input preferential information acquired from the decision maker is a graded pairwise comparison (or ranking) of reference actions. It is based on decision-rule preference model induced from a rough approximation of the graded comprehensive preference relation among the reference actions. The set of decision rules applied to a new set of actions provides a fuzzy preference graph, which can be exploited by an extended fuzzy net flow score, to build a final ranking.

Keywords: Multicriteria choice and ranking, Decision rules, Dominance-based rough sets, Graded preference relations, Fuzzy preference graph, Fuzzy net flow score, Leximax

1 Introduction

Construction of a logical model of behavior from observation of agent's acts is a paradigm of artificial intelligence and, in particular, of inductive learning. The set of rules representing a decision policy of an agent constitutes its *preference model*. It is a necessary component of decision support systems for multicriteria choice and ranking problems. Classically, it has been a utility function or a binary relation – its construction requires some *preference information* from the agent called *decision maker* (DM), like substitution ratios among criteria, importance weights, or thresholds of indifference, preference and veto. In comparison, the preference model in terms of decision rules induced from *decision examples* provided by the DM has two advantages over the classical models: (i) it is intelligible and speaks the language of the DM, (ii) the preference information comes from observation of DM's decisions.

Inconsistency often present in the set of decision examples cannot be considered as simple error or noise – they follow from hesitation of the DM, unstable character of his/her preferences and incomplete determination of the family of criteria. They can convey important information that should be taken into account in the construction of

S. Tsumoto et al. (Eds.): RSCTC 2004, LNAI 3066, pp. 510–522, 2004.

the DM's preference model. Rather than correct or ignore these inconsistencies, we propose to take them into account in the preference model construction using the *rough set* concept [14, 15]. For this purpose, the original version of rough set theory has been extended in two ways : (i) substituting the classical indiscernibility relation with respect to attributes by a dominance relation with respect to criteria, and (ii), substituting the data table of actions described by attributes, by a pairwise comparison table, where each row corresponds to a pair of actions described by binary relations on particular criteria, which permits approximation of a comprehensive preference relation in multicriteria choice and ranking problems. The extended rough set approach is called dominance-based rough set approach [3,5,6,8,9,11,16].

Given a finite set A={x,y,z,...} of actions evaluated by a family of criteria $G=\{g_1,\ldots,g_n\}$, we consider the preferential information in the form of a pairwise comparison table (PCT) including pairs of some *reference actions* from a subset A'$\subseteq$A. In addition to evaluation on particular criteria, each pair (x,y)$\in$A'$\times$A' is characterized by a *comprehensive preference relation* which is graded (true or false to some grade). Using the rough set approach to the analysis of the PCT, we obtain a rough approximation of the graded preference relation by a dominance relation. More precisely, the rough approximation concerns unions of graded preference relations, called upward and downward cumulated preference relations. The rough approximation is defined for a given level of consistency, changing from 1 (perfect separation of certain and doubtful pairs) to 0 (no separation of certain and doubtful pairs). The rough approximations are used to induce "*if ..., then ...*" decision rules. The resulting decision rules constitute a preference model of the DM. Application of the decision rules on a new set $M\subseteq A\times A$ of pairs of actions defines a preference structure in *M* in terms of fuzzy four-valued preference relations. In order to obtain a recommendation, we propose to use a Fuzzy Net Flow Score (FNFS) exploitation procedure adapted to the four-valued preference relations.

The paper is organized as follows. In section 2, we define the pairwise comparison table from the decision examples given by the DM. In section 3, we briefly sketch the variable-consistency dominance-based rough set approach to the analysis of PCT, for both cardinal and ordinal scales of criteria. Section 4 is devoted to induction of decision rules and section 5 characterizes the recommended procedure for exploitation of decision rules on a new set of actions. An axiomatic characterization of the FNFS procedure is presented in section 6. Section 7 includes an illustrative example and the last section groups conclusions.

2 Pairwise Comparison Table (PCT) Built of Decision Examples

For a representative subset of reference actions A'$\subseteq$A, the DM is asked to express his/her comprehensive preferences by pairwise comparisons. In practice, he/she may accept to compare the pairs of a subset $B\subseteq A'\times A'$. For each pair (x,y)$\in B$, the comprehensive preference relation $\succ$ assumes different grades h of intensity, hence denoted by $\succ^h$. Let H be the finite set of all admitted values of h, and H^+ (resp. H^-) the subset of strictly positive (resp., strictly negative) values of h. It is assumed that $h\in H^+$ iff $-h\in H^-$ and $h\in(0,1]$. Finally $H = H^-\cup\{0\}\cup H^+$ and $H\subset[-1,1]$.

For each pair $(x,y) \in A' \times A'$, the DM is asked to select one of the four possibilities:

1. action x is comprehensively preferred to y in grade h, i.e. $x \succ^h y$, where $h \in H^+$,
2. action x is comprehensively *not* preferred to y in grade h, i.e. $x \succ^h y$, where $h \in H^-$,
3. action x is comprehensively indifferent to y, i.e. $x \succ^0 y$,
4. DM refuses to compare x to y.

Although the intensity grades are numerically valued, they may be interpreted in terms of linguistic qualifiers, for example: "*very weak preference*", "*weak preference*", "*strict preference*", "*strong preference*" for h=0.2, 0.3, 0.7, 1.0, respectively. A similar interpretation holds for negative values of h. Let us also note that $x \succ^h y$ does not necessarily imply $y \succ^{-h} x$ and $x \succ^0 y$ does not necessarily imply $y \succ^0 x$.

An m×(n+1) *Pairwise Comparison Table* S_{PCT} is then created on the base of this information. Its first n columns correspond to criteria from set G. The last, (n+1)-th column of S_{PCT}, represents the comprehensive binary relation $\succ^h$ with $h \in H$. The m rows are pairs from *B*. If the DM refused to compare two actions, such a pair does not appear in S_{PCT}.

In the following we will distinguish two kinds of criteria – *cardinal* and *ordinal* ones. In consequence of this distinction, for each pair of actions in an S_{PCT} we have either a difference of evaluations on cardinal criteria or pairs of original evaluations on ordinal criteria. The difference of evaluations on a cardinal criterion needs to be translated into a graded marginal intensity of preference. For any cardinal criterion $g_i \in G$, we consider a finite set $H_i \equiv (H_i^- \cup \{0\} \cup H_i^+)$ of marginal intensity grades such that for every pair of actions $(x,y) \in A \times A$ exactly one grade $h \in H_i$ is assigned.

1. $x \succ_i^h y$, $h \in H_i^+$, means that action x is preferred to action y in grade h on criterion g_i,
2. $x \succ_i^h y$, $h \in H_i^-$, means that action x is *not* preferred to action y in grade h on criterion g_i,
3. $x \succ_i^0 y$, means that action x is similar (asymmetrically indifferent) to action y on criterion g_i.

Within the preference context, the similarity relation $\succ_i^0$, even if not symmetric, resembles indifference relation. Thus, in this case, we call this similarity relation "asymmetric indifference". Of course, for each cardinal criterion $g_i \in G$ and for every pair of actions $(x,y) \in A \times A$, $[\exists h \in H_i^+ : x \succ_i^h y] \Rightarrow [\nexists k \in H_i^+ : y \succ_i^k x]$ as well as $[\exists h \in H_i^- : x \succ_i^h y] \Rightarrow [\nexists k \in H_i^- : y \succ_i^k x]$. Observe that the binary relation $\succ^0$ is reflexive, but neither necessarily symmetric nor transitive, and $\succ^h$ for $h \in H \backslash \{0\}$ are neither reflexive nor symmetric and not necessarily transitive. $\bigcup_{h \in H} \succ^h$ is not necessarily complete.

Consequently, PCT can be seen as decision table $S_{PCT} = \langle B, G \cup \{d\} \rangle$, where $B \subseteq A \times A$ is a non-empty set of pairwise comparisons of reference actions and d is a decision corresponding to the comprehensive pairwise comparison (comprehensive graded preference relation).

3 Rough Approximation of Comprehensive Graded Preference Relations Specified in PCT

Let G^N be the set of cardinal criteria, and G^O – the set of ordinal criteria, such that $G^N \cup G^O = G$ and $G^N \cap G^O = \emptyset$. Moreover, for each $P \subseteq G$, we denote by P^N, P^O the same partitioning of P, i.e. $P^O = P \cap G^O$ and $P^N = P \cap G^N$. In order to define the rough approximations of comprehensive graded preference relations we need the concept of dominance relation between two pairs of actions with respect to (w.r.t.) a subset of criteria. This concept is defined below, separately for subsets of cardinal criteria and for subsets of ordinal criteria. In the case of cardinal criteria, the dominance is built on graded preference relations, and in the case of ordinal criteria, the dominance is built directly on pairs of evaluations.

A. Cardinal Criteria Let $P = P^N \subseteq G$ ($P \neq \emptyset$). Given $(x,y),(w,z) \in A \times A$, the pair of actions (x,y) is said to dominate (w,z) w.r.t. subset of cardinal criteria P (denoted by $(x,y)D_P(w,z)$) if x is preferred to y at least as strongly as w is preferred to z w.r.t. each $g_i \in P$. Precisely, "*at least as strongly as*" means "*in at least the same grade*", i.e. for each $g_i \in P$ and $k \in H_i$ such that $w \succ_i^k z$, there exist $h \in H_i$ such that $h \geq k$ and $x \succ_i^h y$. Let $D_{\{i\}}$ be the dominance relation confined to the single criterion $g_i \in P$. The binary relation $D_{\{i\}}$ is a complete preorder on $A \times A$. Since the intersection of complete preorders is a partial preorder and $D_P = \bigcap_{g_i \in P} D_{\{i\}}$, then the dominance relation D_P is a partial preorder on $A \times A$. Let $R \subseteq P \subseteq G$ and $(x,y),(u,v) \in A \times A$; then the following implication holds: $(x,y)D_P(u,v) \Rightarrow (x,y)D_R(u,v)$.

Given $P \subseteq G$ and $(x,y) \in A \times A$, we define:

- a set of pairs of actions dominating (x,y), called P-*dominating set*, $D_P^+(x,y) = \{(w,z) \in A \times A\text{: } (w,z)D_P(x,y)\}$,
- a set of pairs of actions dominated by (x,y), called P-*dominated set*, $D_P^-(x,y) = \{(w,z) \in A \times A\text{: } (x,y)D_P(w,z)\}$.

To approximate the comprehensive graded preference relation, we need to introduce the concept of *upward cumulated preference* (denoted by $\succ^{\geq h}$) and *downward cumulated preference* (denoted by $\succ^{\leq h}$), having the following interpretation:

- $x \succ^{\geq h} y$ means "x is comprehensively preferred to y by *at least* grade h", i.e. $x \succ^{\geq h} y$ if $x \succ^k y$, where $h \leq k \in H$,
- $x \succ^{\leq h} y$ means "x is comprehensively preferred to y by *at most* grade h", i.e. $x \succ^{\leq h} y$ if $x \succ^k y$, where $h \geq k \in H$.

The P-dominating sets and the P-dominated sets defined on *B* for all pairs of reference actions from *B* are "granules of knowledge" that can be used to express P-lower and P-upper approximations of cumulated preference relations $\succ^{\geq h}$ and $\succ^{\leq h}$, respectively:

- for $h \in H$, $\underline{P}(\succ^{\geq h}) = \{(x,y) \in B\text{: } D_P^+(x,y) \subseteq \succ^{\geq h}\}$, $\overline{P}(\succ^{\geq h}) = \bigcup_{(x,y) \in \succ^{\geq h}} D_P^+(x,y)$.
- for $h \in H$, $\underline{P}(\succ^{\leq h}) = \{(x,y) \in B\text{: } D_P^-(x,y) \subseteq \succ^{\leq h}\}$, $\overline{P}(\succ^{\leq h}) = \bigcup_{(x,y) \in \succ^{\leq h}} D_P^-(x,y)$.

It has been proved in [3] that for $h\in H$, $\underline{P}(\succ^{\geq h}) \subseteq \succ^{\geq h} \subseteq \overline{P}(\succ^{\geq h})$ and $\underline{P}(\succ^{\leq h}) \subseteq \succ^{\leq h} \subseteq \overline{P}(\succ^{\leq h})$. Furthermore, one has also that, for $h\in H$, $\underline{P}(\succ^{\geq h}) = B - \overline{P}(\succ^{\leq h})$ and $\underline{P}(\succ^{\leq h}) = B - \overline{P}(\succ^{\geq h})$. From the definition of the P-boundaries (P-doubtful regions) of $\succ^{\geq h}$ and of $\succ^{\leq h}$ for any $h\in H$, $Bn_P(\succ^{\geq h}) = \overline{P}(\succ^{\geq h}) - \underline{P}(\succ^{\geq h})$ and $Bn_P(\succ^{\leq h}) = \overline{P}(\succ^{\leq h}) - \underline{P}(\succ^{\leq h})$, it follows that $Bn_P(\succ^{\geq h})=Bn_P(\succ^{\leq h})$.

The concepts of the quality of approximation, reducts and core can be extended also to the approximation of cumulated preference relations. In particular, the *quality of approximation* of $\succ^{\geq h}$ and $\succ^{\leq h}$ for all $h\in H$, by $P\subseteq G$ is characterized by the coefficient $\gamma_P = \left|B - \left(\bigcup_{h\in H} Bn_P(\succ^{\geq h})\right)\right| / |B| = \left|B - \left(\bigcup_{h\in H} Bn_P(\succ^{\leq h})\right)\right| / |B|$, where $|\ |$ denotes cardinality of a set. It expresses the ratio of all pairs of actions $(x,y)\in B$ correctly assigned to $\succ^{\geq h}$ and to $\succ^{\leq h}$ by the set P of criteria to all the pairs of actions contained in B. Each minimal subset $P\subseteq G$, such that $\gamma_P = \gamma_G$, is a *reduct* of G (denoted by $RED_{S_{PCT}}$). Let us remark that S_{PCT} can have more than one reduct. The intersection of all B-reducts is the *core* (denoted by $CORE_{S_{PCT}}$).

In fact, for induction of decision rules, we consider the Variable Consistency Model on S_{PCT} [12,16] relaxing the definition of P-lower approximation of the cumulated preference relations $\succ^{\geq h}$ and $\succ^{\leq h}$, for any $h\in H$, such that $(1-l)\times 100$ percent of the pairs in P-dominating or P-dominated sets may not belong to the approximated cumulated preference relation: $\underline{P}^l(\succ^{\geq h}) = \left\{(x,y)\in B : \left|D_P^+(x,y)\cap \succ^{\geq h}\right| / \left|D_P^+(x,y)\right| \geq l\right\}$ and $\underline{P}^l(\succ^{\leq h}) = \left\{(x,y)\in B : \left|D_P^-(x,y)\cap \succ^{\leq h}\right| / \left|D_P^-(x,y)\right| \geq l\right\}$ where $l\in(0,1]$ is the required level of consistency.

B. Ordinal Criteria. In the case of ordinal criteria, the dominance relation is defined directly on pairs of evaluations $g_i(x)$ and $g_i(y)$, for all pairs of actions $(x,y)\in A\times A$. Let $P=P^O$ and $P^N=\emptyset$, then, given $(x,y),(w,z)\in A\times A$, the pair (x,y) is said to dominate the pair (w,z) w.r.t. subset of ordinal criteria P (denoted by $(x,y)D_P(w,z)$) if, for each $g_i\in P$, $g_i(x)\geq g_i(w)$ and $g_i(z)\geq g_i(y)$. Let $D_{\{i\}}$ be the dominance relation confined to the single criterion $g_i\in P^O$. The binary relation $D_{\{i\}}$ is reflexive, transitive, but non-necessarily complete (it is possible that *not* $(x,y)D_{\{i\}}(w,z)$ and *not* $(w,z)D_{\{i\}}(x,y)$ for some $(x,y),(w,z)\in A\times A$). Thus, $D_{\{i\}}$ is a partial preorder. Since the intersection of partial preorders is a partial preorder and $D_P=\bigcap_{g_i\in P} D_{\{i\}}$, $P=P^O$, then the dominance relation D_P is a partial preorder.

C. Cardinal and Ordinal Criteria. If subset of criteria $P\subseteq G$ is composed of both cardinal and ordinal criteria, i.e. if $P^N\neq\emptyset$ and $P^O\neq\emptyset$, then, given $(x,y),(w,z)\in A\times A$, the pair (x,y) is said to dominate the pair (w,z) w.r.t. subset of criteria P, (denoted by $(x,y)D_P(w,z)$) if (x,y) dominates (w,z) w.r.t. both P^N and P^O. Since the dominance relation w.r.t. P^N is a partial preorder on $A\times A$ and the dominance w.r.t. P^O is also a partial preorder on $A\times A$, then also the dominance D_P, being the intersection of these two dominance relations, is a partial preorder. In consequence, all the concepts related to rough approximations introduced in 3.1 can be restored using this specific definition of dominance relation.

4 Induction of Decision Rules from Rough Approximations

Using the rough approximations of relations $\succ^{\geq h}$ and $\succ^{\leq h}$, defined in Section 3, it is then possible to induce a generalized description of the preferential information contained in a given S_{PCT} in terms of decision rules. The syntax of these rules is based on the concept of *upward cumulated preferences w.r.t. criterion* g_i (denoted by $\succ_i^{\geq h}$) and *downward cumulated preferences w.r.t. criterion* g_i (denoted by $\succ_i^{\leq h}$), having similar interpretation and definition as for the comprehensive preference. Let also $G_i=\{g_i(x),\ x\in A\}$, $g_i\in G^O$, be a set of different evaluations on ordinal criterion g_i. The decision rules induced from S_{PCT} have then the following syntax:

1) $\mathbf{D}_{\geq}$***-decision rules***, which are induced with the hypothesis that all pairs from $\underline{P}^l(\succ^{\geq h})$ are positive and all the others are negative learning examples:

   if $x\succ_{i1}^{\geq h(i1)}y$ *and* ... $x\succ_{ie}^{\geq h(ie)}y$ *and* $g_{ie+1}(x)\geq r_{ie+1}$ *and* $g_{ie+1}(y)\leq s_{ie+1}$ *and* ... $g_{ip}(x)\geq r_{ip}$ *and* $g_{ip}(y)\leq s_{ip}$, *then* $x\succ^{\geq h}y$,

2) $\mathbf{D}_{\leq}$***-decision rules***, which are induced with the hypothesis that all pairs from $\underline{P}^l(\succ^{\leq h})$ are positive and all the others are negative learning examples:

   if $x\succ_{i1}^{\leq h(i1)}y$ *and* ... $x\succ_{ie}^{\leq h(ie)}y$ *and* $g_{ie+1}(x)\leq r_{ie+1}$ *and* $g_{ie+1}(y)\geq s_{ie+1}$ *and* ... $g_{ip}(x)\leq r_{ip}$ *and* $g_{ip}(y)\geq s_{ip}$, *then* $x\succ^{\leq h}y$,

   where $P=\{g_{i1},\dots,g_{ip}\}\subseteq G$, $P^N=\{g_{i1},\dots,g_{ie}\}$, $P^O=\{g_{ie+1},\dots,g_{ip}\}$, $(h(i1),\dots,h(ie))\in H_{i1}\times\dots\times H_{ie}$ and $(r_{ie+1},\dots,r_{ip})$, $(s_{ie+1},\dots,s_{ip})\in G_{ie+1}\times\dots\times G_{ip}$;

Since we are working with variable consistency approximations, it is enough to consider the lower approximations of the upward and downward cumulated preference relations, namely $\underline{P}^l(\succ^{\geq h})$ and $\underline{P}^l(\succ^{\leq h})$. To characterize the quality of the rules, we say that a pair of actions *supports* a decision rule ρ if it matches both the condition and decision parts of ρ. On the other hand, a pair is *covered* by a decision rule ρ as soon as it matches the condition part of ρ. Let *Cover(ρ)* denote the set of all pairs of actions covered by the rule ρ. Finally, we define the credibility $\alpha_\rho(\succ^{\geq h})$ of $D_{\geq}$-decision rule ρ as $\alpha_\rho(\succ^{\geq h})=\dfrac{|Cover(\rho)\cap\succ^{\geq h}|}{|Cover(\rho)|}$. For $D_{\leq}$-decision rules, the credibility is defined analogously.

Let us remark that the decision rules are induced from P-lower approximations whose composition is controlled by user-specified consistency level l. It seems reasonable to require that the smallest accepted credibility of the rule should not be lower than the currently used consistency level l. Indeed, in the worst case, some pairs of actions from the P-lower approximation may create a rule using all criteria from P thus giving a credibility $\alpha_\rho\left(\succ^{\geq h}\right)\geq l$. The user may have a possibility of increasing this lower bound for credibility of the rule but then decision rules may not cover all pairs of actions from the P-lower approximations. Moreover, we require that each decision rule is minimal. Since a decision rule is an implication, by a *minimal* decision rule we understand such an implication that there is no other implication with an antecedent of at least the same weakness and a consequent of at least the same strength with a not worse credibility $\alpha_\rho\left(\succ^{\geq h}\right)\geq l$. The induction of variable-consistency decision rules can be done using the rule induction algorithm for VC-DRSA, which can be found in [13].

5 Use of Decision Rules for Decision Support

Application of the set of decision rules on a new subset M=M×M⊆A×A of pairs of actions induces a specific preference structure in set M. In fact, each pair of actions (u,v)∈M can match several decision rules. The matching rules can state different grades of preference and have various credibilities. A synthesis of the matching rules for a given pair of actions results in a graded (fuzzy) four-valued preference relation of level 2 [2]. This means that not only the relation is a graded one but also that its α-cuts are fuzzy four-valued preference relations, because of information about preference and non-preference. The three steps of the exploitation procedure lead to final ranking in the set of actions M.

Step 1. By application of the decision rules on M, we get for each pair (u,v)∈M a set of different covering rules (possibly empty) stating different conclusions in the form of cumulated preference relations $\succ^{\geq h}$ and $\succ^{\leq h}$. For all pairs (u,v)∈M, the cumulated preference relations are stratified into preference relations $\succ^{h}$ of grade h∈H and for each pair $u\succ^{h}v$ a confidence degree $\beta(u\succ^{h}v)$ is calculated. This means that, for each h∈H, $\succ^{h}$ is a fuzzy relation in M, which may be represented by a fuzzy preference graph.

In general, several decision rules assigning pair (u,v) to different cumulated preference relations are taken into account. For each h∈H, a confidence $\beta\left(u\succ^{h}v\right)$ is committed to the pair $u\succ^{h}v$ computed as the difference between the positive and negative arguments $\beta\left(u\succ^{h}v\right)=\beta^{+}\left(u\succ^{h}v\right)-\beta^{-}\left(u\succ^{h}v\right)$ where $\beta^{+}\left(u\succ^{h}v\right)$ takes into account rules ρ_i matching the pair (u,v) (i=1,…,k) that assign (u,v) to the cumulated preference relation $\succ^{\geq s}$ (or $\succ^{\leq q}$) such that h≥s (or h≤q):

$$\beta^{+}\left(u \succ^{h} v\right)=\frac{\left|(\mathrm{Cover}(\rho_1)\cap \succ^{h})\cup\ldots\cup(\mathrm{Cover}(\rho_k)\cap \succ^{h})\right|^2}{\left|\mathrm{Cover}(\rho_1)\cup\ldots\cup \mathrm{Cover}(\rho_k)\right|\left|\succ^{h}\right|}$$

$\beta^{+}\left(u \succ^{h} v\right)$ can be interpreted as a product of the credibility of the rule and its relative strength w.r.t. the graded preference relation. The confidence $\beta^{-}\left(u \succ^{h} v\right)$ is defined for matching decision rules ρ_i (i=k+1,…,m) that assign (u,v) to different graded preference relations than $\succ^h$ ($r_{k+1},\ldots,r_p > h$ and $r_{p+1},\ldots,r_m < h$).

Step 2. Pairs of relations ($\succ^h$, $\succ^{-h}$) are considered as providing information about both preference and non-preference in grade h. These contradictory pieces of information induce a four-valued relation for each $h\in H^+$. An advisable procedure to exploit any of these four-valued relations is an extension of the Fuzzy Net Flow Score. For each action $x\in M$: the net flow score is computed as $S^h_{nf}(x)=S^h_{++}(x)-S^h_{+-}(x)+S^h_{-+}(x)-S^h_{--}(x)$, where $S^h_{++}(x)=\sum_{y\in M}\beta(x\succ^h y)$, $S^h_{+-}(x)=\sum_{y\in M}\beta(y\succ^h x)$, $S^h_{-+}(x)=\sum_{y\in M}\beta(y\succ^{-h} x)$ and $S^h_{--}(x)=\sum_{y\in M}\beta(x\succ^{-h} y)$. This builds up a complete preorder $\trianglerighteq^h$ for each $h\in H^+$, such that $u\trianglerighteq^h v \Leftrightarrow S^h_{nf}(u)\geq S^h_{nf}(v)$

Step 3. The preorders $\trianglerighteq^h$, $h\in H^+$, are aggregated by the leximax procedure, i.e. resolving indifference in a preorder of grade h by a preorder of grade $k\in H^+$, where k is the highest grade among the grades smaller than h.

$$u \triangleright v \quad\Leftrightarrow\quad \exists h\in H^+ : \begin{cases}\forall k\in H^+ \text{ such that } k>h,\ u\trianglerighteq^k v \text{ and } v\trianglerighteq^k u\\ \qquad u\trianglerighteq^h v \text{ and not } v\trianglerighteq^h u\end{cases}$$

$$u\equiv v \quad\Leftrightarrow\quad \forall h\in H^+ : u\trianglerighteq^h v \text{ and } v\trianglerighteq^h u$$

where $\triangleright$ is the asymmetric part of $\trianglerighteq$ and $\equiv$ is the symmetric part of $\trianglerighteq$.

This lexicographic approach considers the set of preorders $\trianglerighteq^h$ for $h\in H^+$ as providing consistent hierarchical information on the comprehensive graded preference relation. Therefore, it gives priority to preorders $\trianglerighteq^h$ with high values of grade h. Indeed, the preorders with lower values of h are only called to break ties from high h-value preorders. For this reason, this lexicographic approach is called *leximax* procedure.

The final recommendation in ranking problems consists of the total preorder $\trianglerighteq$; in choice problems, it consists of the maximal action(s) of $\trianglerighteq$.

6 Axiomatic Characterization of the Fuzzy Net Flow Score procedure

In the context of four-valued relation, a ranking method resulting in the complete preorder $\trianglerighteq^h$ on A can be viewed as a function $\trianglerighteq(\succ^h, \succ^{-h})$ aggregating the pair of valued relations $\succ^h$, $\succ^{-h}$ on A×A into a single ranking. In the previous section, we proposed to rank alternatives by means of an extended Fuzzy Net Flow Score (FNFS) procedure, i.e. $u \trianglerighteq(\succ^h, \succ^{-h})\, v \;\Leftrightarrow\; S^h_{nf}(u) \geq S^h_{nf}(v)$. It can be shown that the axioms proposed in [1] (neutrality, strong monotonicity, circuit-independency) can be naturally extended to characterize the FNFS dealing with pairs of relations.

7 Illustrative Example

Let us consider the case of a Belgian citizen wishing to buy a house in Poland for spending his holidays there. The selling agent approached by the customer wants to rank all the available houses to present them in a relevant order to the customer. Thereby, the latter is proposed first to have a look at a short list of 7 houses (the reference actions), characterized by three criteria that seem important to the customer: Distance to the nearest airport, Price and Comfort (Table 1). While the two first criteria are cardinal (expressed in km and in , respectively), the last one is represented on a three-level ordinal scale (*Basic*, *Medium*, *Good*). The customer is then asked to give – even partially – his preferences on the set of 7 proposed houses, in terms of a comprehensive graded preference relation.

Table 1. Short list of the houses (reference actions).

Location of the house	Distance to the nearest airport (A1: [km])	Price (A2: [€])	Comfort (A3: [ ])
0: Poznan	3	60	*Good*
1: Kapalica	35	30	*Good*
2: Krakow	7	85	*Medium*
3: Warszawa	10	90	*Basic*
4: Wroclaw	5	60	*Medium*
5: Malbork	50	50	*Medium*
6: Gdansk	5	70	*Medium*

The customer gives his preferences by means of the graph presented in Fig. 1, where a thin arc represents a weak preference, and a bold arc, a strong preference. Thereby, this is a comprehensive graded preference relation, with 2 positive grades of preference, weak and strong ones. One may observe that the customer preference is allowed to be both not complete (there may exist pairs of houses without an arc; e.g., 5 and 4) and not completely transitive (e.g., 6 is preferred to 4 and 4 is preferred to 3, without evident preference between 6 and 3).

In order to build the PCT, differences of evaluations on cardinal criteria have been encoded in marginal graded preference relations ($\succ^h_i$), with H_i={–1, –0.5, 0, 0.5, 1}, i=1,2. While comparing two alternatives, x and y, a difference in Distance criterion

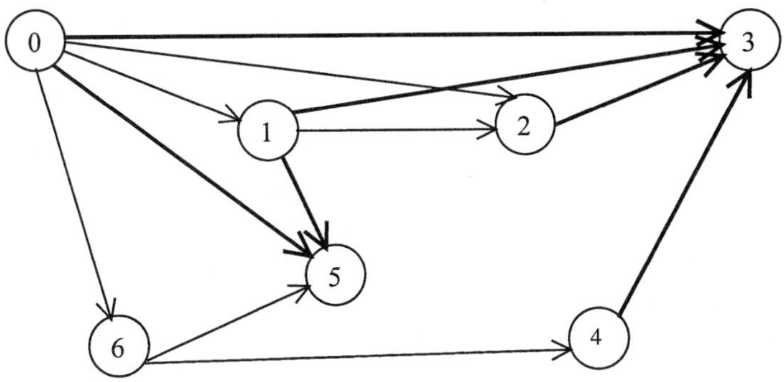

Fig. 1. Graph representation of the comprehensive graded preference relation in the set of reference actions.

smaller (in absolute value) than 3km is considered as non significant ($x \succ_1^0 y$ and $y \succ_1^0 x$). If the difference is between 4 and 10km in favor of x, then one weakly prefers x to y ($x \succ_1^{0.5} y$); finally, the preference is strong as soon as the difference is strictly greater than 10km ($x \succ_1^1 y$). As far as the Price criterion is concerned, an absolute difference smaller than 10 leads to indifference ($x \succ_2^0 y$ and $y \succ_2^0 x$), and the weak (resp. strong) preference appears as soon as the difference is strictly greater than 10 (resp. 30). For the sake of simplicity, we have assumed in this example that the marginal graded preference relations are symmetric, e.g. $x \succ_i^{0.5} y \Leftrightarrow y \succ_i^{-0.5} x$. As the Comfort criterion is ordinal, we have to take into account the pair of evaluations on this criterion instead of their difference. The piecewise comparison table (PCT) resulting from the above preference information is sketched in Table 2.

Table 2. A partial PCT corresponding to customer's preferences on the set of reference actions.

Pairs of reference actions (x,y)	h on A1: $x \succ_1^h y$	h on A2: $x \succ_2^h y$	Evaluations of (x;y) on A3	h on comprehensive preference relation: $\succ^h$
(0,0)	0	0	*(Good; Good)*	0
(0,1)	1	-0.5	*(Good; Good)*	0.5
(0,2)	0.5	0.5	*(Good; Medium)*	0.5
(0,3)	0.5	0.5	*(Good; Basic)*	1
(0,5)	1	0	*(Good; Medium)*	1
(0,6)	0	0	*(Good; Medium)*	0.5
…				

25 rules have been induced using the variable-consistency rule inducer [13], with a minimal consistency level l=0.85. Two examples of such rules are

if $x \succ_1^{\geq 1} y$ *and* $(x;y) \geq_3 (Good;Medium)$, *then* $x \succ^{\geq 1} y$;

if $x \succ_1^{\leq -1} y$ *and* $x \succ_2^{\leq 0.5} y$, *then* $x \succ^{\leq -0.5} y$

Suppose that the selling agent has found four other houses, presented in Table 3, and would like to see how these houses will be ranked by the customer. He may use to this end the preference model of the customer in form of the above decision rules on the set of new houses. According to Step 1 of our exploitation procedure presented in section 5, application of the rules on all possible pairs of the new houses results in fuzzy relation $\succ^h$, corresponding to fuzzy preference graphs (h=1 and 0.5). Then, according to Step 2, complete preorder $\trianglerighteq^h$ in the set of new houses is obtained by the Fuzzy Net Flow Score procedure. The fuzzy net flow score for h=1 and the corresponding complete preorder $\trianglerighteq^1$ are shown in the two last columns of Table 3. In fact, according to Step 3, since no pair of actions (x,y) have the same fuzzy net flow score at grade h=1, this grade is sufficient to define the final ranking of the new houses ($\trianglerighteq = \trianglerighteq^1$).

The dominance-based rough set approach gives a clear recommendation:

- for the **choice problem**, it suggests to **select house 2'** having the highest score,
- for the **ranking problem**, it suggests the **ranking** presented in the last column of Table 3:
  (2') → (3') → (0') → (1')

Table 3. The set of new houses and their ranks in the final ranking.

Location of the house	Distance to the nearest airport (A1: [km])	Price (A2: [€])	Comfort (A3: [ ])	Fuzzy Net Flow Score (h=1)	Final rank
0': Kornik	50	40	*Medium*	0.23	3
1': Rogalin	15	50	*Basic*	-5.17	4
2': Lublin	8	60	*Good*	3.42	1
3': Torun	100	50	*Medium*	1.52	2

8 Summary and Conclusions

We presented a complete methodology of multicriteria choice and ranking based on decision rule preference model. By complete we mean that it starts from acquisition of preference information, then it goes through analysis of this information using the Dominance-based Rough Set Approach (DRSA), followed by induction of decision rules from rough approximations of preference relations, and ends with a recommendation of the best action in a set or of a ranking of given actions.

The preference information is given by the Decision Maker (DM) in form of pairwise comparisons (or ranking) of some reference actions – comparison means specification of a grade of comprehensive preference of one reference action on another. DRSA aims at separating consistent from inconsistent preference information, so as to express certainly (P-lower approximation) or possibly only (P-upper approximation) the comprehensive graded preference relations for a pair of actions in terms of evaluations of these actions on particular criteria from set P. The inconsistency concerns the basic principle of multicriteria comparisons that says: if for two pairs of actions, (x,y) and (w,z), action x is preferred to action y at least as much as action w is preferred to z on all criteria from P, then the comprehensive preference of x over y should not be weaker than that of w over z. The rough approximations of comprehensive graded preference relations prepare the ground for induction of decision rules with a warranted credibility. Upon acceptance of the DM, the set of decision rules constitutes the preference model of the DM, compatible with the pairwise comparisons of reference actions. It may then be used on a new set of actions, giving as many fuzzy preference relations $\succ^h$ in this set (fuzzy preference graphs) as there are grades of the comprehensive graded preference relation. Exploitation of these relations with the Fuzzy Net Flow Score procedure leads to complete preorders $\trianglerighteq^h$ for particular grades. Aggregation of these preorders using the leximax procedure gives the final recommendation, that is, the best action or the final ranking $\trianglerighteq$.

Acknowledgements

The research of the second author has been supported by the Italian Ministry of University and Scientific Research (MURST). The third author wishes to acknowledge financial support from the Ministry of Science and from the Foundation for Polish Science.

References

1. Bouyssou, D.: "Ranking methods based on valued preference relations: a characterization of the net-flow method". *European Journal of Operational Research* 60 (1992) no.1, 61-68
2. Dubois, D., Ostasiewicz W., Prade H.: "Fuzzy sets: history and basic notions". [In]: D. Dubois and H. Prade (eds.), *Fundamentals of Fuzzy Sets*. Kluwer Academic Publishers, Boston, 2000, 21-124
3. Greco S., Matarazzo, B., Slowinski, R.: *"Rough approximation of a preference relation by dominance relations"*, ICS Research Report 16/96, Warsaw University of Technology, Warsaw, 1996, and in: *European Journal of Operational Research* 117 (1999) 63-83
4. Greco, S., Matarazzo, B., Slowinski, R., Tsoukias, A.: "Exploitation of a rough approximation of the outranking relation in multicriteria choice and ranking". In: T.J.Stewart and R.C. van den Honert (eds.), *Trends in Multicriteria Decision Making*. LNEMS vol. 465, Springer-Verlag, Berlin, 1998, 45-60
5. Greco, S., Matarazzo B. and Slowinski R.: "The use of rough sets and fuzzy sets in MCDM". Chapter 14 in: T. Gal, T. Stewart and T. Hanne (eds.), *Advances in Multiple Criteria Decision Making*. Kluwer Academic Publishers, Dordrecht, 1999, 14.1-14.59
6. Greco, S., Matarazzo, B., Slowinski, R., "Extension of the rough set approach to multicriteria decision support". *INFOR* 38 (2000) no.3, 161-196
7. Greco, S., Matarazzo, B., Slowinski, R., "Conjoint measurement and rough set approach for multicriteria sorting problems in presence of ordinal criteria". [In]: A.Colorni, M.Paruccini, B.Roy (eds.), *A-MCD-A: Aide Multi Critère à la Décision – Multiple Criteria Decision Aiding*, European Commission Report EUR 19808 EN, Joint Research Centre, Ispra, 2001, pp. 117-144
8. Greco, S., Matarazzo, B., Slowinski, R., "Rough sets theory for multicriteria decision analysis". *European J. of Operational Research* 129 (2001) no.1, 1-47

9. Greco, S., Matarazzo, B., Slowinski, R., "Rule-based decision support in multicriteria choice and ranking". [In] S. Benferhat, Ph. Besnard (eds.), *Symbolic and Quantitative Approaches to Reasoning with Uncertainty*. Lecture Notes in Artificial Intelligence, vol. 2143, Springer-Verlag, Berlin, 2001, pp. 29-47
10. Greco, S., Matarazzo, B., Slowinski, R.: "Preference representation by means of conjoint measurement and decision rule model". In: D. Bouyssou, E.Jacquet-Lagreze, P.Perny, R.Slowinski, D.Vanderpooten, Ph.Vincke (eds.), *Aiding Decisions with Multiple Criteria-Essays in Honor of Bernard Roy*. Kluwer, Boston, 2002, pp. 263-313
11. Greco, S., Matarazzo, B., Slowinski, R.: "Multicriteria classification". Chapter 16.1.9 [in]: W.Kloesgen and J.Zytkow (eds.), *Handbook of Data Mining and Knowledge Discovery*, Oxford University Press, New York, 2002, pp. 318-328.
12. Greco S., Matarazzo B., Slowinski R., Stefanowski J.: "Variable consistency model of dominance-based rough set approach". [In]: W.Ziarko, Y.Yao: *Rough Sets and Current Trends in Computing*, Lecture Notes in Artificial Intelligence, vol. 2005, Springer-Verlag, Berlin, 2001, pp. 170-181
13. Greco S., Matarazzo B., Slowinski R., Stefanowski J.: "An algorithm for induction of decision rules consistent with dominance principle". [In]: W.Ziarko, Y.Yao: *Rough Sets and Current Trends in Computing*, Lecture Notes in Artificial Intelligence, vol. 2005, Springer-Verlag, Berlin, 2001, pp. 304-313.
14. Pawlak Z.: "Rough sets". *Int. J. of Information & Computer Sciences* 11 (1982) 341-356
15. Slowinski, R., Stefanowski, J., Greco, S., Matarazzo, B.: "Rough sets based processing of inconsistent information in decision analysis". *Control and Cybernetics* 29 (2000) no.1, 379-404
16. Slowinski, R., Greco, S., Matarazzo, B.: "Mining decision-rule preference model from rough approximation of preference relation". [In]: Proc. 26th IEEE Annual Int. Conference on *Computer Software & Applications* (*COMPSAC 2002*). Oxford, England, 2002, pp. 1129-1134
17. Stefanowski, J.: "On rough set based approaches to induction of decision rules". [In]: A. Skowron and L. Polkowski (eds.): *Rough Sets in Data Mining and Knowledge Discovery*. Vol.1, Physica-Verlag, Heidelberg, 1998, pp.500-529

Measuring the Expected Impact of Decision Rule Application

Salvatore Greco[1], Benedetto Matarazzo[1], Nello Pappalardo[2], and Roman Słowiński [3,4]

[1] Faculty of Economics, University of Catania, Corso Italia 55, 95129 Catania, Italy
{salgreco,matarazz}@unict.it
[2] Faculty of Agriculture, University of Catania, Via S. Sofia 100, 95123 Catania, Italy
npappala@unict.it
[3] Institute of Computing Science, Poznan University of Technology, 60-965 Poznan
[4] Institute for Systems Research, Polish Academy of Sciences, 01-447 Warsaw, Poland
slowinsk@sol.put.poznan.pl

Abstract. Decision rules induced from a data set allow to particularize the relationships between condition and decision factors. Several indices can be used to characterize the most significant decision rules based on "historical" data, but they are not able to measure the impact that these rules (or strategies derived from these rules) will produce in the future. Thus, in this paper, a new methodology is introduced to quantify the impact that a strategy derived from decision rules may have on a real life situation in the future. The utility of this approach is illustrated by an example.

1 Introduction

Knowledge discovered from data is often represented in the form of "*if...,then...*" decision rules which are easily interpretable. In machine learning and rough set theory [3] such rules are induced from data sets containing information about a set of objects described by a set of attributes. A decision maker (DM) can use these induced rules to support decision making in the future. In fact, evaluating particular factors characterizing the rules, like *confidence* and *support*, the DM can choose the most significant rules to take into account for the next decisions. In general, these quantitative measures may help the user to interpret the discovered rules, use them, or to select the most interesting subset if the number of rules is too large.

In fact, when the DM makes a decision (or implements a strategy) according to a decision rule, he expects some improvement deriving from this decision. For example, a doctor who wants to increase the number of patients being healed, applies a particular treatment of which he doesn't know what will be the final result. Another typical example concerns the manager of a supermarket who wishes to implement a strategy on the prices to increase the number of customers. Therefore, in this paper, we introduce a new methodology for estimating the "real" impact that could result from a strategy derived from a decision rule.

The paper is organized as follows. In the next section, we briefly remind representation of decision rules and the quantitative measures to evaluate their significance. In Section 3, we present a new methodology for measuring the impact that a strategy

S. Tsumoto et al. (Eds.): RSCTC 2004, LNAI 3066, pp. 523–528, 2004.

derived from decision rules may have on a real life situation in the future. Final Section 4 presents the conclusions.

2 Measures Evaluating Decision Rules Induced from Examples

In this paper, we take into account decision rules induced from a *decision table*. In particular, a decision table is composed of a set U of examples (objects) described by a set of attributes (Q) used for object description. The attributes are divided into *condition attributes* (independent variables) and *decision attribute* (dependent variable). Formally, let DT be a decision table represented as follows:

$$DT = (U, A \cup \{d\}) , \tag{1}$$

where U is a set of examples (objects), A is a set of condition attributes describing examples such that a: $U \rightarrow V_a$ for every $a \in A$. The set V_a is a domain of a. $d \notin A$ is a decision attribute that partitions examples into a set of decision classes (concepts) $\{K_j$: $j = 1,...,k\}$. A decision rule (r) expresses the relationship between condition attribute(s) and a generic class K_j. It can be represented in the following form:

$$\Phi \rightarrow \Psi , \tag{2}$$

where $\Phi = \Phi_1 \wedge \Phi_2 \wedge \ldots \wedge \Phi_m$ is a condition part of the rule and Ψ is a decision part of the rule indicating that an example should be assigned to class K_j. Up to now, several algorithms for generating such rules have been proposed (for a review concerning the rough set approach see [4], [5]).

The above mentioned statement allows to identify the objects satisfying condition and decision part of the rule. However, any rule is not necessarily or always represented as a strict consequence relation. So, several quantitative measures are associated with the rule for measuring its various properties (see, for example, [2] and [6] for exhaustive reviews of the subject). To define these measures, we take into account the set-theoretic interpretation of rules. Let Φ the condition part of the rule; $m(\Phi)$ denotes the set of objects of U that satisfy the conditions expressed by Φ. Similarly, the set $m(\Psi)$ consists of objects satisfying the decision expressed by Ψ. Now, we can define an index, called *confidence* (or certainty) of the rule, represented as follows:

$$conf(r,U) = \frac{|m(\Phi) \cap m(\Psi)|}{|m(\Phi)|} , \tag{3}$$

where $|\cdot|$ denotes the cardinality of a set, i.e., $|m(\Phi) \cap m(\Psi)|$ denotes the number of objects satisfying both parts Φ and Ψ and $|m(\Phi)|$ is the number of objects satisfying the condition Φ only. The range of this measure is $0 \le conf(r,U) \le 1$, and shows the degree to which Φ is related to Ψ. If $conf(r,U) = \alpha$, then $(100 \cdot \alpha)\%$ of objects satisfying Φ also satisfy Ψ. It can be interpreted as the probability to obtain a particular decision class Ψ if condition Φ holds.

Moreover, each decision rule is characterized by its *strength*, defined by the number of objects satisfying condition and decision part of the rule, i.e. $strength(r,U) = |m(\Phi) \cap m(\Psi)|$. Confidence and strength are often used to choose the most important rules induced from a decision table.

3 A New Idea for Analysing the Interest of Rules

In the previous section, we have recalled the concept of confidence and strength of the rules, interpreted as useful measures able to help in the choice of the most important decision rules. The different meanings of these indices imply to consider both indicators in the choice of the rules. These indices do not allow, however, evaluating the improvement produced by a decision strategy based on application of a considered decision rule. So, we introduce a new index that can be considered as a measure of "efficiency" of the rule. The idea is the following.

Let us suppose that we have a decision rule $r \equiv \Phi \rightarrow \Psi$ with a confidence $conf(r,U) = \alpha$. Let us suppose also that we want to implement a decision strategy aiming at increasing the number of objects satisfying Ψ. An example in a medical context is the following. Let Φ be the condition "presence of component A in the blood" and Ψ be the decision "not sick". In this context $\Phi \rightarrow \Psi$ is the decision rule "if component A is present in the blood of x, then x is not sick" with a credibility $conf(r,U)$. Suppose to experiment now the treatment T = "inject component A in the blood of x if x has not it and he/she is sick". The question is: what is the expected increase (in %) of non sick patients after application of treatment T?

Let us consider now U' being a new universe where the experiment is performed. The set of objects satisfying condition Γ in universe U' is denoted by $m'(\Gamma)$. Therefore, $m'(\Phi)$ is the set of objects satisfying condition Φ in universe U'. Analogous interpretation holds for $m'(\neg\Phi)$, $m'(\Psi)$ and $m'(\neg\Psi)$.

After applying treatment T, universe U' will be transformed to universe U''.

The set of objects satisfying condition Γ in universe U'' is denoted by $m''(\Gamma)$. Therefore, $m''(\Phi)$ is the set of objects satisfying condition Φ in universe U''. Analogous interpretation holds for $m''(\neg\Phi)$, $m''(\Psi)$ and $m''(\neg\Psi)$.

We assume that universe U' and U'' are homogeneous with universe U. This means that if the decision rule $r \equiv \Phi \rightarrow \Psi$ holds in U with confidence $conf(r,U)$, then it holds also in the transition from U' to U'' in the following sense: if we modify condition "$\neg\Phi$" to condition "Φ" in the set $m'(\neg\Phi \wedge \neg\Psi)$, we may reasonably expect that $conf(r,U) \times |m'(\neg\Phi \wedge \neg\Psi)|$ elements from $m'(\neg\Phi \wedge \neg\Psi)$ will satisfy decision "Ψ" in universe U''. With respect to our example, this means that in universe U'' the non sick patients are

$$m''(\Psi) = |m'(\Phi \wedge \Psi)| + |m'(\neg\Phi \wedge \Psi)| + |m'(\neg\Phi \wedge \neg\Psi)| \times conf(r,U) =$$
$$= |m'(\Phi \wedge \Psi)| + |m'(\neg\Phi \wedge \Psi)| + |m'(\neg\Phi \wedge \neg\Psi)| \times \frac{|m(\Phi) \cap m(\Psi)|}{|m(\Phi)|}. \tag{4}$$

Therefore the expected increment in the percentage of non sick patients from universe U' to universe U'' due to treatment T is given by:

$$\delta(\Psi) = \frac{|m''(\Psi)|}{|U'|} - \frac{|m'(\Psi)|}{|U'|} = \frac{|m'(\neg\Phi) \cap m'(\neg\Psi)|}{|U'|} \times conf(r,U) = \tag{5}$$

$$=\frac{|m'(\neg\Phi)\cap m'(\neg\Psi)|}{|U'|}\times\frac{|m(\Phi)\cap m(\Psi)|}{|m(\Phi)|}.$$

Let us observe that $\delta(\Psi)$ can be rewritten as follows:

$$\delta(\Psi)=\frac{|m'(\neg\Phi)\cap m'(\neg\Psi)|}{|m'(\neg\Psi)|}\times\frac{|m'(\neg\Psi)|}{|U'|}\times\frac{|m(\Phi)\cap m(\Psi)|}{|m(\Phi)|} \tag{6}$$

or

$$\delta(\Psi)=\frac{|m'(\neg\Phi)\cap m'(\neg\Psi)|}{|m'(\neg\Phi)|}\times\frac{|m'(\neg\Phi)|}{|U'|}\times\frac{|m(\Phi)\cap m(\Psi)|}{|m(\Phi)|}. \tag{7}$$

The above decompositions (6) and (7) of the increment $\delta(\Psi)$ have a very nice interpretation:

- the ratio $\frac{|m'(\neg\Phi)\cap m'(\neg\Psi)|}{|m'(\neg\Psi)|}$ = $conf(s,U')$ is the confidence of rule $s \equiv \neg\Psi \rightarrow \neg\Phi$ in universe U';
- the ratio $\frac{|m'(\neg\Phi)\cap m'(\neg\Psi)|}{|m'(\neg\Phi)|}$ = $conf(t,U')$ is the confidence of rule $t \equiv \neg\Phi \rightarrow \neg\Psi$ in universe U';
- the ratio $\frac{|m'(\neg\Psi)|}{|U'|}$ is the percentage of objects which do not satisfy decision Ψ in universe U';
- the ratio $\frac{|m'(\neg\Phi)|}{|U'|}$ is the percentage of objects which do not satisfy condition Φ in universe U'.

The above results are interesting from two different viewpoints:

1) they permit to give an idea of the result of application of a decision rule: in the considered example, $\delta(\Psi)$ gives an indication of the results of application of treatment T based on decision rule Ψ;
2) they permit to define two measures of interest of a decision rule with respect to its application: let us remark that from the considered viewpoint the interest of a decision rule $r \equiv \Phi \rightarrow \Psi$ is related to its confidence but also to the confidence of the contrapositive decision rule $s \equiv \neg\Psi \rightarrow \neg\Phi$ in universe U', as explained by (6), or to the inverse decision rule $t \equiv \neg\Phi \rightarrow \neg\Psi$ in universe U', as explained by (7). On the basis of above considerations we further define an index $E^c(r,U,U')$ of efficiency with respect to consequent of a decision rule $r = \Phi \rightarrow \Psi$ induced in universe U and applied in universe U':

$$E^c(r,U,U')=conf(r,U)\times conf(s,U')=\frac{|m(\Phi)\cap m(\Psi)|}{|m(\Phi)|}\times\frac{|m'(\neg\Phi)\cap m'(\neg\Psi)|}{|m'(\neg\Psi)|}. \tag{8}$$

Let us remark that from (6) the increment $\delta(\Psi)$ can be expressed as

$$\delta(\Psi) = E^C(r,U,U') \times \frac{|m'(\neg\Psi)|}{|U'|} . \tag{9}$$

On the basis of above considerations, we can also define an index $E^A(r,U,U')$ of efficiency with respect to antecedent of decision rule $r \equiv \Phi\rightarrow\Psi$ induced in universe U and applied in universe U':

$$E^A(r,U,U') = conf(r,U) \times conf(t,U') = \frac{|m(\Phi) \cap m(\Psi)|}{|m(\Phi)|} \times \frac{|m'(\neg\Phi) \cap m'(\neg\Psi)|}{|m'(\neg\Phi)|} . \tag{10}$$

Let us remark that from (7) the increment $\delta(\Psi)$ can be expressed as

$$\delta(\Psi) = E^A(r,U,U') \times \frac{|m'(\neg\Phi)|}{|U'|} . \tag{11}$$

Let us observe that for each decision rule $r \equiv \Phi \rightarrow\Psi$ and its contrapositive rule $s \equiv\neg\Psi\rightarrow\neg\Phi$, we have

$$E^C(r,U,U') = E^C(s,U',U) , \tag{12}$$

while for each decision rule $r = \Phi \rightarrow\Psi$ and its inverse rule $t \equiv\neg\Phi \rightarrow\neg\Psi$, we have

$$E^A(r,U,U') = E^A(t,U',U) . \tag{13}$$

Finally, let us observe that for each decision rule $r \equiv \Phi \rightarrow\Psi$ the following property is always satisfied:

$$E^C(r,U,U') \times |m'(\neg\Psi)| = E^A(r,U,U') \times |m'(\neg\Phi)| . \tag{14}$$

4 Conclusions

In this paper, we presented a methodology to quantify the impact of decision rules when these are taken into consideration by a decision maker to implement a decision strategy. Some indices, such as confidence, allow to estimate the probability of obtaining a particular decision Ψ considering the condition Φ. This index can be interpreted as a characteristic of the present universe U and does not estimate the impact of the decision strategy based on this rule on a possibly different universe U'. Therefore the new indices we proposed take into consideration both the characteristics of the universe U from which the decision rules are induced, but also the universe U' in which the decision rules are applied.

The validity of the proposed measure relies on the assumption of homogeneity requiring that the confidence of a rule is the same in the universe of origin U and in the universe of destination U'. While such an assumption may seem strong, it is difficult to imagine a possible use of decision rules induced from a data table without making a similar assumption in practice. If this assumption would not be satisfied, it would mean that rule $r \equiv$ "*if A, then B*" induced in universe U, is completely useless in universe U' because once applied in situation A, one could get an unexpected consequence C, different from B.

It is possible and useful to extend the proposed methodology to decision rules of the form [1]:

$$r = \Phi_1 \wedge \Phi_2 \wedge \ldots \wedge \Phi_n \rightarrow \Psi \,. \tag{15}$$

An example in a medical context is the following. Let Φ_i, $i \in N$ and $N = \{1,\ldots,n\}$, be the condition "presence of component A_i in the blood". Moreover, let Ψ be the decision "not sick". In this context $r = \Phi_1 \wedge \Phi_2 \wedge \ldots \wedge \Phi_n \rightarrow \Psi$ is the decision rule "if components A_1 and A_2 … and A_n are present in the blood of x, then x is not sick" with a credibility $conf(r, U)$.

Acknowledgements

The fourth author wishes to acknowledge financial support from the State Committee for Scientific Research and the Foundation for Polish Science.

References

1. Greco, S., Matarazzo, B, Pappalardo, N., Slowinski, R.: *Some indices to measures the expected effects of decision rule applications*, manuscript, (2004)
2. Hilderman, R.J. and Hamilton, H.J.: *Knowledge Discovery and Measures of Interest*, Kluwer Academic, Boston (2002)
3. Pawlak, Z.: *Rough Sets. Theoretical Aspects of Reasoning about Data.* Kluwer, Dordrecht (1991)
4. Skowron, A., Polkowski, L.: Decision algorithms: a survey of rough set-theoretic methods. *Fundamenta Informaticae* 27 (3/4) (1997) 345-358
5. Stefanowski, J.: "On rough set based approaches to induction of decision rules". In: A. Skowron, L. Polkowski (eds.): *Rough Sets in Data Mining and Knowledge Discovery*, Physica-Verlag, Heidelberg (1998) 500-529
6. Yao, Y.Y., and Zhong, N.: An analysis of quantitative measures associated with rules. [In]: N. Zhong and L. Zhou (eds.), *Methodologies for Knowledge Discovery and Data Mining.* Lecture Notes in Artificial Intelligence, 1574, Springer-Verlag, Berlin (1999) 479-488

Detection of Differences between Syntactic and Semantic Similarities

Shoji Hirano and Shusaku Tsumoto

Department of Medical Informatics
Shimane University, School of Medicine
Enya-cho Izumo City, Shimane 693-8501 Japan
hirano@ieee.org, tsumoto@computer.org

Abstract. One of the most important problems with rule induction methods is that it is very difficult for domain experts to check millions of rules generated from large datasets. The discovery from these rules requires deep interpretation from domain knowledge. Although several solutions have been proposed in the studies on data mining and knowledge discovery, these studies are not focused on similarities between rules obtained. When one rule r_1 has reasonable features and the other rule r_2 with high similarity to r_1 includes unexpected factors, the relations between these rules will become a trigger to the discovery of knowledge. In this paper, we propose a visualization approach to show the similarity relations between rules based on multidimensional scaling, which assign a two-dimensional cartesian coordinate to each data point from the information about similiaries between this data and others data. We evaluated this method on two medical data sets, whose experimental results show that knowledge useful for domain experts could be found.

1 Introduction

One of the most important problems with rule induction methods is that it is very difficult for domain experts to check millions of rules generated from large datasets. Moreover, since the data collection is deeply dependent on domain knowledge, rules derived by datasets need deep interpretation made by domain experts. For example, Tsumoto and Ziarko reported the following case in analysis of a dataset on meningitis [1].

Even though the dataset is small, the number of records is 141, they obtained 136 rules with high confidence and high support. Here are the examples which are unexpected to domain experts.

```
1. [WBC 12000] & [Gender=Female] & [CSFcell 1000] => Virus meningitis
   (Accuracy: 0.97, Coverage: 0.55)
2. [Age > 40] & [WBC > 8000] => Bacterial meningitis
   (Accuracy: 0.80, Coverage: 0.58)
3. [WBC > 8000] & [Gender=Male] => Bacterial menigits
   (Accuracy: 0.78, Coverage: 0.58)
4. [Gender=Male] & [CSFcell>1000] => Bacterial meningitis
   (Accuracy: 0.77, Coverage: 0.73)
```

S. Tsumoto et al. (Eds.): RSCTC 2004, LNAI 3066, pp. 529–538, 2004.

The factors in these rules unexpected to domain experts are gender and age, which have not been pointed out in the literature on meningitis [2].

Since these detected patterns may strongly depend on the characteristics of data, Tsumoto and Ziarko searched for the hidden factors. For this analysis, several groupings of attributes are processed into the dataset.

The results obtained from the secondary analysis of processed data show that both [*Gender* = *male*] and [*Age* > 40] are closely related with chronic diseases, which is a risk factor of bacterial meningitis. The first attribute-value pair, [*Gender* = *male*] is supported by 70 cases in total 198 records: 48 cases are bacterial meningitis, all of which suffered from chronic diseases (25 cases: diabetes mellitus, 17 cases: liver cirrhosis and 6 cases: chronic sinusitis.) On the other hand, [*Age* > 40] is supported by 121 cases: 59 cases are bacterial meningitis, 45 cases of which suffered from chronic diseases (25 cases: diabetes mellitus, 17 cases: liver cirrhosis and 3 cases: chronic sinusitis.) Domain explanation was given as follows: chronic diseases, especially diabetes mellitus and liver cirrhosis degrade the host-defence to microorganisms as immunological deficiency and chronic sinusitis influences the membrane of brain through the cranial bone. Epidemiological studies show that women before 50 having mensturation suffer from such chronic diseases less than men.

This example illustrates that deep interpretation based on data and domain knowledge is very important for discovery of new knowledge. Especially, the above example shows the importance of similarities between rules. When one rule r_i has reasonable features and the other rule r_j with high similarity to r_i includes unexpected factors, the relations between these rules will become a trigger to the discovery of knowledge.

In this paper, we propose a visualization approach to show the similarity relations between rules based on multidimensional scaling, which assign a two-dimensional cartesian coordinate to each data point from the information about similiaries between this data and others data. We evaluated this method on three medical data sets. Experimental results show that several knowledge useful for domain experts could be found.

2 Preliminaries

2.1 Defintions from Rough Sets

Preliminaries. In the following sections, the following notations introduced by Grzymala-Busse and Skowron [3], are used which are based on rough set theory [4]. These notations are illustrated by a small database shown in Table 1, collecting the patients who complained of headache.

Let U denote a nonempty, finite set called the universe and A denote a nonempty, finite set of attributes, i.e., $a : U \to V_a$ for $a \in A$, where V_a is called the domain of a, respectively. Then, a decision table is defined as an information system, $A = (U, A \cup \{d\})$.

The atomic formulas over $B \subseteq A \cup \{d\}$ and V are expressions of the form $[a = v]$, called descriptors over B, where $a \in B$ and $v \in V_a$. The set $F(B, V)$ of formulas over B is the least set containing all atomic formulas over B and closed with respect to disjunction, conjunction and negation. For example, [*location* = *occular*] is a descriptor of B.

For each $f \in F(B,V)$, f_A denotes the meaning of f in A, i.e., the set of all objects in U with property f, defined inductively as follows.

1. If f is of the form $[a = v]$ then, $f_A = \{s \in U | a(s) = v\}$
2. $(f \wedge g)_A = f_A \cap g_A$; $(f \vee g)_A = f_A \vee g_A$; $(\neg f)_A = U - f_a$

By the use of the framework above, classification accuracy and coverage, or true positive rate is defined as follows.

Definition 1.
Let R and D denote a formula in $F(B,V)$ and a set of objects whose decision class is d. Classification accuracy and coverage(true positive rate) for $R \to d$ is defined as:

$$\alpha_R(D) = \frac{|R_A \cap D|}{|R_A|} (= P(D|R)), \text{ and } \kappa_R(D) = \frac{|R_A \cap D|}{|D|} (= P(R|D)),$$

where $|S|$, $\alpha_R(D)$, $\kappa_R(D)$ and $P(S)$ denote the cardinality of a set S, a classification accuracy of R as to classification of D and coverage (a true positive rate of R to D), and probability of S, respectively.

Probabilistic Rules. According to the definitions, probabilistic rules with high accuracy and coverage are defined as:

$$R \overset{\alpha,\kappa}{\to} d \text{ s.t. } R = \vee_i R_i = \vee \wedge_j [a_j = v_k], \quad \alpha_{R_i}(D) \geq \delta_\alpha \text{ and } \kappa_{R_i}(D) \geq \delta_\kappa,$$

where δ_α and δ_κ denote given thresholds for accuracy and coverage, respectively.

3 Similarity of Rules

As shown in the subsection 2.1, rules are composed of (1) relation between attribute-value pairs (proposition) and (2) values of probabilistic indices (and its supporting sets). Let us call the former component a **syntactic** part and the latter one a **semantic** part. Two similarities are based on the characteristics of these parts.

3.1 Syntactic Similarity

Syntatic similarity is defined as the similarity between conditional parts of the same target concept. In the example shown in Section 1, the following two rules have similar conditional parts:

```
R2. [Age > 40] & [WBC > 8000]  => Bacterial meningitis
   (Accuracy: 0.80, Coverage: 0.58)

R3. [WBC > 8000] & [Gender=Male] => Bacterial menigits
   (Accuracy: 0.78, Coverage: 0.58)
```

Table 1. Contingency Table for Similarity

		$Rule_j$		
		Observed	*Not Observed*	Total
$Rule_i$	*Observed*	a	b	$a+b$
	Not Observed	c	d	$c+d$
	Total	$a+c$	$b+d$	$a+b+c+d$

The difference between these two rules are $[Age > 40]$ and $[Gender = Male]$. To measure the similarity between these two rules, we can apply several indices of two-way contigency tables. Table 1 gives a contingency table for two rules, $Rule_i$ and $Rule_j$. The first cell a (the intersection of the first row and column) shows the number of matched attribute-value pairs. From this table, several kinds of similarity measures can be defined. The best similarity measures in the statistical literature are four measures shown in Table 2 [5]. For further reference, readers may refer to [6]. It is notable that these indices satisfies the property on symmetry shown in the beginning of this section.

Table 2. Definition of Similarity Measures

(1) Matching Number	a
(2) Jaccard's coefficient	$a/(a+b+c)$
(3) χ^2-statistic	$N(ad-bc)^2/M$
(4) point correlation coefficient	$(ad-bc)/\sqrt{M}$

$N = a+b+c+d$, $M = (a+b)(b+c)(c+d)(d+a)$

3.2 Semantic Similarity: Covering

The other similarity which can be defined from the definition of the rule is based on the *meaning* of the relations between formulas f_i and f_j from the viewpoint of set-theoretical point of view. Let us assume that we have two rules:

$$f_i \to D\ (\alpha_{f_i}(D), \kappa_{f_i}(D))$$
$$f_j \to D\ (\alpha_{f_j}(D), \kappa_{f_j}(D))$$

As shown in the last subsection, syntactic similarity is defined as $sim(f_i, f_j)$ from the viewpoint of syntactic representations. Since f_i and f_j have meanings (supporting sets), ${f_i}_A$ and ${f_j}_A$, respectively, where A denotes the given attribute space. Then, we can define $sim({f_i}_A, {f_j}_A)$ by using a contingency table: Table 1. While this table is used in the last subsection as the number of matched number of attribute-value pairs.

3.3 Semantic Similarity: Accuracy and Coverage

The similarity defined in the last subsection is based on the supporting sets of two formulas.

Table 3. Two way Contingency Table

	$R_1 = 0$	$R_1 = 1$	
$R_2 = 0$	a	b	$a + b$
$R_2 = 1$	c	d	$c + d$
	$a + c$	$b + d$	$a + b + c + d$ $(= \|U\| = N)$

However, to calculate these similarities, we should go back to the dataset, which may be time-consuming for huge datasets. In such cases, we can use the combination of accuracy and coverage to measure the similarity between two rules. Let us return the definition of accuracy and coverage. From the viewpoint of a two-way contingency table, accuracy and coverage are defined as follows. Let R_1 and R_2 denote a formula in $F(B, V)$. A contingency tables is a table of a set of the meaning of the following formulas: $|[R_1 = 0]_A|$,$|[R_1 = 1]_A|$, $|[R_2 = 0]_A|$,$|[R_1 = 1]_A|$, $|[R_1 = 0 \wedge R_2 = 0]_A|$,$|[R_1 = 0 \wedge R_2 = 1]_A|$, $|[R_1 = 1 \wedge R_2 = 0]_A|$,$|[R_1 = 1 \wedge R_2 = 1]_A|$, $|[R_1 = 0 \vee R_1 = 1]_A|(= |U|)$. This table is arranged into the form shown in Table 1. From this table, accuracy and coverage for $[R_1 = 0] \to [R_2 = 0]$ are defined as:

$$\alpha_{[R_1=0]}([R_2 = 0]) = \frac{a}{a+c}, and \kappa_{[R_1=0]}([R_2 = 0]) = \frac{a}{a+b}.$$

It is easy to show that accuracy and coverage do not hold the symmetric relation, that is, $\alpha_{[R_1=0]}([R_2 = 0]) \neq \alpha_{[R_2=0]}([R_1 = 0])$ nor $\kappa_{[R_1=0]}([R_2 = 0]) \neq \kappa_{[R_2=0]}([R_1 = 0])$.

However, combinations of these two indices give several types of similarity indices [7], as shown in Table 4. Since $a/(a + b)$ and $a/(a + c)$ are accuracy and coverage, they can be represented by these two indices. For example, Kulczyski's measure is written as $\frac{1}{2}(\alpha_R(D) + \kappa_R(D))$, where R and D denotes $[R1 = 0 \ or \ 1]$ and $[D = 0 \ or \ 1]$, respectively.

Table 4. Definition of Similarity Measures (2)

(5) Kulczynski	$\frac{1}{2}(\frac{a}{a+b} + \frac{a}{a+c})$
(6) Ochiai	$\frac{a}{\sqrt{(a+b)(a+c)}}$
(7) Simpson	$\frac{a}{min\{(a+b),(a+c)\}}$

4 Multidimensional Scaling

4.1 How MDS Works

Metric MDS. The most important function of MDS is to recover cartesian coordinates (usually, two-dimensional) from a given similarity matrix. For recovery, we assume that a similarity is given as an inner product of two vectors for objects. Although we need three points to recover coordinates, but one point is fixed as the origin of the plane.

Let us assume that the coordinates of two objects x_i and x_j are given as: $(x_{i1}, x_{i2}, \cdots, x_{ip})$ and $(x_{j1}, x_{j2}, \cdots, x_{jp})$, where p is the number of dimension of the space. Let k denote the origin of the space $(0, 0, \cdots, 0)$. Then, here, we assume that the distance betweeen x_i and x_j d_{ij} is given as the formula of distance, such as Eucledian, Minkowski, and so on. MDS based on this assumption is called *metric MDS*. Then, the similarity between i and j s_{ij} is given as:

$$s_{ij} = d_{ik}d_{jk}\cos\theta = \sum_{m=1}^{p} x_{im}x_{jm}$$

From the triangle ijk, the following formula holds:

$$d_{ij}^2 = d_{ik}^2 + d_{jk}^2 - 2d_{ik}d_{jk}\cos\theta.$$

Therefore, similarity should hold the following formula.

$$s_{ij} = \frac{d_{ik}^2 + d_{jk}^2 - d_{ij}^2}{2}$$

Since s_{ij} is given as $\sum_{m=1}^{p} x_{im}x_{jm}$, the similarity matrix for s_{ij} is given as:

$$\mathbf{Z} = \mathbf{X}\mathbf{X}^{\mathbf{T}},$$

where $\mathbf{X}^{\mathbf{T}}$ denotes the transposition matrix of $\mathbf{X}$. To obtain $\mathbf{X}$, we consider the minimization of an objective function Q defined as:

$$Q = \sum_i \sum_j \left(z_{ij} - \sum_{m=1}^{p} x_{im}x_{jm} \right)^2.$$

For this purpose, we apply *EckartandYoung* decomposition [8] in the following way. first, we calculate eigenvalues, denoted by $\lambda_1, \cdots, \lambda_p$, and eigenvectors of $\mathbf{Z}$, denoted by $\mathbf{v^1}, \cdots, \mathbf{v^p}$. Then by using a diagnoal matrix of eigenvalues, denoted by $\mathbf{\Lambda}$ and a matrix with eigenvectors, denoted by $\mathbf{Y}$, we obtain the following formula:

$$\mathbf{X} = \mathbf{Y}\mathbf{\Lambda}\mathbf{Y}^{\mathbf{T}},$$

where

$$\mathbf{\Lambda} = \begin{pmatrix} \lambda_1 & 0 & \ldots\ldots\ldots & & 0 \\ 0 & \lambda_2 & 0 \ldots & \ldots & 0 \\ \ldots\ldots & & \lambda_i & \ldots\ldots\ldots & \\ 0 & 0 & \ldots & \lambda_{p-1} & 0 \\ 0 & 0 & \ldots & 0 & \lambda_p \end{pmatrix},$$

and

$$\mathbf{Y} = \left(\mathbf{v^1}, \mathbf{v^2}, \cdots, \mathbf{v^p}\right).$$

From this decomposition, we obtain $\mathbf{X}$ as

$$\mathbf{X} = \mathbf{Y}\Lambda^{1/2}.$$

Nonmetric MDS. The above metric MDS can be applied to the case only when the difference between similarities has the meaning. In other words, the similarity index holds the property of interval calculus (interval scale).

If the similarity index holds the property of order, we should not apply the above calculus to the similarity matrix, but we should apply nonmetric MDS method. Here, we will introduce Kruskal method, which is one of the most well-known nonmetric MDS method [7]. First, we calculate given similarities s_{ij} into distance data d^*_{ij} (dissimilarity). Next, we estimate the coordinates of x_i and x_j from the minimization of *Stress* function, defined as:

$$S = \sqrt{\frac{\sum\sum_{i<j}(d_{ij} - d^*_{ji})^2}{\sum\sum d^2_{ij}}},$$

where the distance d_{ij} is defined as a Minkowski distance:

$$d_{ij} = \left(\sum_{m=1}^{P} |x_{im} - x_{jm}|^t\right)^{1/t},$$

where t denotes the Minkowski constant. For the minimization of S, optimization methods, such as gradient method are applied and the dimensionality and t will be estimated.

Since the similarity measures given above do not hold the property of distance (triangular inequality), we adopt nonmetric MDS method to visualize similarity relations.

5 Experimental Results

We applied the combination of rule induction and nonmetric MDS to two medical databases on meningits in order to confirm the characteristics of rules obtained by Tsumoto and Ziarko's method [1]. For similarity measures, we adopt Kulczynski's similarity and calculate similarity measures from accuracy and coverage of rules obtained from data.

Figure 1 and 2 shows the two-dimensional and three-dimensional assignments of the rules, respectively.

On the other hand, Figure 3 and 4 shows the two-dimensional and three-dimensional assignments of the rules, respectively.

These four figures suggest that two axes should be considered for visualization: one is differences in visualized patterns between 2-D and 3-D spaces of synctactic or semantic similarity. The other one is differences in patterns between two similarities.

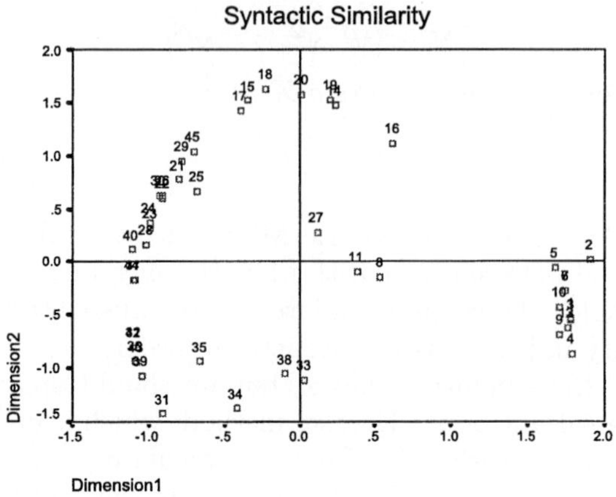

Fig. 1. Two-dimensional Visualization of Rules (Syntactic Similarity)

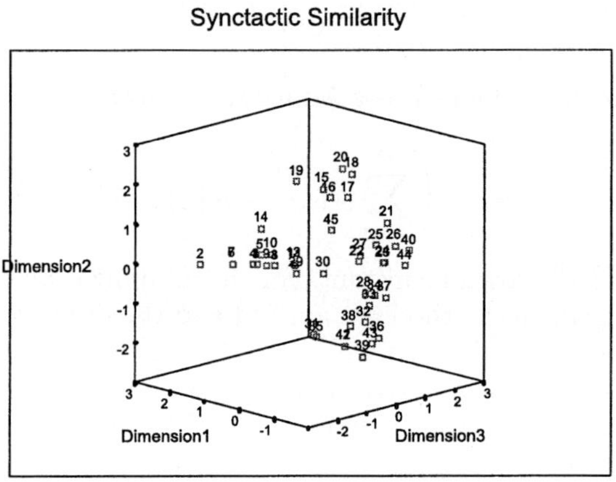

Fig. 2. Three dimensional Visualization of Rules (Synctactic Similarity)

6 Conclusion

In this paper, we propose a visualization approach to show the similar relations between rules based on multidimensional scaling, which assign a two-dimensional cartesian coordinate to each data point from the information about similiaries between this data and others data. As similarity for rules, we define three types of similarities: syntactic, semantic (covering based) and semantic (indice based). Syntactic similarity shows the difference in attribute-value pairs, semantic similarity gives the similarity of rules from the viewpoint of supporting sets. MDS assigns each rule into the point of two-dimensional plane with distance information, which is useful to capture the intuitive dissimilarities between rules. Since the indices for these measures may not hold the property of distance (transitivity), we adopt nonmetric MDS, which is based on the stress function.

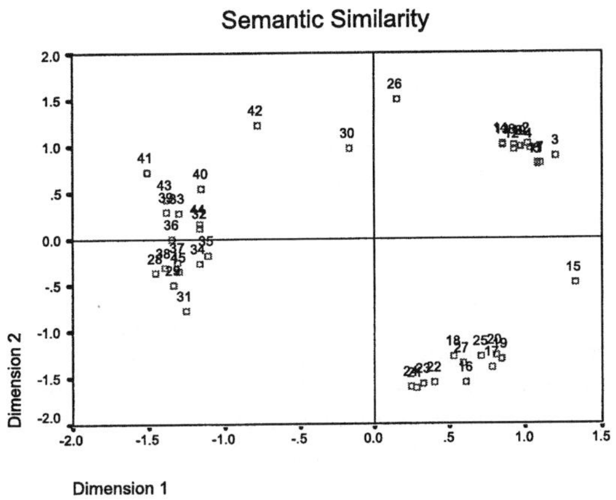

Fig. 3. Two-dimensional Visualization of Rules (Semantic Similarity)

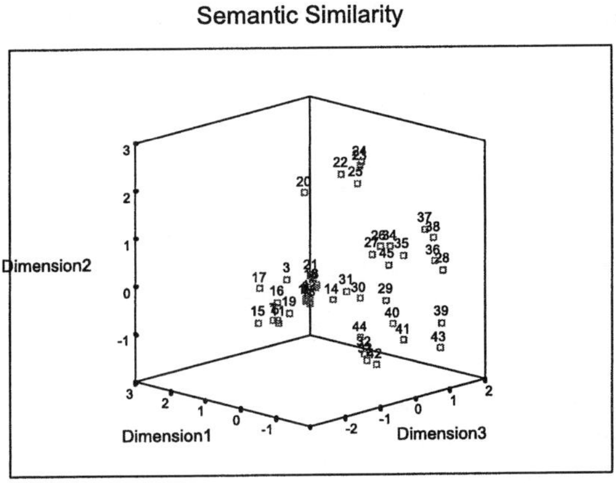

Fig. 4. Three dimensional Visualization of Rules (Semantic Similarity)

Finally, we evaluated this method on a medical data set, whose experimental results show that several knowledge useful for domain experts could be found. This study is a preliminary study on the visualization of rules' similarity based on MDS. Further analysis of this method, such as studies on computational complexity, scalability will be made and reported in the near future.

Acknowledgement

This work was supported by the Grant-in-Aid for Scientific Research (13131208) on Priority Areas (No.759) "Implementation of Active Mining in the Era of Information Flood" by the Ministry of Education, Science, Culture, Sports, Science and Technology of Japan.

References

1. Tsumoto, S., Ziarko, W.: The application of rough sets-based data mining technique to differential diagnosis of meningoenchepahlitis. In Ras, Z.W., Michalewicz, M., eds.: Foundations of Intelligent Systems, 9th International Symposium, ISMIS '96, Zakopane, Poland, June 9-13, 1996, Proceedings. Volume 1079 of Lecture Notes in Computer Science., Springer (1996) 438–447
2. Adams, R., Victor, M.: Principles of Neurology 5th Edition. McGraw-Hill, New York (1993)
3. Skowron, A., Grzymala-Busse, J.: From rough set theory to evidence theory. In Yager, R., Fedrizzi, M., Kacprzyk, J., eds.: Advances in the Dempster-Shafer Theory of Evidence. John Wiley & Sons, New York (1994) 193–236
4. Pawlak, Z.: Rough Sets. Kluwer Academic Publishers, Dordrecht (1991)
5. Everitt, B.: Cluster Analysis. 3rd edn. John Wiley & Son, London (1996)
6. Yao, Y., Zhong, N.: An analysis of quantitative measures associated with rules. In Zhong, N., Zhou, L., eds.: Methodologies for Knowledge Discovery and Data Mining, Proceedings of the Third Pacific-Asia Conference on Knowledge Discovery and Data Mining. Volume 1574 of Lecture Note in AI., Berlin, Springer (1999) 479–488
7. Cox, T., Cox, M.: Multidimensional Scaling. 2nd edn. Chapman & Hall/CRC, Boca Raton (2000)
8. Eckart, C., Young, G.: Approximation of one matrix by another of lower rank. Psychometrika **1** (1936) 211–218

Processing of Musical Data Employing Rough Sets and Artificial Neural Networks

Bozena Kostek, Piotr Szczuko, and Pawel Zwan

Gdansk University of Technology, Multimedia Systems Department
Narutowicza 11/12, 80-952 Gdansk, Poland
{bozenka,szczuko,zwan}@sound.eti.pg.gda.pl
http://www.multimed.org

Abstract. This paper presents system assumptions for automatic recognition of music and musical sounds. An overview of the MPEG-7 standard, focused on audio information description, is given. The paper discusses some problems in audio information analysis related to efficient MPEG-7-based applications. The effectiveness of the implemented low-level descriptors for automatic recognition of musical instruments is presented on the basis of experiments. A discussion on the influence of the choice of descriptors on the recognition score is included. Experiments are carried out basing on a decision system employing Rough Sets and Artificial Neural Networks. Conclusions are also included.

Keywords: Music Information Retrieval, MPEG-7 low-level descriptors, rough sets, Artificial Neural Networks (ANN), decision systems

1 Introduction

Recently defined MPEG-7 standard is designed to describe files containing digital representations of sound, video, images and text information allowing the contents to be automatically queried in a number of multimedia databases that can be accessed via the Internet. MPEG-7 standard specifies the description of features related to the audio-video (AV) content as well as information related to the management of AV content. In order to guarantee interoperability for some low-level features, MPEG-7 also specifies part of the extraction process. MPEG-7 descriptions take two possible forms: a textual XML form (high-level descriptors) suitable for editing, searching, filtering, and browsing and a binary form (low-level descriptors) suitable for storage, transmission, and streaming.

For many applications, the mapping between low-level descriptions and high-level queries will have to be done during the description process. The search engine or the filtering device will have to analyze the low-level features and, on this basis, perform the recognition process. This is a very challenging task for audio analysis research [4]. The technology related to intelligent search and filtering engines using low-level audio features, possibly together with high-level features, is still very limited. A major question remains open what is the most efficient set of low-level descriptors that

S. Tsumoto et al. (Eds.): RSCTC 2004, LNAI 3066, pp. 539–548, 2004.

have to be used to allow a certain class of recognition tasks to be performed on the description itself. Of importance is the fact that the parameters of MPEG-7 musical sounds were selected based on many, however, separately carried on, experiments, hence the need to test the quality of the parameters in a process of automatic identification of musical instrument classes. The experiments will be based on a decision-making system employing learning algorithms.

The paper will discuss a number of parametrization methods that are used for describing musical objects. First, assumptions of the engineered database are presented. Problems discussed in the paper are related to how musical objects are saved and searched for in the engineered sound database. Despite the standard relatively clear-cut instructions on how musical objects should be described (e.g. using the features vector), it mainly covers the indexing of files in databases rather than focus on the algorithmic tools for searching these files.

Generally, it could be said that music could be searched using a so-called "query-by-example" scheme. A musical signal including single and polyphonic sounds and human voice sounds (speech and singing), music, scores (graphical form), MIDI code or verbal description, each comes as a different representation. The paper will give examples of features vector based on time, spectral, time- frequency musical signals representations.

However, the problem of how to effectively query multimedia contents applies to search tools, as well. To address that, many research centers focus on this problem. Earlier research at the Department of Sound and Vision at the Gdansk University of Technology showed that for automatic search of musical information intelligent decision-making systems works much better than typical statistical or topological methods. Rough sets allow for searching databases with incomplete information and inconsistent entries. This theory, founded by Pawlak [14], and applications based on rough sets are now extremely well developed [3],[8],[9],[13],[14],[15],[16]. For the purpose of experiments the RSES system was used, developed by the Warsaw University [1],[2],[5]. Rough Set Exploration System has been created to enable multi-directional practical investigations and experimental verification of research in decision support systems and classification algorithms, in particular of those with application of rough set theory [1],[2].

Artificial Neural Networks are computing structures that adjust themselves to a specific application by training rather than by having a defined algorithm. The network is trained by minimizing the error of network classification. When a specific threshold error is reached, the learning process is considered complete. The use of rough sets and artificial neural networks help to effectively identify musical objects, even if during training decision systems are given only a limited number of examples.

2 Low-Level MPEG-7 Descriptors

Development of streaming media on the Internet caused huge demand to make audio-visual material searchable in the same way as text is. Audio and video contain a lot of information that can be used in indexing and retrieval applications. Many research efforts have been spent to describe the content of an audio and video signals, using specific indexing parameters and extraction techniques. The MPEG-7 standard provides a uniform and standardized way of describing the multimedia content. A part of this standard is specifically dedicated to the description of the audio content. The MPEG-7 Audio framework consists of two description levels: low-level audio descriptors, and high-level ones related to semantic information and *metadata. Metadata* are compiled from collections of low-level descriptors that are the result of detailed analysis of the content actual data samples and signal waveforms. MPEG-7 expresses these descriptions in XML, thereby providing a method of describing the audio or video samples of the content in textual form [4],[6],[12].

The MPEG-7 standard defines six categories of low-level audio descriptors. Generally, it may be said that the division of these parameters is related to the need to visualize the sound, and to extract significant signal parameters regardless of the audio signal type (e.g. musical sounds, polyphonic signals, etc.). In addition a so-called "silence" parameter is also defined. They measure several characteristics of sound, which can be stored as an XML file that serves as a compact representation of the analyzed audio. These six categories contain the following parameters [6]:

I. Basic
1. Audio Waveform
2. Audio Power

II. Basic spectral
3. Audio Spectral Envelope
4. Audio Spectral Centroid
5. Audio Spectrum Spread
6. Audio Spectrum Flatness

III. Signal parameters
7. Audio Fundamental Frequency
8. Audio Harmonicity

IV. Timbral temporal
9. Attack Time
10. Temporal Centroid

V. Timbral spectral
11. Harmonic Spectrum Centroid
12. Harmonic Spectral Deviation
13 Harmonic Spectral Spread
14 Harmonic Spectral Variation
15 Spectral Centroid

VI. Spectral Basis
16. Audio Spectrum Basis
17. Audio Spectrum Projection

3 System Assumptions

A very interesting example of musical databases is CDDB that contained over 1 million CDs [7]. However, apart from world-wide known databases there exist many local databases. An example of such a musical database is the one created at the Multimedia Systems Department of the Gdansk University of Technology. Musical database consists of three sub-databases, each related to different format of music. Therefore, the first one contains musical sounds, the second one - MIDI files, and the third one fragments of music from CDs. Searching for music, MIDI-based recording or a sound signal (audio type) in a music database includes the following tasks:

- registration – employing a sound card,
- uploading the pattern file,
- playing back the pattern file,
- automatic parameterization of the pattern file,
- defining query criteria (*Metadata* description),
- searching in the parameter database based on the *Metadata* description and vector parameter similarity with the following options:
- searching for the specific file and not downloading it
- script compiled in Server environment / downloading the file with parameters from the server,
- review and playback of query results,
- downloading the file selected.

Fig. 1 shows the general system operation principle making a clear distinction between MIDI queries and those containing musical sounds. Additional categories of files are for complex sounds (e.g. musical duets) and polyphonic sounds. Sound signals are introduced into system, which applies some preprocessing, then extracts certain features from each sound, generating a representation of those features using MPEG-7 low-level descriptors.

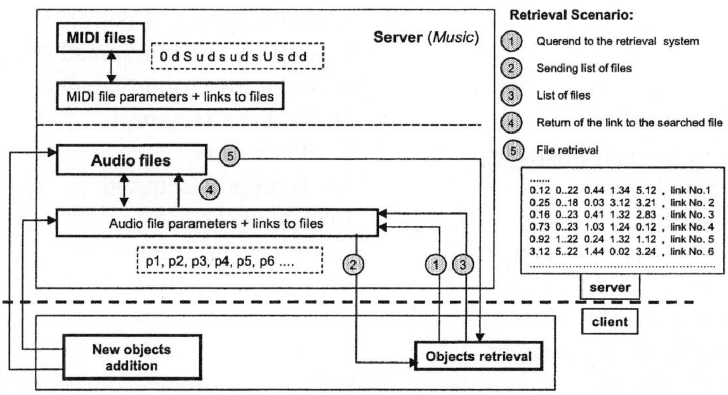

Fig. 1. General system operation principle.

A database record consists of the following components: category, [parameter vector], *Metadata* description and resource link. The parameter file includes a parametric description, and a *Metadata* description is added for each database object. The query process does not parameterize all database objects (this is done when introducing a new object to the database). The search is for a file that matches the description. In this way, audio file can be specifically described in a standardized form that can be stored in a database. This provides a reliable way to identify a particular piece of content without actually decoding its essence data or analyzing its waveform, but rather by simply scanning its description.

3.1 MPEG-7 Based Parameters Applied to Musical Sounds

Before automatic parameter extraction can be done, the sound fundamental frequency must be estimated. A modified Schroeder's histogram was applied for this purpose [11]. The effectiveness of detection of the musical sound fundamental frequency is very high for the chosen instruments (98%), thus the calculation of signal parameters would not suffer from the erroneous pitch detection.

The parametrization consists in calculation of some MPEG-7-based descriptors. Since they were recently reviewed by the authors in other publication [11], thus they are only listed below:

- *Spectral centroid* (m_1):
- *Audio harmonicity* (m_2):
- *Harmonic Spectral Spread* (m_3);
- *Harmonic Spectral Deviation* (m_4);
- *Harmonic Spectral Centroid* (m_5);
- *Audio Spectral Flatness* - spectral Power Density Function calculated on the basis of the *N*-point FFT algorithm (m_6):

$$FM = 10 \cdot \log \frac{\left(\prod_{i=1}^{N/2} P_i \right)^{\frac{2}{N}}}{\frac{2}{N} \cdot \sum_{i=1}^{N/2} P_i} \tag{1}$$

where: P_i – consecutive sample amplitude

N – analysis resolution.

For practical calculation Eq. (1) adopts the form:

$$FM = 10 \left\{ \left[\frac{2}{N} \left(\log_{10} P_1 + \ldots\ldots + \log_{10} P_{N/2} \right) \right] - \log_{10} \left[\frac{2}{N} \cdot \left(P_1 + \ldots\ldots + P_{N/2} \right) \right] \right\} \tag{2}$$

By analyzing sound envelope, two additional parameters were determined [11]:

- *LogAttack Time* (m_7), defined as the time during which the envelope changes its value from 0.1 to 0.9 of the maximum value in units of multiplicity of the length of the frame of envelope averaging (in the experiments the value was 512 samples);
- *Temporal Centroid Descriptor* (m_8).

The parameters and fundamental frequency of the sound were then the basis for the vector of sound description given in the format as seen below:

$$v = \lfloor m_1 \quad m_2 \quad m_3 \quad m_4 \quad m_5 \quad m_6 \quad m_7 \quad m_8 \quad f_p \rfloor \tag{3}$$

3.2 ANN-Based MPEG-7-Based Parameter Quality Testing

To test the parameters for their usefulness for musical instruments classification process, an artificial neural network algorithm was used (ANN). The neural musical predictor was implemented using the Matlab system. The neural network had three layers with 8 neurons in the input layer, 14 neurons in the hidden layer and 6 neurons in the output layer. Activation functions were unipolar. Feature vectors were fed to the network input. Vectors of parameters were randomly divided into two sets: training and validation vectors. Each set contained 50% of all vectors. Error back-propagation algorithm was used to train the neural network. The process of training was considered as finished when the value of the cumulative error of network responses for the set of testing vectors had dropped below the assumed threshold value or when the cumulative error of network responses for the validation set of vectors had been rising for more then 10 cycles in a row. The recognized class of the instrument was determined by the highest value of the output signals of neurons in the output layer. The training procedure was repeated 10 times and the best-trained network was chosen for further experiments. Results obtained were shown in Table 1. As shown in Tab. 1 cello sound recognition effectiveness was 100%, violin sounds were recognized with approx. 93% accuracy (some mix-up with clarinet sounds occurred), that of clarinet and trombone sounds was more than 84%. Trombone sounds that were incorrectly recognized were classified by the system as trumpet sounds; trumpet and saxophone sounds were confused with each other (more than 40% of cases).

Table 1. Recognition effectiveness of the MPEG-7-based descriptors.

[%]	clarinet	trumpet	violin	sax	trombone	Cello
clarinet	**84.2**	5.3	5.3	0.0	5.3	0.0
trumpet	0.0	**53.8**	0.0	46.2	0.0	0.0
violin	6.3	0.0	**93.8**	0.0	0.0	0.0
sax	0.0	23.1	0.0	**46.2**	30.8	0.0
trombone	0.0	17.6	0.0	0.0	**82.4**	0.0
cello	0.0	0.0	0.0	0.0	0.0	**100**

3.3 Wavelet-Based and Joint Representation Quality Testing

Because MPEG-7 parameters were calculated for the steady state of sound, the decision was made to enhance the description by adding descriptors based on the transient phase of sound. Earlier research on wavelet parameters for the transient state of musical sounds allowed for easy calculation of such parameters [10]. One of the main advantages of wavelets is that they offer a simultaneous localization in time and frequency domain. Frames consisting of 2048 samples taken from the transient of a sound were analyzed. Several filters such as proposed by Daubechies, Coifman, Haar, Meyer, Shannon, etc., were used in analyses and their order was varied from 2 up to 8. It was found that Daubechies filters (2nd order) have the computational load considerably lower than while employing other types of filters, therefore they were used in the analysis. For the purpose of the study several parameters were calculated. They were derived by observing both energy and time relations within the wavelet subbands. Energy-related parameters are based on energy coefficients computed for the wavelet spectrum sub-bands normalized with regard to the overall energy of the parameterized frame corresponding to the starting transient. On the other hand, time-related wavelet parameters refer to the number of coefficients that have exceeded the given threshold. Such a threshold helps to differentiate between "tone-like" and "noise-like" characteristics of the wavelet spectrum [10].

To assess the quality of wavelet-based feature vectors, the musical sounds underwent recognition for wavelet parameters (8 parameters), and later for a combined representation of the steady and transient states (simultaneous MPEG-7 and wavelet parameterization resulting in 16 parameters). To that end, ANNs were used again. System results for the wavelet-based representation are given by the diagonal of Tab. 2 (correctly recognized class of instrument). The other values denote the errors made in the recognition process. As seen from Tab. 2 results, the system recognition effectiveness was 100% in the case of trumpet. Other musical instrument sounds were recognized in some cases incorrectly. It can be seen that the wavelet parameterization helped to correctly recognize trumpet sounds and much better results were obtained for other instruments, especially for saxophone, while the cello did not do that well.

Because dimensions of the input vector increased for the combined representation, thus the neural structure increased. There were 16 neurons in the input layer, 16 in the hidden layer and 6 in the output layer. Recognition results are given in Table 3. As seen in Table 3 musical instrument sounds were properly classified for the most part (the values of the neurons are equal to or close to 1). There were some errors in the case of trombone, violin and sax sounds.

Table 2. Recognition effectiveness of the wavelet-based descriptors.

[%]	Clarinet	trumpet	violin	sax	trombone	Cello
clarinet	**94.7**	0.0	0.0	0.0	5.3	0.0
trumpet	0.0	**100**	0.0	0.0	0.0	0.0
violin	6.3	0.0	**87.5**	0.0	0.0	12.5
sax	7.7	15.4	0.0	**76.9**	0.0	0.0
trombone	0.0	0.0	0.0	5.9	**88.2**	5.9
cello	0.0	0.0	10.0	0.0	0.0	**90.0**

The combined FFT and wavelet representation ensures much better recognition results for each group of instruments. This is because the parameterization process covers both the transient and steady state of sound, and the resulting features of the parameter vector complement each other. In addition, another experiment was performed, this time much larger number of instrument sounds was tested, however, there were only three groups of instrument classes classified by the ANN. As seen from Table 4 the ANN-based system performed very well. This was due to the fact that the extended feature vector representation (joint representation) was used. Moreover, instrument of similar timbre were assigned to the same instrument groups, thus the system was not confused.

Table 3. Recognition effectiveness of the MPEG-7+wavelet-based descriptors.

[%]	clarinet	trumpet	violin	sax	trombone	Cello
clarinet	**94.7**	0.0	0.0	5.3	0.0	0.0
trumpet	0.0	**92.3**	0.0	7.7	0.0	0.0
violin	0.0	0.0	**93.8**	6.3	0.0	0.0
sax	0.0	0.0	0.0	**100**	0.0	0.0
trombone	5.9	5.9	0.0	0.0	**88.2**	0.0
cello	0.0	0.0	0.0	0.0	0.0	**100**

Table 4. Recognition effectiveness for instrument groups.

Instrument group	Number of sounds	Erroneous recognition	Effectiveness
string	276	4	98.55%
woodwind	561	6	98.93%
brass	495	6	97.79%
all	1332	16	97.80%

3.4 Rough Set-Based Feature Vector Quality Testing

For the purpose of experiments RSES system was employed [5]. RSESlib is a system containing library of functions for performing various data exploration tasks such as: data manipulation and edition, discretization of numerical attributes, calculation of reducts. It allows for generation of decision rules with use of reducts, decomposition of large data into parts that share the same properties, search for patterns in data, etc. Data are represented as a decision table in RSES [1], [5]. Since the system was presented very thoroughly at the rough set society forum, thus no detail will be shown here, however, a reader interested in the system may visit its homepage [5].

Recognition effectiveness for rough set-based decision system is shown in Table 5. Denotations in Table 5 are as follows: alto_trombone(1), altoflute (2), Bach_trumpet (3), bass_clarinet (4), bass_trombone (5), bassflute (6), bassoon (7), Bb_clarinet (8), C_trumpet, (9), CB (10), cello (11), contrabass_clarinet (12), contrabassoon (13), Eb_clarinet (14), English_horn (15), flute (16), French_horn (17), oboe (18), piccolo (19), trombone (20), tuba (21), viola (22), violin (23), violin_ensemble (24). Most errors were due to similarity in timbre of instruments, for example: such pairs of instruments clarinet and bass clarinet, trombone and bass trombone and also contrabass (CB) and cello were often misclassified due to their timbre similarity. In overall, system accuracy was equal to 0.78. In addition, an experiment similar to the one performed previously, based on ANN, was carried out. Instruments were assigned to three classes, and classification was performed once again. Results obtained were gathered in Table 6. As seen from Table 6 the system accuracy was very good, and comparable to ANN-based system, even if in this case twice as many instrument sounds were being classified Therefore, it could be said that common (joint) feature vector representation containing both MPEG-7-based and wavelet-based parameters is more effective than the one based on MPEG-7 representation, alone.

Table 5. Recognition effectiveness for instrument based on rough sets.

No.	1	2	3	4	5	6	7	8	9	10	11	12
Eff.	0.67	0.71	0.88	0.57	0.5	0.83	0.88	0.8	0.88	0.79	0.81	0.83
No.	13	14	15	16	17	18	19	20	21	22	23	24
Eff.	0.75	0.63	0.88	0.44	0.74	0.75	1	0.59	1	0.87	0.81	1

Table 6. Recognition effectiveness for instrument groups based on rough sets.

Instrument group	Number of sounds	Erroneous recognition	Effectiveness
string	411	6	98.54%
woodwind	902	17	98.12%
brass	712	18	97.47%
all	2025	41	97.98%

Conclusions

In the paper an overview of the MPEG-7 standard audio descriptors has been presented. The aim of the carried out study was to automatically classify musical instrument sounds on the basis of a limited number of parameters, and to test the quality of musical sound parameters that are included in the MPEG-7 standard. It has been seen that MPEG-7-based features alone are not fully sufficient for the correct audio retrieval, mainly due to the lack of information about the signal time features. The use of the wavelet-based parameters has led to better audio retrieval efficiency. This has been verified further by extending experiments for the case of audio retrieval based on rough sets. Therefore, there is a continuing need for further work on the selection and effectiveness of parameters for the description of musical sounds, and audio signals in general.

Acknowledgement

The research is sponsored by the Committee for Scientific Research, Warsaw, Grant No. 4T11D 014 22, and the Foundation for Polish Science, Poland.

References

1. Bazan, J., Szczuka, M.: RSES and RSESlib - A Collection of Tools for Rough Set Computations, Proc. of RSCTC'2000, LNAI 2005, Springer Verlag, Berlin (2001)

2. Bazan, J., Szczuka, M, Wroblewski, J..: A New Version of Rough Set Exploration System, Proc. RSCTC LNAI 2475, In J.J. Alpigini et al. (Eds), Springer Verlag, Heidelberg, Berlin (2002) 397-404
3. Bazan, J.G, Nguyen, H.S., Skowron, A., Szczuka, M.: A View on Rough Set Concept Approximations. In G. Wang, Q. Liu, Y. Yao, A. Skowron (Eds.): Proc. of RSFD, Chongqing, China, Lecture Notes in Computer Science 2639, Springer (2003) 181-188
4. Hunter, J.: An overview of the MPEG-7 Description Definition Language (DDL), IEEE Transactions on Circuits and Systems for Video Technology, 11 (6), June (2001) 765-772
5. http://logic.mimuw.edu.pl/~rses/ (RSES homepage)
6. http://www.meta-labs.com/mpeg-7-aud
7. http://www.freedb.org
8. Komorowski, J., Pawlak, Z., Polkowski, L., Skowron, A.: Rough Sets: A Tutorial, Rough Fuzzy Hybridization: A New Trend in Decision-Making. Pal, S. K., Skowron, A. (eds.), Springer-Verlag (1998) 3-98
9. Kostek, B.: Soft Computing in Acoustics, Applications of Neural Networks, Fuzzy Logic and Rough Sets to Musical Acoustics, Physica Verlag, Heidelberg, NY (1999).
10. Kostek, B., Czy ewski, A.: Representing Musical Instrument Sounds for their Automatic Classification, J. Audio Eng. Soc., Vol. 49, 9, (2001) 768 – 785
11. Kostek, B., Zwan, P.: Wavelet-based automatic recognition of musical instruments, 142nd Meeting of the Acoustical Soc. of Amer., Fort Lauderdale, Florida, USA, No. 5, Vol. 110, 4pMU5, Dec. 3-7. (2001) 2754
12. Lindsay, A.T., Herre, J.: MPEG-7 and MPEG-7 Audio – An Overview, J. Audio Eng. Soc., Vol. 49, 7/8, (2001) 589-594
13. Pal, S. K., Polkowski, L., Skowron, A.: Rough-Neural Computing. Techniques for Computing with Words. Springer Verlag, Berlin, Heidelberg, New York (2004)
14. Pawlak, Z.: Rough Sets, International J. Computer and Information Sciences, No. 11 (5) (1982)
15. Pawlak, Z.: Probability, Truth and Flow Graph. Electronic Notes in Theoretical Computer Science, International Workshop on Rough Sets in Knowledge Discovery and Soft Computing, Satellite event of ETAPS 2003, Warsaw, Poland, April 12-13, (2003) Elsevier, Vol. 82 (4) (2003)
16. Pawlak, Z.: Elementary Rough Set Granules: Towards a Rough Set Processor. In: Rough-Neural Computing. Techniques for Computing with Words. Pal, S.K., Polkowski L., Skowron A. (eds.). Springer Verlag, Berlin, Heidelberg, New York (2004) 5-13

Integration of Rough Set and Neural Network for Application of Generator Fault Diagnosis

Wei-ji Su, Yu Su, Hai Zhao, and Xiao-dan Zhang

School of Information Science & Engineering, Northeastern University
110004 Shenyang, P.R.China
suweiji_2003@163.com

Abstract. In the paper, integration of rough set and neural network for fault is put forward and used in generator fault diagnosis. At first, rough set theory is utilized to reduce attributes of diagnosis system. Set in accordance with the practical needs, optimized decision attribute set acts as the input of artificial neural network used for fault diagnosis, which has been used for Fengman hydroelectric power station and testified the feasibility of integration of rough set and neural network. Given enough data, this method could be popularized to other generators.

1 Introduction

1.1 Rough Set

Rough set theory is a mathematical tool for dealing with uncertainty, which was introduced and studied by Pawlak (1982). Unlike other methods such as fuzzy set theory, Dempster--Shafer theory or statistical methods, rough set analysis requires no external parameters and uses only the information presented in the given data. It could analyze and deal with inaccurate, inconsistent and imperfect data effectively and discovery hidden knowledge and rules [4-5].

U is a nonempty limited set. Region R is an equipollence relationship family of U. Then K=(U,R) compose of an approximation space. Ind(K) is defined as an equipollence relationship family of K. R disport U to an equipollence class and empty set R. If subset X of U could not be expressed exactly by R, called X as rough set. Rough set usually is described by lower approximation and upper approximation.

1.2 Decision and Reduction

Being important in data process, knowledge expression system could express equipollence relationship expediently. In knowledge system data table, column expresses attribute and row expresses object (such as state, procedure), and each row expresses a piece of information of the object. Data is gained by observation and measurement. In the table, an attribute corresponds an equipollence relationship, and a table could be considered as an equipollence relationship family, namely knowledge database.

S. Tsumoto et al. (Eds.): RSCTC 2004, LNAI 3066, pp. 549–553, 2004.

Decision table is a kind of special knowledge expression system. It tells how to decide when requirements of certain conditions are met. According to knowledge expression system, decision table could be defined as follows: suppose K=(U, A) is a knowledge expression system, C and D are two attributes subsets named condition attribute and decision attribute respectively. Then, the knowledge expression system that includes condition attributes and decision attributes could be defined as decision table.

1.3 Characteristic and Application of Artificial Neural Networks

Dealing with complex mode function, association function, speculation function, memory function, better robusticity and expansibility, artificial neural networks is widely used in practice. However, long training time is a factor that restricts application of ANN. Based on integration rough set and neural network, the paper puts forward system figure and applies it to generator fault diagnosis. In the following, work principle and applications of the system are introduced with some conclusions drawn[1-3].

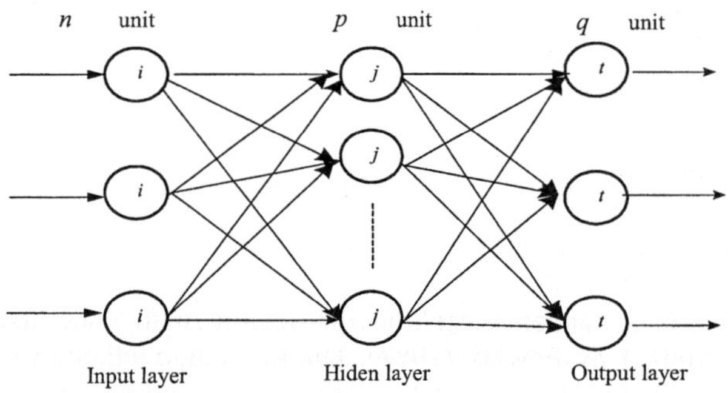

Fig. 1. Artificial neural network.

2 The Structure of Rough Set Neural Network System

RNN system figure as follow:

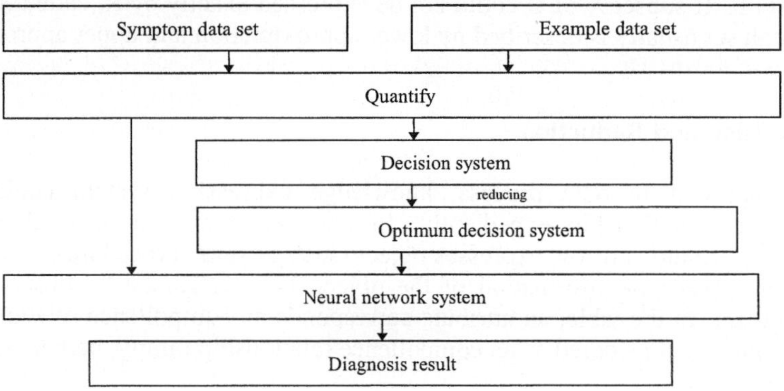

Fig. 2. The structure of rough set neural network system.

Working principle of each part:

1) Example data set: it comes from original data. For generators, original data include essential attributes such as excitation current, excitation voltage, phase voltage, wire voltage, wire current, stator number, impedance and so on. Some information collected by sensor such as temperature of iron core, loop and cooler is also included.

2) Quantify: rough set is a kind of symbolized analysis method which has to discretize continuous variable. Often used methods are rough function and neural network. Critical value corresponding to each correlative technology could be calculated by utilizing correlative field knowledge. Based on the calculated critical value, example data could be quantified

3) Decision system: Based on rough set method, a two dimensions table by quantified attributes could be created. Each row describes an object while each column describes an attribute of the object (attribute includes condition attribute and decision attribute). Decision is mainly composed of decision attribute.

4) Reduction: reducing decision table includes: reducing condition attribute. If decision table is consistent, the compatibility will be examined and the attribute will be deleted until the decision is the simplest; reducing decision rules: the least decision algorithms could be obtained by deleting those redundant information and reduplicate information in the simplest decision table. Of course, we could first reduce each decision rules, then reduce condition attribute, and at last form the least condition attribute set.

5) Optimum decision system: it is a new study example formed by adopting reduced least condition attribute set and original data. The example deletes all redundant condition attributes and only reserves important attributes which influence classification.

6) Neural network system: neural network is practiced and trained by using examples after being reduced. BP neural network could be selected as the main function of neural network is to map in mode classification and feature picking-up. In artificial neural network, learning rules are algorithm to modify weight value. At present, there are three neural network learning rules: correlation rules, correction rules and no teacher learning rules. We could use learning rules to gain appropriate mapping function or expectant output and increase capability of system. At last based on least condition attribute set and corresponding original data form testing example to test network and output classification result[6].

3 Application of Integration of Rough Set and Neural Network for Generator Fault Diagnosis

The steps of using this system to diagnosis generator's fault are as following:

Picking-up original information: form information table by selecting system measurable character of the generator and measuring character signals; Discretization based on different condition discretizes each condition attribute's value range. The optimal attribute's value range is the least attribute's value set that is able to right distinguish all fault character and forms fault decision table; Such as A_1 is excitating Current, A_2 is excitating voltage, A_3 is power, $A_4 \sim A_{12}$ are three-phase currents and voltages of generator, A_{14} is a breaker and so on.

Table 1. Discretization table.

Condition attribute	Discretization region		
	0	1	2
A_1	0 A	[0,660A]	(660A,+∞)
A_2	0 V	[0,135V]	(135V,+∞)
A_3	0 MW	(0,75MW]	(75MW, +∞)
A_4	[0 KV,7.5KV]	(7.5KV,7.967KV]	(7.967KV, +∞)
…	…	…	…
A_{14}	open	close	

Table 2. Fault kind and its symptom.

Fault kind	Fault symptom
1-lost magnetism fault	Excitating Voltage and Current, Ia, Ib, Ic are zero;The other conditions are not changed.
2-Over voltage fault	Output Voltage is too high.
3-low voltage over current fault	Output voltage too high, Current too low.
4-differential fault	differential relay alarm, currents of three phases are different.
5-one phase grounding fault	One phase current too high, voltage too low.
6-two phases grounding short circuit fault	Some two phases current too high, voltage too low.
7-three phases grounding short circuit fault	Three phases currents too high, three phases voltage too low.
8- loop short circuit fault	Some one phase current too high.
9-stator entire grounding	The grounding phase voltage is zero, the others voltage are more than 1.73 times of rating voltage.
10-over load fault	Current is more than 1.1 times of rating current; Power is more than rating power.

Table 3. Decision table of generator.

	Condition attribute														
U	A_1	A_2	A_3	A_4	A_5	A_6	A_7	A_8	A_9	A_{10}	A_{11}	A_{12}	A_{13}	A_{14}	m
1	0	0	0	1	1	1	1	1	1	0	0	0	0	1	1
2	1	1	1	2	2	2	2	2	2	1	1	1	1	1	2
3	1	1	2	0	0	0	0	0	0	2	2	2	2	1	3
4	1	1	1	1	1	1	1	1	1	0	1	2	1	1	4
5	1	1	1	0	1	1	0	1	1	2	1	1	2	1	5
6	1	1	1	1	0	1	1	0	1	1	2	1	2	1	6
7	1	1	1	0	1	0	0	1	0	2	1	2	2	1	7
8	1	1	1	0	2	2	0	0	2	2	1	1	2	1	8
9	1	1	1	0	2	2	0	0	2	0	0	0	1	1	9
10	1	1	2	1	1	1	1	1	1	2	2	2	2	1	10

Table 4. The least decision rules.

U	A_1	A_3	A_4	A_5	A_6	A_{10}	A_{11}	A_{12}	A_{13}	m
1	0	0	1	1	1	0	0	0	0	1
2	1	1	2	2	2	1	1	1	1	2
3	1	2	0	0	0	2	2	2	2	3
4	1	1	1	1	1	0	1	2	1	4
5	1	1	0	1	1	2	1	1	2	5
6	1	1	0	0	1	2	2	1	2	6
7	1	1	0	0	0	2	2	2	2	7
8	1	1	0	2	2	2	1	1	2	8
9	1	1	0	2	2	0	0	0	1	9
10	1	2	1	1	1	2	2	2	2	10

Form optimal decision table, namely least solution of decision, on the basis of optimal reduction of decision table which is obtained by reducing condition attributes.

The method is effective as when the system is examined by fact data, the result is in accordance with the fact.

Conclusion

The merit of rough set and neural network theory is integrated by the methods introduced in the paper: firstly, by using rough set theory, condition attribute of example could be reduced and fault diagnosis could be speeded up; secondly, by using rough set theory, condition attribute is reduced, redundant data in example is eliminated and the veracity is increased; by using the method, redundant data is decreased, the cost of computing is reduced and real time is enhanced; as BP neural network boasts of better robusticity and expansibility, error diagnosis and lost diagnosis could be eliminated effectively. The method is effective in fact application.

References

1. Hao LN: Rough set neural network intelligent hybrid system and its applications in engineering [D]. Shenyang: Northeastern University, (2001) 21:47-49.
2. He Y, Wang G H: Multisensor information fusion with applications. [M]. Beijing: Publishing House of Electronics Industry.(2000) 156-160.)
3. Zhang X J, Liu X B, Yan C P, et al: Power System Fault Diagnosis Based on the Forward and Backward Reasoning Automation of Electric Power Systems, (1998),22(5): 30-32.
4. Pawlak Z: Rough set theory and its application to data analysis [J]. Cybernetics and Systems, (1998),29(9):611-668.
5. Pawlak Z: Rough Sets, Rough Relations and Rough Functions. Fundamental Information, (1996), 27(2,3):103-108.
6. Su Y, Zhao H, Wang G, Su W J: A Fused Neural Network Based on BP Algorithm [J] Journal of Northeastern University (Natural Science), 2003,11:1037- 1040.

Harnessing Classifier Networks – Towards Hierarchical Concept Construction

Dominik Ślęzak[1,2], Marcin S. Szczuka[3], and Jakub Wróblewski[2]

[1] Department of Computer Science, University of Regina
Regina, SK, S4S 0A2, Canada
[2] Polish-Japanese Institute of Information Technology
Koszykowa 86, 02-008 Warsaw, Poland
[3] Institute of Mathematics, Warsaw University
Banacha 2, 02-097 Warsaw, Poland
{slezak,jakubw}@pjwstk.edu.pl, szczuka@mimuw.edu.pl

Abstract. The process of construction and tuning of classifier networks is discussed. The idea of relating the basic inputs with the target classification concepts via the internal layers of intermediate concepts is explored. Intuitions and relationships to other approaches, as well as the illustrative examples are provided.

1 Introduction

In the standard approach to classification, we use hypothesis formation (learning) algorithm to find a possibly direct mapping from the input values to decisions. Such an approach does not always result in success. We address the situation when the desired solution should have an internal structure. Although possibly hard to find and learn, such architecture provide significant extensions in terms of flexibility, generality and expressiveness of the yielded model. We attempt to show our view on the process of construction and tuning of hierarchical structures of concepts. We address these structures as *classifier networks*, where the input concepts correspond to the classified objects or their behavior with respect to the standard classifiers, and the output concept reflects the final classification. The relationship between input and output concepts is not direct but based on the internal layers of intermediate concepts, which help in more reliable transition from the basic information to possibly compound classification goal. We strive against formalization of this approach with use of analogies rooted in other areas, such as artificial neural networks [2, 3], ensembles of classifiers [1, 10], and layered learning [9]. We present the formalism that describes our classifier networks and illustrate them with examples of actual models.

2 Hierarchical Learning and Classification

In general, a **concept** is an element of a parameterized concept space. By a proper setting of these parameters we choose the right concept. In our approach,

S. Tsumoto et al. (Eds.): RSCTC 2004, LNAI 3066, pp. 554–560, 2004.

a concept represents a basic element acting on the information originating from other concepts or the data source. As an analogy, consider the case of neural networks (NN), where a concept corresponds to a signal transmitted through a neuron. Dependencies between concepts and their importance are represented by weighted node connections. Similarly to the feedforward NN, operations can be performed from bottom to top. They can correspond to the following goals:

Construction of compound concepts from the elementary ones. It can be observed in case-based reasoning [4], layered learning [9], as well as rough mereology [6] and rough neurocomputing [5], where we approximate target concepts step by step, using the simpler ones that are easier to learn from data.

Construction of simple concepts from the advanced ones. It can be considered for the synthesis of classifiers, where we start from compound concepts reflecting the behavior of a given object with respect to particular, often compound classification systems, and we tend to obtain a very simple concept of a decision class where that object should belong to. This corresponds to the instantiation of general concept in a simpler, more specialized concept.

The above are not the only possible types of constructions. In a classification problem, decision classes can have a compound semantics requiring gradual specification corresponding to the first type of construction. When considering hierarchical structures at the general level one has to make choices with respect to homogeneity and synchronization:

Homogeneous vs. heterogeneous. At each level of hierarchy we make choice of the concept space to be used. In the simplest case each node implements the same type of mapping. The nodes differ only by choice of parameters [8]. First step towards heterogeneity is by permitting different types of concepts to be used at various levels in hierarchy, but retaining any single layer uniform (the layered learning model [9]). Finally, we may remove all restrictions on the uniformity of the neighboring nodes; such structure is more general but harder to control.

Synchronous vs. asynchronous. This issue is concerned with the layout of connections between nodes. If it has easily recognizable layered structure we regard it to be synchronized. If we permit the connections to be established on less restrictive basis, the synchronization is lost. Then, the nodes from non-consecutive levels may interact and the whole idea of simple-to-compound precedence of concepts becomes less usable. Restricting ourselves to the two easier architectures, we can consider the following notion concerning feedforward networks transmitting the concepts:

Definition 1. *By a* hierarchical concept scheme *we mean a tuple* $(\mathcal{C}, \mathcal{MAP})$. $\mathcal{C} = \{C_1, \ldots, C_n, C\}$ *is a collection of the* concept spaces, *where* C *is called the target concept space. The* concept mappings $\mathcal{MAP} = \{map_i : C_i \to C_{i+1} : i = 1, \ldots, n, C_{n+1} = C\}$ *are the functions linking consecutive concept spaces.*

Any classifier network corresponds to $(\mathcal{C}, \mathcal{MAP})$, i.e. each i-th layer provides us with the elements of C_i. In case of total homogeneity, we have $C_i = C$ and $map_i = identity$. For partly homogeneous case the mappings may be nontrivial.

Following the structure of feedforward neural network, the inputs to each next layer are linear combinations of the concepts from the previous one. In general, we cannot apply the traditional definition of a linear combination.

Definition 2. Feedforward concept scheme *is a triple* $(\mathcal{C}, \mathcal{MAP}, \mathcal{LIN})$, *where* $\mathcal{LIN} = \{lin_i : 2^{C_i \times W_i} \to C_i : i = 1, \ldots, n\}$ *defines* generalized linear combinations *over the concept spaces* C_i. *For any* $i = 1, \ldots, n$, W_i *denotes the space of the* combination parameters. *If* W_i *is a partial or total ordering, then we interpret its elements as* weights *reflecting the relative importance of particular concepts in construction of the resulting concept.*

Let us denote by $m(i) \in \mathbb{N}$ the number of nodes in the i-th network layer. For any $i = 1, \ldots, n$, the nodes from the i-th and $(i+1)$-th layers are connected by the links labeled with parameters $w_{j(i+1)}^{j(i)} \in W_i$, for $j(i) = 1, \ldots, m(i)$ and $j(i+1) = 1, \ldots, m(i+1)$. For any collection of the concepts $c_i^1, \ldots, c_i^{m(i)} \in C_i$ occurring as the outputs of the i-th network's layer in a given situation, the input to the $j(i+1)$-th node in the $(i+1)$-th layer takes the following form:

$$c_{i+1}^{j(i+1)} = map_i \left(lin_i \left(\left\{ \left(c_i^{j(i)}, w_{j(i+1)}^{j(i)} \right) : j(i) = 1, \ldots, m(i) \right\} \right) \right) \qquad (1)$$

Consider the case of Fig. 1a, where map_i and lin_i are stated separately. Parameters $w_{j(i+1)}^{j(i)}$ could be also used directly in a *generalized concept mapping* $genmap_i : 2^{C_i \times W_i} \to C_{i+1}$ as in figure 1b. These two possibilities reflect construction tendencies described in Section 2. Function $genmap_i$ can be applied to construction of more compound concepts parameterized by the elements of W_i, while the usage of Definitions 1 and 2 results rather in potential syntactical simplification of the new concepts.

3 Weighted Compound Concepts

Beginning with the input layer of the network, we expect it to provide the concepts-signals $c_1^1, \ldots, c_1^{m(1)} \in C_1$, which will be then transmitted towards the target layer using (1). If we learn the network related directly to real-valued training sample, then we get $C_1 = \mathbb{R}$, lin_i can be defined as classical linear combination (with $W_i = \mathbb{R}$), and map_i as identity.

Example 1. [8] Let us assume that the input layer nodes correspond to various classifiers and the task is to combine them within a general system, which synthesizes the input classifications in an optimal way. For any object, each input classifier induces possibly incomplete vector of beliefs in the object's membership to decision classes. Let DEC denote the set of decision classes specified for a given classification problem. By the *weighted decision space* $WDEC$ we mean the family of subsets of DEC with elements labeled by their beliefs. Any *weighted decision* $\widetilde{\mu} = \{(k, \mu_k) : k \in X_{\widetilde{\mu}}, \mu_k \in \mathbb{R}\}$ corresponds to a subset $X_{\widetilde{\mu}} \subseteq DEC$ of decision classes for which the beliefs $\mu_k \in \mathbb{R}$ are known.

Example 2. Let $DESC$ denote the family of logical descriptions, which can be used to define rough-set-based decision rules for a given classification problem [10]. Every *rule* is labeled with its *description* $\alpha_{rule} \in DESC$ and *decision information*, which takes – in the most general framework – the form of $\widetilde{\mu}_{rule} \in WDEC$. For a new object, we measure its degree of satisfaction of the rule's description (usually zero-one), combine it with the number of training objects satisfying α_{rule}, and come out with the number $app_{rule} \in \mathbb{R}$ expressing the level of rule's *applicability* to this object. As a result, by the *decision rule set space* $RULS$ we mean the family of all sets of elements of $DESC$ labeled by weighted decision sets and the degrees of applicability.

Definition 3. *By a* weighted compound concept space C *we mean a space of collections of* sub-concepts *from some* sub-concept space S, *labeled with the* concept parameters *from a given space* V, *i.e.*, $C = \bigcup_{X \subseteq S} \{(s, v_s) : s \in X, v_s \in V\}$. *For a given* $c = \{(s, v_s) : s \in X_c, v_s \in V\}$, *where* $X_c \subseteq S$ *is the* range *of* c, *parameters* $v_s \in V$ *reflect relative importance of sub-concepts* $s \in X_c$ *within* c_i.

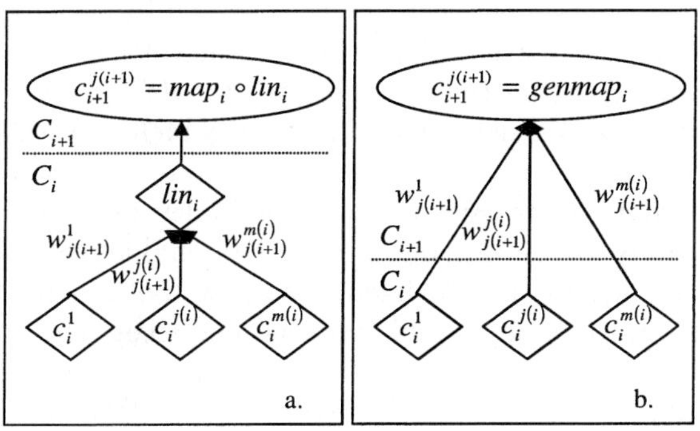

Fig. 1. Production of new concepts in consecutive layers.

Just like in case of combination parameters W_i in Definition 2, we can assume a partial or total ordering over the concept parameters.

Definition 4. *Let the i-th network layer correspond to the weighted compound concept space* C_i *based on sub-concept space* S_i *and parameters* $V_i = \mathbb{R}$. *Consider the* $j(i+1)$*-th node in the next layer. We define its input as follows:*

$$\begin{aligned} lin_i\left(\left\{\left(c_i^{j(i)}, w_{j(i+1)}^{j(i)}\right) : j(i) = 1, \ldots, m(i)\right\}\right) = \\ = \left\{\left(s, \sum_{j(i): s \in X_{j(i)}} w_{j(i+1)}^{j(i)} v_s^{j(i)}\right) : s \in \bigcup_{j(i)=1}^{m(i)} X_{j(i)}\right\} \end{aligned} \tag{2}$$

where $X_{j(i)} \subseteq S_i$ *is simplified notation for the range of the weighted compound concept* $c_i^{j(i)}$ *and* $v_s^{j(i)} \in \mathbb{R}$ *denotes the importance of sub-concept* $s \in S_i$ *in* $c_i^{j(i)}$.

Formula (2) can be applied both to $WDEC$ and $RULS$. In case of $WDEC$, the sub-concept space equals to DEC. The sum $\sum_{j(i):s\in X_{j(i)}} w^{j(i)}_{j(i+1)} v^{j(i)}_s$ gathers the weighted beliefs of the previous layer's nodes in the given decision class $s \in DEC$. In the case of $RULS$ we do the same with the weighted applicability degrees for the elements-rules belonging to the sub-concept space $DESC \times WDEC$.

4 Activation Functions

In rule-based classifier network, we initiate the input layer with the degrees of applicability of the rules in particular rule-sets to a new object. After processing with these type of concept along (possibly) several layers, we use the concept mapping function

$$map(ruls) = \left\{ \left(k, \sum_{(\alpha,\widetilde{\mu},app)\in ruls:k\in X_{\widetilde{\mu}}} app \cdot \mu_k\right) : k \in \bigcup_{(\alpha,\widetilde{\mu},app)\in ruls} X_{\widetilde{\mu}} \right\} \quad (3)$$

that is we simply summarize the beliefs (weighted by the rules' applicability) in particular decision classes. Similarly, we finally map the weighted decision to the decision class, which is assigned with the highest resulting belief.

The intermediate layers are designed to help in voting among the classification results obtained from particular rule sets. Traditional rough set approach assumes specification of a fixed voting function, which – in our terminology – would correspond to the direct concept mapping from the first $RULS$ layer into DEC, with no hidden layers and without possibility of tuning the weights of connections. An improved adaptive approach [10] enables us to adjust the rule sets, but the voting scheme is still fixed. The new method provides us with a framework for tuning the weights and learning adaptively the voting formula.

Still, the scheme based only on generalized linear combinations and concept mappings is not adjustable enough. The reader may check that composition of functions (2) for elements of $RULS$ and $WDEC$ with (3) results in the collapsed single-layer structure corresponding to the most basic weighted voting among decision rules. This is exactly what happens with classical feedforward neural network models with linear activation functions.

Definition 5. Neural concept scheme *is a quadruple* $(\mathcal{C}, \mathcal{MAP}, \mathcal{LIN}, \mathcal{ACT})$, *where the first three entities are provided by Definitions 1, 2, and* $\mathcal{ACT} = \{act_i : C_i \to C_i : i = 2, \ldots, n+1\}$ *is the set of activation functions, which can be used to relate the inputs to the outputs within each i-th layer of a network.*

It is reasonable to assume a kind of monotonicity of $\mathcal{ACT}$ (a relative importance of parts of concept remains roughly unchanged). It is expressible for weighted compound concepts introduced in Definition 3. Given a concept $c_i \in C_i$ represented as the weighted collection of sub-concepts, we claim that its more important (better weighted) sub-concepts should keep more influence on the concept $act_i(c_i) \in C_i$ than the others. In [8] we introduced sigmoidal activation function, which can be generalized as $act^{\alpha}_{\mathcal{C}}(c) = \left\{ \left(s, e^{\alpha \cdot v_s} / \sum_{(t,v_t)\in c} e^{\alpha \cdot v_t}\right) : (t, v_t) \in c \right\}$

(see [7]). By composition of lin_i and map_i with functions act^{α}_{i+1} modifying the concepts within the entire nodes, we obtain a classification model with a satisfiable expressive and adaptive power. If we apply this kind of function to the rule sets, we modify the rules' applicability degrees by their internal comparison. Such performance cannot be obtained using the classical neural networks with the nodes assigned to every single rule. Moreover, the decision rules which inhibit influence of other rules (so called *exceptions*) can be easily achieved by negative weights and proper activation functions.

5 Learning in Classifier Networks

The proper choice of connection weights in the network can be learned similarly to backpropagation technique for neural networks. Backpropagation is a method for reducing the global error of a network by performing local changes in weights' values. The key issue is to have a method for dispatching the value of the network's global error functional among the nodes [3]. This method, when shaped in the form of an algorithm, should provide the direction of the weight update vector, which is then applied according to the learning coefficient (see [2] for classical setting). In the more complicated models which we are dealing with, the idea of backpropagation transfers into the demand for a general method of establishing weight updates. This method should comply to the general principles postulated for the rough-neural models [5, 6, 10]. Namely, the algorithm for the weight updates should provide a certain form of *mutual monotonicity* i.e. small and local changes in weights should not rapidly divert the behavior of the whole scheme and, at the same time, a small overall network error should result in merely cosmetic changes in the weight vectors.

We do not claim to have discovered the general principle for constructing backpropagation-like algorithms for classifier networks. In [8] we have been able to construct generalization of gradient-based method for the homogeneous schemes based on the weighted decision concept space $WDEC$. The step to partly homogeneous schemes is natural for the class of weighted compound concepts, which can be processed using the same type of activation function.

6 Conclusions

Although we have some experience with neural networks transmitting non-trivial concepts [8], this is definitely the very beginning of more general theoretical studies. The most emerging issue is the extension of the proposed framework onto more advanced structures than the introduced weighted compound concepts, without losing a general interpretation of monotonic activation functions, as well as relaxation of some quite limiting mathematical requirements. We are going to challenge these problems in further works.

Acknowledgements

Supported by grant 3T11C00226 from Polish Ministry of Scientific Research. Authors also supported by the Faculty of Science at the University of Regina, and Polish-Japanese Institute of Information Technology.

References

1. Dietterich, T.: Machine learning research: four current directions. *AI Magazine* **18/4** (1997) pp. 97–136.
2. Hecht-Nielsen, R.: Neurocomputing. Addison-Wesley, New York (1990).
3. le Cun, Y.: A theoretical framework for backpropagation. In: Neural Networks – concepts and theory. IEEE Computer Society Press, Los Alamitos (1992).
4. Lenz, M., Bartsch-Spoerl, B., Burkhard, H.-D., Wess, S. (eds.): Case-Based Reasoning Technology – From Foundations to Applications. LNAI 1400, Springer (1998).
5. Peters, J., Szczuka, M.: Rough neurocomputing: a survey of basic models of neurocomputation. In: Proc. of RSCTC'02. LNAI 2475, Springer (2002) pp. 309–315.
6. Polkowski, L., Skowron, A.: Rough Mereology in Information systems. A Case Study: Qualitative Spatial Reasoning. In: Polkowski, L., Tsumoto, S., Lin, T.Y. (eds.): Rough Set Methods and Applications. Physica-Verlag, Heidelberg (2000).
7. Ślęzak, D.: Normalized decision functions and measures for inconsistent decision tables analysis. *Fundamenta Informaticae* **44/3** (2000) pp. 291–319.
8. Ślęzak, D., Wróblewski, J., Szczuka, M.: Constructing Extensions of Bayesian Classifiers with use of Normalizing Neural Networks. In: Zhong, N., Raś, Z., Tsumoto, S., Suzuki, E. (eds.), Proc. of ISMIS'2003. LNAI 2871, Springer (2002) pp. 408–416.
9. Stone, P.: Layered Learning in Multiagent Systems: A Winning Approach to Robotic Soccer. MIT Press, Cambridge MA (2000).
10. Wróblewski, J.: Adaptive aspects of combining approximation spaces. In: Pal, S.K., Polkowski, L., Skowron, A. (eds.): Rough-Neural Computing: Techniques for Computing with Words. Springer, Heidelberg (2003) pp. 139–156.

Associative Historical Knowledge Extraction from the Structured Memory

JeongYon Shim

Division of General Studies, Computer Science, Kangnam University
San 6-2, Kugal-ri, Kihung-up,YongIn Si, KyeongKi Do, Korea
mariashim@kangnam.ac.kr
Tel: +82 31 2803 736

Abstract. For the intelligent automatic information processing, the efficient memory structure and intelligent knowledge extraction mechanism using this structure should be studied. Accordingly, we propose structured memory with the mechanism for extracting the historical knowledge. In a retrieval stage, the empirical historic factor effects on the reaction of a certain class. This system is applied to the area for estimating the purchasing degree from the type of customer's tastes, the pattern of commodities and the evaluation of a company.

1 Introduction

Pavlov discovered the conditional reflex through the experiment with dogs. He put meal powder in a dog's mouth and measured salivation. The basic methodology with a biologically significant unconditioned stimulus, which reflexively evokes some unconditioned response. For instance, food is a unconditioned stimulus and salivation is a unconditioned response. The unconditioned stimulus is paired with a neutral conditioned stimulus, such as a bell. After a number of such pairings, the conditioned stimulus acquires the ability to evoke the response by itself. When the response occurs to the conditioned stimulus, it is called a conditioned response. Although Pavlov's original research involved food and salivation, a variety of unconditioned stimulus and unconditioned responses have been used to develop conditional responses[DR].

Pavlov's theory can be applied to construct the memory and to control the operation of the structured memory.The repeated relations between the unconditioned stimulus and unconditioned response make the association of conditioned response and form the historical prior knowledge in the memory. The prior knowledge effects on the perception and decision making for a certain thing by producing a preconception. If he has a prior knowledge in his memory, he reacts very strongly on the input pattern related to this. The positive Historical prior knowledge has a positive effects on the perception and negative one has a negative effects. This Historical prior knowledge comes from the complex experience,namely, the environmental cause, teaching signal, the Historical memory from the award and punishment and etc.. This Historical prior knowledge can

S. Tsumoto et al. (Eds.): RSCTC 2004, LNAI 3066, pp. 561–566, 2004.

be a kind of a wisdom as well as conditional reaction by experience. For this reason, it can help to perform the effective precise perception and inference.

Accordingly, in this paper, as one of method for implementing the brain function, Structured Memory with historical prior knowledge is proposed. We define the Historical knowledge as Empirical Historic Sensory factor. Structured Memory which has five layered hierarchical structure is controlled by mechanisms of memory called acquisition stage, retention stage and retrieval stage.

In a retrieval stage, the Empirical Historic Sensory Factor effects on the reaction of a certain class. We apply this system to the area for estimating the purchasing degree from the type of customer's tastes, the pattern of commodities and the evaluation of a company.

2 Structured Memory: CRHM(Conditional Reactive Hierarchical Memory)

2.1 The Structure

According to the study of brain,we designed the structured memory, CRHM. As shown in Fig. 1, CRHM has three dimensional hierarchical structure which consists of five layers,namely, Input layer, Reaction layer, Learning-Perception layer, Associative layer and S/O layer.

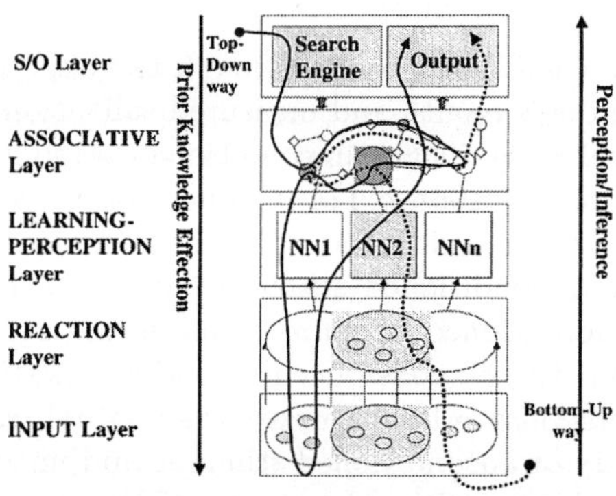

Fig. 1. Structured Memory:CRHM

The overview of the processing mechanism in CRHM is as follows. Input layer which corresponds to the sensory cell, takes part in the function of getting the data from the environment. The different classified cells in the Input layer get the data and pass them to Reaction layer. The data which belong to the different classes, can be mixed. If the mixed data come in to the Input layer, they are propagated to the Reaction layer. In the Reaction layer, the mixed data are filtered by filtering function and activate the corresponding cells. Then the corresponding Neural network(NN) of the fired class is selected and performs its function in the Learning-Perception layer. It processes learning or perception mechanism in that step. The output values are passed to the nodes in the Associative layer. The Associative layer consists of knowledge cells that are connected by the associative relations and that contribute to process the unified associative functions. The activating state of the cells fired by the NN is propagated to the connected cells according to the associative relations horizontally. In this step, the related facts can be extracted as much as user wants. Finally,the outputs from the Associative layer are passed to S/O layer in which produces the results[JC]. In the knowledge acquisition step, historical prior knowledge are formed and they effect the reaction layer during inferential process.

3 Conditional Reactive Mechanism by the Empirical Historic Sensory Factor

3.1 Empirical Historic Sensory Factor

It is generally known that human brain strongly reacts on the familiar facts which are experienced before. In a similar way, this concept can be adopted to the intelligent system and used for developing the more efficient mechanism. To implement this concept, we define the value that represents the Historical prior knowledge as Empirical Historic Sensory Factor. Empirical Historic Sensory Factor is the value which represents the Historical prior knowledge in the memory. This factor affects the reactive degree of a certain class for the input data in the Reaction layer.

Associative layer consists of nodes and their relations. These nodes are connected to their neighbors according to their associative relations horizontally and connected to NN of the previous layer vertically. Each node has two factors of P(Property) and EV(Historical Value). P has the property of a class and EV retains the Historical value obtained by the mechanism. The Historical value represents the preference or the strength of activation. The relation between the two nodes is represented by both linguistic term and its associative strength. which has a real value of [-1,1]. The positive value denotes the excitatory strength and the negative value represents the inhibitory relation between the nodes. It is used for extracting the related facts. The relational graph is transformed to the forms of AM(Associative Matrix) and vector B in order to process the knowledge retrieval mechanism. AM has the values of associative strengths in the matrix form and vector B denotes the EV of the nodes.

For example, the relational graph can be transferred to the associative matrix A and vector B as follows.

The associative matrix,A, is :

$$A = \begin{bmatrix} 1.0 & 1.0 & 1.0 & 0.0 & 0.0 \\ -1.0 & 1.0 & 0.9 & 0.0 & 0.0 \\ -1.0 & -0.9 & 1.0 & 0.7 & 0.3 \\ 0.0 & 0.0 & -0.7 & 1.0 & 0.0 \\ 0.0 & 0.0 & -0.3 & 0.0 & 1.0 \end{bmatrix}$$

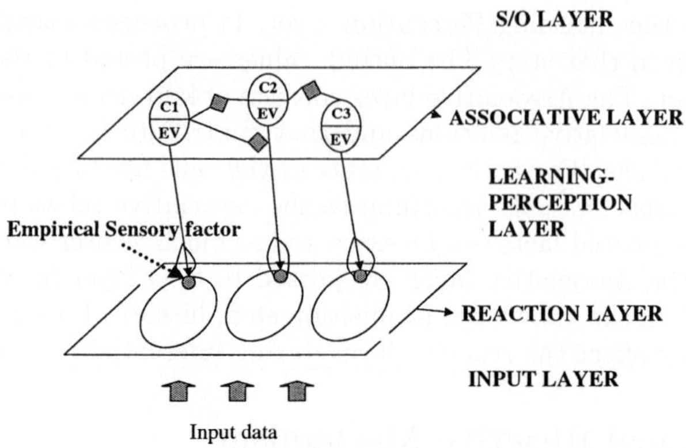

Fig. 2. Empirical Historic Sensory factor

The matrix, A, has the form of $A = [R_{ij}]$. The associative strength,R_{ij}, between C_i and C_j is calculated by equation (2).

$$R_{ij} = P(a_i|a_j)D \tag{1}$$

where D is the direction arrow, $D = 1 or - 1$, $i = 1, \ldots, n$, $j = 1, \ldots, n$.

The vector B is :

$B = \begin{bmatrix} -0.9 \; 1.0 \; 0.3 \; 0.8 \; 0.2 \end{bmatrix}$

It consists of the Historical value,V_i.

Using this Associative Matrix,A, and vector B, this system can extract the related facts by following knowledge retrieval algorithm.

3.2 Conditional Reactive Mechanism in the Knowledge Retrieval Stage

The extracting algorithm retrieves the facts related to the activated nodes. The conditional reactive algorithm for the knowledge retrieval is as following Algorithm 1.

Algorithm 1: Conditional reactive algorithm

Step 1: Get EV(Historical Value) of the node in the Associative layer.
Step 2: Get the input data in the input layer.
Step 3: Calculate the Empirical Historic Sensory Factor,E_i,

$$E_i = \frac{1 - exp^{-V_i}}{1 + exp^{-V_i}}$$

Step 4: Calculate the Firing factor,F_i,

$$F_i = P(C_i|e_1, e_2, \ldots, e_n) = \prod_{k=1}^{n}(C_i|e_k)$$

Step 5: Calculate the Historical accessing factor,H_i,

$$H_i = \frac{1}{1+e^{-A}}, A = \begin{cases} A+1 \text{ if } \textit{accessed} \\ A-1 \text{ otherwise} \end{cases}$$

Step 6: Calculate the Reaction degree,S_i,

$$S_i = \frac{E_i + F_i + H_i}{3}$$

Step 7: Evaluate the activating state through reaction degree, S_i .
If $S_i \geq 0.5$
activation state = 1
ELSE
activation state = 0

Step 8: Activate the corresponding NNi of a class i of if activation state is 1 and $F_i \geq q_i$.

Step 9: Propagate the output value to the connected node in the Associative layer.

$$O_i = Y_i * S_i$$

where O_i is the output value of a class NNi,Y_i is the actual output and S_i is the reaction degree.

Step 10: Extract the related fact in the Associative layer.

Step 11: Produce the output in S/O interface.

Step 12: Stop

4 Experiments

This system is applied to the area for estimating the purchasing degree from the type of customer's tastes(C1), the pattern of commodities(C2) and the evaluation of a company(C3). We tested with three classes. First class consists of ten customer's input term - four types of customer's tastes, second class consists of five input factors - three patterns of commodities and third class consists of eight evaluating terms. Fig.3 denotes the variation of output O_i according to the Historical Value of the node in Associative layer where V_i is Historical Value, E_i is Empirical Historic Sensory Factor, S_i is reaction degree, Historical Accessing factor H_i is 0.7311, Filtering factor F_i is 1.0 and the output value of NNi is 0.998201. As shown in the figure, this memory is reacted by the Empirical Historic Sensory Factor sensitively and produces the different output values according to the Empirical Historic Sensory Factor.

```
Empirical Historic Sensory Factor:

   C1          C2          C3
 0.245670   0.670894   0.067804

C1(the pattern of commodities) is fired.

Ei=0.576890  Fi=1.000000 Hi=0.895407
Reaction degree= 0.824099

Actual output of NN2
Type1     Type2     Type3
0.009876 0.456032 0.908765

Output value : Type3 0.748912
```

Fig. 3. Knowledge retrieval step: output value from the mechanism

5 Conclusion

We designed Structured Memory with Empirical Historic Sensory Factor. In a retrieval stage, the Empirical Historic Sensory Factor effects on the reaction of a certain class. This system is applied to the area for estimating the purchasing degree from the type of customer's tastes, the pattern of commodities and the evaluation of a company.

As a result of testing, we could find that it can extract the related data easily. This system is expected to be applicable to many areas as data mining, pattern recognition and circumspect decision making problem considering associative concepts and prior knowledge.

References

[E] E. Bruce Goldstein,Sensation and Perception,BROOKS/COLE

[JP] Judea Pearl : Probabilistic reasoning in intelligent systems, networks plausible inference,Morgan kaufman Publishers (1988)

[LF] Laurene Fausett: Fundamentals of Neural Networks,Prentice Hall

[SH] Simon Haykin: Neural Networks,Prentice Hall

[DR] David Robinson: Neurobiology,Springer

[JC] Jeong-Yon Shim, Chong-Sun Hwang,Data Extraction from Associative Matrix based on Selective learning system,IJCNN'99, Washongton D.C

[DR] John R. Anderson,Learning and Memory,Prentice Hall

Utilizing Rough Sets and Multi-objective Genetic Algorithms for Automated Clustering

Tansel Özyer, Reda Alhajj, and Ken Barker

Advance Database Systems and Applications Lab
Department of Computer Science
University of Calgary, Calgary, Alberta, Canada
{ozyer,alhajj,barker}@cpsc.ucalgary.ca

Abstract. This paper addresses the problem of estimating the number of clusters for web data by using a multi-objective evolutionary algorithm, NSGA-II (non-dominated sorting genetic algorithm) to eliminate the assignment of subjective weights. Clustering algorithms in general need the number of clusters as a priori and mostly it is hard for the domain experts to estimate the number of clusters. By applying a heuristic, among the existing solutions, feasible solutions are chosen for each clustering and minimum number of clusters satisfying our heuristic can be chosen as the actual number of clusters. As a last stage, a domain expert can analyze the results and take a decision. For the experiments, we used a course web site from the Department of Computer Science at University of Calgary.

1 Introduction

Data mining methods and techniques are designed for revealing previously unknown significant relationships and regularities out of huge heaps of details in large data collections [2]. The World Wide Web (WWW) is a fertile area for data mining research. This shows the necessity for analyzing and discovering the web. Web mining is the intersection of many research areas (AI and especially the sub-areas of machine learning and natural language processing, among others) [3]. Inefficient design of the web site will result in unhappy visitors. One of the main leverages, web logs is used to achieve tasks for the web mining.

Clustering is one of the data mining tasks; it involves determining the classes from the data themselves. Clustering is used to describe methods to group unlabeled data.

Our approach presented in this paper is based on clustering web users' sessions by using rough set clustering as explained in [6, 7]. In general, the number of clusters is given a-priori; however, Web visits and site content may vary. The proposed method is based on multi-objective optimization clustering where each sub goal function is given a subjective weight value. The user should be able to view and choose one of the pareto-optimal points. This led us to the idea of using NSGA-II algorithm to present to the user several alternatives without taking the weight values into account within the given number of clusters value range. Otherwise, the user will have several trials weighting with different values until a satisfactory result is obtained.

S. Tsumoto et al. (Eds.): RSCTC 2004, LNAI 3066, pp. 567–572, 2004.

The proposed approach has been tested using a second year course web site of the Department of Computer Science at the University of Calgary. We analyzed the web log during one month and conducted our experiments over 450,000 entries. The obtained results are promising and demonstrate the effectiveness and applicability of the proposed approach.

The rest of the paper is as follows. Section 2 is an overview of the background necessary to understand the proposed approach. Section 3 describes the NSGA-II multi-objective algorithm. Section 4 explains the proposed approach. Section 5 includes the experimental results. Section 7 is the conclusions.

2 Using Rough Set Theory with Clustering

The rough set approach was proposed in [8]; it is a mathematical approach to imprecision, vagueness and uncertainty. Indiscernibility is the basis for the rough set theory. Due to the granularity of knowledge, some objects of interest cannot be discerned and appear as the same (or similar). The basic concept of the rough set theory is the notion of approximation space, which is an ordered pair $A=(U, R)$, where U is nonempty set of objects called the universe, and R is equivalence relation on U, called *indiscernibility relation.* If x, y $\in$ U and xRy then x and y are indistinguishable in A. The vague concept is assumed to have a pair of precise concepts: lower bound (denoted $\underline{A}(x)$) and upper bound (denoted $\overline{A}(x)$) [9]. All objects in the lower bound are believed to be in the concept, whereas objects in the upper bound possibly belong to the concept. The difference between the lower and upper bounds is the boundary region. Consider

$$X \subseteq U: \quad \begin{array}{l} \underline{A}(X) = \{x \in U : A(x) \subseteq X\} \\ \overline{A}(X) = \{x \in U : A(x) \cap X \neq \phi\} \end{array} \tag{1}$$

Several clustering approaches have been proposed so far [4]. The author in [6, 7] propose using genetic algorithm for rough set clustering. In [7] for mining web log data; students enrolled in Computing Science Department are clustered. Each session is represented by on/off campus (1/0), day time/night time access (1/0), accessing lab day/non lab day (1/0), number of downloads and number of hits attributes; number of downloads and hits are normalized. Both papers use genetic algorithm where each genome consists of partition of all the objects. [6] describes the application of the same solution to cluster the highway sections as another example to demonstrate rough set theoretic evolutionary computing. Here, the proposed approach uses two sub goals as to maximize the number of objects in the lower bound of the clusters and minimize the intra-cluster distance assigned with subjective weight values.

3 NSGA-II: A Multi-objective Evolutionary Algorithm

One of the traditional methods being used is weighting each objective and scalarize the result. The target is to find an optimal solution which can be defined as: a solution which is not dominated by any other solution; such a solution is called *Pareto optimal*, and the entire set of optimal trade-offs is called the *Pareto-optimal front.*

At the end of each run, pareto-optimal front may be obtained. But it actually represents one single point. Decision making process may require considering all the alternatives. In the application of NSGA-II on the rough set clustering problem, no constraint is specified. Solutions to a multi-objective optimization method are mathematically expressed in terms of non-dominated or superior points. In a minimization problem, a vector $x^{(1)}$ is partially less than another vector $x^{(2)}$, denoted $x^{(1)} \prec x^{(2)}$, when no value of $x^{(2)}$ is less than $x^{(1)}$ and at least one value of $x^{(2)}$ is strictly greater than $x^{(1)}$. If $x^{(1)}$ is partially less than $x^{(2)}$, we say that $x^{(1)}$ dominates $x^{(2)}$ or the solution $x^{(2)}$ is inferior to $x^{(1)}$. Any member of such vectors which is not dominated by any other is said to be non-dominated or non-inferior. The optimal solutions to a multi-objective optimization problem are non-dominated solutions [11].

NSGA was proposed in [10]. The idea behind NSGA is that ranking selection method is used to emphasize good points and a niche method is used to maintain stable subpopulations of good points. It is based on non-dominated sorting procedure. NSGA received lot of criticism because of its high computational complexity of non-dominated sorting, lack of elitism and the need for specifying the sharing parameter. As a result, the work described in [1] proposed NSGA-II algorithm.

4 The Proposed Approach

Using the same fitness evaluations, it is proposed to use the NSGA-II algorithm. The most important benefit of NSGA-II is to provide a diverse set of solutions. It helps the user finding alternative solutions among the individuals at the pareto-optimal front. We believe this will help more to look at the clustering result from many perspectives according to the automatically generated importance weights to sub-goals.

We also propose a heuristic by using cluster validity index. Briefly, the user enters the maximum number of clusters, say n. For each number of clusters, say c=2..n, we run NSGA-II algorithm to get the several pareto-optimal front individuals for each cluster.

The cluster validity index functions are identified as the under-partition measure function and over-partition measure functions [5]. The under-partition measure function produces a break point at the optimal cluster number c^*. It has a very small value when $c \geq c^*$ and relatively large values when $c < c^*$. So, it determines whether under-partitioned case occurred in clustering or not. The under-partition measure function is expressed as:

$$v_u(c) = \frac{1}{c}\sum_{i=1}^{c} MD_i \qquad 2 \leq c \leq n \tag{2}$$

where MD_i is the mean intra-cluster distance; its formula is:

$$\sum_{x \in X_i} \frac{dist\ (v_i - x)}{n_i} \tag{3}$$

X_i in Formula 3 is the dataset belonging to cluster i and n_i is the number of objects in cluster i. The mean of cluster v_i is given as:

$$v_i = \frac{\sum_{x \in \underline{A}(X_i), x \notin \overline{A}(X_i)} r_1 x + \sum_{x \in \underline{A}(X_i), x \in \overline{A}(X_i)} r_2 x}{r_1 \,|\, x \in \underline{A}(X_i) \wedge x \notin \overline{A}(X_i) \,| + r_2 \,|\, x \in \underline{A}(X_i) \wedge x \in \overline{A}(X_i) \,|} \tag{4}$$

While determining v_i, given r_1 and r_2 ($r_1 > r_2$) as the values that show the contribution of the point to the cluster, it is known that objects existing in lower bound but not in the upper approximation are believed to be in the cluster. However, objects existing only in the upper approximation are possibly in the cluster, we assigned $r_1 = 1$ and $r_2 = 0.5$ [12].

The over-partition measure function produces a break point at the optimal cluster number c^*. It has a very large value when $c > c^*$ and relatively small values when $c \leq c^*$. So, it determines whether the over-partitioned case occurred in clustering or not. The over-partition measure function is expressed as:

$$v_o(c) = \frac{c}{d_{\min}} \qquad 2 \leq c \leq n \tag{5}$$

where d_{min} is the minimum distance between the cluster centers.

In determining the optimal number of clusters, one instance for each c $(2 \leq c \leq n)$ is used in determining the optimal cluster, since we will have several instances for each c value. Therefore, we take the average value of under-partition and over-partition measure functions of individuals in the pareto-optimal front for each c. Average values of $v_u(c)$ and $v_o(c)$ are shown as $\overline{v_u}(c)$ *and* $\overline{v_o}(c)$.

For each cluster, the minimum and maximum values are computed as:

$$\bar{v}_{\max\_u} = \max_c \overline{v_u}(c) \text{ and } \bar{v}_{\min\_u} = \min_c \overline{v_u}(c) \text{ where } 2 \leq c \leq n \tag{6}$$

$$\bar{v}_{\max\_o} = \max_c \overline{v_o}(c) \text{ and } \bar{v}_{\min\_o} = \min_c \overline{v_o}(c) \text{ where } 2 \leq c \leq n \tag{7}$$

We normalize $\overline{v_u}(c)$ *and* $\overline{v_o}(c)$ as follows:

$$\bar{v}_{Nu}(c) = \frac{\bar{v}_u(c) - \bar{v}_{\min\_u}(c)}{\bar{v}_{\max\_u}(c)} \tag{8}$$

$$\bar{v}_{No}(c) = \frac{\bar{v}_o(c) - \bar{v}_{\min\_o}(c)}{\bar{v}_{\max\_o}(c)} \tag{9}$$

Finally we formalize the cluster validity index, v_{sv} as:

$$v_{SV} = \bar{v}_{Nu}(c) + \bar{v}_{No}(c) \tag{10}$$

The cluster validity index is the key value to decide which pareto-optimal front of cluster c will be selected as optimal. The minimum of the cluster validity indices gives the optimum pareto-optimal front solution.

5 Experiments

We conducted our experiments on Intel Xeon 1.40 GHz CPU, 512 MB RAM Windows XP Dell PC. First, we compiled the web accesses of a second year course from the Computer Science Department at the University of Calgary during one month (20 minutes threshold). All accesses are grouped under 1227 user visits. After preparing the data, we modified the source code of NSGA-II [1]. In the experiments, we used population size as 100, the number of generations as 120, and the pair (0.9, 0.01) is assigned as (crossover, mutation). We run the algorithm within a pre-specified range for the number of clusters, *c*=2…5. Under the same parameters, *c*=4 gives us the best pareto-optimal front indicating individuals are good results for analyzing at the pareto-optimal front. Explicitly, the value for (number of pareto optimal fronts, cluster validity index) pair for different number of clusters, namely 2, 3, 4 and 5 are, respectively, (21, 1.0), (18, 0.71), (16, 0.394), and (33, 1.0).

In this section, we show the three clustering results. Table 1 displays the average (on\off campus, day time\night time, lab\no lab days, number of hits, number of downloads) of each lower and upper bounds of *c* according to our analysis. The main point here is that the user can choose any best from his\her point of view and what is more, we recommend the end user which of the pareto-optimal fronts of *c* is best by checking the cluster validity index.

Table 1. Three solutions among the first pareto-optimal front(c=2..5).

	C=2	C=3	C=4	C=5
	($\underline{A}$, $\overline{A}$,B, $\overline{B}$)	($\underline{A}$, $\overline{A}$,B, $\overline{B}$,C, $\overline{C}$)	($\underline{A}$, $\overline{A}$,B, $\overline{B}$, C, $\overline{C}$, D, $\overline{D}$)	($\underline{A}$, $\overline{A}$,B, $\overline{B}$,C, $\overline{C}$,D $\overline{D}$,E, $\overline{E}$)
(1)	((.28,.82,.71,16.9,3.34), (.31,.80,.78,15.8,3.09), (.35,.77,.85,17.3,3.29), (.34,.78,.85,16.25,3.31))	((.38,.80,.86,17.2,3. 5), (.34,.83,.84,15.2,3.25), (.26,.71,.73,17.25,3.48), (.29,.81,.82,14.41,3.08), (.35,.75,.74,17.1,3.23), (.30,.81,.81,16.7,3.11))	((.32,.71,.82,15.89,3.4), (.31,.84,.85,17,3.33), (.33,.70,.79,13.64,3.08), (.30,.84,.82,17.20,3.11), (.36,.68,.73,14.5,4.86), (.31,.84,.81,14.9,5.25), (.36,.60,.77,14.2,2.7), (.30,.82,.81,14.6,3.1))	((.26,.69,.71,23,4.2), (.26,.81,.83,14.8,3.2), (.38,.81,.74,23,4.1), (.31,.85,.83,15.3,3.2) (.46,.7,.7,15,3.55), (.32,.82,.84,15.2,3.49) (.23,.55,.63,9.6,2.1), (.28,.81,.83,14.1,3.08) (.37,.78,.80,25,2.5), (.33,.85,.86,16.9,3.2))
(2)	((.31,.81,.77,17.6,3.42), (.31,.80,.79,16.4,3.44), (.34,.78,.82,16.54,3.17), (.32,.78,.82,15.79,3.27))	((.38,.82,.82,15.8,3.32), (.32,.83,.84,16.05,3.2), (.32,.73,.79,15.0,2.96), (.31,.80,.84,14.2,3.01), (.32,.74,.69,19,4.1), (.32,.80,.80,15,3.3))	((.38,.69,.76,21.8,4.7), (.33,.83,.84,18.52,3.46), (.29,.75,.74,11.9,2.7), (.28,.83,.81,7,3.24), (.36,.69,.82,12.26,2.8), (.30,.82,.83,15.15,3.3), (.40,.72,.77,12.42,2.2), (.29,.83,.81,14.9,3.29))	((.30,.76,.76,10,2.6), (.29,.94,.98,14,3), (.35,.85,.73,17.9,4.1) (.31,.83,.84,16,3.3) (.41,.75,.75,17.5,3.7) (.33,.80,.83,15.8,3.2) (.25,.62,.70,17.4,3.7) (.30,.80,.84,15,3.2) (.31,.81,.83,25,3.7) (.33,.84,.85,17,3.4)
(3)	((.28,.82,.74,16.7,3.47), (.29,.81,.77,16.81,3.56), (.39,.76,.86,12,2.7), (.34,.78,.84,15.4,2.72))	((.38,.83,.83,16.1,3.36), (.36,.85,.85,15.5,3.30), (.26,.72,.78,15.4,3.0), (.30,.80,.83,14.6,3.0), (.30,.72,.67,17.0,4.1), (.32,.81,.80,16.0,3.3))	((.35,.71,.78,15,5.2) (.31,.84,.83,18.31,4.49), (.30,.69,.73,12,2.7), (.30,.83,.83,17,3.24), (.32,.70,.77,13.4,4.14), (.31,.82,.82,16.02,4.42), (.37,.71,.78,13.7,2.1), (.29,.85,.82,14.05,2.1))	((.25,.72,.75,9,2.3), (.27,.81,.81,16,3.0), (.39,.84,.76,18.7,4.1), (.31,.83,.81,16.6,3.3), (.37,.75,.77,15.6,3.5), (.33,.80,.83,16.3,3.3), (.33,.69,.69,14.9,3.4), (.30,.81,.83,16.02,3.2), (.36,.84,.82,14.7,3.5), (.32,.83,.85,16.84,3.4))

It is not claimed that the results show a straight difference between *c* values, here we only try to find the pareto-optimal front where optimal clusters likely to occur by checking the average cluster validity indexes. It turned out that *c*=4 makes more sense in terms of the number of hits and downloads features.

6 Conclusion

We used a revised version of NSGA-II algorithm instead of the traditional multi-objective evolutionary algorithms. This gives the user the opportunity to let the system determine the convenient alternative results without assigning subjective weights after several trials. After that, we look up the average cluster validity index value of a pareto-optimal front of each c value and decide where optimal clusters are most likely to occur. Experimental results demonstrated the applicability and effectiveness of the proposed approach.

References

1. Deb K. et al., A Fast Elitist Non-Dominated Sorting Genetic Algorithm for Multi-Objective Optimization:NSGA-II. Proceedings of the Parallel Problem Solving from Nature. Springer Lecture Notes in Computer Science No. 1917, (2000), Paris, France.
2. Grabmeier J. et al, Techniques of Cluster Algorithms in Data Mining, Kluwer Academic Publishers, Data Mining and Knowledge Discovery, Volume 6, (2003), pp.303–360.
3. Kosala R. et al., Web Mining Research: A Survey. SIGKDD: SIGKDD Explorations: Newsletter of the Special Interest Group (SIG) on Knowledge Discovery & Data Mining. ACM, Volume 2, (2000).
4. Jain A. K. et al. Data Clustering: A Review. ACM Surveys, Volume 31, No.3, (1999).
5. Kim Do-Jong et al. A Novel Validity Index for Determination of the Optimal Number of Clusters. IEICE Trans. Inf. & Syst, Volume E84-D, (2001).
6. Lingras P., Unsupervised Rough Set Classification Using GAs, Journal of Intelligent Information Systems. Volume:16, (2001), pp. 215-228.
7. Lingras P., Rough set clustering for Web mining. FUZZ-IEEE'02. Proceedings of the 2002 IEEE International Conference on Fuzzy Systems, Volume:2, (2002), pp.1039 –1044.
8. Pawlak Z., Rough Sets. International Journal of Computer and Information Sciences, Volume 11, (1982), pp.341-356.
9. Pawlak Z. et al., Rough Sets. Communications of the ACM, Volume 38, pp. 88-95, 1995.
10. Srinivas N. et al., Multiobjective Optimization Using Nondominated Sorting Genetic Algorithms. Journal of Evolutionary Computation, Volume 2, No 3, pp. 221-248, 1994.
11. Tamura K. et al., Necessary and Sufficient Conditions for Local and Global Non-Dominated Solutions in Decision Problems with Multi-objectives. Journal of Optimization Theory and Applications, Vol:27, (1979), 509-523.
12. Yao, Y.Y. et al., A review of rough set models, in: Rough Sets and Data Mining: Analysis for Imprecise Data, Lin, T.Y. and Cercone, N. (Eds.), Kluwer Academic Publishers, Boston, (1997), pp. 47-75.

Towards Missing Data Imputation: A Study of Fuzzy K-means Clustering Method*

Dan Li[1], Jitender Deogun[1], William Spaulding[2], and Bill Shuart[2]

[1] Department of Computer Science & Engineering
University of Nebraska-Lincoln, Lincoln NE 68588-0115
[2] Department of Psychology
University of Nebraska-Lincoln, Lincoln NE 68588-0308

Abstract. In this paper, we present a missing data imputation method based on one of the most popular techniques in Knowledge Discovery in Databases (KDD), i.e. clustering technique. We combine the clustering method with soft computing, which tends to be more tolerant of imprecision and uncertainty, and apply a fuzzy clustering algorithm to deal with incomplete data. Our experiments show that the fuzzy imputation algorithm presents better performance than the basic clustering algorithm.

1 Introduction

The problem of missing (or incomplete) data is relatively common in many fields of research, and it may have different causes such as equipment malfunctions, unavailability of equipment, refusal of respondents to answer certain questions, etc. These types of missing data are unintended and uncontrolled by the researchers, but the overall result is that the observed data cannot be analyzed because of the incompleteness of the data sets. A number of researchers over last several decades have investigated techniques for dealing with missing data [1–4]. Methods for handling missing data can be divided into three categories. The first is *ignoring and discarding data*, and *listwise deletion* and *pairwise deletion* are two widely used methods in this category [2]. The second group is *parameter estimation*, which uses variants of the *Expectation-Maximization* algorithms to estimate parameters in the presence of missing data [1]. The third category is *imputation*, which denotes the process of filling in the missing values in a data set by some plausible values based on information available in the data set [4].

Among all imputation approaches, there are many options varying from simple method such as mean imputation, to some more robust and complicated methods based on the analysis of the relationships among attributes. Principal imputation methods in practice include (a) Mean imputation; (b) Regression imputation; (c) Hot deck imputation; and (d) Multiple imputation [3]. Clustering

* This work was supported, in part, by a grant from NSF (EIA-0091530), a cooperative agreement with USADA FCIC/RMA (2IE08310228), and an NSF EPSCOR Grant (EPS-0091900).

S. Tsumoto et al. (Eds.): RSCTC 2004, LNAI 3066, pp. 573–579, 2004.

algorithms have been widely used in hot deck imputation. One of the most well known clustering algorithms is the K-means method, which takes the number of desirable clusters, K, as input parameter, and outputs a partitioning of K clusters on a set of objects. The conventional clustering algorithms are normally crisp. However, it is sometimes not the case in reality, i.e., an object could be assigned to more than one clusters. Therefore, a fuzzy membership function can be applied to the K-means clustering, which models the degree of an object belonging to a cluster. This brings the basic idea of soft computing, which is tolerant of imprecision, uncertainty and partial truth [5]. In this paper, we present a hot deck missing data imputation method based on soft computing.

2 Missing Data Imputation with K-means Clustering

A fundamental problem in missing data imputation is to fill in missing information about an object based on the knowledge of other information about the object. As one of the most popular techniques in data mining, clustering method facilitates the process of solving this problem. Given a set of objects, the overall objective of clustering is to divide the data set into groups based on similarity of objects, and to minimize the intra-cluster dissimilarity. In K-means clustering, the intra-cluster dissimilarity is measured by the summation of distances between the objects and the centroid of the cluster they are assigned to. A cluster centroid represents the mean value of the objects in the cluster.

Given a set of N objects $X = \{x_1, x_2, ..., x_N\}$ where each object has S attributes, we use x_{ij} ($1 \leq i \leq N$ and $1 \leq j \leq S$) to denote the value of attribute j in object x_i. Object x_i is called a *complete* object, if $\{x_{ij} \neq \phi \mid \forall\ 1 \leq j \leq S\}$, and an *incomplete* object, if $\{x_{ij} = \phi \mid \exists\ 1 \leq j \leq S\}$, and we say object x_i has a missing value on attribute j. For any incomplete object x_i, we use $R = \{j \mid x_{ij} \neq \phi, 1 \leq j \leq S\}$ to denote the set of attributes whose values are available, and these attributes are called *reference* attributes. Our objective is to obtain the values of non-reference attributes for the incomplete objects. By K-means clustering method, we divide data set X into K clusters, and each cluster is represented by the centroid of the set of objects in the cluster. Let $V = \{v_1, v_2, ..., v_K\}$ be the set of K clusters, where v_k ($1 \leq k \leq K$) represents the centroid of cluster k. Note that v_k is also a vector in an S-dimensional space. We use $d(v_k, x_i)$ to denote the distance between centroid v_k and object x_i.

The algorithm for missing data imputation with K-means clustering method can be divided into three processes. First, randomly select K complete data objects as K centroids. Second, iteratively modify the partition to reduce the sum of the distances for each object from the centroid of the cluster to which the object belongs. The process terminates once the summation of distances is less than a user-specified threshold ε. The last process is to fill in all the non-reference attributes for each incomplete object based on the cluster information. Data objects that belong to the same cluster are taken as nearest neighbors of each other, and we apply a nearest neighbor algorithm to replace missing data.

We use generalized L_P norm distance [6] to measure the distance between a centroid and a data object in the cluster, as shown in Equation (1):

$$d(v_k, x_i) = \left(\sum_{j=1}^{S} |x_{i,j} - v_{k,j}|^p \right)^{1/p}. \tag{1}$$

The Euclidean distance is actually L_2 distance and the Manhattan distance is L_1 distance. Another choice is the Cosine based distance which is calculated from Cosine Similarity, as shown in Equation (2):

$$Sim(v_k, x_i) = \frac{\sum_{j=1}^{S} x_{i,j} * v_{k,j}}{\sqrt{\sum_{j=1}^{S} {x_{i,j}}^2 \sum_{j=1}^{S} {v_{k,j}}^2}}, \quad \text{and} \quad d(v_k, x_i) = e^{-Sim(v_k, x_i)}. \tag{2}$$

3 Missing Data Imputation with Fuzzy K-means Clustering

Now we want to extend the original K-means clustering method to a fuzzy version to impute missing data. The reason for applying fuzzy approach is that fuzzy clustering provides a better description tool when the clusters are not well-separated, as is the case in missing data imputation. Moreover, the original K-means clustering may be trapped in a local minimum status if the initial points are not selected properly. However, continuous membership values in fuzzy clustering make the resulting algorithms less susceptible to get stuck in local minimum situation.

In fuzzy clustering, each data object x_i has a membership function which describes the degree that this data object belongs to certain cluster v_k. The membership function is defined in Equation (3):

$$U(v_k, x_i) = \frac{d(v_k, x_i)^{-2/(m-1)}}{\sum_{j=1}^{K} d(v_j, x_i)^{-2/(m-1)}}, \tag{3}$$

where $m > 1$ is the fuzzifier, and $\sum_{j=1}^{K} U(v_j, x_i) = 1$ for any data object x_i $(1 \leq i \leq N)$ [7]. Now we can not simply compute the cluster centroids by the mean values. Instead, we need to consider the membership degree of each data object. Equation (4) provides the formula for cluster centroid computation:

$$v_k = \frac{\sum_{i=1}^{N} U(v_k, x_i) * x_i}{\sum_{i=1}^{N} U(v_k, x_i)}. \tag{4}$$

Since there are unavailable data in incomplete objects, we use only reference attributes to compute the cluster centroids.

The algorithm for missing data imputation with fuzzy K-means clustering method also has three processes. Note that in the initialization process, we pick K centroids which are evenly distributed to avoid local minimum situation. In the second process, we iteratively update membership functions and centroids until the overall distance meets the user-specified distance threshold ε. In this process, we cannot assign the data object to a concrete cluster represented by a cluster centroid (as did in the basic K-mean clustering algorithm), because each data object belongs to all K clusters with different membership degrees. Finally, we impute non-reference attributes for each incomplete object. We replace non-reference attributes for each incomplete data object x_i based on the information about membership degrees and the values of cluster centroids, as shown in Equation (5):

$$x_{i,j} = \sum_{k=1}^{K} U(x_i, v_k) * v_{k,j}, \text{ for any non-refence attribute } j \notin R. \quad (5)$$

4 Experiments and Analysis

We test our algorithms on two types of data sets. One is weather related databases for drought risk management. The other type of data is the Integrated Psychological Therapy (IPT) outcome databases for psychotherapy study. A common property in these two types of data sets is that missing data are present either due to the malfunction (or unavailability) of equipment or caused by the refusal of respondents. We use the Root Mean Squared Error (RMSE) to evaluate the overall performance of the imputation algorithms. For each experiment with user-specified parameters, we randomly remove amount of data from test set, and use them as missing data. We run each experiment ten times and the experimental results are based on the average values of testing. Since each data attribute has different domain, to fairly test our algorithms, we first normalize the data set so that all the data values are between 0 and 100.

4.1 Mean Substitution vs. K-means

We first compare the non-fuzzy K-means imputation algorithm with mean substitution method, as shown in Figure 1. For K-means algorithm, we select Manhattan distance metric to compute the distance between any two data objects, and the numbers of clusters are 4 (left) and 7 (right), respectively. Each experiment is conducted ten times. From Figure 1, it is obvious that imputation with K-means clustering method outperforms widely used mean substitution method. This indicates that it is reasonable to fill in missing (non-reference) attributes based on the information from reference attributes. Given two or more data objects, if they are similar (close) with regard to reference attributes, other non-reference attributes should be similar (close) too. This is the essential assumption based on which our K-means imputation algorithm works.

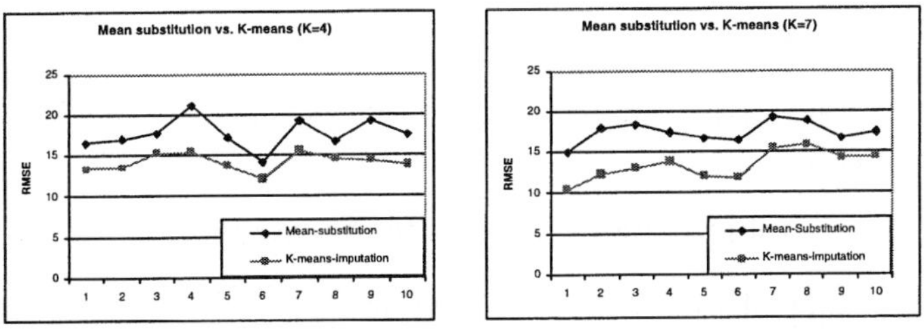

Fig. 1. Mean substitution vs. non-fuzzy K-means imputation.

4.2 K-means vs. Fuzzy K-means

We evaluate and analyze the performance of the basic K-means and the fuzzy K-means imputation algorithms from two aspects. First, we want to see how the percentage of missing data influences the performance of the algorithms. Second, we test on various input parameters (e.g. distance metrics, the value of fuzzifier m, and cluster number K), and conclude with the best values.

Percentage of Missing Data. Table 1 summarizes the results for varying percentages of missing values in the test cases. The experiments are based on two groups of input parameters. First, we select Euclidean distance metric, assume 8 clusters, and set the value of fuzzifier for fuzzy algorithm to 1.5. In the second group of experiments, we use Manhattan distance as the dissimilarity measure, assume 7 clusters, and set the value of fuzzifier to 1.3. We make two observations from Table 1. First, as the percentage of missing values increases, the overall error also increases considering both the basic K-means and the fuzzy K-means imputation algorithms. This is reasonable because we lose more useful information when the amount of missing data increases. The second observation is that the fuzzy K-means algorithm provides better results than the basic K-means method. Especially, when the percentage reaches 20%, the basic K-means algorithm cannot work properly.

Table 1. RMSE for varying percentages of missing values.

	Euclidean Distance, K=8, m=1.5				Manhattan Distance, K=7, m=1.3				
	5%	10%	20%	30%	1%	2%	5%	10%	15%
K-means	14.08	15.93	NA	NA	13.18	13.39	13.94	15.31	15.86
Fuzzy K-means	11.77	12.05	14.41	14.79	10.17	11.51	12.32	13.23	14.57

Effect of Input Parameters. Now, we design experiments to evaluate two missing data imputation algorithms by testing on different input parameters. First, we select three different distance metrics, i.e. Euclidean distance, Manhattan distance, and Cosine-based distance, as shown in Equation (1) and (2).

Table 2 presents the effect of these metrics. We can see that Manhattan distance provides the best result, and the Cosine-based distance is the worst. Again, it can be seen that the fuzzy imputation algorithm outperforms K-means algorithm for all three distance metrics.

Table 2. RMSE for varying distance metrics.

	Manhattan Distance	Euclidean Distance	Cosine-based Distance
K-means	13.37	14.08	17.65
Fuzzy K-means	11.12	11.77	14.99

Next, we want to test on the effect of the value of fuzzifier, which has been used in Equation (3). Since fuzzifier is only a parameter used in fuzzy imputation algorithm, as shown in Table 3, the K-means clustering method does not present much change as the value of m changes. However, for fuzzy algorithm, the change in performance is obvious, and the best value of m is 1.3. When the value of fuzzifier goes to 2, the basic K-means algorithm even outperforms the fuzzy K-means algorithm. This indicates that selecting a proper parameter value is important for system performance.

Table 3. RMSE for varying the values of fuzzifier.

	Euclidean Distance, K=8, 5% missing			
	m=1.1	m=1.3	m=1.5	m=2.0
K-means	13.81	13.71	14.08	13.58
Fuzzy K-means	12.49	10.07	11.77	17.23

5 Conclusion

In this paper, we investigate missing data imputation techniques with the aim of constructing more accurate algorithms. We borrow the idea from fuzzy K-means clustering, and apply it to the problem of missing data imputation. The experimental results demonstrate the strength of this method. We evaluate the performance of the algorithms based on the RMSE error analysis. We discover that the basic K-means algorithm outperforms the mean substitution method, which is a simple and common approach for missing data imputation. Experiments also show that the overall performance of the fuzzy K-means method is better than the basic K-means method, especially when the percentage of missing values is high. We test the performance of our algorithms based on difference input parameters, and find the best value for each parameter.

References

1. Dempster, A.P., Laird, N.M., Rubin, D.B.: Maximum likelihood from incomplete data via the EM algorithm. J. of Royal Statistical Society Series **39** (1977) 1–38

2. Gary, K., Honaker, J., Joseph, A., Scheve, K.: Listwise deletion is evil: What to do about missing data in political science (2000) http://GKing.Harvard.edu.
3. Little, R.J., Rubin, D.B.: Statistical Analysis with Missing Data. Wiley, New York (1987)
4. Myrtveit, I., Stensrud, E., Olsson, U.H.: Analyzing data sets with missing data: an empirical evaluation of imputation methods and likelihood-based methods. IEEE Transactions on Software Engineering **27** (2001) 999–1013
5. (Zadeh, L.A.) http://www.cs.berkeley.edu/projects/Bisc/bisc.memo.html.
6. Akleman, E., Chen, J.: Generalized distance functions. In: Proceedings of the '99 International Conference on Shape Modeling. (1999) 72–79
7. Krishnapuram, R., Joshi, A., Nasraoui, O., Yi, L.: Low-complexity fuzzy relational clustering algorithms for web mining. IEEE Trans. on Fuzzy Syst. **9** (2001) 595–607

K-means Indiscernibility Relation over Pixels

James F. Peters and Maciej Borkowski

Department of Electrical and Computer Engineering
University of Manitoba, Winnipeg, Manitoba R3T 5V6 Canada
{jfpeters,maciey}@ee.umanitoba.ca

Abstract. This article presents a new form of indiscernibility relation based on K-means clustering of pixel values. The end result is a partitioning of a set of pixel values into bins that represent equivalence classes. The proposed approach makes it possible to introduce a form of upper and lower approximation specialized relative to sets of pixel values. This approach is particularly relevant to a special class of digital images for power line ceramic insulators. Until now the problem of determining when a ceramic insulator needs to be replaced has relied on visual inspection. With the K-means indiscernibility relation, it is now possible to automate the detection of faulty ceramic insulators. The contribution of this article is the introduction of an approach to classifying power line insulators based on a rough set methods and K-means clustering in analyzing digital images.

Keywords: Approximation, classification, digital image processing, K-means clustering, rough sets.

1 Introduction

Considerable work on the application of rough set theory [1] in classifying various kinds of images has been reported (see, e.g., [2-3]) . This article introduces an approach to image classification based on rough set theory and an application of classical K-means clustering [4]. In this paper, partition of an object universe is carried out using what is known as a K-means indiscernibility relation, identification of decision classes, and synthesis of upper and lower approximations of pixel sets provide a basis for the classification method described in this article. The basic approach is to use the Moody and Darken [4] K-means clustering algorithm to separate pixels in an image into bins relative a set of selected image features such as hue and saturation. Once pixels have been separated into bins, then a modified form of the traditional indiscernibility relation is used to identify a partition of image pixels that provides a basis for image classification. The proposed approach to image classification has an application in classifying powerline equipment images.

This paper has the following organization. To help make this article self-contained, a brief presentation of basic concepts from rough sets and K-means clustering is given in Section 2. The approximation image classification method based on rough sets and K-means clustering is introduced and illustrated in

S. Tsumoto et al. (Eds.): RSCTC 2004, LNAI 3066, pp. 580–585, 2004.

Section 3. A very brief description of a toolset that automates the proposed image classification method is given in Section 4.

2 Basic Concepts

This section gives a brief introduction to rough sets and K-means clustering, which provide a basis for the approach to classifying images and pattern recognition presented in this article. In addition, this section introduces a new form of equivalence relation useful in expressing our approximate knowledge of the information represented by the grey levels of pixels in a digital image.

2.1 K-means Clustering

The basic problem in clustering is to find a set of centres which accurately reflect the distribution of data points congregating around the centres. With the K-means clustering algorithm the number of centres is decided in advance. Given N data points, the K-means algorithm partitions the data points $\{x_n\}$ into K disjoint subsets S_j, so that $J = \sum_{j=1}^{K} \sum_{n \in S_j} \|x_n - \mu_j\|^2$ is minimized, and where μ_j is the mean of the data point in bin S_j and is computed using $\mu_j = \frac{1}{|S_j|} \sum_{n \in S_j} x_n$.

In the case where the set of data points consists of pixels, the K-means algorithms divides the space of all grey levels into K bins. The idea is to create these bins in such a way that each point lies closest to the mean value of all points from the bin in which this point belongs.

2.2 K-means Indiscernibility Relation

This section introduces a new form of equivalence relation useful in expressing our approximate knowledge of the information represented by the grey levels of pixels in a digital image. We use here the fact that each equivalence relation defines a partitioning of the universe (e.g., all pixel values for an image are partitioned into non-intersecting sets). This partitioning can be accomplished using K-means clustering. Let $IS = (U, A)$ be an information system where U is a set of objects (e.g., pixel grey-levels) and A is a set of attributes (e.g., pixel coordinates, hue, saturation, intensity). K-means clustering gives us partitioning of gray-level space into K bins. For each bin i, where i is integer number from 1 to K, we can find the bin centre and diameter. Let C_i denote the centre of the ith bin and let D_i denote the diameter of the ith bin. Then the indiscernibility relation is defined in (3).

$$\mathrm{Ind}_{IS,K}(B) = \{(x, x') \in U^2 \mid \forall a \in B, \exists i \in \{1, ..., K\}. |a(x) - C_i| \leq D_i \wedge |a(x') - C_i| \leq D_i\} \quad (3)$$

In other words, two points x and x' are indiscernible if all their attribute values lie in the same bins resulting from K-means clustering. Let $B_{C,D}(x)$ denotes a bin with centre C, diameter D of B-indiscernible objects containing

x. Now upper and lower approximation of a set X of pixels can be defined relative to K-means bins where $B^*(X) = \{x \in U \mid B_{C,D}(x) \cap X \neq \emptyset\}$ and $B_*(X) = \{x \in U \mid B_{C,D}(x) \subseteq X\}$.

3 Sample Classification of Ceramic Insulator Images

The main steps in classifying a digital image using upper and lower approximations are presented in this section.

3.1 Pixel Attributes and Decision Class

Each pixel gives values for an image stored in one byte, e.g. one byte for red, one for blue and one for green. The resulting Hue, Saturation, Intensity (HIS), Hue, Saturation, Lightness (HSL) and Hue, Saturation, Value (HSV) values are also stored in one byte. This gives us nine attributes each with values ranging from 0 to 255. Small values are visualized using dark grey levels and high values using bright grey levels. The grey levels of the pixels of an image are then sifted into K bins.

3.2 Upper and Lower Approximation

To compute the upper and lower approximation of a set of pixels, the information from all the attributes is combined into one image. Upper and lower approximation are given by $B^*(X) = \{x \in U \mid B_{C,D}(x) \cap X \neq \emptyset\}$ and $B_*(X) = \{x \in U \mid B_{C,D}(x) \subseteq X\}$. The set X is the decision class which was defined in the preceding section. The equivalence relation $B_{C,D}(x)$ is the equivalence relation defined by the partitioning from K-means clustering and $B \subseteq A$ is the set of all nine colour channels. To construct an upper approximation, we find all intervals (bins) which have non-empty intersection with the decision class. This must be done for each attribute separately. A point belongs to the upper approximation only if bins for all its attributes have non-empty intersection with corresponding decision intervals. By analogy, the lower approximation can be constructed in similar manner. The resulting image is in black and white. Points belonging to the upper and lower approximation are denoted by a black colour and those not belonging to either the upper or lower approximation by a white colour.

3.3 Entropy

The deterioration of an insulator's surface results in visual colour changes in the image showing the insulator. The purpose of this step is to identify those areas in the insulator image with high frequencies of change. This leads to the identification of areas that indicate potential deterioration. We use the concept of entropy to identify areas of high change in an insulator image. The formula for the entropy is -$\sum_{i=1,d} p_i \log_2 p_i$, where p_i denotes the probability of occurrences of the $i-th$ decision in the data set, and d is number of all decisions. We then apply a three by three pixels entropy filter. This means that for each pixel in the image, we take its 3-by-3 neighbourhood and calculate the entropy for obtained set of zeros and ones. In our case d equals 2, since we have only black and white pixels. Let p_1 be the number of all black pixels divided by the area of the filter. By analogy, let p_2 be the number of all white pixels divided by the area of the filter. Since the number of all pixels equals to the sum of white and black pixels, the equation $p_1 + p_2 = 1$ holds true. The entropy is highest in the case where the number of black pixels equals to the number of white pixels. In an insulator image, high entropy values are represented by dark grey levels, whereas small entropy values are denoted by bright grey levels. Thus, the entropy yields high values only for areas with some points belonging to the upper or lower approximation and some outside the approximation region. This makes it possible to identify regions with high changes and this points to the onset of insulator surface deterioration.

3.4 Selection of Decision Classes

The optimal decision class intervals are not known a priori. Hence, it is necessary to introduce some method that can be used to select appropriate intervals for decision classes. Nevertheless, we know that degraded areas of the insulator's surface (due to their high change rates) yield on average higher entropy, even when the decision class is not set optimally. Therefore, we integrate the image over all possible values of the interval's centre to find the optimal intervals for decision classes. Let F denote the image on the input of this step, then define the integral $\hat{F} = (1/256) \int_{\upsilon} F$, where υ is the set of decision class interval centres. Since we deal only with a finite number of decision class interval centres, $\hat{F}$ is implemented as a summation. Also observe that the diameter of each interval can be fine-tuned to better suit a given training set.

3.5 Computation of Average Pixel Brightness

To obtain a more compact description of an image, we need to calculate the average pixel brightness in an image. Let $G(x, y) \in I^{m*n}$ be image I^{m*n} obtained from $\widehat{F}((I^{m*n})^3) \rightarrow I^{m*n}$. The average brightness of a pixel is calculated using $damage = \sum \sum_{y=0,m,x=0,n} G(x, y)$, where m and n are an image's dimensions, $I \in \{0, 1, \ldots, 255\}$, and $x, y \in N, 0 \leq x < n$ and $0 \leq y < m$. From the process of recreation of image G it is clear that high values of the *damage* parameter correspond to highly deteriorated insulator's surface and low values to the surface in a good condition.

Example 3.1 In this example images are reconstructed relative to lower approximation of the pixel sets in original images. We will use 7-means clustering. A histogram for a typical bad insulator image is shown in Fig. 1, where the dashed vertical lines denote borders of the bins. This means that all pixels from a bin will be indistinguishable for the purpose of calculating the lower approximation.

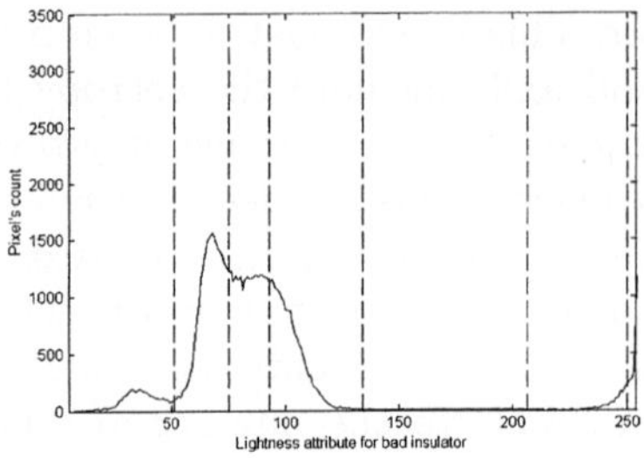

Fig. 1. Histogram for bad insulator

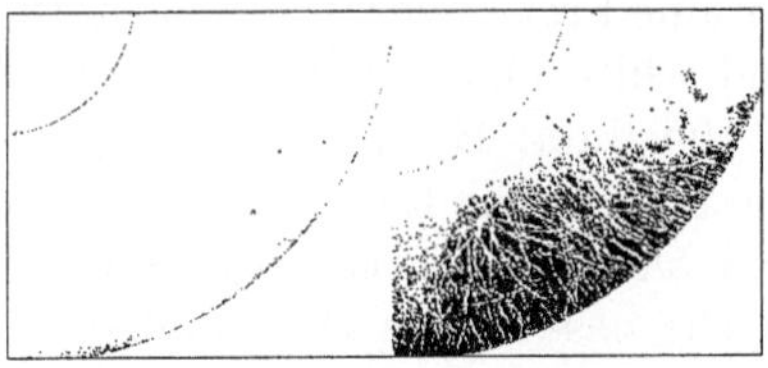

Fig. 2. Lower approx. of sample images

The image in Fig. 2 represents arbitrarily selected decision classes. It shows the result of applying lower approximation to reconstruct the original images. In the case of the lower approximation of the sample images shown in Fig. 2, it can be seen that the lower approximation for a bad (severely cracked) insulator is darker than the lower approximation for a good insulator. From visual inspection of Fig. 2, we can conclude from patterns revealed by the lower approximation that the ceramic insulator is suspect, and requires replacement.

4 Image Classification Toolset

The approximation classification method described in this article has been automated. A sample user interface panel is shown in the snapshot in Fig. 3. Using this tool, it is possible to select the feature set to be used in obtaining approximate knowledge about the condition of insulators exhibited in images. The hue feature has been selected in the snapshot for the image classification toolset shown in Fig. 3. Instead of declaring that an insulator is either good or bad, the

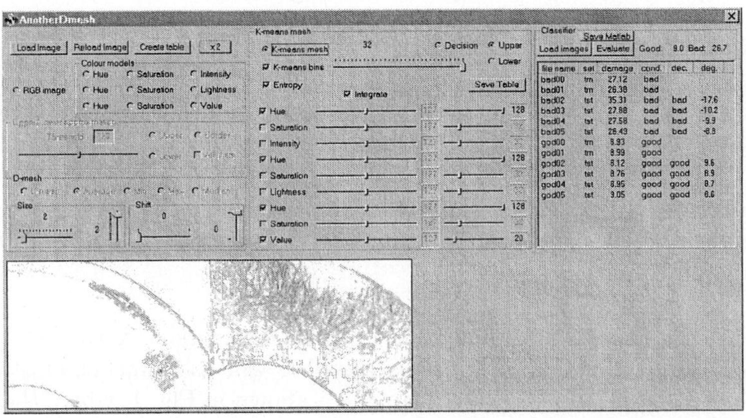

Fig. 3. Snapshot of sample use of Image Classification Toolset

degree of goodness or badness is measured. This is in keeping with recent research on approximate reasoning and an adaptive calculus of granules (see, e.g., [5]), where inclusion measurements of one granule in another represent being a part of *to a degree* (see last column in Fig. 3). This toolset is important, since it makes it easier to schedule maintenance on power line insulators with respect to those insulators requiring immediate attention vs. those insulators that are damaged but do not require immediate replacement. To evaluate the classification algorithm described in this article, k-fold cross-validation method has been used to compare the error rate ε of a traditional image classification method (see, e.g., [6]) using the Fast Fourier Transform ($\varepsilon = 0.0121$) and the proposed image classification method ($\varepsilon = 0.0006$) with k = 10.

5 Conclusion

This paper has presented an approach to approximate classification of images based on a K-means indiscernibility relation and traditional rough set theory. This approach has been illustrated in the context of classifying ceramic insulators used on high voltage powerlines, which has been traditionally done by visual inspection of insulator images or by physical inspection of insulators. In the context of classifying insulator images, the classification method introduced in this article has been automated. The results obtained during k-fold cross-validation for the proposed classification method are encouraging.

Acknowledgements

The research of James Peters and Maciej Borkowski has been supported by grants from Manitoba Hydro, and the research of James Peters has also been supported by Natural Sciences and Engineering Research Council of Canada (NSERC) grant 185986.

References

1. Z. Pawlak, Rough sets, Int. J. of Information and Computer Sciences, vol. 11, no. 5, 1982, 341-356, 1982
2. WITAS project homepage: http://www.ida.liu.se/ext/witas/
3. M. Borkowski, Digital Image Processing in Measurement of Ice Thickness on Power Transmission Lines: A Rough Set Approach, M.Sc. Thesis, Supervisor: J.F. Peters, Department of Electrical and Computer Engineering, University of Manitoba, 2002.
4. J. Moody, C.J. Darken, Fast learning in networks of locally-tuned processing units, Neural Computation 1(2), 1989, 281-294.
5. L. Polkowski, A. Skowron, Towards adaptive calculus of granules. In: Proc. of the Sixth Int. Conf. on Fuzzy Systems (FUZZ-IEEE'98), Anchorage, Alaska, 4-9 May 1998, 111-116.
6. R.C. Gonzalez, R.E. Woods, Digital Image Processing, NJ, Prentice-Hall, 2002.

A New Cluster Validity Function Based on the Modified Partition Fuzzy Degree

Jie Li, Xinbo Gao, and Li-cheng Jiao

School of Electronic Engineering, Xidian Univ., Xi'an 710071, P.R.China

Abstract. The cluster validity is an important topic of cluster analysis, which is often converted into the determination of the optimal cluster number. Most of the available cluster validity functions are limited for the analysis of numeric data set and ineffective for the categorical data set. For this purpose, a new cluster validity function is presented in this paper, namely the modified partition fuzzy degree. By combining the partition entropy and the partition fuzzy degree, the new cluster validity can be applied to any data set with numeric attributes or categorical attributes. The experimental results illustrate the effectiveness of the proposed cluster validity function.

1 Introduction

Cluster analysis is one of multivariant statistical analysis and an important branch of unsupervised pattern recognition. It has been widely applied in the fields of data mining and computer vision. For a given data set, one should first judge whether or not there exists clustering structures, which belongs to the topic of cluster tendency. Then, if necessary, one need to determine these clustering structures, which is the topic of cluster analysis. After obtain the structures, one also needs further to analysis the rationality of the clustering result, which is the topic of cluster validity. While, the cluster validity can be converted to the determination of the optimal cluster number.

The available studies of cluster validity can be divided into 3 groups [1, 2]. The first group is based on the fuzzy partition of data set, for instance, the separation degree, the partition entropy, and the proportional coefficient. These methods are simple and easy to implement. However, the disadvantage lies in lacking of direct relationship with the structure features of data set, which leads to some limitations. The second group is based on the geometric structure of data set, such as, partition coefficient, separation coefficient, Xie-Beni index and graph-theory-based validity function. These methods possess close relationship with the structure of data but difficult for applications for their high complexity. The final group is based on the statistic information of the data set, for examples, PFS clustering, Boosting method, and validity functions with entropy forms. These methods bases on the fact that the optimal classification can provide good statistic information of the data structure. So, their performance depends on the consistency between the statistic hypothesis and the data set distribution.

S. Tsumoto et al. (Eds.): RSCTC 2004, LNAI 3066, pp. 586–591, 2004.

The above cluster validity functions are designed for the data set with numeric attributes. However, in the applications of data mining, data set with categorical attributes are often encountered. Since the categorical domain is not ordered, it cannot always get the effective result by converting the categorical values into numeric values. There are some cluster analysis methods for data set with categorical attributes, such as k-modes algorithm [3], ROCK algorithm [4], and CLOPE algorithm [5], but lacks of cluster validity methods.

For this purpose, we propose the concept of partition fuzzy degree (PFD), which is related to both the information of the fuzzy partition and geometric structure of the data set. By combining the partition entropy and partition fuzzy degree, a new modified PFD function is defined for the cluster validity function for both the data set with numeric attributes and with categorical attributes.

2 The Modified PFD Function

Let $X = \{x_1, x_2, \ldots, x_n\}$ denote a data set, and $x_i = [x_{i1}, x_{i2}, \ldots, x_{ip}]^T$ represent the p features of the i-th sample. The fuzzy clustering can be described the following mathematical programming problem.

$$\min J_m(U, V) = \sum_{i=1}^{c}\sum_{j=1}^{n} u_{ij}^m d_{ij}^2 \tag{1}$$

For a pre-specified cluster number c, an alternative optimization technique, such as fuzzy c-mean algorithm, can be used to obtain the optimal partition matrix U of the data set. To evaluate the partition effect, the fuzzy partition entropy and partition fuzzy degree were proposed as criteria of cluster validity.

Definition 2.1. For a given cluster number c and fuzzy partition matrix U, the fuzzy partition entropy is defined as Eq.(2).

$$H(U; c) = -\frac{1}{n}\sum_{i=1}^{c}\sum_{j=1}^{n} u_{ij}\log_a(u_{ij}) \tag{2}$$

Bezdek used the fuzzy partition entropy to construct a cluster validity criterion for determining the optimal cluster number c^*.

$$H(U, c^*) = \min_c\{\min_{\Omega_c} H(U; c)\}$$

Definition 2.2. For a given cluster number c and fuzzy partition matrix U, the partition fuzzy degree is defined as Eq.(3).

$$P_f(U; c) = \frac{1}{n}\sum_{i=1}^{c}\sum_{j=1}^{n} |u_{ij} - (u_{ij})_H| \tag{3}$$

where, we have

$$(u_{ij})_H = \begin{cases} 1 & u_{ij} = \max_{1\le k\le c}\{u_{ij}\} \\ 0 & otherwise \end{cases}$$

that is, $(u_{ij})_H$ is the defuzzifying result of the fuzzy partition matrix.

Partition fuzzy degree (PFD) can also used as a criterion to judge the fuzziness of a classification result. Like the fuzzy partition entropy , the more distinct the cluster result, the less the value of $P_f(U;c)$ is. Therefore, to obtain the optimal cluster number c, we hope to get the least value of $P_f(U;c)$ for the fuzzy partition. Unfortunately, the function of $H(U;c)$ and $P_f(U;c)$ has the increasing tendency with the increasing of cluster number c, which will interfere the detection of the optimal number. For this purpose, by combining $H(U;c)$ and $P_f(U;c)$, we present a new modified PFD function, $M_{pf}(U;c)$.

Definition 2.3. For a given cluster number c and fuzzy partition matrix U, the modified partition fuzzy degree of a data set is defined as Eq.(4).

$$M_{pf}(U;c) = \frac{P_f(U;c)}{\widetilde{H}(U;c)} \tag{4}$$

Where $\widetilde{H}(U;c) = Smooth(H(U;c))$ is the smoothed fuzzy partition entropy by the 3-point smoothing operator or median filter. Moreover, we assume that $M_{pf}(U;c) = 0$ in the case of U is a crisp partition matrix.

In this way, by compensating the increasing tendency of PFD function with the increasing of cluster number, the modified PFD function can be easily used to select the optimal cluster number.

3 The MPFD-Based Optimal Choice of Parameters

Based on the proposed modified PFD function, we will discuss how to determine the optimal cluster number for the numeric data and categorical data.

3.1 The Optimal Choice of Cluster Number c^* for Numeric Data

For the numeric data, the most popular cluster analysis method is the fuzzy c-means (FCM) algorithm. Like other clustering algorithm, the FCM algorithm also asks the specification of cluster number c in advance. To determine the optimal cluster number c^*, we define a criterion function as

$$M_{pf}(U,c^*) = \min_{c}\{\min_{\Omega_c} M_{pf}(U,c)\} \tag{5}$$

where Ω_c is a finite set of all possible optimal partition matrix with different cluster number c, and c^* corresponds to the optimal cluster number.

3.2 The Optimal Choice of Cluster Number c^* for Categorical Data

For the cluster analysis for categorical data, we adopt the CLOPE algorithm. Let $X = \{x_1, x_2, \cdots, x_n\}$ denote a set of data set with n samples, and all the features of sample x_j are categorical type. $\{X_1, X_2, \cdots, X_c\}$ represents the c-partition of data set X, and $D(X_i)$ is the statistic histogram of X_i respect to different categorical attributes. We define

$$S(X_i) = \sum_{x_j \in X_i} |x_j| \tag{6}$$

in which $|x_j|$ represents the dimensionality of sample x_j, and

$$W(X_i) = |D(X_i)| \tag{7}$$

where $|D(X_i)|$ denotes the number of categorical attributes in the set of $D(X_i)$.

In the CLOPE algorithm, the clustering objective function is defined as

$$Profit_r(X) = \frac{1}{n} \sum_{i=1}^{c} \frac{S(X_i)}{W(X_i)^r} \times |X_i| \tag{8}$$

where, $|X_i|$ is the cardinality of the set of X_i, *i.e.*, the number of elements. r is a positive real number, called repulsion, which is used to control the similarity within clusters. For any a r, one can find a optimal partition $\{X_i^*\}$ and cluster number c^* to maximize Eq.(8). Thus, the optimal choice of cluster number c^* is converted to the optimal choice of repulsion r^*.

Like Eq.(5), we can also construct a criterion based the MPFD to determine the optimal repulsion r^* for the CLOPE algorithm.

$$M_{pf}(U^*, r^*) = \min_{r}\{\min_{\Omega_r} M_{pf}(U, r)\} \tag{9}$$

After finding the optimal repulsion r^*, it will be easy to obtain the corresponding optimal cluster number c^*.

4 Experimental Results

In this section, we conduct several experiments with the numeric and categorical data to verify the effectiveness of the proposed cluster validity function.

Experiment with numeric data: In this experiment, we adopt a set of synthetic data as shown in Fig.1(a), which consists of 1050 points in 2D plane belonging to 9 Gaussian distributed subsets with the variance of 1.6. Let c takes from 2 to $c_{\max}$ (here, we takes $c_{\max} = 20$). The FCM algorithm is used to obtain the optimal partition matrix with $m = 2$, and the MPFD function is computed versus to the cluster number c as shown in Fig.1(b).

Based on the intuition, we find that this data set can be divided into 3 subsets from the global viewpoint, and 9 subsets from the local viewpoint. By analyzing the minima of the MPFD function in Fig.1(b), we can conclude that the first optimal choice of cluster number c is 3, and the second optimal choice of cluster number c is 9, which is in accordance to the real condition.

Meanwhile, we plot the partition entropy and PFD functions in Fig.1(c). Although both of them also have local minima at $c = 3$ and $c = 9$, the increasing tendency of curves versus c makes it difficult to automatically extract the local minima. Fig.1(d) shows the curve of the ratio of PFD to the partition entropy, in which the increasing tendency of the PFD is also compensated to some degree. The two global minima can be obtained at $c = 3$ and $c = 9$ by setting a threshold $T = 0.7$. However, it is obvious that the PFD and the partition entropy occur the local minima at the same values of c, the direct compensation of PFD with partition entropy will blur the positions of the global minima and even make the global minima vanishing. It is the reason why we use the smoothed partition entropy to compensate the PFD rather than the partition entropy itself.

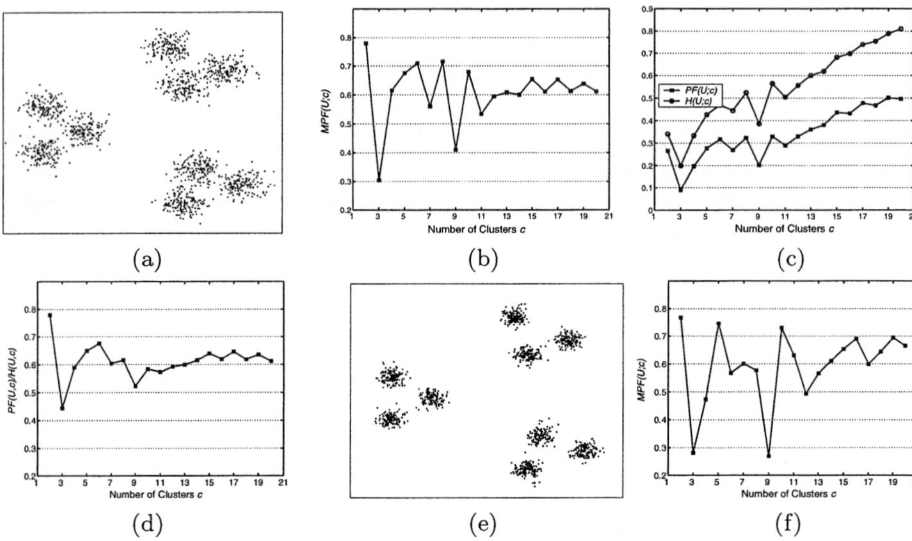

Fig. 1. (a) Test data ($\sigma^2 = 1.6$), (b) The plot of the $M_{pf}(U;c)$ vs. c, (c) The plots of the $P_f(U;c)$ and $H(U;c)$ vs. c, (d) The plot of the ratio of the $P_f(U;c)$ to the $H(U;c)$ vs. c., (e) Test data ($\sigma^2 = 1$), (f) The plot of the $M_{pf}(U;c)$ vs. c.

To evaluate the sensitiveness of the MPFD to the cluster tendency of data set, we decrease the variance of the above data set from 1.6 to 1 as test data shown in Fig.1(e). The plot of the MPFD vs. c for the second test data is presented in Fig.1(f). Compared the Fig.1(b) and Fig.1(f), it can be found that with the decreasing of the scatter degree of the data set, the global minima of the MPFD are also decreased. Moreover, with the data subset becoming compact, the optimal choice of cluster number changes from 3 to 9, which is also in accordance with human intuition. Hereby, the proposed MPFD can be used to choice the optimal cluster number as well as to compare the separability degree of the given data sets.

Experiment with categorical data: In this experiment, we use the bean disease data as test-bed [6]. We also apply the proposed cluster validity function to get the optimal cluster number of this data set. The obtained partition entropy and the PFD are plotted in Fig.2(a), in which both of them are increased with the repulsion r. So, it is impossible to get the optimal cluster number with the partition entropy and the PFD. While the plot of the MPFD is shown in Fig.2(b) for the same data set. For the convenience of visualizing the relationship between

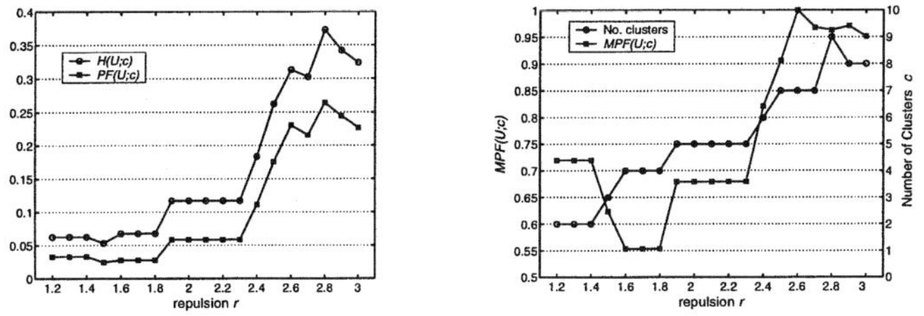

(a) (b)

Fig. 2. (a)Plots of $P_f(U;c)$ and $H(U;c)$ vs. r, (b)Plots of $M_{pf}(U;c)$ and c vs. r.

the parameters r and c, we plot the function of the cluster number c with the repulsion r at the same plot. From the Fig.2(b), we can draw a conclusion that the MPFD get the minimum at $r = 1.6 \sim 1.8$, which corresponds to the optimal cluster number 4. The conclusion agrees with the real condition.

5 Conclusions

This paper presents a modified partition fuzzy degree and uses it as a cluster validity function. The experimental results with the synthetic data and real data show that it can effectively analyze the numeric data as well as the categorical data to obtain the optimal cluster number. Moreover, it can also be used to compare the separability degree of the given data sets.

References

1. Bezdek,J.C., Pattern Recognition with Fuzzy Objective Function Algorithms. New York: Plenum Press, 1981
2. Gao Xinbo and Xie Weixin, Advances in theory and applications of fuzzy clustering. Chinese Science Bulletin, **45(11)** (2000), 961–970
3. Zhexue Huang, Michael,K.Ng., A Fuzzy k-modes Algorithm for clustering categorical Data, IEEE Trans. on Fuzzy Systems. **7(4)** (1999), 446–452
4. Sudipto,G., Rajeev,R., Kyuseok,S., ROCK: A Robust Clustering Algorithm for Categorical Attributes. Proceedings of the IEEE International Conference on Data Engineering, Sydney, March. (1999)
5. Yiling Yang, Xudong Guan, Jinyuan You, CLOPE: A Fast and Effective Clustering Algorithm for Transactional Data. Proceedings of the Eighth ACM SIGKDD International Conference on Knowledge Discovery and Data Mining, Edmonton, Alberta, Canada July. (2002)
6. Michalski,R.S., Stepp,R.E., Automated construction of classifications: Conceptual clustering versus numerical taxonomy. IEEE Trans. on PAMI, **5** (1983), 396–410

On the Evolution of Rough Set Exploration System

Jan G. Bazan[1], Marcin S. Szczuka[2], Arkadiusz Wojna[2], and Marcin Wojnarski[2]

[1] Institute of Mathematics, University of Rzeszów
Rejtana 16A, 35-959 Rzeszów, Poland
bazan@univ.rzeszow.pl

[2] Faculty of Mathematics, Informatics and Mechanics, Warsaw University
Banacha 2, 02-097, Warsaw, Poland
{szczuka,wojna}@mimuw.edu.pl, mwojnars@ns.onet.pl

Abstract. We present the next version (ver. 2.1) of the Rough Set Exploration System – a software tool featuring a library of methods and a graphical user interface supporting variety of rough-set-based and related computations. Methods, features and abilities of the implemented software are discussed and illustrated with examples in data analysis and decision support.

1 Introduction

Research in decision support systems, classification algorithms, in particular those concerned with application of rough sets requires experimental verification. To be able to make thorough, multi-directional practical investigations and to focus on essential problems one needs an inventory of software tools that automate basic operations. Several such software systems have been constructed by various researchers, see e.g. [13, vol. 2]. That was also the idea behind creation of the Rough Set Exploration System (**RSES**).

It is already almost a decade since the first version of RSES appeared. After several modifications, improvements and removal of detected bugs it was used in many applications. Comparison with other classification systems (see [12, 1]) proves its value. The RSESlib, which is a computational backbone of RSES, was also used in construction of the computational kernel of ROSETTA — an advanced system for data analysis (see [19]).

The first version of Rough Set Exploration System (RSES v. 1.0) in its current incarnation and its further development (RSES v. 2.0) were introduced approximately four and two years ago, respectively (see [3, 4]). The present version (v. 2.1) introduces several changes, improvements and, most notably, several new algorithms – the result of our recent research developments in the area of data analysis and classification systems.

The RSES software and its computational kernel maintains all advantages of previous versions. The algorithms have been re-mastered to provide better flexibility and extended functionality. New algorithms added to the library follow

S. Tsumoto et al. (Eds.): RSCTC 2004, LNAI 3066, pp. 592–601, 2004.

the current state of our research. Improved construction of the system allows further extensions and supports augmentation of RSES methods into other data analysis tools.

The re-implementation of the RSES core classes in Java^{TM} 2 and removal of legacy code is further fostered in the RSES v. 2.1. The computational procedures are now written in Java using its object-oriented paradigms. The migration to Java simplifies some development operations and, ultimately, leads to improved flexibility of the product permitting migration of RSES software to operating systems other than Windows (currently e.g. Linux).

In this paper we briefly show the features of the RSES software, focusing on recently added algorithms and methods. The changes in GUI and improvements in existing components are also described. We illustrate the presentation of new methods with examples of applications in the field of classification systems.

2 Basic Notions

To give the reader a better understanding of the RSES' description, we bring here some basic notions that are further used in the presentation of particular methods.

The structure of data that is the central point of our work is represented in the form of *information system* or, more precisely, the special case of an information system called *decision table.*

Information system is a pair of the form $\mathbf{A} = (U, A)$ where U is a *universe* of *objects* and $A = \{a_1, ..., a_m\}$ is a set of *attributes* i.e. mappings of the form $a_i : U \rightarrow V_{a_i}$, where V_{a_i} is called *value set* of the attribute a_i. The decision table is also a pair of the form $\mathbf{A} = (U, A \cup \{d\})$ with a distinguished attribute d. In the case of decision table the attributes belonging to A are called *conditional attributes* or simply *conditions* and d is called *decision.* We will further assume that the set of decision values is finite. The i-th *decision class* is a set of objects $C_i = \{o \in U : d(o) = d_i\}$, where d_i is the i-th decision value taken from the decision value set $V_d = \{d_1, ..., d_{|V_d|}\}$

A reduct is one of the most essential notions in rough sets. $B \subset A$ is a *reduct* of information system if it carries the same indiscernibility information as the whole A, and no proper subset of B has this property. In case of decision tables a *decision reduct* is a set of attributes $B \subset A$ such that it cannot be further reduced and carries the same indiscernibility information as the decision.

A *decision rule* is a formula of the form $(a_{i_1} = v_1) \wedge ... \wedge (a_{i_k} = v_k) \Rightarrow d = v_d$, where $1 \leq i_1 < ... < i_k \leq m$, $v_i \in V_{a_i}$. Atomic subformulae $(a_{i_1} = v_1)$ are called *conditions.* We say that the rule r is *applicable* to an object, or alternatively, an object *matches* a rule, if its attribute values satisfy the premise of the rule. With a rule we can connect some numerical characteristics such as *matching* and *support*, that help in determining rule quality (see [1, 2]).

By *cut* for an attribute $a_i \in A$, such that V_{a_i} is an ordered set we will denote a value $c \in V_{a_i}$. With the use of a cut we may replace the original attribute a_i with a new, binary attribute which depends on whether the original attribute value for an object is greater or lower than c (more in [10]).

Template of **A** is a propositional formula $\bigwedge(a_i = v_i)$ where $a_i \in A$ and $v_i \in V_{a_i}$. A generalised template is the formula of the form $\bigwedge(a_i \in T_i)$ where $T_i \subset V_{a_i}$. An object *satisfies* (matches) a template if for every attribute a_i occurring in the template the value of this attribute on the considered object is equal to v_i (belongs to T_i in case of a generalised template). The template induces in natural way the split of original information system into two distinct subtables. One of those subtables contains objects that satisfy the template, the other the remainder. Decomposition tree is a binary tree, whose every internal node is labelled by a certain template and external node (leaf) is associated with a set of objects matching all templates in a path from the root to the leaf (see [10]).

3 Contents of RSES v. 2.1

3.1 Input/Output Formats

During operation certain functions belonging to RSES may read and write information to/from files. Most of these files are regular ASCII files.

Slight changes from the previous RSES versions were introduced in the format used to represent the basic data entity i.e. the decision table. The new file format permits attributes to be represented with use of integer, floating point number or symbolic (text) value. There is also a possibility of using "virtual" attributes, calculated during operation of the system, for example derived as a linear combinations of existing ones. The file format used to store decision tables includes a header where the user specifies size of the table, the name and type of attributes. The information from header is visible to the user in the RSES GUI e.g., attribute names are placed as column headers when the table is being displayed.

RSES user can save and retrieve data entities such as rule sets, reduct sets etc. The option of saving the whole workspace (project) in a single file is also provided. The project layout together with underlying data structures is stored using dedicated, optimised binary file format.

3.2 The Algorithms

The algorithms implemented in RSES fall into two main categories.

First category gathers the algorithms aimed at management and edition of data structures. It covers functions allowing upload and download of data as well as derived structures, procedures for splitting tables, selecting attributes etc. There are also procedures that simplify preparation of experiments, such as an automated n fold cross-validation.

The algorithms for performing rough set based and classification operations on data constitute the second essential kind of tools implemented inside RSES.

Most important of them are:
Reduction algorithms i.e. algorithms allowing calculation of the collections of reducts for a given information system (decision table). In the version 2.1 the method for calculation of dynamic reducts (as in [1]) is added.
Rule induction algorithms. Several rule calculation algorithms are present. That includes reduct-based approaches (as in [2]) as well as evolutionary and covering methods (cf. [17, 8]). Rules may be based on both classical and dynamic reducts. Calculated rules are accompanied with several coefficients that are further used while the rules are being applied to the set of objects.
Discretisation algorithms. Discretisation permits discovery of cuts for attributes. By this process the initial decision table is converted to one described with simplified, symbolic attributes; one that is less complex and contains the same information w.r.t. discernibility of objects (cf. [1, 10]).
Data completion algorithms. As many real-life experimental data contains missing data, some methods for filling gaps in data are present in RSES. For more on data completion techniques see [9].
Algorithms for generation of new attributes. New attributes can be generated as linear combinations of existing (numerical) ones. Such new attributes can carry information that is more convenient in decision making. The proper linear combinations are established with use of methods based on evolutionary computing (cf. [4, 14]).
Template generation algorithms provide means for calculation of templates and generalised templates. Placed side by side with template generation are the procedures for inducing table decomposition trees (cf. [11]).
Classification algorithms used to determine decision value for objects with use of decision rules, templates and other means (cf. [1, 2, 11]). Two major new classification methods have been added in RSES version 2.1. They belong to the fields of instance-based learning and artificial neural networks, respectively. They are described in more detail further in this paper (Sections 4.1 and 4.2). The classification methods can be used to both verifying classifiers on a test sample with given decision value and classifying new cases for which we do not know decision value.

3.3 The RSES GUI

To simplify the use of RSES algorithms and make it more intuitive the RSES graphical user interface was further extended. It is directed towards ease of use and visual representation of workflow. Version 2.0 (previous one) undergone some face lifting. There are some new gadgets and gizmos as well. Project interface window has not change much (see Fig. 1). As previously, it consists of two parts. The visible part is the project workspace with icons representing objects created during our computation. Behind the project window there is the history window, reachable via tab, and dedicated to messages, status reports, errors and warnings. While working with multiple projects, each of them occupies a separate workspace accessible via tab at the top of workplace window.

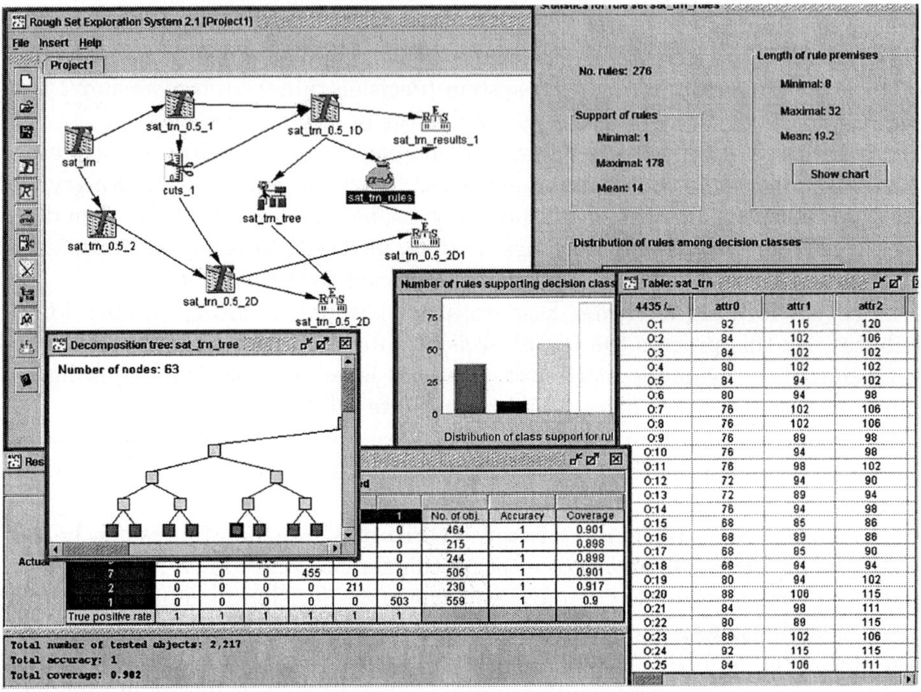

Fig. 1. The project interface window

It was designers' intention to simplify the operations on data within project. Therefore, the entities appearing in the process of computation are represented in the form of icons placed in the upper part of workplace. Such an icon is created every time the data (table, reducts, rules,...) is loaded from the file. User can also place an empty object in the workplace and further fill it with results of operation performed on other objects. Every object appearing in the project have a set of actions associated with it. By right-clicking on the object the user invokes a context menu for that object. It is also possible to invoke an action from the general pull-down program menu in the main window. Menu choices allow to view and edit objects as well as include them in new computations. In many cases a command from context menu causes a new dialog box to open. In this dialog box the user can set values of parameters used in desired calculation. If the operation performed on the object leads to creation of a new object or modification of existing one then such a new object is connected with edge originating in object(s) which contributed to its current state. Placement of arrows connecting icons in the workspace changes dynamically as new operations are being performed. In the version 2.1 the user has the ability to align objects in workspace automatically, according to his/her preferences (eg. left, horizontal, bottom).

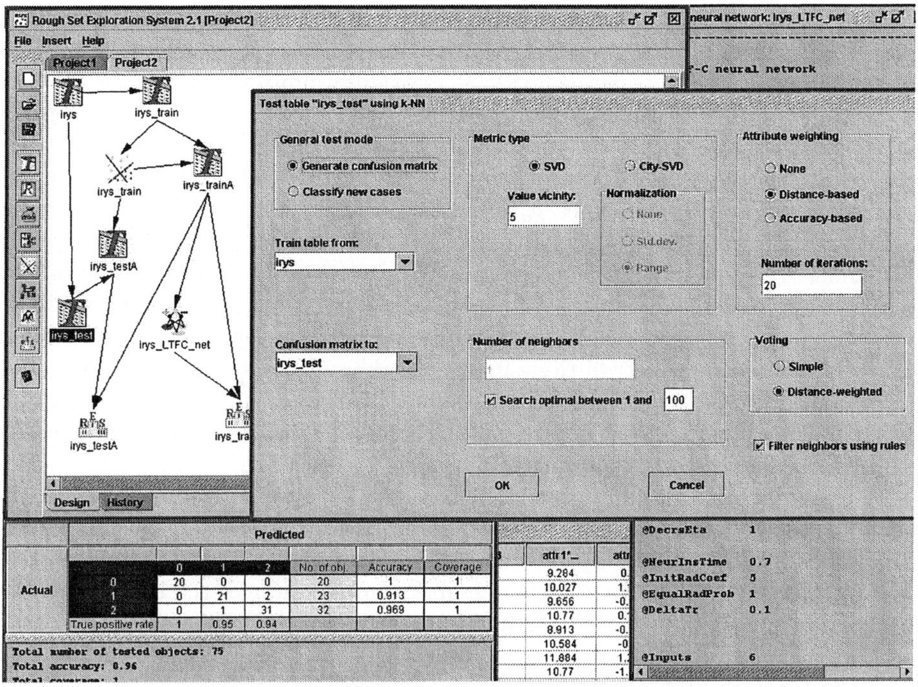

Fig. 2. Instance based classification in the RSES GUI

An important new GUI feature added in the version 2.1 is the possibility to display some statistical information about tables, rules and reducts in a graphical form (see Fig.1).

4 New Methods

In the current version two new classification methods have been added.

4.1 Instance Based Method

As an instance based method we implemented the special, extended version of the k nearest neighbours (k-nn) classifier [6]. First the algorithm induces a distance measure from a training set. Then for each test object it assigns a decision based on the k nearest neighbours of this object according to the induced distance measure.

The distance measure ρ for the k-nn classifier is defined as the weighted sum of the distance measures ρ_a for particular attributes $a \in A$:

$$\rho(x, y) = \sum_{a \in A} w_a \cdot \rho_a(a(x), a(y)).$$

Two types of a distance measure are available to the user. The City-SVD metric [5] combines the city-block Manhattan metric for numerical attributes with the Simple Value Difference (SVD) metric for symbolic attributes.

The distance between two numerical values $\rho_a(a(x), a(y))$ is the difference $|a(x) - a(y)|$ taken either as an absolute value or normalised with the range $a_{\max} - a_{\min}$ or with the doubled standard deviation of the attribute a on the training set. The SVD distance $\rho_a(a(x), a(y))$ for a symbolic attribute a is the difference between the decision distributions for the values $a(x)$ and $a(y)$ in the whole training set. Another metric type is the SVD metric. For symbolic attributes it is defined as in the City-SVD metric and for a numerical attribute a the difference between a pair of values $a(x)$ and $a(y)$ is defined as the difference between the decision distributions in the neighbourhoods of these values. The neighbourhood of a numerical value is defined as the set of objects with similar values of the corresponding attribute. The number of objects considered as the neighbourhood size is the parameter to be set by a user.

A user may optionally apply one of two attribute weighting methods to improve the properties of an induced metric. The distance-based method is an iterative procedure focused on optimising the distance between the training objects correctly classified with the nearest neighbour in a training set. The detailed description of the distance-based method is described in [15]. The accuracy-based method is also an iterative procedure. At each iteration it increases the weights of attributes with high accuracy of the 1-nn classification.

As in the typical k-nn approach a user may define the number of nearest neighbours k taken into consideration while computing a decision for a test object. However, a user may use a system procedure to estimate the optimal number of neighbours on the basis of a training set. For each value k in a given range the procedure applies the leave-one-out k-nn test and selects the value k with the optimal accuracy. The system uses an efficient leave-one-out test for many values of k as described in [7].

When the nearest neighbours of a given test object are found in a training set they vote for a decision to be assigned to the test object. Two methods of nearest neighbours voting are available. In the simple voting all k nearest neighbours are equally important and for each test object the system assigns the most frequent decision in the set of the nearest neighbours. In the distance-weighted voting each nearest neighbour vote is weighted inversely proportional to the distance between a test object and the neighbour. If the option of filtering neighbours with rules is checked by a user, the system excludes from voting all the nearest neighbours that produce a local rule inconsistent with another nearest neighbour (see [7] for details).

The k-nn classification approach is known to be computationally expensive. The crucial time-consuming task is searching for k nearest neighbours in a training set. The basic approach is to scan the whole training set for each test object. To make it more efficient an advanced indexing method is used [15]. It accelerates searching up to several thousand times and allows to test datasets of a size up to several hundred thousand of objects.

Table 1. Classification error of k-nn classifiers with the estimation of the optimal value of k from a training set

Nearest neighbors voting Filtering with rules			Simple No filtering		Dist-weighted No filtering		Simple Filtering		Dist-weighted Filtering	
Dataset	Trn set	Test set	est. k	error	est. k	error	est. k	error	est. k	error
segment	1 540	770	1	2,47%	1	2,47%	1	2,47%	4	2,73%
splice (DNA)	2 000	1 186	1	5,99%	1	5,99%	1	5,99%	1	5,99%
chess	2 131	1 065	1	2,45%	1	2,45%	1	2,45%	20	1,6%
satimage	4 435	2 000	5	9,45%	4	9,85%	5	9,45%	4	9,35%
mushroom	5 416	2 708	1	0%	1	0%	1	0%	1	0%
pendigits	7 494	3 498	1	2,84%	5	2,26%	1	2,84%	4	2,29%
nursary	8 640	4 320	13	1,95%	15	0,75%	19	0,91%	13	0,31%
letter	15 000	5 000	1	3,22%	5	2,92%	1	3,22%	8	2,82%
census94	30 162	15 060	27	15,95%	151	16,44%	76	16,27%	160	16,29%
shuttle	43 500	14 500	1	0,06%	3	0,06%	1	0,06%	2	0,05%

Table 1 presents the classification accuracy for 10 data sets from the UCI repository [21]. The data sets provided as a single file (*segment, chess, mushroom, nursery*) have been randomly split into a training and a test part with the ratio 2 to 1. The remaining data sets (*splice, satimage, pendigits, letter, census94, shuttle*) have been tested with the originally provided partition. In the experiment the City-SVD metric with the distance based attribute weighting method were used. We tested four k-nn based classifiers: all combinations of simple and distance weighted voting with and without filtering neighbours with rules. To make the results comparable all classifiers were tested with the same instance of a distance measure and the same partition for each data set. The values of k used in the experiments were selected from the range between 1 and 200 by the procedure delivered with the system.

The results from Table 1 show that the accuracy of the k-nn classifiers is comparable to other well-known classifiers like C5.0 [7]. The classification error is similar for different parameter setting but in general the k-nn with distance-weighted voting and rule-based filtering seems to have a little advantage over the k-nn classifiers with the other setting.

4.2 Local Transfer Function Classifier

Local Transfer Function Classifier (LTF-C) is a neural network solving classification problems [16]. Its architecture is very similar to this of Radial Basis Function neural network (RBF) or Support Vector Machines (SVM) – the network has a hidden layer with gaussian neurons connected to an output layer of linear units. There are some additional restrictions on values of output weights that enable to use an entirely different training algorithm and to obtain very high accuracy in real-world problems.

The training algorithm of LTF-C comprises four types of modifications of the network, performed after every presentation of a training object:

1. changing positions (means) of gaussians,
2. changing widths (deviations) of gaussians, separately for each hidden neuron and attribute,
3. insertion of new hidden neurons,
4. removal of unnecessary or harmful hidden neurons.

As one can see, the network structure is dynamical. The training process starts with an empty hidden layer, adding new hidden neurons when the accuracy is insufficient and removing the units which do not positively contribute to the calculation of correct network decisions. This feature of LTF-C enables automatic choice of the best network size, which is much easier than setting the number of hidden neurons manually. Moreover, this helps to avoid getting stuck in local minima during training, which is a serious problem in neural networks trained with gradient-descend.

LTF-C shows a very good performance in solving real-world problems. A system based on this network won the first prize in the EUNITE 2002 World Competition "Modelling the Bank's Client behaviour using Intelligent Technologies". The competition problem was to classify bank customers as either active or non-active, in order to predict if they would like to leave the bank in the nearest future. The system based on LTF-C achieved 75.5% accuracy, outperforming models based on decision trees, Support Vector Machines, standard neural networks and others (see [20]) .

LTF-C performs also very well in other tasks, such as handwritten digit recognition, breast cancer diagnosis or credit risk assessment (details in [16]).

5 Perspective

The RSES toolkit will further grow as new methods and algorithms emerge. More procedures are still coming from current state-of-the-art research. Most notably, the work on a new version of the RSESlib library of methods is well under way. Also, currently available computational methods are being integrated with DIXER - a system for distributed data processing.

The article reflects the state of software tools at the moment of writing, i.e. beginning of March 2004. For information on most recent developments visit the Web site [18].

Acknowledgement

Many persons have contributed to the development of RSES. In the first place Professor Andrzej Skowron, the supervisor of all RSES efforts from the very beginning. Development of our software was supported by grants 4T11C04024 and 3T11C00226 from Polish Ministry of Scientific Research and Information Technology.

References

1. Bazan, J.: A Comparison of Dynamic and non-Dynamic Rough Set Methods for Extracting Laws from Decision Tables, In [13], vol. 1, pp. 321–365
2. Bazan, J.G., Nguyen, S.H, Nguyen, H.S., Synak, P., Wróblewski, J.: Rough Set Algorithms in Classification Problem. In: Polkowski, L., Tsumoto, S., Lin, T.Y. (eds), Rough Set Methods and Applications, Physica-Verlag, Heidelberg, 2000 pp. 49–88.
3. Bazan, J., Szczuka, M.,: RSES and RSESlib - A Collection of Tools for Rough Set Computations. Proc. of RSCTC'2000, LNAI 2005, Springer-Verlag, Berlin, 2001, pp. 106–113
4. Bazan, J., Szczuka, M., Wróblewski, J.: A New Version of Rough Set Exploration System. Proc. of RSCTC'2002, LNAI 2475, Springer-Verlag, Berlin, 2002, pp. 397–404
5. Domingos, P.: Unifying Instance-Based and Rule-Based Induction. Machine Learning, Vol. 24(2), 1996, pp. 141–168.
6. Duda, R.O., Hart, P.E.: Pattern Classification and Scene Analysis, Wiley, New York, 1973.
7. Góra, G., Wojna, A.G.: RIONA: a New Classification System Combining Rule Induction and Instance-Based Learning. Fundamenta Informaticae, Vol. 51(4), 2002, pp. 369–390.
8. Grzymała-Busse, J.: A New Version of the Rule Induction System LERS. Fundamenta Informaticae, Vol. 31(1), 1997, pp. 27–39
9. Grzymała-Busse, J., Hu, M.: A Comparison of Several Approaches to Missing Attribute Values in Data Mining. Proc. of RSCTC'2000, LNAI 2005, Springer-Verlag, Berlin, 2001, pp. 340–347
10. Nguyen Sinh Hoa, Nguyen Hung Son: Discretization Methods in Data Mining. In [13] vol.1, pp. 451-482
11. Hoa S. Nguyen, Skowron, A., Synak, P.: Discovery of Data Patterns with Applications to Decomposition and Classfification Problems. In [13] vol.2, pp. 55-97.
12. Michie, D., Spiegelhalter, D.J., Taylor, C.C.: Machine Learning, Neural and Statistical Classification. Ellis Horwood, London, 1994
13. Skowron A., Polkowski L.(ed.): Rough Sets in Knowledge Discovery vol. 1 and 2. Physica-Verlag, Heidelberg, 1998
14. Ślęzak, D., Wróblewski, J.: Classification Algorithms Based on Linear Combinations of Features. Proc. of PKDD'99, LNAI 1704, Springer-Verlag, Berlin, 1999, pp. 548–553.
15. Wojna, A.G.: Center-Based Indexing in Vector and Metric Spaces. Fundamenta Informaticae, Vol. 56(3), 2003, pp. 285-310.
16. Wojnarski, M.: LTF-C: Architecture, Training Algorithm and Applications of New Neural Classifier. Fundamenta Informaticae, Vol. 54(1), 2003, pp. 89–105
17. Wróblewski, J.: Covering with Reducts - A Fast Algorithm for Rule Generation. Proceeding of RSCTC'98, LNAI 1424, Springer-Verlag, Berlin, 1998, pp. 402-407
18. Bazan, J., Szczuka, M.: The RSES Homepage, `http://logic.mimuw.edu.pl/~rses`
19. Ørn, A.: The ROSETTA Homepage, `http://www.idi.ntnu.no/~aleks/rosetta`
20. Report from EUNITE World competition in domain of Intelligent Technologies, `http://www.eunite.org/eunite/events/eunite2002/competitionreport2002.htm`
21. Blake, C.L., Merz, C.J.:UCI Repository of machine learning databases. Irvine, CA: University of California, 1998, `http://www.ics.uci.edu/~mlearn`

Discovering Maximal Frequent Patterns in Sequence Groups

J.W. Guan[1,2], David A. Bell[1], and Dayou Liu[2]

[1] School of Computer Science
The Queen's University of Belfast
BT7 1NN, Northern Ireland, U.K.
{j.guan,da.bell}@qub.ac.uk

[2] College of Computer Science and Technology
Jilin University
130012, Changchun, P.R. China
dyliu@mail.jlu.edu.cn

Abstract. In this paper, we give a general treatment for some kind of sequences such as customer sequences, document sequences, and DNA sequences, etc. Large collections of transaction, document, and genomic information have been accumulated in recent years, and embedded latently in it there is potentially significant knowledge for exploitation in the retailing industry, in information retrieval, in medicine and in the pharmaceutical industry, respectively. The approach taken here to the distillation of such knowledge is to detect strings in sequences which appear frequently, either within a given sequence (eg for a particular customer, document, or patient) or across sequences (eg from different customers, documents, or patients sharing a particular transaction, information retrieval, or medical diagnosis; respectively).

Keywords: Rough Sets, Data Mining, Sales Data, Document Retrieval, DNA sequences/profiles, Bioinformatics

Introduction

Progress in bar-code technology has made it possible for retail organisations to collect and store massive amounts of sales data. Large amounts of data are also being accumulated in information retrieval, biological and genomic information systems. For example, Celera reportedly maintains a 70 Tbyte database which grows by 15-20 gbytes every day. Another organization in the pharmaceutical industry is pooling 1 Tbyte of data at each of 4 sites and the volume doubles every 8-9 months. Making full use of this data to gain useful insights into, for example, health issues, presents a tremendous challenge and opportunity. For example, we can potentially inform diagnoses and treatments for the patient in a hospital by taking careful account of patterns in the DNA sequences in a group of a patient's genes. *Data mining* is the computer-based technique of discovering interesting, useful, and previously unknown patterns from massive

S. Tsumoto et al. (Eds.): RSCTC 2004, LNAI 3066, pp. 602–609, 2004.

databases (Frawley Piatetsky-Shapiro Matheus 1991) – such as those generated in gene expression. Exploiting the similarity between DNA sequences can lead to significant understanding in bioinformatics (Kiem Phuc 2000).

Patterns in a group of genes (DNA sequences) can be considered as phrases of a collection of documents (Kiem Phuc 2000). This suggests that text mining techniques (eg Feldman *et al* 1997, 1998, 1998a; Landau *et al* 1998) can be used for finding patterns and discovering knowledge about patterns, and ultimately ailments and treatments.

Mining sequential patterns is an attractive and interesting issue, there are various and extensive areas of exploration and application to which it is related. Some existing results for other applications can be extended to this area. For example, Srikant and Agrawal (1995-1996) have addressed and solved a general problem of finding maximal patterns from large datasets; Feldman *et al* (1997-1998) have investigated maximal association rules for mining for keyword co-occurrences in large document collection and proposed an integrated visual environment for text mining; etc. Here we present a genenal method to treat general sequences.

We develop general theory and algorithms for discovering patterns and maximal patterns systematically. The paper is organised as follows.

Section 1 introduces what we need to know of sequences, and the definition of frequent patterns in a group of sequences is presented in section 2. Theorems and Algorithm Appending for discovering patterns with certain support or levels of occurrence in the group of sequences are proposed in section 3. This section also proposes Algorithm Checking for finding higher support patterns with lower computational cost. Section 4 is to find maximal patterns.

1 Sequences and Containing Relations

Sequences appear in various data and convey information to be mined. Customer, document, and DNA sequences are examples. Investigation of sequences is on the containing relation between sequences, patterns from sequences.

Generally, sequences can be defined as follows. Given a non-empty set $\mathcal{B}$, we call elements in it as items. A *sequence* s over $\mathcal{B}$ is an ordered list of non-empty subsets of $\mathcal{B}$, expressed as $s = A_1A_2...A_n...A_N$, where $\emptyset \subset A_n \subseteq \mathcal{B}$ for $n = 1, 2, ..., N$ and $N > 0$.

We call N the *length* of sequence s and denote $|s| = N$. Let us denote the set of sequences over $\mathcal{B}$ as $\mathcal{S}_\mathcal{B}$ and denote the set of sequences over $\mathcal{B}$ with length N as $\mathcal{S}_{\mathcal{B},N}$.

Example 1.1 (*Customer sequences*). Consider a large database of customer transactions. Each transaction consists of three fields: transaction Date, customer Id, transaction Items. The following example is given in (Agrawal Srikant 1994).

Date	*Id*	*Items*
10/6/93	2	10, 20
12/6/93	5	90
15/6/93	2	30
20/6/93	2	40, 60, 70
25/6/93	4	30
25/6/93	3	30, 50, 70
25/6/93	1	30
30/6/93	1	90
30/6/93	4	40, 70
25/7/93	4	90

This database can be expressed as a group of customer sequences as follows.

Customers i	Sequences s_i	Length $\|s_i\|$
1	$\{30\}\{90\}$	2
2	$\{10,20\}\{30\}\{40,60,70\}$	3
3	$\{30,50,70\}$	1
4	$\{30\}\{40,70\}\{90\}$	3
5	$\{90\}$	1

where $\mathcal{B} = \{10, 20, 30, 40, 50, 60, 70, 90\}$.

Example 1.2 (*Document sequences*). Consider a large collection of documents. Each document consists of several fields: document Id, term Categories (e.g., country names, topics, people names, organisations, stock exchanges, etc.). The following example is given by Feldman et al in their paper (Feldman et al 1997) to investigate maximal association rules and mining for keywords co-occurrences in document collection, where collection D consists of 10 documents $d_1, d_2, ..., d_{10}$; and Categories T_1, T_2 are *countries, topics*; respectively.

$D\backslash 2^{T_k}$	$T_1 = countries$	$T_2 = topics$
d_1, d_2	$\{Canada, Iran, USA\}$	$\{crude, ship\}$
d_3	$\{USA\}$	$\{earn\}$
d_4, d_5	$\{USA\}$	$\{jobs, cpi\}$
d_6	$\{USA\}$	$\{earn, cpi\}$
d_7	$\{Canada\}$	$\{sugar, tea\}$
d_8, d_9	$\{Canada, USA\}$	$\{trade, acq\}$
d_{10}	$\{Canada, USA\}$	$\{earn\}$

Example 1.3 (*DNA sequences/Profiles*). Let $\mathcal{B}$ be the set of nucleotides A,C, G,T. Then, a sequence formed by singletons (one element subsets) is a DNA sequence (Kiem Phuc 2000, Bell Guan 2003, Guan Bell Liu 2003). For example, let $\mathcal{U} = \{u_1, u_2, u_3, u_4\}$, where

$u_1 = ACGTAAAAGTCACACGTAGCCCCACGTACAGT$,
$u_2 = CGCGTCGAAGTCGACCGTAAAAGTCACACAGT$,
$u_3 = GGTCGATGCACGTAAAATCAGTCGCACACAGT$,
$u_4 = ACGTAAAAGTAGCTACCCGTACGTCACACAGT$.

It is interesting that DNA sequences are usually used in scientific area of biology and medicine while DNA profiles are frequently used by journalists to report crime events.

Now, let us define some containing relations in $\mathcal{S}_{\mathcal{B}}$.

First of all, sequence $a = A_1A_2...A_n$ $(n > 0)$ is said to be *contained in* sequence $b = B_1B_2...B_m$ $(m > 0)$ and denoted by $a \preceq b$, if there exist n integers $1 \le i_1 < i_2 < ... < i_n \le m$ such that

$$A_1 \subseteq B_{i_1}, A_2 \subseteq B_{i_2}, ..., A_n \subseteq B_{i_n}.$$

In this case, we say that a is a *sub*-sequence of b and that b is a *super* sequence or an *extension* of a. Obviously, we have $|a| \le |b|$.

Usually, sequence $a = A_1A_2...A_n$ $(n > 0)$ is said to be usually *contained in* sequence $b = B_1B_2...B_m$ $(m > 0)$, if there exist n integers $1 \le i_1 < i_2 < ... < i_n \le m$ such that

$$A_1 = B_{i_1}, A_2 = B_{i_2}, ..., A_n = B_{i_n}.$$

In this case, we say that a is a usual *sub*-sequence of b and that b is a usual *super* sequence or *extension* of a.

In particular, the strong containing relation in $\mathcal{S}_{\mathcal{B}}$ means that sequence $A_1A_2...A_n$ is said to be strongly *contained in* sequence $B_1B_2...B_m$ and denoted by $A_1A_2...A_n \le B_1B_2...B_m$, if there exist n *contiguous* integers $1 \le i < i+1 < ... < i+n-1 \le m$ such that

$$A_1 = B_i, A_2 = B_{i+1}, ..., A_n = B_{i+n-1}.$$

In this case, we say that a is a strong *sub*-sequence of b and that b is a strong *super* sequence or *extension* of a.

For DNA sequences, we only consider the strong containing relation.

Given a sequence s, the set of sub-sequences of s is said to be the *language from* the sequence, denoted by $\mathcal{L}(s)$, which is equal to $\{v | v \preceq s, |s| > 0\}$. A sub-sequence of s is said to be a *pattern in* the sequence.

Let $\mathcal{U}$ be a group (set) of sequences, $\mathcal{U} = \{s_1, s_2, ..., s_k, ..., s_K\}, K = |\mathcal{U}|$. Denote $L = \max(|s_1|, |s_2|, ..., |s_k|, ..., |s_K|)$.

The union $\mathcal{L}(\mathcal{U}) = \cup_{k=1}^{K} \mathcal{L}(s_k) = \cup_{k=1}^{K} \{v | v \preceq s_k, |v| > 0\}$ is said to be the *language from* the group, denoted by $\mathcal{L}(\mathcal{U})$.

2 Frequent Patterns Contained in a Sequence Group

A particular sequence can be contained (or can "co-occur") in many sequences of a group as their common sub-sequence, i.e., common pattern.

First of all, for a sequence $w \in \mathcal{L}(\mathcal{U})$ in the language from group $\mathcal{U}$, we need to know how many sequences in $\mathcal{U}$ containing w. The number, denoted by t and so $t \le |\mathcal{U}| = K$, of such sequences is called its *support/occurrence number* and it is said to be a *t-support/occurrence* pattern. Of course, a t-support/occurrence pattern is a t'-support/occurrence pattern whenever $t' \le t$, and we prefer the number is a maximal one.

Furthermore, for a sequence $w \in \mathcal{L}(\mathcal{U})$ in the language from group $\mathcal{U}$, we need to know what sequences in $\mathcal{U}$ containing w. For a sequence $w \in \mathcal{L}(\mathcal{U})$ in the language from group $\mathcal{U}$, the sub-group (subset) of sequences in $\mathcal{U}$ containing w is $\{u \in \mathcal{U} | u \succeq w\}$, denoted by $w^{\mathcal{U}}$. Sub-group $w^{\mathcal{U}}$ consists of sequences in group $\mathcal{U}$ in which sequence w is contained, and is called the *support/occurrence group* of sequence w. So w is a $|w^{\mathcal{U}}|$-support/occurrence pattern. We also call w a $|w^{\mathcal{U}}|/|\mathcal{U}|$-*frequent* pattern.

In one word, for a given group $\mathcal{U}$ of sequences and a given pattern w, it is foremost to know its support/occurrence group $w^{\mathcal{U}}$ in $\mathcal{U}$. When a pattern w is given, we also want to indicate its its support/occurrence group $w^{\mathcal{U}}$ simultaneously. Therefore, a particular notation is necessarily introduced for patterns. We call this notation the *occurring notation* for patterns. In this notation, pattern w is written as $w\{w^{\mathcal{U}}\}$ with its support/occurrence group $w^{\mathcal{U}}$ added and detailed to indicate the group when $w^{\mathcal{U}} \subset \mathcal{U}$. Notice that, in this notation, a naked pattern w means that its support/occurrence group is the whole group $\mathcal{U}$, i.e., $w^{\mathcal{U}} = \mathcal{U}$. In this case, w is abbreviated from $w\mathcal{U}$.

Theorem 2.1. Let $\mathcal{U}$ be a group of sequences over $\mathcal{B}$. For two patterns $w, v \in \mathcal{L}(\mathcal{U})$, if $v \preceq w$ then $v^{\mathcal{U}} \supseteq w^{\mathcal{U}}$. That is, subsequence has super support/occurrence group, and super sequence has support/occurrence subgroup.

Generally, given a threshold $\tau > 0$, sequence $w \in \mathcal{L}(\mathcal{U})$ is called a τ-*frequent pattern* if $|w^{\mathcal{U}}|/|\mathcal{U}| \geq \tau$. Here τ is called the *minimum support rate* or *minimum frequency*, and w is said to be a pattern with minimum support (rate) τ or (Agrawal Srikant 1994, Kiem Phuc 2000).

Notice that $0 \leq |w^{\mathcal{U}}|/|\mathcal{U}| \leq 1$. Thus, a threshold τ should take a value satisfying $0 < \tau \leq 1$. Usually, τ is given by a percentage.

In this paper, the frequency of a pattern is defined as the support/occurrence rate of the pattern in the group of sequences. Repeatedly, we say pattern w is $|w^{\mathcal{U}}|$-support/occurrence or $|w^{\mathcal{U}}|/|\mathcal{U}|$-frequent.

The set of *τ-frequent patterns* with length l is denoted by $M(\mathcal{U}, \tau, l) = \{w \mid w \in \mathcal{L}(\mathcal{U}), |w^{\mathcal{U}}|/|\mathcal{U}| \geq \tau, |w| = l\}$, where $l \leq L$.

Denote $M(\mathcal{U}, \tau) = \cup_{l=1}^{L} M(\mathcal{U}, \tau, l)$.

3 Theorems for Finding Patterns

1-length patterns are called *units*. A 1-length pattern $w \in (2^{\mathcal{B}} - \{\emptyset\})$ is in $M(\mathcal{U}, \tau, 1)$ if and only if $|w^{\mathcal{U}}|/|\mathcal{U}| \geq \tau$.

Theorem 3. 1. $M(\mathcal{U}, k/|\mathcal{U}|, 1) = \{z \in (2^{\mathcal{B}} - \{\emptyset\}) \mid |z^{\mathcal{U}}| \geq k\}$.

2. In $M(\mathcal{U}, k/|\mathcal{U}|, l+1)$, every pattern w can be expressed as either left or right concatenation $w = zx$ or $w = yz$ of such a unit z that $z \in M(\mathcal{U}, k/|\mathcal{U}|, 1)$ and $x, y \in M(\mathcal{U}, k/|\mathcal{U}|, l)$.

Conversely, given $z \in M(\mathcal{U}, k/|\mathcal{U}|, 1)$ and $x, y \in M(\mathcal{U}, k/|\mathcal{U}|, l)$, their concatenation $w = zx$ or $w = yz$ is in $M(\mathcal{U}, k/|\mathcal{U}|, l+1)$ if its frequency is not decreased.

Algorithm Appending for constructing $\tau = k/|\mathcal{U}|$-frequent patterns

begin

1. Find all 1-length patterns in $M(\mathcal{U}, k/|\mathcal{U}|, 1)$ from $z \in (2^{\mathcal{B}} - \{\emptyset\})$ by checking its occurring/support group $|z^{\mathcal{U}}| \geq k$.

2. Find $M(\mathcal{U}, k/|\mathcal{U}|, l+1)$ from $M(\mathcal{U}, k/|\mathcal{U}|, l)$ as follows.

begin

For all patterns in $M(\mathcal{U}, k/|\mathcal{U}|, l)$ of length l keep concatenating either left or right with 1-length patterns z in $M(\mathcal{U}, k/|\mathcal{U}|, 1)$

For each resultant pattern w of length $l+1$ compute its support group $w^{\mathcal{U}}$

Add w to $M(\mathcal{U}, k/|\mathcal{U}|, l+1)$ if $|w^{\mathcal{U}}| \geq k$

end

end

In the case where there is nothing known at the beginning, Algorithm Appending is a possible way to construct k-support/occurrence patterns for a given k. However, its computational cost is rather high. Fortunately, there is an easier way to find higher occurrence patterns, when we know all k-support/occurrence patterns at the outset.

Algorithm Checking for finding higher occurrence patterns

For each pattern w in $M(\mathcal{U}, (k-1)/|\mathcal{U}|, l)$ of length l

check its support/occurrence group $w^{\mathcal{U}}$

add w to $M(\mathcal{U}, k/|\mathcal{U}|, l)$ if $|w^{\mathcal{U}}| \geq k$

4 Maximal Patterns

For the group of sequences $\mathcal{U}$ and its containing relation, there are two kinds of maximum to be considered: the first is maximal sequences over the group $\mathcal{U}$, the second is maximal patterns over the set of τ-frequent patterns for a given τ.

Given a threshold τ, in the set of τ-frequent patterns, we say that a τ-frequent pattern w is *maximal* if it cannot be τ-frequently extended further, i.e., if there is no τ-frequent pattern w' other than w such that $w' \succ w$. A maximal τ-frequent pattern is also called a τ-*key*. The set of τ-*keys* is denoted by $\max M(\mathcal{U}, \tau) = \max\{w | w \in M(\mathcal{U}, \tau)\}$.

Our conjecture is that keys play as an important role as that of the most important attributes and keys in databases and rough set theory, keywords and terms in text mining and information retrieval, etc. Therefore, our research on the mining of patterns focuses on keys.

All sub-sequences in a τ-key are τ-patterns that can be extended to the τ-key, and every τ-pattern can be extended to a τ-key.

Let the support group be set $\mathcal{U}$ of sequences $u_1, u_2, ..., u_K; K > 0$. A sequence u is called a *maximal sequence* in $\mathcal{U}$ if there is no other extension sequence of u; i.e., there is no other sequence u' in $\mathcal{U}$ such that $u' \succ u$. The set of maximal sequences in $\mathcal{U}$ is denoted by $\max(\mathcal{U}) = \max\{u | u \in \mathcal{U}\}$.

If u is a maximal sequence then $u^{\mathcal{U}} = \{u\}$, i.e., its support/occurrence group consists of itself alone. In fact, u occurs in sequence u, so $u \in u^{\mathcal{U}}$. Moreover, u cannot occurs in other sequence s so that $u \prec s$ since then s would be a further sequence extension of u to contradict the sequence maximum of u in $\mathcal{U}$.

Let us denote the set of maximal sequences in $\mathcal{U}$ by

$\max(\mathcal{U}) = \{u_{i_1}\{u_{i_1}\}, u_{i_2}\{u_{i_2}\}, ..., u_{i_k}\{u_{i_k}\}\}$, where $u_i\{u_i\}$ is sequence u_i expressed in the occurring notation $u_i\{u_i^{\mathcal{U}}\}$ with $u_i^{\mathcal{U}} = \{u_i\}$.

We suggest the following method to find maximal sequences in $\mathcal{U}$.

Algorithm Comparing

begin

Compare each sequence u in $\mathcal{U}$

with every sequence v in $\mathcal{U} - \{u\}$

to see if $u \prec v$

if not then u is maximal and put it into $\max(\mathcal{U})$.

end

Let the support group be $\mathcal{U} = \{u_1, u_2, ..., u_K\}, K > 0$. Then a pattern w is a $1/|\mathcal{U}|$-key if and only if w is a maximal sequence in $\mathcal{U}$. That is, $\max M(\mathcal{U}, 1/|\mathcal{U}|) = \max(\mathcal{U})$.

It is remarkable that keys for $\tau = 1/|\mathcal{U}|$ are very easy to find, whereas finding the set of patterns in $M(\mathcal{U}, 1/|\mathcal{U}|)$ is very complicated since its size is the biggest over all τ.

Notice that the complexity for computing $\max M(\mathcal{U}, 1/|\mathcal{U}|)$ is only $O(K(K-1)L^2)$ while that for computing $M(\mathcal{U}, 1/|\mathcal{U}|)$ is much greater up to

1. $O((2^{|\mathcal{B}|} - 1)^L KL^2)$ for customer sequences;
2. $O(4^L KL^2)$ for DNA sequences;
3. $O((2^{|T_1|} - 1)(2^{|T_2|} - 1)...(2^{|T_N|} - 1)KN^2)$ for document sequences.

So, to find maximal patterns of $\tau = 1/|\mathcal{U}|$ is rather easy. We now only need to find maximal patterns, keys, of $\tau = k/|\mathcal{U}|$ for $k \geq 2$.

We suggest the following method to find maximal patterns $\max M(\mathcal{U}, k/|\mathcal{U}|)$ for $k \geq 2$ based on the fact that $M(\mathcal{U}, k/|\mathcal{U}|)$ is obtained in hand:

Algorithm Comparing

begin

Compare each sequence w in $M(\mathcal{U}, k/|\mathcal{U}|)$

with every sequence v in $M(\mathcal{U}, k/|\mathcal{U}|) - \{w\}$

to see if $w \prec v$

if not then w is maximal and put it into $\max M(\mathcal{U}, k/|\mathcal{U}|)$

end

5 Summary and Future Work

We have given a general treatment for some kind of sequences such as customer sequences, document sequences, and DNA sequences, etc. We have presented algorithms based on theorems developed here to find maximal frequent patterns in sequences. Further work and applications to discover knowledge about patterns in sequences are currently in process.

References

1. Agrawal, R.; Srikant, R. 1994-1995, Mining sequential patterns, in *Proceedings of the 11th International Conference on Data Engineering, Taipei, Taiwan, March 1995; IBM Research Report RJ 9910, October 1994 (expanded version).*
2. Bell, D.A.; Guan, J. W. (1998). "Computational methods for rough classification and discovery", *Journal of the American Society for Information Science, Special Topic Issue on Data Mining,* Vol.49(1998), No.5, 403-414.
3. Bell, D.A.; Guan, J. W. 2003, "Data mining for motifs in DNA sequences", in G. Wang *et al* (ed.) *Proceedings of the 9th International Conference on Rough Sets, Fuzzy Sets, Data Mining and Granular Computing (RSFDGrC'2003),* Chongqing, China, October 19-22, 2003.
4. Feldman, R.; Aumann, Y.; Amir, A.; Zilberstain, A.; Kloesgen, W. Ben-Yehuda, Y. 1997, Maximal association rules: a new tool for mining for keyword co-occurrences in document collection, in *Proceedings of the 3rd International Conference on Knowledge Discovery (KDD 1997),* 167-170.
5. Frawley, W.J., Piatetsky-Shapiro, G., & Matheus, C.J. (1991). Knowledge discovery in databases: an overview. In G. Piatetsky-Shapiro, W.J. Frawley (eds). Knowledge Discovery in Databases (pp. 1-27). AAAI/MIT Press.
6. Guan, J. W. ; Bell, D. A. (1998), "Rough computational methods for information systems", *Artificial Intelligence – An International Journal,* Vol.105(1998), 77-104.
7. Kiem, H.; Phuc, D. 2000, "Discovering motif based association rules in a set of DNA sequences", in W. Ziarko & Y. Yao (ed.) *Proceedings of the Second International Conference on Rough Sets and Current Trends in Computing (RSCTC'2000),* Banff, Canada, October 16-19, 2000; 348-352. ISBN 0828-3494, ISBN 0-7731-0413-5
8. Pawlak, Z. (1991). Rough sets: theoretical aspects of reasoning about data. Kluwer.
9. Srikant, R.; Agrawal, R. 1995-1996, Mining sequential patterns: generalizations and performance improvements, in *Proceedings of the Fifth International Conference on Extending Database Technology (EDBT), Avignon, France, March 1996; IBM Research Report RJ 9994, December 1995 (expanded version).*

Fuzzy Taxonomic, Quantitative Database and Mining Generalized Association Rules

Hong-bin Shen[1], Shi-tong Wang[2,3], and Jie Yang[1]

[1] Institute of Image Processing & Pattern Recognition, Shanghai Jiaotong Univ. Shanghai, China, 200030
zjshenhongbin@yahoo.com.cn, jieyang@sjtu.edu.cn
[2] Dept. of Information, Southern Yangtse University, Jiangsu, China, 214036
[3] Dept. of Computing, HongKong Polytechnic University, HongKong

Abstract. Mining association rules and the relative knowledge from databases has been a focused topic in recent data mining fields. This paper focuses on the issue of how to mine generalized association rules from quantitative databases with fuzzy taxonomic structure, and a new fuzzy taxonomic quantitative database model has been proposed to solve the problem. The new model is demonstrated effective on a real-world databases.

Keywords: data mining, association rule, fuzzy taxonomic structure

1 Introduction

Data mining is a key step of knowledge discovery in large databases. Since algorithm Apriori for mining association rules was proposed by Agrawal etc [1], various efforts have been made to improve or to extend the algorithm [2–4]. In [3], J. Han and Y. Fu extended the algorithm Apriori to allow the discovery of the so-called generalized Boolean association rules that represent the relationships between basic data items, as well as between the items of higher levels of the taxonomic structure in the crisp taxonomic structure. A noticeable feature of their algorithm [3] is that different support thresholds were used for different levels of abstraction.

However, in many real world applications, the related taxonomic structures may not be necessarily crisp, rather, certain fuzzy taxonomic structures reflecting partial belonging of one item to another may pertain. For example, soybean may be regarded as both food plants and oil bearing crops, but to different degrees. In [5], Q. Wei and G. Chen addressed the problem of mining generalized Boolean association rules based on the fuzzy taxonomic structure.

As to our concern, the information in many, if not most, databases is not limited to categorical attributes, but also contains much quantitative data, and many scholars have proposed different definitions of quantitative association rules and the mining algorithms accordingly [3,6]. But unfortunately, all these researches are carried out based on crisp taxonomic structures. Therefore, how to mine generalized quantitative association rules based on fuzzy taxonomic structure is a heated problem needed to be solved. In this paper, we will propose a new specific fuzzy taxonomic quantitative database model, based on which, the approach to mine generalized quantitative association rules will be discussed. Moreover, we will introduce the concept of

S. Tsumoto et al. (Eds.): RSCTC 2004, LNAI 3066, pp. 610–617, 2004.

multiple minimum supports into fuzzy taxonomic quantitative database model, and will present a new adaptive method to compute minimum support threshold with regard to different itemsets of the fuzzy taxonomic quantitative database.

2 On Fuzzy Taxonomic Structure

Association rules express the relationships between attributes. Often, there are multiple levels of abstraction among the attributes of the databases, such as pen $\prec$ stationary, shirt $\prec$ clothes.

Definition 1. A concept hierarchy H is defined on one or a set of attribute domains. Suppose a hierarchy H is defined on a set of domains $D_i,...,D_k$, in which different levels of concepts are organized into a hierarchy using partial order: $H_l : D_i \times ... \times D_k \Rightarrow H_{l-1} \Rightarrow ... \Rightarrow H_0$, where H_l represents the set of concepts at the primitive level, H_{l-1} stands for the concepts at one level higher than those at H_l, etc., and H_0 is the highest level.

Then a concept hierarchy consists of a set of nodes organized in partial order. A node is a leaf node if it has no child, or a nonleaf node otherwise.

Definition 2. A crisp taxonomic structure H is a concept hierarchy and every node in H has only one parent node, that is to say, every node belongs to its parent node with degree 1.

Definition 3. A fuzzy taxonomic structure H is a concept hierarchy and one or more nodes in H have at least two parent nodes, and $\sum_y \mu_{xy} = 1$ is satisfied for each node x, where y is the parent of x, and μ_{xy} is the degree of x belonging to its parent node y.

Fig.1 shows a simple example of the crisp taxonomic structure and Fig.2 is an example of the fuzzy taxonomic structure.

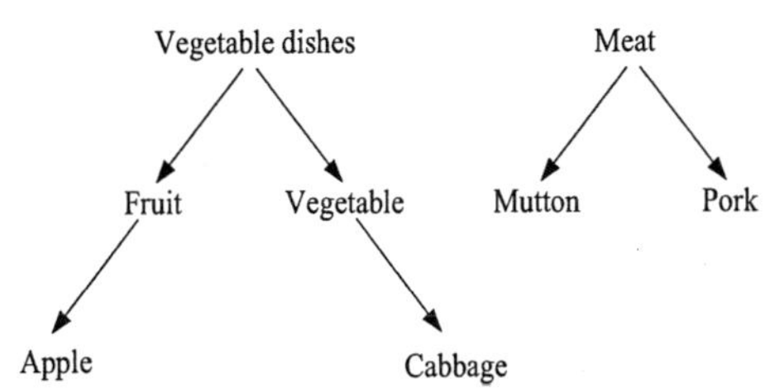

Fig. 1. An example of crisp taxonomic structure.

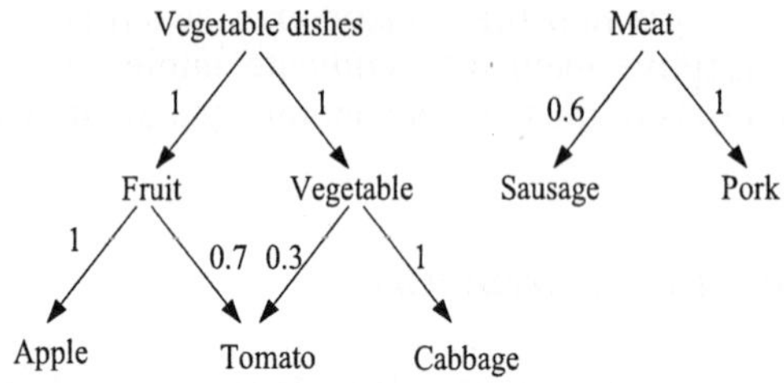

Fig. 2. An example of Fuzzy taxonomic structure.

3 A New Fuzzy Taxonomic Quantitative Database Model

In the case of mining generalized quantitative association rules, the measure for counting the support degree of nonleaf-nodes used in [7] is hardly applied, due to the different definitions between quantitative association rules and Boolean ones. Quantitative association rules are defined on the limited intervals of domain of every numeric attribute [5], so it is hard to decide the degree and which interval of the items at higher concept level every record should support using the method in [7]. Therefore, two problems below should be effectively solved while mining generalized quantitative association rules with fuzzy taxonomic structure.

1) How to decide the confidence degree of every nonleaf-nodes with fuzzy taxonomic structure.
2) How to count the support degree of every interval of the nonleaf-nodes.

For these purposes, we will address a new computation function below to determine the confidence degree of nonleaf-nodes in a fuzzy taxonomic structure, and a new fuzzy taxonomic quantitative database model is also proposed, based on which, we can easily count the support degree of every interval of the nonleaf-nodes, and generalized quantitative association rules can accordingly be generated.

As the fuzzy taxonomic structure only represents the partial degrees of the edges, the confidence degree μ_x of attribute-node x (nonleaf-node) needs to be newly derived based on fuzzy reasoning theory [8]. Specially, we take

$$\mu_x = \underset{\forall y}{\otimes}\left\{ \underset{\forall l:x\to y}{\oplus} \left(\underset{\forall e on l}{\otimes} \mu_{le} \right) \right\} \tag{1}$$

where x is an attribute node(nonleaf-node) , y is a leaf-node that can be reached from x , $l:x\to y$ is one of the accesses(paths) of attribute-node x and y , e on l is one of the edges on access l , μ_{le} is the degree on the edge e on l . Operator $\oplus$ stands for *max* operator, $\otimes$ for *min*.

For a leaf-node, its confidence degree is 1,and the confidence degree for every nonleaf-node can be obtained according to the formula (1).

Definition 4. Suppose the original quantitative database T is the form as $I_1 \times I_2 \times \cdots \times I_n = \{(d_1, d_2, \cdots, d_n) \mid d_i \in D_i, i = 1,2,\cdots,n\}$, where $I_1, I_2, \cdots, I_n \in I$, I is the set of attributes of T , $n = |I|$, D_i is the domain of I_i . Given a fuzzy taxonomic structure H and if the following partial order ($\prec$) exists:

$$I_l(\mu_{lP}), I_r(\mu_{rP}), \cdots, I_k(\mu_{kP}) \prec P, I_v(\mu_{vQ}), I_f(\mu_{fQ}), \cdots, I_j(\mu_{jQ}) \prec Q, \cdots\cdots$$
$$P(\mu_{PF}), \cdots, Q(\mu_{QF}) \prec F, \cdots\cdots$$

where μ_{mn} denotes the degree of node m belonging to node n, if there is no path between m and n, μ_{mn} =0,and P, Q denotes the nodes at the closest higher level than those at primitive level, F denotes the node at higher level than P, Q and so on. Then we define a new database model T' as follows:

$I_1(\mu_1) \times I_2(\mu_2) \times \cdots \times I_n(\mu_n) \times P(\mu_P) \times Q(\mu_Q) \times \cdots \times F(\mu_F) \times \cdots = \{(d_1(\mu_1), d_2(\mu_2), \cdots, d_n(\mu_n), d_P(\mu_P), d_Q(\mu_Q), \cdots, d_F(\mu_F), \cdots) \mid d_i \in D_i, i = 1,2,\cdots,n, d_P \in D_P, d_Q \in D_Q, \cdots, d_F \in D_F \cdots\}$, where $D_i, i=1,2,\cdots,n$ has the same meaning as above, D_P is the domain of d_P, and $d_P = d_l + d_r + \cdots + d_k$ ($\mu_{iP} \neq 0$, $i = l, r, \cdots, k$), D_Q is the domain of d_Q, and $d_Q = d_v + d_f + \cdots + d_j$ ($\mu_{iQ} \neq 0$, $i = v, f, \cdots, j$), D_F is the domain of d_F, and $d_F = \sum_i d_i$,where $d_i (i \in n)$ is the value of the leaf-node attribute I_i that can be reached from nonleaf-node F. For leaf-nodes, the confidence degree μ =1, and the confidence degree μ for nonleaf-nodes can be obtained from the formula (1). The new database model T' will be called the fuzzy taxonomic quantitative database model.

Table 2 shows the fuzzy taxonomic quantitative database of table 1 according to the fuzzy taxonomic structure shown in Fig.2.

Table 1. Original database.

RID	Apple	Tomato	Cabbage	Sausage	Pork
1	15	18	29	30	81
2	26	57	46	21	24

Table 2. Fuzzy taxonomic quantitative database of Table 1.

RID	Apple (1.0)	......	Pork (1.0)	Fruit (0.7)	Vegetable (0.3)	Meat (0.6)	Vegetable dishes (0.7)
1	15	......	81	33	47	111	62
2	26	......	24	83	103	45	129

Based on the discussion above, to extend the original quantitative database to a fuzzy taxonomic quantitative database, we must compute the confidence degrees μ of each itemset and the domain value V for the itemsets of higher levels of abstraction. For instance, because apple is a leaf-node item, so the confidence degree is μ (apple)=1.0. Similarly, the confidence degree of fruit and vegetable dishes can be obtained using function (1) as below:

μ (fruit)=min(1.0,0.7)=0.7, μ (vegetable dishes)=*min*(*min*(1.0,1.0), *max*(*min* (1.0, 0.7), *min*(1.0,0.3)), *min*(1.0,1.0))=0.7. For the first record of Table 2, V (vegetable dishes)= V (apple)+ V (tomato)+ V (cabbage)= 15 + 18 + 29 = 62.

4 Mining Generalized Quantitative Association Rules from Fuzzy Taxonomic Quantitative Database

4.1 Partitioning Numeric Attributes Dynamically

To simplify the problem of mining quantitative association rules, a feasible method is to map this problem into the problem of mining Boolean association rules. Therefore, quantitative association rule should be appropriately defined. A type of definition based on intervals of the domain of numeric attribute was introduced by Srikant R,etc [9]. The key idea of such a definition is to partition the domain of every numeric attribute into several intervals according to some proper methods [5,10]. For example, if the domain of the attribute apple in Table 1 is [7,26], suppose we can partition the domain into two intervals: <apple:7…16>, <apple:17…26>, then each of the two intervals is regarded as a Boolean attribute. After all the numeric attributes are partitioned into intervals, a database only containing Boolean attributes (intervals) can be obtained, and based on the new database, $\sum count$ operator [7] may be used to sum the total support degree of all the itemsets. Each record in the new database supports every interval with degree μ ($0<\mu\leq 1$), which equals to the confidence degree of the interval, 1 for leaf-node attribute and for nonleaf-node attribute, μ can be computed from formula (1), e.g. μ (<apple:7…16>)=1.0, μ (<fruit:14…40>)=0.7. Specially, while computing the confidence degree of an itemset containing more than one interval, the confidence degree of such an itemset is equal to the minimum confidence degree of all the intervals. e.g., if an itemset *A* contains two intervals, such as <apple:7…16>,<fruit:14…40>,then:

μ (*A*)=*min*(μ (<apple:7…16>), μ (<fruit:14…40>))=*min*(1.0,0.7)=0.7.

4.2 Selecting Minimum Support Threshold Adaptively

After extending the original quantitative database to the fuzzy taxonomic quantitative database, the leaf-node attributes will be of the same importance with the attributes of higher level, the only difference is that every record will support the intervals of leaf-node attributes with degree 1, but μ ($0<\mu\leq 1$) for the intervals of nonleaf- node attributes. That is to say, the support degree of an interval is related with its confidence degree. The larger confidence degree, the greater the total final support degree. Therefore, the minimum support threshold for the itemsets with larger confidence degree should be greater than those with lower confidence degree. Considering this, we propose a new minimum support threshold select function below to compute the minimum support threshold for different itemsets in fuzzy taxonomic quantitative database model. We define:

$$minsup(t) = \gamma - ((\gamma - \kappa)\times(1-\mu)) \quad (2)$$

where t is an itemset containing one or more intervals, γ is the user-defined upper-minimum support, κ is the user-defined lower-minimum support, μ is the confidence degree of the itemset.

Theorem 1. function (2) increases monotonically with μ

Proof: Suppose there are two itemsets: t_1, t_2, and the condition $1 \geq \mu_1 > \mu_2 > 0$ is satisfied, where μ_1 is the confidence degree of t_1, μ_2 is the confidence degree of t_2, therefore, $1-\mu_1 < 1-\mu_2$. Because γ and κ are constants, we can obtain the following result easily: $(\gamma-\kappa)\times(1-\mu_1) < (\gamma-\kappa)\times(1-\mu_2)$,
then $\gamma-((\gamma-\kappa)\times(1-\mu_1)) > \gamma-((\gamma-\kappa)\times(1-\mu_2))$ □

In terms of theorem 1, with the increasing of μ, the minimum support threshold increases accordingly. For example, if we set γ=0.5, κ=0.2, then we can compute the minimum support threshold of the itemset *A* using function (2), i.e.
minsup(*A*) = 0.5-((0.5-0.2)×(1.0-0.7))=0.41. Similarly, we can select the minimum support threshold adaptively according to the confidence degrees of different itemsets.

5 Experimental Study

In order to study the effectiveness of the fuzzy taxonomic quantitative database model discussed above, we take the testbed consisting of a realistic Chinese databases DB. DB is the database of Yield of Major Farm Crops of China from 1985 to 1999. There are 20 attributes and 448 records in DB and the fuzzy taxonomic structure of DB is shown in Fig.3.

We firstly extend the original quantitative database to the fuzzy taxonomic quantitative database, then partition the new database using the method introduced in [9,10]. Experimental results show that different types of association rules can be obtained using the new fuzzy taxonomic quantitative database with relative small cost. Table 3 shows some of the interesting rules obtained. For instance, for the rule: fruit [3628.0 ,528594.8] ⇒ wheat [1.0 ,280.9], *sup*=0.39, *conf*=0.66, it means if the output of fruit is between 3628.0 and 528594.8 tons, the output of wheat will be between 1.0 and 280.9 tons, and the support degree of this rule is 0.39, the confidence degree of this rule is 0.66,and this is a cross-level rule. Such a rule is very useful to decisioners, when they want to limit the output of wheat between 1.0 and 280.9 tons this year because a great deal is left from several previous years, controlling the planting area of fruit to limit the output of it between 3628.0 and 528594.8 tons is an effective way.

6 Conclusions

In this paper, we present a new fuzzy taxonomic quantitative database model for mining generalized quantitative association rules with fuzzy taxonomic structures. The approach of counting the support degree is discussed, furthermore, a new minimum support threshold select function was proposed according to the confidence degree of different itemsets, so that the minimum support can be selected adaptively.

A real-life database is used to test the new model, and the experimental results have shown the flexibility and validity of the new fuzzy taxonomic quantitative database model.

Table 3. Part of the interesting generalized quantitative association rules mined from DB.

ID	Generalized rules	Sup	Conf	Rules type
1	fruit[3628.0 ,528594.8] ⇒ wheat [1.0 ,280.9]	0.39	0.66	Cross-level rule
2	rice[465.1,2495.8] ∧ citrus [199.0,2120078.0] ⇒ tea[27.0 ,118157.2]	0.36	0.97	Leaf-level rule
3	Oil-bearing crops[0.1 ,324874.9] ⇒ fruit[3628.0 ,528594.8]	0.26	0.74	Abstraction-Level rule

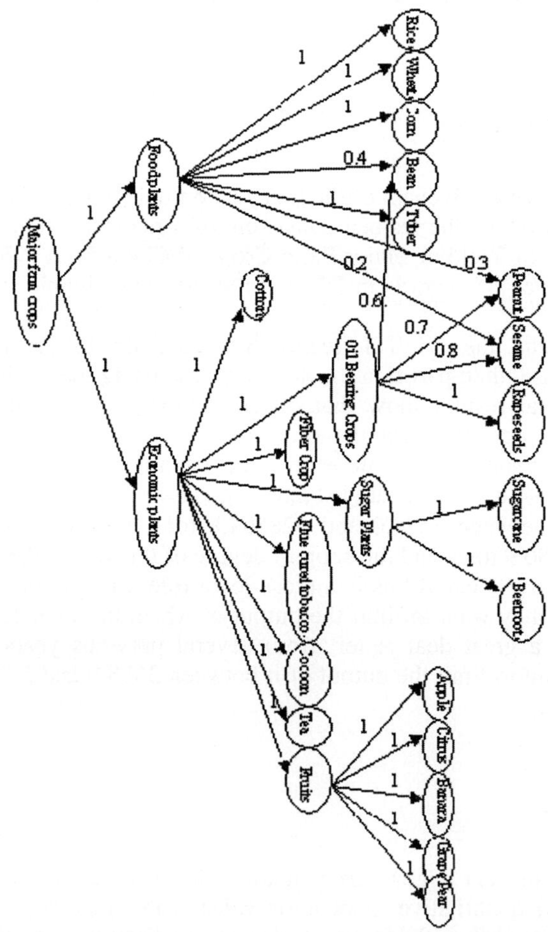

Fig. 3. The fuzzy taxonomic structure information of DB.

References

1. R.Agrawal, T.Imielinski and A.Swami. Mining association rules between sets of items in large databases. In Proc. Of the 1993 ACM SIGMOD Intl. Conference on Management of Data,(1993) 207~216.
2. Rakesh Agrawal, Heikki Mannila, Ramakrishnan Srikant, hannu Toivonen,A. Inkeri Verkamo. Fast Discovery of Association Rules. In Advances in Knowledge Discovery and Data Mining , AAAI Press/ The MIT Press, (1996) 307~328.
3. Jiawei Han and Yongjian Fu. Mining Multiple-Level Association Rules In Large Databases. IEEE Transaction on knowledge and Data Engineering, September, 5(11) (1999) 798~805.
4. Savasere, E.Omiecinski, S.Navathe. An Efficient Algorithm for Mining Association Rules in Large Databases.In Proceedings of the VLDB Conference, Zurich, Switzerland, September (1995).
5. C.L.Lui. Mining generalized association rules in fuzzy taxonomic structures. PHD thesis, Hong Kong Polytechnic University, (2001).
6. Y. Aumann and Y. Lindell. A statistical theory for quantitative association rules. In Proceedings of the fifth ACM SIGKDD international conference on Knowledge discovery and data mining, San Diego, CA, USA, August (1999) 15~18.
7. Qiang Wei, Guoqing Chen. Mining Generalized Association Rules with Fuzzy Taxonomic Structures. In Proceedings of the North America Fuzzy Information Processing Society (NAFIPS99), New York, (1999) 477~481.
8. Shitong Wang. Fuzzy Inference Theory and Fuzzy Expert System. Shanghai Science and Technology publisher. (1994).
9. Srikant R, Agrawal R. Mining quantitative association rules in large relational tables. In Proceedings of the ACM SIGMOD Conference on Management of Data. (1996).
10. Han J, Fu Y. Dynamic generation and refinement of concept hierarchies for knowledge discovery in databases. In Proceedings of the KDD'94, Seattle ,WA ,(1994) 157~168.

Pattern Mining for Time Series Based on Cloud Theory Pan-concept-tree

Yingjun Weng and Zhongying Zhu

Department of Automation, Shanghai Jiaotong University, Shanghai 200030, China
{Stephen_weng,zyzhu}@sjtu.edu.cn

Abstract. One important series mining problems is finding important patterns in larger time series sets. Two limitations of previous works were the poor scalability and the robustness to noise. Here we introduce a algorithm using symbolic mapping based on concept tree. The slope of subsequence is chosen to describe series data. Then, the numerical data is transformed into low dimension symbol by cloud models. Due to characteristic of the cloud models, the loss of data in the course of linear preprocessing is treated. Moreover, it is more flexible for the local noise. Second, cloud Boolean calculation is realized to automatically produce the basic concepts as the leaf nodes in pan-concept-tree which leads to hierarchal discovering of the knowledge .Last, the probabilistic project algorithm was adapted so that comparison among symbols may be carried out with less CPU computing time. Experiments show strong robustness and less time and space complexity.

1 Introduction

Recently, there has been much work on adapting data mining algorithms to time series databases. There exists a vast body of works on efficiently locating *known* patterns in time series [1-2]. Here, however, we must be able to *discover* them without any prior knowledge about the regularities of the data under study. Moreover, these methods discover some form of patterns that are application specific, scalability is not addressed, and more importantly they completely disregard the problem of noise. The importance of noise when attempting to discover patterns cannot be overstated. Even small amounts of noise can dominate distance measures, including the most commonly used data mining distance measures, such as the Euclidean distance. Robustness to such situations is non-trivial.

In this paper, we introduce a novel time- and space-efficient algorithm to discover *matching* patterns. Our method is based on a recent algorithm for pattern discovery in DNA sequences [3]. The intuition behind the algorithm is to project the data objects (in our case, time series), onto lower dimensional subspaces, based on a randomly chosen subset of the objects features. Before obtaining trend of series, we do linear boundary reduction (LBR), which results in dismissing some raw data. The symbolic representation, in this paper, is based on the cloud models, which allows for linguistic symbol expression for features (slope) of segments. Moreover it can solve dismissing as it supports the randomness and fuzziness integration on boundary.

S. Tsumoto et al. (Eds.): RSCTC 2004, LNAI 3066, pp. 618–623, 2004.

2 Definitions

Here we generalize the definition to allow for matching under the presence of noise, and to eliminate a special, degenerate case of a pattern.

***Definition* 1 *Match*:** Given a positive real number R (called *range*) and a time series T containing a subsequence C beginning at position p and a subsequence M beginning at q, if distance measure $D(C, M) \leq R$, then M is called a *matching* subsequence of C.

Whereas one can observe that the best matches to a subsequence (apart from itself) tend to be located one or two points to the left or the right of the subsequence in question. Intuitively, any definition of pattern should exclude the possibility of over-counting these trivial matches, which we define more concretely below.

***Definition* 2 *Trivial Match*:** Given a time series T, containing a subsequence C beginning at position p and a matching subsequence M beginning at q, we say that M is a *trivial match* to C if either $p = q$ or there does not exist a subsequence M' beginning at q' such that $Dist\ (C, M') > R$, and either $q < q' < p$ or $p < q' < q$.

We can now define the problem of enumerating the K most significant patterns in a time series.

***Definition* 3 *K-Pattern* (*n, R*):** Given a time series T, a subsequence length n and a range R, the most significant pattern piecewise in T (hereafter called the *1-Pattern* (*n, R*)) is the subsequence C_1 that has highest count of non-trivial matches (ties are broken by choosing the pattern whose matches have the lower variance). The Kth most significant pattern in T is the subsequence C_K that has the highest count of non-trivial matches, and satisfies $D(C_K, C_i) > 2R$, for all $1 \leq i < K$.

Note that this definition forces the set of subsequences in each match to be mutually exclusive. This is important because otherwise two matches might share the majority of their elements, and thus be essentially the same.

3 Symbolic Pan-concept-trees

Follow [4] the slope of line reflects the series tendency. But it still has some shortcoming. First, the LBR algorithm using linear regression may produce a very disjointed linking on series data. Thus, the interval between piecewise segments would be the place that raw data lost.

It is obviously that the representation becomes an essential and fundamental issue. Compatibility clouds theory offers a flexible path to integrate qualitative and quantitative knowledge [5]. In view of this theorem, the concept of linguistic variable provides a means of approximate linguistic concepts, which are not amenable to description in precise quantitative terms such as time series and etc. We use the cloud to construct a slope concept tree whose nodes are linguistic variables describing segments' trend [6]. These linguistic variables are consisted of a set of linguistic atoms A_i (E_{xi}, E_{ni}, H_{ei}), i. e.

$$A = \{A_1(Ex_1, En_1, He_1), \cdots\cdots, A_m(Ex_m, En_m, He_m)\} \tag{1}$$

Where $A_i(i=1,\ldots\ldots,m)$ is concept atom represented by cloud models. According to the cloud generator algorithm, we can produce many drops of cloud corresponding to different slope breakpoints. Figure1 shows the transformation.

$$A_{level1} = \{Down, Normal, Up\}$$
$$A_{level2} = \{Sharp-Down, Mid-Down, Gentle-Down, Normal, Gentle-Up, Mid-Up, Sharp-Up\} \quad (2)$$

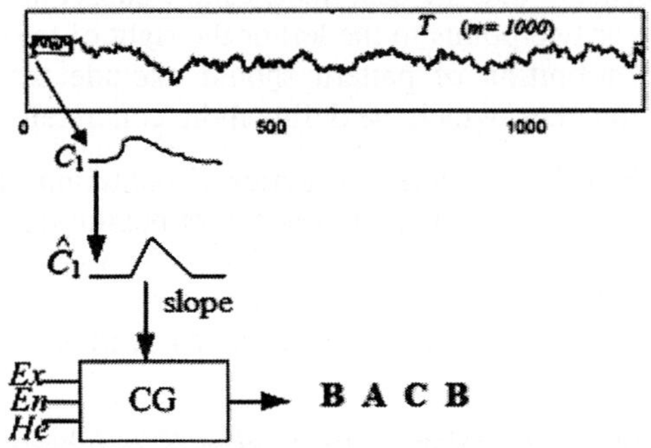

Fig. 1. Symbolic representation of subsequence shape.

Concept hierarchy plays a fundamentally important role in data mining. Through automatically generating the concept hierarchies, the mining efficacy is improved, and the knowledge is discovered at different abstraction levels. In this paper, the Boolean calculation of cloud models is used to generate the concept hierarchies, that is, cloud transform is realized to automatically produce the basic numerical concepts as the leaf nodes in pan-concept tree [7]. Figure 2 shows a two-level pan-concept tree instance.

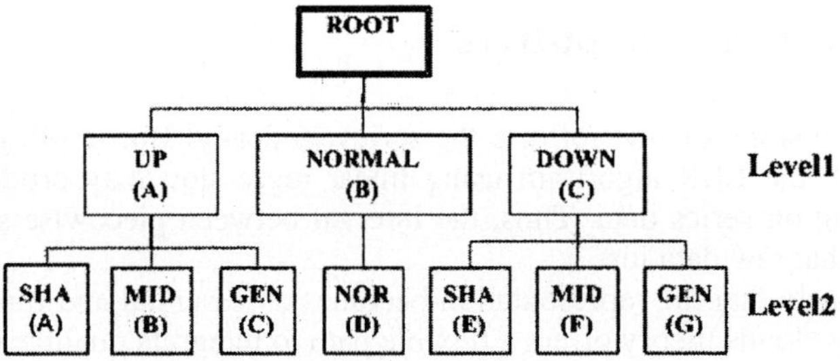

Fig. 2. Concept tree for slope representation.

It seems that one slope value may be mapped to several memberships, so that we only choose the corresponding concept that has the biggest membership. After these, the raw series data are transferred into qualitative representation by linguistic concept. These processing reduce subsequences from N dimensions to m dimensions, the data is dimensionality-reduced representation. After transformed a time series into the linguistic variable representation, we eventually obtain a discrete representation for subsequences of time series.

Definition 4 *Word*: A subsequence C of length N can be represented as a *word* $\hat{C} = \hat{C}_1, \cdots \hat{C}_m$. Then the mapping from linguistic variable to a word is obtained as corresponding alphabet shown in Fig. 2.

4 Projection Searching Algorithm

Our pattern discovery algorithm is best elucidated step by step.

***Step* 1:** extracting subsequences using a sliding window across raw data, converting them into symbolic form as Fig.2, and placing them into matrix S. Note that each row index of points backs to the original location of the subsequence.

***Step* 2:** We randomly select 2 columns of S to act as a mask as shown in Fig.3. If two words corresponding to subsequences i and j are hashed to the same bucket, we increase the count of cell (i,j) in a *matching score matrix*, which has been previously initialized to all zeros.

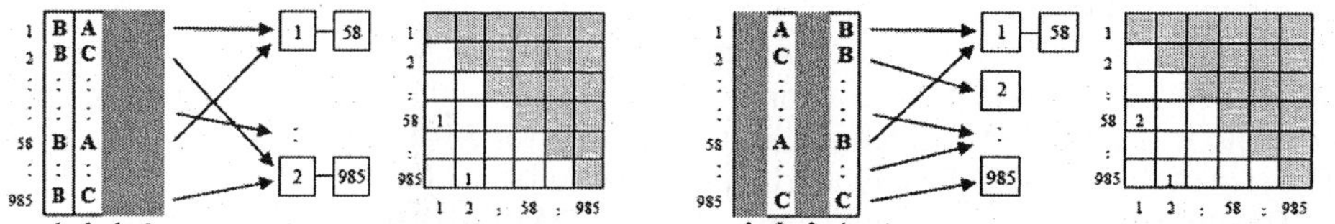

Fig. 3. Random matching and matching score matrix.

***Step* 3:** Repeating the process an appropriate number of times. It is important to note that the buckets cannot be reused at different iteration. We examine the matching matrix. If the entries in matrix were relatively uniform, it would suggest that there are no patterns to be found in our dataset. But if there have some significant values in the matching matrix, the clue of matching segments has been found out.

We can stop when the largest value in the matching matrix is no greater than we would have expected by chance. In order to do this we need to be able to calculate what values we should expect to find in the *matching score matrix*, assuming there are no patterns, for any given set of parameters. Following [4], we observe that given two randomly-generated words of size m over an linguistic atom number l, the probability that they match with up to errors is

$$p(l, m, \varepsilon) = \sum_{i=0}^{\varepsilon} C_i^m \left(\frac{l-1}{l}\right)^i \left(\frac{1}{l}\right)^{m-i} \tag{3}$$

The equation (4) assumes that each symbol of the variable has equal probability, which is guaranteed by our discrete procedure. Since random string projection is a locality-sensitive hashing scheme in the sense defined by, we have the probability of two words of projecting to the same value as

$$q(m, \varepsilon, t) = \sum_{i=0}^{\varepsilon} \left(1 - \frac{i}{m}\right)^t \tag{4}$$

where t is the length of the projected string. We conclude that if we have k random strings of size n, an entry of the similarity matrix will be hit on average times in each step of iteration.

$$Expect = C_2^k \sum_{i=0}^{\varepsilon} \left(1 - \frac{i}{m}\right)^t C_t^m \left(\frac{l-1}{l}\right)^i \left(\frac{1}{l}\right)^{m-i} \tag{5}$$

***Step* 4:** retrieving the two original time series subsequences corresponding to the indices of the largest value cell in our matching matrix. We can measure the distance between them. Assuming that the two sequences are within R of each other, they form a tentative pattern. However there may be other subsequences which are also within R of the subsequences, and thus need to be added to this provisional pattern.

***Step* 5:** Once discovering all matching subsequences within R, we can report them to the user, and begin iteratively examining the *matching score matrix* for the next largest value which has not been previously examined, and which is not within R of a previously reported pattern.

The *matching score matrix* also appears to be quite demanding in terms of space requirements. In general, however, we can expect it to be extremely sparse, and thus worth the slight time overhead to implement it as a sparse matrix. In the worst case, the number of cells which have a non-zero entry is times the number of iterations i (in practice, it is much less), since a reasonable value for i is on the order of 10 to 100. The size of the sparse collision matrix it is linear in $|T|$.

To summarize, the time complexity of noise TIME SERIES PROJECTION is $O(i\,|S|)$, which is $O(|T|)$. In contrast, the time complexity of the brute force approach is $O(|T|^2)$. Both algorithms have $O(|T|)$ space complexity.

5 Experiments

To answer the noise influencing, we performed the following experiment. We took the dataset of monthly-closings of the Dow-Jones industrial index, Aug. 1968 - Aug. 1981. We used normal random noise, which was added to the entire length of the dataset. We began with noise which had a standard deviation that was a tiny fraction the standard deviation of the original data. Fig.4 (a), (b) shows that although a typical amount of noise added to raw data, it still can be tolerated by our algorithm. In this experiment, we use k=1, N=15, m=3 as inputs. The patterns discovered by our algorithm are subsequence No.1 and No.15, subsequences No.1 and No.16, which implemented under added noise.

6 Conclusions

In this work we have formalized the problem of finding time series patterns, with noise subsections. We introduced a novel, scalable algorithm for discovering these patterns. Our algorithm is much faster than the brute force algorithm, and as a further benefit, is an anytime algorithm, producing rapid approximate results very quickly,

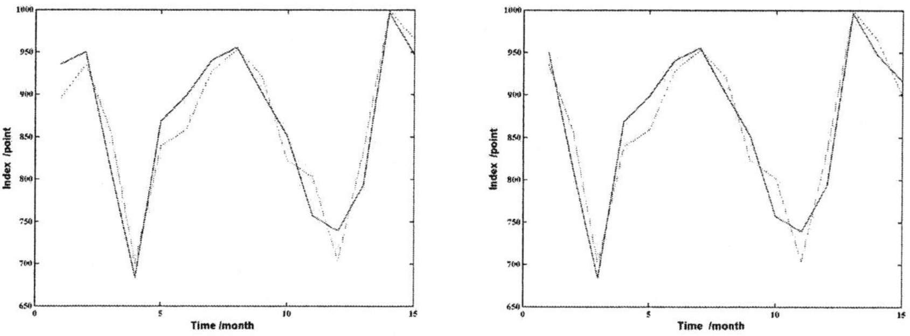

(a) (b)

Fig. 4. Experiment for noise influencing (a) Pattern discovered from raw data without noise; (b) Pattern discovered from raw data with noise.

and using additional computational time to refine the results. Being the cloud models transformation, series trend was expressed in linguistic variable that holds fuzziness and randomness. Not only the dimension reduction, but robustness to the noise of this algorithm was achieved.

Several directions for future research suggest themselves. A more detailed theoretical analysis with allow us to prove bounds on our algorithm. It may be interesting to extend our work to the discovery of motifs in multidimensional time series, and to the discovery of motifs under different distance measures such as Dynamic Time Warping.

References

1. Hegland, M., Clarke, W., Kahn, M. Mining the MACHO dataset. Computer Physics Communications. 2002,142 (1-3): 22-28.
2. Engelhardt, B., Chien, S. Mutz, D. Hypothesis generation strategies for adaptive problem solving. Proceedings of the IEEE Aerospace Conference, Big Sky, MT. 2000.
3. Tompa, M. & Buhler, J. Finding motifs using random projections. Proceedings of the 5th Int'l Conference on Computational Molecular Biology. Montreal, Canada: 2001. 67-74.
4. Keogh E, Chakrabarti K, Pazzani M. et al. Dimensionality reduction for fast similarity search in large time series databases. Journal of Knowledge and Information Systems. 2000, 3(3): 263-286.
5. Li D Y, Cheung D, Shi X M. et al. Uncertainty reasoning based on cloud models in controllers. Computer Math. Applic, 1998, 35(3):99-123.
6. Weng Y J, Zhu Z Y. Research on Time Series Data Mining Based on Linguistic Concept Tree Technique. Proceeding of the IEEE Int'l Conference on Systems, Man & Cybernetics. Washington, D.C.: 2003:1429-1434.
7. Jiang R, Li D Y. Similarity search based on shape representation in time-series data sets. Journal of computer research & development. 2000, 37(5):601-608.

Using Rough Set Theory for Detecting the Interaction Terms in a Generalized Logit Model

Chorng-Shyong Ong[1], Jih-Jeng Huang[1], and Gwo-Hshiung Tzeng[2]

[1] Institute of Information Management, No. 1, Sec. 4
Roosevelt Rd., Taipei 106, Taiwan, R.O.C.
ongcs@im.ntu.edu.tw, u5460637@ms16.hinet.net

[2] Institute of Technology Management, 1001 Ta-Hsueh Road, Hsinchu 300, Taiwan, ROC.
ghtzeng@cc.nctu.edu.tw

Abstract. Although logit model has been a popular statistical tool for classification problems it is hard to determine interaction terms in the logit model because of the *NP*-hard problem in searching all sample space. In this paper, we provide another viewpoint to consider interaction effects based on information granulation. We reduce the sample space of interaction effects using decision rules in rough set theory, and then use the procedure of stepwise selection method is used to select the significant interaction effects. Based on our results, the interaction terms are significant and the logit model with interaction terms performs better than other two models.

1 Introduction

Logit model is one of the most popular statistical tools for classification problems. Logit model can suit various kinds of distribution functions [1] and is more suitable for the real-world problems. In additional, in order to increase its accuracy and flexibility, several methods have been proposed to extend the traditional binary logit model, including multinomial logit model [2-6] and logit model for ordered categories [7]. Therefore, the generalized logit model is the general form of binary logit model and multinomial logit model.

Although the concept of logit model has proposed by McFadden [8-11] since 1970's, there are still some issues which have been discussed recently. These issues can be divided into two types. One is the problem of model building, and the other is the problem of data structure [12]. This paper proposes a solution to overcomes the problem of the interaction effects and the viewpoint of information granulation is adopted to solve the above problems using rough set theory.

The interaction effects exist when the effect of an explanatory variable on a response variable depends on the third variable. The traditional method used to conduct the interaction effect is to incorporate a moderator variable to test the significance [13]. However this method is usually heuristic and must have prior knowledge or theory support about the moderator [13]. It is also difficult to apply to the field of data mining or machine learning when the characterization of the data set is completely unknown at all.

S. Tsumoto et al. (Eds.): RSCTC 2004, LNAI 3066, pp. 624–629, 2004.

Even though this method is too arbitrary for researchers to assign a moderator variable, it seems compelling to do so. The hard problem can be described as if the logit model has n explanatory variables, then the sample space of interaction effects contain $\sum_{i=2}^{n}\binom{n}{i}$ terms. In this situation, it is impractical to conduct the *NP*-hard problem, when we have amount explanatory variables even with today's computer technique.

In this paper, we provide another viewpoint to look interaction effects based on information granulation. First, we reduce the sample space of interaction effects using decision rules in rough set theory, and then the procedure of stepwise selection method is used to select the significant interaction effects in logit model. A data set is used to show the procedures of our concept and compared to other models with the criteria of the predictive power. Based on our results, the interaction terms are significant statistically and the logit model with interaction terms is better than the other two models according to the criteria of predictive power.

2 Review of the Logit Model

Let a p-dimensional explanatory variables $\boldsymbol{x}' = (x_1, x_2, \ldots, x_p)$ and Y be the response variable with categories 1,2,…,r. Then the generalized logit model is given by the equation

$$\text{logit}(\boldsymbol{\pi}) = ln[\frac{P(Y=j\,|\,\boldsymbol{x})}{P(Y=k\,|\,\boldsymbol{x})}] = \boldsymbol{x}'\beta_j \quad 0 \le j \le r, \quad j \ne k. \tag{1}$$

where β_j is a (p+1) vector of the regression coefficients for the jth logit.

In order to evaluate logit models, several statistics have been provided to measure predictive power, including generalized R^2, association and classification rate. These statistical measurements are compared, here, to evaluate various logit models.

In additional, the stepwise technique is used to detect the interaction terms when we had known the possible sample space [12], and it is suggested for exploratory research or purely predictive research [15-17]. Although various forms of stepwise technique have been proposed, backward stepwise elimination is suggested for using because of its ability to detect the suppressor effect [15] and used here. In this paper, all the explanatory variables and the possible interaction terms will be in the logit model, and the backward stepwise elimination is used to select important variables with p=0.15. Next, we discuss the concept of information granulation and rough set theory to link the logit model.

3 Information Granulation and Rough Set Theory

Based on the concept of Zadeh [20], information granulation involves dividing a complex object into subsets, and a granule is a subset of the objects. Each granule is drawn together by indistinguishability, similarity or functionality in the objects. In this paper, the granule is associated with decision rules. For example, given an information system $\boldsymbol{I}=(U,A)$, then we can calculate the indiscernibility relation $U/IND(A)$ and the elements obtained in each indiscernibility are called granules.

Let a granule $G=\{u_1,u_2,\ldots,u_n\}$ satisfies the decision rule $\varphi \Rightarrow \theta$, then it indicates the granule has a common property when the conditional attribute equals φ, and then the decision attribute will equal θ. This property is used for detecting interaction effects in the logit model.

Recently, rough sets have been a useful tool to retrieval granules of knowledge [21-22], and the relationship between rough sets and information granulation has been discussed in [23]. Rough set theory is used, in this paper, to induce decision rules. Rough sets, originally proposed by Pawlak in [24], is a mathematical tool to deal with vagueness or uncertainty. It has been used in the area of multicriteria decision analysis [25,26], variable reduction [27], knowledge acquisition [28,29], etc. to solve uncertain problems in the real world.

The original concept of approximation space in rough sets can described as follows. Given an approximation space

$$apr=(U,A)$$

where U is the universe which is a finite and nonempty set and A is the set of attributes. Then based on the approximation space, we can define the lower and upper approximations of a set.

$$\underline{apr}(A)=\{x \mid x\in U, U/Ind(A)\subset X\} \tag{2}$$

$$\overline{apr}(A)=\{x \mid x\in U, U/Ind(A)\cap X\neq \phi\} \tag{3}$$

An information system may contain many reducts, and the interaction of all reducts is called the core, which indicates the most relevant attributes in the system. To derive the reduct is a non-trivial task and has been proved to be a *NP*-hard problem [36,37]. It is impractical to use an exhaustive algorithm to compute reducts when many attributes exist. Genetic algorithms has been shown a useful tool to find the reduct effectively [38,39] and is adopt in this paper.

Once the reducts have been derived, overlaying the reducts on the information system can induce the decision rules. A decision rule can be expressed as $\varphi \Rightarrow \theta$, where φ denotes the conjunction of elementary conditions, => denotes indicates, and θ denotes the disjunction of elementary decisions. A traditional rough set is used to classify new samples according to the decision rules. In this paper, the decisional rules are used for detecting the interaction effects.

$$If \quad \vee(\wedge des[A_i]) \quad then \quad \vee des[D_j] \tag{4}$$

where $des[A_i]$ and $des[D_j]$ denote the value in the conditional attribute A and the decision attribute D. We can consider $des[A_i]$ as providing information or the explanatory ability to $des[D_j]$ (i.e. the value of D is determined by the intersection of A_i). Based on this viewpoint, we can define the degree of contribution to D, ϕ, and

$$\vee(des[D_j]) = \sum \phi(des[A_i]) + \sum \phi(\wedge des[A_i]) \quad \forall i = 1,2,...,k \tag{5}$$

indicates the decision attribute can be classified or predicted by the sum of main effects and interaction effects of conditional attributes.

4 Implementation

In this section, one data set is used to show the effectiveness of the proposed method. According to the type of response variable, we use the multinomial logit model in this data set for detecting interaction terms. In additional, since calculating the reducts is a *NP*-hard problem, genetic algorithms is used to obtain the reducts in this paper. There are 4 reducts with the same support and length in the first data set and we can choose one of four to be the final reduct to induce the decision rules. Usually, the principle of parsimony is used for choosing the reduct. In this paper, the first reduct is used to induce decisional rules.

Next we can set a threshold to obtain a possible simple space of interaction terms using decision rules. Here, we focus on the conditional attributes and set the threshold equal 10 to obtain the possible interaction terms in the first data set. Note that the threshold can vary depending on the situation of decision rules. Then, we put 18 possible interaction terms into the multinomial logit model and use the backward elimination method to determine the significant terms. The results of parameter estimation in Table 1 show that there are 8 interaction terms which are significant (with p=0.15).

Table 1. Results of fitting multinomial logit model in first data set.

Explanatory Variable	Logistic Coefficient	Standard Error	Wald Chi-square	*P*-value
School*Money	0.05250	0.03240	2.6273	0.1050
Age*School*Sports	-0.01540	0.00584	6.9621	0.0083
Age*School*Grades	-0.01150	0.00491	5.4766	0.0193
Gender*Race*School	-0.19870	0.12390	2.5706	0.1089
School*Grades*Sports	0.05240	0.02380	4.8573	0.0275
Gender*School*Grades	-0.67930	0.28970	5.4980	0.0190
Gender*Age*School*Grade	0.10610	0.04730	5.0359	0.0248
Gender*Grades*School*Grade	-0.07580	0.04830	2.4669	0.1163

The model is compared with other two models, of which one incorporates all variables and the other incorporates all variables using backward technique. The valuated criteria, including Tau-a, Gamma, Generalized R^2 and classification rate, all indicate that the proposed our model is better then the other two models in Table 3.

Table 2. The comparison with various models.

Model	Tau-a	Gamma	Generalized R^2	Classification Rate
Multinomial logit model with all variables	0.182	0.299	0.0923	64.6%
Multinomial logit model with all variables using backward technique	0.167	0.297	0.0796	59.6%
Multinomial logit model with interaction effects using backward technique	0.200	0.328	0.1266	66.1%

5 Conclusions

Logit model is a useful classification method which does not need any assumption of distribution in explanatory variables. As we know, when important interaction terms are lost, the predictive or interpretive power will decrease. However it is hard to determine the interaction terms according to theory or subject experience, and it is impossible to search the entire sample space of interaction terms.

In this paper, we provide another method for detecting interaction effects in a logit model. A multinomial logit model is used to test the effectiveness with one data set. Based on the results, the interaction terms can actually be found using rough sets, and they are statistically significant. In additional, the criteria of predictive power are best in our proposed model, indicating that it is more accurate than the other two models.

References

1. Press, S. J., Wilson S.: Choosing between Logistic Regression and Discriminant Analysis. J am. Stat. Assoc. 73 (1978) 699-705.
2. Aldrich, J. H., Nelson F. D.: Linear Probability, Logit, and Probit Models. Sage, CA (1984).
3. DeMaris, A.: Logit Modeling. Sage, CA (1992).
4. Knoke, D., Burke P. J.: Log-linear Models. Sage, CA (1980).
5. Liao, T. F.: Interpreting Probability Model: Logit, Probit, and Other Generalized Linear Models. Sage, CA (1994).
6. McCullagh, P.: Regression Model for Ordinal Data. J. Roy. Stat. Soc. A Sta. 42 (1980) 109-142.
7. Zarembka, P. (ed.): Frontiers in Econometrics. Conditional Logit Analysis of Qualitative Choice Behavior. Academic Press, New York (1974).
8. Manski, C. F., McFadden D. (eds.) Structural Analysis of Discrete Data with Econometric Applications. Econometric Models of Probabilistic Choice. MIT Press, MA (1981).
9. Hildebrand, W. (ed.) Advances in Econometrics. Qualitative Response Models. Cambridge University Press, Cambridge (1982).
10. McFadden, D., Econometric Analysis of Qualitative Response Models, in: Z. Griliches and M. D. Intriligator (Eds), Handbook of Econometrics, Vol. II, pp. 1395-1457, Amsterdam: North-Holland, 1984.
11. Menard, S.: Applied Logistic Regression Analysis. 2nd. Sage, CA (2001).
12. Jaccard, J.: Interaction Effects in Logistic Regression. Sage, CA (2001).
13. Argesti, A., Finlay B.: Statistical Methods for the Social Science. 3rd. Prentice-Hall, NJ (1997).
14. Hosmer, D. W., Lemeshow S.: Applied Logistic Regression. Wiley, New York (1989).

15. Wofford, S., Elliott D. S., Menard S.: Continuities in Marital Violence. Journal of Family Violence 9 (1994) 195-225.
16. Gupta, M., Ragade R., Yager R. (Eds.) Advances in Fuzzy Set Theory and Applications. Fuzzy Sets and Information Granularity. Amsterdam, North-Holland (1979).
17. Zhong, N., Skowron A., Ohsuga S. (Eds.) New Directions in Rough Sets, Data Mining, and Granular-Soft Computing. Calculi of Granules Based on Rough Set Theory: Approximate Distributed Synthesis and Granular Semantics for Computing with Words. Springer-Verlag, Berlin Heidelberg New York (1999).
18. Peter, J. F., Pawlak Z., Skowron A.: A Rough Set Approach to Measuring Information Granules. Proceedings of the 26th Annual International Computer Software and Application Conference, (2002) 1135-1139.
19. Pawlak, Z.: Granularity of Knowledge, Indiscernibility and Rough Set. IEEE International Conference on Fuzzy Systems, (1998) 106-110.
20. Pawlak, Z.: Rough Set. Int. J. Comput. Inf. Sci. (1982) 341-356.
21. Greco, S., Matarazzo B., Slowinski R.: Rough Sets Theory for Multicriteria Decesion Analysis. Eur. J. Oper. Res. 129 (2001) 1-47.
22. Pawlak, Z. Slowinski R.: Rough Set Approach to Multi-Attribute Decision Analysis. Eur. J. Oper. Res. 72 (2001) 1–47.
23. Beynon, M.: Reducts Within the Variable Precision Rough Sets Model: A Further Investigation. Eur. J. Oper. Res. 134 (2001) 592-605.
24. Pawlak, Z.: Rough Set Approach to Knowledge-Based Decision Support. Eur. J. Oper. Res. 99 (1997) 48-57.
25. Grzymala-Busse, J. W.: Knowledge Acquisition under Uncertainty- A Rough Set Approach. J. Intell. Robot. Syst. 1 (1988) 3-16.
26. Pal, S. K., Skowron A. (Eds.) Rough Fuzzy Hybridization: A New Trend in Decision Making. Rough Sets: A Tutorial. Singapore (1999) 1-98.
27. Slowinski, R. (Ed.) Intelligent Decision Support- Handbook of Applications and Advances of the Rough Sets Theory. The Discernibility Matrices and Function in Information Systems. Kluwer Academic Publishers, Dordrecht (1992) 331-362.
28. Wang, P. P. (Ed.) Preceedings of the International Workshop on Rough Sets Soft Computing at Second Annual Joint Conference on Information Sciences. Finding Minimal Reducts Using Genetic Algorithms. Wrightsville Beach, NC (1995) 186-189.
29. Polkowski, L. Skowron A. (Eds,) Rough Sets in Knowledge Discovery 2: Applications, Case Studies and Software Systems. Genetic Algorithm in Decomposition and Classification Problems. Physica-Verlag, Heidelberg (1998) 472–492.

Optimization of the ABCD Formula for Melanoma Diagnosis Using C4.5, a Data Mining System

Ron Andrews[1], Stanislaw Bajcar[2], Jerzy W. Grzymała-Busse[3,4], Zdzisław S. Hippe[5], and Chris Whiteley[1]

[1] Department of Electrical Engineering and Computer Science, University of Kansas, Lawrence, KS 66045, USA

[2] Regional Dermatology Center, 35-310 Rzeszow, Poland

[3] Department of Electrical Engineering and Computer Science, University of Kansas, Lawrence, KS 66045, USA

[4] Institute of Computer Science, Polish Academy of Sciences, 01-237 Warsaw, Poland

Jerzy@ku.edu

http://lightning.eecs.ku.edu/index.html

[5] Department of Expert Systems and Artificial Intelligence University of Information Technology and Management, 35-225 Rzeszow, Poland

ZHippe@wenus.wsiz.rzeszow.pl

Abstract. Our main objective was to improve the diagnosis of melanoma by optimizing the ABCD formula, used by dermatologists in melanoma identification. In our previous research, an attempt to optimize the ABCD formula using the LEM2 rule induction algorithm was successful. This time we decided to replace LEM2 by C4.5, a tree generating data mining system. The final conclusion is that, most likely, for C4.5 the original ABCD formula is already optimal and no further improvement is possible.

1 Introduction

The number of diagnosed cases of melanoma, one of the most dangerous skin cancers, is increasing. Thus any improvement of melanoma diagnosis is crucial to save human lives. Nowadays melanoma is routinely diagnosed with help of the so-called ABCD formula (A stands for Asymmetry, B for border, C for color, and D for diversity of structure) [2],[12]. Results of successful optimization of the ABCD formula, using the LEM2 rule induction algorithm (Learning from Example Module, version 2), a component of the data mining system LERS (Learning from Examples using Rough Sets) [4], [5] were reported in [1], [3], [6], [7]. Rough set theory was initiated in 1982 [9], [10].

In this paper we report results on yet another attempt to optimize the ABCD formula, this time using a different, well-known data mining system C4.5 [11]. The data on melanoma, consisting of 410 cases, were collected at the Regional Dermatology Center in Rzeszow, Poland [8]. In our current research we evaluated all attributes from this data set, one attribute at a time, checking their

S. Tsumoto et al. (Eds.): RSCTC 2004, LNAI 3066, pp. 630–636, 2004.

significance for diagnosis using the number of errors determined by ten-fold cross validation and C4.5. Then we used sequences of 30 experiments of ten-fold cross validations, also using C4.5, in our attempt to look for the optimal ABCD formula. Note that in previous research using LERS [1], [3], [6], [7], a substantial improvement in melanoma diagnosis was accomplished. However, this time our final conclusion is that the original ABCD formula, used for diagnosis with C4.5, is, most likely, already optimal. Moreover, the sequence of 30 different experiments of ten-fold cross validation was not sufficient. This conclusion was reached using 300 and 3,000 experiments of ten-fold cross validation.

2 ABCD Formula

In diagnosis of melanoma an important indicator is TDS (Total Dermatoscopic Score), computed on the basis of the ABCD formula, using four variables: *Asymmetry*, *Border*, *Color* and *Diversity*. The variable *Asymmetry* has three different values: *symmetric spot*, *one axial symmetry*, and *two axial symmetry*. *Border* is a numerical attribute, with values from 0 to 8. A lesion is partitioned into eight segments. The border of each segment is evaluated; the sharp border contributes 1 to *Border*, the gradual border contributes 0. *Color* has six possible values: *black*, *blue*, *dark brown*, *light brown*, *red* and *white*. Similarly, *Diversity* has five values: *pigment dots*, *pigment globules*, *pigment network*, *structureless areas* and *branched streaks*. In our data set *Color* and *Diversity* were replaced by binary single-valued variables. The TDS is traditionally computed using the following formula (known as the ABCD formula):

$$TDS = 1.3 * Asymmetry + 0.1 * Border + 0.5 * \Sigma Colors + 0.5 * \Sigma Diversities,$$

where for *Asymmetry* the value *symmetric spot* counts as 0, *one axial symmetry* counts as 1, and *two axial symmetry* counts as 2, Σ *Colors* represents the sum of all values of the six color attributes and Σ *Diversities* represents the sum of all values of the five diversity attributes.

3 C4.5 Testing of Single Attributes

The significance of individual attributes, or testing the importance of specific attributes as part of the ABCD formula, was conducted by changing the coefficient associated with an attribute from 0 to 2, by 0.05 increments, and keeping values of all twelve remaining coefficients equal to one. Therefore, the original data set was transformed into a new data set, without TDS, and with values of all attributes, except one attribute, equal to one. For all attributes, except *Border*, the total number of errors, a result of ten-fold cross validation, was between 70 and 80. Note the total number of errors, again determined by ten-fold cross validation for the original data set without TDS (with values of all remaining attributes unchanged), was equal to 85.

For *Border* the number of errors was between 12 and 73 when its coefficient was between 0 and 1, and then leveled out to between 70 and 80 when its coefficient was between 1 and 2.

Intuitively, this test shows that when the coefficient associated with *Border* is much smaller than all other coefficients the number of errors is smaller. Obviously, creators of the ABCD formula were familiar with this fact since in the ABCD formula the coefficient for *Border* is much smaller than for other attributes.

4 Main Experiments

The most important performance criterion for all methods of data mining is the total number of errors. To discover the error number we used ten-fold cross validation: all cases were randomly re-ordered, and then the set of all cases was divided into ten mutually disjoint subsets of approximately equal size. For each subset, all remaining cases were used for training, i.e., for rule induction, while the subset was used for testing. Thus, each case was used nine times for training and once for testing. Note that using different re-orderings of cases causes slightly different error numbers. The original C4.5 system is not equipped with any way to randomly re-order a data set, so we added a mechanism to accomplish this task.

Previous experiments attempted at looking for the optimal ABCD formula while using LEM2, an algorithm of LERS, were successful [1], [3], [6], [7]. Our current experiments were aimed towards the same goal: to find the optimal ABCD formula, however, this time we used the C4.5 system. Similarly as in [1], [3], [6], [7], we assumed that the optimal ABCD formula, for computing a new TDS, should be also a linear combination of 13 attributes:

$$\begin{aligned}
&new_TDS = c_1 * Asymmetry + c_2 * Border + c_3 * Color_black + \\
&c_4 * Color_blue + c_5 * Color_dark_brown + c_6 * Color_light_brown + \\
&c_7 * Color_red + c_8 * Color_white + c_9 * Diversity_pigment_dots + \\
&c_{10} * Diversity_pigment_globules + c_{11} * Diversity_pigment_network + \\
&c_{12} * Diversity_structureless_areas + c_{13} * Diversity_branched_streaks.
\end{aligned}$$

Our objective was to find optimal values for coefficients $c_1, c_2, ..., c_{13}$. The criterion of optimality was the smallest total number errors for sequences of 30 ten-fold cross validations with different re-ordering of examples in the data set.

Thus for each vector $(c_1, c_2, ..., c_{13})$ the corresponding new_TDS was computed, the sequence of 30 re-orderings of the data set was performed, and then for each new data set ten-fold cross validation was used for the evaluation of the number of errors.

Since the original ABCD formula yielded relatively small number of errors, we set the base value of coefficients to the same value as in the original ABCD formula. Then we run sequences of 30 experiments of ten-fold cross validation for vectors $(c_1, c_2, ..., c_{13})$ of coefficient values close to original, with increments of 0.01, running altogether over 73,000 experiments.

Table 1. Explored coefficient ranges for thirteen attributes from the melanoma data set

Attribute	Tested range
Asymmetry	1.28 – 1.38
Border	0.02 – 0.12
Color_black	0.41 – 0.59
Color_blue	0.42 – 0.53
Color_dark_brown	0.41 – 0.55
Color_light_brown	0.41 – 0.59
Color_red	0.51 – 0.59
Color_white	0.50 – 0.50
Diversity_pigment_dots	0.42 – 0.57
Diversity_pigment_globules	0.41 –0.59
Diversity_pigment_network	0.44 – 0.50
Diversity_structureless_areas	0.41 – 0.59
Diversity_branched_streaks	0.52 – 0.58

The smallest error obtained from such a sequence of 30 ten-fold cross validation experiments indicated the optimal choice of $(c_1, c_2, ..., c_{13})$. A special script was created to compute the new_TDS given ranges for all 13 coefficients $c_1, c_2, ..., c_{13}$, see Table 1. Due to computational complexity, not all combinations of coefficients that are implied by Table 1 were tested.

During testing with C4.5 using ten- fold cross-validation, we discovered that certain orderings of the data set could cause the system to core dump. This fault did not seem to have a single definitive cause, but during initial testing this issue was a cause for concern with respect to automating the system. Not wanting to spend time debugging the problem in the decision tree generation system, we opted to work around it by computing averages of successful runs of C4.5.

Since the total number of errors for trees was larger than the total number of errors for rules, we used the latter as a guide for identification the best ABCD formula. The best results were obtained from the following formula

$$new\_TDS = 1.3 * Asymmetry + 0.03 * Border + 0.5 * \Sigma Colors$$
$$0.5 * Diversity\_pigment\_dots + 0.5 * Diversity\_pigment\_globules +$$
$$0.47 * Diversity\_pigment\_network + 0.5 * Diversity\_structureless\_areas +$$
$$0.5 * Diversity\_branched\_streaks.$$

Results of running our experiments are presented in Tables 2–3.

Using the well-known statistical test for the difference between two averages, with the level of significance specified at 0.05, initially we concluded that new_TDS was better than the original, mostly due to small standard deviations. However, with a difference between averages being so small, we decided to run additionally 300 and then 3,000 experiments to test the same hypothesis. Surprisingly, the same test for the difference between two averages, with the same level of significance equal to 0.05, yielded quite opposite conclusions: the difference between the new_TDS and original one was not significant. Since the test

Table 2. Number of errors – preliminary experiments

TDS	Rules	Unpruned trees	Pruned trees
Original TDS	9	9	9
New TDS	11	13	14
No TDS	85	89	88

Table 3. Number of errors for rules

TDS	Length of a sequence of ten-fold cross validations	Number of errors	Standard deviation
Original TDS	30	6.20	0.41
New TDS	30	5.97	0.18
Original TDS	300	8.51	1.55
New TDS	300	8.45	2.00
Original TDS	3,000	8.51	9.32
New TDS	3,000	8.45	10.13

with more experiments is more reliable, our final conclusion is that there is no significant difference in performance between the new_TDS and original.

The unpruned decision tree generated by C4.5 from the data with TDS computed by the original ABCD formula is presented below.

```
TDS <= 4.8 :
| C_BLUE = 1: Blue_nevus (66.0/1.0)
| C_BLUE = 0:
| | D_b_STREAKS = 1: Benign_nev (71.0)
| | D_b_STREAKS = 0:
| | | D_PIGM_DOTS = 1: Benign_nev (48.0/1.0)
| | | D_PIGM_DOTS = 0:
| | | | D_PIGM_NETW = 1: Benign_nev (8.0)
| | | | D_PIGM_NETW = 0:
| | | | | C_WHITE = 0: Blue_nevus (5.0/1.0)
| | | | | C_WHITE = 1: Benign_nev (2.0)
TDS > 4.8 :
| TDS <= 5.4 : Suspicious (81.0)
| TDS > 5.4 :
| | C_BLUE = 1: Malignant (16.0/1.0)
| | C_BLUE = 0:
| | | C_RED = 1: Malignant (41.0)
| | | C_RED = 0:
| | | | C_WHITE = 1: Malignant (17.0)
| | | | C_WHITE = 0:
| | | | | ASYMMETRY = 0: Malignant (0.0)
| | | | | ASYMMETRY = 2: Malignant (5.0)
```

```
| | | | | ASYMMETRY = 1:
| | | | | | TDS > 5.6 : Malignant (4.0)
| | | | | | TDS <= 5.6 :
| | | | | | | TDS <= 5.5 : Malignant (2.0)
| | | | | | | TDS > 5.5 : Suspicious (3.0/1.0)
```

As a result of pruning of the tree generated by C4.5 from the data set with TDS computed by the original ABCD formula, the following tree was obtained:

```
TDS <= 4.8 :
| C_BLUE = 0: Benign_nev (134.0/7.3)
| C_BLUE = 1: Blue_nevus (66.0/2.6)
TDS > 4.8 :
| TDS <= 5.4 : Suspicious (81.0/1.4)
| TDS > 5.4 : Malignant (88.0/5.0)
```

5 Conclusions

This paper presents an attempt to find the optimal ABCD formula that is widely used by physicians to diagnose melanoma. Our assumption was that the diagnosis will be supported by C4.5, a data mining system. Therefore, all experiments aimed at optimizing the ABCD formula were conducted using C4.5. First, all thirteen attributes from our data set describing melanoma were tested for significance, with a total number of errors determined by ten-fold cross validation using C4.5. The only conclusion was that the coefficient, associated with the attribute *Border* should be small. Our main experiments were designed to look for an optimal ABCD formula while preserving the original form of linear combination of attributes, characteristic for the ABCD formula. This optimization was conducted by applying many thousands of vectors of values of the thirteen coefficients and processing each such vector by a sequence of 30 experiments of ten-fold cross validation, each with a different re-ordering of the data sets. As a result, the optimal ABCD formula was found. Nevertheless, after additional experiments, running ten-fold cross validation for the data containing TDS computed by the original ABCD formula and data containing TDS computed by the optimal ABCD formula 300 times and 3,000 times, each ten fold cross-validation with different re-ordering of both data sets, we observed that – statistically – there is no significant difference in the total number of errors for both formulas, with the level of significance = 0.05. Thus, our final conclusion is that, most likely, for C4.5 the original ABCD formula is already optimal.

References

1. Alvarez, A., Brown, F. M., Grzymala-Busse, J. W., and Hippe, Z. S.: Optimization of the ABCD formula used for melanoma diagnosis. Proc. of the IIPWM'2003, Int. Conf. On Intelligent Information Processing and WEB Mining Systems, Zakopane, Poland, June 2–5, 2003, 233–240.

2. Friedman, R. J., Rigel, D. S., and Kopf, A. W.: Early detection of malignant melanoma: the role of physician examination and self-examination of the skin. *CA Cancer J. Clin.* **35** (1985) 130–151.
3. Grzymala-Busse, J. P., Grzymala-Busse, J. W., and Hippe Z. S.: Melanoma prediction using data mining system LERS. Proceeding of the 25th Anniversary Annual International Computer Software and Applications Conference COMPSAC 2001, Chicago, IL, October 8–12, 2001, 615–620.
4. Grzymala-Busse, J. W.: LERS – A system for learning from examples based on rough sets. In Intelligent Decision Support. Handbook of Applications and Advances of the Rough Sets Theory. Slowinski, R. (ed.), Kluwer Academic Publishers, Dordrecht, Boston, London (1992) 3–18.
5. Grzymala-Busse J. W.: A new version of the rule induction system LERS. *Fundamenta Informaticae* **31** (1997) 27–39.
6. Grzymala-Busse J. W. and Hippe Z. S.: Postprocessing of rule sets induced from a melanoma data set. Proc. of the COMPSAC 2002, 26th Annual International Conference on Computer Software and Applications, Oxford, England, August 26–29, 2002, 1146–1151.
7. Grzymala-Busse J. W. and Hippe Z. S.: A search for the best data mining method to predict melanoma. Proceedings of the RSCTC 2002, Third International Conference on Rough Sets and Current Trends in Computing, Malvern, PA, October 14–16, 2002, Springer-Verlag,Berlin, Heidelberg, New York (2002) 538–545.
8. Hippe, Z. S.: Computer database NEVI on endargement by melanoma. *Task Quarterly* **4** (1999) 483–488.
9. Pawlak, Z.: Rough Sets. *International Journal of Computer and Information Sciences* **11** (1982) 341–356.
10. Pawlak, Z.: Rough Sets. Theoretical Aspects of Reasoning about Data. Kluwer Academic Publishers, Dordrecht, Boston, London (1991).
11. Quinlan, J. R.: C4.5: Programs for Machine Learning, Morgan Kaufmann Publishers, San Mateo, CA (1988).
12. Stolz, W., Braun-Falco, O., Bilek, P., Landthaler, A. B., Cogneta, A. B.: Color Atlas of Dermatology, Blackwell Science Inc., Cambridge, MA (1993).

A Contribution to Decision Tree Construction Based on Rough Set Theory*

Xumin Liu[1,2], Houkuan Huang[1], and Weixiang Xu[3]

[1] School of Computer and Information Technology, Beijing Jiaotong University, 100044
[2] School of Information Engineering, Capital Normal University, Beijing 100037
[3] School of Traffic and Transportation, Beijing Jiaotong University, 100044
liuxmxxxy@263.net

Abstract. In this paper, the algorithm of building a decision tree is introduced by comparing the information gain or entropy. The produced process of univariate decision tree is given as an example. According to rough sets theory, the method of constructing multivariate decision tree is discussed. Using the algorithm, the complexity of decision tree is decreased, the construction of decision tree is optimized and the rule of data mining could be built.

1 Introduction

Classification is an important task in Data Ming. Methods of Decision Tree, Neural Network and statistics methods etc. are used to finish the important task of classification. Decision tree has many advantages, such as its fast speed, high accuracy as well as easy mode of production, which attracts many researchers in data mining.

The theory of Rough Set (RS) put forward by Professor Z.Pawlak in 1982, which identifies the knowledge from a new angle and associates knowledge with classification, provides a mathematical tool which are more sharable for human's recognition to deal with the inaccurate and uncompleted data classifying problems. The theory, which has been widely used in many fields, is mainly applied to reduce knowledge and analyze knowledge dependence.

In this paper, a data-mining algorithm of building a decision trees is introduced by comparing the gain or entropy. According to the theory of rough sets, the method to construct multivariate decision tree is discussed. The problem of choosing the initial attribute during the test is solved based on the concept of relative core of the RS theory. The producing process of decision tree is given by way of comparison between univariate decision tree and multivariate decision tree through examples.

2 Decision Tree

The method of decision tree[1] is a data mining method that finds out the classification knowledge in training sets by building a decision tree. Its core is how to build a decision tree with high accuracy and a small scale.

* This paper is supported by Beijing Educational Committee under Grant No. KM200410028013

S. Tsumoto et al. (Eds.): RSCTC 2004, LNAI 3066, pp. 637–642, 2004.

A decision tree is a flow-chart-like tree structure, where each internal node denotes a test on an attribute, each branch represents an outcome of the test, and leaf nodes represent classes or class distributions. The basic algorithm for decision tree induction is a greedy algorithm that constructs decision tree in a top-down recursive and divide-and-conquer manner.

There are many algorithms of decision tree. In 1986 J.Ross Quinlan discovered the famous decision tree induction algorithm, ID3 version, which caused much effect. Making supplement and improvement on it in 1993, he raised the popular C4.5 algorithm. Later C5.0 algorithm appeared as an improved commercial version of C4.5. Besides some scalability algorithms like SLIQ[2], SPRINT[3] and RainForest algorithms[4] also have wide application.

3 Foundation of RS Theory

RS theory defines the knowledge from a new angle[5]. It regards knowledge as the partition of domain, supposes it has granularity and discusses knowledge by introducing the equivalence relation in algebra.

3.1 Attribute Choice

It's hoped that noise and irrelevant attributes can be eliminated so that the number of attributes decrease to improve the understanding of decision trees. For most of the data sets, it's impossible to find out the best combination by trying all the combinations of the attributes, because the number of combinations of the attribute increases on an exponential curve. Consequently some heuristics must be used when choosing attribute. RS theory can be used to choose multivariate testing attribute.

Let U be a limited set called domain, composed of interested subjects. R is an equivalence relation defined on U, U/R means the partition of R on U. $[x]_R$ is an equivalence class of R of x, x∈U. In RS theory, ordered pair (U,R) is called a approximation space, and any subset X⊆U is called a concept. Each concept X can be defined as lower and upper approximation:

$$\underline{R}X = \bigcup\{x \in U : [x]_R \subseteq X\} \qquad \overline{R}X = \bigcup\{x \in U : [x]_R \cap X \neq \Phi\} \tag{1}$$

$\underline{R}X$ is a set composed of elements that certainly belong to concept X by the owned knowledge R. $\overline{R}X$ is a set composed of elements that may belong to concept X. For R and Q, two equivalence relations on U, P-positive region of Q can be defined as:

$$POS_P(Q) = \bigcup_{X \in U/Q} \underline{P}X \tag{2}$$

Where $POS_P(Q)$ is the set made up of all the elements that must be partitioned to class U/Q by knowledge P.

Let U be a domain. P and Q are two equivalence relation sets defined on U. If equation (3) is true, we call the equivalence relation R∈P Q-unnecessary, otherwise Q-necessary.

$$POS_{IND(P)}(IND(Q)) = POS_{IND(P-\{R\})}(IND(Q)) \tag{3}$$

Where IND(P)=∩P (call the intersection belonging to equivalence relation of P) is also a equivalence relation, and is called an indiscernibility relation on P.

The set composed by all the Q-necessary equivalence relations in P is called Q-core of P, written as $CORE_Q(P)$.

With P and Q indicate respectively the condition attribute and the decision attribute in an information system, if an attribute R∈P is Q-unnecessary, the decision of the original information system will not change when attribute R is removed from D. While the decision will change when attribute in $CORE_Q(P)$ is removed. Therefore attribute in $CORE_Q(P)$ is very important to the decision. Attributes in relative core can be chosen as attributes for multivariate tests.

3.2 Definition of Relative Generalization

The definition of relative generalization is used to build multivariate test. Simple conjunction of the chose attributes for multivariate test might lead to the problem of over-fitting of data, so we can define one equivalence relation as relative generalization corresponding to another one.

Definition: Let P and Q be two equivalence relation sets on U.

$$U / IND(P) = \{X_1, X_2, \cdots, X_n\} \qquad U / IND(Q) = \{Y_1, Y_2, \cdots, Y_m\} \tag{4}$$

$$Z_i = \bigcup_{X_j \in U / IND(P)} \{X_j : X_j \in Y_i\} \quad i = 1,2,\cdots,m \tag{5}$$

$$Z_{m+1} = \bigcup_{X_j \in U / IND(P)} \{X_j : X_j \not\subset Y_i, \forall i\} \tag{6}$$

Then the definite equivalence relation P of $\{Z_1, Z_2, ..., Z_{m+1}\}$ on U is called relative generalization corresponding to Q, written as $GEN_Q(P)$. The rationality of the definition above can be illustrated by the following proposition.

Proposition: $\{Z_1, Z_2 ..., Z_{m+1}\}$ build a partition of U, where Z_i(i=1,2,...,m+1) is defined by (5) and (6).

4 Construction of Univariate Decision Trees

Take an information system as an example. Table 1 presents training data tuples. Take attribute Class as the testing subject, namely the main attribute (independent variable). Then check out the relationship between this attribute and other ones. Letting main attribute have value Y or N divides all the data into two sets.

We discuss calculation of information entropy partition decision tree in ID3 algorithm, and construct a univariate decision tree by comparing information gain. Since "outlook" has the highest information gain among the attributes, it is selected as the test attribute. A node is created and labeled with outlook, and branches are grown for each of the attribute's values. The samples falling into the partition for out look="overcast" all belong to the same class Y. A leaf should therefore be created by the end of this branch and labeled with Y. Similarly with the other two branches, sample decision tree for each partition is built recursively. The final decision tree is shown in Fig. 1.

Table 1. Training data tuples from an information system.

U	Condition attributes(C)				Decision attribute(D)
	Outlook(a_1)	temperature(a_2)	humidity(a_3)	windy(a_4)	Class(D)
1	sunny	hot	high	false	N
2	sunny	hot	high	true	N
3	overcast	hot	high	false	Y
4	rain	mild	high	false	Y
5	rain	cool	normal	false	Y
6	rain	cool	normal	true	N
7	overcast	cool	normal	true	Y
8	sunny	mild	high	false	N
9	sunny	cool	normal	false	Y
10	rain	mild	normal	false	Y
11	sunny	mild	normal	true	Y
12	overcast	mild	high	true	Y
13	overcast	hot	normal	false	Y
14	rain	mild	high	true	N

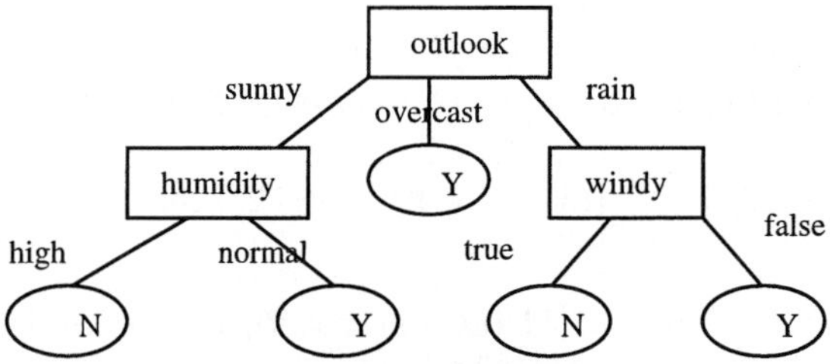

Fig. 1. Univariate Decision Tree.

The complexity of this tree (the number of all nodes) is 8. From the process of decision tree building, we know that when all the nodes of a leaf are Y or N, there's no need to partition, thus the downward recursive process stops. In the process of subtree production, the earlier such "pure" nodes appear, the better.

5 Building a Multivariate Decision Tree

The difference between univariate decision tree and multivariate decision tree is that test of the former is based on a single attribute, while the latter is based on one or more attributes. When choosing attributes on each node of a decision tree, ID3 algorithm does not give enough emphasis on relation between attributes. This disadvantage might cause repetition of sub trees, so other optimized algorithms of decision trees are considered[6]. We'll discuss how to construct a multivariate decision tree with RS theory.

The algorithm leads decision trees out from data expressed with information system. In form an information system S is defined as a four tuple S=<U,A,V,f>. where U is domain; A is a set of all attributes, which can be further classified into condition attribute C and decision attribute D, $C \cap D = \Phi$, $V = \cup V_P$ $(P \in A)$, V_P is value scale of attribute P f U×A→V is called an information function. First choose the best test according to a certain partition, and then partition training sets with the chosen test, which means for each result of the test comes out a branch. The algorithm is applied recursively to each partition led out by the test. If all the samples of a certain partition come from the same class, a leaf node labeled with the name of class is produced.

The partition ability of attributes is used as measurement standard of partition. According to the definition of relative core, we know that attributes of core in condition attribute set, compared with those in decision attributes set is crucial for making decisions. Using some definitions of RS, the process of building a multivariate test is as follows:

(1) Compute the core of condition attribute set C corresponding to decision attribute set D. namely $CORE_D(C)$, if $CORE_D(C) = \Phi$, turn to (2), otherwise let $CORE_D(C) = \{a_1,a_2,...,a_k\}$, turn to (3).

(2) Use ID3 algorithm to choose a best attribute as test for the node.

(3) Let $P = a_1 \wedge a_2 \wedge ... \wedge a_k$, compute the relative generalization of P corresponding to Q $GEN_D(P)$ and use it as a test for the node. For the information system shown in Table 1, we now build a multivariate decision tree with this algorithm. First in the given information system compute the core of condition attribute set C corresponding to decision attribute set D. We can computer that

$U/IND(C) = \{\{1\},\{2\},\{3\},\{4\},\{5\},\{6\},\{7\},\{8\},\{9\},\{10\},\{11\},\{12\},\{13\},\{14\}\}$
$U/IND(D) = \{\{1,2,6,8,14\},\{3,4,5,7,9,10,11,12,13\}\}$

According to Equation (2)

$POS_{IND(C)}(D) = \{1,2,3,4,5,6,7,8,9,10,11,12,13,14\}=U$

Check that if a_i (I = 1,2,3,4) is necessary in C corresponding to D. Remove a_1 from C,$POS_{IND(C-\{a1\})}(D) = \{2,5,9,10,11,13\} \neq POS_{IND(C)}(D)$

According to Equation (3), a_1 is D-necessary in C.

Similarly a_4 is D-necessary, while a_2 and a_3 are D-unnecessary, from which we gain $CORE_D(C) = \{a_1, a_4\}$.

After choosing important attributes, we should construct multivariate test using the chosen attributes. First let $P = a_1 \wedge a_4$,

$U/P = \{\{1,8,9\}, \{2,11\},\{3,13\},\{4,5,10\},\{6,14\},\{7,12\}\}$

Then using equation (5) and (6), we compute the partition on U of generalization of P corresponding to D.

$\{\{1,2,8,9,11\},\{3,4,5,7,10,12,13\},\{6,14\}\}$

Because partitions correspond to attributes one by one, this partition defines the only new attribute of U, namely the constructed multivariate test $GEN_D(P)$.

Taking $GEN_D(P)$ as the root of the decision tree with the algorithm above, the subjects in the information system are divided into different subsets according to the values of attributes. Multivariate decision tree produced from the given information system with RS method is shown in fig. 2.

As is shown in the figure, this multivariate decision tree can classify all the training samples correctly. But it has two fewer nodes than the univariate decision tree. The method of multivariate decision tree based on RS decreases the complexity of the tree.

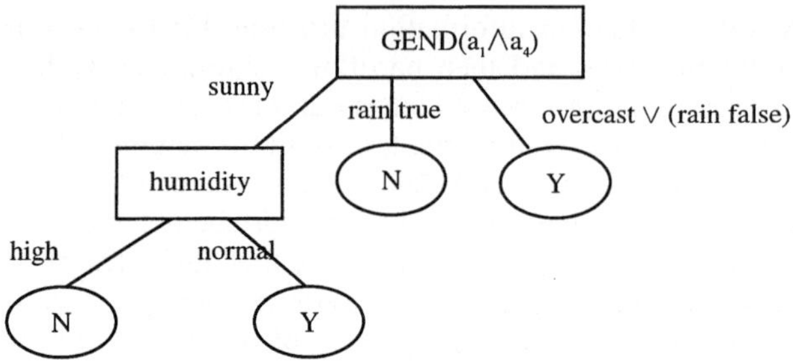

Fig. 2. Multivariate Decision Tree.

6 Conclusion

The new method of building decision tree based on RS theory, which made use of core of condition attribute set according to decision attribute set, solve problems of choosing attribute in multivariate test. For the building of a multivariate test, using generalization of one equivalence relation corresponding to another one makes the multivariate test not be simple conjunction of the chosen attributes, but produce a new attribute from it. This algorithm can decrease the complexity, optimize the structure of the decision tree and mine better regulation information. Especially the more data are mined by decision tree algorithm, the better efficiency and function the algorithm has, and the more evident superiority the algorithm has.

References

1. Jiawei Han, Micheline Kamber. Data Mining Concepts and Techniques. Beijing. China Machine Press, (August.2000) (in Chinese)
2. M. Mehta, R. Agrawal, and J. Rissanen. SLIQ: A fast scalable classifier for data mining. 1996 Int. Conf. Extending Database Technology (EDBT'96), Avignon, France, (Mar.1996)
3. J. Shafer, R. Agrawal, and M.Mehta. SPRINT: A scalable parallel classifier for data mining. 1996 Int. Conf. Very Large Data Bases (VLDB'96), Bombay, India, (Sept. 1996) 544-555
4. J. Gehrke, R. Ramakrishnan, and V. Ganti. Rainforest: A framework for fast decision tree construction of large datasets. Very Large Data Bases (VLDB'98), New York, (Aug. 1998)
5. Liu Tongming. Data Mining Techniques and Its Application. Beijing. Publishing House of National Defence Industry, (Sept.2001) (in Chinese)
6. Miao Duoqian. Rough Sets Based on Approach for Multivariate Decision Tree Construction. Journal of Software, (Jun.1997) 425-431 (in Chinese)

Domain Knowledge Approximation in Handwritten Digit Recognition

Tuan Trung Nguyen

Polish-Japanese Institute of Computer Techniques
ul. Koszykowa 86, 02-008 Warsaw, Poland
nttrung@pjwstk.edu.pl

Abstract. Pattern recognition system on large sets of complex objects often have to deal with atypical samples that defy most traditional classifiers. Such samples can be handled with additional domain knowledge from an human expert. We propose a framework for the transfer of knowledge from the expert and incorporating it into the learning process of our recognition system using the rough mereology methods. We also show how this knowledge acquisition can be conducted in an interactive manner, with a large dataset of handwritten digits as an example.

Keywords: Rough mereology, concept approximation, machine learning, handwritten digit recognition.

1 Overview

A typical pattern recognition system attempts to describe the characteristic features of the target recognition classes so that new samples could be identified when checked against those features. Most existing systems employ some kind of hierarchical descriptions of complex patterns built from *primitives*, elemental blocks that can be extracted directly from input data. For this task, in most cases, a descriptive language, or a reasoning scheme, adopted beforehand is used for the learning process and only final quantitative parameters for the description are extracted from data. The development of rough set methods, however, have shown that the language, or the scheme itself can, and should, be determined by the data rather than provided *a priori*. Recent experiments confirmed that this approach can allow to gain significant improvement in classification results. We show that this process can be further refined using background knowledge provided by a human expert.

The second problem covered in this paper involves the treatment of a typical samples. The extensive development of computer techniques for the automatic recognition of complex graphical objects like handwritten digits often or characters is often based on machine learning methods that allow to capture the essential characteristics of the studied objects from training sets. It is can be however observed that there usually is a portion of training samples that defies this learning process, and therefore are referred to as 'atypical' or 'hard' samples. Until recently, understanding these samples had nor received much investigation

S. Tsumoto et al. (Eds.): RSCTC 2004, LNAI 3066, pp. 643–652, 2004.

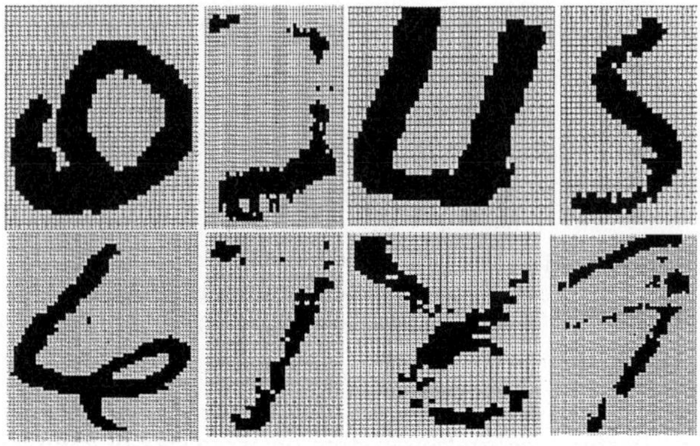

Fig. 1. Hard Digit Samples

as most researches considered them as mere statistical error or a kind of unavoidable noise in the training data. But there is currently an observable trends in the optical character recognition (OCR) research community which attempts to address this problem and give the atypical samples a more adequate treatment, most usually by means of multilayered hybrid recognition systems.

In this paper, we present a scheme for incorporating domain knowledge about handwritten digit samples into the learning process. The knowledge is provided by an hypothetical expert that will interact with the classification system during a later phase of the learning process, providing certain 'guidance' to the difficult task of adaptive searching for correct classifiers. The main underlying assumption is that when the feature space is as large as in the case of handwritten digits, algorithms seeking to approximate human reasoning functions will perform better if equipped with domain knowledge provided by a human expert.

In distinction to most popular domain knowledge based approaches widely used in recognition systems, ours concentrates on specific difficult, error-prone samples encountered during the learning phase. The expert will pass the correct classification of such cases to the system along with his explanation on how he arrived at his decision on the class identity of the sample. The system then attempts to translate this knowledge into its own descriptive language and primitives, to rebuild its classifiers.

We describe the process of transferring the expert's reasoning scheme into the recognition system, based on the rough mereology approach to concept's approximation [7], [11]. We also present the mechanism of interaction between expert and the classifier construction system presented in [1]. This is a development and extension of the methods and results described in [5]. In particular, we show how complex spatial relations between parts of graphical objects can be approximated.

2 Description of the Handwritten Recognition System

For the research in this paper we use a handwritten digit recognition engine based on the Enhanced Loci coding scheme, which assigns to every image's pixel a code reflecting the topology of its neighborhood. Codes for neighboring regions then can be combined to reflect the internal structure of the digit's image. Loci coding, though simple, has proved to be very successful in digit recognition. For a detailed description of this coding scheme, consult [3].

Once the Loci coding is done, the digit image is segmented into regions consisting of pixels with the same code value. These regions then serve as *primitives* to build the graph representation of the image [6].

Typical digit recognition systems classify an unknown sample by computing its 'distance' or 'similarity' to a collection of prototypes established during the training phase. This is often done on an uniform basis, irrespective to the 'difficulty' of the investigated sample, whereas it is obvious that not all samples are equally easy to classify. Samples that are far from the 'centers' of the class prototypes tend to fall on the boundaries between classes, are more error-prone and hence can be regarded as more 'difficult'. While existing recognition algorithms perform well on most 'regular' digit subclasses, the majority of 'difficult' samples can only be recognized with additional knowledge, most often provided by a human expert.

A straightforward criteria to detect such samples can be defined as follows:

Let PG_k be the prototype set constructed for class k during the training phase and d_k be the distance function established for that class. An unknown digit sample u_k of class k is considered 'difficult', 'hard' or 'atypical' if:

$$d_k(u_k, PG_k) \geq \rho \max\{(v, PG_K) : v \in TR \wedge CLASS(v) = k\}$$

where $\rho \in (0, 1]$ is some cut-off threshold and TR is the training table.

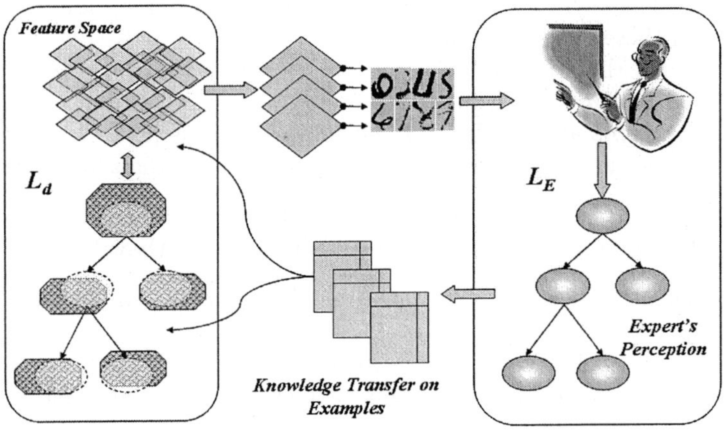

Fig. 2. System's Overview

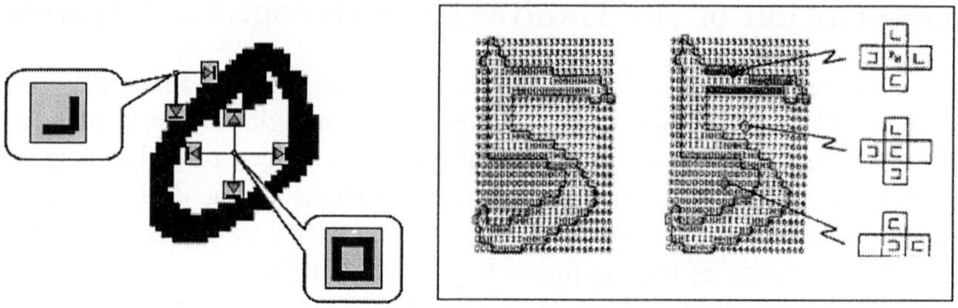

Fig. 3. The Loci coding scheme

A more refined approach assumes samples repeatedly misclassified during cross-validation tests in the training phase as 'difficult'. Since class identity of all digit samples are known during the training phase, we can detect the 'hard' ones beforehand and submit them to the expert for review.

3 Expert's Knowledge Transfer

3.1 General Scheme

Now suppose that at some point during the training phase, we detect a number of samples of class k that are misclassified. The samples are submitted to the expert, which returns not only the correct class identity, but also an explanation on *why*, and perhaps more importantly, *how* he arrived at his decision. This is denoted in the form of a rule:

$$[CLASS(u) = k] \equiv \Im(EFeature_1(u), ..., EFeature_n(u))$$

where $EFeature_i$ represents the expert's perception of some characteristics of the sample u, while synthesis operator $\Im$ represents his perception of some relations between these characteristics.

It is assumed that the expert's reasoning scheme, and therefore, the actual structure of $EFeature_i$ in general is not flat, but can be multi-layered with various sub-concepts at subsequent levels of abstractions [9].

For example, the expert may express his perception of digit '5' as (See Fig.4):

$[CLASS(u) =$'5'$] \equiv a, b, c, d$ are parts of u; 'Above_Right'(a,b); 'HStroke'(a); $b = Compose(c, d)$; 'VStroke'(c); 'WBelly'(d); 'Above'(c, d),

where *Compose* is an assembling operator that produces a bigger part from smaller components.

The above means if there is a west-open belly below a vertical stroke and the two have a horizontal stroke above-right in the sample's image, then the sample is a '5'.

The main challenge here is that the expert explanation is expressed in his own descriptive language, intrinsically related to his natural perception of images

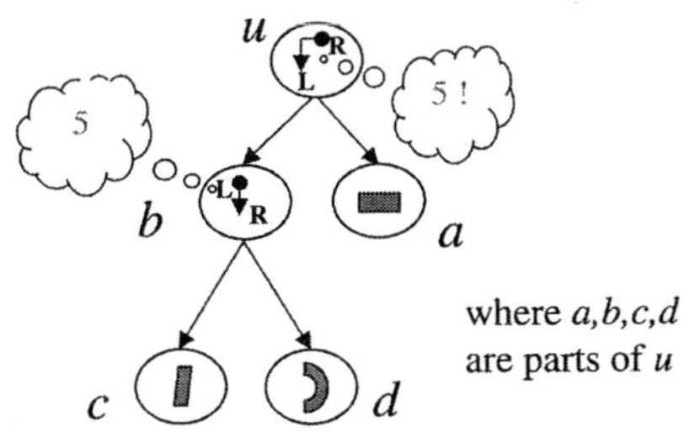

Fig. 4. Object Perception Provided by Expert

and often heavily based on natural language constructs (a *foreign language* L_f), while classifiers have a different language designed to, for example, facilitate the computation of physical characteristics of the images (a *domestic language* L_d). For example, the expert may view sample images as a collection of shapes or strokes ("A '6' is something that has a neck connected with a circular belly") while the recognition system regards the samples as graphs of Loci-based nodes. The knowledge passing process hence can be considered as approximating of expert's concept by the classifier construction system.

It is essential here that the concept matching should not be 'crisp', but expressed by some rough inclusion measures, determining if something is satisfying the concept to a certain degree [1]. For instance, a stroke at 85 degree to the horizontal can still be regarded as a vertical stroke, though obviously with a degree less than 1.0. The extent of such variations may be provided by the expert (e.g., by providing samples that represent 'extreme' instances of a given concept).

Let us further assume that such an inclusion measure is denoted by $Match(p, C) \in [0, 1]$, where p is a pattern (or a set of patterns) encoded in L_d and C is a concept expressed in L_f. An example of concept inclusion measures would be:

$$Match(p, C) = \frac{|\{u \in T : Found(p, u) \wedge Fit(C, u)\}|}{|\{u \in T : Fit(C, u)\}|}$$

where T is a common set of samples used by both the system and the expert to communicate with each other on the nature of expert's concepts, $Found(p, u)$ means a pattern p is present in u and $Fit(C, u)$ means u is regarded by the expert as fit to his concept C.

Our principal goal is, for each expert's explanation, find sets of patterns Pat, Pat_1,...,Pat_n and a relation $\Im_d$ such that

$$\textbf{if } (\forall i : Match(Pat_i, EFeature_i) \geq p_i) \wedge (Pat = \Im_d(Pat_1, ..., Pat_n))$$
$$\textbf{then } Quality(Pat) > \alpha$$

where $p, p_i : i \in \{1, .., n\}$ and α are certain cutoff thresholds, while the *Quality* measure, intended to verify if the target pattern *Pat* fits into the expert's concept of digit class k, can be any, or combination, of the following criteria:

– $Support_{CLASS=k}(Pat) = |\{u \in U : Found(Pat, u) \wedge CLASS(u) = k\}|$

– $Confidence_{CLASS=k}(Pat) = \dfrac{Support(Pat)}{|\{u \in U : Found(Pat, u)\}|}$

– $Coverage_{CLASS=k}(Pat) = \dfrac{Support(Pat)}{|\{u \in U : CLASS(u) = k\}|}$

where U is the training set.

In other words, we seek to translate the expert's knowledge into the domestic language so that to generalize the expert's reasoning to the largest possible number of physical digit samples. The requirements on inclusion degrees ensure the stability of the target reasoning scheme, as the target pattern Pat retains its quality regardless of deviations at input patterns Pat_i as long as they still approximate the expert's concept $EFeature_i$ to degrees at least p_i. This may also be described as *pattern robustness.*

Another important aspect of this process is its *concept approximation robustness*, meaning not only does it ensure that the target pattern Pat will retain its quality with regard to input patterns deviations in inclusion degrees, but it also should guarantee that if we have some input patterns Pat'_i equally "close" or "similar" to $EFeature_i$, then the target pattern $Pat' = \Im_d(Pat'_1, ..., Pat'_n)$ will meet the same quality requirements as Pat to a satisfactory degree. This leads to an approximation of $EFeature_i$ that is independent from particular patterns Pat_i, allowing us to construct approximation schemes that focus on inclusion degrees p_i rather than on a specific input patterns Pat_i.

3.2 Basic Pattern Approximation

One can observe that the main problem that poses here is how to establish the interaction between the expert who reasons in L_f and the classifier construction system that uses L_d. Here, once again, the system has to learn (with the expert's help) "what he meant when he said what he said." More precisely, the system will have to construct the measure $Match$ and the relation $\Im_d$.

In order to learn the measure $Match$, which essentially means we are trying to learn the expert's concept of $EFeature_i$, we will ask the expert to examine a given set of samples U and provide a decision table (U, d) where d is the expert decision whether $EFeature_i$ is present in a particular sample from U, for instance, whether a sample has a "WBelly" or not. We then try to select a set of features in the system's domestic language that will approximate the decision d, for example, number of pixels with the NES Loci code. For example:

In the above table, #NES is the number of white pixels that are bounded in all directions except to the West.

In the next step, the expert will , instead of just answer whether a particular feature is present or not, express how strong his belief in his perception of the feature, using some 'soft' degree like 'Strong','Fair','Weak' etc. He might be asked by the system to provide reference samples with such degrees of belief, as well as to pick from samples presented to him by the system those he considered fit into his concept in a particular degree.

Table 1. Pattern approximation

	WBelly
u_1	yes
u_2	no
...	...
u_n	yes

$\Rightarrow$

	#NES	WBelly
u_1	252	*Strong*
u_2	4	*Weak*
...	...	...
u_n	90	*Fair*

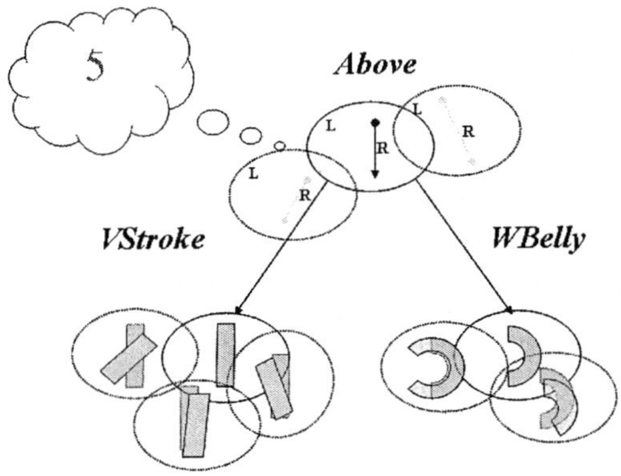

Fig. 5. Confidence degrees expressed by expert

Since the sample set U comprises mostly of 'difficult' cases and other special cases that need to be examined by an expert, it is assumed that U is not too large. Experiments conducted have shown that basic level features can be effectively approximated with high coverage, using straightforward greedy heuristics. A typical set of about 20–30 samples allows to approximate basic concept such as 'Belly' or 'Vertical Stroke' within seconds.

3.3 Pattern Relation Approximation

Having approximated the concepts $EFeature_i$, we can try to translate the expert's relation $\Im$ into our $\Im_d$ by asking the expert to go through U and provide us with the additional attributes of whether he found the $EFeature_i$ and a decision d if the relation $\Im$ holds.

We then replace the attributes corresponding to $EFeature_i$ with the characteristic functions of the domestic feature sets that approximate those concepts and try to add other features, possibly induced from original domestic primitives, in order to approximate the decision d. Again, this task should be resolved by means of adaptive or evolutionary search strategies without too much computing burden.

Here is an example how the concept of a 'vertical stroke' 'above' a 'west-open belly' would be approximated:

In the above table, #V_S is the number of black pixels having the Loci code characterizing a vertical stroke and $S_y < B_y$ tells whether the median center of

Table 2. Pattern relation approximation

	VStroke	WBelly	Above
u_1	yes	yes	yes
u_2	yes	no	no
...	...	...	...
u_n	yes	yes	no

⇒

	#V_S	#NES	$S_y < B_y$	Above
u_1	34	252	yes	yes
u_2	45	4	no	no
...	...	...	...	...
u_n	40	150	no	no

⇓

	Match(#V_S,VStroke)	*Match* (#NES,WBelly)	*Match* ($S_y < B_y$)	*Match*(Above)
u_1	0.85	0.95	(yes,1.0)	(yes, 0.9)
u_2	0.95	1.0	(no, 0.1)	(no, 0.05)
...	...	...	...	...
u_n	0.90	0.70	(no, 0.3)	(no, 0.15)

Table 3. Reasoning with soft matching degrees

	Match(VStroke)	*Match* (WBelly)	*Match* (Above)	*Is* 5?
u_1	*Fair*	*Strong*	*Strong*	*Strong*
u_2	*Strong*	*Strong*	*Weak*	*Fair*
...	...	...	...	...
u_n	*Fair*	*Weak*	*Weak*	*Weak*

the stroke is placed closer to the upper edge of the image than the median center of the belly. The third table shows degrees of inclusion of these domestic features in the original expert's concept "VStroke", "WBelly" or "Above" respectively.

Similarly to the procedure described in the previous subsection, the expert can express his degree of belief and help the system approximate his belief's scale in an interactive procedure. This is to enhance the pattern matching process with soft degrees of concept matching. Instead of implicit numeric degrees of inclusion, we can ask the expert to provide us with a description on of how he perceives a particular feature on a particular subsets of samples. This, as experiments show, sometimes proves crucial in allowing the search for the approximation to succeed, as well as to significantly reduce the time needed to do so.

The Table 2 now becomes Table 3.

The main idea behind pattern relation approximation is the observation that while "crisp" learning essentially requires a search through the product space of many $EFeature_i$, which is often complex and computationally prohibitive, the additional relation $\Im$ will provide a "guidance" that helps navigate throughout the possible feature space and ultimately will allow a more successful search result.

It is noteworthy that the concept approximation process should work under a requirement to the quality of the searched global pattern Pat, which should have a substantial support among other samples, not examined by the expert, from the training collection. This will ensure the knowledge passed by the expert on a particular example is actually generalized into more global concept.

4 Experiments

In order to illustrate the developed methods, we conducted a series of experiments on the U.S. National Institute of Standards and Technology (NIST) Handwritten Segmented Character Special Database 3, a major reference base within the handwritten character recognition community (For details see [2]). We compared the performances gained by a standard learning approach, described in [6] with and without the aid of the domain knowledge. The additional knowledge, passed by an human expert on popular classes as well as some atypical samples allowed to reduce the time needed by the learning phase from 205 minutes to 168 minutes, which means an improvement of about 22 percent without loss in classification quality. The representational samples found are also slightly simpler than those found without using the background knowledge.

5 Conclusion

An interactive method for incorporating domain knowledge into the design and development of a classification system is presented. We have demonstrated how approximate reasoning scheme can be used in the process of knowledge transfer from human expert's ontology, often expressed in natural language, into computable pattern features. Developed schemes ensure stability and adaptability of constructed classifiers. We have shown how granular computing, equipped with rough mereology concepts can be effectively applied to a highly practical field such as OCR and handwritten digit recognition. Preliminary experiments conducted showed that presented methods can help improve the learning process and provides a better understanding of the dataset investigated.

Acknowledgment

The author would like to relay his gratitude to professor Andrzej Skowron of Warsaw University for his insights and profound comments on approximate reasoning schemes as well as his invaluable encouragements with the development of the presented experimental system.

This work has been partly supported by Grant 3 T11C 002 26 funded by the Ministry of Scientific Research and Information Technology of the Republic of Poland.

References

1. P. Doherty, W. Lukasiewicz, and A. Skowron. *Knowledge Engineering: Rough Set Approach.* Physica Verlag, in preparation.
2. J. Geist, R. A. Wilkinson, S. Janet, P. J. Grother, B. Hammond, N. W. Larsen, R. M. Klear, C. J. C. Burges, R. Creecy, J. J. Hull, T. P. Vogl, and C. L. Wilson. The second census optical character recognition systems conference. *NIST Technical Report NISTIR 5452*, pages 1–261, 1994.

3. K. Komori, T. Kawatani, K. Ishii, and Y. Iida. A feature concentrated method for character recognition. In Bruce Gilchrist, editor, *Information Processing 77, Proceedings of the International Federation for Information Processing Congress 77*, pages 29–34, Toronto, Canada, August 8-12, 1977. North Holland.
4. Z.C. Li, C.Y. Suen, and J. Guo. Hierarchical models for analysis and recognition of handwritten characters. *Annals of Mathematics and Artificial Intelligence*, pages 149–174, 1994.
5. Tuan Trung Nguyen and Andrzej Skowron. Rough set approach to domain knowledge approximation. In G. Wang, Q. Liu, Y. Yao, and A. Skowron, editors, *Proceedings of the 9th International Conference: Rough Sets, Fuzzy Sets, Data Mining, and Granular Computing, RSFDGRC'03. Lecture Notes in Computer Science Vol. 2639*, pages 221–228, Chongqing, China, Oct 19-22, 2003. Springer Verlag.
6. Tuan Trung Nguyen. Adaptive classifier construction: An approach to handwritten digit recognition. In J.J. Alpigini, J.F. Peters, A. Skowron, and N. Zhong, editors, *Proceedings of the Third International Conference on Rough Sets and Current Trends in Computing,RSCTC 2002. Lecture Notes in Computer Science Vol. 2475*, pages 578–585, Malvern, PA, USA, October 14-16, 2002, 2002. Springer Verlag.
7. L. Polkowski and A. Skowron. Rough mereology: A new paradigm for approximate reasoning. *Journal of Approximate Reasoning*, 15(4):333–365, 1996.
8. L. Polkowski and A. Skowron. Towards adaptive calculus of granules. In L.A. Zadeh and J. Kacprzyk, editors, *Computing with Words in Information/Intelligent Systems*, pages 201–227, Heidelberg, 1999. Physica-Verlag.
9. L. Polkowski and A. Skowron. Constructing rough mereological granules of classifying rules and classifying algorithms. In B. Bouchon-Meunier, J.Rios-Gutierrez, L. Magdalena, and R.R. Yager, editors, *Technologies for Constructing Intelligent Systems I*, pages 57–70, Heidelberg, 2002. Physica-Verlag.
10. Robert J. Schalkoff. *Pattern Recognition: Statistical, Structural and Neural Approaches.* John Wiley & Sons, Inc., 1992.
11. A. Skowron and L. Polkowski. Rough mereological foundations for design, analysis, synthesis, and control in distributed systems. *Information Sciences*, 104(1-2):129–156, 1998.

An Automatic Analysis System for Firearm Identification Based on Ballistics Projectile

Jun Kong[1,2], Dongguang Li[1], and Chunnong Zhao[1]

[1] School of Computer and Information Science, Edith Cowan University
2 Bradford Street, Mount Lawley 6050 Perth, Western Australia
[2] School of Computer Science, Northeast Normal University
138 Renmin Street, Changchun, Jilin, China
kongjun@nenu.edu.cn

Abstract. Characteristic markings on the cartridge and projectile of a bullet are produced when a gun is fired. Over thirty different features within these marks can be distinguished, which in combination produce a "fingerprint" for identification of a firearm. Given a means of automatically analyzing features within such a firearm fingerprint, it will be possible to identify not only the type and model of a firearm, but also each individual weapon as effectively as human fingerprint identification can be achieved. In this paper, a new analytic system based on fast Fourier transform (FFT) for identifying the projectile specimens digitized using the line-scan imaging technique automatically is proposed. Experimental results show that the proposed system has the ability of efficient and precise analysis and identification for projectiles specimens.

1 Introduction

The analysis of marks on bullet casings and projectiles provides a precise tool for identifying the firearm from which a bullet is discharged [1] [2]. Characteristic markings on the cartridge and projectile of a bullet are produced when a gun is fired. Over thirty different features within these marks can be distinguished, which in combination produce a "fingerprint" for identification of a firearm. This forensic technique is the vital element for legal evidence, in cases where the use of firearms is involved. Projectile bullets fired through the barrel of a gun will exhibit extremely fine striation markings, some of which are derived from minute irregularities in barrel produced during the manufacturing process. The examination of these striations on land marks and groove marks of the projectile is difficult using conventional optical microscopy. However, digital imaging techniques have the potential to detect the presence of striations on ballistics specimens for identification. Given a means of automatically analyzing features within such a firearm "fingerprint", it will be possible to identify not only the type and model of a firearm, but also each individual weapon as effectively as human fingerprint identification can be achieved. Due to the skill required and intensive nature of ballistics identification, law enforcement agencies around the world have expressed considerable interest in the application of ballistics imaging identification systems to both greatly reduce the time for identification and to introduce reliability (or repeatability) to the process.

S. Tsumoto et al. (Eds.): RSCTC 2004, LNAI 3066, pp. 653–658, 2004.

The papers on the automatic identification of a cartridge cases and projectiles are hardly to be found. L. P. Xin [3] proposed a cartridge cases based identification system for firearm authentication. C. Kou et al. [4] described a neural network based model for the identification of the chambering marks on cartridge cases.

In this paper, a new analytic system based on fast Fourier transform (FFT) for identifying the projectile specimens captured using the line-scan imaging technique automatically is proposed. In Section 2, the line-scan imaging technique for projectiles capturing is described. The analytic approach based on FFT for identifying the projectile characteristics and the experimental results are presented in Section 3. And Section 4 gives a short conclusion.

2 Line-Scan Imaging Technique for Projectile Capturing

The proposed analysis system for identifying the projectiles is composed of three parts (shown in **Fig. 1**), and each part is described in detail in following sections.

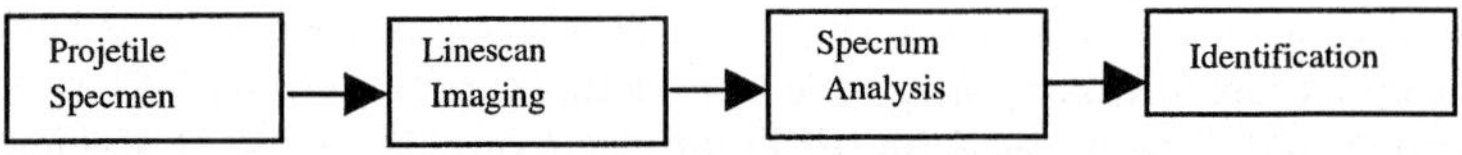

Fig. 1. The diagram of proposed analysis system.

Line-Scan Imaging. The traditional light microscopy technique for imaging the cylindrical shapes of ballistics specimen is inherently unsuitable for high contrast imaging. It is difficult to maintain image quality from oblique lighting on a cylindrical surface, from low magnification microscopy because of loss of focus and definition as the specimen is translated and rotated [5]. However, we can obtain the surface information from a cylindrical shaped surface using a line-scan imaging technique by scanning consecutive columns of picture information and storing the data in a frame buffer to produce a 2D image of the surface of the cylindrical specimen. Relative motion between the line array of sensors in the line-scan camera and the surface being inspected is the feature of the line-scan technique. With the line-scan technique, because the cylindrical ballistics specimen is rotated about an axis of rotation relative to a stationary line array of sensor, then all points on the imaging line of the sample are in focus. Hence, all points on the rotating surface will be captured on the collated image during one full rotation of the cylindrical ballistics specimen [5].

The projectile specimens in our study are provided by Western Australia Police Station including four classes (belonging to four guns). They are: 1) Browning, semi-automatic pistol, in caliber 9mm. 2) Norinco, semiautomatic pistol, in caliber 9mm. 3) and 4) Long Rifle, semiautomatic pistol, in caliber 22. All the projectile specimens in our study are recorded using the line-scan imaging technique discussed above. Some line-scanned images of four class in our study are shown **Fig. 2**.

In the real application, the line-scanned image of a projectile specimen could be affected and noised by many factors such as the lighting conditions, the material, and the original texture on the surface of specimen. All these can bring strong noise into the line-scanned image and would bring many difficulties to extract and identify the important features used for identifying the individual specimen, such as the contours, edges, the directions and the width (or distance) of land and groove marks. In order to remove or decrease the affection mentioned above, we need image pre-processing operations on the line-scanned images obtained above.

Contrast Enhancement and Feature Extraction. The images (the effective regions in original images) shown in **Fig. 3** a, b, c, and d are transformed versions corresponding to the images in **Fig. 2** by region selecting and contrast enhancement transformation. We adopt the *Sobel* operators to extract the contours and edges of the land and groove marks on line-scanned images of projectile specimens. For the reason that the directions of the land and the groove marks of the projectile specimens are all or almost along 90 degree in the line-scanned images, we only adopted the vertical direction mask for extracting the features, shown in **Fig. 3** e, f, g, and h, of the line-scanned images.

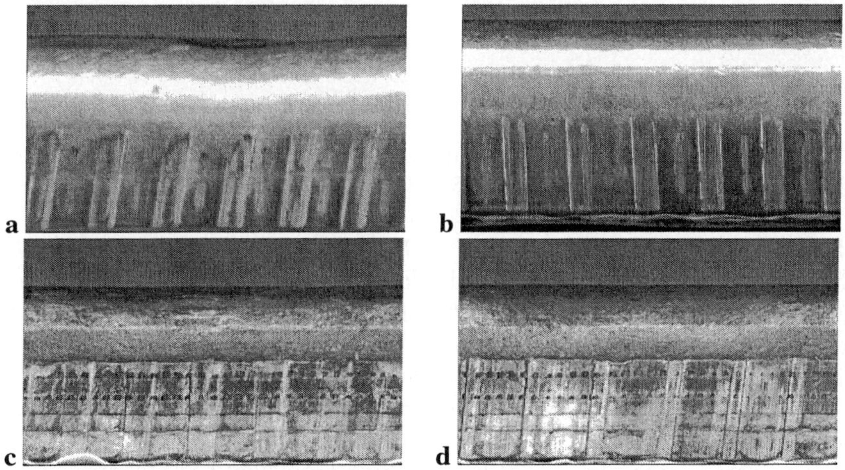

Fig. 2. Four class line-scanned images in our study (with code: a, 101; b, 201; c, 301; d, 401).

3 FFT-Based Analysis for Projectile Identification

The Fourier spectrum is ideally suited for describing the directionality of periodic or almost periodic 2-D patterns in an image. These global texture patterns, although easily distinguishable as concentrations of high-energy burst in the spectrum, generally are quite difficult to detect with spatial methods because of the local nature of these techniques.

The plots of radius and angle spectrum corresponding to images in **Fig. 3** a, b are shown in **Fig. 4** a, b, c and d, respectively. The results clearly exhibit directional 'energy' distributions of the surface texture between class one and two. Comparing **Fig. 4** a and b, the plots of radius spectrum, the former contains six clear peaks in the range of low frequencies (r <20), the later has only three peaks in the same range and is smooth in shape, this indicates that 'energy' of the class one specimen is distributed in several permanent positions, and also reveals that the class one specimens has a coarse surface texture and the wide land and groove marks, while the surface texture of class two is fine and the wide of land and groove marks is thin.

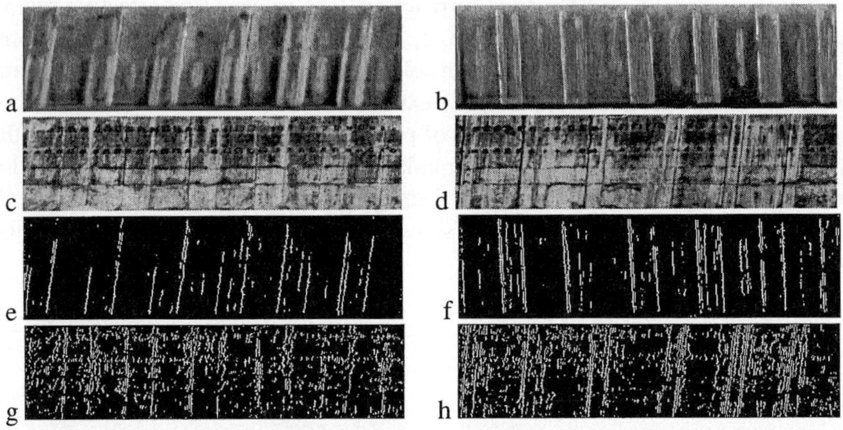

Fig. 3. Contrast enhancement results (a, b with size 400×110, and c, d with size 400×100), and the contours and edges extracting using Sobel operator.

The angular spectrums (**Fig. 4** c and d) display a great distinctness in position of prominent peaks between class one and two. Further study reveals that the angular spectrum is able to clearly indicate the angular position of periodic grooves or scratches on the surface with respect to the measurement coordinate. It can be seen from the angular spectrum there is a maximum peak at bout 81 degree in **Fig. 4** c. This is indicative of scratches (the land or groove marks) oriented in the direction 81 degree on the surface of projectiles , while the maximum peak in **Fig. 4** d at bout 95 degree. In addition, the former plot has a second prominent peak (corresponding to small or shallow marks on the projectiles surface) at about 100 degree. However, the second peak of **Fig. 4** d is at about 85 degree.

The characteristics of projectile specimen surface textures can also be revealed by examining quantitative differences of spectrums using a set of features. To compare and analyze the spectrums differences of class one and two easily, a set of features is used, and the quantitative results are shown in Table 1(where r_1 and a_2, Max; r_2 and a_3, Mean; r_3 and a_4, Std; r_4 and a_5, Max**:** Median; and a_1, Position of maximum peak).

It can be observed from **Table 1** that the Max, Mean, and Std of class one have a relatively small than class two, while the relative variation for radio between Max and Mean is greater. And the difference of prominent peaks (corresponding to the orientations of land and groove marks) of class one and two is 14 degrees. This provides evidence that FFT spectrum analysis, in the form of quantification, can reveal characteristic and directional surface textures of projectile specimen.

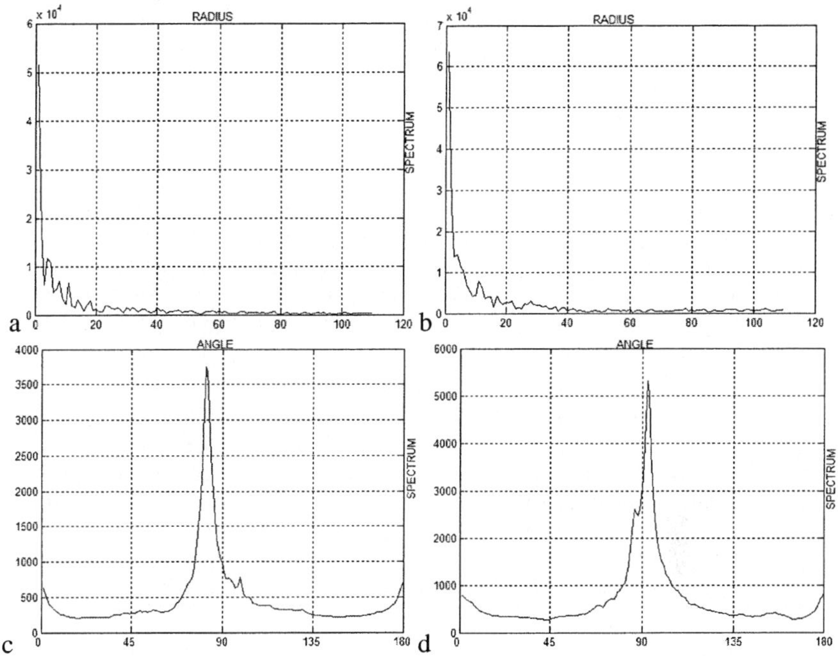

Fig. 4. Radial spectrum (a, b) and Angular spectrum (c, d) of the images (a, b) in Fig. 3.

Table 1. Radial spectrum and angular spectrum statistics results of **Fig. 3** a and b.

Class	Code	Radial spectrum				Angular spectrum				
		r_1	r_2	r_3	r_4	a_1	a_2	a_3	a_4	a_5
1	101	51517	1728	5372	29.81	81	3753	475.2	546.2	7.898
2	201	63646	2538	6809	25.07	95	5308	697.9	794.7	7.600

All experimental results of projectiles in our study are listed in **Table 2**.

Identification. Observing **Table 2** and recalling that the calibers of type one and two are same, and so are the type three and four, we can easily identify the projectiles using any one of features listed in Table 2. For example, all the values of r_4 for type one are greater than 28.0, while for type two, no one is greater than 26.0. Same result can be obtained using others features in **Table 2**.

4 Conclusion

In this paper, a new analytic system for identifying the projectile specimens is proposed. We not only present an approach for capturing the surface image of projectile at high resolution using line-scan imaging technique, but also presented a novel and effective FFT-based analysis technique for projectiles analyzing and identifying. The characteristics we used in spectrum analysis can be formed as a set of features vectors

Table 2. Radial spectrum and angular spectrum statistics results of specimens in our study.

Class	Code	Radial spectrum				Angular spectrum				
		r_1	r_2	r_3	r_4	a_1	a_2	a_3	a_4	a_5
1	101	51517	1728	5372	29.81	81	3753	475.2	546.2	7.898
	102	51162	1591	5187	32.16	81	3709	437.6	545.6	8.487
	103	51200	1520	5087	33.68	81	3583	418.2	509.8	8.571
	104	51556	1699	5348	30.34	81	3589	467.3	514.1	7.685
	105	62715	1962	6299	31.96	81	4219	539.5	617.8	7.827
2	201	63646	2538	6809	25.07	95	5308	697.9	794.7	7.600
	202	64381	2738	7038	23.51	95	5257	752.9	777.7	6.990
	203	64059	2545	6707	25.16	95	5193	700.0	794.0	7.419
3	301	63959	2899	6942	22.06	86	2514	724.7	451.9	3.469
	302	64448	2478	6889	26.01	86	2714	719.4	445.5	3.774
	303	64288	2743	7090	23.43	86	2517	685.8	439.9	3.669
	304	63694	3011	6999	21.23	86	2750	752.7	512.8	3.657
4	401	76059	4040	8554	18.27	79	4965	1010	787.8	4.916
	402	76406	5026	8982	15.20	79	4972	1256	835.6	3.959
	403	75607	3735	8035	20.23	79	4897	933.9	753.3	5.249
	404	76796	3786	8498	20.28	79	4135	946.3	738.6	4.371

for the building of an intelligent system for projectile automatic identification in further works. This system can make a significant contribution towards the efficient and precise analysis of firearm identification based on ballistics projectiles. The study demonstrates that different types of land and groove marks generated by different guns have distinctive surface textures, and these textures can be measured and identified effectively by spectral analysis. This makes it clear that spectral analysis is an effective method to study line-scanned images of projectile specimen. This technique can surmount difficulties with descriptions in the normal spacial domain in identifying texture features formed by land and groove marks in the surface of projectile.

References

1. C.L. Smith, and J.M. Cross, (1995): Optical Imaging Techniques for Ballistics Specimens to Identify Firearms. Proceedings of the 29th Annual 1995 International Carnahan Conference on Security Technology, pp. 275-289, Oct. 1995, England.
2. R. Saferstein (ED), (1988) Forensic Science Handbook: Volume 2. Englewood Cliffs: Prentice Hall, 1988.
3. Le-Ping Xin, (2000): A Cartridge Identification System for Firearm Authentication. WCCC_ICSP 2000. 5th International Conference on Volume: 2, P1405-1408.
4. Chenyuan Kou, Cheng-Tan Tung and H. C. FU, (1994): FISOFM: Firearms Identification based on SOFM Model of Neural Network. Institute of Electrical and Electronics Engineers 28th Annual 1994 International Carnahan Conference on , 12-14 Oct. Pages: 120-125.
5. C.L. Smith, Robinson, M. and Evans, P.: Line-scan Imaging for the positive identification of ballistics. International Carnahan Conference on Security Technology, 269-275. 2000.

Granulation Based Image Texture Recognition

Zheng Zheng, Hong Hu, and Zhongzhi Shi

Key Laboratory of Intelligent Information Processing, Institute of Computing Technology
Chinese Academy of Sciences, Beijing, China
Graduate School of the Chinese Academy of Sciences, Beijing, China
Bao_zhengzheng@263.net

Abstract. Granular computing as an enabling technology and as such it cuts across a broad spectrum of disciplines and becomes important to many areas of applications. In this paper, we present our model of information granulation that is more suitable to image recognition. Then, we construct an image granule framework and present a granulation based image texture recognition algorithm. We compare our algorithm with some other algorithms and the results show that our algorithm is effective and efficient.

1 Introduction

Information granules, as the name itself stipulates, are collections of entities, usually originating at the numberic level, that are arranged together due to their similarity, functional adjacency, indistinguishability, coherency or alike [1,2]. Information granules as all abstraction of our reality are aimed at building efficient and user-centered views of the external world and supporting and facilitating our perception of the surrounding physical and virtual world. Granular computing as an enabling technology and as such it cuts across a broad spectrum of disciplines and becomes important to many areas of applications.

Multiple-scale texture-shape recognition approach tries to cluster textures and shapes. In a multi-resolution approach, texture and shape should be analyzed at different levels. Usually texture can be viewed as a random field [3] or fractals [4]. In this paper, we construct an image granulation model. By using our granulation model, we extract features from image set and use our image relation to select some important features. Then, we use the selected features to recognize new samples. The results of experiments show that our algorithm is efficient and effective.

2 Framework of Image Granulation

When people recognize images, they don't bury in a minute analysis completed at the level of individual pixels. They concentrate to identity some higher level entities. Besides, when they find the key features to recognize images, they often find some big differences rather than small ones. These phenomenons inspire us to use granular computing to image recognition. Based on these, we define the image granulation that can take our algorithm's concentration on higher level entities of image.

S. Tsumoto et al. (Eds.): RSCTC 2004, LNAI 3066, pp. 659–664, 2004.

Definition 1. Image G can be viewed as nested framework. To construct the framework of image granulation is to simplify G, that is, to arrange the pixels in G to different granules due to their similarity, their adjacency, indistinguishability, coherency or alike. According to these, we can construct a triple set $<G\ F,\ >$ and a granular domain $[G]$. we define the function $[G]$—>$[Y]$ as $[F]$, where [Y] is the new feature set of the granules in $[G]$ and $[\Gamma]$ is a new structure of the granules in $[G]$. The first level of an image is a set of quintuplet $IG^0_{GL_0} = (x^0, y^0, q^0_0, q^0_1, .q^0_2)$, where $IG^0_{GL_0}$ can be viewed as a pixel of image. $L_0 = (x^0, y^0)$ is the pixel's location and $(q^0_0, q^0_1, .q^0_2)$ is its RGB values. Besides, we define $X^0_G = \{IG^0_{GL_0}\}$ and $X^0 = \bigcup_G X^0_G$.

Definition 2. Suppose $IG^l_{GL_l 1}, IG^l_{GL_l 2}$ are two image granules of level l and a vector $T^l_{IG^l_{GL_l j}} = (t^l_{j1}, t^l_{j2}, ..., t^l_{jn})$ is assigned to $IG^l_{GL_l j}$ that is computed from $IG^{l-1}_{GL_{l-1}}$. L_l is the location of $IG^l_{GL_l}$. $SIMILAR^l(IG^l_{GL_l 1}, IG^l_{GL_l 2})$ is a similar relation. Based on this, higher level granules can be defined as

$IG^{l+1}_{GL_{l+1} 1} = [IG^l_{GL_l 1}] = \{IG^l_{GL_l j} \mid IG^l_{GL_l j}\ \text{SIMILAR}^l IG^l_{GL_l 1}\}$. $IG^{l+1}_{GL_{l+1} 1}$ is a set of l level granules near $IG^l_{GL_l 1}$ and feature vector $T^{l+1}_{[IG^l_{GL_l 1}]}$ can be computed from $IG^l \in [IG^l_{GL_l 1}]$.

3 Granulation Based Multiple-Scale Texture-Shape Recognition

Based on above definitions, we develop a granulation based multiple-scale texture-shape recognition algorithm. And accompany with the presentation of algorithm, we define some image granulation related concepts.

Algorithm. Granulation based multiple-scale texture-shape recognition algorithm (GTRA)
Step 1. Initiallization $X^0_G = \{IG^0_{GL_1}\}$ and $X^0 = \bigcup_G X^0_G$;

Step 2. Constructing image granules
While (condition)
{For $IG^l_{GL_1} \in X^l_g$, $IG^{1++}_{GL_{l+1}} = [IG^l_{GL_l}] = \{IG^l_{GL'_l} \mid IG^l_{GL'_l}\ \text{SIMILAR}^l IG^l_{GL_l}\}$ };

Here, we define $SIMILAR^l(\cdot) = dis^l(I^l_{gL^1_0}, I^l_{gL^2_0} \mid w_i) < r^l$ and

$$dis^0(Y, Z \mid w_i) = \sum_{i=0}^{n-1} w_i \cdot | y_i - z_i |, \text{ where } w_i = (1,1,0,0,0).$$

When $l>0$, there are two kinds of $SIMILAR^l(\cdot)$ relations. The first is same as that of level 0, that is $SIMILAR^l(IG^l_{GL_l 1}, IG^l_{GL_l 2}) = dis(IG^l_{GL_l 1}, IG^l_{GL_l 2} \mid W) < r^l$, where $W = \{w_0, w_1, ..., w_{n-1}\}$ and $dis(IG^l_1, IG^l_2 \mid W) = \sum_i w_i \mid t^l_{1i} - t^l_{2i} \mid$.

The second is called as "module-matching similar relation" and it is defined as *SM*.

We define small image blocks $M^l = \{m^l_0, m^l_1, ..., m^l_n\}$ as modules, where m^l_i belongs to an element of X^l, where $X^l = \bigcup_G X^l_G, X^l_G = \bigcup_{L_l} \{IG^l_{GL_l}\}$.

1	2	3
8	9	4
7	6	5

Fig. 1. Module.

$$SM^l(\mathrm{a, b}) = \begin{cases} 1, \text{if } \forall \mathrm{m} \in M^l(mDis(a,m) = mDis(b,m)) \\ 0, \quad \text{otherwise} \end{cases}$$

In our experiments, we only take binary 3×3 module as example. If $a \in \mathrm{X}^l_{\mathrm{G}}$, I_i is a pixel of a and I'_i is a pixel of m. The relative location i is showed in Fig. 1.

$$mDis(a,m) = \begin{cases} 1, \ if \forall((i<9) \wedge (dis(I_i, I_9 \mid w_M) > thr) \leftrightarrow (I'_i = 1)) \\ 0, \ \text{otherwise} \end{cases}$$,where $w_M = (0,0,1,....,1)$.

We define $[m^l_i]_{IG^{l+1}_{L_{l+1}}} = \{\mathrm{y} \mid \mathrm{y} \in IG^{l+1}_{L_{l+1}}, \mathrm{y}\ SM^l\ m^l_i\}$ and $T^{l+1}_{IG^{l+1}_{L_{l+1}}} = (L_{l+1}, \mid [m^l_0]_{IG^{l+1}_{L_{l+1}}} \mid, \mid [m^l_1]_{IG^{l+1}_{L_{l+1}}} \mid, ..., \mid [m^l_{n-1}]_{IG^{l+1}_{L_{l+1}}} \mid)$ is assigned to $IG^{l+1}_{L_{l+1}}$.

$T^{l+1}_{IG^{l+1}_{L_{l+1}}}$ is the spectrum of module-matching in $IG^{l+1}_{L_{l+1}}$.

We also define the spectrum of module-matching as $[M^l]_G = \{[m^l_0]_{\mathrm{X}^{l+1}_G}, [m^l_1]_{\mathrm{X}^{l+1}_G}, ..., [m^l_{n-1}]_{\mathrm{X}^{l+1}_G}\}$, where $[m^l_k]_{\mathrm{X}^{l+1}_G} = \bigcup_{L_{l+1}} [m^l_k]_{IG^{l+1}_{L_{l+1}}}$.

$[M^l] = \{[M^l]_G \mid \text{for all } \mathrm{G}\}$ is the set of all spectrums of all images.

Step 3. Constructing modules

While (condition)

{For each $[M^l]_G$ in $[M^l]$, $M^{l+1}_G = \{[M^l]_{G_1} \mid [M^l]_{G_1}\ SIMLAR^l [M^l]_G\}$;

Here, we define $dis^l([M^l]_{G_1}, [M^l]_{G_2} \mid w_i) = \sum_{i=0}^{n-1} w_i(\|[m^l_i]^2_{X^1_{G1}}\| - \|[m^l_i]^2_{X^1_{G2}}\|)^2$ (*).

Definition 3. Suppose U is a set of H typical images (seed images) and for each $G \in U$, M^{l+1}_G denotes a class of image that is similar with G. Each G_i belonging to class M_G^{l+1} has a m dimension vector $x_i^G = [M^l]_G$ that is $x_i^G = (x_{i1}^G, x_{i2}^G, \ldots, x_{im}^G)$ (i=1,2,..., n_G) and the size of class M_G^{l+1} is n_G,. We denote the class center of $M_{G_j}^{l+1}$ as $\bar{x}_k^{G_j} = \frac{1}{n_G}\sum_{i=1}^{n_G} x_{ik}^{G_j}$ (k=1, 2,..., m) and the center of all classes of images in U is $\bar{x}_k = \frac{1}{H}\sum_{j=1}^{H} x_k^{G_j}$.

Definition 4. The importance degree of each module is defined as:

$$\lambda_q = \frac{\sum_{j=1}^{r} n_{G_j} | x_q^{G_j} - \bar{x}_q |}{\sum_{j=1}^{r}\sum_{i=1}^{n_j} | x_{iq}^{G_j} - \bar{x}_q^{G_j} |}$$, which is the importance degree of each features.

Another key problem is how to define the thredhold β of the distance in formula (*).

Definition 5. We define $\beta = \theta \times \frac{\sum_{q=1}^{m} \max | x_{iq}^{G_j} - x_{i'q}^{G_{j'}} |}{m}$, where $i \neq i'$, $j \neq j'$ and θ is a constant.

Using β defined before, we can ignore some small between-class difference and concern greater differences. In our experiment, we define θ=0.618 that is the gold division point.

Step 4. *Result*={1,......,*m*};

Step 5. Sorting modules according to the value of λ_i (i=1to$n$) in decreasing order;

Step 6. Selecting effect module

For i=1 to n

{Delete $[m_i^l]_{X_G^{l+1}}$ from $[M^l]_G$;

If every two images (G_1 and G_2) in the same class satisfy G_1 *SIMLAR* ^{l} G_2,

then *Result=Result*-{i};

else Complete $[m_i^l]_{X_G^{l+1}}$ to $[M^l]_G$ };

The numbers in *Result* are the subscripts of modules selected.

Step 7. Result's evaluation

We use classification gain to evaluate the selected module set. The classification gain is computed by $cr = \frac{\sum_{i=1}^{C} n_i}{M}$.

Here, M is the total examples' number in for all classes to be classified, and n_i is the number of examples being correctly clustered in $[M^l]_G$.

4 Experiments

In the following experiments, 6 texture class groups ($TCG_0 \sim TCG_5$) are used and every image class group is created by a random affine transformation of a seed image. Every seed image creates a texture class that contains 10 affined texture images. Some seed images are showed in Fig. 2. The number of texture classes in these 6 groups are 10,20,30,41,51and 61 and TCG_i is a subset of TCG_{i+1}. An image *G* is classified to class *d*, if its feature vector has nearest distance with the feature vector of the seed image *S* of the class *d*. If *G* is just created by an affine transformation of *S*, the classified result is right, otherwise, it is wrong.

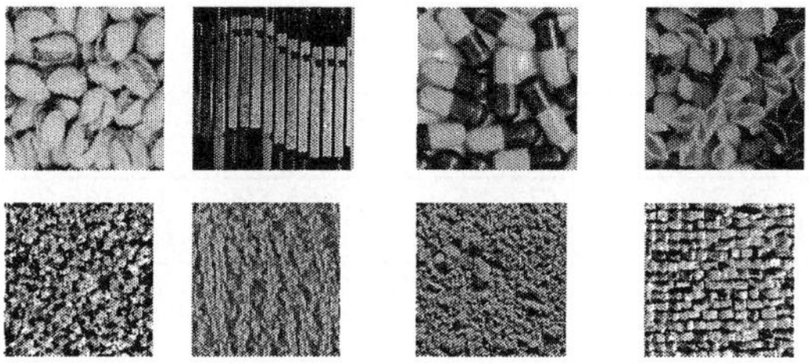

Fig. 2. Some seed images. Above 4 images from TCG_i, below 4 from DLTG.

The classification gain for above 6 texture classes group is showed in the table 1. Every item in the table 1 has 3 parts. The first part is the selected feature dimension when the highest classification gain appears, and the following two parts are two classification gains. The first classification gain is the highest gain of the selected feature and the second is the classification gain before feature selection.

The first row is the parameters of our algorithm and the others are about some popular multiple-scale texture-shape recognition algorithms[5]. We can find satisfied classification gain, but the selected features are often a little more than other methods. And our algorithm **GTRA** is more efficient than most of other algorithms because it can find final selected features once.

5 Conclusion

The concept of information granulation was first introduced by Zadeh in the context of fuzzy sets in 1979. The basic ideas of information granulation have appeared in fields, such as rough set theory, fuzzy set, quotient space and many others. There is a fast growing and renewed interest in the study of information granulation and computations under the umbrella term of *Granular Computing*(GrC). In this paper, we present a model of information granulation that is more suitable to image recognition. Based on it, we present an information granulation based image texture recognition algorithm and compare it with some other algorithms. The results show that our algorithm is effective and efficient.

Table 1. The classification gain for 6 texture class groups.

	TCG_0	TCG_1	TCG_2	TCG_3	TCG_4	TCG_5
GTRA	18(79%, 75%)	20(75.5%, 76%)	17(79.7%, 77%)	25(72.9%, 72.9%)	19(67.1%, 68.8)	16(69.0%, 70.2%)
CMIG	21(76%, 75%)	121(78%, 76%)	118(82.7%, 77%)	121(75.4%, 72.9%)	122(67.6%, 68.8)	117(68.9%, 70.2%)
ABM	4(71.0%, 60.0%)	40(50.0%, 50.0 %)	66(55.7%, 55.7%)	55(47.3%, 47.1%)	32(45.7%, 43.7%)	70(46.6%, 46.6%)
SRPM	2(47.0%, 40.0)	52(52.5%, 49.5%)	17(54.0,. 46.7%)	17(49.3%, 44.6%)	12(49.8%, 45.3%)	22(48.8%, 46.1%)
RPM1	11(73.0%, 69.0%)	16(69.0%, 68.0%)	16(77.7%, 77.7%)	31(73.2%, 73.2%)	11(71.6%, 69.8%)	32(70.3%, 70.3%)
RPM2	10(78%, 78%)	6(75.0%, 74.0%)	27(76.3%, 76.3)	32(72.7%, 72.7%)	33(67.8%, 67.8%	83(68.3%, 68.3%)
GFBM	12(79.0%, 78.0%)	2(73.5%, 68.5%)	20(75.0%, 74.7%)	15(71.0%, 69.3%)	24(69.6%, 69.6)	24(68.4%, 68.4)
GMM	1(82%, 80%)	49(88%, 88%)	43(87%, 86%)	43(82%, 80%)	78(81.2%, 80.8%)	78(81.9%, 81.2%0
GarbT	3(83%, 77%)	22(81.5%, 76%)	19(85.3%, 85.3%)	19(80.1%, 79.3%)	23(75.5%, 75.3%)	43(76.3%, 76.3%)
GibMV	2(78%, 84%)	20(71%, 71%)	29(70%, 70%)	40(67%, 67%)	10(70.6%, 68.3%)	53(67.4%, 67.2%)
MIG	103(76%, 75%)	127(75.5%, 76%)	119(78.7%, 77%)	121(72.4%, 72.9%)	10(65.5%, 68.8)	121(68.2%, 70.2%)

Acknowledgement

This paper is partially supported by National Natural Science Foundation of P.R. China(No. 90104021, No. 60173017), and National 863 Project of P.R. China(No. 2003AA115220)

References

1. Zadeh, L.A., Fuzzy sets and inforamtion granularity, Advances in fuzzy set theory and applications, pp. 3-18, 1979
2. Pedrycz, W., Granular computing: an emerging paradigm, pringer-Verlag, 2001.
3. Tuceryan, M., Texture analysis, Handbook of Pattern Recognition and Computer Vision(2nd Edition), pp.207-248.
4. Keller, J.M., Chen, S., Texture description and segmentation through fractal geometry, Computer Vsion, Granphics, and Image Processing, 45, pp.150-166, 1989.
5. Hu, H., Zheng, Z., Shi, Z.P., Li, Q.Y., Shi, Z.Z., Texture classification using multi-scale rough module_matching and module_selection, to appear.

Radar Emitter Signal Recognition Based on Resemblance Coefficient Features

Gexiang Zhang[1,3], Haina Rong[2], Weidong Jin[1], and Laizhao Hu[3]

[1] School of Electrical Engineering, Southwest Jiaotong University,
Chengdu 610031 Sichuan, China
dylan7237@sina.com

[2] School of Computer and Communication Engineering, Southwest Jiaotong University
Chengdu 610031 Sichuan, China

[3] National EW Laboratory, Chengdu 610031 Sichuan, China

Abstract. Resemblance coefficient (RC) feature extraction approach for radar emitter signals was proposed. Definition and properties of RC were given. Feature extraction algorithm based on RC was described in detail and the performances of RC features were also analyzed. Neural network classifiers were designed. Theoretical analysis results and simulation experiments of 9 typical radar emitter signal feature extraction and recognition show that RC features are not sensitive to noise and average accurate recognition rate rises to 99.33%, which indicates that the proposed approach is effective.

1 Introduction

Radar emitter signal recognition is the key process in ELINT, ESM and RWR systems. Although some intra-pulse feature extraction methods were presented [1-4] in recent years, the methods have some drawbacks: (i) they focused mainly on qualitative analysis instead of quantitative analysis; (ii) they did not involve the case of changing signal-to-noise rate (SNR); (iii) they could recognize only two or three radar emitter signals. So we propose a novel feature extraction approach called resemblance coefficient approach (RCA). We present definition and properties of resemblance coefficient (RC) and describe detailed algorithm of extracting RC features from radar emitter signals. After stability and noise-suppression of RCA are analyzed, RC features of 9 radar emitter signals are extracted and recognition experiment are made using neural network classifiers. Experimental results show that RC features are not sensitive to noise and RCA is an effective and efficient method.

2 Resemblance Coefficient Feature Extraction

Definition 1. Suppose that one-dimension functions *f(x)* and *g(x)* are continuous, positive and real, i.e. $f(x) \geq 0, g(x) \geq 0$. If the integral domains of *f(x)* and *g(x)*

S. Tsumoto et al. (Eds.): RSCTC 2004, LNAI 3066, pp. 665–670, 2004.

are their definable domains of the variable x and the value of function $f(x)$ or $g(x)$ cannot be always equal to 0 when x is within its definable domain. Resemblance coefficient of functions $f(x)$ and $g(x)$ is defined as

$$C_{rc} = \frac{\int f(x)g(x)dx}{\sqrt{\int f^2(x)dx} \cdot \sqrt{\int g^2(x)dx}} \tag{1}$$

Because $f(x)$ and $g(x)$ are positive functions, according to the famous Schwartz inequation, we can obtain

$$0 \leq \int f(x)g(x)dx \leq \sqrt{\int f^2(x)dx} \cdot \sqrt{\int g^2(x)dx} \tag{2}$$

Obviously, we can get $0 \leq C_{rc} \leq 1$. According to the condition of Schwartz inequation, if $f(x)$ equals to $g(x)$, RC of $f(x)$ and $g(x)$ gets the maximal value 1. In fact, if and only if the $f(x)$-to-$g(x)$ ratio in every point is constant, C_{rc} equals to 1. If and only if the integral of product of $f(x)$ and $g(x)$ is zero, C_{rc} equals to the minimal value 0. From the definition of RC, if function $f(x)$ or $g(x)$ is multiplied by a non-zero constant value, C_{rc} is not changed. Definition 1 gives the RC of two continuous functions only. The following description discusses RC of two discrete signal sequences.

Definition 2 Suppose that discrete signal sequences $\{S_1(i), i=1,2,\ldots,N\}$ and $\{S_2(j), j=1,2,\ldots,N\}$ are one-dimensional and positive, i.e. $S_1(i) \geq 0, S_2(i) \geq 0, i = 1,2,\ldots, N$. RC of $\{S_1(i), i=1,2,\ldots,N\}$ and $\{S_2(j), j=1,2,\ldots,N\}$ is defined as

$$C_r = \frac{\sum S_1(i)S_2(i)}{\sqrt{\sum S_1^2(i)} \cdot \sqrt{\sum S_2^2(i)}} \tag{3}$$

In equation (3), all points of signal sequences $\{S_1(i), i=1,2,\ldots,N\}$ and $\{S_2(j), j=1,2,\ldots,N\}$ are not zero. The value domain of C_r is the same as C_{rc}, i.e. $0 \leq C_r \leq 1$. Similarly, if and only if the ratio of $\{S_1(i)\}$ to $\{S_2(j)\}$ in every point is constant, the value of C_r gets to the maximal value 1. According to the above definition of RC, the algorithm of RC feature extraction of radar emitter signals is given as follows.

(i) Preprocessing of radar emitter signals includes Fourier transform, normalization of signal energy to eliminate effect of distance of radar emitter and solving the center frequency. Finally, the preprocessed signal $\{G(j), j=1,2,\ldots,N\}$ is obtained.

(ii) Computing the RC of signal sequences $\{G(j), j=1,2,\ldots,N\}$ and a unit signal $\{U(k), k=1,2,\ldots,N\}$. The RC of $\{G(j)\}$ and $\{U(k)\}$ can be calculated using the following formula.

$$C_{r1} = \frac{\sum U(i)G(i)}{\sqrt{\sum U^2(i)} \cdot \sqrt{\sum G^2(i)}} \tag{4}$$

(iii) Computing the RC of signal sequences $\{G(j), j=1,2,\ldots,N\}$ and an isosceles triangle signal $\{T(k), k=1,2,\ldots,N\}$. RC of $\{G(j)\}$ and $\{T(k)\}$ is

$$C_{r2} = \frac{\sum T(i)G(i)}{\sqrt{\sum T^2(i)} \cdot \sqrt{\sum G^2(i)}} \tag{5}$$

(iv) C_{r1} and C_{r2} are used to construct a feature vector $CR = [C_{r1}, C_{r2}]$.

3 Performance Analysis of RC Features

Suppose that preprocessed radar emitter signal is $\{G(k), k=1,2,\ldots,N\}, G(k)=S(k)+N(k), k=1,2,\ldots,N$, where $\{S(k)\}$ is useful signal, $\{N(k)\}$ is additive Guassian white noise and N is the length of signal sequences. Because the energy of noise distributes evenly in whole frequency band and the energy of radar emitter signal is mainly within valid frequency band, in energy spectrum of pulse signal, the energy of noise in valid frequency band is 5% of the total energy of noise at most and about 90% of the total energy of useful signal is mainly in valid frequency band. Thus, SNR can be enhanced greatly after the signal intercepted is preprocessed. The following analysis only discusses a bad situation in which SNR is 5dB. When SNR=5dB, SNR_1 of preprocessed signal is $SNR_1 = 10\log(18 \cdot 10^{(SNR/10)})$. Then, we can obtain

$$\sum N^2(i) = b \sum S^2(i) \tag{6}$$

where b=0.0176. Without noise, C_{r1} and C_{r2} are respectively

$$C_{r1} = \frac{\sum U(i)S(i)}{\sqrt{\sum U^2(i)} \cdot \sqrt{\sum S^2(i)}} = \frac{\sum S(i)}{\sqrt{N} \cdot \sqrt{\sum S^2(i)}} \tag{7}$$

$$C_{r2} = \frac{\sum T(i)S(i)}{\sqrt{\sum T^2(i)} \cdot \sqrt{\sum S^2(i)}} = \frac{\sum iS(i)}{\sqrt{\sum i^2} \cdot \sqrt{\sum S^2(i)}} \tag{8}$$

Because $\{T(k)\}$ is a lateral symmetry signal, it is enough to contain the left side of signal $\{T(k)\}$. When considering noise, C'_{r1} and C'_{r2} can also be computed.

$$C'_{r1} = \frac{\sum U(i)[S(i)+N(i)]}{\sqrt{\sum U^2(i)} \cdot \sqrt{\sum [S(i)+N(i)]^2}} = \frac{C_{r1}}{\sqrt{1+2\sum S(i)/N^2 b}} + \frac{bC_{r1} \cdot \sum S^2(i)}{\sum S(i)} \approx C'_{r11} + C'_{r12} \tag{9}$$

In equation (9), normalization is made in preprocess of signal, so $\sum S(i) \leq 1$. Obviously, N^2 is a very big integer. Thus, $C'_{r11} \approx C_{r1}$. Because $0 \leq C_{r1} \leq 1$, the value of b is very small and $\sum S^2(i) \leq \sum S(i)$, C'_{r12} is much smaller than C'_{r11} and can be ignored. Therefore, the sum of C'_{r11} and C'_{r12} equals approximately to C_{r1}.

$$C'_{r2} = \frac{\sum T(i)[S(i)+N(i)]}{\sqrt{\sum T^2(i)} \cdot \sqrt{\sum [S(i)+N(i)]^2}} = \frac{C_{r2}}{\sqrt{1+2b\sum S(i)/N}} + \frac{b\sum T(i) \cdot \sum S(i)}{N\sum T(i)S(i)} \approx C'_{r21} + C'_{r22} \tag{10}$$

Obviously, in equation (10), $C'_{r21} \approx C_{r2}$, $C'_{r22} \approx 0$, so $C'_{r21} + C'_{r22} \approx C_{r2}$. According to the above analysis, RC is not nearly affected by noise when SNR is 5dB. Of course, RC is more stable when SNR is greater than 5dB.

4 Experimental Results

To demonstrate the feasibility and effectiveness of the proposed approach, 9 typical radar emitter signals are chosen to make the simulation experiment. They are CW, BPSK, MPSK, LFM, NLFM, FD, FSK, IPFE and CSF, respectively. Frequency of radar emitter signals is 700MHz. Sampling frequency and pulse width are 2GHz and 12.8 μs, respectively. Frequency shift of LFM is 50MHz. 31-bit pseudo-random code is used in BPSK and Barker code is used in IPFE and FSK. Huffman code is applied in MPSK and stepped-frequency in CSF is 20MHz.

Recent vast research activities in neural classification have established that neural networks (NN) are a promising alternative to various conventional classification methods. NN have become an important tool for classification because neural networks have many advantages in theoretical aspects. [5-6] So in the experiment, classifiers are designed also using NN. Feed-forward NN is used to design classifiers, which is composed of three layers: the first layer is the input layer that has 2 neurons corresponding to the inputs of two RC features; the second layer is hidden layer that has 20 neurons. '*tansig*' is chosen as the transfer functions in the hidden layer. The last layer is output layer that has the same number of neurons as radar emitter signals to be recognized. Transfer function in output layer is '*logsig*'. The ideal outputs of neural network are "1". The output tolerance is 0.05 and output error is 0.001.

For every radar emitter signal, 150 feature samples are extracted in each SNR point of 5dB, 10dB, 15dB and 20dB. So 600 samples in total are generated when SNR varies from 5dB to 20dB. The samples are classified into two groups: training group and testing group. Training group, one third of the total samples generated, is applied to train NN classifers and testing group, two third of the total samples generated, is used to test trained NN classifers. Mean values and variance values of the samples in training group are shown in Table 1. To illustrate the distribution of the features intuitively in pattern space, 200 feature samples of each of radar emitter signals are used to draw a feature distribution graph. Thus, 1800 feature samples in total are achieved and are shown in Fig.1. From Table 1 and Fig.1, conclusions can be drawn that noise has little effect on resemblance features when SNR varies in a wide range and the features of different radar emitter signals have good separations from those of other radar emitter signals.

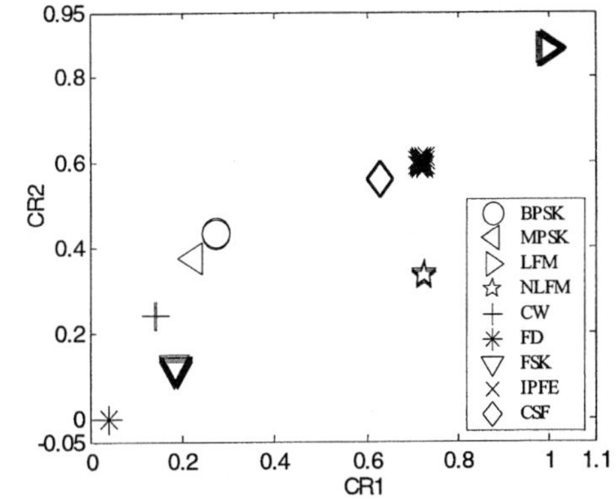

Fig. 1. Feature distribution of radar emitter signals.

Table 1. Means and variances in testing group of radar emitter signals.

Types of radar signals	C_{r1}		C_{r2}	
	Means	Variances	Means	Variances
CW	0.1417	4.8243×10^{-7}	0.2437	4.3645×10^{-8}
BPSK	0.2716	9.6950×10^{-7}	0.4356	8.6719×10^{-7}
MPSK	0.2256	2.7199×10^{-7}	0.3748	4.3270×10^{-7}
LFM	0.9959	3.9890×10^{-5}	0.8617	2.9688×10^{-5}
NLFM	0.7262	7.1475×10^{-7}	0.3337	1.0518×10^{-5}
FD	0.0400	1.7276×10^{-7}	3.2536×10^{-4}	1.3388×10^{-7}
FSK	0.1868	2.1261×10^{-5}	0.1219	4.8410×10^{-5}
IPFE	0.7180	1.2913×10^{-4}	0.5982	1.9219×10^{-4}
CSF	0.6276	6.4220×10^{-6}	0.5584	4.8736×10^{-6}

1800 samples in training group are applied to train NN classifer. The samples in testing group, 3600 feature samples, are used to test the trained NN classifer and testing results are shown in Table 2. To verify the good performances of RC features and NN classifers, the samples of only 10dB SNR are employed to train NN classifer and then the samples in testing group are used to test the trained NN classifer and testing results are shown in Table 3. In Table 2, average recognition rate arrives at 99.33% and the average recognition rate also rises to 99.28% in Table 3.

Table 2. Accurate recognition rates (ARR) of radar emitter signals.

ARR	BPSK	MPSK	LFM	NLFM	CW	FD	FSK	IPFE	CSF
5 dB	100.0	88.80	100.0	100.0	100.0	100.0	100.0	87.80	100.0
10 dB	100.0	100.0	100.0	100.0	100.0	100.0	100.0	99.20	100.0
15 dB	100.0	100.0	100.0	100.0	100.0	100.0	100.0	100.0	100.0
20 dB	100.0	100.0	100.0	100.0	100.0	100.0	100.0	100.0	100.0

Table 3. Accurate recognition rates (ARR) of NN calssifer trained using 10 dB SNR samples.

ARR	BPSK	MPSK	LFM	NLFM	CW	FD	FSK	IPFE	CSF
5 dB	85.20	99.60	100.0	99.75	99.87	100.0	100.0	100.0	89.80
10 dB	100.0	100.0	100.0	100.0	100.0	100.0	100.0	100.0	100.0
15 dB	100.0	100.0	100.0	100.0	100.0	100.0	100.0	100.0	100.0
20 dB	100.0	100.0	100.0	100.0	100.0	100.0	100.0	100.0	100.0

5 Concluding Remarks

Because features extracted from time and frequency domain are sensitive to noise in traditional methods, it is very difficult to recognize accurately radar emitter signals affected by plenty of noise in the process of transmission and processing in scout. To meet the requirements of modern electronic warfare, a novel feature extraction approach is proposed in this paper. Experimental results and analysis in theory demonstrate that the features are very effective in identifying different radar signals because they have good performances of noise-suppression, clustering the same radar signals and separating the different radar signals.

References

1. Zhang Q.R., Shan P.J.: Spectrum Correlation of Intrapulse Feature Analysis of Radar Signal. Electronic Warfare. Vol.19, No.4. (1993) 1-6
2. Yan X.D., Zhang Q.R., Lin X.P.: A Recognition Method of Pulse Compression Radar Signal. Electronic Warfare. Vol.20, No.1, (1994) 28-34
3. Liu A.X.: A Novel Radar Signal Recognition Method. Spaceflight Electronic Warfare. (2003) 14-16
4. Huang Z.T., Zhou Y.Y., Jiang W.L.: The Automatic Analysis of Intra-pulse Modulation Characteristics Based on the Relatively Non-Ambiguity Phase Restore. Journal of China Institute of Communications. Vol.24, No.4. (2003) 153-160
5. Zhang G.P.: Neural Networks for Classification: A Survey. IEEE Transaction on System, Man, and Cybernetics-Part C: Application and Reviews. Vol.30, No.4. (2000) 451-462
6. Kavalov D., Kalinin V.: Neural Network Surface Acoustic Wave RF Signal Processor for Digital Modulation Recognition. IEEE Transaction on Ultrasonics, Ferroelectrics, and Frequency Control. Vol.49, No.9. (2002) 1280-1290

Vehicle Tracking Using Image Processing Techniques

Seung Hak Rhee[1], Seungjo Han[1], Pan koo Kim[1],
Muhammad Bilal Ahmad[2], and Jong An Park[1]

[1] College of Electronics and Information Engineering
Chosun University, Gwangju, Korea
japark@chosun.ac.kr
[2] Signal and Image Processing Lab, Dept. of Mechatronics
Kwangju Institute of Science and Technology, Gwangju, Korea
bilal@kjist.ac.kr

Abstract. A real time vehicle tracking in image sequences is presented. The moving vehicles are segmented by the method of differential image followed by the process of morphological dilation. The vehicles are recognized and tracked using statistical moments. The straight lines in the moving vehicles are found with the help of Radon transform. The direction of the moving object is calculated from the orientation of the straight lines in the direction of the principal axes of the moving objects. The direction of the moving object and the displacement of the object in the image sequence are used to calculate the velocity of the moving objects.

1 Introduction

Object tracking is an important problem in the field of content-based video processing. When a physical object appears in several consecutive frames, it is necessary to identify its appearances in different frames for purposes of processing. Object tracking attempts to locate, in successive frames, all objects that appear in the current frame. The most straightforward approach to this task is to consider objects as rectangular blocks and use traditional block matching algorithms [1]. However, since objects may have irregular shapes and deformations in different frames, video spatial segmentation and object temporal tracking can be combined [2]-[3]. In object tracking, pattern recognition is to deal with the geophysical data based on the information contained in the image sequences. An automatic interpretation or recognition of geophysical data is very difficult from the image sequences [4]. A lot of efforts have been found in the literature [5]-[9], and still a lot of research is needed for automatic recognition of moving objects in the image sequences. Most methods of object tracking such as optical flow [10], block matching [3], etc are highly computational and hence difficult to apply in the run time applications. In this paper, we have proposed an effective moving object tracking based on the orientation of the moving objects. Moving objects locations are found in the image sequence by the method of differential edge image followed by morphological dilation. After locating the moving objects in the image sequences, we extract different high-level features directly from the regions of pixels in the images, and describe them by various statistical measures. Such measures are usually represented by a single value. Measurements of area, length, perimeter, elongation, compactness, moments of inertia are usually called statistical geomet-

S. Tsumoto et al. (Eds.): RSCTC 2004, LNAI 3066, pp. 671–678, 2004.

rical descriptions [11]. We use the statistical geometrical descriptions to recognize the moving objects in the image sequences. The principal axes of inertia for the moving objects in the image sequences are used for extracting the direction of the moving objects. The straight lines in the moving objects are determined by the Radon transform [12]. The straight lines in the moving objects that are almost aligned with the principal axes are averaged to find the direction of the moving objects. We assumed that the velocity of the moving objects is not too high, and we restrict the search area for tracking of the individual moving objects within the most probable range.

This paper is organized as follows. Section 2 describes the segmentation of the moving objects using differential edge images followed by the process of morphological dilation. Section 3 describes the different statistical descriptors that will be utilized for tracking and recognizing the objects. Section 4 explains the Radon transform to find the direction of the moving objects. Simulation results are shown in section 5.

2 Segmentation of Moving Objects in the Image Sequences

We first segment the moving objects in the input image sequence. Edge detector is applied on the two input image sequence. For removing the background (still part) in the images, we find the binary difference image from the resulting two input edge maps, as:

$$D(x, y) = ABS(E2(x,y) - E1(x,y)), \tag{1}$$

where E2(x,y), E1(x,y) are the two binary edge maps of the input image sequence, and D(x,y) is the resulting binary difference image. The resulting binary difference image D(x,y) gives us the possible location of moving objects. To find the areas of moving objects, we binary dilate the difference image D(x,y) as:

$$DL = dilate(D), \tag{2}$$

where DL is the dilated image of the difference binary image D. The dilated image DL detects the areas of moving objects in the image sequence. In the dilated image DL, all possible moving objects (both real and erroneous moving objects) are detected. The erroneous moving objects are detected due to the presence of noise in the images. We applied a thresholding method to extract the real moving objects from the dilated image DL. We first label the moving objects in the dilated image DL and then calculate the binary areas of each of the moving objects. We threshold the real moving objects that have considerable area in the dilated image as:

$$\begin{array}{ll} \text{if } A[DL(j)] > T_{area} & \\ & \text{Real Moving Object (keep it)} \\ \text{else} & \\ & \text{Erroneous Moving Object (discard it)} \end{array} \tag{3}$$

where A[DL(j)] calculates the binary area of jth labeled object in DL, and T_{area} is the threshold, the value of which depends on the size of input images, and the distance of camera from the scene. We discard the erroneous moving objects by replacing 1s with 0s in that area. Finally, we get the image, which contains only real moving objects in the image sequence. We then calculate the statistical descriptors in those actual moving areas.

3 Vehicle Tracking

After segmenting the moving objects from the input image sequence, a matching algorithm is needed between the regions in the two consecutive images for tracking and recognizing the moving objects. A region matching or similarity is obtained by comparing the statistical descriptors of the two regions. Since the images may have translational, rotational, and scaling differences (objects may move further or closer to the camera), the region or shape measures should be invariant with respect to translational, rotation and scaling. One kind of such invariants belongs to statistical moments, called statistical invariant descriptors.

3.1 Statistical Moments and Invariant Descriptors

The moment invariants are moment-based descriptors of planar shapes, which are invariant under general translation, rotational and scaling transformations. Such statistical moments work directly with regions of pixels in the image using statistical measures. Such measures are usually represented by a single value. These can be calculated as a simple by-product of the segmentation procedures. Such statistical descriptors usually find area, length, perimeter, elongation, Moments of Inertia, etc. The moments of a binary image b(x, y) are calculated as:

$$\mu_{pq} = \sum_x \sum_y b(x,y) x^p y^q, \tag{4}$$

where p and q define the order of moment. Where b(x,y) can be omitted as it has only 1 and 0 values, so sums are only taken where b(x,y) has values 1. The center of gravity of the object can be found from moments as:

$$\bar{x} = \frac{\mu_{10}}{\mu_{00}}, \qquad \bar{y} = \frac{\mu_{01}}{\mu_{00}}, \tag{5}$$

where $(\bar{x}, \bar{y})$ are the coordinates of the center of gravity. The pqth discrete central moment m_{pq} of a region is defined by

$$m_{pq} = \sum_x \sum_y (x-\bar{x})^p (y-\bar{y})^q \tag{6}$$

where the sums are taken over all points (x,y). Hu [13] proposed seven new moments from the central moments that are invariant to changes of position, scale and orientation of the object represented by the region using central moments of lower orders. All the seven moments are translational, rotational and scale invariants. These invariants will help us in the object tracking of the moving objects.

The principal axes of inertia define a natural coordinate system for a region. Let θ be the angle that the x-axis of the natural coordinate system (the principal axes) makes with the x-axis of the reference coordinate system. Then θ is given by

$$\theta = \frac{1}{2}\tan^{-1}\left[\frac{2m_{11}}{m_{20}-m_{02}}\right] \tag{7}$$

From the principal axes of inertia, we can find the direction of the moving objects.

3.2 Tracking of Moving Objects

For tracking of moving objects, the seven statistical descriptors are calculated for the detected moving regions of the input image sequence. There are translation and rotation of moving objects due to motion from one image frame to another image frame, and also the object can move far or closer from the camera, which results in the different size of the object in terms of pixels for the fixed camera position. The next step is the comparison of the statistical descriptors in the two images. Here we have assumed that either the motion of the objects are very small, or the frame rate is very high, so that we can restrict the search area for tracking of the individual moving objects within the most probable range. With the help of the statistical descriptors, we recognize and track different kinds of moving objects. We found the statistical invariant descriptors for every detected moving region in the two images, and then track the moving objects within the search region by comparing the statistical descriptors.

4 Velocity Vectors of the Moving Objects

After tracking the moving objects in the input image sequence, we determine the principle axes using Eq. (7) for each of the segmented moving objects. The principal axes do not give the true direction of the moving object, because of 2D image representation of 3D objects. However, the principal axes give the rough estimate of the direction of the moving objects. To find the true direction, we need to determine the straight lines in the object. The Radon transform is used to find the straight lines in the moving objects.

4.1 Straight Lines Using the Radon Transform

Radon transform can be efficiently used to search the straight lines in the images. It transforms two dimensional images with lines into a domain of possible line parameters, where each line in the image will give a peak positioned at the corresponding line parameters. The Radon transformation shows the relationship between the 2-D object and the projections. Let us consider a coordinate system shown in Fig. 1. The function $g(s,\theta)$ is a projection of f(x,y) on the axis s of θ direction. The function $g(s,\theta)$ is obtained by the integration along the line whose normal vector is in θ direction. The value $g(0,\theta)$ is defined that it is obtained by the integration along the line passing the origin of (x,y)-coordinate. The general Radon transformation is given as:

$$g(s,\theta) = \int \int_{-\infty}^{\infty} f(x,y)\delta(x\cos\theta + y\sin\theta - \rho)dxdy \tag{8}$$

The Eq. (8) is called Radon transformation from the 2-D distribution f(x,y) to the projection $g(s,\theta)$.

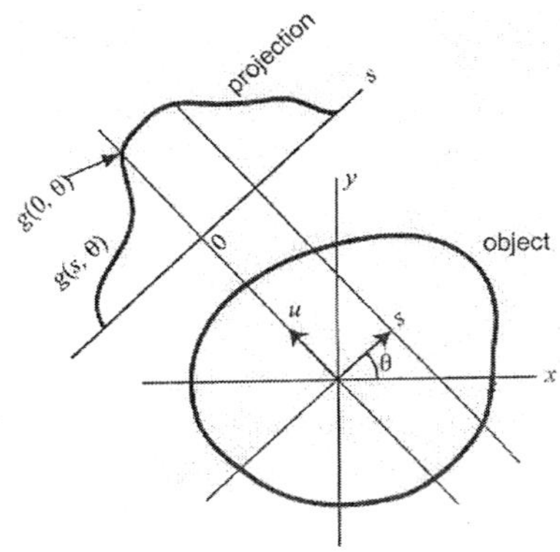

Fig. 1. Radon Transformation.

Although the Radon transformation expresses the projection by the 2-D integral on the x,y-coordinate, the projection is more naturally expressed by an integral of one variable since it is a line integral. Since, the s,u-coordinate along the direction of projection is obtained by rotating the x,y-coordinate by θ, the Radon transform, after a change of axes transformation, is given as:

$$g(s,\theta) = \int \int_{-\infty}^{\infty} f(s\cos\theta - u\sin\theta, s\sin\theta + u\cos\theta)\delta(0)dsdu \quad (9)$$

Since the δ-function in Eq. (9) is a function of variable s, we get

$$\int_{-\infty}^{\infty} \delta(0)ds = 1$$

It follows from the above that the Radon transformation $g(s,\theta)$ in Eq. (8) is translated into the following integral of one variable u,

$$g(s,\theta) = \int \int_{-\infty}^{\infty} f(s\cos\theta - u\sin\theta, s\sin\theta + u\cos\theta)du \quad (10)$$

This equation expresses the sum of f(x,y) along the line whose distance from the origin is s and whose normal vector is in θ direction. This sum, $g(s,\theta)$, is called ray-sum.

The Radon transform could be computed for any angle, and could be displayed as an image. From Fig. 1, the Radon transform of the input images can be computed for any angle. In practice, we compute the Radon transform at angles from 0 to 179 degree, in 1 degree increment. The procedure to find the straight lines using the radon transform is as follows:

- Compute the binary edge image of input image using the edge detector
- Compute the Radon transform of the edge image at angles from 0 to 179
- Find the locations of strong peaks in the Radon transform matrix. The location of these peaks corresponds to the location of straight lines in the original image.
- The straight lines are drawn in the image space from the information obtained through the strong peaks in the Radon transform.

4.2 Object Orientation

We determined all the straight lines using the Radon transform for the every tracked object in the image sequence. The orientation of the moving object is determined from the straight lines and the principal axes of the object. The x-axis of the principal axes is selected as the reference axis. The straight lines that make a greater angle than the threshold angle are discarded. The angles that the remaining straight lines in the object make with the principal axes are averaged. The average angle thus determined is the true orientation of the 3D moving objects.

The direction of moving object is found from the law of cosines from the orientation angles of the individual moving object in the two consecutive images. From Fig.2, we can find the direction of the moving object. In Fig.2, let L_1 and L_2 be the two lines making angle θ_1 and θ_2 with respect to x-axis of the reference frame, respectively. L_1 and L_2 correspond to the true orientation of the moving object. The mathematical derivation for the moving object direction θ_3 with respect to x can be derived as:

$$\text{For L1}: \; y = m_1 x + c_1$$

$$\text{For L2}: \; y = m_2 x + c_2$$

By solving the above equations, the intersection point of L_1 and L_2 can be found as:

$$x_{\text{int}} = \frac{c_2 - c_1}{m_1 - m_2}, \qquad y_{\text{int}} = m_1 x_{\text{int}} + c_1 \tag{11}$$

The origin in Fig.2 is the center of gravity of the object in the previous image frame. From law of cosines

$$l_3^2 = l_1^2 + l_2^2 - 2l_1 l_2 \cos(\pi + \theta_1 - \theta_2) \quad \text{and} \tag{12}$$

$$\cos(\theta_3 - \theta_1) = \frac{l_1^2 + l_3^2 - l_2^2}{2l_1^2 l_3^2} \tag{13}$$

The angle θ_3 gives the direction of the moving object. The small l_1, l_2, l_3, are the magnitudes of L_1, L_2 and L_3 lines. For calculating the magnitude of the velocity vector, the Euclidean distance of the two centers of gravity is measured. From the angle

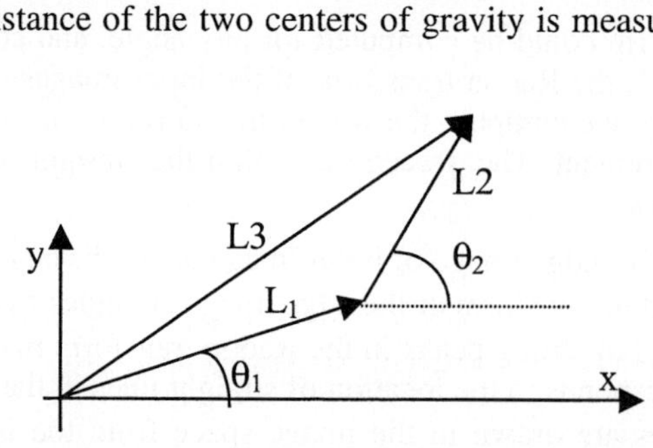

Fig. 2. Determining the direction of the moving object.

θ_3, and Euclidean distance of the centers of gravity, we calculate the velocity vectors of the moving objects. Same method is applied for extracting the velocity vectors of each individual moving object.

5 Simulation Results

For simulation, 256 x 256 gray-level image sequences are used. One test sequence is shown in Fig.3. First we segment the moving objects from the input image sequence using the proposed differential edge algorithm. The statistical descriptors are calculated for the segmented moving regions only. The moving objects are recognized using the similarity of statistical descriptors. The direction of the moving object is determined using the Radon transform and the principal axes. The principal axes doesn't give the right direction of the 3D object, whereas the direction obtained by using the Radon transform represents more accurate direction of the moving object. Figure 4 shows the tracking result of different test image sequences. The three test moving objects are accurately tracked in the image sequences.

Fig. 3. A test sequence.

Fig. 4. Object tracking using the proposed algorithm on three test image sequences.

6 Conclusions

In this work, a new algorithm is proposed for segmenting, recognizing, tracking and finding the velocity vectors for moving objects in a video stream. There are many popular techniques for finding velocity vectors, such as optical flow, and block matching algorithm, but they are time-consuming algorithms. Our method is computationally fast and gives compact information about the moving objects. From the input video stream, we segment the moving objects using the edge differential algorithm. For tracking of the moving objects, we proposed method based on the statistical invariant moments or descriptors, which are invariant to translation, rotation and scaling transformation. After tracking, we found the orientation of the moving scaling transformation. After tracking, we found the orientation of the moving objects using the principal axes of inertia and the Radon transform. From the knowledge of the orientation of the moving object in the consecutive image frames, we found the direction of the moving objects. From the displacement of the center of gravity, we found the Euclidean distance of the moving objects. The final velocity vector for a moving object is calculated from the orientation angles, and the Euclidean distance of the centers of gravity of the object. The process of edge detection and segmentation accurately find the location and areas of the real moving objects, and hence the extractions of moving information are very easy and accurate. The orientation of the objects is more accurately determined from the Radon transform.

Acknowledgements

This study was supported by research grant from the Chosun University, Gwangju, Korea (2002).

References

1. A.M. Tekalp, Digital Video Processing, Parentice Hall, 1995.
2. R.C. Gonzalez and R. E. Woods, Digital Image Processing, Prentice Hall, 1993.
3. Berthold Klaus Paul Horn, Robot Vision, McGraw-Hill, 1986.
4. N. Diehl, "Object Oriented Motion Estimation and Segmentation in Image Sequences," Signal Processing: Image Communication, Vol. 3, No. 1, pp. 23-56, Feb. 1991.
5. C. Cafforio and F. Rocca, "Tracking Moving Objects in Television Images," Signal Processing, Vol. 1, pp. 133-140, 1979.
6. Willium B. Thompson, "Combining motion and contrast for segmentation," IEEE Trans. Pattern Anal. Machine Intelligence, pp. 543-549, Nov. 1980.
7. M. Etoh et. al., "Segmentation and 2D motion estimate by region fragments," Proc. 4th Int. Conf. Computer Vision, pp.192~199, 1993.
8. P.J. Butt, J.R. Bergen, R. Hingorani, R. Kolczinski, W.A. Lee, A. Leung, J. Lubin, and H. Shvaytser, "Object tracking with a moving camera, an application of dynamic motion analysis,". in IEEE Workshop on Visual Motion, pp. 2-12, Irvine, CA, March 1989.
9. Chao He, Yuan F. Zheng, and Stanley C. Ahalt, "Object tracking using the Gabor wavelet transform and the golden section algorithm," IEEE transactions on multimedia, vol. 4, No. 4, December 2002.
10. B. K. P. Horn and B. G. Schunck, "Determining optical flow," Artificial Intelligence,. 17, pp.185~203, 1981.
11. Robert M. Haralick, Linda G. Shapiro, Computer and Robot Vision, vol. 1, Addison Wesely, 1992.
12. S. R. Deans, The Radon Transform and some of its applications, Kreiger, 1983.
13. M. K. Hu, "Visual pattern recognition by moment invariants," IEEE Trans. Information Theory, Vol. IT-8, No. 2, pp. 179-187, 1962.

Classification of Swallowing Sound Signals: A Rough Set Approach

Lisa Lazareck[1] and Sheela Ramanna[2]

[1] Department of Engineering Science, Oxford University
Oxford, OX1 3PJ, UK
lisa.lazareck@eng.ox.ac.uk

[2] Department of Applied Computer Science, University of Winnipeg
Winnipeg, Manitoba R3B 2E9, Canada
s.ramanna@uwinnipeg.ca

Abstract. This paper introduces an approach to classifying swallowing sound signals to detect those patients at risk of aspiration, or choking using rough set methods. An important contribution of a recent study of segmenting the waveform of swallowing sound signals has been the use of the waveform dimension (WD) to describe signal complexity and major changes in signal variance. Prior swallowing sound classification studies have not considered discretization in the extraction of features from swallow sound data tables. In addition, derivation of decision rules for classifying swallowing sounds have not been considered. In the study reported in this paper, both discretization (quantization of real-valued attributes) and non-discretization have been used to achieve attribute reduction and decision rule derivation.

1 Introduction

This paper presents the results of classifying swallowing sound signals using rough sets [7], which is an application of the methods described in [9]. Considerable work has already been done in classifying swallowing sounds [2],[5-6],[8]. The approach presented in this paper represents an advance over what has already been reported in earlier studies, since it considers discretization to achieve attribute reduction and it uses rough set methods to derive rules [9], which makes it possible to automate swallowing sound signal classification. The current gold-standard method for the assessment of aspiration (or choking) is the videofluorosopic swallow study (VFSS) which is a radiologic procedure, whereby subjects ingest small amounts of barium-coated boluses while x-rays penetrate the subject and resultant images are video-recorded. However, VFSS is time-consuming and results in some radiation exposure. Because of the x-ray exposure and lack of portability, the VFSS cannot be used repeatedly when assessing/monitoring intervention strategies for a patient or assessing an evolving neurological condition of a patient. In the late 1990's, the majority of acoustical swallow studies were mainly concerned with the timing of the swallow within the breath cycle. The later studies focused on basic characteristics of the swallowing sound

S. Tsumoto et al. (Eds.): RSCTC 2004, LNAI 3066, pp. 679–684, 2004.

and whether it could be used as an indicator of abnormalities [2],[5]. Given the fact that swallowing sounds are non-stationary by nature, a waveform dimension (WD) fractal dimension has been used to segment swallowing sound signal [5]. WD is a measurement describing the underlying signal complexity or major changes in the signal's variance. This paper reports classification of 350 swallowing sound signals obtained from a total of 26 subjects: 23 from the Children's Hospital and 3 from the St. Amant Center in Winnipeg, Manitoba.

This paper is organized as follows. A brief introduction to swallow sound signals is given in Sections 2 and 3. Swallowing sound signal classification results using the rough set methods are presented in Section 4. A comparison of the results presented in this paper and earlier results are given in Section 5.

2 Swallowing Sound Signals

A normal swallow consists of an oral, pharyngeal and esophageal phase. A bolus (food) enters the mouth and is consciously pushed toward the back of the throat, involuntarily passes through the epiglottis and into the esophagus and transfers to the stomach through peristaltic waves. It is speculated that from the opening of the cricoipharynx and return of the epiglottis, "clicking" sounds or "clicks" can be heard. In between the initial and final click, quieter sounds are heard and we refer them as "non-clicks". A swallowing signal is non-stationary by nature. Hence, preliminary studies began by analyzing normal swallowing sound signals by dividing the signal into stationary segments using fractal dimension concept [5]. In particular, variance fractal dimension (VFD), which is a fractal-based measurement describing the underlying signal complexity was used. In the later work, waveform dimension (WD) was employed [4] as a tool for segmentation instead of VFD. Loosely based on the principle of fractal dimension, WD is also a measurement of the degree of complexity or meandering between the points of a signal in time domain. WD is a measurement calculated for a specified window size where a window is moved over the entire signal creating a waveform dimension trajectory (WDT). Let n, d, L, and a be the number of steps in a waveform, planar extent or diameter of a waveform which is the farthest distance between the starting point "1" and any other point "i" of the waveform, the total length of the waveform, and the average distance between successive points , respectively [4]. In effect, L = sum(distance(i, i+1), a = mean(distance(i, i+1), n = L/a, and d = max(distance(1, i+1)). Then compute WD = log n/(log n + log d/L). The characteristic signal features used in this paper are based on the WDT calculation procedure, which is reportedly fairly insensitive to noise. Time, frequency, audio and video domain analyses are required to fully identify, extract and compare swallowing sound signals.

3 Sound Signal Features

To investigate its characteristic features, it is necessary to divide the signal into stationary segments. A swallowing sound signal is segmented using a waveform

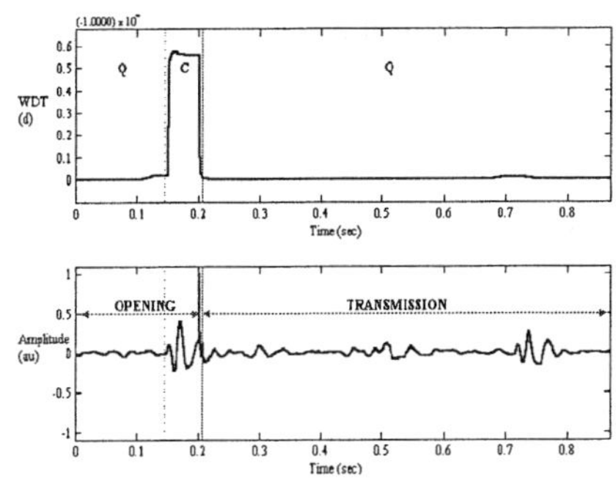

Fig. 1(a). Normal Swallow Signal

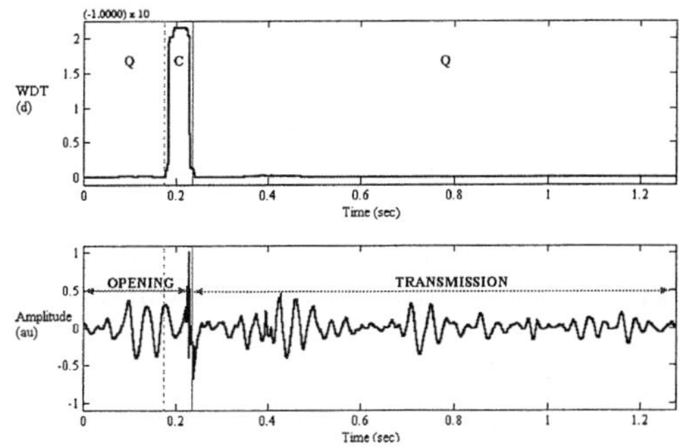

Fig. 1(b). Abnormal Sound Signal

dimension that results in a corresponding (1:1 mapped) signal that depicts major changes in signal variance. Sample normal and abnormal swallowing sound signals with their corresponding waveform dimension labeled WDT (Waveform Dimension Trajectory) are shown in Fig. 1. An adaptive segmentation method based on the aforementioned waveform dimension (WD) was applied to the 350 swallowing sound signals. Before extracting signal features, each swallowing sound is divided into two characteristic segments: *opening* and *xmission* (transmission). Physiologically, *opening* starts with the onset of the swallow and ends with the first click noise. *xmission* starts directly after the first click noise and ends preceding the final click noise. If the entire signal is under review, *total* is used as the reference. The *opening* and *xmission* sections are labeled accordingly in Fig. 1, as are *click* ('C') and *quiet* ('Q') segments. A *quiet* segment does not contain any extraneous noises, such as *gulp* or *clack.* Stemming from time transcriptions, WD trajectories, and the swallowing sound signal magnitude, three sets of features were computed for each of the *opening*, *xmission* and *total* sections. The first feature set was 'time duration,' or length of swallowing sound signal in the time domain per section. The second feature set was 'waveform dimension,' the maximum value of WDT for *opening* and *xmission* sections and the mean value of WDT for *total* section. The third feature set was 'magnitude,' or mean rectified value of the swallowing sound in time domain for *opening*, *xmission* and *total* sections. Following the initial intuitive features, more were selected and designated for the *opening* section only, as *opening* was the least contaminated by extraneous noises, such as *gulp* and *clack.* Using Fast Fourier Transform, the power spectrum was calculated for every 100 ms segment of the signal with 50% overlap between adjacent segments. Then from the spectrum of the *opening* section, 'Fpeak,' 'Fmax,' 'Fmean,' 'Fmedian' and 'Pave' were calculated. In addition, the average frequencies in seven specified frequency bands were calculated.

A total of 24 attributes and one decision d $\in$ {normal, abnormal} have been identified [6]. These are: a1 - Opening Duration (sec), a2 - Xmission Duration (sec), a3 - Total Duration (sec), a4 - MaxOpening (waveform), a5 - MaxXmission (waveform), a6 - MeanTotal (waveform), a7 - MeanOpening (signal), a8 - MeanXission (signal), a9 - MeanTotal (signal), a10 - FreqPeak (Hz), a11 - Freq-

Max (Hz), a12 - FreqMean (Hz), a13 - FreqMedian (Hz), a14 - Pavg150 (150-300 dB), a15 - Pavg300 (300-450 dB), a16 - Pavg450 (450-600 dB), a17 - Pavg600 (600-750 dB), a18 - Pavg750 (750-900 dB), a19 - Pavg900 (900-1050 dB), a20 - vg1050 (1050-1200 db), a21 - OpeningSkewness, a22 - XmissionSkewness, a23 - OpeningKurtosis, a24 - XmissionKurtosis. Out of these 24 attributes, a1 to a6 can be considered as a group (T) representing 'time duration and waveform dimension' features, a7 to a9 belonging to a group (M) representing 'magnitude' features, a10 to a13 to group (F) representing 'frequency' features, a14 to a20 belonging to a group (P) representing 'average band frequency' features, and a21 to a24 to group(N) representing 'normality' features.

4 Swallowing Sound Signal Classification Results

Two groups of subjects participated in the study, including 15 healthy (a mix of children and adults) and 11 patients with swallowing dysfunction. For both experiments, subjects were fed three textures, 'semi-solid,' 'thick liquid,' and 'thin liquid' in the same order. Both the discretized and non-discretized cases have been considered for each of the three types of swallowing using RSES [1]. In each case, both the *genetic GA* and *lem2* [3] methods have been considered in rule derivation. Previously, training sets were selected using the leave-one-out method [6]. In this study, 10-fold cross-validation has been used to obtain training and testing sets. We use the definitions for accuracy and coverage from RSES with the error rate ε being computed as 1 – (#test items correctly classified/card(test set)). A comparison of both discretized and non-discretized methods for the three types of bolus textures has been summarized in Table 1.

The discretized method outperforms the nondiscretized method in terms of error rate, accuracy, coverage as well as the size of the rule set for all bolus textures. The training set accuracies for both discretized and non-discretized cases are 100% (error rate of 0 and 100% coverage) for both genetic and lem2

Table 1. Comparison of Classification Results

Method	Avg. Correct: GA/LEM2	Avg. Error rate: GA/LEM2	Avg. Incorrect: GA/LEM2	Avg. Accuracy: GA/LEM2	Avg. Coverage: GA/LEM2	Avg. # of rules: GA/LEM2
			Thick Liquid Classification Results			
Disc	11.1/ 9.9	0.18/ 0.27	2.3/ 2.3	81.6/ 81.5	99.2/ 91.3	74.2/ 21.5
Non-Disc	8.8/ 3.7	0.34/ 0.72	4.3/ 0.7	67.5/ 84.2	98.2/ 33.23	1216/ 76
			Thin Liquid Classification Results			
Disc	9.4/ 8.6	0.12/ 0.14	1.3/ 1.0	88.3/ 89.8	100/ 98.4	9.5/ 6.2
Non-Disc	9.1/ 4.2	0.15/ 0.58	1.6/ 0.5	85.2/ 76.1	100/ 45.4	825.7/ 34.5
			Semi-Solid Classification Results			
Disc	9.3/ 8.1	0.13/ 0.25	1.5/ 0.9	87.0/ 90.5	100/ 83.3	65.5/ 10.6
Non-Disc	7.5/ 2.4	0.3/ 0.8	2.5/ 2.6	77.8/ 65.2	94/ 28	913/ 56

algorithms. The average number of rules used by the Lem2 classifier is significantly less than those used by genetic algorithm classifier. For instance, in the discretized case for thick liquids (see Table 1), using GA technique, the average error rate is 0.18, the average accuracy is 82% and the average coverage over the ten-fold is 99%. Using the Lem2 algorithm, the average error rate is 0.27, the average accuracy is 82% and the average coverage is 91.3%. This means that on an average about 18% of the cases are being misclassified in both cases.

5 Comparison with Earlier Results

In the earlier study, discriminant analysis with SPSS was employed for classification with the system trained and tested using leave-one-out approach [6]. The experiments reported in this paper included all measurements (both normal and abnormal cases) for each bolus texture. It is interesting to compare results, even though separate experiments were conducted for normal and abnormal swallowing sounds in the previous study. In terms of optimal feature set, the discriminant method considered *time duration* features more important than *waveform dimension* features. This matches RSES results, whereas both a5 and a6 are considered redundant for both normal and abnormal cases. In addition, both techniques find Total Duration (a3) feature irrelevant, except in the case of Semi-Solid texture with RSES. Next, both studies consider *magnitude* features important and find FredMedian (a13) redundant. The largest set of redundant features were found in group (P), average band frequencies, where lower bands (a14 to a18) are considered irrelevant. This corroborates the earlier study which reveals the dominating characteristic of high frequency components of a swallow within the breath and swallowing sound signal. The results of group (N) are quite inconclusive from both studies. Overall, the results reported in this paper (10-fold approach) compare quite well with earlier studies (leave-one-out approach) if we look at average error rates. We correctly classify 11 of 13, 9 of 11 and 9 of 11 cases in the test set for Thick Liquid, Thin Liquid, and Semi-Solid textures respectively. The final screen algorithm used in earlier studies correctly classified 13 of 15 normal subjects and 11 of 11 subjects with some degrees of dysphagia and/or neurological impairments.

6 Conclusion

This paper presents the results of classifying swallowing sound signals using rough sets on a set of 350 swallowing sound signals obtained from a total of 26 subjects. It can be seen that the discretized method outperforms the nondiscretized method in terms of error rate, accuracy, coverage as well as the size of the rule set with both genetic and Lem2 algorithms. Both algorithms yield high classification accuracy with a small rule set. The coverage in the case of genetic algorithm technique is slightly better than those of Lem2; however, the Lem2 classifier is more accurate than the genetic classifier in the discretized case. In terms of error rates, the results reported in this article compare well with earlier studies.

Acknowledgements

The research by Lisa Lazareck and Sheela Ramanna has been supported by Natural Sciences and Engineering Research Council of Canada (NSERC). The authors would like to acknowledge the help of the following researchers: J.F. Peters, Z. Moussavi, and G. Rempel from the University of Manitoba and Z. S. Hippe at University of Technology and Management, Rzeszów, Poland.

References

1. Bazan, J.G., Szczuka, M.S., Wroblewski, J. 2002. A new version of the rough set exploration system. In: J.J. Alpigini, J.F. Peters, A. Skowron, N. Zhong, Eds., Rough Sets and Current Trends in Computing, Lecture Notes in Artificial Intelligence, No. 2475. Springer-Verlag, Berlin, 397-404.
2. I.H. Gewolb, J.F. Bosma, V.L. Taciak, F.L. Vice, Abnormal Developmental Patterns of Suck and Swallow Rhythms During Feeding in Preterm Infants with Bronchopulmonary Dysplasia, *Developmental Medicine and Child Neurology*, vol. 43, no. 7, pp. 454-459, July, 2001
3. J.W. Gryzmala-Busse, LERS: A knowledge discovery system. In: L. Polkowski, A. Skowron (Eds.),Rough Sets in Knowledge Discovery, vol. 2, Physica-Verlag, Berlin, Germany, 1998, 562-565.
4. M.J., Katz, "Fractals and the Analysis of Waveforms," *Computers in Biology and Medicine*, vol. 18, no. 3, pp. 145-156, 1998.
5. L.J. Lazareck, Z.K. Moussavi, Adaptive Swallowing Sound Segmentation By Variance Dimension, *Proc. EMBEC 02 European Medical and Biological Engineering Conference* 1, 2002, 492-493.
6. L.J. Lazareck, Classification of Normal and Dysphagic Swallows by Acoustical Means, MSc. Thesis, ECE Department, University of Manitoba, 2003.
7. Z. Pawlak, Rough sets, Int. J. of Information and Computer Sciences, 11(5), 1982, 341-356, 1982
8. J.B. Palmer, K.V. Kuhlemeier, D.C. Tippett, C., Lynch, A protocol for the videofluorographic swallowing study, *Dysphagia*, 8, 1993, 209-214.
9. J.F. Peters, S. Ramanna, Software change classification system: A rough set approach, *Software Quality Journal* 11(2), June 2003, 121-148.

Emotional Temporal Difference Learning Based Multi-layer Perceptron Neural Network Application to a Prediction of Solar Activity

Farzan Rashidi[1] and Mehran Rashidi[2]

[1] Control Research Department, Engineering Research Institute, Tehran, Iran
P.O.Box: 13445-754, Tehran
f.rashidi@ece.ut.ac.ir
[2] Hormozgan Regional Electric Co. Bandar-Abbas, Iran
mrashidi@mehr.sharif.edu

Abstract. Nonlinear time series prediction has in recent years, been the subjects of many methodological and applied studies in the fields of system identification and nonlinear prediction. An important benchmark has been the prediction of solar activity with the markup increase in the practical importance of space weather forecasting; its motivation has risen far beyond more methodological concerns. In this paper, we have used a bounded rationality decision-making procedure, whose utility has been demonstrated in several identification and control tasks, for predicting sunspot numbers. An emotional temporal difference learning based multi layer perceptron neural network is introduced and applied to the prediction task.

1 Introduction

Predicting the future has been an interesting important problem in human mind. Alongside great achievements in this endeavor there remain many natural phenomena the successful predictions of which have so far eluded researchers. Some have been proven unpredictable due to the nature of their stochasticity. Others have been shown to be chaotic: with continuous and bounded frequency spectrum resembling noise and sensitivity to initial conditions attested via positive Lyapunov exponents resulting in long term unpredictability of the time series. Although important progress has been made in model based prediction; e.g. advanced methods now exist that can decimate chaotic time series, bounded rationality, behavioral, and generally non model based approaches are gaining popularity because of the possibility of their application to varied class of tasks without charges.

The emotional learning algorithm is a model-free method, which has three distinctive properties in comparison with other neurofuzzy learning algorithms. For one thing, one can use very complicated definitions for emotional signal without increasing the computational complexity of algorithm or worrying about differentiability or render ability into recursive formulation problems. For another, the parameters can be adjusted in a simple intuitive way to obtain the best performance. Besides, the training is very fast and efficient. As can be seen these properties make the method preferable in real time applications like control tasks, as have been presented in literature [1-4].

S. Tsumoto et al. (Eds.): RSCTC 2004, LNAI 3066, pp. 685–690, 2004.

In this paper emotional temporal difference learning has been used as new training procedures for the networks having MLP structure. A set of data about the time series of sunspots has been used in comparing the results. Paying attention to the characteristics and importance of the issue, the error signal has been employed as emotional signal in learning MLP networks with TD rules [6]. The results show that emotional temporal difference learning based MLP neural network is capable of improving the prediction accuracy and presenting better predictions in comparison with ANFIS neuro-fuzzy models.

2 Emotional Temporal Difference Learning Based Multi-layer Perceptron Neural Network

2.1 Temporal Difference Learning

Temporal difference (TD) learning is a type of reinforcement learning for solving delayed-reward prediction problems. Unlike supervised learning, which measures error between each prediction and target, TD uses the difference of two successive predictions to learn that is Multi Step Prediction. The advantage of TD learning is that it can update weights incrementally and converge to a solution faster [8]. In a delay-reward prediction problem, the observation-outcome sequence has the form $x_1, x_2, x_3, \ldots, x_m, z$ where each x_t is an observation vector available at time $t, 1 \le t \le m$ and z is the outcome of the sequence. For each observation, the learning agent makes a prediction of z, forming a sequence: $P_1, P_2, P_3, \ldots, P_m$. Assuming the learning agent is an artificial neural network, update for a weight w of the network with the classical gradient descent update rule for supervised learning is:

$$\Delta w = -\alpha \nabla_w E \tag{1}$$

Where α is the learning rate, E is a cost function and $\nabla_w E$ is the gradient vector. A simple form of E can be

$$E = \frac{1}{2}\sum_{t=1}^{m}(P_t - z)^2 \tag{2}$$

where P_t and z have been described at above. From equations (1) and (2), Δw will be calculated as follows:

$$\Delta w = -\alpha \sum_{t=1}^{m}(P_t - z)\nabla_w P \tag{3}$$

In [9] Sutton derived the incremental updating rule for equation (4) as:

$$\Delta w_t = \alpha(P_{t+1} - P_t)\sum_{k=1}^{t}\nabla_w P_k, \ t = 1,2,\ldots,m \text{ and } P_{m+1} \overset{def}{=} z \tag{4}$$

To emphasize more recent predictions, an exponential factor λ is multiplied to the gradient term:

$$\Delta w_t = \alpha(P_{t+1} - P_t)\sum_{k=1}^{t}\lambda^{t-k}\nabla_w P_k \tag{5}$$

Where $0 \leq \lambda \leq 1$. This results in a family of learning rules, $TD(\lambda)$, with constant values of λ. But there are two special cases:

First, when $\lambda = 1$, equation (5) falls back to equation (4), which produces the same training result as the supervised learning in Equation (3). Second, when $\lambda = 0$, equation (5) becomes

$$\Delta w_t = \alpha(P_{t+1} - P_t)\nabla_w P_k \tag{6}$$

Which has a similar form as equation (3). So the same training algorithm for supervised learning can be used for $TD(0)$.

2.2 TDMLP Neural Network

Multilayer perceptrons are an important class of neural networks that have been applied successfully to solve some difficult and diverse problems by training them in a supervised manner with some learning algorithms such as error correction learning rule, delta rule and etc. The classical generalized delta rule for multi-layer feedforward network is [7]:

$$\Delta w_l = \alpha y_{l-1}^T \delta_l \tag{7}$$

Where w_l is a $m \times n$ weight matrix connecting layer $l-1$ and l, m is the size of layer $l-1$ and n is the size of layer l, α is the learning rate (a scalar), y_{l-1}^T is transpose of the column vector y_{l-1} which is the output in layer $l-1$, δ_l is a column vector of error propagated from layer l to $l-1, l=0$ for the input layer. For output layer and for hidden layer the vector of backpropagated error, δ_l, is deferent and defined as:

$$\delta_l = \begin{cases} (T-Z) * f_l'(net_l) & \text{if } l \text{ is an output layer} \\ f_l'(net_l) * w_{l+1}\delta_{l+1} & \text{if } l \text{ is a hidden layer} \end{cases} \tag{8}$$

Where $f_l'(.)$ is the derivative of transfer function, f_l, in layer l, net_l is the weighted sum in layer l, δ_{l+1} is the delta value backpropagated from the upper layer of layer l, * denotes the element-wise vector multiplication, *T* is the target vector, *Z* is the output vector. To applying TD learning to the multi-layer feedforward network, we extract the term $(T-Z)$ from the original δ_l and obtain the δ_l^* as a new delta rule. So we define δ_{k+1}^* as:

$$\delta_{k+1}^* = diag[f'_{k+l}(net_{k+l})] \tag{9}$$

Where *diag* is the diagonal matrix and l is the output layer. If l is a hidden layer, equation (9) can be written as:

$$\delta_l^* = f_l'(net_l) * w_{l+1}.\delta_{l+1}^* \tag{10}$$

With the new delta, equation for change of each weight is rewritten as:

$$[\Delta w_l]_{ij} = \alpha[y_{l-1}]_i[\delta_l]_j = \alpha(T-Z)^T.([y_{l-1}]_i[\delta_l^*]_j) \tag{11}$$

Where $\left[\delta_l^*\right]_j$ is the *jth* element in vector δ_l^* and $\left[y_{l-1}\right]_i$ is the *ith* element in vector y_{l-1}. Unlike the original delta which is a vector backpropagated from an upper to a lower layer, now the new delta, δ_l^* is a $m \times n$ matrix where m is the size of output layer and n is the size of layer l. The error term $(T-Z)$ is needed for calculation of every weight increment. Comparing gradient decent in supervised learning in equation (3) and the backpropagation with new delta in equation (9) $\nabla_w P(t)$, the gradient term at time t for weight w' is:

$$\nabla_{w'} P_t = \left(\left[y_{l-1}\right]_i \left[\delta_l^*\right]_j\right)^T \tag{12}$$

Where $w' = \left[w_l(l)\right]_{ij}$ is the *ijth* element in the weight matrix w_l at the time t. By substituting this result to the formula of $TD(\lambda)$ learning in equation (6), we have:

$$\left[\Delta w_{lt}\right]_{ij} = \alpha\left(P_{t+1} - P_t\right)^T \sum_{k=1}^{t} \lambda^{t-k} \left(\left[y_{l-1}(k)\right]_i \left[\delta_l^*(k)\right]_{j,:}\right)^T \tag{13}$$

Where Δw_{lt} is the matrix of increment of weight connecting layer l and $l-1$ for prediction P_t. The term inside summation is called the history vector, denoted by $\left[h_l(t)\right]_{ij}$. We now obtain updating rules of TD learning by backpropagation. The weight update is performed by equation (13) with the new delta.

3 Predicting the Amount of Solar Activity

The time series of the number of sunspots which accounts for the amount of solar activity has been a good field for testing different methods of modeling and prediction for a long time. The amount of solar activity, as the sun is the nearest star, controls space climate events. The effect of these events on earth, satellites, weather and communication have been studied and the time series predictions related to it has been improved from university researchers to important international applied issues. Paying attention to the past decades events that caused trouble for invaluable satellites and the nine day Quebec electrical supply going out in 1989 shows the importance of predicting space climate events. Physicists, engineering and astrologers have developed different methods of predicting solar activity via the time series of sunspots.

In this paper, emotional temporal difference learning algorithm has been applied to MLP neural network for predicting annual and monthly time series predictions of the number of sunspots. A viewed in fig.1. solar activity is an alternative chaotic event with an approximation time of eleven years. The error index in predicting the sunspot number in this paper, the normalized mean square error (NMSE), is defined as follow

$$NMSE = \left(\frac{\sum_{i=1}^{n} (y - \hat{y})^2}{\sum_{i=1}^{n} (y - \bar{y})^2} \right) \tag{14}$$

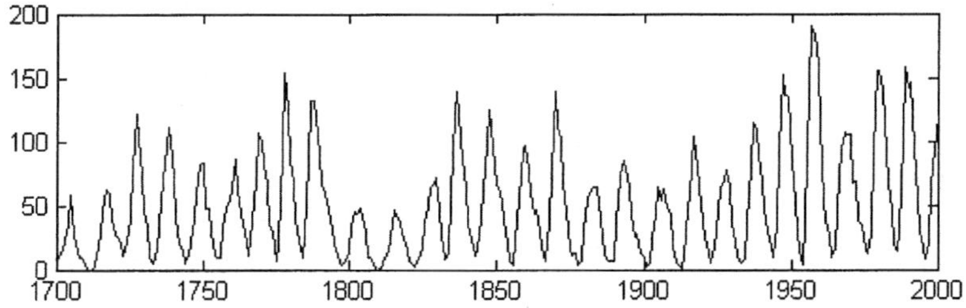

Fig. 1. The yearly averaged sunspot number.

In which $y, \hat{y}$ and $\overline{y}$ are observed data, predicted data and the average of observed data respectively. The prediction system has been developed with emotional temporal difference learning algorithm based on double layer MLP network. The emotional signal is computed via subtracting the successful prediction. Then this signal, with attention to (13) formula and temporal difference learning, is useful in updating network weights. Figure 2 shows the predictions by ETDLMLP. This diagram is a part of test set, especially the cycle 19 which has an above average peak in 1957. Table 1 presents the results obtained from ANFIS, RBF, ELFIS and ETDLMLP. According to this table, it is observable that ETDLMLP generates the most accurate prediction in the solar maximum; however the NMSE of ANFIS, RBF, ELFIS, are the least. Noticeably it's more important to predict the peak points with small errors rather than the points in minimum regions. This is a result of the emotions of critic in the solar maximum.

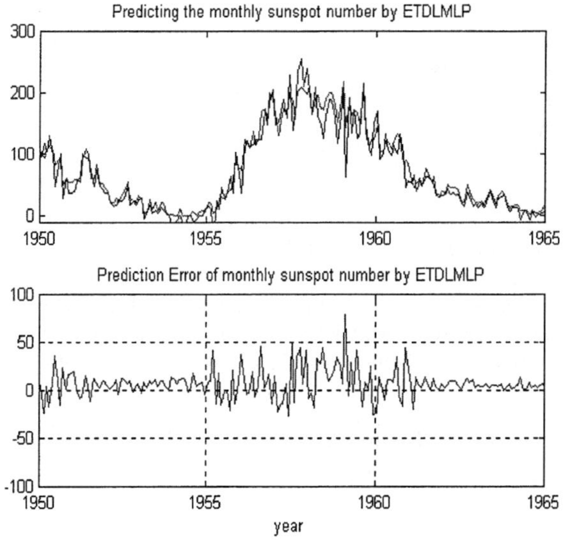

Fig. 2. Predicting the sunspot number by Emotional temporal difference learning based Multi layer perceptron.

Table 1. Comparison of predictions by selected neural and neurofuzzy models.

	Specifications	Computation Time	NMSE
ANFIS	8 rules and 165 epochs	89.5790 sec.	0.1702
RBF	7 neurons in hidden layer	84.7820 sec.	0.1314
ELFIS	3 Sugeno type fuzzy rules	47.3320 sec.	0.1386
ETDLMLP	12 neurons in hidden layer, ($\lambda = 0.5$)	35.2800 sec.	0.1037

4 Conclusion

In this paper, the proposed emotional temporal difference learning based MLP neural network has been used in the prediction of solar activity (the sunspot number time series). The emotional signal is determined with emphasis on the solar maximum regions (the peak points of sunspot numbers) and it has shown better results in comparison with adaptive network based fuzzy inference system.

References

1. Eppler W., Beck H.N.,"Peicewise linear networks (PLN) for function approximation", Proc. of IEEE Int. Con. on neural networks, Washington, 1999
2. Rashidi. F., Rashidi M., Hashemi Hosseini A., "Emotional Temporal Difference Learning Based Intelligent Controller", IEEE Coference, CCA, pp.341-346, 2003.
3. Rashidi, M., Rashidi, F., Monavar, H., "Peak load forecasting in power systems using emotional learning based fuzzy logic", IEEE Conference on System Man and Cybernetics, Vol. 2, pp. 1985-1988, 2003
4. Kavli T. "ASMOD: An algorithm for adaptive spline modeling of observation data", Int. J. of Control, 58(4), pp. 947-967, 1993
5. Ali Gholipour, Ali Abbaspour, Caro Lucas, Babak N. Araabi, Mehrdad Fatourechi, "Enhancing the Performance of Neurofuzzy Predictors by Emotional Learning Algorithm", Submitted to informatica Journal, 2003
6. Tomaso Poggio and Federico Girosi, "A Theory of Networks for Approximation and Learning", A. I. Memo 1140, MIT, 1989
7. D.E.Rumelhart, G.E.Hinton, and R.J.Williams, "Learning Internal Representations by Error Propagation", Parallel Distributed Processing (PDP): Exploration in Microstructure of Recognition, Vol. 1, Chapter 8, MIT Press, Cambridge, Massachusetts, 1986
8. Weigend A., Huberman B., Rumelhart D.E, "Predicting the future: a connectionist approach", Int. J. Of Neural systems, vol. 1, pp. 193-209, 1990
9. Weigend A., Huberman B., Rumelhart D.E., "Predicting sunspots and exchange rates with connectionist networks", in Nonlinear Modeling and Forecasting, Casdagli, Eubank: Editors, Addison-Wesley, pp. 395-432, 1992

Musical Metadata Retrieval with Flow Graphs

Andrzej Czyzewski and Bozena Kostek

Gdansk University of Technology, Multimedia Systems Department
Narutowicza 11/12, 80-952 Gdansk, Poland
{andcz,bozenka}@sound.eti.pg.gda.pl
http://www.multimed.org

Abstract. The CDDB database available in the Internet is widely used for the retrieval of metadata associated with almost any CD record. The database is queried automatically each time a CD is copied on a computer with appropriate software installed. However, this database could be used also for musical recording searching. An advanced query algorithm was prepared to that end employing the concept of inference rule derivation from flow graphs introduced recently by Pawlak. The searching engine utilizes knowledge acquired in advance and stored in flow graphs in order to enable searching CD records database. The experimental results showing the effectiveness of analyzing musical metadata with this method are presented in the paper.

1 Introduction

Rapid growth of interest is observed in the so-called "semantic Web" concepts [3]. The Semantic Web provides the representation of data on the World Wide Web. Zdzislaw Pawlak in his recent papers [5], [6] promotes his new mathematical model of flow networks which can be used to mining knowledge in databases. Recently his finding were also generalized [4]. Given the increasing amount of music information available online, the aim is to enable an efficient access to such information sources. We applied these concepts to the domain of semantic Web content analysis, namely to a musical metadata querying. We demonstrate how to apply this conceptual framework based on flow graphs to improve music information retrieval efficiency.

The experiments that were performed by us consisted in constructing a music database collecting music recordings together with semantic description. A searching engine is designed, which enables querying for a particular musical piece utilizing the knowledge on the entire database content and relations among its elements contained in the flow graphs constructed following Pawlak's ideas. As we demonstrate in the paper, these goals could be achieved efficiently provided the searching engine uses the knowledge of database content acquired a priori and represented by distribution ratios between branches of the flow graph which in turn can be treated as a prototype of a rule-based decision algorithm.

2 The Database

2.1 CDDB Service

CDDB service is the industry standard for music recognition services. It contains the largest online database of music information in the world (currently more than 22

S. Tsumoto et al. (Eds.): RSCTC 2004, LNAI 3066, pp. 691–698, 2004.

million tracks), and is used by over 30 million people in more than 130 countries every month. Seamless handling of soundtracks data provide music listeners both professional and amateurs with access to a huge store of information on recorded music [1], [2]. The large database queried so frequently by users from all over the world provides also a very interesting material for research experiments in the domain of searching engine optimizing. The organization of metadata related to a compact disc indexed in the CDDB database is presented in Tab. 1.

Table 1. Metadata fields in the *CDDB* database.

Album Data Fields:	
Album Title	Can be a multi-word expression (string)
Album Artist	as above
Record Label	The label or publisher of the CD
Year	The year the CD was recorded or published
Genre	Every album can have both a primary and a secondary genre
Compilation	Indicates whether tracks have different artists
Number/Total Set	Can identify a CD as a member of a box sets
Language	Used to help display in appropriate character set
Region	To identify where the CD was released
Certifier	Authorized party (artist or label) who has certified the data accuracy
Notes	General notes such as dedications, etc.
Track Data Fields:	
Track Title	Can be a multi-word expression (string)
Track Artist	Vital for compilations, such as soundtracks or samplers
Record Label	May be different from track to track for compilations
Year	May be different from track to track
Beats/Minute	Used for special purposes (synchronizing with special devices)
Credits	E.g. guest musicians, songwriter, etc.
Genre	Every track can have both a primary and a secondary genre
ISRC	The International Standard Recording Code number for the CD track
Notes	General track notes such as "recorded in ...", etc.
Credits	Can be entered for entire album, for individual tracks or segments
Credit Name	Can be person, company, or place such as recording location
Credit Role	Instrument, composer, songwriter, producer, recording place, etc.
Credit Notes	E.g. to specify unusual instruments, etc.
Genres	Can be entered for entire album or applied to individual tracks
Metagenres	General classification. e.g. Rock; Classical; New Age; Jazz...
Subgenres	More specific style. e.g. Ska; Baroque, Choral; Ambient; Bebop, Ragtime...
Segments	Each segment can have its own name, notes, and credits

The content of the world-wide CDDB was targeted in our experiments as the principal material for experiments. However, because of the large volume of this database we decided that initially we will construct and use much smaller local database utilizing the CDDB data format. Consequently, a database was constructed especially for the purpose of this study containing approximately 500 compact discs textual data stored together with fragments of music corresponding to various categories. This database provided a material for initial experiments with searching music employing the proposed method. Subsequently, the huge CDDB database containing metadata related to majority of compact disks hitherto produced in the world was utilized.

2.2 CDDB Database Organization and Searching Tools

A sample record from the CDDB database is presented in Fig. 1. The field denoted as "frames" needs some explanation. It contains the frame numbers, because the CDDB protocol defines beginning of each track in terms of track lengths and the number of preceding tracks. The most basic information required to calculate these values is the CD table of contents (the CD track offsets, in "MSF" [Minutes, Seconds, Frames]). That is why tracks are often addressed on audio CDs using "MSF" offsets. The combination determines the exact disc frame where a song starts. The process of CDDB database querying begins with submitting the content of the "frames" field to a database searching engine. It is assumed that this numerical data string is unique for each CD, because it is improbable that the numerical combination could be repeated for different albums. Sending this numerical string to a remote CDDB database results with transmitting back all data related to the album stored in the database, namely artist, title,..., genre, etc. This feature is exploited by a huge number of clients worldwide. However, as results from above, such a query can be made, provided users possess a copy of the CD record which metadata are searched for. If so, their computers can automatically get data from the CDDB database and display these data. Consequently, local catalogs of records (phonotecs) can be built up fast and very efficiently with the use of this system.

CDDBID: eb117b10 [22164FD]
artist=Céline DION
title=Let's Talk About Love
numtracks=16
compilationdisc=no
genre=Pop
year=1997
comment=this is her bestselling album
0=The Reason
1=Immortality
2=Treat Her Like A Lady
3=Why, Oh Why ?
4=Love Is On The Way
5=Tell Him (Avec Barbra Streisand)
6=Amar Haciendo El Amor
7=When I Need You
8=Miles To Go (Before I Sleep)
9=Us
10=Just A Little Bit Of Love
11=My Heart Will Go On (Chanson D'amour Du Film Titanic)
12=Where Is The Love ?
13=Be The Man
14=I Hate You Then I Love You (Avec Luciano Pavarotti)
15=Let's Talk About Love
frames=0,22580,41415,59812,81662,101655,123540,142347,161295,182290,208287,226792,247817,
270010,290987,312245,335675
order=0 1 2 3 4 5 6 7 8 9 10 11 12 13 14 15

Fig. 1. Sample CDDB database record.

A possible benefit from the universal and unrestricted access to CDDB could be, however, much higher than just obtaining the textual information while having a copy of a record at a disposal. Namely, provided an adequate searching engine is employed, CDDB users could submit various kinds of queries in this largest set of data on recorded sound, without the necessity to gain an access to any CD record in advance. A typical situation concerning database records is that the CDDB database may contain many records related to the same CD. That is because all CDDB users possessing records ale allowed to send and store remotely metadata utilizing various software tools. Consequently, textual information related to the same CD records can be spelled quite much differently.

3 Data Mining in the CDDB Database

The weakness of typical data searching techniques lays in lacking or not using any a priori knowledge concerning the queried dataset.

The abundant literature on techniques for searching data in databases describes many methods and algorithms for probabilistic search and data mining techniques, including decision trees application. There are no reports, however, on successful application of any of them to representing knowledge contained in the CDDB database.

As a method of data mining in the CDDB database we propose a system application which uses logic as mathematical foundations of probability for the deterministic flow analysis in flow networks. As was said, the new mathematical model of flow networks underlying the decision algorithm in question was proposed recently by Zdzislaw Pawlak [5], [6]. The decision algorithm allowed us to build an efficient searching engine for the CDDB database.

Two databases prepared in the CDDB format were selected as objects of our experiments: a local database containing metadata related to approximately 500 CD disks and the original CDDB imported from *freedb.org* website (*rev. 20031008*). At first the much smaller local database was used in order to allow experiments without engaging too much computing power for flow graph modeling. Moreover, only 5 most frequently used terms were selected as labels of node columns. These are:

- **Album title** (optional *ASCII* string not exceeding 256 letters)
- **Album artist** (up to 5 words separated by spaces)
- **Year** of record issuing (4 decimal digits)
- **Genre** (type of music that can be according to CDDB standard: Blues,...,Classical,...,Country,..., Folk,..., Jazz,..., Rock,...,Vocal). It is together 148 kinds of musical genres
- **Track title** (optional ASCII string not exceeding 256 letters)
- The term **Number** was considered a decision attribute – in the CDDB database it is represented by unique digit/letter combination of the length equal to 8 (for example: *0a0fe010, 6b0a4b08, etc.*).

Once the number of a record is determined, which is associated with a concrete CD, it allows a retrieval of all necessary metadata from the database (as presented in Fig. 1) and render them by automatic filling/replacing the fields of an electronic questionnaire. The graph designed to represent data relations between chosen terms is illustrated in Fig. 2.

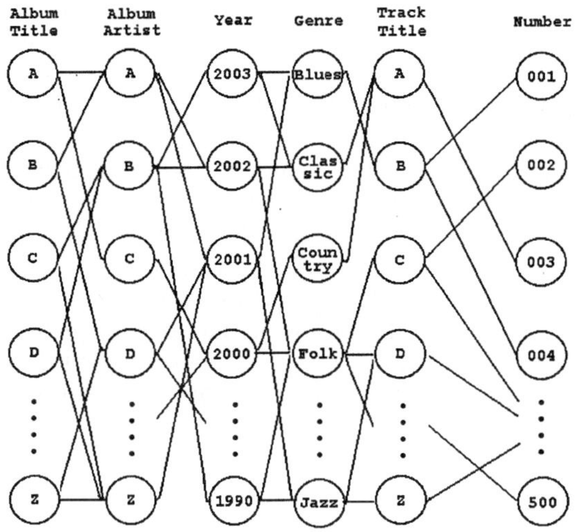

Fig. 2. Flow graph representing knowledge relevant to frequently made CDDB queries.

The process of knowledge acquisition is initiated for the smaller CDDB database with analyzing first letters of terms "Album Title", "Album Artist" and "Track Titles". This temporary solution was adopted because of the small size of the experimental database. Otherwise the number of paths between nodes would be too small and the problem of CD records searching would be hard-defined in practice for most objects. Above restriction does not concern the full CDDB database containing many records of selected performers as well as many records metadata of which contain the same words in the fields related to album or track titles. A software implementation of the algorithm based on theoretical assumptions proposed by Pawlak was prepared and implemented to a server having the following features: 2 *Athlon MP* 2,2 GHz processors, *Windows 2000*™ OS *MySQL* database server, *Apache*™ WWW server. The result of branch-related factors calculation is illustrated in Fig. 3.

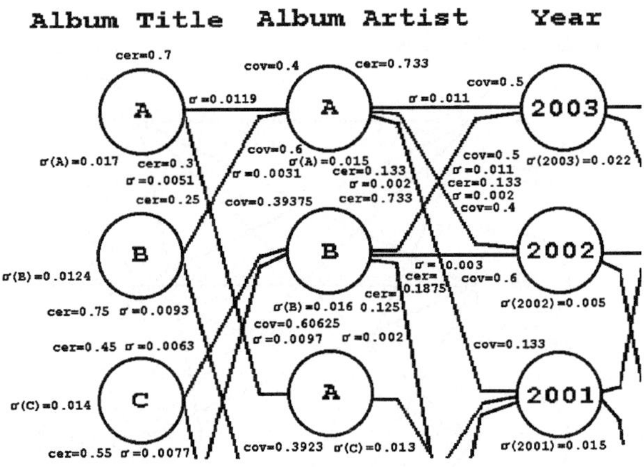

Fig. 3. Fragment of flow graph with marked values of **certainty**, **coverage** and **strength** calculated for branches.

The process of knowledge acquisition does not finish with determining the values of **certainty**, **coverage** and **strength** for each branch. The knowledge base should be prepared for servicing queries with any reduced term set. Correspondingly, the graph should be simplified in advance in order to determine data dependencies applicable to such cases. The knowledge base should be prepared in advance to serve such queries rather than assuming calculating new values of factors related to shorter paths each time a term is dropped (field left empty by the user). That is why in order to shorten the time needed for calculations made in response to a query, all terms are left-out consecutively, one of them at a time while the values of branch factors are calculated each time and stored. This solution lets users to get ready answer for each question almost immediately, independently on the amount of knowledge they possess on the CD record which is searched for. An example of a simplified flow graph is illustrated in Fig. 4. The dropping of the term "Album Artist" node layer entails among others the following calculations:

A -> A -> 2003 ==> B -> 2003
0.0087=0.733*0.0119
C -> B -> 2002 ==> C -> 2002
0.0012=0.1875*0.0063

The decision rules can be derived from flow graphs. Correspondingly, the following sample inference rules can be obtained from the graph showed in Fig. 2, whose fragment is depicted in Fig. 3:

If *Album Title=B* **and** *Album Artist=A* **and** *Year=2003* **and** *Genre=genre_value* **and** *Track Title=track_title_value* **then** *Number=number_value*

If *Album Title=C* **and** *Album Artist=B* **and** *Year=2002* **and** *Genre=genre_value* **and** *Track Title=track_title_value* **then** *Number=number_value*

The values of: *genre_value, track_title_value and number_value* can be determined from the parts of the graph that are not covered by the figure (for captions resolution limitations). If the user did not provide *Album Artist* value, the direct data flows from the nodes *Album Title* to nodes *Year* can be analyzed as in Fig. 4. The inference rules are shorter in this case and adequate values of **certainty**, **coverage** and **strength** have to be adopted.

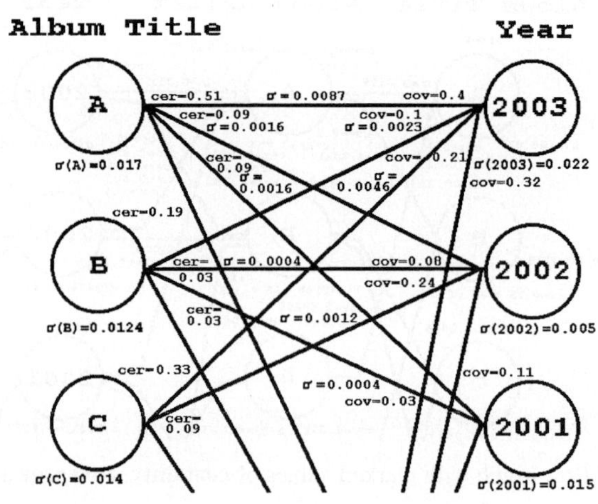

Fig. 4. Simplified flow graph (from Fig. 3) after leaving-out the term: "Album artist".

For example the value of rule strength associated with the paths determined by node values: *Album Title=B -> Album Artist=A* (as in Fig. 3) equal to σ=0.0031 and σ=0.0011 are replaced by the new value of σ=0.0023 associated with the path: *Album Title=B -> Year=2003*. The shortened rules corresponding to the previous examples given above are as follows:

If *Album Title=B* **and** *Year=2003* **and** *Genre=genre_value* **and** *Track Title=track_title_value* **then** *Number=number_value*
If *Album Title=C* **and** *Year=2002* **and** *Genre=genre_value* **and** *Track Title=track_title_value* **then** *Number=number_value*

The latter inference rules may adopt the same decision attribute (the number of the same CD record), however the rule strength (σ value) can be different in this case. The rule strength is a decisive factor for ordering searching results in the database. The principle of ordering matches is simple: the bigger the rule strength value, the higher is the position of the CD record determined by the rule in the ordered rank of matches. This principle allows for descending ordering of queried CD's basing on the rules derived from the analysis of optimal data flow in the graphs representing available knowledge on CD records.

4 Conclusions

An application of the knowledge extraction algorithm to the CDDB case is practically justified provided it is possible to complete all computing tasks on a typical server (full set of inference rule derivation) in time shorter that 1 day. This demand is entirely fulfilled in the case of flow graphs application.

The assumption made in the original flow graphs model requires that the rows of the decision table represent rules that are mutually exclusive in the sense that they are supported by disjoint sets of objects. Since it is not always true for musical records data, we plan to consider the model proposed recently in the literature [4] in which the condition of independence of decision rules is relaxed.

Acknowledgments

The research is sponsored by the State Committee for Scientific Research, Warsaw, Grant No. 4T11D 014 22, and the Foundation for Polish Science, Poland.

References

1. http://www.freedb.org
2. http://www.gracenote.com
3. http://www.semanticweb.org/
4. Greco S., Pawlak Z. and Slowinski R.: Generalized Decision Algorithms, Rough Inference Rules and Flow Graphs. [In]: J.J. Alpigini, J.F. Peters, A. Skowron, N. Zhong (eds.), Rough Sets and Current Trends in Computing. Lecture Notes in Artificial Intelligence, vol. 2475, Springer-Verlag, Berlin, 2002, pp. 93-104

5. Pawlak, Z.: Probability, Truth and Flow Graph. Electronic Notes in Theoretical Computer Science, International Workshop on Rough Sets in Knowledge Discovery and Soft Computing, Satellite event of ETAPS 2003, Warsaw, Poland, April 12-13, (2003) Elsevier, Vol. 82 (4) (2003)
6. Pawlak, Z.: Elementary Rough Set Granules: Towards a Rough Set Processor. In: Rough-Neural Computing. Techniques for Computing with Words. Pal, S.K., Polkowski L., Skowron A. (eds.). Springer Verlag, Berlin, Heidelberg, New York (2004) 5-13.

A Fuzzy-Rough Method for Concept-Based Document Expansion

Yan Li[1], Simon Chi-Keung Shiu[1], Sankar Kumar Pal[2], and James Nga-Kwok Liu[1]

[1] Department of Computing, Hong Kong Polytechnic University, Kowloon, HongKong
{csyli,csckshiu,csnkliu}@comp.polyu.edu.hk

[2] Machine Intelligence Unit, Indian Statistical Institute, Kolkata, 700 035, India
sankar@isical.ac.in

Abstract. In this paper, a novel approach of fuzzy-rough hybridization is developed for concept-based document expansion to enhance the quality of text information retrieval. Firstly, different from the traditional way of document representation, a given set of text documents is represented by an incomplete information system. To discover the relevant keywords to be complemented, the weights of those terms which do not occur in a document are considered missing instead of zero. Fuzzy sets are used to take care of the real-valued weights in the term vectors. Rough sets are then used to extract the potentially associated keywords which convey a concept for text retrieval in this incomplete information system. Finally, through incorporating Nearest Neighbor mechanism, the missing weights of the extracted keywords of a document can be filled by searching the corresponding weights of the most similar document. Thus, the documents in the original text dataset are expanded, whereas the number of total keywords is reduced. Some experiments are conducted using part of data from Ruters21578. Since the concept-based method is able to identify and supplement the potentially useful information to each document, the performance of information retrieval in terms of recall is greatly improved.

1 Introduction

The Internet and World Wide Web are making vast amounts of information easily accessible, in which text is the most prevalent medium for expressing information and knowledge. Locating and extracting useful information from texts has long been the main goal in the information retrieval (IR) community. To evaluate the performance of a given IR system, a concept *Recall* is usually used. It is a measure of , given a search criterion, how many documents are returned versus how many documents should have been returned. To improve the retrieval quality in terms of recall, automatic query expansion and document expansion are developed by some researchers [1-3]. Through the detecting of potentially associated keywords using these techniques, the queries and documents are more specifically expressed and therefore more effective retrieval can be achieved. Most current work is based on statistical theory, user feedback as well as additional thesaurus, which often require large text corpus

S. Tsumoto et al. (Eds.): RSCTC 2004, LNAI 3066, pp. 699–707, 2004.

and extra domain knowledge. Furthermore, due to the term-based rather than concept-based expansion, the performance of document expansion is not satisfactory [4]. In this paper, rough set theory is incorporated to identify the essential missing keywords which potentially convey different concepts to describe the documents. Without using extra heuristics and domain knowledge, the text retrieval performance can be enhanced through complementing the important missing information to given text datasets.

In the context of IR, a document in a text corpus is often represented by a term vector using the vector space model (VSM). Each term vector consists of the weights, through the *term frequency-inverted document frequency* (tf-idf) computation, of the corresponding terms of a document. Traditionally, the weights of those terms which do not occur in a given document are considered to be zero. However, some potentially relevant information would be lost due to this document representation. From the prospective of information system, it is more natural to consider the text corpus as an incomplete information system instead of a complete one. That is, instead of assigning zero to the weights of those terms which are absent in a document, these weights are considered missing. Based on this idea, a method of representing document as an incomplete term vector is proposed. Using this method, an incomplete information system can be constructed consisting of the term vectors with some missing term weights. The information loss can be avoided to some extent and thereby improve the text retrieval quality.

In the framework of incomplete information system, document expansion can be effectively dealt with using rough sets. After the development of rough set theory by Pawlak in 1982 [5], many researchers have developed rough set-based concepts and methods to select the most important features and generate decision rules in incomplete information systems [6-9]. In this paper, rough sets are used to extract keywords as well as reduce the redundancy for the document corpus including the incomplete document vectors. In order to implement this process, fuzzy sets are incorporated to take care of the real-valued weights in each incomplete document vector. Only the regular term weights (i.e., the term weights which are not missing) are fuzzified. The mechanism of Nearest Neighbor is then applied to predict the missing weights, thereby to complete the task of document expansion. Through applying rough sets in incomplete information system, the essential part of the potentially useful information is detected and expanded. The greatest merit of our approach is that, although the potential relevant keywords for text retrieval are added to a document, the number of the total keywords is reduced through rough set-based feature selection in the incomplete information system.

The reminder of this paper is organized as follows. In Section 2, the tf-idf weight computation is described and the new document representation method is proposed, where each document in a text document dataset is represented by an incomplete term vector with missing weights. This is followed by Section 3 in which we describe how the incomplete term vectors are fuzzified. Three triangular membership functions are used for each term, denoted by “low”, “medium”, and “high” to describe the term frequency. In Section 4, potentially associated keywords are extracted under the incomplete information system environment. This is done by incorporating some new concepts of rough set theory. Section 5 deals with the document expansion through predicting the missing weights of the selected keywords. The mechanism of Nearest Neighbor is applied in missing weight prediction. The experimental analysis is given in Section 6.

2 Document Representation

Assume that there are N documents and n different terms in a text corpus. Using VSM, each document is represented by an n-dimensional term vector. Each different term which occurs in the text corpus is considered as a dimension in the term vector. The corresponding value of a term dimension in the vector is the weight of the term in question. Here the weight of each term in each document is computed using tf -idf.

The weight of the kth term in the ith document is given as $w_{ik}' = -\log(N_k/N)f_{ik}$, where N_k is the number of documents containing term k; N is the total number of documents; f_{ik} is the frequency of term k in document i. After normalized by dividing $\max_{ik}\{w_{ik}'\}$, the N documents in the text corpus can be represented by an $N\times n$ matrix, $DW = [w_{ij}]$, where $w_{ij} = w_{ij}'/\max_j\{w_{ij}'\}$, if the jth term t_j occurs in the ith document; otherwise, $w_{ij} = 0$. Together with decision attributes, say, the topic of documents, the matrix can be considered as a decision table or a complete information system. Note that, according to the weight computation, if the jth term t_j is absent in the ith document d_i, the jth dimension of the ith document, w_{ij}, is equal to zero.

This way of assigning the weights to absent terms is not very reasonable because it is possible that some potential useful information will be lost. In this paper, to complement the documents with potentially relevant terms (i.e., document expansion), using incomplete information systems to represent the text dataset is preferred. An example is given in Section 4 to demonstrate that transforming an incomplete information system to a complete one would cause information loss and therefore degrade the retrieval performance.

3 Fuzzify Term Weights

In order to use rough sets to select keywords, the real-valued weights have to be discretized. The most often used method in IR is using "0" and "1" to represent the weights which are equal to zero or not equal to zero, respectively. After using this discretized method, the term vectors cannot reflect the extent of how frequent it is for each term. Thus, the computed similarity measure of the documents cannot well reflect the actual similarity between documents. To reduce the information loss, fuzzy sets are incorporated to refine the representation of term vectors through discretizing the weights for each term to three fuzzy sets "Low", "Medium", "High", denoted by L, M, H, respectively.

Based on the document representation mentioned in Section 2, each element in the term vectors w_{ij} is given by $w_{ij} = w_{ik}/ \max_k\{w_{ik}'\} \in [0, 1]$. Let the center of the fuzzy sets L, M, and H be c_L, c_M and c_H, respectively. The triangular membership functions are described in Fig.1.

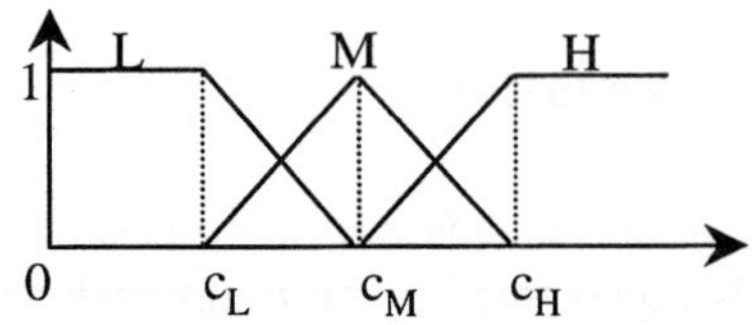

Fig. 1. Membership functions of fuzzy sets for term weights.

Note that in this paper, without using any domain knowledge to determine the centers for the three fuzzy sets, we set $c_L = 0.25$, $c_M = 0.5$, and $c_H = 0.75$. These parameters can be given beforehand or be tuned during the process of training according to the output performance.

4 Rough Set Theory in Incomplete Information System

4.1 Document Representation by Incomplete Information System

After the real-valued weights are fuzzified using the membership function given in Section 3, the text document dataset can be represented by an incomplete information system with missing weights. Such an incomplete information system is described in Table 1. t1, t2, t3, and t4 are the terms which occur in the 6 documents, the computed term weights using tf –idf are fuzzified to three fuzzy labels. "*" denotes the missing weights.

Table 1. An incomplete information system.

Document	t1	t2	t3	t4	topic
1	high	low	high	Low	{T1}
2	low	*	high	Low	{T1}
3	*	*	low	Low	{T3}
4	high	*	high	High	{T1, T2}
5	*	*	high	High	{T1, T2}
6	low	high	high	*	{T1, T2}

If the documents are represented in the traditional way, the missing weights should be labeled as "low" after the process of fuzzifying. If we replace all "*" with "low", the information system become a complete one as in Table 2, which is a complete extension of the incomplete information system in Table 1.

Table 2. A complete information system.

Document	**t1**	**t2**	**t3**	**T4**	**topic**
1	high	low	high	low	{T1}
2	low	low	high	low	{T1}
3	low	low	low	low	{T3}
4	high	low	high	high	{T1, T2}
5	low	low	high	high	{T1, T2}
6	low	high	high	low	{T1, T2}

Using rough set theory, it is easy to know that each attribute in Table 2 is indispensable. {t1, t2, t3, t4} is the only reduct of the complete information system. 6 rules R = {r1, r2, ..., r6} can be extracted from each record in Table 2. On the other hand, from the original incomplete information system (Table 1), {t1, t3, t4} is the only reduct. The corresponding rules in R' = {r1', r2', ..., r6'} are:

r1': IF (t1 = high) AND (t3 = high) AND (t4 = low) THEN topic = T1.
r2': IF (t1 = low) AND (t3 = high) AND (t4 = low) THEN topic = T1.
r3': (t1 = *) AND (t3 = low) AND (t4 = low) THEN topic = T3.
r4': (t1 = high) AND (t3 = high) AND (t4 = high) THEN topic = T1 or T2.
r5': (t1 = *) AND (t3 = high) AND (t4 = high) THEN topic = T1 or T2.
r6': (t1 = low) AND (t3 = high) AND (t4 = *) THEN topic = T1 or T2.

Now we demonstrate that it is possible to lose important information if treating missing values as being absent. Consider a query document: (t1 = low) AND (t2 = high) AND (t3 = low) AND (t4 = high). According to rule set R, there is no matching rule and therefore no decision can be provided. According to rule set R', r6' is the rule which can completely match the query document, therefore the decision for the query is "T1 or T2". It is possible that this result is reasonable through the statistical observations from document 4 and 5.

4.2 Some Related Concepts

As mentioned before, due to the existence of missing values in an incomplete information system, some new concepts are required in order to use rough sets to identify the essential information in an incomplete system. Corresponding to the concepts of equivalence relation, equivalence class and lower and upper approximations in rough set theory for complete information system, the new set of concepts of similarity relation, maximal consistent block, and set approximations is introduced [7]. Here we introduce the corresponding concepts in the text IR domain. An incomplete information system for a document corpus is represented as IIS = $(D, TM \cup \{Topic\}, f)$, where D is the set of documents, each document is an object $d \in D$; TM is the set of total terms which occur in the document set, *Topic* is the decision attribute, i.e., the class label of the documents.

Similarity relation is a tolerance relation which satisfies reflexivity and symmetry. For a subset of *TM*, $T \subseteq TM$, a similarity relation *SM*(*S*) on *D* is defined as

$SM(T) = \{(d_x, d_y) \in D \times D | \forall t \in TM, f_t(d_x) = f_t(d_y) \text{ or } f_t(d_x) = * \text{ or } f_t(d_y) = *\}$.

Consequently, ***Similarity class*** of a document d_x with respect to $T \subseteq TM$, $S_T(d_x)$, is the set of documents which are indiscernible to d_x, i.e., $S_T(d_x) = \{ d_y \in D | (d_x, d_y) \in SM(T)\}$.

A subset documents $X \subseteq D$ is said to be ***consistent*** with respect to a subset of terms *T*, if: $\forall (d_x, d_y) \in X, (d_x, d_y) \in SM(T)$.

Based on these concepts, the ***lower and upper set approximations*** can be redefined as

$$\underline{T}(X) = \{d_x \in D \mid S_T(d_x) \subseteq X\}$$

$$\overline{T}(X) = \{d_x \in D \mid S_T(d_x) \cap X \neq \phi\}$$

A ***maximal consistent block*** of $T \subseteq TM$, denoted by MCB_T, is the maximal subset of *D* which is consistent with respect to *T*, $MCB_T = \{X \subseteq D$, *X* is consistent with respect to $T \mid \neg\exists\ Y \subseteq D$, Y is consistent with respect to *T* and $Y \supset X\}$. The maximal consistent block of *T* with respect to a document $d \in D$ is the set of maximal consistent blocks which include *d*, denoted by $MCB_T(d)$.

A subset of terms $T \subseteq TM$ is called a **reduct** of *TM* if $MCB_T = MCB_{TM}$.

4.3 Generate Reducts in Incomplete Information System

In this paper, the focus is to discover hidden associated keywords for a set of documents for document expansion instead of categorizing the documents. Therefore, we propose a method to generate reducts in the incomplete information system without considering the decision attribute *topic*. According to the theoretic results in [7], a reduct can be computed as follows.

Step 1. Compute the discernibility matrix of the incomplete information system.
Step 2. Compute MCB_{TM}.
Step 3. Compute the prime implicant of discernibility function

$$\Delta = \prod_{(X,Y) \in MCB_{TM} \times MCB_{TM}} \alpha_{TM}(X,Y) \text{, where } \alpha_{TM}(X,Y) = \prod_{(x,y) \in (X,Y)} \sum \alpha(x,y) \text{,}$$

and $\alpha(x,y) = \{t \in TM \mid f_t(x) \neq "*", f_t(y) \neq "*", f_t(x) \neq f_t(y)\}$.

Step 3 can be completed through several computations. Let REDU represent the reduct of *TM*.

(1) Select the most frequent term $t \in TM$, add t to REDU.
(2) Set $TM = TM - \{t\}$.
(3) If REDT$\subseteq X$, for $\forall X \in$ MCB_{TM}, stop; else, turn to (1).

5 Document Expansion through Predicting Missing Weights Based on 1-NN

After the reduct of the original set of terms is generated in Section 4, the essential part of information (i.e., the most important keywords) is identified. There are some missing weights of these extracted keywords in the term vectors. Document expansion is addressed through predicting these missing weights using the methodology of 1-NN. The best values of these missing weights are determined by retrieving the most similar term vector with the same topic through the similarity computation among the regular keywords. Thus, the missing values of the most important terms for document classification are predicted and complemented in the documents.

For example, consider the incomplete information system described in Table 1. After the process of generating reduct, the only reduct is identified as {t1, t3, t4}, which shows that keywords t1, t3 and t4 are the most important information for the document set. The missing values of t1 for document 3, document 5, t4 for document 6, should be predicted. Since there does not exist a document with the same topic, T3, of document 3, its missing value for t1 cannot be predicted. Document 3, therefore, is not expanded. For document 5, the missing value of t1 can be predicted by the most similar document, document 4, with the same topic T1 or T2. That is, "*" is replaced with "high" in document 5. Similarly, the missing value of t4 in document 6 is replaced with "high" from document 5.

Note that the similarity measure used here is the similarity between two term vectors, which is computed based on the weighted distance $Sim\ (d_x, d_y) = 1 - \sum_k w_k |w_{ik} - w_{jk}|$. The corresponding fuzzy term vectors are not used in similarity computation because it involves the similarity calculation between two fuzzy sets.

6 Experimental Analysis

To evaluate and demonstrate the effectiveness of our proposed method for document expansion, some experiments are conducted on a randomly selected subset of text data from the Reuters21578 dataset. There are 30 documents and 4 topics in the dataset. Since the topic of "earn" is the most popular one in Reuters21578, we use this in our example. The results and analysis are given as follows.

After the weight computation and reduct generation, two example weight vectors of the topic "earn", W1 and W2, are

Table 3. Two example weight vectors for the topic "earn".

W1	t1	t2	t3	t4	t5	t6	t7
	0.6327	0.0000	0.2109	1.0000	0.2109	0.5714	0.5714
	t8	t9	t10	t11	t12	t13	t14
	0.2293	0.0000	0.0000	0.4286	0.4286	0.4286	0.2109
W2	t1	t2	t3	t4	t5	t6	t7
	0.0000	0.0000	0.1845	0.0000	0.0000	0.0000	0.0000
	t8	t9	t10	t11	t12	t13	t14
	0.0000	0.0000	0.0000	0.0000	0.0000	0.0000	0.0923

After applying our proposed document expansion method, W2 is expanded as

W2	t1	t2	t3	t4	t5	t6	t7
	0.6327	0.0000	0.1845	1.0000	0.2109	0.5714	0.5714
	t8	t9	t10	t11	t12	t13	t14
	0.2293	0.0000	0.0000	0.4286	0.4286	0.4286	0.0923

There are 14 feature terms in the reduct, which are t1= "pct", t2= "oil", t3= "mln", t4= "Jaguar", t5= "price", t6= "Egan", t7= "car", t8= "sales", t9= "official", t10= "OPEC", t11= "XJ", t12= "John", t13= "stg" and t14= "net". After expanded, only the most important 12 terms, t1, t2, t4 - t13 are supplemented in W2 which make it more meaningful and more relevant to the topic "earn". In this paper, the recall of the text information retrieval is used to evaluate the performance. The definition of recall is given as

Recall = No. of retrieved relevant documents/ No. of total relevant documents

Note that there are totally 12 relevant documents for the topic "earn" in the dataset. When the type of queries similar to W1 (Type1) is used, 9 documents can be retrieved without document expansion (i.e., recall = 9/12 = 75%); when the type of queries similar to W2 (Type2) is used, 3 documents are returned as results without document expansion (i.e., recall = 3/12 = 25%). After using our document expansion method, all the 12 relevant documents will be retrieved using any of the two type queries. The average recall using the two types of queries increase from 62.5% to 100%. Here the proportion of the two types of queries is the same to that of the relevant documents in the dataset, i.e., number of Type1 queries/ number of Type2 queries = 9 /3 = 3:1. Average recall = (75% * 3 + 25%*1)/4 = 62.5%. These results are listed in Table 4.

Table 4. Recall without expansion versus with expansion.

Query	Recall (without expan.)	Recall (with expan.)
Type1	75%	100%
Type2	25%	100%
Average	62.5%	100%

7 Conclusions

In this paper, to improve the text retrieval performance in terms of recall, a novel approach of fuzzy-rough hybridization is developed for the task of document expansion. In this context, a given set of documents is represented by an incomplete information system. Fuzzy sets are used to discretize the real-valued weights through tf-idf computation. Rough set theory in incomplete information system environment is applied to detect the most relevant terms which need to be supplemented in a particular document. Different from other methods for document expansion, our method can identify the potential associated terms which convey a concept (here a concept is a topic of a document) using rough sets. Therefore, the most relevant information can be located and added to a document. From the experimental results and analysis, the recall of text retrieval is greatly improved. Another observation is that, since only the terms in the reduct are considered as the candidates to be appended to the documents, the computational load for document expansion is very minimal. Future work includes developing more efficient algorithm for document expansion using larger text database.

Acknowledgement

This work is supported by the CERG research grant BQ-496.

References

1. Chung, Y. M. and Lee, J. Y., A corpus-based approach to comparative evaluation of statistical term association measures. *Journal of the American Society for Information Science and Technology*, vol. 52, no. 4, pp. 283-296, 2001.
2. Haines, D. and Croft, W. B., Relevance feedback and inference networks. In *Proceedings of the 16th annual international ACM-SIGIR conference on research and development in information retrieval*, pp. 2-11, ACM Press, NY, 1993.
3. Mandala, R., Tokunaga, T., and Tanaka, H., Query expansion using heterogeneous thesauri. *Information Processing and Management*, vol. 36, no. 3, pp. 361-378, 1998.
4. Qiu, Y. and Frei, H. P., Concept based query expansion. In *Proceedings of the 16th annual international ACM-SIGIR conference on research and development in information retrieval*, pp. 160-169, ACM Press, NY, 1993.
5. Pawlak Z., Rough sets, *International Journal of Computer and Information Science*, vol. 11, pp. 341-356, 1982.
6. Pawlak Z., *Rough sets: Theoretical aspects of reasoning about data*, Dordrecht: Kluwer, 1991
7. Leung, Y. and Li, D., Maximal consistent block technique for rule acquisition in incomplete information systems. *Information Sciences*, vol. 153, pp. 85-106, 2003.
8. Kryszkiewica, M., Rules in incomplete information systems, *Information Sciences*, vol. 113, pp. 271-292, 1999.
9. Orlowska E. (ed.), *Incomplete information: Rough set analysis*, Heidelberg: Physica-Verlag, 1998.

Use of Preference Relation for Text Categorization

Hayri Sever[1], Zafer Bolat[1], and Vijay V. Raghavan[2]

[1] Department of Computer Engineering
Baskent University
06530 Ankara, Turkey
{sever,zafer}@baskent.edu.tr

[2] The Center for Advanced Computer Studies
The Department of Computer Science
University of Louisiana
Lafayette, LA 70504, USA
raghavan@cacs.lousiana.edu

Abstract. The sudden expansion of the web and the use of the Internet has caused some research fields to regain (or even increase) its old popularity. Of them, text categorization aims at developing a classification system for assigning a number of predefined topic codes to the documents based on the knowledge accumulated in the training process. In this paper, we investigate a text categorization method based on steepest descent induction algorithm combined with multi-level preference relation over retrieval output that is especially suitable for inducing classifiers over non-exclusive data set. Our framework enables us to define a threshold value for relativeness such a way that it becomes specific for each category. Furthermore, a cache memory of a category, which is obtained when training the classifier, makes text categorization adaptive. We have found out that a cache memory based on 8-4-2 (positive-boundary-negative) examples yielded almost true classifiers over Reuters-2178 data set.

Keywords: Text Categorization, Perceptron, Adaptive Text Filtering.

1 Preliminaries

We propose a framework for the *Text Categorization* (TC) problem based on *Steepest Descent Algorithm SDA* [1], which is an induction method combined with a multi-level preference relation on profile output. In literature, the *SDA* algorithm was used to handle clusters of past optimal queries [2], to create an optimal query based on two-level preference relation over retrieval output (i.e., a user judges the documents returned by the system as either relevant or irrelevant) [3, 1, 4], and to induce classifier for text filtering [5, 6]. The main theme of this article deals with text categorization in which it is typical to entertain with non-exclusive examples (i.e., an example might be assigned to more than one category). This implies at least three regions, namely positive, boundary,

S. Tsumoto et al. (Eds.): RSCTC 2004, LNAI 3066, pp. 708–713, 2004.

negative for which a two-level preference relation would not be answer to induce classifiers.

Our objective is to formulate an optimal profile, p_{opt}, that discriminates more preferred documents from less preferred ones. With this objective in mind, we define a preference relation $\succ$ on a set of partially-ordered documents, Δ, in a profile output as follows. For $d, d' \in \Delta, d \succ d'$ is interpreted as d is preferred to d'. It is assumed that the user's preference relation on Δ yields a weak order where the following conditions are hold [1]:

$d \succ d'$ or $d' \succ d$.

$d \succ d'$ and $d' \succ d'' \Rightarrow d \succ d''$.

The essential motivation is that p_{opt} provides an acceptable profile output; that is, for all $d, d' \in \Delta$, there exists $p_{opt} \in \Im$ such that $d \succ d' \Rightarrow \alpha(p_{opt}, d) > \alpha(p_{opt}, d')$, where $f : \Im \times D \rightarrow R^{\geq 0}$ denotes a preference status function.

In this paper, optimal profile, p_{opt}, is formulated inductively by SDA as described in [1]. Let $B = \{b = d - d' : d \succ d'\}$ be the set of difference vectors in a profile output. To obtain p_{opt} from any profile $q \in \Im$, we solve following linear inequalities

$$p^T b > 0 \qquad (1)$$

for all $b \in B$. A steepest descent algorithm is used to find a solution vector p_{opt} for Eq. (1). We define total error, which is to be minimized, in our linear system as follows.

$$J(p) = \sum_{b \in \Gamma(p)} -p^T b, \qquad (2)$$

where

$$\Gamma(p) = \{b = d - d' : p^T b \leq 0\} \subseteq B.$$

We define the steps of the algorithm as follows.

1. Choose a starting profile vector p_0; let $k = 0$.
2. Let p_k be a profile vector at the start of the (k+1)*th* iteration; identify the following set of difference vectors:

   $$\Gamma(p_k) = \{b = d - d' : d \succ d' \text{ and } \alpha(p_k, b) \leq 0\};$$

   if $\Gamma(p_k) = \emptyset, p_{opt} = p_k$ is a solution vector and exit the loop, otherwise,
3. Let

   $$p_{k+1} = p_k - \alpha_k \bigtriangledown J(p_k)$$

   where: α_k is a positive number that sets the step size and assumed to be one here; $\bigtriangledown J(p_k) = -\sum_{b \in \Gamma(p_k)} b$
4. $k = k + 1$; go back to Step (2).

Theoretically it is known that SDA terminates only if the set of retrieved documents is linearly separable. Therefore, a practical implementation of the algorithm should guarantee that the algorithm terminates whether or not the retrieved set is linearly separable. In this paper, we use a pre-defined iteration number and R_{norm} measure for this purpose [7]. The algorithm is terminated if the iteration number reaches the pre-defined limit or the R_{norm} value of the current profile is higher than or equal to some pre-defined value.

Predicted Label	Actual Label	
	relevant	irrelevant
Relevant	a	b
Irrelevant	c	d

(a)

	Training	Test
With at least one topic	7,775	3,019
With no topic	1,828	280
Total	9,603	3,299

(b)

Fig. 1. (a) Measures of system effectiveness. (b) Number of documents in the collection.

2 Experiment

In this section, we describe the experimental set up in detail. First, we describe how the Reuters-21578 dataset is parsed and the vocabulary for indexing is constructed. Upon discussion of our approach to training, the experimental results are presented.

2.1 Method

To experimentally evaluate the proposed TC method, we have used the Modified Apte split of Reuters-21578 corpus that has 9,603 training documents, 3,299 test documents, and 8,676 unused documents. Figure 1(b) shows some statistics about the number of documents in the collection.

We have produced a dictionary of single words excluding numbers as a result of pre-processing the corpus including performing parsing and tokenizing the text portion of the title as well as the body of both training and unused documents. We have used a universal list of 343 stop words to eliminate functional words from the dictionary[1]. The Porter stemmer algorithm was employed to reduce each remaining words to word-stems form[2]. Since any word occurring only a few times is statistically unreliable, the words occurring less than five times were eliminated. Our TC framework is based on the Vector Space Model (VSM) in which documents and profiles are represented as vectors of weighted terms. We have used the *tf*idf* weighting scheme and then, normalized document vectors (i.e., making documents unit vectors).

A document is assigned to a topic by a particular classifier if its relativeness assertion is verified by holding multi-level preference relation over cache of documents of that topic. When an error occurs the cache memory is updated accordingly. If it is type one error (fail to accept document as relevant), then we replace the positive example with the biggest preference status value in the cache by the document that just caused that error; if it is type two error (fail to reject irrelevant document), then the document replaces the one with the smallest preference status value in negative examples of the concept cache. Once an error occurs and concept cache is re-organized, then SDA is applied to the cache

[1] The stop list is available at: http://www.iiasa.ac.at/docs/R_Library/libsrchs.html

[2] The source code for the Porter Algorithm is found at: http://www.tartarus.org/ martin/PorterStemmer [8]

to update the threshold value of corresponding concept. Note that if incoming document does not decrease the R_{norm} value (or threshold value, of course), then it is judged as relevant to the concept at hand.

The breakeven point is the value at which precision and recall becomes equal. If no values of precision and recall are exactly equal, interpolated breakeven is computed as the average of the values at the closest point. In simple terms, compute recall value at the rank of m, where m is equal to total number of relevant documents and then, without changing the value of recall find the best possible value for precision; finally, take average of them to get breakeven point. The breakeven point is included in our results for historical reasons (to compare with others'results), but we emphasize on precision and recall values, where the precision and recall are equal to $a/(a+b)$ and $a/(a+c)$, respectively. In reporting results, as shown in Figure 1(a), we also disclosed the values of dichotomous table to let one interpret the results from different perspectives, e.g., fallout or F measure value of classifiers.

2.2 Training

In our past work [5], we have experimentally found that a better classifier can be built if negative examples are in the range of $50 - 80\%$ of positive examples. Hence, we added negative examples in the amount of 50% of positive ones to the training set of a topic. During training, we did not discriminate positive examples based on their exclusiveness. That is, we used the SDA algorithm (with two-preference level) as described in [5]. Giving consideration to the growing evidence of incorporating just a number of top irrelevant documents into the error function to lessen up common term weights of a profile, we developed a TC framework for learning a concept efficiently, effectively, and adaptively.

A cache consists of a three tuple of $(l - m - n)$ documents, where l, m, and n indicate the number of exclusively positive (positive region), non-exclusively positive (boundary region), and negative (negative region) documents, respectively. Once an initial classifier is obtained using two-level preference relation over training set of a concept, it re-runs against the same training set to establish initial cache organization. The top documents are picked up for corresponding regions of the cache and then, average preference status values of documents in the boundary region is accepted as initial threshold value. Specifically, we entertained with 8-4-2, 12-6-3, 16-8-4, and 20-10-5 cache; all of them did not make any difference within the range of 2% enhancement in effectiveness from one to another. The results with respect to the 8-4-2 cache are reported here because of obvious efficiency benefit.

3 Discussion

Our findings indicate that breakeven point cannot be used as composite measurement especially when difference between precision and recall is high. In Table 1, effectiveness values of adaptive classifiers over test set as well as that of retrospective classifier (i.e., run adaptive classifiers over test data set second time

Table 1. Adaptive and Retrospective Classifiers. All topics in the data set are included as long as they have at least 12 exclusively (document belonging to a single concept) and 6 non-exclusively (document belonging to multiple concepts). The symbols *S and M* stand for *single* and *multiple* category labels. Similarly, the symbols *a,b,c, and d* denote values dichotomous table for a given topic. As usual *P, R, and be* stand for precision (a/(a+b)), recall (a/(a+c)), and breakeven points of the classifier for a topic.

Topic	Training		Test		Adaptive Classifier							Retrospective Classifier		
	S	M	S	M	a	b	c	d	P	R	be1	P	R	be2
cocoa	46	9	15	3	18	6	0	2995	0.75	1.00	0.94	0.82	1.00	1.00
grain	41	392	11	138	112	25	37	2845	0.82	0.75	0.81	0.93	0.96	0.95
veg-oil	19	68	16	21	22	13	15	2969	0.63	0.59	0.59	0.67	0.89	0.84
earn	2840	37	1083	4	1020	73	67	1859	0.93	0.94	0.93	0.98	0.97	0.97
acq	1596	54	696	23	570	76	149	2224	0.88	0.79	0.87	0.99	0.81	0.95
copper	31	16	5	13	15	1	3	3000	0.94	0.83	0.89	1.00	0.89	0.97
money-supply	123	17	28	6	20	9	14	2976	0.69	0.65	0.73	1.00	0.68	0.90
coffee	90	21	22	6	26	3	2	2988	0.90	0.93	0.93	1.00	0.89	0.96
ship	108	89	36	53	62	14	27	2916	0.82	0.70	0.71	0.66	0.91	0.92
sugar	97	29	25	11	26	11	10	2972	0.70	0.72	0.64	0.45	0.92	0.89
trade	251	118	74	43	62	38	55	2864	0.62	0.53	0.63	0.97	0.59	0.89
reserves	37	18	12	6	9	12	9	2989	0.43	0.50	0.61	0.88	0.78	0.83
cotton	15	24	13	7	14	7	6	2992	0.67	0.70	0.78	0.47	0.90	0.87
livestock	13	62	5	19	12	13	12	2982	0.48	0.50	0.54	0.77	0.83	0.79
crude	253	136	121	68	146	29	43	2801	0.83	0.77	0.82	0.93	0.95	0.93
nat-gas	24	51	12	18	14	18	16	2971	0.44	0.47	0.53	0.95	0.60	0.83
cpi	54	15	17	11	14	15	14	2976	0.48	0.50	0.45	0.75	0.70	0.75
gnp	58	43	15	20	21	8	14	2976	0.72	0.60	0.74	1.00	0.80	0.94
money-fx	206	332	87	92	109	42	70	2798	0.72	0.61	0.68	0.72	0.96	0.87
interest	190	157	81	50	75	46	56	2842	0.62	0.57	0.63	0.80	0.72	0.76
bop	22	53	9	21	16	17	14	2972	0.48	0.53	0.60	0.60	0.83	0.77
rubber	31	6	9	3	9	6	3	3001	0.60	0.75	0.88	0.83	0.83	0.87
gold	70	24	20	10	22	9	8	2980	0.71	0.73	0.81	1.00	0.67	0.90
ipi	33	8	11	1	7	11	5	2996	0.39	0.58	0.52	0.46	0.92	0.75
iron-steel	26	14	12	2	8	8	6	2997	0.50	0.57	0.70	1.00	0.43	0.86
jobs	37	9	12	9	17	6	4	2992	0.74	0.81	0.76	1.00	0.76	0.95
pet-chem	13	7	6	6	4	14	8	2993	0.22	0.33	0.42	0.83	0.42	0.83
Total	6324	1809	2453	664	2450	530	667	77866	0.82	0.79	0.71	0.90	0.88	0.88

with no learning mode) are shown. The relative effectiveness of retrospective classifier over the one without cache can be regarded as the power of learning, which is roughly equal to the factor of 1.32. The closeness of effective values of adaptive and non-adaptive classifiers strongly indicate poor quality of training set of Reuters 21578 data set. Because of space limitation, we did not include comparison table here, but the performance of our retrospective classifier over top eight categories (namely, earn, acq, money-fx, grain, crude, trade, interest, ship) is 0.91, which is better than that of SVM (Support Vector Machine) [9], a well-known TC technique.

References

1. Wong, S.K.M., Yao, Y.Y.: Query Formulation in Linear Retrieval Models. Journal of the American Society for Information Science **41** (1990) 334–341
2. Raghavan, V.V., Sever, H.: On the reuse of past optimal queries. In Fox, E.A., ed.: Proceedings of ACM SIGIR'95, Seattle, WA (1995) 344–351
3. Bollmann, P., Wong, S.K.M.: Adaptive linear information retrieval models. In: Proceedings of the Tenth International Conference on Research and Development in Information Retrieval, New Orleans, LA (1987) 157–163
4. Wong, S.K.M., Yao, Y.Y., Salton, G., Buckley, C.: Evaluation of an adaptive linear model. Journal of the American Society for Information Science **42** (1991) 723–730
5. Alsaffar, A., Deogun, J., Sever, H.: Optimal queries in information filtering. In Ras, Z., Ohsuga, S., eds.: Foundations of Intelligent Information Systems. Lecture notes in computer science (LNCS). Springer-Verlag, Berlin, Germany (2000) 435–443
6. Sever, H., Bolat, Z.: A text filtering method for digital libraries. In: Proceedings of Libraries and Education in the Networked Information Environment. Volume 13., Ankara,TR, International Association of Technological University Libraries (2003) www.iatul.org/conference/proceedings/vol13/.
7. Raghavan, V., Jung, G., Bollmann, P.: A critical investigation of recall and precision as measures of retrieval system performance. ACM Transactions on Information Systems **7** (1989) 205–229
8. Porter, M.F.: An algorithm for suffix stripping. Program **14** (1980) 130–137
9. Dumais, S., Platt, J., Heckerman, D., Sahami, M.: Inductive learning algorithms and representations for text categorization. In: Proceedings of the seventh international conference on Information and knowledge management, ACM Press (1998) 148–155

An Expert System for the Utilisation of the Variable Precision Rough Sets Model

Malcolm J. Beynon and Benjamin Griffiths

Cardiff Business School, Cardiff University
Colum Drive, Cardiff, CF10 3EU, Wales, UK
BeynonMJ@cardiff.ac.uk

Abstract. The variable precision rough sets model (VPRS) is a development of the original rough set theory (RST) and allows for the partial (probabilistic) classification of objects. This paper introduces a prototype VPRS expert system. A number of processes for the identification of the VPRS related β-reducts and their respective β intervals over the domain of the β parameter are included. Three data sets are utilised in the exposition of the expert system.

1 Introduction

The variable precision rough sets model (VPRS) introduced in [7], is a development on rough set theory (RST, see [5]), to accommodate for probabilistic decision rules to be constructed. The prototype expert system introduced here attempts to allow the effective application of VPRS. This utilises a β interval for which a subset of condition attributes (β-reduct) has the same level of quality of classification as the whole set of condition attributes [2]. An inclusion is the utilisation of β-reduct graphs [2], which allow a choice of β-reduct to be made and elucidates the asymmetric nature of the level of correct classification and the quality of classification.

2 Fundamentals of VPRS

Central to VPRS (and RST) is the information system, which contains a universe U of objects (o_1, o_2, ...), characterised by a set condition attributes C (c_1, c_2, ...) and classified to a set decision attributes D (d_1, d_2, ...). With equivalence classes $E(\cdot)$ of objects, for a given proportionality value β, the β-positive region corresponding to a subset of the objects $Z \subseteq U$ is defined:

β-positive region of the set $Z \subseteq U$: $POS_P^\beta(Z) = \bigcup_{\Pr(Z \mid X_i) \geq \beta} \{X_i \in E(P)\}$.

Here the value β is defined to lie between 0.5 and 1 [1]. Other expressions, β-boundary and β-negative regions for $Z \subseteq U$ and $P \subseteq C$ are given by:

S. Tsumoto et al. (Eds.): RSCTC 2004, LNAI 3066, pp. 714–720, 2004.

$$BND_P^\beta(Z) = \bigcup_{1-\beta<\Pr(Z\mid X_i)<\beta}\{X_i \in E(P)\},\ NEG_P^\beta(Z) = \bigcup_{\Pr(Z\mid X_i)\le 1-\beta}\{X_i \in E(P)\}.$$

These are general definitions, they are particularly useful when Z is a decision class ($Z \in E(D)$). Having defined and computed measures relating to the ambiguity of classification, [7] introduced the measure of *quality of classification*, defined by:

$$\gamma^\beta(P, D) = \frac{\operatorname{card}\left(\bigcup_{\Pr(Z|X_i)\ge\beta}\{X_i \in E(P)\}\right)}{\operatorname{card}(U)},\text{ where } Z \in E(D) \text{ and } P \subseteq C,$$

for a specified value of β. The value $\gamma^\beta(P, D)$, measures the proportion of objects in the universe U for which classification is possible subject to the specified value of β. VPRS applies these ideas by seeking $P \subseteq C$, which are capable of explaining allocations given by C subject to the majority inclusion relation, defined *β-reducts* [7].

The original utilisation of VPRS centred around the selection of a β value with a β-reduct then identified and the subsequent rule set constructed [7]. A $\beta_{\min}$ value was utilised in a criterion to select a β-reduct and introduced the concept of an associated β interval with every identified β-reduct [2]. These intervals also contributed to a criterion for the possible selection of β-reducts [3].

Anomalies between β-reduct selection and β values were identified, resulting in the definition of external and internal β values and hidden (or extended) β-reducts. That is, if an external β value is imposed independently of any calculation, with a knowledge of the $\gamma^\beta(P, D)$ required then hidden β-reducts would not be identified. An internal β value used could allow smaller sized β-reducts with rules of higher certainty of correct classification. These are exposited in the proposed expert system.

3 Description of VPRS Expert System

Here, the prototype expert system (denoted ES) is introduced through its application to a small data set presented in [2], see Table 1, defined IS_1.

Table 1. Cut points and number of objects in the intervals for each condition attribute.

	c_1	c_2	c_3	c_4	c_5	c_6	d_1		c_1	c_2	c_3	c_4	c_5	c_6	d_1
o_1	1	1	1	1	1	1	1	o_5	1	0	1	0	1	1	2
o_2	1	0	1	0	1	1	1	o_6	0	0	0	1	1	0	2
o_3	0	0	1	1	0	0	1	o_7	1	0	1	0	1	1	2
o_4	1	1	1	0	0	1	2								

The IS_1 has 13 associated β-reducts (see [2]), two ways of considering β-reducts are; *i*) Subject to expert choice of β value and *ii*) Visual representation of the β-reducts (through β-reduct graphs). Here these options are incorporated in the ES, which includes the construction of the β-reduct graph for IS_1, see Fig. 1.

Fig. 1 reports all possible β-reducts and their associated β intervals, in a β-reduct graph window (left side of window), as well as the different levels of $\gamma^{\beta}(C, D)$ and their respective β. Each β-reduct is presented with its β interval(s). The solid and dashed lines are the intervals of β for which β-reducts exist when an external β value is considered and β intervals associated with hidden β-reducts respectively.

The selection of a β-reduct can be performed through a simple choice by a user. Along with the β-reduct also presented are; the number of rules, number of objects given a classification, number of objects correctly classified and associated percentage correct. Two β-reducts deserve particular attention in Fig. 1.

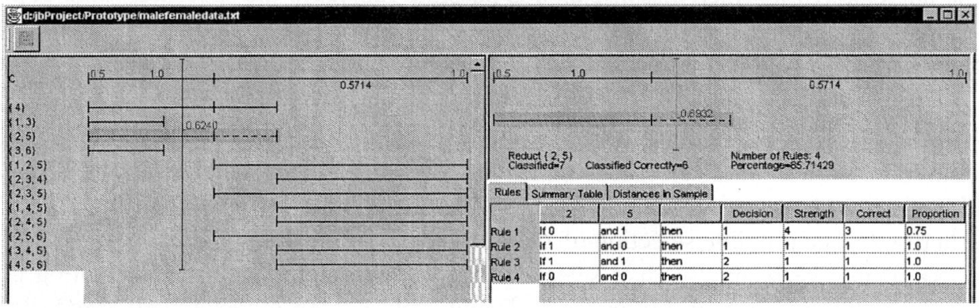

Fig. 1. β-reduct graph window for IS_1.

The first β-reduct considered is $\{c_2, c_5\}$ (only set {2, 5} given on left side), which has a solid and dashed line. That is, a β value clicked on this interval (dashed line) would describe the same results as if a β value was picked on the solid line for this β-reduct. For the β-reduct $\{c_2, c_5\}$ its set of decision rules are presented (in right sub-window), which shows all objects are given a classification.

The second β-reduct is $\{c_4\}$, which has two solid lines and thus indicates two β intervals that would give different sets of rules etc. This multiplicity of $\{c_4\}$ as a β-reduct is exposited in the constructed rules. The selection of either of these two β intervals is presented in snapshots of sub-regions of an ES window, see Fig. 2

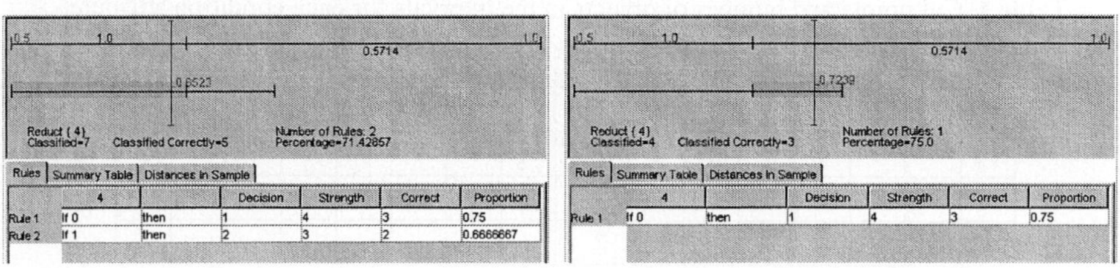

Fig. 2. Individual β-reduct choice and constructed rules for $\{c_4\}$ from IS_1.

Apart from the constructed rules, a summary table of classification accuracy as well as a breakdown of the classification of each object including the distances of each rule to represent an object's classification can be given.

4 Application of Expert System to Wine Data Set

In this section the ES is utilised on the well-known wine data set (found at http://www.ics.uci.edu/~mlearn/MLRepository.html). Here the first 10 condition attributes were considered, which are all continuous in nature, hence granularity in the information is large. The ES offers a number of continuous value discretisation (CVD) approaches, for brevity a simple equal width CVD was adopted, which produced two intervals for each condition attribute (not discussed). The resultant IS_2 was partitioned into in-sample and out-of-sample proportions of 0.8 and 0.2 (choice of proportions allowed for with ES). The associated β-reduct graph for IS_2 is presented in Fig. 3, based on an in-sample of 142 objects.

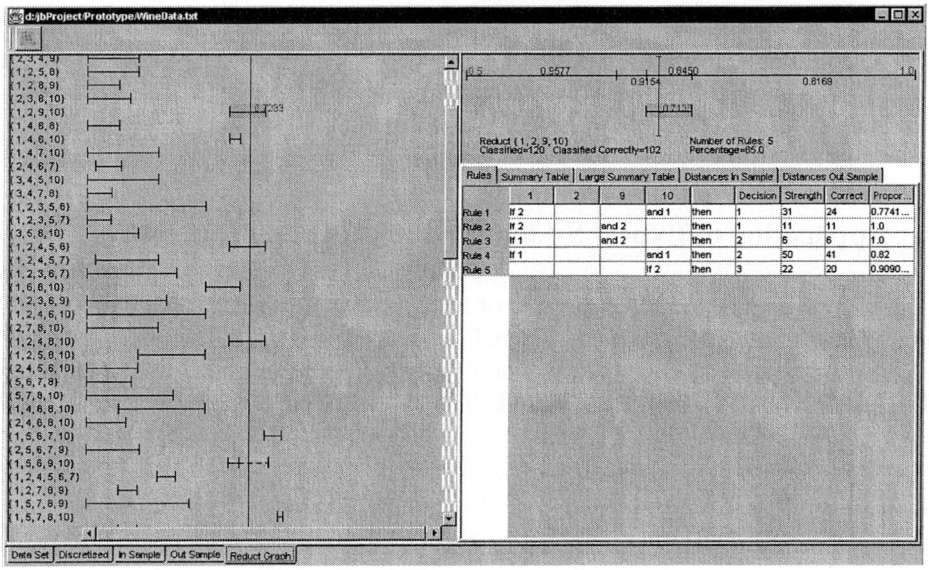

Fig. 3. β-reduct graphs window for IS_2.

In Fig. 3, a similar ES window to that in Fig. 1 is presented, for the IS_2 in-sample the noticeable feature is the large number of identified distinct sets of condition attributes which are β-reducts (55 in this case). Some of these may be multiple β-reducts for different (distinct) β intervals. All of these can be viewed on the left hand side of the window using the scroll bar and any one β-reduct chosen for further analysis. The right hand side of the ES window in Fig. 3 indicates the β-reduct $\{c_1, c_2, c_9, c_{10}\}$ was chosen. The resultant rules for this β-reduct are also presented.

Fig. 4 reports snapshots of the ES which give a summary table of classification accuracy including rule distances of individual objects in the in-sample.

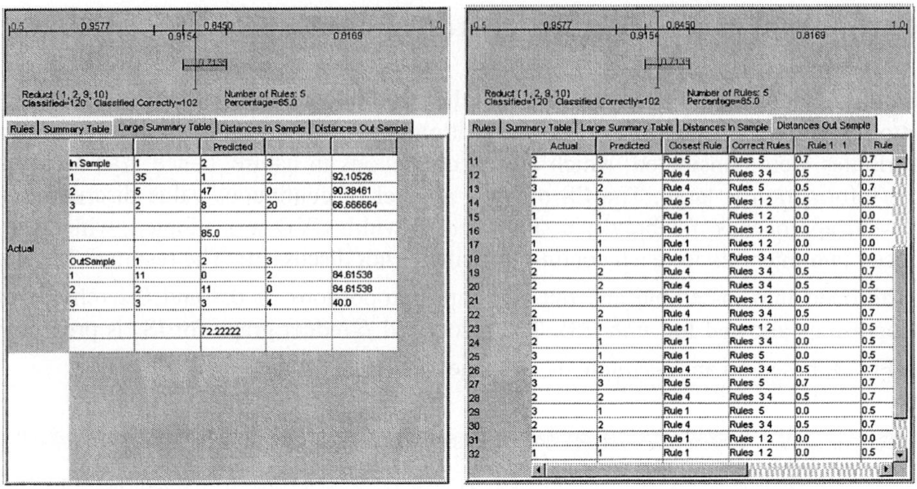

Fig. 4. Summary and Distance sub-windows for β-reduct $\{c_1, c_2, c_9, c_{10}\}$ with IS_2.

5 Application of Expert System to Bank Rating Problem

This section applies the ES in the area of bank ratings. In particular the Bank Financial Strength Rating (BFSR) is considered, introduced in 1995, by Moody's Investors Services. It represents Moody's opinion of a bank's intrinsic safety and soundness. Using data from Bankscope, 132 large U.S. banks were found to have a BFSR rating. As in the extant credit rating literature these characteristics covered the well known areas of profitability, leverage, liquidity and risk and were included in [6]: c_1 - Net Income Revenue/Average Assets, c_2 - Non Interest Expense/Average Assets, c_3 - Equity/Assets, c_4 - Net Loans/Assets, c_5 - Loan Loss Reserves/Gross Loans, c_6 - Dividend Pay-Out.

The decision attribute here was binary and based on the linguistic interpretation of the partition of the banks BFSR rating (using definitions from [4]) and is:

"*whether a bank is considered to posses at least strong intrinsic financial strength to that of no more than adequate financial strength*"

From the above definition, it follows 65 and 67 banks are in the respective groups, referring to less than of greater than strong BFSR, respectively. A level of CVD was undertaken on the six condition attributes, in this case as in section 4 an equal width CVD approach was undertaken, with two equal widths found for each condition attribute (not discussed). Defining the resultant information IS_3, as in the previous applications of ES the associated β-reduct graph is presented in Fig. 5.

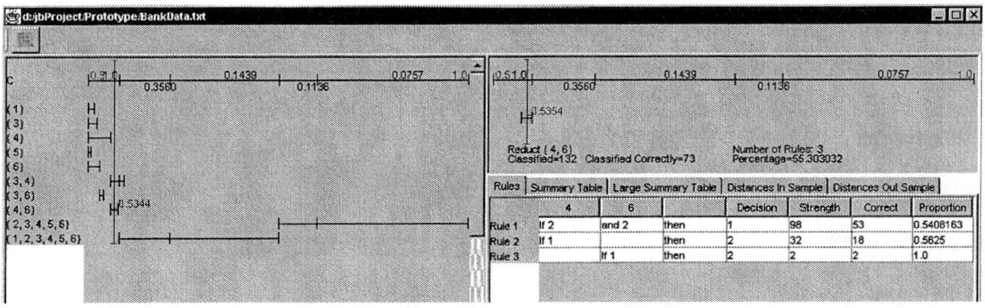

Fig. 5. β-reduct graphs window for IS_3.

In Fig. 5, the majority of the β intervals associated with β-reducts near the lower limit of the whole β domain (near 0.5). One of these β-reduct $\{c_4, c_6\}$ is highlighted and its associated rules reported. In this case there are three rules which classify 132 (out of 132) banks, with only 73 (55.3030%) banks correctly classified. The 132 banks classified enforces the notion that for this β-reduct then $\gamma^{0.5354}(C, D) = \gamma^{0.5354}(\{c_4, c_6\}, D) = 1.0$ as reported. There are two subsets of condition attributes which cover the majority of the β domain (C and $\{c_2, c_3, c_4, c_5, c_6\}$). The $\{c_2, c_3, c_4, c_5, c_6\}$ can be considered a different β-reduct over two distinct β intervals, the resultant rules are presented in snapshots of the ES window, see Fig. 6.

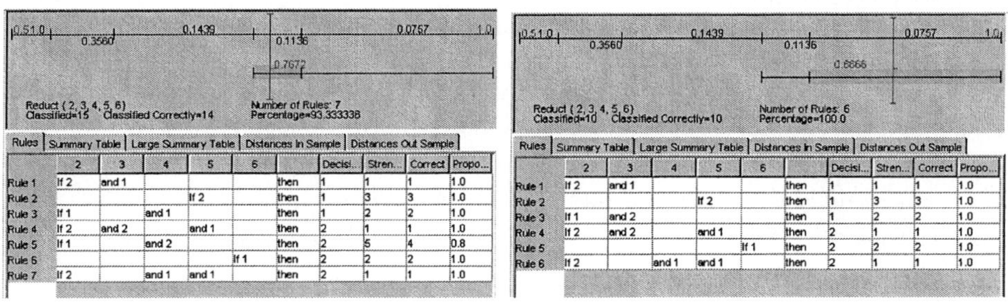

Fig. 6. Individual β-reduct choice and constructed rules for $\{c_2, c_3, c_4, c_5, c_6\}$ from IS_3.

In Fig. 6, the effect of the choice of a β value in two different intervals is apparent, with the set of rules associated with the higher β interval (right sub-window) a subset of the set of rules associated with lower β interval (left sub-window).

6 Conclusions

This paper has introduced a prototype of an expert system (ES) for the utilisation of the variable precision rough sets model (VPRS) for data mining. This includes the characterisation of the associated β intervals including whether they are external or internal. The development of ES includes the incorporation of other approaches to the selection of β-reducts and specific β value. This study highlights its possible role in a bagging approach to object classification. That is, for a β value, different numbers of β-reducts exist, the principle of bagging would allow a collective 'predicted' decision of an object to a decision outcome.

References

1. An, A., Shan, N., Chan, C., Cercone, N., Ziarko, W.: Discovering rules for water demand prediction: An enhanced rough-set approach. Engineering Application and Artificial Intelligence 9 (1996) 645–653.
2. Beynon, M.: Reducts within the Variable Precision Rough Set Model: A Further Investigation. European Journal of Operational Research 134 (2001) 592–605.
3. Beynon, M.J.: The Identification of Low-Paying Workplaces: An Analysis Using the Variable Precision Rough Sets Model. In Proc. RSCTC'2002, LNAI 2475, Sringer, Berlin (2002) 530–537.
4. Moody's. Rating Definitions - Bank Financial Strength Ratings, Internet site www.moodys.com. Accessed on 27/11/2003
5. Pawlak, Z.: Rough sets. International Journal of Information and Computer Sciences 11 (5) (1982) 341–356.
6. Poon, W.P.H., Firth, M., Fung, M.: A multivariate analysis of the determinants of Moody's bank financial strength ratings. Journal of International Financial Markets Institutions and Money 9 (1999) 267-283.
7. Ziarko, W.: Variable precision rough set model. Journal of Computer and System Sciences 46 (1993) 39–59.

Application of Decision Units in Knowledge Engineering

Roman Siminski and Alicja Wakulicz-Deja

University of Silesia, Institute of Computer Science
Poland, 41-200 Sosnowiec, Bedzinska 39
{siminski,wakulicz}@us.edu.pl
Phone (+48 32) 2 918 381 ext. 768, Fax (+48 32) 2 918 283

Abstract. In this paper we shall present the decision units idea that, allow us to divide a set of rules into subsets - decision units. This paper gives attention to decision units in chosen problems of knowledge engineering. We present our own rule base verification method based on decision unit conception. The decision units are simple and intuitive models describing relations in rule knowledge base, being direct superstructure of a rule-base model. The unit's usage offers the knowledge engineer's support on the technical design and base realization level.

1 Introduction

Modularity is one of advantages that knowledge representation posses [9] – each rule is a component of certain elements describing chosen part of domain knowledge. Rules can undergo formation and modification processes independently. The outcome of design and realisation process of rule knowledge base is a set of rules. For rule knowledge bases the total number can count up to hundreds or thousands of the rules. In such cases the verification and maintenance process [2] are difficult. The reason for these problems could be modularity and independence of the rules – when the number of rules increases, the dependence between rules is less clear and its reconstruction requires from a knowledge engineer lots of work and attention.

The aim, which allows avoiding legibility loss of connections between rules, can be the introduction of syntactic elements of a higher level than rules, into the knowledge representation language. As an example of such a classical solution in expert system domain we can present knowledge sources implemented together with expert system tables (blackboard architecture) [4] [5] and other methods described in papers [1] [16] [17].

In this paper we shall present the decision units idea, [13] [14] that allow us to divide a set of rules into subsets according to a simple and useful criterion. Such a division depends mainly on a specific knowledge representation language. The division can be used in the majority of rule-based systems using rules similar to the Horn clause. This paper gives attention to decision units in chosen problems of knowledge engineering.

S. Tsumoto et al. (Eds.): RSCTC 2004, LNAI 3066, pp. 721–726, 2004.

2 Decision Units

In the real-world rule knowledge bases literals are often coded using *attribute-value* pairs. In this chapter we shall introduce conception of decision units determined on a rule base containing the Horn clause rules, where literals are coded using attribute-value pairs. We assume a backward inference.

A decision unit U is defined as a triple $U = (I, O, R)$, where I denotes a set of input entries, O denotes a set of output entries and R denotes a set of rules fulfilling given grouping criterion. These sets are defined as follows:

$$I = \{ (attr_i, val_{ij}) : \exists r \in R \ (attr_i, val_{ij}) \in antec(r) \}$$
$$O = \{ (attr_i, val_{ij}) : \forall r \in R \ attr_i = conclAttr(r) \}$$
$$R = \{ r : \forall i \neq j, r_i, r_j \in R \ conclAttr(r_i) = conclAttr(r_j) \}$$

Two functions are defined on a rule r: $conclAttr(r)$ returns attribute from conclusion of rule r, $antec(r)$ is a set of conditions of rule r.

As it can be seen, decision unit U contains the set of rules R, each rule $r \in R$ contains the same attribute in the literal appearing in the conclusion part. All rules grouped within a decision unit take part in an inference process confirming the aim described by attribute, which appears in the conditional part of each rule. The process given above is often considered to be a part of decision system, thus it is called — a *decision unit.*

All pairs (*attribute*, *value*) appearing in the conditional part of each rule are called decision unit input entries, whilst all pairs (*attribute*, *value*) appearing in the conclusion part of each set rule R are called decision unit *output entries.*

3 Decision Units in Knowledge Base Verification

Knowledge base verification is currently one of the most important knowledge engineering issues, because the verification problem of expert systems is limited to its knowledge base verification. This paper has a limited volume; thus a discussion on basic knowledge base verification issues shall by omitted. More information can be found in review papers [10] [12] and quoted references.

3.1 Local Verification at the Decision Unit Level

A single decision unit can be considered as a model of an elementary, partial decision that has been worked out by the system. The reason for this situation is that all rules being a constitution of a decision unit have the same conclusion attribute. All conclusions create a set of unit output entries specifying possible to confirm inference aims. A decision unit can be considered as:

- a unit, knowing only input and output entries, omitting rules that are an integral part of a unit — so called black box approach [3];
- a decision unit, knowing its internal structure, i.e. considering both input and output entries and rules — so called glass box approach [3].

Using a black box technique it is possible to test functionality of a given decision unit by activation of the inference run. This can be performed not only in interaction with a system user, but using an input mode as well, and by using automatically generated testing sets defined on the basis of input and output entries knowledge. It is significant to find out whether the unit is complete on the local level or not.

A glass box technique takes into account an internal structure of a decision unit hence we obtain the possibility to verify anomalies by using the classical detection method [6] [7] [8]. Decomposition of the base can cause that the number of rules covering given unit can be relatively low, which enables efficient usage of classical verification algorithms based on different methods, but giving an opportunity to use these methods interchangeable, in the same way as an internal unit structure can be conceived.

Summarising:

1. Input and output entry knowledge allows matching testing data without a user presence. It is possible to make unit verification with no user presence.
2. Independently from the possibilities of testing process automation, the user can by himself evaluate the unit efficiency and can individually select the testing data.
3. At the unit level the verification based on the effective algorithms and anomalies location can be performed.
4. Decision unit is a convenient medium that allows making a presentation — user focuses on partial decision method, omitting integral structure or specific rules.

3.2 Net Decision Units Global Verification

The decision unit net allows us to formulate the global verification method. On the strength of connections between decision unit analysis it is possible to detect local anomalies in rules, such as deficiency, redundancy, incoherence or circularity, creating chains during an inference process. We can apply considerations at the unit level using black box and glass box techniques. Digressing from an integral unit structure, which creates a net, allows us to detect characteristic symptoms of global anomalies. This can give us a push to do a detailed analysis, making allowance for an integral structure of each unit. This analysis is nevertheless limited to a given fragment of a net, having been tipped previously through a black box verification method.

As an example of the global relationship detection technique shall be presented a circular relationship detection technique. Figure 1a presents such an example. A net can be described as a directed graph. After exclusion of input and output entries discrimination and after rejection of vertexes which stand for disjointed input and output entries the graph assumes shape like the one presented by Figure 1b. Such graph shall be called a global relationship decision unit graph. As it can be seen, there are two cycles: 1-2-3-1 and 1-3-1.

The presence of cycles can indicate appearance of a cycle relationship in a considered rule base. Figure 1c presents example where there is no cyclical relationship – the arcs define proper rules. To make the graph more clear a text description has been omitted. On the contrary, the figure 1d presents case where both cycles previously present at figure 1b now stand for real cycles in a base rule.

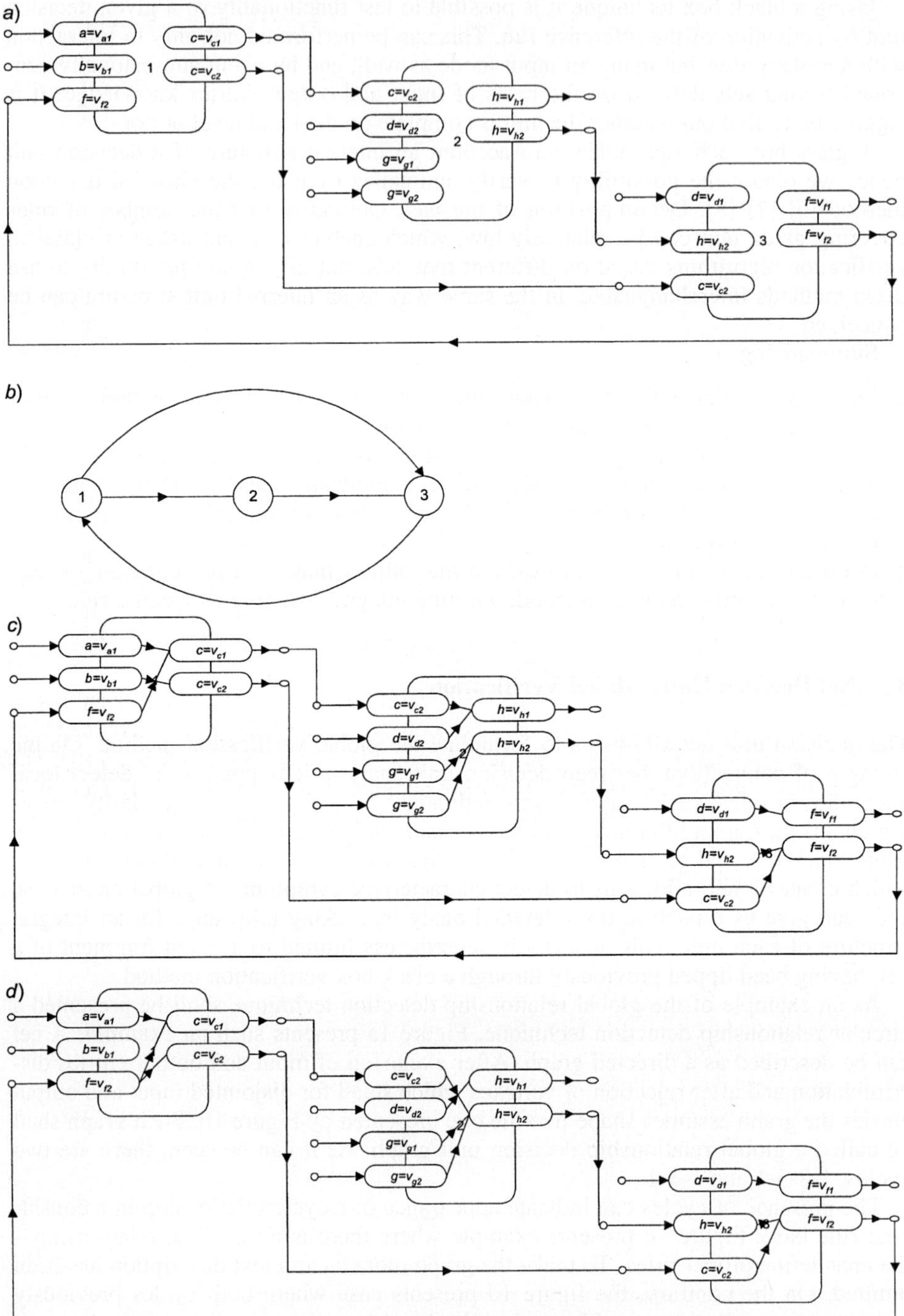

Fig. 1. Reduced reason-result graphs.

Thus, the presence of cyclical relationship on a decision unit relationship graph is an indication to carry out a cyclical relationship presence inspection on a global level. This can be achieved by creating a suitable reason-result graph, representing relations between input and output entries of units causing cyclical relations described by decision unit relationship diagram. Scanned graph shall consist of only nodes and arcs necessary to determine a circularity causing limitations in scanned area

4 The Decision Units Net as a Decision Model

A single decision unit can be considered as a medium created by elementary decision system, and decision units net can be considered as global decision model presented by a given system. It describes a confirmation way of assumed conclusions targets. Thus, in a given moment a current decision model presents a decision unit net. Taking into consideration the simplicity of decision unit idea, easiness of graphic presentation, and intuition the knowledge base presentation can be interesting way of making comparison whether a current decision model is a function of an intended model. The net of the decision units may be considered as a global model of decisions produced by the system, giving no consideration to the local structure of connections. Digressing from an integral unit structure allows observing the model of obtaining the goals of inference without the necessity of going into details and making no obstacles to get the detailed level. It seems that thanks to the simplicity of the idea, such approach shall assure the possibility of knowledge base assumption verification, without implementing new concepts, structures or methods.

The decision units are thus simple and intuitive models describing relations in knowledge base-rule, being direct superstructure of a rule-base model. The decision unit's usage does not impose a composed method of creating the knowledge base. The unit's usage offers the knowledge engineer's support on the technical design and base realisation level. It is possible to take some advantages of other methods of knowledge modelling during a design process and if so, the decision unit can be a supplement to those methods.

5 Summary

The decision units are simple and intuitive models describing relations in knowledge base-rule, being direct superstructure of a rule-base model. Thus, the decision units can be considered as a simple agenda in knowledge base-rule modelling. The decision unit technique allows us to elaborate own knowledge base verification method that combine anomaly static analysis technique with knowledge base testing in close to real-world conditions. The difficulties with rule-base verification have been described in a natural and intuitive way.

The works that has been carried out made it possible to realise the prototype version of an assistance system that helps to realise and verify knowledge rule-base. This system is known as the *kbBuilder* [11] [15] system and allows creating knowledge bases founded upon specialised base edition tools, running current verification and inspection of data input correctness, automatic knowledge base source text generation, and knowledge protection.

References

1. Antoniou G., Wachsmuth I., Structuring and Modules for Knowledge Bases: Motivation for a New Model, Knowledge-Based Systems, (1994), 7 (1), 49-51.
2. Coenen F. Bench-Capon T., Maintenance of Knowledge-Based Systems, Academic Press Inc. San Diego, (1993).
3. IEEE, Standard for Software Reviews and Audits, IEEE Std 1028-1986, (1986).
4. Michalik K., Package Sphinx 2.3 – user guide, AITECH – Artificial Intelligence Laboratory, Katowice, (in polish), (1999).
5. Michalik K., Siminski R., The Hybrid Architecture Of The AI Software Package Sphinx, Proceedings of CAI'98 – Colloquia in Artificial Intelligence, Poland, (1998).
6. Preece A.D., Methods for Verifying Expert System Knowledge Base, apreece@csd.abdn.ac.uk, (1991)
7. Preece A.D., Verifying expert system knowledge bases: An example, apreece@csd.abdn.ac.uk, (1991).
8. Preece A.D., Foundation and Application of Knowledge Base Verification. International, Journal of Intelligent Systems, 9, (1994).
9. Reichgelt Han, Knowledge Representation: An AI Perspective., Ablex Publishing Corporation, Norwood, New Jersey, (1991).
10. Siminski R., Methods and Tools for Knowledge Bases Verification and Validation, Proceedings of CAI'98 – Colloquia in Artificial Intelligence, Poland, (1998).
11. Siminski R., O pewnym praktycznym aspekcie weryfikacji regułowych baz wiedzy, Proceedings of V KNIWSE, Poland (in polish), (2003).
12. Siminski R., Wakulicz-Deja A., Principles and Practice in Knowledge Bases Verification, Proceedings of IIS'98 – Intelligent Information Systems VII, Poland, (1998).
13. Siminski R., Wakulicz-Deja A., Dynamic Verification Of Knowledge Bases, Proceedings of IIS'99, Intelligent Information Systems VIII, Poland, (1999).
14. Siminski R., Wakulicz-Deja A., Verification of Rule Knowledge Bases Using Decision Units, Advances in Soft Computing, Intelligent Information Systems, Physica–Verlag, Springer Verlag Company, (2000).
15. Siminski R., Wakulicz-Deja A., kbBuilder - system wspomagania tworzenia i weryfikacji regułowych baz wiedzy, Proceedings of V KNIWSE, Poland (in polish), (2003).
16. Vanthienen J., Moreno García A. M., Illustrating Knowledge Base Restructuring and Verification in a Real World Application,www.econ.kuleuven.ac.be/tew/academic/infosys/Members/vthienen/PUB/EUROVAV99/EUROVAV99.DOC, (1999).
17. Vestli, M., Nordbi I., Silvberg, A., Modeling Control in Rule-based Systems, IEEE Software, 11 (3), (1994).

Fuzzy Decision Support System with Rough Set Based Rules Generation Method

Grzegorz Drwal[1] and Marek Sikora[2]

[1] Institute of Mathematics
Silesian Technical University, Kaszubska 23, 44-101 Gliwice, Poland
gdrwal@gmt.com.pl
[2] Institute of Computer Sciences
Silesian Technical University, Akademicka 16, 44-101 Gliwice, Poland
msikora@iinf.polsl.gliwice.pl

Abstract. This paper presents system which tries to combine the advantages of rough sets methods and fuzzy sets methods to get better classification. The fuzzy sets theory supports approximate reasoning and the rough sets theory is responsible for data analyzing and process of automatic fuzzy rules generation. The system was designed as a typical knowledge based system consisting of four main parts: rule extractor, knowledge base, inference engine, user interface and occurs to be useful tool in various decision problems and fuzzy control.

1 Introduction

In real situations many decisions have to be made on the basis of imprecise, incomplete, uncertain and/or vague information. Many theories provided a decision maker with tools which enable him to cope with uncertain (imprecise) and vague data present in many real decision tasks.

One of them - fuzzy sets theory [11] represents such imprecise knowledge by means of fuzzy linguistic terms. This representation makes it possible to carry out quantitative processing in the course of inference based on compositional rule of inference which is used for handling uncertain (imprecise) knowledge, called fuzzy reasoning. The main disadvantage of fuzzy reasoning systems is the difficulty in preparing knowledge bases for such systems. The several methods for automatically generating fuzzy if-then rules have been proposed (e.g. gradient descent learning method [5], genetic algorithm based method [6], least squares methods [10]), unfortunately, obtained results are often unsatisfactory.

On the other hand the rough sets theory [7] has been implemented in many applications of incomplete, imprecise and uncertain data analysis. The use of rough sets theory doesn't need any additional information about data and permits, without loss of accuracy, minimizing of knowledge base, represented as a set of decision rules. The rough sets theory gives also the tools which enable to estimate the quality of approximation of classification. This paper suggest rough sets theory's methods [9] in order to automate the process of generation of fuzzy rules for fuzzy reasoning systems.

S. Tsumoto et al. (Eds.): RSCTC 2004, LNAI 3066, pp. 727–732, 2004.

2 Induction of Decision Rules Based upon Rough Sets Theory

Rough sets theory can be treated as a tool for data table analysis. Table data are representing as decision table $\boldsymbol{DT}=(U, A\cup\{d\})$, where U is a set of objects, A is a set of features describing these objects called conditional attributes and d is a decision attribute ($d\notin A$). Each attribute can be treated as a function $a : U \rightarrow X_a$ ($d : U \rightarrow Y$), where X_a is a set of attribute a values. For every decision attribute value $v \in Y$, set $C_v=(x\in U: d(x)=v\}$ is called a decision class.

In rough sets theory the rules of the following form are considered:

$$\text{if } a_1 \in V_a \text{ and ... and } a_N \in V_{a_N} \text{ then } d = v \tag{1}$$

where: $\{a_1,..,a_N\}\subseteq A$, $\forall_{i\in\{1,..,N\}}\ V_{a_i} \subseteq X_{a_i}$. Each expression $a\in V_a$ is called a descriptor, especially in standard rough sets model [7], descriptors are in $a = v$ form, where $v\in V_a$.

The set of attributes occurred in conditional part of the rule consists of the attributes belonging to relative reduct [7]. Depends on induction rules method it is object-related relative reduct or relative reduct for whole decision table.

Below, we introduce the essential definitions allow to present our methods of generating the decision rules. With any subset of attributes $B\subseteq A$, an equivalence relation denoted by $IND(B)$ called the B-indiscernibility relation, can be associated and defined by $IND(B)=\{\ (x,y)\in U\times U : \forall_{a\in B}\ (\ a(x)=a(y)\ )\}$. By $[x]_{IND(B)}$ we denote the equivalence class of $IND(B)$ defined by $x\in U$. For every $x\in U$, each minimal attribute set $B\subseteq A$ satisfying the condition $\{y\in[x]_{IND(B)} : d(x)\neq d(y)\}=\{y\in[x]_{IND(A)} : d(x)\neq d(y)\}$ is called the relative reduct for object x.

Application of rough set theory to data containing numerical attributes required their previous discretization [3] or tolerance based rough sets model use [9], in which the B-indiscernibility relation $IND(B)$ is replaced by tolerance relation $\tau(B)$ (equivalence classes $[x]_{IND(B)}$are replaced by tolerance sets $I_B(x)$)in the following way:

$$\forall_{x,y\in U}\ ((x,y) \in \tau(B) \Leftrightarrow \forall a_i \in B[\delta_{a_i}(a_i(x), a_i(y)) \leq \varepsilon_{a_i}]) \tag{2}$$

$$\forall_{y\in U}\ (y \in I_B(x) \Leftrightarrow (x,y) \in \tau(B)) \tag{3}$$

where: $\delta_{a_i}$is a distance function (e.g. $\delta_{a_i}(a_i(x), a_i(y)) = \frac{|a(x)-a(y)|}{\max X_a - \min X_a}$, ε_{a_i} are fixed numbers called tolerance thresholds.

The relative reducts set for object x can be determined based on analysis the corresponding row (column) in the discernibility matrix modulo d. The discernibility matrix modulo d is a square matrix $(c_{xy})_{x,y\in U}$ with the elements defined as follows:

$$c_{xy} = \begin{cases} a \in A : (y \notin I_{\{a\}}(x)) \wedge (d(x_i) \neq d(x_j)) \\ \phi : \quad d(x_i) = d(x_j) \end{cases} \tag{4}$$

In consideration of their computational complexity, algorithms of generating object-related relative reducts using discernibility matrix can be employed for tables consisting of several thousand objects. In [4, 9], the algorithms of finding the minimal relative reduct without using the discernibility matrix are presented.

We use the tolerance model of rough sets in our researches. Before rules calculation, we discretize the numerical data using the entropy method [3], then we look for similarities between data that have been already discretized. We take a simple algorithm of finding the proper values of tolerance thresholds [8].

Rough sets tolerance model application leads to approximate rules calculation. For calculation the quality of each rule one compute the values of quality evaluation function [1]. We use the function known as the χ^2 Pearson function q_p [1] in our experiments. Usually, high accuracy and coverage are requirements of decision rules. Then, the probability that dependence representing by a rule is standing not only for analyzed table but also for objects from outside of the table increases.

Taking into account the above considerations, finally, we propose the following approximate rules generation algorithm:

input: **DT**$= (U, A \cup \{d\})$, `tolerance thresholds vector` $(\varepsilon, \varepsilon, .., \varepsilon), q_p$– `Pearson quality evaluation function, x-object, rule generator, an order of conditional attributes` $(a_{i_1}, a_{i_2}, .., a_{i_{card(A)}})$ `so as the attribute the most frequently appearing in` c_x `is the first (attribute appearing the most rarely is the last)`
begin
  `create rule r, which has the decision descriptor d=d(x) only;`
  $r_{best} := r$;
  for every `j := 1, ... ,card(A)`
    `add descriptor` $a_{i_j} \in V_{a_{i_j}}$ `to conditional part of rule r (where` $V_{a_{i_j}} = \{a_{i_j}(y) \in X_{a_{i_j}} : y \in I_{a_{i_j}}(x)\}$)
    if $q_p(r) > q_p(r_{best})$ **then** $r_{best} := r$
return r_{best}

The algorithm generates one rule for every object from U. Next descriptor adding causes an increasing of rule accuracy. Quality evaluation function is particular about rule fitting to training data.

After all rules generation, we make a filtration of rules set choosing only these rules, that will be enough to cover the training set U, beginning from the strongest rules (at the same time, after adding a new rule into filtered set, there are remove from input rules set all rules generated from objects covered by added rule). Such approach ensures that there are the strongest rules in output rules set and usually this set is relatively small.

3 The Fundamentals of Fuzzy Reasoning

In our system, called FClass, we assume knowledge to be a collection of rules consisting of linguistic statements that link conditions (situations) with conclusions (decisions). Such knowledge, expressed by a finite number (k=1,2,..,K) of heuristic fuzzy rules of the MISO type (multiple input single output), may be written in the form:

$$R^{(k)} : if\ a_1\ is\ A_1^{(k)}\ and\ a_2\ is\ A_2^{(k)}\ and\ ...\ and\ a_N\ is\ A_N^{(k)}\ then\ d\ is\ B^{(k)} \quad (5)$$

where $A_1^{(k)}$, $A_2^{(k)}$,..., $A_N^{(k)}$ denote the values of linguistic variables a_1,a_2,...,a_N of the antecedent defined in the following universes of discourse: X_1, X_2, ..., X_N, and $B^{(k)}$ stands for the value of linguistic variable d of the consequent in universe of discourse Y.

For the sake of generality and simplicity we use the membership function representation of different variants of the compositional rule of inference (CRI) of FITA method (First Inference Then Aggregate) in the formulas written below:

$$\mu_{B'}(y) = \begin{pmatrix} \bigwedge_k \\ \bigvee_k \end{pmatrix} \sup_{\boldsymbol{x}\in \boldsymbol{X}} *_T \left[\mu_{A'}(\boldsymbol{x}), I\left(\mu_{A^{(k)}}(\boldsymbol{x}), \mu_{B^{(k)}}(y)\right)\right] \quad (6)$$

where I denotes a fuzzy relation (implication) ,(∨, ∧) is a rule aggregation operator (connective also), A' and B' denote respectively fuzzy values of observation and classification result, $*_T$ stands for any t-norm, $\mu_{A^{(k)}}(\boldsymbol{x})$ denotes $*_T\left(\mu_{A_1^{(k)}}(x_1), \mu_{A_2^{(k)}}(x_2), ..., \mu_{A_N^{(k)}}(x_N)\right)$ and $\mu_{A'}(\boldsymbol{x})$ stands for $*_T(\mu_{A'_1}(x_1)$, $\mu_{A'_2}(x_2), ..., \mu_{A'_N}(x_N))$.

In the FClass system we implemented both constructive and destructive interpretation of fuzzy decision rules. Table 1 an table 2 present all possible combinations of operations implemented in constructive and destructive parts of the FClass system.

In order to determine the discrete representative value of the final membership function $\mu_{B'}(y)$, and therefore obtain a crisp classification result, various methods of defuzzification can be applied. In the FClass system, the most frequently used defuzzification methods are employed [2]: center of gravity (COG),

Table 1. Options of constructive part of FClass inference mechanism

Connective $also_r$	Fuzzy relation	T-norm operator
MAX, $x \vee y$	MIN, $x \wedge y$	MIN, $x \wedge y$
MAX, $x \vee y$	PROD, $x * y$	PROD, $x * y$

Table 2. Options of destructive part of FClass inference mechanism

Connective $also_r$	Fuzzy implication	T-norm operator
MIN, $x \wedge y$	Kleene-Dienes, $\neg x \vee y$	MIN, $x \wedge y$
MIN, $x \wedge y$	Zadeh, $x \wedge y \vee \neg x$	MIN, $x \wedge y$
MIN, $x \wedge y$	Lukasiewicz, $1 \wedge (\neg x + y)$	BOLD_PROD, $(x + y - 1) \vee 0$
MIN, $x \wedge y$	Fodor , $\begin{cases} 1, & if\ x \le y \\ \neg x \vee y, & otherwise \end{cases}$	MIN_0 , $\begin{cases} 0, & if\ x + y \le 1 \\ x \wedge y, & otherwise \end{cases}$
MIN, $x \wedge y$	Reichenbach, $1 - x + x * y$	PROD, $x * y$

mean of maxima (MOM), height method (HM) for the constructive part and indexed center of gravity (ICOG) defuzzifier, modified indexed center of gravity defuzzifier ($MICOG_\alpha$) for destructive part.

4 The Numerical Example

To present the abilities of our methods we used the data set of digital fundus eye images. In this set there are eight conditional attributes and each of them is of real type. The attributes mean the features, which numerically characterize eye-disc structures of examined patients. Decision attribute allows to define two classes: normal and glaucomatous patients. This set has been chosen on account of difficulties with direct (experimental) fuzzy rules set definition based on them. It is because, based on visual data analysis one is not able to give even approximate form of fuzzy rules in a simple way.

The scheme of rule induction can be written as:

1. the data were put through discretization (entropy method)
2. then, values of tolerance thresholds have been found (as a tolerance threshold vector evaluating function we used the formula (5))
3. in the presented rule generation algorithm the quality evaluation function q_p has been used.
4. choice of rules sufficient to cover a training set gave us, finally, the 15 decision rules.
5. next, the rules were put through fuzzyfication scheme - each value $< k1, k2 >$ of attribute q is exchanged by linguistic value of the pseudotrapeziodal membership functions defined as (see fig.1):

- condition attributes: m1=k1, m2=k2, a=$minX_q$, b=$maxX_q$, h=1
- decision attribute: m1=number of class, m2=number of class, a=number of class-1, b=number of class+1, h=strength of rule

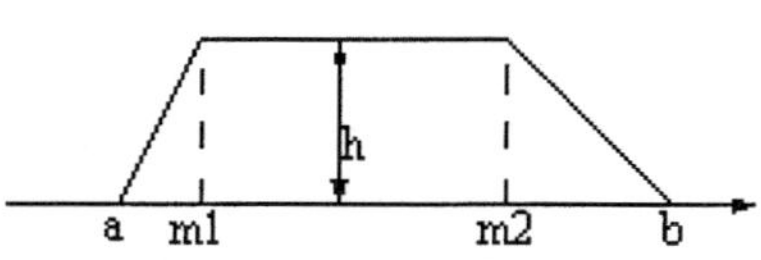

Fig. 1. Pseudotrapeziodal membership function

The application of decision algorithm for not fuzzy rules (various ways of voting were tested in the case of classification conflict) gave at best the classification accuracy 65%. By the same methods classification after fuzzyfication gave the result better by 7% (data classification by means of the methods rendered accessible in Rosetta program allowed to gain 60%, and using Cee5 program, 64% classification accuracy).

5 Conclusions

Based on decision rules, fuzzy rules generation may improve classification results obtained by decision algorithm. Presented by us process of obtaining decision rules and, next, fuzzy rules needs further investigations - we want to search an answer the following questions:

- whether application of the known fuzzy rules automatic generation (adaptation) methods [5, 6, 10] may improve the classification abilities of rules obtained by us
- since fuzzy classifier works quick based on relatively not many rules, we want to search if an application for classification only certain small number of the best rules from each decision class, significantly influences on classification results

Acknowledgement

This research was supported by Polish State Committee of Scientific Research under the grant No. 5 T12A 001 23.

References

1. Bruha I. "*Quality of Decision Rules: Definitions and Classification Schemes for Multiple Rules*", Nakhaeizadeh G., Taylor C. C. (ed.) "Machine Learning and Statistics, The Interface", John Wiley and Sons, 1997;
2. Drwal G. "*FClass/RClass Systems - the Fuzzy Sets and Rough Sets Based Approaches to Classification under Uncertainty*", Archive of Theoretical and Applied Computer Science, Polish Academy of Science, vol. 2, 2000;
3. Fayyad U. M., Irani K. B. "*Multi-Interval Discretization of Continuous-Valued Attributes for Classification Learning*", Proceedings of the 13th International Joint Conference on Artificial Intelligence. Morgan Kaufmann, pp. 1022-1027, 1993;
4. Nguyen H. S., Nguyen S. H. "*Some Efficient Algorithms for Rough Set Methods*", Proc. of the IPMU'96 Conference, vol. 2, Granada, Spain, pp. 1451-1456, 1996;
5. Nomura H., Hayashi I., Wakami N. "*A Learning Method of Fuzzy Inference Rules by Descent Method*", Proceedings of the FUZZ-IEEE'92 International Conference, pp. 203-210, 1992;
6. Nomura H., Hayashi I., Wakami N. "*A Self-tuning Method of Fuzzy Reasoning by Genetic Algorithm*", Proceedings of the International Fuzzy Systems and Intelligent Control Conference, pp. 236-245, 1992;
7. Pawlak Z. "*Rough Sets*", International Journal of Information and Computer Sciences 11 (5), pp. 341-356, 1982;
8. Sikora M., Proksa P. "*Algorithms for generation and filtration of approximate decision rules, using rule-related quality measures*", Bulletin of International Rough Set Society, vol. 5, no. 1/2, Proc. of the RSTGC-2001 Conference, 2001;
9. Stepaniuk J. "*Knowledge Discovery by Application of Rough Set Models*", ICS PAS Reports, no. 887, Warszawa, 1999;
10. Tagaki T., Sugeno M. "*Fuzzy Identification of Systems and its Applications to Modeling and Control*", IEEE Trans. System, Man and Cybernetics, vol. 15, pp. 116-132, 1985;
11. Zadeh L.A. "Fuzzy Sets", Information and Control, vol. 8, pp. 338-353, 1965;

Approximate Petri Nets for Rule-Based Decision Making

Barbara Fryc[1], Krzysztof Pancerz[1], and Zbigniew Suraj[1,2]

[1] Chair of Computer Science Foundations
University of Information Technology and Management
Sucharskiego Str. 2, 35-225 Rzeszów, Poland
{bfryc,kpancerz,zsuraj}@wenus.wsiz.rzeszow.pl
[2] Institute of Mathematics, Rzeszów University
Rejtana Str. 16A, 35-310 Rzeszów, Poland

Abstract. This paper describes a new Petri net model named approximate Petri net. Approximate Petri nets can be used for knowledge representation and approximate reasoning. The net model presented in the paper is defined on the base of the rough set theory, fuzzy Petri nets and coloured Petri nets.

Keywords: approximate reasoning, approximate Petri nets, decision systems.

1 Introduction

Modelling of approximate reasoning has earlier been presented in a literature (cf. [6], [7], [8]). The aim of the research has been the transformation of the information or decision system and derived rules into corresponding concurrent models. In [4] we used a matrix representation of fuzzy Petri nets. This representation has been used in a fuzzy reasoning algorithm which was simple to implement in modern programming languages and the MATLAB environment. The proposed algorithm allowed parallel firing of independent rules in one reasoning step. However, the reasoning models in the form of fuzzy Petri nets, even for relatively small decisions systems, become very large. A new approach proposed in this paper decreases significantly a size of reasoning models. It is characteristic of high-level nets. In our approach we assume that a decision table represents the knowledge base for an expert system. We extract two types of rules from a decision system using the rough set methods. First type of rules represents the relationship between the values of conditional attributes and the decision. The second type of rules represents relationship between the values of conditional attributes. On the base of a set of all rules extracted from a given decision system we construct an approximate Petri net as an approximate reasoning model. Using the conditional rules we can compute a decision for unknown values of attributes, especially, when the decision has to be made immediately and the values of attributes are read from sensors in the unknown time interval. Using the net model we can also compute decisions for new objects.

S. Tsumoto et al. (Eds.): RSCTC 2004, LNAI 3066, pp. 733–742, 2004.

In Section 2 we introduce basic notions and notation used in the paper. Section 3 presents the approximate Petri net. In Section 4 the approximate reasoning model is presented. Conclusions and further works are presented in Section 5.

2 Basic Notions and Notation

In this section we recall basic notions and introduce notation related to the fuzzy set theory [2] and the rough set theory [5].

2.1 Fuzzy Sets

A *fuzzy set* A in a universe of discourse X, written A_X, is defined as a set of pairs $(\mu_A(x), x)$, where $\mu_A : X \to [0,1]$ is a *membership function* of A_X and $\mu_A(x) \in [0,1]$ is the *grade of membership* of $x \in X$ in A_X. A membership function $\mu_A(x)$ is the degree to which an element $x \in X$ belongs to the fuzzy set A_X.

It is very often assumed that X is finite, i.e., $X = \{x_1, \ldots, x_n\}$. The pair $(\mu_A(x), x)$ is called a *fuzzy singleton* and denoted by $\mu_A(x)/x$. Then, the fuzzy set A_X can be written as $A_X = \{(\mu_A(x), x) : x \in X\}$ or $A_X = \mu_A(x_1)/x_1 + \ldots + \mu_A(x_n)/x_n = \sum_{i=1}^{n} \mu_A(x_i)/x_i$. Pairs $\mu_A(x)/x$ with $\mu_A(x) = 0$ are omitted.

A fuzzy set A_X is said to be empty, written $A_X = \emptyset$, if and only if $\mu_A(x) = 0$ for each $x \in X$. The family of all fuzzy sets defined in X will be denoted by $\mathcal{A}_X$. The family $\mathcal{A}_X$ includes among others the empty fuzzy set as well as the whole universe of discourse X written as $X = 1/x_1 + \ldots + 1/x_n$. The fundamental operations and relations for fuzzy sets are understood in a classical way.

In the sequel, we will use the operation of removing elements from a given fuzzy set, defined as follows.

Definition 1 (Removing elements from a fuzzy set). *Let A_X be a fuzzy set in a universe of discourse X and let $X' \subseteq X$. Then $A_X \backslash X'$ is the fuzzy set A'_X in a universe of discourse X such that:*

$$\mu_{A'}(x) = \begin{cases} 0 & \text{if } x \in X', \\ \mu_A(x) & \text{otherwise.} \end{cases}$$

2.2 Rough Sets

Information Systems. An *information system* is a pair $S = (U, A)$, where U is a nonempty, finite set of *objects*, called the *universe*, A is a nonempty, finite set of attributes. Every attribute $a \in A$ is a total function $a : U \to V_a$, where V_a is the set of values of a, called the *domain* of a. The set $V = \bigcup_{a \in A} V_a$ is said to be the domain of A.

A *decision system* is any information system of the form $S = (U, A \cup D)$, where $A \cap D = \emptyset$. D is a set of distinguished attributes called *decisions*. The elements of A are called *conditional attributes* (or *conditions*, in short).

Let $S = (U, A')$ be a decision system, where $A' = A \cup D$ and let V' be the domain of A'. Pairs (a, v), where $a \in A'$, $v \in V'$ are called *descriptors* over A' and V' (or over S, in short). Instead of (a, v) we write also $a = v$ or a_v.

For the sets of descriptors we assume the following notation: $DESC_A(S)$ - the set of all descriptors corresponding to conditions from A in S, $DESC_a(S)$ - the set of all descriptors corresponding to a given condition $a \in A$ in S, $DESC_D(S)$ - the set of all descriptors corresponding to decisions from D in S, $DESC_d(S)$ - the set of all descriptors corresponding to a given decision $d \in D$ in S.

The set of terms over A' and V' is the least set of descriptors (over A' and V') and closed with respect to the classical propositional connectives such that: NOT (negation), OR (disjunction), AND (conjunction), i.e., if τ, τ' are terms over A' and V', then (NOT τ), (τ AND τ'), (τ OR τ') are terms over A' and V'. The meaning $||\tau||_S$ (or $||\tau||$, in short) of a term τ in S is defined inductively as follows: if τ is of the form $a = v$ then $||\tau|| = \{u \in U : a(u) = v\}$, $||\tau \text{ OR } \tau'|| = ||\tau|| \cup ||\tau'||$, $||\tau \text{ AND } \tau'|| = ||\tau|| \cap ||\tau'||$, $||\text{NOT } \tau|| = U - ||\tau||$.

Indiscernibility Relation. Let $S = (U, A)$ be an information system. With any subset of attributes $B \subseteq A$ we associate a binary relation $ind(B)$, called an *indiscernibility relation*, which is defined by $ind(B) = \{(u, u') \in U \times U : \underset{a \in B}{\forall} [a(u) = a(u')]\}$. The indiscernibility relation $ind(B)$, as an equivalence relation, splits the given universe U into a family of equivalence classes $\{U_1, \ldots, U_r\}$. Objects belonging to the same equivalence class U_i, where $i = 1, \ldots, r$, are indiscernible, otherwise objects are discernible with respect to attributes from B only. An equivalence class including an object u is denoted by $[u]_B$ and defined as $[u]_B = \{u' \in U : (u, u') \in ind(B)\}$.

Rough Membership Function. Some subsets of objects in an information system cannot be distinguished in terms of some available subset of attributes. They can only be roughly defined. Let $S = (U, A)$ be an information system. A given subset of attributes $B \subseteq A$ determines the approximation space $AS = (U, ind(B))$ in S. For a given subset $X \subseteq U$ (called a concept X), a *rough membership function* of an object u to the set X is defined as: $\mu_X^B(u) = \frac{card([u]_B \cap X)}{card([u]_B)}$. The value of a membership function $\mu_X^B(u)$ can be interpreted as a degree of certainty to which u belongs to X.

Rules in Decision Systems. Rules express the relationships between values of attributes in decision systems.

Let $S = (U, A')$ be a decision system, where $A' = A \cup D$ and let V' be the domain of A'. Any implication r : IF ϕ THEN ψ, where ϕ and ψ are terms over A' and V', is called a rule in S. ϕ is referred to as the *predecessor* of r and denoted by $Pred(r)$. ψ is referred to as the *successor* of r and denoted by $Succ(r)$.

In the sequel we will distinguish two kinds of rules in a given decision system. The rules expressing some relationships between values of conditions are called *conditional rules.* Formally, a *conditional rule* in S is any expression of the following form:

$$\text{IF } a_{i_1} = v_{i_1} \text{ AND } \ldots \text{ AND } a_{i_r} = v_{i_r} \text{ THEN } a_p = v_p$$

or

$$\text{IF } a_{i_1} = v_{i_1} \text{ OR } \ldots \text{ OR } a_{i_r} = v_{i_r} \text{ THEN } a_p = v_p$$

where $a_{i_j} \in A$, $v_{i_j} \in V_{a_{i_j}}$ for $j = 1, \ldots, r$, $a_p \in A$ and $v_p \in V_{a_p}$.

The rules expressing some relationships between the values of conditions and the decision are called *decision rules.* A *decision rule* in S is any expression of the following form:

$$\text{IF } a_{i_1} = v_{i_1} \text{ AND } \ldots \text{ AND } a_{i_r} = v_{i_r} \text{ THEN } d_k = v_k$$

or

$$\text{IF } a_{i_1} = v_{i_1} \text{ OR } \ldots \text{ OR } a_{i_r} = v_{i_r} \text{ THEN } d_k = v_k$$

where $a_{i_j} \in A$, $v_{i_j} \in V_{a_{i_j}}$ for $j = 1, \ldots, r$ and $d_k \in D$, $v_k \in V_{d_k}$.

Several numerical factors can be associated with a given rule. In the paper we need a so called *certainty factor.*

Let $S = (U, A')$ be a decision system, where $A' = A \cup D$ and IF ϕ THEN ψ be a rule in S. The number $\frac{card(||\phi|| \cap ||\psi||)}{card(||\phi||)}$ is called the *certainty factor* (CF) of the given rule. It is easy to see that $CF \in [0, 1]$. If $CF = 1$ then we will say that a given rule is deterministic. Otherwise (i.e., if $CF < 1$), we will say that the given rule is non-deterministic.

Let $S = (U, A')$ be a decision system, where $A' = A \cup D$. The set of all conditional rules extracted from S we denote by $RUL^c(S)$. This set includes the set $RUL^c_d(S)$ of deterministic rules and the set $RUL^c_n(S)$ of non-deterministic rules. Analogously, we denote by $RUL^d(S)$ the set of all decision rules extracted from S with the sets $RUL^d_d(S)$ and $RUL^d_n(S)$. Finally, the set of all rules in S we denote by $RUL(S)$. So we have:

$$RUL(S) = RUL^c(S) \cup RUL^d(S) = RUL^c_d(S) \cup RUL^c_n(S) \cup RUL^d_d(S) \cup RUL^d_n(S).$$

In order to generate the foregoing sets of rules we can use the standard rough set methods.

3 Approximate Petri Nets

This section contains the formal definition of approximate Petri nets (AP-nets) and describes briefly their behaviour. The main idea of approximate Petri nets derives from coloured Petri nets introduced by Jensen [3] and fuzzy Petri nets used by Chen et al. [1].

3.1 The Structure of *AP*-Nets

By a *closed expression* we understand an expression without variables. By **B** we denote the Boolean type ($\mathbf{B} = \{false, true\}$) with the standard operations of propositional logic. Moreover, we will use notation as follows. $Type(v)$ - the type of a variable v, $Type(expr)$ - the type of an expression $expr$, $Var(expr)$ - the set of all variables in an expression $expr$, $Type(Vars)$ - the set of types of variables from the set $Vars$, $expr < b >$ - the value obtained by evaluating an expression $expr$ in a binding b.

Definition 2. *An approximate Petri net (AP-net) is a tuple:*

$$APN = \{\Sigma, P, T, A_{in}, A_{out}, N_{in}, N_{out}, C, G, E_{in}, E_{out}, I, f\}$$

where: Σ is a finite set of non-empty types (colour sets), P is a finite set of places, T is a finite set of transitions, A_{in} is a finite set of input arcs, A_{out} is a finite set of output arcs, N_{in} is an input node function, N_{out} is an output node function, C is a colour function, G is a guard function, E_{in} is an input arc expression function, E_{out} is an output arc expression function, I is an initialization function, f is a certainty factor function.

The sets P, T, A_{in} and A_{out} must be pairwise disjoint.

An input node function $N_{in} : A_{in} \to P \times T$ maps each input arc to a pair such that the first element is a place and the second one is a transition.

An output node function $N_{out} : A_{out} \to T \times P$ maps each output arc to a pair such that the first element is a transition and the second one is a place.

A colour function $C : P \to \Sigma$ maps each place to a colour set $C(p)$ from Σ.

A guard function T maps each transition to an expression $G(t)$ such that: $\underset{t \in T}{\forall} Type(G(T)) = \mathbf{B} \wedge Type(Var(G(T))) \subseteq \Sigma$, i.e. $G(t)$ must be of the Boolean type. Moreover, all variables in $G(t)$ must have types that belong to Σ.

An input arc expression function E_{in} maps each input arc to an expression $E_{in}(a)$ such that: $\underset{a \in A_{in}}{\forall} Type(E_{in}(a)) = 2^{C(p(a))} \wedge Type(Var(E_{in}(a))) \subseteq \Sigma$, where $p(a)$ is the place of $N_{in}(a)$. Each evaluation of $E_{in}(a)$ must yield a subset of the colour set $C(p(a))$ that is attached to the corresponding place. Moreover, all variables in $E_{in}(a)$ must have types that belong to Σ.

An output arc expression function E_{out} maps each output arc to an expression $E_{out}(a)$ such that: $\underset{a \in A_{out}}{\forall} Type(E_{out}(a)) = \mathcal{A}_{C(p(a))} \wedge Type(Var(E_{out}(a))) \subseteq \Sigma$, where $p(a)$ is the place of $N_{out}(a)$. Each evaluation of $E_{out}(a)$ must yield a fuzzy set in a universe of discourse $C(p(a))$, where $C(p(a))$ is attached to the corresponding place. Moreover, all variables in $E_{out}(a)$ must have types that belong to Σ.

An initialization function I maps each place to a closed expression $I(p)$ such that: $\underset{p \in P}{\forall} Type(I(p)) = \mathcal{A}_{C(p)}$, i.e., $I(p)$ must be a fuzzy set in a universe of discourse $C(p)$.

A certainty factor function $f : T \to [0, 1]$ maps each transition to a real value between zero and one (called a certainty factor value).

3.2 The Behaviour of *AP*-Nets

First we introduce the following notation for $t \in T$:

- $A_{in}(t) = \{a \in A_{in} : N_{in}(a) \in P \times \{t\}\}$,
- $A_{out}(t) = \{a \in A_{out} : N_{out}(a) \in \{t\} \times P\}$,
- $In(t) = \{p \in P : \underset{a \in A_{in}}{\exists} N(a) = (p,t)\}$,
- $Out(t) = \{p \in P : \underset{a \in A_{out}}{\exists} N(a) = (t,p)\}$,
- $Var(t) = \{v : v \in Var(G(t)) \vee \underset{a \in A_{in}(t)}{\exists} v \in Var(E_{in}(t)) \vee \underset{a \in A_{out}(t)}{\exists} v \in Var(E_{out}(t))\}$.

Moreover, we assume that $a(p,t)$ denotes the arc $a \in A_{in}$ such that $N_{in}(a) = (p,t)$ and $a(t,p)$ denotes the arc $a \in A_{out}$ such that $N_{out}(a) = (t,p)$.

A binding of a transition t is a function b defined on $Var(t)$ such that $\underset{v \in Var(t)}{\forall} b(v) \in Type(v)$ and $G(t) < b >$ is true, where $G(t) < b >$ denotes evaluation of the guard expression $G(t)$ in a binding b. By $B(t)$ we denote the set of all bindings for t.

Any transition $t \in T$ is enabled to fire if and only if $B(t) \neq \emptyset$.

A marking M of APN is a function defined on P such that: $\underset{p \in P}{\forall} M(p) \in \mathcal{A}_{C(p)}$.

If a transition $t \in T$ fires with a given binding $b \in B(t)$ in a given marking M then a new marking M' appears such that:

$$M'(p) = \begin{cases} M(p) \backslash E(a(p,t)) < b > & \text{if } \ p \in In(t), \\ M(p) + E(a(t,p)) < b > & \text{if } \ p \in Out(t), \\ M(p) & \text{otherwise,} \end{cases}$$

where "\" denotes removing elements from a fuzzy set (defined in subsection 2.1) and "+" is the union of two fuzzy sets.

4 Approximate Reasoning Models

Below we give an algorithm for constructing an approximate reasoning model APN_S in the form of an approximate Petri net, corresponding to a decision system S.

Let $S = (U, A')$ be a decision system, where $A' = A \cup D$ and let $RUL(S)$ be a set of all rules in S.

ALGORITHM for constructing an approximate reasoning model APN_S in the form of an AP-net, corresponding to a decision system S.
INPUT: A decision system S with a set $RUL(S)$ of rules.
OUTPUT: An approximate reasoning model APN_S corresponding to S.
begin
create a set P of places;

```
P = ∅;
create a set Σ of types;
Σ = ∅;
create a set T of transitions;
T = ∅;
create a set A_in of input arcs;
A_in = ∅;
create a set A_out of output arcs;
A_out = ∅;
for each attribute a_i ∈ A' do
begin
   create a place p_{a_i};
   create a type a_i;
   for each descriptor τ_k ∈ DESC_{a_i} do
   begin
      create a colour τ_k;
      add τ_k to a_i;
   end;
   add a_i to Σ;
   add a_i to p_{a_i};
   set an initial marking "∅" for p_{a_i};
   add p_{a_i} to P;
end;
for each rule r_i ∈ RUL(S) do
begin
   create a transition t_{r_i};
   set a certainty factor value for t_{r_i} equal to CF of r_i;
   create a guard expression G_{t_i};
   add G_{t_i} to t_{a_i};
   for each descriptor (a_j = v_j) ∈ Pred(r_i) do
   begin
      create a bidirectional arc δ(p_{a_j}, t_{r_i}) from p_{a_j} to t_{r_i};
      create a variable xa_j of the type a_j;
      create an input arc inscription ε_j;
      add ε_j to δ(p_{a_j}, t_{r_i});
      add δ(p_{a_j}, t_{r_i}) to A_in;
   end;
   for each descriptor (a_j = v_j) ∈ Succ(r_i) do
   begin
      create an output arc δ(t_{r_i}, p_{a_j}) from t_{r_i} to p_{a_j};
      create a variable ya_j of the type a_j;
      create an output arc inscription ε_j;
      add ε_j to δ(t_{r_i}, p_{a_j});
      add δ(t_{r_i}, p_{a_j}) to A_out;
   end;
```

add t_{r_i} to T;
end;
end.

Each place p_{a_i} of APN_S corresponds to one attribute (conditional or decision) of S. For each place p_{a_i}, its colour set consists of colours corresponding to individual values of the attribute a_i. Each transition t_{r_i} of APN_S represents one rule (conditional or decision) extracted from the decision system S. The forms of input arc expressions, output arc expressions and guard expressions will be shown in the example below.

Table 1. A decision system.

$U\backslash A$	a	b	c	d
u_1	5	1	3	0
u_2	1	2	1	1
u_3	3	3	2	1
u_4	2	2	4	1
u_5	4	3	2	0

Example 1. Let us consider a decision system $S = (U, A \cup \{d\})$ presented in Table 1, where $U = \{u_1, u_2, u_3, u_4, u_5\}$, $A = \{a, b, c\}$ and d is a decision. Using the standard rough set methods for generating rules and computing certainty factors, we can extract all decision and conditional rules from S with CF. The set $RUL^d(S)$ of decision rules with the appropriate CFs is the following:

IF $b = 1$ OR $c = 3$ OR $a = 5$ THEN $d = 0$ $(CF = 1)$,
IF $b = 2$ OR $c = 1$ OR $a = 1$ THEN $d = 1$ $(CF = 1)$,
IF $a = 3$ THEN $d = 1$ $(CF = 1)$,
IF $b = 2$ OR $c = 4$ OR $a = 2$ THEN $d = 1$ $(CF = 1)$,
IF $a = 4$ THEN $d = 0$ $(CF = 1)$,
IF $b = 3$ OR $c = 2$ THEN $d = 1$ $(CF = 0.5)$,
IF $b = 3$ OR $c = 2$ THEN $d = 0$ $(CF = 0.5)$.
The set $RUL^c(S)$ of conditional rules with the appropriate CFs is the following:
IF $b = 1$ OR $c = 3$ THEN $a = 5$ $(CF = 1)$,
IF $c = 1$ THEN $a = 1$ $(CF = 1)$,
IF $c = 4$ THEN $a = 2$ $(CF = 1)$,
IF $b = 1$ OR $a = 5$ THEN $c = 3$ $(CF = 1)$,
IF $a = 1$ THEN $c = 1$ $(CF = 1)$,
IF $b = 3$ OR $a = 3$ OR $a = 4$ THEN $c = 2$ $(CF = 1)$,
IF $a = 2$ THEN $c = 4$ $(CF = 1)$,
IF $c = 3$ OR $a = 5$ THEN $b = 1$ $(CF = 1)$,
IF $c = 1$ OR $a = 1$ THEN $b = 2$ $(CF = 1)$,
IF $c = 2$ OR $a = 3$ THEN $b = 3$ $(CF = 1)$,
IF $c = 4$ OR $a = 2$ THEN $b = 2$ $(CF = 1)$,

IF $c = 2$ OR $a = 4$ THEN $b = 3$ $(CF = 1)$,
IF $b = 2$ THEN $a = 1$ $(CF = 0.5)$,
IF $b = 3$ OR $c = 2$ THEN $a = 3$ $(CF = 0.5)$,
IF $b = 2$ THEN $a = 2$ $(CF = 0.5)$,
IF $b = 3$ OR $c = 2$ THEN $a = 4$ $(CF = 0.5)$,
IF $b = 2$ THEN $c = 1$ $(CF = 0.5)$,
IF $b = 2$ THEN $c = 4$ $(CF = 0.5)$.

After execution of the Algorithm we obtain an approximate reasoning model in the form of *AP*-net for the decision system S. A part of it is shown in Figure 1 and shortly described below.

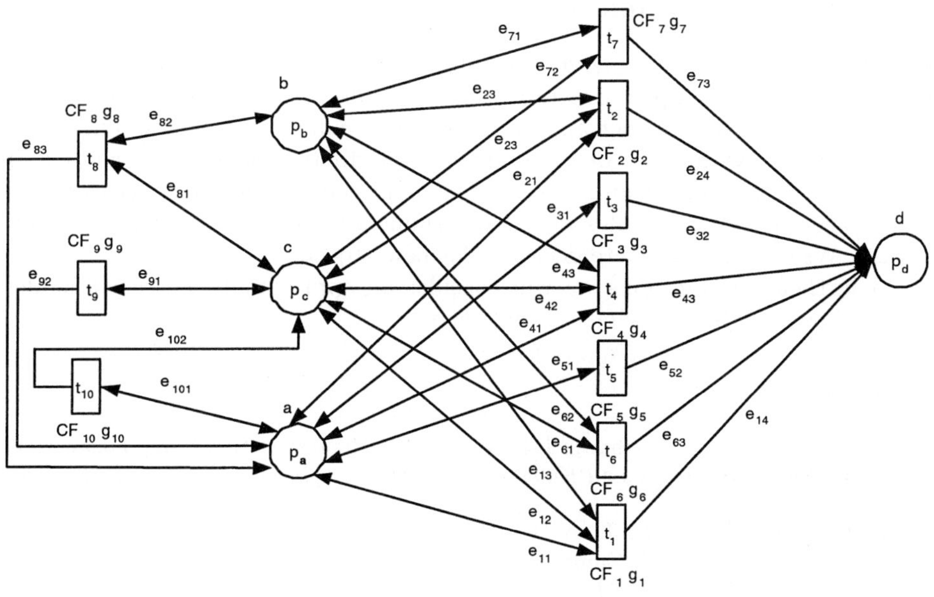

Fig. 1. Approximate reasoning model for S.

On the foregoing model places p_a, p_b, p_c represent conditional attributes a, b, c, respectively. However, the place p_d represents a decision. The transitions $t_1, \ldots, t_7$ represent the decision rules, transitions t_8, t_9, t_{10} represent several deterministic conditional rules. Transitions representing the rest of deterministic conditional rules and the non-deterministic conditional rules have been omitted. Bidirectional input arcs used in the constructed net check only the membership function of suitable elements in the fuzzy sets of input places but do not remove them from there. The colour sets (types) are the following: $a = \{a_1, a_2, a_3, a_4, a_5\}$, $b = \{b_1, b_2, b_3\}$, $c = \{c_1, c_2, c_3, c_4\}$, $d = \{d_0, d_1\}$. For example, transition t_1 represents the decision rule: IF $b = 1$ OR $c = 3$ OR $a = 5$ THEN $d = 0$ $(CF = 1)$. The input arc expressions are the following: $e_{11} = \{x_a\}$, $e_{12} = \{x_c\}$, $e_{13} = \{x_b\}$, where x_a, x_c, x_b are variables of the type a, c, b, respectively. The output arc expression has the form $e_{14} = CF * max(\mu(x_a), \mu(x_c), \mu(x_b))/y_d$, where y_d is a variable of the type d. The guard expression for t_1 is the following: $g_1 = [x_a = a_5 \wedge x_c = c_3 \wedge x_b = b_1 \wedge x_d = d_0]$. Moreover, $CF_1 = 1$. Analogously we can describe other transitions and arcs.

The initial marking of each place is an empty set. During the reasoning we read values of conditional attributes (for example on the base of measurements) and set marking of places corresponding to these attributes. It is possible that some values of conditional attributes are unknown, then having values of remained attributes we can compute them by firing conditional transitions. In the next step we compute markings of places corresponding to decisions.

5 Concluding Remarks

The approximate Petri net model presented in this paper makes possible designing and simulation of approximate reasoning on the base of the decision system. Using the coloured Petri net approach we reduce number of places. The net is more legible if we have a lot of conditional attributes. Another advantage of this approach is the reasoning based on the knowledge coded in a decision system. Using a conditional rules we can determine unknown values in the decision system. We can also compute decisions for new objects.

In further investigations we will consider an approximate Petri net model with a time and the behaviour of that model.

References

1. Chen, S.-M., Ke, J.-S., Chang, J.-F.: Knowledge Representation Using Fuzzy Petri Nets. *IEEE Transactions on Knowledge and Data Engineering*, Vol. 2, No. 3, 1990, pp. 311-319.
2. Fedrizzi, M., Kacprzyk, J.: A Brief Introduction to Fuzzy Sets and Fuzzy Systems. In: J. Cardoso, H. Camargo (Eds.), *Fuzziness in Petri Nets*, Physica-Verlag, Heidelberg, 1999, pp. 25-51.
3. Jensen, K.: *Coloured Petri Nets. Basic Concepts, Analysis Methods and Practical Use.* Vol. 1. Springer-Verlag, Berlin Heidelberg, 1996.
4. Fryc, B., Pancerz, K., Peters, J.F., Suraj, Z.: On Fuzzy Reasoning Using Matrix Representation of Extended Fuzzy Petri Nets. *Fundamenta Informaticae*, (to appear in 2004).
5. Pawlak, Z.: *Rough Sets - Theoretical Aspects of Reasoning About Data. Kluwer Academic Publishers*, Dordrecht, 1991.
6. Pedrycz, W., Peters, J.F., Ramanna, S., Furuhashi, T.: From Data to Fuzzy Petri Nets: Generalized Model and Calibration Abilities. In: *Proceedings of the IFSA'97*, Vol. III, 1997, pp. 294-299.
7. Peters, J.F., Skowron, A., Suraj, Z., Pedrycz, W., Ramanna, S.: Approximate Real-Time Decision Making: Concepts and Rough Fuzzy Petri Net Models. *International Journal of Intelligent Systems*, 14-4, 1998, pp. 4-37.
8. Skowron A., Suraj Z.: A Parallel Algorithm for Real-Time Decision Making: A Rough Set Approach. *Journal of Intelligent Information Systems 7*, Kluwer Academic Publishers, Dordrecht, 1996, pp. 5-28.

Adaptive Linear Market Value Functions for Targeted Marketing

Jiajin Huang[1], Ning Zhong[2], Chunnian Liu[1], and Yiyu Yao[3]

[1] College of Computer Science and Technology, Beijing University of Technology
Beijing Municipal Key Laboratory of Multimedia and Intelligent Software Technology
100022, Beijing, China
hjj@emails.bjut.edu.cn

[2] Department of Information Engineering, Maebashi Institute of Technology
Maebashi-City 371-0816, Japan
zhong@maebashi-it.ac.jp

[3] Department of Computer Science, University of Regina
Regina, Saskatchewan, Canada S4S 0A2
yyao@cs.uregina.ca

Abstract. This paper presents adaptive linear market value functions to solve the problem of identification of customers having potential market value in targeted marketing. The performance of these methods is compared with some standard data mining methods such as simple Naive Bayes. Experiments on real world data show that the proposed methods are efficient and effective.

1 Introduction

The identification of customers having potential market value is one of the key problems of targeted marketing [10, 14]. If the problem is solved well, marketers can only send advertisements to these customers. For customers, they can get the information which they really want, and for marketers, they can reduce labor and communication costs for advertising their products. Targeted marketing is an important area of applications for data mining [4, 9, 14]. It is also one of dominant trends in Web Intelligence for developing e-business and e-commerce portals [11–13]. Although standard data mining techniques have been widely used to solve the problem by building models to predict worthy customers for promotion, most of these techniques are based on classification rules mining such as decision tree system [4], ProbRough system [5], and so on. There may be some difficulties with these techniques. On the one hand, the selection of significant rules may not be an easy task. On the other hand, we may get too many or too few potential customers by using these derived rules [10, 14].

A linear market value function model is an alternative solution for the above targeted marketing problems [10, 14]. In this model, each customer can be assigned to a market value to indicate the likelihood of buying the product. Thus a ranked list can be produced according to the market values and a cut-off point

S. Tsumoto et al. (Eds.): RSCTC 2004, LNAI 3066, pp. 743–751, 2004.

of the ranked list can be chosen based on various criteria such as financial constraints. The market value of each customer can be measured by a market value function which is a linear combination of a set of utility functions. One of the key techniques in this model is the estimation of attribute weights. Training a linear market value function mainly means using training data to find the weights of attributes to calculate market values of the customers. Several methods of estimating weights of attributes have been discussed in [2, 10, 14]. However, these methods only are based on information-theoretic measures of attribute importance. In this paper, we discuss other alternative methods of estimating weights of attributes in this model. An adaptive linear market value function based on acceptable ranking strategy is presented. The adaptive linear model has been used in the areas of Information Retrieval [7, 8] and Information Filtering [1]. To best of our knowledge, no papers report this method in targeted marketing. Through our investigations, we will provide useful insights for developing a more effective market value function model for targeted marketing.

The rest of the paper is organized as follows. Section 2 discusses related work. Section 3 presents an adaptive linear market value function model and related methods by extending its result. Section 4 evaluates the result by using real world examples. Section 5 gives conclusions.

2 Related Work

In the above introduction section, we have discussed the shortcoming of methods based on classification rules mining. In this section, we will focus on other related methods.

It is well-known that nowadays most customers information is given by information table [10, 14]. Each row of the table gives a customer related information, each column corresponds to an attribute of customers, and each cell is the value of a customer with respect to an attribute. Formally, an information table is a 4-tuple:

$$S = (U, At, I_a | a \in At, V_a | a \in At) \tag{1}$$

where U is a finite nonempty set of customers, At is a finite nonempty set of attributes and $At = C \bigcup D$, C is a finite set conditional attributes, D is a finite set of decision attributes, V_a is a nonempty set of values for $a \in At$, and $I_a : U \rightarrow V_a$ is an information function for $a \in At$.

According to values of decision attributes, we can divide U into P and N, where P and N denote positive and negative examples, respectively. For our applications, P is the set of current customers, and N is the set of people who have not buy the product. We can estimate some functions from P to predict the potential customers in N. A ranked list can be produced according to these functions and a cut-off point of the ranked list can be chosen based on various criteria such as financial constraints. One of the functions is as follows:

$$r(x) = Pr(P|x) \tag{2}$$

where x is an element in U and can be described by the tuple of attribute values $(v_1, \ldots, v_i, \ldots, v_n)$, $v_i \in V_i$. It means we can rank customers according to the probability that x is in P. The top customers in the ranked list are the targeted customers. Eq.(2) can be represented as following based on Naive Bayes methods [6]:

$$r(x) = \frac{Pr(P) \prod_{i \in At, v_i \in V_i} Pr(v_i|P)}{Pr(x)} \tag{3}$$

$Pr(P)$ denotes the probability of observing a positive instance. $Pr(v_i|P)$ denotes the probability of observing attribute value v_i on attribute i in P, $Pr(x)$ denotes the probability of observing x in U.

We have the following method named simple Naive Bayes (SNB for short) under the assumption that the probability of observing each customer is the same.

$$r(x) \propto Pr(P) \prod_{i \in At, v_i \in V_i} Pr(v_i|P) \tag{4}$$

However, sometimes we need other information such as the degree of attributes importance to predict the potential customers more effectively. We cannot obtain these information only by using the Naive Bayes method. A linear market value function model is an alternative solution [10, 14]. In this model

$$r(x) = \sum_{a \in At} \omega_a u_a(I_a(x)) \tag{5}$$

where ω_a is the weight of an attribute $a \in At$, u_a is a utility function defined on V_a for an attribute $a \in At$. There are two key techniques for building the linear model. They are the estimation of individual utility functions and attribute weights. The utility of an attribute value is determined by the number of existing members (more details see [10, 14]). And the attributes weights are drawn from information-theoretic measures such as the Information Gain:

$$\omega_a = H(a) - H_P(a) \tag{6}$$

where $H(a)$ and $H_P(a)$ denote the entropy of attribute a in U and P, respectively. They can be defined as follows:

$$H(a) = -\sum_{v \in V_a} Pr(v) \log Pr(v) \tag{7}$$

$$H_P(a) = -\sum_{v \in V_a} Pr(v|P) \log Pr(v|P) \tag{8}$$

where $Pr(v)$ denotes the probability of observing attribute value v on attribute a in U, and $Pr(v|P)$ denotes the probability of observing attribute value v on attribute a in P.

3 Adaptive Market Value Function Model

From Eqs. (7) and (8), we can see that the attribute weights are based on a probability distribution of attribute values. The underlying assumption is that the probability distribution is correct.

In this paper, we will estimate the attribute weights by using an alternative method. The proposed market value function model is an adaptive one. It is similar to the adaptive linear model in Information Retrieval [7, 8] and Information Filtering [1].

We can define a marketer's preference using a binary relation $\preceq$ in U. If the marketer is more likely to send an advertisement to x' than x, we have

$$x \preceq x' \quad x, x' \in U. \tag{9}$$

It is obvious that

$$x \preceq x' \Leftrightarrow x \in N, x' \in P. \tag{10}$$

In the market value function model, our primary objective is to find a market value function r defined on U such that

$$x \preceq x' \Rightarrow r(x) < r(x') \; x, x' \in U. \tag{11}$$

According to the market value function model, a customer $x \in U$ can be represented as a vector $\mathbf{x} = (x_1, \ldots, x_i, \ldots, x_n)$, where x_i is the utility function value defined on V_a for attribute $i \in At$. Moreover, we have a weight vector $\mathbf{w}$ $= (w_1, \ldots, w_n)$. Thus Eq. (5) can be represented as follows:

$$r(\mathbf{x}) = \mathbf{w} \cdot \mathbf{x}. \tag{12}$$

According to Eq. (11), we have

$$\mathbf{x} \preceq \mathbf{x}' \Rightarrow r(\mathbf{x}) < r(\mathbf{x}') \Leftrightarrow \mathbf{w} \cdot \mathbf{x} < \mathbf{w} \cdot \mathbf{x}'. \tag{13}$$

Let

$$\mathbf{B} = \{\mathbf{b} = \mathbf{x}' - \mathbf{x} | \mathbf{x}', \mathbf{x} \in U \; and \; \mathbf{x} \preceq \mathbf{x}'\}. \tag{14}$$

According to Eq. (13), we have

$$\mathbf{w} \cdot \mathbf{b} > 0, \quad for \; \forall \mathbf{b} \in \mathbf{B}. \tag{15}$$

We can see that if Eq. (15) holds, $\mathbf{w}$ is correct, and if $\exists \mathbf{b}' \in \mathbf{B}, \mathbf{w} \cdot \mathbf{b}' < 0$, an error occurs. In this case, the value $-\mathbf{w} \cdot \mathbf{b}'$ is a measure of the error. Let $\mathbf{B}' =$ $\{\mathbf{b}' | \mathbf{w} \cdot \mathbf{b}' < 0, \mathbf{b}' \in \mathbf{B}\}$. We aim to minimize the total errors $\sum_{\mathbf{b}' \in \mathbf{B}'} (-\mathbf{w} \cdot \mathbf{b})$. Based on the above analysis, we can get an algorithm, namely AMV (Adaptive Market Value), to search the weight vector $\mathbf{w}$ by using gradient descent to minimize the total errors. Furthermore, if the gradient descent is to consider the total error defined for each instance in P, we can get the algorithm SAMV (Stochastic Adaptive Market Value). Compared with AMV, SAMV updates attribute weights upon examining each positive instance. In AMV and SAMV, η is a positive number that sets the step size.

```
AMV (P, N)
Input: a positive set P, a negative set N;
Output: an attribute weight vector w.
    (1) Choose an initial attribute weight vector w
    (2) do{
          for each customer x' in P
              for each customer x in N
                  if w·x'<w·x
                  then vector b=b+η(x'-x)
          w=w+b;
    }while Eq. (15) holds
```

```
SAMV (P, N)
Input: a positive set P, a negative set N;
Output: an attribute weight vector w.
    (1) Choose an initial attribute weight vector w
    (2) do{
          for each customer x' in P{
              for each customer x in N
                    if w·x'<w·x
                    then vector b=b+η(x'-x)
              w=w+b;
          }

    }while Eq. (15) holds
```

In real world, we, sometimes, want to update the current weight when a new instance occurs and Eq. (15) does not also always hold during the loop. The first problem can be solved by only repeating one time in the algorithm SAMV (called SAMV1). In general, there are too few positive instances and too many negative instances in U [4]. Under the assumption that the current negative instances are enough, the attribute weights can be updated by the algorithm SAMV1 when a new positive instance occurs. The second problem can be solved by setting the iteration numbers.

4 Experiments

Two datasets on potential customers have been used for our approaches. These datasets are divided into the training set and the testing set, respectively. The training set is used to learn the above market value functions and the learned functions are used to rank the testing examples. In the first dataset, each member is described by 96 attributes, such as hobby, income, etc. We selected randomly 18964 (894 positive instances) as the training set and 24134 (647 positive instances) as the testing set, respectively. In the second dataset [3], each customer

Table 1. Lift value results on two datasets ($\eta = 1$)

Datasets	SAMV1	AMV	MV	SNB
Dataset 1	63.1%	62.8%	63.2%	50.3%
Dataset 2	71.7%	73.0%	71.7%	58.8%

has 85 attributes. The dataset is divided into a training set with 5822 examples and a testing set with 4000 examples, respectively.

The lift index [4] is used as the evaluation criterion. After all testing examples are ranked using the proposed algorithms, we divided the ranked list into 100 equal deciles. Let S_i denote how many positive examples are in the ith deciles. The lift index is defined as

$$S_{lift} = (1 \times S_1 + 0.99 \times S_2 + \ldots + 0.01 \times S_{100}) / \sum S_i \qquad (16)$$

Thus, we can show the distribution of the positive examples in the ranked list for the intuitive evaluation.

Table 1 shows the lift index results of the algorithms SAMV1, AMV, the market value model (MV) and SNB on the two datasets. From this table, we can see that the lift index of MV is a little better than AMV and is similar to SAMV1 on dataset 1, and the AMV outperforms other methods on dataset 2.

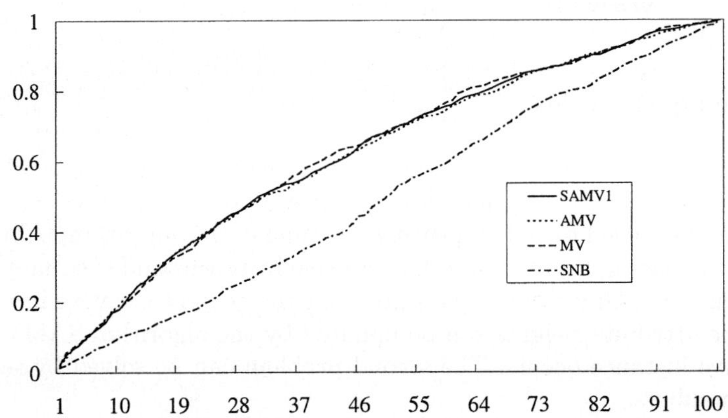

Fig. 1. The lift curve of four methods on dataset 1 ($\eta = 1$)

Figures 1 and 2 show the lift curves [9] of the above four methods on the two datasets, respectively. The horizontal axis shows the top proportion of customers in the ranked list and the vertical axis shows the proportion of responses based on the total positive instances in the testing set. In Fig. 1, the SAMV1 and AMV are better than MV over the targeting range between 11% and 24% on dataset 1. In Fig. 2, the results of AMV are better than SAMV1 and MV between about 15% and 48% of targeted customers.

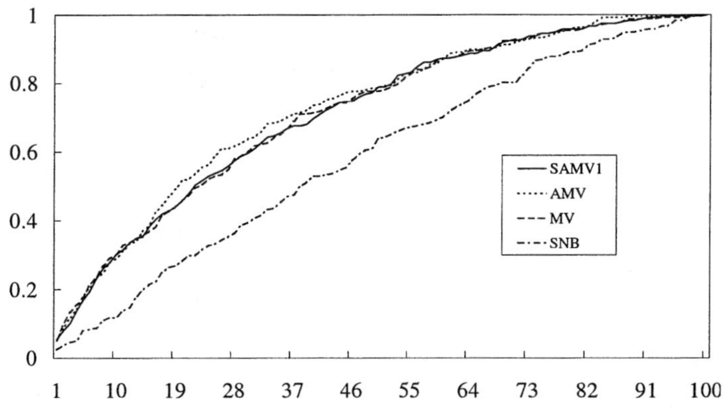

Fig. 2. The lift curve for four methods on dataset 2 ($\eta = 1$)

Figures 3 and 4 show the ROC curves [9] of the above four methods on the two datasets, respectively. The horizontal axis shows a percentage of the total number of negatives and the vertical axis shows a percentage of the total number of positives. In Fig. 3, the results of AMV, SMV1 and MV are similar on dataset 1. In Fig. 4, the results of AMV are better than SAMV1 and MV if marketers aim to cover about between 36% and 77% of positives because the AMV gives less false positive rate than others.

In total, we can get the approximate results by using SAMV1, AMV and MV, respectively. These methods outperform simple Naive Bayes. The SAMV1 and AMV provide a new method to estimate market value function. Under the assumption that the current negative instances are enough, the SAMV1 can be regarded as an incremental algorithm.

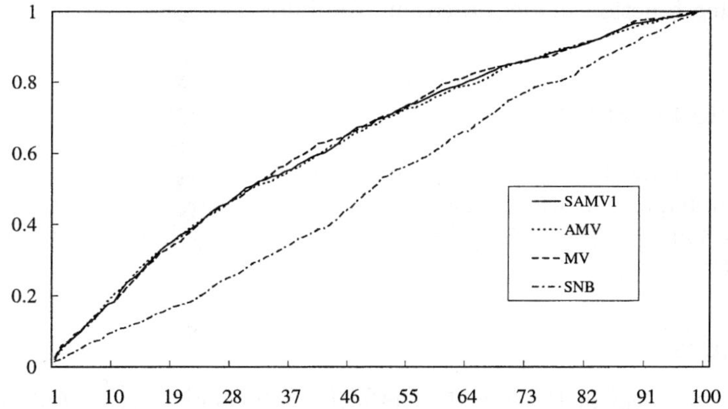

Fig. 3. The ROC curves for four methods on dataset 1 ($\eta = 1$)

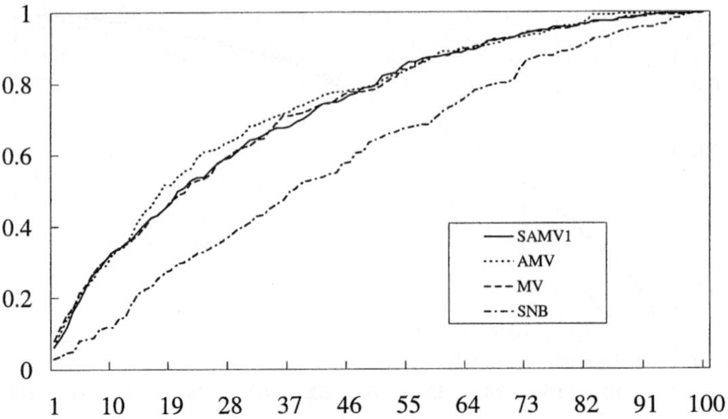

Fig. 4. The ROC curves for four methods on dataset 2 ($\eta = 1$)

5 Conclusion

In this paper, we studied the adaptive market value functions in targeted marketing. Algorithms AMV, SAMV and SAMV1 are presented. These methods are evaluated using real world examples. Experiments show that these methods are effective in targeted marketing. The AMV and SAMV are new methods to estimate the market value function model. And under the assumption that the current negative instances are enough, the SAMV1 can also be regarded as an incremental algorithm for targeted marketing.

However, the proposed methods in this paper are based on two classes (buy or not buy). In fact, there is multi-level preference (i.e. multi-class) in sets of customers such as buy, not buy, likely buy, and so on. In the future, we will research the multi-level preference in the market value function model. Furthermore, targeted marketing based on Web information system is one of dominant trends in Web Intelligence for e-business. In the future, we will also develop the market value function model based on Web information system.

Acknowledgement

This work is supported by the Natural Science Foundation of China (60173014), Beijing Municipal Natural Science Foundation (4022003) and Multimedia and Intelligent Software Technology Beijing Municipal Key Laboratory Open Foundation.

References

1. Alsaffar, A., Deogun J., Sever, H. "Optimal Queries in Information Filtering", *Proc. 12th International Symposium on Methodologies for Intelligent Systems (ISMIS 2000)*, Springer LNAI 1932 (2000) 435-443.

2. Huang, J., Liu, C., Ou, C., Yao, Y.Y., Zhong, N. "Attribute Reduction of Rough Sets in Mining Market Value Funtions" *Proc. 2003 IEEE/WIC International Conference on Web Intelligence (WI'03)*, IEEE-CS Press (2003) 470-473.
3. Kim, Y.S., Street, W.N. "Coil challenge 2000: Choosing and Explaining Likely Caravan Insurance Customers", Technical Report 2000-09. Sentient Machine Research and Leiden Institute of Advanced Computer Science, June 2000. http://www.wi.leidenuniv.nl/ putten/library/cc20000/.
4. Ling C.X., Li, C. "Data Mining for Direct Marketing: Problems and Solution", *Proc of KDD'98* (1998) 73-79.
5. Poel, D., Piasta, Z. "Purchase Prediction in Database Marketing with the ProbRough System", L. Polkowski and A. Skowron (eds.) *Rough Stes and Current Trends in Computing*, Springer LNAI 1424 (1998) 593-600.
6. Mitchell, T.M. *Machine Learning*, China Machine Press (2003)
7. Wong, S.K.M., Yao., Y.Y. "Query Formulation in Linear Retrieval Models", *Jounral of the American Society for Information Science*, 41(5) (1990) 334-341.
8. Wong, S.K.M., Yao., Y.Y. "Evaluation of an Adaptive Linear Model", *Jounral of the American Society for Information Science*, 42(10) (1991) 723-730.
9. Witten, I, Frank, E. *Data Mining Practical Machine Learning Tools and Techniques with Java Implementations*, China Machine Press (2003).
10. Yao, Y.Y., Zhong, N., Huang, J., Ou, C., Liu, C. "Using Market Value Functions for Targeted Marketing Data Mining" *International Journal of Pattern Recognition and Artigicial Intelligence*, 16(8) (2002) 1117-1131.
11. Zhong, N., Liu, J., Yao, Y.Y., "Web Intelligence (WI): A New Paradigm for Developing the Wisdom Web and Social Network Intelligence", Zhong, N., Liu, J., and Yao, Y.Y. (eds) *Web Intelligence*, Springer Monograph (2003) 1-16.
12. Zhong, N., Liu, J., Yao, Y.Y. (eds.) Web Intelligence, Springer (2003)
13. Zhong, N., "Towards Web Intelligence", E. Menasalvas Ruiz, J. Segovia, P.S. Szczepaniak (eds) Advances in Web Intelligence, LNAI 2663, Springer (2003) 1-14.
14. Zhong, N., Yao, Y.Y., Liu, C., Huang, J., Ou, C., "Data Mining for Targeted Marketing", Intelligent Technologies for Information Analysis, Springer (2004).

Using Markov Models to Define Proactive Action Plans for Users at Multi-viewpoint Websites

Ernestina Menasalvas[1,*], Socorro Millán[2], and P. Gonzalez[1]

[1] Facultad de Informática UPM, Madrid, Spain
[2] Universidad del Valle. Cali. Colombia

Abstract. Deciding about the best action plan to be tailored to and carried out for each user is the key for personalization. This is a challenging task as the maximum number of elements of an environment have to be taken into account when making decisions such as type of user, actual behaviour or goals to fulfil. The difficulty is even greater when dealing with web users and when decisions have to be taken on-line and salesmen are not involved. In this paper, we propose an approach that integrates user typologies and behaviour patterns in a multidepartamental organization to decide the best action plan to be carried out at each particular moment. The key idea to do this is based on detecting users behaviour changes by means of Behaviour Evolution Models (a combination of Discrete Markov Models). Besides, an agent based architecture has been proposed for the implementation of the whole method.

1 Introduction

Relationships with the users are paramount when trying to competitively develop activities in any web environment. It is difficult to manage customers when no information about them is available since this causes the lost of the one-to-one relationship with customers and this tends to make businesses less competitive.

In maintaining a relationship with the user, both objective data about the user (gender, age, likes and dislikes) as well as subjective information about the current context of the user (his/her behaviour, goals at each particular moment) have to be taken into account. In web environments, many enterprises have been very worried about getting hold of the identity of the navigator in terms of personal data. However, though knowing the user (his/her profile, what he/she wants, his/her goals, likes and dislikes) is important, what it is really important is the information about they way he/she wants to fulfil his/her goals, his/her particular behaviour: his/her preferences and the context are important factors that determine the way he/she behaves in each particular navigation. All this, integrated with information related to the business, preferences and goals of the organization behind will result in a successful e-CRM.

Nevertheless, the behaviour of a web user is not generally something stable but variable while navigating. Hence, detecting and capturing the user behaviour evolution so to accordingly and successfully act at each particular moment is the unavoidable

* Research is partially supported by Universidad Politécnica de Madrid (project Web-RT) and MCYT under project DAWIS.

S. Tsumoto et al. (Eds.): RSCTC 2004, LNAI 3066, pp. 752–761, 2004.

commitment that web-site sponsors must face. But user behaviour evolution depends not only on his/her present situation but on his/her profile. Thus, when deciding about the best set of actions to undertake, action plan, different users typologies have to be taken into account too.

Dynamic models such as the Markov models have shown to be an appropriate tool for extracting and exploring dynamic behaviour and for modelling a page access pattern when successfully applied to problems such as link prediction and path analysis. Some authors have stated that there is some evidence that web surfing behavior may be a non-Markovian process in nature [9], and consequently, Markov models can not be used as true data generating tools. Nevertheless, they provide a mechanism to describe a useful and meaningful view of a dynamic web behaviour.

Once we are able to characterize the behaviour of the user the challenge is to recognize at each particular moment the department of the company for which the session is or could be more profitable so that an appropriate and personalized action plan can be tailored.

In this paper, we present an approach to identify, among available action plans, the best plan to be carried out depending on the actions and behaviour of the user as he/she navigates on the web. The approach is based on a Markov model. In this sense, we propose a method to characterize user behaviours and model his possible evolutions on a site as a Markovian process. We also propose an agent architecture to deploy the present approach.

The remainder of the paper is organized as follows. Section 3 presents the preliminaries of the method. Section 4 presents the proposed Markov model. In section 7 the proposed architecture is given. In section 2 related works are briefly shown. Finally, in section 8 main conclusions and further developments are included.

2 Related Work

Information collected and stored by Web servers is the main source of data for analyzing user navigation patterns. A successful e-CRM depends mainly on the capabilities of businesses to identify and classified users in order to model and predict her/his behaviour on the site and generate action plans geared to make him/her a frequent customer. Web site personalization is one of the keys to do it [3], [12].

Different web mining approaches and techniques have been proposed in order to improve the sites by creating adaptive Web sites, based mainly on the analysis of user access logs [5], [15].

An important aspect of web mining for analyzing web user access logs is related to categories and clusters. Clustering users, based on their common properties, and analyzing features in each cluster, can provide more appropriate services to the users.

To group and characterize similar web site users, several clustering techniques have been proposed [21], [13], [7], [12], [10], [14].

In [7] clustering of Web users based on their access patterns is analyzed. According to these patterns, pages are later organized so that users of a cluster will find these pages easy to access.

An algorithm, PageGather, for semi-automatically improving site organization by learning from visitor access patterns is proposed in [16]. Using page co-occurrence frequencies clusters of related but unlinked pages are found. Based on PageGather, index pages are created for easier navigation.

[21] describes a remote Java agent that captures client's selected links and page orders, accurate page viewing time, and cache references. Link path sequences are enumerated and clustering, in this path space, is done using the cosine angle distance metric.

On the other hand, Markov models have been used, among other things, to improve pre-fetching strategies for web caches [22], to classify browsing sessions [10], to influence caching priorities between primary, secondary and tertiary storages [11], and to predict web page accesses [4] ,[20], [17], [2].

3 Markov Models Preliminaries

As stated in [19], a DMM (Discrete Markov Model) can be defined by the tuple $< S, A, \lambda >$. S corresponds to the state space, physical or observable event, A is a matrix representing transition probabilities from one state to another. λ is the initial probability distribution of the states in S. An element of the matrix A, say $A[s, s']$ can be interpreted as the probability of transitioning from state s to s' in one step. Similarly, an element of $A * A$ will denote the probability of transitioning from one state to another in two steps, and so on.

The fundamental property of Markov models is the dependency on previous states together with order [18]. Order refers to the way previous states affect a sequence of observations. Thus, a first order model is the one in which the following state depends only on the previous one in the sequence, while in higher orders, it depends on the 2, 3, ..., previous states.

Low-order Markov models of web navigation are used in [1] to estimate purchases probabilities of a user based on clicks sequences so to dynamically classify a user's visit as buy visit, non-buy visit.

Higher order models, much more precise than low-order, have limitations related to the complexity of the state-space. As the number of states increases, the coverage of the states and the transitions between them can be considerably reduced in the training set. On the other hand, the complexity of the state space can also negatively affect the model precision [4].

In [17] authors propose to combine different order Markov models to solve the coverage problem, though this approach further increases the problem of state-space complexity. Thus, they propose to obtain 1,2,3, ... order Markov models (All-Kth-Order Markov models) using the training set. As some sequences of states will not be present in the training set, when applying the model the most precise model (higher order) will be chosen first.

There are certain approaches that can be used to reduce state-space complexity [17] but they may also reduce the accuracy of prediction of the resulting model.

A proposed method for combining different order Markov models obtaining a global model that will reduce the state-space complexity, retaining at the same time the coverage of the All-Kth-Order Markov models and even improving accuracy of prediction is proposed in [4].

4 Behaviour Evolution Model

The behaviour of a user while navigating in a web site evolves even while in the same session. Changes in behavior can be of a different nature: pages visited, environment, mood. No matter what the reason for the change can be, what really matters is discovering when the behaviour has varied and, consequently, act.

4.1 Preliminaries

We propose to build a behavior evolution model. As different users can be classified in different typologies according to their previous relationship with the site, data from previous navigations, we propose to have different evolution models for each typology.

Once typologies or profiles of users are obtained, we proceed to identify the different observable behaviour in each kind of user. In order to make the process computable, we define certain moments in which we observe the behaviour to see if it has changed. In our case, these points correspond to web pages of the site, in which changes in user behaviour can be observed. We will call these points Breaking Points (BK from now on). Hence, the model we propose is based on three basic concepts:

- User typology: each possible profile that is identified by segmenting the user database taking objective information of the relationship between the user and the enterprise into account.
- User behavior: each possible observable behaviour of the relationship between the user and the site in each navigation. Subjective information representing user context and goals such as inter-click times, amount of time spent by a customer on the site in the past and so on are taken into account.
- Breakpoint: point in which the behaviour of a user is analyzed to see its evolution or tendency.

Thus, the model will help to estimate not only the probability of going to the next BK but also to predict the behaviour a particular user will show when arriving at that particular BK.

4.2 The Proposed Model

Let $BK = \{BK_1, \ldots, BK_R\}$ be the set of Breakpoint identified in the site, let $U = \{U_1, \ldots, U_M\}$ be the set of possible user typologies and let $T_i = \{T_1, \ldots, T_M\}$ the set of observed behaviours for particular typology of user T_i. We define states of the first order DMM, $S = \{S_1, \ldots, S_N\}$, as all the possible combinations of BK and T_i that are present in the training set. Then the maximum number of possible states of the model will be $N = R \times M$.

Let us illustrate the model with an example: let us assume that we have three breaking points $\{BK_1, BK_2, BK_3\}$, and two different kinds of behavior observed, $\{T_1, T_2\}$ for those users in typology U_1. Then, the possible states of the first order Markov model will be: $S = \{S_1, S_2, S_3, S_4, S_5, S_6\}$ (6 states), where $S_1 = BK_1T_1$, $S_2 = BK_1T_2$, $S_3 = BK_2T_1$, $S_4 = BK_2T_2$, $S_5 = BK_3T_1$ and $S_6 = BK_3T_2$.

Assuming that BK are certain web pages of the site, then the state transitions will depend both on the topology of the site and on the historical navigation data.

In the example, if we assume that the set of possible transitions for the typology given is: $\{BK_1BK_2, BK_1BK_3, BK_2BK_3, BK_3BK_3\}$, we can represent the transitions graphically as in figure 1.

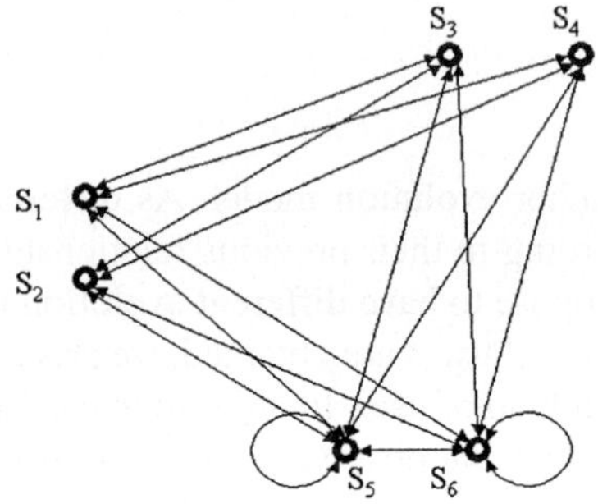

Fig. 1. Example of a Discrete Markov Model

Once the status of the model is defined, the transition matrix A can be filled with the estimated frequencies found in the training set. Having a number N of states the size of the transition matrix will be $N \times N$. Let $t_{i,j}$ be a cell of the matrix. The resulting matrix takes the form of the one represented in the following table:

$$A = \begin{matrix} S_1 \\ S_2 \\ \cdots \\ S_N \end{matrix} \begin{bmatrix} t_{1,1} & t_{1,2} & \dots & t_{1,N} \\ t_{2,1} & t_{2,2} & \dots & t_{2,N} \\ \dots & \dots & \dots & \dots \\ t_{N,1} & t_{N,2} & \dots & t_{N,N} \end{bmatrix}$$

In the case of the example, each cell is interpreted in the following way. For example, cell$t_{2,3}$ stores the probability of going from S_2, BK_1T_2, to S_3, BK_2T_1. In other words, the probability of going from BK_1 to BK_2 changing the behaviour classified as T_2, to behaviour T_1.

Once we have the transition matrix, then some problems can be solved. For example, given an on-line session, we could find the probability of arriving at a certain page with a certain behaviour (state in the model). This way for example, given session $\{\dots, S_L, S_M\}$, we could find the probability of reaching state S_N. The answer is as simple as looking for the information kept in the cell $t_{M,N}$ of the transition matrix, that is, $P(S_N/\{S_M\})$.

Once the first order model is obtained and depending on the training set, higher order models can be obtained. The combination of all the models for the different user typologies will result in a model of user behaviour evolution.

In the example, for order 2 model, the number of possible transitions will be $V_{6,2} + 2 = 30{+}2 = 32$ (Variations without repetition , the order counts, of 6 elements taken two by two plus two transitions with repetition: $\{S_5, S_5\}$ y $\{S_6, S_6\}$). The matrix would have all these combinations as entry point for the rows and the simple status or observations as columns and would take the form of the following figure:

$$A^2 = \begin{matrix} \{S_1, S_3\} \\ \{S_1, S_4\} \\ \cdots \\ \{S_6, S_6\} \end{matrix} \begin{bmatrix} t^2_{1,1} & t^2_{1,2} & \cdots & t^2_{1,6} \\ t^2_{2,1} & t^2_{2,2} & \cdots & t^2_{2,6} \\ \cdots & \cdots & \cdots & \cdots \\ t^2_{32,1} & t^2_{32,2} & \cdots & t^2_{32,6} \end{bmatrix}$$

Now, problems that we were solving with the order 1 model can be solved with higher precision as not only the previous state count but also two previous states.

In the example, having an on-line session $\{S_1, S_3\}$, to find the probability of reaching BreakPoint BK_3 and then change behaviour to T_2 we will have to calculate $P(S_6/\{S_1, S_3\})$. That is the element $t^2_{1,6}$ of A^2.

As we have already mentioned in section 3 the main problem related to higher order models has to do with coverage. We propose to use the techniques of intelligent combination of Markov models proposed in [4].

For an efficient on-line deployment of the proposed model, we propose to store in trees the estimated frequencies. Hence, a tree for each possible state of a 1-order model will be obtained. For the example, figure 2 shows part of the tree for S_6 state. In this case, level 0 keeps information to the probability of that state λ (is the initial probability distribution of the states in S). Level 1 nodes, for example for S_3, will store $t_{3,6}$, this is the transition from S_3 to S_6. Level 2 nodes will store in the same fashion second order transitions, this way S_1 will store the value of $t^2_{1,6}$ from A^2 transition matrix.

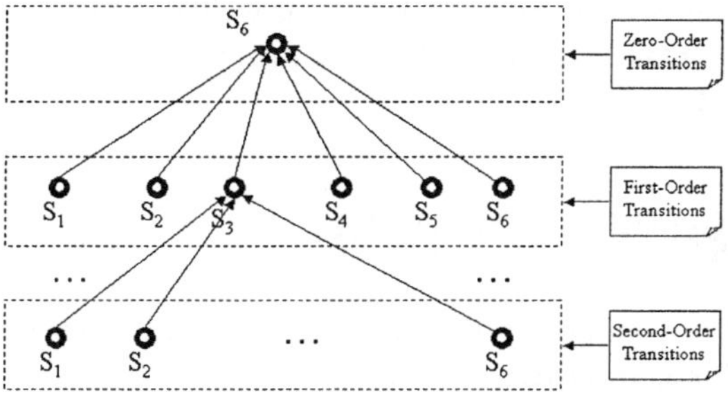

Fig. 2. Behaviour Evolution Model Tree

5 Obtaining the Models

In order to obtain the evolution behaviour model, a preprocessing stage in which historical session data is analyzed to identify user typologies, behaviours, and breaking points, is needed.

Present tasks needed in the process are presented below. All of them, when related to preprocessing of logs common in any other web mining procedure, are taken for granted. In [8] a detailed description of the process to generate breakpoints can be found.

5.1 Data Preparation

After the weblogs have been properly preprocessed and sessions have been obtained, information in the logs is enriched in order to obtain user behaviour typologies. In our case, logs are enriched with information related both to the context of the user and the navigation itself. To take care of this latter part in our approach, the algorithm presented in [6]) has been used.

With logs enriched this way, the next step is to obtain user behaviour typologies for each possible user profile.

To identify behaviours we make use of the breakpoints calculated according to [8] and for all possible BK we calculate the possible behaviours according to navigation information and value of session [6]. Thus, according to all this information, sessions are classified and subsessions are segmented for later classification.

5.2 Model Development

Once sessions and subsessions are properly identified and classified, the next step is to obtain the Markov evolution behaviour model.

A model of evolution of behaviour will be obtained for each user typology. The model will be the result of the combination of DMM of different orders in which $< S, A, \lambda >$ has been estimated. States, S, depend on the BKs (that are common for every typology in the site) and on the behaviours of each user typology. Initial probabilities of each state , λ, transition matrices of each order $A, A^2, \ldots,$ as well as the maximun order for which probabilities can be obtained will be calculated taking into account the original dataset already preprocessed.

6 Online Application of the Model

Once the model of behaviour is estimated, it can be applied on-line. The process for applying the model is as follows:

1. User Typology identification. When entering the site, a user is assigned his/her typology. This, can be the one kept in the profile of the user, if this is a registered user, or the result of a classification method used for new navigators.
2. User Behaviour Model Construction. For each event in a navigation a model is built to keep the user behavior. The model will later be used when applying a Markov behaviour model at BK's.
3. Check the behaviour at the Breaking Point. Each time a user visits a breakpoint, taking into account both the user typology and the user behaviour up to this point, the Markov model is used to estimate the possible change of behaviour and the next breakpoint that the user will probably visit.
4. Better Action Plan Determination. Considering the user typology and its behaviour model, and according to the results presented in [6], the better action plan to be followed is determined.

The dynamic nature of the web itself added to the fact that we are dealing with user typologies, user model behavior, user lifecycle models and, in general, probabilistic models based on the data being gathered on-line by the web server, requires a continuous process of refining and reviewing the models and action plans in order to keep alive the intelligent component of the CRM system. Due to the implicit cost of the refining process, the benefit of improving the models will have to be balanced with the cost of loosing customers because of a bad model response, so that the exact moment to refine the model is estimated.

7 Architecture Overview

For the implementation of the system, a multiagent architecture based on a three-layer architecture proposed in [6] has been used.

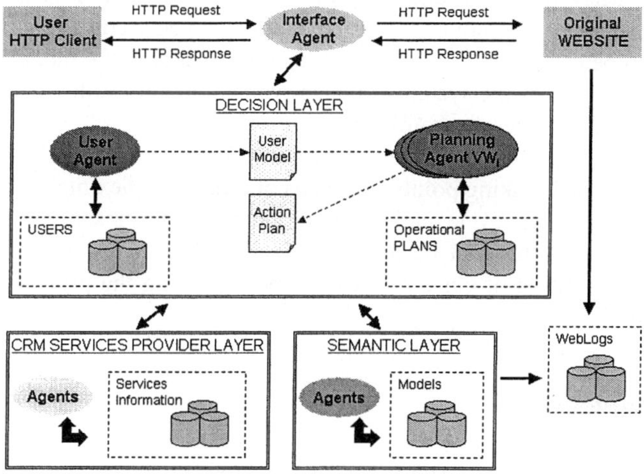

Fig. 3. Multiagent architecture

Figure 3 illustrates the agents involved and the interactions between them. The new architecture we are proposing is composed of 4 layers:

- Decision Layer. This layer includes agents that make decisions depending on the information supplied by the semantic layer. There are two main kind of agents:
  - User Agents. Represent each navigation on the site. The interaction User-Interface Agent and Interface Agent-User agent will make it possible together with the data being already stored to calculate the user model.
  - Planning Agents or Agents of strategy. The main task of these agents is to determine the strategy to be followed.They will collaborate with the Interface agents and CRM Services Provider Layer agents to elaborate the best action plan.

- Semantic Layer. This layer contains agents related to the logic of the algorithms and method used. We will have different agents, each of which will specialize in the application of the different models needed for decision making process. Models will be stored in a repository from which they will be updated, deleted or improved when needed. For the latter we will have refining agents.
- CRM Services Provider Layer. It offers an interface, which will be used by any agent asking for a service. Each agent will offer only one particular service, so that, a particular Action Plan selected for a particular session at a particular moment will involve several agents that will act, collaborate and interact among them in order to reach the proposed goals.

8 Conclusions

A model for analyzing user behaviour changes has been presented. The model combines different order Markov models and integrates different user typologies. The main advantage of the model is that not only user navigation can be predicted but the behaviour shown can also be estimated. An agent architecture to deploy the model has also been proposed. A prototype of the system is under evaluation and results obtained at one of the teaching university site are promising.

The presented approach can be used as basis for a personalized web site. Issues such as obtaining the breaking points by means of other complex methods, evolution of typologies, typologies life cycle analysis would improve the present method.

These open issues that can be developed and addressed by multiple alternatives have been the motivation of current research for improving the proposed method and forthcoming work.

Acknowledgments

The research has been partially supported by Universidad Politécnica de Madrid under Project WEB-RT Doctorado con Cali.

References

1. Mersereau AJ Bertsimas DJ and Patel NR. Dynamic classification of online customers. In *Proceedings of the SIAM International Conference on Data Mining, San Francisco, California*, May.
2. D. Weld C. Anderson, P. Domingos. Relational markov models and their applications to adaptive web navigation. *Proc. of The Eighth ACM SIGKDD International Conference on Knowledge Discovery and Data Mining (KDD2002)*, 2002.
3. H. Dai and B. Mobasher. A road map to more effective web personalization: Integrating domain knowledge with web usage mining. In *Proc.of the International Conference on Internet Computing 2003 (IC'03), Las Vegas, Nevada*, June 2003.
4. M. Deshpande and G. Karypis. Selective markov models for predicting web-page accesses, 2001.

5. Oren Etzioni. The world-wide web: Quagmire or gold mine? *Communications of the ACM*, 39(11):65–68, 1996.
6. M. Pérez E. Hochsztain V. Robles O.Marbán J. Peña A. Tasistro E. Menasalvas, S. Millán. Beyond user clicks: an algorithm and an agent-based architecture to discover user behavior. *1st European Web Mining Forum, Workshop at ECML/PKDD-2003, 22 September 2003, Cavtat-Dubrovnik, Croatia*, 2003.
7. Y. Fu, K. Sandhu, and M. Shih. Clustering of web users based on access patterns, 1999.
8. M. Hadjimichael, O. Marbán, E. Menasalvas, S. Millan, and J.M. Peña. Subsessions: a granular approach to click path analysis. In *Proceedings of IEEE Int. Conf. On Fuzzy Systems 2002 (WCCI2002), Honolulu, U.S.A.*, pages 878–883, May 2002.
9. Bernardo A. Huberman, Peter L. T. Pirolli, James E. Pitkow, and Rajan M. Lukose. Strong regularities in World Wide Web surfing. *Science*, 280(5360):95–97, 1998.
10. C. Meek P. Smyth S.White I. Cadez, D. Heckerman. Visualization of navigations patterns on a web site using model-based clustering. *Proc. of The Sixth ACM SIGKDD International Conference on Knowledge Discovery and Data Mining (KDD2000)*, 2000.
11. Achim Kraiss and Gerhard Weikum. Integrated document caching and prefetching in storage hierarchies based on Markov-chain predictions. *VLDB Journal: Very Large Data Bases*, 7(3):141–162, 1998.
12. B. Mobasher, H. Dai, T. Luo, M. Nakagawa, and J. Witshire. Discovery of aggregate usage profiles for web personalization. In *Proceedings of the WebKDD Workshop*, 2000.
13. O. Nasraoiu, R. Krisnapuram, and A. Joshi. Mining web access logs using a fuzzy relational clustering algorithm based on a robust estimator. 1998.
14. O. Nasraoui, H. Frigui, A. Joshi, and R. Krishnapuram. Mining web access logs using relational competitive fuzzy clustering.
15. Mike Perkowitz and Oren Etzioni. Adaptive web sites: Automatically synthesizing web pages. In *AAAI/IAAI*, pages 727–732, 1998.
16. Mike Perkowitz and Oren Etzioni. Towards adaptive Web sites: conceptual framework and case study. *Computer Networks (Amsterdam, Netherlands: 1999)*, 31(11–16):1245–1258, 1999.
17. James E. Pitkow and Peter Pirolli. Mining longest repeating subsequences to predict world wide web surfing. In *USENIX Symposium on Internet Technologies and Systems*, 1999.
18. Lawrence R. Rabiner.
19. Ramesh R. Sarukkai. Link prediction and path analysis using markov chains. In *Computer Networks, Volume 33, Issues 1-6, Pages 377-386.*
20. R. Sarukkai. Link prediction and path analysis using markov chains. *Ninth International World Wide Web Conference*, 2000.
21. C. Shahabi, A. M. Zarkesh, J. Adibi, and V. Shah. Knowledge discovery from user's web-page navigation. In *Proceedings of the Seventh International Workshop on Research Issues in Data Engineering, High Performance Database Management for Large-Scale Applications (RIDE'97), Washington- Brussels - Tokyo, IEEE*, pages 20–31, 1997.
22. J.C. Mogul V.N. Padmanabhan. Using predictive prefetching to improve world wide web latency. *Computer Communication Review*, 1996.

A Guaranteed Global Convergence Particle Swarm Optimizer

Zhihua Cui and Jianchao Zeng

Division of system simulation and computer application
Taiyuan Heavy Machinery Institute, Shanxi, P.R.China, 030024
cui_zhi_hua_7645@sohu.com

Abstract. The standard Particle Swarm Optimizer may prematurely converge on suboptimal solutions that are not even guaranteed to be local extrema. A new particle swarm optimizer, called stochastic PSO, which is guaranteed to convergence to the global optimization solution with probability one, is presented based on the analysis of the standard PSO. And the global convergence analysis is made using the F.Solis and R.Wets' research results. Finally, several examples are simulated to show that SPSO is more efficient than the standard PSO.

1 Introduction

The "Particle Swarm Optimizer" algorithm is included in the field of swarm intelligence, and was first introducted by Russel C.Eberrhart and James Kennedy[1][2] in 1995 as a substitute for GA. The PSO algorithm was invented with reference to bird flocks social behavior. Unlike the GA technique that employs genetic manipulations, subsequent actions of respective individuals are influenced by their own movements and those of their companions. It has been proven that PSO can perform on even ground using GA techniques with reference to the problem of function optimization, based on studies after the launch of the theory.

The current canonical particle swarm algorithm loops through a pair of formulas, one for assigning the velocity and another for changing the particle's position:

$$v_i(t+1) = wv_i(t) + c_1r_1(p_i - x_i(t)) + c_2r_2(p_g - x_i(t)) \tag{1}$$

$$x_i(t+1) = x_i(t) + v_i(t) \tag{2}$$

where $x_i(t)$ and $v_i(t)$ are vectors representing the current position and velocity respectively, $0 \leq w < 1$ is an inertia weight determining how much of the particle's previous velocity is preserved, and $c_1, c_2$are two positive acceleration constants, $r_1, r_2$are two uniform random sequences sampled from U(0,1), p_i is the personal best position found by the ith particle and p_g is the best position found by the entire swarm so far.

The stochastic nature of the particle swarm optimizer makes it more difficult to prove (or disprove) like global convergence. Ozcan and Mohan have

S. Tsumoto et al. (Eds.): RSCTC 2004, LNAI 3066, pp. 762–767, 2004.

published the first mathematical analysises regarding the trajectory of a PSO particle[3][4]. From the theoretical analysis[5], the trajectory of the particle $x_i(t)$ converges onto a weighted mean of p_i and p_g. F.Solis and R.Wets[6]have studied the convergence of stochastic search algorithms, most notably that of pure random search algorithms, providing criteria under which algorithms can be considered to be global search algorithms, or merely local search algorithms. Frans Van Den Bergh[7] used their definitions extensively in the study of the convergence characteristics of the PSO and the guaranteed convergence PSO (GCPSO), he proved the PSO is not even guaranteed to be local extrema, and GCPSO can converge on a local extremum.

The convergence behavior of the standard PSO is discussed, and a new particle swarm optimizer, called stochastic PSO (SPSO), that is guaranteed to convergence to the global optimization solution with probability one, is presented in Section 2. Section 3 provides the global convergence analysis of SPSO using the F.Solis and R.Wets' research results. Finally, several examples are simulated to show that SPSO is more efficient than the standard PSO.

2 Analysis of the PSO and Introduction of SPSO

Let w equal zero, the update equations (1) and (2) can be combined as follow:

$$x_i(t+1) = x_i(t) + c_1 r_1 (p_i - x_i(t)) + c_2 r_2 (p_g - x_i(t)) \tag{3}$$

This formula reduces the global search capability, but increases the local search capability. So, if $x_j(t) = p_j = p_g$, particle j will "flying" at the velocity zero. To improve the global search capability, we conserve the current best position of the swarm p_g, and randomly initialize particle j's position $x_j(t+1)$, and other particles are manipulated according to (3), this means

$$p_j = x_j(t+1) \tag{4}$$

$$p_i = p_i, if(f(p_i) < f(x_i(t+1))) \tag{5}$$

$$p_i = x_i(t+1), if(f(p_i) \geq f(x_i(t+1))) \tag{6}$$

$$p_g^{'} = argmin\{f(p_i), i = 1, 2, ..., s\} \tag{7}$$

$$p_g = argmin\{f(p_g^{'}), f(p_g)\} \tag{8}$$

If $p_j = p_g$, then particle j's position $x_j(t+1)$ needs to continue initialize randomly and other particles are manipulated according to (3); if $p_j \neq p_g$, and does not change, then all particles are manipulated according to (3); if $p_j \neq p_g$, and changes p_g, there exists an integer k1j, which is satisfied $x_k(t+1) = p_k = p_g$, then particle k's position $x_k(t)$needs to continue initialize randomly and other particles are manipulated according to (3), thus the global search capability enhanced. Because of the particle's position need to uniformly sample from the domain when $x_j(t) = p_j = p_g$, the modified PSO algorithm called stochastic PSO (SPSO).

3 Convergence Analysis of SPSO Algorithm

3.1 Trajectories Analysis of SPSO Algorithm

To make the problem more tractable, the stochastic components of the update equations, as well as the personal best position of the particle p_i and the best position of the entire swarm p_g, were held constant.

By (3), we have

$$x_i(t+1) = (1-\varphi)x_i(t) + \varphi_1 p_i + \varphi_2 p_g \tag{9}$$

when the initial condition $x_i(0) = x_{i0}$have been specified, the closed form of (6) can be obtained using any suitable technique for solving non-homogeneous recurrence relations. A complete derivation of the equation is given by

$$x_i(t) = k + (x_{i0} - k)(1-\varphi)^t \tag{10}$$

where

$$k = \frac{\varphi_1 p_i + \varphi_2 p_g}{\varphi} \tag{11}$$

Note that the above equations assume that p_g and p_i remain constant while t changes. The actual SPSO algorithm will allow p_g and p_i to change through update equation respectively. Thus the closed form of the update equation presented above remains valid until a better position is discovered, after which the above equations can be used again after recompuing the new values of k. The exact time step at which this will occur depends on the objective function, as well as the values of p_g and p_i. To allow the extrapolation of the sequence it is convenient to rather keep p_g and p_i constant.

Theorem 1. *If* $|1-\varphi| < 1$,

$$\lim_{t\to+\infty} x_i(t) = p_g \tag{12}$$

Proof. By (9),if $|1-\varphi| < 1$,$\lim_{t\to+\infty} x_i(t) = k = \frac{\varphi_1 p_i + \varphi_2 p_g}{\varphi}$,and

$$x_i(t+1) = x_i(t) - (\varphi_1+\varphi_2)x_i(t) + \varphi_1 p_i + \varphi_2 p_g \tag{13}$$

when $t \to +\infty$, $\lim_{t\to+\infty} x_i(t+1) = \lim_{t\to+\infty} x_i(t)$,so

$$-(\varphi_1+\varphi_2)x_i(t) + \varphi_1 p_i + \varphi_2 p_g = 0 \tag{14}$$

because of φ_1, φ_2 are random variables, formula (12) true if and only if $\lim_{t\to+\infty}$ $x_i(t) = p_i = p_g$.

3.2 Global Convergence Analysis of SPSO

For convenience, the relevant definitions proposed by F.Solis and R.Wets have been reproduced below.

Lemma 1. *$f(D(z,\xi)) \leq f(z)$ and if $\xi \in S$,then $f(D(z,\xi)) \leq f(\xi)$*

Where D is a function that constructs a solution to t he problem, ξ is a random vector based on probability space (R^n, B, μ_k), f is the objective function, S is the search space, $\mu_k$is a probability measure on B and B is the σ-algebra of subset of R^n.

Lemma 2. *For any (Borel) subset A of S with v[A]¿0, we have that*

$$\prod_{k=0}^{+\infty}(1 - \mu_k[A]) = 0 \tag{15}$$

Theorem 2. *Suppose that f is a measurable function, S is a measurable subset of R^n and (Lemma1) and (Lemma2) are satisfied. Let $\{Z_k\}_{k=1}^{+\infty}$ be a sequence generated by the algorithm. Then*

$$\lim_{k \to +\infty} P[z_k \in R_\varepsilon] = 1 \tag{16}$$

where $P[z_k \in R_\varepsilon]$ is the probability that at step k, the point z_k generated by the algorithm is in R_ε (the set of global points).

The proof presented here casts the SPSO into the framework of a global stochastic search algorithm, thus allowing the use of Theorem2 to prove convergence. Thus it remains to show that the SPSO satisfies both (Lemma) and (Lemma2).

Let $\{p_{g,t}\}$ be a sequence generated by the SPSO algorithm, where $p_{g,t}$ is the current best position of the swarm at time t. Define function D

$$D(p_{g,t}, x_i(t)) = p_{g,t}, iff(p_{g,t}) \leq f(x_i(t)) \tag{17}$$
$$D(p_{g,t}, x_i(t)) = x_i(t), iff(p_{g,t}) > f(x_i(t)) \tag{18}$$

The definition of D above clearly complies with Lemma1, since the sequence $x_i(t)$is monotonic by definition.

If the SPSO algorithm satisfies the Lemma2, the union of the sample spaces of the particles must cover S, so that

$$S \subseteq \bigcup_{i=1}^{s} M_{i,t} \tag{19}$$

at time step t, where $M_{i,t}$ denotes the support of the sample space of particle i. If$x_j(t) = p_i = p_g$,$M_{j,t} = S$. For other particles, the shape of $M_{j,t}$ is defined as follows:

$$M_{i,t} = x_i(t-1) + \varphi_1(p_i - x_i(t-1)) + \varphi_2(p_g - x_i(t-1)) \tag{20}$$

where $0 \le \varphi_1 \le c_1, 0 \le \varphi_2 \le c_2$. $M_{i,t}$is a hyper-rectangle parameterized by $\varphi_1$and φ_2, with one corner specified by $\varphi_1 = \varphi_2 = 0$ and the other by $\varphi_1 = c_1, \varphi_2 = c_2$. Regardless of the location of these corners it is clear that $v[M_{i,t} \bigcap S] < v[S]$whenever

$$max\{c_1|p_i - x_i(t-1)|, c_2|p_g - x_i(t-1)|\} < 0.5 \times diam(S) \tag{21}$$

where diam(S) denotes the length of S, and v(S) is a closure of S. By theorem1, the lengths of $M_{i,t}$tend to zero as t tends to infinity. Since the volume of each individual $M_{i,t}$ becomes smaller with increasing k values, it is clear that the volume of their union, $v[\bigcup_{i \neq j} M_{i,t}]$, must also decrease. This shows that, except for $k < k'$, with k' finite,

$$v[\bigcup_{i \neq j} M_{i,t} \bigcap S] < v[S] \tag{22}$$

so that the $M_{i,t}$ cannot cover S. Therefore there exists a finite k' so that for all $t \ge k'$ there will be a set $A \subset S$ with $\sum_{i \neq j} \mu_{i,t}[A] = 0$.

But $M_{j,t} = S$, so $\bigcup_{i=1}^{s} M_{i,t} = S$, define the Borel subset A of S, and $A = M_{i,t}$, then $v[A] > 0, \mu_t[A] = \sum_{i=1}^{s} \mu_{i,t}[A] = 1$, thus Lemma2 satisfied, by theorem2, SPSO can be convergent to global best solution with probability one.

4 Performance Evaluation

For the performance evaluation of the SPSO, we will use two functions. They are usual test functions in global optimization.

Goldstein-Price Function:

$f_1(X) = [1 + (1 + x_1 + x_2)^2(19 - 14x_1 + 3x_1^2 - 14x_2 + 6x_1x_2 + 3x_2^2)]$
$\times [30 + (2x_1 - 3x_2)^2(18 - 32x_1 + 12x_1^2 + 48x_2 - 36x_1x_2 + 27x_2^2)]$,

$$x_j \in [-2.0, 2.0] \tag{23}$$

J.D.Schaffer Function:

$$f_2(X) = \frac{\sin^2 \sqrt{x_1^2 + x_2^2} - 0.5}{[1 + 0.001 \times (x_1^2 + x_2^2)]^2} - 0.5, x_j \in [-100.0, 100.0] \tag{24}$$

In the experiments the size of population are all 20, inertia weight decreased from 1.0 to 0.4, acceleration constants and are 1.8 in PSO, and 0.5 in SPSO, max generation is 500, stop critetria is the expression $|F^* - F^{best}| < \varepsilon \times F^*$ (if F*=0, it will be $|F^* - F^{best}| < \varepsilon$). Here F^* is the global optimum and F^{best} denotes the function value of the best individual in current generation. The experimental results are shown in Table 1. Each result was obtained through 50 random runs.

*F_{eval} denotes the function evaluation number.

*F_{per} denotes the function convergence radio.

Table 1. Comparison of *PSO* and *SPSO*

Function	Algorithm	Error	F_{per}	F_{eval}
F1	PSO	0.0001	100	157
F1	SPSO	0.0001	100	16
F2	PSO	0.01	30	68
F2	SPSO	0.01	62	234

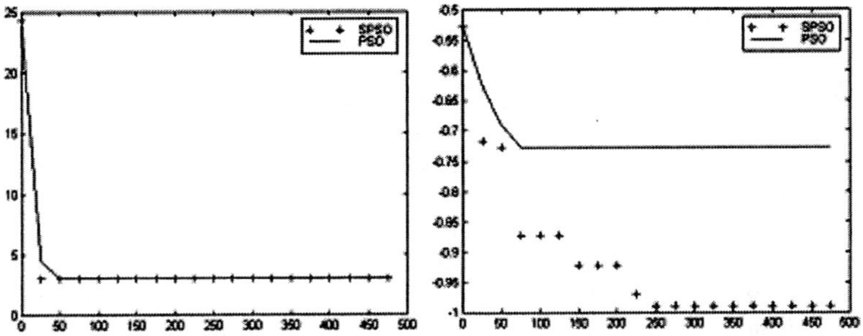

Fig. 1. Comparison of PSO and SPSO

The author suggested the structure of a new PSO algorithm, stochastic PSO (SPSO) in this paper. From the above table, SPSO is a better algorithm than PSO from evaluation number and convergence radio. Future research will include the foundation of more effective and widely used methods of updating equations, carrying out the non-numeric implementation of SPSO and the management of knowledge in SPSO.

References

1. Kennedy, J., Eberhart, R.C.: Particle Swarm Optimization. IEEE International Conference on Neural Networks. (1995) 1942–1948
2. Kennedy, J., Eberhart, R.C.: A New Optimizer Using Particle Swarm Theory. Proceedings of the 6th International Symposium on Micro Machine and Human Science. (1995) 39–43
3. Ozcan,E.,Mohan,C.K.: Analysis of A Simple Particle Swarm Optimization System. Intelligence Engineering Systems Through Artificial Neural Networks (1998) 253–258
4. Ozcan,E.,Mohan,C.K.: Particle Swarm Optimization: Surfing the waves Proc. Of the Congress on Evolutionary Computation 1999 1939–1944
5. Clerc,M.,Kennedy,J.: The Particle Swarm: Explosion, Stability and Convergence in a Multi-Dimensional Complex Space. IEEE Trans. on Evolutionary Computation **16** 2002 58–73
6. Solis,F.,Wets,R.: Minimization by Random Search Techniques. Mathematics of Operations Research. **6** (1981) 19–30
7. Van den Bergh,F.: An Analysis of Particle Swarm Optimizers. Ph.D thesis, University of Pretoria. 2000

Adaptive Dynamic Clone Selection Algorithms

Haifeng Du, Li-cheng Jiao, Maoguo Gong, and Ruochen Liu

Institute of Intelligent Information Processing, Xidian University
710071, Xi'an, China
{haifengdu72,lchjiao1}@163.com

Abstract. Based on the Antibody Clonal Selection Theory of immunology, a novel artificial immune system algorithm, adaptive dynamic clone select algorithm, is put forward. The new algorithm is intended to integrate the local searching with the global and the probability evolution searching with the stochastic searching. Compared with the improved genetic algorithm and other clonal selection algorithms, the new algorithm prevents prematurity more effectively and has high convergence speed. Numeric experiments of function optimization indicate that the new algorithm is effective and useful.

1 Introduction

Clone means repsroducing or propagating asexually. A group of genetically identical cells are descended from a single common ancestor, such as a bacterial colony whose members arose from a single original cell as a result of binary fission. The idea attracts such great attentions that some new algorithms based on clonal selection theory are proposed successively[1][2][3].

A novel clonal selection operator based on Antibody Clonal Selection Theory is presented in this paper, and a corresponding algorithm, Adaptive Dynamic Clone Selection Algorithm (ADCSA), is put forward. Based on the antibody-antibody affinity, antibody–antigen affinity and their dynamic allotting memory units along with the scale of antibody populations, ADCSA can combine the stochastic searching methods with evolutionary searching based on the probability. Furthermore, by using clone selection operator, the algorithm can integrate the global searching and local searching. Simulations of function optimization indicate that ADCSA has better performance than the classical evolutionary algorithm and the Clonal Selection Algorithm in reference[1].

2 Clonal Selection Operator

Just as the same as the Evolutionary Algorithms(EAs)[4], the Artificial Immune System Algorithms work on the encoding of the parameter set rather than the parameter set itself (except where the real-valued individuals are used). Without the loss of

S. Tsumoto et al. (Eds.): RSCTC 2004, LNAI 3066, pp. 768–773, 2004.

universality, we consider maximizing the function $\varphi : \prod_{i=1}^{m}[d_i, u_i] \rightarrow R(d_i < u_i)$, where m is the number of variants to be optimized, namely $X = \{x_1, x_2 \cdots x_m\}$. Set the antigen $\varphi : R^m \rightarrow R$ an objective function. For the binary code, antibody $A \in S^l$, $S^l = \{0,1\}^l$ denotes all binary cluster set with the same length l. $\vec{A} = \{A_1, A_2 \cdots A_n\}$ is the antibody population, and antibody $A_i = \{a_{i1}, a_{i2}, \cdots a_{il}\}$. The binary cluster is divided into m segments with the length l_i, $l = \sum_{i=1}^{m} l_i$, where each segment is expressed as $x_i \in [d_i, u_i]$ $\quad i = 1,2,\cdots,m$ respectively.

The antibody-antigen affinity function f is generally the objective function. Antibody-antibody affinity function is defined as the following equation:

$$D_{ij} = \left\| X_i - X_j \right\| \qquad i, j = 1,2,\cdots,n \tag{1}$$

$\|\bullet\|$ is an arbitrary norm, generally taking Euclidean distance for real-valued coding and Hamming distance for binary coding. $D = (D_{ij})_{n \times n}$ $\quad i, j = 1,2,\cdots,n$ is the affinity matrix of antibody-antibody. D is a symmetrical matrix, which indicates the diversity of the antibody population.

Inspired by the Antibody Clonal Selection Theory of Immunology, the major elements of Clonal Selection Operator are presented as Fig. 1, and the detail explanations of the Clonal Operating, Immune Genetic Operating and Clonal Selection Operating just like reference [3].

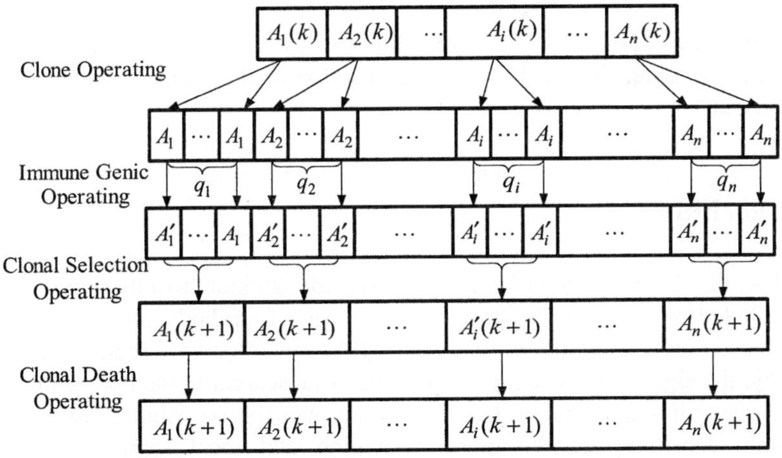

Fig. 1. The main operating processing of the Clonal Selection Operator.

After the clonal selection, the new antibody population is:

$$\vec{A}(k+1) = \{A_1(k+1), A_2(k+1), \cdots, A_i'(k+1), \cdots, A_n(k+1)\} \tag{2}$$

Where, $A_i'(k+1)=A_j(k+1), i\neq j$ and $f(A_i'(k+1))=f(A_j(k+1))$.

One of $A'_i(k+1)$ and $A_j(k+1)$ should be canceled according to the death probability p_d. The death strategies can be either generating a new antibody randomly to replace $A'_i(k+1)$ or $A_j(k+1)$, or using crossover or mutation strategy to generate a new antibody to replace them.

After the action of clonal selection operator, we can acquire the corresponding new antibody populations $\vec{A}(k+1)=\{A_1(k+1), A_2(k+1)\cdots A_n(k+1)\}$, which are equivalent to the memory cells and plasma cell after biologic clonal selection. Here we make no special division about that.

The Clonal Selection Operator is to produce a variation population around the parents according to their affinity, which enlarges the searching area accordingly.

In Eas, for the mutation operator:

$$P\{a\rightarrow b\}=p_m^{d(a,b)}(1-p_m)^{l-d(a,b)} \tag{3}$$

p_m is normally small , the less the Hamming distance $d(a,b)$ is, the bigger $P\{a\rightarrow b\}$. Then the searching area is enlarged.

But in clonal selection operator, the probability that all of the q clone individual is changed to b is:

$$P_1\{\Phi(A_i)\rightarrow b\}=\prod_{i=1}^{q-1}P\{A_i'\rightarrow b\}=\left(p_m^{d(A_i,b)}(1-p_m)^{l-d(A_i,b)}\right)^{q-1} \tag{4}$$

Under the condition of equal probability, the probability that one of the q clone individual is changed to b is:

$$P_2\{\Phi(A_i)\rightarrow b\}=\sum_{i=1}^{q-1}P\{A_i'\rightarrow b\}=(q-1)\times\left(p_m^{d(A_i,b)}(1-p_m)^{l-d(A_i,b)}\right) \tag{5}$$

The bigger q is, the less P_1 and the bigger P_2. As a result, the searching scope extends. Furthermore, the local optimizing function of the clonal selection can realize local search.

3 Algorithm

Based on the antibody-antibody affinity, antibody–antigen affinity and their dynamically allotted memory units along with the scale of antibody populations, Adaptive Dynamic Clone Selection Algorithm (ADCSA) can adaptively regulate its evolution. Thereby, the algorithm can combine the stochastic searching methods with evolutionary searching based on the probability. Synchronously, by using clone selection, the algorithm can integrate the global searching and local searching. The mutate probability, the scale of both memory units and generic antibody units evolve adaptively along with antibody-antibody affinity and antibody-antigen affinity. Using the Clonal Selection Operator, ADCSA is implemented as Fig. 2. Memory unit M (k) records the best antibodies, which include the solution for the problem during algorithm process. Since different mutate probability for the memory unit and generic antibody unit are adopted and p_m^M is less than $p_m^{A_b}$, actually the evolutionary search-adopted and p_m^M is less than $p_m^{A_b}$, actually the evolutionary searching with a certain probability analogous to the genetic algorithm is performed on the memory unit; the stochastic searching is applied to the generic antibody unit. ADCSA adopts the cross-over operator to increase population diversity and improve the convergent speed.

ALGORITHM Adaptive Dynamic Clone Selection Algorithm

Step1: initiate the antibody population $\vec{A}(0)$, enact algorithm parameters.

Step2: Calculate the affinity $f(\varphi(\vec{A}(k)))$.

Step3: Allot adaptively the antibody populations, namely: according to the affinity, the antibody population is disparted to memory unit and generic antibody unit,

$$A(k) = \{M(k), A_b(k)\}$$

Where $M(k) = \{A_1(k), A_2(k), \cdots A_t(k)\}$, $A_b(k) = \{A_{t+1}(k), A_{t+2}(k), \cdots A_n(k)\}$, $t = fix[n \times (s_c + D_{is})]$. *fix*(*) is the integral function below, *fix*(*x*) denotes the most integer less than *x*; s_c is a constant set to assure the size of memory units. Otherwise:

$$D_{is} = \frac{\sqrt{\frac{1}{(n-1)\times n}\sum_{j=1}^{n}\sum_{i=1}^{n} D_{ij}}}{\max_i\{|u_i - d_i|\}}$$

which is used to measure the diversity of antibody population, $0 \le D_{is} \le 1$, the bigger D_{is} is, the better is the diversity.

Step4: regulate the mutate probability: according to the following equation, the corresponding mutate probability of each antibody can be calculated.

$$p_m^i(k) = p_m^c + \left[1 + \exp\left(l \frac{f(\varphi(A_i(k)))}{\sum_{j=1}^{n} f(\varphi(A_j(k)))}\right)\right]^{-1} \qquad i = 1,2,\cdots n$$

A further amendment is made as follows:

$$p_m^i(k) = \begin{cases} p_m^M & p_m^i(k) > p_m^M \quad i = 1,2,\cdots t \\ p_m^{A_b} & p_m^i(k) < p_m^{A_b} \quad i = t+1 \cdots n \end{cases}$$

Where p_m^M and $p_m^{A_b}$ are mutate threshold value of memory unit and generic antibody unit respectively, generally, $p_m^M << p_m^{A_b} < 1$.

Step5: according to the affinity and the clone scale, Perform the clonal operator and get the new antibody population $\vec{A}(k+1)$;

Step6: *k*=*k*+1; if satisfy the halt condition, end, or else return to step2.

Fig. 2. Adaptive Dynamic Clone Selection Algorithms.

Combining the enactment iterative times with hunting condition, here the algorithm is halted at the following criterion:

$$\left| f^{*} - f^{best} \right| < \varepsilon \tag{6}$$

Where f^{*} is the global optimum of f, f^{best} is the current best function value.

4 Numerical Experiments and Discussion

From Eq. (7) to Eq. (10), the test functions are used to test the performance of ADCSA.

$$f_1(x,y) = 1 + x \times \sin(4\pi x) - y \times \sin(4\pi y + \pi) + \frac{\sin(6\sqrt{x^2+y^2})}{6\sqrt{x^2+y^2} + 10^{-15}} \quad x, y \in [-1,1] \tag{7}$$

$$f_2(x,y) = \left(\frac{3}{0.05 + (x^2+y^2)} \right)^2 + (x^2+y^2)^2 \quad x, y \in [-5.12, 5.12] \tag{8}$$

$$f_3(x,y) = -(x^2+y^2)^{0.25} \left(\sin^2 50 (x^2+y^2)^{0.1} + 1.0 \right) \quad x, y \in [-5.12, 5.12] \tag{9}$$

$$f_4(x,y) = 0.5 - \frac{\sin^2 \sqrt{x^2+y^2} - 0.5}{1 + 0.001 \times (x^2+y^2)^2} \quad x, y \in [-10, 10] \tag{10}$$

The comparison of ADCSA and MGA [5] is shown in the table 1. The initial population of ADCSA and MGA are produced randomly, the bracket gives the number of population, the code length of each variable is 22, and the maximum evolutionary generation is 1000. For MGA, the ratio of producing new individual is 90%, the crossover probability and mutate probability are 0.7 and $0.7/l$ respectively. For ADCSA, $p_m^c = 0.005$, $p_m^M = 1/l$, $p_m^{A_b} = 0.3$ $n_c = 0.3$.

The statistic results of T_{av} (the evaluation number of reaching the optimal value) and N_{lov}(the number of immersing into the local optimal value) over all independently repeated for 20 times are shown in table 1. It clearly shows that the performance of ADCSA is much better than MGA. ADCSA has more strong ability to break away the local optimum than MGA; and the convergent speed of ADCSA is faster than MGA. T_{av} in table 1 is only the statistic results without immersing into the local optimal value. It needs to point out that, in 20 tests, there are actually only two times for MGA to break away from the local optimal triumphantly when optimizing function f_4, the mean of evaluation number is 46305. The other two times should owe to the properly chosen initial populations, and the mean evaluation number is 630.

Since function f_4 is very easy to get into the local optimal value, its further comparisons among ADCSA, CSA[1]and MGA is shown in table 2. The condition of CSA is the same as that of ADCSA.

Table 1. The comparison of ADCSA and MGA.

Test functions	ε	n/N_C	T_{av}		N_{lov}	
			ADCSA	MGA	ADCSA	MGA
f_1	0.04	20/30(40)	486	156	0	11
f_2	0.1	20/30(40)	2,832	5,917	0	0
f_3	0.1	20/30(40)	6,737	6,329	0	4
f_4	0.005	20/100(100)	12,218	23,468	0	16

Table 2. The performance comparison of ADCSA, CSA and MGA for function f_4(ε=0.005).

	MGA		ADCSA			CSA		
n/N_C	50	500	20/30	50/75	100/500	20/30	50/75	100/500
T_{av}	/	3,650	7,364	13,110	27,981	7,192	16,668	32,633
N_{lov}	20	11	2	0	0	13	2	0

Table 2 shows that the success of MGA mostly depends on the initial population, and CSA, ADCSA have strong ability to break away from the local optimal value. The choice of initial population has a rather weak influence on their performances. CSA and ADCSA overcome the prematurity to some degree. On the other hand, the antibody scale and clonal scale affect the performance of CSA and ADCSA: the smaller the antibody scale and clonal scale are, the larger the probability of immersing into the local optimal values is. However, the contrary conclusion doesn't hold, if the antibody scale and clonal scale exceed a certain range, the influence becomes weak. Furthermore, the performance of ADCSA is better than that of CSA.

The algorithm using clonal selection Operator is called Immune Clonal Computing (ICC) in our research. More than a simply improved Evolutionary Algorithm (EAs), ICC is essentially different from EAs in both biologic mechanic and manipulated processes.

References

1. L. N. De Castro, F. J. Von Zuben.: The Clonal Selection Algorithm with Engineering Applications, Proc. of GECCO'00, Workshop on Artificial Immune Systems and Their Applications, (2000) 36–37
2. J. Kim, P.J. Bentley.: Towards an artificial immune system for network intrusion detection: an investigation of clonal selection with a negative selection operator. Proceedings of the 2001 Congress on Evolutionary Computation, 2 (2001) 1244 –1252
3. Haifeng DU, Licheng JIAO, Sun'an Wang.: Clonal Operator and Antibody Clone Algorithms. Proceedings of the First International Conference on Machine Learning and Cybernetics, Beijing, (2002) 506–510
4. Michalewicz, Z.: Genetic Algorithms + Data Structures = Evolution Programs. 3rd edn. Springer-Verlag, Berlin Heidelberg New York (1996)
5. Andrew Chipperfield, Peter Fleming, Hartmut Pohlheim, Carlos Fonseca..: Genetic Algorithm TOOLBOX for Use with MATLAB. http://clio.mit.csu.edu.au/subjects/itc554/Src

Multiobjective Optimization Based on Coevolutionary Algorithm

Jing Liu, Weicai Zhong, Li-cheng Jiao, and Fang Liu

Institute of Intelligent Information Processing, Xidian University, Xi'an, 710071 China
neouma@163.com

Abstract. With the intrinsic properties of multiobjective optimization problems in mind, multiobjective coevolutionary algorithm (MOCEA) is proposed. In MOCEA, a Pareto crossover operator, and 3 coevolutionary operators are designed for maintaining the population diversity and increasing the convergence rate. Moreover, a crowding distance is designed to reduce the size of the nondominated set. Experimental results demonstrate that MOCEA can find better solutions at a low computational cost. At the same time, the solutions found by MOCEA scatter uniformly over the entire Pareto front.

1 Introduction

Lots of multiobjective evolutionary algorithms (MOEAs) have been proposed, such as, FFGA [1], NSGA [2], SPEA [3], and so on. At present, all MOEAs are proposed from the following two aspects: (a) Design the fitness of an individual and the selection method such that the population can converge to the Pareto-optimal set. (b) Design the method that can maintain the population diversity such that a well distributed and well spread nondominated set can be obtained.

As well known, premature convergence is a bottleneck problem of EAs. Therefore, when the problem dimension is high, MOEAs are prone to be trapped in the local Pareto-optimal set. Moreover, the convergence rate is slow, which also prevent MOEAs from being applied to practical applications. So what should be also noted is: With the intrinsic properties of MOPs in mind, design the method that not only can prevent premature convergence, but also can increase the convergence rate. Based on this, we propose multiobjective coevolutionary algorithm (MOCEA).

2 Problem Definition

The optimization goal of a general MOP is

$$\min_{\mathbf{x}\in\Omega} \ \mathbf{y}=\boldsymbol{f}(\mathbf{x})=(f_1(\mathbf{x}),f_2(\mathbf{x}),\ldots,f_k(\mathbf{x})) \quad s.t. \ \boldsymbol{e}(\mathbf{x})=(e_1(\mathbf{x}),e_2(\mathbf{x}),\ldots,e_m(\mathbf{x}))\le 0 \tag{1}$$

where $\mathbf{x}=(x_1,x_2,\ldots,x_n)\in \boldsymbol{X}$ is the decision vector, $\mathbf{y}=(y_1,y_2,\ldots,y_k)\in \boldsymbol{Y}$ is the objective vector. $\boldsymbol{X}$ represents the decision space, and $\boldsymbol{Y}$ the objective space. The feasible set

S. Tsumoto et al. (Eds.): RSCTC 2004, LNAI 3066, pp. 774–779, 2004.

X_f={x∈X | e(x) ≤ 0} is defined as the set of decision vectors **x** that satisfy the constraint e(**x**). The image of X_f is denoted as Y_f={f(x) | x∈X_f}.

Definition 1: For any two objective vectors u and v,

$$\boldsymbol{u} < \boldsymbol{v} \;\; iff \;\; \forall i \in \{1,\ldots,n\},\; u_i \le v_i \;\; and \;\; \exists i \in \{1,\ldots,n\},\; u_i < v_i \tag{2}$$

Definition 2: For decision vectors $\boldsymbol{a}$ and $\boldsymbol{b}$, $\boldsymbol{a} \succ \boldsymbol{b}$ ($\boldsymbol{a}$ *dominates* $\boldsymbol{b}$) iff $f(\boldsymbol{a})<f(\boldsymbol{b})$.

Definition 3: x∈X_f is nondominated regarding a set of $A \subseteq X_f$ iff $\nexists \boldsymbol{a} \in A : \boldsymbol{a} \succ \mathbf{x}$.

Definition 4: Let $A \subseteq X_f$. $p(A)$ gives the set of nondominated decision vectors in A:

$$p(A) = \{\boldsymbol{a} \in A \,|\, \boldsymbol{a} \text{ is nondominated regarding } A\} \tag{3}$$

Definition 5: Consider a set of decision vectors $A \subseteq X_f$

(a) The set A is denoted as a local Pareto-optimal set iff

$$\forall \boldsymbol{a} \in A,\; \nexists \mathbf{x} \in X_f,\; \mathbf{x} \succ \boldsymbol{a} \wedge \|\mathbf{x} - \boldsymbol{a}\| < \varepsilon \wedge \| f(\mathbf{x}) - f(\boldsymbol{a}) \| < \delta \tag{4}$$

where $\|\bullet\|$ is a corresponding distance metric and $\varepsilon>0$, $\delta>0$.

(b) The set A is called a global Pareto-optimal set iff $\forall \boldsymbol{a} \in A,\; \nexists \mathbf{x} \in X_f,\; \mathbf{x} \succ \boldsymbol{a}$.

3 Multiobjective Coevolutionary Algorithm

Let P_t represent the current population.

(a) Determine the set of individuals, $p(P_t)$, in P_t. The decision vectors of $p(P_t)$ are nondominated regarding P_t. The fitness of each individual i in $p(P_t)$ is

$$S(i) = \left|\{j \,|\, j \in P_t \wedge i \succ j\}\right| / (N+1) \tag{5}$$

(b) The fitness of each individual j in $P_t \backslash p(P_t)$ is [3]

$$F(j) = 1 + \sum_{i \in p(P_t), i \succ j} S(i) \tag{6}$$

Let $P_{t+1} \leftarrow \varnothing$. The corresponding selection method is described as: (a) Select two individuals i, j at random; (b) If $F(i)<F(j)$ then $P_{t+1} \leftarrow P_{t+1}+\{i\}$, else $P_{t+1} \leftarrow P_{t+1}+\{j\}$.

The external set $\overline{P}_t$ has $\overline{N}$ individuals, and its decision vectors are nondominated among all solutions generated so far. P_t represents the current population, $O_t=p(P_t)$ is the nondominated set regarding P_t, and $\overline{P}_t$ is the external set. We update $\overline{P}_t$ as: (a) Copy O_t to $\overline{P}_t$, obtaining $\overline{P'}_t$, i.e., $\overline{P'}_t \leftarrow \overline{P}_t + O_t$; (b) Determine the nondominated set regarding $\overline{P'}_t$, and assign it to $\overline{P}_{t+1}$, i.e., $\overline{P}_{t+1} \leftarrow p(\overline{P'}_t)$.

$\overline{P}_t$ be the current external set with $\overline{M}(>\overline{N})$ individuals, where $\overline{N}$ is the maximum size of the external set. To get an estimate of the density of solutions surrounding a particular point in the population, we introduce a parameter i_{dist} (called the crowding distance [4]). The crowding distances of the first and the last points along each objective are set to ∞. Thereafter, the solutions are sorted according to the crowding distance and the first $\overline{N}$ points are picked.

Let $\boldsymbol{P}_t$ be the current population, and $\boldsymbol{O}_t = p(\boldsymbol{P}_t)$ be the nondominated set regarding $\boldsymbol{P}_t$. $\boldsymbol{O}_t^a$ and $\boldsymbol{O}_t^b$ are nondominated sets regarding $\boldsymbol{P}_t^a$ and $\boldsymbol{P}_t^b$.

Pareto neighborhood crossover operator: Let $(x_1, x_2, \ldots, x_n) \in \boldsymbol{P}_t$, select an individual $(r_1, r_2, \ldots, r_n)$ in $\boldsymbol{O}_t$ at random, and then generate a new individual $(z_1, z_2, \ldots, z_n)$ according (7) to replace $(x_1, x_2, \ldots, x_n)$, where $U(\bullet, \bullet)$ is a uniform random number.

$$z_i = r_i + U(-1,1) \times (r_i - x_i), \quad i = 1, \ldots, n \tag{7}$$

Cooperating operator: $\boldsymbol{P}_t^a = (\mathbf{x}_1^a, \ldots, \mathbf{x}_M^a)$ and $\boldsymbol{P}_t^b = (\mathbf{x}_1^b, \ldots, \mathbf{x}_N^b)$. For each $(x_1^a, x_2^a, \ldots, x_n^a)$ in $\boldsymbol{P}_t^a$, select an individual $(r_1^b, r_2^b, \ldots, r_n^b)$ in $\boldsymbol{O}_t^b$, then generate a new individual $(z_1^a, z_2^a, \ldots, z_n^a)$ according to (8), which form the next generation $\boldsymbol{P}_{t+1}^a$.

$$z_i^a = r_i^b + U(-1,1) \times (r_i^b - x_i^a), \quad i = 1, \ldots, n \tag{8}$$

Analogously, for each individual $(x_1^b, x_2^b, \ldots, x_n^b)$ in $\boldsymbol{P}_t^b$, select an individual $(r_1^a, r_2^a, \ldots, r_n^a)$ in $\boldsymbol{O}_t^a$ at random, then generate a new individual $(z_1^b, z_2^b, \ldots, z_n^b)$ according to (9), which form the next generation $\boldsymbol{P}_{t+1}^b$.

$$z_i^b = r_i^a + U(-1,1) \times (r_i^a - x_i^b), \quad i = 1, \ldots, n \tag{9}$$

Annexing operator: $\boldsymbol{P}_t^a = (\mathbf{x}_1, \ldots, \mathbf{x}_M)$ and $\boldsymbol{P}_t^b = (z_1, \ldots, z_N)$. If (10) is true,

$$\forall \mathbf{x} \in \boldsymbol{O}_t^a, \ \exists z \in \boldsymbol{O}_t^b, \ z \succ \mathbf{x} \tag{10}$$

(labeled as $\boldsymbol{O}_t^b \rhd \boldsymbol{O}_t^a$), then $\boldsymbol{P}_t^b$ annexes $\boldsymbol{P}_t^a$ to generate $\boldsymbol{P}_{t+1}^b(\boldsymbol{l}_1, \ldots, \boldsymbol{l}_{N+M})$ as follow: $\boldsymbol{l}_i = z_i$, $i=1,\ldots,N$; $\boldsymbol{l}_i$, $i=N+1, \ldots, N+M$ are determined by (11).

$$l_{i,j} = r_j + U(-1,1) \times (r_j - x_{i-N,j}), \; j = 1, \ldots, n \tag{11}$$

Splitting operator: $P_t = (\mathbf{x}_1, \ldots, \mathbf{x}_M)$ is split into two child populations $\boldsymbol{P}_{t+1}^a$ and $\boldsymbol{P}_{t+1}^b$ as follow: randomly select $M/2$ individuals from $\boldsymbol{P}_t$ to create $\boldsymbol{P}_{t+1}^a = (z_1^a, \ldots, z_{M/2}^a)$, and the remainder form $\boldsymbol{P}_{t+1}^b = (z_1^b, \ldots, z_{M/2}^b)$. Then perform the mutation in (12) on one of two populations. Given that $\boldsymbol{P}_{t+1}^a$,

$$z_i^a = \begin{cases} z_i^a & U(0,1) < \frac{1}{n} \\ z_i^a + G(0, \frac{1}{t}) & \text{otherwise} \end{cases}, \quad k = 1, \cdots, n \tag{12}$$

ALGORITHM 1 describes the details of MOCEA.

ALGORITHM 1 Multiobjective Coevolutionary Algorithm

$\boldsymbol{P}^a$ and $\boldsymbol{P}^b$ be two populations and $|\boldsymbol{P}^a| = |\boldsymbol{P}^b| = N$. $\boldsymbol{O}^a$ and $\boldsymbol{O}^b$ are two nondominated sets regarding $\boldsymbol{P}^a$ and $\boldsymbol{P}^b$, respectively. $\overline{\boldsymbol{P}}$ represents the external set, and $|\overline{\boldsymbol{P}}| = \overline{N}$.

Step 1: Initialize $\boldsymbol{P}_0^a$ and $\boldsymbol{P}_0^b$, determine $\boldsymbol{O}_0^a$ and $\boldsymbol{O}_0^b$, $\overline{\boldsymbol{P}}_0 \leftarrow \varnothing$, and $t \leftarrow 0$;

Step 2: Update the external set $\overline{\boldsymbol{P}}_t$ with $\boldsymbol{O}_t^a$ and $\boldsymbol{O}_t^b$, obtaining $\overline{\boldsymbol{P}}_{t+1}$; If $|\overline{\boldsymbol{P}}_{t+1}| > \overline{N}$, then the size of $\overline{\boldsymbol{P}}_{t+1}$ is reduced to $\overline{N}$;

Step 3: Divide $\overline{\boldsymbol{P}}_t$ into two parts: $\overline{\boldsymbol{P}}_t^a$ and $\overline{\boldsymbol{P}}_t^a$, then perform the elitism on $\boldsymbol{P}_t^a$ and $\boldsymbol{P}_t^b$, obtaining the mid-populations $\boldsymbol{P}_t'^a$ and $\boldsymbol{P}_t'^b$;

Step 4: Calculate the fitness of each individual in $\boldsymbol{P}_t'^a$ and $\boldsymbol{P}_t'^b$, obtaining two new populations $\boldsymbol{P}_{t+1/2}^a$ and $\boldsymbol{P}_{t+1/2}^b$;

Step 5: If the termination criterion are reached, output $\overline{\boldsymbol{P}}_{t+1}$ and stop;

Step 6: Perform the Pareto neighborhood operator on each individual in $\boldsymbol{P}_{t+1/2}^a$ and $\boldsymbol{P}_{t+1/2}^b$, obtaining $\boldsymbol{P}_{t+1/2}'^a$ and $\boldsymbol{P}_{t+1/2}'^b$;

Step 7: Perform the mutation in (12) on each individual in $\boldsymbol{P}_{t+1/2}^a$ and $\boldsymbol{P}_{t+1/2}^b$ with probability P_m, obtaining $\boldsymbol{P}_{t+1/2}''^a$ and $\boldsymbol{P}_{t+1/2}''^b$;

Step 8: If $\boldsymbol{O}_{t+1/2}''^a \rhd \boldsymbol{O}_{t+1/2}''^b$, then $\boldsymbol{P}_{t+1/2}''^a$ annexes $\boldsymbol{P}_{t+1/2}''^b$, obtaining $\boldsymbol{P}_{t+1/2}'''^a$; otherwise if $\boldsymbol{O}_{t+1/2}''^b \rhd \boldsymbol{O}_{t+1/2}''^a$, then $\boldsymbol{P}_{t+1/2}''^a$ annexes $\boldsymbol{P}_{t+1/2}''^b$, obtaining $\boldsymbol{P}_{t+1/2}'''^b$; otherwise, perform the cooperating operator on $\boldsymbol{P}_{t+1/2}''^a$ and $\boldsymbol{P}_{t+1/2}''^b$, obtaining $\boldsymbol{P}_{t+1/2}'''^a$ and $\boldsymbol{P}_{t+1/2}'''^b$;

Step 9: If the size of $\boldsymbol{P}_{t+1/2}'''^a$ (or $\boldsymbol{P}_{t+1/2}'''^b$) is equal to $2N$, then perform the splitting operator on $\boldsymbol{P}_{t+1/2}'''^a$ (or $\boldsymbol{P}_{t+1/2}'''^b$), obtaining $\boldsymbol{P}_{t+1}^a$ (or $\boldsymbol{P}_{t+1}^b$); otherwise, let $\boldsymbol{P}_{t+1}^a \leftarrow \boldsymbol{P}_{t+1/2}'''^a$, $\boldsymbol{P}_{t+1}^b \leftarrow \boldsymbol{P}_{t+1/2}'''^b$, $t \leftarrow t+1$, and go to Step 2.

4 Simulation Experiments

The problem dimension is 30 for MO2 and 10 for MO3. The parameters of MOCEA are: N=50, P_m=0.3, $\overline{N}=100$. The parameters of SPEA: the population size is 100, p_m is 0.3, the crossover probability is 0.8, and the size of the external set is 100.

In following experiments, the modified version of $\mathcal{C}$ measure is adopted as (16):

$$\text{MO1: } \min f_1(\mathbf{x}) = 2\sqrt{x_1},\ \min f_2(\mathbf{x}) = x_1(1-x_2)+5,\ s.t.\ 1 \le x_1 \le 4, -20 \le x_2 \le 20 \tag{13}$$

$$\begin{aligned} \text{MO2: } & \min f_1(\mathbf{x}) = x_1,\ \min f_2(\mathbf{x}) = 1-(f_1/g)^2,\ g(\mathbf{x}) = 1+9\cdot(\textstyle\sum_{i=2}^{n} x_i)/(n-1) \\ & s.t.\ 0 \le x_i \le 1,\ i=1,\dots,n \end{aligned} \tag{14}$$

$$\begin{aligned} \text{MO3: } & \min f_1(\mathbf{x}) = x_1,\ \min f_2(\mathbf{x}) = 1-\sqrt{f_1/g}, \\ & g(\mathbf{x}) = 1+10(n-1)+\textstyle\sum_{i=2}^{n}(x_i^2 - 10\cos(4\pi x_i)), \\ & s.t.\ \ 0 \le x_1 \le 1,\ -5 \le x_i \le 5,\ i=2,\dots,n \end{aligned} \tag{15}$$

$$\mathcal{C}(\boldsymbol{A},\boldsymbol{B}) = |\{\boldsymbol{b} \in \boldsymbol{B} : \exists \boldsymbol{a} \in \boldsymbol{A}, \boldsymbol{a} \succ \boldsymbol{b}\}| / |\boldsymbol{B}| \tag{16}$$

where $\boldsymbol{A}, \boldsymbol{B} \subseteq \boldsymbol{X}_f$ are two decision vector sets.

Fig.1~Fig.3 show the comparison between MOCEA and SPEA for MO1~MO3. Fig.1(a) shows that the value of C(MOCEA, SPEA) is large when t is small. When t increases up, the value of C(MOCEA, SPEA) becomes small. From Fig.1(b) and (c) we can see that SPEA converges to the ideal Pareto front only after 10 generations, while SPEA needs 50 generations.

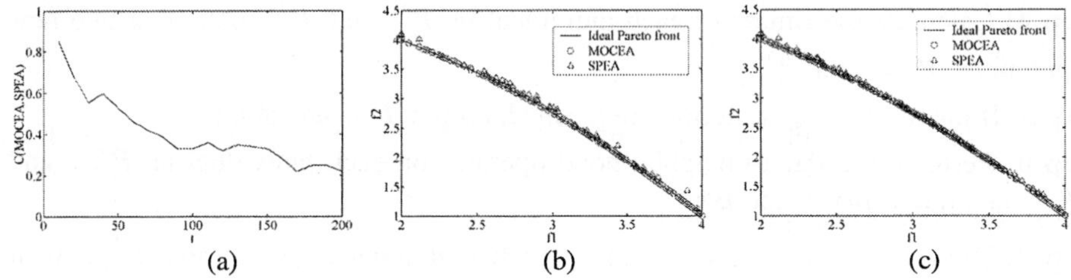

Fig. 1. The comparison between MOCEA and SPEA for MO1. (b) and (c) are the Pareto fronts obtained at 10th and 50th generations, respectively.

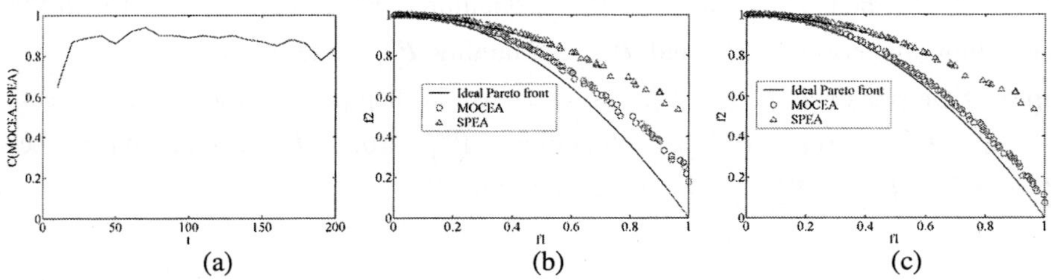

Fig. 2. The comparison between MOCEA and SPEA for MO2. (b) and (c) are the Pareto fronts obtained at 100th and 200th generations, respectively.

Fig.2(a) shows that C(MOCEA, SPEA) keeps a large value throughout the evolutionary process. From Fig.2(b) and (c) we can see that MOCEA approaches to ideal Pareto front gradually, while SPEA is trapped into a local Pareto optimal set.

Fig.3(a) shows that C(MOCEA, SPEA) keeps a large value (about 0.6) throughout the evolutionary process. From Fig.3(b) and (c) we can see that MOCEA converges to the ideal Pareto front after 100 generations, while SPEA needs over 200 generations.

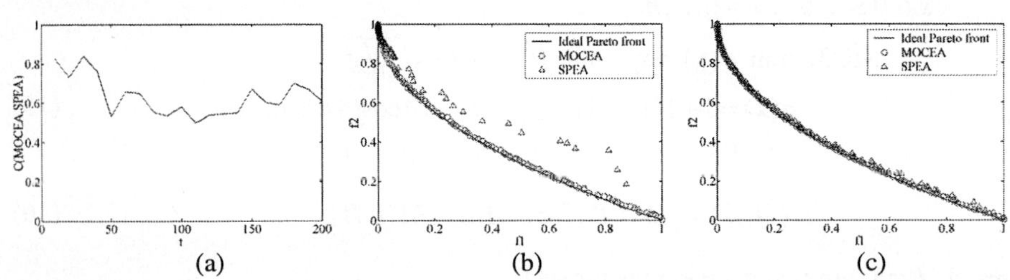

Fig. 3. The comparison between MOCEA and SPEA for MO3. (b) and (c) are the Pareto fronts obtained at 100th and 200th generations, respectively.

5 Conclusion

Experimental results show that MOCEA can effectively maintain the population diversity and obtain a Pareto front distributed uniformly. In addition, for the high dimensional MOPs, MOCEA can obtain high quality solutions.

References

1. C. M. Fonseca, P. J. Fleming, Multiobjective optimization and multiple constraint handling with evolutionary algorithms—part I: A unified formulation. IEEE Trans. on Systems, Man, and Cybernetics 28(1), 1998: 26–37.
2. N. Srinivas, K. Deb, Multiobjective optimization using nondominated sorting in genetic algorithms. Evolutionary Computation, 2(3), 1994: 221–248.
3. E. Zitzler, L. Thiele, Multiobjective evolutionary algorithms: A comparative case study and the strength pareto approach. IEEE Trans. on Evolutionary Computation. 3(9), 1999: 257-271.
4. K. Deb, S. Agrawal, A. Pratap, T. Meyarivan, A Fast Elitist Non-Dominated Sorting Genetic Algorithm for Multi-Objective Optimization: NSGA-II, Indian Institute of Technology Kanpur Kanpur, India, KanGAL Rep.200001, 2000.

Extracting Protein-Protein Interaction Sentences by Applying Rough Set Data Analysis

Filip Ginter[1,2], Tapio Pahikkala[1,2], Sampo Pyysalo[1,2], Jorma Boberg[1,2], Jouni Järvinen[1,2], and Tapio Salakoski[1,2]

[1] Turku Centre for Computer Science (TUCS)
[2] Department of Information Technology, University of Turku
Lemminkäisenkatu 14 A, FIN-20520 Turku, Finland

Abstract. In this paper, we introduce a way to apply rough set data analysis to the problem of extracting protein-protein interaction sentences in biomedical literature. Our approach builds on decision rules of protein names, interaction words, and their mutual positions in sentences. In order to broaden the set of potential interaction words, we develop a morphological model which generates spelling and inflection variants of the interaction words. We evaluate the performance of the proposed method on a hand-tagged dataset of 1894 sentences and show a precision-recall break-even performance of 79,8% by using leave-one-out cross-validation.

1 Protein-Protein Interactions

The amount of published knowledge in the biomedical domain is overwhelming, and due to the introduction of high-throughput methods it grows at an unprecedented rate. While there are a number of efforts to identify and store information in databases [1, 2], most knowledge remains available only in unstructured text form in scientific articles and their abstracts. The premier bibliographic database in the field, PubMed[1], contains over 14 million citations and more than 7 million abstracts. The amount of data makes manual information extraction a formidable task and is enough to deluge computationally expensive automatic information extraction systems such as those based on sentence parsing [3].

A number of projects have focused on the development of methods for extracting protein-protein interactions (see e.g. [4] for a recent survey). While most of the previous work has concentrated on extraction on the level of publication abstracts, we present a method for extracting sentences actually describing protein-protein interactions. The proposed method is highly efficient and it is additionally capable of explaining the decisions that have been made.

2 Information Systems and Decision Rules

This section is devoted to some basic concepts of rough set data analysis. We adopt here the notation used by Pawlak in [5]. An *information system* is a pair $\mathcal{S} = (U, A)$,

[1] `http://www.ncbi.nlm.nih.gov/PubMed/`

S. Tsumoto et al. (Eds.): RSCTC 2004, LNAI 3066, pp. 780–785, 2004.

where U is a finite nonempty sets of *objects* called the *universe* and A is a finite sets of *attributes*. With every attribute $a \in A$, we associate a set V_a of its *values*. Furthermore, each attribute $a \in A$ is a mapping $a\colon U \to V_a$.

Let $\mathcal{S} = (U, A)$ be an information system. With every subset $B \subseteq A$, we may associate a language For(B). Formulas of For(B) are built up of attribute-value pairs (a, v), where $a \in B$ and $v \in V_a$, by means of logical connectives $\vee$, $\wedge$, and $\neg$ in a canonical way.

For any $\Phi \in$ For(B), we denote by $\|\Phi\|_{\mathcal{S}}$ the set of all objects $x \in U$ satisfying Φ in $\mathcal{S}$, and refer it to as the *meaning* of Φ in $\mathcal{S}$. The meaning $\|\Phi\|_{\mathcal{S}}$ of Φ in $\mathcal{S}$ is defined inductively as follows:

$$\begin{aligned}
\|(a,v)\|_{\mathcal{S}} &= \{x \in U \mid a(x) = v\};\\
\|\Phi \vee \Psi\|_{\mathcal{S}} &= \|\Phi\|_{\mathcal{S}} \cup \|\Psi\|_{\mathcal{S}};\\
\|\Phi \wedge \Psi\|_{\mathcal{S}} &= \|\Phi\|_{\mathcal{S}} \cap \|\Psi\|_{\mathcal{S}};\\
\|\neg\Phi\|_{\mathcal{S}} &= (\|\Phi\|_{\mathcal{S}})^{\mathsf{C}}.
\end{aligned}$$

If we distinguish in an information system $\mathcal{S} = (U, A)$ two subsets C and D of A, called *condition* and *decisions attributes*, respectively, then the system will be called a *decision table*. We assume that $C \cap D = \emptyset$ and $C \cup D = A$. A *decision rule* in $\mathcal{S}$ is an expression $\Phi \to \Psi$, where $\Phi \in$ For(C) and $\Psi \in$ For(D), and C and D are the condition and the decision attributes of $\mathcal{S}$, respectively. With every decision rule $\Phi \to \Psi$, we associate a *certainty factor*

$$\mathrm{cer}_{\mathcal{S}}(\Phi \to \Psi) = \frac{\mathrm{card}(\|\Phi \wedge \Psi\|_{\mathcal{S}})}{\mathrm{card}(\|\Phi\|_{\mathcal{S}})}.$$

We will also use a *coverage factor* of the decision rule $\Phi \to \Psi$ defined by

$$\mathrm{cov}_{\mathcal{S}}(\Phi \to \Psi) = \frac{\mathrm{card}(\|\Phi \wedge \Psi\|_{\mathcal{S}})}{\mathrm{card}(\|\Psi\|_{\mathcal{S}})}.$$

The certainty factor is the frequency of objects having the property Ψ among the objects which have the property Φ, and the coverage factor is the frequency of the objects having the property Φ in the set of objects which have the property Ψ.

3 Decision Rules Based on Interaction Words

The set of interaction words is "rough" (or "fuzzy") in a sense that some instances of a certain word describe a protein-protein interaction, but other instances do not. *Potential interaction words* are the words that have at least once acted as an interaction word in some sentence describing an interaction.

We assume that protein-protein interaction sentences always contain at least two *proteins* that are interacting, and an interaction word describing the type of the interaction. Therefore, in this paper we concentrate only on sentences which contain at least two protein names. For each potential interaction word appearing in such a sentence, we consider three possibilities how the word can be related to the proteins of the sentence:

Table 1. A simple decision table

U	WORD	POSITION	INTERACTION
x_1	activity	after	no
x_2	link	after	no
x_3	repair	after	no
x_4	required	after	no
x_5	binds	middle	yes
x_6	form	middle	yes
x_7	link	middle	yes
x_8	regulate	middle	yes

a potential interaction word may appear *before* all the proteins, in the *middle* of some proteins, or *after* all the proteins. For example, let us consider the following sentences; the first can be found in [6] and the second in [7].

1. "All our data are consistent with models in which `RAD17`, `RAD24` and `MEC3` are coordinately *required* for the *activity* of one or more DNA *repair* pathways that *link* DNA damage to cell cycle arrest."
2. "The head domain of `talin` thus *binds* to `integrins` to *form* a *link* to the `actin` cytoskeleton and can thus *regulate* `integrin` function."

The first sentence contains three proteins `MEC3`, `RAD17`, and `RAD24`, and four words *activity*, *link*, *repair*, and *required* that are potential interaction words, but this sentence does not describe an interaction. The second sentence contains the proteins `actin`, `integrins`, and `talin`, and the potential interaction words *binds*, *form*, *link*, and *regulate*. This sentence describes several protein-protein interactions.

Let us now consider more formally the structure of the decision table $\mathcal{S} = (U, A)$. The set of objects U is such that each object in U corresponds to one instance of one potential interaction word. The attribute set of $\mathcal{S}$ contains the condition attributes WORD and POSITION and the decision attribute INTERACTION. The value set of the attribute WORD contains all known potential interaction words and the value set of POSITION contains the values "before", "middle", and "after". The decision attribute INTERACTION may have the values "yes" or "no". The above sentences can be represented by a decision table given in Table 1. Note that the word *link* has now two roles: *link* describes an interaction in the second sentence, but not in the first one.

Next we will describe how we build up the decision table $\mathcal{S}$. Suppose that we have a training set of sentences, labeled as either interaction or non-interaction sentences. It is also essential that the protein names are tagged in the sentences. Note that there exist several methods for automatic identification of protein names in biomedical text, many of which are evaluated in [4]. Furthermore, the training sentences that are labeled as interaction sentences must be tagged to recognize the words that actually describe protein-protein interactions – these words form the set of potential interaction words V_{WORD}. After obtaining the set V_{WORD}, the set of training sentences must be re-tagged to further identify all potential interaction words in them (even though these potential interaction words do not necessarily describe interactions in these sentences). After the tagging phase the decision table $\mathcal{S}$ can be formed as described above.

We end this section by presenting how we actually make the decisions. Let us assume that we have a decision table $\mathcal{S}$ obtained by examining some training set of sentences. Let us then consider a sentence Σ, not belonging to the set of training examples, which contains at least two protein names. We can represent each instance of a potential interaction word in Σ by a formula $\Phi \in \mathrm{For}(C)$, where C is the set of condition attributes of $\mathcal{S}$, that is, $C = \{\textsc{Word}, \textsc{Position}\}$. For instance, if Σ contains the potential interaction word *bind* in the middle of some protein names of Σ, we may represent this situation by the formula $(\textsc{Word}, \mathrm{bind}) \wedge (\textsc{Position}, \mathrm{middle})$. We also expand all these formulas Φ to a decision rule of the form $\Phi \to (\textsc{Interaction}, \mathrm{yes})$. Since each instance of a potential interaction word induces one such rule, we may attach a set $R(\Sigma)$ of decision rules to the sentences Σ. Further, for each decision rule $\Phi \to \Psi \in R(\Sigma)$, we may now compute the certainty factor $\mathrm{cer}_{\mathcal{S}}(\Phi \to \Psi)$ and the coverage factor $\mathrm{cov}_{\mathcal{S}}(\Phi \to \Psi)$ determined by $\mathcal{S}$. In our experiments we assumed that $R(\Sigma)$ can possibly be a multiset, because a potential interaction word can appear twice in a similar position in the same sentence.

Because there are usually several rules that can be applied for a sentence Σ, the problem is now how to combine the information given by the certainty and the coverage factors of the rules in $R(\Sigma)$. Of course, there are several ways to do this. Suppose that Σ contains k instances of potential interaction words; this means that $R(\Sigma)$ contains k rules, that is, $R(\Sigma) = \{\Phi_i \to \Psi_i \mid 1 \leq i \leq k\}$. We introduce the following aggregate value of the rules related to the sentence Σ:

$$\mathrm{agg}_{\mathcal{S}}(\Sigma) = \sum_{i=1}^{k} \mathrm{cer}_{\mathcal{S}}(\Phi_i \to \Psi_i) \cdot \mathrm{cov}_{\mathcal{S}}(\Phi_i \to \Psi_i).$$

This value can be interpreted so that the greater $\mathrm{agg}_{\mathcal{S}}(\Sigma)$ is, the more likely the sentence Σ describes an interaction.

Let us also define for the sake of generality that if Σ is a sentence that does not contain at least two protein names or $R(\Sigma) = \emptyset$, then $\mathrm{agg}_{\mathcal{S}}(\Sigma) = 0$.

4 Morphological Model of Interaction Words

The set of potential interaction words $V_{\textsc{Word}}$ needs to be as broad as possible. We start with a set consisting of words that describe a protein-protein interaction in some training sentence labeled as an interaction sentence – in our experiments, which are described in Section 5, the set $V_{\textsc{Word}}$ originally contained 354 unique words. Initially the set $V_{\textsc{Word}}$ contains only the inflected forms occurring in the corpus. Thus, for example, the set $V_{\textsc{Word}}$ might contain the word *activated*, but not the words *activates, activate*, or *activating*. A straightforward way to extend the set is to consider all inflected forms of the words, as opposed to only the forms in which they actually appear in the corpus. It is further important to consider spelling variations like *localize/localise*, *labeled/labelled*, *coactivate/co-activate*.

We develop a two-level morphological model, a formalism introduced by Koskenniemi [8], which we use to generate the various inflections, spelling variants, and derivations of the words in the set $V_{\textsc{Word}}$ obtaining a set of 158 verb stems, 41 noun stems, and 14 adjective or adverb stems. From these 213 stems, our model generates 1304 forms, considerably extending the set $V_{\textsc{Word}}$.

5 Experimental Setting

We compiled a corpus of 1894 sentences manually annotated as containing an interaction (1114 sentences) or not containing an interaction (780 sentences). Additionally the proteins were identified in all sentences, and in the interaction sentences also the interaction words were marked up.

We used the leave-one-out crossvalidation to evaluate the proposed method. We excluded each sentence Σ in turn from the corpus and obtained from the remaining sentences the decision table S so that first we formed the set V_{WORD} consisting of interaction words of interaction sentences and then expanded V_{WORD} by applying the morphological model of Section 4. Then we re-tagged the sentences by marking each word from the expanded V_{WORD} as a potential interaction word, and finally we formed the actual table S from these tagged sentences. When computing the $\text{agg}_S(\Sigma)$-value for the excluded sentence Σ, we first searched all the words of V_{WORD} of S which can be found in Σ. Then we constructed $R(\Sigma)$ and for each rule $\Phi \to \Psi \in R(\Sigma)$ we computed the certainty and the coverage factors that were used to compute $\text{agg}_S(\Sigma)$.

A straightforward way to construct a classifier is to use a suitable threshold for $\text{agg}_S(\Sigma)$ when deciding whether an unseen sentence is an interaction sentence. However, the selection of such a threshold is a non-trivial and vague task. Therefore, we proceed in a different manner to find out the capability of our method. Namely, we may order the sentences in a descending order with respect to their $\text{agg}_S(\Sigma)$-values to obtain a list L of sentences ordered in such a manner that if a sentence Σ_1 appears in L before a sentence Σ_2, then Σ_1 is more likely an interaction sentence than Σ_2. We noticed in our experiments that if we take the first 50 sentences from L, 49 of them are interaction sentences. Similarly, when selecting 100, 150, and 200 leading sentences of L, we obtain 95, 140, and 189 interaction sentences, respectively.

We also compute the precision-recall curve from this ordered list L of sentences in such a way that we move sentences one by one from the beginning of L to the set of sentences classified as interaction sentences, and the sentences remaining in L form the set of sentences classified as non-interaction sentences. At each step we compute the corresponding precision and recall values based on the current classification. The precision-recall curve is presented in Figure 1. The value of the precision-recall break-even point, the point at which precision and recall values are equal, is 79.8%.

Conclusions

In this paper, we introduced a way to apply rough set data analysis to the protein-protein interaction extraction problem. The method was based on decision rules of proteins, interaction words, and their mutual locations in sentences. We also presented a way to combine information given by the certainty and coverage factors of the rules related to a certain sentence. Our method is efficient and it also has the advantage that it is capable of explaining the decisions that have been made.

Acknowledgment

This work was supported by Tekes, the National Technology Agency of Finland.

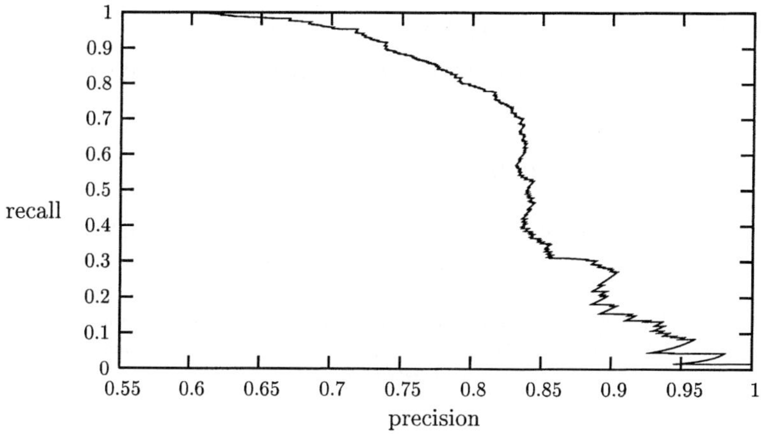

Fig. 1. The precision-recall curve

References

1. Bader, G., Donaldson, I., Wolting, C., Ouellette, B., Pawson, T., Hogue, C.: BIND – the biomolecular interaction network database. Nucleic Acids Research **29** (2001) 242–245
2. Xenarios, I., Rice, D., Salwinski, L., Baron, M., Marcotte, E., Eisenberg, D.: DIP: The database of interacting proteins. Nucleic Acids Research **28** (2000) 289–291
3. Temkin, J., Gilder, M.: Extraction of protein interaction information from unstructured text using a context-free grammar. Bioinformatics **19** (2003) 2046–2053
4. Bunescu, R., Ge, R., Kate, R., Marcotte, E.M., Mooney, R., Ramani, A.K., Wong, Y.W.: Comparative experiments on learning information extractors for proteins and their interactions. Artificial Intelligence in Medicine. Special Issue on Summarization and Information Extraction from Medical Documents (2004) (to appear)
5. Pawlak, Z.: Rough sets, decision algorithms and Bayes' theorem. European Journal of Operational Research **136** (2002) 181–189
6. Lydall, D., Weiner, T.: G2/M checkpoint genes of saccharomyces cerevisiae: further evidence for roles in DNA replication and/or repair. Molecular and General Genetic **256** (1997) 638–651
7. Calderwood, D., Zent, R., Grant, R., Rees, D., Hynes, R., Ginsberg, M.: The talin head domain binds to integrin beta subunit cytoplasmic tails and regulates integrin activation. The Journal of Biological Chemistry **274** (1999) 28071–28074
8. Koskenniemi, K.: Two-level model for morphological analysis. In Bundy, A., ed.: Proceedings of the Eighth International Joint Conference on Artificial Intelligence, 8-12 August 1983, Karlsruhe, West Germany, William Kaufmann, Inc. (1983) 683–685

Feature Synthesis and Extraction for the Construction of Generalized Properties of Amino Acids

Witold R. Rudnicki[1] and Jan Komorowski[2]

[1] Interdisciplinary Centre for Mathematical and Computational Modelling, Warsaw University
Pawinskiego 5a, 02-106, Warsaw, Poland
W.Rudnicki@icm.edu.pl
[2] The Linnaeus Centre for Bioinformatics, Uppsala University
BMC, Box 598, Husargatan 3, SE-751 24 Uppsala, Sweden
Jan.Komorowski@lcb.uu.se

Abstract. Amino acid similarity matrices are used for protein sequence comparison. It has been shown previously that they can be reconstructed from equivalence classes between amino acids. The goal of the current study is to propose an algorithm for identification of the properties that generate these equivalence classes. An approximate reasoning method for feature extraction and synthesis is developed to this end. It is shown that these equivalence classes are related with the amino acid properties that are important for the formation of the protein structure. The algorithm presented in this study works best for bit-patterns, which are frequently encountered in bit-vector representations.

1 Introduction

Discovering similarity between protein sequences is one of the most important fields of bioinformatics. Algorithms, which are used for this goal, such as BLAST [1] or FASTA [2] utilize the so-called amino acid similarity matrices (AAS matrices). In a very general sense, these matrices are an experimental record of how often the amino acids are substituted for each other during molecular evolution. Each element of the matrix is indexed by two amino acids and its value is related to the probability of substituting one of the amino acids with the other one.

AAS matrices belonging to the PAM [3] and BLOSUM [4] families are used most often. They are based on the frequencies of amino acids substitution in related protein sequences. An example of an AAS matrix and its application in the sequence alignment is given in the supplementary material available on the web at [5]. Each AAS matrix is suitable for a comparison of sequences at a certain evolutionary distance. AAS matrices can be considered to be a source of generalized information about evolution on the molecular level. It is interesting which properties of amino acids are conserved in evolution and which seem to be less important. It has been shown that elements of AAS matrices are correlated with the hydrophobicity and size of amino acids [6-8]. All AAS matrices exhibit similar correlations with amino acid properties (see e.g. [6]). The subtle differences in correlations between amino acid properties and AAS matrices are not suitable for the analysis of importance of amino acid prop-

S. Tsumoto et al. (Eds.): RSCTC 2004, LNAI 3066, pp. 786–791, 2004.

erties at various evolutionary distances. We explore an alternative approach here that enables such analysis. AAS matrices are reconstructed with the help of specially defined equivalence classes between amino acids. We assume that equivalence classes arise from the amino acid properties. In a previous study [9], we have shown that using equivalence classes of amino acids, it is possible to reconstruct the experimental AAS. The goal of the current study is to find generalized amino acid properties that lead to the equivalence classes obtained previously. Generalized properties are defined here as subsets of the amino acid property space. The ultimate goal in this line of research is the analysis of the variability of the generalized properties that are used for reconstructing the AAS matrices that are suitable for sequence comparisons at various evolutionary distances.

2 Methods

Equivalence classes are represented by bit-patterns. Several equivalence classes are required to represent the amino acids in the reconstruction of the AAS matrices from the BLOSUM and PAM families. Hence, each amino acid is represented by a bit–vector, where each position of the bit-vector corresponds to some equivalence class. Elements of the AAS matrices are obtained as a scalar product of bit-vectors representing a given pair of amino acids. Several hundred physical, conformational and bio-statistical parameters of amino acids were reported to date. Kanehisa et al [6] collected 437 properties in the AAindex database. All properties from this database are used in our analysis.

In the first step, bit patterns are extracted from all bit-vector representations of AAS matrices, separately for the PAM and BLOSUM families. All unique bit patterns are collected and stored for further use. Significant variability in bit-vector representations of amino acids [9] does not allow for an exact derivation of the generalized properties. Instead, approximate reasoning methods based on approximate data sets are needed.

2.1 Non-randomness of Equivalence Classes

The simplest equivalence class for amino acids may be defined by requiring that the value of a certain property should be contained between some limiting values. If it is the case, sorting amino acids according to the values of this property should reveal a bit-pattern with a continuous block of 1s. In a more complicated case, the equivalence class could be defined as a product of two properties. In such case, the pattern mentioned earlier may contain gaps consisting of amino acids that did not fulfill conditions for the second property. However, the number of the gaps should not be too high. A procedure utilizing this reasoning is applied to all representations of the AAS matrices. For each bit-pattern, we record properties that lead to a block with the smallest number of gaps in the ordered pattern. Properties that appear most often are recorded. Then, the same procedure is repeated with a randomized property database, in order to check validity of the results.

2.2 Construction of the Generalized Properties

The heuristic procedure described above is able to detect relations between bit-patterns and amino acid properties. However, it is not suitable for the generation of the generalized properties that would explain equivalence classes. It is therefore extended and refined so as to allow constructing subsets in the amino acid property space. These subsets contain generalized properties consistent with the observed equivalence classes.

One should note that each bit-pattern defines two equivalence classes: amino acids that were assigned 1s, and amino acids that were assigned 0s. In principle, one cannot exclude that a generalized property may be more naturally defined for the equivalence class defined by 0s. Hence, the generalized properties should be created both for the initial pattern and its complement (inverted pattern). It may be also noted that by defining a property as an interval on the property scale, we create two subsets – inside and outside of the interval. Neither in this case can one exclude the possibility that a given bit-pattern would be related to the outside of the interval. Therefore, for a single bit-pattern the generalized property based on the single amino acid property is defined in four ways:

$$(\text{Original pattern or Inverted pattern}) \times (\text{Inside or Outside})$$

Obviously, the definitions of the generalized properties may be also defined by more than a single property. In such a case, the number of possible combinations is higher. One should note, however, that a combination of the original pattern for one property, with the inverted pattern for the other property leads to the empty set. For example, for a generalized property built from two basic properties, the number of possible combinations is eight:

$$\text{Original pattern} \times (\text{Inside or Outside})_1 \times (\text{Inside or Outside})_2$$
$$\text{Inverted pattern} \times (\text{Inside or Outside})_1 \times (\text{Inside or Outside})_2$$

In this study, generalized properties are constructed with at most three basic properties, which leads to 16 possible combinations.

PROCEDURE: Construction of generalized properties:

```
For each pattern BPi {
 Create BPiinverse
 For each property pj{
  For BPi and BPiinverse {
   Construct generalized property PINSj and POUTj
   Check if pattern can be explained by PINSj or POUTj
   For each property pk {
    Construct generalized property PINSk and POUTk
    Check if pattern can be explained by
     (PINSj or POUTj) X (PINSk or POUTk)
    For each property pk {
     Construct generalized property PINSl and POUTl
     Check if pattern can be explained by
     (PINSj or POUTj) X (PINSk or POUTk) X (PINSl or POUTl)
}}}}}
```

The algorithm outlined above utilizes two elementary operations. In the first one, a minimal interval for the basic property is found so that all amino acids in the equivalence class are included in this interval. The false positives – amino acids for which the property is inside the minimal interval, but which are not included in the equivalence class – are then found. If the set of false positives is empty, then the generalized property that is compatible with the equivalence class coded by the bit-pattern is found. Another elementary operation is used for the generalized properties that are defined with two or three basic properties. In this case, a set of common false positives (a product of the sets containing false positives for each property) is found. Again, if this set is empty, the generalized property defined by the combination of the basic properties is compatible with the equivalence class coded with the bit-pattern.

3 Results

3.1 Non-randomness of the Equivalence Classes

The properties that are selected most often as related to the bit-patterns are: the normalized frequency of alpha-helix, the normalized frequency of alpha-helix in all-alpha classes, the average reduced distance for the side chain, the normalized relative frequency of the helix end, the conformational parameter of the beta-structure, the average flexibility indices and the residue volume. All these properties are strongly correlated with either hydrophobicity or the size of the molecule. This result is in a good agreement with the previous findings [5].

Patterns that are associated with these properties are found in almost all bit-vector representations of AAS matrices. For a majority of the matrices, these properties are observed at least 200 times for each AAS matrix with the maximum number of hits exceeding 500. In the case of a randomly shuffled database, patterns associated with random properties appear with a much lower frequency. The number of hits never exceeded 100 and only very few properties scored more than 50 hits for a single AAS matrix. This suggests that relations between bit-patterns and amino acid properties are not random artifacts of the data.

3.2 Construction of the Generalized Properties

The amino acid property database compiled by Kanehisa et al (AAindex) [6], the Z-scale descriptors derived by Sandberg et al. [8] and the principal components derived by Venkatarajan and Braun [7] (referred to as E-scale) are used to find generalized properties related to bit-patterns. It has been reported in the literature that almost all variability of the amino acid property space can be explained by five independent orthogonal coordinates [7, 8]. Obviously, 437 properties in the AAindex database are highly correlated. A subset of 5 uncorrelated properties, with the correlation coefficient between each pair lower than 0.2, is selected as a representation of the database. Properties related to the bit-patterns obtained from the bit-vector representations of the amino acids are used to construct this subset. The following five properties are chosen: the normalized frequency of alpha-helix, the average reduced distance for the side chain, the normalized composition of membrane proteins, the transfer free energy from vap to chx and the normalized frequency of the extended structure.

Generalized properties are derived separately for the BLOSUM and PAM families for patterns that appear at least 200-, 50- and 10 times in the bit-vector representations of amino acids. To check the consistency of the procedure, generalized properties are also derived for the database in which values of the properties are randomly shuffled between amino acids. Initially, the properties that should be used in the generation of the generalized properties were obtained with the minimal entropy approach but it turned out that in our case it could lead to over-fitting. This effect was strongest when a set of correlated properties was used. This finding led us to a procedure that uses a set of a priori defined generalized properties. Even with this approach, a significant number of false generalized properties are discovered for all patterns. The discrimination between shuffled and original database was most clear for the e-scales of Venkatarajan and Braun.

Procedure developed in our study reproduces almost all equivalence classes using the 5 orthogonal properties (see Table 1). Initial tests showed that extending the database beyond 5 properties does not give much improvement above the level of statistical noise. The reconstruction achieved the highest degree of success for the bit-patterns that appear most frequently, and the reconstruction quality is best for these bit-patterns. Almost all of them can be reconstructed using only two properties. In most of the cases, the procedure described above produces several alternative generalized properties for the same bit-pattern. Therefore, a careful analysis is required in the interpretation of the results. We may assume that similar equivalence classes should be explained by generalized properties based on the same basic properties, differing by small differences between borders of the defining intervals. Generalized properties that can be extended to cover several equivalence classes by slight modifications of the thresholds levels in their definitions should be considered as realistic explanations of the bit-patterns. On the other hand, the generalized properties, which are artifacts of the construction procedure, need not be easily extended. A procedure for the automated extraction of the generalized properties is a subject of further studies.

Table 1. The number of bit-patterns reconstructed from generalized properties obtained from the physical properties. The generalized properties were based on three properties at most. The number of reconstructed bit-patterns based on at most two properties is shown in parenthesis.

	Z-scales		*E-scales*		*AAindex5*	
	PAM	BLOSUM	PAM	BLOSUM	PAM	BLOSUM
			n>200			
all patterns	76	112	76	112	76	112
reconstructed	76 (72)	112 (110)	75 (72)	112 (109)	76 (64)	111 (109)
			n>50			
all patterns	214	468	214	468	214	468
reconstructed	209 (179)	464 (415)	210 (171)	465 (415)	206(166)	458 (410)
			n>10			
all patterns	648	1460	648	1460	648	1460
reconstructed	594 (438)	1417 (1099)	594 (427)	1431 (1119)	605 (425)	1406 (1113)

4 Conclusions

We have introduced a method for extracting relationships between AAS matrices and amino acid properties. We effectively perform feature extraction and synthesis from proteomic data. The method is based on a broadly treated approximate reasoning methodology. It is demonstrated that the equivalence classes arising from the bit-vector representations of the amino acids may be reconstructed from the generalized properties of amino acids. The properties are defined as suitable subsets of the amino acid property space. Elucidation of the biologically important generalized properties remains a subject of current studies.

Acknowledgements

This research receives partial support from the Human Research Potential & the Socio-economic Knowledge Base: Access to Research Infrastructures program under the HPRI-CT-2001-00153 contract, The Knut and Alice Wallenberg Foundation and The Swedish Foundation for Strategic Research. The computations were carried out at the Interdisciplinary Centre for Mathematical and Computational Modelling, Warsaw University (ICM), grant G26-11.

References

1. Altschul, S.F., Gish, W., Miller, W., Myers, E.W. and Lipman D.J. (1990) Basic local alignment search tool, *J. Mol. Biol.*, **215**, 403-410.
2. Pearson, W.R. and Lipman, D.J. (1988) Improved tools for biological sequence comparison, *P. Natl* Acad. Sci. USA, 85, 2444-2448.
3. Dayhoff, M.O., Schwartz, R.M., Orcutt, B.C. (1978) A model of evolutionary change in proteins. In Dayhoff, M.O. (ed.), Atlas of Protein Sequence and Structure, Vol. 5, Suppl. 3. National Biomedical Research Foundation, Washington, DC, pp. 345–352.
4. Henikoff, S. and Henikoff, J.G. (1992) Amino acid substitution matrices from protein blocks, *Proc. Natl. Acad. Sci. USA*, **89**, 10915–10919.
5. http://www.icm.edu.pl/home/rudnicki/RSCTC2004/AppendixA.doc
6. Tomii, K. and Kanehisa, M. (1996) Analysis of amino acid indices and mutation matrices for sequence comparison and structure prediction of proteins, *Protein Eng.* **9**, 27-36.
7. Venkatarajan, M.S. and Braun, W. (2001) New quantitative descriptors of amino acids based on multidimensional scaling of a large number of physical–chemical properties. *J. Mol. Model.* 7, 445–453.
8. Sandberg, M., Eriksson, L., Jonsson, J. Sjöström, M., and Wold, S., (1998) New Chemical Descriptors Relevant for the Design of Biologically Active Peptides: A Multivariate Characterization of 87 Amino Acids *J. Med. Chem.* **41**, 2481-2491.
9. Rudnicki, W.R., *unpublished data.*

Improvement of the Needleman-Wunsch Algorithm

Zhihua Du and Feng Lin

Nanyang Technological University, Singapore
{pg02318276,asflin}@ntu.edu.sg

Abstract. This paper provides a novel approach to improve the Needleman-Wunsch algorithm, one of the most basic algorithms in Protein or DNA sequence pairwise alignment. In the first part, the problem of this algorithm is outlined. Later, a general introduction of related work is described. Finally, a modified Needleman-Wunsch algorithm and experimental results are presented. The importance of this process lies on its effect of keeping common patterns in sequences to be aligned accurately.

1 Introduction

Pairwise alignment aims to find the best match between two DNA or protein sequences. It provides computer tools to directly compare two sequences, either nucleic acid or peptide. They are starting points for all kinds of sequence analysis. The most basic algorithm, Needleman-Wunsch algorithm, to align two sequences was developed by S.A.Needleman and C.D.Wunsch [1]. This algorithm will maximize the number of matches between the sequences along the entire length of the sequences. So this algorithm is also called global sequence alignment. For two sequences a=$a_1a_2...a_n$ and b=$b_1b_2...b_n$, where$S_{i,j}$=S($a_1a_2...a_i$,$b_1b_2...b_j$) then [2][3].

$$S_{ij} = \begin{cases} S_{i-1,j-1} + S(a_ib_j) \\ max(S_{i-x,j} - w_x),\ x \geq 1 \\ max(S_{i,j-y} - w_y),\ y \geq 1 \end{cases} \tag{1}$$

Where $S_{i,j}$ is the score at position i in sequence a and position j in the 1 sequence b, $S(a_ib_j)$ is the score for aligning the characters at positions i and j, these values can be obtained through PAM [11] or BLOSUM [12] amino acid substitution matrices. w_x is the penalty for a gap of length x in sequence a, and w_y is the penalty for a gap of length y in sequence b.

The essential problem is that this algorithm incorporates no external knowledge of the sequences being aligned, such as BLOCKs+ [4][5], eBlocks [7] database, pattern, motif or structural information. So this algorithm can not ensure the similar structures align or align common patterns in sequences. It only aligns patterns when they occur in the regions of highest similarity between the two sequences [6]. But when common patterns in the two sequences do not appear in the regions of high similarity, these algorithms do not always match the patterns.

S. Tsumoto et al. (Eds.): RSCTC 2004, LNAI 3066, pp. 792–797, 2004.

In the following section, we will do some attempts and implementation to improve sequence alignment accuracy by using a modified Needleman-Wunsch algorithm. The algorithm presented here is incorporating BLOCKs+ database information into the Needleman-Wunsch algorithm. It brings the method used by biologists which consists in forcing the alignment of occurrences of blocks into the Needleman-Wunsch algorithm.

2 Related Work

There are two efforts attempting to meld motif and sequence alignments: PHI-BLAST [8] and SWP [6]. PHI-BLAST(Pattern-Hit Initiated BLAST) is a search program that combines matching of regular expressions with local alignments surrounding the match. Given a protein sequences S and a regular expression pattern P occurring in S, PHI-BLAST will search a database for other sequences that include the pattern and have significant similarity to the sequence. SWP(Smith-Waterman algorithm with Patterns) is an algorithm designed specifically to incorporate patterns into the Smith-Waterman algorithm. It compares subsequences letter by letter like the Smith-Waterman but attributes a supplementary bonus/reward when patterns are matched. Firstly, it finds all the patterns in the two sequences by searching the databank PROSITE [10]. Secondly, it aligns occurrences of patterns. Because the same PROSITE regular expression in two sequences can contain variable length subpatterns such as x[5,8]. In order to do hypothetical pattern match, it seeks possible positions of insertions/deletions in the patterns. Finally, implements a modified dynamic programming algorithm for determining which patterns will be aligned according to the strength of the matches between the two patterns.

3 Modified Needleman-Wunsch Algorithm

In this section, we provide a novel method to improve the Needleman-Wunsch algorithm. The implementing details are presented.

Step 1: Locatation of Two Instances of the Same Block
At the first step, we locate all the blocks in the two sequences by searching BLOCKs+ database. Using the Block Searcher compares a DNA or protein query sequence with each block in the database of BLOCKs+ being searched. For example, take the sequence, RTCB_ECOLI in the Prosite family PS01288. We can search from the BLOCKs+ database to find a set of blocks hidden in this sequence in Figure 1 [9].

The lower the E-Value for a block, the less reasonable to insert a gap in the block.

Step 2: Global Alignment with Blocks
After having two lists of the blocks presented in both sequences, we use a modified Needleman-Wunsch algorithm to maximize the score by dynamic programming algorithm. There are several situations when blocks are shared by two

Block	Frame	Location (aa)	Block E-value
IPB001233A	0	29-64	2.4e-20
IPB001233B	0	65-78	1.1e-06
IPB001233C	0	159-172	7.4e-09
IPB001233D	0	176-215	9.5e-22
IPB001233E	0	216-247	5e-15

Fig. 1. Block searcher result

sequences, such as inversion, appearing several times in the same sequences. Like SWP algorithm, we modify the Needleman-Wunsch algorithm to take maximum among all alignments. Let A and B are two sequences of length m and n, blockp is a shared block between the two sequences. The modified algorithm is as following:

$$S_{ij} = \begin{cases} S_{i-1,j-1} + S(a_i b_j) \\ max(S_{i-x,j} - w_x) \\ max(S_{i,j-y} - w_y) \\ max(\text{blocks ending at(i,j)}) S_{i-len,j-len} \\ \quad +|score(blockp)| \times reward + score(blockp) \end{cases} \tag{2}$$

Where len is the length of the block in the two sequences, $s(a_i b_j)$ is the score for aligning the characters at positions i and j, w_x is the penalty for a gap of length x in sequence A, w_y is the penalty for a gap of length y in sequence B. Score(blockp) is the score of alignment a shared block, which is obtained by adding similarity score of each $s(a_x b_y)$ where $i - len < x \leq i$, $j - len < y \leq j$. In the position(i,j), its score is determined by four paths, three of them are the same with the original algorithm: match, insertion and deletion. Another path is the match of the shared block beginning at the (i-len+1,j-len+1). Figure 2 shows the dependency. In order to favor the alignment of blocks, the modified algorithm gives an additive reward to the score when a block matching.

It is possible to find two occurrences of a block for which the alignment score is negative, so we do some tricky computing instead of times reward simply. We use absolute value of a block alignment score times reward, then adding to the score value to ensure a positive increase instead of the negative block alignment score. It also can relate with the strength of match among blocks.

When doing trace back, it also needs consider a block path. If the current maximum score is determined by a block score with reward, the trace back path should be along the diagonal to trace back len steps. Construct an optimal alignment of these regions, the score of this alignment is reported as optimal.

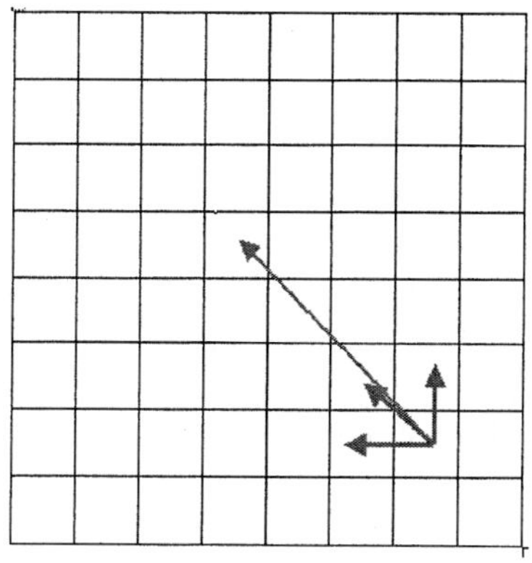

Fig. 2. Block dependency

4 Experimental Results

We use two sequences: RTCB_ECOLI and Y682_METJA in the PROSITE family PS01288 as our test data, which share five blocks: IPB001233A, IPB001233B, IPB001233C, IPB001233D, IPB001233E. In our experiment, the gap penalty is 16, gap extension is 4, substitution matrix is Blosum30 and reward is 2. Using the normal Needleman-Wunsch algorithm, it only can align three blocks correctly, which are IPB001233B, IPB001233D and IPB001233E. It inserts long gaps between IPB001233A and IPB001233C. Figure 3 and Figure 4 show the results.

```
                                               11111111
MNYELLTTEN-------------APVKMWTKGV---PVEADARQQLINT 33
|   |                  |             |     |  |
MKDVLKRVSDVVWELPKDYKDCMRVPGRIYLNEILLDELEPEVLEQIANV 50
                                              11111
11111111111111111111111111111   1112222222222222222
AKMPFIFKHIAVMPDVHLGKGSTIGSVI---PTKGAIIPAAVGVDIGC-- 78
|  | | |     ||||| | |  || |       | | |  || || |
ACLPGIYKYSIAMPDVHYGYGFAIGGVAAFDQREGVISPGGVGFDINCLT 100
11111111111111111111111111111111   22222222222222
```

```
         3                                 3333333333333
---------KH--------------------------LGTLGTGNHFIEICLD-- 175
         |                           || || ||||| |
KEDLEFIEEHGCLKDADASYVSDKAKERGRVQLGSLGSGNHFLEVQYVEK 700
                                    33333333333333
```

Fig. 3. NW result

In the modified algorithm, all blocks can be matched perfectly in the Figure 5 and 6.

5 Conclusions

The modified Needleman-Wunsch algorithm presented here is similar to the existing SWP algorithm and PHI-BLAST algorithm with some important differences. The most important difference is that the SWP algorithm didn't handle a situation that the alignment score of two occurrences of a pattern is negative.

```
                                             11111
MNYELLTTEN--------------APVKMWTKGV---PVEADARQQLINT 33
|   |                    |             |     |  |
MKDVLKRVSDVVWELPKDYKDCMRVPGRIYLNEILLDELEPEVLEQIANV 50
                                             11111

1111111111111111111111111111111   22222222222222
AKMPFIFKHIAVMPDVHLGKGSTIGSVIPTK---GAIIPAAVGVDIGC-- 78
|  | | |    ||||| | |  || |       | | |  || || |
ACLPGIYKYSIAMPDVHYGYGFAIGGVAAFDQREGVISPGGVGFDINCLT 100
1111111111111111111111111111111   22222222222222
```

```
                               33333333333333
-------------------------------HLGTLGTGNHFIEI----- 172
                                || || |||| |
KEDLEFIEEHGCLKDADASYVSDKAKERGRVQLGSLGSGNHFLEVQYVEK 700
                               33333333333333
            44444444444444444444444444444444444444
CLD---------ESDQVWIMLHSGSRGIGNAIGTYFIDLAQKEMQETLET 213
  |         |  ||    | |||| |  | |       |
VFDEEAAEIYGIEENQVVVLVHTGSRGLGHQICTDYLRIMEKAAKNYGIK 750
            44444444444444444444444444444444444444
4455555555555555555555555555555555
LPSRDLAYFMEGTEYFDDYLKAVAWAQLFASLNRDAMMENVVTALQSITQ 263
|| |  ||      |    |  ||       |  ||      |
LPDRQLACAPFESEEGQSYFKAMCCGANYAWANRQMITHWVRESFEEVFK 800
4455555555555555555555555555555555
```

Fig. 4. The modified result

It simply uses a weight times the score which will lead to decrease the alignment of occurrences instead of favoring it. But in our method, we have considered this situation to avoid the problem. Secondly, our method uses BLOCKs+ database instead of regular expression database. So in our method the occurrences of the blocks in the two sequences are of the same length, which can reduce some hypothetical affects when doing variable length pattern matching. At last, the publicly BLOCKs+ database seems to be more comprehensive than many regular expression databases. The collection of protein families in PROSITE is incomplete.

Our algorithm effectively brings the information now available in BLOCKs+ database into the Needleman-Wunsch global sequence alignment. This makes it very convenient for researchers pay more attention on the biological characters on sequence alignment than common string sequence alignment. As an increase of protein-coding sequences, the blocks-based tools become more important for interpreting the large volume of sequence data. we anticipate blocks-based tools play a very important role at protein sequence alignment.

References

1. Needleman,S.B. and Wunsch,C.D.: A general method applicable to the search for similarities in the amino acid sequence of two proteins. J.Mol.Biol. **48** (1970) 443-453
2. Smith,T.F. and Waterman,M.S.: Identification of common molecular subsequences. J.Mol.Biol. **147** (1981) 195-197
3. Smith,T.F. and Waterman,M.S.:Comparison of biosequences. Adv.Appl.Math. **2** (1981)
4. Henikoff,S. and Henikoff,J.G. and Pietrokovski,S.:Blocks+: A non-redundant database of protein alignment blocks dervied from multiple compilations. Bioinformatics. **15(6)** (1999) 471-479
5. Henikoff,J.G. and Greene,E.A. and Pietrokovski,S. and Henikoff,S.:Increased coverage of protein families with the blocks database servers. Nucleic Acids. Res. **28** (2000) 228-230
6. Comet,J.-P. and Henry,J.:Pairwise sequence alignment using a PROSITE pattern-derived similarity score. Computers and Chemistry. **26** (2002) 421-436
7. Su,Q. and Lu,L. and Brutlab,D.:eBlocks. http://fold.stanford.edu/eblocks (2002)

8. Altschul,S.F. and Madden,T.L. and schaffer,A. and Zhang,J. and Zhang,Z. and Miller,W. and Lipman,D.J.:Gapped BLAST and PSI-BLAST: a new generation of protein database search programs. Nucleic Acids Res. **25** (1997) 3389-3402
9. Henikoff,S. and Henikoff,J.G.:The prosite database. Nucleic Acids Res. **19(23)** (1999) 6565-6572
10. Hofmann,K. and Bucher,P. and Falquet,L. and Bairoch,A.:Automated assembly of protein blocks for database searching. Nucleic Acids Res. **27** (1991) 215-219
11. Dayhoff,M.O.:Survey of new data and computer methods of analysis. In Atlas of protein sequence and structure. **5** (1978) suppl.3. National Biomedical Research Foundation, Georgetown University, Washington,D.C.
12. Henikoff,S. and Henikoff,J.G:Amino acid substitution matrics from protein blocks. Proc.Natl.Acad.Sci. **89** (1992) 10915-10919

The Alignment of the Medical Subject Headings to the Gene Ontology and Its Application in Gene Annotation

Henrik Tveit[1,2], Torulf Mollestad[1,3], and Astrid Lægreid[2]

[1] Norwegian University of Science and Technology, Department of Computer and Information Science, Sem Sælands vei 7-9, NO-7491 Trondheim, Norway
[2] Norwegian University of Science and Technology, Department of Cancer Research and Molecular Medicine, MTS, NO-7489 Trondheim, Norway
[3] SAS Institute AS Norway, Pb 2666 Solli, NO-0203 Oslo, Norway

Abstract. The Gene Ontology (GO) is a controlled vocabulary used for annotation of genes. Assigning such terms to uncategorized genes is time-consuming work, and a recurring task in biomedicine. The biomedical citations of the literature database MEDLINE are indexed with terms from the Medical Subject Headings (MeSH). We studied whether MeSH terms from gene-related MEDLINE entries could be translated to GO, and be used automatically for annotation purposes. We explored three MeSH to GO alignments: pairing similar MeSH and GO term synonyms, indirect linking through MeSH's associations with Enzyme Commission (EC) terms and the official EC2GO translation table, and using association analysis to indicate which MeSH and GO terms that co-occurred most frequently for existing annotations. We here show that an alignment can be found, and, despite inconsistency in the use of MeSH terms as MEDLINE indexes, we conclude that GO annotation prediction using this alignment is useful in manual annotation of genes.

Introduction

Large-scale gene expression analysis allows biologists to gather more molecular data than ever before. This enables the biologists to perform more comprehensive experiments and faster, and more effective, research. However, the interpretation of such data is a comprehensive task due to the complexity introduced by the large number of involved genes and proteins. To assist in this work several standards for the description of gene roles and functions have been proposed. The Gene Ontology (GO) Consortium [1] provides the preferred controlled vocabulary for use in gene annotation. A gene may be annotated with at least one term from each of the three GO sub-ontologies: molecular function, biological process and cellular component. Various databases offer GO gene annotations, but none of these are complete. The biologists are forced to study the literature to acquire the existing information for their candidate gene lists. This annotation process is time-consuming, and a recurring task as new aspects of the annotated genes are discovered. The situation has challenged computer scientists to find automatic annotation procedures. Lægreid [2] and Hvidsten [3] applied rough sets prediction techniques based on gene expression data, while Ray-

S. Tsumoto et al. (Eds.): RSCTC 2004, LNAI 3066, pp. 798–804, 2004.

chaudhuri [4] focused on biomedical article abstracts using Maximum entropy modeling, naïve Bayes classification and nearest neighbour classification.

National Library of Medicine's (NLM) MEDLINE database contains 12 million biomedical citations. Each entry contains an article's title, abstract, author(s) and publication data. In addition, NLM has manually assigned each entry several key terms denoting the article content. Medical Subject Headings (MeSH) [5] is NLM's own controlled vocabulary thesaurus. It is constructed as a directed acyclic graph and contains main MeSH descriptors with associated cross-references assisting users to find appropriate MeSH descriptors. MeSH is the main indexing terminology of the MEDLINE entries, which often contains 15-25 MeSH descriptors each.

Our study aimed at exploring whether MeSH terms of MEDLINE entries that related to experiment genes could be used for annotation purposes. This would require an alignment of MeSH to GO, resulting in a translation table. The downloaded MEDLINE entries would have to relate to the genes in question, and the entry MeSH terms would have to describe the gene of the document. If these requirements were met, we could automate the annotation process by letting computers download relevant entries and use the translation table to translate the MEDLINE entries' MeSH terms to GO annotations. Ideally, MeSH and GO experts should construct a manually assessed translation table. However, since this is currently unavailable, we are forced to automate this process. We explored three approaches to the alignment of MeSH and GO, let biological experts validate the resulting translation tables, and predicted annotations and manually evaluated the predictions of a test set of 40 genes.

Methods

We downloaded the Gene Ontology of April 2003 containing 6854 biological process terms with 1072 synonyms, and 5110 molecular function terms with 1529 synonyms. We focused on these branches only, as cellular component annotations can be inferred from annotations in these two. We also downloaded the Medical Subject Headings of 2003 with 21973 main descriptors and 126862 cross-references. Due to the wide scope of MeSH, we limited our study to 23 relevant sub-trees. The used MeSH vocabulary contained 8023 MeSH entries, together with 35472 cross-references.

Alignment Based on Implicit Relations

Raychaudhuri et al [4] obtained training data by fetching MEDLINE citations indexed with MeSH terms directly corresponding to 21 selected target GO terms. They were convinced that equal MeSH and GO terms had the same biological interpretation. In our first approach, we explored this concept more thoroughly. To increase the probability of finding co-occurrences between the two terminologies, we included term synonyms: GO synonyms from an official synonym list and from translation tables linking GO to other terminologies (e.g. SwissProt Keywords), and MeSH synonyms from MeSH cross-references. We removed duplicates and general terms.

A simple comparison step found all equal GO and MeSH synonyms. Matches would indicate an implicit relation between the two, reflecting our assumption of equal terms having equal meaning. The identified implicit relations constituted a MeSH2GOimplicit translation table mapping MeSH to GO.

Alignment Based on Indirect Relations

The downloaded MeSH distribution contained many attributes for each MeSH entry. One attribute associated some MeSH entries with terms from the Enzyme Commission (EC) [6]. In our second approach, we investigated whether the MeSH terms could be indirectly linked to the Gene Ontology through the EC terms and the official EC2GO translation table. We extracted and studied EC term-containing MeSH entries from the MeSH entries. The EC references, scattered over all four levels of the EC hierarchy, were transformed into leaf node references in order to be compatible with the EC2GO translation table. This increased the number of EC references per MeSH entry with a high-level EC reference. All transformations were marked with the original EC level. The EC2GO table was applied to the list of MeSH terms with EC leaf node references. Based on the EC identifiers, a simple assembly step merged the two tables into a MeSH2GOindirect translation table.

Alignment Based on Association Rules

Finally, we generated rules reflecting frequently co-occurring MeSH and GO terms in a training set. Thus, the last alignment contained translations relevant for annotation purposes and not necessarily synonym pairs as in the preceding approaches. The training set consisted of European Bioinformatics Institute's GO Annotations (GOA) and MeSH terms associated with the annotated genes. Using the gene symbols of the annotations as individual PubMed search strings, we extracted these MeSH terms from the fetched MEDLINE entries. The training data was stored in a two-column table: The first column containing a MEDLINE identifier, the second column containing either a MeSH term or a GO identifier. A single MEDLINE identifier could occur one or many times, depending on how many GO annotations (1-N) and MeSH terms (0-N) that were associated with it.

To find the frequently co-occurring MeSH terms and GO identifiers from this training set, we applied association analysis. Association rule mining aims at the discovery of relationships between items in a dataset. Based on Argawal et al [7] we present a short formal framework of this technique. Let $I = \{i_1, i_2, \ldots i_k\}$ be a set of binary attributes called items. A transaction T with a transaction identifier T_{ID} in a database D of transactions consists of an item set such that $T \subseteq I$. Let X be an item set of $|X|$ items such that $X \subseteq I$. A transaction T satisfies X if $X \subseteq T$. An association rule is an implication of the form $X \Rightarrow Y$, where $X \subset I$, $Y \subset I$, and $X \cap Y = \emptyset$. The percentage of transactions in D that satisfy both X and Y is known as the Support s% of the rule $X \Rightarrow Y$ (and of the rule $Y \Rightarrow X$). The percentage of transactions in D satisfying X that also satisfy Y is known as the Confidence c% of the rule $X \Rightarrow Y$ (not the same as for $Y \Rightarrow X$). The rule $X \Rightarrow Y$ is satisfied if *s% > minsupport* and *c% > minconfidence*. The thresholds *minsupport* and *minconfidence* are manually set.

Employing SAS Association Analysis with our training set as input, we set the MEDLINE identifier as T_{ID}, and used the MeSH terms and the GO identifiers as items, I. The returned rules had $|X| \leq 3$ and $|Y| \leq 3$, where both X and Y could include both MeSH terms and GO identifiers. We excluded all rules but those of the format $X_{\text{MeSH term(s)}} \Rightarrow Y_{\text{GO identifier(s)}}$, which we ranked according to their confidence. The highest-ranking rules constituted the MeSH2GOassociation translation table.

Annotation Based on MeSH Terms

In order to test whether MeSH terms of gene-related MEDLINE documents could be used for annotation using our MeSH2GO translation tables, we constructed a test set of gene annotations from GOA and the Dept. of Cancer Research and Molecular Medicine, Norwegian University of Science and Technology (NTNU). Through PubMed, we acquired all MEDLINE documents containing one of the gene symbols and extracted the MeSH terms. The final test set consisted of the gene identifiers and their associated GO identifiers (from GOA and NTNU) and MeSH terms (from the MEDLINE entries). The MeSH terms would be used to predict annotations for the test genes, and the manually assessed annotations would be used for validation.

To annotate the test set genes, we simply matched a document's MeSH terms with a MeSH2GO table and translated them into GO terms. Next, we let each document vote for its associated GO terms and ranked the GO terms according to its number of document votes. The top n GO terms were used as annotation predictions. This annotation process was repeated three times, one for each alignment.

Results

Evaluation of the Alignment of MeSH to GO

Biological experts evaluated the three alignments individually by categorising each term pair into three groups. A term pair of the implicit and indirect alignments was *positive* if the two terms were biological synonyms, *possibly positive* if the terms were synonyms under certain circumstances, or *negative* if the terms never referred to the same biological phenomenon. The term alignments based on association rules were considered positive if the biological concepts reflected by the involved MeSH terms truly would imply the annotations reflected by the involved GO terms. An alignment based on association analysis was possibly positive if such a relationship could be true for special cases, or negative if there was no biological relationship.

The MeSH2GOimplicit translation table consisted of 1377 implicit relations mapping 907 MeSH terms to 1093 GO terms. Manual examination revealed a fairly good alignment. 85% of the proposed synonyms were positive and 12% were possibly positive. Only 4% categorised as negatives.

The MeSH2GOindirect translation table contained 14079 indirect relations between MeSH and GO. The table mapped 730 MeSH terms to 1666 GO terms via 1528 EC terms. 661 of the indirect relations stemmed from MeSH2EC links at the fourth level. Due to indications of preliminary results the biological experts considered these alignments only. 81% were characterised as positives, 15% as possibly positives, and 5% as negatives.

The size of the training set directly affects the quality and quantity of the resulting rules of an association analysis. Unfortunately, the availability of GO annotations with associated MEDLINE identifiers was limited during our work, and we settled with 18212 annotations from GOA and NTNU. These were associated with 8815 unique MEDLINE entries indexed with 92158 MeSH terms. The limited availability of training data forced the analysis thresholds to be low: *minsupport > 0.5%*, *minconfidence > 2%*. SAS generated 38357 association rules, of which 1282 were of the desired form. 27% were positive, 35% possibly positive and 38% negative.

Validation of the Annotation Predictions

We randomly selected 40 test genes from the GOA and NTNU annotation collections. These were associated with 354 reference annotations that were used for prediction validation purposes. The biologists considered an annotation prediction *correct* if it corresponded directly to a gene's reference annotation, or any of the GO terms' predecessors. The highest and more general GO levels were not used. A prediction corresponding to reference annotation's successor in GO was termed *possibly correct.* Since there are many missing annotations in existing gene annotation sets [2], biologists evaluated all predictions not matching any reference annotation. Correct and possibly correct predictions were termed *new annotations* and included. All other predictions were termed *wrong*. To quantify our validations, we define *precision* (*precision'*) as the ratio of annotations found correct (correct and possibly correct). We define *recall* (*recall'*) as the fraction of the reference annotations represented among the correct (correct and possibly correct) predictions. We calculated these measures using the 10, 15 and 20 GO terms most frequently proposed by a gene's MeSH terms as annotations. The prediction results are illustrated in Figure 1:

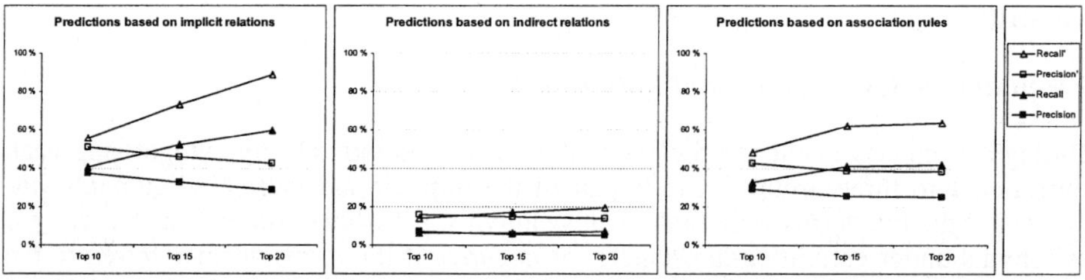

Fig. 1. The results of annotation prediction based on implicit relations (left) and association rules (left). Precision and Recall were calculated with the top 10, top 15 and top 20 proposed GO terms per gene as predictions.

The alignment based on implicit relations between MeSH and GO resulted in the best annotation predictions in our study (Figure 1, left). 130 of 354 known annotations were identified and 82 new annotations could be found based on the predictions. The annotation predictions covered a wide range of different annotations within the subtrees biological process and molecular function. The biological experts regarded these annotation predictions as being of high value as an aid in manual annotation.

The prediction based on indirect relations performed poorer than expected recalling 22 of the 354 known annotations and finding 3 new (Figure 1, middle). Due to the use of EC, the prediction was limited to molecular function terms describing enzymatic functions. Within this category, the predictions would be a valuable help.

The prediction using association rules identified 84 of the 354 known annotations and 64 new (Figure 1, right). The range of predicted annotations was somewhat limited as only 31 unique terms were predicted (e.g. *cell adhesion*, *cell proliferation*, *cell-cell signalling*, *development*, *immune response*, *neurogenesis*, *signal transduction*). Only 199 of the 1282 association rules lead to an annotation prediction, and all of these but one were of the simple format $X_{\text{MeSH term}} \Rightarrow Y_{\text{GO identifier}}$. The biologists considered the predictions of this method to be of limited value.

Discussion

The results indicate that aligning MeSH to GO is possible, with the best performance achieved through synonym-based MeSH to GO relations. Indirect alignment is almost as correct, but the implicit set is by far larger. Furthermore, 431 of the used indirect rules constitute a subset of the implicit alignment. The two sets together contain only 1607 unique synonym pairs, covering just a fraction of GO. This will improve with future releases of MeSH and GO with more terms, synonyms, and translation tables. The development and refinement of EC, as well as new versions of the EC2GO, should improve the indirect alignment. The association analysis clearly suffered from limited training data. However, when more training data becomes available, this approach could reveal undiscovered biological relationships, and reflect complicated relations between several MeSH terms and a GO term; $X_{\text{MeSH terms}} \Rightarrow Y_{\text{GO identifier}}$.

Annotation prediction based on the implicit alignment had the better performance of the three presented methods. Its high numbers of correct predictions correlate well with the quality of the corresponding translation table. For the other two prediction methods used, such a correlation was poorer. Using the indirect alignment, substantially fewer annotations were recalled. This is most likely due to the use of enzymatic MeSH terms only. With the indirect relations, more predictions were classified as wrong. Manual investigation of some of the used documents revealed that enzymatic MeSH terms often reflect enzymes used in the methodological approach, rather than the genes mentioned in the article. Thus, despite good translation table quality, the usage of enzymatic MeSH terms in MEDLINE entries introduces too much noise in this prediction. MeSH2GOassociation gave more correct predictions than the quality of the translation table would indicate. However, it connected MeSH terms with GO terms at higher, more general GO-levels, which obviously lack the more detailed information of lower level predictions.

In MEDLINE entries, some MeSH terms may be marked as *major MeSH headings*. These reflect the main subject of the corresponding article. Raychaudhuri [4] prioritised these when searching for relevant training data. We rerun our experiments emphasising a MEDLINE entry's major MeSH headings. However, no significant improvement was achieved. Actually, Funk and Reid [8] found that major MeSH headings were assigned with only a 61.1% consistency. Only 33.8% of the MEDLINE entries had consistency among all of their respective MeSH terms. Funk and Reid concluded that the MeSH terms described central concepts better than peripheral points. Our own inspections of our predictions correlate with Funk and Reid's findings; Unless a specific function of a given gene is the main subject of a MEDLINE entry, the way MeSH terms are used to index MEDLINE leads to noise during gene annotation. This seems to be a larger problem than the alignment quality. An example is the correct synonym pair *Transcription Factors* (MeSH) and *GO:0003700 transcription factor activity* (GO). Appearing in the implicit and indirect translation tables, this pair was the source of numerous misclassifications. This confirms the notion that the use of MeSH terms is not optimal, and it implies that we cannot disqualify alignments based on prediction performance. Another source of prediction error was the actual gene-relevance of the downloaded MEDLINE entries. Unfortunately, there is no proper solution to ensure such relevance as of today.

We conclude that aligning MeSH to GO can be done automatically. Although the current translation tables do not cover all possible relations, we expect this to improve with future releases of MeSH and GO. The annotation predictions based on MeSH terms represent a valuable aid in manual annotation work.

Visit http://www.goat.no for the MeSH2GO annotation tool and the complete paper.

References

1. Ashburner M, Ball CA, Blake JA, Botstein D, Butler H, Cherry JM, Davis AP, Dolinski K, Dwight SS, Eppig JT, et al. Gene ontology: Tool for the unification of biology. The Gene Ontology Consortium. Nat. Genet. 25: 25-29. 2000.
2. Lægreid A, Hvidsten TR, Midelfart H, Komorowski J, Sandvik AK. Predicting gene ontology biological process from temporal gene expression patterns. Genome Res. 13(5): 965-79. 2003.
3. Hvidsten TR, Lægreid A, Komorowski J. Learning rule-based models from gene expression time profiles annotated using Gene Ontology. Bioinformatics, 19:1116-23. 2003
4. Raychaudhuri S, Chang JT, Sutphin PD, Altman RB. Associating genes with gene ontology codes using a maximum entropy analysis of biomedical literature. Genome Res. 12: 203-214. 2002.
5. National Library of Medicine. Medical Subject Headings. http://www.nlm.nih.gov/mesh/meshhome.html
6. Nomenclature Committee of the International Union of Biochemistry and Molecular Biology. Enzyme Nomenclature. http://www.chem.qmul.ac.uk/iubmb/enzyme/
7. Agrawal R, Imielinski T, Swami A. Mining association rules between sets of items in large databases. In Proceedings of the ACM SIGMOD Conference on Management of Data, 207-216. 1993.
8. Funk ME, Reid CA. Indexing Consistency in MEDLINE. Bulletin of the Medical Library Association, 71(2):176-83. 1983.

Rough Set Methodology in Clinical Practice: Controlled Hospital Trial of the MET System

Ken Farion[1], Wojtek Michalowski[2],
Roman Słowiński[3], Szymon Wilk[3], and Steven Rubin[1]

[1] Children's Hospital of Eastern Ontarion, Ottawa, Canada
{farion,rubin}@cheo.on.ca
[2] University of Ottawa, Ottawa, Canada
wojtek@management.uottawa.ca
[3] Poznan University of Technology, Poznan, Poland
{roman.slowinski,szymon.wilk}@cs.put.poznan.pl

Abstract. Acute abdominal pain in childhood is a common but diagnostically challenging problem facing Emergency Department personnel. Experienced physicians use a combination of key clinical attributes to assess and triage a child, but residents and inexperienced physicians may lack this ability. In order to assist them, we used knowledge discovery techniques based on rough set theory to develop a clinical decision model to support the triage. The model was implemented as a module for the Mobile Emergency Triage system – a clinical decision support system for the rapid emergency triage of children with acute pain. The abdominal pain module underwent a clinical trial in the Emergency Department of a teaching hospital. The trial allowed us to compare in a prospective manner the accuracy of the system to the triage performance of the physicians and the residents. The preliminary results are very encouraging and they demonstrate validity of developing computer-based support tools for a clinical triage.

Keywords: Rough set theory; Emergency triage; Clinical trial; Clinical decision support systems; Handheld computers

1 Introduction

Acute abdominal pain in children is a common but diagnostically challenging problem facing Emergency Department (ED) personnel. There are many possible causes for the pain. Some patients have serious illnesses requiring urgent treatment, and possibly surgery. Most patients, however, have non-serious causes, or the pain resolves before a cause is determined.

Experienced physicians use a combination of key historical information and physical findings to assess and triage children. These attributes frequently occur in recognizable patterns, allowing the physician to make the correct assessment quickly and efficiently. Medical residents and other inexperienced physicians may lack the acumen to know what information to collect or recognize the patterns.

S. Tsumoto et al. (Eds.): RSCTC 2004, LNAI 3066, pp. 805–814, 2004.

This may lead to delays in definitive care for those who are unwell, while expensive, time-consuming tests and observation might be carried unnecessarily.

In order to assist the inexperienced ED physicians and residents we used knowledge discovery techniques based on rough set theory to develop a clinical decision model that uses easily determined attributes to support the triage by distinguishing between three disposition categories: *discharge*, *observation/further investigation*, and *consult.* The clinical decision model was implemented as a module in the Mobile Emergency Triage (MET) system – a modular clinical decision support system aimed at supporting the emergency triage of children with acute pain. The system is intended to be used by the ED clinicians to help them in evaluating patients and making triage decisions.

The MET abdominal pain module underwent a clinical trial in the ED of the Children's Hospital of Eastern Ontario (CHEO)[1]. When the complete analysis of trial data is finished, its results will allow us to compare thoroughly the triage accuracy of the system with the performance of the clinicians.

The paper is organized as follows – we start by describing the process of triaging a child in ED. Then we explain the development of the clinical decision model and describe the MET system. Further, we give details on the clinical trial and present preliminary results obtained after the first 3 months. We finish with conclusions.

2 Triage of Abdominal Pain

Medical personnel in the ED makes triage decisions in order to assess whether a patient requires urgent attention from a specialist, or some other course of action needs to be taken. Based upon information from the patient's complaint, history, physical examination, and the results of laboratory tests clinicians make decisions about the severity of the patient's presenting condition, and the management process that follows.

The process of triaging non-trauma cases in the ED is illustrated in Figure 1. It involves two assessment phases, which answer the following questions: how quickly does a patient need to receive medical attention, and what type of management is necessary.

The first phase, called prioritization, is done by a triage nurse who evaluates severity of patient's clinical condition and assigns her an appropriate priority level that determines waiting time in the ED. Patients with high priority are immediately seen by physicians, while the other may wait for longer period of time.

The second phase – disposition involves physicians who on a basis of examinations and laboratory tests triage a patient. In the teaching hospital, patients are also often assessed by residents and then reviewed by staff physicians. Disposition leads to one of the following recommendations: *discharge*, *observation/further investigation* (*observation* in short), and *consult.*

[1] CHEO is a teaching hospital that is a part of the University of Ottawa.

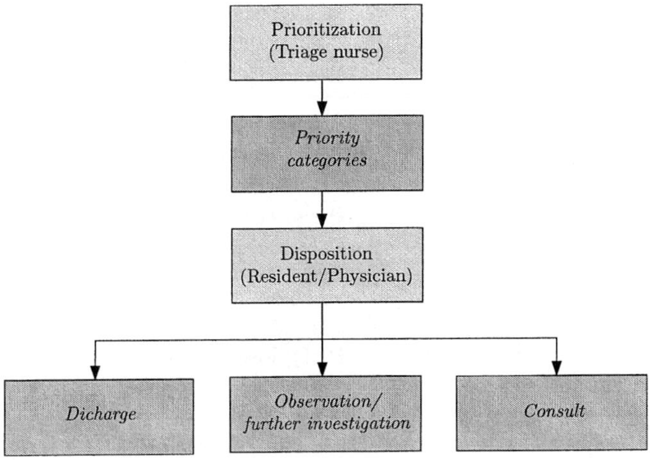

Fig. 1. Prioritization and disposition as a part of the triage

Focus of the research described here is on supporting the disposition phase only that is further referred to as triage.

3 Development of the Clinical Decision Model

There are several possible ways of represent clinical reasoning – decision rules being one of them. The decision rules constitute a convenient way of representing clinical knowledge as they are intuitive and easy to interpret by the domain experts. They also offer a comprehensive representation of regularities and patterns present in data. Moreover, they are accepted and used in medical practice [1].

The development of the clinical decision model started with a retrospective chart study to collect clinical data that could be used to induce decision rules. Charts of 623 patients with presenting abdominal pain complaint, seen during the 1996 – 2002 period in the ED of CHEO were evaluated. The chart of each patient was reviewed with special reference to most common clinical symptoms and signs evaluated in the ED (see Table 1). The final discharge diagnosis (not the ED disposition) was used in order to ensure accuracy of the clinical outcomes that were used for developing and evaluating the clinical decision model. As our goal was to develop a triage algorithm as opposed to the diagnostic tool, we used discharge diagnosis to assign each patient to appropriate triage category that corresponds to a disposition decision in ED (e.g., if the discharge diagnosis was appendicitis, then the triage category was *consult* because such a patient needs to be seen by pediatric surgeon).

The data set created from the charts was studied for regularities using knowledge discovery techniques based on rough set theory [2]. As the clinical data were incomplete (for some attributes, such as rebound tenderness or WBC, the number of missing values was close to 25% of cases) we used extended rough set

Table 1. Attributes and their domains

Attribute	Domain[2]
Age	0–5 years, $\geq$ 5 years
Sex	male, female
Duration of pain	$\leq$ 24 hours, 1–7 days, > 7 days
Site of pain	RLQ, lower abdomen, other
Type of pain	continuous, intermittent
Shifting of pain	yes, no
Previous visit	yes, no
Vomiting	yes, no
Site of tenderness	RLQ, lower abdomen, other
Rebound tenderness	yes, no
Localized guarding	yes, no
Temperature	< 37 C, 37–39 C, $\geq$ 39 C
WBC (white blood cells)	$\leq$ 4, 4–12, $\geq$ 12

approach that deals with incomplete data without need to modify the original information [3]. This extended approach replaces indiscernibility by a new relation – cumulative indiscernibility[3].

The data set was analyzed using ROSE software [4]. We started with checking all attributes given by medical experts and then attempted to reduce this set, however this did not produce satisfactory results (number of the attributes in a reduct diminished from 13 to 12). Considering our earlier experience with the analysis of the smaller abdominal pain data set [5] when it was possible to generated good classification rules using a reduced set of attributes (9 out of 12), we decided to expand evaluation of the attributes. We used an approach based on a fuzzy measure[4] to assess information value of attributes [6]. Specifically, we used Shapley value [7] that interprets the quality of rough approximations of the triage in terms of the fuzzy measure. This permits to estimate how well an attribute explains relationships in data. Shapley values for all single attributes are presented in Figure 2 (the greater the value, the more information an attribute carries).

To identify a minimal set of attributes for which accurate decision rules could be created, we iteratively tested subsets of them in an order determined by their Shapley values – starting from the top 4 ones (the minimal subset resulting in the non-zero quality of the approximation of the triage) and ending with all 13

[2] Domains of real-valued attributes (age, duration of pain, temperature and WBC) were discretized according to medical practice.

[3] The relation assumes two objects are indiscernible if their values for considered attributes are equal or at least one is missing (in other words, it is assumed a missing value is equal to any specified one).

[4] Fuzzy measure is a set function that satisfies the property of monotonicity [6]. Quality of the approximation of the triage fulfills this property and thus can be considered a fuzzy measure.

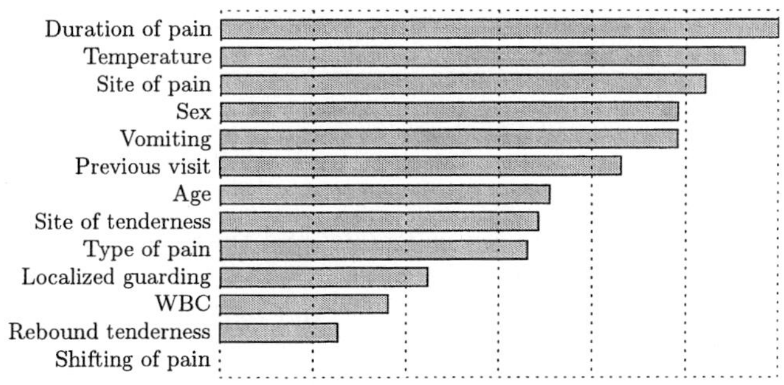

Fig. 2. Attributes and their Shapley values

attributes. For each subset we assessed classification capabilities of corresponding decision rules (in terms of their classification accuracy) using cross-validation tests [8]. Results of the tests suggested that rules based on all 13 attributes offered the highest accuracy. This contradiction of our earlier findings [5] can be explained by the fact that the initial analysis was conducted on a much smaller set of patients (175 records) divided into two categories – *consult* and *discharge*. Clearly, more specific classification requires that all attributes are considered.

A clinical decision model for triage of abdominal pain patients that was ultimately created consists of 172 rules induced from the complete set of attributes, sample ones are presented in Table 2.

4 The MET System

The MET system [9] currently has two clinical modules - scrotal pain and abdominal pain, and research is under way to develop a hip pain module. The clinical decision model described in the previous section forms the core of the abdominal pain module. The system's design, illustrated in Figure 3, follows the principles of extended client-server architecture [10] with the client running on a mobile device – a handheld computer. Mobility of the system is imposed by the specificity of the clinical setting (no room for a desktop workstation in ED and no time to leave triage area for consulting the system) and it significantly improves the usability of the system by offering support directly at a point of care [11].

The desired functionality of the MET is accomplished through a clear division of tasks and functions to be executed on the server and on the client side. The server performs two functions: it provides integration with a hospital information system (IS) using HL7 protocol[5], and it communicates with mobile clients using local and remote (wireless) connections. The mobile client is used for entering clinical data and triaging a patient.

[5] HL7 (Health Level 7) is the standard protocol for exchanging information between medical applications [12].

Table 2. Sample decision rules

Triage	Conditions
discharge	site of pain is in lower abdomen, and vomiting occurred, and there was a previous visit
observe	age is under 5 years, sex is female, and there was a previous visit, and localized guarding is found
consult	sex is male, and pain is constant, and temperature is above 39 C, and site of pain is in RLQ

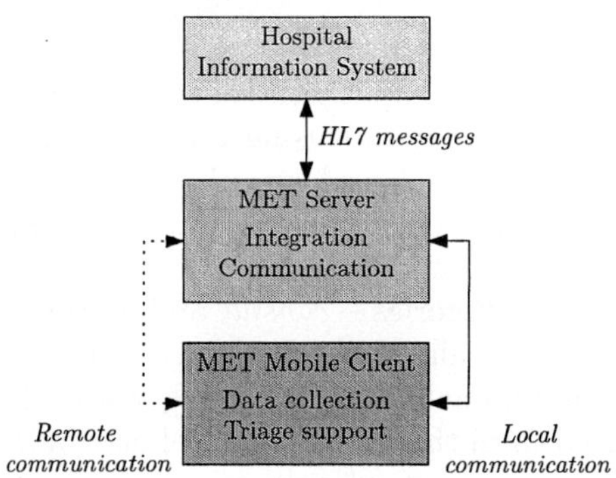

Fig. 3. MET architecture

As soon as a patient is admitted to the ED and recorded in the hospital IS, it transmits to the MET server a record containing patient's demographic information and the presenting complaint. If the complaint is supported by any of the modules, the server transfers a patient record to the client. Then the client is used to collect values of clinical attributes and to generate triage recommendation.

One of the unique features of the MET client is its adaptability to the type of captured clinical information [13]. For example, the results of the physical examination of the abdomen are entered, using pictograms (see Figure 4), while the temperature is entered using a numeric keypad to minimize the amount of data typed-in manually (see Figure 5). For most of the clinical symptoms and signs, the system allows for a free entry of any additional comments about the patient's condition. There is reported evidence that such structured data collection usually contributes to the improved triage and diagnosis of a patient [14].

The triage function on a client can be invoked at any time, and it uses the patient's most current data to provide a triage recommendation. Depending on the information currently available, the distance-based classifier [15] embedded in the MET system invokes the most suitable part of the clinical decision model, that is, a subset of rules providing the best overall match. The system gives a triage recommendation by prioritizing the outcome that according to the model represents the strongest triage recommendation. Even if the model does not have rules exactly matching the available data, the system will consult the most closely matching rules.

When collection of information about the patient's condition is completed, all the information gathered to date is transferred to the MET server, thus updating the patient's record, and when the triage phase is finished, the completed record is moved back to the hospital IS.

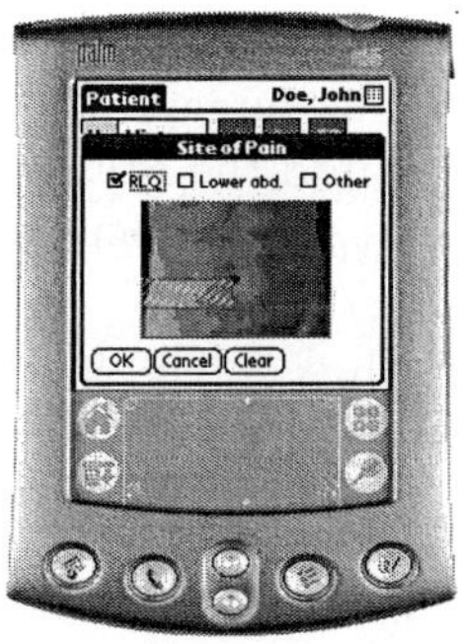

Fig. 4. Data capture using the pictogram

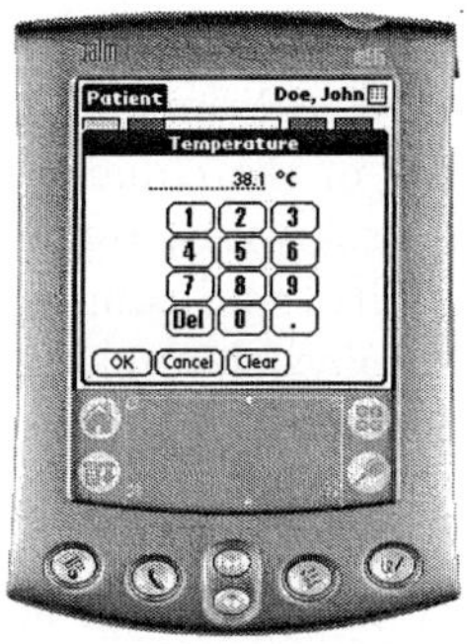

Fig. 5. Data capture using the numeric keypad

5 Design of the Clinical Trial

The purpose of clinical trial is to verify and compare triage performance of the ED personnel (physicians and residents are considered as two separate groups) and the MET system. It is one of the first clinical trails involving clinical support system that was conducted during normal operation of the ED and involved all residents and staff physicians (together over 50 people). The design, following the recommendations appropriate for any clinical trial in the ED, and information flow captured by the trial is presented in Figure 6. Upon arrival to the ED, patient is admitted and assessed in the usual fashion. When a patient is registered, the main presenting complaint is recorded. If it is abdominal pain, then a patient record created by the hospital IS is flagged accordingly, thus enabling the MET server to filter these patients who should be potentially included in the trial.

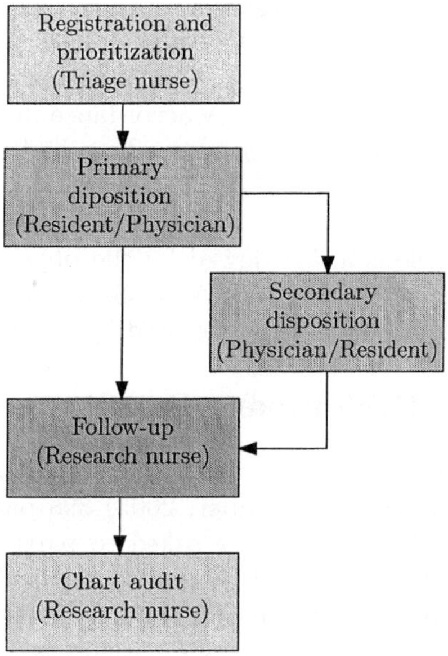

Fig. 6. Design and information flow of the clinical trial

A physician or a resident starts the primary disposition phase by asking for a consent to participate in the trial (a physician who performs the primary disposition is denoted as the primary observer). Positive answer triggers check if the patient is eligible for the trial. The patient can be included if she is between 1 and 17 years of age and abdominal pain lasts up to 10 days. Exclusion criteria encompass abdominal pain as the result of trauma, pain caused by an acute disease or a chronic illness, and direct referral to surgery. If the patient is eligible, values of the clinical attributes are entered into the MET client as the examination progresses. Regardless of the eligibility, paper documentation (an ED chart) is filled and completed.

When the physician makes a disposition decision, it is entered into the system indicating the end of the triage and locking the patient's data. The MET client runs the triage function to create a triage recommendation, but this recommendation is not accessible to the user. Keeping the triage recommendation blinded from the physician addresses one of the main ethical concerns raised before starting the trial, namely that use of MET at this stage does not affect the way a patient is managed in the ED.

When possible, another physician (denoted as the secondary observer) repeats the triage process collecting clinical data through independent examination of the patient and entering triage decision. The information is handled in the same manner as during the primary observation, however the secondary observer is not able to view the patient data collected by the primary one. As the patient's condition change with time, the secondary observer is considered to be valid only if patient is seen within 1 hour from completing the primary observation. The purpose of such a setup (typical for regular clinical trials) is to assess inter-observers accordance in evaluating the patients.

Each eligible patient who a had triage decision is followed-up at 7 – 14 days after her visit in the ED. For patients admitted to hospital, the hospital chart is retrieved to assist in determining the patient's final diagnosis. All categorization decisions are reviewed by the physicians for accuracy and, where necessary, to resolve ambiguities. All decisions are made without the knowledge of the triage recommendation generated by MET.

6 Preliminary Results

The clinical trial was designed to last for 6 months. During the first 3 months (August – September, 2003) 898 patients with abdominal pain visited the ED in CHEO, 420 were asked to participate in the trial and 400 agreed. 328 patients were eligible and were included in the study. For 230 included patients the follow-up and the chart audit phases have been already completed, thus the final categorization for these patients is established and verified. 178 verified patients were examined by physicians and 150 – by residents (98 patients were seen by both).

The accuracy of triage decisions is presented in Table 3. We focused on the records of patients seen and evaluated by the ED physicians, as they were fully verified, thus could be used for a reliable comparison. For those records MET gave better overall accuracy and the accuracy for *discharge* and *consult* categories, but it had difficulties with triaging the patients requiring *observation* – the majority of them were incorrectly triaged as *discharge*. This prompts for revising the classification strategy embedded in the system, as such mistakes should be minimized.

Table 3. Accuracy of disposition for ED physicians and MET

	Overall	Discharge	Observation	Consult
Physicians	64.6%	64.8%	63.0%	65.2%
MET	66.3%	75.8%	18.5%	69.6%

7 Conclusions

Knowledge discovery techniques based on rough set theory and its extensions allowed us to mine incomplete clinical data, to estimate the information content of attributes and to express patterns found in data in form of decision rules. The rules constitute the clinical decision model to support the triage of children with abdominal pain which was implemented in the MET system.

The system underwent the clinical trial in the ED of CHEO. Preliminary results show that the system offers the triage accuracy comparable to the one achieved by the ED physicians. Preliminary analysis of the results also shows that quality of data is very important for providing an acceptable level of support. While MET mimics physicians' reasoning and works well on data collected by the ED physicians, at the same time it is less accurate when used on data collected by the residents who are less accurate in correctly evaluating patient's symptoms and sign and also are more prone to give "spot diagnosis" that does not have solid justification in the collected information. This observation underlines the synergy between the physicians and MET and clearly shows the system is not a competitor for humans, but a sophisticated tools that requires experienced users to operate properly.

The overall evaluation of the system by participating physicians and residents is favorable with both groups emphasizing the usefulness of the MET system by providing structured and easy-to-use information-gathering facilities and its available directly at a point of care.

Acknowledgments

The research reported in this paper was supported by the grants from the Natural Sciences and Engineering Research Council of Canada and the Polish Committee for Scientific Research. Authors would like to thank Rhonda Correll, Nataliya Millman, Mathieu Chiasson and Bernard Plouffe for their work on the MET system development and organization and management of the clinical trial.

References

1. Glas, A., Pijnenburg, B., Lijmer, J., Bogaard, K., de Roos, M., Keeman, J., Butzelaar, R., Bossuyt, P.: Comparison of diagnostic decision rules and structured data collection in assessment of acute ankle injury. Canadian Medical Association Journal **166** (2002) 727–733

2. Pawlak, Z., Slowinski, R.: Rough set approach to multi-attribute decision analysis. European Journal of Operational Research **72** (1994) 443–459
3. Greco, S., Matarazzo, B., Slowinski, R.: Dealing with missing data in rough set analysis of multi-attribute and multi-criteria decision problems. In Zanakis, S., Doukidis, G., Zopounidis, C., eds.: Decision Making: Recent Developments and Worldwide Applications, Kluwer Academic Publishers (2000) 295–316
4. Predki, B., Wilk, S.: Rough set based data exploration using rose system. In Ras, Z., Skowron, A., eds.: Foundations of Intelligent Systems, Springer-Verlag (1999) 172–180
5. Michalowski, W., Rubin, S., Slowinski, R., Wilk, S.: Triage of the child with abdominal pain: A clinical algorithm for emergency patient management. Journal of Paediatrics and Child Health **6** (2001) 23–28
6. Greco, S., Matarazzo, B., Slowinski, R.: Fuzzy measures as a technique for rough set analysis. In: Proc. 6th European Congress on Intelligent Techniques and Soft Computing (EUFIT'98), Aachen (1998) 99–103
7. Shapley, L.: A value for n-person games. In Kuhn, H., Tucker, A., eds.: Contributions to the Theory of Games II, Princeton University Press (1953) 307–317
8. Mitchell, T.: Machine Learning. McGraw Hill (1997)
9. Michalowski, W., Rubin, S., Slowinski, R., Wilk, S.: Mobile clinical support system for pediatric emergencies. Decision Support Systems **36** (2003) 161–176
10. Jing, J., Helal, A., Elmagarmid, A.: Client-server computing in mobile environments. ACM Computing Surveys **32** (1999) 117–157
11. Ammenwerth, E., Buchauer, A., Bludau, B., Haux, R.: Mobile information and communication tools in the hospital. International Journal of Medical Informatics (2000) 21–40
12. Quinn, J.: An HL7 (Health Level Seven) overview. Journal of American Health Information Management Association **7** (1999) 32–34
13. Kersten, M., Michalowski, W., Wilk, S.: Designing man-machine interactions for mobile clinical systems: Met triage support on palm handheld. In Bisdorff, R., ed.: 14th Mini-EURO Conference HCP'2003 Human centered processes. Distributed decision making and man-machine cooperation, Luxembourg (2003)
14. Korner, H., Sondenaa, K., Soreide, J.: Structured data collection improves the diagnosis of acute appendicitis. British Journal of Surgery **85** (1998) 341–344
15. Stefanowski, J.: Classification support based on the rough sets. Foundations of Computing and Decision Sciences **18** (1993) 371–380

An Automated Multi-spectral MRI Segmentation Algorithm Using Approximate Reducts

Sebastian Widz[1], Kenneth Revett[2], and Dominik Ślęzak[3,1]

[1] Polish-Japanese Institute of Information Technology, Warsaw, Poland
[2] University of Luton, Luton, UK
[3] Department of Computer Science, University of Regina, Regina, Canada

Abstract. We introduce an automated multi-spectral MRI segmentation technique based on approximate reducts derived from the data mining paradigm of the theory of rough sets. We utilized the T1, T2 and PD MRI images from the Simulated Brain Database as a "gold standard" to train and test our segmentation algorithm. The results suggest that approximate reducts, used alone or in combination with other classification methods, may provide a novel and efficient approach to the segmentation of volumetric MRI data sets.

Keywords: MRI segmentation, approximate reducts, genetic algorithms

1 Introduction

In Magnetic Resonance Imaging (MRI) data, segmentation in a 2D context entails assigning labels to pixels (or more properly voxels), where the labels correspond to primary parenchymal tissue types: usually white matter (WM), gray matter (GM), and cerebral spinal fluid (CSF). It has been demonstrated repeatedly that the relative distributions of and/or changes in the levels of primary brain tissue classes are diagnostic for specific diseases such as stroke, Alzheimer's disease, various forms of dementia, and multiple sclerosis to name a few [3, 4]. Segmentation process is usually performed by an expert who visually inspects a series of MRI films. In a clinical setting, it may be difficult for a doctor on-call or a radiologist to have sufficient time and/or the requisite experience to analyze the potentially voluminous and variable nature of MRI that is produced in a busy hospital setting. Therefore, any tool which provides detailed and accurate information regarding MRI analysis in an automated manner may be valuable.

The segmentation accuracy is estimated as a similarity measure between the results of the algorithm and the expert's evaluation. Therefore, a kind of "gold standard" – an objective and verifiable MRI data set where every voxel is classified with respect to tissue class with 100% accuracy, is helpful. One such gold standard is the Simulated Brain Database (SBD) [1]. It contains a series of

[1] The SBD data sets were provided by the Brain Imaging Centre, Montreal Neurological Institute (http://www.bic.mni.mcgill.ca/brainweb).

S. Tsumoto et al. (Eds.): RSCTC 2004, LNAI 3066, pp. 815–824, 2004.

3D volumetric multi-spectral MRI data sets (T1, T2, PD) with axial orientation. Every set consists of 181 slices (1mm slice thickness), where each slice is $181*217$ voxels, with no inter-slice gaps. A number of different data sets are available with varying with slice thickness, noise ratios and field inhomogeneity (INU) levels which can be set to the user defined values.

SBD provides an opportunity to investigate segmentation algorithms in a supervised manner. One can generate a classification system using the classified volume for training and then test on volumes not included in the training set. Traditionally, MRI segmentation methods have been performed using cluster analysis, histogram extraction, and neural networks [1, 5, 7, 15]. In this paper, we present an approach based on the concept of approximate reducts [10–12] derived from the data mining paradigm of the theory of rough sets [6, 9]. We utilize T1, T2, and PD MRI modalities from SBD for training and testing. Decision tables are generated as basing on the set of 10 attributes extracted from the training volumes (1mm horizontal slices) where the classification is known. Using an order based genetic algorithm (o-GA) (cf. [2, 14]), we search through the decision table for approximate reducts resulting in the simple "if..then.." decision rules.

After training, we test the rule sets for segmentation accuracy across all imaging modalities along three variables: slice thickness, noise level and intensity of inhomogeneity (INU). The segmentation accuracy varies from 95% (T1, 1mm slices, 3% noise, and 20 % INU) to 75% (PD, 9 mm, 9% noise, and 40% INU) using training set 1mm 3preprocessing, these data agree favorably with more traditional and complicated approaches. It suggests that approximate reducts may provide a novel approach to MRI segmentation.

The article is organized as follows: In section 2, we describe the data preparation technique, which involves attribute selection and quantification. In section 3, we describe the algorithms employed to find approximate reducts and decision rules used in the testing phase of the segmentation process. Next we present the results of this analysis in section 4 and a brief discussion follows in section 5.

2 Data Preparation

In the rough set theory the sample of data takes the form of an *information system* $\mathbb{A} = (U, A)$, where each attribute $a \in A$ is a function $a : U \to V_a$ from the universe U into the value set V_a. In our case the elements of U are voxels taken from MR images. There are $181 * 217 * k$ objects, where k denotes the number of MRI slices for a specified thickness. The set A contains the attributes labelling the voxels with respect to the MRI modalities illustrated in Figure 2.

The goal of MRI segmentation is to classify voxels into their correct tissue classes using the available attributes A. We trained the classifier using a *decision table* $\mathbb{A} = (U, A \cup \{d\})$, where the additional *decision attribute* $d \notin A$ represents the ground truth. We can consider five basic decision classes corresponding to the following types: background, bone, white matter (WM), gray matter (GM), and cerebral spinal fluid (CSF) (cf. Figure 1). In our approach we restrict our classification algorithm to WM, GM, and CSF voxels. Below we characterize the method we employed to extract the attributes in A from the MRI images.

Magnitude: *Magnitude attributes*, denoted by $mag_{T1}, mag_{T2}, mag_{PD}$, have the values derived from frequency histograms for T1, T2, and PD modalities. Figure 1 below graphically displays the total voxel content of a single SBD T1-weighted slice. There are several peaks which can be resolved using standard polynomial interpolation techniques. We used a set of Matlab Polynomial Toolbox functions (Polyfit and Polyval) and normalized the y-axis to smooth out the histogram in order to find the peaks. We extracted the Full-Width Half-Maximum (FWHM) interval for each peak (which is approximately centered about the mean). We labelled the objects-voxels belonging to each such FWHM with specific values of mag_{T1} in our decision table. In the same way, we labelled the objects belonging to the gaps between those intervals with some intermediate values. The same procedure was invoked for the T2 and PD image magnitude attributes.

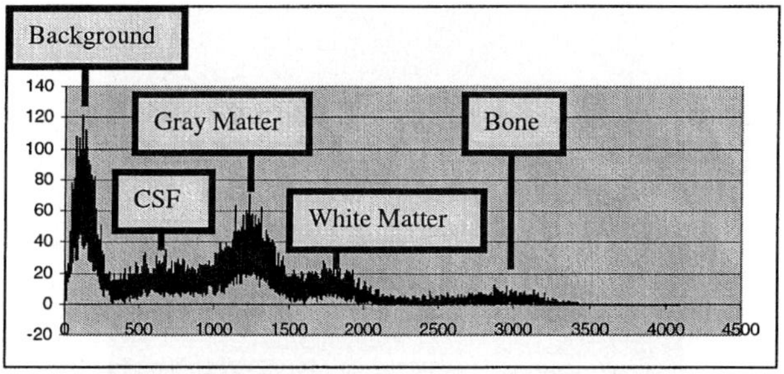

Fig. 1. A single bin frequency histogram from a T1 SBD slice #81 (1mm slice thickness, 3% noise and 20% INU). The x-axis values are 12 bit-unsigned integers, corresponding to the magnitude of the voxels from the raw image data. The histogram's peaks are likely to correspond to particular decision/tissue classes.

Discrete Laplacian and Neighbor: *Discrete Laplacian attributes*, denoted by $lap_{T1}, lap_{T2}, lap_{PD}$, have values derived by a general non-directional gradient operator, which is used in this context to determine whether the neighboring voxels have enough homogenous values. For instance, lap_{T1} takes the value 0 for a given voxel, if its neighborhood for T1 is homogeneous, and 1 otherwise. We use a threshold determined by the variance of this image which varies according to noise and INU. The associated *neighbor attributes*, denoted by $nbr_{T1}, nbr_{T2}, nbr_{PD}$, replace the original values of magnitudes mag_{T1}, mag_{T2}, and mag_{PD} using the following approach:

```
If (lap == 1)
    nbr = magnitude value from the decision table
Else // (then we want to adjust the middle voxel to its neighbors)
    If (there is unique most frequent value in neighborhood)
        nbr = the most frequent value in neighborhood
    Else
        nbr = the value of a randomly chosen neighboring voxel
```

Mask: The *mask attribute*, denoted by msk, is a rough estimation of the position of a voxel within the brain. First we isolate the brain region by creating a binary mask. On a histogram we find a frequency value below which every magnitude value corresponds to background. After artifact removal and hole filling, we are left with a single solid masked brain region. Then a central point is calculated which is an average of x and y coordinates of masked voxels. We divide the mask into 4 parts by drawing two orthogonal lines that cross at the center. Then 3 translations are made of all 4 parts: by 10, 20, and 50 voxels towards central point, as displayed in Figure 2.D. It yields concentric circles defining the approximations of bone, GM, WM, and CSF. The values of $msk \in A$ in our decision table $\mathbb{A} = (U, A \cup \{d\})$ are defined by membership of voxels to particular regions (GM = 1, WM = 2, and CSF = 3).

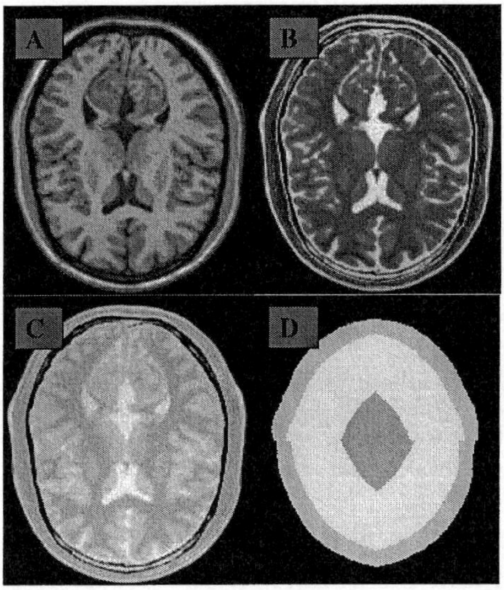

Fig. 2. Modalities T1 (Picture A), T2 (B), and PD (C) from the SBD data set, generated for slice thickness 1mm, 3% noise, and 20% field inhomogeneity (INU). Picture D presents the mask obtained for these modalities.

3 Approximate Reduction

When modelling complex phenomena, one must strike a balance between accuracy and computational complexity. In the current context, this balance is achieved through the use of a *decision reduct*: an irreducible subset $B \subseteq A$ *determining* d in decision table $\mathbb{A} = (U, A \cup \{d\})$. The obtained decision reducts are used to produce the decision rules from the training data. For smaller reducts we generate shorter and more general rules, better applicable to new objects. Therefore, it is worth searching for reducts with a minimal number of attributes.

Sometimes it is better to remove more attributes to get even shorter rules at the cost of slight inconsistencies. One can specify a measure $\mathcal{M}(d/\cdot) : \mathcal{P}(A) \to \mathbb{R}$ which evaluates the degree of influence $\mathcal{M}(d/B)$ of subsets $B \subseteq A$ on d. Then one can decide which attributes may be removed from A without a *significant* loss of the level of $\mathcal{M}$. Given decision table $\mathbb{A} = (U, A \cup \{d\})$, accuracy measure $\mathcal{M}(d/\cdot) : \mathcal{P}(A) \to \mathbb{R}$, and approximation threshold $\varepsilon \in [0, 1)$, let us say that $B \subseteq A$ is an $(\mathcal{M}, \varepsilon)$-*approximate decision reduct*, if and only if it satisfies inequality $\mathcal{M}(d/B) \geq (1 - \varepsilon)\mathcal{M}(d/A)$ and none of its proper subsets does it. For a more advanced study on such reducts we refer the reader to [10]. In this article, we consider the *multi-decision relative gain measure* (cf. [12]):

Definition 1. *Let $\mathbb{A} = (U, A \cup \{d\})$ and $\varepsilon \in [0, 1)$ be given. We say that $B \subseteq A$ is an (R, ε)*-approximate decision reduct, *if and only if it is irreducible set of attributes that satisfies inequality*

$$R(d/B) \geq (1 - \varepsilon)R(d/A) \tag{1}$$

where

$$R(d/B) = \sum_{\textit{rules } \mathrm{r} \textit{ induced by } \mathrm{B}} \left(\frac{\textit{number of objects recognizable by } \mathrm{r}}{\textit{number of objects in } \mathrm{U}} * \max_i \frac{\textit{probability of the } \mathrm{i}\textit{-th decision class induced by } \mathrm{r}}{\textit{prior probability of the } \mathrm{i}\textit{-th decision class}} \right) \tag{2}$$

Measure 2 expresses the average gain in determining decision classes under the evidence provided by the rules generated by $B \subseteq A$ [12]. It can be used, e.g., to evaluate the potential influence of a particular attributes on the decision. The quantities of $R(d/\{a\})$, $a \in A$, reflect the average information gain obtained from one-attribute rules. They are, however, not enough to select the *subsets* of relevant attributes. For instance, several attributes $a \in A$ with low values of $R(d/\{a\})$ can create together a subset $B \subseteq A$ with high $R(d/B)$ – they may represent complementary knowledge about decision which should be put together while constructing the decision rules.

The problems of finding approximate reducts are NP-hard (cf. [10]). Therefore, even for the case of decision table $\mathbb{A} = (U, A \cup \{d\})$ with only 10 attributes

$$A = \{mag_{T1}, lap_{T1}, nbr_{T1}, msk, mag_{T2}, lap_{T2}, nbr_{T2}, mag_{PD}, lap_{PD}, nbr_{PD}\}$$

described in the previous section, it means that one would prefer to consider the use of a heuristic rather than an exhaustive search for the best reducts, in the light of computational complexity. We extend the *order based genetic algorithm (o-GA)* for searching for minimal decision reducts [14], to find heuristically (sub)optimal reducts specified by Definition 1. We follow the same way of extension as that proposed in [11] for searching for reducts approximately preserving the measure of information entropy.

Each genetic algorithm simulates the evolution of *individuals* within a population [2, 14]. The result of evolution is an increase in the average fitness of members of a population, which strives towards some global optimum. In the computational version of evolution, the fittest individual(s) within a given population are taken to be nearly as optimal as the global optimum of the given problem. Its behavior depends on the specification of the *fitness function*, which evaluates individuals and determines which of them are likely to survive. As a *hybrid algorithm* [2], our o-GA consists of two parts:

1. *Genetic part*, where each chromosome encodes a permutation of attributes
2. *Heuristic part*, where permutations τ are put into the following algorithm:

(R, ε)-REDORD algorithm (cf. [11, 14]):

1. Let $\mathbb{A} = (U, A \cup \{d\})$ and $\tau : \{1, .., |A|\} \rightarrow \{1, .., |A|\}$ be given; Let $B_\tau = A$;
2. For $i = 1$ to $|A|$ repeat steps 3 and 4;
3. Let $B_\tau \leftarrow B_\tau \setminus \{a_{\tau(i)}\}$;
4. If B_τ does not satisfy condition (1), undo step 3.

We define fitness of a given permutation-individual τ due to the quality of B_τ resulting from (R, ε)-REDORD. The reduct quality is usually based on its length (cf. [6, 14]). Therefore, we use the following measure for a reduct [14]:

$$fitness(\tau) = 1 - card(B_\tau) \,/\, card(A) \tag{3}$$

To work on permutations-individuals, we use the order cross-over (OX) and the standard mutation switching randomly selected genes [2, 8]. The results are *always* (R, ε)-approximate decision reducts, i.e. satisfy criterion (1) and cannot be further reduced without its failure.

4 Results of Experiments

The experimental results were obtained using 150 segmentation test cases. For each test a training set was generated using 10 random brain slices chosen from the slice range (61-130) in SBD database. For each thickness 1/3/5/7/9mm and the noise levels (noise/INU) 3/20, 9/20, and 9/40, we performed the classification tests based on the following procedure:

1. Generate all (R, ε)-approximate decision reducts using o-GA based on (R, ε)-REDORD algorithm for a given $\varepsilon \in [0, 1)$;
2. For each obtained (R, ε)-approximate decision reduct $B \subseteq A$ generate decision rules with conditions induced by B and its values in the universe;
3. Sort decision rules according to their support, in order to choose the most significant rules which recognize each given object;
4. For a new unclassified object choose α most significant applicable rules;
5. Choose a decision which is overall best supported within the set of the most significant rules.

		Noise 3% / INU 20%			Noise 9% / INU 20%			Noise 9% / INU 40%		
		$\alpha = 1$	$\alpha = 3$	$\alpha = 5$	$\alpha = 1$	$\alpha = 3$	$\alpha = 5$	$\alpha = 1$	$\alpha = 3$	$\alpha = 5$
Th 1	$\varepsilon =$									
	0.002	94.65	94.67	94.42	83.54	82.54	83.04	76.72	76.44	77.81
	0.004	94.83	94.73	95.05	82.92	82.31	82.20	78.08	77.09	75.63
	0.006	94.46	94.79	94.73	82.30	81.84	81.36	**78.72**	76.39	76.46
	0.008	94.53	94.82	**95.10**	82.68	82.46	82.95	77.47	77.72	74.37
	0.010	94.45	94.71	94.90	82.09	**84.35**	81.42	76.89	77.19	78.34
Th 3	$\varepsilon =$									
	0.002	87.76	87.80	**88.54**	83.77	84.01	84.01	80.96	81.12	**81.61**
	0.004	87.80	87.81	87.86	84.06	84.19	84.10	79.04	79.08	79.08
	0.006	87.80	88.35	88.35	84.06	84.03	84.03	79.04	79.08	79.08
	0.008	87.80	88.24	88.34	84.07	84.04	**84.19**	79.05	78.89	79.06
	0.010	87.80	88.35	88.35	84.06	84.03	84.03	79.01	76.40	78.92
Th 5	$\varepsilon =$									
	0.002	75.19	83.12	81.94	**82.73**	81.91	81.91	80.31	80.31	80.31
	0.004	83.23	83.72	83.72	81.66	81.62	81.62	80.33	80.37	80.37
	0.006	83.23	83.60	83.23	81.66	81.85	81.85	80.36	80.26	80.23
	0.008	83.23	83.72	83.72	81.66	81.69	81.85	80.33	80.37	80.37
	0.010	83.23	83.60	**83.72**	81.66	80.54	80.54	80.32	79.90	**80.56**
Th 7	$\varepsilon =$									
	0.002	78.77	78.77	78.77	78.75	78.69	78.46	77.52	77.52	77.52
	0.004	78.84	79.25	79.25	78.85	78.79	78.85	77.81	78.03	78.03
	0.006	78.84	79.25	79.25	78.85	**79.06**	78.89	77.81	78.03	78.03
	0.008	78.84	79.25	79.20	78.85	78.79	78.85	77.52	77.52	77.52
	0.010	78.84	79.25	**79.25**	78.86	78.01	78.01	77.81	77.34	**78.04**
Th 9	$\varepsilon =$									
	0.002	77.21	77.22	**79.19**	75.29	75.66	75.40	74.50	74.67	74.74
	0.004	77.20	77.21	77.31	76.49	76.65	76.56	74.82	74.90	74.90
	0.006	77.22	77.54	77.54	76.49	76.65	76.65	74.82	74.82	74.82
	0.008	77.22	77.54	77.54	76.49	76.54	**76.67**	74.82	75.02	**75.18**
	0.010	77.21	77.33	77.22	76.36	76.08	76.55	74.54	74.51	74.95

Fig. 3. Application of (R, ε)-approximate reducts extracted from slices with noise 3% and INU 20%. We test cases with noise 3% / INU 20%, noise 9% / INU 20%, and noise 9% / INU 40%, considered for thickness varying from 1mm to 9mm.

The above procedure was more challenging when applied to slices which possessed a higher thickness/noise/INU level. For each of such levels, we considered 15 tests parameterized by the choice of ε and α as illustrated by Figure 3.

The results from Figure 3 were obtained by testing 20 random slices (range 61-130) from the same image volumes (across all 3 imaging modalities). For the slice thicknesses higher than 1mm we tested on all given slices within the specified range above because of decreasing number of slices when thickness increases.

For each level of $\varepsilon \in [0, 1)$, we calculated the average length of (R, ε)-approximate reducts obtained for various data sets. By varying from $\varepsilon = 0,002$ to $0,010$, this length decreases from $3,82$ to $2,35$, without dramatic changes in the average accuracy (practically the same result of 80,88% for $\varepsilon = 0,002$ and $0,010$, with the best intermediate average accuracy 81,03% for $\varepsilon = 0,004$). It shows that using o-GA with (R,ε)-REDORD algorithm enables us to reduce thoroughly the number of attributes necessary for reasonable classification.

The results also show that the proposed reduction procedure can yield better classification model than in case of selection of attributes, which seem to provide the highest information gain separately. Figure 4 shows that the attributes with high values induced by measure (2) are not necessarily those most frequently occurring in the reducts and, therefore, decision rules used for classification. For instance, for $\varepsilon = 0,004$ which has the best average accuracy level, attributes msk, nbr_{T2}, mag_{PD} loose their importance, although their relative gain values are higher than, e.g., that of lap_{T1}, which starts to be crucial in decision rules. Moreover, for $\varepsilon \geq 0,004$, the most frequently occurring (R,ε)-approximate reducts were always $\{mag_{T1}\}$ and $\{lap_{T1}, nbr_{T1}, mag_{T2}\}$. It suggests that modalities $T1, T2$ are fairly enough for the MRI segmentation.

a	$R(d/a)$	$\varepsilon = 0.002$	$\varepsilon = 0.004$	$\varepsilon = 0.006$	$\varepsilon = 0.008$	$\varepsilon = 0.010$
mag_{T1}	2.87	65	32	23	20	20
lap_{Tl}	1.39	22	28	20	36	37
nbr_{T1}	2.80	24	29	20	36	37
msk	1.53	38	7	1	5	7
mag_{T2}	2.00	29	32	21	19	10
lap_{T2}	1.31	2	6	1	0	5
nbr_{T2}	2.09	49	7	1	17	13
mag_{PD}	1.53	20	3	0	1	4
lap_{PD}	1.13	18	4	0	0	1
nbr_{PD}	1.12	5	2	0	3	0

Fig. 4. Decision information gains induced by particular attributes evaluated using measure (2) for the exemplary considered data, as well as the numbers of occurrences of attributes within (R,ε)-approximate reducts extracted for various settings of $\varepsilon \in [0,1)$.

The second phase of our experiments concerned comparison with other approaches to the MRI segmentation. Since the results in the literature are usually stated for slightly different (less varied) settings of noise, INU, and thickness, we recalculated our classification models appropriately. Given the experience, resulting from Figure 3 and other statistics, we were trying to use possibly optimal settings for $\varepsilon \in [0,1)$ and the number rules α used in the voting procedure. The obtained comparison is illustrated in Figure 5. It shows that our approach is competitive with the other, often much more complicated methods.

5 Conclusions and Discussion

An automated image segmentation must be quick (on the order of seconds) and have a reliable level of accuracy across all tissue classes. Our results indicate

Thickness	Phantom Accuracy	Our Accuracy	
1	90.0%	90.0%	91.9%
3	84.0%	87.1%	89.3%
5	74.0%	82.8%	86.2%
Noise	**Phantom Accuracy**	**Our Accuracy**	
0	89.0%	90.0%	91.9%
3	91.0%	95.5%	95.7%
5	84.0%	92.8%	29.0%
7	84.0%	88.0%	85.3%
9	81.0%	82.4%	74.2%
INU	**Phantom Accuracy**	**Our Accuracy**	
0	90.0%	9.00%	91.9%
20	91.0%	9.40%	95.2%
40	86.0%	9.33%	92.4%

Fig. 5. "Phantom Accuracy" from SBD at the default values for noise 3% and INU 20% (http://www.bic.mni.mcgill.ca/users/kwan/vasco.html). "Our Accuracy" for 3% noise and 20% INU (1st sub-column), as well as 0% noise and 0% INU (2nd sub-column).

that with a reasonable amount of noise (3-5%), typical field inhomogeneities (20% or less), and a reasonable slice thickness (3-5mm), our approximate reduct algorithm is capable of yielding segmentation accuracy on the order of 90+ %, consistent – if not more accurate than other approaches. Not only our algorithm achieve a high segmentation accuracy, but it works across all 3 major imaging modalities (T1, T2, PD). This is a contrast to most other segmentation algorithms which classify on a single modality [5, 7, 15].

Our results are obtained without any image pre-processing such as median filtering and other smoothing operations. We are pursuing investigating the segmentation accuracy when various standardized filtering and averaging processes are embedded into the algorithm. The results indicate that the major impediment to accurate segmentation is slice thickness and noise. They display a reduction of just 18% from the best to the worst case. This problem may not be solved with technological advances, but may instead, require a fresh computational perspective, one such as that provided by the rough set theory.

There are numerous issues which should be additionally taken into account. First of all, we considered only healthy brain images with constant number of histogram peaks. In future, we will focus on some pathologies and extend the system to read most of known MRI data standards. Secondly, our algorithm is a supervised method. In a real live data, however, we would not have a known segmented phantom. This could be coped by using more training data sets generated from, e.g., some brain atlas data sets. Finally, we have a number of technical problems to be solved. For instance, images with high INU have a general "speckled" appearance. This may be due in part to the variance threshold applied to the Laplacian function. In general, we use some parameters chosen manually. In future, we will extend our o-GA to optimize them adaptively.

Acknowledgments

We would like to thank Mr. Łukasz Budkiewicz for help in preprocessing the MRI data, as well as Dr. Jakub Wróblewski for valuable comments on implementation and usage of the order based genetic algorithms.

The third author was supported by the grant awarded from the Faculty of Science at the University of Regina, as well as by the internal research grant of Polish-Japanese Institute of Information Technology.

References

1. Cocosco, C.A., Zijdenbos, A.P., Evans, A.C.: Automatic Generation of Training Data for Brain Tissue Classification from MRI. In: Proc. of MICCAI'2002 (2002).
2. Davis, L. (ed.): Handbook of Genetic Algorithms. Van Nostrand Reinhold (1991).
3. Kamber, M., Shinghal, R., Collins, L.: Model-based 3D Segmentation of Multiple Sclerosis Lesions in Magnetic Resonance Brain Images. IEEE Trans Med Imaging 14(3) (1995) pp. 442–453.
4. Kaus, M., Warfield, S.K., Nabavi, A., Black, P.M., Jolesz, F.A., Kikinis, R.: Automated Segmentation of MRI of Brain Tumors. Radiology 218 (2001) pp. 586–591.
5. Kollokian, V.: Performance Analysis of Automatic Techniques for Tissue Classification in Magnetic Resonance Images of the Human Brain. Master's thesis, Concordia University, Montreal, Canada (1996).
6. Komorowski, J., Pawlak, Z., Polkowski, L., Skowron, A.: Rough sets: A tutorial. In: S.K. Pal, A. Skowron (eds): Rough Fuzzy Hybridization – A New Trend in Decision Making. Springer Verlag (1999) pp. 3–98.
7. Kovacevic N., Lobaugh N.J., Bronskill M.J., Levine B., Feinstein A. and Black, S.E.: A Robust Extraction and Automatic Segmentation of Brain Images. NeuroImage 17 (2002) pp. 1087–1100.
8. Michalewicz, Z.: Genetic Algorithms + Data Structures = Evolution Programs. Springer-Verlag (1994).
9. Pawlak, Z.: Rough sets – Theoretical aspects of reasoning about data. Kluwer (1991).
10. Ślęzak, D.: Approximate Entropy Reducts. Fundamenta Informaticae (2002).
11. Ślęzak, D., Wróblewski, J.: Order-based genetic algorithms for the search of approximate entropy reducts. In: Proc. of RSFDGrC'2003. Chongqing, China (2003).
12. Ślęzak, D., Ziarko, W.: Attribute Reduction in Bayesian Version of Variable Precision Rough Set Model. In: Proc. of RSKD'2003. Elsevier, ENTCS 82(4) (2003).
13. Vannier, M.W.: Validation of Magnetic Resonance Imaging (MRI) Multispectral Tissue Classification. Computerized Medical Imaging and Graphics 15(4) (1991).
14. Wróblewski, J.: Theoretical Foundations of Order-Based Genetic Algorithms. Fundamenta Informaticae 28(3-4) (1996) pp. 423–430.
15. Xue J.H., Pizurica A., Philips W., Kerre E., Van de Walle R., Lemahieu, I.: An Integrated Method of Adaptive Enhancement for Unsupervised Segmentation of MRI Brain Images. Pattern Recognition Letters, Vol 24(15) (2003) pp. 2549–2560.
16. Zijdenbos, A.P., Dawant, B.M., Margolin, R.A., Palmer, A.C.: Morphometric Analysis of White Matter Lesions in MR Images: Method and Validation. IEEE Trans. Med. Imaging 13(4) (1994) pp. 716–724.

Rough Set-Based Classification of EEG-Signals to Detect Intraoperative Awareness: Comparison of Fuzzy and Crisp Discretization of Real Value Attributes

Michael Ningler[1], Gudrun Stockmanns[2], Gerhard Schneider[1], Oliver Dressler[1], and Eberhard F. Kochs[1]

[1] Department of Anesthesiology, Klinikum rechts der Isar
Technische Universität München, Ismaninger Straße 22, D-81675 München, Germany
{m.ningler,gerhard.schneider,e.f.kochs}@lrz.tu-muenchen.de
http://www.anaesth.med.tu-muenchen.de

[2] Institute of Information Technology, University Duisburg – Essen
Bismarckstr. 90, D-47057 Duisburg, Germany
gudrun.stockmanns@uni-duisburg.de
http://iit.uni-duisburg.de

Abstract. Automated classification of calculated EEG parameters has been shown to be a promising method for detection of intraoperative awareness. In the present study, rough set-based methods were employed to generate classification rules. For these methods, discrete attributes are required. We compared a crisp and a fuzzy discretization of the real parameter values. Fuzzy discretization transforms one real attribute value to several discrete values. By combining the different (discrete) values of all attributes, several sub-objects were produced from a single original object. Rule generation from a training set of objects and classification of a test set provided good classification rates of approximately 90% for both crisp and fuzzy discretization. Fuzzy discretization resulted in a simpler and smaller rule set than crisp discretization. Therefore, the simplicity of the resulting classifier justifies the higher computational effort caused by fuzzy discretization.

1 Introduction

Recently, electroencephalogram (EEG) analysis has attained increasing interest for detection of intraoperative awareness during general anesthesia. As continuous visual analysis of raw EEG is not feasible during anesthesia, automated classification of EEG data is highly desired. For this purpose, we used rough set theory to build a classifier that discerns the patient states "unconscious" and "aware" by employing EEG-derived parameters.

Rough set theory provides methods to create rule-based classifiers, and has successfully been employed in different fields particularly in medical applications (e.g. [11]). Rough set methods require discrete attributes. As the EEG signal and its derived attributes are continuous, a preprocessing step is necessary to discretize those

S. Tsumoto et al. (Eds.): RSCTC 2004, LNAI 3066, pp. 825–834, 2004.

attributes. This paper presents a crisp and a fuzzy discretization method, both compared with respect to their classification performance (measured by classification rate) and to the simplicity of the related classifiers (measured by the number and length of the generated rules).

2 Basic Concepts

Rough set theory, as developed by Pawlak [6], is applied to objects which are described by a set of condition attributes and assigned to certain decisions (classes). In general, some objects may be indistinguishable using only the knowledge given by the condition attributes. When such objects are assigned to different classes, it is not possible to imply the decision based only on the condition attributes. Rough set theory solves that problem by employing approximate sets. Methods based on this concept allow:

1. to reduce the set of condition attributes to a smaller set called (relative) reduct, which provides the same classification performance as the entire set, and
2. to create decision rules to classify new objects.

The original rough set methods create decision rules that classify the entire training set of objects correctly. This procedure assumes exact input data. Corruption of attribute values or of classes caused by noise is not tolerated at all. Variable precision rough set model is an extension of the original concept that allows a small error in object classification, denoted by β, and produces more general reducts and decision rules [14].

Decision rules have the form $c_1 = v_{c1} \wedge c_2 = v_{c2} \wedge \ldots \rightarrow d$, where c_1, c_2, ... are condition attributes, v_{c1}, v_{c2}, ... are values of condition attributes and d is a decision. An object *matches* a rule, if the values of all condition attributes c_i given by the rule are equal to the values of the corresponding attributes of the object. The *length* of a rule is determined by the number of given attribute-value pairs of this rule. A rule is called *minimal*, if it is not possible to remove an attribute-value pair from the rule without loosing classification performance [8].

Tsumoto introduced two measures to assess a decision rule R [12]:

accuracy: $$\alpha_R = \frac{|X_R \cap D_R|}{|X_R|}, \quad (1)$$

coverage: $$\kappa_R = \frac{|X_R \cap D_R|}{|D_R|}, \quad (2)$$

where X_R is the set of all objects matching rule R, D_R is the set of all objects having the same decision as the rule R, and $|X_R|$ denotes the magnitude of a set X_R. Accuracy is a measure of the probability of a correct classification for an object that matches the rule. Coverage measures the number of correctly classified objects over the number of all objects with the same decision as the rule.

In the present approach, all minimal rules are generated that provide a previously determined minimal accuracy δ_α. During generation of the rules, α_R and κ_R are calculated for each rule and stored for further processing.

3 Discretization

As rough set theory requires discrete attributes, a preprocessing step is necessary to discretize the real value attributes. In the present paper crisp and fuzzy discretization methods were performed to compare their influence on the resulting classifier.

Generally, crisp discretization is performed by dividing the domain of the real value attribute into several intervals. Many different discretization methods exist in literature [3]. Even rough set methods can be used for discretization (see e.g. [5]). For the present application, the following requirements should be fulfilled by the particular discretization method:

- The original attributes should be preserved, to facilitate the interpretation of the resulting rule set.
- The discretization of one attribute should be independent from the discretization of other attributes, to allow incremental execution and modification.
- The discretization should be unsupervised – i.e. no class information is used – to allow the discretization of the entire set of objects before partitioning into training and test set.

These requirements narrow the choice of discretization methods. In our approach, the boundaries of the intervals were determined by equal frequency method, i.e. each interval includes approximately the same number of objects. The intervals were assigned to integer numbers, which are used as discrete attribute values.

Crisp discretization is very strict and does not take into account the distances or similarities between objects in an adequate way. Thus, objects with similar real values may be assigned to different intervals and objects with a significant difference in the real domain may be indiscernible in the discretized domain. Fuzzy discretization solves that problem by assigning a real attribute value not only to one but to several discrete values with a *degree of membership*. This softens the strict interval boundaries and results in a more flexible representation of the objects' properties.

For this purpose, the set of interval numbers is interpreted as a set of *linguistic terms* according to fuzzy set theory. A real attribute value is related to each linguistic term k with a *degree of membership* μ_k. μ_k can be interpreted as a degree of association of the real value with the linguistic term k. For each linguistic term k a *membership function* f_k is defined. The *membership function* determines the degree of membership μ_k of the linguistic term k for a real attribute value.

In the present approach, the membership functions have triangular form with a maximum (1) at the center of the according crisp interval and minima (0) at the centers of previous and next interval. As a result, only the membership functions of neighboring intervals overlap and the sum of all membership functions is 1 at any arbitrary real value (see figure 1). Therefore, every real attribute value is assigned to at most two linguistic terms (interval numbers) with μ_k>0. After fuzzy discretization a single value of attribute c_i has turned into multiple values with degrees of membership μ_{c_ik}. An attribute c_i with multiple values is called a *multiple descriptor* [10].

This procedure is illustrated by an example: One object is described by the two real value attributes c_1 and c_2. The fuzzy linguistic terms are given by (1 / 2 / 3) for both attributes. The degrees of membership for attribute c_1 μ_{c_1k} are (0.1 / 0.9 / 0.0) and for attribute c_2 μ_{c_2k} are (0.0 / 0.7 / 0.3). These values are provided by membership functions not presented here. The values of the attributes c_1 and c_2 turn to multiple descriptors (see table 1).

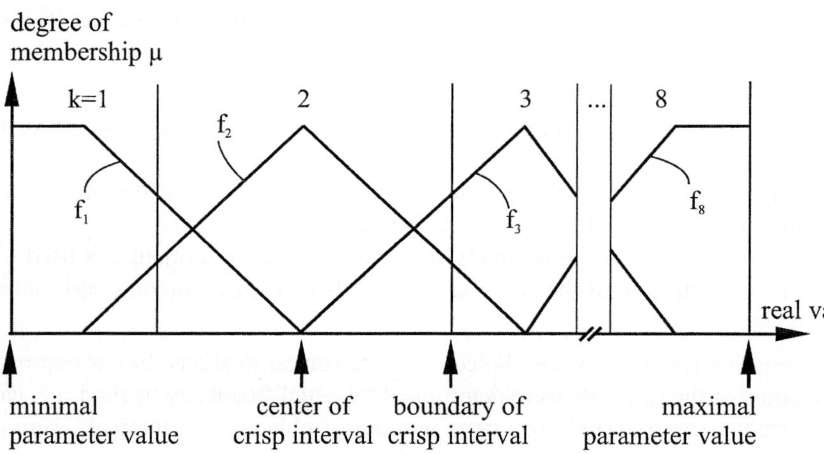

Fig. 1. Construction of membership functions f_k using interval boundaries of crisp discretization. In the present approach, 8 intervals were used.

Table 1. Example for multiple descriptors after fuzzy discretization of the single attributes.

object	c_1		c_2	
	k	μ_{c_1k}	k	μ_{c_2k}
1	1	0.1	1	0.0
	2	0.9	2	0.7
	3	0.0	3	0.3

This type of attributes cannot be handled by rough set methods. Slowinski and Stefanowski proposed a method to transform one object with multiple descriptors into several *sub-objects* with single discrete attribute values and an additional real number called *degree of realization* [10]. Sub-objects are built by all possible combinations of the linguistic terms k with $\mu_{c_ik} > 0$ of all attributes.

In our example, this procedure results in four sub-objects as depicted in column 1-5 of table 2. To calculate the degree of realization of a certain sub-object m, at first the degrees of membership μ_{c_ik} are averaged over all attributes c_i. This results in an aggregated degree of membership μ_m (see column 6 of table 2):

$$\mu_m = \frac{1}{|C|}\sum_{c_i \in C} \mu_{c_ik}\,, \tag{3}$$

where C is the set of all attributes.

Table 2. Creation of sub-objects from a single object by combination of all linguistic terms of all attributes.

sub-object m	c_1	μ_{c_1k}	c_2	μ_{c_2k}	μ_μ
1	1	0.1	2	0.7	0.4
2	1	0.1	3	0.3	0.2
3	2	0.9	2	0.7	0.8
4	2	0.9	3	0.3	0.6
				Sum μ_m	2.0

The degree of realization π_m of a sub-object is calculated by normalizing μ_m:

$$\pi_m = \frac{\mu_m}{\sum_{m=1}^{M} \mu_m}\,, \tag{4}$$

where M is the number of all sub-objects constructed from the considered original object. For rule generation, only discretized attributes and the degree of realization π_m are used (see table 3).

Table 3. Resulting representation of sub-objects after fuzzy discretization.

sub-object m	c_1	c_2	π_m
1	1	2	0.2
2	1	3	0.1
3	2	2	0.4
4	2	3	0.3

The same procedure is repeated for each original object. The structure of sub-objects is similar to an information system commonly used in rough set theory, except for the existence of π_m. Rough set methods as described in the previous section require only slight modification before they can be applied to sub-objects. In the original rough set theory the magnitude of a set of objects is given by the number of objects. The magnitude of a set of sub-objects X is calculated as the sum of the π_x over all elements of X:

$$|X| = \sum_{x \in X} \pi_x\,. \tag{5}$$

Now a sub-object is denoted by x instead of m to indicate that sub-objects can result from several original objects.

4 Classification of New Objects

To classify a new object y by a set of decision rules, we applied fuzzy inference (e.g. [13]), irrespective of the discretization method (crisp or fuzzy): The value of each attribute of the new object y is separately fuzzy discretized as described in the previous section (table 1). In the following, a rule R of the form $c_1 = v_{c1} \wedge c_2 = v_{c2} \wedge ... \rightarrow d$ is considered. An attribute value v_{ci} of the rule corresponds to a linguistic term k of attribute c_i of the object y and therefore to the according degree of membership μ_{c_ik}. Fuzzy inference does not simply check whether an object matches a rule or not. Instead a *degree of fulfillment* μ_R is calculated as the minimum of the μ_{c_ik} of all attributes employed by rule R:

$$\mu_R = MIN(\{\mu_{c_ik} \mid k = v_{ci}\}) . \tag{6}$$

Example: R is given by $c_1 = 1 \wedge c_2 = 3 \rightarrow d$ and object y is given by the example of table 1. Then $\mu_R = MIN(\mu_{c_1 1}, \mu_{c_2 3}) = MIN(0.1, 0.3) = 0.1$.

Each rule of the rule set is weighted with a weighting factor $w_R = \mu_R \cdot \kappa_R$, where κ_R is the coverage of rule R, as calculated when generating the rules. Subsequently, all rules are grouped by their decision d resulting in a set of rules for each decision. To classify the object y all w_R are summed up separately for each decision and the decision with the highest sum is assigned to object y.

If this highest sum is equal for several decisions, the object is classified as "unknown" and treated as misclassified. The same applies, if $\mu_R = 0$ for all rules.

5 Clinical Data

Rough set methods were applied to segments of EEG signals from anesthetized and aware patients. The data were taken from a clinical study on 40 patients who underwent surgery under general anesthesia [7]. The recording of EEG signals was started several minutes before induction of anesthesia and stopped several minutes after return of consciousness after surgery. After loss of consciousness and intubation, hypnotic agent was stopped until awareness occurred. Then administration of the hypnotic was resumed and surgery was performed. As the result, there were three phases of patient state "aware" and two phases of state "unconscious".

Signal segments with a length of 8 seconds were taken immediately before and after loss of consciousness as well as before and after awareness (return of consciousness) and were associated to the two classes "unconscious" / "aware", respectively. Additional segments were taken from the "aware" state and supplemented by the same number of segments from the "unconscious" state. A clinical expert visually assessed the artifact contamination of the segments, and severely distorted segments were disregarded. The resulting set of segments consists of 224 segments from "aware" state and 251 segments of "unconscious" state. This data set is very challenging due to the selection of segments close to the transitions between patient states, where EEG signals were similar for the different classes.

6 Data Processing

52 parameters were calculated from the EEG segments using spectral analysis, statistical methods, complexity measures and basic signal processing methods such as maximum absolute amplitude. Each parameter provided one real value for each segment. The selection of the parameters was done in several steps.

At first, the parameters were separately assessed for their ability to distinguish between the two classes "unconscious" / "aware" through Receiver Operator Characteristics (ROC) analysis [4]. ROC analysis calculates sensitivity and specificity for each possible threshold given by the mean of two consecutive parameter values. The ROC curve is a plot of sensitivity against 1 - specificity. The area under ROC curve is a real number in the range of 0 – 1. This area is a measure for the ability of the parameter to distinguish between the two classes, whereas 0.5 means that the classes can not be distinguished at all. If the classes can be perfectly separated by the considered parameter, the ROC area is 0 or 1.

Then, multiple correlation clustering was applied [2]. This method decomposes the set of parameters into subsets of similar, i.e. highly correlated, parameters. From highly correlated parameters, parameters revealing the poorer discrimination of the patient states – measured by the area under ROC curve – were removed.

The resulting set of 10 parameters was further reduced by calculating relative reducts using variable precision rough set model based on crisp discretized data (8 intervals, equal frequency method). The objects were given by the EEG segments and the decision classes by the two patient states "unconscious" and "aware". The admissible classification error β was varied from 0 to 0.40 in steps of 0.05. The final parameter set was selected based on the most frequent relative reducts and comprises five parameters (see table 4).

For the rule generation, both crisp and fuzzy discretization (with 8 intervals / linguistic terms) were performed, as previously described. The fuzzy discretization resulted in 13424 sub-objects. The following calculations were independently performed for crisp and fuzzy discretization.

Classification rates were calculated by three-fold cross validation [11], as described in the following. The set of objects was divided into 3 subsets. The segments of a single patient were assigned to only one of these subsets. Each subset contained approximately the same number of objects of each class. Two of the subsets were used as a training set to create a rule set. The objects of the remaining set (test set) were classified using these rules and a classification rate was calculated as the ratio of correctly classified objects over the number of all objects of the test set.

Each of the three subsets of objects was used as a test set with the remaining two sets as training set. Results of the three calculations were averaged.

For rule creation, the minimal required accuracy δ_α was varied from 1 to 0.60 in steps of 0.05. Only rules with a minimal coverage of 0.01 were considered for the classification of the objects of the test set.

Table 4. Selected parameter set for rule creation.

Analysis Type	Parameter Name
Basic Signal Processing	1. Derivative: Crest Factor
Complexity Analysis	Lempel-Ziv Complexity Measure
Spectral Analysis	Band 30.00 – 127.99 Hz Absolute Power
Statistical Analysis	Normed Kurtosis
Statistical Analysis	Normed Skewness

7 Results

The main results for the comparison of crisp and fuzzy discretization are classification rates, number of rules and rule lengths. Presented results are averages of the three calculations from the three-fold cross validation.

For crisp discretization, the best classification rate was 90.1% with $\delta_\alpha = 0.90$. The best classification rate for fuzzy discretization was 90.3% with $\delta_\alpha = 0.85$. The classification rates are very close for both crisp and fuzzy discretization. For comparison we also developed a classifier based on self organizing feature maps. The classification rates of this classifier were approximately 89%.

The number of rules with a coverage of at least 0.01 was 139 for crisp and 56 for fuzzy discretization. Table 5 presents the distribution of the number of rules over the rule length. In the case of fuzzy discretization, more than 96% of all rules have a rule length shorter than 3, while for crisp discretization this applies for only 63% of all rules. That means, fuzzy discretization produces a reduced number of rules which are simpler.

Table 5. Frequency of rules with different rule lengths for crisp and fuzzy discretization.

	crisp ($\delta_\alpha = 0.90$)		fuzzy ($\delta_\alpha = 0.85$)	
rule length	numb. rules	ratio %	numb. rules	ratio %
1	12	8.6	11	19.6
2	75	54.0	43	76.8
3	51	36.7	2	3.6
4	1	0.7	0	0.0
sum	139	100.0	56	100.0

8 Conclusions

Both crisp and fuzzy discretization result in satisfying classification rates. Rough set methods and discretization techniques presented here have been proven to be appropriate for the separation of awareness from consciousness using EEG parameters.

As fuzzy discretized input data causes the creation of shorter rules, these rules are more general. Consequently, a smaller number of rules is necessary to describe the data set and the classifier is much simpler.

Alternatively, other crisp discretization methods could be applied such as equal width or more intelligent entropy-based or clustering-based methods. However, all these methods suffer from their insufficiency to represent similar objects in different intervals disjoint by strict boundaries, particularly when the attributes values are uniformly distributed over a wide range. Any crisp discretization can be used as the basis for the fuzzy discretization presented here.

In our approach, the degrees of membership in fuzzy discretization were aggregated by averaging, instead of employing Yager's t-norm, as proposed by Slowinski and Stefanowski [10]. We also tested an aggregation by the minimum operator, which is a special case of Yager's t-norm [10]. Since this resulted in slightly poorer classification rates, we decided to use averaging.

In further investigations improvements related to the feature selection procedure should be done, as the selection of the most frequent relative reduct is not very specific. Calculation of dynamic relative reducts [1] or searching for frequential reducts using probability distributions [9] for the attribute values might have advantages.

The computational effort is much higher for fuzzy than for crisp discretization, since this method results in 13424 sub-objects instead of 475 objects in the present approach. A careful selection of a small attribute set is crucial to avoid creation of too many sub-objects which may cause tremendous computation time. The classification of new objects with the completed rule set can become time critical, when on-line application is the goal. Therefore, it is more important to minimize the computational effort for classification than for rules generation. A smaller and simpler rule set justifies the higher computation time of fuzzy discretization for creation of the rules.

References

1. Bazan, J., Skowron, A., Synak, P.: Dynamic Reducts as a Tool for Extracting Laws from Decision Tables. International Symposium on Methodologies for Intelligent Systems ISMIS. Lecture Notes in Artificial Intelligence, Vol. 869. Springer-Verlag, Berlin Heidelberg New York (1994) 346-355
2. Doyle, J.R.: MCC - Multiple Correlation Clustering. International Journal of Man-Machine Studies, 37(6) (1992) 751-765
3. Liu, H., Hussain, F., Tan, C.L., Dash, M.: Discretization: An Enabling Technique. Data Mining and Knowledge Discovery 6(4) (2002) 393-423
4. Metz, C.E.: Basic Principles of ROC Analysis. Seminars in Nuclear Medicine 8(4) (1978) 283-298

5. Nguyen, H.S., Nguyen, S.H.: Discretization Methods in Data Mining. In: Polkowski, L., Skowron, A. (eds.): Rough Sets in Knowledge Discovery 1 - Methodology and Applications. Physica-Verlag, Heidelberg (1998) 451-482
6. Pawlak, Z.: Rough Sets. International Journal of Computer and Information Sciences, 11(5) (1982) 341-356
7. Schneider, G., Marcu, T., Stockmanns, G., Schäpers, G., Kochs, E.F.: Detection of Awareness during TIVA and Balanced Anesthesia Based on Wavelet-Transformed Auditory Evoked Potentials. www.asa-abstracts.com: A297 (2002)
8. Shan, N., Ziarko, W.: Data-based Acquisition and Incremental Modification of Classification Rules. Computational Intelligence 11(2) (1995) 357-370
9. Slezak, D.: Searching for Frequential Reducts in Decision Tables with Uncertain Objects. In: Polkowski, L., Skowron, A. (eds.): Rough Sets and Current Trends in Computing. Lecture Notes in Computer Science, Vol. 1424. Springer-Verlag, Berlin Heidelberg New York (1998) 52-59
10. Slowinski, R., Stefanowski, J.: Rough-Set Reasoning about uncertain data. Fundamenta Informaticae 27(2-3) (1996) 229-243
11. Tsumoto, S., Tanaka, H.: PRIMEROSE: Probabilistic Rule Induction Method Based on Rough Sets and Resampling Methods. Computational Intelligence 11(2) (1995) 389-405
12. Tsumoto, S., Tanaka, H.: Automated Discovery of Medical Expert System Rules from Clinical Databases Based on Rough Sets. Proceedings of the 2nd International Conference on Knowledge Discovery and Data Mining. AAAI Press, Menlo Park, California (1996) 63-69
13. Watanabe, H., Detloff, W.D.: VLSI fuzzy chip and inference accelerator board systems. In: Zadeh, L.A., Kacprzyk, J. (eds.): Fuzzy Logic for the Management of Uncertainty. John Wiley & Sons Inc., New York (1992) 211-243
14. Ziarko, W.: Variable Precision Rough Set Model. Journal of Computer and System Sciences, 46 (1993) 39-59

Fuzzy Logic-Based Modeling of the Biological Regulator of Blood Glucose

José-Luis Sánchez Romero, Francisco-Javier Ferrández Pastor, Antonio Soriano Payá, and Juan-Manuel García Chamizo

Department of Computing and Information Technology, University of Alicante
Apdo. 99, E-03080 Alicante, Spain
{sanchez,fjferran,soriano,juanma}@dtic.ua.es

Abstract. This paper proposes the utilisation of fuzzy logic so as to design a system which models the biological regulator of blood glucose. That system consists of several fuzzy relations, each one of them modeling a component of the biological glycemia regulator, that is, pancreatic insulin production, net hepatic glucose balance, insulin dependent and independent glucose uptake, and kidney function. A set of experiments has been carried out by means of a simulation of the proposed model, checking that fuzzy control provides good results for the studied cases. The system could be a basis for developing artificial glycemia control mechanisms to be applied as a therapy for different pathologies, as well as for the development of simulators and monitors to aid diagnosis.

1 Introduction

Glucose is essential for cellular nutrition; its normal concentration in blood is within the range of 3.9-6.7 mmol/l. Hyperglycemia (high glucose level) can damage patients' health in the long term; hypoglycemia (low level) can make complications arise in the short term [1, 2]. The pancreas plays a main role in glycemia regulation: it secretes insulin, a hormone which reduces glycemia by enabling glucose to penetrate cells, thus maintaining normoglycemia [2]. A common illness related to an impaired glycemia regulation is Diabetes Mellitus (DM), mainly due to an insufficient insulin secretion or action. DM patients must control their diet and, frequently, follow a therapy to regulate glycemia externally that, in case of insulin dependent DM patients, usually consists of daily injection of insulin to compensate their own inefficient production of this hormone [3, 4]. The financial costs related to DM therapies are high, both for the patient and for the National Health System [3].

In this paper, we will first describe some significant aspects regarding the biological glycemia regulation system. Next we will review some artificial methods for achieving the same aim. Finally, we will propose a Fuzzy Logic model which enables the glycemia regulation system to be studied in different conditions and show the results obtained from simulations carried out with Matlab©. Despite its strong medical basic, the development of the study is closely related to Artificial Intelligence.

S. Tsumoto et al. (Eds.): RSCTC 2004, LNAI 3066, pp. 835–840, 2004.

1.1 The Biological Blood Glucose Regulation System

Insulin takes part in insulin-dependent glucose utilisation, performed mostly by muscle and adipose tissue. There is also an insulin-independent glucose utilisation carried out mainly by the central nervous system and red blood cells.

Glucose enters the extracellular space via both intestinal absorption and hepatic production. In the first case, glucose is absorbed by the gut to enter the portal circulation, with a rate related to ingested carbohydrates. Depending on glucose and insulin levels, the liver removes glucose from blood to synthesize glycogen or spills glucose to blood by means of glycogen breakdown and gluconeogenesis. The kidney excretes glucose through the urine when glycemia surpasses a threshold (about 9 mmol/l).

1.2 Artificial Blood Glucose Regulators and Regulation Models

Most research related to Diabetes is addressed to improve the metabolic control by using artificial regulation mechanisms that compensate the biological regulating system. The most usual mechanism is the injection of several daily doses of insulin [3]. This therapy does not achieve good results: it is difficult to adapt the insulin a patient needs along the day with punctual external supplies of it, so hypoglycaemic and hyperglycaemic episodes appear in an alternated way. In order to adapt the insulin supply to the patient's necessities, the *insulin pump* has been designed [3, 4]. This device supplies previously and remotely programmed insulin doses. Despite the positive results of this therapy, it lacks a feedback in the insulin infusion related to the glucose level. This non-autonomous operation points out the possibility of designing a device that was able to measure the glucose level and to react for achieving normoglycemia.

We must consider how much each regulation model fits the system we deal with. Its dynamics is not well-known, so the behaviour and the application results of a classical PID regulator could be inadequate [5]. Models based on neural networks or genetic algorithms can be applied to poorly structured systems, but they need a wide set of empiric data to infer regulation mechanisms based on their typical learning algorithms [6, 7]. Regulation models based on fuzzy sets are mainly applied to systems whose knowledge base could be virtually equal to the one a specialist has, where decisions are made depending on the combination of values of some factors [6, 7]. We will apply these fuzzy inference features to the problem of glycemia regulation.

2 Model Specification Oriented to Fuzzy Design

We will base on the components described in subsection 1.1 so as to model the glycemia regulation system. The model (shown in figure 1) consists of five fuzzy modules, each one representing a component of the biological system. Five fuzzy variables connect the modules: *Iout*, *Ghep*, *Gdep*, *Gind*, and *Gren*; these variables provide three derived ones: *Gin*, *Gadd*, and *Gout*. An input variable, *Gpre*, is assumed to be a previous glucose absorption by the gut (carbohydrate ingestion). We will use the equations appeared in [8] with some corrections proposed in [9] to model the carbohydrate ingestion. The summation of *Gpre* and *Gout* results in the variable *Gin*, which causes insulin production (*Iout*); *Gin* and *Iout* regulate the hepatic glucose balance, that is, a positive (addition) or negative (consumption) value for the variable *Ghep*. By summing both variables a new one results, *Gadd*, which regulates renal glucose elimination and insulin-independent glucose utilisation; *Gadd* and *Iout* regulate insulin-dependent glucose utilisation. The composition of the functions of these three subsystems gives the final glycemic level, *Gout*, which is back propagated.

In the next subsections we will describe the modules and the related variables. Each input variable is given a suffix to indicate the module where it acts as a parameter. For example, Gin^{IP} represents the different subsets of *Gin* when it is used as the input variable for the *Insulin Production* module.

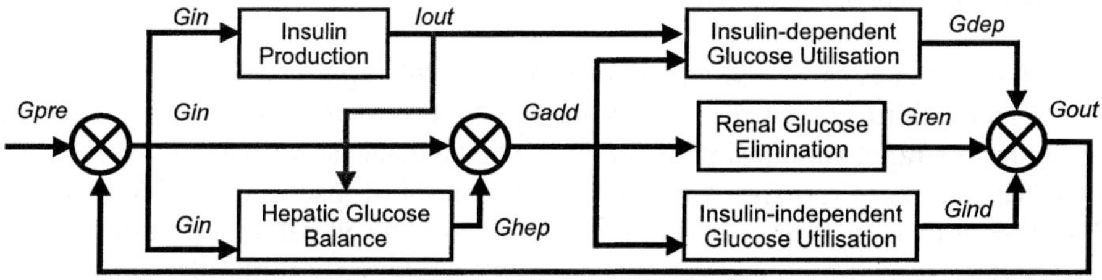

Fig. 1. The model of the blood glucose regulation system, with its modules and related variables.

2.1 Insulin Production

This module consists of a fuzzy set corresponding to the input variable Gin^{IP}, another one corresponding to the output variable *Iout*, and a series of fuzzy rules to relate them. We had a database with several pairs <*glucose level-insulin secretion*> to find a relationship between glucose level (ranging from 0.0 to 25.0 mmol/l) and expected insulin secretion (20.38-114.70 mU/l) [1, 2]. We divided those ranges into some fuzzy partitions. Figure 2 shows the membership function μGin^{IP} and the fuzzy rules.

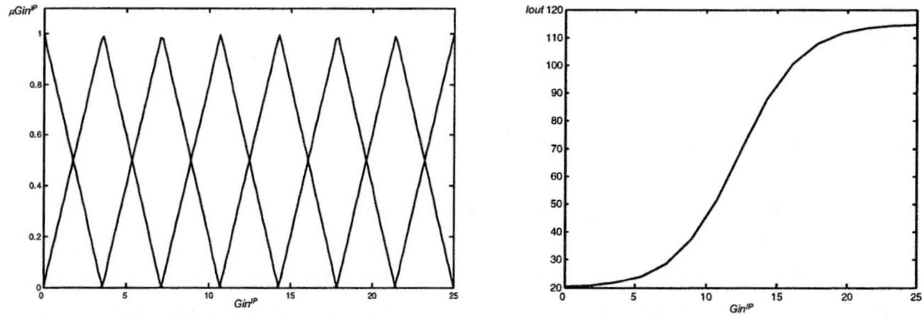

Fig. 2. The membership function μGin^{IP} for the input variable Gin^{IP} (left) and the curve resulting from the application of the fuzzy rules that relate Gin^{IP} and *Iout*.

2.2 Hepatic Glucose Balance

This module consists of two fuzzy sets corresponding to the input variables Gin^{HGB} and $Iout^{HGB}$, and a third one for the output variable *Ghep*; a collection of fuzzy rules relates the two input variables with the output variable. We used a set of data which relates glucose and insulin levels (ranging from 1.1 to 4.4 mmol/l and from 0.0 to 100.0 mU/l respectively) with hepatic glucose absorption/production (–1.56 to 4.25 mmol/h) [8]. Each input variable is partitioned into eight fuzzy sets, so *Ghep* is divided into sixty-four fuzzy sets corresponding to the full combination of the input fuzzy sets. The 3D curve in figure 3 left shows the fuzzy associative memory (FAM) containing the sizty-four rules.

2.3 Insulin-Dependent Glucose Utilisation

This module consists of two sets that correspond to the input variables $Gadd^{IDGU}$ and $Iout^{IDGU}$, and a third one corresponding to the output variable *Gdep*; a set of fuzzy rules relates the input variables with *Gdep*. We had a database with expected relationship between glucose (ranging from 0.0 to 20.0 mmol/l), insulin (20.0-100.0 mU/l), and glucose utilisation (0.0-3.75 mmol/h) [8]. Each input variable is partitioned into eight fuzzy sets so the output variable is divided into sixty-four fuzzy sets corresponding to the full combination of the input fuzzy sets. The FAM which contains the sixty-four combination rules is shown by means of the 3D curve in figure 3 right.

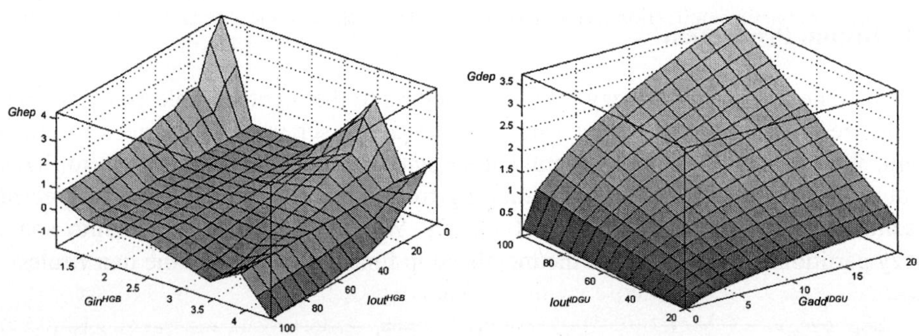

Fig. 3. The graphs showing the values of the FAM for output variables *Ghep* (left) and *Gdep*.

2.4 Insulin-Independent Glucose Utilisation

This module consists of a fuzzy partition corresponding to the input variable $Gadd^{IIGU}$ (mmol/l) and another one corresponding to the output variable *Gind* (mmol/h), and a set of fuzzy rules to relate them. Internally, a subsystem calculates the relation between glycemia and red blood cells glucose utilisation giving the output variable *Grbc*; the other determines the relation between glycemia and central nervous system glucose utilisation giving the output variable *Gcns*. Both results are added to give the global insulin-independent glucose utilisation *Gind*. The membership function $\mu Gadd^{IIGU}$ is similar to $\mu Gadd^{IDGU}$. Figure 4 left shows the fuzzy rules.

2.5 Renal Glucose Elimination

This module consists of a fuzzy set corresponding to the input variable $Gadd^{RGE}$ (mmol/l) and another one corresponding to the output variable *Gren* (mmol/h), and a collection of fuzzy rules to relate them. The membership function $\mu Gadd^{RGE}$ is similar to $\mu Gadd^{IDGU}$ and the fuzzy rules are shown in the curve in figure 4 right.

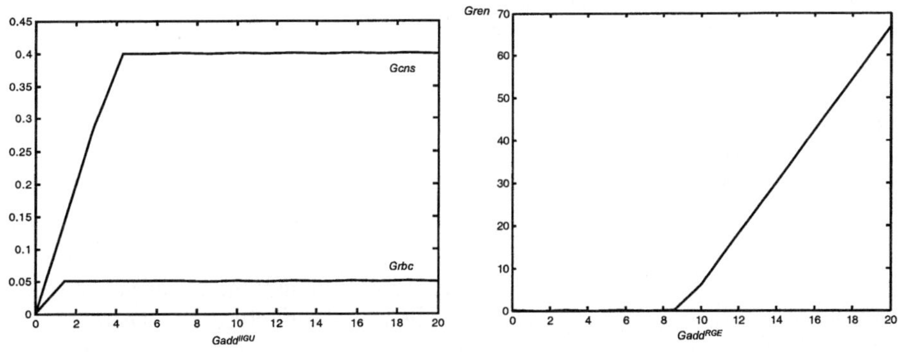

Fig. 4. Left: Curves that show the fuzzy rules which relate $Gadd^{IIGU}$ to *Gcns* and to *Grbc*. Right: Curve that shows the application of the fuzzy rules which relate $Gadd^{RGE}$ to *Gren*.

3 Experimentation

A set of experiments were performed so as to check the correctness of the proposed model. We used the simulation tool Simulink, integrated into Matlab©. In the first type of experiments, we tested the reaction of the system on a punctual and instantaneous change in blood glucose (with no glucose ingestion). We caused a fast glycemia increase to 18.0 mmol/l. The system reacts to achieve normoglycemia in some minutes. Next, we caused a glycemia decrement to 3.0 mmol/l; again, the system performed the necessary actions to achieve normoglycemia in some minutes. In the second type of experiments, we tested the behavior of the system on a daytime, that is, considering glucose ingestion from breakfast, lunch, dinner, and after-dinner (280 mmol glucose at 7:00, 14:00, and 20:00; 70 mmol at 22:30) and we obtained the blood insulin and glucose levels along the 24 hours course. Glycemia remains at any time between 5.0 and 9.0 mmol/l, thus avoiding severe hypoglycemia and hyperglycemia. Figure 5 shows the glycemia time course from both types of experiments.

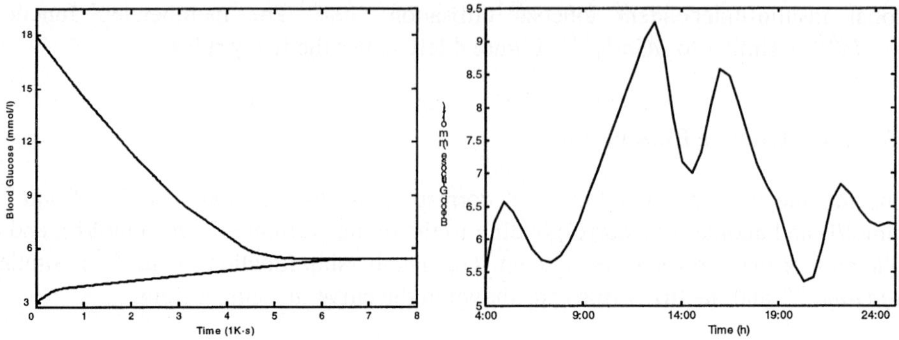

Fig. 5. Left: time course of glycemia variations starting from 18 (upper curve) and from 3 mmol/l. Right: the same along a full daytime (showed from 4:00 to 24:00) from 5.5 mmol/l.

4 Conclusions

We have proposed a fuzzy regulator model to control glycemia and simulated it with modeling software. Some evidences indicate the model correctness. On the one hand, the curves showing the application of the rules in the fuzzy modules match the empiric data used by other models [1, 2, 8]. On the other hand, the experiments results show how the system adequately reacts to achieve normoglycemia. Therefore, the application of Fuzzy Logic techniques facilitates the design of regulating mechanisms for complex systems. A future work consists of transferring the simulation results to a hardware architecture [6, 7], so as to study the viability of implementing a fuzzy regulator on an electronic device. In the long term, we can focus on developing a device to be implanted in human body for compensating the biological glycemia regulating system, also considering its use for diagnosis. This would require a multidisciplinary study of the biocompatibility and the biological reactions to the device implantation.

References

1. Schmidt, R. F., Thews, G.: Fisiología Humana. McGraw-Hill Interamericana (1993)
2. Guyton, A. C., Hall, J.: Tratado de Fisiología Médica. McGraw-Hill Interamericana (2001)
3. Klarenbach, S. W., Jacobs, P.: International Comparison of Health Resource Utilization In Subjects With Diabetes. Diabetes Care, Vol. 26 (2003) 1116-1122
4. Scavini, M., Schade, D. S.: Implantable Insulin Pumps. Clinical Diabetes, Vol. 14.2 (1996)
5. Ogata, K.: Ingeniería de Control Moderna. Prentice-Hall (1998)
6. Driankov, D., Hellendom, H.: An Introduction to Fuzzy Control. Springer-Verlag (1993)
7. Conner, D.: Fuzzy-logic Control Systems. EDN (1993) 77-88
8. Lehmann, E. D., Deutsch, T.: A physiological model of glucose-insulin interaction in type 1 diabetes-mellitus. Journal of Biomedical Engineering, Vol. 14 (1992) 235-242
9. Sánchez, J. L., Soriano, A., García, J. M.: Implementación de un modelo fisiológico para regulación de la glucemia mediante inyección de insulina. Proceedings of the XXI Annual Conference of the Spanish Biomedical Engineering Society (2003) 367-370

The Rough Set Database System: An Overview

Zbigniew Suraj[1,2] and Piotr Grochowalski[2]

[1] Chair of Computer Science Foundations
University of Information Technology and Management, Rzeszow, Poland
zsuraj@wenus.wsiz.rzeszow.pl
[2] Institute of Mathematics, Rzeszow University, Poland
piotrg@univ.rzeszow.pl

Abstract. The paper describes the "Rough Sets Database System" (called in short the RSDS system) for the creation of bibliography on rough sets and their applications. This database is the most comprehensive online rough sets bibliography and accessible under the following web-site address: http://rsds.wsiz.rzeszow.pl
The service has been developed in order to facilitate the creation of rough sets bibliography, for various types of publications. At the moment the bibliography contains over 1400 entries from more than 450 authors. It is possible to create the bibliography in *HTML* or *BibTeX* format. In order to broaden the service contents it is possible to append new data using specially dedicated form. After appending data online the database is updated automatically. If one prefers sending a data file to the database administrator, please be aware that the database is updated once a month.
In the current version of the RSDS system, there is the possibility for appending to each publication an abstract and keywords. As a natural consequence of this improvement there exists a possibility for searching a publication by keywords.

Keywords: rough sets, fuzzy systems, neural networks, evolutionary computing, data mining, knowledge discovery, pattern recognition, machine learning, database systems.

1 Introduction

Rough sets, introduced by Professor Zdzislaw Pawlak in 1981 [16], are a rapidly developing discipline of theoretical and applied computer science. It has become apparent during the last years that a bibliography on this subject is urgently needed as a tool for both the efficient research on, and the use of rough set theory.

The aim of this paper is to present the RSDS system for the creation of bibliography on rough sets and their applications; papers on other topics have been included whenever rough sets play a decisive role for the presented matters, or in case outstanding applications of rough set theory are discussed. Compiling the bibliography for the database we faced the fact that many important ideas

S. Tsumoto et al. (Eds.): RSCTC 2004, LNAI 3066, pp. 841–849, 2004.

and results are contained in reports, theses, memos, etc.; we have done our best to arrive at a good compromise between the completeness of the bibliography and the restriction to generally available publications.

Another difficulty we hade to cope with was the sometimes extremely different alphabetizing of author's names.

The following served among others as the sources for the bibliography database:

- The publications in the journal Fundamenta Informaticae and others.
- Books on the rough set theory and applications as well as proceedings of the international conferences on rough sets mentioned in the references at the end of this article.
- Other materials available at the of International Rough Set Society.
- Queries for "rough sets" in the website of the databases.

The service has been developed in order to facilitate the creation of rough sets bibliography, for various types of publications. At present it is possible to create the bibliography in *HTML* or *BibTeX* format. In order to broaden the service contents it is possible to append new data using specially dedicated form. After appending data online the database is updated automatically. If one prefers sending a data file to the database administrator, please be aware that the database is updated once a month.

There are following types of publications available in the service: article, book, booklet, inbook, incollection, inproceedings, manual, mastersthesis, phdthesis, proceedings, techreport, unpublished.

This paper is organized as follows. Section 2 presents an overview of information used to characterize the RSDS system. The future plans for the RSDS system are discussed in section 3. Conclusions are given in section 4.

2 Description of the RSDS System

2.1 Home Page

Having the system activated on a display appears the English version home page. The service menu comprises several options allowing moving around the whole system. The menu includes the following: *Home page*, *Login*, *Append*, *Search*, *Download*, *Send*, *Write to us*, *Statistics*, *Help*.

2.2 Appending Data

In order to append a new data to the bibliographic database at first one shall go to the *Append* section. Before appending a new data, user must login in the system using a special form. That form includes the fields allowing to insert user *id* and user *password*. If a user inserts a wrong user *id* or *password* then a message describing the mistake displays on the screen. If user wants to login at first, then one must use the other special form, by clicking the *First login* button. That form includes the fields allowing to insert: user's *name* and user's *surname*, *e–mail*, user *id* and user's *password*. Next, the entered data is verified in the database. If all data is correct, the account for the user is created at once, and then the user is logged into the system automatically with a new data number in the database. This information helps at the implementation of existing data changes. After login, the special form displays and it is then possible to type a new data (excluding data about authors; another form is dedicated to entering the authors data). After providing an information concerning the publication type, the form is updated with fields required for inputting specific data. The fields required for proceeding with data input are marked with the star character (*). The required fields described are by the *BibTeX* format specification. After entering the required data, it is possible to proceed to the next step - which is inputting authors or editors data. The authors data inputting form be reloaded until the last author data record is entered. A user decides when to stop entering the authors data by clicking the *End* button. For the entered data verification, all the data is displayed prior to sending to the database. After accepting, the data is sent.

The list concerning publication types together with describing them fields follows.

Publication	**Description**
article	An article from a journal. *Fields required:* author, title, journal, year. *Optional fields:* volume, number, pages, month, note.
book	A book with the known, given publisher. *Fields required:* author or editor, title, publisher, year. *Optional fields:* volume, series, address, edition, month, note.
booklet	Printed and bound matter, whilst the publisher is unknown. *Fields required:* title. *Optional fields:* author, address, month, year, note.
inbook	A part of a book, could be chapter or given pages. *Fields required:* author or editor, title, chapter or pages, publisher, year. *Optional fields:* volume, series, address, edition, month, note.
incollection	A part of a book with its own title. *Fields required:* author, title, book title, publisher, year. *Optional fields:* editor, chapter, pages, address, month, note.
inproceedings	An article published in conference proceedings. *Fields required:* author, title, book title, year. *Optional fields:* author, organization, publisher, address, month, note.

manual	Manual or documentation. *Fields required:* title. *Optional fields:* author, organization, address, edition, month, year, note.
mastersthesis	M.Sc. thesis. *Fields required:* author, title, school, year. *Optional fields:* address, month, note.
phdthesis	Ph.D. thesis. *Fields required:* author, title, school, year. *Optional fields:* address, month, note.
proceedings	Proceedings. *Fields required:* title, year. *Optional fields:* editor, publisher, organization, address, month, note.
techreport	Report, usually with a given number, being periodically issued. *Fields required:* author, title, institution, year. *Optional fields:* number, address, month, note.
unpublished	A document with a given author and title data, unpublished. *Fields required:* author, title, note. *Optional fields:* month, year.

Explanation on existing fields.

address	Publisher's address.
author	Forename and surname of an author (or authors).
booktitle	Title of a quoted in part book.
chapter	The chapter number.
edition	Issue, edition.
editor	Forenames and surnames of editors. If there also exists the field "author", the "editor" denotes the editor of a larger entity, of which the quoted work is a part.
institution	Institution publishing the printed matter.
journal	Journal's name.
month	Month of issue or completion of the manuscript.
note	Additional information useful to a reader.
number	The journal or the report number. Usually journals are being identified by providing their year and a number within the year of issue. A report, in general, has only a number.
organization	Organization supporting a conference.
pages	One or more page numbers; for example 42-11, 7,41,73-97.
publisher	Publisher's name.
school	University college, where the thesis be submitted.

series	A name of book series. If one quotes a book from given series, then the "title" field denotes the title of a book whilst the "series" field should contain the entire series name.
title	The title of the work.
volume	The periodical's or the book's volume.
year	Year of issue. In case of unpublished work, the year of completing writing. Year only in number format e.g. 1984.
URL	The WWW Universal Resource Locator that points to the item being referenced. This often is used for technical reports to point to the ftp site where the postscript source of the report is located.
ISBN	The International Standard Book Number.
ISSN	The International Standard Serial Number. Used to identify a journal.
abstract	An abstract of a publication.
keywords	Key words attached to a publication. This can be used for searching a publication.

Note: All data must be appended in the Latin alphabet – without national marks.

2.3 Searching Data

For the database searching go to the *Search* section. An alphabetical searching and an advanced searching options are possible. The advanced searching allows for providing the title, the author and key words of a publication. The required data can be sent to a user in two formats: at first *HTML* format data is displayed and then after clicking the *BibTeX* link, the *BibTeX* format file is created. It is then possible to download the created file with the **.tex* extension (with an entered file name). Two file downloading methods have been applied for user's comfort:

– Saving directly to a user's local hard drive.
– Sending the file as an e-mail attachment.

Before editing existing data into the database, user must login in the system and then using the *Search* option display *HTML* format chosen data on the screen. After clicking the *Edit* button, the special form displays with existing data and it is then possible to edit this data. A user decides when to stop editing the data by clicking the *Submit entry* button. After that the data is sent to the database administrator. If user logins as administrator, then there exists possibility for deleting redundant data in the database.

2.4 Downloading a File

Before saving data to the file, one must specify the operating system for which the file with the entered file name and the *.*tex* extension should be created. Two methods for downloading the file in the RSDS system have been implemented:

- Save to user's local hard drive.
- Send as an e-mail attachment.

2.5 Sending a File

It is possible to submit a file with the bibliographic data to the database administrator, who has the software allowing for appending automatically a large data to the database. In order to do it one can use a special dedicated form. Submissions in the form of *BibTeX* files are preferred. Please note that submissions are not immediately available as the database is updated in batches once a month.

2.6 Write to Us

This section allows to write and send the comments on the service to us by using the special dedicated form. This form includes a field for comments and the *Send* button. Any comments about our service will be helpful and greatly appreciated. Please post them to the database administrator who permanently carries out work on improving the service and broadening of its possibilities.

2.7 Statistics

This section allows to display two type of statistics about the bibliographic data in the form of the dynamic graphs:

- Amount and types of publications included in the database.
- Distribution of publication dates.

Moreover, this section provides information concerning:

- How many times the service has been visited by the users.
- The number of registered users.
- The number of authors in the database.

3 Future Plans for the RSDS System

We plan to extend the RSDS system possibilities to the following, among others:

- Implementation of new methods for searching data.
- Implementation of new visualization methods of data statistics.
- Adding the database FAQ.
- Updating of the bibliographic database.

4 Conclusions

We have created the RSDS system by applying some of the basic possibilities of computer tools which are needed in the bibliography database systems. Those tools support a user in searching of rough sets publications as well as downloading files in a natural and very effective way.

The main point of the RSDS system is its extensibility: it is easy to connect other methods and tools to the system.

It seems that our system presented in the paper is a professional database system which offers a stable platform for extensions.

Using the RSDS system is an opportunity for information exchange between scientists and practitioners who are interested in the foundations and applications of rough sets.

The developers of the RSDS system hope that the increase in the dissemination of results, methods, theories and applications based on rough sets will stimulate further development of the foundations and methods for real-life applications in intelligent systems.

For future updating of the bibliography we will appreciate receiving all forms of help and advice. In particular, we would like to become aware of relevant contributions which are not referred to in this bibliography database. All submitted material will also be included in the RSDS system.

The RSDS system has been designed and implemented at Rzeszow University, and installed at University of Information Technology and Management in Rzeszow.

The RSDS system runs on any computer with any operating system connected to the Internet. The service is based on the Internet Explorer 6.0, Opera 7.03 as well as Mozilla 1.3 (correct operation requires the web browser with the accepting cookie option enabled).

Acknowledgments

We are grateful to Professor Andrzej Skowron from Warsaw University (Poland) for stimulating discussions about this work and providing bibliographic data for the RSDS system. We wish to thank our colleagues from the Logic Group of Warsaw University for their help in searching data, especially Rafal Latkowski, Piotr Synak and Marcin Szczuka. Our deepest thanks go to the staff of the Chair of Computer Science Foundations of University of Information Technology and Management in Rzeszow as well as the staff of the Computer Science Department of Rzeszow University for their support and their infinite patience. We are all obliged to the Editors of this book for making the publication of this article possible.

References

1. J.J. Alpigini, J.F. Peters, A. Skowron, N. Zhong (Eds.): Rough Sets and Current Trends in Computing. Third International Conference, RSCTC 2002, Malvern, PA, USA, October 14-16, 2002, Lecture Notes in Artificial Intelligence 2475, Springer-Verlag, Berlin 2002.

2. Cios, K.J., Pedrycz, W., Swiniarski, R.W.: Data Mining. Methods for Knowledge Discovery. Kluwer Academic Publishers, Dordrecht 1998.
3. Demri, S.P., Orlowska, E.,S.: Incomplete Information: Structure, Inference, Complexity. Springer-Verlag, Berlin 2002.
4. L. Czaja (Ed.): Proceedings of the Workshop on Concurrency, Specification and Programming, CS&P'2003, Vol. 1-2, Czarna, Poland, September 25-27, 2003, Warsaw University, 2003.
5. S. Hirano, M. Inuiguchi, S. Tsumoto (Eds.): Proceedings of International Workshop on Rough Set Theory and Granular Computing (RSTGC'2001), Matsue, Shimane, Japan, May 20-22, 2001. Bulletin of International Rough Set Society 5/1-2 (2001).
6. M. Inuiguchi, S. Miyamoto (Eds.): Proceedings of the First Workshop on Rough Sets and Kansei Engineering in Japan, December 14-15, 2002, Tokyo, Bulletin of International Rough Set Society 7/1-2 (2003).
7. M. Inuiguchi, S. Hirano, S. Tsumoto (Eds.): Rough Set Theory and Granular Computing, Studies in Fuzziness and Soft Computing, Vol. 125, Springer-Verlag, Berlin 2003.
8. T.Y. Lin (Ed.): Proceedings of the Third International Workshop on Rough Sets and Soft Computing (RSSC'94). San Jose State University, San Jose, California, USA, November 10-12, 1994.
9. T.Y. Lin, A.M. Wildberger (Eds.): Soft Computing: Rough Sets, Fuzzy Logic, Neural Networks, Uncertainty Management, Knowledge Discovery. Simulation Councils, Inc., San Diego, CA, 1995.
10. T.Y. Lin (Ed.): Proceedings of the Workshop on Rough Sets and Data Mining at 23rd Annual Computer Science Conference, Nashville, Tenessee, March 2, 1995.
11. T.Y. Lin (Ed.): Journal of the Intelligent Automation and Soft Computing 2/2 (1996) (special issue).
12. T.Y. Lin (Ed.): International Journal of Approximate Reasoning 15/4 (1996) (special issue).
13. T.Y. Lin, N. Cercone (Eds.): Rough Sets and Data Mining. Analysis of Imprecise Data. Kluwer Academic Publishers, Dordrecht 1997.
14. E. Orlowska (Ed.): Incomplete information: Rough set analysis. Physica-Verlag, Heidelberg, 1997.
15. S.K. Pal, A. Skowron (Eds.): Rough Fuzzy Hybridization: A New Trend in Decision-Making. Springer-Verlag, Singapore 1999.
16. Pawlak, Z.: Rough Sets – Theoretical Aspects of Reasoning about Data. Kluwer Academic Publishers, Dordrecht 1991.
17. S.K. Pal, L. Polkowski, A. Skowron (Eds.): Rough-Neural Computing. Techniques for Computing with Words. Springer-Verlag, Berlin 2004.
18. W. Pedrycz, J.F. Peters (Eds.): Computational Intelligence in Software Engineering. World Scientific Publishing, Singapore 1998.
19. Polkowski, L.: Rough Sets. Mathematical Foundations. Springer-Verlag, Berlin 2002.
20. L. Polkowski, A. Skowron (Eds.): Rough Sets in Knowledge Discovery 1. Methodology and Applications. Physica-Verlag, Heidelberg 1998.
21. L. Polkowski, A. Skowron (Eds.): Rough Sets in Knowledge Discovery 2. Applications, Case Studies and Software Systems. Physica-Verlag, Heidelberg 1998.
22. L. Polkowski, A. Skowron (Eds.): Proceedings of the First International Conference on Rough Sets and Current Trends in Computing (RSCTC'98), Warsaw, Poland, 1998, Lecture Notes in Artificial Intelligence 1424, Springer-Verlag, Berlin 1998.

23. L. Polkowski, S. Tsumoto, T.Y. Lin (Eds.): Rough Set Methods and Applications. New Developments in Knowledge Discovery in Information Systems. Physica-Verlag, Heidelberg, 2000.
24. A. Skowron, S.K. Pal (Eds.): Pattern Recognition Letters 24/6 (2003) (special issue).
25. A. Skowron, M. Szczuka (Eds.): Proceedings of an International Workshop on Rough Sets in Knowledge Discovery and Soft Computing, RSDK, Warsaw, Poland, April 5-13, 2003, Warsaw University, 2003.
26. R. Slowinski, J. Stefanowski (Eds.): Proceedings of the First International Workshop on Rough Sets: State of the Art. And Perspectives. Kiekrz – Poznan, Poland, September 2-4, 1992.
27. R. Slowinski (Ed.): Intelligent Decision Support – Hanbook of Applications and Advances of the Rough Sets Theory. Kluwer Academic Publishers, Dordrecht 1992.
28. R. Slowinski, J. Stefanowski (Eds.), Foundations of Computing and Decision Sciences 18/3-4 (1993) 155-396 (special issue).
29. Z. Suraj (Ed.): Proceedings of the Sixth International Conference on Soft Computing and Distributed Processing (SCDP 2002), June 24-25, 2002, Rzeszow, Poland, University of Information Technology and Management Publisher, Rzeszow 2002.
30. S. Tsumoto, S. Kobayashi, T. Yokomori, H. Tanaka, and A. Nakamura (Eds.): Proceedings of the Fourth International Workshop on Rough Sets, Fuzzy Sets and Machine Discovery (RSFD'96). The University of Tokyo, November 6-8, 1996.
31. S. Tsumoto (Ed.): Bulletin of International Rough Set Society 1/1 (1996).
32. S. Tsumoto (Ed.): Bulletin of International Rough Set Society 1/2 (1997).
33. S. Tsumoto, Y.Y. Yao, and M. Hadjimichael (Eds.): Bulletin of International Rough Set Society 2/1 (1998).
34. P.P. Wang (Ed.): Proceedings of the International Workshop on Rough Sets and Soft Computing at Second Annual Joint Conference on Information Sciences (JCIS'95), Wrightsville Beach, North Carolina, 28 September – 1 October, 1995.
35. P.P. Wang (Ed.): Proceedings of the Fifth International Workshop on Rough Sets and Soft Computing (RSSC'97) at Third Annual Joint Conference on Information Sciences (JCIS'97). Duke University, Durham, NC, USA, Rough Set & Computer Science 3, March 1-5, 1997.
36. G. Wang, Q. Liu, Y.Y. Yao, A. Skowron (Eds.). Rough Sets, Fuzzy Sets, Data Mining, ad Granular Computing. 9th International Conference, RSFDGrC 2003, Chongqing, China, May 26-29, 2003, Lecture Notes in Artificial Intelligence 2639, Springer-Verlag, Berlin 2003.
37. W. Ziarko (Ed.): Proceedings of the Second International Workshop on Rough Sets and Knowledge Discovery (RSKD'93). Banff, Alberta, Canada, October 12-15, 1993.
38. W. Ziarko (Ed.): Rough Sets, Fuzzy Sets and Knowledge Discovery (RSKD'93). Workshops in Computing, Springer-Verlag & British Computer Society, London, Berlin 1994.
39. W. Ziarko (Ed.): Computational Intelligence: An International Journal 11/2 (1995) (special issue).
40. W. Ziarko (Ed.): Fundamenta Informaticae 27/2-3 (1996) (special issue)
41. W. Ziarko, Y.Y. Yao (Eds.): Rough Sets and Current Trends in Computing. Second International Conference, RSCTC 2000, Banff, Canada, October 16-19, 2000, Lecture Notes in Artificial Intelligence 2005, Springer-Verlag, Berlin 2001.

Author Index

Lecture Notes in Artificial Intelligence (LNAI)

Vol. 2782: M. Klusch, A. Omicini, S. Ossowski, H. Laamanen (Eds.), Cooperative Information Agents VII. XI, 345 pages. 2003.

Vol. 2780: M. Dojat, E. Keravnou, P. Barahona (Eds.), Artificial Intelligence in Medicine. XIII, 388 pages. 2003.

Vol. 2777: B. Schölkopf, M.K. Warmuth (Eds.), Learning Theory and Kernel Machines. XIV, 746 pages. 2003.

Vol. 2752: G.A. Kaminka, P.U. Lima, R. Rojas (Eds.), RoboCup 2002: Robot Soccer World Cup VI. XVI, 498 pages. 2003.

Vol. 2741: F. Baader (Ed.), Automated Deduction – CADE-19. XII, 503 pages. 2003.

Vol. 2705: S. Renals, G. Grefenstette (Eds.), Text- and Speech-Triggered Information Access. VII, 197 pages. 2003.

Vol. 2703: O.R. Zaïane, J. Srivastava, M. Spiliopoulou, B. Masand (Eds.), WEBKDD 2002 - MiningWeb Data for Discovering Usage Patterns and Profiles. IX, 181 pages. 2003.

Vol. 2700: M.T. Pazienza (Ed.), Extraction in the Web Era. XIII, 163 pages. 2003.

Vol. 2699: M.G. Hinchey, J.L. Rash, W.F. Truszkowski, C.A. Rouff, D.F. Gordon-Spears (Eds.), Formal Approaches to Agent-Based Systems. IX, 297 pages. 2002.

Vol. 2691: V. Mařík, J.P. Müller, M. Pechoucek (Eds.), Multi-Agent Systems and Applications III. XIV, 660 pages. 2003.

Vol. 2684: M.V. Butz, O. Sigaud, P. Gérard (Eds.), Anticipatory Behavior in Adaptive Learning Systems. X, 303 pages. 2003.

Vol. 2671: Y. Xiang, B. Chaib-draa (Eds.), Advances in Artificial Intelligence. XIV, 642 pages. 2003.

Vol. 2663: E. Menasalvas, J. Segovia, P.S. Szczepaniak (Eds.), Advances in Web Intelligence. XII, 350 pages. 2003.

Vol. 2661: P.L. Lanzi, W. Stolzmann, S.W. Wilson (Eds.), Learning Classifier Systems. VII, 231 pages. 2003.

Vol. 2654: U. Schmid, Inductive Synthesis of Functional Programs. XXII, 398 pages. 2003.

Vol. 2650: M.-P. Huget (Ed.), Communications in Multiagent Systems. VIII, 323 pages. 2003.

Vol. 2645: M.A. Wimmer (Ed.), Knowledge Management in Electronic Government. XI, 320 pages. 2003.

Vol. 2639: G. Wang, Q. Liu, Y. Yao, A. Skowron (Eds.), Rough Sets, Fuzzy Sets, Data Mining, and Granular Computing. XVII, 741 pages. 2003.

Vol. 2637: K.-Y. Whang, J. Jeon, K. Shim, J. Srivastava, Advances in Knowledge Discovery and Data Mining. XVIII, 610 pages. 2003.

Vol. 2636: E. Alonso, D. Kudenko, D. Kazakov (Eds.), Adaptive Agents and Multi-Agent Systems. XIV, 323 pages. 2003.

Vol. 2627: B. O'Sullivan (Ed.), Recent Advances in Constraints. X, 201 pages. 2003.

Vol. 2600: S. Mendelson, A.J. Smola (Eds.), Advanced Lectures on Machine Learning. IX, 259 pages. 2003.

Vol. 2592: R. Kowalczyk, J.P. Müller, H. Tianfield, R. Unland (Eds.), Agent Technologies, Infrastructures, Tools, and Applications for E-Services. XVII, 371 pages. 2003.

Vol. 2586: M. Klusch, S. Bergamaschi, P. Edwards, P. Petta (Eds.), Intelligent Information Agents. VI, 275 pages. 2003.

Vol. 2583: S. Matwin, C. Sammut (Eds.), Inductive Logic Programming. X, 351 pages. 2003.

Vol. 2581: J.S. Sichman, F. Bousquet, P. Davidsson (Eds.), Multi-Agent-Based Simulation. X, 195 pages. 2003.

Vol. 2577: P. Petta, R. Tolksdorf, F. Zambonelli (Eds.), Engineering Societies in the Agents World III. X, 285 pages. 2003.

Vol. 2569: D. Karagiannis, U. Reimer (Eds.), Practical Aspects of Knowledge Management. XIII, 648 pages. 2002.

Vol. 2560: S. Goronzy, Robust Adaptation to Non-Native Accents in Automatic Speech Recognition. XI, 144 pages. 2002.

Vol. 2557: B. McKay, J. Slaney (Eds.), AI 2002: Advances in Artificial Intelligence. XV, 730 pages. 2002.

Vol. 2554: M. Beetz, Plan-Based Control of Robotic Agents. XI, 191 pages. 2002.

Vol. 2543: O. Bartenstein, U. Geske, M. Hannebauer, O. Yoshie (Eds.), Web Knowledge Management and Decision Support. X, 307 pages. 2003.

Vol. 2541: T. Barkowsky, Mental Representation and Processing of Geographic Knowledge. X, 174 pages. 2002.

Vol. 2533: N. Cesa-Bianchi, M. Numao, R. Reischuk (Eds.), Algorithmic Learning Theory. XI, 415 pages. 2002.

Vol. 2531: J. Padget, O. Shehory, D. Parkes, N.M. Sadeh, W.E. Walsh (Eds.), Agent-Mediated Electronic Commerce IV. Designing Mechanisms and Systems. XVII, 341 pages. 2002.

Vol. 2527: F.J. Garijo, J.-C. Riquelme, M. Toro (Eds.), Advances in Artificial Intelligence - IBERAMIA 2002. XVIII, 955 pages. 2002.

Vol. 2522: T. Andreasen, A. Motro, H. Christiansen, H.L. Larsen (Eds.), Flexible Query Answering Systems. X, 383 pages. 2002.

Vol. 2514: M. Baaz, A. Voronkov (Eds.), Logic for Programming, Artificial Intelligence, and Reasoning. XIII, 465 pages. 2002.

Vol. 2507: G. Bittencourt, G.L. Ramalho (Eds.), Advances in Artificial Intelligence. XIII, 417 pages. 2002.

Vol. 2504: M.T. Escrig, F. Toledo, E. Golobardes (Eds.), Topics in Artificial Intelligence. XI, 427 pages. 2002.

Vol. 2499: S.D. Richardson (Ed.), Machine Translation: From Research to Real Users. XXI, 254 pages. 2002.

Vol. 2484: P. Adriaans, H. Fernau, M. van Zaanen (Eds.), Grammatical Inference: Algorithms and Applications. IX, 315 pages. 2002.

Vol. 2479: M. Jarke, J. Koehler, G. Lakemeyer (Eds.), KI 2002: Advances in Artificial Intelligence. XIII, 327 pages. 2002.

Vol. 2475: J.J. Alpigini, J.F. Peters, A. Skowron, N. Zhong (Eds.), Rough Sets and Current Trends in Computing. XV, 640 pages. 2002.

Vol. 2473: A. Gómez-Pérez, V.R. Benjamins (Eds.), Knowledge Engineering and Knowledge Management. Ontologies and the Semantic Web. XI, 402 pages. 2002.